...There's No Pl

The History Place

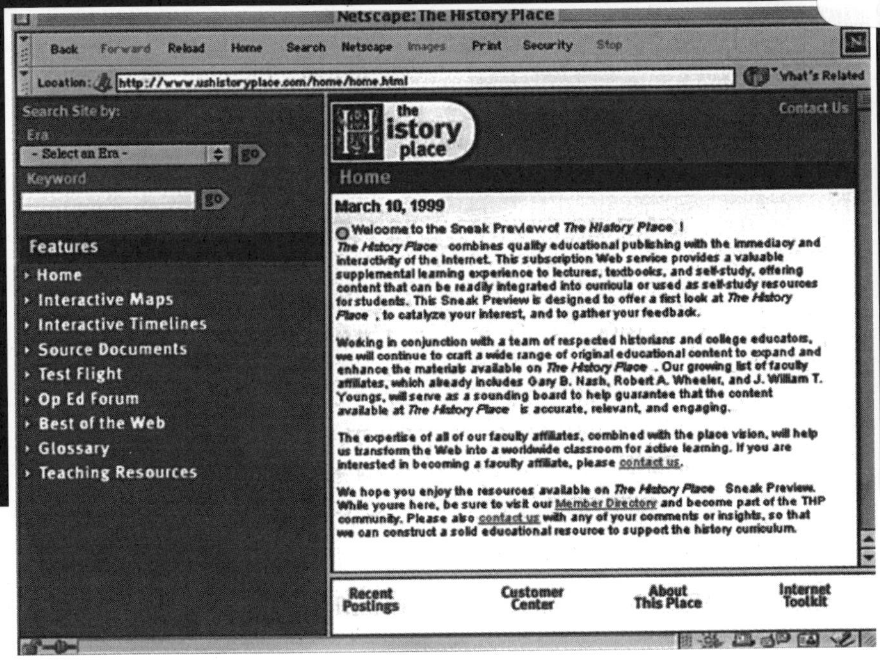

http://www.ushistoryplace.com

Welcome to The History Place, a new online resource for students and instructors of the United States History survey. The pedagogical mission of The History Place is to introduce the lessons of the past using the innovative technological tools of today. The History Place features a variety of learning tools and references designed to make study easier, more engaging, and more rewarding.

The History Place is developed by Peregrine Publishers in partnership with a growing number of historians and writers, including Gary Nash of UCLA, Saul Cornell of the Ohio State University, and John Nicols and Jim Mohr of the University of Oregon.

Congratulations!

With your purchase of *The American People, Fifth Edition*, Addison Wesley Longman is pleased to provide you with a twelve-month subscription to The History Place, a unique Web resource for history students. At The History Place, you'll find a continually enriched learning resource that includes interactive maps, timelines, and other learning activities; a rich collection of source documents; the powerful TestFlight testing tool for self-assessment; and much more.

To explore this valuable teaching and learning resource:

1. Go to www.awl.com/nash
2. Click on The History Place login icon
3. Follow the instructions to register your subscription using the following access code:

WSNV-CHOTT-THOLE-STRUT-BROOM-LOBES

4. During the registration process, you will choose a personal user ID and password for use in logging into the site. Once your subscription is confirmed, you can begin using The History Place immediately.

Your pre-assigned access code can be used only once to establish your subscription, which is not transferable and is limited to twelve months from the date of activation. If you purchased a used textbook, this access code may have already been used. However, you can find information on how to purchase a subscription on The History Place registration page.

ISBN: 0-321-08493-4

The
AMERICAN PEOPLE

PACIFIC OCEAN
WASHINGTON
OREGON
IDAHO
MONTANA
WYOMING
NEVADA
UTAH
COLORADO
CALIFORNIA
ARIZONA
NEW MEXICO
NORTH DAKO
SOUTH DAKO
NEBRASKA
KANS
OKLA
TEXAS
MEXICO
Cape Flattery
Puget Sound
Tacoma
Seattle
Olympia
Mt. St. Helens 8,366 ft. (2,550 m)
Mt. Rainier 14,410 ft. (4,300 m)
Spokane
Columbia River
Portland
Salem
Eugene
Cape Blanco
CASCADE RANGE
COAST RANGES
ROCKY MOUNTAINS
Great Falls
Helena
Missouri River
Billings
Bismarck
Grand
Boise
Idaho Falls
Snake River
Pocatello
Rapid City
Pierre
BLACK HILLS
Casper
Cape Mendocino
Sacramento River
CENTRAL
SIERRA NEVADA
GREAT BASIN
Great Salt Lake
Ogden
Salt Lake City
Provo
Reno
Carson City
Lake Tahoe
Sacramento
San Francisco Bay
San Francisco
Oakland
San Jose
San Joaquim River
Fresno
Mt. Whitney 14,500 ft. (4,400 m)
DEATH VALLEY
Las Vegas
North Platte River
Laramie
Cheyenne
Longs Peak 14,256 ft. (4,344 m)
South Platte River
Grand Island
Platte River
Denver
Green River
Colorado River
Mt. Elbert 14,433 ft. (4,400 m)
Colorado Springs
Pikes Peak 14,110 ft. (4,300 m)
Pueblo
Arkansas River
COLORADO PLATEAU
Bakersfield
MOJAVE DESERT
Los Angeles
Long Beach
Anaheim
Santa Ana
Salton Sea
San Diego
Colorado River
Santa Fe
Albuquerque
Oklahon
Lawt
Phoenix
Mesa
Tucson
Rio Grande
Brazos River
LLANO ESTACADO
Las Cruces
El Paso
Fort
San Anton
Corpu
130°W
120°W
115°W
110°W
105°W
100°W
125°W
50°N
45°N
40°N
35°N
30°N
25°N
Tropic of Cancer
N
S
E
W
KAUAI
OAHU
Honolulu
MOLOKAI
MAUI
HAWAII
PACIFIC OCEAN
Hilo
HAWAII
22°N
155°W
160°W
19°N
0 100 Miles
0 100 Kilometers
RUSSIA
Bering Strait
ARCTIC OCEAN
70°N
180°
170°W
160°W
150°W
140°W
130°W
BROOKS RANGE
Arctic Circle
ALASKA
Fairbanks
ALASKA RANGE
Mt. McKinley 20,320 ft. (6,194 m)
Anchorage
CANADA
60°N
KENAI PENINSULA
Gulf of Alaska
Juneau
KODIAK I.
BERING SEA
170°E
PACIFIC OCEAN
ALEUTIAN ISLANDS
0 250 Miles
0 250 Kilometers

The United States: Physical-Political
Land Elevation
Feet
Meters
10,000
3,000
7,000
2,000
3,000
1,000
700
200
(Sea Level) 0
0 (Sea Level)
Below Sea Level
Below Sea Level
International boundaries
State boundaries
National capital
State capital
CANADA
ATLANTIC OCEAN
Gulf of Mexico
CUBA
Lake Superior
Lake Huron
Lake Ontario
Lake Erie
St. Lawrence River
Bay of Fundy
Cape Cod
LONG ISLAND
DELMARVA PENINSULA
Chesapeake Bay
Cape Hatteras
Cape Fear
Cape Canaveral
Florida Keys
Straits of Florida
Lake Okeechobee
Mississippi Delta
ADIRONDACK MTS.
ALLEGHENY MTS.
BLUE RIDGE MTS.
PIEDMONT
COASTAL PLAIN
CENTRAL PLAINS
Mt. Mitchell 6,684 ft. (2,030 m)
Mississippi River
Missouri River
Illinois River
Ohio River
Tennessee River
Alabama River
Hudson River
Susquehanna River
James River
MAINE
VT
NH
MA
CT
RI
NEW YORK
PENNSYLVANIA
NEW JERSEY
DELAWARE
MARYLAND
WASHINGTON, D.C.
WEST VIRGINIA
VIRGINIA
NORTH CAROLINA
SOUTH CAROLINA
GEORGIA
FLORIDA
ALABAMA
MISSISSIPPI
TENNESSEE
KENTUCKY
OHIO
INDIANA
ILLINOIS
WISCONSIN
MINNESOTA
IOWA
MISSOURI
ARKANSAS
LOUISIANA
Augusta
Lewiston
Portland
Burlington
Montpelier
Concord
Manchester
Boston
Worcester
Providence
Hartford
Bridgeport
New York City
Jersey City
Newark
Trenton
Albany
Syracuse
Rochester
Buffalo
Harrisburg
Philadelphia
Pittsburgh
Wilmington
Dover
Baltimore
Annapolis
Richmond
Newport News
Norfolk
Charleston
Huntington
Wheeling
Winston-Salem
Greensboro
Raleigh
Charlotte
Greenville
Columbia
Charleston
Savannah
Atlanta
Macon
Columbus
Jacksonville
Tallahassee
Tampa
St. Petersburg
Fort Lauderdale
Miami
Birmingham
Huntsville
Montgomery
Mobile
Jackson
Meridian
Biloxi
Nashville
Knoxville
Memphis
Louisville
Frankfort
Lexington
Cincinnati
Columbus
Cleveland
Akron
Toledo
Detroit
Lansing
Grand Rapids
Indianapolis
Fort Wayne
Gary
Chicago
Rockford
Peoria
Springfield
St. Louis
Jefferson City
Kansas City
Springfield
Milwaukee
Madison
Green Bay
Duluth
St. Paul
Minneapolis
Cedar Rapids
Davenport
Des Moines
Little Rock
Fort Smith
Pine Bluff
Shreveport
Baton Rouge
New Orleans
50°N
40°N
35°North Latitude
20°N
95°W
90°W
85°W
80°W
75°W
70°W
65°W
70° West Longitude
0
200 Miles
0
200 Kilometers
ATLANTIC OCEAN
PUERTO RICO (U.S.)
San Juan
0
100 Miles
0
100 Kilometers

The AMERICAN PEOPLE

CREATING A NATION AND A SOCIETY

Volume One   To 1877

fifth edition

General Editors

GARY B. NASH
University of California, Los Angeles

JULIE ROY JEFFREY
Goucher College

JOHN R. HOWE
University of Minnesota

PETER J. FREDERICK
Wabash College

ALLEN F. DAVIS
Temple University

ALLAN M. WINKLER
Miami University of Ohio

Longman

New York San Francisco Boston
London Toronto Sydney Tokyo Singapore Madrid
Mexico City Munich Paris Cape Town Hong Kong Montreal

Publisher:	Priscilla McGeehon
Senior Acquisitions Editor:	Jay O'Callaghan
Development Manager:	Lisa Pinto
Development Editor:	Karen Helfrich
Executive Marketing Manager:	Sue Westmoreland
Supplement Editor:	Jennifer Ackerman
Media Supplement Editor:	Mark Toews
Senior Production Manager:	Valerie Zaborski
Project Coordination, Text Design, and Electronic Page Makeup:	Elm Street Publishing Services, Inc.
Cover Designer/Manager:	Nancy Danahy
Cartographer:	Magellan Geographix, Inc.
Photo Researcher:	PhotoSearch, Inc.
Senior Manufacturing Buyer:	Dennis J. Para
Printer and Binder:	Quebecor-World-Taunton
Cover Printer:	The Lehigh Press, Inc.

Library of Congress Cataloging-in-Publication Data

The American people : creating a nation and a society / general editors, Gary B. Nash . . . [et al.]. —
5th ed.
p. cm.
Includes bibliographical references and index.
ISBN 0-321-07106-9 (volume one)
1. United States—History. I. Nash, Gary B.
E178.1 .A49355 2001
973—dc21 99-087019

Please visit our website at http://www.awl.com

Single Volume Edition ISBN 0-321-07104-2
Volume One ISBN 0-321-07106-9
Volume Two ISBN 0-321-07626-5

1 2 3 4 5 6 7 8 9 10—WCT—03 02 01 00

Brief CONTENTS

Detailed CONTENTS

Part Two
A REVOLUTIONARY PEOPLE, 1775–1828

Part Three
AN EXPANDING PEOPLE, 1820–1877

Specialized CONTENTS

RECOVERING *the* PAST

TECHNOLOGY CHANGES *the* AMERICAN PEOPLE

DIAGRAPHICS

MAPS

FIGURES

TABLES

PREFACE

The Yoruba people of West Africa have an old saying, "However far the stream flows, it never forgets its source." Why, we wonder, do such ancient societies as the Yoruba find history so important, whereas today's American students question its relevance? This book aims to end such skepticism about the usefulness of history.

As we begin the twenty-first century, in an ethnically and racially diverse society caught up in an interdependent global society, history is of central importance in preparing us to exercise our rights and responsibilities as free people. History cannot make good citizens, but without history we cannot understand the choices before us and think wisely about them. Lacking a collective memory of the past, we lapse into a kind of amnesia, unaware of the human condition and the long struggles of men and women everywhere to deal with the problems of their day and to create a better society. Unfurnished with historical knowledge, we deprive ourselves of knowing about the huge range of approaches people have taken to political, economic, and social life; to solving problems; and to conquering the obstacles in their way.

History has a deeper, even more fundamental importance: the cultivation of the private person whose self-knowledge and self-respect provide the foundation for a life of dignity and fulfillment. Historical memory is the key to self-identity, to seeing one's place in the long stream of time, in the story of humankind. "It is true that history cannot satisfy our appetite when we are hungry, nor keep us warm when the cold wind blows," says the New York Chinatown History Project. "But it is also true that if younger generations do not understand the hardships and triumphs of their elders, then we will be a people without a past. As such, we will be like water without a source, a tree without roots."

When we study our own history, that of the American people, we see a rich and extraordinarily complex human story. This country, whose written history began with a convergence of Native Americans, Europeans, and Africans, has always been a nation of diverse peoples—a magnificent mosaic of cultures, religions, and skin shades. This book explores how American society assumed its present shape and developed its present forms of government; how as a nation we have conducted our foreign affairs and managed our economy; how as individuals and in groups we have lived, worked, loved, married, raised families, voted, argued, protested, and struggled to fulfill our dreams and the noble ideals of the American experiment.

Several ways of making the past understandable distinguish this book from most textbooks written in the last twenty years. The coverage of public events like presidential elections, diplomatic treaties, and economic legislation is integrated with the private human stories that pervade them. Within a chronological framework, we have woven together our history as a nation, as a people, and as a society. When, for example, national political events are discussed, we analyze their impact on social and economic life at the state and local level. Wars are described not only as they unfolded on the battlefield and in the salons of diplomats but also on the home front, where they are history's greatest motor of social change. The interaction of ordinary Americans with extraordinary events runs as a theme throughout this book.

Above all, we have tried to show the "humanness" of our history as it is revealed in people's everyday lives. The authors have often used the words of ordinary Americans to capture the authentic human voices of those who participated in and responded to epic events such as war, slavery, industrialization, and reform movements.

GOALS AND THEMES OF THE BOOK

Our primary goal is to provide students with a rich, balanced, and thought-provoking treatment of the American past. By this, we mean a history that treats the lives and experiences of Americans of all national origins and cultural backgrounds, at all levels of society, and in all regions of the country. It also means a history that seeks connections between the many factors—political, economic, technological, social, religious, intellectual, and biological—that have molded and remolded American society over four centuries. And, finally, it means a history that encourages students to think about how we have all inherited a complex past filled with both notable achievements and thorny problems. The only history befitting a democratic nation is one that inspires students to initiate a frank and searching dialogue with their past.

To speak of a dialogue about the past presumes that history is always under revision and is always interpretive rather than simply an agreed-upon account of what happened in the past. Historians continually revise their understanding of what happened in the past. This is true in every country and has been true since Herodotus and Thucydides wrote the first histories of ancient Greece. Historians reinterpret history both because they find new evidence on old topics and also because new sensibilities inspire them to ask questions about the past that did not interest earlier historians. It is this continual questioning of the past that has led to historical research and writing on many topics previously ignored or scanted.

Through this book, we also hope to promote class discussions, which can be organized around seven questions that we see as basic to the American historical experience:

1. How has this nation been peopled, from the first inhabitants to the many groups that arrived in slavery or servitude during the colonial period down to the voluntary immigrants of today? How have these waves of newcomers contributed to the American cultural mosaic? To what extent have different immigrant groups preserved elements of their ethnic, racial, and religious heritages? How have the tensions between cultural assimilation and cultural preservation been played out, in the past and today?
2. To what extent have Americans developed a stable, democratic political system flexible enough to address the wholesale changes occurring in the last two centuries and to what degree has this political system been consistent with the principles of our nation's founding?
3. How have economic and technological changes affected daily life, work, family organization, leisure, sexual behavior, the division of wealth, and community relations in the United States?
4. How did the European settlement of the Americas alter the landscape? How have environmental factors shaped American society, and how have Americans changed in their attitudes and policies concerning the natural environment?
5. Has American religion served more to promote or retard social reform in our history? Whatever their varied sources, how have the recurring reform movements in our history dealt with economic, political, and social problems in attempting to square the ideals of American life with the reality?
6. What has been the role of our nation in the world? To what extent has the United States served as a model for other peoples, as an interventionist savior of other nations around the globe, and as an interfering expansionist in the affairs of other nations?
7. How have American beliefs and values changed over more than four hundred years of history, and how have they varied between different groups—women and men; Americans of many colors and cultures; people of different regions, religions, sexual orientations, ages, and classes?

In writing a history that revolves around these themes, we have tried to convey two dynamics that operate in all societies. First, we observe people continuously adjusting to new developments, such as industrialization and urbanization, over which they seemingly have little control; yet we realize that people are not paralyzed by history but are the fundamental creators of it. They retain the ability, individually and collectively, to shape the world in which they live and thus in considerable degree to control their own lives.

Second, we emphasize the connections that always exist among social, political, economic, and cultural events. Just as our individual lives are never neatly parceled into separate spheres of activity, the life of a society is made up of a complicated and often messy mixture of forces, events, and accidental occurrences. In this text, political and economic, technological and cultural factors are intertwined like strands in a rope.

STRUCTURE OF THE BOOK

Part Organization

The chapters of this book are grouped into six parts that relate to major periods in American history. The title of each part suggests a major theme that helps to characterize the period.

Chapter Structure

Every chapter begins with a *personal story* recalling the experience of an ordinary or lesser-known American. Chapter 1, for example, is introduced with the tragic account of Opechancanough, a Powhatan tribesman whose entire life of nearly ninety years was consumed by a struggle for his land and against hunger and alien values brought by Spanish and English newcomers. This brief anecdote introduces the overarching themes and major concepts of the chapter, in this case the meeting of three societies—Native American, European, and African—in the North American wilderness, each with different cultural values, life-styles, and aspirations. In addition, the personal story launches the chapter by engaging the student with a human account, suggesting that history was shaped by ordinary as well as extraordinary people. Following the personal story and easily identifiable by its visual separation from the anecdote and the body of the chapter, a *brief chapter overview* links the biographical sketch to the text. Students should read these crucial transition paragraphs carefully for two reasons: first, to identify the three or four major themes of the chapter; and second, to understand the organizational structure of the chapter.

We aim to facilitate the learning process for students in other ways as well. Every chapter ends with pedagogical features to reinforce and expand the presentation. A *Timeline* reviews the major events and developments covered in the chapter. A *Conclusion* briefly summarizes the main concepts and developments elaborated in the chapter and serves as a bridge to the following chapter. A list of *Recommended Readings* provides supplementary sources for further study or research; an annotated selection of novels and films is included. Finally, a special annotated section of *Suggested Web Sites* follows the print sources, offering students information on electronic sources relating to chapter themes. Each map, figure, and table has been chosen to relate clearly to the narrative.

SPECIAL FEATURES

A distinctive feature of this book is the two-page *Recovering the Past* presented in each chapter. These RTPs, as the authors affectionately call them, introduce students to the fascinating variety of evidence—ranging from household inventories, folk tales, and diaries to tombstones, advertising, and popular music—that historians have learned to employ in reconstructing the past. Each RTP gives basic information about the source and its use by historians and then raises questions for students to consider as they study the example reproduced for their inspection.

In addition to the "Recovering the Past" sections, we have provided other elements that will facilitate learning for students.

- *Technology Changes the American People* is a new feature that helps students understand the ways in which scientific and technological changes have come about and the impact they have had on the character of American life. The feature shows that the process of invention and change is not confined by national boundaries; technological and scientific innovations in the United States have often been connected with and dependent on developments elsewhere in the world. While many of the ideas and technological advances discussed came from outside the United States, each feature highlights the ways in which innovations have affected and often transformed the daily life of ordinary Americans. The flush toilet, the bicycle, plastic, and more recently the World Wide Web are some of the innovations discussed in the new feature. All have changed the way Americans lived in their homes, spent their free time, worked at their jobs, and did their shopping.
- In a series of *Diagraphics* we bring together, in visually engaging ways, economic data that portrays how political, social, and technological changes are closely intertwined at particular moments in American history. One diagraphic, for example, suggests the broad impact of new methods of steel production during the nineteenth century on the ways in which Americans worked, travelled, constructed their buildings, and waged war.
- The program of *color illustrations*—paintings, cartoons, photographs, maps, and figures—amplifies important themes while presenting visual evidence for student reflection and analysis. Captions on all photographs, maps, and figures are designed to help students understand and interpret the information presented. Summary tables, which we refer to as "talking boxes," recap points discussed in the narrative, pulling the material together in a format designed for ease of student study. Examples of such "talking boxes" include "Significant Factors Promoting Economic Growth, 1820–1860" in Chapter 10 and "Conflicting Aims During the Cold War" in Chapter 27.
- The comprehensive timeline developed for this edition includes the important political, diplomatic, social, economic, cultural, and technological events of the past 400 years. This six-page, full-color timeline, with illustrations as well as a listing of significant events, is designed to be hung on a wall and used throughout the semester. It is available free with every purchase of a new copy of the book.

THE FIFTH EDITION

The fifth edition of *The American People* has benefited from both the helpful comments of scholars and the experience of teachers and students who used previous editions of the book. While some of the modifications are small, others, like the revision and updating of Chapter 30, are substantial. Another major effort of this edition has been the coverage of science and technology. Aware of the importance of this aspect of our history, we have paid careful attention not only to the process and character of scientific and technological change but also to its social consequences. Much of the treatment of science and technology has been woven into the text, but the new feature, *Technology Changes the American People,* provides detailed analyses of significant developments that have had a substantial impact on

American life. This edition also features several substantially revised and some entirely new RTPs, a feature of the book that has been one of the favorites over the years. An expanded map program as well as carefully selected new visual materials provide students with additional ways of understanding chapter discussions. Revised bibliographies with new annotated sections on film and fiction and a list of helpful Web sites provide avenues for further explorations outside of the classroom. The foldout timeline, described above, is also a new feature of this edition.

Major Changes in the Fifth Edition

- *Chapter 3* revises the discussion of African slavery and the Atlantic slave trade and features a new section on slavery in the French and British colonies of North America
- *Chapter 4* includes the RTP on household inventories, moved from Chapter 5; *Technology Changes the American People* discusses the lightning rod
- *Chapter 5* has a new RTP that focuses on poetry and the work of African American writer, Phillis Wheatley; small pox inoculation is the subject of the new feature, *Technology Changes the American People*
- *Chapter 6* has been shortened and reorganized; the discussion of the American Revolution has been enriched by placing it within the larger context of the other Democratic revolutions of the period; a revised RTP on Patriotic Paintings (moved from Chapter 8) appears in this chapter with a discussion of artist John Trumbull and his painting *The Death of General Warren at the Battle of Bunker's Hill*
- *Chapter 7* blends material on revolutionary politics, once part of Chapter 6, into the analysis of the continuing ambiguities of politics in the post-war 1780s, thus making Chapters 6 and 7 more balanced in length; the analysis of the republican community makes clear the hardening of racial attitudes
- *Chapter 8* treats domestic events, like the American response to the French Revolution and the Alien and Sedition Acts, in the context of the broad theme of trans-Atlantic Democratic revolutions; highlights the contributions made by radical Irish, among them ardent Irish nationalists, and other immigrants to the Jeffersonian opposition during the hectic politics of the 1790s; a significantly revised RTP on European Travel Journals (moved from Chapter 12) now appears in this chapter, with a substantial journal selection from the French visitor, Moreau de Saint Mery; a *Technology Changes the American People* essay focuses on the development of wooden machinery and the role of this early technology in the first stirrings of the industrial revolution
- *Chapter 9* concludes the new theme of the age of Democratic revolutions in the discussion of the domestic fallout over the Haitian revolution and the emotional, ideological, and diplomatic connections between the United States and Latin American independence movements; the chapter now emphasizes the hardening of northern racial attitudes as northerners ended slavery in that region; an analysis of Eli Whitney and the Cotton Gin is the focus of the new section, *Technology Changes the American People*
- *Chapter 11* includes more material on the importance of outwork during the early industrial period
- *Chapter 12* has a new RTP on slave narratives that not only provides an introduction to slave narratives as an historical source but also places them in the context of the abolitionist campaign to end slavery; the development of a practical sewing machine and its impact are the basis for the section *Technology Changes the American People*
- *Chapter 14* has changes, especially in terminology, that reflect the contributions of the New Western History
- *Chapter 18* includes an expanded analysis of the technological advances of the industrial age and provides insight into the factors that helped to spark change; the flush toilet is the focus of *Technology Changes the American People*
- *Chapter 19* looks at the bicycle in the section *Technology Changes the American People*
- *Chapter 21* shows the link between scientific theories and racism
- *Chapter 22* features a new discussion of the great Flu Epidemic of 1918 and has included some new material on scientific and technical research during the war
- *Chapter 23* includes new material on the technology of flood control to accompany the new section on the Great Mississippi flood of 1927 and enriched sections on household technology and the impact of the automobile; the development and impact of the wireless radio is the subject of *Technology Changes the American People*
- *Chapter 24* points out the limitations of the New Deal for African Americans
- *Chapter 25* has a new RTP on historical monuments and their relationship to history and

memory and discusses the development of plastics in *Technology Changes the American People*

- *Chapter 26* has increased coverage of computers in connection with the edition's goal of highlighting technology; features new material on the experiences of Native American, Latino, and African American communities in the postwar United States; the chapter also focuses on the development and significance of air conditioning in the new feature, *Technology Changes the American People*
- *Chapter 27* refocuses the analysis of the Cold War as a result of new materials now available to scholars; provides additional material on Eisenhower and on anti-Communism at home, including the ways in which an anti-homosexual effort played a part in the anti-Communist crusade
- *Chapter 29* has stronger coverage of the Civil Rights Movement and additional material on Native American rights; as part of the effort to highlight the importance of science and technology, there is an expanded discussion of birth control and the development of the pill and more material on nuclear regulation
- *Chapter 30* has been significantly revised and updated; it opens with a new anecdote, revealing the experience of a working-class family in the 1990s; the section on the economy discusses the recent boom period and notes the significance of the merger movement and the soaring stock market; sections on foreign policy (including Kosovo) and the Clinton presidency (including impeachment efforts) have been updated; new materials have been added on declining voter turnouts, the end of Affirmative Action, the environmental movement, and immigration laws; in keeping with the emphasis on science and technology this chapter features the World Wide Web as the subject for *Technology Changes the American People*

Our aim has been to write a balanced and vivid history of the development of the American nation and its society. We have also tried to provide the support materials necessary to make teaching and learning enjoyable and rewarding. The reader will be the judge of our success. The authors welcome your comments.

Gary B. Nash
Julie Roy Jeffrey

NOTE *to the* STUDENT

FEATURES OF THIS BOOK

The authors have included a number of tools to help you in your study of American history.

- Each chapter begins with a *personal story* recalling the experience of an ordinary or lesser-known American. A *brief chapter overview* links this opening story to the major themes of the chapter.
- An *outline* provides an overview of the chapter topics and organization.
- *Summary* tables ("talking boxes") recap points discussed in the chapter for easy reference.
- Special icons in every chapter mark general and specific topics also addressed on *The History Place Web Site* that you have access to with the purchase of this text: http://www.ushistoryplace.com. This teaching and learning Web-based resource for students and instructors of American history provides interactive maps; timelines; a rich collection of primary sources, secondary sources, and links to related American history sites; an Op-Ed forum to spark classroom discussion; and Updated News presented with historical perspective.
- *Recovering the Past* essays in each chapter examine different kinds of historical evidence ranging from household inventories, folktales, and diaries to tombstones, advertising, and popular music.
- Eleven *Technology Changes the American People* essays focus on the development of science and new technologies (such as the cotton gin and the flush toilet) and their impact on peoples' everyday lives.
- A carefully selected program of *illustrations*—paintings, cartoons, photographs, maps, and figures—amplifies important themes while presenting visual evidence for your reflection and analysis.
- A *timeline* reviews the major events and developments covered in the chapter.
- Also included with this text is a full-color *timeline poster,* designed to be hung on a wall and used throughout the semester. This comprehensive timeline includes numerous important political, diplomatic, social, economic, cultural, and technological events of the past 400 years of American history.
- A *Conclusion* briefly summarizes the main concepts and developments discussed in the chapter.
- *Recommended Readings* are included at the end of every chapter, offering you research suggestions for scholarly resources, as well as a brief list of fiction and film (feature films and documentaries) related to chapter topics and themes.
- At the end of each chapter there is also an annotated list of *Suggested Web Sites* that relate to chapter topics and themes. Though these Web addresses were checked for accuracy before publication of this text, the changing nature of Web sites suggests that at least a few might be outdated links by the time you investigate them. These and additional Web suggestions will be updated regularly on the text's Web site (*http://www.awl.com/nash*) and The History Place site.

In addition to the specific Web sites recommended for the chapters, you may also want to visit some of the following *major history Web sites* that have content that relates to all periods of American history.

Smithsonian Institution—National Museum of American History
http://americanhistory.si.edu/

Library of Congress Web Site
http://www.loc.gov/

Library of Congress American Memory Project
http://memory.loc.gov/ammem/amhome.html

National Archives and Records Administration Home Page
http://www.nara.gov

"The Digital Classroom"
http://www.nara.gov/education/teaching/teaching.html

"The Exhibit Hall"
http://www.nara.gov/exhall/

Documents for the Study of American History (AMDOCS)
http://www.ukans.edu/carrie/docs/amdocs_index.html

United States Census Bureau
http://www.census.gov/

The African-American Mosaic—A Library of Congress Resource Guide
http://lcweb.loc.gov/exhibits/african/intro.html

National Women's History Project
http://www.nwhp.org

National Gallery of Art
http://www.nga.gov/home.htm

Historical Maps: The Perry Castaneda Library Map Collection
http://www.lib.utexas.edu/Libs/PCL/Map_collection/historical/history_main.html

University of California—Berkeley Library Digital Map Collection
http://www.lib.berkeley.edu/EART/digital/tour.html

SUPPLEMENTS

FOR QUALIFIED COLLEGE ADOPTERS

Companion Web Site, Nash Online, http://www.awl.com/nash. This online course companion provides a wealth of resources for both students and instructors using *The American People,* Fifth Edition. Instructors will find the instructor's manual, teaching links, downloadable figures and photos, animated maps, thematic timelines, and narrated photo essays.

The History Place Premium Web Site, http://www.ushistoryplace.com. Available at no additional cost for students who purchase a new copy of the textbook, the site is a continually updated American history Web site of extraordinary breadth and depth, which features unmatched interactive maps, timelines, and activities; hundreds of source documents, images, and audio clips; a powerful TestFlight student self-assessment tool; and much more.

Instructor's Manual. Neal Brooks and Ingrid Sabio, Essex Community College. This guide was written based on ideas generated in "active learning" workshops and is tied closely to the text. In addition to suggestions on how to generate lively class discussion and involve students in active learning, this supplement also offers a file of exam questions and lists of resources, including films, slides, photo collections, records and audiocassettes.

Comprehensive American History Transparency Set. This vast collection of American history map transparencies includes over two hundred map transparencies ranging from the first Native Americans to the end of the Cold War, covering wars, social trends, elections, immigration and demographics. Also included are a reproducible set of student map exercises, teaching tips, and correlation charts.

American Impressions: A CD-ROM for U.S. History. This unique CD-ROM for the U.S. History course is organized in a topical and thematic framework which allows in-depth coverage with a media-centered focus. Hundreds of photos, maps, works of art, graphics, and historical film clips are organized into narrated vignettes and interactive activities to create a tool for both professors and students. Topics include "The Encounter Period," "Revolution to Republic," "A Century of Labor and Reform," and "The Struggle for Equality." A guide for instructors provides teaching tips and suggestions for using advanced media in the classroom. The CD-ROM is available in both Macintosh and Windows formats.

Visual Archives of American History, 2/e. This two-sided video laserdisc explores history from the meeting of three cultures to the present. It is an encyclopedic chronology of U.S. history offering hundreds of photographs and illustrations, a variety of source and reference maps—several of which are animated—plus fifty minutes of video. For ease in planning lectures, a manual listing barcodes for scanning and frame numbers for all the material is available.

Discovering American History Through Maps and Views. Created by Gerald Danzer, University of Illinois at Chicago, the recipient of the AHA's 1990 James Harvey Robinson Prize for his work in the development of map transparencies—this set of 140 four-color acetates is a unique instructional tool. It contains an introduction on teaching history through maps and a detailed commentary on each transparency. The collection includes cartographic and pictorial maps, views and photos, urban plans, building diagrams, and works of art.

A Guide to Teaching American History Through Film. Written by Randy Roberts, Purdue University, this guide provides instructors with a creative and practical tool for stimulating classroom discussion. The sections include "American Films: A Historian's Perspective," a list of films, practical suggestions and bibliography. The film listing is presented in narrative form, developing connections between each film and the topics being discussed.

Video Lecture Launchers. Prepared by Mark Newman, University of Illinois at Chicago, these video lecture launchers (each two to five minutes in duration) cover key issues in American history from 1877 to the present. The launchers are accompanied by an *Instructor's Manual.*

Transparencies. A set of 40 map transparencies drawn from the text.

"This Is America" *Immigration Video.* Produced by the American Museum of Immigration, this video tells the story of American immigrants, relating their personal stories and accomplishments. By showing how the richness of our culture is due to the contributions of millions of immigrant Americans, the videos make the point that America's strength lies in the ethnically and culturally diverse backgrounds of its citizens.

Telecourse Package. America in Perspective: U.S. History Since 1877—produced and distributed by the LeCroy Center for Educational Telecommunications, Dallas Country Community College District—are designed as a component of a comprehensive learning package consisting of the 26-lesson telecourse program, *The American People,* and a telecourse study guide. *Telecourse Study Guide for America in Perspective* contains numerous study aids, self-tests, enrichment ideas, and suggested readings, all keyed to specific pages in *The American People.* The study guide can be ordered through your Longman representative. In addition, *The American Adventure Telecourse Study Guide* has been updated to include a new pagination key to better correlate to this new edition of *The American People.*

Test Bank. This test bank, prepared by Jeanne Whitney, Salisbury State University, contains more than 3,500 objective, conceptual, and essay questions. All questions are keyed to specific pages in the text.

Test Gen Computerized Testing System. This flexible, easy-to-master computer test bank includes all the test items in the printed test bank. The software allows you to edit existing questions and add your own items. Tests can be printed in several different formats and can include figures such as graphs and tables.

FOR STUDENTS

Companion Web Site, Nash Online, http://www.awl.com/nash. This online course companion provides a wealth of resources for both students and instructors using *The American People,* Fifth Edition. Students will find chapter summaries, test questions, interactive Web exercises, animated maps, primary sources, and thematic timelines.

The History Place Premium Web Site, http://www.ushistoryplace.com. Available at no additional cost for students who purchase a new copy of the textbook, the site is a continually updated American history Web site of extraordinary breadth and depth, which features unmatched interactive maps, timelines, and activities; hundreds of source documents, images, and audio clips; a powerful TestFlight student self-assessment tool; and much more.

Interactive Edition CD-ROM. This unique CD-ROM offers students a complete multimedia learning experience. It contains the full text of the book, plus photos, figures, maps, video, web links, practice tests, and primary sources. The easy-to-use navigation makes it simple to search the text, take notes, and highlight key sections. *Free* when packaged with the text.

Study Guide. This two-volume study guide, created by Neal Brooks and Ingrid Sabio, Essex Community College, includes chapter outlines, significant themes and highlights, a glossary, learning enrichment ideas, sample test questions, exercises for identification and interpretation, and geography exercises based on maps in the text.

Study Wizard Computerized Tutorial. Prepared by J. Patrick McCarthy, University of Georgia, this interactive program features chapter outlines and multiple-choice, true-false, and short-answer questions. It also contains a glossary and gives users immediate test scores and answer explanations.

Longman American History Atlas. This full color historical atlas includes more than 100 maps, all designed especially for this volume. This valuable reference tool is available shrinkwrapped with *The American People* at low cost.

America Through the Eyes of Its People: Primary Sources in American History, Second Edition. This one-volume collection of primary documents portrays the rich and varied tapestry of American life. It contains documents by women, Native Americans, African Americans, Hispanics, and others who helped to shape the course of U.S. history along with student study questions and contextual headnotes.

Sources of the African American Past. Edited by Roy Finkenbine, University of Detroit at Mercy, this collection of primary sources covers key themes in the African-American experience from the West African background to the present. Balanced between political and social history, it offers a vivid snapshot of the lives of African Americans in different historical periods, and includes documents representing women and different regions of the United States. Available at a minimum cost when bundled with the text.

Women and the National Experience. Edited by Ellen Skinner, Pace University, this primary source reader contains both classic and unusual documents describing the history of women in the United States. The documents provide dramatic evidence that outspoken women attained a public voice and participated in the development of national events and policies long before they could vote. Chronologically organized and balanced between social and political history, this reader offers a striking picture of the lives of women across American history. Available at a minimum cost when bundled with the text.

Reading the American West. Edited by Mitchel Roth, Sam Houston State University, this primary source reader uses letters, diary excerpts, speeches, interviews, and newspaper articles to let students experience how historians research and how history is written. Every document is accompanied by a contextual headnote and study questions. The book is divided into chapters with extensive introductions. Available at a minimum cost when bundled with the text.

Retracing the Past, Third Edition. This two-volume set of readers is edited by Ronald Schultz, University of Wyoming, and Gary B. Nash. These secondary source readings cover economic, political, and social history with special emphasis on women, racial and ethnic groups, and working-class people.

Learning to Think Critically: Films and Myths About American History. Randy Roberts and Robert May, Purdue University, use well-known films such as *Gone with the Wind* and *Casablanca* to explore some common myths about America and its past. This short handbook subjects some popular beliefs to historical scrutiny in order to help students develop a method of inquiry for approaching the subject of history in general.

Mapping America: A Guide to Historical Geography. This workbook by Ken Weatherbie, Del Mar College, was revised specifically for this new edition. Each volume contains 18 exercises corresponding to the map program in the text; each exercise concludes with interpretive questions about the role of geography in American history. This free item is designed to be packaged with *The American People.*

Mapping American History: Student Activities. Written by Gerald Danzer, University of Illinois at Chicago, this free map workbook for students features exercises designed to teach students to interpret and analyze cartographic materials as historical documents. This free item is designed to be packaged with *The American People.*

ACKNOWLEDGMENTS

The authors wish to thank the following reviewers who gave generously of their time and expertise and whose thoughtful and constructive work have contributed greatly to this edition:

Cara Anzilotti, *Loyola Marymount University*
Virginia H. Bellows, *Tulsa Community College*
S. Charles Bolton, *University of Arkansas at Little Rock*
William Furdell, *University of Great Falls*
David J. Grettler, *Northern State University*
David Gutzke, *Southwest Missouri State University*
Craig Hendricks, *Long Beach City College*
Anne Klejment, *University of St. Thomas*
Larry Lowther, *Central Washington University*
Robert F. Marcom, *San Antonio College*
Thomas M. McLuen, *Spokane Falls Community College*
Cassandra L. Newby-Alexander, *Norfolk State University*
Sean O'Neill, *Grand Valley State University*
Gene B. Preuss, *Texas Tech University*
Dale J. Schmitt, *East Tennessee State University*
John A. Trickel, *Richland College*
Michael P. White, *Temple College*

Over the years, as previous editions of this text were being developed, many of our colleagues read and criticized the various drafts of the manuscript. For their thoughtful evaluations and constructive suggestions, the authors wish to express their gratitude to the following reviewers:

Richard H. Abbott, *Eastern Michigan University*
John Alexander, *University of Cincinnati*
Kenneth G. Alfers, *Mountain View College*
Terry Alford, *North Virginia Community College*
Gregg Andrews, *Southwest Texas State University*
Robert Asher, *University of Connecticut, Storrs*
Harry Baker, *University of Arkansas at Little Rock*
Michael Batinski, *Southern Illinois University*
Gary Bell, *Sam Houston State University*
Virginia Bellows, *Tulsa Community College*
Spencer Bennett, *Siena Heights College*
Jackie R. Booker, *Western Connecticut State University*
James Bradford, *Texas A&M University*
Neal Brooks, *Essex Community College*
Jeffrey P. Brown, *New Mexico State University*
Dickson D. Bruce, Jr., *University of California, Irvine*
David Brundage, *University of California, Santa Cruz*
Colin Calloway, *Dartmouth University*
D'Ann Campbell, *Indiana University*
Jane Censer, *George Mason University*
Vincent A. Clark, *Johnson County Community College*
Neil Clough, *North Seattle Community College*
Matthew Ware Coulter, *Collin County Community College*
David Culbert, *Louisiana State University*
Mark T. Dalhouse, *Northeast Missouri State University*
Bruce Dierenfield, *Canisius College*
John Dittmer, *DePauw University*
Gordon Dodds, *Portland State University*
Richard Donley, *Eastern Washington University*
Dennis B. Downey, *Millersville University*
Robert Downtain, *Tarrant County Community College*
Robert Farrar, *Spokane Falls Community College*
Bernard Friedman, *Indiana University–Purdue University at Indianapolis*
Bruce Glasrud, *California State University, Hayward*
Brian Gordon, *St. Louis Community College*
Richard Griswold del Castillo, *San Diego State University*
Carol Gruber, *William Paterson College*
Colonel Williams L. Harris, *The Citadel Military College*
Robert Haws, *University of Mississippi*
Jerrold Hirsch, *Northeast Missouri State University*
Frederick Hoxie, *University of Illinois*
John S. Hughes, *University of Texas*
Link Hullar, *Kingwood College*
Donald M. Jacobs, *Northeastern University*
Delores Janiewski, *University of Idaho*
David Johnson, *Portland State University*
Richard Kern, *University of Findlay*

Robert J. Kolesar, *John Carroll University*
Monte Lewis, *Cisco Junior College*
William Link, *University of North Carolina, Greensboro*
Patricia M. Lisella, *Iona College*
Paul K. Longmore, *San Francisco State University*
Rita Loos, *Framingham State College*
Ronald Lora, *University of Toledo*
George M. Lubick, *Northern Arizona University*
Suzanne Marshall, *Jacksonville State University*
John C. Massman, *St. Cloud State University*
Vern Mattson, *University of Nevada at Las Vegas*
Art McCoole, *Cuyamaca College*
John McCormick, *Delaware County Community College*
Sylvia McGrath, *Stephen F. Austin University*
James E. McMillan, *Denison University*
Otis L. Miller, *Belleville Area College*
Walter Miszczenko, *Boise State University*
Norma Mitchell, *Troy State University*
Gerald F. Moran, *University of Michigan, Dearborn*
William G. Morris, *Midland College*
Marian Morton, *John Carroll University*
Roger Nichols, *University of Arizona*
Paul Palmer, *Texas A&I University*
Al Parker, *Riverside City College*
Judith Parsons, *Sul Ross State University*
Carla Pestana, *Ohio State University*
Neva Peters, *Tarrant County Community College*
James Prickett, *Santa Monica College*
Noel Pugash, *University of New Mexico*
Juan Gomez-Quiñones, *University of California, Los Angeles*
George Rable, *Anderson College*
Joseph P. Reidy, *Howard University*
Leonard Riforgiato, *Pennsylvania State University*
Randy Roberts, *Purdue University*
Mary Robertson, *Armstrong State University*
David Robson, *John Carroll University*
Jud Sage, *Northern Virginia Community College*
Phil Schaeffer, *Olympic College*
Sylvia Sebesta, *San Antonio College*
Herbert Shapiro, *University of Cincinnati*
David R. Shibley, *Santa Monica College*
Ellen Shockro, *Pasadena City College*
Nancy Shoemaker, *University of Connecticut*
Bradley Skelcher, *Delaware State University*
Kathryn Kish Sklar, *State University of New York at Binghampton*
James Smith, *Virginia State University*
John Snetsinger, *California Polytechnic State University, San Luis Obispo*
Jo Snider, *Southwest Texas State University*
Stephen Strausberg, *University of Arkansas*
Katherine Scott Sturdevant, *Pikes Peak Community College*
Nan M. Sumner-Mack, *Hawaii Community College*
Cynthia Taylor, *Santa Rosa Junior College*
Tom Tefft, *Citrus College*
John A. Trickel, *Richland College*
Donna Van Raaphorst, *Cuyahoga Community College*
Morris Vogel, *Temple University*
Michael Wade, *Appalachian State University*
Jackie Walker, *James Madison University*
Paul B. Weinstein, *University of Akron—Wayne College*
Joan Welker, *Prince George's Community College*
Kenneth H. Williams, *Alcorn State University*
Mitch Yamasaki, *Chaminade University*
Charles Zappia, *San Diego Mesa College*

ABOUT *the* AUTHORS

GARY B. NASH received his Ph.D. from Princeton University. He is currently Director of the National Center for History in the Schools at the University of California, Los Angeles, where he teaches colonial and revolutionary American history. Among the books Nash has authored are *Quakers and Politics: Pennsylvania, 1681–1726* (1968); *Red, White, and Black: The Peoples of Early America* (1974, 1982, 1992, 2000); *The Urban Crucible: Social Change, Political Consciousness, and the Origins of the American Revolution* (1979); and *Forging Freedom: The Black Urban Experience in Philadelphia, 1720–1840* (1988). A former president of the Organization of American Historians, his scholarship is especially concerned with the role of common people in the making of history. He wrote Part I and served as a general editor of this book.

JULIE ROY JEFFREY earned her Ph.D. in history from Rice University. Since then she has taught at Goucher College. Honored as an outstanding teacher, Jeffrey has been involved in faculty development activities and curriculum evaluation. She was Fulbright Chair in American Studies at the University of Southern Denmark, 1999–2000. Jeffrey's major publications include *Education for Children of the Poor* (1978); *Frontier Women: The Trans-Mississippi West, 1840–1880* (1979, 1997); *Converting the West: A Biography of Narcissa Whitman* (1991); and *The Great Silent Army of Abolitionism: Ordinary Women in the Antislavery Movement* (1998). She is the author of many articles on the lives and perceptions of nineteenth-century women. Her research continues to focus on abolitionism as well as on history and film. She wrote Parts III and IV in collaboration with Peter Frederick and acted as a general editor of this book.

JOHN R. HOWE received his Ph.D. from Yale University. At the University of Minnesota, his teaching interests include early American politics and relations between Native Americans and whites. His major publications include *The Changing Political Thought of John Adams* (1966) and *From the Revolution Through the Age of Jackson* (1973). He is presently completing a book on conceptions of language in American Revolutionary political writing, and has launched a project dealing with the social politics of verbal discourse in revolutionary America. Howe wrote Part II of this book.

PETER J. FREDERICK received his Ph.D. in history from the University of California, Berkeley. His career has focused on innovative student-centered teaching in American history at California State University, Hayward, and since 1970 at Wabash College (1992–1994 at Carleton College). Recognized nationally as a distinguished teacher and for numerous articles and workshops for faculty on learning and teaching, Frederick has also written several articles on biography and autobiography, and a book, *Knights of the Golden Rule: The Intellectual as Christian Social Reformer in the 1890s*. He coordinated and edited all the "Recovering the Past" sections and coauthored Parts III and IV.

ALLEN F. DAVIS earned his Ph.D. from the University of Wisconsin. A former president of the American Studies Association, he is a professor of history at Temple University and editor of *Conflict and Consensus in American History* (9th edition, 1997). He is the author of *Spearheads for Reform: The Social Settlements and the Progressive Movement* (1967) and *American Heroine: The Life and Legend of Jane Addams* (1973). He is coauthor of *Still Philadelphia* (1983), *Philadelphia Stories* (1987), and *One Hundred Years at Hull-House* (1990). He is currently working on a book on masculine culture in America. Davis wrote Part V of this book.

ALLAN M. WINKLER received his Ph.D. from Yale University. He has taught at Yale and the University of Oregon, and is now Distinguished Professor of History at Miami University of Ohio. An award-winning teacher, he has also published extensively about the recent past. His books include *The Politics of Propaganda: The Office of War Information, 1942–1945* (1978); *Modern America: The United States from the Second World War to the Present* (1985); *Home Front U.S.A.: America During World War II* (1986, 2000); and *Life Under a Cloud: American Anxiety About the Atom* (1993, 1999.). His research centers on the connections between public policy and popular mood in modern American history. Winkler wrote Part VI of this book.

The
AMERICAN PEOPLE

1

THREE WORLDS MEET

CHAPTER OUTLINE

In the late 1550s, a few years after Catholic King Philip II and Protestant Queen Elizabeth assumed the thrones in Spain and England, respectively, Opechancanough was born in Tsenacommacah. In the Algonquian language, the word *tsenacommacah* meant "densely inhabited land." Later, English colonizers would rename this place Virginia after their monarch, the virgin queen Elizabeth. Before he died in the 1640s, in the ninth decade of his life, Opechancanough had seen light-skinned, swarthy, and black-skinned newcomers from a half-dozen European nations and African kingdoms swarm into his land. Like thousands of other Native Americans, he was witnessing the early moments of European expansion across the Atlantic Ocean.

Opechancanough was only an infant when Europeans first reached the Chesapeake Bay region. A small party of Spanish had explored the area in 1561, but they found neither gold nor silver nor anything else of value. Upon departing, they took with them the brother of one of the local chieftains, who was a member of Opechancanough's clan. They left behind something of unparalleled importance in the history of contact between the peoples of Europe and the Americas: a viral infection that spread like wildfire through a population that had no immunity against it. Many members of Opechancanough's tribe died, although their casualties were light compared with those of other tribes that caught the deadly European diseases.

In 1570, when Opechancanough was young, the Spanish returned and established a Jesuit mission near the York River. Violence occurred, and before the Spanish abandoned the Chesapeake in 1572, they put to death a number of captured Indians, including a chief who was Opechancanough's relative. The Native Americans learned that Europeans, even when they came bearing the crosses of their religion, were a volatile and dangerous people.

Opechancanough was in his forties when three ships of fair-skinned settlers disembarked in 1607 to begin the first permanent English settlement in the New World. For several months, he watched his half brother Powhatan, high chief of several dozen loosely confederated tribes in the region, parry and fence with the newcomers. Then Powhatan sent him to capture the English leader John Smith and escort him to the Indians' main village. Smith was put through a mock execution but then released. He later got the best of Opechancanough, threatening him with a pistol, humiliating him in front of his warriors, and assaulting one of his sons, whom Smith "spurned like a dog."

Opechancanough nursed his wounds for years while Powhatan grew old and the English settlements slowly spread in the Chesapeake region. Then, in 1617, he assumed leadership of the Powhatan Confederacy. Two years later, a Dutch trader sold 20 Africans to the settlers after docking at Jamestown. Three years after that, Opechancanough led a determined assault on the English plantations that lay along the rivers and streams emptying into the bay. The Indians killed nearly one-third of the intruders. But they paid dearly in the retaliatory raids that the colonists mounted in succeeding years.

As he watched the land-hungry settlers swarm in during the next two decades, Opechancanough's patience failed him. Finally, in 1644, now in his eighties, he galvanized a new generation of warriors and led a final desperate assault on the English. It was a suicidal attempt, but the "great general" of the Powhatan Confederacy, faithful to the tradition of his people, counseled death over enslavement and humiliation. Though the warriors inflicted heavy casualties, they could not overwhelm the colonizers, who vastly outnumbered them. For two years, Opechancanough was kept prisoner by the Virginians. Nearly blind and "so decrepit that he was not able to walk alone," he was fatally shot in the back by an English guard in 1646.

Over a long lifetime, Opechancanough painfully experienced the meeting of people from three continents. His land was one of many that would be penetrated by Europeans over the next three centuries, as Christian civilization girdled the globe. On the Chesapeake Bay, this clash of cultures formed the opening chapter of what we know as American history. That history, in turn, was one scene in a much broader drama of European colonization and exploitation of many indigenous cultures thousands of miles from the Old World. The nature of this violent intermingling of Europeans, Africans, and Native Americans is an essential part of early American history. But to understand how the destinies of red, white, and black people became intertwined in Opechancanough's land, we must look at the precontact history and cultural foundations of life in the homelands of each of them.

The French, under Jean Ribault, discovering the River of May in Florida on May 1, 1564. Engraving by Theodore De Bry, 1591, after a painting by Jacques Le Moyne, who accompanied the expedition in 1564. *(The Granger Collection, New York)*

THE PEOPLE OF AMERICA BEFORE COLUMBUS

Thousands of years before the European voyages of discovery, the history of humankind in North America began. Nomadic bands from Siberia, hunting big game animals such as bison, caribou, and reindeer, began to migrate across a land bridge connecting northeastern Asia with Alaska. Geologists believe that this land bridge, perhaps 600 miles wide, existed most recently between 25,000 and 14,000 years ago, when massive glaciers locked up much of the earth's moisture and left part of the Bering Sea floor exposed. Ice-free passage through Canada was possible only briefly at the beginning and end of this period, however. At other times, melting glaciers flooded the land bridge and blocked foot traffic to Alaska. Scholars are divided on the exact timing, but the main migration apparently occurred between 11,000 and 14,000 years ago, although possibly much earlier. Some new archaeological finds suggest multiple migrations, both by sea and land, from several regions of Asia and even from Europe.

Hunters and Farmers

For thousands of years, the early hunters trekked southward and eastward, following vegetation and game. In time, they reached the tip of South America and the eastern edge of North America. Thus did people from the "Old World" discover the "New World" thousands of years before Columbus.

Archaeologists have excavated ancient sites of early life in the Americas, unearthing tools, ornaments, and skeletal remains that can be scientifically dated. In this way, they have tentatively reconstructed the dispersion of these first Americans over an immense land mass. Although much remains unknown, archaeological evidence suggests that as centuries passed and population increased, the earliest inhabitants evolved into separate cultures, adjusting to various environments in distinct ways. Europeans who rediscovered the New World thousands of years later would lump together the myriad societies they found. But by the 1500s, the "Indians" of the Americas were enormously diverse in the size and complexity of their societies, the languages they spoke, and their forms of social organization.

Archaeologists and anthropologists have charted several phases of "Native American" history. The Beringian period of initial migration ended about 14,000 years ago. During the Paleo-Indian era, 14,000 to 10,000 years ago, big-game hunters flaked hard stones into spear points and chose "kill sites" where they slew herds of Pleistocene mammals. This more reliable food source allowed population growth, and

Migration Routes from Asia to the Americas

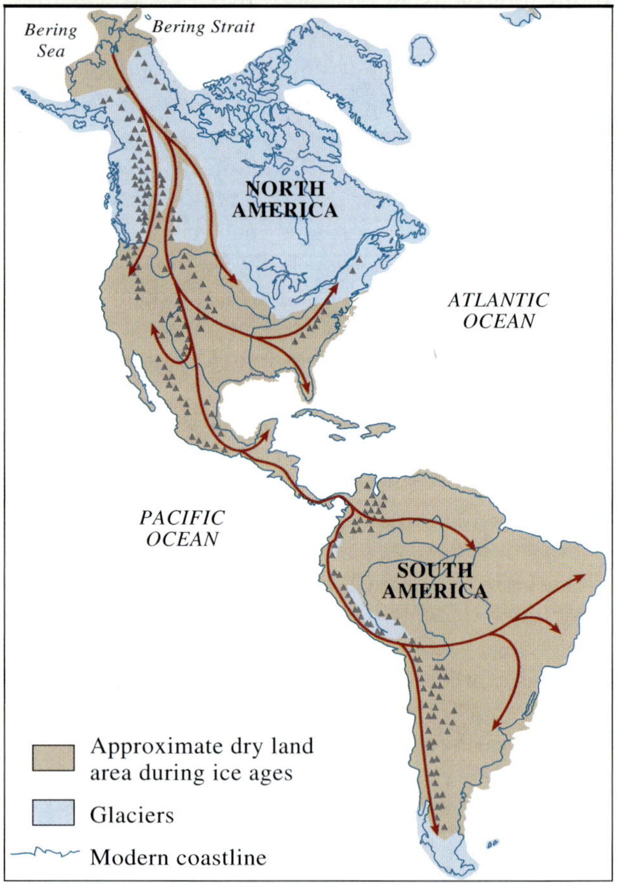

The red arrows indicate the general flow of migrating societies over thousands of years before Europeans reached the Americas. Based on fragile archaeological evidence, these migratory patterns are necessarily tentative, and new discoveries support early Stone Age arrivals by boat.

nomadism began to give way to settled habitations or local migration within limited territories.

Then during the Archaic era, from about 10,000 to 2,500 years ago, great geological changes brought further adaptations to the land. As the massive Ice Age glaciers slowly retreated, a warming trend turned vast grassland areas from Utah to the highlands of Central America into desert. The Pleistocene mammals were weakened by more arid conditions, but human populations ably adapted. They learned to exploit new sources of food, especially plants. In time, a second technological breakthrough, the "agricultural revolution," occurred.

We have sometimes imagined that these early people lived in a primordial paradise in harmony with their surroundings. But recent archaeological evidence points to examples of environmental devastation that severely damaged the biodiversity of the Americas. The first wave of intruders found a wilderness teeming with so-called megafauna: saber-toothed tigers, woolly mammoths, gigantic ground sloths, huge bison, and monstrous bears. But by about 10,000 years ago, these animals were almost extinct. Both overhunting and a massive shift of climate that deprived the huge beasts of their grazing environment were to blame.

The depletion of the megafauna left the hemisphere with a much restricted catalogue of animals. Left behind were large animals such as elk, buffalo, bear, and moose. But the extinction of the huge beasts forced people to prey on new sources of food such as turkeys, ducks, and guinea pigs. Their reduced food supply may have gradually reduced their population.

Over many centuries in the Americas, salinization and deforestation put the environment under additional stress. For example, in what is today central Arizona, the Hohokam civilization collapsed hundreds of years ago, much like that in ancient Mesopotamia, when the irrigation system became too salty to support agriculture. At New Mexico's Chaco Canyon, the fast-growing Anasazi denuded a magnificently forested region in their search for firewood and building materials. This, in turn, led to the erosion of rich soil that impoverished the region for the Anasazi.

When Native Americans learned to domesticate plant life, they began the long process of transforming their relationship to the physical world. Learning how to plant, cultivate, and harvest allowed them certain control over once-ungovernable natural forces. Anthropologists believe that this process began independently in widely separated parts of the world—Africa, Asia, Europe, and the Americas—about 9,000 to 7,000 years ago. Though agriculture developed very slowly, it eventually brought dramatic changes in human societies everywhere.

Pre-Columbian Societies of the Americas

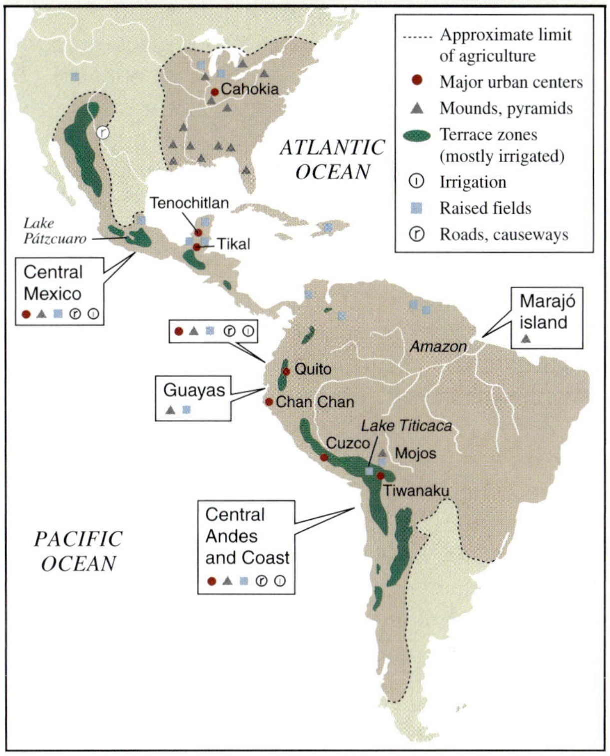

Once described as nomadic hunter-gatherers, indigenous peoples in the Americas were agriculturalists and urban dwellers in many areas and populated the land as densely as did people in many other parts of the world.

Over the millennia, humans progressed from doorside planting of a few wild seeds to systematic clearing and planting of bean and maize fields. As

The ruins of Pueblo Bonita in Chaco Canyon, New Mexico, mark the center of Anasazi culture in the twelfth century A.D. This San Juan River basin town may have contained 1,000 people living in apartment-like structures larger than any built in North America until the late nineteenth century. (© *David Muench*)

the production of domesticated plant food ended dependence on gathering wild plants and pursuing game, settled village life began to replace nomadic existence. Increases in food supply brought about by agriculture triggered other major changes. As more ample food fueled population growth, large groups split off to form separate societies. Greater social and political complexity developed because not everyone was needed as before to secure the society's food supply. Men cleared the land and hunted game, and women planted, cultivated, and harvested crops. Many societies empowered religious figures, who organized the common followers, directed their work, and exacted tribute as well as worship from them. In return, the community trusted them to ward off hostile forces.

Everywhere in the Americas, regional trading networks formed. Along trade routes carrying commodities such as salt for food preservation, obsidian rock for projectile points, and copper for jewelry also traveled technology, religious ideas, and agricultural practices. By the end of the Archaic period, about 500 B.C., hundreds of independent kin-based groups, like people in other parts of the world, had learned to exploit the resources of their particular area and to trade with other groups in their region.

Native Americans in 1600

The last epoch of pre-Columbian development, the post-Archaic phase, occurred during the 2,000 years before contact with Europeans. It involved a complex process of growth and environmental adaptation among many distinct societies—and crisis in some of them. In the American Southwest, for example, the ancestors of the present-day Hopi and Zuni developed carefully planned villages composed of large, terraced, multistoried buildings, each with many rooms. By the time the Spanish arrived in the 1540s, the indigenous Pueblo people were using irrigation canals, dams, and hillside terracing to water their arid maize fields. In their agricultural techniques, their skill in ceramics, their use of woven textiles for clothing, and their village life, Pueblo society resembled that of peasant communities in many parts of Europe and Asia.

Far to the east were the mound-building societies of the Mississippi and Ohio valleys. When European

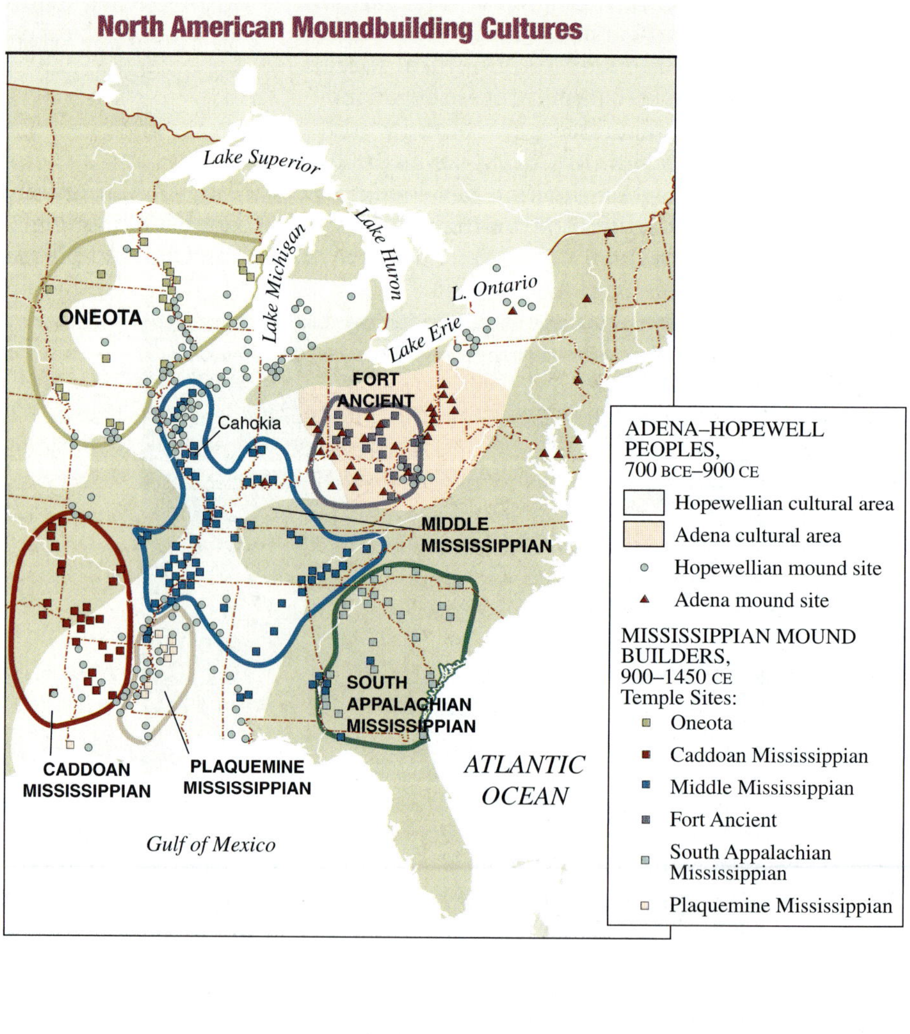

Plows, shovels, and bulldozers have obliterated many of the earthworks created at hundreds of moundbuilding sites in the eastern half of North America.

One of the hundreds of symbolic mounds built by people of the Hopewell culture, this one, in the shape of a serpent, is near present-day Cincinnati. *(National Museum of the American Indian, New York)*

settlers first crossed the Appalachian Mountains a century and a half after arriving on the continent, they were amazed to find hundreds of ceremonial mounds and gigantic sculptured earthworks in geometric designs or in the shapes of huge humans, birds, or writhing serpents. Believing all "Indians" to be forest primitives, they reasoned that these were the remains of an ancient civilization that had found its way to North America—perhaps Phoenicians, survivors of the sunken island of Atlantis, or the Lost Tribes of Israel spoken of in European mythology.

The mound-building societies of the Ohio valley declined many centuries before Europeans reached the continent, perhaps attacked by other tribes or damaged by severe climatic changes that undermined agriculture. But about A.D. 600, another mound-building agricultural society arose in the Mississippi valley. Its center, the city of Cahokia with perhaps 40,000 inhabitants, stood near present-day St. Louis. Great ceremonial plazas, flanked by a temple that rose in four terraces to a height of 100 feet, marked this first metropolis in America. This was the urban center of a far-flung Mississippi culture that encompassed hundreds of villages from Wisconsin to Louisiana and from Oklahoma to Tennessee.

Before the mound-building cultures of the continental heartlands mysteriously declined, their influence was already transforming the woodlands societies along the Atlantic coastal plain. The numerous small tribes that settled from Nova Scotia to Florida never equaled the larger societies of the midcontinent in earthwork sculpture, architectural design, or development of large-scale agriculture. But they were far from the "savages" that the first European explorers described. They had added limited agriculture to their skill in using natural plants for food, medicine, dyes, and flavoring and had developed food procurement strategies that exploited all the resources around them—cleared land, forests, streams, shore, and ocean.

Most of the eastern woodlands tribes lived in waterside villages. Locating their fields of maize near fishing grounds, they often migrated seasonally between inland and coastal village sites or situated themselves astride two ecological zones. In the Northeast, their birchbark canoes, light enough to be carried by a single man, helped them trade and communicate over immense territories. In the Southeast, population was denser and social and political organization more elaborate.

On the eve of European exploration of the Americas, the continent north of the Rio Grande contained at least 3 to 4 million people, of whom perhaps 500,000 lived along the eastern coastal plain and in the piedmont region accessible to the early European settlers. Though estimates vary widely, perhaps 40 to 60 million people lived in the entire hemisphere when Europeans first arrived. This contrasted with some 70 to 90 million in Europe about 1500 and about 50 to 70 million in Africa. The colonizers were not coming to a "virgin wilderness," as they often described it, but to a land inhabited for thousands of years by people whose village existence in many ways resembled that of the arriving Europeans.

In some important ways, however, Indian culture differed sharply from that of Europeans. Horses and oxen, for example, did not exist in the New World. Without large draft animals, Indians had no incentive to develop wheeled vehicles or, for that matter, the

Recovering the Past

ARCHAEOLOGICAL ARTIFACTS

The recovery of the past before there were extensive written records is the domain of archaeology. Virtually our entire knowledge of Indian societies in North America before the arrival of European colonizers is drawn from the work of archaeologists who have excavated the ancient living sites of the first Americans. Many Native Americans today strongly oppose this rummaging in the ancient ancestral places; they particularly oppose the unearthing of burial sites. But the modern search for knowledge about the past goes on.

Archaeological data have allowed us to overcome the stereotypic view of Native Americans as a primitive people whose culture was static for thousands of years before Europeans arrived in North America. This earlier view allowed historians to argue that the tremendous loss of Native American population and land accompanying the initial settlement and westward migration of white Americans was more or less inevitable. When two cultures, one dynamic and forward-looking and the other static and backward, confronted each other, historians have frequently maintained, the more advanced or "civilized" culture almost always prevailed.

Much of the elaborate early history of people in the Americas is unrecoverable. But many fragments of this long human history are being recaptured through archaeological research. Particularly important are studies that reveal how Indian societies were changing during the few centuries immediately preceding the European arrival in the New World. These studies give us a much better chance to interpret the seventeenth-century interaction of Native Americans and Europeans because they provide an understanding of Indian values, social and political organization, material culture, and religion as they existed when the two cultures first met.

One such investigation has been carried out over the last century at the confluence of the Mississippi and Missouri Rivers near modern-day East St. Louis, Illinois. Archaeologists have found the center of a vast Mississippi culture that began about A.D. 600, reached its peak about 300 years before Columbus's voyages, and then declined through a combination of drought, dwindling food supplies, and internal tensions. Cahokia is the name given to

Pottery effigy vessels in the shape of human heads. *(National Museum of the American Indian, New York)*

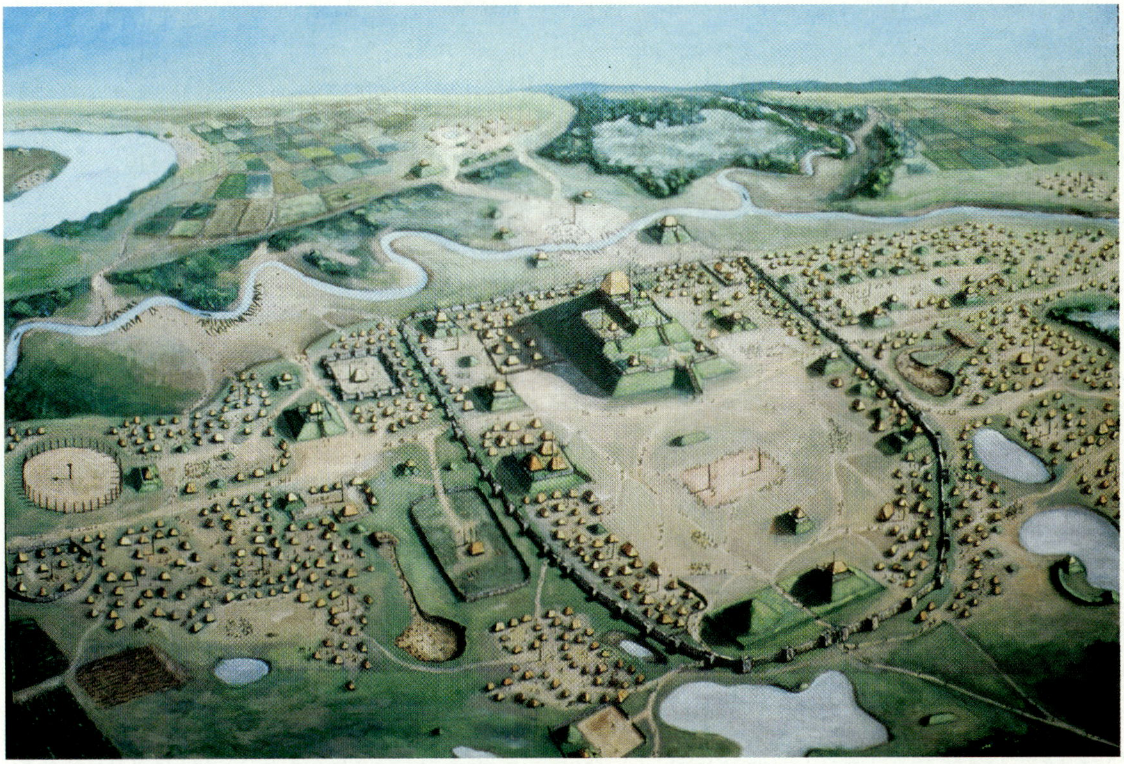

A reconstructed view of Cahokia, the largest town in North America before European arrival, painted by William R. Iseminger. An estimated 50 million cubic feet of earth was used to construct the ceremonial and burial mounds. *(Cahokia Mounds State Historic Site)*

the urban center of a civilization that at its height dominated an area as large as New York State. At the center of Cahokia stood one of the largest earth constructions built by ancient man anywhere on the planet. Its base covering 15 acres, this gigantic earthen temple rises in four terraces to a height of 100 feet, as tall as a ten-story modern office building. The drawing shown above indicates some of the dozens of smaller geometric mounds discovered near this major temple. Notice the outlying farms, a sure sign of the settled (as opposed to nomadic) existence of the people who flourished ten centuries ago in this region. How does this depiction of ancient Cahokia change your image of Native American life before the arrival of Europeans?

By recovering artifacts from Cahokia burial mounds, archaeologists have pieced together a picture, still tentative, of a highly elaborate civilization along the Mississippi bottomlands. Cahokian manufacturers mass-produced salt, knives, and stone hoe blades for both local consumption and export. Cahokian artisans made sophisticated pottery, ornamental jewelry, metalwork, and tools. They used copper and furs from the Lake Superior region, black obsidian stone from the Rocky Mountains, and seashells from the Gulf of Mexico, demonstrating that the people at Cahokia were involved in long-distance trade. In fact, Cahokia was a crucial crossroads of trade and water travel in the heartland of North America.

The objects shown on page 8, unearthed from graves by archaeologists, are an example of the culture of the Mississippi Mound Builders. The round-faced pottery bottles in the form of heads, each about 6 inches tall and wide, show a sense of humor in early Mississippi culture. Holes in the ears of the bottles once held thongs so that the objects could be hung or carried. Other objects, such as a figure of a kneeling woman found in Tennessee, had holes under the arms for a similar purpose. What other conclusions about Cahokian culture can you draw from figures such as these? Are there archaeological sites in your area that contain evidence of Native American civilization?

The fact that some graves uncovered at Cahokia contain large caches of finely tooled objects and that other burial mounds contain many skeletons unaccompanied by any artifacts leads archaeologists to conclude that this was a more stratified society than those the first settlers encountered along the Atlantic seaboard. Anthropologists believe that some of the Mississippi culture spread eastward before Cahokia declined, but much mystery still remains concerning the fate and cultural diffusion of these early Americans.

potter's wheel. Many inventions—such as the technology for smelting iron, which had diffused widely in the Old World—had not crossed the ocean barrier to reach the New World. The opposite was also true: Valuable New World crops, such as corn and potatoes, which had been developed by Indian agriculturists, were unknown in the Old World before Columbus.

Contrasting Worldviews

Colonizing Europeans called themselves "civilized" and typically described the people they met in the Americas as "savage," "heathen," or "barbarian." The gulf separating people in Europe and North America was defined not only by their material cultures but also by the way they viewed their relationship to the environment and defined social relations in their communities. Having evolved in complete isolation from each other, European and Indian cultures exhibited a wide difference in values.

Regarding land as a resource to be exploited for human benefit, Europeans believed that it should be privately possessed. From this belief developed much that Europeans took for granted: property lines often demarcated by fences, inheritance customs for transmitting land from one generation to another within the same family, and courts to settle resulting disputes. Property was the basis not only of sustenance but also of independence, wealth, status, and identity. The social structure directly mirrored patterns of land ownership, with a land-wealthy elite at the apex of the social pyramid and a propertyless mass at the bottom.

Native Americans also had concepts of property and boundaries. But they believed that land had sacred qualities and should be held in common. As one German missionary explained the Indian view in the eighteenth century, the Creator "made the Earth and all that it contains for the common good of mankind. Whatever liveth on the land, whatsoever groweth out of the earth, and all that is in the rivers and waters . . . was given jointly to all and everyone is entitled to his share."

Communal ownership sharply limited social stratification and increased a sense of sharing in most Indian communities, much to the amazement of Europeans accustomed to wide disparities of wealth. Observing the Iroquois of the eastern woodlands in 1657, a French Jesuit noted with surprise that they had no almshouses because "their kindness, humanity and courtesy not only makes them liberal with what they have, but causes them to possess hardly anything except in common. A whole village must be without corn, before any individual can be obliged to endure privation." Not all Europeans were acquisitive, competitive individuals. The majority were peasants scratching a subsistence living from the soil, living in kin-centered villages with little contact with the outside world, and exchanging goods and labor through barter. But in Europe's cities, a wealth-conscious, ambitious individual who valued and sought wider choices and greater opportunities to enhance personal status was coming to the fore. In contrast, Native American traditions stressed the group rather than the individual and valor rather than wealth.

There were exceptions. The empires of the Aztec in Central America and the Inca in South America were highly developed, populous, and stratified. So, in North America, were a few tribes such as the Natchez. But on the eastern and western coasts of the continent and in the Southwest—the regions of contact in the sixteenth and seventeenth centuries—the European newcomers encountered a people whose cultural values differed strikingly from theirs.

European colonizers in North America also found disturbing the matrilineal organization of many tribal societies. Contrary to European practice, family membership among most tribes was determined through the female line. A typical family consisted of an old woman, her daughters with their husbands and children, and her unmarried granddaughters and grandsons. When a son or grandson married, he moved from this female-headed household to one headed by the matriarch of his wife's family. Divorce was also the woman's prerogative. If she desired it, she merely set her husband's possessions outside their dwelling door. Clans were composed of several matrilineal kin groups related by a blood connection on the mother's side. To Europeans, this was a peculiar and dangerous reversal of their male-dominated sexual hierarchy.

In Native American societies, women also held subordinate positions, but not nearly to the extent found among European women. For example, European women were almost entirely excluded from political affairs. But in many Native American villages, designated men sat in a circle to deliberate and make decisions, and the senior women of the village stood behind them, lobbying and instructing. Village chiefs were male, but they were often chosen by the elder women of their clans, as was the case with the Iroquois. If they moved too far from the will of the women who appointed them, these chiefs were removed—or "dehorned." "Our ancestors," the Oneida chief Giod Peter explained, "considered it a great transgression to reject the counsel of their women, particularly the female governesses. Our ancestors considered them mistresses of the soil. . . . The women, they are the life of the nation."

The role of women in the tribal economy reinforced the sharing of power between male and female.

Indian Societies During the Period of Early European Settlement

The great number of Indian societies within the present-day boundaries of the United States—each with its own language—indicates the cultural diversity of the first peoples of North America at the time Europeans arrived.

Men hunted, fished, and cleared land, but women controlled the cultivation, harvest, and distribution of crops, supplying probably three-quarters of their family's nutritional needs. When the men were away hunting, women directed village life. Europeans, imbued with the idea of male superiority and female subordination, perceived such sexual equality as another mark of "savagery."

In economic relations, Europeans and Indians differed in ways that sometimes led to misunderstanding and conflict. Over vast stretches of the continent, Indians had built trading networks for centuries before Europeans arrived, making it easy for them to trade with arriving Europeans and incorporate new metal and glass trade items into their culture. But trade for Indian peoples was also a way of preserving interdependence and equilibrium between individuals and communities. This principle of reciprocity displayed itself in elaborate ceremonies of gift giving and pipe smoking that preceded the exchange of goods. Europeans saw trade largely as economic exchange, with the benefit of building good will between two parties sharply limited in comparison with Indians.

In the religious beliefs of Native Americans, the English saw a final damning defect. Europeans built their religious life around the belief in a single divinity, written scriptures, a trained and highly literate clergy, and churches with structured ceremonies. Native American societies, sharing no literary tradition, had less structured religious beliefs. Believing that human life could be affected, positively or negatively, by the mysterious power pervading everything in nature—in rocks, water, the sun, the moon, and animals—Indian people sought to conciliate these spirits and maintain proper relationships with them, even the spirits of the fish, beaver, and deer they hunted. Pueblo people, for example, living in arid lands where rainfall dictated their well-being, expressed their thanks for rain by performing frequent ritual dances.

For Europeans, the Indians' polytheism was pagan and devilish. Europeans understood that Indians had religious leaders called shamans, who used medicinal plants and magical chants to heal the sick and facilitated the people's quests to communicate with the spiritual world. But Europeans regarded the shamans as especially dangerous because they occupied powerful roles among a spiritually misled people. Their fear and hatred of infidels intensified by the Protestant Reformation, Europeans saw a holy necessity to convert—or destroy—these enemies of their God.

The city of Loango, at the mouth of the Congo River on the west coast of Africa, was larger at the time of this drawing in the mid-eighteenth century than all but a few seaports in the British colonies in North America. *(The Granger Collection, New York)*

AFRICA ON THE EVE OF CONTACT

Half a century before Columbus reached the Americas, a Portuguese sea captain, Antam Gonçalves, made the first European landing on the west coast of sub-Saharan Africa. If he had been able to travel the length and breadth of the immense continent, he would have encountered a rich variety of African states, peoples, and cultures. African "backwardness" and cultural impoverishment was a myth perpetuated after the slave trade had begun transporting millions of Africans to the New World. During the period of early contact with Europeans, Africa, like pre-Columbian America, was recognized as a diverse continent with a long history of cultural evolution.

The Kingdoms of Africa

The estimated 50 million peoples in fifteenth-century Africa lived in vast deserts, grasslands, and tropical forests. As in Europe and the Americas at that time, most people tilled the soil. Part of their skill in farming derived from the development of iron production, which began in present-day Nigeria about 450 B.C., long before it reached Europe. More efficient iron implements increased agricultural productivity, in turn spurring population growth. The pattern was repeated in other parts of the world—the Americas, Europe, the Far East, and the Middle East—when the agricultural revolution began.

Before fifteenth-century Europeans reached the west coast of Africa, a number of large empires had risen there. The first was the kingdom of Ghana, which embraced an immense territory between the Sahara and the Gulf of Guinea and stretched from the Atlantic Ocean to the Niger River.

The development of large towns, skillfully designed buildings, elaborate sculpture and metalwork, long-distance commerce, and a complex political structure marked the Ghanaian kingdom from the sixth to eleventh centuries. A thriving caravan trade with Arab peoples across the Sahara to Morocco and Algeria brought extensive Muslim influence by the eleventh century, when the king of Ghana boasted an army of 200,000, maintained trading contacts as far east as Cairo and Baghdad, and was furnishing, through Muslim middlemen in North Africa, two-thirds of the gold supply for the Christian Mediterranean region.

An invasion of North African Muslim warriors beginning in the eleventh century introduced a period of religious strife that eventually destroyed the kingdom of Ghana. But in the same region arose the Islamic kingdom of Mali. Prospering through its control of the gold trade, Mali flourished until the early sixteenth century. Its city of Timbuktu contained a distinguished faculty of scholars to whom North Africans and even southern Europeans came to study. Traveling there in the 1330s, the Arab geographer Ibn-Battuta wrote admiringly of "the discipline of its officials and provincial governors, the excellent condition of public finance, and . . . the respect accorded to the decisions of justice and to the authority of the sovereign."

Elsewhere along the Atlantic coast, other kingdoms such as Kongo, Songhay, and Benin grew in the centuries before seaborne Europeans reached Africa.

In their towns, rivaling those of Europe in size, lived people skilled in metalworking, weaving, ceramics, architecture, and aesthetic expression. Codes of law, regional trade, and effective political organization all developed by the fifteenth century. Finding their way to Africa south of the Sahara, Europeans encountered not a backward area but a densely settled region with an ancient history of long-distance trade and cultural exchange with other peoples.

Population growth and cultural development in Africa, as elsewhere in the world, proceeded at different rates in different regions. Where soil was rich, rainfall adequate, and minerals abundant, as in western Sudan, population grew and cultures changed rapidly. Where inhospitable desert or impenetrable forest ruled, societies remained small and changed very slowly. Isolation from other cultures retarded development, whereas contact with other regions encouraged change. For example, cultural innovation accelerated in East African Swahili-speaking societies facing the Indian Ocean after trading contacts began with the Eastern world in the ninth century. Around the same time, traders from Arabia, India, and the East Indies began to spread Muslim influence in West Africa.

The African Ethos

The many peoples of Africa, who were to supply at least two-thirds of all the immigrants who crossed the ocean to the Western Hemisphere in the three centuries after Europeans began colonizing there, came from a rich diversity of cultures. But most of them shared certain ways of life that differentiated them from Europeans.

As in Europe, the family was the basic unit of social organization. Unlike European societies, however, African societies were organized in a variety of kinship and political systems. In many African societies, like many Native American ones, the family was matrilineal. Property rights and political inheritance descended through the mother rather than the father. The son of a chief's sister inherited his position, and a married man joined his bride's people.

West Africans believed in a Supreme Creator and in lesser deities associated with natural forces such as rain, fertility, and animal life. Because these deities could intervene in human affairs, they were elaborately honored. Like most North American Indian societies, West Africans held that spirits dwelt in the trees, rocks, and rivers around them, and hence they exercised care in the treatment of these natural objects.

Africans also worshiped ancestors, who were believed to mediate between the Creator and the living. Because the dead played such an important role for the living, relatives held elaborate funeral rites to ensure the proper entrance of a deceased relative into the spiritual world. The more ancient an

(Left) Before Europeans reached West Africa, Niger River craftsmen were producing terra cotta figures such as this horseman. With outstretched arms, the rider holds the reins. His helmet, heavy necklace, shoulder quiver, and dagger fastened to his arm all signify his warrior nobility. *(Equestrian Figure, Inland Niger Delta region, Mali, Possibly 13–15th century, Terracotta, H. 70.5 (27¾ in.), Museum purchase, 86–12–2, Photograph by Frank Khoury, National Museum of African Art, Smithsonian Institution)* (Right) In the Benin kingdom of West Africa, people celebrated the leopard as "king of the bush." Copper alloy leopards of this kind were usually placed at the king's side when he sat in state to symbolize the king's ominous power combined with prudent reserve. (© *Dirk Bakker, 1978*)

West African Slaving Forts

Europeans fought lustily for control of slaving forts on the West African coast, and many forts changed hands several times during the long period of the Atlantic slave trade.

ancestor, the greater was this person's power to affect the living; thus the "ancient ones" were devoutly worshiped. Deep family loyalty and regard for family lineage flowed naturally from ancestor worship. Finally, West Africans believed in spirit possession, where gods spoke to men and women through priests and other religious figures.

Social organization in much of West Africa by the time Europeans arrived was as elaborate as in fifteenth-century Europe. At the top of society stood nobles and priests, usually elderly men. Beneath them were the great masses of people, mostly farmers, but also some craftsmen, traders, teachers, and artists. At the bottom of society resided slaves. As in ancient Greece and Rome, they were "outsiders"—war captives, criminals, or sometimes people who sold themselves into servitude to satisfy a debt. The rights of slaves were restricted, and their opportunities for advancement were narrow. Nevertheless, as members of the community, they were entitled to protection under the law and allowed the privileges of education, marriage, and parenthood. Their servile condition was not permanent, nor was it automatically inherited by their children, as would be the fate of Africans enslaved in the Americas.

EUROPE IN THE AGE OF EXPLORATION

In the ninth century, about the time that the mound builders of the Mississippi valley were constructing their urban center at Cahokia and the kingdom of Ghana was rising in West Africa, western Europe was an economic and cultural backwater. The center of political power and economic vitality in the Old World had shifted eastward to Christian Byzantium, which controlled Asia Minor, the Balkans, and parts of Italy. The other dynamic culture of this age, Islam, had spread through the Middle East, spilled across North Africa, and penetrated Spain and West Africa south of the Sahara.

Over the next six centuries, an epic revitalization of western Europe occurred, creating the conditions that enabled its leading maritime nations vastly to extend their oceanic frontiers. By the late fifteenth century, a 400-year epoch of militant European expansion was under way. Only in the twentieth century was this process of Europeanization reversed, as colonized people regained their autonomy and cultural identity through wars of national liberation.

The Rise of Europe

The rebirth of western Europe, which began around A.D. 1000, owed much to a revival of long-distance trading from Italian ports on the Mediterranean and the rediscovery of ancient knowledge that these contacts permitted. The once mighty cities of the Roman Empire had stagnated for centuries, but now Venice, Genoa, and other Italian ports began trading with peoples facing the Adriatic, the Baltic, and the North Seas. These new contacts brought wealth and power to the Italian commercial cities, which gradually evolved into merchant-dominated city-states that freed themselves from the rule of feudal lords in control of the surrounding countryside.

While merchants led the emerging city-states, western Europe's feudal system was gradually weakening. For centuries, feudal lords, not kings, had exercised the normal powers of the state—the power to tax, wage war, and administer the law. In the thirteenth and fourteenth centuries, however, kings began to reassert their political authority and to undertake efforts to unify their realms. One of their primary goals was to curb the power of the great lords who dominated entire regions and to force lesser nobles into dependence on and obedience to the crown.

The Black Death (bubonic plague), which devastated western Europe and Africa from 1348 to 1354, promoted the unification of old realms into early modern states. The plague killed one-third of the population, a blow from which Europe did not recover demographically for centuries. The nobilities with which monarchs had to contend were reduced in size, for the plague defied class distinction. Ironically, feudal lords treated their peasants better for a time because their labor, tremendously reduced by the plague, became more valuable.

Early developments in England led to a distinctive political system. In 1215, the English aristocracy curbed the powers of the king when they forced him to accept the Magna Carta. On the basis of this charter, a parliament composed of elective and hereditary members eventually gained the right to meet regularly to pass money bills. Parliament was thus in a position to act as a check on the crown, an arrangement unknown on the Continent. During the sixteenth century, the crown and Parliament worked together toward a more unified state, with the English kings wielding less political power than their European counterparts.

Economic changes of great significance also occurred in England during the sixteenth century. To practice more profitable agriculture, great landowners began to "enclose" (consolidate) their estates, throwing peasant farmers off their plots and turning many of them into wage laborers. The formation of this working class was the crucial first step toward industrial development.

Continental Europe lagged behind England in two respects. First, it was far less affected by the move to "enclose" agricultural land. Part of the explanation lies in the values of continental aristocrats, who regarded the maximization of profit as unworthy of gentlemen. French nobles could lose their titles for commercial activities. Second, continental rulers were less successful in engaging the interests of their nobilities, and these nobles never shared governance with their king, as did English aristocrats through their participation in Parliament. In France, a noble faction assassinated Henry III in 1589, and the nobles remained disruptive for nearly another century. In Spain, the final conquest of the Muslims and expulsion of the Jews, both in 1492, strengthened the monarchy's hold, but regional cultures and leaders remained strong. The continental monarchs would thus warmly embrace doctrines of royal absolutism developed in the sixteenth century.

The New Monarchies and the Expansionist Impulse

In the second half of the fifteenth century, ambitious monarchs coming to power in France, England, and Spain sought social and political stability in their kingdoms. Louis XI in France, Henry VII in England, Isabella of Castile, and Ferdinand of Aragon all created armies and bureaucratic state machinery strong enough to quell internal conflict, such as the English War of the Roses, and to raise taxes sufficient to support their regimes. In these countries, and in Portugal as well, economic revival and the reversal of more than a century of population decline and civil disorder nourished the impulse to expand. This impulse was also fed by Renaissance culture. Ushering in a new, more secular age, the Renaissance (Rebirth) encouraged freedom of thought, richness of expression, and an emphasis on human abilities. Beginning in Italy and spreading northward through Europe, the Renaissance peaked dramatically in the late fifteenth century when the age of exploration began.

The exploratory urge had two initial objectives: first, to circumvent Muslim traders by finding an eastward oceanic route to Asia; and second, to tap the African gold trade at its source. Since the tenth century, Muslim middlemen in North Africa had brought the precious metal to Europe from Guinea. Now the possibility arose of bypassing these non-Christian traffickers. Likewise, Christian Europeans dreamed of eliminating Muslim traders from the commerce with Asia. Since 1291, when Marco Polo returned to Venice with

European Exploration of the Americas, 1492–1610

Within one century, Europeans had mapped most of the coasts of the Americas and the islands of the Caribbean Sea.

tales of Eastern treasures—spices, silks, perfumes, drugs, and jewels—Europeans had bartered with the Orient. But the difficulties of the long eastward overland route through the Muslim world kept alive the hopes of Christian Europeans that an alternative water route existed. Eventually, Europe's mariners found they could voyage to Cathay by both eastward and westward water routes.

Portugal seemed the least likely of the rising nation-states to lead the expansion of Europe outside its continental boundaries, yet it forged into the lead at the end of the fifteenth century. A poor and insignificant country of only one million inhabitants, Portugal had gradually overcome Moorish control in the twelfth and thirteenth centuries and, in 1385, had wrenched itself free of domination by neighboring Castile. Led by Prince Henry the Navigator, for whom trade was secondary to the conquest of the Muslim world, Portugal breached the unknown. In the 1420s, Henry began dispatching Portuguese mariners to probe the unknown Atlantic "sea of darkness." His intrepid sailors were aided by important improvements in navigation, mapmaking, and ship design, all promoted by the prince.

Portuguese captains operated at sea on three ancient Ptolemaic principles: that the earth was round, that distances on its surface could be measured by degrees, and that navigators could "fix" their position on a map by measuring the position of the stars. The invention in the 1450s of the quadrant, which allowed a precise measurement of star altitude necessary for determining latitude, represented a leap forward from the chart-and-compass method of navigation. Equally important was the design of a lateen-rigged caravel, adapted from a Moorish ship design. Its triangular sails permitted ships to sail into the wind, allowing them to beat southward along the African coast—a feat the square-rigged European vessels could never perform—and return northward against prevailing winds.

By the 1430s, the ability of Prince Henry's captains to break through the limits of the world known to Europeans had carried them to Madeira, the Canaries, and the Azores, lying off the coasts of Portugal and northwestern Africa. These were soon developed as the first European agricultural plantations, located on the continent's periphery. From there, the Portuguese sea captains pushed farther south.

By the time of Prince Henry's death in 1460, Portuguese mariners had reached the west coast of Africa, where they began a profitable trade in ivory, slaves, and especially gold. By 1500, they had captured control of the African gold trade monopolized for centuries by North African Muslims. The gleaming metal now traveled directly to Lisbon by sea rather than by camel caravan across the Sahara to North African Muslim ports such as Tunis and Algiers. In 1497, Vasco da Gama became the first European to sail around the Cape of Africa, allowing the Portuguese to colonize the Indian Ocean and to reach modern Indonesia and south China by 1513. By forcing trade concessions in the islands and coastal states of the East Indies, the Portuguese unlocked the fabulous Asian treasure houses that since Marco Polo's time had whetted European appetites.

Reaching the Americas

The marriage of Ferdinand and Isabella in 1469 united the independent states of Aragon and Castile and launched the Spanish nation into its golden age. Leading the way for Spain was an Italian sailor, Christopher Columbus. The son of a poor Genoese weaver, Columbus had married into a prominent family of Lisbon merchants, thus making important contacts at court.

Celebrated for hundreds of years as the intrepid explorer who initiated permanent contact between Europe and the Americas, Columbus is attacked by some today as the ruthless exploiter of Indian peoples and lands. But Columbus is best understood in the context of his own times—an age of great brutality and violence and also an age in which Catholic Spain was engaged in the final stages of expelling the Moorish people who had controlled southern Spain for centuries. Columbus's urge to explore was nourished by ideas and questions about the geographic limits of his world, and he was inspired by notions of contributing to the reconquest of Moorish Spain. The Latin inscription on the tomb of his monarchs, Isabella and Ferdinand, captures the mood of the era: "Overthrowers of the Mahometan sect and repressors of heretical stubbornness."

Like many sailors, Columbus had listened to sea tales about lands to the west. He may have heard Icelandic sagas about the voyages of Leif Eriksson and several thousand Norse immigrants who reached Newfoundland five centuries before. Other ideas circulated that the Atlantic Ocean stretched to India and eastern Asia. Could one reach the Indies by sailing west rather than by sailing east around Africa, as the Portuguese were attempting? Columbus hungered to know.

For nearly ten years, Columbus tried unsuccessfully to secure financial backing and royal sanction in Portugal for exploratory voyages. Many mocked his modest estimates of the distance westward from Europe to Japan. Finally, in 1492, Queen Isabella of Spain commissioned him, and he sailed west with three tiny ships and a crew of about 90 men. Strong winds, lasting ten days, blew the ships far into the Atlantic. There they were becalmed. In the fifth week at sea—longer than any European sailors had been out of the sight of land—mutinous rumblings swept through the crews. But Columbus pressed on. On the seventieth day, long after Columbus had calculated he would reach Japan, a lookout sighted land. On October 12, 1492, the sailors clambered ashore on a tiny island in the Bahamas, which Columbus named San Salvador (Holy Savior). Grateful sailors "rendered thanks to Our Lord, kneeling on the ground, embracing it with tears of joy."

Believing he had reached Asia, Columbus explored the island-speckled Caribbean for ten weeks. After landing on a heavily populated island that he named Hispaniola (shared today by Haiti and the Dominican Republic) and on Cuba (which he thought was the Asian mainland), he set sail for Spain with cinnamon, coconuts, a bit of gold, and several kidnapped natives.

the History place

Homeward bound, he penned a report of what he believed were his Asian discoveries: hospitable people, fertile soils, magnificent harbors, and gold-filled rivers.

The First Columbian Voyage of 1492

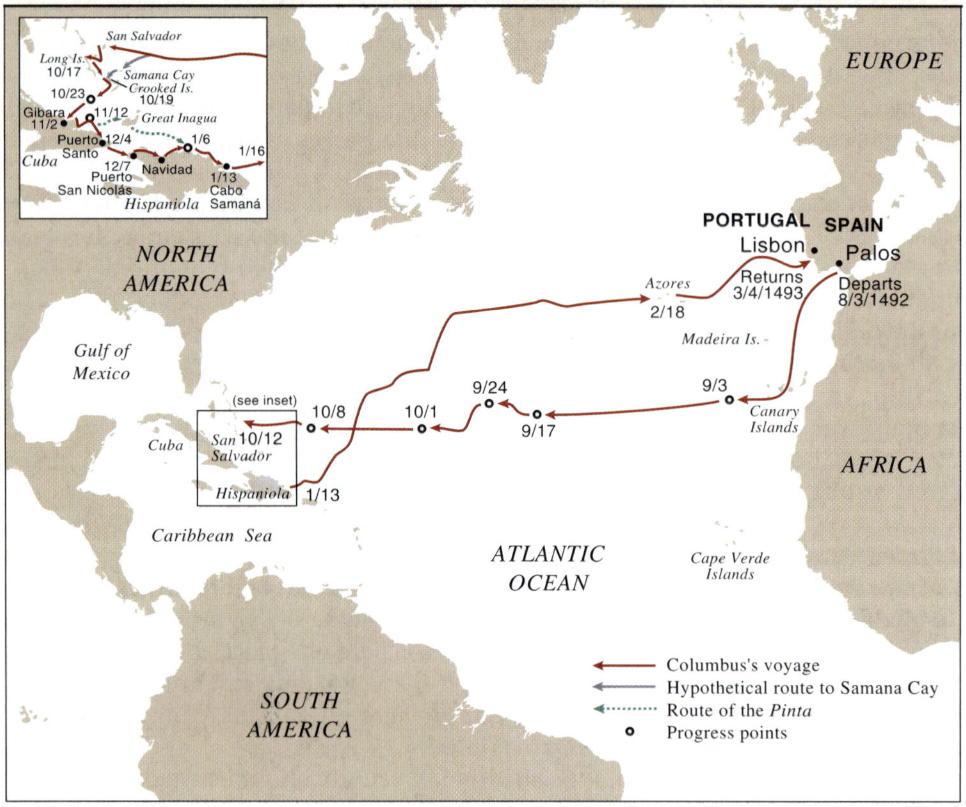

In Columbus's 70-day voyage from Spain to San Salvador, it took thirty days to reach the Canary Islands off the coast of West Africa.

Quickly printed and distributed throughout Europe, Columbus's report brought him financing between 1494 and 1504 for three much larger expeditions to explore the newfound lands. The second voyage, carrying over 1,200 Spanish in 17 ships, initiated the first extended contact between Europeans and Native Americans. In an ominous display of what was to come, Columbus's men captured some 1,600 Tainos on Hispaniola and carried 550 of them back to Spain as slaves in 1495. Only 350 survived the stormy voyage to Spain. Here began the Atlantic slave trade that would alter the history of the world, though it began in the reverse direction of what would soon become its dominant flow. Although his discoveries seemed less significant than the Portuguese exploits in the South Atlantic, Columbus led Spain to the threshold of a mighty empire. He reaped few rewards, however, dying unnoticed and penniless in 1506. To the end, he believed that he had found the water route to Asia.

The expansion of Spain and Portugal into new areas of the world profoundly affected patterns of economic activity in Europe. Its commercial center now shifted away from the ports of the Mediterranean to the Atlantic ports facing the New World.

The New World also beckoned as a field of religious contest. The heavily populated Americas offered millions of potential Christian converts. But the Catholic-Protestant division within Christianity complicated Christian dreams of converting a "heathen" continent. The people of western Europe, just as they were unlocking the secrets of the new worlds to the east and west in the sixteenth century, were torn by religious schisms that magnified national rivalries.

Religious Conflict During the Reformation

At the heart of Europe's religious strife was a continental movement to cleanse the Christian church of corrupt practices and return it to the purer ways of early Christianity. Criticism of the worldliness of the Catholic church mounted during the Renaissance. Then a German friar, Martin Luther, became the first to break successfully with Rome, initiating a Protestant Reformation of theology and practice. As Protestant sects multiplied, a Catholic Reformation grew up within the church, and the two groups began a long battle for the souls of Europeans.

Luther was preparing for a legal career in 1505 when a bolt of lightning nearly struck him during a violent thunderstorm. Trembling with fear, he vowed to become a monk. But in the religious order of Saint Augustine, he lost faith in the power of the age-old rituals of the church—prayer, the Mass, confession, pilgrimages to holy places, even crusades against Muslim infidels. He reasoned that salvation came through an inward faith, or "grace," that God conferred on those he chose. Good works, Luther believed, did not earn grace but were only the external evidence of grace won through faith. Luther had taken the revolutionary step of rejecting the church's elaborate hierarchy of officials, who presided over the rituals intended to guide individuals along the path toward salvation.

Luther's doctrine of private "justification by faith" did not immediately threaten the church. But in 1517, he openly attacked the sale of "indulgences" for sins by which the pope raised money for the building of St. Peter's in Rome. By purchasing indulgences, individuals had been told, they could reduce their time (or that of a deceased relative) in purgatory. Luther drew up 95 arguments against this practice and called on Christians to practice true repentance. The spread of printing, invented less than 70 years before, allowed the rapid circulation of his ideas. The printed word and the ability to read it were to become revolutionary weapons throughout the world.

Luther's cry for reform soon inspired Germans of all classes. He denounced five of the seven sacraments of the church, calling for a return to baptism and communion alone. He attacked the upper clergy for luxurious living and urged priests, who were nominally celibate but were often involved in irregular sexual relations, to marry respectably. He railed against the "detestable tyranny of the clergy over the laity" and called for a priesthood of all believers. He urged people to seek faith individually by reading the Bible, which he translated into German and made widely available for the first time in printed form. Most dangerously, he called on the German princes to assume control over religion in their states, directly challenging the authority of Rome and further undermining the functions of its clergy.

The basic issue dividing Catholics and Protestants thus centered on the source of religious authority. To Catholics, religious authority resided in the organized Church, headed by the pope. To Protestants, the Bible was the sole authority, and access to God's word or God's grace did not require the mediation of the Church.

Building on Luther's redefinition of Christianity, John Calvin, a Frenchman, brought new intensity and meaning to the Protestant Reformation. In 1536, at age 26, he published a ringing appeal to every Christian to form a direct, personal relationship with God. By Calvin's doctrine, God had saved a few souls at random before Creation and damned the rest. Human beings could not alter this predestination, but those who were good Christians must struggle to understand and accept God's saving grace if he chose to import it. Without mediation of ritual or priest but by "straight-walking," one was to behave as one of God's elect, the "saints." This radical theology, even more insistent on individual godliness than Luther's, spread among all classes throughout Europe.

John Calvin (1509–1564), painted by Hans Holbein the Younger, is portrayed as a man of letters, books, and solemn religiosity. "What I have taught and written," wrote Calvin, "did not grow in my brain, but that I hold it from God." *(The Granger Collection, New York)*

Calvin proposed reformed Christian communities structured around the elect few. To remake the corrupt world and follow God's will, communities of "saints" must control the state, rather than the other way around. Elected bodies of ministers and dedicated laymen, called presbyteries, were to govern the church, directing the affairs of society down to the last detail so that all, whether saved or damned, would work for God's ends.

Calvinism, as a fine-tuned system of self-discipline and social control, was first put into practice in the

1550s in the city-state of Geneva, near the French border of Switzerland. Here the brilliant and austere leader established what he intended to be a model Christian community. A council of 12 elders drove nonbelievers from the city, rigidly disciplined daily life, and stripped the churches of every appeal to the senses—images, music, incense, and colorful clerical gowns. Religious reformers from all over Europe flocked to the new holy community, and Geneva soon became the continental center of the reformist Christian movement and a haven for refugee Protestant leaders. The city was, wrote John Knox of Scotland in 1556, "the most perfect school of Christ that ever was in the earth since the days of the apostles."

Calvin's radical program converted large numbers of people to Protestantism throughout Europe. Like Lutheranism, it recruited most successfully among the privileged classes of merchants, landowners, lawyers, and the nobility and among the rising middle class of master artisans and shopkeepers.

Sixteenth-century monarchs initially regarded attacks on the Catholic Church with horror. But many local princes adopted some version of the reformed faith. The most important monarch to break with Catholicism was Henry VIII of England. When Pope Clement VII refused him permission to divorce and remarry, Henry declared himself head of the Church of England, or Anglican church. Although it retained many Catholic features, the Church of England moved further in a Protestant direction under Henry's son Edward. But when Mary, Henry's older Catholic daughter, came to the throne, she vowed to reinstate her mother's religion by suppressing Protestants. Her policy created Protestant martyrs, and many were relieved when she died in 1558, bringing Henry's younger Protestant daughter, Elizabeth, to the throne. During her long rule, the flinty Elizabeth steered Anglicanism along a middle course between the radicalism of Geneva and the Catholicism of Rome.

The countries most affected by the Reformation—England, Holland, and France—were slow in trying to colonize the New World, so Protestantism did not gain an early foothold in the Americas. Catholicism in Spain and Portugal remained almost immune from the Protestant Reformation. Thus, even while under attack, Catholicism swept across the Atlantic almost unchallenged during the century after Columbus's voyages.

THE IBERIAN CONQUEST OF AMERICA

From 1492 to 1518, Spanish and Portuguese explorers opened up vast parts of Asia and the Americas to European knowledge. Yet during this age of exploration, only modest attempts at settlement were made, mostly by the Spanish on the Caribbean islands of Cuba, Puerto Rico, and Hispaniola. The three decades after 1518, however, became an age of conquest. In some of the bloodiest chapters in recorded history, the Spanish nearly exterminated the native peoples of the Caribbean islands, toppled and plundered the great inland empires of the Aztec and Inca in Mexico and Peru, discovered fabulous silver mines, and built an oceanic trade of enormous importance to all of Europe. This short era of conquest had immense consequences for global history.

Portugal, meanwhile, restricted by one of the most significant lines ever drawn on a map, concentrated mostly on building an eastward oceanic trade to southeastern Asia. In 1493, to settle a dispute, the pope had demarcated Spanish and Portuguese spheres of exploration in the Atlantic. Drawing a north–south line 100 leagues (about 300 miles) west of the Azores, the pope confined Portugal to the eastern side. One year later, in the Treaty of Tordesillas, Portugal obtained Spanish agreement to move the line 270 leagues farther west. Nobody knew at the time that a large part of South America, as yet undiscovered by Europeans, bulged east of the new demarcation line and therefore fell within the Portuguese sphere. In time, Portugal would develop this region, Brazil, into one of the most profitable areas of the New World.

The Spanish Onslaught

Within a single generation of Columbus's death in 1506, Spanish conquistadores explored, claimed, and conquered most of South America (except Brazil), Central America, and the southern parts of North America from Florida to California. Led by audacious explorers and military leaders, and usually accompanied by enslaved Africans, they established Spanish authority and Catholicism over an area that dwarfed their homeland in size and population. They were motivated by religion, growing pride of nation, and dreams of personal enrichment. "We came here," explained one Spanish foot soldier in Cortés's legion, "to serve God and the king, and also to get rich."

In two bold and bloody strokes, the Spanish overwhelmed the ancient civilizations of the Aztec and Inca. In 1519, Hernando Cortés set out with 600 soldiers from coastal Veracruz and marched over rugged mountains to attack Tenochtitlán (modern-day Mexico City), the capital of Montezuma's Aztec empire. At its height, centuries before, the ancient city in the valley of Mexico had contained perhaps 200,000 people. But in 1521, following two years of tense relations between the Spanish and Aztec, it fell before Cortés's assault. The Spanish use of horses and firearms provided an important advantage; so did a

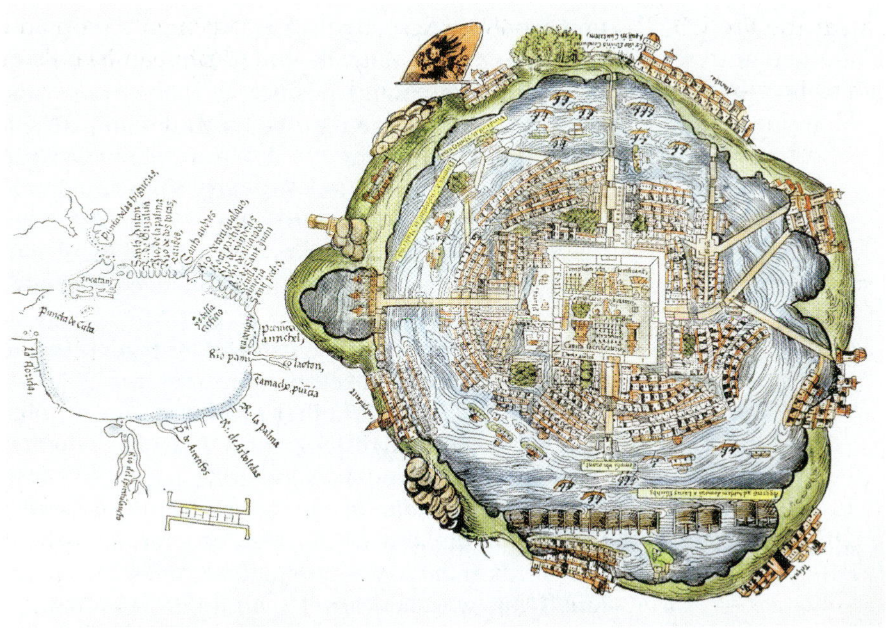

The plan of Tenochtitlán, later Mexico City, is from the Latin edition of Cortés's "Second Letter," on his conquest of the Aztec. Cortés's account was widely published in Europe, where Germans, French, and English were astounded to hear of such an extraordinary Aztec metropolis with floating gardens, causeways, and monumental architecture. *(The Granger Collection, New York)*

murderous smallpox epidemic in 1520 that felled thousands of Aztec. Support from local peoples oppressed by Montezuma's tyranny was also indispensable in overthrowing the Aztec ruler. From the valley of Mexico, the Spanish extended their dominion over the Mayan people of the Yucatán and Guatemala in the next few decades.

In the second conquest, the intrepid Francisco Pizarro, marching from Panama through the jungles of Ecuador and into the towering mountains of Peru with a mere 168 men, most of them not even soldiers, toppled the Inca empire. Like the Aztec, the populous Inca lived in a highly organized social system. But also like the Aztec, they were riddled by smallpox and weakened by violent internal divisions. This ensured Pizarro's success in capturing their capital at Cuzco in 1533. From there, Spanish soldiers marched farther afield, plundering other gold- and silver-rich Inca cities. Further expeditions into Chile, New Granada (Colombia), Argentina, and Bolivia in the 1530s and 1540s brought under Spanish control an empire larger than any in the Western world since the fall of Rome.

By 1550, Spain had overwhelmed the major centers of native population throughout the Caribbean, Mexico, Central America, and the west coast of South America. Spanish ships carried gold, silver, dyewoods, and sugar east across the Atlantic and transported African slaves, colonizers, and finished goods west. In a brief half century, Spain had exploited the advances in geographic knowledge and marine technology of its Portuguese rivals and brought into harsh but profitable contact with each other the people of three continents. The triracial character of the Americas was already firmly established by 1600.

For nearly a century after Columbus's voyages, Spain enjoyed almost unchallenged dominion over the fabulous hemisphere newly revealed to Europeans. Greedy buccaneers of various nations snapped at the heels of homeward-bound Spanish treasure fleets with cargoes of silver, but this was only a nuisance. France made gestures of contesting Spanish or Portuguese control by planting small settlements in Brazil and Florida in the mid-sixteenth century, but they were quickly wiped out. England remained island-bound until the 1580s. Until the seventeenth century, only Portugal, which staked out important claims in Brazil in the 1520s, challenged Spanish domination of the New World.

The Great Dying

Spanish conquest of major areas of the Americas set in motion two of the most far-reaching processes in modern history. One involved microbes; the other, silver.

Spanish contacts with the natives of the Caribbean basin, central Mexico, and Peru in the early sixteenth century triggered the most dramatic and disastrous population decline in recorded history. The population of the Americas on the eve of European arrival had grown to an estimated 50 to 60 million or more. In some areas, such as central Mexico, the highlands of Peru, and certain Caribbean islands, population density exceeded that of most of Europe. But though they were less populous than the people of the Americas, the European colonizers had one extraordinary biological

Spanish and Portuguese Conquests in the Americas

Never before the Spanish and Portuguese arrived in the Americas had such small numbers of people established their dominance over such a large and populous area.

advantage: for centuries Old World peoples had been exposed to nearly every lethal microbe that infects humans on an epidemic scale in the temperate zone. Over the centuries, Europeans had built up immunities to these diseases. Such biological defenses did not eliminate smallpox, measles, diphtheria, and other afflictions, but they limited their deadly power. Geographic isolation, however, had kept these diseases from the peoples of the Americas. So, too, did the Native Americans' lack of large domesticated animals, which were the major disease carriers. Arriving Europeans therefore unknowingly encountered a huge component of the human race that was utterly defenseless against the "domesticated" infections the Europeans and their animals carried inside their bodies.

The results were catastrophic. On Hispaniola, a population of about one million that had existed when Columbus arrived had only a few thousand survivors by 1530. Of some 15 million inhabitants in central Mexico before Cortés's arrival, nearly half perished within fifteen years. Demographic disaster also struck the populous Inca peoples of the Peruvian Andes, speeding ahead of Pizarro's conquistadores. Smallpox "spread over the people as great destruction," an old Indian told a Spanish priest in the 1520s. "There was great havoc. Very many died of it. They could not stir, they could not change position, nor lie on one side, nor face down, nor on their backs. And if they stirred, much did they cry out. . . . And very many starved; there was death from hunger, [for] none could take care of [the sick]." Such terrifying sickness led many natives to believe that their gods had failed them, and this belief left them ready to acknowledge the greater power of the Spainards' God.

In most areas where Europeans intruded in the hemisphere for the next three centuries, the catastrophe repeated itself. Whether Protestant or Catholic, whether French, English, Spanish, or Dutch, whether male or female, every newcomer from the Old World participated accidentally in the spread of disease that typically eliminated, within a few generations, at least two-thirds of the native population. Millions of Native Americans who had never seen a European died of European diseases, which swept like wildfire through densely populated regions.

The enslavement and brutal treatment of the native people intensified the lethal effects of European diseases. After their spectacular conquests of the Inca and Aztec, the Spanish enslaved thousands of native people and assigned them work regimens that severely weakened their resistance to disease. Some priests like Bartolomé de Las Casas waged lifelong campaigns to reduce the exploitation of the Indians, but they had only limited power to control the actions of their colonizing compatriots.

Silver, Sugar, and Their Consequences

The small amount of gold that Columbus brought home from the West Indies raised hopes that this metal, which along with silver formed the standard of wealth in Europe, might be found in the transatlantic paradise. Some gold was gleaned from the Caribbean islands and later from Colombia, Brazil, and Peru. But though men pursued it fanatically to the far corners of the hemisphere, more than three centuries would pass before they found gold in windfall quantities in North America. Silver proved most abundant—so plenteous, in fact, that when bonanza strikes were made in Bolivia in 1545 and then in northern Mexico in the next decade, much of Spain's New World enterprise focused on its extraction. The Spanish empire in America, for most of the sixteenth century, was a vast mining community.

Native people, along with some African slaves, provided the first labor supply for the mines. The Spaniards permitted the highly organized Indian societies to maintain control of their own communities but exacted from them huge labor drafts for mining. By imposing themselves at the top of a highly stratified

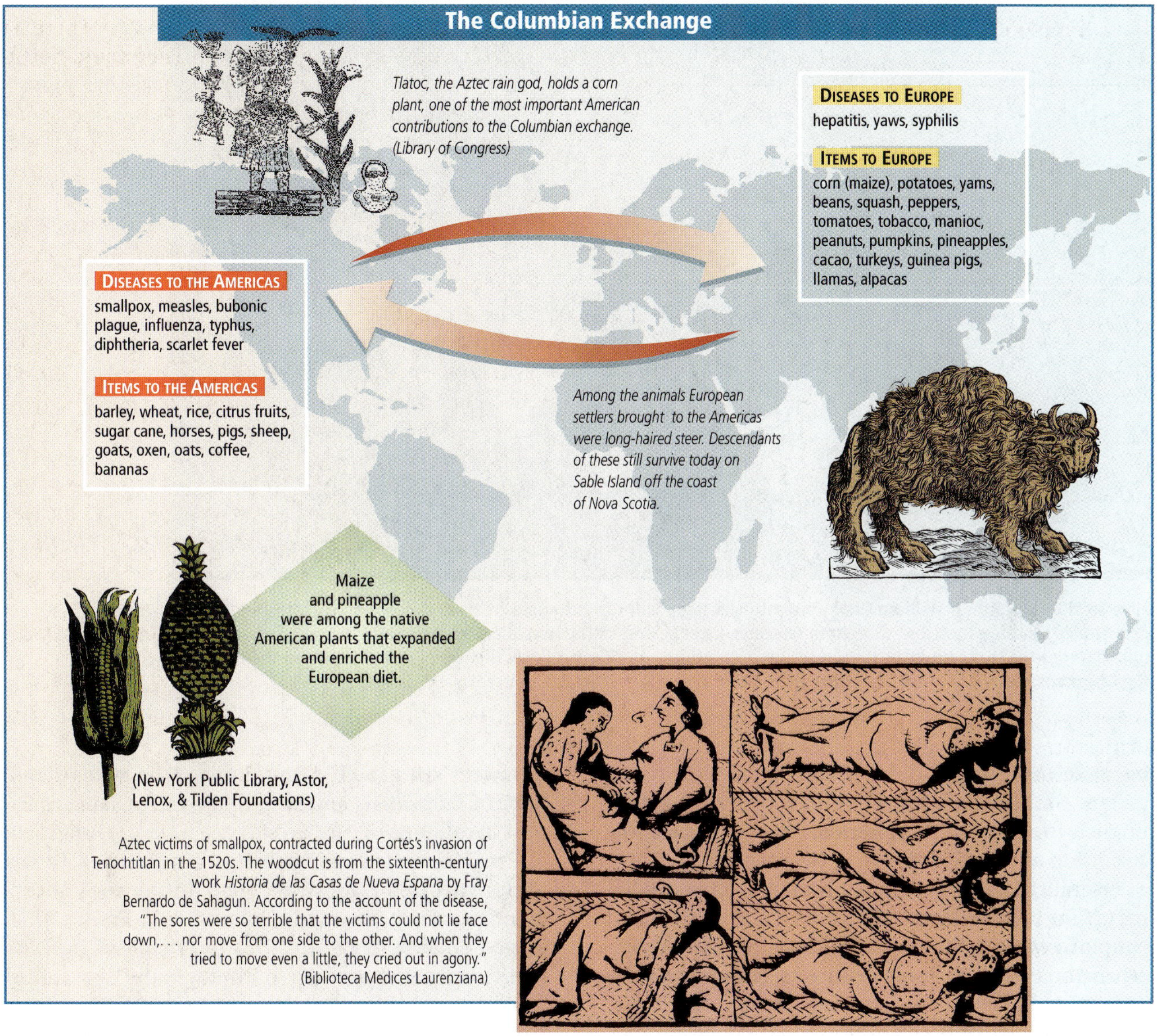

Tlatoc, the Aztec rain god, holds a corn plant, one of the most important American contributions to the Columbian exchange. (Library of Congress)

Among the animals European settlers brought to the Americas were long-haired steer. Descendants of these still survive today on Sable Island off the coast of Nova Scotia.

(New York Public Library, Astor, Lenox, & Tilden Foundations)

Aztec victims of smallpox, contracted during Cortés's invasion of Tenochtitlan in the 1520s. The woodcut is from the sixteenth-century work *Historia de las Casas de Nueva Espana* by Fray Bernardo de Sahagun. According to the account of the disease, "The sores were so terrible that the victims could not lie face down,. . . nor move from one side to the other. And when they tried to move even a little, they cried out in agony." (Biblioteca Medices Laurenziana)

social order that had previously been organized around tributary labor, the Spanish enriched themselves beyond the dreams of even the most visionary explorers. At Potosí, in Bolivia, 58,000 workers labored at elevations of up to 13,000 feet to extract the precious metal from a fabulous sugarloaf "mountain of silver." The town's population reached 120,000 by 1570, making it larger than any in Spain at the time. Thousands of other workers toiled in the mines of Zacatecas, Taxco, and Guanajuato. By 1660, they had scooped up more than 7 million pounds of silver from the Americas, tripling the entire European supply.

The massive flow of bullion from the Americas to Europe triggered profound changes. It financed further conquests and settlement in Spain's American empire, spurred long-distance trading in luxury items such as silks and spices from East Asia, and capitalized agricultural development in the New World of sugar, coffee, cacao, and indigo. The bland diet of Europeans gradually changed as items such as sugar and spices, previously luxury articles for the wealthy, became accessible to ordinary people.

The enormous increase of silver in circulation in Europe after the mid-sixteenth century also caused a "price revolution." As the supply of silver increased faster than the volume of goods and services that Europeans could produce, the value of the metal declined. Put differently, prices rose. Between 1550 and 1600, they doubled in many parts of Europe and then rose another 50 percent in the next half century. Land-owning farmers got more for their produce, and merchants thrived on the increased circulation of goods. But artisans, laborers, and landless agricultural workers (the vast majority of the population) suffered

This 1823 lithograph by William Clark romanticizes gang labor in the sugar fields of the British West Indies by decorously clothing men and women in trousers, jackets, and skirts. In reality, enslaved Africans worked seminaked under the punishing sun. However, this depiction accurately reflects the use of female labor in the harvesting of sugar cane. *(By Permission of the British Library)*

because their wages did not keep pace with rising prices. Skilled artisans, lamented one of the first English immigrants to America, "live in such a low condition as is little better than beggary."

Overall, the price revolution brought a major redistribution of wealth and increased the number of people in western Europe living at the margins of society. It thus built up the pressure to emigrate to the Americas, Europe's new frontier. At the same time, rising prices stimulated commercial development. Expansion overseas fed expansion at home and intensified changes toward capitalist modes of production already under way in the sixteenth century.

While the Spaniards organized their overseas empire around the extraction of silver from the highlands of Mexico, Bolivia, and Peru, the Portuguese staked their future on sugar production in the lowlands of Brazil. Spanish colonial agriculture supplied the huge mining centers, but the Portuguese, adapting techniques of cultivation worked out earlier on their Atlantic islands, produced sugar for export markets.

Whereas the Spanish mining operations rested primarily on the backs of the native labor force, the lowland Portuguese sugar planters scattered the indigenous people and replaced them with platoons of African slaves. By 1570, this regimented work force was producing nearly 6 million pounds of sugar annually; by the 1630s, output had risen to 32 million pounds per year. High in calories but low in protein, the sweet "drug food" revolutionized the tastes of millions of Europeans and stimulated the oceanic transport of millions of African slaves across the Atlantic.

From Brazil, sugar production jumped to the island-speckled Caribbean. Here, in the early seventeenth century, England, Holland, and France challenged Spain and Portugal for the riches of the New World. Once they secured footholds in the West Indies, Spain's enemies stood at the gates of the Hispanic New World empire. This ushered in a long period of conflict "beyond the line"—where European treaties had no force. Through contraband trading with Spanish settlements, piratical attacks on Spanish treasure fleets, and outright seizure of Spanish-controlled islands, the Dutch, French, and English in the seventeenth century gradually sapped the strength of the first European empire outside of Europe.

Spain's Northern Frontier

The crown jewels of Spain's New World empire were silver-rich Mexico and Peru, with the islands and coastal fringes of the Caribbean representing lesser, yet valuable, gemstones. Distinctly third in importance were the northern borderlands of New Spain—the present-day Sun Belt of the United States. Yet the early Spanish influence in Florida, the Gulf region, Texas, New Mexico, Arizona, and California indelibly marked the history of the United States. Spanish control of the southern fringes of North America began in the early 1500s and did not end for three centuries, when Mexico wrested independence from Spain in 1821. Far outlasting Spanish rule were the plants and animals they introduced to North America, ranging from sheep, cattle, and horses to various grasses and weeds that crowded out native plants.

Spanish explorers began charting the southeastern region of North America in the early sixteenth century, beginning with Juan Ponce de León's expeditions to Florida in 1515 and 1521 and Lucas Vasquez d'Ayllon's short-lived settlement at Winyah Bay in South Carolina in 1526. For the next half century, Spaniards planted small settlements along the coast as far north as the Chesapeake Bay, where their temporary encampment included many enslaved Africans. The Spanish traded some with the natives, but the North American coast, especially Florida, was chiefly important to the Franciscan priests, who attempted to gather the local tribes into mission villages and convert them to Catholicism.

The Spanish made several attempts to bring the entire Gulf of Mexico region under their control. From 1539 to 1542, Hernando de Soto, a veteran of Pizarro's conquest of the Inca, led a military expedition deep into the homelands of the Creeks and Choctaws and explored westward from Tampa Bay across the Mississippi to Arkansas.

De Soto's expedition at first found receptive natives, but his men could not provide what the Spanish most wanted—gold. Pillaging Indian villages and seizing food supplies, de Soto's men cut a brutal swath as far north as North Carolina and as far west as Arkansas. Disease followed the Spanish explorers everywhere they went. Little could the English know that their Spanish enemies were paving the way for them in North America's southeastern sector by spreading lethal microbes that devastated Indian societies and broke up the great chiefdoms of the lower South.

In 1559, Spaniards again marched northward from Mexico in an attempt to establish their authority in the lower Gulf region. Everywhere they went, they enslaved Indians to carry provisions. In 1565, they sought to secure Florida. Building a fort at St. Augustine, they evicted their French rivals at Fort Caroline, 40 miles to the north. St. Augustine became the center of Spain's northeastern frontier, and Florida remained a Spanish possession for more than two centuries.

The Southwest became a more important region of early Spanish activity in North America. Francisco Vásquez de Coronado explored the region from 1540 to 1542, leading an expedition of several hundred Spanish soldiers, a number of Africans, and a baggage train of 1,300 friendly Indians, servants, and slaves. Coronado never found the Seven Cities of Cíbola, reported by earlier Spanish explorers to be fabulously decorated in turquoise and gold. But he opened much of Arizona, New Mexico, and Colorado to eventual Spanish control, happened upon the Grand Canyon, and probed as far north as the Great Plains. His interior explorations, together with the nearly simultaneous expedition of de Soto in the Southeast, established Spanish claims to the southern latitudes of North America and gave them contacts, often bloody, with the populous corn-growing Indian societies of the region.

The Southwest, like Florida and the Gulf region, had no golden cities. In New Mexico, however,

James Walker's *Vaqueros in a Horse Corral* speaks beautifully of the Spanish origins of the cowboy in the American West. *(Gilcrease Museum of American Art, Tulsa, OK)*

Franciscan priests tried to harvest souls. A half century after Coronado's exploratory intrusions, Juan de Onate led 400 Spanish soldiers and ten Franciscan friars up the Rio Grande in 1598 to find some 60,000 Pueblo gathered in scores of settled towns where they had practiced agriculture for centuries. For the next 80 years, the Franciscans tried to graft Catholicism onto Pueblo culture by building churches on the edges of ancient native villages. As long as the priests were content to overlay Indian culture with a veneer of Catholicism, they encountered little resistance because the Pueblo found advantage in Spanish military protection from their Apache enemies and valued access to mission livestock and grain during years of drought. So, outwardly, they professed the Christian faith. But secretly the Pueblo still practiced their traditional religion in the underground Pueblo ceremonial chambers called kivas.

ENGLAND LOOKS WEST

By the time England awoke to the promise of the New World, Spain and Portugal were firmly entrenched there. But by the late sixteenth century, the conditions necessary to propel England overseas had ripened. During the seventeenth century, the English, as well as the Dutch and French, began overtaking their southern European rivals. The first challenge came in the Caribbean, where between 1604 and 1640 the English planted several small colonies producing tobacco and later sugar. Few guessed that some secondary and relatively unproductive settlements then being planted on the North American mainland would in time be among England's most prized possessions.

England Challenges Spain

England was the slowest of the Atlantic powers to begin exploring and colonizing the New World. Although far more numerous than the Portuguese, the English in the fifteenth century had little experience with long-distance trade and few contacts with cultures beyond their island aside from the French, against whom they had waged the Hundred Years' War (1337–1453). Only the voyages of John Cabot (the Genoa-born Giovanni Caboto) gave England any claim in the New World sweepstakes. But Cabot's voyages to Newfoundland and Nova Scotia a few years after Columbus's first voyage—the first northern crossing of the Atlantic since the Vikings—were never followed up.

At first, England's interest in the far side of the Atlantic centered primarily on fish. This high-protein food, basic to the European diet, was the gold of the North Atlantic. Early North Atlantic explorers found the waters off Newfoundland and Nova Scotia teeming with fish—not only the ordinary cod but also the delectable salmon. But the fishermen of Portugal, Spain, and France, more than those of England, began making annual spring trips to the offshore fisheries in the 1520s. Not until the end of the century would the French and English drive Spanish and Portuguese fishermen from the Newfoundland Banks.

Exploratory voyages along the eastern coast of North America hardly interested the English. It was for the French that Cartier and Verrazano sailed between 1524 and 1535. Looking for straits westward to India, through the northern land mass that was still thought to be a large island, they made contact with many Indian tribes and charted the coastline from the St. Lawrence River to the Carolinas. They established the northern latitudes as a suitable place for settlement but found nothing of immediate value to take home. The time had not yet arrived when Europeans would leave their homelands to resettle in America rather than go there merely to extract its riches.

Changes in the late sixteenth century, however, propelled the English overseas. The rising production of woolen cloth, a mainstay of the English economy, had sent merchants scurrying for new markets after 1550. Their success in establishing trading companies in Russia, Scandinavia, the Middle East, and India vastly widened England's commercial orbit and raised hopes for developing still other spheres. Meanwhile, population growth and rising prices depressed the economic conditions of ordinary people and made them look across the ocean for new opportunities.

The cautious policy of Queen Elizabeth I, who ruled from 1558 to 1603, did not include promoting overseas colonies. She favored Protestantism partly as a vehicle of national independence. Ambitious and talented, she had to contend with Philip II, king of Spain and her fervently Catholic brother-in-law, whose long reign nearly coincided with hers. Regarding Elizabeth as a Protestant heretic, Philip plotted incessantly against her. The pope added to Catholic–Protestant tensions in England by excommunicating Elizabeth in 1571 and absolving her subjects from paying her allegiance—in effect, inciting them to overthrow her.

The smoldering conflict between Catholic Spain and Protestant England broke into open flames in 1587. Two decades before, Philip II had sent 20,000 Spanish soldiers into his Netherlands provinces to suppress Protestantism. Then, in 1572, he had helped arrange the massacre of thousands of French Protestants. By the 1580s, Elizabeth was providing covert aid to the Protestant Dutch revolt against Catholic rule. Philip vowed to crush the rebellion and

Under the leadership of Elizabeth I, here displayed in royal finery and resting her hand on the globe, England challenged and ultimately overturned Spain's domination of worldwide sea trade. Behind the placid face was a determined and sometimes ruthless ruler. *(By kind permission of the Marquess of Tavistock and Trustees of the Bedford Estate)*

decided as well to launch an attack on England to wipe out this growing center of Protestant power.

Elizabeth fed the flames of the international Catholic–Protestant conflict in 1585 by sending 6,000 English troops to aid the Dutch Protestants. Three years later, Philip dispatched a Spanish armada of 130 ships carrying 30,000 men and 2,400 artillery pieces. Sails blazing with crusaders' crosses, the fleet set forth to conquer Elizabeth's England. For two weeks in the summer of 1588, a sea battle raged off the English coast. A motley collection of smaller English ships, with the colorful sea dog Francis Drake in the lead, defeated the Armada, sinking many of the lumbering Spanish galleons and then retiring as the legendary "Protestant wind" blew the crippled Armada into the North Sea.

The Spanish defeat prevented a crushing Catholic victory in Europe and brought a temporary stalemate in the religious wars. It also solidified Protestantism in England and brewed a fierce nationalistic spirit there. Shakespeare's love of "this other Eden, this demi-paradise" spread among the people; and with Spanish naval power checked, both the English and the Dutch found the seas more open to their rising maritime and commercial interests.

The Westward Fever

In the last decades of the sixteenth century, the idea of overseas expansion captured the imagination of important elements of English society. Urging them on were two Richard Hakluyts, uncle and nephew. In the 1580s and 1590s, they devoted themselves to advertising the advantages of colonizing on the far side of the Atlantic. For nobles at court, colonies offered new baronies, fiefdoms, and estates. For merchants, the New World promised exotic produce to sell at home and a new outlet for English cloth and other goods. For militant Protestant clergy, there awaited a continent filled with heathen people to be saved from devilish savagery and Spanish Catholicism. For the commoner, opportunity beckoned in the form of bounteous land, almost for the taking. The Hakluyts' pamphlets publicized the idea that the time was ripe for England to break the Iberian monopoly on the riches of the New World.

England first attempted colonizing, however, in Ireland. In the 1560s and 1570s, the English gradually extended control over the island through brutal military conquest. Ireland became a turbulent frontier for thousands of career-hungry younger sons of gentry families as well as landless commoners. Many of the leaders first involved in New World colonizing served in Ireland, and many of their ideas of how to deal with a "savage" and "barbaric" people stemmed from their Irish experience.

The first English attempts at overseas settlement were small, feeble, and ill-fated. Whereas the Spanish encountered unheard-of wealth and scored epic victories over ancient and populous civilizations, the English at first met only failure in relatively thinly settled lands. Beginning in 1583, they mounted several unsuccessful attempts to settle Newfoundland. Other settlers, organized by Walter Raleigh, planted a settlement from 1585 to 1588 at Roanoke Island, off the North Carolina coast. They apparently perished in attacks by a local tribe after killing a tribal leader and displaying his head on a pike. Small groups of men sent out to establish a tiny colony in Guiana, off the

South American coast, failed in 1604 and 1609, and another group that set down in Maine in 1607 lasted only a year. Even the colonies founded in Virginia in 1607 and Bermuda in 1612, although they would flourish in time, floundered badly for several decades.

English merchants, sometimes supported by gentry investors, undertook these first tentative efforts. They risked their capital hoping that small-scale ventures in North America might produce the profits of their other overseas commercial ventures. They had their queen's blessing though little royal backing in subsidies, ships, and naval protection. The Spanish and Portuguese colonizing efforts were national enterprises, sanctioned, capitalized, and coordinated by the crown. The English colonies were private ventures, organized and financed by small partnerships of merchants who pooled their slender resources.

English colonization could not succeed until these first merchant adventurers solicited the wealth and support of the prospering middle class. This support grew steadily in the first half of the seventeenth century, but even then, investors were drawn far more to the quick profits promised in West Indian tobacco production than to the uncertainties of mixed farming, lumbering, and fishing on the North American mainland. In the 1620s and 1630s, most of the English capital invested overseas went into establishing tobacco colonies in tiny Caribbean islands, including St. Christopher (1624), Barbados (1627), Nevis (1628), Montserrat (1632), and Antigua (1632).

Apart from the considerable financing required, the vital element in launching a colony was a suitable body of colonists. About 80,000 streamed out of England between 1600 and 1640, as economic, political, and religious developments pushed them from their homeland at the same time that dreams of opportunity and adventure pulled them westward. In the next 20 years, another 80,000 departed.

Economic difficulties in England prompted many to try their luck in the New World. The changing agricultural system, combined with population growth and the unrelenting increase in prices caused by the influx of New World silver, produced a surplus of unskilled labor, squeezed many small producers, and spread poverty and crime. By the late 1500s, the roads, wrote Richard Hakluyt, were swarming with "valiant youths rusting and hurtful for lack of employment," and the prisons were "daily pestered and stuffed full of them."

A generation later, beginning in 1618, the renewed European religious wars between Protestants and Catholics devastated the continental market for English woolen cloth, bringing unemployment and desperate conditions to the textile regions. Probably half of England's households lived on the edge of poverty. "This land grows weary of her inhabitants," wrote John Winthrop of East Anglia, "so as a man, which is the most precious of all creatures, is near more vile among us than a horse or a sheep."

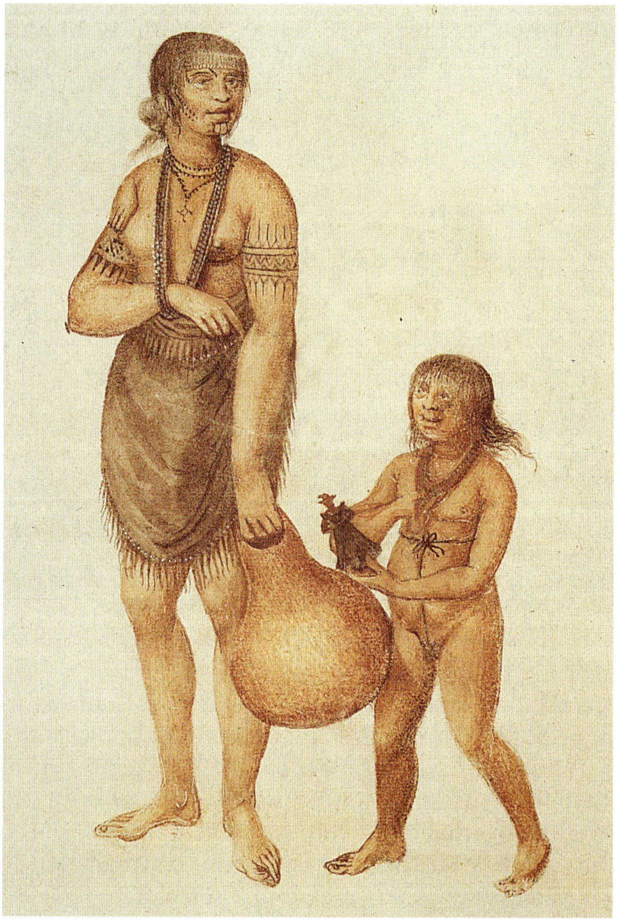

John White, governor of the second expedition to Virginia in 1587, rendered the first pictorial records of native life in the Americas. This watercolor of a tattooed noblewoman of Pomeiock shows her right arm resting in a chain of pearls or copper beads. Her young daughter holds a prized English doll in an Elizabethan dress. *(Copyright The British Museum)*

Religious persecution and political considerations intensified the pressure to emigrate from England in the early seventeenth century. How this operated in specific situations will be considered in the next chapter. The largest number of emigrants went to the West Indies. The North American mainland colonies attracted perhaps half as many, and the Irish plantations in Ulster and Munster still fewer. For the first time in their history, large numbers of English people were abandoning their island homeland to carry their destinies to new frontiers.

Anticipating North America

The early English settlers in North America were far from uninformed about the indigenous people of the New World. Beginning with Columbus's first description of the New World, published in several European cities in 1493 and 1494, reports and promotional accounts circulated among the participants in early voyages of discovery, trade, and settlement. This literature became the basis for anticipating the world that had been discovered beyond the setting sun.

Colonists who read or listened to these accounts got a dual image of the native people. On the one hand, the Indians were depicted as a gentle people who eagerly received Europeans. Columbus had written of the "great amity toward us" that he encountered in San Salvador in 1492 and had described the Arawaks there as "a loving people" who "were greatly pleased and became so entirely our friends that it was a wonder to see." Verrazano, the first European to touch the eastern edge of North America, wrote optimistically about the native people in 1524. The natives, graceful of limb and tawny-colored, he related, "came toward us joyfully uttering loud cries of wonderment, and showing us the safest place to beach the boat."

This positive image of the Native Americans reflected both the friendly reception that Europeans often actually received and the European vision of the New World as an earthly paradise where war-torn, impoverished, and persecuted people could build a new life. The strong desire to trade with the native people also encouraged a favorable view because only a friendly Indian could become a suitable partner in commercial exchange.

A counterimage of a savage, hostile Indian, however, also entered the minds of settlers coming to North America. Like the positive image, it originated in the early travel literature. As early as 1502, Sebastian Cabot had paraded in England three Eskimos he had kidnapped on an Arctic voyage. They were described as flesh-eating savages and "brute beasts" who "spake such speech that no man could understand them." Many other accounts portrayed the New World natives as crafty, brutal, loathsome halfmen, who lived, as Amerigo Vespucci put it, without "law, religion, rulers, immortality of the soul, and private property."

The English had another reason for believing that all would not be friendship and amiable trading when they came ashore. For years they had read accounts of the Spanish experience in the Caribbean, Mexico, and Peru—and the story was not pretty. Many books described in gory detail the wholesale violence that occurred when Spaniard met Mayan, Aztec, or Inca. Accounts of Spanish cruelty, even genocide, were useful to Protestant pamphleteers, who labeled the Catholic Spaniards "hell-hounds and wolves." Immigrants embarking for North America wondered whether similar violent confrontations awaited them.

Timeline

	Pre-Columbian Epochs
12,000 B.C.	Beringian epoch ends
6000 B.C.	Paleo-Indian phase ends
500 B.C.	Archaic era ends
500 B.C.–c. 1000	Post-Archaic era in North America
	Norse seafarers establish settlements in Newfoundland
A.D. 1000–1500	Kingdoms of Ghana, Mali, Songhay in Africa
1420s	Portuguese sailors explore west coast of Africa
1492	Christopher Columbus lands on Caribbean islands
	Spanish expel Moors (Muslims) and Jews
1494	Treaty of Tordesillas
1497–1585	French and English explore northern part of the Americas
1498	Vasco da Gama reaches India after sailing around Africa
1513	Portuguese explorers reach China
1515–1565	Spanish explore Florida and southern part of North America
1520s	Luther attacks Catholicism
1521	Cortés conquers the Aztec
1530s	Calvin calls for religious reform
1533	Pizarro conquers the Inca
1540–1542	Coronado explores the Southwest
1558	Elizabeth I crowned queen of England
1585	Roanoke Island settlement
1588	English defeat the Spanish Armada
1603	James I succeeds Elizabeth I
1607	English begin settlement at Jamestown, Virginia

Another factor nourishing negative images of the Indian stemmed from the Indians' possession of the land necessary for settlement. For Englishmen, rooted in a tradition of the private ownership of property, this presented moral and legal, as well as practical, problems. As early as the 1580s, George Peckham, an early promoter of colonization, had admitted that the English doubted their right to take the land of others. In 1609, Anglican minister Robert Gray wondered, "By what right can we enter into the land of these savages, take their rightful inheritance from them, and plant ourselves in their places, being unwronged or unprovoked by them?"

The problem could be partially solved by arguing that English settlers did not intend to take the Indians' land but wanted only to share it with them. In return, they would offer the natives the advantages of a more advanced culture and, most important, the Christian religion. This argument would be repeated for generations. As the governing council in Virginia put it in 1610, the settlers "by way of merchandizing and trade, do buy of [the Indians] the pearls of earth, and sell to them the pearls of heaven."

A more ominous argument arose to justify English rights to native soil. By denying the humanity of the Indians, the English, like other Europeans, claimed that the native possessors of the land disqualified themselves from rightful ownership of it. "Although the Lord hath given the earth to children of men," one Englishman reasoned, "the greater part of it [is] possessed and wrongfully usurped by wild beasts and unreasonable creatures, or by brutish savages, which by reason of their godless ignorance and blasphemous idolatry, are worse than those beasts which are of the most wild and savage nature."

Defining the Native Americans as "savage" and "brutish" did not give the English arriving in Opechancanough's land the power to dispossess his people of their soil, but it armed them with a moral justification for doing so when their numbers became sufficient. Few settlers arriving in North America doubted that their technological superiority would allow them to overwhelm the indigenous people. For their part, people like Opechancanough probably perceived the arriving Europeans as impractical, irreligious, aggressive, and strangely intent on accumulating material wealth.

Conclusion

Converging Worlds

The English immigrants who began arriving on the eastern edge of North America in the early seventeenth century came late to a New World that other Europeans had been colonizing for more than a century. The first English arrivals, the immigrants to Virginia, were but a small advance wave of the large, varied, and determined fragment of English society that would flock to the western Atlantic frontier during the next few generations. Like Spanish, Portuguese, and French colonizers before them, they would establish new societies in the newfound lands in contact with the people of two other cultures—one made up of ancient inhabitants of the lands they were settling and the other composed of those brought across the Atlantic against their will. We turn now to the richly diverse founding experience of the English latecomers in the seventeenth century.

Recommended Reading

The People of America Before Columbus

Brian M. Fagan, *The Great Journey: The Peopling of Ancient America* (1987) and *Ancient North America: The Archaeology of a Continent* (1991); Alvin M. Josephy, Jr., *America in 1492: The World of the Indian Peoples Before the Arrival of Columbus* (1992); Philip Kopper, *The Smithsonian Book of North American Indians: Before the Coming of Europeans* (1986); Kenneth Macgowan and Joseph A. Hester, Jr., *Early Man in the New World* (1983); Lynne Sebastian, *The Chaco Anasazi: Sociopolitical Evolution in the Prehistoric Southwest* (1994); Lynda N. Shaffer, *Native Americans Before 1492: The Moundbuilding Centers of the Eastern Woodlands* (1992); Dean Snow, *The Archaeology of North America: American Indians and Their Origins* (1976).

Africa on the Eve of Contact

George E. Brooks, *Landlords and Strangers: Ecology, Society, and Trade in Western Africa, 1000–1630* (1993); Basil Davidson, *The African Genius* (1969); Paul E. Lovejoy, *Transformations in Slavery: A History of Slavery in Africa* (1983); Roland Oliver and Anthony Atmore, *The African Middle Ages, 1400–1800* (1981); John Thornton, *Africa and Africans in the Making of the Atlantic World, 1400–1600* (1992).

Europe in the Age of Exploration

Carlo M. Cipolla, *Guns, Sails, and Empires: Technological Innovations and the Early Phases of European Expansion, 1400–1700* (1966) and *Before the Industrial Revolution: European Society and Economy, 1000–1700* (1976); Ralph Davis, *The Rise of the Atlantic Economies* (1973); J. H. Elliot, *The Old World and the New, 1492-1650* (1970); W. H. McNeill, *The Rise of the West* (1963); William D. Phillips, Jr., and Carla Rahn Phillips, *The Worlds of Christopher Columbus* (1992); Eric Wolf, *Europe and the People without History* (1982).

The Iberian Conquest of America

Inga Clendinnen, *The Aztecs* (1991); Alfred Crosby, Jr., *The Columbian Exchange: Biological and Cultural Consequences of 1492* (1972); Charles Gibson, *The Aztecs Under Spanish Rule* (1964); Charles Hudson, *Knights of Spain, Warriors of the Sun: Hernando de Soto and the South's Ancient Chiefdoms* (1997); James Lockhart and Stuart B. Schwartz, *Early Latin America* (1983); R. C. Padden, *The Hummingbird and the Hawk: Conquest and Sovereignty in the Valley of Mexico, 1503–1541* (1962); M. Leon Portilla, *The Broken Spears: The Aztec Account of the Conquest of Mexico* (1962); David E. Stannard, *American Holocaust: Columbus and the Conquest of the New World* (1992).

England Looks West

Kenneth R. Andrews, *Trade, Plunder, and Settlement: Maritime Enterprise and the Genesis of the British Empire, 1480–1630* (1985); Nicholas P. Canny, *The Elizabethan Conquest of Ireland* (1976); De Lamar Jensen, *Reformation Europe, Age of Reform and Revolution* (1981); Karen Kupperman, *Roanoke: The Abandoned Colony* (1984); Peter Laslett, *The World We Have Lost* (1971); David B. Quinn, *England and the Discovery of America, 1481–1620* (1974) and *Set Fair for Roanoke: Voyages and Colonies, 1584–1606* (1985); A. L. Rowse, *The Expansion of Elizabethan England* (1955); Keith Wrightson, *English Society, 1580–1680* (1982).

Fiction and Film

Search of the First Americans (1992), part of the Nova series produced by the Public Broadcasting System (PBS), provides a fascinating introduction to the peopling of the Americas before the Columbian voyages. *Secrets of the Lost Red Paint People,* also in this series, shows how archaeologists have reconstructed—always tentatively—the ancient world of the Americas. In a feature film titled *Conquest of Paradise* (1992) Gerard Depardieu plays Christopher Columbus, but Boston's WGBH seven-part *Columbus and the Age of Discovery* (1991) is much more comprehensive and more authentic. In *Roanoke,* a miniseries, PBS has also explored the friction between Indians and colonizers in the first attempt of the English to plant a North American settlement.

Suggested Web Sites

http://www.anthro.mankato.msus.edu/prehistory/vikings/vikhome.html

Vikings in the New World. This site explores the history of some of the earliest European visitors to America.

http://www.mcn.org/2/oseeler/drake.htm

Sir Francis Drake. This comprehensive site covers much of Drake's life and voyages.

http://lcweb.loc.gov/exhibits/1492/intro.html

1492: An Ongoing Voyage. An exhibit of the Library of Congress, Washington DC, this site provides brief essays and images about early civilizations and contact in the Americas.

http://marauder.millersv.edu/~columbus/

The Computerized Information Retrieval System on Columbus and the Age of Discovery. The History Department and Academic Computing Services of Millersville University of Pennsylvania provide this text retrieval system containing over 1,000 text articles from various magazines, journals, newspapers, speeches, official calendars, and other sources relating to various encounter themes.

http://www.angelfire.com/ca/humanorigins/index.html

Ancient Mesoamerican Civilizations. Kevin L. Callahan of the University of Minnesota Department of Anthropology maintains this page that supplies information regarding Mesoamerican civilizations with well-organized essays and photos.

http://medicine.wustl.edu/~mckinney/cahokia/cahokia.html

Cahokia Mounds. The Cahokia Mounds state historical site gives information about a fascinating pre-Columbian culture in North America.

http://www.mexonline.com/precolum.htm

Mexico Pre-Columbian History. This site provides information on the Aztec, Maya, Mexica, Olmec, Toltec, Zapotec, and other pre-European cultures, as well as information on museums, archaeology, language, and education.

http://www.acs.ucalgary.ca/HIST/tutor/eurvoya/

The European Voyages of Exploration. This University of Calgary site has images and texts for nearly every facet of European exploration.

http://www.ushistoryplace.com

the History place A richly detailed on-line learning environment complete with interactive maps, timelines, history activities, primary source documents, and links to related American history sites.

2

COLONIZING *a* CONTINENT

CHAPTER OUTLINE

By 1637, after five years in New England, John Mason knew both the prospects and perils of England's new overseas frontier. In his early thirties, Mason had emigrated from southeastern England. He was part of the flock of John Warham, a Puritan minister from the village of Dorchester. In Massachusetts, the group commemorated their origins by giving the name Dorchester to the area assigned to them. Here, six miles south of Boston, they built a simple church, assigned town lots and outlying farms, and began the work of serving their God in the wilderness of North America.

Like many Puritans, Mason had thrilled at the sight of southern New England's game-filled forests and fish-filled streams, the fields cleared and tilled by Algonquian agriculturists, the lush meadows available for grazing stock. Though the winters were inhospitable, it seemed this might be the Promised Land where Puritan refugees could plant their New World Zion. But Mason also recognized that these lands were not vacant. From the earliest days of the Pilgrim settlers at Plymouth in 1620, it was evident that the native occupiers of the region, whose claim went back a hundred generations, stood in the way of the Puritan "errand into the wilderness."

In the fall of 1636, Mason followed many of his Dorchester friends out of Massachusetts. Desirous of better land and restless with the political squabbling in the Massachusetts Bay Colony, the Dorchester settlers set out for the Connecticut River, 100 miles to the west. For 14 days, nipped by the frost of late autumn, they trekked wearily along Indian paths, carrying their meager possessions. At their journey's end, they founded the town of Windsor, on the west bank of the Connecticut.

Six months later, when his new village was no more than a collection of crude lean-tos, militia captain John Mason marched south against the Pequots. He owed his officership to military experience in the Netherlands, where thousands of English soldiers had gone in the 1620s to help the Protestant Dutch break the yoke of Catholic Spain in the Lowlands. Now he commanded several hundred men whom the fledgling Connecticut River towns had dispatched to drive the Pequots from the area. In the years before the English arrival, the powerful Pequots had formed a network of tributary tribes. Finding it impossible to placate the English as they swarmed into the Connecticut River valley, the Pequots chose resistance.

At dawn on May 26, 1637, Captain Mason and his troops approached a Pequot village on the Mystic River. Supported by Narragansett allies, the English slipped into the town. After a few scuffles in the half-light, Mason cried out, "We must burn them," and his men began torching the Pequot wigwams. Then they rushed from the fortified village. As flames engulfed the huts, the Pequots fled the inferno, only to be cut down with musket and sword by the English soldiers, who had ringed the community. Most of the terrified victims were noncombatants—old men, women, and children—for the Pequot warriors were preparing for war at another village about five miles away.

Before the sun rose, a major portion of the Pequot tribe had been exterminated. The resistance of the others crumbled when they learned the fate of their families. "It was a fearful sight to see them thus frying in the fire," wrote one Puritan, "and horrible was the stink and scent thereof; but the victory seemed a sweet sacrifice, and they gave the praise thereof to God, who had wrought so wonderfully for them." Mason himself wrote that God had "laughed at his enemies and the enemies of his people, . . . making them as a fiery oven."

Captain John Mason was a God-fearing Puritan and a man highly esteemed by his fellow colonists. His actions at the Mystic River, just seven years after the great Puritan migration to New England had begun in 1630, testify that the European colonization of America involved a violent confrontation of two cultures. We often speak of the "discovery" and "settlement" of North America by English and other European colonists. But the penetration of the eastern edge of what today is the United States might more accurately be called the "invasion of America."

Yet mixed with violence was utopian idealism. In the New World, Puritans—and countless waves of immigrants who followed them—sought both spiritual and economic renewal. Settlement in America represented a chance to escape European war, despotism, material want, and religious corruption. The New World was a place to rescue humankind from the ruins of the Old World. This chapter reconstructs the manner of settlement and the character

Cecil Calvert grasping a map of Maryland held by his grandfather, the second Lord Baltimore; detail of a painting by Gerard Soest, court painter to Charles II. (*Enoch Pratt Free Library, Baltimore*)

of immigrant life in six areas of early colonization: the Chesapeake Bay, southern New England, the French and Dutch area from the St. Lawrence River to the Hudson River, the Carolinas, Pennsylvania, and the Spanish toeholds on the southern fringe of the continent. A comparison of these various colonies will show how the colonizers' backgrounds, ideologies, goals, and modes of settlement produced distinctly different societies in North America in the seventeenth century.

THE CHESAPEAKE TOBACCO COAST

In 1585, England gained a first foothold in a hemisphere dominated by Spanish and Portuguese colonizers. A reconnaissance expedition organized by Walter Raleigh, one of Queen Elizabeth's favorite courtiers, scouted the Carolina coast and hastened homeward carrying two natives and a string of tales about rich soil, friendly Indians, and mineral wealth. A second voyage in 1585 and a third in 1587, composed of 91 men, 17 women, and 9 children, planted a small colony on Roanoke Island. But the enterprise failed. The voyages to Roanoke were too small and poorly financed to establish successful settlements. They served only as tokens of England's rising challenge to Spain in North America and as a source of valuable information for colonists later settling the area.

The Roanoke colony also failed resoundingly as the first sustained contact between English and Native American peoples. Although one member of the first expedition reported that "we found the people most gentle, loving, and faithful, void of all guile and treason," relations with the local tribes quickly soured and then turned violent. Charges flew back and forth, the English believing that the local Indians had stolen a silver cup and the Indians angered by English raids on their winter supply of corn. Aware of their numerical disadvantage and afraid of a coordinated attack against them, the English turned their muskets on a local leader to intimidate the natives with their superior technology. In 1591, when a relief expedition reached Roanoke, none of the settlers could be found. Most likely these "lost colonists" succumbed to Indian attacks. It was an ominous beginning for England's overseas ambitions.

Jamestown

In 1607, a generation after the first Roanoke expedition, a group of merchants established England's first permanent colony in North America at Jamestown, Virginia. Under a charter from James I, they operated as a joint-stock company, an early form of a modern corporation that allowed them to sell shares of stock in their company and use the pooled investment capital to outfit and supply overseas expeditions. Although the king's charter to the Virginia Company of London began with a concern for bringing Christian religion to native people who "as yet live in darkness and miserable ignorance of the true knowledge of God," most of the settlers probably agreed with Captain John Smith, who emerged as their strongest leader. "We did admire," he wrote, "how it was possible such wise men could so torment themselves with such absurdities, making religion their colour, when all their aim was profit."

Profits in the early years proved elusive, however. Expecting to find gold and other minerals, anticipating a rewarding trade with Indians for beaver and deer skins, and, best of all, hoping to discover the fabled passage through the North American continent to China, the original investors and settlers received a rude shock. Rather than duplicating the remarkable success of the Spanish and Portuguese in Mexico, Peru, and Brazil, the early Virginia colonists died miserably of dysentery, malaria, and malnutrition. More than 900 settlers, mostly men, arrived in the colony between 1607 and 1609; only 60 survived.

Seeking occupational diversity, the Virginia Company sent French silk artisans, Italian glassmakers, and Polish potash burners to Jamestown. But one-third of the first three groups of immigrants were gold-seeking adventurers with unroughened hands, a proportion of gentlemen six times as great as in the English population. Many others were unskilled servants, some with criminal backgrounds, who "never did knowe what a days work was," observed John Smith. Both types adapted poorly to wilderness conditions, leaving Smith begging for "but thirty carpenters, husbandmen, gardeners, fishermen, and blacksmiths" rather than "a thousand such gallants as were sent to me, that would do nothing but complain, curse and despair, when they saw . . . all things contrary to the report in England."

The Jamestown colony was also hampered by the common assumption that Englishmen could exploit the Indians of the region. Cortés and Pizarro had conquered the mighty Aztec and Inca empires with a few hundred soldiers and then turned the labor of thou sands of natives to Spanish advantage. Why not, the early settlers mused, in Virginia?

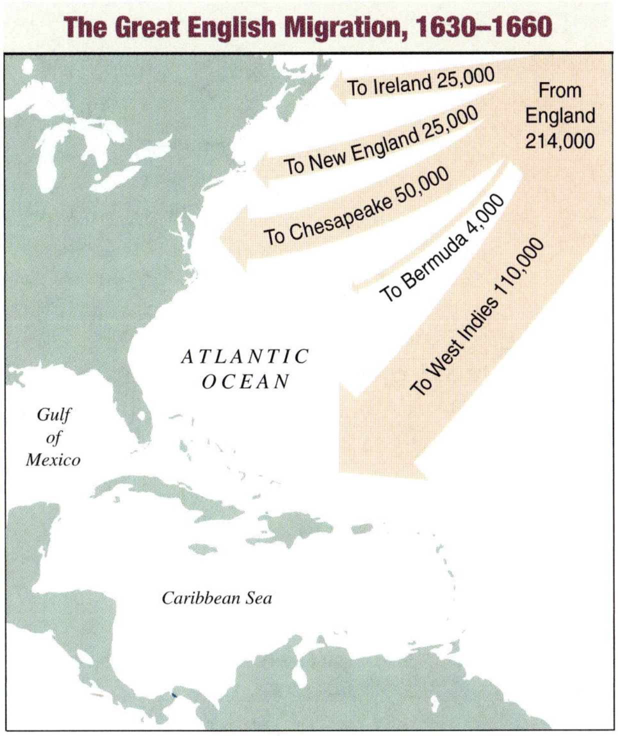

This figure shows that more than half of all the early English immigrants to the Americas went to the West Indies. Even a larger proportion of the Africans brought to the English colonies found themselves sold in England's Caribbean islands.

But the English found that the indigenous peoples were not densely settled and could not be easily subjugated. Contrary to expectations, no wealthy Indian empire lay waiting to be conquered. Nor could the Virginians mold the 20,000 Powhatan Indians of the region into a servile labor force, because, unlike the Spanish, the English settlers brought neither an army of conquistadores nor an army of priests to subdue the natives.

Instead, relations with some 40 small groups that the able Powhatan had united into a confederacy turned bitter almost from the beginning. Powhatan brought supplies of corn to the sick and starving Jamestown colony during the first autumn. However, John Smith, whose military experience in eastern Europe had schooled him in dealing with people he regarded as "barbarians," raided Indian corn supplies and tried to cow the local tribes by shows of force. In response, Powhatan withdrew from trade with the English and sniped at their flanks. Many settlers died in the "starving times" of the first years.

Despite these early failures, the Virginia Company of London poured more money and settlers into the venture. Understanding the need for ordinary farmers who could raise the food necessary to sustain the colony, they reorganized the company in 1609. They enticed many new settlers by promising free land at the end of seven years' labor for the company. In 1618, they sweetened the terms by offering 50 acres of land outright to anyone journeying to Virginia. To thousands of people on the margins of English society, such an offer was irresistible. More than 9,000 crossed the Atlantic between 1610 and 1622 to begin life anew in Virginia. Yet only 2,000 remained alive at the end of that period. "Instead of a plantation," wrote one English critic, "Virginia will shortly get the name of a slaughter house."

No one knows exactly what the Jamestown settlement looked like in its early years; this twentieth-century mural by Stanley King is a conjectured rendering based on archaeological evidence. New archaeological findings at the site of the Jamestown fort are adding to our knowledge of the first English Virginians. *(National Park Service, Colonial National Historical Park)*

Sot Weed and Indentured Servants

Even though the colony proved a burial ground for most immigrants within a few years of arrival, the promise of free land lured a steady stream of settlers to Virginia. Also crucial to the continued migration was the discovery that tobacco grew splendidly in Chesapeake soil. Frenchmen had first brought tobacco from Florida to Portugal in the 1560s. But it was Francis Drake's boatload of the "jovial weed" (so named for its intoxicating effect), procured in the West Indies in 1586, that popularized it among the upper class and launched a long history of addiction that still ravages the world.

Even James I's denunciation of smoking as "loathsome to the eye, hateful to the nose, harmful to the brain, and dangerous to the lungs" failed to halt the smoking craze. The "sot weed" became Virginia's salvation. Planters shipped the first crop in 1617, and tobacco cultivation spread rapidly. Commanding the handsome price of three shillings per pound in England, tobacco allowed a profit sufficient for settlers to plant it even in the streets and marketplace of Jamestown. By 1624, Virginia exported 200,000 pounds of the "stinking weed"; by 1638, though the price had plummeted, the crop exceeded three million pounds. Tobacco became to Virginia in the 1620s what sugar was to the West Indies and silver to Mexico and Peru. In London, men gibed that Virginia was built on smoke.

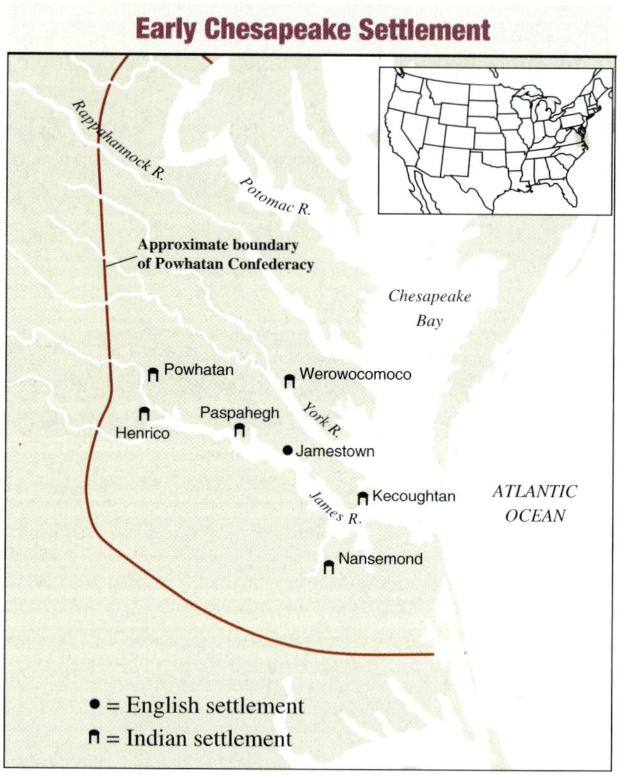

Only the major Indian villages in the early 1600s are indicated on this map. Note that the town sites are all oriented to the rivers—the source of both food and transportation.

By the end of the 1600s, most young European males were addicted to tobacco. Like the young Dutchmen shown in this painting, they practiced various tricks such as the "ring," "whiffle," "gulp," and "retention" as part of the smoking cult. (*Adriaen Brouwer, "The Smokers," The Metropolitan Museum of Art, Bequest of Michael Friedsam, 1931, The Friedsam Collection*)

While launching Virginia on an era of sustained growth, the cultivation of tobacco also obliged Virginia's planters to find a reliable supply of cheap labor. Tobacco required intensive care through the various stages of planting, weeding, thinning, suckering, worming, cutting, curing, and packing. To fill their need, planters recruited immigrants in England and Ireland and a scattering from Sweden, Portugal, Spain, Germany, and even Turkey and Poland. Such people, called indentured servants, willingly sold a portion of their working lives in exchange for free passage to America. About four of every five seventeenth-century immigrants to Virginia—and later, Maryland—were indentured. Nearly three-quarters of them were male, and mostly between 15 and 24 years old.

Many of the indentured servants came from the armies of the unemployed. Others were orphans, political prisoners, or common criminals who escaped the gallows by going abroad. Some were of the "middling sort," younger sons unlikely to inherit a father's farm or shop, or young men eager to leave behind an unfortunate marriage. Others were drawn simply by the prospect of adventure in a "strange new land." But overwhelmingly, indentured servants came from the lower rungs of the social ladder at home.

Life for indentured servants often turned into a nightmare. Only a handful, perhaps one in 20, realized the dream of achieving freedom and acquiring land. If malarial fevers or dysentery did not quickly kill them, servants often succumbed to the brutal work routine imposed by harsh masters. Even by the middle of the seventeenth century, when the starving times were only a memory, about half died during the first few years of "seasoning." Masters bought and sold their servants as property, gambled for them at cards, and worked them to death because there was little motive for keeping them alive beyond their term of labor. "My Master Adkins," wrote one servant in 1623, "hath sold me for £150 like a damned slave." When servants neared the end of their contract, masters found ways to add time and were backed by courts that they controlled.

Contrary to English custom, masters often put women servants to work at the hoe. Sexual abuse by masters was common, and servant women paid dearly for illegitimate pregnancies. The courts fined them heavily and ordered them to serve an extra year or two to repay the time lost during pregnancy and childbirth. They also deprived mothers of their illegitimate children, indenturing them out at an early age. For many servant women, marriage was the best release from this hard life. Many willingly accepted the purchase of their indenture by any man who suggested marriage.

Robert Vaughan's scenes for John Smith's memoirs (1624) get some of the story right but are fanciful in some respects. Here, Smith takes the gigantic Powhatan by the scalplock. The close combat between Indians and Englishmen in the background is dramatic but hardly accurate. (*From* The Generall Historie of Virginia, *1624, by Captain John Smith/Library of Congress*)

Expansion and Indian War

As Virginia's population increased, spurred by the growth of tobacco production, violence mounted between white colonizers and the Powhatan tribes. In 1614, the sporadic hostility of the early years ended temporarily with the arranged marriage of Powhatan's daughter, the fabled Pocahontas, to planter John Rolfe. However, the profitable cultivation of tobacco created an intense demand for land. As more and more settlers pushed up the rivers flowing into Chesapeake Bay, the local tribes worried that the previous abrasive and sometimes bloody contact might become a disastrous one.

In 1617, when Powhatan retired, the leadership of the Chesapeake tribes fell to Opechancanough. This proud and talented leader began building military strength for an all-out attack on his English enemies. The English murder of Nemattanew, a Powhatan war captain and religious prophet, triggered a fierce Indian assault on Good Friday in 1622 that dealt Virginia a staggering blow. More than one-quarter of the white population fell before the marauding tribesmen; the casualties in cattle, crops, and buildings were equally severe.

The devastating attack bankrupted the Virginia Company. As a result, the king annulled its charter in 1624 and established a royal government, which allowed the elected legislative body established in 1619, the House of Burgesses, to continue lawmaking in concert with the royal governor and his council.

The Indian assault of 1622 fortified the determination of the surviving planters to pursue a ruthless new Indian policy. John Smith, writing from England two years later, noted the grim satisfaction that had followed the Indian attack. Many, he reported, believed that it "will be good for the plantation, because now we have just cause to destroy them by all means possible." Bolstered by instructions from London to "root out [the Indians] from being any longer a people," the Virginians conducted annual military expeditions

Painted at the time she was presented to the court of King James I, Pocahontas appears in a red velvet jacket over a dark dress with gold buttons. She holds a fan of three ostrich feathers. We can only imagine how her elaborate shoulder collar of white lace must have felt for a 22-year-old woman accustomed to loose-fitting, comfortable clothes. *(National Portrait Gallery, Smithsonian Institution/Art Resource, NY)*

against the native villages west and north of the settled areas. The "flood of blood," as the English poet John Donne called it in 1622, had cost the colony dearly and doomed the Virginia Company of London. Yet it justified a policy of "perpetual enmity," even though several leaders admitted that the Indians had attacked in 1622 because of "our own perfidious dealing with them."

Population growth after 1630 and the recurrent need for fresh acreage by settlers who planted soil-exhausting tobacco intensified the pressure on Indian land. The tough, ambitious planters soon encroached on Indian territories, provoking war in 1644 and again in 1675. In each of these conflicts, the colonizers proved superior. Greatly outnumbering their opponents, they reduced the native population of Virginia to less than 1,000 by 1680. The Chesapeake tribes, Virginians came to believe, were merely obstacles to be removed from the path of English settlement.

Proprietary Maryland

By the time Virginia had achieved commercial success in the 1630s, another colony on the Chesapeake took root. The founder's main aim was not profit but a refuge for Catholics and a New World version of the English manorial countryside.

George Calvert, an English nobleman, designed and promoted Virginia's Chesapeake neighbor. Closely connected to the royal family, he had received a huge grant of land in Newfoundland in 1628, just three years after James I had elevated him to the peerage as Lord Baltimore. In 1632, Charles I, James's son, prepared to grant him a more hospitable domain of 10 million acres. Calvert named it Terra Maria after the king's Catholic wife, Queen Henrietta Maria. In English it became Maryland.

Catholics were an oppressed minority in England, and Lord Baltimore planned his colony as a haven for them. But knowing that he needed more than a small band of Catholic settlers, the proprietor invited others too. Catholics, never a majority in his colony, were quickly overwhelmed by Protestants who jumped at the offer of free land with only a modest yearly fee to the Calverts.

Lord Baltimore died while the charter for his colony was being drawn up in 1632, leaving his 26-year-old son, Cecilius, to carry out his plans. The charter guaranteed the proprietor control over all branches of government, but young Calvert learned that his colonists

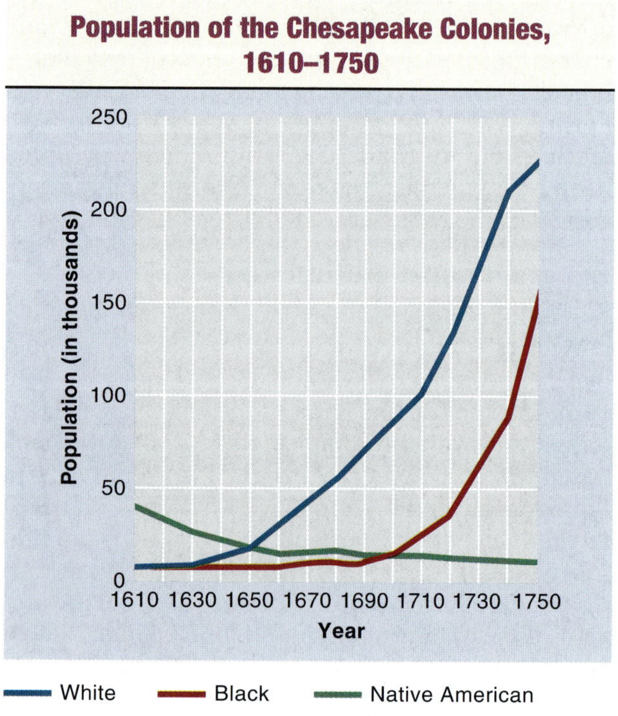

As indicated in this chart, it was not until the 1690s, when Chesapeake planters began turning to Africa for their labor, that the black population in the Chesapeake colonies began to rise rapidly. Source: U.S. Bureau of the Census.

would not be satisfied with fewer political liberties than they enjoyed at home or could find in other colonies. Hence, the Lords Baltimore were obliged to give up their charter-given right to initiate all colonial laws, subject only to the advice and consent of the people.

In land policy, Calvert's heirs found it impossible to carry out his plan for establishing feudalism in the woodlands of eastern North America. Arriving in 1634, immigrants blithely ignored his design of 6,000-acre manors for his relatives and 3,000-acre manors for lesser aristocrats, each to be ruled by provincial nobles and worked by flocks of serflike tenants. The settlers took up their free land, imported as many indentured servants as they could afford, maintained generally peaceful relations with local Indian tribes, grew tobacco on scattered riverfront plantations like their Virginia neighbors, and governed themselves locally as much as possible. In time, they created their own social hierarchy, not with assigned social roles but with status determined by the ability of some to rise above others in the competitive tobacco economy. Although Maryland grew slowly at first—in 1650, it had a population of only 600—it developed rapidly in the second half of the seventeenth century. By 1700, its population of 33,000 was half that of Virginia.

Daily Life on the Chesapeake

Though immigrants to the Chesapeake Bay region dreamed of bettering the life they had known in England, existence for most of them was dismally difficult. Only a minority could expect to marry and rear a family, because marriage had to be deferred until the indenture was completed; also, there were three times more men than women. Once made, marriages were fragile. Either husband or wife was likely to succumb to disease within about seven years. The vulnerability of pregnant women to malaria frequently terminated marriages in the first few years, and death claimed half the children born before they reached adulthood. Few children had both parents alive while growing up. Grandparents were almost unknown.

In a society so numerically dominated by men, widows were prized and remarried quickly. Such conditions produced complex families, full of stepchildren and stepparents, half-sisters and half-brothers. In the common case of marriage between a widow and a widower, each with children from a previous marriage, the web of family life became particularly complex, and the tensions attending child rearing unusually thick.

The household of Robert Beverley of Middlesex County illustrates the tangled family relationships in this death-filled society. When Beverley married Mary Keeble in 1666, she was a 29-year-old widow who had borne seven children during her first marriage. At least four of them were still alive to join the household of their mother's new husband. They gained five half-brothers and half-sisters during their mother's 12-year marriage to Beverley. When Mary Keeble Beverley died at age 41, her husband quickly remarried a recent widow, Katherine Hone. Beverley's second wife brought her son into the household and in the next nine years produced four more children with Beverley before his death in 1687. Thus, between 1666 and 1687, Beverley had married two widows who bore him nine children and had been stepfather to the eight children his two wives had produced with previous husbands. Not one of these 17 children, from an interlocking set of four marriages, reached adulthood with both a living mother and father.

We think of the churches of the colonial South as handsome, steepled, red brick buildings, but this unpainted clapboard church is typical of the rudimentary buildings erected by early colonists in the Chesapeake region. (*Harold Wickliffe Rose Papers, Yale University Library, New Haven, CT*)

Plagued by such mortality, the Chesapeake remained, for most of the seventeenth century, a land of immigrants rather than a land of settled families. Churches and schools took root very slowly amid such fluidity. The large number of indentured servants further destabilized community life. Strangers in a household, they served their time and moved on, replaced by other strangers, purchased as they clambered off boats fresh from England.

The fragility of life in the tobacco-growing Chesapeake world showed clearly in the region's architecture. As in most New World colonies, the settlers at first erected only primitive huts and shanties, hardly more than windbreaks. After establishing crops, planters improved their habitats but still built ramshackle one-room dwellings. "Their houses," it was observed in 1623, "stand scattered one from another, and are only made of wood . . . so as a firebrand is sufficient to consume them all." Even as Virginia and Maryland matured, cheaply built and cramped houses, usually no larger than 16 by 24 feet, remained the norm. Life was too uncertain, the tobacco economy too volatile, and the desire to invest every available shilling in field labor too great for men to build grandly. In England, solidly framed buildings erected on stone foundations had become the rule several centuries before. But throughout the Chesapeake, settlers erected "earthfast" flimsy cabins and houses directly on the ground or on posts.

Even by the early eighteenth century, most Chesapeake families were "pigg'd lovingly together," as one planter said, in a crude house without interior partitions. Eating, dressing, working, and loving all took place with hardly a semblance of privacy. For nearly two centuries, most ordinary Virginians and Marylanders lived in such quarters. "Like a flock of sheep in a fold," an eighteenth-century traveler described the family he bedded down with, 16 to a room, on the Virginia frontier. Even prosperous planters did not begin constructing fully framed, substantial homesteads until a century after the colony was founded.

The crudity of life also showed in the household possessions of the Chesapeake colonists. Struggling farmers and tenants were likely to own only a straw mattress, a simple storage chest, and the tools for food preparation and eating—a mortar and pestle to grind corn, knives for butchering, a pot or two for cooking stews and porridges, wooden trenchers and spoons for eating. Most ordinary settlers owned no chairs, no dressers, no plates or silverware. Among middling planters, the standard of living was raised only by possession of a flock mattress, coarse earthenware for milk and butter, a few pewter plates and porringers, a frying pan or two, and a few rough tables and chairs.

Even one of Virginia's wealthiest planters, the prominent Robert Beverley, had "nothing in and about his house but what was necessary . . . good beds . . . but no curtains, and instead of cane chairs, he hath stools made of wood." To be near the top of Chesapeake society meant having three or four rooms, sleeping more comfortably, sitting on chairs rather than squatting on the floor, and acquiring such ordinary decencies as chamber pots, candlesticks, bed linen, a chest of drawers, and a desk. Only a few boasted such luxury items as clocks, books, punch bowls, wine glasses, and imported furniture. Four generations elapsed in the Chesapeake settlements before the frontier quality of life slowly gave way to more refined living.

MASSACHUSETTS AND ITS OFFSPRING

While some English settlers in the reign of James I (1603–1625) scrambled for wealth on the Chesapeake, others in England looked to the wilds of North America as a place to build a tabernacle to God. The society they fashioned aimed at unity of purpose and utter dedication to reforming the corrupt world. American Puritanism would powerfully affect the nation's history, especially in planting the seeds of a belief in America's special mission in the world. Yet the "New England way" only partially prefigured the pathways of American development because Puritanism represented a visionary attempt to banish diversity on a continent where the arrival of streams of immigrants from around the globe was destined to become a primary phenomenon.

Puritanism in England

England had been officially Protestant since 1558. Many English in the late sixteenth century, however, thought the Church of England was still ridden with Catholic vestiges. Detesting such remnants of Catholicism as vestments and rituals that lingered on in the reign of Elizabeth (1558–1603), some demanded the end of every taint of "the Bishop of Rome and all his detestable enormities." Because they wished to purify the Church of England, they were dubbed Puritans.

The people attracted to the Puritan movement were not only religious reformers but also men and women who hoped to find in religion an antidote to the changes sweeping over English society. Many feared for the future, as they witnessed the growth of turbulent cities, the increase of wandering poor, rising prices, and accelerating commercial activity. In general, they disapproved of the growing freedom from the restraints of gentry-dominated medieval institutions such as the church, guilds, and local government.

The concept of the individual operating as freely as possible, maximizing both opportunities and personal potential, is at the core of our modern system of beliefs and behavior. But many in Elizabethan England dreaded the crumbling of traditional restraints. They worried that individualistic behavior would undermine the notion of community—the belief that people were bound together by reciprocal rights, obligations, and responsibilities. Especially they decried the "degeneracy of the times," which they saw in the defiling of the Sabbath by maypole dancing, card playing, fiddling, bowling, and all the rest of the roistering and erotic behavior reflected in Shakespeare's dramatic portrayals of "Merrie England." Puritans vowed to reverse the march of disorder, wickedness, and disregard for community by imposing a new discipline.

One part of their plan was a social ethic stressing work as a primary way of serving God. Derived from the Calvinist concept of "calling," this emphasis on work made the religious quest of every member of society equally worthy. The labor of a mason was just as valuable in God's sight as that of a merchant, and so was his soul. The "work ethic" would banish idleness and impart discipline throughout the community. Second, Puritans organized themselves into religious congregations where each member hoped for personal salvation but also supported all others in their quest. Third, Puritans assumed responsibility for the "unconverted" people around them. They were convinced that others who could not find Christian truth in their hearts might have to be coerced and controlled, as in Calvin's Geneva. Religious reform and social vision were in this way interlocked.

When King James VI of Scotland succeeded the childless Elizabeth as James I of England in 1603, he spoke stridently for the divine right of the monarch and his own role as head of the church. Claiming responsibility only to God, James collided with the rising power of the Puritans. They had occupied the pulpits in hundreds of churches, gained control of several colleges at Oxford and Cambridge, and recruited many followers. Translating their religious appeal into political power, the Puritans obtained many seats in Parliament and aggressively challenged the king's power. James responded by harassing them, removing dozens of Puritan ministers from their pulpits, and threatening many others. "I will harry them out of the land," he vowed, "or else do worse."

When Charles I succeeded to the throne in 1625, the situation worsened for Puritans. Determined to strengthen the monarchy and stifle dissent, the king summoned a new Parliament in 1628 and one year later adjourned this venerable body (which was the Puritans' main instrument of reform) when it would not accede to royal demands. The king then appointed William Laud, the bishop of London, to high office and turned him loose on the Puritans, whom Laud called "wasps" and the "most dangerous enemies of the state."

By 1629, when the king began ruling without Parliament, many Puritans were turning their eyes to northern Ireland, Holland, the Caribbean islands, and, especially, North America. They were convinced that God intended them to carry their religious and social reforms beyond the reach of persecuting authorities. A declining economy added to their discouragement about England, for the depression in the cloth trades was most severe in Puritan strongholds. To some distant shore, many Puritans decided, they should transport a fragment of English society and complete the Protestant Reformation. As they understood history, God had assigned them a special task in his plan for the redemption of humankind.

Puritan Predecessors in New England

Puritans were not the first Europeans to reach northeastern North America. Fishermen of various European nations had been working the fishing banks off Newfoundland and drying the cod they caught on the coast of Cape Cod and Maine since the early 1500s. They frequently made contact with the Algonquian-speaking tribes of the area. A short-lived attempt at settlement on the coast of Maine had also been made in 1607. Seven years later, the aging Chesapeake war dog John Smith, hired to hunt whales off the North American coast, coined the term "New England" after visiting the area. In his *Description of New England,* published in 1616, he excited considerable interest in the "Paradise of these parts."

No permanent settlement took root, however, until the Pilgrims—actually outnumbered by non-Pilgrims—arrived in Plymouth in 1620. Unlike the Puritans who followed, these humble Protestant farmers did not expect to convert a sinful world. Rather, they wanted to be left alone to realize their radical vision of a pure and primitive life. Instead of reforming the Church of England, they left it and hence were called Separatists. They had first fled from England to Amsterdam in 1608, then to Leyden when they found the commercial capital of Holland too corrupt, and, finally, in 1620, to North America.

When they arrived at the northern tip of Cape Cod in November 1620, the Pilgrims were weakened by a stormy nine-week voyage and ill-prepared for the harsh winter ahead. Misled by John Smith's glowing report of a warm, fertile country, they discovered instead a severe climate and a rockbound coast. By the following spring, half the Mayflower passengers were dead, including 13 of the 18 married women.

Recovering the Past

HOUSES

Homesteading is central to our national experience. For 300 years after the founding of the first colonies, most Americans were involved in taming and settling the land. On every frontier, families faced the tasks of clearing the fields, beginning farming operations, and building shelter for themselves and their livestock. The kinds of structures they built depended on available materials, their resources and aspirations, and their notions of a "fair" dwelling. The plan of a house and the materials used in its construction reveal much about the needs, resources, priorities, and values of the people who built it.

By examining archaeological remains of early ordinary structures and by studying houses that are still standing, historians are reaching new understandings of the social life of pioneering societies. Since the 1960s, archaeologists and architectural historians have been studying seventeenth-century housing in the Chesapeake Bay and New England regions. They have discovered a familiar sequence of house types—from temporary shanties and lean-tos to rough cabins and simple frame houses to larger and more substantial dwellings of brick and finished timber. This hovel-to-house-to-home pattern existed on every frontier, as sodbusters, gold miners, planters, and cattle raisers secured their hold on the land and then struggled to move from subsistence to success.

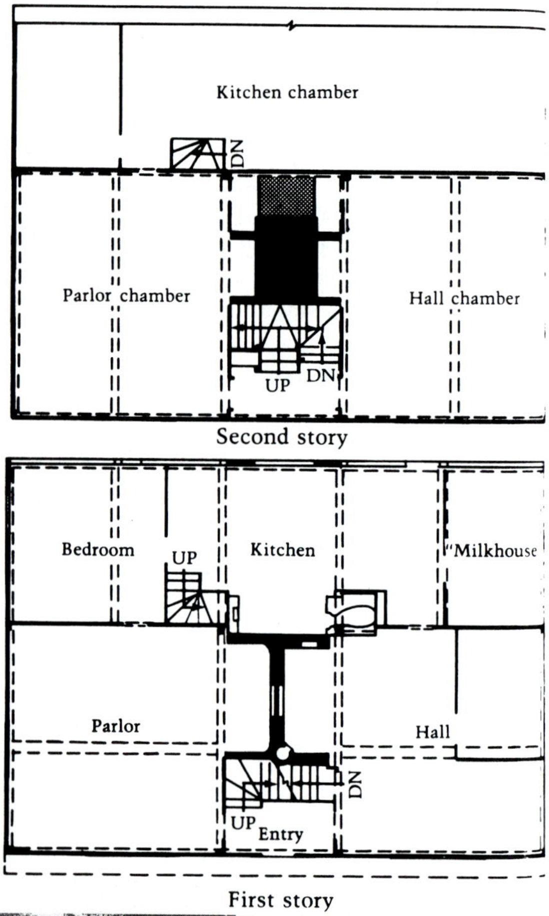

William Boardman house, Saugus, Massachusetts, c. 1687; a floor plan of the house is shown above. *(The Society for the Preservation of New England Antiquities)*

Reconstructed Chesapeake planter's house, typical of such simply built and unpainted structures in the seventeenth century. *(Photograph by Julie Roy Jeffrey)*

What is unusual in the findings of the Chesapeake researchers is the discovery that the second phase in the sequence—the use of temporary, rough-built structures—lasted for more than a century. Whereas many New Englanders had rebuilt and extended their temporary clapboard houses into timber-framed, substantial dwellings by the 1680s, Chesapeake settlers continued to construct small, rickety buildings that had to be repaired continually or abandoned altogether every 10 to 15 years.

The William Boardman house shown at left, built around 1687, is an example of the "orderly, fair, and well-built" houses of late-seventeenth-century Massachusetts. Its plan shows a typical arrangement of space: the hall, used for cooking, eating, working, and socializing; the parlor; a sleeping room for the parents; and a lean-to for kitchen chores and activities such as dairying. The great central chimney warmed the main downstairs room. Upstairs were two rooms used for both storage and sleeping. As you examine the exterior of the building, note the materials that have been used and the arrangement and treatment of windows, doors, and chimney. What impression of the Boardman family might visitors have as they approached the house? What kind of privacy and comfort did the house provide for family members?

The house shown above is a typical reconstructed tobacco planter's house. It has some of the same features as the Boardman house, for both are products of an English building tradition. But there are some major differences between the two. In the Chesapeake house, the chimney is not built of brick but of mud and wood; there is no window glass, only small shutters. The exterior is rough, unfinished planking. The placement of doors and windows and the overall dimensions indicate that this house has only one room downstairs and a loft above. The builders of this house clearly enjoyed less privacy and comfort than the Boardmans.

Historians have puzzled over this contrast between the architecture of the two regions. Part of the explanation may lie in the different climatic conditions and different immigration patterns of New England and the Chesapeake. In the southern region, disease carried off thousands of settlers in the early decades. The imbalance of men and women produced a stunted and unstable family life, hardly conducive to an emphasis on constructing fine homes. In New England, good health prevailed almost from the beginning, and the family was at the heart of society. It made more sense, in this environment, to make a substantial investment in larger and more permanent houses. Some historians argue, moreover, that the Puritan work ethic impelled New Englanders to build solid homes—a compulsion unknown in the culturally backward, "lazy" South.

Archaeological evidence combined with data recovered from land, tax, and court records, however, suggests another reason for the impermanence of housing in the Chesapeake region. Living in a labor-intensive tobacco world, it is argued, planters large and small economized on everything possible in order to buy as many indentured servants and slaves as they could. Better to live in a shanty and have ten slaves than to have a handsome dwelling and nobody to cultivate the fields. As late as 1775, the author of *American Husbandry* calculated that in setting up a tobacco plantation, five times as much ought to be spent on purchasing 20 black fieldhands as on the "house, offices, and tobacco-house."

Only after the Chesapeake region had emerged from its prolonged era of mortality and gender imbalance and a mixed economy of tobacco, grain, and cattle had replaced the tobacco monoculture did the rebuilding of the region begin. Excavated house sites indicate that this occurred in the period after 1720. New research is revealing that the phases of home building and the social and economic history of a society were closely interwoven. What do houses today reveal about the resources, economic livelihood, priorities, and values of contemporary Americans? Do class and regional differences in house design continue?

The survivors, led by the staunch William Bradford, settled at Plymouth. Squabbles soon erupted with local Indians, whom Bradford considered "savage and brutish men, which range up and down, little otherwise than the wild beasts." In 1622, they found themselves nearly overwhelmed by the arrival of 60 non-Pilgrims, sent out by the London Company, which had helped the Pilgrims finance their colony. For two generations, the Pilgrims tilled the soil, fished, and tried to keep intact their religious vision. But with the much larger Puritan migration that began in 1630, the Pilgrim villages nestled on the shores of Cape Cod Bay became a backwater of the thriving, populous Massachusetts Bay Colony, which absorbed them in 1691.

Errand into the Wilderness

In 11 ships, about a thousand Puritans set out from England in 1630 for the Promised Land. They were the vanguard of a movement that by 1642 brought about 18,000 colonizers to New England. Led by John Winthrop, a talented Cambridge-educated member of the English gentry, they operated under a charter from the king to the Puritan-controlled Massachusetts Bay Company. The Puritans set about building their utopia convinced they were carrying out a divine task. "God hath sifted a nation," wrote one Puritan, "that he might send choice grain into this wilderness."

Their intention was to establish communities of pure Christians who collectively swore a covenant with God to work for his ends. To accomplish this, the Puritan leaders agreed to employ severe means. Civil and religious transgressors must be rooted out and severely punished. They emphasized homogeneous communities where the good of the group outweighed individual interests. "We must delight in each other, make others' conditions our own, rejoice together, mourn together, labor and suffer together," counseled Winthrop.

To realize their utopian goals, the Puritans willingly gave up freedoms that their compatriots sought. An ideology of rebellion in England, Puritanism in North America became an ideology of control. Much was at stake, for as Winthrop reminded the first settlers, "we shall be as a city upon a hill [and] the eyes of all people are upon us." That visionary sense of mission would help to shape a distinctive American self-image in future generations.

As in Plymouth and Virginia, the first winter tested the strongest souls. More than 200 of the first 700 settlers perished, and 100 others, disillusioned and sickened by the forbidding climate, returned to England the next spring. But Puritans kept coming. They "hived out" along the Back Bay of Boston, the port capital of the colony, along the rivers that emptied into the bay, south into what became Connecticut and Rhode Island a few years later, and north along the rocky Massachusetts coast.

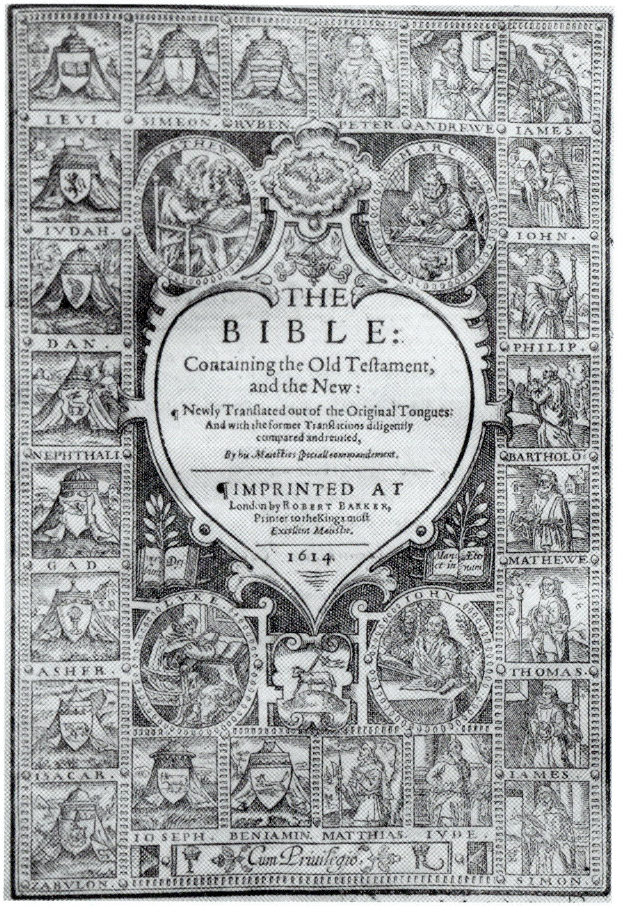

Fundamental to reformed Protestantism was each person having direct access to the Gospel. Literacy was therefore widespread in New England. London printers turned out thousands of Bibles in a variety of sizes and forms. John Winthrop carried this Bible across the Atlantic. The engraved title page shown here presents the emblems of the chiefs of the twelve tribes of Israel and the twelve apostles of Christ. *(Courtesy of the Massachusetts Historical Society)*

Motivated by their militant work ethic and sense of mission, and led by men experienced in local government, law, and exhortation, the Puritans thrived almost from the beginning. The early leaders of Virginia were soldiers of fortune or roughneck adventurers with predatory instincts, men who had no families or had left them at home. The ordinary Chesapeake settlers were mostly young men with little stake in English society who sold their labor to cross the Atlantic. But the early leaders in Massachusetts were university-trained ministers, experienced members of the lesser gentry, and men with a compulsion to fulfill God's prophecy for New England. Most ordinary settlers came as freemen in families. Trained artisans and farmers from the middle rank of English society, they established tight-knit communities in which, from the outset, the brutal exploitation of labor rampant in the Chesapeake had no place.

An Elusive Utopia

The Puritans built a sound economy based on agriculture, fishing, timbering, and trading for beaver furs with local Indians. Even before leaving England, the directors of the Massachusetts Bay Company transformed their commercial charter into a rudimentary government and transferred the charter to New England. There they laid the foundations of self-government. Free male church members annually elected a governor and deputies from each town, who formed one house of a colonial legislature, the General Court. The other house was composed of the governor's assistants, later to be called councillors. Consent of both houses was required to pass laws.

The Puritans also established the first printing press in the English colonies and planted the seed of a university, Harvard College, which opened its doors in 1636 to train clergymen. The Puritan leaders also launched a brave attempt in 1642 to create a tax-supported school system so that all children might gain the "ability to read and understand the principles of religion and the capital laws of this country." In 1647, the government ordered every town with 50 families to establish an elementary school and every town with 100 families a secondary school as well, open to all who wanted an education.

In spite of these accomplishments, the Puritan colony suffered many of the tensions besetting people bent on human perfection. Nor did Puritans prove any better than their less religious countrymen on the Chesapeake at reaching an accommodation with the Native Americans. Surrounded by seemingly boundless land, Puritans found it difficult to stifle acquisitive instincts and to keep families confined in compact communities. Restless souls looked to more distant valleys. "An over-eager desire after the world," wrote an early leader, "has so seized on the spirits of many as if the Lord had no farther work for his people to do, but every bird to feather his own nest." Those remaining at the nerve center in Boston agitated for broader political rights and even briefly ousted Winthrop as governor in 1635, when the colony's clergy backed the stiff-necked Thomas Dudley. After a few years, Governor Winthrop wondered if the Puritans had not gone "from the snare to the pit."

Winthrop's troubles multiplied in 1633 when Salem's Puritan minister, Roger Williams, began to voice disturbing opinions on church and government policies. Now the colony's leaders faced a contentious and visionary young man who argued that the Massachusetts Puritans were not truly pure because they would not completely separate from the polluted Church of England (which most Puritans still hoped to reform). Williams also denounced mandatory worship, which he said "stinks in God's nostrils," and argued that government officials should not interfere with religious matters but confine themselves to civil affairs. "Coerced religion," he warned, "on good days produces hypocrites, on bad days rivers of blood." Today honored as the earliest spokesman for the separation of church and state, Williams seemed in 1633 to strike at the heart of the Bible commonwealth, whose leaders regarded civil and religious affairs as inseparable. Williams also charged the Puritans with illegally intruding on Indian land.

Winthrop and others spent two years plying Williams alternately with sweet reason and threats, but they could not quiet the determined young man. Convinced that he would split the colony into competing religious groups and undermine authority, the magistrates vowed to deport him to England. Warned by Winthrop, Williams fled southward through winter snow with a small band of followers to found Providence, a settlement on Narragansett Bay in what would become Rhode Island.

Even as they were driving Williams out, the Puritan authorities confronted another threat: a magnetic woman of extraordinary talent and intellect. Anne Hutchinson was as devoted a Puritan as any who came to the colony. Arriving in 1634 with her husband and seven children, she gained great respect among Boston's women as a midwife, healer, and spiritual counselor. She soon began to discuss religion, suggesting that the "holy spirit" was absent in the preaching of some ministers. Before long Hutchinson was leading a movement labeled "antinomianism," an interpretation of Puritan doctrine that stressed the mystical nature of God's free gift of grace while discounting the efforts the individual could make to gain salvation.

By 1636, Boston was dividing into two camps—those who followed the male clergy and those who cleaved to the theological views of a gifted though untrained woman with no official standing. Her followers included most of the community's malcontents—merchants who chafed under the price controls the magistrates imposed in 1635, young people resisting the rigid rule of their elders, women disgruntled by male authority, and artisans who resented wage controls designed to arrest growing inflation. Hutchinson doubly offended the male leaders of the colony because she boldly stepped outside the subordinate position expected of women. "The weaker sex" set her up as a "priest" and "thronged" after her, wrote one male leader. Another described a "clamour"

Early New England

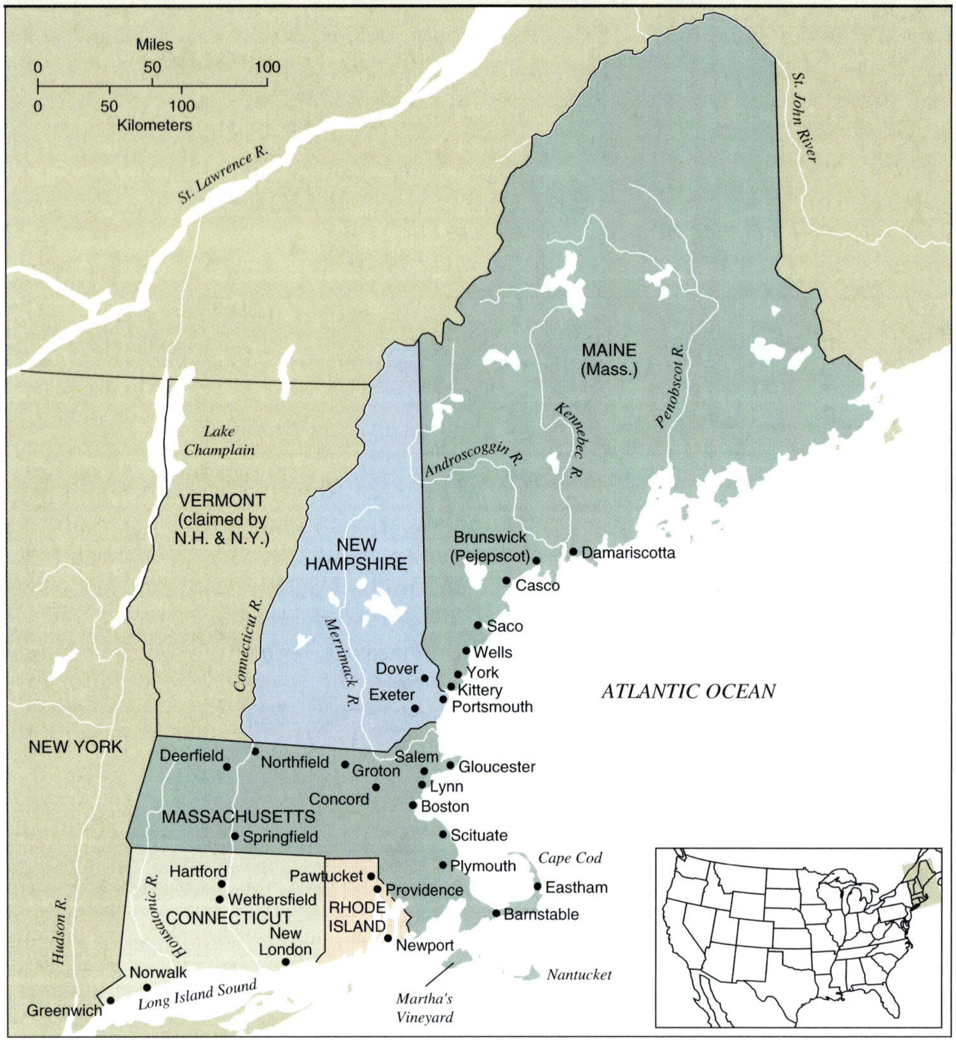

Maine and New Hampshire became the frontier to which New England settlers migrated when their towns and farmlands became too crowded.

in Boston that "New England men . . . usurp over their wives and keep them in servile subjection."

Determined to remove this thorn from their sides, the clergy and magistrates put Hutchinson on trial in 1637. After two long interrogations, they convicted her of sedition and contempt in a civil trial and banished her from the colony "as a woman not fit for our society." Six months later, the Boston church excommunicated her for preaching 82 erroneous theological opinions. She had "highly transgressed and offended and troubled the church," intoned the presiding clergyman, and "therefore in the name of our Lord Jesus Christ, I do cast you out and deliver you up to Satan and account you from this time forth to be a heathen and a leper." In the last month of her eighth pregnancy, Hutchinson, with a band of supporters, followed Roger Williams's route to Rhode Island, the catch basin for Massachusetts Bay's dissidents.

Ideas proved harder to banish. The magistrates could never enforce uniformity of belief nor curb the appetite for land. Growth, geographic expansion, and commerce with the outside world all eroded the ideal of integrated, self-contained communities filled with piety. Leaders never wearied of reminding Puritan settlers that the "care of the public must oversway all private respects." But they faced the nearly impossible task of containing land-hungry immigrants in an expansive region. By 1636, groups of Puritans had swarmed not only to Rhode Island but also to Hartford and New Haven, where Thomas Hooker and John Davenport led new Puritan settlements in what became Connecticut.

New Englanders and Indians

The charter of the Massachusetts Bay Company proclaimed that the "principal end of this plantation" was "to win and incite the natives to the knowledge and obedience of the only true God and Saviour of mankind and the Christian faith." But the instructions that Governor John Winthrop carried from England reveal other Puritan thoughts about the native inhabitants. According to Winthrop's orders, all men were to receive training in the use of firearms, a reversal of the sixteenth-century English policy of disarming the citizenry in order to quell public disorders. New England magistrates prohibited Indians from entering Puritan towns and threatened to deport any colonist selling arms to an Indian or instructing one in their use.

Only sporadic conflict with local tribes occurred at first because disease had catastrophically struck the Native Americans of New England, who may have numbered 125,000 in 1600, and left much of their land vacant. English fishermen, stopping along the coast in 1616, triggered a ferocious outbreak of respiratory viruses and smallpox that wiped out three-quarters of the population. Five years later, an Englishman exploring the area wrote that the Indians "died on heapes, as they lay in their houses" and described walking through a forest where human skeletons covered the ground.

When smallpox returned in 1633, killing thousands more natives, it again relieved pressure for land. The Puritans saw the disease as proof that God had intervened on their side, just when a flood of new settlers was causing trouble over rights to land. "Without this remarkable and terrible stroke of God upon the natives," reported the Charlestown settlers, "[we] would with much more difficulty have found room, and at far greater charge have obtained and purchased land." Many surviving Indians welcomed the Puritans because they now had surplus land and through trade hoped to gain English protection against tribal enemies to the north.

The settler pressure for new land, however, soon reached into areas untouched by disease. Land hunger mingled with the Puritan sense of mission made an explosive mix. To a people brimming with messianic zeal, the heathen Indians represented a mocking challenge to the building of a religious commonwealth that would "shine as a beacon" back to decadent England. A failure to convert the natives to civility and Christianity would have represented a failure by the Puritans to control the land to which God had directed them. God, they knew, would punish them with his wrath for this failure.

Making the "savages" of New England strictly accountable to the ordinances that governed white behavior was part of this quest for fulfilling their mission. The Puritans succeeded with the smaller, disease-ravaged tribes of eastern Massachusetts. But their attempts to control the stronger Pequots led to the bloody war in 1637 in which John Mason was a leader. The Puritan victory in that war assured English domination over all the tribes of southern New England except the powerful Wampanoags and Narragansetts of Rhode Island and removed the last obstacle to expansion into the Connecticut River valley. Missionary work, led by John Eliot, began among the remnant tribes in the 1640s. After a decade of effort, about 1,000 Indians had been settled in four "praying villages," learning to live according to the white man's ways.

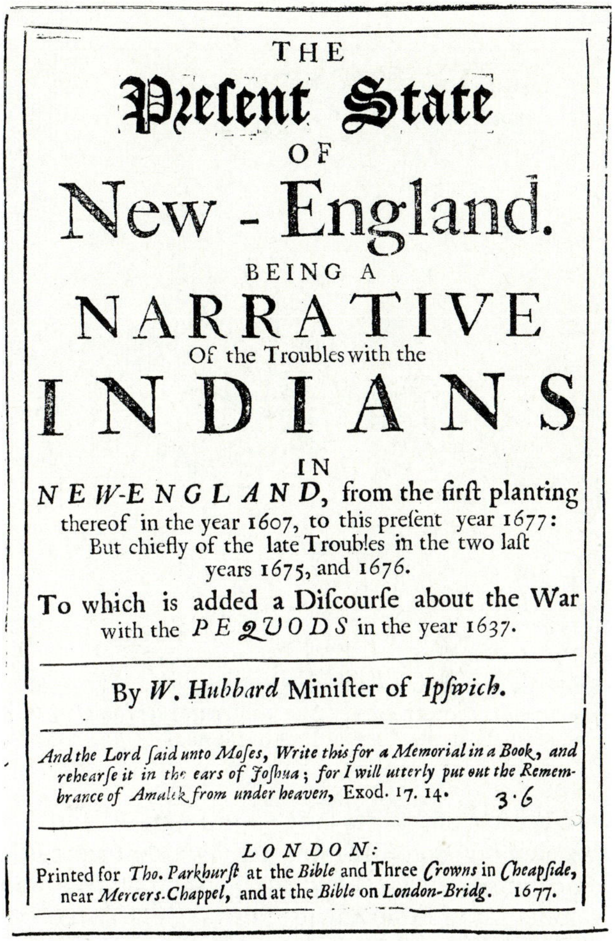
THE
Preſent State
OF
New - England.
BEING A
NARRATIVE
Of the Troubles with the
INDIANS
IN
NEW-ENGLAND, from the firſt planting thereof in the year 1607, to this preſent year 1677: But chiefly of the late Troubles in the two laſt years 1675, and 1676.
To which is added a Diſcourſe about the War with the *PEQUODS* in the year 1637.

By *W. Hubbard* Miniſter of *Ipſwich*.

And the Lord ſaid unto Moſes, Write this for a Memorial in a Book, and rehearſe it in the ears of Joſhua; for I will utterly put out the Remembrance of Amalek from under heaven, Exod. 17. 14. 3·6

LONDON:
Printed for *Tho. Parkhurſt* at the *Bible* and Three *Crowns* in *Cheapſide*, near *Mercers-Chappel*, and at the *Bible* on *London-Bridg*. 1677.

New England's leaders were always troubled by their difficult relations with the native inhabitants of the region. Histories of these tensions, like this one published in Boston and London in 1677, often appeared after Indian wars and usually defended the colonists' actions. (*The New York Public Library*)

The Web of Village Life

The village was the vital center of Puritan life. Unlike the Chesapeake tobacco planters, who dispersed along the streams and rivers of their area, the Puritans established small, tightly settled villages. Most pursued "open field" agriculture, trudging out from the

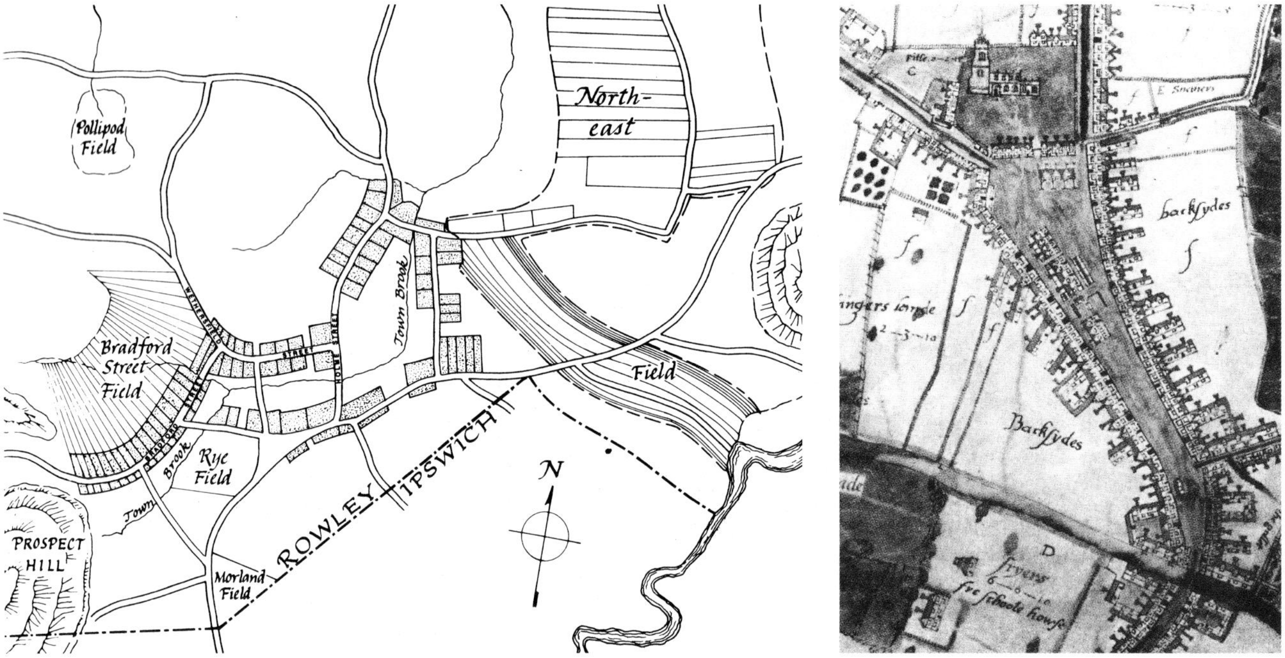

(Left) The similarity in settlement patterns between England and New England can be seen in a modern rendering of early seventeenth-century Rowley, Massachusetts (*Reprinted by permission of David Grayson Allen, ©1981. All rights reserved*), and (right) a plan of Chelmsford, Essex, in 1591 (*Essex Record Office, Essex, England*).

village each morning to farm narrow strips of land that radiated out from the town. They grazed their cattle on common meadow and cut firewood on common woodland. In other towns, Puritans employed the "closed field" system of self-contained farms that they had known at home. Both systems re-created agricultural life in many parts of England.

In either system, families lived close together in compact towns built around a common, with its meetinghouse and tavern. These small, communal villages kept families in close touch so that each could be alert not only to its own transgressions, but also to those of its neighbors. "In a multitude of counsellors is safety," Puritan ministers were fond of advising, and the little villages of 50 to 100 families perfectly served the need for moral surveillance, or "holy watching." To achieve godliness and communal unity, Puritans also prohibited single men and women from living by themselves, beyond patriarchal authority and group observation. Left to themselves, men and women would stray from the path, for, as Thomas Hooker put it, "every natural man and woman is born full of sin, as full as a toad of poison." Virginia planters counted the absence of restraint as a blessing. New Englanders feared it as the Devil.

At the center of every Puritan village stood the meetinghouse. These plain wooden structures, sometimes called "Lord's barns," gathered in every soul in the village, not just once but twice a week—on the Lord's day and during midweek as well. No man stood higher in the community than the minister. He was the spiritual leader in these small, family-based, community-oriented settlements, which viewed life as a Christian pilgrimage.

The unique Puritan mixture of strict authority and incipient democracy, of hierarchy and equality, can be seen in the way the Massachusetts town distributed land and devised local government. Each town was founded by a grant of the colony's General Court, sitting in Boston. Only groups of Puritans who had signed a compact signifying their unity of purpose received settlement grants. "We shall by all means," read the town of Dedham's covenant, "labor to keep off from us such as are contrary minded, and receive only such unto us as may be probably of one heart with us."

After receiving a grant, townsmen met to parcel out land. They awarded individual grants according to the size of a man's household, his wealth, and his usefulness to the church and town. Such a system perpetuated existing differences in wealth and status. Yet some towns wrote language into their covenants that to the modern ear has an almost socialistic ring. "From each according to his ability to each as need shall require," read one. It was not socialism that the Puritans had in mind. Rather, they believed that the community's welfare transcended individual ambitions or accomplishments and that unity demanded limits on the accumulation of wealth. Every family should have enough land to sustain it, and prospering men were expected to use their wealth for the community's benefit, not for conspicuous consumption. Repairing the meetinghouse, building a school, aiding a widowed neighbor—such were the proper uses of wealth.

Having felt the sting of centralized power in church and state, Puritans emphasized local exercise of authority. Until 1684, only male church members could vote, and as the proportion of males who were church members declined, so did the proportion of men who could vote. These voters elected selectmen, who allocated land, passed local taxes, and settled disputes. Once a year, all townsmen gathered for the town meeting, called later by Thomas Jefferson the "wisest invention ever devised by the wit of man for the perfect exercise of self-government." At the town meeting, the citizens selected town officers for the next year and decided matters large and small: Should the playing of football in the streets be prohibited? Might Widow Thomas be allowed £10 for a kidney stone operation for her son? What salary should the schoolteacher be paid?

The appointment of many citizens to minor offices—surveyors of hemp, informers about deer, purchasers of grain, town criers, measurers of salt, fence viewers, and many others—bred the tradition of local government. Complaints about officialdom rarely grew into political bitterness in such a system. All officeholders were annually subject to electoral approval, and about one out of every ten adult males in many towns was selected each year for some office, large or small. In New England, nobody could acquire a reputation for sobriety and industry without finding himself elected to a local post.

The predominance of families also lent cohesiveness to Puritan village life. Strengthening this family orientation was the remarkably healthy environment of the Puritans' "New Israel." Whereas the germs carried by English colonizers devastated neighboring Indian societies, the effect on the newcomers of entering a new environment was the opposite. The low density of settlement prevented infectious diseases from spreading, and the isolation of the New England villages from the avenues of Atlantic commerce, along which diseases as well as cargo flowed, minimized biological hazards.

The result was a spectacular natural increase in the population and a life span unknown in Europe. At a time when the population of western Europe was barely growing—deaths almost equaled births—the population of New England, discounting new immigrants, doubled every 27 years. The difference was not due to a higher birthrate. New England women typically bore about seven children during the course of a marriage, but this barely exceeded the European norm. The crucial factor was that chances for survival after birth were far greater than in England because of the healthier climate and better diet. In most of Europe, only half the babies born lived long enough to produce children themselves. Life expectancy for the population at large was less than 40 years. In New England, nearly 90 percent of the infants born in the seventeenth century survived to marriageable age, and life expectancy exceeded 60 years—longer than for the American population as a whole at any time until the early twentieth century. About 25,000 people immigrated to New England in the seventeenth century, but by 1700, they had produced a population of 100,000. By contrast, some 75,000 immigrants to the Chesapeake colonies had yielded a population of only about 70,000 by the end of the century.

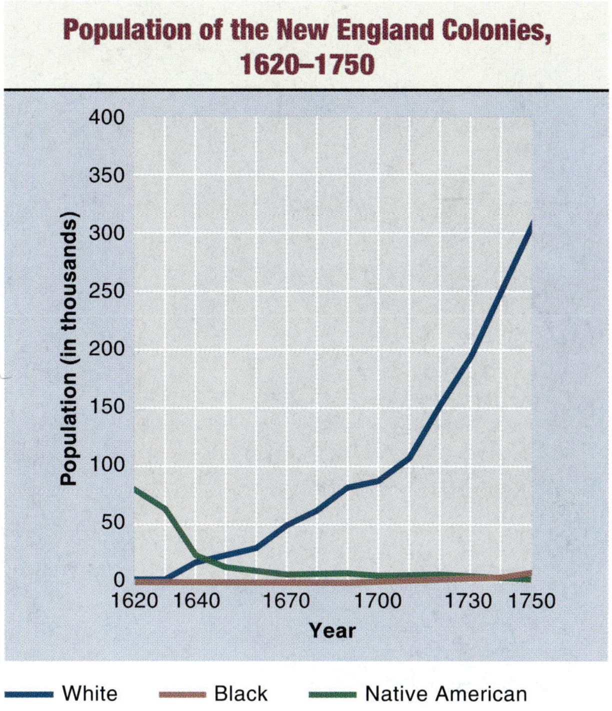

The far more rapid white population growth in New England than in the Chesapeake region reflected higher birthrates, a healthier environment, and a reliance on free labor. Source: U.S. Bureau of the Census.

Women played a vital role in this family-centered society. The Puritan woman was not only wife, mother, and housekeeper; she also kept the vegetable garden; salted and smoked meats; preserved vegetables and dairy products; and spun yarn, wove cloth, and made clothes.

The presence of women and a stable family life strongly affected New England's regional architecture. As communities formed, the Puritans converted early economic gains into more substantial housing rather than investing in bound labor as Chesapeake colonists

Three of Arthur and Joanna Mason's five children were captured in this 1670 painting. The nine-year-old boy on the left holds a silver-headed walking stick, signifying his status as male heir. His six-year-old sister in the middle holds a yellow fan and red and yellow ribbons. The four-year-old sister to the right holds a rose, which Puritans used as a symbol of innocence associated with childhood. (*Fine Arts Museum of San Francisco, Gift of Mr. and Mrs. John Rockefeller 3rd, 1979.7.3*)

did, retarding family formation and rendering the economy unstable. In New England, well-constructed one-room houses with sleeping lofts quickly replaced the early "wigwams, huts, and hovels." Families then added parlors and lean-to kitchens as soon as they could. Within a half century, New England immigrants accomplished a general rebuilding of their living structures, whereas the Chesapeake lagged far behind.

A final binding element in Puritan communities was the stress on literacy and education, eventually to become a hallmark of American society. Placing religion at the center of their lives, Puritans emphasized the ability to read catechisms, psalmbooks, and especially the Bible. Literacy could instill the basic precepts of life. "Thy life to mend, this book attend" went one verse in a children's schoolbook. In literacy, Puritans saw guarantees that they would not succumb to the savagery they perceived all around them in the new land. Through education, they could preserve the central values of their struggle to redeem humankind in the North American wilderness.

An event in England in 1642 affected the future development of the New England colonies. King Charles I pushed his people into revolution by violating the country's customary constitution and continuing earlier attacks against Puritans. By 1649, the ensuing civil war climaxed with the trial and beheading of the king. Thereafter, during the so-called Commonwealth period (1649–1660), Puritans in England could complete the reform of religion and society at home. Meanwhile, migration to New England abruptly ceased.

The 20,000 English immigrants who had come to New England by 1649 were scattered from Maine to Long Island. Governor Winthrop of Massachusetts lamented the dispersion, and Roger Williams condemned the "depraved appetite" for new and better land. Yet, in a terrain so rock-strewn that its pastures were said to produce Yankee sheep with sharpened noses, it was natural that farmers should seek better plow land.

To combat the problems of dispersion, Puritan leaders established a broad intercolony political structure in 1643 called the Confederation of New England. Designed to coordinate government among the various Puritan settlements (Rhode Island was pointedly excluded) and especially to provide greater defense against the French, the Dutch, and the Indians, the pact bound together Massachusetts, Plymouth, the small colony of New Haven, and the river towns of Connecticut. This first American attempt at federalism managed to function fitfully for a generation, though Massachusetts, the strongest and largest member, often refused to abide by group decisions when they ran counter to its objectives.

Although the Puritans fashioned stable communities, developed the economy, and constructed effective government, their leaders, as early as the 1640s, complained that the founding vision of Massachusetts Bay was faltering. Material concerns seemed to transcend religious commitment; the individual prevailed over the community. In 1638, the General Court declared a day of humiliation and prayer to atone for the colony's "excess idleness and contempt of authority." A generation later, the synod of 1679—a convention of Puritan Churches—cried out that the "church, the commonwealth and the family are being destroyed by self-assertion." By this time, Puritans rarely mentioned the work of salvaging English Protestantism by example. Instead, they concentrated on keeping their children on the straight and narrow road.

But despite such complaints about moral laxness, New England had achieved economic success and political stability by the end of the seventeenth century. Towns functioned efficiently, poverty was uncommon, public education had been mandated, and family life was stable. If social diversity increased and the religious zeal of the founding generation waned, that was only to be expected. One second-generation Bay colonist put the matter bluntly. His minister had noticed his absence in church and found him late that day at the docks, unloading a boatload of cod. "Why were you not in church this morning?" asked the clergyman. Back came the reply: "My father came here for religion, but I came for fish."

FROM THE ST. LAWRENCE TO THE HUDSON

The New Englanders were not the only European settlers in the northern region, for both France and Holland created colonies there. While English settlers founded Jamestown, the French were settling Canada, where they had failed in the 1540s.

France's America

Henry IV, the first strong French king in half a century, sent Samuel de Champlain to explore deep into the territory even before the English had obtained a foothold on the Chesapeake. Champlain established a small settlement in Port Royal, Acadia (later Nova Scotia), in 1604 and another at Quebec, in 1608. Already established French fish-drying stations in Newfoundland had initiated trading with Indians for furs, and Champlain's settlers hoped for easy profits on beaver. But the holders of the fur monopoly in France did not encourage immigration to the colony, because settlement would reduce the forests from which the furs were harvested. New France therefore remained so lightly populated that English marauders easily seized and held Quebec from 1629 to 1632.

In 1609–1610, Champlain allied with the Algonquian Indians of the St. Lawrence region in attacking their Iroquois enemies to the south, earning their eternal enmity. This drove the Iroquois to trade furs for European goods with the Dutch on the Hudson River, and when the Iroquois exhausted the furs of their own territory, they turned north and west, determined to seize the forest-rich resources from the Hurons, French allies in the Great Lakes region.

When the fury of the Iroquois descended on them in the 1640s, the Hurons were a people already decimated by a decade of epidemics that had spread among them as they accepted Jesuit priests in their villages. In the "beaver wars" of the 1640s and 1650s, the Iroquois used Dutch guns to attack Huron parties carrying beaver pelts to the French. By mid-century, Iroquois attacks had scattered the Hurons, all but ending the French fur trade and reducing the Jesuit influence to a few villages of Christianized Hurons.

The bitterness bred in these years colored future colonial warfare, driving the Iroquois to ally with the English against the French. But for the time being, in the mid-seventeenth century, the English remained unhindered by the beleaguered French colonists, who numbered only about 400.

England Challenges the Mighty Dutch

By 1660, the Chesapeake and New England regions each contained about 30,000 settlers. Between them lay the mid-Atlantic area controlled by the Dutch, who had planted a small colony named New Netherland at the mouth of the Hudson River in 1624 and in the next four decades had extended their control to the Connecticut and Delaware river valleys. South of the Chesapeake lay a vast territory where only the Spanish, on their mission frontier in Florida, challenged the power of Native American tribes.

These two areas, north and south of the Chesapeake, became strategic zones of English colonizing activity after the end of England's civil war in 1660 brought the restoration of the English monarchy. Commercial rival of the Dutch and religious and economic enemy of the Spanish, England moved to cement its claims on the North American coast.

Although for generations they had been the Protestant bulwarks in a mostly Catholic Europe, England and Holland became bitter commercial rivals in the mid-seventeenth century. By the time the Puritans arrived in New England, the Dutch had become the mightiest carriers of seaborne commerce in western Europe. By one contemporary estimate, Holland owned 16,000 of Europe's 20,000 merchant ships. The Dutch had also muscled in on Spanish and

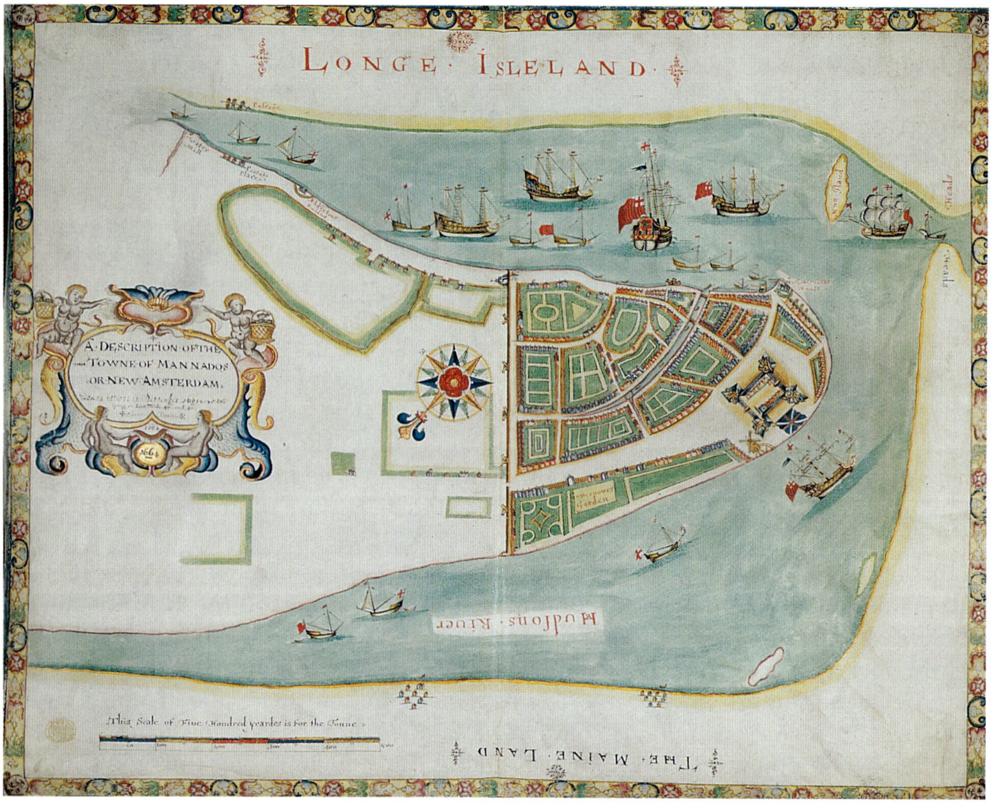

The fort at the tip of Manhattan, flying an English flag, shows prominently in this 1664 map of Dutch New Amsterdam just after it had been bloodlessly conquered by a small English fleet. The park-filled city and the Governor's garden fronting on the Hudson River were separated by a wall from the farmlands of "upper" Manhattan. *(By Permission of the British Library)*

Portuguese transatlantic commerce, trading illegally with Iberian colonists who gladly violated their government's commercial policies to obtain cloth and slaves more cheaply.

By 1650, the Dutch had temporarily overwhelmed the Portuguese in Brazil, and soon their vast trading empire reached the East Indies, Ceylon, India, and Formosa. The best shipbuilders, mariners, and businessmen in western Europe, they validated the dictum of Sir Walter Raleigh that "whosoever commands the sea commands the trade; whosoever commands the trade of the world commands the riches of the world, and consequently the world itself."

In North America, the Dutch West India Company's New Netherland colony was small but profitable. Agents fanned out from Fort Orange (Albany) and New Amsterdam (New York City) into the Hudson, Connecticut, and Delaware river valleys. There they established a lucrative fur trade with local tribes by hooking into the sophisticated trading network of the Iroquois Confederacy, which stretched to the Great Lakes. The Iroquois welcomed the Dutch presence. The newcomers were few in number, they did not have voracious appetites for land, and they were willing to exchange desirable goods for the pelts of animals that were abundant in the vast Iroquois territory. At Albany, the center of the Dutch–Iroquois trade, relations remained peaceful and profitable for several generations because both peoples admirably served each other's needs.

Although the Dutch never settled more than 10,000 people in their mid-Atlantic colonies, their commercial and naval powers were impressive. The Virginians learned as much in 1667 when brazen Dutch raiders captured 20 tobacco ships on the James River and confiscated virtually the entire tobacco crop for that year.

By 1650, England was ready to challenge Dutch maritime supremacy. Three times between 1652 and 1675, war broke out between the two Protestant competitors for control of the emerging worldwide capitalist economy. In the second and third wars, the Dutch colony on the Hudson River became an easy target for the English. They captured it in 1664 and then, after it fell to the Dutch in 1673, recaptured it almost immediately. By 1675, the Dutch had been permanently dislodged from the North American mainland. But they remained mighty commercial competitors of the English around the world.

New Netherland—where from the beginning Dutch, French Huguenots, Walloons from present-day Belgium, Swedes, Portuguese, Finns, English, refugee Portuguese Jews from Brazil, and Africans had commingled in a babel of languages and religions—now

Restoration Colonies: New York, the Jerseys, Pennsylvania, and the Carolinas

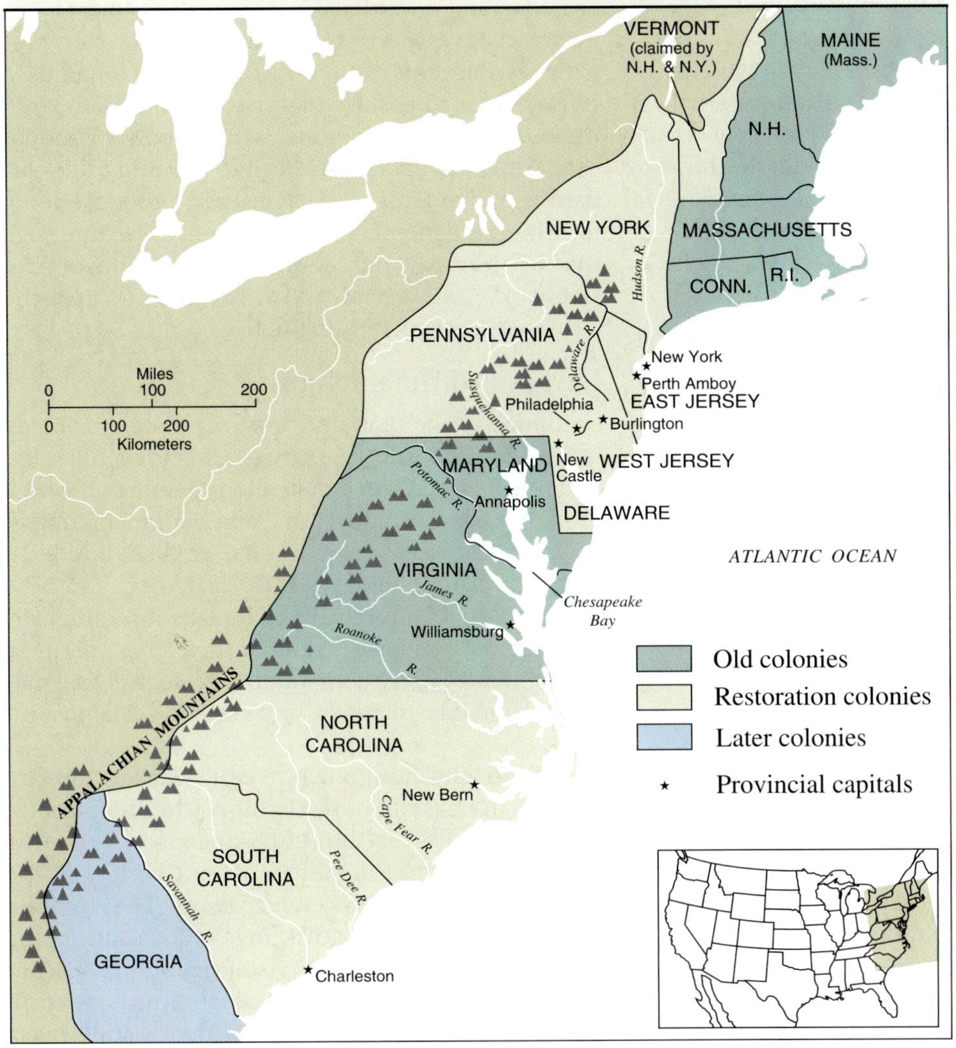

After founding the Restoration colonies from the 1660s to the 1680s, England's colonists claimed the entire seaboard between Spanish Florida and French Canada.

became New York. It was so named because Charles II made a proprietary grant of the territory, along with the former Dutch colonies on the Delaware River, to James, duke of York, his brother and heir to the English throne.

Under English rule, the Dutch colonists remained ethnically distinct for several generations, clinging to their language, their Dutch Reformed Calvinist churches, and their architecture. In time, however, English immigrants overwhelmed the Dutch, and gradual intermarriage among the Dutch, French Huguenots (Protestants), and the English—the three main groups—diluted ethnic loyalties. But New York retained its polyglot, religiously tolerant character, and its people never allowed religious concerns or utopian plans to interfere with the pragmatic conduct of business.

PROPRIETARY CAROLINA: A RESTORATION REWARD

In 1663, three years after he was restored to his father's throne, England's Charles II granted a vast territory named Carolina to a group of supporters during his years of exile. Its boundaries extended from Virginia southward to central Florida and westward to the Pacific. Within this potential empire, eight proprietors, including several involved in Barbados sugar plantations, gained large powers of government and semifeudal rights to the land. For settling their royal reward, they constructed a system of government with both feudal and modern features. To lure settlers, they promised religious freedom and offered land free for the asking. But onto this generous land offer they grafted plans for a semimedieval government in which they, their deputies, and a few noblemen would monopolize political power. Reacting to a generation of violence and radical social experiments during the English civil war (1642–1649), they designed Carolina as a model of social and political stability in which a hereditary aristocracy would check boisterous small landholders.

Carolina realities bore faint resemblance to these hopes. The rugged sugar and tobacco planters who streamed in from Barbados and Virginia, where depressed economic conditions made a new beginning in Carolina seem attractive, claimed their 150 acres of free land (and additional acreage for each family member or servant they brought). But they ignored proprietary regulations about settling in compact rectangular patterns and reserving two-fifths of every county for an appointed nobility. In government, they also did as they pleased. Meeting in assembly for the first time in 1670, they refused to accept the proprietors' Fundamental Constitutions of 1667 and ignored the orders of the governor appointed in London. Most of the settlers already knew how to run a slave society from having lived in Barbados, and from that experience they shaped local government.

The Indian Debacle

Carolina was the most elaborately planned colony in English history but the least successful in achieving amicable relations with the natives. The proprietors in London had intended otherwise. Mindful of the violence that had plagued other settlements, they projected a well-regulated Indian trade run exclusively by their appointed agents. But the aggressive settlers from the West Indies and the Chesapeake flouted all this. Those from Barbados, accustomed to exploiting African slave labor, saw that if the major tribes of the Southeast—the Cherokee, Creek, and Choctaw—could be drawn into trade, the planters might reap vast wealth. The Spanish in Florida had done little to tap this potential gold mine; their main goal was to protect their territorial claim by establishing missions that gathered local Indians into a sedentary, agricultural life.

It was not the beaver that beckoned in the Indian trade, as in the North, but the deerskin, much desired in Europe for making warm and durable clothing. In the villages of the southeastern tribes, where natives farmed as well as hunted, the Carolina colonies found a people eager to obtain European trade goods. But what began as a trade for the skins of deer soon became a trade for the skins of Indians. To the consternation of the London proprietors, capturing Indians for sale in New England and the West Indies became the cornerstone of commerce in Carolina in the early years.

The Indian slave trade plunged Carolina into a series of wars. Planters and merchants selected a tribe, armed it, and rewarded it handsomely for bringing in enemy captives. Even strong tribes that allied for trade with the Carolinians found that after they had used English guns to enslave their weaker neighbors, they themselves were sometimes scheduled for elimination. The colonists claimed that "thinning the barbarous Indian natives" was necessary to make room for white settlement. The "thinning" was so thorough that by the early eighteenth century the two main tribes of the coastal plain, the Westos and the Savannahs, were nearly extinct.

Early Carolina Society

Carolina's fertile land and warm climate convinced many that it was a "Country so delicious, pleasant, and fruitful that were it cultivated doubtless it would prove a second Paradize." In came Barbadians, Swiss, Scots, Irish, French Huguenots, English, and even migrants from New England, New York, and New Jersey. But far from creating paradise, this ethnically and religiously diverse people clashed abrasively in an atmosphere of fierce competition, ecological exploitation, brutal race relations, and stunted social institutions.

For the land-hungry white cattle raisers and rice growers of coastal South Carolina, the Indian slave trade had no direct benefits, because the profits flowed entirely to the merchants of Charleston, the main port and seat of government. They reaped important secondary advantages, however. As the Indian population of the coastal region fell sharply, expansion from the initial settlements around Charleston became easier. Along the twisting rivers that flowed to the coast, planters staked out claims and experimented with a variety of exotic crops, including sugar, indigo, tropical fruits, tobacco, and rice. After much experimentation, planters found that rice was the staple crop on which a flourishing economy could be built.

Rice cultivation required backbreaking labor to drain the swampy lowlands, build dams and levees, and hoe, weed, cut, thresh, and husk the crop. Many early settlers had owned African slaves in Barbados, so their early reliance on slave labor came naturally. On widely dispersed plantations, black labor came to predominate. In 1680, four-fifths of South Carolina's population was white. But by 1720, when the colony had grown to 18,000, black slaves outnumbered whites two to one.

As in Virginia and Maryland, the low-lying areas of coastal Carolina were so disease-ridden that population grew only slowly in the early years. "In the spring a paradise, in the summer a hell, and in the autumn a

This painting of Mulberry Plantation in South Carolina shows the mansion house, built in 1708, and rows of slave huts constructed in an African style. Most enslaved Africans lived in far more primitive structures in the eighteenth century. (*Gibbes Museum/Carolina Art Association*)

hospital," remarked one traveler. Malaria and yellow fever, especially dangerous to pregnant women, were the main killers that retarded population growth, and the scarcity of women further limited natural increase. Like the West Indies, the rice-growing region of Carolina was at first more a place to accumulate a fortune than to rear a family.

In healthier northern Carolina, a different kind of society emerged amid pine barrens along a sandy coast. Settled largely by small tobacco farmers from Virginia seeking free land, the Albemarle region developed a mixed economy of livestock grazing, tobacco and food production, and the extraction of naval stores—lumber, turpentine, resin, pitch, and tar. Slavery took root only slowly in North Carolina, which was still 85 percent white in 1720. A land of struggling white settlers (called "Lubberland" by one prosperous Virginia planter), its healthier climate and settlement by families rather than by single men with servants and slaves gave it a greater potential for sustained growth.

In 1701, North and South Carolina became separate colonies, their distinctiveness having already divided them. But in North as well as South Carolina, several factors inhibited the growth of a strong corporate identity: the pattern of settlement, ethnic and religious diversity, and a lack of shared assumptions about social and religious goals.

THE QUAKERS' PEACEABLE KINGDOM

Of all the utopian dreams imposed on the North American landscape in the seventeenth century, the most remarkable was the Quakers'. During the English civil war, the Society of Friends, as the Quakers called themselves, had sprung up as one of the many radical sects searching for a juster society and a purer religion. Their visionary ideas and defiance of civil authority cost them dearly in fines, brutal punishment, and imprisonment. After Charles II and Parliament stifled radical dissent in the 1660s, they, too, sent many converts across the Atlantic. The society they founded in Pennsylvania foreshadowed more than any other colony the future religious and ethnic pluralism of the United States.

The Early Friends

Like Puritans, the Quakers regarded the Church of England as corrupt and renounced its formalities and rituals, which smacked of Catholicism. They also foreswore all Church officials and institutions, persuaded that every believer could find grace through the "inward light," a redemptive spark in every human soul. Rejecting original sin and eternal predestination, Quakers offered a radical alternative to the reigning Calvinist doctrine.

Quakers were persecuted in England after their movement, led by George Fox and Margaret Fell, gathered momentum in the 1650s. Other Protestants regarded them as dangerous fanatics, for the Quakers' egalitarian doctrine of the "light within" took precedence even over scripture and elevated all lay people to the position of the clergy.

Garbing themselves in plain black cloth and practicing civil disobedience, the Quakers also threatened social hierarchy and order. They refused to observe the customary marks of deference, such as doffing one's hat to a superior, believing that God made no social distinctions. They used the familiar "thee" and "thou" instead of the formal and deferential "you," they resisted taxes supporting the Church of England,

and they refused to sign witnesses' oaths on the Bible, regarding this as profane. Most shocking, they renounced the use of force in human affairs and therefore refused to perform militia service.

Quakers also affronted traditional views when they insisted on the spiritual equality of the sexes and the right of women to participate in church matters on an equal, if usually separate, footing with men. Quaker leaders urged women to preach and to establish separate women's meetings. Among Quakers who fanned out from England to preach the doctrine of the inward light, 26 of the first 59 to cross the Atlantic were women. All but four of them were unmarried or without their husbands and therefore living, traveling, and ministering outside the bounds of male authority.

Intensely committed to converting the world, Quakers ranged westward to North America and the Caribbean in the 1650s and 1660s. Nearly everywhere, they were reviled, mutilated, imprisoned, and deported. Puritan Massachusetts warned them that their liberty in that colony consisted of "free liberty to keep away from us and such as will come to be gone as fast as they can, the sooner the better." Hungering to serve in what they called "the Lamb's War" (the crusade of the meek), the Quakers vowed to test the Puritans' resolve and kept coming.

The Bay Colony magistrates were desperate to eliminate this dangerous threat to religious conformity and civil authority. Finally, in 1659, they hanged two Quaker men on the Boston Common and threatened to hang Mary Dyer, an old woman who had followed Anne Hutchinson a quarter century before. Escorted from the colony, she returned the next year, undaunted, to meet her death at the end of a rope.

Early Quaker Designs

By the 1670s, the English Quakers were looking for a place in the New World to carry out their millennial dreams. In England, royal fears of a Catholic conspiracy led to severe religious repression of all dissenting groups in the late 1670s. Thousands of Quakers were jailed and fined heavily for practicing their faith.

Emerging as their leader in this dark period was William Penn, the son of Admiral Sir William Penn, who by capturing Jamaica from the Spanish in 1654 had placed in English hands one of the most productive sugar-growing sites in the world. Young William had been groomed for life in the English aristocracy, but he rebelled against his parents' designs for him in one of the professions. At age 23, he was converted by a spellbinding speech about the power of the Quaker inward light. After joining the Society of Friends in 1666, Penn devoted himself to their cause.

In 1674, Penn joined other Friends in establishing their own colony, on former Dutch territory, between the Hudson and Delaware rivers. They purchased the land, known as West Jersey, from Lord John Berkeley. Penn now helped fashion a constitution, extraordinarily liberal for its time, that allowed virtually all free males to vote annually for legislators and local officials. Settlers were guaranteed freedom of religion and trial by jury. As Penn and the other trustees of the colony explained, "We lay a foundation for [later] ages to understand their liberty as men and Christians, that they may not be brought in bondage, but by their own consent; for we put the power in the people."

The last phrase, summing up the document, would have shocked anyone of property and power in England or America at the time. Most regarded "the people" as ignorant, dangerous, and certain to bring society to a state of anarchy if entrusted with the right to rule themselves. Nowhere in the English world had ordinary citizens, especially those who owned no land, enjoyed such extensive privileges. Nowhere had a popularly elected legislature received such broad authority.

Despite these idealistic plans, West Jersey sputtered at first. Only 1,500 immigrants arrived in the first five years, and the colony for several decades was caught up in legal complications caused by the tangled claims to the land and government. The center of Quaker hopes lay across the Delaware River, where in 1681, Charles II granted William Penn a territory almost as large as England itself. The grant extinguished a large royal debt to Penn's father, but the crown also benefited by getting the pesky Quakers out of England. To the Quakers' great fortune, the territory granted to Penn, the last unassigned segment of the eastern coast of North America, was also one of the most fertile.

Pacifism in a Militant World: Quakers and Indians

On the day Penn received his royal charter for Pennsylvania, he wrote a friend, "My God that has given it to me will, I believe, bless and make it the seed of a nation." The nation that Penn envisioned was unique among colonizing schemes. Penn intended to make his colony an asylum for the persecuted, a refuge from arbitrary state power. Puritans had striven for social homogeneity and religious uniformity, excluding all not of like mind. In the Chesapeake and Carolina colonies, aggressive, nonidealistic men sought to exploit the region's resources and bondspeople. But Penn dreamed of inviting to his forested colony people of all religions and national backgrounds and blending them together in peaceful coexistence. His state would claim no authority over the consciences of its citizens nor demand military service of them.

The Quakers who began streaming into Pennsylvania in 1682 quickly absorbed earlier Dutch,

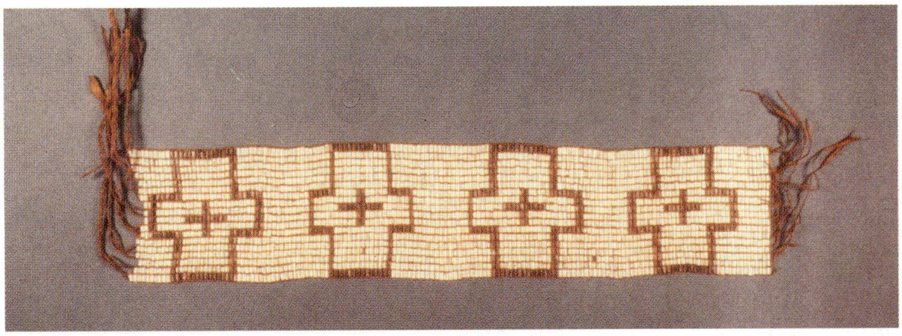

Just as a deed finalized a land exchange to Europeans, the wampum belt signified an agreement to the Indians. This Lenape belt, made of leather and simple shell beads, is said to have been given to William Penn at the signing of the Treaty of Shackamaxon in 1682. (*National Museum of the American Indian, New York*)

Finnish, and Swedish settlers. They participated in the government by electing representatives who initiated laws. They were primarily farmers, and like colonists elsewhere they avidly acquired land, which Penn sold at reasonable rates. But unlike other colonizers, the Quakers practiced pacifism, holding the ethic of love and nonresistance embodied in the Sermon on the Mount as literally binding on them.

Even before arriving, Penn laid the foundation for peaceful relations with the Delaware tribe inhabiting his colony. "The king of the Country where I live, hath given me a great Province," he wrote to the Delaware chiefs, "but I desire to enjoy it with your Love and Consent, that we may always live together as Neighbors and friends." In this single statement Penn dissociated himself from the entire history of European colonization in the New World and from the widely held negative view of Indians. Recognizing the Indians as the rightful owners of the land included in his grant, Penn pledged not to sell one acre until he had first purchased it from local chiefs. He also promised strict regulation of the Indian trade and a ban on the sale of alcohol.

The Quaker accomplishment is sometimes disparaged with the claim that there was little competition for land in eastern Pennsylvania between the natives and the newcomers. However, a comparison between Pennsylvania and South Carolina, both established after the restoration of Charles II to the English throne in 1660, shows the power of pacifism. A quarter century after initial settlement, Pennsylvania had a population of about 20,000 whites. Penn's peaceful policy had so impressed Native American tribes that Indian refugees began migrating into Pennsylvania from all sides. During the same 25 years, South Carolina had grown to only about 4,000 whites, while becoming a cauldron of violence. Carolinians spread arms through the region to facilitate slave dealing, shipped some 10,000 members of local tribes off to New England and the West Indies as slaves, and laid waste to the Spanish mission frontier in Florida.

As long as the Quaker philosophy of pacifism and friendly relations with the Delawares and Susquehannocks held sway, interracial relations in the Delaware River valley contrasted sharply with those in other parts of North America. But ironically, the Quaker policy of toleration, liberal government, and exemption from military service attracted to the colony, especially in the eighteenth century, thousands of immigrants whose land hunger and disdain for Indians undermined Quaker trust and friendship. Germans and Scots-Irish flooded in, swelling the population to 31,000 by 1720. Neither shared Quaker idealism about racial harmony. Driven from their homelands by hunger and war, they pressed inland and, sometimes encouraged by the land agents of Penn's heirs, encroached on the lands of the local tribes. This created conflict with the natives who had sought sanctuary in Pennsylvania. By the mid-eighteenth century, a confrontation of displaced people, some red and some white, was occurring in Pennsylvania.

Building the Peaceable Kingdom

Although Pennsylvania came closer to matching its founder's goals than any other European colony, Penn's dreams never completely materialized. Nor could he convince people to settle in compact villages, which he believed necessary for his "holy experiment." The plain Quaker farmers scattered across the countryside and built simple farmsteads. Instead of agricultural villages with meetinghouses at their centers, as in New England, they created open country networks without any particular centers or boundaries. Yet a sense of common endeavor persisted.

Quaker farmers prized family life and emigrated almost entirely in kinship groups. This helped them maintain their distinctive identity. So did other practices such as allowing marriage only within their society, carefully providing land for their offspring, and guarding against too great a population increase (which would cause too rapid a division of farms) by limiting the size of their families.

Settled by religiously dedicated farming families and favored by rich grainlands, Pennsylvania's countryside blossomed. The colony's port capital of Philadelphia also grew rapidly. By 1700, it overtook

Edward Hicks painted *Penn's Treaty with the Indians* in the nineteenth century. It is a romanticized version of the Treaty of Shackamaxon by which the Lenape chiefs ceded the site of Philadelphia to Penn. The treaty was actually made in 1682, but Hicks was correct in implying that the Lenape held Penn in high regard for his fair treatment of them. (*Hicks, Edward,* Penn's Treaty with the Indians, *Gift of Edgar William and Bernice Chrysler Garbisch, ©2000 Board of Trustees, National Gallery of Art, Washington, c. 1840/1844, canvas, .617 x .765 [24¼ x 30⅛]*)

New York City in population, and a half century later it was the largest city in the colonies, bustling with a wide range of artisans, merchants, and professionals.

The Limits of Perfectionism

Despite commercial success and peace with Native Americans, not all was harmonious in early Pennsylvania. Politics were often turbulent, in part because of Pennsylvania's weak leadership. Penn was a much-loved proprietor, but he did not tarry long in his colony to guide its course. He returned to England in 1684, visited his colony briefly in 1700, and then left forever. The leadership vacuum he left was never filled.

A more important cause of disunity resided in the Quaker attitude toward authority. In England, balking at authority was almost a daily part of Quaker life. To be a Quaker was to refuse to bear arms, to disobey the law prohibiting nonconformists to hold religious services, to deny the Bible as revealed truth, to reject the traditional role assigned women, and to violate social custom obliging inferiors to defer to their superiors. But in Pennsylvania, the absence of persecution eliminated a crucial binding element. The factionalism that developed among them demonstrated that people never unify so well as when under attack. Rather than looking inward and banding together, they looked outward to an environment filled with opportunity. Their squabbling filled Penn with dismay. Why, he asked, were his settlers so "governmentish, so brutish, so susceptible to scurvy quarrels that break out to the disgrace of the Province?"

Meanwhile, Quaker industriousness and frugality led to such material success that after a generation, social radicalism and religious evangelicalism began to fade. As in other colonies, settlers discovered the door to prosperity wide open, and in they surged.

Where Pennsylvania differed from New England and the South was in its relations with Native Americans, at least for the first few generations. It also departed from the Puritan colonies in its immigration policy. Pennsylvania, it is said, was the first community since the Roman Empire to allow people of different national origins and religious persuasions to live together under the same government on terms of near equality. English, Highland Scots, French, Germans, Irish, Welsh, Swedes, Finns, and Swiss all settled in Pennsylvania. This ethnic mosaic was further complicated by a medley of religious groups, including Mennonites, Lutherans, Dutch Reformed, Quakers, Baptists, Anglicans, Presbyterians, Catholics, Jews, and a sprinkling of mystics. Their relations may not always have been friendly, but few attempts were made to discriminate against dissenting groups. Pennsylvanians thereby laid the foundations for the pluralism that was to become the hallmark of American society.

NEW SPAIN'S NORTHERN FRONTIER

Spain's outposts in Florida and New Mexico, preceding all English settlements on the eastern seaboard, fell into disarray between 1680 and the early eighteenth century just as the English colonies were sinking deep roots. Trying to secure a vast northern frontier with only small numbers of settlers, the Spanish relied on forced Indian labor. This reliance proved to be their undoing in Florida and New Mexico.

Popé's Revolt

During the 1670s, when the Franciscan priests developed a new zeal to root out traditional Indian religious ceremonies, the Pueblo people turned on the Spanish intruders. In years of harsh rule, the Spanish had extracted tribute labor from the Pueblo, who at the same time suffered the ravaging effects of European diseases. Both of these punishing long-term effects contributed to Pueblo alienation. But pushing the Pueblo to the edge was an assault on their religion. Launching a campaign to restrict native religious ceremonies in the 1670s, the Spanish friars began to seize the Pueblo kivas (underground ceremonial religious chambers), to forbid native dances, and to destroy priestly Indian masks and prayer sticks. In August 1680, led by Popé, a much-persecuted medicine man from San Juan pueblo, about two dozen Pueblo villages scattered over several hundred miles rose up in fury. They burned Spanish ranches and government buildings, systematically destroyed Spanish churches, lay waste to Spanish fields, and killed half of the friars. As the Spanish governor in Santa Fe watched the church go up in flames, he reported his shock at the "scoffing and ridicule which the wretched and miserable Indian rebels made of the sacred things, intoning . . . prayers of the church with jeers."

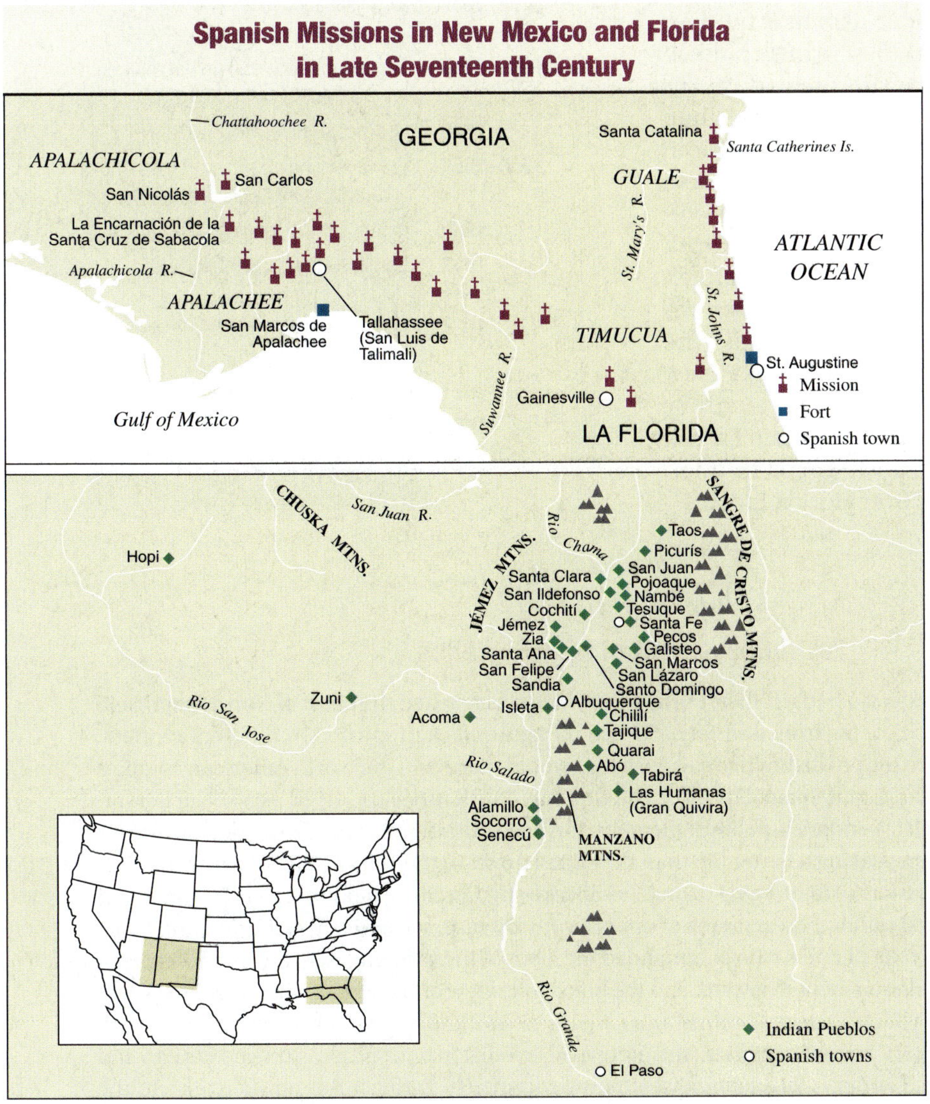

The extensive Spanish missionary activity in Florida and New Mexico had no English parallel.

Spanish settlers, soldiers, and friars streamed back to El Paso, abandoning their northern frontier in the Southwest for more than a decade. Only in 1694 did a new Spanish governor, the intrepid Diego de Vargas, regain Santa Fe and gradually subdue most of the Pueblo. Learning from Popé's rebellion, the Spanish declared a kind of cultural truce, easing their demands for Pueblo labor tribute and tolerating certain Pueblo rituals in return for nominal acceptance of Christianity. Periodic tension and animosity continued, but the Pueblo had to come to terms with the Spanish because of their need for defense against their old enemies—the Navajo, Ute, and Apache.

Decline of Florida's Missions

The Franciscan missions in Florida were as severely pummeled as those in New Mexico in the late seventeenth and early eighteenth centuries. Rapidly settling in South Carolina, the English were eager to use Indian allies to attack the Spanish Indian villages and sell the captives into slavery. The resentment of missionized Indians, wearying under demands on their labor, further weakened the tenuous Spanish hold on them. The attacks of Carolinians in the early 1680s destroyed a number of Spanish missions. When England and Spain went to war in 1701—called Queen Anne's War in the colonies—the Carolinians attacked St. Augustine by land and sea. Burning mission villages to the ground, they slaughtered the Spanish friars and captured some 4,000 women and children to be sold as slaves. The Spanish mission frontier was thoroughly devastated, with only St. Augustine remaining as a Spanish stronghold. Unlike New Mexico, no Spanish reconquest of the territory occurred. From this time forward, English and French traders, with more attractive trade goods to offer, would have the main influence over Florida Indians.

Timeline

1590	Roanoke Island colony fails
1607	Jamestown settled
1616–1621	Native American population in New England decimated by European diseases
1617	First tobacco crop shipped from Virginia
1619	First Africans arrive in Jamestown
1620	Pilgrims land at Plymouth
1622	Powhatan tribes attack Virginia settlements
1624	Dutch colonize mouth of Hudson River
1630	Puritan immigration to Massachusetts Bay
1632	Maryland grant to Lord Baltimore (George Calvert)
1633–1634	Native Americans in New England again struck by European diseases
1635	Roger Williams banished and flees to Rhode Island
1636	Anne Hutchinson exiled to Rhode Island
1637	New England wages war against the Pequot people
1642–1649	English civil war ends great migration to New England
1643	Confederation of New England
1659–1661	Puritans hang two Quaker men and one Quaker woman on Boston Common
1660	Restoration of King Charles II in England
1663	Carolina charter granted to eight proprietors
1664	English capture New Netherland and rename it New York
	Royal grant of the Jersey lands to proprietors
1680	Popé's revolt in New Mexico
1681	William Penn receives Pennsylvania grant

Conclusion

The Achievement of New Societies

Nearly 200,000 immigrants who had left their European homelands reached the coast of North America in the seventeenth century. Coming from a variety of social backgrounds and spurred by different motives, they represented the rootstock of distinctive societies that would mature in the North American colonies of England, France, Holland, and Spain. For three generations, North America served as a social laboratory for religious and social visionaries, political theorists, fortune seekers, social outcasts, and, most of all, ordinary men and women seeking a better life than they had known in their European homelands.

Nearly three-quarters of them came to the Chesapeake and Carolina colonies. Most of them found this region a burial ground rather than an arena of opportunity. Disease, stunted family life, and the harsh work regimen imposed by the planters who commanded the labor of the vast majority ended the dreams of most who came. Yet population inched upward, and the bone and sinew of a workable economy formed. In the northern colonies, to which the fewest immigrants came, life was more secure. Organized around family and community, favored by a healthier climate, and motivated by religion and social vision, the Puritan and Quaker societies thrived. Utopian expectations were never completely fulfilled. But nowhere else in the

Western world at that time could they even have been attempted. What did succeed was the rooting of agricultural life based on family farms and the establishment of locally oriented political institutions marked by widespread participation. Thus, as the seventeenth century progressed, the scattered settlements along the North American coast, largely isolated from one another, as well as a few inland French and Spanish settlements, pursued their separate paths of development.

Recommended Reading

The Chesapeake Tobacco Coast

Philip D. Morgan and Jean Russo, eds., *Colonial Chesapeake Society* (1989); Edmund S. Morgan, *American Slavery, American Freedom: The Ordeal of Colonial Virginia* (1975); David B. Quinn, ed., *Early Maryland in a Wider World* (1982); Darrett B. Rutman and Anita H. Rutman, *A Place in Time: Middlesex County, Virginia, 1650–1750* (1984); Karen Kupperman, *Settling with the Indians: The Meeting of English and Indian Cultures in America, 1580–1640* (1980); Kathleen M. Brown, *Good Wives, Nasty Wenches, and Anxious Patriarchs: Gender, Race, and Power in Colonial Virginia* (1996); Alden Vaughan, *American Genesis: Captain John Smith and the Founding of Virginia* (1975).

Massachusetts and Its Offspring

Christopher Hill, *Society and Puritanism in Pre-Revolutionary England*, 2d ed. (1967); Perry Miller, *Errand into the Wilderness* (1956); David Cressy, *Coming Over: Migration and Communication Between England and New England in the Seventeenth Century* (1987); David D. Hall, *Worlds of Wonder, Days of Judgment: Popular Religious Belief in Early New England* (1989); John Demos, *A Little Commonwealth: Family Life in Plymouth Colony* (1970); Kenneth Lockridge, *A New England Town (1970); Stephen Innes, Labor in a New Land* (1983); Darrett B. Rutman, *Winthrop's Boston* (1965); Edmund S. Morgan, *The Puritan Dilemma: The Story of John Winthrop* (1958); Robert Middlekauff, *The Mathers* (1971); Roger Thompson, *Sex in Middlesex: Popular Mores in a Massachusetts County, 1649–1699* (1986); Stephen Innes, *Creating the Commonwealth: The Economic Culture of Puritan New England* (1995); Virginia D. Anderson, *New England's Generation: The Great Migration and the Formation of Society and Culture in the Seventeenth Century* (1991).

From the St. Lawrence to the Hudson

Robert C. Ritchie, *The Duke's Province: A Study of Politics and Society in Colonial New York, 1660–1691* (1977); Daniel K. Richter and James H. Merrell, eds., *Beyond the Covenant Chain: The Iroquois and Their Neighbors in Indian North America, 1600–1800* (1987); Joyce Goodfriend, *Before the Melting Pot: Society and Culture in Colonial New York City, 1664–1730* (1992); Daniel K. Richter, *The Ordeal of the Longhouse: The Peoples of the Iroquois League in the Era of European Colonization* (1992); Bruce G. Trigger, *Children of the Aataentsic: A History of the Huron People, 1600–1664* (1976); James Axtell, *The Invasion Within: The Contest of Cultures in Colonial North America* (1985).

Proprietary Carolina

M. Eugene Sirmans, *Colonial South Carolina* (1966); Verner Crane, *The Southern Frontier, 1670–1732* (1929); Robert M. Weir, *Colonial South Carolina* (1983); Richard Waterhouse, *A New World Gentry: The Making of a Merchant and Planter Class in South Carolina, 1670–1770* (1989); Daniel C. Littlefield, *Rice and Slaves: Ethnicity and the Slave Trade in Colonial South Carolina* (1981).

The Quakers' Peaceable Kingdom

Frederick B. Tolles, *Meeting House and Counting House: The Quaker Merchants of Colonial Philadelphia* (1948); Gary B. Nash, *Quakers and Politics: Pennsylvania,* 1681–1726 (1968); J. William Frost, *The Quaker Family in Colonial America* (1972); Sharon V. Salinger, *"To Serve Well and Faithfully": Labor and Indentured Servitude in Pennsylvania* (1987); Sally Schwartz, *A Mixed Multitude: The Struggle for Toleration in Colonial Pennsylvania* (1987); Barry J. Levy, *Quakers and the American Family* (1988).

New Spain's Northern Frontier

David J. Weber, *The Spanish Frontier in North America* (1992); Ramon A. Gutiérrez, *When Jesus Came, the Corn Mothers Went Away: Marriage, Sexuality, and Power in New Mexico, 1500–1846* (1991); Marvin T. Smith, *Archaeology of Aboriginal Culture Change in the Interior Southeast: Depopulation During the Early Historical Period* (1987); Andrew L. Knout, *The Pueblo Revolt of 1680* (1995); Jerald T. Milanich, *Florida Indians and the Invasion of Europe* (1995); Jane Landers, *Black Society in Spanish Florida* (1999).

Fiction and Film

Nathaniel Hawthorne's *The Scarlet Letter* (1850) is an American classic on Puritan love, infidelity, and morality; Hollywood's version, by the same title, features Demi Moore and Gary Oldman (1995). John Barth's *The Sotweed Factor* (1960) is a rollicking and ribald novel about indentured servitude, tobacco planting, love, and brutishness in seventeenth-century Maryland. *Black Robes* (1991), a gripping film made in Canada, evokes all the cruelty of the contact between early French Jesuit missionaries and the Iroquois people. The film is based on Brian Manning's novel of the same name. Werner Herzog's *Aguirre: The Wrath of God* (1972) is a surreal film about the early Spanish conquest of much of the Americas in the sixteenth century. A much milder film on early Indian–European contact is *Squanto: A Warrior's Tale* (1994), featuring Adam Beach.

Suggested Web Sites

http://www.apva.org.

Jamestown Rediscovery. This site mounted by the Association for the Preservation of Virginia Antiquity has excellent material on archaeological excavations at Jamestown.

http://etext.virginia.edu/users/deetz

The Plymouth Colony Archive Project at the University of Virginia. This site contains comprehensive and fairly extensive information about late seventeenth-century Plymouth Colony.

http://xroads.virginia.edu/~CAP/PENN/pnhome.html

William Penn, Visionary Proprietor. William Penn had an interesting life, and this site is a good introduction to the man and some of his achievements.

http://www.hanksville.org/NAresources

Index of Native American Resources on the Internet. A comprehensive source for Native American history and art.

http://www.ushistoryplace.com

the History place A richly detailed on-line learning environment complete with interactive maps, timelines, history activities, primary source documents, and links to related American history sites.

3

MASTERING *the* NEW WORLD

CHAPTER OUTLINE

Anthony Johnson, an African, arrived in Virginia in 1621 with only the name Antonio. Caught as a young man in the Portuguese slave-trading net, he had passed from one trader to another in the New World until he reached Virginia. There he was purchased by Richard Bennett and sent to work at Warrasquoke, Bennett's tobacco plantation situated on the James River. In the next year, Antonio was brought face-to-face with the world of triracial contact and conflict that would shape the remainder of his life. On March 22, 1622, the Powhatan tribes of tidewater Virginia fell on the white colonizers in a determined attempt to drive them from the land. Of the 57 people on the Bennett plantation, only Antonio and four others survived.

Antonio—his name anglicized to Anthony—labored on the Bennett plantation for some 20 years, slave in fact if not in law, for legally defined bondage was still in the formative stage. During this time, he married Mary, another African trapped in the labyrinth of servitude, and fathered four children. In the 1640s, Anthony and Mary Johnson gained their freedom after half a lifetime of servitude. Probably at this point they chose a surname, Johnson, to signify their new status. Already past middle age, the Johnsons began carving out a niche for themselves on Virginia's eastern shore. By 1650, they owned 250 acres, a small herd of cattle, and two black servants. In a world in which racial boundaries were not yet firmly marked, the Johnsons had entered the scramble of small planters for economic security.

By schooling themselves in the workings of the English legal process, carefully cultivating white patronage, and working industriously on the land, the Johnsons gained their freedom, acquired property, established a family, warded off contentious neighbors, and hammered out a decent existence. But by the late 1650s, as the lines of racial slavery tightened, the customs of the country began closing in on Virginia's free blacks.

In 1664, convinced that ill winds were blowing away the chances for their children and grandchildren in Virginia, the Johnsons began selling their land to white neighbors. The following spring, most of the clan moved north to Maryland, where they rented land and again took up farming and cattle raising. Five years later, Anthony Johnson died, leaving four children and his wife. The growing racial prejudice of Virginia followed Johnson beyond the grave. A jury of white men in Virginia declared that because Johnson "was a Negroe and by consequence an alien," the 50 acres he had deeded to his son Richard before moving to Maryland should be awarded to a local white planter.

Johnson's children and grandchildren, born in America, could not duplicate the modest success of the African-born patriarch. By the late seventeenth century, people of color faced much greater difficulties in extricating themselves from slavery. When they did, they found themselves forced to the margins of society. Anthony's sons never rose higher than the level of tenant farmer or small freeholder. John Johnson moved farther north into Delaware in the 1680s, following a period of great conflict with Native Americans in the Chesapeake region. Members of his family married local Indians and became part of a triracial community that has survived to the present day. Richard Johnson stayed behind in Virginia. When he died in 1689, just after a series of colonial insurrections connected with the overthrow of James II in England, he had little to leave his four sons. They became tenant farmers and hired servants, laboring on plantations owned by whites. By now, in the early eighteenth century, slave ships were pouring Africans into Virginia and Maryland to replace white indentured servants, the backbone of the labor force for four generations. To be black had at first been a handicap. Now it became a fatal disability, an indelible mark of degradation and bondage.

Mastering the North American environment involved several processes that would echo down the corridors of American history. Prominent among them were the molding of an African labor force and the gradual subjection of Native American tribes who contested white expansion. Both developments occurred in the lifetimes of Anthony and Mary Johnson and their children. Both involved a level of violence that made this frontier of European expansion not a zone of pioneer equality and freedom but one of growing inequality and servitude.

This chapter surveys the fluid, conflict-filled era from 1675 to 1715, a time when five overlapping struggles for mastery occurred. First, in determining to build a slave labor force, the colonists struggled to establish their mastery over resistant African captives. Second, the settlers

Slave Deck of the Albanoz, watercolor done by a young naval officer in a Spanish slave ship captured by the *HMS Albanoz.* (*National Maritime Museum, Greenwich, England*)

sought mastery over Native American tribes, both those that stood in the way of white expansion and those that were their trading and military partners. Third, the colonists resisted the attempts of English imperial administrators to bring them into a more dependent relationship. Fourth, within colonial societies, emerging elites struggled to establish their claims to political and social authority. Finally, the colonizers, aided by England, strove for mastery over French, Dutch, and Spanish contenders in North America.

AFRICAN BONDAGE

For almost four centuries after Columbus's voyages to the New World, European colonizers transported Africans out of their homelands in the largest forced migration in history. Estimates vary widely, but the number of Africans brought to the New World was probably not less than 12 million. Millions more perished while being marched from the African interior to coastal trading forts or during the passage across the Atlantic. Nearly as many were traded across the Sahara to Red Sea and Indian Ocean slave markets during the centuries from 650 to 1900.

African peoples, fed into the merciless slave trade, were crucially important in building the first transoceanic European colonial empires. Once the slave trade began, locales for producing desired commodities such as sugar, coffee, rice, and tobacco moved from the Old World to the Americas. This gradually shifted Europe's orientation from the Mediterranean Sea to the Atlantic Ocean. Africa became an essential part of the Atlantic-basin system of trade and communication by providing Europeans with the human labor needed to unlock the profits buried in productive American soils. Without African labor, the overseas colonies of European nations would never have flourished as they did.

While the economic importance of enslaved Africans can hardly be overstated, it is equally important to understand the cultural interchange that occurred when some 12 million Africans arrived in the Western hemisphere. Of all the newcomers who peopled the New World between the late fifteenth and early nineteenth centuries, the Africans were by far the most numerous, probably outnumbering Europeans two or three to one. As a result, African slavery became the context in which European life would evolve in many parts of the Americas. At the same time, the slave trade etched lines of communication for the movement of crops, agricultural techniques, diseases, and medical knowledge among Africa, Europe, and the Americas.

European slave traders carried most Africans to the West Indies, Brazil, and Spanish America. Fewer than one out of every 20 reached North America, which remained a fringe area for slave traders until the early eighteenth century. Yet those who came to the American colonies, about 10,000 in the seventeenth century and 350,000 in the eighteenth, profoundly affected the destiny of North American society. In a prolonged period of labor scarcity, their labor and skills were indispensable to colonial economic development while their African customs mixed continuously with that of their European masters. Moreover, the racial relations that grew out of slavery so deeply marked society that the problem of race has continued to be one of this nation's most difficult problems.

The Slave Trade

The African slave trade did not begin as a part of the colonization of the Americas but as an attempt to fill a labor shortage in the Mediterranean world. As early as the eighth century, Arab and Moorish traders had driven slaves across Saharan caravan trails for delivery to Mediterranean ports. Seven centuries later, Portuguese merchants became the first European slave traders. For Africans, the Portuguese were nothing more than a new trading partner who could provide guns, horses, copper and brass, rum, and especially textiles.

When Portuguese ship captains reached the west coast of Africa by water, they tapped into a slave-trading network that had operated in central and west Africa for many generations. Slaveholding was deeply rooted in African societies, regarded as a natural part of human organization, and was important in enhancing one's status and augmenting one's ability to produce wealth. However, slaves were employed in a wide variety of occupations, often serving as soldiers, administrators, and even occasionally as royal advisors.

Many Africans were relegated to slavery by judicial decree for crimes they had committed, but far more were victims of military enslavement, captives in the wars between the numerous states of central and west Africa. For example, Songhay—the largest state in Africa in the 1500s—waged wars of territorial conquest recurrently, capturing slaves as it expanded its empire. The economy of the kingdom of Dahomey leaned heavily for several centuries on commerce in slaves. One former slave, Francisco Feliz de Sousa, came to own a fleet of slave ships. But the carrying trade was mainly in the hands of Europeans.

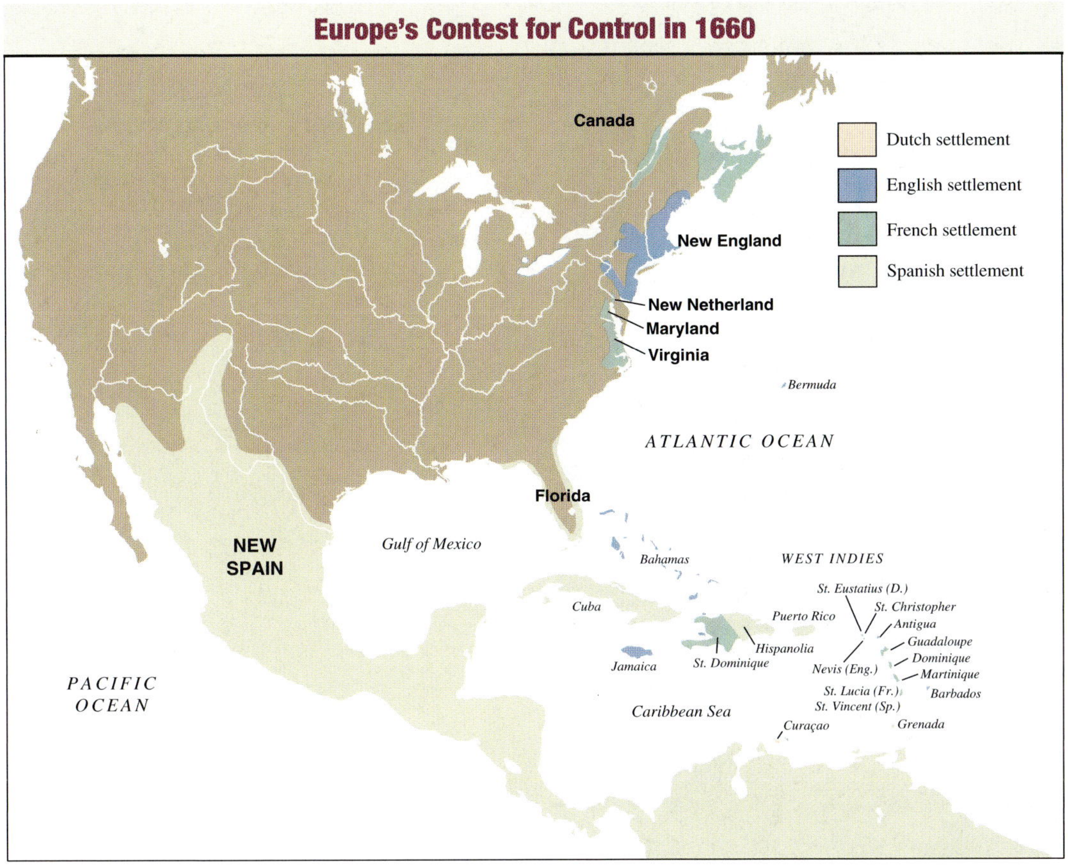

While the English clung to part of North America's eastern coast, they battled with their European rivals for control of the more valuable Caribbean.

More than anything else, sugar transformed the African slave trade. For centuries, sugarcane had been grown in the Mediterranean countries to sweeten the diet of the wealthy. As sugar's popularity grew, the center of production shifted to Portugal's Atlantic island of Madeira, off the coast of Africa. Here in the sixteenth century, a European nation for the first time established an overseas colony organized around slave labor. From Madeira, the cultivation of sugar spread to Portuguese Brazil and Spanish Santo Domingo. By the seventeenth century, with Europeans developing a taste for sugar almost as insatiable as their craving for tobacco, they vied fiercely for the tiny islands dotting the Caribbean and for control of the trading forts on the West African coast. African kingdoms, eager for European trade goods, fought each other to supply the "black gold" demanded by white ship captains.

Many European nations competed for trading rights on the West African coast. In the seventeenth century, when slave traders brought about one million Africans to the New World, the Dutch replaced the Portuguese as the major supplier. The English, meanwhile, hardly counted in the slave trade. Not until the 1690s, when they began their century-long rise to maritime greatness, did the English challenge the Dutch. But by the 1790s, the English were the foremost European slave traders.

In the eighteenth century, European traders carried at least six million Africans to the Americas. By this time African slave labor figured so importantly in the colonial world that one Englishman called slavery the "strength and the sinews of this western world."

Once established on a large scale, the Atlantic slave trade dramatically altered slave recruitment in Africa. When criminals and "outsiders" were insufficient in number to satisfy the growing European demand, African kings waged war against neighboring tribes. European guns abetted the process. By 1730, Europeans were providing some 180,000 weapons a year, spreading kidnapping and organized violence while strengthening the most militarily effective kingdoms. Again and again, coastal and interior kings invaded the hinterlands of western and central Sudan to procure slaves. Perhaps three-quarters of the slaves transported to English North America came from the part of western Africa that lies between the Senegal and Niger rivers and the Gulf of Biafra.

The pain of a slave coffle, in which enslaved Africans were tied together with forked branches and bark rope, shows in this eighteenth-century print. About one-eighth of the slaves marched toward coastal holding pens were children. (*The Mansell Collection*)

In this forcible recruitment of slaves, young males—most of them 10 to 24 years old—were preferred over women. This was the preference of New World plantation owners for male field laborers, but it also reflected the decision of vanquished African villagers to yield up more men than women to raiding parties because women were the chief agriculturists in their society and, in matrilineal and matrilocal kinship systems, were too valuable to be sacrificed.

Even the most vivid accounts of the slave trade cannot convey the pain and demoralization that accompanied the initial capture and subsequent march to slave-trading forts on the West African coast or the dreaded "middle passage" across the Atlantic. Olaudah Equiano, an eighteenth-century Ibo from what is now Nigeria, described how raiders from another tribe kidnapped him and his younger sister when he was only 11 years old. He passed from one trader to another while being marched to the coast. Many slaves attempted suicide or died from exhaustion or hunger on these forced marches. But Equiano survived. Reaching the coast, he encountered the next humiliation, confinement in barracoons, fortified enclosures on the beach, where a surgeon from an English slave ship inspected him. Equiano was terrified by the light skins, language, and long hair of the English and was convinced that he "had got into a world of bad spirits and that they were going to kill me."

More cruelties followed. European traders often branded the African slaves they purchased with a hot iron to indicate which company had procured them. The next trauma came with the ferrying of slaves in large canoes to the ships anchored in the harbor. An English captain recounted the desperation of Africans who were about to lose touch with their ancestral homeland and embark on a vast unknown ocean. "The Negroes are so loath to leave their own country," he wrote, "that they have often leaped out of the canoes, boat and ship, into the sea, and kept under the water till they were drowned."

Conditions aboard the slave ships were miserable, even though the traders' goal was to deliver alive as many slaves as possible to the other side of the Atlantic. Equiano recounted the scene below decks, where manacled slaves were crowded together like corpses in coffins. "With the loathsomeness of the stench, and crying together, I became so sick and low that I was not able to eat, nor had I the least desire to taste anything." The refusal to take food was so common that ship captains devised special techniques to cope with slaves who were determined to starve themselves to death rather than reach the New World in chains. Slavers flogged their captives brutally and applied hot coals to their lips. If this did not suffice, they force-fed the slaves with a mouth wrench.

The Atlantic passage usually took four to eight weeks, so physically depleting and psychologically wrenching that one of every seven captives died en route. Many others arrived in the Americas deranged or near death. In all, the relocation of any African may have averaged about six months from the time of capture to the time of arrival at the plantation of a colonial buyer. During this protracted personal crisis, the slave was completely cut off from the moorings of a previous life—language, family and friends, tribal religion, familiar geography, and status in a local community. Still awaiting these victims of the European demand for cheap labor was adaptation to a new physical environment, a new language, a new work routine, and a life of unending bondage for themselves and their children.

Slavery in the Spanish and French Borderlands

Before a single enslaved African touched soil in the English colonies, thousands of slaves were already present in North America. They came first with fifteenth-century Spanish explorers such as Ponce de Leon, Vasquez de Ayllon, de Soto, and Coronado. Estevancio, born in Morocco, was indispensable to Coronado's expedition in North America's Southwest, serving as guide, healer, linguist, and diplomat to Indian tribes. The importance of Africans on these arduous expeditions gave slavery a distinct character in the early Spanish colonies. Laboring in fields, in fort and church construction, and on supply trains, they were also valuable as soldiers, guides, and linguistic go-betweens with Indian people. In this way, slavery had little of the castelike character it developed in the English colonies. Also contributing to the greater flexibility of Spanish slavery was the frequent crossing of blood among Spaniards, Indians, and Africans.

French slaves were as important to the development of Louisiana as they were to Spanish Florida and New Mexico. Arriving with skills as rice growers, indigo processors, metal workers, river navigators, herbalists, and cattle keepers, West Africans became the backbone of the economy. Like male slaves in the Spanish colonies, they mingled extensively with Indian women, producing mixed-race children known locally as *grifs*. African women sometimes made interracial liaisons with French immigrants, often soldiers in search of partners. Always precariously in charge of limited numbers of French settlers, French governors in Louisiana used enslaved Africans extensively as militiamen and sometimes granted them freedom for military service. All in all, the chance of gaining freedom in fluid French Louisiana exceeded that of any other colony in North America's Southeast, and the absorption of free blacks into white society, particularly if they were of mixed-race descent, was shockingly common from the English point of view.

The Southern Transition to Black Labor

Although they were familiar with Spanish, Dutch, Portuguese, and French use of black slaves, English colonists on the mainland of North America turned only slowly to Africa to solve their labor problem. Like other Europeans, they first regarded Native Americans as the obvious source of labor. But European diseases ravaged native societies, and Indians, more at home in the environment than the white colonizers, proved difficult to subjugate. Indentured white labor proved the best way to meet the demand for labor during most of the seventeenth century. Beginning in 1619, a small number of Africans entered Virginia and Maryland to labor in the tobacco fields alongside white servants. But as late as 1671, when some 30,000 slaves toiled in English Barbados, fewer than 3,000 served in Virginia. They were still outnumbered there at least three to one by white indentured servants.

Only in the last quarter of the seventeenth century did the southern labor force begin to change into one in which black slaves performed most of the field labor. Three reasons explain this shift. First, the rising commercial power of England, at the expense of the Spanish and Dutch, swelled English participation in the African slave trade. Beginning in the 1680s, southern planters could purchase slaves more readily and cheaply than before. Second, the supply of white servants from England began drying up, and those who did arrive fanned out among a growing number of colonies. Third, white servant unrest and a growing population of landless, discontented, and potential rebellious former servants led white planters to seek a more pliable labor force. Consequently, by the 1730s, the number of white indentured servants had dwindled to insignificance. Black hands, not white, tilled and harvested Chesapeake tobacco and Carolina rice. Nothing had greater priority in starting a plantation than procuring slave labor. "If any one designs to make a plantation in this province," wrote Thomas Nairne from South Carolina in 1710, "the first thing to be done is, after having cut down a few trees, to split palisades or clapboards and therewith make small houses or huts to shelter the slaves."

In enslaving Africans, English colonists merely copied their European rivals in the New World. Making it all the more natural for American planters to adopt this labor system was the precedent their countrymen had set in the English West Indies. From

The African Slave Trade

For every African brought to North America, more than nine were sold as slaves in the West Indies and more than eight in Brazil.

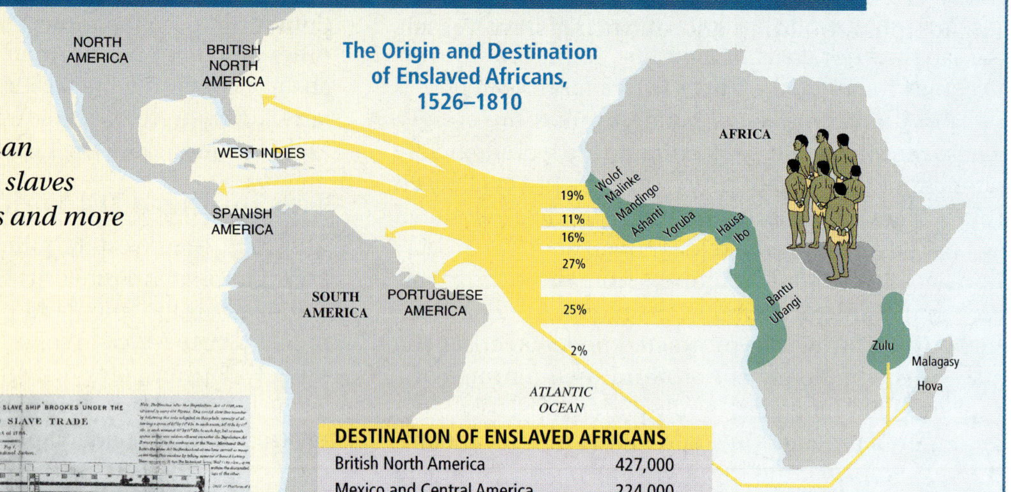

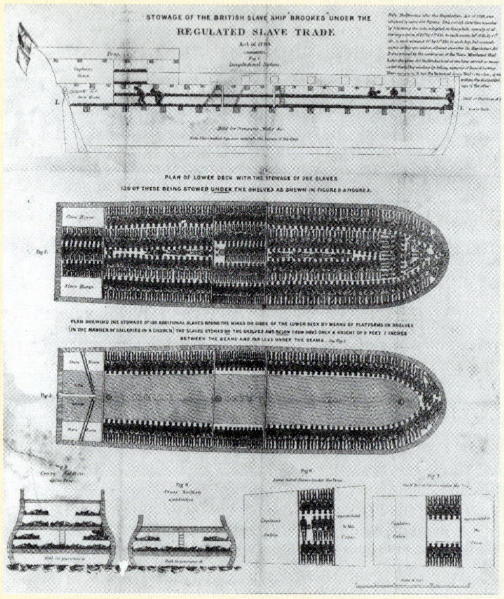

The illustration above, from an eighteenth-century pamphlet, demonstrates British regulations for stowing the human cargo aboard slave ships. The Brooks, a 320-ton slave-trading ship, was built to accommodate 451 persons. However, because it was expected that many slaves would die en route, shipcaptains sometimes attempted to increase their profits by crowding even more slaves into the hold than regulations allowed (The Library of Congress).

DESTINATION OF ENSLAVED AFRICANS	
British North America	427,000
Mexico and Central America	224,000
West Indies	4,040,000
Spanish America	746,000
Portuguese America	3,647,000

SOURCE: Data from Phillip D. Curtin, *The Atlantic Slave Trade*

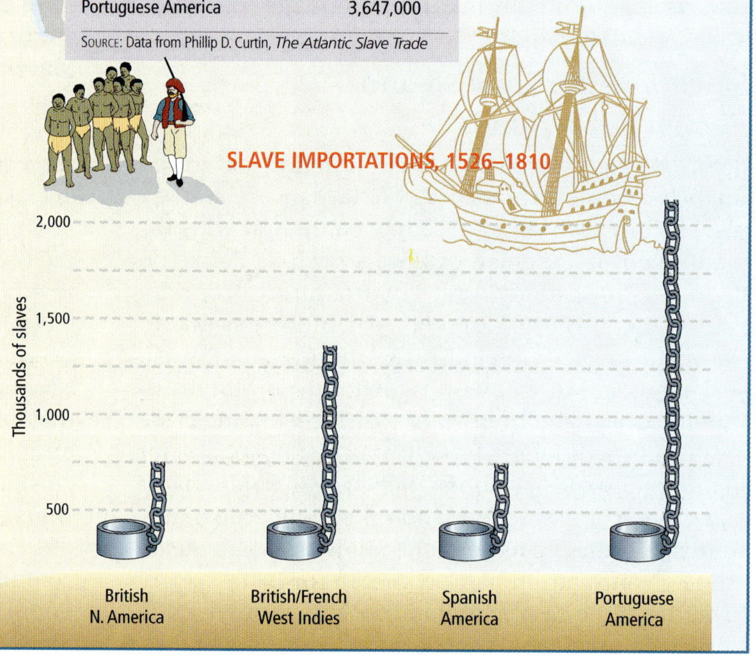

the 1630s onward, the English imported Africans in droves in Barbados, Jamaica, and the Leeward Islands. Through brutal repression, they molded them into a sugar-producing slave labor force. Human bondage would later become the subject of intense moral debate, but in the seventeenth century, all but a few whites accepted it without question.

Slavery in the Northern Colonies

Slavery never became the foundation of the northern colonial workforce, for labor-intensive crops such as sugar and rice would not grow in colder climates. On the smaller family farms, household labor and occasional hired hands sufficed. Only in the cities, where slaves worked as artisans and domestic servants, and in a few scattered rural areas did slavery take substantial root.

Although the northern colonists employed few slaves, their economies became enmeshed in the Atlantic commercial network, which depended on slavery and the slave trade. New England's merchants eagerly pursued profits in the slave trade as early as the 1640s, when their ships began supplying Barbados with Africans. By 1676, New England slavers were packing their holds with slaves from Madagascar, off the coast of East Africa, and transporting them 6,000 miles to the western side of the Atlantic. By 1750, half the merchant fleet of Newport, Rhode Island, reaped profits from carrying human cargo. In New York and Philadelphia, building and outfitting slave vessels proved profitable.

New England's involvement in the international slave trade deepened with the growth of its seaports as centers for the distilling of rum—the "hot, hellish and terrible liquor." Made from West Indian sugar, rum became one of the principal commodities traded for slaves on the African coast. As the number of slaves to be fed in the Caribbean multiplied—from about 50,000 in 1650 to 500,000 in 1750—the West Indies became a favorite market for the codfish hauled in by New England's extensive fishing fleet. Wheat from the middle colonies and barrel staves and hoops from North Carolina also fed into the slave-based West Indies economy. Hence, as the plantation South became most directly involved in an international system of racial exploitation, every other North American colony also participated in it.

The System of Bondage

The first Africans brought to the American colonies came as bound servants. They served their term, and if (like Anthony and Mary Johnson) they survived, they gained their freedom. Once released, they could own land, hire out their labor, and move as they pleased. Their children, like those of white indentured servants, were born free.

But gradually, seventeenth-century, Chesapeake planters began to draw tighter lines around the activities of black servants. By the 1640s, Virginia forbade blacks, free or bound, to carry firearms. In the 1660s, marriages between white women and black servants were called "shameful matches" and the "disgrace of our Nation." Bit by bit, white settlers strengthened the association between black skin and slave status.

By the mid-seventeenth century, most white colonists were convinced that perpetual bondage was the appropriate status for black servants. By the end of the century, when incoming Africans increased from a trickle to a torrent, even the small number of free blacks found themselves pushed to the margins of society. Slavery, which had existed for centuries in many societies as the lowest social status, was in the Americas becoming a caste reserved for those with black skin. Step by step, white society was turning the black servant from a human being into a chattel.

In this dehumanization of Africans, which the English largely copied from their colonial rivals, the key step was instituting hereditary lifetime service. Once servitude became perpetual, relieved only by death, all other privileges quickly vanished. When a mother's slave condition legally passed on to her newborn black infant (not the case in other forms of slavery, such as in Africa), slavery became self-perpetuating, passing automatically from one generation to the next.

Slavery was not only a system of forced labor but also a pattern of human relationships legitimated by law. By the early eighteenth century, most provincial legislatures were enacting laws for limiting black rights and controlling black activities. Borrowed largely from England's Caribbean colonies, "black codes" forced Africans into an ever narrower world. Slaves were forbidden to testify in court, engage in commercial activity, hold property, participate in the political process, congregate in public, travel without permission, and legally marry or be parents. Nearly stripped of human status, they became defined as property; gradually all legal restraints on the master's treatment of them disappeared.

Eliminating slave rights had both pragmatic and psychological dimensions. With every African in chains a potential rebel, the rapid increase in the slave population brought anxious demands for strict control. The desire to stifle black rebelliousness mingled with a need to justify brutal behavior toward slaves by defining them as less than human. "The planters," wrote one Englishman in Jamaica, "do not want to be told that their Negroes are human creatures. If they believe them to be of human kind, they cannot regard them as no better than dogs or horses."

Dehumanizing slaves involved one of the great paradoxes of modern history. Many Old World immigrants imagined the Americas as a liberating and regenerating arena. Yet the opportunity to exploit its resources led to a historic world process by which masses of people were wrenched from their homelands and forced into a system of slavery that could be maintained only by increasing intimidation and brutality.

SLAVE CULTURE

The basic struggle for Africans toiling on plantations 5,000 miles from their homes was to create strategies for living as satisfactorily as possible despite horrifying treatment. The master hoped to convert the slave into a mindless drudge who obeyed every command and worked efficiently for his profit. But the attempt to cow slaves rarely succeeded completely. Masters could set the external boundaries of existence for their slaves, controlling physical location, work roles, diet, and shelter. But the authority of the master class impinged far less on how slaves established friendships, fell in love, formed kin groups, reared children, worshiped their gods, buried their dead, and organized their leisure time.

In these aspects of daily life, slaves in America drew on their African heritage to shape their existence to some degree. In doing so, they laid the foundations for an African American culture. At first, this culture had many variations because slaves came from many areas in Africa and lived under different conditions in the colonies. But common elements emerged, led by developments in the South, where about 90 percent of American slaves labored in the colonial period.

The Growth of Slavery

Arriving in North America, Africans entered a relatively healthy environment compared with other areas of the New World. The West Indies became a graveyard for both whites and blacks. In South America, tropical diseases swept away slaves like leaves in a windstorm. In the southern colonies, where the ghastly mortality of the early decades had subsided by the time Africans were arriving in large numbers, their chances for survival were much better. A simple comparison makes the point. Colonizers in Virginia and Jamaica each owned about 200,000 slaves in 1775. But to attain that number, more than three times as many Africans had been imported into Jamaica as into Virginia during the eighteenth century.

This environmental advantage, combined with a more even sex ratio, led to a natural increase in the North American slave population unparalleled elsewhere. In 1675, about 4,000 slaves were scattered across Virginia and Maryland. Most were men. They toiled with their masters and a larger number of white indentured servants, clearing the land, planting, hoeing, and harvesting tobacco. A half century later, with the decline of white servitude, 45,000 slaves labored on Chesapeake plantations. By 1760, when the number of slaves exceeded 185,000, the Chesapeake plantations relied almost entirely on black labor.

Although slave codes severely restricted the lives of slaves, the possibility for family life increased as the southern colonies matured. Larger plantations employed dozens and even hundreds of slaves, many of the men laboring in skilled crafts, and the growth of roads and market towns permitted them greater opportunities to forge relationships beyond their own plantation. By the 1740s, a growing proportion of Chesapeake slaves were American-born, had established families, and lived in plantation outbuildings where from sundown to sunup they could fashion personal lives—and a distinct black culture—of their own.

In South Carolina, African slaves drew on agricultural skills they had practiced on the other side of the Atlantic and made rice the keystone of the coastal economy by the early eighteenth century. Their numbers increased rapidly, from about 4,000 in 1708 to 90,000 by 1760. Working mostly on large plantations in swampy lowlands, they endured the most life-sapping conditions on the continent. But in the coastal low country, they outnumbered whites three to one by 1760 and hence were able to maintain more of their African culture than slaves in the Chesapeake region. South Carolina, one European observed in 1737, "looks more like a negro country than like a country settled by white people." Many slaves spoke Gullah, a "pidgin" mixing several African languages. They often gave African names to their children—names like Cudjoe, Cuffe, Quashey, and Phibbi—and kept alive their African religious customs.

In the northern colonies, where no labor shortage existed and the climate did not allow the cultivation of staple crops, slaves made up less than 10 percent of the population. They typically worked as artisans, farmhands, or personal servants. Mingled among them were occasional Indian slaves. Whereas about two-thirds of all southern slaves worked on plantations with at least ten of their fellows by the 1720s, in the North the typical slave labored alone or with only a few others. Living in the same house as the master, slaves adapted to European ways much faster than in the South, where the slave quarters were places for

Africans as a Percentage of the Total Population in the British Colonies, 1650–1770

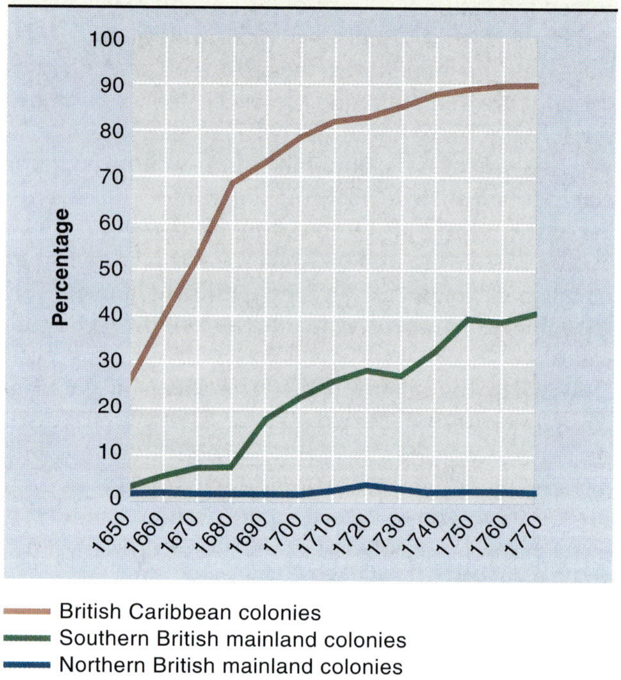

Variations in the racial composition of Britain's American colonies led to distinct differences in cuisine, dress, language, music, and other cultural characteristics. Source: Robert W. Fogel and Stanley L. Engerman, *Time on the Cross* (Boston: Little, Brown, 1974), 21.

perpetuating African folkways. Slavery was also less repressive in the North. Slaves were more widely dispersed among the white population, and black–white contact was so extensive that African culture faded more quickly.

Slavery spread more extensively in the northern ports than across the countryside. Artisans found it profitable to invest in slaves whom they could work on a year-round basis. Ship captains purchased them for maritime labor. And an emerging urban elite of merchants, lawyers, and landlords displayed its wealth and status by employing slaves as liveried coachmen and house servants. By the beginning of the eighteenth century, more than 40 percent of New York City's households owned slaves. Even in Quaker Philadelphia, slaveholding increased sharply in the eighteenth century. Struggling white artisans resented slave workers for undercutting their wages, and the white citizenry felt threatened by potential black arsonists and rebels. Yet where labor demand was high, the desire for lifelong servants, who could be purchased for a mere two years of a free white laborer's wages, outweighed these reservations.

Resistance and Rebellion

While struggling to adapt to bondage in various regions of British America, slaves also resisted and rebelled in ways that constantly reminded their masters that slavery's price was eternal vigilance. Slaveowners preferred to interpret rebelliousness as evidence of the "barbarous, wild savage natures" of Africans, as a South Carolina law of 1712 phrased it. Some planters, like Virginia's Landon Carter, believed that "slaves are devils and to make them free is to set devils free." But from the African point of view, the struggle against enslavement was essential to maintaining meaning and dignity in a life of degrading toil. Resisters' goals varied: to rejoin family members, to flee, to convince masters to improve their condition, or to avenge sadistic overseers.

"Saltwater" Africans, those fresh from their homelands, often resisted slavery fiercely. "You would really be surprized at their perseverance," wrote one observer. "They often die before they can be conquered." Commonly, this initial resistance took the form of escaping to the frontier to begin renegade settlements, to Indian tribes in the interior that sometimes offered refuge, or to Spanish Florida. Open rebellions, such as those in New York City in 1712 and at Stono, South Carolina, in 1739, mostly involved newly arrived slaves.

There was no North American parallel, however, for the massive slave uprisings that erupted periodically in the West Indies and Brazil. Nor was there an American parallel to the semistates in the South Atlantic sugar world, where runaway slaves built their own communities and resisted periodic assaults by colonial troops. Slaves had far better chances to mount successful rebellions in these areas because they vastly outnumbered their masters and, in the case of Brazil, could flee to the rugged interior to join unconquered Indian tribes. "The greater number of blacks which a frontier has," remarked one colonist, "and the greater the disproportion is between them and her white people, the more danger she is liable to."

In North America, slaves rarely outnumbered whites except in South Carolina, and the master class tried to cultivate tension between local Indians and slaves so that they would be a "check upon each other," as one worried planter explained. When rebellion did occur, white colonizers stopped at nothing to quell it. They tried to intimidate all slaves by torturing, hanging, dismembering, and even burning captured rebels at the stake. After an uprising was disclosed near Charleston, South Carolina, in 1739, for example, city officials tortured and hanged 50 blacks. Their decapitated heads, impaled on posts, gave warning to other potential insurrectionists. In New York City a year later, officials responded to a rumored insurrection by hanging 18 slaves and four white allies and burning 13 other slaves at the stake.

Open rebelliousness often gave way to more subtle forms of resistance as slaves learned English; adjusted to the routines of shop, farm, and plantation; and began forming families. Dragging out the job, shamming illness, pretending ignorance, and breaking tools were strategies for avoiding physical exhaustion and also indirect forms of opposing slavery itself.

Slaves resisted more directly through truancy, arson directed against the master's barns and houses, crop destruction, pilfering to supplement their food supply, and direct assaults on masters, overseers, and drivers. Slave masters extracted labor and obedience from their slaves in an overall sense. If they had not, the slave system would have collapsed. But they did so only with difficulty. Masters learned that to push slaves too hard could be costly. One South Carolina planter drove his slaves late into the night cleaning and barreling a rice crop in 1732. When he awoke in the morning, he found his barn, with the entire harvest in it, reduced to ashes.

Black Religion and Family

Resistance and rebellion represented attacks on the institution of slavery. But the balance of power was always massively stacked against the slaves. Only the most desperate were willing to challenge the system directly. Of greater importance was the struggle of black slaves to find meaning and worth in their existence, no matter how brutal and discouraging the slave system that manacled them. In this quest, religion and family played a central role—one destined to continue far into the postslavery period.

Africans brought a complex religious heritage to the New World. No amount of desolation or physical abuse could wipe out these deeply rooted beliefs. People enduring the daily travail that accompanied slavery typically turned for relief to their deepest emotional sources. Coming from cultures where the division between sacred and secular activities was less clear than in Europe, slaves made religion central to their existence. But until the mid-eighteenth century, most slaves died strangers to Christianity. Only slowly would slaves blend African religious practices with the religion of the master class. Partly this was because slave masters were not eager to see their slaves exposed to Christianity because of its potentially dangerous notions of brotherhood and its prohibition against enslaving other Christians. Yet Christianity's emphasis on meekness and obedience might restrain black rebelliousness. Gradually slaves gained exposure to Christianity, using it both to light the spark of resistance and to find comfort from oppression.

The religious revival that began in the 1720s in the northern colonies and spread southward thereafter made important contributions to African American religion. Evangelicalism stressed personal rebirth, used music and body motion, and caught individuals up in an intense emotional experience. The dancing, shouting, rhythmic clapping, and singing that came to characterize slaves' religious expression represented a creative mingling of West African and Christian religions.

Besides religion, the slaves' greatest refuge from their dreadful fate lay in their families. In West Africa, all social relations were centered in kinship, which stretched backward to include dead ancestors. Torn from their native societies, slaves placed great importance on rebuilding extended kin groups.

Most English colonies prohibited slave marriages. But in practice, domestic life was an area in which slaves and masters struck a bargain. Masters found that slaves would work harder if they were allowed to form families. Moreover, family ties stood in the way of escape or rebellion, for few slaves wanted to leave loved ones at the mercy of an angry master. For their part, slaves valued family life so highly that they were willing to risk almost everything to secure the right to marry and parent children.

Slaves fashioned a family life only with difficulty, however. The general practice of importing three male slaves for every two females stunted family formation. Female slaves, much in demand, married in their late teens, but males usually had to wait until their mid- to late twenties. As natural increase swelled the slave population in the eighteenth century, however, the sex ratio became more even.

Slave marriages were rarely secure because they could be abruptly severed by the sale of either party. This happened repeatedly, especially when a deceased planter's estate was divided among his heirs or his slaves were sold to his creditors to satisfy debts. Young children usually stayed with their mothers until about age eight; then they were frequently torn from their families through sale, often to small planters needing

This eighteenth-century watercolor depicts slaves in South Carolina dancing the "juba," a West African dance. The gourdlike banjo and the twisted leather drumsticks are of African design, reflecting the cultural heritage of Africa transplanted to the American colonies. *(Abby Aldrich Rockefeller Folk Art Center, Williamsburg, VA)*

This portrait, painted about 1780 after Equiano had purchased his freedom, shows him as a successful Londoner with hair and clothes in the style of a fashionable Englishman. In 1792, Equiano married an English woman and had two daughters with her. He died five years later. *(Robert Albert Memorial Museum, Exeter, Devon England/The Bridgeman Art Library)*

only a hand or two. Few slaves escaped separation from family members at some time during their lives.

White male exploitation of black women represented another assault on family life. How many black women were coerced or lured with favors into sexual relations with white masters and overseers cannot be known. But the sizable mulatto (racially mixed) population at the end of the eighteenth century indicates that the number was large. Interracial liaisons, frequently forced, were widespread, especially in the Lower South. In 1732, the *South-Carolina Gazette* called racial mixing an "epidemical disease." It was a malady that had traumatic effects on slave attempts to build stable relationships.

In some interracial relationships, the coercion was of a more subtle nature. In some cases, black women sought the liaison to gain advantages for themselves or their children. These unions nonetheless threatened both the slave community and the white plantation ideal. They bridged the supposedly unbridgeable gap between slave and free society and produced children who plagued whites because they did not fit into the separate racial categories that the colonists wished to maintain.

Despite such obstacles, slaves fashioned intimate ties as husband and wife, parent and child. If monogamous relationships did not last as long as in white society, much of the explanation lies in the conditions of slave life: the shorter life span of African Americans, the shattering of marriage through sale of one or both partners, and the call of freedom that impelled some slaves to run away.

Whereas slave men struggled to preserve their family role, many black women assumed a position in the family that differed from that of white women. Plantation mistresses usually worked hard in helping manage estates, but nonetheless the ideal grew that they should remain in the house to guard white virtue and set the standards for white culture. In contrast, the black woman remained indispensable to both the work of the plantation and the functioning of the slave quarters. She toiled in the fields and worked in the slave cabins. Paradoxically, black women's roles, which required constant labor, made them more equal to men than was the case of women in white society.

Above all, slavery was a set of power relationships designed to extract the maximum labor from its victims. Hence, it regularly involved cruelties that filled family life with tribulation. But slaves in America were unusually successful in establishing families because they lived in a healthier environment; toiled in less physically exhausting circumstances than slaves on sugar and coffee plantations; and were better clothed, fed, and treated than Africans in the West Indies, Brazil, and other parts of the hemisphere. In these more tropical areas, plantation owners imported large numbers of male slaves, literally worked them to death, and then purchased replacements from Africa. Family life in the American colonies brimmed with uncertainty and sorrow, but slaves nonetheless made it the greatest monument to their will to endure captivity and eventually gain their freedom.

THE STRUGGLE FOR LAND

As slavery became entrenched in North America, New England, Virginia, and, later, South Carolina fought major wars against Native Americans. All resulted from settler desire for land, and all left legacies of widespread destruction, heavy casualties, and bitterness. The coastal tribes suffered disastrous defeat and decline; for the colonists, the wars added to the turbulence of the late seventeenth and early eighteenth centuries. Sometimes, as in Virginia, Indian war overlapped with a power struggle within white society.

King Philip's War in New England

Following the Pequot War of 1637 in New England, the Wampanoags and Narragansetts, whose fertile land lay within the boundaries of Plymouth and Rhode Island, tried to keep their distance from the New England colonists. But the New Englanders coveted

The Wampanoags led New England tribes in a tenacious campaign of resistance against the white settlers. Paul Revere engraved this picture of the Wampanoag chief Metacomet, called King Philip by the English. The musket held by Metacomet bespeaks the Indian adoption of European weaponry. *(American Antiquarian Society)*

Indian territories. As they quarreled among themselves over provincial boundaries, they gradually reduced the Indians' land base.

By the 1670s, when New England's population had grown to about 50,000, younger Indians began brooding over their situation. Their leader, Metacomet (named King Philip by the English), was the son of Massasoit, the Wampanoag chief who had allied with the first Plymouth settlers in 1620. Metacomet had watched his older brother preside over the deteriorating position of his people after their father's death in 1661. A year later, Metacomet's brother died mysteriously while Plymouth officials questioned him about a rumored Indian conspiracy. Becoming chief in his turn, Metacomet faced one humiliating challenge after another, climaxing in 1671, when Plymouth forced him to surrender a large stock of guns and accept his people's subjection to English law. Convinced that more setbacks would follow and humiliated by the discriminatory treatment of Indians brought before English courts, Metacomet began recruiting for a resistance movement.

The triggering incident of King Philip's War was the trial of three Wampanoags who were dragged before a Puritan court for an act of tribal revenge against John Sassamon, a Christianized Indian educated at Harvard and Metacomet's aide. Sassamon was a man caught between two cultures. Though he had fled white society after his college years, he warned the Plymouth government in 1675 that the Wampanoags were preparing a general attack on the English settlements. When Sassamon was found murdered shortly afterward, Plymouth officials produced an Indian who claimed he had witnessed the murder and could identify the felons. As a result, three Wampanoags swung at the end of English ropes in June 1675.

The execution of the three tribesmen was the catalyst, but the root cause of the war that erupted was the rising anger of the young Wampanoag males. As would happen repeatedly in the next two centuries as Americans pushed westward, younger Native Americans refused to imitate their fathers, who had tolerated the colonizers' encroachments and abridgment of their sovereignty. Rather than submit further, they attempted a pan-Indian offensive against an intruder with far greater numbers and a much larger arsenal of weapons. For the young tribesmen, revitalization of their ancient culture through war became as important a goal as defeating the enemy.

In the summer of 1675, the Wampanoags unleashed daring hit-and-run attacks on villages in the Plymouth colony. By autumn, many New England tribes, including the powerful Narragansetts, had joined Metacomet's warriors. Towns all along the frontier reeled under Indian attacks. "We were too ready to think that we could easily suppress that flea," confessed John Eliot, who had worked to convert the Indians to Christianity, "but now we find that all the craft is in catching them, and that in the meantime they give us many a sore nip." By the time the first snow fell in November, mobile Indian warriors had devastated the entire upper Connecticut River valley.

By March 1676, Metacomet's forces were attacking less than 20 miles from Boston and Providence. Assumptions about English military superiority faded. Desperate to reverse the course of the war, New England officials passed America's first draft laws. Evasion was widespread, however, with eligible men—all those between ages 16 and 60—"skulking from one town to another." Political friction among the New England colonies also hampered a united counteroffensive.

Metacomet's offensive faltered in the spring of 1676. Food shortages and disease sapped Indian strength, and the powerful Mohawks, with their own

King Philip's War, 1675–1676

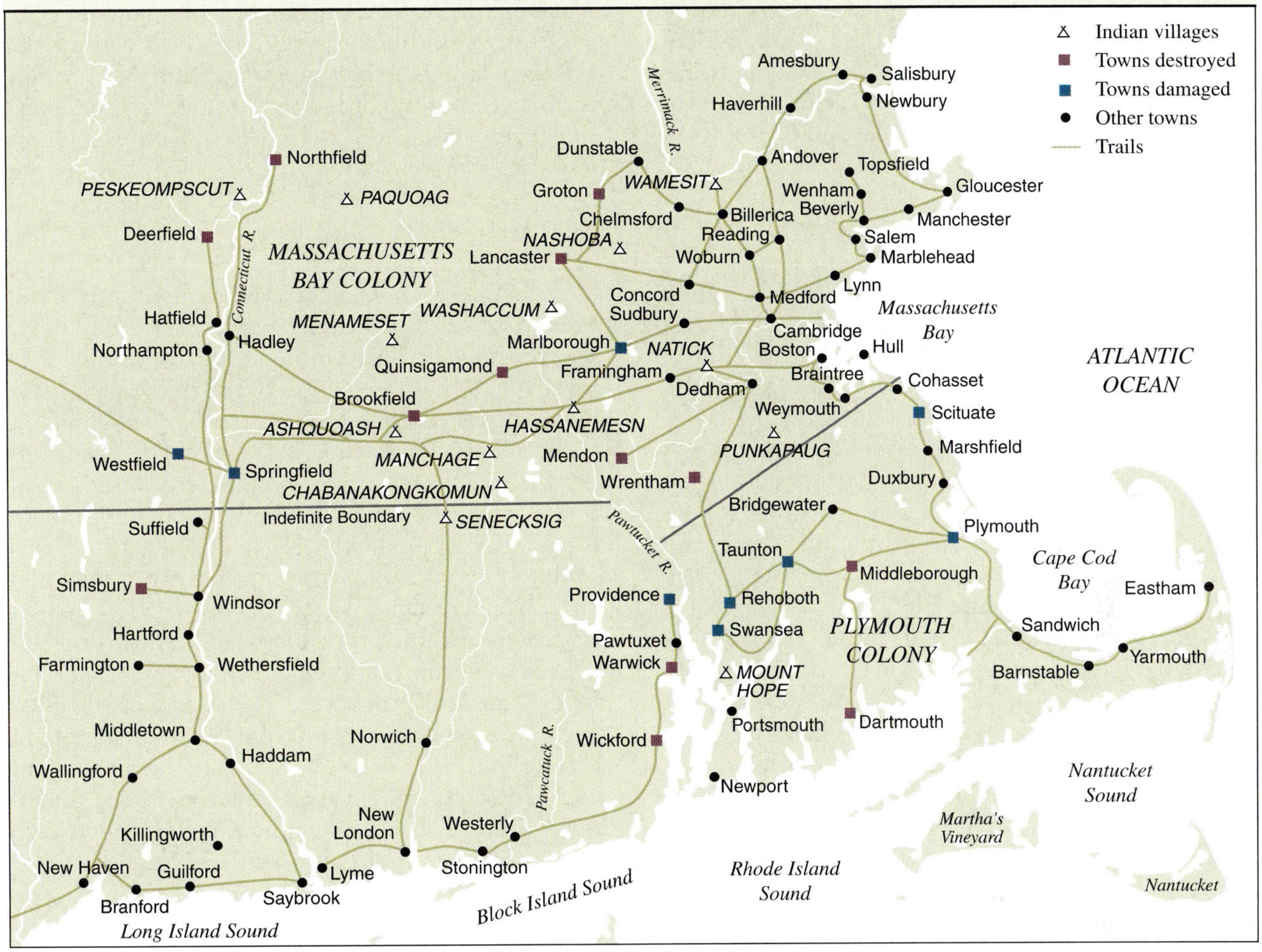

The home base of Metacomet, or King Philip, was within the Plymouth Colony, but he carried the war to the westernmost Massachusetts towns.

advantages in the fur trade to protect, refused to support the New England tribes. By summer, groups of Indians were surrendering, while some moved westward seeking shelter among other tribes. Then Metacomet fell in a battle near the Wampanoag village in Rhode Island where the war had begun. The head of this "hell-hound, fiend, serpent, caitiff and dog," as one colonial leader branded him, was carried triumphantly back to Plymouth, where it remained on display for 25 years.

At war's end, several thousand colonists and perhaps twice as many Indians lay dead. Of some 90 Puritan towns, 52 had been attacked and 13 completely destroyed. Some 1,200 homes lay in ruins and 8,000 cattle were dead. The estimated cost of the war exceeded the value of all personal property in New England. Not for 40 years would the frontier advance beyond the line it had reached in 1675. Indian towns were devastated even more completely, including several inhabited by "praying Indians" who had converted to Christianity and allied with the whites. An entire generation of young men had been nearly annihilated. Many of the survivors, including Metacomet's wife and son, were sold into slavery in the West Indies.

Bacon's Rebellion Engulfs Virginia

While New Englanders fought local tribes in 1675 and 1676, the Chesapeake colonies became locked in a struggle involving both a war between the red and white populations and civil war among the colonizers. Before it ended, hundreds of whites and Indians lay dead in Virginia and Maryland, Virginia's capital of Jamestown lay smoldering, and English troops were crossing the Atlantic to suppress what the king labeled an outright rejection of his authority. This deeply tangled conflict was called Bacon's Rebellion after the headstrong Cambridge-educated planter Nathaniel Bacon, who arrived in Virginia at age 28.

Bacon and many other ambitious young planters detested the Indian policy of Virginia's royal governor, Sir William Berkeley. In 1646, after the second Indian uprising against the Virginians, the Powhatan tribes had accepted a treaty granting them exclusive rights to territory north of the York River, beyond the limits of white settlement. Stable Indian relations suited the established planters, some of whom traded profitably with the Indians, but became obnoxious to new settlers. Nor did the harmonious conditions please the white indentured servants who had served their time and were hoping to find cheap frontier land.

Land hunger and dissatisfaction with declining tobacco prices, rising taxes, and lack of opportunity erupted into violence in the summer of 1675. A group of frontiersmen used an incident with a local tribe as an excuse to attack the Susquehannocks, whose rich land they coveted. Governor Berkeley denounced the attack, but few supported his position. He faced, he said, "a people where six parts of seven at least are poor, indebted, discontented, and armed."

Although badly outnumbered, the Susquehannocks prepared for war. Virginians girded themselves for the southern version of what they heard was occurring in New England. Rumors swept the colony that the Susquehannocks were offering large sums to gain western Indian allies, or that King Philip would support them.

Thirsting for revenge, the Susquehannocks attacked during the winter of 1675–1676 and killed 36 Virginians. That spring, the hot-blooded Nathaniel Bacon became the frontiersmen's leader. Joined by hundreds of runaway servants and some slaves, he attacked friendly and hostile Indians alike. When Governor Berkeley refused to sanction these attacks, Bacon ignored his authority. The governor then declared Bacon a rebel and sent out 300 militiamen to drag him to Jamestown for trial. Bacon headed into the wilderness for "a more agreeable destiny" and recruited more followers, including many substantial planters. Frontier skirmishes with Indians had turned into civil war.

During the summer of 1676, Bacon's and Berkeley's troops maneuvered around each other, while Bacon's men continued their forays against local Indian tribes. In one bold move, Bacon and his followers captured the capital at Jamestown. They razed the statehouse, church, and other buildings and put Governor Berkeley to flight across Chesapeake Bay.

Virginians at all levels had chafed under Berkeley's rule. High taxes, an increase in the governor's powers at the expense of local officials, and the monopoly that Berkeley and his friends held on the Indian trade were especially unpopular. This opposition surfaced in the summer of 1676 as Berkeley's and Bacon's troops pursued each other through the wilderness. Berkeley tried to rally public support by holding new assembly elections and extending the vote to all freemen, whether they owned property or not. But the new assembly turned on the governor, passing a set of reform laws intended to make government more responsive to the common people and to end rapacious officeholding. It also made legal the enslaving of Native Americans.

Time was on the governor's side, however. Having crushed the Indians, Bacon's followers began drifting home to tend their crops. Meanwhile, Berkeley's reports of the rebellion brought the dispatch of 1,100 royal troops from England. By the time they arrived in January 1677, Nathaniel Bacon lay dead of swamp fever and most of his followers had melted back into the frontier. After Bacon's death in October 1676, Berkeley rounded up 23 rebel leaders and hanged them without benefit of trial.

Royal investigators who arrived in 1677 remarked on the genocidal mentality of Bacon's followers, whom they denounced as the "inconsiderate sort of men who so rashly and causelessly cry up a war and seem to wish and aim at an utter extirpation of the Indians." Even a royal governor could not restrain such men, bent on pursuing their hopes of land ownership and independence. To them, Indians were only "wolves, tigers, and bears," as Bacon charged, "which daily destroyed our harmless and innocent lambs."

Hatred of Indians, bred into white society during the war, became a permanent feature of Virginia life. A generation later, in 1711, the legislature spurned the governor's plea for quieting the Indian frontier with educational missions and regulated trade, instead voting military appropriations of £20,000 "for extirpating all Indians without distinction of Friends or Enemys." The remnants of the once populous Powhatan Confederacy lost their last struggle for the world they had known. Now they moved farther west or submitted to a life on the margins of white society as tenant farmers, day laborers, or domestic servants.

After Bacon's Rebellion, an emerging planter aristocracy annulled most of the reform laws of 1676. But the war relieved much of the social tension among white Virginians. Newly available Indian land created fresh opportunities for small planters and former servants. Equally important, Virginians with capital to invest were turning from the impoverished rural villages of England and Ireland to the villages of West Africa to supply their labor needs. This halted the influx of poor white servants who, once free, had formed a discontented mass at the bottom of Chesapeake society. A racial consensus, uniting whites of different ranks in the common pursuit of a prosperous, slave-based economy, began to take shape.

Bacon's Rebellion caused insurrectionary rumblings north and south of Virginia. Many of Bacon's followers took refuge after his death in North Carolina's Albemarle County, the "backside of Virginia." There they joined dissident tobacco farmers, who were distressed by recent Indian uprisings, export duties on tobacco, and quitrents controlled by a mercenary elite. Led by George Durant and John Culpeper, they drove the governor from office and briefly seized the reins of power.

In Maryland, Protestant settlers chafed under high taxes; quitrents; and officeholders regarded as venal, Catholic, or both. Declining tobacco prices and a fear of Indian attacks increased their touchiness. A month after Bacon razed Jamestown, insurgent small planters tried to seize the Maryland government. Two of their leaders were hanged for the attempt. In 1681, Josias Fendall and John Coode, "two rank Baconists" according to Lord Baltimore, led another abortive uprising. After their attempt to kidnap the Catholic proprietor failed, the authorities executed Fendall and banished Coode from the colony.

In all three southern colonies, the volatility of late-seventeenth-century life owed much to the region's peculiar social development. Where family formation was retarded by imbalanced sex ratios and fearsome mortality, and where geographic mobility was high, little social cohesion or attachment to community could grow. Missing in the southern colonies were the stabilizing power of mature local institutions, a vision of a larger purpose, and the presence of experienced and responsive political leaders.

AN ERA OF INSTABILITY

A dozen years after the major Indian wars in New England and Virginia, a series of insurrections and a major witchcraft incident convulsed colonial society. The rebellions were triggered by the Revolution of 1688, known thereafter to Protestants in England as the Glorious Revolution because it ended forever the notion that kings ruled by a God-given "divine right" and marked the last serious Catholic challenge to Protestant supremacy. But these colonial disruptions also signified a struggle for social and political dominance in the expanding colonies. So did the Salem witchcraft trials in Massachusetts.

Organizing the Empire

From the beginning of colonization, the English assumed that overseas settlements existed to promote the national interest at home. According to this mercantilist theory, colonies served as outlets for English manufactured goods, provided foodstuffs and raw materials, stimulated trade (and hence promoted a larger merchant navy), and filled royal coffers by exporting commodities such as sugar and tobacco on which duties were paid. In return, colonists benefited from English military protection and guaranteed markets.

England proceeded slowly in the seventeenth century to regulate its colonies and mold them into a unified empire. A first small step was taken in 1621, when the king's council forbade tobacco growers to export their crop to anywhere but England. Three years later, when the Virginia Company of London plunged into bankruptcy, the crown made Virginia a royal colony, the first of many. However, not until 1651, when the colonists traded freely with the commercially aggressive Dutch, did Parliament consider regulating colonial affairs. It passed a navigation act requiring that English or colonial ships, manned by English or colonial sailors, carry all goods entering England, Ireland, and the colonies, no matter where those goods originated. These first steps toward a regulated empire were also the first steps to place England's power behind national economic development.

In 1660, after the monarchy was restored, Parliament passed a more comprehensive navigation act that listed colonial products (tobacco, sugar, indigo, dyewoods, and cotton) that could be shipped only to England or other English colonies. Like its predecessor, the act took dead aim at Holland's domination of Atlantic commerce while increasing England's revenues by imposing duties on the enumerated articles. Later navigation acts closed loopholes in the 1660 law and added other enumerated articles. Nevertheless, this regulation bore lightly on the colonists because the laws lacked enforcement mechanisms.

After 1675, international competition and war led England to impose greater imperial control. That year marked the establishment of the Lords of Trade, a committee of the king's privy council vested with power to make and enforce decisions regarding the management of the colonies. Their chief goal was to create more uniform governments in North America and the West Indies that would do the crown's will. Although this movement toward the central administration of empire often sputtered, the trend was unmistakable, especially to colonists who felt the sting of royal customs agents sent to enforce the navigation acts. England was becoming the shipper of the world, and its state-regulated policy of economic nationalism, duplicating that of the Dutch, was essential to this rise to commercial greatness.

The Glorious Revolution in New England

When Charles II died in 1685, his brother, the duke of York, became King James II. This set in motion a chain

Recovering the Past

TOMBSTONES

Historians have used funeral orations, gravestone designs and inscriptions, and handbooks on how to die to gain insight into early American culture. Tombstone markings—"graven images," they have been called—provide a particularly fascinating body of evidence. At first, Puritans in New England marked their graves only with wooden rails and posts. But in the 1670s, carved headstones filled with symbolic images began to appear, and they became a regular feature of New England graveyards after that. Hardly any Puritan family thereafter, one historian noted, was "ready to commit its loved ones to the cold earth without an appropriate cluster of symbols hovering protectively over the grave." How the symbols carved on tombstones changed tells much about how people's attitudes and values shifted. "There is no better place in all New England to stand face to face with the past," it has been said, "than in the old burying grounds."

The tombstone shown below shows vividly the intensity with which Puritans faced death. To die was to be called to final account by a just and merciful God, and the way one died gave evidence of one's self-discipline and faith. The scrolled pediment on this gravestone signifies the doorway between earthly life and spiritual rebirth through which Joseph Tapping's relatives hoped he passed. The grim winged skull represents the soul of the dying man in transition. This death's-head motif was widely used on seventeenth-century gravestones. It conveys much of the Puritans' intense concern that life is transitory (note the hourglass above the skull) and that salvation is not automatically granted to those who believe in Christ. This emphasis on life as a preparation for afterlife is reinforced by the Latin mottoes on the right side of the stone: *Vive memor loethi* ("Live mindful of death") and *Fugit hora* ("The hour flies"). At bottom center of the stone is an image of Time fending off Death as Death tries to snuff out the candle of Life.

Joseph Tapping headstone, Boston, 1678. (*From the Daniel and Jessie Lie Farber Collection of Gravestone Photographs, American Antiquarian Society*)

The Puritans' fixation on death has also been noted in the elaborate and expensive funerals they often conducted and in the content of funeral sermons and handbooks on how to die well. In a popular book on advice for the young, *Token for Children*, published first in England in 1671 and in an American edition in 1700, James Janeway described the "Joy and holy Triumph" of a 12-year-old girl's death. As a model of faith in God's mercy, without yielding to pride or certainty of salvation in her last hours, this young girl

> spake with a holy Confidence in the Lord's Love to her Soul, and was not in the least daunted when she spake of her Death, but seemed greatly delighted in the Apprehension of her nearness to her Father's House: And it was not long before she was fill'd with Joy unspeakable in believing.

Also obsessed with death, but with a less joyful view, was Michael Wigglesworth's *Day of Doom* (1662), an account of the Judgment Day in verse intended to reinvigorate Puritan spirituality. *Day of Doom* was New England's first best-seller. The verses reprinted here may suggest why.

By the second quarter of the eighteenth century, attitudes toward death were changing, as the gravestone iconography after about 1730 attests. The epitaphs stressing mortality appeared much less frequently, and

Betsy Shaw headstone, Plymouth, 1795. (*From the Daniel and Jessie Lie Farber Collection of Gravestone Photographs, American Antiquarian Society*)

the ever-present foreboding death's-head, shovels, and hourglass symbols of the seventeenth century began to be replaced by smiling cherubs, angels, natural objects, and sentimentalized willow and urn motifs.

Note the details shown above from an eighteenth-century gravestone compared with those on the Tapping stone. A winged image of Mrs. Betsy Shaw (Plymouth, Massachusetts, 1795) optimistically represents the flight of her soul heavenward. This romantic design tells us much about the secularization of New England society and the passing of the early Puritans' intense seriousness about their godly mission in America to redeem humankind.

As the funerary handiwork of stonecarvers reveals, the Puritans' early providential self-image had been transformed. Less piety and morbid introspection, more worldliness and individual hopefulness had spread through the Puritan Holy Commonwealth. Can you point out how these changes are reflected on the Shaw and Tapping gravestones? What do the markings, inscriptions, and design of tombstones in cemeteries near you reveal about the changing experience and values of later Americans?

Day of Doom
Michael Wigglesworth (1662)

56

Now it comes in, and every sin unto men's
charge doth lay;
It judgeth them and doth condemn, though all
the world say nay.
It so stingeth and tortureth, it worketh such
distress,
That each man's self against himself is forced
to confess.

57

It's vain moreover for men to cover the least
iniquity;
The Judge hath seen, and privy been to all
their villainy.
He unto light and open sight the work of
darkness brings;
He doth unfold both new and old, both known
and hidden things.

58

All filthy facts and secret acts, however closely
done
And long concealed, are there revealed before
the mid-day sun.
Deeds of the night, shunning the light, which
darkest corners sought,
To fearful blame and endless shame are there
most justly brought.

59

And as all facts and grosser acts, so every word
and thought,
Erroneous notions and lustful motion, are
unto judgment brought,
No sin so small and trivial but hither it must
come,
Nor so long past, but now at last it must
receive a doom....

188

The Judge is strong; doers of wrong cannot his
power withstand.
None can be flight run out of sight nor 'scape out
of his hand.
Sad is their state, for advocate to plead their
cause there's none–
None to prevent their punishment, or misery
bemoan.

189

O dismal day! wither shall they for help and
succor flee?
To God above, with hopes to move their
greatest enemy?
His wrath is great, whose burning heat no
floods of tears can slake:
His word stands fast, that they be cast into the
burning lake.

of events that nearly led to civil war. Like his brother, James II professed the Catholic faith. But unlike Charles II, who had disclosed this only on his deathbed, the new king announced his faith immediately on assuming the throne. Consternation ensued. Protestant England recoiled when James issued the Declaration of Indulgence, which granted liberty of worship to all. Although religious toleration is cherished today, it was unacceptable to most English Protestants 300 years ago. Belief that the declaration was primarily a concession to Catholics hardened when the king began creating Catholic peerages to fill the House of Lords; appointed Catholics to high government posts, including command of the English navy; and demanded that Oxford and Cambridge open their doors to Catholic students. In 1687, the king dismissed a resistant Parliament. When his wife, believed to be too old for further childbearing, gave birth to a son in 1688, a Catholic succession loomed.

Convinced that James was trying to seize absolute power and fearing a Catholic conspiracy, a group of Protestant leaders secretly plotted the king's downfall. In 1688, led by the earl of Shaftesbury, they invited William of Orange, a prince of the Netherlands, to invade England and take the throne with his wife, Mary, James's Protestant daughter. James abdicated rather than fight. It was a bloodless victory for Protestantism, for parliamentary power and the limitation of kingly prerogatives, and for the propertied merchants and gentry of England who stood behind the revolt.

The response of New Englanders to these events stemmed from their previous experience with royal authority and their fear of "papists." In 1676, New England became a prime target for efforts to reorganize the empire and crack down on smuggling, which had prevailed there for two generations. In 1684, Charles II had annulled the Massachusetts charter. Two years later, James II appointed Sir Edmund Andros, a crusty professional soldier and former governor of New York, to rule over the newly created Dominion of New England. Soon the Dominion gathered under one government the colonies of New Hampshire, Massachusetts, Connecticut, Plymouth, Rhode Island, New York, New Jersey, and part of Maine. Puritans now had to swallow the bitter fact that they were subjects of London bureaucrats who cared more about shaping a disciplined empire than about the special religious vision of one group of overseas subjects.

At first, New Englanders accepted Andros, though coolly. But he soon earned their hatred by invading freedoms they had come to cherish. He imposed taxes without legislative consent, ended trial by jury, abolished the General Court of Massachusetts (which had met annually since 1630), muzzled Boston's town meeting, and challenged the validity of all land titles. He mocked the Puritans by converting a Boston Puritan church into an Anglican chapel, held services there on Christmas Day—a gesture that to Puritans stank of popery—and overturned their practice of suppressing religious dissent.

When news reached Boston in April 1689 that William of Orange had landed in England, ending James II's hated Catholic regime, Bostonians streamed into the streets to the beat of drums. They imprisoned

The center of government and official news in colonial New England was Boston's town house, built in 1657. Note the stocks and whipping post at lower left. (*From* Boston's First Town House, 1657–1711, *1930, by Charles A. Lawrence/ The Bostonian Society*)

Andros, a suspected papist, and overwhelmed the fort in Boston harbor, which held most of the governor's small contingent of red-coated royal troops. Andros escaped, disguised in women's clothing, but was quickly recaptured. Boston's ministers, along with merchants and former magistrates, led the rebellion, but city folk of the lower orders supplied the foot soldiers. For three years, an interim government ruled Massachusetts while the Bay colonists awaited a new charter and a royal governor.

Although Bostonians had dramatically rejected royal authority, which to them represented the "bloody Devotees of Rome" as well as arbitrary power, no internal revolution occurred. However, growing social stratification and the emergence of a political elite led some citizens to argue that men of modest means but common sense might better be trusted with power. "Anarchy" was the word chosen by Samuel Willard, minister of Boston's Third Church, to tar the popular spirit he saw unloosed in Boston in the aftermath of Andros's ouster. But such egalitarian rumblings came to little.

Leisler's Rebellion in New York

In New York, the Glorious Revolution was similarly bloodless at first but far more disruptive. It was not necessary to overthrow royal government when news arrived of James II's abdication. It simply melted away. When a local militia captain, the German-born Jacob Leisler, appeared at Fort James at the lower tip of Manhattan, Governor Francis Nicholson made only a token show of resistance before quietly stepping down. Displacing the governor's "popishly affected dogs and rogues," Leisler established an interim government and ruled with an elected Committee of Safety for 13 months until a governor appointed by King William arrived.

Leisler's government enjoyed popularity among small landowners and urban laboring people. Most of the upper echelon, however, detested him. They remembered that he had come to New Amsterdam in 1660 as a common foot soldier of the Dutch West India Company and three years later had leapfrogged into the merchant class by marrying a wealthy widow. After the English took over the Dutch colony in 1664, he was often at odds with New Yorkers of the upper rank. "Up jump into the saddle hott brain'd Capt. Leisler," sneered one aristocrat after Leisler's takeover. Thereafter, the Leislerians were often labeled as people of "mean birth, and sordid education and desperate fortunes."

Such antipathy was returned in kind by lower- and middle-class Dutch inhabitants, who felt a smoldering resentment toward the town's English elite. Many Dutch merchants had readily adjusted to the English conquest of New Netherland in 1664, and many incoming English merchants had married into Dutch families. But beneath the upper class, where economic success softened ethnic friction, incidents of Anglo-Dutch hostility were common. Ordinary Dutch families felt that the English were crowding them out of the society they had built.

The Glorious Revolution was the spark igniting this smoldering social conflict. Leisler shared Dutch hostility toward New York's English elite, and his sympathy for the common people, mostly Dutch, earned him the hatred of the city's oligarchy. Leisler freed imprisoned debtors, planned a town-meeting system of government for New York City, and replaced merchants with artisans in important offices. By the autumn of 1689, Leislerian mobs were attacking the property of some of New York's wealthiest merchants. Two merchants, refusing to recognize Leisler's authority, were jailed.

Leisler's opponents, accustomed to controlling government, were horrified at the power of what they called the "rabble" or the "tumultuous multitude." They believed that ordinary people had no right to rebel against authority or to exercise political power. When a new English governor arrived in 1691, the anti-Leislerians embraced him and charged Leisler and seven of his assistants with treason for assuming the government without royal instructions.

In the ensuing trial, Leisler and Jacob Milbourne, his son-in-law and chief lieutenant, were convicted of treason by an all-English jury and hanged. Leisler's popularity among the artisans of the city was evident when his wealthy opponents could find no carpenter in the city who would furnish a ladder to use at the scaffold. After his execution, peace gradually returned to New York, but for years provincial and city politics reflected the deep rift between Leislerians and anti-Leislerians.

Southern Rumblings

The Glorious Revolution also focused dissatisfactions in several southern colonies. Because Maryland was ruled by a Catholic proprietor, the Protestant majority seized power on word of the Glorious Revolution and used it for their own purposes. Lord Baltimore had returned to England in 1684. In 1688, when his instructions to his colony to honor William and Mary were delayed, leading officials and planters formed a Protestant Association. Seizing control of the government in July 1689, they vowed to cleanse Maryland of popery and to reform a corrupt customs service, cut taxes and fees, and extend the rights of the representative assembly. The militant Protestant John Coode, formerly a fiery Anglican minister who, as we have seen, had been involved in a brief rebellion in 1681, assumed the reins of government and held them until the arrival of Maryland's first royal governor in 1692.

In neighboring Virginia, the wounds of Bacon's Rebellion were still healing when word of the Glorious Revolution arrived. The fact that Virginia lived under a Catholic governor, Lord Howard of Effingham, and a number of Catholic officials he had installed fostered rumors of a Catholic plot. News of the revolution in England led a group of planters, suffering a prolonged drop in tobacco prices, to attempt an overthrow of the governor. The uprising quickly faded when the governor's council asserted itself and took its own measures to remove Catholics from positions of authority.

The Glorious Revolution brought lasting political changes to several colonies. The Dominion of New England collapsed. Connecticut and Rhode Island regained the right to elect their own governors, but Massachusetts (now including Plymouth) and New Hampshire became royal colonies with governors appointed by the king. In Massachusetts, a new royal charter in 1691 eliminated Church membership as a voting requirement. The Maryland proprietorship was abolished (to be restored in 1715 when the Calverts became Protestant), and Catholics were barred from office. Everywhere Protestant Englishmen celebrated their liberties.

The Social Basis of Politics

Although the colonial insurrections associated with the Glorious Revolution sought primarily to overthrow arbitrary royal governors and foil papist plots (most of them imaginary), they revealed social and political tensions that accompanied the transplanting of English society to the North American wilderness. Still hardly beyond the frontier stage, the immature societies along the coast were fluid, unruly, and competitive. They lacked the stable political systems and acknowledged leadership class thought necessary for maintaining social order.

The colonial elite tried, of course, to foster social and political stability. The best insurance of this, they believed, was the maintenance of a stratified society where children were subordinate to parents, women to men, servants to masters, and the poor to the rich. Amid the barbarizing conditions of the New World, where anarchy lurked just beyond every threshold, it was especially vital—in the eyes of the upper echelon—to reproduce the social arrangements of the Old World.

Hence, in every settlement, leaders tried to maintain a system of social gradations and subordination. Puritans did not file into church on Sundays and occupy the pews in random fashion. Rather, the seats were "doomed," or assigned according to customary yardsticks of respectability—age, parentage, social position, wealth, and occupation. Even in fluid Virginia, lower-class people were hauled before courts for horse racing because this was a sport by law reserved for men of social distinction.

But this social ideal proved difficult to maintain. Regardless of previous rank, settlers rubbed elbows so frequently and faced such raw conditions together that those without pedigrees often saw little reason to defer to men of superior rank. "In Virginia," explained John Smith, "a plain soldier that can use a pickaxe and spade is better than five knights." Colonists everywhere gave respect not to those who claimed it by birth, but to those who earned it by deed.

Adding to the difficulty of reproducing a traditional social order in the colonies was the social fluidity in frontier society. A native elite gradually formed, but it had no basis, as in Europe, in legally defined and hereditary social rank. Planters and merchants, accumulating large estates, aped the English gentry by cultivating the arts, building fine houses, and acquiring symbols of respectability such as libraries, coaches, and racehorses. Yet their place was rarely secure. In the race to drag wealth from the resource-rich environment, new competitors nipped constantly at their heels.

Amid such social flux, the elite could never command general allegiance to the ideal of a fixed social structure. Ambitious men on the rise such as Nathaniel Bacon and Jacob Leisler, and thwarted men below them who followed their lead, rose up against the constituted authorities, which they almost certainly would not have dared to do so in their homelands. When they gained power during the Glorious Revolution, in every case only briefly, the leaders of these uprisings linked themselves with a tradition of English struggle against tyranny and oligarchical power. They vowed to make government more responsive to the ordinary people, who composed most of their societies.

In both North and South, this earned parvenu leaders the epithet "Masaniello," after the peasant fish seller of Naples who in 1647 had mobilized ordinary people against exploitation by the rich. Masaniello briefly controlled the city, momentarily stood the political order on its head, and became an Italian Robin Hood. In America, Virginia's royal governor likened Bacon's Rebellion to Masaniello's revolt. In New York, Leisler was labeled a local Masaniello by his wealthy enemies. In Maryland, John Coode proudly called himself a Chesapeake Masaniello. The comparisons were far from exact, but references to the Italian folk hero indicate that colonists from all ranks recognized that social relations in their competitive and open society were subject to violent alterations that violated the ideal of a fixed, orderly social system.

Witchcraft in Salem

The ordinary people in the colonies, for whom Bacon and Leisler tried to speak, could sometimes be misled, as the tragic events of the Salem witch hunts demonstrated. In Massachusetts, the deposing of Governor Andros left the colony in political limbo for three years, and this allowed what might have been a brief outbreak of witchcraft in the little community of Salem to escalate into a bitter and bloody battle. The provincial government, caught in transition, reacted only belatedly.

On a winter's day in 1692, 9-year-old Betty Parris and her 11-year-old cousin Abigail Williams began to play at magic in the kitchen of a small house in Salem, Massachusetts. They enlisted the aid of Tituba, the slave of Betty's father, Samuel Parris, the minister of the small community. Tituba told voodoo tales handed down from her African past and baked "witch cakes." The girls soon became seized with fits and began making wild gestures and speeches. Soon other young girls in the village were behaving strangely. Village elders extracted confessions that they were being tormented by Tituba and two other women, both social outcasts.

What began as the innocent play of young girls turned into a ghastly rending of a farm community capped by the execution of 20 villagers accused of witchcraft. In the seventeenth century, people still took literally the biblical injunction "Thou shalt not suffer a witch to live." For centuries throughout western Europe, people had believed that witches followed Satan's bidding and did evil to anyone he designated. Communities had accused and sentenced women to death for witchcraft far more often than men. In Massachusetts, more than 100 people, mostly older women, had been accused of witchcraft before 1692, and more than a dozen had been hanged.

In Salem, the initial accusations against three older women quickly multiplied. Within weeks, dozens had been charged with witchcraft, including several prominent members of the community. But formal prosecution of the accused witches could not proceed because neither the new royal charter of 1691 nor the royal governor to rule the colony had yet arrived. For three months, while charges spread, local authorities could only jail the accused without trial. When Governor William Phips arrived from England in May 1692, he ordered a special court to try the accused. By then events had careened out of control.

All through the summer, the court listened to testimony. By September it had condemned about two dozen villagers. The authorities hanged 19 of them on barren "Witches Hill" outside the town and crushed 80-year-old Giles Corey to death under heavy stones. The trials rolled on into 1693, but by then, colonial leaders, including many of the clergy, recognized that a feverish fear of one's neighbors, rather than witchcraft itself, had possessed the little village of Salem.

Many factors contributed to the hysteria. Among them were generational differences between older Puritan colonists and the sometimes less religiously motivated younger generation, old family animosities, population growth and pressures on the available farmland, and tensions between agricultural Salem Village and the nearby commercial center called Salem Town. An outbreak of food poisoning may also have caused hallucinogenic behavior. Probably nobody will ever fully understand the exact mingling

Witch hangings, usually of women, were numerous in Europe as well as the colonies; this woodcut appeared in *England's Grievance Discovered* (1655), a book on injustices in England's coal industry. Identified by letter in the picture are the hangman (A), town crier (B), sheriff (C), and magistrate (D).

of causes, but the fact that most of the individuals charged with witchcraft were women underscores the relatively weak position of women in Puritan society. The relentless spread of witchcraft accusations reflects the anxiety of this tumultuous era. War, economic disruption, the political takeover of the colony by Andros and then his overthrow, and erosion of the early generation's utopian vision all became a deadly mix.

CONTENDING FOR A CONTINENT

At the end of the seventeenth century, Indian wars and internal upheaval gave way to protracted international war. The smoldering struggle for mastery of the New World among four contending European powers—Holland, Spain, France, and England—now became overt. North America was less an arena of armed rivalry among the European powers than were the Carribbean sugar islands. Nonetheless, the global struggle for control of land and sea that erupted late in the seventeenth century—beginning nearly 100 years of conflict—reached the doorsteps of those who thought that in immigrating to North America they had left war behind.

Anglo-French Rivalry

In 1661, the French king, Louis XIV, ushered in a new era for New France. Determined to make his country the most powerful in Europe, the king regarded North America and the Caribbean with renewed interest. New France's timber resources would build the royal navy, its fish would feed the growing mass of slaves in the French West Indies, and its fur trade, if greatly expanded, would fill the royal coffers.

Under able governors such as Count Frontenac, New France grew in population, economic strength, and ambition in the late seventeenth century. In the 1670s, Louis Jolliet and Father Jacques Marquette, a Jesuit priest, explored an immense territory watered by the Mississippi and Missouri rivers, previously unknown to Europeans. A decade later, military engineers and priests began building forts and missions, one complementing the other, throughout the Great Lakes region and the Mississippi valley.

Visions of a mighty inland empire grew in the 1680s when René Robert de La Salle canoed down the Mississippi all the way to the Gulf of Mexico and planted a settlement in Texas at Matagorda Bay. The dream of connecting Canada and Louisiana by a chain of forts and trading posts would not be realized for another half century. But it was the French, with a colonial population of only 12,000, rather than the English, with colonies inhabited by 200,000, whom the Indian tribes permitted to settle in the interior of North America. Traders and missionaries from France seemed very different in Indian villages than land-hungry, expansionist English settlers.

The growth of French strength and ambitions brought New England and New France into deadly conflict for a generation, beginning in the late seventeenth century. Religious hostility overlaid commercial rivalry. Protestant New Englanders regarded Catholic New France as a satanic challenge to their divinely sanctioned mission. When the European wars began in 1689, precipitated by Louis XIV's territorial aggression in western and central Europe, armed conflict between England and France quickly extended into every overseas theater where the two powers had colonies. In North America, the battle zone was New York, New England, and eastern Canada.

In two wars, from 1689 to 1697 and 1702 to 1713, the English and French, while fighting in Europe, also sought to oust each other from the New World. The zone of greatest importance was the Caribbean, where slaves produced huge sugar fortunes. Both home governments understood that the North American colonies were important chiefly as a source of the timber and fish that sustained the sugar-producing tropical economy of the West Indies. On the North American mainland, problems of weather, disease, transport, and supply were so great that only irregular warfare was possible.

The English struck three times at the centers of French power—Port Royal, which commanded the access to the St. Lawrence River, and Quebec, the administrative center of New France. In 1690, during King William's War (1689–1697), their small flotilla captured Port Royal, the hub of Acadia (which was returned to France at the end of the war). The English assault on Quebec, however, failed disastrously. In Queen Anne's War (1702–1713), New England attacked Port Royal three times before finally capturing it in 1710. A year later, when England sent a flotilla of 60 ships and 5,000 men to conquer Canada, the land and sea operations foundered before reaching their destinations.

With European-style warfare miserably unsuccessful in America, both England and France attempted to subcontract military tasks to their Indian allies. Here was a new aspect of the meeting of cultures—the use of Native Americans as mercenaries in an international conflict. This policy occasionally succeeded, especially with the French, who gladly sent their own troops into the fray alongside Indian partners. The French and their Indian allies wiped out the frontier outpost of Schenectady, New York, in 1690; razed Wells, Maine, and Deerfield, Massachusetts, in 1703; and battered other towns along the New England frontier during both wars.

Visiting French Louisiana in 1735, Alexander de Batz painted members of the Illinois tribe who traded at New Orleans. Note the hatted African, who apparently has been adopted by the Illinois. (*Alexander de Batz, Desseins de Sauvages de Plusieurs Natims, 1735, Peabody Museum, Harvard University, Photograph by: Hillel Burger*)

In retaliation, the Iroquois, supplied by the English, stung several French settlements and left New France "bewildered and benumbed" after a massacre near Montreal in 1689. Assessing their own interests, and too powerful to be bullied by either France or England, the Iroquois sat out the second war in the early eighteenth century. Convinced that neutrality served their purposes better than acting as mercenaries for the English, they held to the principle that "we are a free people uniting ourselves to whatever sachem [chief] we wish."

The Results of War

The Peace of Utrecht in 1713, which ended Queen Anne's War, capped the century-long rise of England and the decline of Spain in the rivalry for the sources of wealth outside Europe. England, the big winner, received Newfoundland and Acadia (renamed Nova Scotia), and France recognized English sovereignty over the fur-rich Hudson Bay territory. France retained Cape Breton Island, controlling the entrance to the St. Lawrence River. In the Caribbean, France yielded St. Kitts and Nevis to England. Spain lost its provinces in Italy and the last of its holdings in the Netherlands to the Austrian Habsburgs. Spain also surrendered Gibraltar and Minorca to England and awarded the English the lucrative privilege of supplying the Spanish empire in America with African slaves, a favor formerly enjoyed by the French Senegal Company.

The French were the big losers in these wars, but they did not abandon their New World ambitions. Soon after Louis XIV died in 1715, his successors tried to regain lost time in America by mounting a huge

Timeline

1600–1700	Dutch monopolize slave trade
1619	First Africans imported to Virginia
1637	Pequot War in New England
1640s	New England merchants enter slave trade
	Virginia forbids blacks to carry firearms
1650–1670	Judicial and legislative decisions in Chesapeake colonies solidify racial lines
1651	Parliament passes first navigation act
1664	English conquer New Netherland
1673–1685	French expand into Mississippi valley
1675–1677	King Philip's War in New England
1676	Bacon's Rebellion in Virginia
1682	La Salle canoes down Mississippi River and claims Louisiana for France
1684	Massachusetts charter recalled
1688	Glorious Revolution in England, followed by accession of William and Mary
1689	Overthrow of Governor Andros in New England
	Leisler's Rebellion in New York
1689–1697	King William's War
1690s	Transition from white indentured servant to black slave labor begins in Chesapeake region
1692	Witchcraft hysteria in Salem
1700	Spanish establish first mission in Arizona
1702–1713	Queen Anne's War
1713	Peace of Utrecht

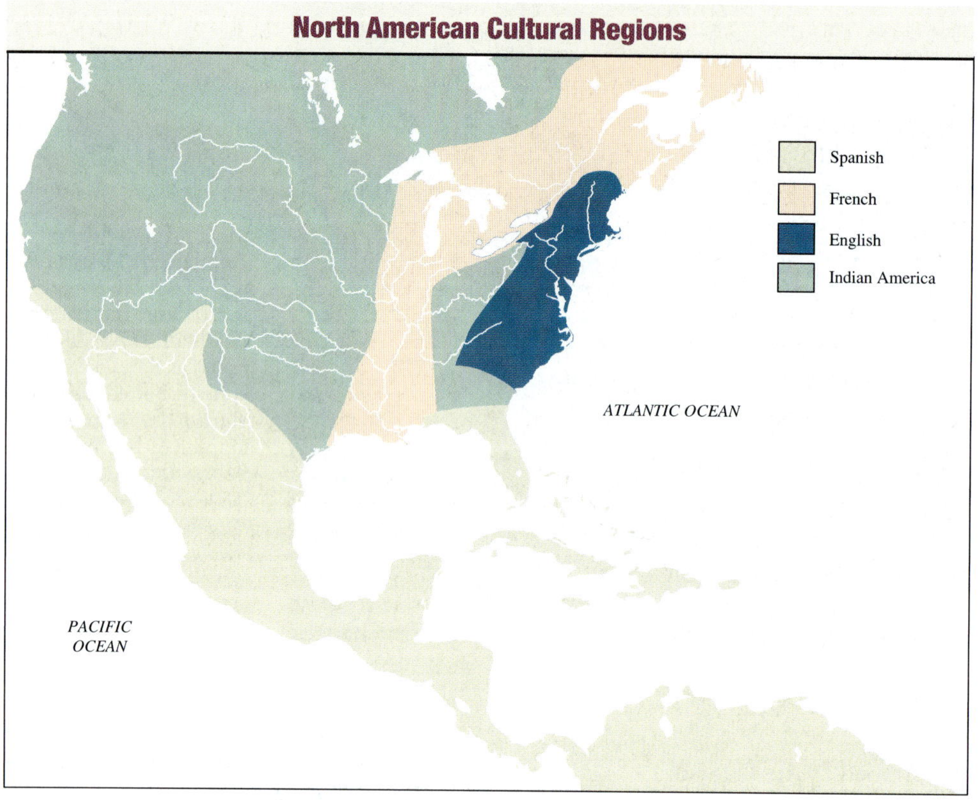

This map of European cultural regions in mid-eighteenth-century North America disguises the cultural influence of hundreds of Indian societies that lived among, between, and beyond the sparsely settled European settlements. Only along the eastern seaboard was European dominance secure.

expedition to settle Louisiana. Because France deported many undesirables to the colony and because the French aristocracy destroyed by wild speculation the stock that financed the project, few French immigrants joined the settlement of New Orleans. French colonies expanded only in the Caribbean, where by 1750, the islands of Hispaniola, Martinique, and Guadeloupe counted 46,000 whites and 250,000 slaves. Although the islands enriched a few, they strengthened the empire little, because slaves could not be armed and the islands were expensive to defend.

After the Peace of Utrecht, Spain still retained—on paper—a vast empire in North America. However, its hold on the southern tier of the continent was very tenuous, and it had learned how easily its thinly peopled missions and frontier outposts could be crippled or destroyed by chafing Native Americans and invading English. In the first half of the eighteenth century, the Spanish settlements stagnated, suffering from Spain's colonial policy that regarded them as marginal, money-losing affairs worth the trouble only as essentially defensive outposts.

Spain's priority was not to expand its presence in North America but to preserve what it had by keeping others away. That in itself would prove to be difficult, for this garrison mentality had to compete with the commercially minded English and French, whose colonial population, especially the former's, was growing rapidly. Small, impoverished Spanish frontier outposts could do little to halt the expansion of British and French America.

Though England had rebuffed France after a generation of war, New England suffered grievous economic and human losses. In time, Nova Scotia would provide a new frontier for Puritan farmers. But the two wars between 1689 and 1713 struck hard at New England's economy. Massachusetts bore the brunt of the burden. Probably one-fifth of all able-bodied males in the colony participated in the Canadian campaigns, and of these, about one-quarter never lived to tell of the terrors of New England's first major experience with international warfare. At the end of the first war, in 1697, one leader bemoaned that Massachusetts was left "quite exhausted and ready to sink under the calamities and fatigue of a tedious consuming war." The war debt was £50,000 sterling in Massachusetts alone, a greater per capita burden than the national debt today.

At the end of the second conflict, in 1713, war widows were so numerous that the Bay Colony faced its first serious poverty problem. In addition, wartime taxes had "much impoverished and enfeebled" the people, and price inflation had eaten deeply into the pocketbooks of most working families. Pamphleteers in New England's principal port wrote of the "present melancholy circumstances" and the "distressed state of the Town of Boston."

The colonies south of New England remained on the sidelines during most of the war. But war at sea between European rivals affected even those who sat out the land war. In Queen Anne's War, New York lost one of its best grain markets when Spain, allied with France, outlawed American foodstuffs in its West Indian colonies. The French navy plucked off nearly 30 New York merchant vessels, about one-quarter of the port's fleet, and disrupted the vital sea lanes between the mainland and the Caribbean to the detriment of Philadelphia's grain merchants.

The burdens and rewards fell unevenly on the participants, as usually happens in wartime. Some low-born men could rise spectacularly. William Phips, the twenty-sixth child in his family, had been a poor sheep farmer and ship's carpenter in Maine who seemed destined to go nowhere. Then he won a fortune by recovering a sunken Spanish treasure ship in the West Indies in 1687. For that feat, he was given command of the expedition against Port Royal in 1690. Victory there catapulted him to the governorship of Massachusetts in 1691; thereafter his status was secure.

Other men, already rich, got richer. Andrew Belcher of Boston, who had grown wealthy on provisioning contracts during King Philip's War (1675–1677), combined patriotism with profit in King William's and Queen Anne's wars by supplying warships and outfitting the New England expeditions to Canada. As one of the favored recipients of the fruits of war, Belcher became a local titan, riding through Boston's crooked streets in London-built coaches, erecting a handsome mansion on State Street, and purchasing slaves to symbolize his rise to the pinnacle of New England society.

Most men, especially those who did the fighting, gained little, however, and many lost all. The least securely placed New Englanders—indentured servants, apprentices, recently arrived immigrants, unskilled laborers, fishermen, and ordinary farmers—supplied most of the voluntary or involuntary troops, and they died in numbers that seem staggering today. Antipopery, dreams of glory, and promises of plunder in French Canada lured most of them into uniform. Having achieved no place on the paths leading upward, they grasped at straws. A hefty percentage of those who sailed in the naval expeditions against Port Royal or plodded overland to attack Montreal and Quebec never lived even to collect their meager wages. None found the advertised booty, which turned out to be only a sugarplum dangled by military recruiters.

Conclusion

Controlling the New Environment

By the second decade of the eighteenth century, the 12 English colonies on the eastern edge of North America had secured footholds in the hemisphere and erected the basic scaffolding of colonial life. With the aid of England, they had ousted the Dutch from their mid-Atlantic perch. They had fought the French to a draw and held their own against the Spanish. The coastal Indian tribes were reeling from disease and a series of wars that secured the colonists' land base along 1,000 miles of coastal plain. Though never controlling the powerful Indian tribes of the interior, the colonists had established a profitable trade with them. The settlers had overcome a scarcity of labor by copying the other European colonists in the hemisphere, who had linked the west coast of Africa to the New World through the ghastly trade in human flesh. Finally, the colonists had engaged in insurrections against what they viewed as arbitrary and tainted governments imposed by England.

The embryo of British America carried into the eighteenth century contained peculiarly mixed features. Still physically isolated from Europe, the colonists developed of necessity a large measure of self-reliance. Slowly, they began to identify themselves as the permanent inhabitants of a new land rather than as transplanted English, Dutch, or Scots-Irish. Viewing land and labor as the indispensable elements of a fruitful economy, they learned to exploit without apologies the land of one dark-skinned people and the labor of another. Yet even as they attained a precarious mastery in a triracial society, they were being culturally affected by the very people to which whose land and labor they laid claim. Although utopian visions of life in America still reverberated in the heads of some, most colonists had awakened to the reality that life in the New World was a puzzling mixture of unpredictable opportunity and sudden turbulence, unprecedented freedom and debilitating wars, racial intermingling and racial separation. It was a New World in much more than a geographic sense, for the people of three cultures who now inhabited it had remade it; and, while doing so, they were remaking themselves.

Recommended Reading

African Bondage

Philip Curtin, *The Atlantic Slave Trade: A Census* (1969) and *The Rise and Fall of the Plantation Complex* (1990); David B. Davis, *The Problem of Slavery in Western Culture* (1966); Carl N. Degler, *Neither Black nor White: Slavery and Race Relations in Brazil and the United States* (1971); Richard S. Dunn, *Sugar and Slaves: The Rise of the Planter Class in the English West Indies, 1624–1713* (1972); H. Hoetink, *Slavery and Race Relations in the Americas* (1973); Patrick Manning, *Slavery and African Life: Occidental, Oriental, and African Slave Trades* (1990); James A. Rawley, *The Transatlantic Slave Trade* (1981); Walter Rodney, *West Africa and the Atlantic Slave Trade* (1969); Frank Tannenbaum, *Slave and Citizen (1956);* Hugh Thomas, *The Slave Trade* (1997); John Thornton, *Africa and Africans in the Making of the Atlantic World, 1440–1680* (1992); Lorena Walsh, *From Calabar to Carter's Grove: The History of a Virginia Slave Community* (1997).

Slave Culture

Ira Berlin, *Many Thousands Gone: The First Two Centuries of Slavery in North America* (1998); T. H. Breen and Stephen Innes, *"Myne Owne Ground": Race and Freedom on Virginia's Eastern Shore, 1640–1676* (1980); Thomas J. Davis, *A Rumor of Revolt: The "Great Negro Plot" in Colonial New York* (1985); Michael A. Gomez, *Exchanging Our Country Marks: The Transformation of African Identities in the Colonial and Antebellum South* (1998); Gwendolyn Midlo Hall, *Africans in Colonial Louisiana* (1992); Winthrop D. Jordan, *White Over Black* (1968); Marvin L. Michael Kay and Lorin Lee Cary, *Slavery in North Carolina, 1748–1775* (1995); Allan Kulikoff, *Tobacco and Slaves: The Development of Southern Cultures in the Chesapeake, 1680–1800* (1986); Philip D. Morgan, *Slave Counterpoint: Black Culture in the Eighteenth-Century Chesapeake and Low-Country* (1998); Gerald Mullin, *Flight and Rebellion: Slave Resistance in Eighteenth-Century Virginia* (1972); Michael Mullin, *Africa in America: Slave Acculturation and Resistance in the American South* (1992); William Piersen, *Black Yankees: The Development of an African-American Subculture in Eighteenth-Century New England* (1988); Mechal Sobel, *The World They Made Together: Black and White Relations in Eighteenth-Century Virginia* (1987); Betty Wood, *Slavery in Colonial Georgia, 1730–1775* (1984); Peter H. Wood, *Black Majority: Negroes in South Carolina from 1670 Through the Stono Rebellion* (1974); Michael A. Gomez, *Exchanging Our Country Marks: The Transformation of African Identities in the Colonial and Antebellum South* (1998); Lorena S. Walsh, *From Calabar to Carter's Grove: The History of a Virginia Slave Community* (1997); Graham Russell Hodges, *Root and Branch: African Americans in New York and East Jersey, 1613–1863* (1999).

The Struggle for Land

James Axtell, *The European and the Indian* (1981); Colin G. Calloway, *New Worlds for All: Indians, Europeans, and the Remaking of Early America* (1997); Francis Jennings, *The Ambiguous Iroquois Empire* (1984); Jill Lepore, *The Name of the War: King Philip's War and the Origins of American Identity* (1998); Calvin Martin, *Keepers of the Game: Indian-Animal Relationships and the Fur Trade* (1978); Gary B. Nash, *Red, White, and Black*, 4th ed. (2000); Daniel Usner, Jr., *Indians, Settlers, and Slaves in a Frontier Exchange Economy: The Lower Mississippi Valley Before 1783* (1992); Wilcomb Washburn, *The Governor and the Rebel* (1957); J. Leitch Wright, *The Only Land They Knew: The Tragic Story of the American Indians in the Old South* (1981).

An Era of Instability

Paul Boyer and Steven Nissenbaum, *Salem Possessed: The Social Origins of Witchcraft* (1974); John P. Demos, *Entertaining Satan: Witchcraft and the Culture of Early New England* (1982); Carol F. Karlsen, *The Devil in the Shape of a Woman* (1987); David Lovejoy, *The Glorious Revolution in America* (1972); Mary Beth Norton, *Founding Mothers and Fathers: Gendered Power and the Forming of American Society* (1996); Richard Weisman, *Witchcraft, Magic, and Religion in 17th-Century Massachusetts* (1984).

Contending for a Continent

Ramon A. Gutiérrez, *When Jesus Came, the Corn Mothers Went Away: Marriage, Sexuality, and Power in New Mexico, 1500–1846* (1992); A. H. Johns, *Storms Brewed in Other Men's Worlds: The Confrontation of Indians, Spanish, and French in the Old Southwest* (1975); Oakah L. Jones, Jr., *Los Paisanos: Spanish Settlers on the Northern Frontier of New Spain* (1979); D. W. Meinig, *The Shaping of America: Atlantic America, 1492–1800* (1986); Edward Spicer, *Cycles of Conquest: The Impact of Spain, Mexico, and the United States on the Indians of the Southwest, 1533–1960* (1962); Ian K. Steele, *Warpaths: Invasions of North America* (1994); David J. Weber, *The Spanish Frontier in North America* (1992); Richard White, *The Middle Ground: Indians, Empires, and Republics in the Great Lakes Region, 1650–1815* (1991).

Fiction and Film

Louise Erdrich's poem titled "Captivity," which can be found in her *Jacklight* collection (1984), is a valuable Indian-centered reading of one of the most popular Indian captivity accounts ever published—Mary Rowlandson's *A Narrative of the Captivity, Sufferings and Removes of Mrs. Mary Rowlandson*, first published in 1682. Boston's WGBH has produced a suberb four-part video series on *Africans in America* (1998). The first two parts cover slavery and slave culture in the seventeenth and eighteenth centuries. Much shorter is *A Son of Africa: The Slave Narrative of Olaudah Equiano*, a half-hour video, produced by the BBC, of the only eighteenth-century slave who wrote an autobiography. *Three Sovereigns for Sarah* (1985), a PBS miniseries starring Vanessa Redgrave, stunningly dramatizes the Salem witchcraft trials. Arthur Miller's play, *The Crucible* (1953) is on the same topic and is as engaging today as it was three decades ago when it played on stages around the country.

Suggested Web Sites

http://etext.virginia.edu/salem/witchcraft

Witchcraft in Salem Village. Extensive archive of the 1692 trials and life in late seventeenth-century Massachusetts.

http://dpls.dacc.wisc.edu/slavedata/index.html

DPLS Archive: Slave Movement During the Eighteenth and Nineteenth Centuries (Wisconsin). This site explores the slave ships and the slave trade that carried millions of Africans to the New World.

http://vi.uh.edu/pages/mintz/primary.htm

*Excerpts From Slave Narratives.*The seventeenth- through nineteenth-century accounts of slavery housed in this site speak volumes about the many impacts of slavery.

http://www.thc.state.tx.us/belle/index.html

La Salle Shipwreck Project. This Texas Historical Commission site is about the archaeological dig to recover the ship of one of America's famous early explorers.

http://www.law.umkc.edu/faculty/projects/ftrials/salem/salem.htm

Salem Witchcraft Trials (1692). Images, chronology, court, and official documents by Dr. Doug Linder at University of Missouri—Kansas City Law School.

http://www.yale.edu/lawweb/avalon/18th.htm

Colonial Documents. The key documents of the Colonial Era are reproduced here, as are some of the important documents from earlier and later time periods in American history.

http://members.aol.com/jeworth/gboindex.htm

Georgia Before Oglethorpe. This resources guide informs the viewer about Native American Georgia in the seventeenth century.

http://www.ushistoryplace.com

the History place A richly detailed on-line learning environment complete with interactive maps, timelines, history activities, primary source documents, and links to related American history sites.

4

The MATURING *of* COLONIAL SOCIETY

CHAPTER OUTLINE

As a youth, Devereaux Jarratt knew only the isolated life of the small southern planter. Born in 1733 on the Virginia frontier, he was the third son of an immigrant yeoman farmer. In New Kent County, where Jarratt grew up, class status showed in a man's dress, his leisure habits, his house, even in his religion. A farmer's "whole dress and apparel," Jarratt recalled later, "consisted in a pair of coarse breeches, one or two shirts, a pair of shoes and stockings, an old felt hat, and a bear skin coat." In a maturing colonial society that was six generations old by the mid-eighteenth century, such simple folk stepped aside and tipped their hats when prosperous neighbors went by. "A periwig, in those days," recollected Jarratt, "was a distinguishing badge of gentle folk, and when I saw a man riding the road, near our house, with a wig on, it would so alarm my fears . . . that, I dare say, I would run off, as for my life."

As the colonies grew rapidly after 1700, economic development brought handsome gains for some, opened modest opportunities for many, but produced disappointment and privation for others. Jarratt remembered that his parents "neither sought nor expected any title, honors, or great things, either for themselves or their children. They wished us all brought up in some honest calling that we might earn our bread, by the sweat of our brow, as they did." But Jarratt was among those who advanced. His huge appetite for learning was apparent to his parents when as a small child he proved able to repeat entire chapters of the Bible before he had learned to read. That earned him some schooling. But at age 8, when his parents died, he had to take his place behind the plow alongside his brothers. Then, at 19, Jarratt was "called from the ax to the quill" by a neighboring planter's timely offer of a job tutoring his children.

Tutoring put Jarratt in touch with the world of wealth and status. Gradually, he advanced to positions in the households of wealthy Virginia planters. His modest success also introduced him to the world of evangelical religion. In the eighteenth century, an explosion of religious fervor dramatically reversed the growing secularism of the settlers. Jarratt first encountered evangelicalism in the published sermons of George Whitefield, an English clergyman.

But it was later, at the plantation of John Cannon, "a man of great possessions in lands and slaves," that he personally experienced conversion under the influence of Cannon's wife. Jarratt later became a clergyman in the Anglican Church, which was dominated in the South by wealthy and dignified planters. He never lost his religious zeal and desire to carry religion to the common people. In this commitment to spiritual renewal, he participated in the first mass religious movement to occur in colonial society.

Colonial North America in the first half of the eighteenth century was a thriving, changing set of regional societies that had developed from turbulent seventeenth-century beginnings. New England, the mid-Atlantic colonies, the Upper and Lower South, New France, and the northern frontier of New Spain were all distinct regions. Even within regions, diversity increased in the eighteenth century as incoming streams of immigrants, mostly from Africa, Germany, Ireland, and France, added new pieces to the emerging American mosaic.

Despite their bewildering diversity and lack of cohesion, the colonies along the Atlantic seaboard were affected similarly by population growth and economic development. Everywhere except on the frontier, class differences grew. A commercial orientation spread from north to south, especially in the towns, as local economies matured and forged links with the network of trade in the Atlantic basin. The exercise of political power of elected legislative assemblies and local bodies produced seasoned leaders, a tradition of local autonomy, and a widespread belief in a political ideology stressing the liberties that freeborn Englishmen should enjoy. All regions experienced a deep-running religious awakening that was itself connected to secular changes. All these themes will be explored as we follow the way scattered frontier settlements developed into mature provincial societies.

Joseph Beekman Smith, *Wesley Chapel on John Street, New York City—1768* (detail), completed 1817–1844 (based on earlier sketches). *(Old John Street United Methodist Church, New York)*

AMERICA'S FIRST POPULATION EXPLOSION

In 1680, some 150,000 colonizers clung to the eastern edge of North America. By 1750, they had swelled sevenfold to top one million. This growth rate, never experienced in Europe, staggered English policymakers. Perceptive observers understood that the population gap between England and its American colonies was closing rapidly. Benjamin Franklin's prediction in 1751—that before his grandchildren died, the colonies would outstrip the mother country in population—proved correct.

The population boom was fed from both internal and external sources. Among the white colonial population, a high marriage rate, large families, and lower mortality than in Europe prevailed by the 1720s. Natural increase accounted for much of the population boom in all the colonies and nearly all of it in New England, where immigrants arrived only in a trickle in the eighteenth century. The black population also began to increase naturally by the 1720s. American-born slaves, forming families and producing as many children as white families, soon began to outnumber slaves born in Africa. The 15,000 Africans in 1690 grew to 80,000 in 1730 and 325,000 in 1760. By then, when they composed one-fifth of the colonial population, their numbers were growing far more from natural increase than from importation.

Population of European Colonies in North America, 1680–1770

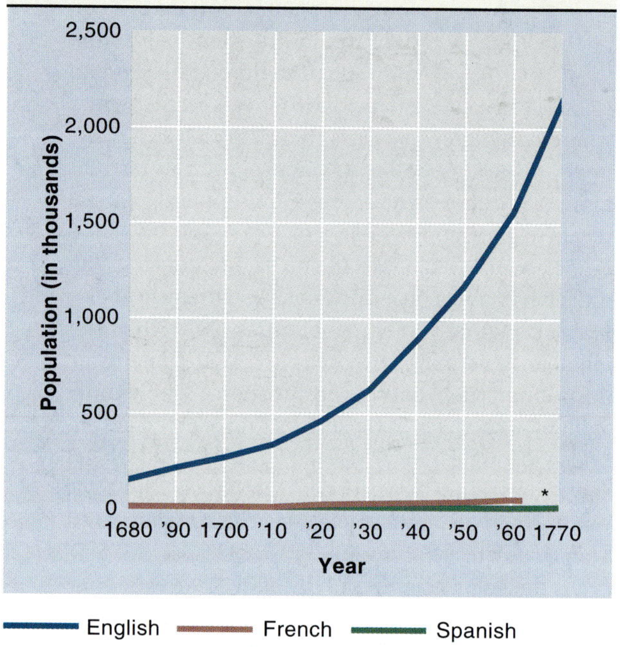

Whereas the population of French and Spanish colonies in North America inched upward (the result of few arriving immigrants and a low birthrate in settlements dominated by males), the population of English colonies soared.

The New Immigrants

While expanding through natural increase, the colonial population also absorbed waves of new immigrants. They were not English, however. The last sizable group of settlers from England had arrived at the end of the seventeenth century. The eighteenth-century newcomers, who far outnumbered those emigrating before 1700, came overwhelmingly from Germany, Switzerland, Ireland, and Africa, and they were mostly indentured servants and slaves. Of all the groups arriving in the eighteenth century, the Africans were the largest.

German-speaking settlers, about 90,000 strong, flocked to the colonies in the eighteenth century. Many were Protestant farmers of Swiss and French extraction, fleeing "God's three arrows"—famine, war, and pestilence. Drifting down the Rhine to Rotterdam, they crowded onto ships and began the long voyage to America. Once in the colonies, they hurried to areas where promoters promised them cheap and fertile land, low taxes, and freedom from military duty. Most settled between New York and South Carolina, with Pennsylvania claiming the largest number of them. Coming mostly in families, they turned much of the mid-Atlantic hinterland into a German-speaking region. Place names still mark their zone of settlement: Mannheim, New Berlin, and Herkimer, New York; Bethlehem, Ephrata, Nazareth, and Hanover, Pennsylvania; Hagerstown and Frederick, Maryland; Mecklenberg and New Hanover, North Carolina.

Even more Protestant Scots-Irish arrived. Several thousand from northern Ireland arrived each year after the Peace of Utrecht in 1713 reopened the Atlantic sea lanes. Mostly poor farmers, they streamed into the same backcountry areas where Germans were settling, though more of them followed the mountain valleys south into the Carolinas and Georgia. Occasionally mingling with the Germans, these Ulster families washed over the ridges of Appalachia until their appetite for land brought them face-to-face with the ancient occupiers of the land. No major Indian wars occurred between 1715 and 1754, but the frontier bristled with tension as the new settlers pushed westward.

In the enormous population growth occurring after 1715, the region southward from Pennsylvania increased most spectacularly. New England nearly tripled in population, but the middle and southern colonies quadrupled, though in the South the fast-growing slave population accounted for much more of

Native American Population Loss, 1500–1700

This map does not show Indian population loss in Central America and the West Indies, but in most of this region the loss by 1700 was at least 80 percent.

the growth than in the mid-Atlantic. Pennsylvania, with its fertile lands and open door policy, grew fastest of all. Between 1720 and 1760, its population mushroomed from 30,000 to 180,000. Virginia, with a population of nearly 340,000 by 1760, remained by far the largest colony.

The social background of these new European immigrants differed substantially from that of their seventeenth-century predecessors. The early settlers included a number of men from the upper levels of the English social pyramid: university-trained Puritan ministers, sons of wealthy gentry, and merchants. In the eighteenth century, few such men arrived.

The seventeenth-century immigrants had also included many from the middle rungs of the English social ladder—yeomen farmers, skilled craftsmen, and shopkeepers. They formed the backbone of the provincial churches and participated actively in community politics. Through "shipboard mobility," they moved up a notch or two on the western side of the Atlantic. Many lived to see their sons enter the professions or embark on a mercantile career in a society

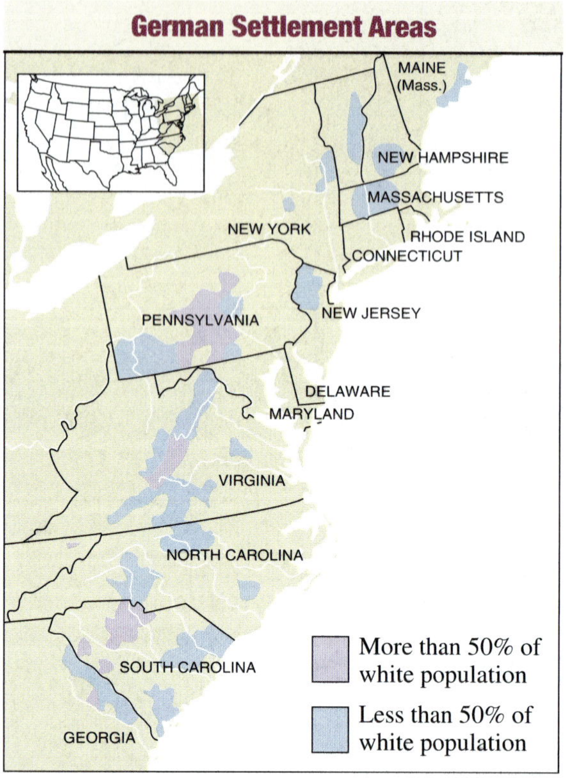

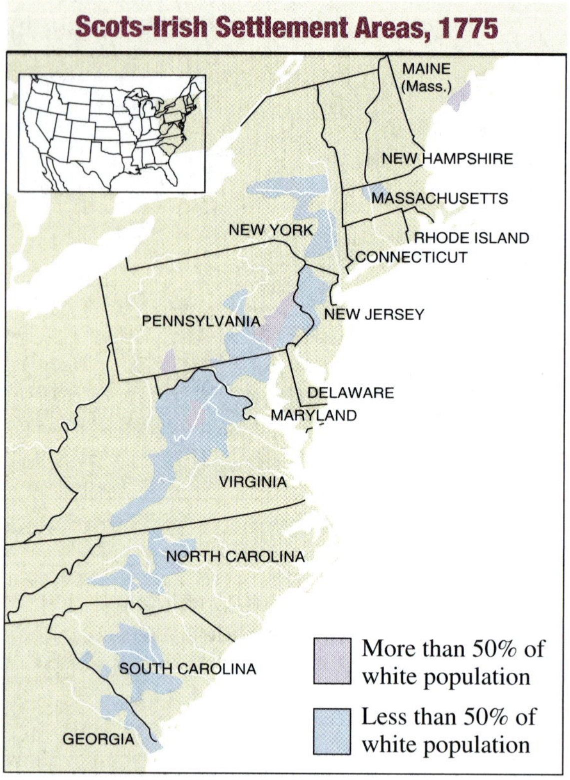

Most German and Scots-Irish immigrants in the 1700s were farmers, and they quickly moved into the interior, where land was cheapest and most available.

with plenty of room at the top. Such people came rarely in the eighteenth century, for religious persecution had waned in England, and material conditions had improved.

Slaves and indentured servants made up most of the incoming human tide after 1713. The traffic in servants became a regular part of the commerce linking Europe and America. Shipowners made their profits fetching sugar, fish, furs, rice, tobacco, and forest products eastward. On the westbound voyages, plenty of room remained for human cargo after loading the less bulky textiles and manufactured products desired by colonists.

Shipboard conditions for servants worsened in the eighteenth century and were hardly better than on slave ships. The wretchedness of the passage can be judged by the attempt at reform in the 1720s, when the British government required an increase in horizontal space to 6 feet by 18 inches per passenger, with no allowance for children.

Such attempts to reduce "tight packing" did little to improve shipboard life. Crammed between decks in stifling air, servants suffered from smallpox and fevers, rotten food, impure water, cold, and lice. "Children between the ages of one and seven seldom survive the sea voyage," bemoaned one German immigrant, "and parents must often watch their offspring suffer miserably, die, and be thrown into the ocean." One expedition of 3,000 Palatinate immigrants in 1717 lost 470 en route; on another, 250 succumbed shortly after reaching port. "I never see such parcels of poor wretches," one Virginia observer remarked of an incoming troop of servants in 1758, "some almost naked and what had clothes was as black as chimney sweepers and almost starved." The misery would be repeated thousands of times in the next two centuries. The shipboard mortality rate of about 15 percent in the colonial era made this the most unhealthy of all times to seek American shores.

Like indentured servants in the seventeenth century, servant immigrants who poured ashore after 1715 came mostly from the bottom of society. As earlier, some were petty criminals, political prisoners, and the castoffs of the cities. Yet they were bold and ambitious souls. "Men who emigrate," an Englishman commented, "are from the nature of their circumstances, the most active, hardy, daring, bold and resolute spirits, and probably the most mischievous also."

Once ashore, most indentured servants, especially males, found the labor system harsh. Merchants sold them, one shocked Britisher reported in 1773, "as they do their horses, and advertise them as they do their

The communalistic Moravian immigrants who came to Pennsylvania in the 1740s dedicated themselves, like the Quakers, to peaceful relations with the Indians. The Prussian John Jacob Schmick and his Norwegian wife, Johanna, were missionaries to the Delawares. *(Moravian Historical Society, Nazareth, PA)*

beef and oatmeal." Facing cruel treatment, thousands of servants ran away. Advertisements for them filled the colonial newspapers alongside notices for escaped slaves. Servants knew the penalties if they were caught: whipping and additional service, usually reckoned at twice the time lost to the master, but sometimes calculated at a 5-to-1 or 10-to-1 ratio, as in Pennsylvania and Maryland. When war came in the mid-eighteenth century, hundreds of servants fled to the British army, not known for its kindly treatment of soldiers but preferable in many servants' eyes to four or five years under a harsh colonial master.

The goal of every servant was to secure a foothold on the ladder of opportunity. "The hope of buying land in America," a New Yorker noted, "is what chiefly induces people into America." However, many servants died before serving out their time. Others won freedom only to toil for years as poor day laborers and tenant farmers. Only a small proportion achieved the dream of becoming independent landholders. The indentured servants in the seventeenth-century Chesapeake world suffered fearful mortality rates, but those who survived often rose in society. Among the eighteenth-century servants, ironically, the chances of living long enough to complete the labor contract were much better, but the opportunity to climb into the propertied ranks became less favorable. The chief beneficiaries of the system of bound white labor were not the laborers but their masters.

Africans in Chains

The most numerous of the thousands of ships crossing the Atlantic in the eighteenth century were those fitted out as seagoing dungeons for slaves. The slave trade to the southern colonies after the Peace of Utrecht expanded so sharply that within two generations what had been a society with many slaves became a society built on slavery. From 1690 to 1715, annual importations rarely exceeded 1,000, but in the next 15 years, the number probably doubled. The generation after 1730 witnessed the largest influx of African slaves in the colonial period, averaging about 5,000 a year. In the entire period from 1700 to 1775, more than 350,000 African slaves entered the American colonies.

Most of these miserable captives were auctioned off to southern planters, but some landed in the northern cities, especially New York and Philadelphia.

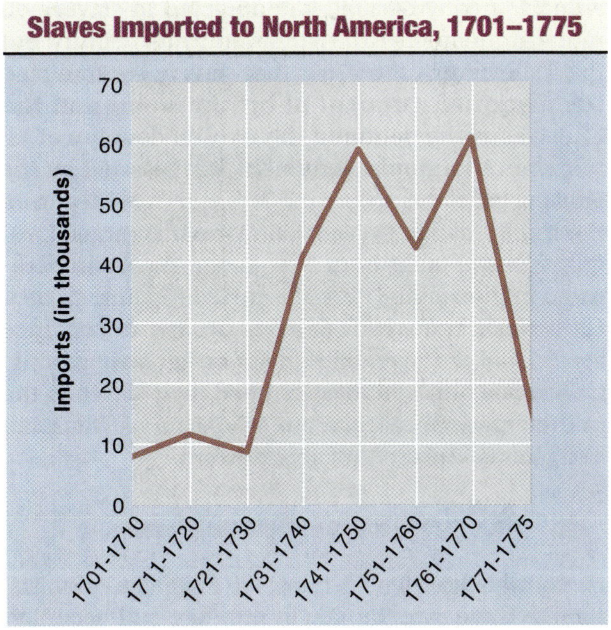

Overwhelmingly, Africans transported to the American colonies arrived from the 1730s to the 1770s. Rapid natural increase, as well as importation, swelled the African population to about 500,000 by the outbreak of the American Revolution. Source: R. C. Simmons, *The American Colonies: From Settlement to Independence,* 1976.

New-Providence Townſhip, Philadelphia County, December 19th, 1772.

RUN AWAY from the ſubſcriber, living in the aforeſaid townſhip, on Monday the fourteenth inſtant, an indented Iriſh ſervant man named BARNABAS KELLY, about five feet three inch... twenty one years of age, ... blind and is near-ſight... other, has long black h... wears tied behind: Had on an old great coat ... cut velvet jacket without buttons, a red o... and a white linen one without ſleeves, an ol... ther breeches, black ſtockings, and a pair ... with ſtrings. He took with him about Four or Five Pounds in money, and his own and his maſter's part of his indentures; alſo a grey HORSE, which trots moſtly and paces a little. Whoever will take up the ſaid ſervant, and ſecure him in any gaol, ſo that I may get him again, ſhall have FORTY SHILLINGS, and FORTY SHILLINGS more for the horſe, and reaſonable charges, paid by

EDWARD ROBERTS.

TO BE SOLD,
The TIME of an *IRISH*
SERVANT GIRL,

WHO has about three years to ſerve. Enquire of the Printers.

Like enslaved Africans, white indentured servants often fled the harsh conditions under which they labored. Advertisements for the recovery of runaway servants (left) filled the colonial newspapers. No explanation is given for the sale of the servant girl's time (right). Was her performance unsatisfactory? Did her master unexpectedly need cash? *(Historical Society of Pennsylvania, Philadelphia)*

Merchants sold them there to artisans, farmers, and upper-class householders seeking domestic servants.

Even as the traffic in slaves peaked, religious and humanitarian opposition to slavery arose. A few individuals, mostly Quaker, had objected to slavery on moral grounds since the late seventeenth century. But the idea grew in the 1750s that slavery contradicted the Christian concept of brotherhood and the Enlightenment notion of the natural equality of all humans. Abolitionist sentiment was also fed by the growing belief that a slave master's authority "depraved the mind," as the Quaker John Woolman argued. An introspective tailor from New Jersey, Woolman dedicated his life in the 1750s to a crusade against slavery. He traveled thousands of miles on foot to convince every Quaker slaveholder of his or her wrongdoing. Only a few hundred masters freed their slaves in the mid-eighteenth century, but men such as Woolman had planted the seeds of abolitionism.

BEYOND THE APPALACHIANS

By the mid-eighteenth century, the American colonists, though increasing rapidly in number, still occupied only a narrow strip of coastal plain in eastern North America. Of about 1.2 million settlers and slaves in 1750, only a tiny fraction lived farther than 100 miles from the Atlantic Ocean. But between them and the Pacific Ocean lay rich soils in the river valleys of the Ohio and Mississippi and beyond that a vast domain that they had not even imagined. Beginning in the 1750s, westward-moving colonists in pursuit of more land would encounter four other groups already established to their west: the populous interior Native American tribes and smaller groups of French Americans, Spanish Americans, and African Americans. Changes already occurring among these groups would affect settlers breaching the Appalachian barrier and, in the third quarter of the eighteenth century, would even reach eastward to the original British settlements.

Cultural and Ecological Changes Among Interior Tribes

During the first half of the eighteenth century, the inland tribes proved their capacity to adapt to the contending European colonizers in their region while maintaining their political independence. Yet extensive contact with the French, Spanish, and English slowly brought ominous changes to Indian ways of life.

The introduction of European trade goods, especially iron implements, textiles, firearms and ammunition, and alcohol, inescapably changed Indian lifeways. Subsistence hunting, limited to satisfying tribal food requirements, turned into commercial hunting, restricted only by the quantity of trade goods desired. Indian males, gradually exhausting the population of deer and beaver east of the Mississippi River, spent far more time away from the villages trapping and hunting.

Women were also drawn into the new economic activities, threatening the matrilineal basis of society. Once killed, the beaver, deer, marten, and fox had to be skinned and the pelts then scraped, dressed, trimmed, and sewn into robes by women. Among some tribes, all this became so time-consuming that they had to procure food resources from other tribes.

The fur trade altered much in traditional Native American life. Spiritual beliefs that the destinies of humans and animals were closely linked eroded when trappers and hunters declared all-out war on the beaver and other fur-bearing animals to provide pelts for the European traders who offered attractive trade goods. Competition for furs sharpened intertribal tensions, often to the point of war. As fur traders of different nationalities competed for client tribes in the fur trade, the tribes were sucked into their patron's rivalry. Also, tribes came to depend on certain trade articles. When furs became depleted in their hunting grounds, they could maintain trade only by conquering more remote tribes with fertile hunting grounds or by forcibly intercepting the furs of other tribes on their way to European trading posts. The introduction of European weaponry, which Indians quickly mastered, further intensified intertribal conflict.

Tribal political organization in the interior also changed in the eighteenth century. Earlier, most tribes had been loose confederations of villages and clans, each exercising local autonomy. The Creek, Cherokee, and Iroquois gave primary loyalty to the village, not to the tribe or confederacy. But trade, diplomatic contact, and war with Europeans required coordinated policies, so villagers gradually adopted more centralized leadership.

Cherokee political organization in the eighteenth century illustrates the changes overcoming tribal societies. Early in the century, the nearly autonomous village formed the basic unit of political authority. But tension with Creek neighbors and intermittent hostilities with English traders and settlers pressed home the need for coordinated decision making. By 1750, the Cherokee had formed an umbrella political organization that under the leadership of Chief Old Hop gathered together the fragmented authority of the villages and formed a more centralized tribal "priest state." When even this proved inadequate, warriors began to assume the dominant role in tribal councils, replacing the civil chiefs. By this process, the Cherokee reorganized their political structure so that dozens of scattered villages could pool their strength.

While incorporating trade goods into their material culture and adapting their economies and political structures to new situations, the interior tribes held fast to tradition in many ways. They saw little reason to replace what they valued in their own culture. What they saw of the colonists' systems of law and justice, religion, education, family organization, and child rearing usually convinced Native Americans that their own ways were superior.

The Indians' refusal to accept the superiority of white culture frustrated English missionaries, eager to win Native Americans from "savage" ways. Some colonists understood that the white behavior observed by natives cast doubts on the notion that Indians were of an inferior race. A Carolinian admitted that "they are really better to us than we are to them. We look upon them with scorn and disdain, and think them little better than beasts in human shape, though if well examined, we shall find that, for all our religion and education, we possess more moral deformities and evils than these savages do."

Despite maintaining many cultural practices, the interior Indian tribes suffered from the commercial, diplomatic, and military contact with the British colonizers. Decade by decade, the fur trade spread epidemic diseases, intensified warfare, depleted game animals, and drew Native Americans into a market economy where their trading partners gradually became trading masters.

France's Inland Empire

While the powerful Iroquois, Cherokee, Creek, and Choctaw tribes interacted with British colonists to their east, they also faced a growing French presence to their west. Between 1699 and 1754, the French developed a system of small forts, trading posts, and agricultural villages throughout the central area of the continent. The aim was to connect French Canada to the Gulf of Mexico and pin the English to the seaboard. French success in this vast region hinged partly on shrewd dealing with the Indian tribes, which retained sovereignty over the land but gradually succumbed to French diseases, French arms, and French-promoted intertribal wars.

Because France's interior empire was organized primarily as a military, trading, and missionizing operation, male French settlers arrived with few French women. This led to a long period when French men encountered Indians in a state of need—not only for trading partners, allies, and souls to be converted but also for wives. From this need came the mingling of French and Indian peoples—what the French called *metissage*—in the vast North American interior. It was almost unthinkable for a French fur trader to do business without an Indian wife who could pave the way for his trading with the Ojibway, Menominee, or any other Great Lakes tribe.

Such interracial marriages, soon to be called "the custom of the country," were desired by the Indians as well as the French. Marital alliances cemented

French North America, 1608–1763

Though thinly settled by colonists, the vast region west of the Proclamation Line claimed by France was held by a combination of forts and trading posts.

trade relations and military alliances. French traders entered Indian kinship circles, making trade flow smoothly, while Indians gained protection against their enemies and access to provisions at the French trading posts. Though the French sometimes descended into fierce warfare with Indian peoples, the North American heartland was a cultural merging ground and marrying ground, as well as marketplace and battleground.

For a full century after 1650, the French Jesuits and fur traders had been building a crescent of settlements and military posts extending down the St. Lawrence River basin, through the Great Lakes, and southward down the Mississippi valley to the Gulf of Mexico. Even though farming communities such as Kaskaskia and Prairie du Chien were thinly dotted, this French presence in the continent's heartland created an effective shield against the expansion-minded British to the east. As the French population grew to about 70,000 by 1750, they demonstrated uniquely how European settlers could coexist with Indian peoples by negotiating incessantly with Indian leaders, respecting Indian ways of conducting trade, and—above all—mingling so thoroughly that almost all French settlements in North America's interior were mixed-race communities. French Louisiana, for example, though thinly populated, had more mixed-race children and more white and black men who lived with Native Americans than any Anglo-American colony.

In 1718, the few hundred early French pioneers of the interior were suddenly inundated when France

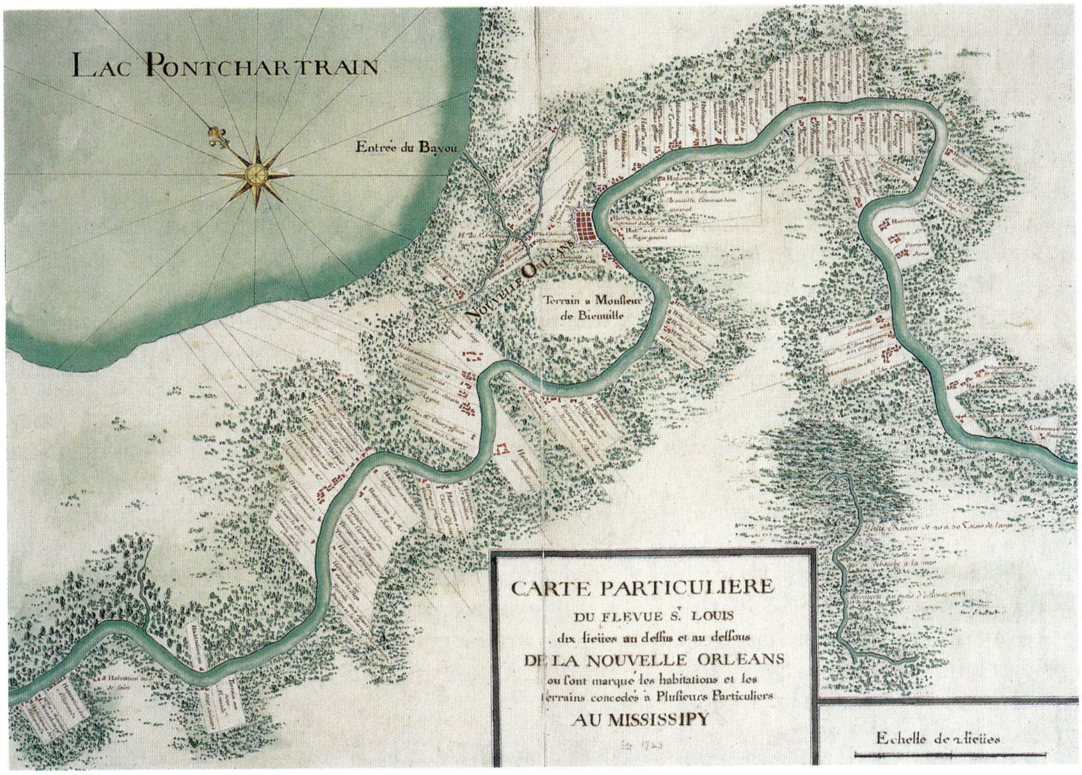

This map of New Orleans Parish in 1723, when the colony was still struggling, shows every plantation fronting on the Mississippi River. *(The Newberry Library)*

settled New Orleans at great cost by transporting almost 7,000 whites and 5,000 African slaves to the mouth of the Mississippi River. Disease rapidly whittled down these numbers, and an uprising of the powerful Natchez in 1729 discouraged further French immigration. Most of the survivors settled around the little town of New Orleans in long, narrow plantations stretching back from the Mississippi River to the endless cypress swamps. Slaves made wood products from cypress and pine for the West Indies and produced indigo, rice, and other crops for France. New Orleans merchants also marketed wheat from the little farming villages taking root in Illinois; bear oil and tobacco from settlements around the western post of Natchitoches; beef from herds in the Mobile River valley; produce from the small upriver German village Les Allemandes; and tens of thousands of deer skins and other pelts delivered annually by Indians for trade goods.

In its economy and society, New Orleans much resembled early Charleston, South Carolina. By contrast, however, French New Orleanians knew nothing of representative political institutions. Ruled by a governor, a commissary and chief judge, and a small appointed council, the people had no elections, no assembly, no newspapers, and no taxes. Because the French king paid dearly to keep the town's troops supplied, he would share power with no one, although he granted planters many favors. A mid-century English observer noted that the planter "is considered as a Frenchman venturing his life, enduring a species of banishment, and undergoing great hardships for the benefit of his country, for which reason he has great indulgence shown." This could not have been said of English planters in Georgia, South Carolina, or Virginia.

From its first introduction in Louisiana in 1719, French plantation slavery grew so rapidly that blacks outnumbered whites by 1765. Most slaves and a majority of whites lived in the New Orleans area. The conditions of life for slaves differed little from the southern English colonies, for slaves also lived in simple cabins and worked under the sun and the lash in a master's fields and swamps. But the French had a paternalistic legal code that gave slaves some protection in courts. When the Spanish took over the colony in 1769, they instituted their own law guaranteeing slaves the right to buy freedom with money earned in their free time. Soon a large free black class emerged, headed by substantial people like Simon Calfat, who ran various enterprises, helped other slaves pay for their freedom, and headed a company of free black militia. When Americans acquired the colony in 1803, they suppressed freedom purchase and discouraged manumission.

Most blacks who lived outside the British colonies labored in New Orleans, but a few could be found pioneering elsewhere beyond the Appalachians. By the early eighteenth century, slaves who escaped Spanish, French, or English masters formed bands in the interior allied with Indian tribes. The Spanish settlers in Texas and California carried a few blacks with them. A supreme expression of the range of possibilities occurred just before the American Revolution when a free black of West Indian parentage, Jean-Baptiste Point du Sable, with his Potawatomi wife, planted the first settlement in what became Chicago. A few years later, the British army arrested Point du Sable and his fellow pioneers as sympathizers with the American rebels.

Spain's America

In the first half of the eighteenth century, the Spanish still possessed by far the largest empire in the Americas. But in North America, the Spanish had great difficulty defending their Florida mission network and military posts, while trying on a shoestring to counter French expansion in the Mississippi River watershed with only a few military posts in Texas and New Mexico. Hispanics, mestizos, and detribalized Indians began to increase modestly in Texas, New Mexico, and California in the first half of the eighteenth century, but they were falling further and further behind in relation to the English and French. The English in South Carolina were ten times as numerous as the Spanish in Florida by 1745, and the gap kept widening. New Mexico's Hispanic population of about 10,000 at mid-century could defend the vast region only because no European challenger appeared.

As in New France, racial intermixture and social fluidity were more extensive in New Spain than in the English colonies. Precisely how much is uncertain because the Spanish never defined racial groups as distinctly as the English. The word *Spaniard* on a census might mean a white immigrant from Mexico or a part-Indian person who "lived like a Spaniard." Social mobility was considerable because the crown was willing to raise even a common person to the status of hidalgo (minor nobleman) as an inducement to settle in New Spain's remote northern frontier. Most of the immigrants became small ranchers, producing livestock, corn, and wheat for export to southward Spanish provinces.

Native Americans had mixed success in resisting Spanish domination in different colonies. In New Mexico, an early nineteenth-century Spanish investigator saw the key to Pueblo cultural autonomy as the underground kivas, which were "like impenetrable temples, where they gather to discuss mysteriously their misfortunes or good fortunes, their happiness or grief. The doors of these *estufas* are always closed to us." The tribes of California, though, were less successful in maintaining cultural cohesion. In the 1770s, the Spanish rapidly completed their western land and sea routes from San Diego to Yerba Buena (San Francisco) to block Russian settlement south of their base in northern California. California's Spanish pioneers were Franciscan missionaries, accompanied by royal soldiers. The priests would choose a good location and then attract a few Indians to be baptized and resettled around the missions, which they helped build. Visiting relatives would then be induced to stay. These Indians lived under an increasingly harsh regimen until they were reduced to a condition of virtual slavery. The California mission, with its extensive and profitable herds and grain crops, theoretically belonged to the Indian converts, but they did not enjoy the profits. Priests even hired them out to immigrant Spaniards. Ironically, the spiritual motives of the priests produced the same reduction and degradation of tribal Americans as elsewhere.

A LAND OF FAMILY FARMS

Population growth and economic development gradually transformed the landscape of eighteenth-century British America. Three variations of colonial society emerged: the farming society of the North, the plantation society of the South, and the urban society of the seaboard commercial towns. Although they shared some important characteristics, each was distinct.

Northern Agricultural Society

In the mid-eighteenth-century northern colonies, especially New England, tightknit farming families, organized in communities of several thousand people, dotted the landscape. New Englanders staked their future on a mixed economy. They cleared forests for timber used in barrels, ships, houses, and barns. They plumbed the offshore waters for fish that fed both local populations and the ballooning slave population of the West Indies. And they cultivated and grazed as much of the thin-soiled, rocky hills and bottomlands as they could recover from the forest.

The farmers of the middle colonies—Pennsylvania, Delaware, New Jersey, and New York—drove their wooden plows through much richer soils than New Englanders. They enjoyed the additional advantage of settling an area cleared by Native Americans who had relied more on agriculture than New England tribes. Thus favored, mid-Atlantic farm families produced modest surpluses of corn, wheat, beef, and pork. By the mid-eighteenth century, New York and Philadelphia ships were carrying these foodstuffs not only to the West Indies, always a primary market, but also to areas that could no longer feed themselves—England, Spain, Portugal, and even New England.

In the North, the broad ownership of land distinguished farming society from every other agricultural region of the Western world. Although differences in circumstances and ability led gradually toward greater social stratification, in most communities, few were truly rich or abjectly poor, and the gap between them was small compared with European society. Except for indentured servants, most men lived to purchase or inherit a farm of at least 50 acres. With their family's labor, they earned a decent existence and provided a small inheritance for each of their children. Settlers valued land highly, for freehold tenure ordinarily guaranteed both economic independence and political rights.

Amid widespread property ownership, a rising population pressed against a limited land supply by the eighteenth century, especially in New England. Family farms could not be divided and subdivided indefinitely, for it took at least 50 acres (of which only a quarter could usually be cropped) to support a family. In Concord, Massachusetts, for example, the founders had worked farms averaging about 250 acres. A century later, in the 1730s, the average farm had shrunk by two-thirds, as farm owners struggled to provide an inheritance for the three or four sons that the average marriage produced.

Decreasing soil fertility compounded the problem of dwindling farm size. When land had been plentiful, farmers planted crops in the same field for three years and then let it lie fallow in pasturage seven years or more until it regained its fertility. But on the smaller farms of the eighteenth century, farmers had reduced fallow time to only a year or two. Such intense use of the soil reduced crop yields, forcing farmers to plow marginal land or shift to livestock production. Such was the process that led Jaret Eliot, New England's first agricultural essayist, to refer to "our old land which we have worn out."

The diminishing size and productivity of family farms drove many New Englanders to the frontier or out of the area altogether in the eighteenth century. "Many of our old towns are too full of inhabitants for husbandry, many of them living on small shares of land," bemoaned one Yankee. In Concord, one of every four adult males migrated from town every decade from the 1740s on, and in many towns out-migration was even greater. Some drifted south to New York and Pennsylvania. Others sought opportunities as artisans in the coastal towns or took to the sea. More headed for the colony's western frontier or north to New Hampshire and the eastern frontier of Maine. Several thousand New England families migrated even farther north, to the Annapolis valley of Nova Scotia. Throughout New England after the early eighteenth century, most farmers' sons knew that their destiny lay elsewhere.

Wherever they took up farming, northern cultivators engaged in agricultural work routines that were far less intense than in the South. The growing season was much shorter, and cereal crops required incessant labor only during spring planting and autumn harvesting. This less burdensome work rhythm led many northern cultivators to fill out their calendars with intermittent work as clockmakers, shoemakers, carpenters, and weavers.

Changing Values

Boston's weather on April 29, 1695, began warm and sunny, noted the devout merchant Samuel Sewall in his diary. But by afternoon, thunder, lightning, and hailstones "as big as pistol and musket bullets" pummeled the town. Sewall dined that evening with Cotton Mather, New England's most prominent Puritan clergyman. Mather wondered why "more ministers' houses than others proportionately had been smitten with lightning." The words were hardly out of his mouth before hailstones began to shatter the windows of Sewall's house, "flying to the middle of the room or farther." Sewall and Mather fell to their knees and broke into prayer together "after this awful Providence."

These two third-generation Massachusetts Puritans understood that God was angry with them as leaders of a people whose piety and moral rectitude were being overtaken by worldliness. Even if farms were getting smaller and open land scarcer, growth and success had undermined early utopian dreams and made Massachusetts "sermon-proof," as one dejected minister put it.

In other parts of the North, the expansive environment and the Protestant emphasis on self-discipline and hard work were also breeding qualities that would become hallmarks of American culture: an ambitious outlook, individualistic behavior, and a love of material things. In Europe, most tillers of the soil expected little from life. With no frontier lands ripe for exploitation, impoverished peasant farmers viewed life not as a quest for achievement but as a perpetual struggle against famine and disease. In America, starvation was almost unknown, and few obstacles held people back from uncharted expanses of land once they had overwhelmed the Native Americans. "Every man," one colonist remarked, "expects one day or another to be upon a footing with his wealthiest neighbor."

Commitment to religion, family, and community did not disappear, but fewer men and women saw daily existence as a preparation for the afterlife. They began to regard land not simply as a source of livelihood but

A proud and prosperous Rhineland immigrant, Martin Van Bergen, had this mural painted over the mantelpiece of his New York farmhouse, giving us a rare view of a colonial farm. *(New York State Historical Association, Cooperstown)*

as a commodity to be bought and sold for profit. "Every man is for himself," sighed a Philadelphia leader only a generation after Penn had planted his "holy experiment." A few decades later, a New Yorker wrote that "the only principle of life propagated among the young people is to get money, and men are only esteemed according to what they are worth, that is, the money they are possessed of."

A slender almanac, written by the twelfth child of a poor Boston candlemaker, captured the new outlook with wit and charm. Born in 1706, Benjamin Franklin had climbed the ladder of success spectacularly. Running away from a harsh apprenticeship to an older brother when he was 16, he abandoned a declining Boston for a rising Philadelphia. By 23, he had learned the printer's trade and was publishing the *Pennsylvania Gazette.* Three years later, he began *Poor Richard's Almanack,* next to the Bible the most widely read book in the colonies.

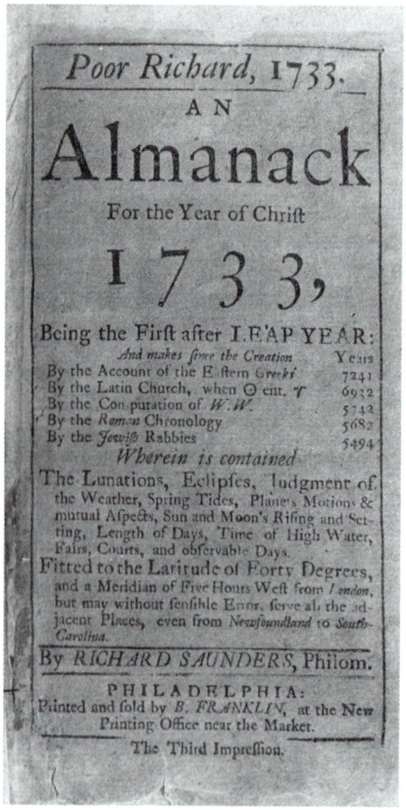

Poor Richard, 1733.

AN

Almanack

For the Year of Chriſt

1733,

Being the Firſt after LEAP YEAR:

And makes ſince the Creation Years
By the Account of the Eaſtern *Greeks* 7241
By the Latin Church, when ☉ ent. ♈ 6932
By the Computation of *W.W.* 5742
By the *Roman* Chronology 5682
By the *Jewiſh* Rabbies 5494

Wherein is contained

The Lunations, Eclipſes, Judgment of the Weather, Spring Tides, Planets Motions & mutual Aſpects, Sun and Moon's Riſing and Setting, Length of Days, Time of High Water, Fairs, Courts, and obſervable Days.

Fitted to the Latitude of Forty Degrees, and a Meridian of Five Hours Weſt from *London*, but may without ſenſible Error, ſerve all the adjacent Places, even from *Newfoundland* to *South-Carolina*.

By *RICHARD SAUNDERS*, Philom.

PHILADELPHIA:
Printed and ſold by *B. FRANKLIN*, at the New Printing Office near the Market.

The Third Impreſſion.

The wit and pragmatic wisdom of Boston-born Benjamin Franklin made his *Poor Richard's Almanack* the most widely read book in the colonies after the Bible. *(Historical Society of Pennsylvania, Philadelphia)*

Franklin spiced his annual almanac—the ordinary person's guide to weather and useful information—with quips, adages, and homespun philosophy. Eventually, this homely material added up to a primer for success published in 1747 as *The Way to Wealth.* "The sleeping fox gathers no poultry" and "Lost time is never found again," advised Poor Richard, emphasizing that time is money. "It costs more to maintain one vice than to raise two children," he counseled, advocating not morality but practicality. "Sloth makes all things difficult but industry all easy," he assured his readers. Ever cocky, Franklin caught the spirit of the rising secularism of the eighteenth century. He embodied the growing utilitarian doctrine that good is whatever is useful and the notion that the community is best served through individual self-improvement and accomplishment.

Women and the Family in Northern Colonial Society

In 1662, Elnathan Chauncy, a Massachusetts schoolboy, copied into his writing book that the soul "consists of two portions, inferior and superior; the superior is masculine and eternal; the feminine inferior and mortal." This lesson had been taught for generations on both sides of the Atlantic. It was part of a larger conception of God's design that assigned degrees of status and stations in life to all individuals. In such a world, women were subordinate, taught from infancy to be modest, patient, and compliant. Regarded by men as weak of mind and large of heart, they existed for and through men. As daughters they were subject to their fathers, as wives to their husbands. John Winthrop reflected the common view that such submission was natural, and hence "a true wife accounts her subjection her honor."

European women usually accepted these narrowly circumscribed roles. Few complained, at least openly, that their work was generally limited to housewifery and midwifery. They silently accepted exclusion from the early public schools and laws that transferred to their husbands any property or income they brought into a marriage. Nor could women speak in their churches or participate in governing them (except in Quaker meetinghouses), and they had no legal voice in political affairs. Most women did not expect to choose a husband for love; parental guidance prevailed in a society in which producing legal heirs was the means of transmitting property. Once wed, women expected to remain so until death, for they could rarely obtain a divorce.

On the colonial frontier, women's lives changed in modest ways. In Europe, about one of ten women did not marry. But in the colonies, where men outnumbered women for the first century, a spinster was almost unheard of, and widows remarried with astounding speed. "A young widow with 4 or 5 children, who among the middling or inferior ranks of people in Europe would have little chance for a second husband," observed one Englishman, "is in America frequently courted as a sort of fortune." *Woman* and *wife* thus became nearly synonymous.

A second difference concerned property rights. Single women and widows in the colonies, as in England, could make contracts, hold and convey property, represent themselves in court, and conduct business. Under English common law, a woman forfeited these rights, as well as all property, when she married. In the colonies, however, legislatures and courts gave wives more control over property brought into marriage or left at their husbands' death. They also enjoyed broader rights to act for and with their husbands in business transactions. In addition, young colonial women slowly gained the right to consent to a marriage partner—a right that came by default to the thousands of female indentured servants who completed their labor contracts and had no parents within 3,000 miles to dictate to them.

Although colonial society did not encourage or reward female individuality and self-reliance, women worked alongside their husbands in competent and complementary ways. Women had limited career choices and rights but broad responsibilities. The work spaces and daily routines of husband and wife overlapped and intersected far more than today. Farm women as well as men worked at planting, harvesting, and milking cows. Women also made candles and soap, butter and cheese, and smoked meat; they made cloth and sometimes marketed farm products. A merchant's wife kept shop, handled accounts when her husband voyaged abroad, and helped supervise the servants and apprentices. "Deputy husbands" and "yoke mates" were revealing terms used by New Englanders to describe eighteenth-century wives.

Despite conventional talk of inferiority, women within their families and neighborhoods nevertheless shaped the world around them. Older women modeled the behavior of young women, aided the needy, and subtly affected menfolk, who held the formal reins of authority. In church life, where they outnumbered men, women worked privately in their families to promote religion in outlying areas, to seat and unseat ministers, and to influence the community's moral life. Periodically, they appeared as visionaries and mystics.

Women held vital responsibilities as midwives. Until the late eighteenth century, the "obstetrick art" was almost entirely in their hands. Midwives such as Anne Hutchinson counseled pregnant women, delivered babies, supervised postpartum recovery, and participated in infant baptism and burial ceremonies. Mrs. Phillips, an immigrant to Boston in 1719, was a familiar figure as she hurried through the streets to attend the lying-in of about 70 women each year. In her 42-year career, she delivered more than 3,000 infants. Because colonial women were pregnant or nursing infants for about half their years between the ages 20 and 40 and because childbirth was dangerous, the circle of female friends and relatives attending childbirth created strong networks of mutual assistance.

In her role as wife and mother, the eighteenth-century northern woman differed somewhat from her English counterpart. Whereas English women married in their mid-twenties, American women typically took husbands a few years earlier. This head start increased their childbearing years. Hence, the average colonial family included five children (two others typically died in infancy), whereas the English family contained fewer than three. Gradually, as the coastal plain filled up in the eighteenth century and older family farms were divided and subdivided among descendants of the early settlers, marriage age crept up and the number of children per family inched down.

Northern child-rearing patterns differed considerably. In the seventeenth century, stern fathers dominated Puritan family life, and few were reluctant to punish unruly children. "Better whip'd than damn'd," advised Cotton Mather, the minister who served as the Puritan conscience of New England. Many parents believed that breaking the young child's will created a pious and submissive personality. In Quaker families, however, mothers played a more active role in child rearing. More permissive, they relied on tenderness and love rather than guilt to mold their children. Attitudes toward choosing a marriage partner also

Childbirth was an oft-repeated event in the lives of most colonial wives. In this portrait of the Cheney family, the older woman is a nanny or mother-in-law; the younger woman holding a baby is Mr. Cheney's second wife. (The Cheney Family, *Gift of Edgar and Bernice Chrysler Garbisch, ©2000 Board of Trustees, National Gallery of Art, Washington, c. 1795, canvas, .490 x .650 [19¼ x 25⅝])*

separated early Puritan and Quaker approaches to family life. Puritan parents usually arranged their children's marriages but allowed them the right to veto. Young Quaker men and women made their own matches, subject to parental veto.

Despite this initial diversity in child rearing, the father-dominated family of New England gradually declined in the eighteenth century. In its place rose the mother-centered family, in which affectionate parents encouraged self-expression and independence in their children. This "modern" approach, on the rise in Europe as well, brought the colonists closer to the methods of parenthood found among the coastal Native Americans, who initially had been widely disparaged for their lax approach to rearing their young.

ECOLOGICAL TRANSFORMATION

Wherever Europeans settled in the Americas, they brought with them animals, plant life, diseases, and ways of viewing the natural resources—all with enormous consequences for the ecosystems they were entering. In New Spain, the introduction of grazing animals—cattle, horses, pigs, sheep, and goats—profoundly altered the landscape. Breeding prolifically in an environment generally free of animal predators, pigs and cattle devoured the tall grasses and most palatable plant species. Within a half century, the domesticated animals left huge areas with little or no ground cover. In this rearranged landscape, new unwelcome plant species took hold—stinging nettle, nightshade, and dandelion.

In England's North American colonies, the rapid increase of settlers after 1715 had different environmental effects. Two were of special importance. First, the demand for wood—for building and heating houses, for producing the charcoal necessary for ironmaking, for shipbuilding and barrelmaking—swiftly depleted coastal forests. Just for heating and cooking, the typical northern farmhouse required an acre of trees each year. An iron furnace needed 20,000 acres of forest to produce a thousand tons of iron. A 40-acre field required 8,000 fence rails. With the population explosion of the eighteenth century, the price of firewood quickly rose as woodcutters ventured farther and farther inland.

Rapid and often wasteful harvesting of the forests had many effects. As the colonists chopped down the forest canopy that had previously moderated the weather, the summers became hotter and winters colder. In deforested areas, snow melted sooner, and, as the winter's melting snow ran off more quickly, watersheds emptied faster. This, in turn, caused soil erosion and periods of drought.

A second ecological transformation occurred when animals brought by Europeans began to replace animals already in North America. European colonists were a livestock people, skilled in mixed farming and herding of domesticated cattle, horses, pigs, sheep, and goats. Such animals provided food, leather, fibers for clothmaking, and the sheer pulling and carrying power relied on by a people who had no other source of energy than their own muscles. Multiplying rapidly in a favorable environment, pigs and cattle "swarm like vermin upon the earth," reported one Virginia account as early as 1700. In some areas, the animals multiplied so rapidly and denuded the native grasses and shrubs so quickly that they actually ate themselves out of subsistence and began to die for lack of grazing land.

While European livestock filled the land, the native fur-bearing animals—beaver, deer, bear, wolf, raccoon, and marten—rapidly became extinct in the areas of settlement. Prized for their skins or hated as predators of domesticated animals, these species were hunted relentlessly as the colonists offered trade goods to Native Americans in exchange for pelts. One broken link in the ecological chain affected others. For example, the dams and ponds of the beaver, which had been breeding grounds for many species of wild ducks, soon were drained and converted to grazing meadows for cattle.

Animals prized for dinner table fare also quickly reached extinction along the East Coast. Wild turkeys were a rarity in Massachusetts by the 1670s. Deer disappeared by the early 1700s in settled areas. "Hunting with us exists chiefly in the tales of other times," wrote Yale's president in the late eighteenth century.

All these environmental changes were linked not only to the numbers of Europeans arriving in North America but also to their ways of thinking about nature. Looking out over wooded hills and fertile valleys, transplanted Europeans could only imagine the possibility of raising valuable crops as if the ecosystem was composed of unconnected elements, each ripe for exploitation. Land, lumber, fish, and fur-bearing animals could be converted into sources of cash that would buy imported commodities that improved one's material condition. The New England writer Edward Johnson described the process perceptively as early as 1653: Who would have imagined, he mused, "that this wilderness should turn a mart for merchants in so short a space, Holland, France, Spain, and Portugal coming hither for trade?" Supplying these Europeans were the farmers, woodcutters, and fishermen who consigned to the marketplace huge portions of the ecosystem that in the world of Native Americans were all-important for sustaining life but not part of a transoceanic system of commercial exchange.

Coming from homelands where land was scarce, the settlers viewed their ability to reap nature's abundance in North America as proof of their success. From their perspective, they were correct because, in fact, colonial agriculture was abundantly successful in terms of what the settlers obliged the land to yield up. Yet the "rage for commerce" and for an improved life produced wasteful practices on farms and in forests and fisheries. "The grain fields, the meadows, the forests, the cattle, etc.," wrote a Swedish visitor in the 1750s, "are treated with equal carelessness." Accustomed to the natural abundance once the native peoples had been driven from the land, and seeing no limits to the land that was available, the colonists embarked on ecologically destructive practices that over a period of many generations profoundly altered the natural world of North America.

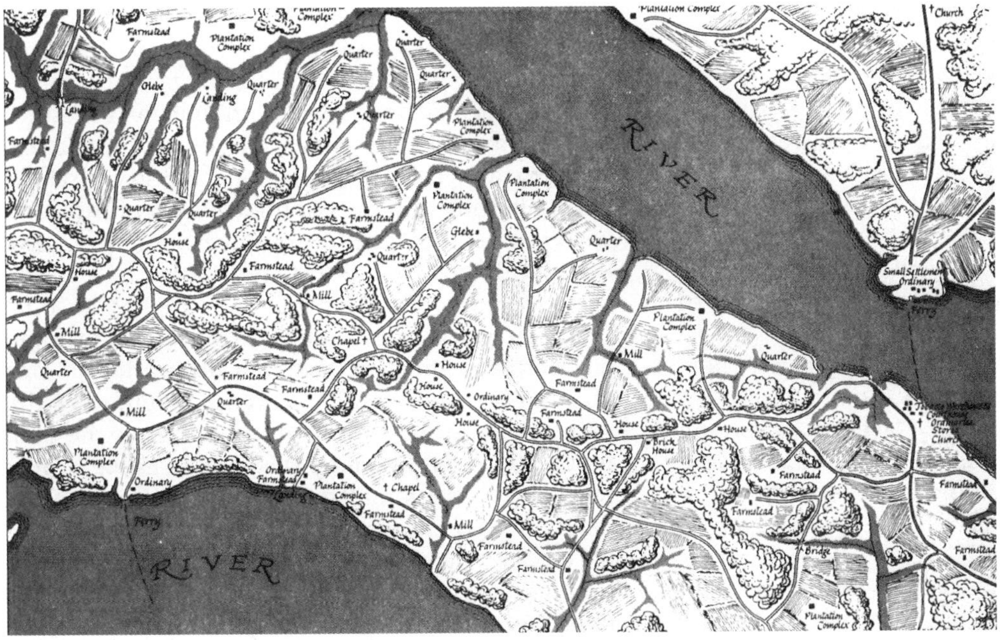

The distribution of cultivated fields, dwellings, and commercial buildings in the tidewater landscape created "communities" without towns (rendered from historical and archaeological evidence). (*From* The Transformation of Virginia, 1740–1790 *by Rhys Isaac. Copyright © 1982 by the University of North Carolina Press. Published for the Institute of Early American History and Culture. Used by permission of the publisher.*)

THE PLANTATION SOUTH

Between 1680 and 1750, the white tidewater settlements of the southern colonies changed from a frontier society marked by high immigration, a surplus of males, and an unstable social organization to a settled society composed mostly of native-born families. After 1715, Scots-Irish and German immigrants flooded into the backcountry of Virginia, the Carolinas, and Georgia, this last intended as a debtors' haven but designed in 1732 as a buffer between Spanish Florida and the Carolinas. But between the piedmont region and the ocean, a mature southern culture took form.

The Tobacco Coast

Tobacco production in Virginia and Maryland expanded rapidly in the seventeenth century, with exports reaching 25 million pounds annually during the 1680s. But then two decades of war in Europe and the Americas, bridging the turn of the century, drove up transportation costs and dampened the demand for tobacco. Stagnation in the tobacco market lasted from the mid-1680s until about 1715.

Yet in this period the Upper South underwent a profound social transformation. First, slaves replaced indentured servants so rapidly that by 1730 the unfree labor force was overwhelmingly black. Second, the planters responded to the depressed tobacco market by diversifying their crops. They shifted some tobacco fields to grain, hemp, and flax; increased their herds of cattle and swine; and became more self-sufficient by developing local industries to produce iron, leather, and textiles. By the 1720s, when a profitable tobacco trade with France created a new period of prosperity, the economy was much more diverse and resilient than a generation before.

Third, the population structure changed rapidly. Black slaves grew from about 7 percent to more than 40 percent of the region's population between 1690 and 1750, and the drastic imbalance between white men and women disappeared. Families rather than single men now predominated. The earlier frontier society of white immigrants who mostly lived short and unrewarding lives as indentured servants grew into an eighteenth-century plantation society of native-born freeholder families.

Notwithstanding the influx of Africans, slave owning was far from universal. As late as 1750, a majority of families owned no slaves at all. Among slave owners, not more than one-tenth held more than 20 slaves. Nonetheless, the common goal was the large plantation where black slaves made the earth yield up profits to support an aristocratic life for their masters. As one Virginia minister observed, "The custom of the country is such that without slaves a man's children stand but a poor chance to marry in reputation."

The Chesapeake planters who acquired the best land and accumulated enough capital to invest heavily in slaves created a gentry lifestyle that set them apart from ordinary farmers such as Devereaux Jarratt's father. By the eighteenth century, the development of the northern colonies had produced prosperous farmers worth several thousand pounds. But such wealth paled alongside the estates of men such as Charles Carroll of Maryland and Robert "King" Carter and William Byrd of Virginia. These Chesapeake planters counted their slaves by the hundreds, their acres by the thousands, and their fortunes by the tens of thousands of pounds.

Ritual display of wealth marked southern gentry life. Racing thoroughbred horses and gambling on them recklessly, sometimes for purses of £100 (at a time when a laboring man earned £40 per year), became common sport for young gentlemen, who had often been educated in England. Planters began to construct stately brick Georgian mansions, some designed by imported English architects. These "greathouses," similar in style to the houses of English gentry, were filled with imported furniture, attended by liveried black slaves, and graced by formal gardens and orchards.

Some observers saw the cultivated aristocratic lifestyle as a veneer. "If a [man] has Money, Negroes, and Land enough," scoffed a Scottish newcomer, "he is a complete Gentleman. These hide all his defects, usher him into the best of company, and draw upon him the smiles of the fair Sex." Affected or not, the emerging Chesapeake planter elite controlled the county courts, officered the local militia, ruled the parish vestries of the Anglican Church, and made law in their legislative assemblies. To their sons, they passed the mantle of political and social leadership.

For all their airs, these southern squires were essentially agrarian businessmen. They spent their days haggling over credit, dealing in land and slaves, scheduling planting and harvesting routines, conferring with overseers, disciplining slaves, and arranging leases with tenants. Cultivating tobacco was a particularly demanding enterprise and a highly personal one. Whereas other staple crops such as wheat and corn required intensive labor only during the planting and harvesting seasons, tobacco demanded the planter's attention throughout the year as the crop moved through the many stages of planting, transplanting, topping, cutting, curing, and packing. A planter's reputation rose and fell with the quality of his crop. So personalized was the culture of tobacco that planters stamped their hogsheads of leaf with their initials or emblem. "Question a planter on the subject," explained one observer, "and he will tell you that he cultivates such or such a kind [of tobacco], as for example, Colonel Carter's sort, John Cole's sort or [that of] some other leading crop master."

Planters' wives also shouldered many responsibilities. They superintended cloth production and the processing and preparation of food while ruling over households crowded with children, slaves, and visitors. An aristocratic veneer gave the luster of gentility to plantations from Maryland to North Carolina, but this could not disguise the fact that these were large working farms, often so isolated from one another that the planter and his wife lived a "solitary and unsociable existence," as one phrased it. With only infrequent contact with the outside world, they learned to be independent as they managed their own little communities of servants, slaves, and family members. Patriarchs on their estates, southern planters were "haughty and jealous of their liberties, impatient of restraint, and can scarcely bear the thought of being controlled by any superior power," noted a mid-eighteenth-century visitor.

The Rice Coast

The plantation economy of the Lower South in the eighteenth century rested on the production of rice and indigo. Rice exports surpassed 1.5 million pounds per year by 1710 and reached 80 million pounds by the eve of the Revolution. Indigo, a smelly blue dye obtained from plants for use in textiles, became a staple crop in the 1740s after Eliza Lucas Pinckney, a wealthy South Carolina planter's wife, experimented successfully with its cultivation. Within a generation, indigo production had spread into Georgia. It soon ranked among the leading colonial exports.

The expansion of rice production transformed the swampy coastal lowlands. In the rice-producing region radiating out from Charleston, planters imported thousands of slaves after 1720; by 1740, slaves composed nearly 90 percent of the region's inhabitants. White population declined as wealthy planters left their estates in the hands of resident overseers. They wintered in cosmopolitan Charleston and summered in Newport, Rhode Island, their refuge from seasonal malaria along the rice coast. Rice converted the eighteenth-century Carolina coast into a tropical plantation regime similar to that of the sugar-producing West Indies. At mid-century, a shocked New England visitor described it as a society "divided into opulent and lordly planters, poor and spiritless peasants, and vile slaves."

Throughout the plantation South, the courthouse became a central gathering place for men. On court days, all classes came to settle debts, dispute land boundaries, sue and be sued. When court was over, a multitude lingered on, drinking, gossiping, and staging horse races, cockfights, wrestling matches, footraces, and fiddling contests. Competition and assertiveness lay at the heart of all these demonstrations of male prowess.

The church, almost always Anglican in the South before 1750, also became a center of community gathering. A visiting northerner described the animated socializing before worship, men "giving and receiving letters of business, reading advertisements, consulting about the price of tobacco and grain, and settling either the lineage, age, or qualities of favourite horses." Then, as the hour of service approached, people filed into church. Reaffirming the social gradation of their rank-conscious society, the lower and middling planters entered first. They stood attentively until the wealthy gentry, striding in together "in a body," took their pews at the front. After church, socializing continued, with young people strolling together and older ones extending invitations to Sunday dinner. The pious Sabbath atmosphere perpetuated in New England was little in evidence.

Rice and Indigo Exports from South Carolina and Georgia, 1698–1775

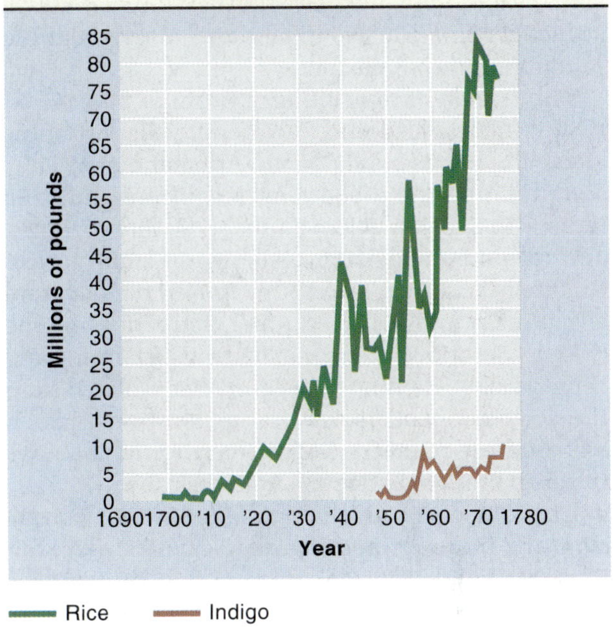

Just as Virginia had been built on tobacco, South Carolina and Georgia were built on rice. Much of it was sent to the West Indies to feed the huge population of enslaved Africans there. Source: U.S. Bureau of the Census.

The Backcountry

While the southern gentry matured along the tobacco and rice coasts, settlers poured into the upland backcountry. As late as 1730, only hunters and Indian fur traders had known this vast expanse of hilly red clay and fertile limestone soils, stretching from Pennsylvania to Georgia. Over the next four decades, it attracted some 250,000 inhabitants, nearly half the southern white population.

Thousands of land-hungry German and Scots-Irish settlers spilled into the interior valleys running along the eastern side of the Appalachians. They squatted on land, lived tensely with neighboring Indians in a region where boundaries were shadowy, and created a subsistence society of small farms. Gradually acquiring slaves, this "mixed medley from all countries and the off scouring of America," as one colonist described them, pursued mixed farming and cattle raising. Their enclaves remained isolated from the coastal region for several generations, which helped these pioneers cling fiercely to the folkways they had brought across the Atlantic.

Crude backcountry life appalled many visitors from the more refined seaboard. In 1733, William Byrd described a large Virginia frontier plantation as a "poor, dirty hovel, with hardly anything in it but children that wallowed about like so many pigs." Charles Woodmason, a stiff-necked Anglican minister who spent three years tramping between settlements in the Carolina upcountry, could hardly find words to express his shock. "Through the licentiousness of the people," he wrote, "many hundreds live in concubinage—swopping their wives as cattle and living in a state of nature more irregularly and unchastely than the Indians."

What Byrd and Woodmason were really observing was the poverty of frontier life and the lack of schools, churches, and towns. Most families plunged into the backcountry with only a few crude household possessions and farm tools, perhaps a pair of oxen, a few chickens and swine, and the clothes on their backs. They lived in rough-hewn log cabins—"cold cabins, unfloored and almost open to the sky," Woodmason observed—and planted their corn, beans, and wheat between the stumps of trees they had felled. Women toiled alongside men, in the fields, forest, and homestead. For a generation, these settlers endured a poor diet, endless work, and meager rewards.

By the 1760s, the southern backcountry had begun to emerge from the frontier stage. Small marketing towns such as Camden, South Carolina; Salisbury, North Carolina; Winchester, Virginia; and Fredericktown, Maryland, became centers of craft activity, church life, and local government. Farms began producing surpluses for shipment east. Density of settlement increased, creating a social life known for harvest festivals, log-rolling contests, horse races, wedding celebrations, dances, and prodigious drinking bouts during which hard cider, whiskey, and apple and peach brandy flowed freely. Class distinctions remained narrow compared with the older seaboard settlements, as many backcountry settlements acquired the look of permanence.

Family Life in the South

As the South emerged from the early era of withering mortality and stunted families, male and female roles gradually became more physically and functionally separated. In most areas, the white gender ratio reached parity by the 1720s, depriving women of their former leverage in the marriage market. The growth of slavery also changed the work role of white women with the wealthy planter's wife becoming the domestic manager in "the great house." In a description of his daughters' daily routine, William Byrd II pointed to the emerging female identity: "They are every day up to their elbows in housewifery, which will qualify them effectually for useful wives and if they live long enough for notable women."

The balanced sex ratio and the growth of slavery also brought changes for southern males. The planter's son had always been trained to operate in the world beyond the plantation-house doors. Learning horsemanship, the use of a gun, and the rhythms of agricultural life was as important a part of a young man's education as lessons with tutors such as Devereaux Jarratt. Ordering and disciplining slaves also became a part of the southern youth's education. Many had slaves of their own before reaching adulthood. Some planters worried that this would lead, as Thomas Jefferson would later write, to "odious peculiarities" in the character of southern men, because slavery involved a "perpetual exercise of the most boisterous passions" by white masters "nursed, educated, and daily exercised in tyranny." But bred to command, southern planters' sons also developed a self-confidence and authority that propelled many of them into leadership roles during the American Revolution.

On the small farms of the tidewater region and throughout the back settlements, women's roles closely resembled those of northern women. Women labored in the fields alongside their menfolk. "She is a very civil woman," noted an observer of a southern frontierswoman, "and shows nothing of ruggedness or immodesty in her carriage; yet she will carry a gun in the woods and kill deer and turkeys, shoot down wild cattle, catch and tie hogs, knock down beeves with an ax, and perform the most manful exercises as well as most men in those parts."

Marriage and family life were more informal in the backcountry. With vast areas unattended by ministers of any religion and courthouses out of reach, most couples married or "took up" with each other in matches unsanctioned by state or church. The arrival of an itinerant clergyman on horseback typically brought forth dozens of couples living in common-law marriage who asked to have vows performed and their children legitimized by baptism. Respectable clergymen saw the frontier settlers living in lascivious abandon. But the poor upcountry hunters and farmers were really only the first of many generations of pioneers who made do as best they could on the forest's edge, where the institutions of settled society had not yet arrived.

THE URBAN WORLD OF COMMERCE AND IDEAS

Only about 5 percent of the eighteenth-century colonists lived in towns as large as 2,500, and none of the commercial centers boasted a population greater than 16,000 in 1750 or 30,000 in 1775. Yet the urban societies were at the leading edge of social change. Almost all the alterations associated with the advent of "modern" life occurred first in the seaport towns and then radiated outward to the villages, farms, and plantations of the hinterland. In the seaboard centers, the transition first occurred from a barter to a commercial economy, from a social order based on achievement rather than assigned status, from rank-conscious and deferential politics to participatory and contentious politics, and from small-scale craftsmanship to factory production. In addition, the cities were the centers of intellectual life and the conduits through which European ideas flowed into the colonies.

Sinews of Trade

In the half century after 1690, Boston, New York, Philadelphia, and Charleston blossomed from urban waterside villages into thriving commercial centers. Their growth accompanied the development of the agricultural interior, to which the seaports were closely linked. As the colonial population rose and spread out, minor seaports such as Salem, Newport, Providence, Annapolis, Norfolk, and Savannah gathered 5,000 or more inhabitants.

Trade was indispensable to colonial economic life, and cities were trade centers. Through them flowed colonial export staples such as tobacco, rice, furs, wheat, timber products, and fish as well as the imported goods that colonists needed: manufactured and luxury goods from England such as glass, paper, iron implements, and cloth; wine, spices, coffee, tea, and sugar from other parts of the world; and the human cargo to fill the labor gap. In these seaports, the pivotal figure was the merchant. Frequently engaged in both retail and wholesale trade, the merchant was also moneylender (for no banks yet existed), shipbuilder, insurance agent, land developer, and often coordinator of artisan production.

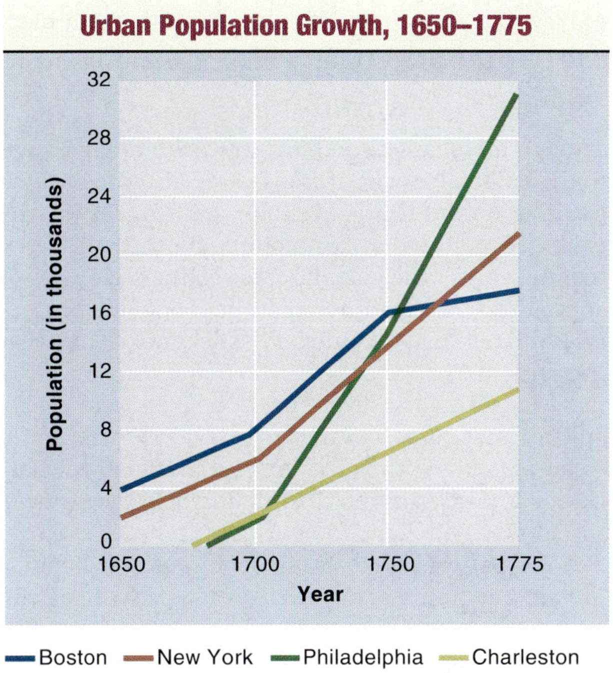

By 1755, Boston had lost its lead as British North America's largest city. Plagued by costly wars and economic difficulties, its population leveled off, whereas that of other cities grew. Source: Gary B. Nash, *The Urban Crucible,* 1979.

By the eighteenth century, the American economy was integrated into an Atlantic basin trading system that connected settlers to Great Britain, western Europe, Africa, the West Indies, and Newfoundland. The rulers of Great Britain, like those of other major trading nations of western Europe, pursued mercantilist trade policies. Mercantilism's core idea was that a country must gain wealth by increasing exports, levying duties on imports, regulating production and trade, and exploiting colonies. The British followed these principles by controlling their colonies' trade; requiring their colonies to supply them with foodstuffs, lumber, and other nonmanufactured products; and selling the colonists British manufactured goods.

The colonists could never produce enough exportable raw materials to pay for the imported goods they craved, so they had to earn credits in England by supplying the West Indies and other areas with foodstuffs and timber products. They also accumulated credit by providing shipping and distribution services. New Englanders became the most ambitious participants in the carrying trade. Sailing from Boston, Salem, Newport, and Providence, Yankee merchant seamen, manning Yankee-built ships, dominated the traffic along the Atlantic seaboard, the Caribbean trade, and the transatlantic commerce. A much higher proportion of New England's population made its living in maritime enterprise than in any other colonial region.

The Artisan's World

Though merchants stood first in wealth and prestige in the colonial towns, artisans were far more numerous. About two-thirds of urban adult males (slaves excluded) labored at handicrafts. By the mid-eighteenth century, the colonial cities contained scores of specialized "leather apron men," not only the proverbial butcher, baker, and candlestick maker but also the carpenters and coopers (who made barrels); shoemakers and tailors; silver-, gold-, pewter-, and blacksmiths; mast and sail makers; masons, plasterers, weavers, potters; and many more. Handicraft specialization increased as the cities matured, but every artisan worked with hand tools, usually in small shops.

Work patterns for artisans were irregular, dictated by weather, hours of daylight, erratic delivery of raw materials, and shifting consumer demand. When ice blocked northern harbors, mariners and dockworkers endured slack time. If prolonged rain delayed the slaughter of cows in the country or made impassable the rutted roads into the city, the tanner and the shoemaker laid their tools aside. The hatter depended on the supply of beaver skins, which could stop abruptly if disease struck an Indian tribe or war disrupted the fur trade. Every urban artisan knew "broken days," slack spells, and dull seasons. Ordinary laborers dreaded winter, for it was a season when cities had "little occasion for the labor of the poor," and firewood to heat even a small house could cost several months' wages.

Urban artisans took fierce pride in their crafts. While deferring to those above them, they saw themselves as the backbone of the community, contributing essential products and services. "Our professions rendered us useful and necessary members of our community," the Philadelphia shoemakers asserted; "proud of that rank, we aspired to no higher." This self-esteem and desire for community recognition sometimes jostled with the upper-class view of artisans as "mere mechanicks," part of the "vulgar herd."

Striving for respectability, artisans placed a premium on achieving economic independence. Every craftsman began as an apprentice, spending five or more teenage years learning the "mysteries of the craft" in a master's shop. After fulfilling his contract, the young artisan became a "journeyman," selling his labor to a master craftsman and frequently living in his house, eating at his table, and sometimes marrying his daughter. The journeyman hoped to complete within a few years the three-step climb from servitude to self-employment. After setting up his own shop, he could control his work hours and acquire the respect that came from economic independence. But in trades requiring greater organization and capital, such as distilling and shipbuilding, the rise from journeyman to master proved impossible for many artisans. Nonetheless, the ideal of the independent craftsman prevailed.

Only a few Boston artisans became prosperous enough to have their portrait painted. But a few did, including Paul Revere and Nathaniel Hurd, the engraver shown here. Hurd came from a long line of artisans: his great-grandfather was a tailor, his grandfather a joiner, and his father a silversmith. Hurd's open collar and rolled-up sleeves show him in his working outfit. This unfinished portrait was probably a study for a more elegant portrait that showed Hurd in an embroidered silk blouse. *(Memorial Art Gallery of the University of Rochester, Marion Stratton Gould Fund)*

In good times, urban artisans did well. They expected to earn a "decent competency" and eventually to purchase a small house. But success was far from automatic, even for those following Poor Richard's advice about hard work and frugal living. An advantageous marriage, luck in avoiding illness, and the size of an inheritance were often the critical factors in whether an artisan moved up or down the ladder of success. In Philadelphia, about half the artisans in the first half of the eighteenth century died leaving enough personal property to have ensured a comfortable standard of living. Another quarter left more, often including slaves and indentured servants. New England's artisans did not fare so well, for their economy was weaker in the eighteenth century. But in all cities, artisans took pride in their life of productive labor. "The meanest [of them] thinks he has a right of civility from the greatest" person in the city, wrote one city dweller.

One of the few contemporary paintings of social activity in colonial taverns, this colorful portrayal of a tavern in Surinam, a Dutch island on the northeastern coast of South America, shows carousing sea captains. American ships went there frequently to trade illegally for shipments of sugar that were quickly transformed into rum—the alcohol of choice in many North American taverns. (*John Greenwood,* Sea Captains Carousing in Surinam, 1758, *The Saint Louis Art Museum*)

URBAN SOCIAL STRUCTURE

Population growth, economic development, and a series of wars that punctuated the period from 1690 to 1765 altered the urban social structure. Stately townhouses rose as testimony to the fortunes acquired in trade, shipbuilding, war contracting, and—probably the most profitable of all—urban land development. "It is almost a proverb," a Philadelphian observed in the 1760s, "that every great fortune made here within these 50 years has been by land." Some merchants amassed fortunes. A merchant's estate of £2,000 sterling was counted impressive in the early eighteenth century. Two generations later, some commercial titans had become North America's first millionaires by accumulating estates of £10,000 to £20,000 sterling.

The rise of Thomas Hancock, on whose fortune his less commercially astute nephew, John Hancock, would later construct a shining political career, provides a glimpse of how war could catapult an enterprising trader to affluence. Hancock, a minister's son, became a bookseller in Boston. An opportune marriage to the daughter of a prosperous merchant provided a toehold in commerce and enough capital to invest in several vessels. By 1735, Hancock had made enough money, much of it from smuggling tea, to build a mansion on Beacon Hill.

When war broke out with Spain in 1739, Hancock used his connections with the governor to obtain lucrative supply contracts for military expeditions to the Caribbean and Nova Scotia. He also invested heavily in privateers, who engaged in private warfare against enemy shipping and auctioned the enemy vessels they overpowered. When peace returned in 1748, all Boston witnessed what war had done for a well-connected merchant. The man who had sold books from a tiny shop on Drawbridge Street 15 years before now imported a four-horse chariot from London with the interior lined in scarlet and the doors emblazoned with a heraldic shield.

Alongside urban wealth grew urban poverty. From the beginning, every city had its disabled, orphaned, and widowed who required aid. But after 1720, poverty marred the lives of many more city dwellers. Many were war widows with numerous children and no means of support. Others were rural migrants seeking opportunities in the city. Some were recent immigrants, who found fewer chances for employment than earlier. Boston was hit especially hard. Its economy stagnated in the 1740s, and taxpayers groaned under the burden of paying for heavy war expenditures. The overseers of the poor lamented that their relief expenditures were double the outlays of any town of equal size "upon the face of the whole earth."

Burdened with mounting poor taxes, cities devised new ways of helping the needy. Rather than support the impoverished in their homes with "outrelief" payments, officials built large almshouses where the poor could be housed and fed more economically. Many of the indigent preferred "to starve in their homes" rather

Recovering the Past

HOUSEHOLD INVENTORIES

Historians use probate records to examine social changes in American society. They include wills, the legal disposition of estates, and household inventories taken by court-appointed appraisers that detail the personal possessions left at death. Inventories have been especially valuable in tracing the transformation of colonial communities.

Like tax lists, inventories can be used to show changes in a community's distribution of wealth. But they are far more detailed than tax lists, providing a snapshot of how people lived at the end of their life. Inventories list and value almost everything a person owned—household possessions, equipment, books, clothes and jewelry, cash on hand, livestock and horses, crops and stored provisions. Hence, through inventories, we can measure the quality of life at different social levels. We can also witness how people made choices about investing their savings—in capital goods of their trade such as land, ships, and equipment; in personal goods such as household furnishings and luxury items; or in real property such as land and houses.

Studied systematically (and corrected for biases, which infect this source as well as others), inventories show that by the early 1700s, ordinary householders were improving their standard of living. Finished furniture such as cupboards, beds, tables, and chairs turn up more frequently in inventories. Pewter dinnerware replaces wooden bowls and spoons, bed linen makes an appearance, and books and pictures are sometimes noted.

Among an emerging elite before the Revolution, much more fashionable articles of consumption appear. The partial inventory of Robert Oliver, a wealthy merchant and officeholder living in a Boston suburb, is reproduced here. You can get some idea of the dignified impression Oliver wished to make by looking at his furniture and dishes and by noticing that he owned a mahogany tea table, damask linen, and a bed with curtains. The inventory further suggests the spaciousness of Oliver's house and shows how he furnished each room.

It is helpful when studying inventories to categorize the goods in the following way: those that are needed to survive (basic cooking utensils, for example); those that make life easier or more comfortable (enough plates and beds for each member of the family, for example); and those that make life luxurious (slaves, silver plates, paintings, mahogany furniture, damask curtains, spices, wine, and so forth). Oliver had many luxury goods as well as items that contributed to his use of leisure time and his personal enjoyment. Which items in his inventory do you think were needed only to survive comfortably? Which were luxuries? What other conclusions can you draw about the lifestyle of rich colonial merchants like Oliver?

Beyond revealing a growing social differentiation in colonial society, the inventories help the historian understand the reaction during the Great Awakening to what many ordinary colonists regarded as sinful pride and arrogance displayed by the elite. By the 1760s, this distrust of affluence among simple folk had led to outright hostility toward men who surrounded themselves with the trappings of aristocratic life. Even the ambitious young John Adams, a striving lawyer, was shocked at what he saw at the house of a wealthy merchant in Boston. "Went over the House to view the Furniture, which alone cost a thousand Pound sterling," he exclaimed. "A seat it is for a noble Man, a Prince. The Turkey Carpets, the painted Hangings, the Marble Tables, the rich Beds with crimson Damask Curtains . . . are the most magnificent of any Thing I have ever seen."

Such a description takes on its full meaning only when contrasted with what inventories tell us about life at the bottom of society. The hundreds of inventories for Bostonians dying in the decade before the American Revolution show that fully half of them died with less than £40 personal wealth and one-quarter with £20 or less. The inventories and wills of Jonathan and Daniel Chandler of Andover, Massachusetts, show the material circumstances of less favored Americans who suffered from the economic distress afflicting New England since the 1730s. Note that Daniel Chandler was a shoemaker. How do the possessions of these brothers compare with Oliver's partial inventory? An examination of these contrasting inventories helps explain the class tension that figured in the revolutionary experience.

Household Inventory of Robert Oliver, Wealthy Merchant

Dorchester Jan.ry 11.th 1763.

Inventory of what Estates Real & Personall, belonging to Coll.o Robert Oliver [Esquire] late of Dorchester Deceased, that has been Exhibited to us the Subscribers, for Apprizement. Viz.t

In the Setting Parlour Viz.tt

a looking Glass		£4.—.—
a Small Ditto		0.6.0
12 Metzitens pictures Glaz'd	@ 6/	3.12.—
8 Cartoons D.o Ditto		4.—.—
11 small Pictures		—.4.—
4 Maps		—.10.—
1 Prospect Glass		—.10.—
2 Escutchons Glaz'd		—.4.—
1 pair small hand Irons		—.6.—
1 Shovel & Tongs		—.8.—
1 Tobacco Tongs		—.1.—
1 pair Bellowes		—.2.—
1 Tea Chest		—.2.—
2 Small Waters		—.1.—
1 Mehogony Tea Table		1.—.—
8 China Cups & Saucers		—.2.—
1 Earthen Cream Pott		—.—.1
1 Ditto. Sugar Dish		—.—.4
1 Black Walnut Table		1.—.—
1 Black Ditto Smaller		0.6.—
1 Round painted Table		0.1.—
7 Leather Bottom Chairs	@ 6/	2.2.—
1 Arm.d Chair Common		1.3.—
1 Black Walnut Desk		1.12.—
1 pair Candlesticks snuffers & Stand Base Mettle		—.4.—
6 Wine Glasses 1 Water Glass		—.1.—
a parcell of Books		1.—.—
a Case with Small Bottles		0.4.—
		22.1.5

In the Entry & Stair Case Viz.t

17 pictures	£0.10.—
	0.10.0

In the Kitchen Chamber Viz.t

a Bedstead & Curtains Compleat		£4.—.—
a Bed Bolster & 2 pillows		5.—.—
a Under Bed & 1 Chair		0.1.—
2 Rugs & 1 Blankett	@ 6/	0.18.—
		09.19.0

In the Dining Room Viz.t

1 pair of andirons	£0.3.—
7 Bass Bottoms Chairs	0.7.—
1 Large Wooden Table	0.3.—
1 Small Ditto Oak	0.1.—
1 Small looking Glass	0.6.—
1 Old Desk	0.6.—
1 Case with 2 Bottles	0.2.—
1 Warming pan	0.12.—
	2. 0. 0

In the Marble Chamber Viz.t

1 Bedstead & Curtains Compleat		£8.—.—
1 feather Bed, Bolster & 2 pillows		8.—.—
1 Chest of Drawers		2.8.—
1 Buroe Table		1.—.—
6 Chairs Leather'd Bottoms	@ 6/	1.16.—
1 Small dressing Glass		—.6.—
1 Small Carpett		1.—.—
1 White Cotton Counterpin		—.18.—
1 pair Blanketts		1.12.—
1 pair holland Sheets		1.4.—
3 pair Dowlases D.o New	@ 12s/pr.	1.16.—
3 pair & 1 Ditto Coarser	@ 4/	0.14.—
3 pair Cotton & Linnen D.o	@ 3/	0.9.—
4 pair Servants Ditto	@ 2/	0.8.—
4 Coarse Table Cloths	@ 1/	0.4.—
10 Ditto Kitchen Towels	@ 1/	0.1.—
5 Diaper Table Cloths	@ 12/	3.—.—
6 Damask Table Cloths	@ 18/	5.8.—
4 N. England Diaper D.o	@ 3	0.12.—
4 pair Linnen pillow Cases	@ 2/	0.8.—
5 Coarser Ditto	@ 1/	0.5.—
6 Diaper Towels	@ 6d	0.3.—
7 Damask Ditto	@ 2/	0.14.—
2 doz.n & 9 Damask Napkins	@ 24/doz.n	3.6.—
1 Gauze Tea Table Cover		0.1.—
		£43.13.0

Household Inventory of Jonathan Chandler (d. 1745)

Cash	£18p
Gun	1p
Psalmbook	8p
	£19p
Debts	£ 5p
Total	£14p

Household Inventory of Daniel Chandler (d. 1752), Shoemaker

Bible
Shoe knife
Hammer — Total £12
Last (shoe shaper)
Various notes

The grid pattern of Philadelphia's straight streets contrasts sharply with Boston's crooked and irregular roads and alleys. Topography had everything to do with this. Surrounded by water creating an irregular shoreline and dominated by three high hills, leveled in the nineteenth century, Boston's streets were laid out in the manner of goat paths. *(Library of Congress Geography & Maps Division)*

than leave their neighborhoods to suffer the discipline and indignities of the poorhouse. Boston's poor women also resisted laboring in the linen factory that was built in 1750 to enable them to contribute to their own support through spinning and weaving. Despite the warnings of Boston's ministers that "if any would not work, neither should they eat," they refused to leave their children at home to labor in America's first textile factory.

The increasing gap between the wealthy and the poor was recorded in the urban eighteenth-century tax lists. The top 5 percent of taxpayers increased their share of the cities' taxable assets from about 30 to 50 percent between 1690 and 1770. The bottom half of the taxable inhabitants saw their share of the wealth shrink from about 10 to 4 percent. Except in Boston, the urban middle classes continued to gain ground. But the growth of princely fortunes amid increasing poverty made some urban dwellers reflect that Old World ills were reappearing in the New.

The Entrepreneurial Ethos

As the cities grew, new values took hold. In the traditional "corporate" view of society, economic life ideally operated according to what was fair, not what was profitable. Citizens usually agreed that government should provide for the general welfare by regulating prices and wages, setting quality controls, licensing providers of service such as tavernkeepers and ferrymen, and supervising public markets where all food was sold. Such regulation seemed natural because a community was defined not as a collection of individuals, each entitled to pursue separate interests, but as a single body of interrelated parts where individual rights and responsibilities formed a seamless web.

But as cities and commerce grew, new values about economic life took hold. Subordinating private interests to the commonweal became viewed as a lofty but unrealistic ideal. Prosperity required the encouragement of acquisitive appetites rather than self-denial, for ambition would spur economic activity as more people sought more goods. The new view held that, if people were allowed to pursue their material desires competitively, they would collectively form a natural, impersonal market of producers and consumers that would operate to everyone's advantage.

As the colonial port towns took their places in the Atlantic world of commerce, merchants became accustomed to making decisions according to the

WEALTH DISTRIBUTION IN COLONIAL AMERICA

Percentage of wealth held by the richest 10% and the poorest 30% of the population in two cities and one rural area

Year	Richest 10%	Poorest 30%
Boston		
1684–1699	41.2	3.3
1700–1715	54.5	2.8
1716–1725	61.7	2.0
1726–1735	65.6	1.9
1736–1745	58.6	1.8
1746–1755	55.2	1.8
1756–1765	67.5	1.4
1766–1775	61.1	2.0
Philadelphia		
1684–1699	36.4	4.5
1700–1715	41.3	4.9
1716–1725	46.8	3.9
1726–1735	53.6	3.7
1736–1745	51.3	2.6
1746–1755	70.1	1.5
1756–1765	60.3	1.1
1766–1775	69.9	1.0
Chester County, Pennsylvania		
1693	23.8	17.4
1715	25.9	13.1
1730	28.6	9.8
1748	28.7	13.1
1760	29.9	6.3
1782	33.6	4.7

Source: Gary B. Nash, *The Urban Crucible,* 1979.

emerging commercial ethic that rejected traditional restraints on entrepreneurial activity. If wheat fetched 8 shillings a bushel in the West Indies but only 5 in Boston, a grain merchant felt justified in sending all he could purchase from local farmers to the more distant buyer. Indifferent to individuals and local communities, the new transatlantic market responded only to the invisible laws of supply and demand.

Tension between the new economic freedom and the older concern for the public good erupted only with food shortages or galloping inflation. Because the American colonies experienced none of the famines that ravaged Europe in this period, such crises occurred rarely, usually during war, when demand for provisions rose sharply.

Such a moment struck in Boston during Queen Anne's War. Merchant Andrew Belcher contracted to ship large quantities of wheat to the Caribbean, where higher prices would yield greater profit than in Boston. Ordinary neighbors, threatened with a bread shortage and angered that a townsman would put profit ahead of community needs, attacked one of Belcher's grain-laden ships in 1710. They sawed through the rudder and tried to run the vessel aground in order to seize the grain. Invoking the older ethic that the public welfare outweighed private interests, they took the law into their own hands. Even the grand jury, composed of substantial members of the community, hinted its approval of the violent action against Belcher by refusing to indict the rioters.

The two conceptions of community and economic life rubbed against each other for many decades. Urban merchants, shopkeepers, land speculators, and ambitious artisans—participants in England's rising commercial empire—cleaved more and more to the new economic formulas, although they continued to voice respect for the old precepts of the corporate community. The clergy continued to preach the traditional message: "Let no man seek his own, but every man another's wealth." But by the mid-eighteenth century, the pursuit of a profitable livelihood, not the social compact of the community, animated most city dwellers.

The American Enlightenment

Ideas about not only economic life but also the nature of the universe and the improvement of the human condition filtered across the Atlantic. In the eighteenth century, an American version of the European intellectual movement called the Enlightenment occurred, and the cities became centers for disseminating these new ideas.

In what is called the Age of Reason, European thinkers rejected the pessimistic Calvinist concept of innate human depravity, replacing it with the optimistic notion that a benevolent God had blessed humankind with the supreme gift of reason. Thinkers like John Locke, in his influential *Essay Concerning Human Understanding* (1689), argued that God had not predetermined the content of the human mind but had instead given it the capacity to acquire knowledge. All Enlightenment thinkers prized this acquisition of knowledge, for it allowed humankind to improve its condition. As the great scientific thinkers Galileo and Isaac Newton demonstrated, systematic investigation could unlock the secrets of the physical universe. Moreover, scientific knowledge could be applied to human institutions to improve society.

The scientific and intellectual advances of the seventeenth and eighteenth centuries encouraged a belief in "natural law" and fostered debate about the "natural" human rights. In Europe, French philosophers Voltaire and Denis Diderot explored the issue of equality. From 1750 to 1772, Diderot published his *Encyclopedia,* which treated such topics as equality,

The American bison, unknown in Europe, was common east of the Mississippi River when European settlers arrived. *(Colonial Williamsburg Foundation)*

liberty, reason, and rights. The ideas of the Enlightenment spread in Europe and the Americas and eventually found expression in movements for reform, democracy, and liberation—all of deep interest to those who were beginning to oppose slavery and the slave trade as abominations.

Though only a small number of educated colonists read the Enlightenment authors, they began in the eighteenth century to make significant contributions to the advancement of science. Naturalists such as John Bartram of Philadelphia gathered and described American plants from all over the eastern part of the continent as part of the transatlantic attempt to classify all plant life into one universal system. Professor John Winthrop III of Harvard made an unusually accurate measurement of the earth's distance from the sun. Standing above them all was Benjamin Franklin, whose spectacular (and dangerous) experiments with electricity, the properties of which were just becoming known, earned him an international reputation.

Franklin's true genius as a figure of the Enlightenment came in his practical application of scientific knowledge. Among his inventions were the lightning rod, which nearly ended the age-old danger of fires when lightning struck wooden buildings; bifocal spectacles; and an iron stove that heated rooms—in an age when firewood was a major item in the household budget—far more efficiently than the usual open fireplace. Franklin also made his adopted city of Philadelphia a center of the American Enlightenment. He led the founding of America's first circulating library in 1731, an artisans' debating club for "mutual improvement" through discussion of the latest ideas from Europe, and an intercolonial scientific association that in 1769 became the American Philosophical Society.

Though most colonists were not educated enough to participate actively in the American Enlightenment, the efforts of men such as Franklin exposed thousands, especially in the cities, to new currents of thought. This led to the growing sense that the colonists, blessed by their abundant environment, might achieve the Enlightenment ideal of a perfect society.

THE GREAT AWAKENING

Many of the social, economic, and political changes occurring in the eighteenth-century colonies converged in the Great Awakening, the first of many religious revivals that would sweep American society during the next two centuries. The timing and character of the Awakening varied from region to region. But everywhere, this quest for spiritual renewal challenged old sources of authority and produced patterns of thought and behavior that helped fuel a revolutionary movement in the next generation.

Fading Faith

Colonial America in the early eighteenth century remained an overwhelmingly Protestant culture. The Puritan, or Congregational, Church dominated all of New England except Rhode Island. Anglicanism held sway in much of New York and throughout the South except the backcountry. In the mid-Atlantic and in the back settlements, German Mennonites, Dunkers, Moravians, and Lutherans; Scots-Irish Presbyterians; and English Baptists and Quakers all mingled.

Yet these diverse groups commanded the allegiance of only about one-third of the colonists. Those who went to no church at all remained the majority. In many areas, ministers and churches were simply unavailable. In Virginia, the most populous colony, only 60 clergymen in 1761 served a population of 350,000—one for every 5,800 people.

Most colonial churches were voluntary or gathered ("congregated") groups, formed for reasons of conscience, not because of government compulsion. Catholics, Jews, and nonbelievers could not vote or hold office. But the persecution of Quakers and Catholics had largely passed, and some dissenting groups by 1720 had gained the right to use long-obligatory church taxes to support their own congregations.

The clergy often administered their congregations with difficulty. Anglicans and several German sects maintained close ties to mother churches across the Atlantic, whereas other denominations attempted to centralize authority. However, most efforts to tighten organization and discipline failed. For example, Anglican ministers had to be ordained in England and regularly report to the bishop of London. But once installed in a Chesapeake parish, an Anglican priest faced wealthy planters who controlled the vestry (the local church's governing body), set his salary, and would drive him out if he challenged them too forcefully. In Connecticut, the Saybrook Platform of 1708 created a network, or "consociation," of Congregational Churches, but individual churches still preserved much of their autonomy.

Though governing their churches frustrated many clergymen, religious apathy was a far more pressing problem in the early eighteenth century. As early as the 1660s, the Congregational clergy of New England had attempted to return wandering sheep to the fold by adopting the Half-Way Covenant. It allowed children of church members, if they adhered to the "forms of godliness," to join the church even if they could not demonstrate that they had undergone a conversion experience. They could not, however, vote in church affairs or take communion.

Adopted in 1662, this compromise kept in the church many children of the founders, and they in turn could pass church membership on to their children. Some ministers took other measures to increase their flocks. Solomon Stoddard, for 60 years patriarch of the Congregational Church in Northampton, Massachusetts, gave communion to every professing Christian and used an emotional style of preaching to reap annual "harvests" of souls.

Despite compromises and innovations, most church leaders saw creeping religious apathy when they surveyed their towns. An educated clergy, its energies often drained by doctrinal disputes within denominations, appealed too much to the mind and not enough to the heart. In such a state, as one Connecticut leader remembered it, "the spirit of God appeared to be awfully withdrawn."

The Awakeners' Message

The Great Awakening was not a unified movement but rather a series of revivals that swept different regions between 1720 and 1760 with varying degrees of intensity. The first stirrings came in the 1720s in New Jersey and Pennsylvania. Theodore Frelinghuysen, a Dutch Reformed minister, excited his congregation through emotional preaching. Avoiding theological abstractions, he concentrated on arousing a need to be "saved." A neighboring Presbyterian, Gilbert Tennent, soon took up the Dutchman's techniques, with similar success.

From New Jersey, the Awakening spread to Pennsylvania in the 1730s, especially among Presbyterians, and then broke out in the Connecticut River valley. There it was led by Jonathan Edwards, who had succeeded his grandfather, Solomon Stoddard, in Northampton's Church. Later a philosophical giant in the colonies, Edwards as a young man gained renown by frightening his parishioners with the fate of "sinners in the hands of an angry God." "How manifold have been the abominations of your life!" Edwards preached. "Are there not some here that have debased themselves below the dignity of human nature, by allowing in sensual filthiness, as swine in the mire . . . ?" Edwards paraded one sin after another before his trembling congregants: "God and your own consciences know what abominable lasciviousness you have practised in things not fit to be named, when you have been alone; when you ought to have been reading, or meditating, or on your knees before God in secret prayer."

After cataloging his parishioners' sins, Edwards drew such graphic pictures of the hell awaiting the unrepentant that his Northampton neighbors were soon preparing frantically for the conversion by which they would be "born again." His *Faithful Narrative of the Surprizing Work of God* (1736), which described his town's awakening, was the first published revival narrative. This literary form would be used many times in the future to fan the flames of evangelical religion.

In 1739, these regional brushfires of evangelicalism were drawn together by a 24-year-old Anglican priest from England, George Whitefield. Inspired by John Wesley, the founder of English Methodism, Whitefield became a master of emotional open-air preaching. Whitefield made seven barnstorming tours along the American seaboard, the first in 1739 and 1740. Thousands turned out to see him, and with each success, his fame and influence grew. In the cities, people fought for places in the churches when he spoke and gathered by the thousands in open fields to hear his message. Even in sedate Philadelphia, he turned skeptics into true believers, "so that one could not walk thro' town, in an evening," claimed the unreligious Benjamin Franklin, "without hearing psalms sung in different families of every street." In Boston, Whitefield preached to 19,000 in three days. Then, at a farewell sermon, he left 25,000 writhing in fear of damnation. In his wake came American preachers, mostly young men like Devereaux Jarratt, whom he had inspired.

Technology Changes the American People

LIGHTNING RODS

In 1746, Benjamin Franklin, already a successful printer, newspaper editor, and civic organizer in Philadelphia, began experimenting with electricity, at that time a mysterious force. Franklin had read about the experiments of Dutchman Pieter van Musschenbroek, who had learned how to condense electricity in a glass bottle (called a Leyden jar) and to produce electrical sparks by attaching a conductor to the two sides of the bottle. Throughout Europe, amateur scientists began to play with Leyden jars, but nobody really understood the source or nature of the mysterious electrical "fluid."

By 1748, Franklin had constructed a number of experiments for producing brilliant sparks from Leyden jars and for measuring the intensity of the sparks. His *Experiments and Observations on Electricity,* published in London three years later, put his name on the lips of scientists all over Europe. His achievements catapulted Franklin to the forefront of the world's scientists and earned him a coveted medal from the Royal Society of London, one of the most advanced scientific bodies in the world. Scientific knowledge had traveled westward across the Atlantic from Europe for two centuries but now went eastward from North America to the amazed Europeans.

In practical terms, Franklin's most important discovery was that lightning produced by thunderstorms was a form of electricity. Devising a common kite of silk stretched across sticks of wood with a thin wire at the top and a metal key tied to the end of the kite string, he proved that "electric fire" would "stream plentifully from the key." His experiment constituted a breakthrough of one of the most formidable barriers of the unknown and opened up an entirely new field of controlled study.

Franklin personified the eighteenth-century Enlightenment in his desire to understand the laws that govern the natural world. He was also an Enlightenment figure in his determination to use these ideas, or what we would call scientific theory, to harness nature. Electricity, in the form of lightning, was a terrifying destructive natural force that for centuries had destroyed buildings, ships, and people with awful regularity. Once Franklin learned the properties of electricity

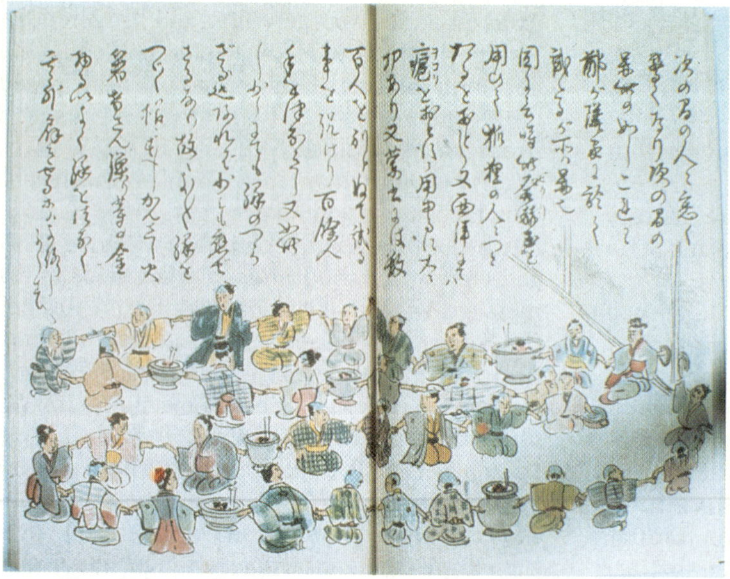

Franklin's global influence reached as far as Japan, as shown in this Japanese electrical parlor game in 1813. *(The Burndy Library, Dibner Institute for the History of Science and Technology)*

Benjamin Franklin's fame in "capturing" the lightning of violent thunderstorms led to dramatic representations of his kite experiment. Here Franklin holds a metal key; through it passes a silk string that leads to the high-flying kite. *(West, Benjamin*—Benjamin Franklin Drawing Lightning from the Sky, *Philadelphia Museum of Art: Gift of Mr. and Mrs. Wharton Sindler)*

and had established that lightning was a form of it, he found it relatively easy to contrive a metal rod, coated to prevent rusting, that would "throw off" the electricity and render it harmless.

By 1753, convinced that he had mastered the theory of electricity and lightning, Franklin went public with an essay that was to make life better for millions of people around the world. In "How to Secure Houses from Lightning" he provided a practical essay that took the terror out of a natural phenomenon and taught people how to use a simple and inexpensive device to protect their lives and property. Soon lightning rods shot up on houses and barns all over the American colonies—and soon all over Europe and other parts of the world. Farmers, homeowners, mariners, and church wardens could soon rest easier, knowing that their barns, houses, ships, and churches were safe. What had seemed to be the wrathful work of an angry God now became a force within the power of humans to control.

In Franklin's premodern world, scientific breakthroughs proceeded slowly. Usually individuals rather than research teams conducted research, and they did so without government sponsorship, without highly capitalized corporate research facilities, even—at least in America—without university laboratories. Franklin conducted his research at home and in the fields surrounding the city of Philadelphia. His was a one-man operation, and his success emanated from what was later called "an ingenious mind and a contriving hand." If the power of Lightning could be harnessed by the son of a Boston candlemaker far from the centers of learning in Europe, what other forces of nature might be understood and brought under rein?

Why do you think Franklin's *Experiments and Observations on Electricity* (1751) were published in London instead of Philadelphia? Do you think that it was advantageous that in the era before patents Franklin's lightning rod could easily be made, leaving him only with honor but no profits from his remarkable invention?

Readings: I. Bernard Cohen, *Benjamin Franklin: Scientist and Statesman* (New York, 1963); Brooke Hindle, *The Pursuit of Science in Revolutionary America, 1735–1789* (Chapel Hill, NC, 1956).

Jonathan Edwards (1703–1758) was the first major philosopher in the American colonies. A leader of the Great Awakening in Massachusetts, he was ousted by his congregation for reprimanding the children of church members for reading *The Midwife Rightly Instructed*, an obstetric guide that was as close as curious children could come to learning about sex. *(Yale University Art Gallery, Bequest of Eugene Phelps Edwards)*

Samson Occom, a Mohegan born in Connecticut, was attracted to Christianity, like so many others who were "outsiders," by the emotional and populistic appeal of the Great Awakening preachers. On a trip to England, Occom raised £12,000 for an evangelical school for Indians, later to become Dartmouth College. *(Courtesy of the Boston Public library, Print Department)*

George Whitefield, who first toured the American colonies in 1739 and 1740, sent thousands of souls "flying to Christ" with his emotional sermons. More Americans heard Whitefield on his many seaboard itineracies, than any other figure in the eighteenth century. *(National Portrait Gallery, London)*

Some of Whitefield's appeal lay in his genius for dramatic performance and some in his ability to simplify theological doctrine and focus people's attention on one facet of religious life, the conversion experience. In electrifying performances, he cast away the conventional written sermons in favor of spontaneous preaching. Using wild body movements and his magnificent voice, he filled thousands with the desire to "fly to Christ."

The appeal of the Awakeners lay both in the medium and the message. They preached that the established, college-trained clergy was too intellectual and tradition-bound to bring faith and piety to a new generation. Congregations were dead, Whitefield declared, "because dead men preach to them." "The sapless discourses of such dead drones," cried another Awakener, were worthless. The fires of Protestant belief could be reignited only if individuals assumed responsibility for their own conversion.

An important form of individual participation was "lay exhorting." "Exhorting" meant that anyone—young or old, female or male, black or white—might spontaneously recount a conversion experience and preach "the Lord's truth." This horrified most established clergymen. Lay exhorting shattered their monopoly on religious discourse and gave new importance to the oral culture of common people, whose spontaneous outpourings contrasted sharply with the controlled literary culture of the gentry. Through lay exhorting, ordinary men and women, and even children, servants, and slaves, crossed class lines and defied assigned roles.

How religion, social change, and politics became interwoven in the Great Awakening can be seen by examining two regions swept by revivalism. Both Boston, the heartland of Puritanism, and interior Virginia, a land of struggling small planters and slave-rich aristocrats, experienced the Great Awakening, but in different ways and at different times.

The Urban North

In Boston, Whitefield-inspired revivalism blazed up amid political controversy. Since 1739, the citizens had argued strenuously about remedies for the severe depreciation of the province's paper currency, which had been issued for years to finance military expeditions against French Canada. The English government insisted that Massachusetts retire all paper money by 1741. Searching for a substitute circulating medium, one group proposed a land bank to issue private bills of credit backed by land. Another group proposed a silver bank to distribute bills of credit backed by silver. Controversy over the land and silver banks swept politics in 1740 and 1741, pitting large merchants, who preferred the fiscally conservative silver bank, against local traders, artisans, and the laboring poor, who preferred the land bank.

Whitefield's arrival in Boston coincided with the currency furor. His stay in Boston overlapped with attacks on merchants as "gripping and merciless usurers" who "heaped up vast estates" at the expense of the common people. At first, Boston's elite applauded Whitefield's ability to call the masses to worship. The master evangelist, it seemed, might restore social harmony by redirecting people from earthly matters such as the currency dispute to concerns of the soul.

When Whitefield left Boston in 1740, he was succeeded by others who were more critical of the "unconverted" clergy and the self-indulgent accumulation of wealth. One was James Davenport, who arrived in 1742. His great-grandfather had been a founder of New Haven, and his father was a respected Congregational minister in Connecticut. But the 25-year-old Davenport, who had been inspired by Whitefield, appeared anything but respectable to the elite.

Finding every church closed to him, even those whose clergy had embraced the Awakening, Davenport preached daily on the Boston Common, aroused religious ecstasy among thousands, and stirred up feeling against Boston's leading figures. Respectable people grew convinced that revivalism had gotten out of hand, for by this time ordinary people were verbally attacking opponents of the land bank in the streets as "carnal wretches, hypocrites, fighters against God, children of the devil, cursed Pharisees." A revival that had begun as a return to religion among backsliding Christians had overlapped with political affairs. Hence, it threatened polite culture, which stressed order and discipline from ordinary people.

The Rural South

The Great Awakening was ebbing in New England and the middle colonies by 1744, although aftershocks continued for years. But in Virginia, where the initial religious earthquake was barely felt, tremors of enthusiasm rippled through society from the mid-1740s onward. As in Boston, the Awakeners challenged and disturbed the gentry-led social order.

Whitefield stirred some religious fervor during his early trips through Virginia. Traveling "New Light" preachers, led by the brilliant orator Samuel Davies, were soon gathering large crowds both in the backcountry and in the traditionally Anglican parishes of the older settled areas. By 1747, worried Anglican clergyman convinced the governor to issue a proclamation restraining "strolling preachers." As in other colonies, Virginia's leaders despised traveling evangelists, for like lay exhorters, these roving Awakeners conjured up a world without properly constituted authority. As one critic put it in 1745, the wandering preachers "have turned the world upside down." When the Hanover County court gave the fiery James Davenport a license to preach in 1750, the governor ordered the suppression of all circuit riders.

New Light Presbyterianism, which challenged the religious monopoly of the gentry-dominated Anglican Church, spread in the 1750s. Then, in the 1760s, came the Baptists. Renouncing finery, attacking ostentatious display, and addressing each other as "brother" and "sister," the Baptists reached out to thousands of unchurched people. Like northern revivalists, they focused on the conversion experience. Many of their preachers were uneducated farmers and artisans who called themselves "Christ's poor." They stressed equality in human affairs and insisted that heaven was always populated more by the humble poor than by the purse-proud rich. Among the poorest of all, Virginia's 140,000 slaves in 1760, the evangelical message began to take hold.

The insurgent Baptist movement in rural Virginia became both a quest for a personal, emotionally satisfying religion among ordinary folk and a rejection of the gentry's social values. Established Anglican pulpits denounced the Awakeners as furiously as had respectable New England divines. In both regions, social changes had weakened the cultural authority of the upper class and, in the context of religious revival, produced a vision of a society drawn along more equal lines.

Legacy of the Awakening

By the time George Whitefield returned to America for his third tour in 1745, the revival had burned out in the North. Its effects, however, were long-lasting. Notably, the Awakening promoted religious pluralism and nourished the idea that all denominations were equally legitimate; none had a monopoly on the truth. Whitefield had anticipated this tendency when he sermonized: "Father Abraham, whom have you in heaven? Any Episcopalians? And the answer came back, No! Any Presbyterians? No! Any Independents or Methodists? No, no, no! Whom have you there? And the final answer came down from heaven, We don't know the names here. All who are here are Christians."

By legitimizing the dissenting Protestant groups that had sprung up in seventeenth-century England, the Great Awakening gave them all a basis for living together in relative harmony. From this framework of denominationalism came a second change—the separation of church and state. Once a variety of churches gained legitimacy, it was hard to justify one denomination claiming special privileges. In the seventeenth century, Roger Williams had tried to sever church and state because he believed that ties with civil bodies would corrupt the church. But during the Awakening, groups such as the Baptists and Presbyterians in Virginia constituted their own religious bodies and broke the Anglican monopoly as *the* Church in the colony. This undermining of the church–state tie would be completed during the revolutionary era.

A third effect of the revival was to legitimate community diversity. Almost from their beginnings, Rhode Island, the Carolinas, and the middle colonies had recognized this. But homogeneity had been prized elsewhere, especially in Massachusetts and Connecticut. There, the Awakening split Congregational Churches into New Lights and Old Lights, and mid-Atlantic Presbyterian Churches were similarly beset by schisms. In hundreds of rural communities by the 1750s, two or three churches existed where only one had stood before. People learned that the fabric of community could be woven from threads of many hues.

New eighteenth-century colonial colleges reflected the religious pluralism symbolized by the Great Awakening. Before 1740, there existed only Puritan Harvard (1636) and Yale (1701) and Anglican William and Mary (1693). To these small seats of higher education were added six new colleges between 1746 and 1769—Dartmouth, Brown, Princeton, and what are now Columbia, Rutgers, and the University of Pennsylvania.

In spite of ties to particular denominations, none of the new colleges was controlled by an established church, all had governing bodies composed of men of different faiths, and all admitted students regardless of religion. Eager for students and funds, they made nonsectarian appeals and constructed classical curricula mixed with natural sciences and natural philosophy.

Last, the Awakening nurtured a subtle change in values that crossed over into politics and daily life. Especially for ordinary people, the revival experience created a new feeling of self-worth. People assumed new responsibilities in religious affairs and became skeptical of dogma and authority. Many, especially the fast-growing Baptists, decried the growing materialism and deplored the new acceptance of self-interested behavior. He who was "governed by regard to his own private interest," Gilbert Tennent preached, was "an enemy to the public," for in true Christian communities, "mutual love is the band and cement." By learning to oppose authority and to take part in creating new churches, thousands of colonists unknowingly rehearsed for revolution.

POLITICAL LIFE

"Were it not for government, the world would soon run into all manner of disorders and confusions," wrote a Massachusetts clergyman early in the eighteenth century. "Men's lives and estates and liberties

COLONIAL COLLEGES

Name	Colony	Founding Date	Denominational Affiliation
Harvard College	Massachusetts	1636	Congregational
College of William and Mary	Virginia	1693	Anglican
Yale College	Connecticut	1701	Congregational
College of New Jersey (Princeton)	New Jersey	1746	Presbyterian
College of Philadelphia (University of Pennsylvania)	Pennsylvania	1754	Secular
King's College (Columbia)	New York	1754	Anglican
College of Rhode Island (Brown)	Rhode Island	1764	Baptist
Queen's College (Rutgers)	New Jersey	1766	Dutch Reformed
Dartmouth College	New Hampshire	1769	Congregational

would soon be prey to the covetous and the cruel," and every man would be "as a wolf" to his neighbors. Few colonists would have disagreed. On both sides of the Atlantic, people believed that government existed to protect life, liberty, and property.

A less easily resolved matter was how political power should be divided—in England, between the English government and the American colonies, and within each colony. Colonists naturally drew heavily on inherited political ideas and institutions, almost entirely English ones, for it was English charters that sanctioned settlement, English governors who ruled, and English common law that governed the courts. But meeting unexpected circumstances in a new environment, colonists modified familiar political forms to suit their needs.

Structuring Colonial Governments

All societies consider it essential to determine the final source of political authority. In England, the notion of the God-given supreme authority of the monarch was crumbling even before the planting of the colonies. In its place arose the belief that stable and enlightened government depended on blending and balancing the interests of monarchy, aristocracy, and democracy. Unalloyed, each of these forms of government would degenerate into oppression. Monarchy, the rule of one, would become despotism. Aristocracy, the rule of the few, would turn into corrupt oligarchy. Democracy, the rule of the many, would descend into anarchy or mob rule. Most colonists believed that the Revolution of 1688 in England, by thwarting the king's pretensions to greater power, had vindicated and strengthened a carefully balanced political system.

In the colonies, political balance was achieved somewhat differently. The governor was the king's agent (or, in proprietary colonies, the agent of the proprietor to whom the king delegated authority). The council, composed of wealthy appointees of the governor in most colonies, was a pale equivalent of the English House of Lords. The assembly, elected by white male freeholders, functioned as a replica of the House of Commons. "The concurrence of these three forms of government," wrote a Bostonian in 1749, "seems to be the highest perfection that human civil government can attain to."

COLONIAL FOUNDATIONS OF THE AMERICAN POLITICAL SYSTEM	
1606	Virginia companies of London and Plymouth granted patents to settle lands in North America.
1619	First elected colonial legislature meets in Virginia.
1634	Under a charter granted in 1632, Maryland's proprietor is given all the authority "as any bishop of Durham" ever held—more than the king possessed in England.
1635	The council in Virginia deports Governor John Harvey for exceeding his power, thus asserting the rights of local magistrates to contest authority of royally appointed governors.
1643	The colonies of Massachusetts, Plymouth, Connecticut, and New Haven draw up articles of confederation and form the first intercolonial union, the United Colonies of New England.
1647	Under a charter granted in 1644, elected freemen from the Providence Plantations draft a constitution establishing freedom of conscience, separating church and state, and authorizing referenda by the towns on laws passed by the assembly.
1677	The Laws, Concessions, and Agreements for West New Jersey provide for a legislature elected annually by virtually all free males, secret voting, liberty of conscience, election of justices of the peace and local officeholders, and trial by jury in public so that "justice may not be done in a corner."
1689	James II deposed in England in the Glorious Revolution and royal governors, accused of abusing their authority, ousted in Massachusetts, New York, and Maryland.
1701	First colonial unicameral legislature meets in Pennsylvania under the Frame of Government of 1701.
1735	John Peter Zenger, a New York printer, acquitted of seditious libel for printing attacks on the royal governor and his faction, thus widening the freedom of the press.
1754	First congress of all the colonies meets at Albany (with seven colonies sending delegates) and agrees on a Plan of Union (which is rejected by the colonies and the English government).
1765	The Stamp Act Congress, the first intercolonial convention called outside England's authority, meets in New York.

Bicameral legislatures developed in most of the colonies in the seventeenth century. The lower houses, or assemblies, represented the local interests of the people at large. The upper houses, or councils (which usually also sat as the highest courts), represented the nascent aristocracy. Except in Rhode Island and Connecticut, every statute required the governor's assent, and all colonial laws required final approval from the king's privy council. This royal check on colonial lawmaking operated imperfectly, however. Laws took months to reach England, and months more passed before word of their final approval or rejection returned. In the meantime, the laws set down in the colonies took force.

Behind the formal structure of politics stood the rules governing who could participate in the political process. In England since the fifteenth century, the ownership of land had largely defined electoral participation (women and non-Christians were uniformly excluded). Only men with property sufficient to produce an annual rental income of 40 shillings could vote or hold office. The colonists closely followed this principle, except in Massachusetts, where until 1691 church membership was the basic requirement. As in England, the poor and propertyless were excluded, for they lacked the "stake in society" that supposedly transformed unpredictable, ignorant creatures into thoughtful and responsible voters.

Whereas in England, the 40-shilling freehold requirement was intended to restrict the size of the electorate, in the colonies, because of the cheapness of land, it conferred the vote on a large proportion of adult males—between 50 and 75 percent in most colonies. As the proportion of landless colonists increased in the eighteenth century, however, the franchise slowly contracted.

Though voting rights were broadly based, most men assumed that only the wealthy and socially prominent should hold positions of political power. Lesser men, it was held, ought to defer to their betters. Balancing this elitist conception of politics, however, was the notion that the entire electorate should periodically judge the performance of those entrusted with political power and reject those who represented them inadequately. Unlike the members of the English House of Commons, who by the seventeenth century thought of themselves as representing the entire nation, the colonial representatives were expected to reflect the views of those who elected them locally. Believing this, their constituents judged them accordingly.

When were citizens entitled to defy those who ruled them? The answer to this vexing question followed English precedent: The people were justified in badgering their leaders, protesting openly, and, in extreme cases of abuse of power, assuming control in order to put things right. The uprisings in the colonies associated with England's Glorious Revolution represented such moments when the deferential mass transformed itself into a purposeful crowd to overthrow those who trampled on their traditional English liberties.

The Crowd in Action

Crowd action, frequently effective, gradually achieved a kind of legitimacy. What gave special power to the common people when they assembled to protest oppressive authority was the general absence of effective police power. In the countryside, where most colonists lived, only the county sheriff, with an occasional deputy, insulated civil leaders from angry farmers. In the towns, the sheriff had only the frail night watch to safeguard public order. As late as 1757, the night watch of New York was described as a "parcell of idle, drinking vigilant snorers, who never quelled any nocturnal tumult in their lives." In theory, the militia stood ready to suppress public disturbances, but both urban and rural crowds usually included many of the very people who composed the militia. Thus, the assembled people became perceived as the watchdog of government, ready to chastise or drive from office those who violated the collective sense of what was right and proper.

Boston's impressment riot of 1747 vividly illustrates the people's readiness to defend their inherited privileges and the weakness of law enforcement. It began when Commodore Charles Knowles brought his Royal Navy ships to Boston for provisioning—and to replenish the ranks of mariners thinned by desertion. When Knowles sent press gangs out on a chill November evening to fill the crew vacancies from Boston's waterfront population, they scooped up artisans, laborers, servants, and slaves, as well as merchant seamen from ships riding at anchor in the harbor.

But before the press gangs could hustle their victims back to the British men-of-war, a crowd of angry Bostonians seized several British officers, surrounded the governor's house, and demanded the release of their townsmen. When the sheriff and his deputies tried to intervene, the mob mauled them. The militia, called to arms by the governor to "suppress the mob by force, and if need be to fire upon 'em with ball," refused to respond. By dusk, a crowd of several thousand defied the governor's orders to disperse, stoned the windows of the governor's house, and dragged a royal barge from one of the British ships into the courtyard of his house, where they burned it amid cheers.

Enraged by the defiant Bostonians, Commodore Knowles threatened to bombard the town. Negotiations averted a showdown, and Knowles released the impressed Bostonians. After the riot, a young politician named Samuel Adams defended Boston's defiance of royal authority. The people, he argued, had a "natural right" to band together against press gangs that deprived them of their liberty. Local magnates who supported the governor in this incident were labeled "tools to arbitrary power."

The Growing Power of the Assemblies

Incidents such as the impressment riot of 1747 demonstrated the touchiness of England's colonial subjects. But a more gradual and restrained change—the growing ambition and power of the legislative assemblies—was far more important. For most of the seventeenth century, royal and proprietary governors had exercised greater power in relation to the elected legislatures than did the king in relation to Parliament. Governors could dissolve the lower houses and delay their sitting, control the election of their speakers, and in most colonies initiate legislation with their appointed councils. Governors also had authority to appoint and dismiss judges at all levels of the judiciary and to create chancery courts, which sat without juries. They also controlled the expenditure of public monies and had authority to grant land to individuals and groups, which they sometimes used to confer vast estates on their favorites.

By the 1730s, royal governments had replaced many of the proprietary governments. In the seventeenth century, Virginia, Massachusetts, and New York had become royal colonies, with governors appointed by the crown. In the eighteenth century, royal government came to New Jersey (1702), South Carolina (1719), and North Carolina (1729), replacing proprietary regimes.

Many royal governors were competent military officers or bureaucrats, but often they were simply recipients of patronage posts. They were rewarded for whom they knew, not what they had done or might accomplish. A few were psychologically damaged, like Sir Danvers Osborn, who committed suicide a week after arriving in New York in 1753. Many were corrupt. Some governors never took up their posts at all, preferring, like the earl of Orkney, Virginia's royal governor from 1705 to 1737, to pocket the salary and pay a part of it to other men who went to the colony as lieutenant governors. But most governors were not crazy, corrupt, or absent; they were merely mediocre.

In the eighteenth century, elected colonial legislatures challenged the swollen executive powers of these colonial governors. The governors lacked the extensive patronage power that enabled ministers of government in England to manipulate elections and buy off opposition groups. They could therefore contest but not prevent encroachments on their power. Bit by bit, the representative assemblies won new rights—to initiate legislation, to elect their own speakers, to settle contested elections, to discipline their membership, and to nominate provincial treasurers who disbursed public funds. Most important, they won the "power of the purse"—the authority to initiate money bills, specifying how much money should be raised by taxes and how it should be spent. Thus the elected assemblies gradually transformed themselves into governing bodies reflecting the interests of the electorate. Governors complained bitterly about the "levelling spirit" and "mutinous and disorderly behavior" of the assemblies, but they could not stop their rise.

Local Politics

Binding elected officeholders to their constituents became an important feature of the colonial political system. In England, the House of Commons was filled with representatives from "rotten boroughs" (ancient places left virtually uninhabited by population shifts) and with men whose vote was in the pocket of the ministry because they had accepted crown appointments, contracts, or gifts. The American assemblies, by contrast, contained mostly representatives sent by voters who instructed them on particular issues and held them accountable for serving local interests.

Royal governors and colonial grandees who sat as councillors often deplored this localist, popular orientation of the people's representatives. The assemblies, sniffed one aristocratic New Yorker, were crowded with "plain, illiterate husbandmen [small farmers], whose views seldom extended farther than the regulation of highways, the destruction of wolves, wildcats, and foxes, and the advancement of the other little interests of the particular counties which they were chosen to represent." In actuality, the voters mostly sent merchants, lawyers, and substantial planters and farmers to represent them in the lower houses, and by the mid-eighteenth century in most colonies, these men had formed political elites. But it was true that they represented the local interests of their constituents. They prided themselves on doing so, for they saw themselves as bulwarks against oppression and arbitrary rule, which history taught them were most frequently imposed by monarchs and their appointed agents.

Local government was usually more important to the colonists than provincial government. In the North, local political authority generally rested in the towns. The New England town meeting decided a

When frontier farmers marched on Philadelphia in 1763 to demand more protection on the frontier, a miniature civil war almost broke out. Philadelphians had little use for the "Paxton Boys," who had murdered 20 harmless Christian Indians in retaliation for frontier raids. (*The Library Company of Philadelphia*)

wide range of matters. In making decisions, the meeting strived for consensus, searching and arguing until it could express itself as a single unit. "By general agreement" and "by the free and united consent of the whole" were phrases denoting a decision-making process that sought participatory assent rather than a democratic competition among differing interests and points of view.

In the South, the county was the primary unit of government. No equivalent of the town meeting existed for placing local decisions before the populace. The planter gentry ruled the county courts and the legislature, and substantial farmers served in minor offices such as road surveyor and deputy sheriff. At court sessions, usually four times a year, deeds were read aloud and then recorded, juries impaneled and justice dispensed, elections held, licenses issued, and proclamations read aloud. On election days, gentlemen treated their neighbors (on whom they depended for votes) to "bumbo," "kill devil," and other alcoholic treats. By the mid-eighteenth century, a landed squirearchy of third- and fourth-generation families had achieved political dominance.

The Spread of Whig Ideology

Whether in local or provincial affairs, a political ideology called Whig, or "republican," had spread widely by the mid-eighteenth century. This body of thought, inherited from England, rested on the belief that concentrated power was historically the enemy of liberty and that too much power lodged in any person or group usually produced corruption and tyranny. The best defenses against concentrated power were balanced government, elected legislatures adept at checking executive authority, prohibition of standing armies (almost always controlled by tyrannical monarchs to oppress the people), and vigilance by the people in watching their leaders for telltale signs of corruption.

Much of this Whig ideology reached the people through the newspapers that began appearing in the seaboard towns in the early eighteenth century. The first was the *Boston News-Letter,* founded in 1704. By 1763, some 23 papers circulated in the colonies. Though limited to a few pages and published only once or twice a week, the papers passed from hand to hand and were read aloud in taverns and coffeehouses. In this way, their contents probably reached most households in the towns and a substantial minority of farmsteads in the countryside.

By the 1730s, newspapers had become an important conduit of Whig ideology. Many reprinted material from English Whig writers who railed against corruption and creeping despotism in the reign of George II (1727–1760). Particularly popular were the essays of John Trenchard and Thomas Gordon, whose *Cato's Letters* and *Independent Whig* found their way into the private libraries of many colonists and were widely reprinted in the newspapers.

The new power of the press and its importance in guarding the people's liberties against would-be tyrants (such as abrasive royal governors) were vividly illustrated in the Zenger case in New York. Young John Peter Zenger, a printer's apprentice, had been hired in 1733 by the antigovernment faction of Lewis Morris to start a newspaper that would publicize the tyrannical actions of Governor William Cosby. In Zenger's *New-York Weekly Journal,* the Morris faction fired salvos at Cosby's interference with the courts and his alleged corruption in giving important offices to his henchmen. New Yorkers believed, said one essay published by Zenger, "that their LIBERTIES and PROPERTIES are precarious, and that SLAVERY is like to be tailed on them and their posterity if some things past are not amended."

Arrested for seditious libel, Zenger was brilliantly defended by Andrew Hamilton, a Philadelphia lawyer hired by the Morris faction to convince the jury that Zenger had been simply trying to inform the people of attacks on their liberties. Although the jury acquitted Zenger, the libel laws remained very restrictive. But the acquittal did reinforce the notion that the government was the people's servant, and it brought home the point that public criticism could keep people with political authority responsible to the people they ruled. Such ideas about liberty and corruption, raised in the context of local politics, would shortly achieve a much broader significance.

Timeline

1662	Half-Way Covenant in New England
1685–1715	Stagnation in tobacco market
1704	*Boston News-Letter,* first regular colonial newspaper, published
1713	Beginning of Scots-Irish and German immigration
1715–1730	Volume of slave trade doubles
1718	French settle New Orleans
1720s	Black population begins to increase naturally
1732	Benjamin Franklin publishes first *Poor Richard's Almanack*
	Impressment riot in Boston
1734–1736	Great Awakening begins in Northampton, Massachusetts
1735	Zenger acquitted of seditious libel in New York
1739–1740	Whitefield's first American tour spreads Great Awakening
	Slaves compose 90 percent of population on Carolina rice coast
1740s	Indigo becomes staple crop in Lower South
1760	Africans compose 20 percent of American population
1760s–1770s	Spanish establish California mission system
1769	American Philosophical Society founded at Philadelphia

Conclusion

America in 1750

The American colonies, robust and expanding, matured rapidly between 1700 and 1750. Transatlantic commerce linked them closely to Europe, Africa, and other parts of the New World. Churches, schools, and towns—the visible marks of the receding frontier—appeared everywhere. A balanced sex ratio and stable family life had been achieved throughout the colonies. Seasoned political leaders and familiar political institutions functioned from Maine to Georgia.

Yet the sinew, bone, and muscle of American society had not yet fully knit together. The polyglot population, one-fifth of it bound in chattel slavery and its Native American component still unassimilated and uneasily situated on the frontier, was a kaleidoscopic mixture of ethnic and religious groups. Its economy, while developing rapidly, showed weaknesses, particularly in New England, where land resources had been strained. The social structure reflected the colonizers' emergence from a frontier stage, but the consolidation of wealth by a landed and mercantile elite was matched by pockets of poverty appearing in the cities and some rural areas. Full of strength, yet marked by awkward incongruities, colonial America in 1750 approached an era of strife and momentous decisions.

Recommended Reading

America's First Population Explosion

Bernard Bailyn, *Voyagers to the West: A Passage in the Peopling of America on the Eve of the American Revolution* (1986); Jon Butler, *The Huguenots in Colonial America* (1983); R. J. Dickson, *Ulster Immigration to Colonial America, 1718–1775* (1966); Aaron S. Fogleman, *Hopeful Journeys: German Immigration, Settlement, and Political Culture, 1717–1775* (1996); James A. Henretta and Gregory Nobles, *Evolution and Revolution: American Society: 1620–1820* (1987); Ned Landsman, *Scotland and Its First American Colony* (1985); John J. McCusker and Russell R. Menard, *The Economy of British America, 1607–1789* (1985); Edwin J. Perkins, *The Economy of Colonial America*, 2d ed. (1988); Stephanie G. Wolf, *Urban Village: Population, Community, and Family Structure in Germantown, Pennsylvania* (1977).

Beyond the Appalachians

Kathryn E. Holland Braund, *Deerskins and Duffels: The Creek Indian Trade with Anglo-America, 1685–1815* (1993); Thomas Ingersoll, *Mammon and Manon in Early New Orleans: The First Slave Society in the Deep South, 1717–1819* (1999); Robert H. Jackson and Edward Castillo, *Indians, Franciscans, and Spanish Colonization* (1995); Marc Simmons, *Coronado's Land: Essays on Daily Life in Colonial New Mexico* (1991); Richard White, *The Middle Ground: Indians, Empires, and Republics in the Great Lakes Region, 1650–1815* (1991); Daniel H. Usner, Jr., *Indians, Settlers, and Slaves in a Frontier Exchange Economy: The Lower Mississippi Valley before 1783* (1992).

A Land of Family Farms

John L. Brooke, *The Heart of the Commonwealth: Society and Political Culture in Worcester County, Massachusetts, 1713–1861* (1989); Richard Bushman, *From Puritan to Yankee* (1967); David W. Conroy, *In Public Houses: Drink and the Revolution of Authority in Colonial Massachusetts* (1995); Cornelia Hughes Dayton, *Women Before the Bar: Gender, Law, and Society in Connecticut, 1639–1789* (1995); Christopher M. Jedrey, *The World of John Cleaveland: Family and Community in Eighteenth-Century New England* (1979); Sung Bok Kim, *Landlord and Tenant in the Colony of New York: Manorial Society, 1664–1775* (1976); James Lemon, *The Best Poor Man's Country: A Geographical Study of Early Southeastern Pennsylvania* (1972); Laurel T. Ulrich, *Good Wives: Image and Reality in the Lives of Women in Northern New England, 1650–1750* (1982); Daniel Vickers, *Farmers and Fishermen: Two Centuries of Work in Essex County, Massachusetts, 1630–1850* (1994).

Ecological Transformation

Alfred Crosby, *Ecological Imperialism: The Biological Expansion of Europe, 900–1900* (1986); Carolyn Merchant, *Ecological Revolutions: Nature, Gender, and Science in New England* (1989); Anthony Penna, *Nature's Bounty: Historical and Modern Environmental Perspectives* (1999); Timothy Silver, *A New Face on the Countryside: Indians, Colonists, and Slaves in South Atlantic Forests, 1500–1800* (1990); Christopher Vecsey and Robert W. Venables, eds., *American Indian Environments: Ecological Issues in Native American History* (1980).

The Plantation South

T. H. Breen, *Tobacco Culture: The Mentality of the Great Tidewater Planters on the Eve of the Revolution* (1985); Joyce E. Chaplin, *An Anxious Pursuit: Agricultural Innovation and Modernity in the Lower South, 1730–1815* (1993); Paul G. E. Clemens, *The Atlantic Economy and Colonial Maryland's Eastern Shore: From Tobacco to Grain* (1980); Carville Earle, *The Evolution of a Tidewater Settlement System* (1975); Rhys Isaac, *The Transformation of Virginia, 1740–1790* (1982); Allan Kulikoff, *Tobacco and Slaves: The Development of Southern Culture in the Chesapeake, 1680–1800* (1986); Daniel Blake Smith, *Inside the Great House: Planter Family Life in Eighteenth-Century Chesapeake Society* (1980); Gregory Stiverson, *Poverty in the Land of Plenty: Tenancy in Eighteenth-Century Maryland* (1980).

The Urban World of Commerce and Ideas

Bernard Bailyn, *The New England Merchants in the Seventeenth Century* (1955); Gary B. Nash, *The Urban Crucible: Social Change, Political Consciousness, and the Origins of the American Revolution* (1979); Billy G. Smith, *The "Lower Sort": Philadelphia's Laboring People, 1750–1800* (1990); G. B. Warden, *Boston, 1687–1776* (1970); Esmond Wright, *Franklin of Philadelphia* (1986).

The Great Awakening

Patricia Bonomi, *Under the Cope of Heaven: Religion, Society, and Politics in Colonial America* (1986); Alan Heimert, *Religion and the American Mind: From the Great Awakening to the Revolution* (1966); Susan Juster, *Disorderly Women: Sexual Politics and Evangelicalism in Revolutionary New England* (1994); Frank J. Lambert, *"Pedlar in Divinity": George Whitefield and the Transatlantic Revivals* (1994); Henry May, *The American Enlightenment* (1976); Perry Miller, *From Colony to Province* (1953); Harry S. Stout, *The Divine Dramatist: George Whitefield and the Rise of Modern Evangelicalism* (1991); Patricia Tracy, *Jonathan Edwards, Pastor* (1979).

Political Life

Bernard Bailyn, *The Origins of American Politics* (1968); Patricia Bonomi, *A Factious People: Politics and Society in Colonial New York* (1977); William Pencak, *War, Politics, and Revolution in Provincial Massachusetts* (1981); Charles Sydnor, *American Revolutionaries in the Making: Political Practices in Washington's Virginia* (1965); Alan Tully, *Forming American Politics: Ideas, Interests, and Institutions in Colonial New York and Pennsylvania* (1994); Robert Zemsky, *Merchants, Farmers, and River Gods: An Essay on Eighteenth-Century American Politics* (1971).

Fiction and Film

Kenneth Roberts, king of historical novelists on eighteenth-century America, movingly describes the Seven Years' War in *Northwest Passage* (1937); Spencer Tracy starred in the Hollywood version with the same title. James Fenimore Cooper's *The Last of the Mohicans* (1836) is another American classic, but much more to the taste of today's students is Hollywood's movie by the same title (1992), starring Daniel Day-Lewis and Madeleine Stowe.

Suggested Web Sites

http://www.historybuff.com/library/refseventeen.html

History Buff's Reference Library. Brief journalistic essays on newspaper coverage of sixteenth- to eighteenth-century American history.

http://www.virginia.edu/~econ/brock.html

The Leslie Brock Center for the Study of Colonial Currency. This site includes both useful primary and secondary documents on early American currency.

http://www.whiteoak.org/

White Oak Fur Post. This site documents an eighteenth-century fur trading post among the Indians in what would become Minnesota.

http://www.english.udel.edu/lemay/franklin/

Benjamin Franklin Documentary History Website. University of Delaware professor J. A. Leo Lemay tells the story of Franklin's varied life in seven parts on this intriguing site.

http://www.civilization.ca/index1e.html

Canada History. Canada and the United States shared a colonial past but developed differently in the long run. This site is a part of the virtual museum of the Canadian Museum of Civilization Corporation.

http://www.jonathanedwards.com/

Jonathan Edwards. Speeches by this famous preacher of the Great Awakening are on this site.

http://www.ushistoryplace.com

the History place A richly detailed on-line learning environment complete with interactive maps, timelines, history activities, primary source documents, and links to related American history sites.

5

BURSTING *the* COLONIAL BONDS

CHAPTER OUTLINE

In 1758, when he was 21 years old, Ebenezer MacIntosh of Boston laid down his shoemaker's awl and enlisted in the Massachusetts expedition against the French on Lake Champlain. The son of a poor Boston shoemaker who had fought against the French in a previous war, MacIntosh had known poverty all his life. Service against the French offered the hope of plunder or at least an enlistment bounty worth half a year's wages. One among thousands of colonists who fought against the "Gallic menace" in the Seven Years' War, MacIntosh contributed his mite to the climactic Anglo-American struggle that drove the French from North America.

But a greater role lay ahead for the poor Boston shoemaker. Two years after the Peace of Paris in 1763, England imposed a stamp tax on the American colonists. In the massive protests that followed, MacIntosh emerged as the street leader of the Boston crowd. In two nights of the most violent attacks on private property ever witnessed in America, a Boston crowd nearly destroyed the houses of two of the colony's most important officials. On August 14, they tore through the house of Andrew Oliver, a wealthy merchant and the appointed distributor of stamps for Massachusetts. Twelve days later, MacIntosh led the crowd in attacking the mansion of Thomas Hutchinson, a wealthy merchant who served as lieutenant governor and chief justice of Massachusetts. "The mob was so general," wrote the governor, "and so supported that all civil power ceased in an instant."

For the next several months, the power of the poor Boston shoemaker grew. Called "General" MacIntosh and "Captain-General of the Liberty Tree" by his townspeople, he soon sported a militia uniform of gold and blue and a hat laced with gold. Two thousand townsmen followed his commands on November 5, when they marched in orderly ranks through the crooked streets of Boston to demonstrate their solidarity in resisting the hated stamps.

Five weeks later, a crowd publicly humiliated stamp distributor Oliver. Demanding that he announce his resignation before the assembled citizenry, they marched him across town in a driving December rain. With MacIntosh at his elbow, he finally reached the "Liberty Tree," which had become a symbol of resistance to England's new colonial policies. There the aristocratic Oliver ate humble pie. He concluded his resignation remarks with bitter words, hissing sardonically that he would "always think myself very happy when it shall be in my power to serve the people."

"To serve the people" was an ancient idea embedded in English political culture, but it assumed new meaning in the American colonies during the epic third quarter of the eighteenth century. Few colonists in 1750 held even a faint desire to break the connection with England, and fewer still might have predicted the form of government that 13 independent states in an independent nation might fashion. Yet in a whirlwind of events, two million colonists moved haltingly toward a showdown with mighty England. Little-known men like Ebenezer MacIntosh as well as his well-known and historically celebrated townsmen Samuel Adams, John Hancock, and John Adams were part of the struggle. Collectively, ordinary people such as MacIntosh influenced—and in fact sometimes even dictated—the revolutionary movement in the colonies. Though we read and speak mostly of a small group of "founding fathers," the wellsprings of the American Revolution can be fully discovered only among a variety of people from different social groups, occupations, regions, and religions.

This chapter addresses the tensions in late colonial society, the imperial crisis that followed the Seven Years' War (in the colonies often called the French and Indian War), and the tumultuous decade that led to the "shot heard round the world" fired at Concord Bridge in April 1775. It portrays the origins of a dual American Revolution. Ebenezer MacIntosh, in leading the Boston mob against crown officers and colonial collaborators who tried to implement a new colonial policy after 1763, helped set in motion a revolutionary movement to restore ancient liberties thought by the Americans to be under deliberate attack in England. This movement eventually escalated into the war for American independence.

But MacIntosh's Boston followers were also venting years of resentment at the accumulation of wealth and power by Boston's aristocratic elite. Behind every swing of the ax, every shattered crystal goblet and splintered mahogany chair, lay the fury of a Bostonian who had seen the city's conservative elite try to dismantle the town meeting, suffered economic hardship, and lost faith that opportunity and just relations still prevailed in his town. This sentiment, which called for the reform of a colonial

A View of the Town of Concord (April 1775), attributed to Ralph Earle. *(Courtesy Concord Museum, Concord, MA)*

society that had become corrupt, self-indulgent, and dominated by an elite, fed an idealistic commitment to reshape American society even while severing the colonial bond. As distinguished from the war for independence, this was the American Revolution.

THE CLIMACTIC SEVEN YEARS' WAR

After a brief period of peace following King George's War (1744–1748), France and England fought the fourth, largest, and by far most significant of the wars for empire that had begun in the late seventeenth century. Known variously as the Seven Years' War, the French and Indian War, and the Great War for Empire, this global conflict in part represented a showdown for control of North America between the Atlantic Ocean and the Mississippi River. In North America, the Anglo-American forces ultimately prevailed, and their victory dramatically affected the lives of all the diverse people living in the huge region east of the Mississippi—English, German, and Scots-Irish settlers in the English colonies; French and Spanish colonizers in Canada, Florida, and interior North America; African slaves in a variety of settlements; and, perhaps most of all, the powerful Native American tribes of the interior.

War and the Management of Empire

After the Glorious Revolution of 1688, England began constructing a more coherent imperial administration. In 1696, a professional Board of Trade replaced the old Lords of Trade; the Treasury strengthened the customs service; and Parliament created overseas vice-admiralty courts, which functioned without juries to prosecute smugglers who evaded the trade regulations set forth in the Navigation Acts. Parliament began playing a more active role after the reign of Queen Anne (1702–1714) and continued to do so when weak, German-speaking King George I came to the throne. Royal governors received greater powers and more detailed instructions and came under more insistent demands from the Board of Trade to enforce British policies. England was quietly installing the machinery of imperial management and a corps of colonial bureaucrats.

The best test of an effectively organized state is its ability to wage war. Four times between 1689 and 1763, England matched its strength against France, its archrival in North America and the Caribbean. These wars of empire had tremendous consequences for all involved—the home governments, their colonial subjects, and the Indian tribes drawn into the bloody conflicts.

We have already seen (in Chapter 3) how the Peace of Utrecht, which ended Queen Anne's War (1702–1713), brought victor's spoils of great importance to England. The generation of peace that followed was really only a time-out, which both England and France used in the years until 1739 to strengthen their war-making capacity. Britain's productive and efficiently governed New World colonies made important contributions. Though known as a period of "salutary neglect," this was actually an era when king and Parliament increased their control over colonial affairs.

Concerned mainly with economic regulation, Parliament added new articles such as fur, copper, hemp, tar, and turpentine to the list of items produced in America that had to be shipped to England before being exported to another country. Parliament also curtailed colonial production of articles important to England's economy: woolen cloth (1699), beaver hats (1732), and finished iron products (1750). Most important, Parliament passed the Molasses Act in 1733. Attempting to stop the trade between New England and the French West Indies, where Yankee traders exchanged fish, beef, and pork for molasses to convert into rum, Parliament imposed a prohibitive duty of 6 pence per gallon on French slave-produced molasses. This turned many of New England's largest merchants and distillers into smugglers and schooled them for a generation—along with their ship captains, crews, and allied waterfront artisans—in defying royal authority.

The generation of peace ended abruptly in 1739 when England declared war on Spain. The immediate cause was the ear of an English sea captain, Robert Jenkins. Spanish authorities had deprived him of that appendage eight years before for smuggling in their colonies. Encouraged by his government, Jenkins publicly displayed his pickled ear in 1738 to whip up war fever against Spain, which English policymakers wanted to chasten for transferring certain commercial privileges from England to France. The real cause of the war, however, was England's determination to continue its drive toward commercial domination of the Atlantic basin.

Five years after the war with Spain began in 1739, it merged into a much larger conflict between England and France, in Europe called the War of Austrian Succession (1744–1748). Its scale far exceeded that of previous conflicts. As military priorities became paramount, the need increased for discipline within the empire. In addition, unprecedented military expenditures led Britain to ask its West Indian and American colonies to share in the costs of defending—and extending—the empire and to tailor their behavior to the needs of the home country.

Outbreak of Hostilities

The tension between English and French colonists in North America, which reached back to the early seventeenth century, was intensified by the spectacular population growth of the English colonies: from 250,000 in 1700 to 1.25 million in 1750, and to 1.75 million in the next decade. Three-quarters of the increase came in the colonies south of New York, propelling thousands of land-hungry settlers toward the mountain gaps in the Appalachians in search of farmland.

Promoting this westward rush were fur traders and land speculators. The fur traders were penetrating a French-influenced region, where they offered native trappers and hunters better prices and higher-quality goods than the French. In the 1740s and 1750s, speculators (including many future revolutionary leaders) formed land companies to capitalize on the seaboard population explosion. The farther west the settlement line moved, the closer it came to the western trading empire of the French and their Indian allies.

Colonial penetration of the Ohio valley in the 1740s established the first English outposts in the continental heartland. This challenged the French where their interest was vital. While the English controlled most of the eastern coastal plain of North America, the French had nearly encircled them to the west by building a chain of trading posts and forts along the St. Lawrence River, through the Great Lakes, and southward into the Ohio and Mississippi valleys all the way to New Orleans.

Challenged by the English, the French resisted. They attempted to block further English expansion by constructing new forts in the Ohio valley and by prying some tribes loose from their new English connections. The English, a French emissary warned a western tribe in the 1750s, "are much less anxious to take away your peltries than to become masters of your lands, and your blindness is so great that you do not perceive that the very hand that caresses you will scourge you like negroes and slaves, so soon as it will have got possession of your lands."

By 1755, the French had driven the English traders out of the Ohio River valley and established forts as far east as the fork of the Ohio River, near present-day Pittsburgh. There, at Fort Duquesne, the French smartly rebuffed an ambitious young Virginia militia colonel named George Washington, dispatched by his colony's government to expel them from the region.

The Iroquois warrior depicted here shows the blending of Indian and European weaponry. His snowshoes and the war club held in his right hand are native in origin. His English musket, slung over his shoulder, and the steel axe fastened at his belt are European trade items. *(© Collection of the New-York Historical Society)*

Men in the capitals of Europe, not in the colonies, made the decision to force a showdown in the interior of North America. England's powerful merchants, supported by American clients, had been emboldened by English success in the previous war against the French. Now, they argued, the time was ripe to destroy the French overseas trade. Convinced, the English ministry ordered several thousand troops to America in 1754; in France, 3,000 regulars embarked to meet the English challenge.

With war looming, the colonial governments attempted to coordinate efforts. Representatives of seven colonies met with 150 Iroquois chiefs at Albany, New York, in June 1754 to woo the powerful Iroquois out of their neutrality and plan a colonial union. Both failed. The Iroquois left the conference with 30 wagonloads of gifts but made no firm commitment to fight against the French. Benjamin Franklin designed a plan for an intercolonial government to manage Indian affairs, provide for defense, and have the power to pass laws and levy taxes. But even the clever woodcut displayed in the *Pennsylvania Gazette* that pictured a chopped-up snake with the insignia "Join or Die" failed to overcome the long-standing jealousies

The Seven Years' War, 1756–1763

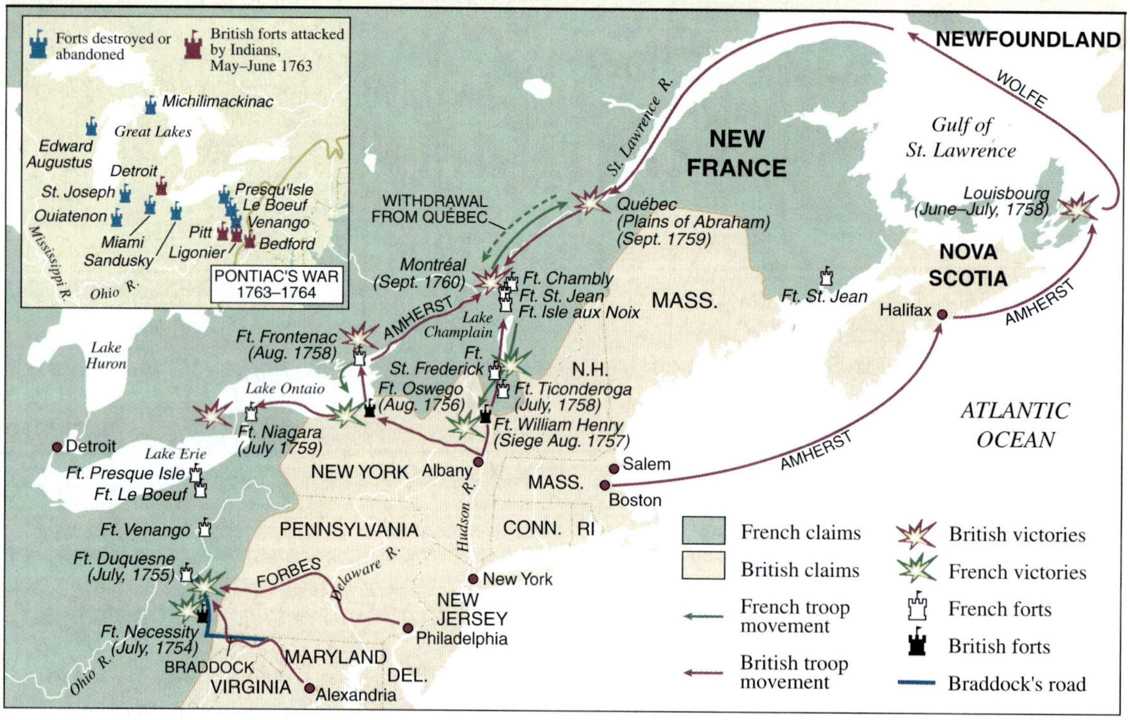

The British-American victory over France and its Indian allies in the Seven Years' War did not bring peace on the western frontier. After the war, Pontiac lead pan-Indian attacks on settlers and British forts. As the map shows, the war began in 1754, two years ahead of the usual date given.

that had thwarted previous attempts at intercolony cooperation. "Everyone cries a union is necessary," sighed Franklin, "but when they come to the manner and form of the union, their weak noodles are perfectly distracted."

With his British army and hundreds of American recruits, General Edward Braddock slogged across Virginia in the summer of 1755, each day cutting a few miles of road through forests and across mountains. A headstrong professional soldier who regarded his European battlefield experience as sufficient for war in the American wilderness, Braddock had contempt for the woods-wise French regiments and their stealthy Indian allies.

As Braddock neared Fort Duquesne, the entire French force and the British suddenly surprised one another in the forest. The French had 218 soldiers and militiamen and 637 Indian allies, while Braddock commanded twice that many redcoats but few Indians. Pouring murderous fire into Braddock's tidy lines, the French and Indians won. Just before he fell, mortally wounded (perhaps by one of his own angry men), Braddock presumably learned that Indians were essential allies and fully capable of pitched battle. Two-thirds of the British and Americans were killed or wounded, and Washington, his uniform pierced by four bullets, had two horses shot from beneath him. Although they had 1,000 men in reserve down the road, the Anglo-American force beat a hasty, ignominious retreat.

Throughout the summer, French-supplied Indian raiders torched the Virginia and Pennsylvania backcountry. "The roads are full of starved, naked, indigent multitudes," observed one officer. One French triumph followed another during the next two years. The victory over Braddock's army had brought almost every tribe north of the Ohio River to the French side. Never was disunity within the English colonies so painfully evident. With its Indian allies, French Canada, only 70,000 inhabitants strong, had badly battered a million and a half colonists supported by the British army.

The turning point in the war came after the energetic William Pitt became England's secretary of state in 1757. "I believe that I can save this nation and that no one else can," he boasted, abandoning Europe as the main theater of action against the French and throwing his nation's military might into the American campaign. The forces he dispatched to America in 1757–1758 dwarfed all preceding commitments: about 23,000 British troops and a huge fleet with 14,000 mariners. But even forces of this magnitude, when asked to engage the enemy in the forests of North America, were not necessarily sufficient to the task without Indian support, or at least neutrality. "A doubt remains not," proclaimed one English official in the colonies, "that the prosperity of our colonies on the continent will stand or fall with our interest and favour among them."

Tribal Strategies

Anglo-American leaders knew that the support of the Iroquois Confederacy and their tributary tribes was crucial. Iroquois allegiance could be secured in only two ways: through purchase or by a demonstration of power that would convince the tribes that the English would prevail with or without their assistance. The Iroquois understood that their interest lay in playing off one European power against the other. "To preserve the balance between us and the French," wrote a New York politician, "is the great ruling principle of modern Indian politics."

The first English stratagem for securing Iroquois support failed in 1754 when colonial negotiators heaped gifts on the Iroquois chiefs at the Albany Congress but received in return only tantalizing half-promises of support against the French. The second alternative fizzled because the English proved militarily inferior to the French in the first three years of the war. Hence, the westernmost of the Iroquois Six Nations, the Seneca, fought on the side of the French in the campaigns of 1757 and 1758, while the Delaware, a tributary tribe, harassed the Pennsylvania frontier.

In 1758, the huge English military buildup began to produce victories. The largest army ever assembled in North America to that point, some 15,000 British and American soldiers, including the Bostonian Ebenezer MacIntosh, suffered terrible casualties and withdrew from the field after attempting to storm Fort Ticonderoga on Lake Champlain in June 1758. Then the tide turned. Troops under Sir Jeffrey Amherst captured Louisbourg, on Cape Breton Island, and Fort Duquesne fell to another army of 6,000 led by General John Forbes. The resolute Pitt had mobilized the fighting power of the English nation and put more men in the field than existed in all of New France. The colonists, in turn, had put aside intramural squabbling long enough to overwhelm the badly outnumbered French.

The victories of 1758 finally moved the Iroquois away from neutrality. Added incentive to join the Anglo-American side came when the English navy bottled up French shipping in the St. Lawrence River, cutting the Iroquois off from French trade goods. By early 1759, foreseeing a French defeat in North America, the Iroquois pledged 800 warriors for an attack on Fort Niagara, the strategic French trading depot on Lake Ontario.

The storming of French Quebec in 1759 was the decisive blow in England's campaign to end the French domination of Canada and the lands west of the Appalachians. The heroic exploits of General James Wolfe made him a hero throughout England and the colonies. (A View of the Taking of Quebec, September 13, 1759, *National Army Museum, London*)

Even dramatic Anglo-American victories did not always guarantee Indian support. In the South, backcountry skirmishes with the Cherokee from Virginia to South Carolina turned into a costly war from 1759 to 1761. In 1760, the Cherokee mauled a British army of 1,300 under Amherst. The following summer, a much larger Anglo-American force invaded Cherokee country, burning towns and food supplies. By this time, English control of the sea had interrupted the Indians' supply of French arms. Beset by food shortages, lack of ammunition, and a smallpox epidemic, the Cherokee finally sued for peace.

Other Anglo-American victories in 1759, the "year of miracles," decided the outcome of the bloodiest war yet known in the New World. The capture of Fort Niagara, the critical link in the system of forts that joined the French inland empire with the Atlantic, was followed by the conquest of sugar-rich Martinique in the West Indies. The culminating stroke came with a dramatic victory at Quebec. Led by 32-year-old General James Wolfe, 5,000 troops scaled a rocky cliff and overcame the French on the Plains of Abraham. The capture of Montreal late in 1760 completed the shattering of French power in North America. The theater of operations shifted to the Caribbean, where fighting continued, as in Europe, for three years longer. But in the American colonies, the old English dream of ridding the continent of the Gallic menace had finally come true.

Consequences of War

The strokes of a few diplomats' pens in 1762–1763 brought astounding changes to European and Indian peoples who for decades had been involved in dizzying complex and shifting relationships that alternated between conflict and cooperation over vast stretches of North American territory. The Spanish, who had tried to check the expansive French southern influence directed from Louisiana, now acquired New Orleans and all of the vast Louisiana territory west of the Mississippi. Although this could provide a buffer against English aspirations in the continent's heartland, Spain's king surrendered Spanish Florida to the British—a pragmatic decision because England agreed to compensate Spain with Havana, which the British had captured during the war.

For the interior Indian tribes, the Treaty of Paris ending the Seven Years' War in 1763 dealt a harsh blow. Unlike the coastal Native Americans, whose population and independence had ebbed rapidly through contact with the colonizers, the inland tribes had maintained their strength and sometimes even grown more unified through relations with settlers. Although they came to depend on European trade goods, Native Americans had turned this commercial connection to their advantage so long as more than one source of trade goods existed.

The Indian play-off system came to a crashing halt when the French ceded Canada and all territory east of the Mississippi, except for New Orleans, to England in the Treaty of Paris. For the interior tribes, only one source of trade goods remained. Two centuries of European rivalry for control of eastern North America ended abruptly. Iroquois, Cherokee, Creek, Ojibway, Shawnee, and scores of other interior tribes were now forced to adjust to this reality.

After making peace, the English government launched a new policy designed to separate Native Americans and colonizers by creating a racial boundary roughly following the crestline of the Appalachian Mountains from Maine to Georgia. The Proclamation of 1763 reserved all land west of the line for Indian nations. White settlers already living beyond the Appalachians were told to withdraw to the east.

Though well intended, this attempt to legislate interracial accord failed completely. Even before the proclamation was issued, the Ottawa chief Pontiac, concerned that the elimination of the French threatened the old treaty and gift-giving system, had gathered together many of the northern tribes that had aided the French assaults on the English forts during the Seven Years' War. Although Pontiac's pan-Indian movement to drive the British out of the Ohio valley collapsed in 1764, it served notice that the interior tribes would not passively watch the invasion of their lands after the French withdrawal from North America.

The English government could sternly command colonial governors to observe the Proclamation of 1763, but it could not enforce its policy. Staggering under an immense wartime debt, England decided to maintain only small army garrisons in America to regulate the interior. Nor could royal governors stop land speculators and settlers from privately purchasing land from trans-Appalachian tribes or from simply encroaching on their land. Under such circumstances, the western frontier seethed after 1763.

Although the epic Anglo-American victory redrew the map of North America, the war also had important social and economic effects on colonial society. It convinced the colonists of their growing strength, yet left them debt-ridden and weakened in manpower. The wartime economy spurred economic development and poured British capital into the colonies, yet rendered them more vulnerable to cyclic fluctuations in the British economy.

Military contracts, for example, brought prosperity to most colonies during the war years. Huge orders for ships, arms, uniforms, and provisions enriched northern merchants and provided good prices for farmers as well. Urban artisans enjoyed full employment and high

At the Treaty of Paris in 1763, France surrendered huge claims west of the Mississippi River to Spain and east of the river to England. England also acquired Florida from Spain.

wages, as tailors' needles flashed to meet clothing contracts, shoemakers stitched for an unprecedented demand for shoes, and bakers found armies clamoring for bread. Privateers—privately outfitted ships licensed by colonial governments to attack enemy shipping—enriched the fortunate few. On a single voyage in 1758, John MacPherson snared 18 French ships. The prize money was lavish enough to allow this son of a Scottish immigrant to pour £14,000 into creating a country estate outside Philadelphia, to which he retired in splendor.

The war, however, required heavy taxes and took a huge human toll. Privateering carried many fortune seekers to a watery grave, and the wilderness campaigns from 1755 to 1760 claimed thousands of lives. Garrison life brought wracking fevers (which claimed more victims than enemy weapons), and battlefield medical treatment was too primitive to save many of the wounded. Boston's Thomas Hancock accurately predicted at the beginning of the war that "this province is spirited to [send] every third man to do the work of the Lord." But the Lord's work was expensive. Thomas Pownall, assuming the governorship of Massachusetts in August 1757, found not the "rich, flourishing, powerful, enterprizing" colony he expected but a province "ruined and undone."

The magnitude of human loss in Boston indicates the war's impact. The wartime muster lists show that nearly every working-class Bostonian tasted military service at some point during the long war. When peace came, Boston had a deficit of almost 700 men in a town of about 2,000 families. The high rate of war widowhood feminized poverty and required expanded poor relief to maintain husbandless women and fatherless children.

Peace ended the amount of new casualties but also brought depression. The British forces in the American theater numbered about 40,000 at the conclusion of the North American campaigns. With their departure for the Caribbean in 1760, the economy slumped badly, especially in the coastal towns. "The tippling soldiery that used to help us out at a dead lift," mused a New York merchant, "are gone to drink [rum]in a warmer region, the place of its production."

The greatest hardships after 1760 fell on laboring people, although even some wealthy merchants went

Recovering the Past

POETRY

Poetry is one of the most ancient and universal of the arts. Making its effect by the rhythmic sound and imagery of its language, poetry often expresses romantic love, grief, and responses to nature. But other kinds of poetry interest historians: reflections of human experience, often expressed with deep emotion; and political verses often written to serve propagandistic goals. For generations, American historians have drawn on poetry to recapture feelings, ideas, and group experiences. For example, American Indian creation myths have often taken poetic form; the poems of Anne Bradstreet and Michael Wigglesworth in seventeenth-century Massachusetts tell us much about Puritan mentality and attitudes on topics running from marriage to death; the poetry of the American Transcendentalists tells us about nineteenth-century notions of heroism and who was admired; and Langston Hughes, Arno Bontemps, and other poets of the Harlem Renaissance have expressed through poetry the bittersweet nature of the African American experience. All this material is grist for the historian's mill.

The revolutionary generation created poetry of great interest to historians. The newspapers of several port cities published weekly "Poet's Corner" satires, drinking songs, and versed commentary on the issues of the day. Verse was widely used to provoke public discussion; in 1767 poets prompted the boycott of British goods to obtain Parliament's reversal of the hated Townshend duties.

A year later, Philadelphia's John Dickinson composed a "Liberty Song" that became the first set of verses learned in all the colonies. Boston's Sons of Liberty began using this "Liberty Song" in annual ceremonies celebrating their resistance to the Stamp Act. Soon the verses were printed in newspapers throughout the colonies and widely used in public gatherings. Set to music and easily learned, the verses cultivated anti-British feeling and a sense of the need for intercolonial cooperation:

> *COME join Hand in Hand, brave AMERICANS all,*
> *And rouse your bold Hearts at fair LIBERTY'S Call;*
> *No* tyrannous *Acts shall suppress your* just Claim,
> *Or stain with* Dishonor *AMEÏRICA's Name.*

Of all the poets of the revolutionary era, none has fascinated today's historians more than Phillis Wheatley, a young slave in Boston who wrote her first poem at age fourteen in 1767. Within six years, she became North America's first published black poet. Boston's "Ethiopian poetess" had been brought from Africa to Boston at age seven and purchased by a prospering tailor named John Wheatley. Soon her master and his wife discovered that she was a prodigy. Learning English in sixteen months so well that she could read the most difficult passages of the Bible, she soon showed an uncanny gift for writing. Much of her writing was inspired by deep religious feelings, but she soon was caught up in the dramatic events in Boston that were bringing revolution closer and closer. In "To the King's Most Excellent Majesty," she saluted King George III in poetry for repealing the Stamp Act; in "On the Death of Mr. Snider [Seider], Murder'd by Richardson," she lambasted the British customs officer who murdered a teenage member of a crowd protesting the British soldiers who occupied Boston in 1768.

Wheatley was anything but radical. She had so thoroughly imbibed Christianity from her master and mistress that she wrote in one of her first poems that "Twas mercy brought me from my *Pagan* land." Many times she used poetry to implore slaves to "fly to Christ." But by 1772, she was inserting a muffled plea for an end of slavery in her odes to American rights and American resistance to British policies.

That Wheatley's poems were published in London in 1773 is remarkable. Women were not supposed to write publicly in the eighteenth century, and certainly not black women. Nonetheless, her master, supported by Boston friends and proud of his slave prodigy, shipped a sheaf of poems to a bookseller in England, who obtained the support of the Countess of Huntingdon for publishing them. They appeared under the title *Poems on Various Subjects, Religious and Moral.* Even more remarkable was that Wheatley, only 20 years old, took ship to London to see her book come off the press. Her master and mistress financed the trip, hoping that sea air would clear her clogged lungs. There she was introduced to important reformers and public dignitaries, received a copy of Milton's *Paradise Lost* from the lord mayor of London, and met with Benjamin Franklin. She returned to Boston in 1774.

Read the two poems below: Wheatley's "On the Death of Mr. Snider [Seider], Murder'd by Richardson," composed

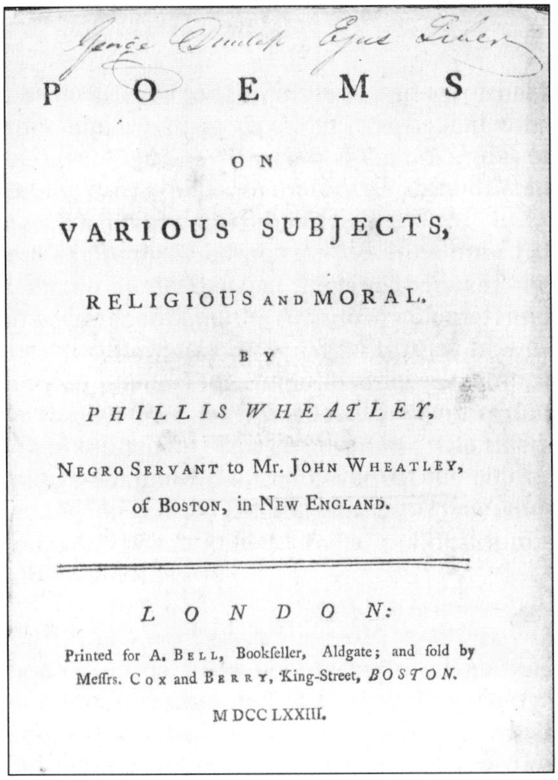

POEMS

ON

VARIOUS SUBJECTS,

RELIGIOUS AND MORAL.

BY

PHILLIS WHEATLEY,

NEGRO SERVANT to Mr. JOHN WHEATLEY,
of BOSTON, in NEW ENGLAND.

LONDON:

Printed for A. BELL, Bookſeller, Aldgate; and ſold by
Meſſrs. COX and BERRY, King-Street, *BOSTON.*

M DCC LXXIII.

(Left) Wheatley worshiped at Old South Meeting House, which held some 5,000 people. In the 1770s, people frequently gathered there for political rallies and deliberations. This partly explains Wheatley's growing interest in the political battles raging in Boston. (Right) Wheatley's patroness in England specifically requested a drawing of Phillis for the frontispiece of this volume of poetry. Scipio Moorhead, slave of Boston's Presbyterian minister, did the drawing. Wheatley's mistress, Susannah Wheatley, called it a fine likeness. *(From the copy in the Rare Book Collection, The University of North Carolina at Chapel Hill)*

in 1770; and her poem addressed to the King's minister in charge of colonial affairs, penned two years later. As modern readers, you may find the poetry stilted, but Wheatley's style was modeled on poetic conventions of the eighteenth century. What change can you discern in Wheatley's political consciousness between 1770 and 1772? Do you consider her poem on Seider's murder by a British customs officer propagandistic? How does she relate the plight of enslaved Africans to the American colonists' struggle? More generally, how effective do you think poetry is in arousing sentiment and mobilizing political energy? Can you think of verse serving as lyrics in popular protest music today?

On the Death of Mr. Snider, Murder'd by Richardson (1770)

In heaven's eternal court it was decreed
How the first martyr for the cause should bleed
To clear the country of the hated brood
We whet his courage for the common good.
Long hid before, a vile infernal here
Prevents Achilles in his mid career
Wherev'r this fury darts his Poisonous breath
All are endanger'd to the shafts of death

To the Right Honourable William,
Earl of Dartmouth, His Majesty's Principal
Secretary of State for North America (1772)

HAIL, happy day, when, smiling like the morn,
Fair Freedom *rose* New-England *to adorn:*
The northern clime beneath her genial ray,
Dartmouth, *congratulates thy blissful sway:*
Elate with hope her race no longer mourns,
Each soul expands, each grateful bosom burns,
While in thine hand with pleasure we behold
The silken reigns, and Freedom's *charms unfold.*
No more, America, *in mournful strain*
Of wrongs, and grievance unredress'd complain,
No longer shalt thou dread the iron chain,
Which wanton Tyranny with lawless hand
Had made, and with it meant t' enslave the land.
Should you, my lord, while you peruse my song,
Wonder from whence my love of Freedom *sprung,*
Whence flow these wishes for the common good,
By feeling hearts alone best understood,
I, young in life, by seeming cruel fate
Was snatch'd from Afric's *fancy'd happy seat:*
What pangs excruciating must molest,
What sorrows labour in my parent's breast?
Steel'd was that soul and by no misery mov'd
That from a father seiz'd his babe belov'd :
Such, such my case. And can I then but pray
Others may never feel tyrannic sway?

bankrupt. Those with the smallest wages had the thinnest savings to cushion them against hard times. How quickly their security could evaporate showed in Philadelphia, where early in the contractionary cycle many poor people, unable to pay their property taxes, were "disposing of their huts and lots to others more wealthy than themselves." The economic security of the middle sector of society also slipped, as established craftsmen and shopkeepers were caught between rising prices and reduced demand for their goods and services. A New York artisan expressed a common lament in 1762. Thankfully, he still had employment, he wrote in the *New-York Gazette.* But despite every effort at unceasing labor and frugal living, he had fallen into poverty and found it "beyond my ability to support my family . . . [which] can scarcely appear with decency or have necessaries to subsist." His situation, he added, "is really the case with many of the inhabitants of this city."

The Seven Years' War paved the way, though not foreseen at the time, for a far larger conflict in the next generation. The legislative assemblies, for example, which had been flexing their muscles at the expense of the governors in earlier decades, accelerated their bid for political power. During wartime, knowing that their governors must obtain military appropriations, they extracted concessions as the price for raising revenues. The war also trained a new group of military and political leaders. In carrying out military operations on a scale unknown in the colonies and in shouldering heavier political responsibilities, men such as George Washington, Samuel Adams, Benjamin Franklin, Patrick Henry, and Christopher Gadsden acquired the experience that would serve them well in the future.

The Seven Years' War, in spite of the severe costs, left many of the colonists buoyant. New Englanders rejoiced at the final victory over the "Papist enemy of the North." Frontiersmen, fur traders, and land speculators also celebrated the French withdrawal, for the West now appeared open for exploitation. This "Garden of the World," trumpeted a Boston almanac publisher, was larger than France, Germany, and Poland combined, "and all well provided with rivers, a very fine wholesome air, a rich soil, . . . and all things necessary for the conveniency and delight of life." A new frontier now seemed to await those whom opportunity had passed by on the crowded seaboard.

The colonists also felt a new sense of identity after the war. Surveying a world free of French and Spanish threats, they could not help but reassess the advantages and disadvantages of subordination to England. The colonists would soon discover, a French diplomat predicted at the war's end, "that they stand no longer in need of your protection. You will call on them to contribute towards supporting the burden which they have helped to bring on you; they will answer you by shaking off all dependence."

Although the American colonists inched toward thinking of themselves as a people capable of standing alone, the British viewed the matter differently at the end of the Seven Years' War. From their perspective, the colonists were unreliable and had fought poorly. Many royal army officers who had fought alongside the Americans had little but contempt for the "martial virtue" of the colonists. "He could take a thousand grenadiers to America," boasted one officer, "and geld all the males, partly by force and partly by a little coaxing."

THE CRISIS WITH ENGLAND

George Grenville became the chief minister of England's 25-year-old king, George III, at the end of the Seven Years' War. He inherited a national debt that had billowed from £75 million to £145 million and a nation of wearied taxpayers. To reduce the debt, Grenville proposed new taxes in England and others in America, asking the colonists to bear their share of running the empire. Grenville's particular concern was financing the 10,000 British regulars left in North America after 1763 to police French-speaking Canada and the frontier and to remind the unruly American subjects that they were still beholden to the crown. Grenville's revenue program initiated a rift between England and its colonies that a dozen years later would become a revolution.

Sugar, Currency, and Stamps

In 1764, Grenville pushed through Parliament several bills that in combination pressed hard on colonial economies. First came the Revenue Act (or Sugar Act) of 1764. While reducing the tax on imported French molasses from six to three pence per gallon, it added a number of colonial products to the list of commodities that could be sent only to England. It also required American shippers to post bonds guaranteeing observance of the trade regulations before loading their cargoes. Finally, it strengthened the vice-admiralty courts, where violators of the trade acts were prosecuted.

Many colonial legislatures grumbled about the Sugar Act because a strictly enforced duty of three pence per gallon on molasses pinched more than the loosely enforced six-pence duty. But only New York objected that any tax by Parliament to raise revenue (rather than to control trade) violated the rights of overseas English subjects who were unrepresented in Parliament.

Next came the Currency Act. In 1751, Parliament had forbidden the New England colonies to issue paper money as legal tender, and now it extended that prohibition to all the colonies. In a colonial economy chronically short of hard cash, this constricted trade.

The move to tighten up the machinery of empire confused the colonists because many of the new regulations came from Parliament. Before, Parliament had let the king, his ministers, and the Board of Trade run overseas affairs. In a world where history taught that power and liberty were perpetually at war, generations of colonists had viewed Parliament as a bastion of English liberty, the bulwark against despotic political rule. Now Parliament began to seem like a violator of colonial rights.

In protesting new parliamentary regulations, colonial leaders were hobbled by uncertainty concerning where Parliament's authority began and ended in administering the colonies. The colonists had always implicitly accepted parliamentary power overseas because it was easier to evade distasteful trade regulations than to contest this power. But the exact limits of that authority were vague.

After Parliament passed the Sugar Act in 1764, Grenville announced his intention to extend to America the stamp duties—already imposed in England—but he gave the colonies a year to suggest alternative ways of raising revenue. The colonies objected strenuously to the proposed stamp tax, but none provided another plan. Knowing that colonial property taxes were slight compared with those in England, Grenville dismissed the petitions that poured in from the colonies and drove the bill through Parliament. The Stamp Act became effective in November 1765. It required revenue stamps on every newspaper, pamphlet, almanac, legal document, liquor license, college diploma, pack of playing cards, and pair of dice.

Colonial reaction to the Stamp Act ranged from disgruntled submission to mass defiance. The breadth of the reaction shocked the British government—and many Americans as well. Lieutenant Governor Hutchinson of Massachusetts believed that "there is not a family between Canada and Pensacola that has not heard the name of the Stamp Act and but very few . . . but what have some formidable apprehensions of it." In many cases, resistance involved not only discontent over England's tightening of the screws on the American colonies but also internal resentments born out of local events. Especially in the cities, the defiance of authority and destruction of property by people from the middle and lower ranks redefined the dynamics of politics, setting the stage for a ten-year internal struggle for control among the various social elements alarmed by the new English policies.

Stamp Act Riots

The Virginia House of Burgesses was the first legislature to react to the news of the Stamp Act, which arrived in April 1765. Virginians were already on edge because a severe decline in tobacco prices and heavy war-related taxes had mired most planters in debt. In late 1764, the burgesses had strenuously objected to the proposed stamp tax, citing the economic hardship it would cause and arguing that it was their "inherent" right to be taxed only by their own consent.

The Stamp Act enraged a group of Virginia's young burgesses. Led by 29-year-old Patrick Henry, a fiery lawyer newly elected from a frontier county, the House of Burgesses in May 1765 debated seven strongly worded resolutions. Old-guard burgesses regarded some of them as treasonable. The legislature finally adopted the four more moderate resolves, including one proclaiming Virginia's right to impose taxes. But they rejected the other resolves, which declared it "illegal, unconstitutional, and unjust" for anybody outside Virginia to lay taxes; asserted that Virginians did not have to obey any externally imposed tax law; and labeled as an "enemy to this, his Majesty's colony" anyone denying Virginia's exclusive right to tax its inhabitants.

Many burgesses had left for home before Henry introduced his resolutions, so less than a quarter of Virginia's legislators voted for the four moderate resolves. But within a month, all seven resolutions were broadcast in the newspapers of other colonies. Henry and the aggressive young burgesses had hurled words of defiance at Parliament for other colonies to reflect on and match.

Governor Francis Bernard of Massachusetts called the Virginia resolves an "alarm bell for the disaffected." Events in Boston in August 1765 amply confirmed his view. On August 14, Bostonians awoke to find an effigy of stamp distributor Andrew Oliver, dressed in rags, hanging from an elm tree in the south end of town. When the sheriff tried to remove it at the order of Lieutenant Governor Thomas Hutchinson, Oliver's brother-in-law, a hostile crowd intervened. In the evening, working men began gathering for a mock funeral. Led by Ebenezer MacIntosh, they cut down Oliver's effigy and boisterously carried it through the streets. Then they leveled Oliver's new brick office on the wharves, rumored to be the distribution point for the hated stamps.

As night fell, the crowd reduced Oliver's luxurious mansion to a shambles. The stamp distributor promptly asked to be relieved of his commission. Twelve days later, MacIntosh led the crowd again in an all-night bout of destruction of the handsomely appointed homes of two British officials and

From the time of his election to the Virginia House of Burgesses at the age of 29, Patrick Henry was an outspoken proponent of American rights. In this portrait, he pleads a case at a county courthouse crowded with local planters. (*Virginia Historical Society, Richmond, VA*)

Hutchinson, a haughty man, who was as unpopular with the common people as his great-great-grandmother, Anne Hutchinson, had been popular. Military men "who have seen towns sacked by the enemy," one observer reported, "declare they never before saw an instance of such fury."

In attacking the property of men associated with the stamp tax, the Boston crowd demonstrated not only its opposition to parliamentary policy but also its resentment of a local elite that for years had disdained lower-class political participation and had publicly denounced the working poor for their supposed lack of industry and frugality. For decades, ordinary Bostonians had aligned politically with the Boston "caucus," which led the colony's "popular party" against conservative aristocrats such as Hutchinson and Oliver. They had also read in the *Boston Gazette* that the new parliamentary legislation had been proposed by "mean mercenary hirelings among yourselves, who for a little filthy lucre would at any time betray every right, liberty, and privilege of their fellow subjects."

But the "rage-intoxicated rabble" had suddenly broken away from the leaders of the popular party and gone further than they had intended. Hutchinson was one of their main targets. Characterized by young lawyer John Adams as "very ambitious and avaricious," Hutchinson was, in the popular view, chief among the "mean mercenary hirelings" of the British. In the aftermath of the destruction of his house—what Governor Bernard called "a war of plunder, of taking away the distinction between rich and poor"—the more cautious political leaders knew that they would have to struggle to regain control of the protest movement.

Violent protests against the Stamp Act also wracked New York and Newport, Rhode Island. Leading the resistance were groups calling themselves the Sons of Liberty, composed mostly of artisans, shopkeepers, and ordinary citizens. Protest took a more dignified form at the Stamp Act Congress, called by Massachusetts and attended by representatives of nine colonies, who met in New York in October 1765. English authorities branded this first self-initiated intercolonial convention a "dangerous tendency." The delegates formulated 12 restrained resolutions that accepted Parliament's right to legislate for the colonies but denied its right to tax them directly.

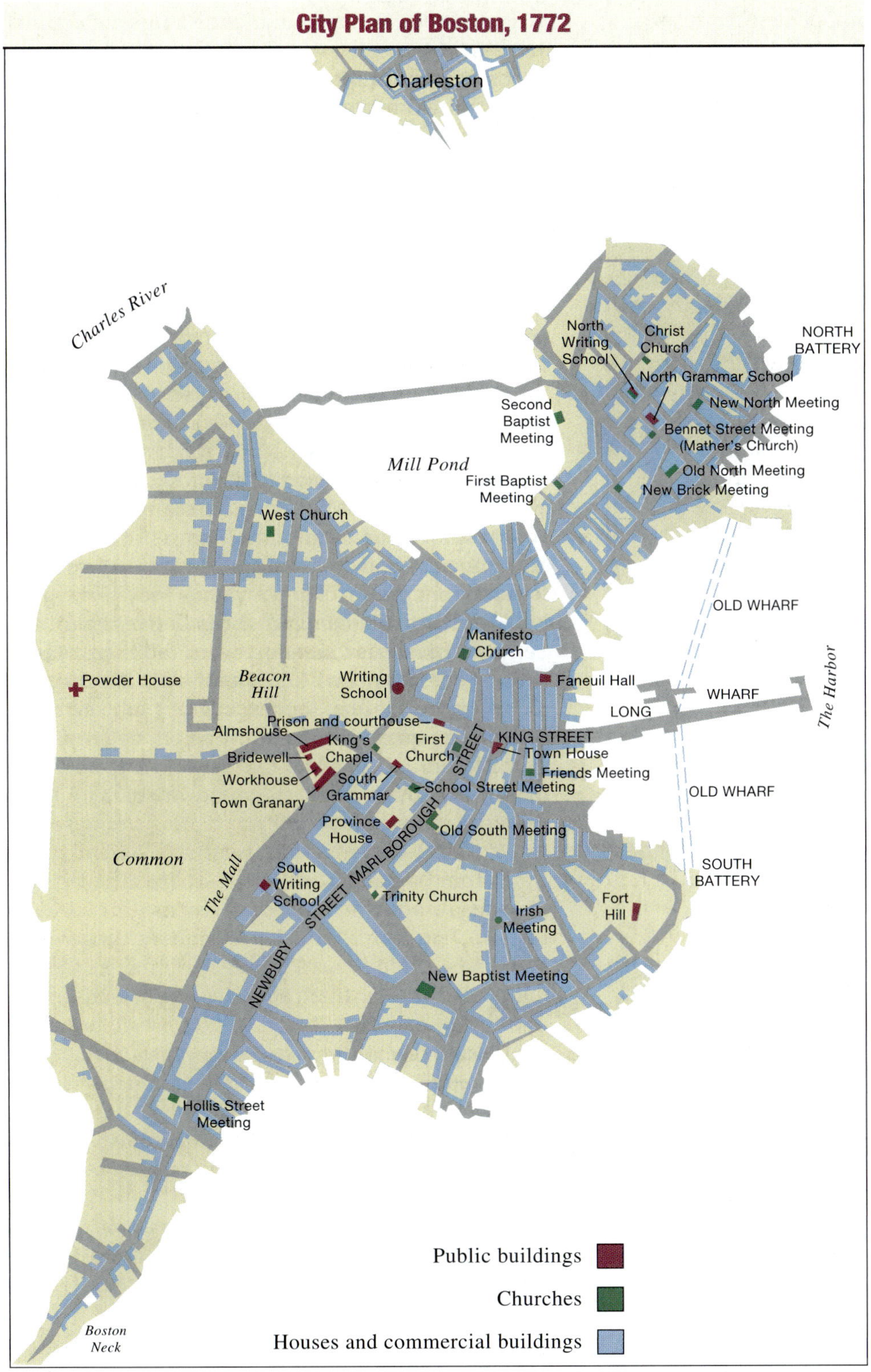

Boston's many churches became important political meeting places in the tumultuous decade leading to the outbreak of war in 1775. Old South Meeting House, holding as many as 5,000 people, became the gathering place of "body of the people." Faneuil Hall was the usual site of town meetings, but when crowds exceeded its capacity of 1,200, meetings were adjourned and reconvened at Old South Meeting House.

By late 1765, effigy-burning crowds all over America were convincing stamp distributors to resign. Colonists defied English authority even more directly by forcing most customs officers and court officials to open the ports and courts for business after November 1 without using the hated stamps required after that date. This often took months of pressure and sometimes mob action, but the Sons of Liberty, often led by new faces in local politics, ultimately got their way by going outside the law.

In March 1766, Parliament debated the surprising American reaction to the Stamp Act. Lobbied by many merchant friends of the Americans, Parliament voted to repeal it. Some members warned that to retreat before colonial defiance of the law would ultimately be fatal. But the legislators bowed to expediency. They satisfied themselves with passing the Declaratory Act, which asserted Parliament's power to enact laws for the colonies in "all cases whatsoever."

The crisis had passed, yet nothing was really solved. Americans had begun to recognize a grasping government trampling its subjects' rights. The Stamp Act, one New England clergyman foresaw, "diffused a disgust through the colonies and laid the basis of an alienation which will never be healed." Stamp Act resisters had politicized their communities as never before. The established leaders, generally cautious in their protests, were often displaced by those beneath them on the social ladder. Men such as New York ship captains Alexander McDougall and Isaac Sears mobilized common citizens and raised political consciousness, employing mass demonstrations and street violence to humble stamp distributors and force open the courts and seaports. Scribbled John Adams in his diary: "The people have become more attentive to their liberties, . . . and more determined to defend them. . . . Our presses have groaned, our pulpits have thundered, our legislatures have resolved, our towns have voted; the crown officers have everywhere trembled, and all their little tools and creatures been afraid to speak and ashamed to be seen."

An Uncertain Interlude

Ministerial instability in England hampered the quest for a coherent, workable American policy. Attempting to be a strong king, George III chose ministers who commanded little respect in Parliament. This led to strife between Parliament and the king's chief ministers; that in turn led to a shuffling of chief ministers and a chaotic political situation at the very time that the king was attempting to overhaul the empire's administration.

To manage the colonies more effectively, the Pitt-Grafton ministry that the king had appointed in 1767 obtained new laws to reorganize the customs service, establish a secretary of state for American affairs, and install three new vice-admiralty courts in the port cities. Still hard-pressed for revenue—for at home the government faced severe unemployment, tax protests, and riots over the high price of grain—the ministry also pushed through Parliament the relatively small Townshend duties on paper, lead, painters' colors, and tea. A final law suspended New York's assembly until that body ceased defying the Quartering Act of 1765, which required public funds for support of British troops garrisoned in the colony since the end of the Seven Years' War. New York knuckled under to save its legislature.

Colonial protests against the Townshend Acts, centered in Massachusetts, were more restrained than in 1765. But the Massachusetts House of Representatives sent a circular letter to each colony objecting to the new Townshend duties, small though they were. Written by Samuel Adams, the letter attacked as unconstitutional the plan to underwrite salaries for royal officials in America from customs duties. Under instructions from England, Governor Bernard dissolved the legislature after it refused to rescind the circular letter. "The Americans have made a discovery," declared Edmund Burke before Parliament, "that we mean to oppress them; we have made a discovery that they intend to raise a rebellion. We do not know how to advance; they do not know how to retreat."

This wood engraving, published in 1829 in a history of the United States, recalls a New Hampshire riot in which townspeople lynched and stoned a stamp distributor in effigy. Cobblestones pried loose from the street seemed to provide the crowd's arsenal. (*The Metropolitan Museum of Art, New York, Bequest of Charles Allen Munn*)

Rather than quelling the disorder as King George III hoped, the occupation of Boston by British troops in 1768 increased tensions. In this engraving by Paul Revere, the red-coated troops are debarking at the Long Wharf. (*Courtesy the Henry Francis du Pont Winterthur Museum*)

Although most colonists only grumbled and petitioned, Bostonians protested stridently. In the summer of 1768, after customs officials seized a sloop owned by John Hancock for a violation of the trade regulations, an angry crowd mobbed them. They fled to a British warship in Boston harbor and remained there for months. Newspapers hounded overeager revenue officers who extracted money for the maintenance of "swarms of officers and pensioners, and an enormous train of underlings and dependents"; they also warned of new measures designed to "suck the life blood" from the people and predicted that troops would be sent to "dragoon us into passive obedience." To many, the belief grew that the English were plotting "designs for destroying our constitutional liberties."

Troops indeed came. The attack on the customs officials brought a resolute response from England, where the government regarded the Bostonians' action as insubordinate and selfish. The ministry dispatched two regiments from England and two more from Nova Scotia. The intention was to bring the Bostonians to a proper state of subordination and make them an example to the rest of the colonies. Now cries went up against maintaining standing armies in peacetime, but radical Bostonians who proposed force to prevent the troops from landing got little support from delegates called to a special provincial convention. On October 1, 1768, red-coated troops marched into Boston without resistance.

After the troops occupied Boston, the colonists' main tactic of protest against the Townshend Acts became economic boycott. First in Boston and then in New York and Philadelphia, merchants and consumers adopted nonimportation and nonconsumption agreements, pledging neither to import nor to use British goods. These measures promised to bring the politically influential English merchants to their aid, for half of British shipping was engaged in commerce with the colonies, and one-quarter of all English exports were consumed there. When the southern colonies also adopted nonimportation agreements in 1768, a new step toward intercolonial union had been taken.

Many colonial merchants, however, especially those tied to the government's interest, saw nonimportation agreements as lacking legal force and refused to be bound by them. They had to be persuaded otherwise by street brigades, usually composed of artisans who warmly supported nonimportation as a boon to home manufacturing. Crowd action welled up again in the seaports, as determined patriot bands attacked the homes and warehouses of offending merchants and "rescued" incoming contraband goods seized by zealous customs officials.

England's attempts to discipline its American colonies and oblige them to share the costs of governing an empire lay in shambles by the end of the 1760s. Using troops to restore order undermined the respect for the mother country on which colonial acceptance of its authority ultimately depended. American newspapers denounced new extensions of British authority. Colonial governors quarreled with their legislatures. Customs officials met with determined opposition and were widely accused of arbitrary actions and excessive zeal in enforcing the Navigation Acts. The Townshend duties had failed miserably, yielding less than £21,000 by 1770 while costing British business £700,000 through the colonial nonimportation movement.

On March 5, 1770, Parliament repealed all the Townshend duties except the one on tea (which the new minister of state, Lord North, explained was retained "as a mark of the supremacy of Parliament and an efficient declaration of their right to govern the colonies"). On that same evening in Boston, British troops fired on an unruly crowd of heckling citizens. For months, Bostonians had been baiting the "lobsterbacks," as they dubbed the red-coated British soldiers. They hated them for competing with townspeople for menial jobs when off duty, as well as for their military presence. On this evening, a taunting crowd had first hurled insults and snowballs and then surged toward a sentry. After a squad of redcoats joined the sentry, someone cried, "Fire!" When the smoke cleared, five bloody bodies, including that of Ebenezer MacIntosh's brother-in-law, stained the snow-covered street. Bowing to furious popular reaction, Thomas Hutchinson, recently appointed governor, ordered the British troops out of town and arrested the commanding officer and the soldiers involved. They were later acquitted, with two young patriot lawyers, John Adams and Josiah Quincy, Jr., providing a brilliant defense.

In spite of the potential of the "Boston massacre" for galvanizing the colonies into further resistance, opposition to English policies, including boycotts, subsided in 1770. Popular leaders such as Samuel Adams in Boston and Alexander McDougall in New York, who had made names for themselves as the standard-bearers of American liberty, had few issues left to exploit. They were further handicapped by the end of the depression that had previously helped sow discontent. Yet the fires of revolution had been not extinguished but merely dampened.

The Growing Rift

From 1770 to 1772, relative quiet descended over the colonies. Then in June 1772, England created a new furor by announcing that it, rather than the provincial legislature, would henceforth pay the salaries of the royal governor and superior court judges in Massachusetts. Even though the measure saved the colony money, it looked like a scheme, undermining a right set forth in the colony's charter, to impose a despotic government on the colony. Judges paid from London presumably would obey London.

Paul Revere was not only a noted silversmith and political activist but also a man who put art to work in the cause of revolutionary politics. This engraving became known throughout the colonies and convinced many people to involve themselves in what had been mainly New England's cause. The smiling British redcoats are reviled in verse: "While faithless P[resto]n and his savage Bonds, / With murd'rous Rancour stretch their bloody Hands, / Like fierce Barbarians grinning o'er their Prey, / Approve the Carnage and enjoy the Day." (*American Antiquarian Society*)

Boston's town meeting protested loudly and created a Committee of Correspondence "to state the rights of the colonists . . . and to communicate and publish the same to the several towns and to the world." Crown supporters called the committee "the foulest, subtlest, and most venomous serpent ever issued from the egg of sedition." By the end of 1772, another 80 towns in Massachusetts had created committees. In the next year, all but three colonies established Committees of Correspondence in their legislatures.

Samuel Adams was by now the leader of the Boston radicals, for the influence of laboring men like Ebenezer MacIntosh had been quietly reduced. Adams was an experienced caucus politicker and a skilled political journalist, and (despite his Harvard degree) he had deep roots among the laboring people. He organized the working ranks through the taverns, clubs, and volunteer fire companies and secured the support of wealthy merchants such as John Hancock, whose ample purse financed patriotic celebrations and feasts that kept politics on everyone's mind and helped build interclass bridges. In England, Adams became known as one of the most dangerous firebrands in America.

In 1772, Rhode Islanders gave Adams new material to work with when they attacked a royal warship. The British commander of the *Gaspee* was roundly hated for hounding the fishermen and small traders of Narragansett Bay. When his ship ran aground while pursuing a suspected smuggler, Rhode Islanders took their revenge, burning the stranded vessel to the waterline. Adding insult to injury, a Rhode Island court convicted the *Gaspee*'s captain of illegally seizing what he was convinced was smuggled sugar and rum. London reacted with cries of high treason. Finding the lips of Rhode Islanders sealed regarding the identity of the arsonists, an investigating committee could do little. The event was tailor-made for Samuel Adams, who used it to "awaken the American colonies, which have been too long dozing upon the brink of ruin."

The final plunge into revolution began when Parliament passed the Tea Act in early 1773. The act allowed the East India Company, which was on the verge of bankruptcy, to ship its tea directly to North America. By eliminating English middlemen and English import taxes, this provided Americans with the opportunity to buy their tea cheaply from the company's agents in the colonies. Even with the small tax to be paid in the colonies, Indian tea would now undersell smuggled Dutch tea. The Americans would get inexpensive tea, the crown would derive a modest revenue, and the East India Company would obtain a new lease on life. The company soon had 600,000 pounds of tea in 2,000 chests ready for shipment to America.

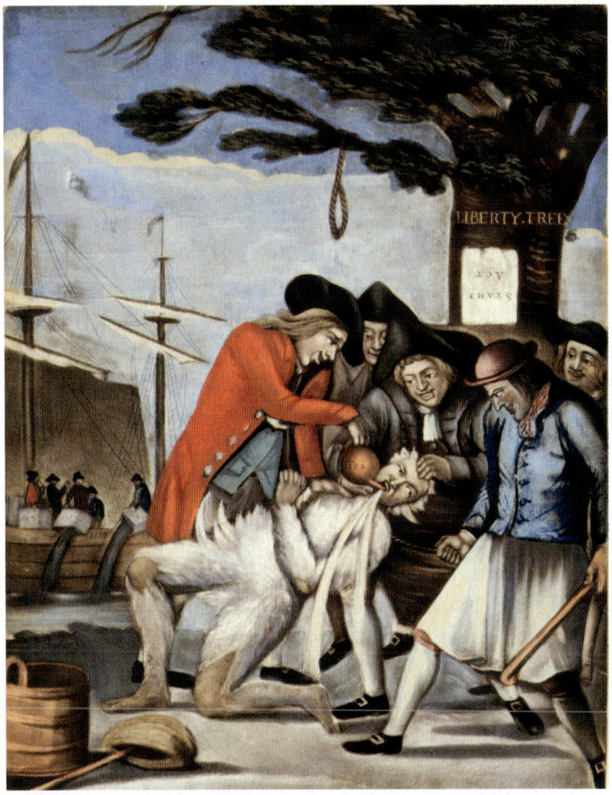

Public sentiment against the importation of tea and other British goods often found expression in a coat of tar and feathers applied to the bare skin of the offending importer. Note the symbols in *The Bostonians Paying the Excise-Man:* the Liberty Tree with a hangman's noose and the overturned copy of the Stamp Act. In the background, Bostonians dump chests of tea into the harbor. (*Library of Congress*)

Parliament monumentally miscalculated the American response. For several years, merchants in Philadelphia and New York had been flagrantly smuggling Dutch tea. As a consequence, imports of English tea in the two seaports plummeted from 500,000 pounds in 1768 to a mere 650 pounds in 1772. The merchants bitterly denounced the new act for giving the East India Company a monopoly on the American tea market. Other monopolies would follow, they predicted, and middlemen of all kinds would be eliminated. The colonists also objected that the government was shrewdly trying to gain acceptance of Parliament's taxing power. As Americans drank the taxed tea, they would also be swallowing the English right to tax them.

The colonists quickly demonstrated that their principles were not entirely in their pocketbooks. Mass meetings in the port towns soon forced the resignation of the East India Company's agents, and citizens vowed to stop the obnoxious tea at the water's edge.

Governor Hutchinson of Massachusetts brought the tea crisis to a climax, convinced that to yield again to popular pressure would forever cripple English sovereignty in America. The popular party led by Samuel Adams had been urging the citizens to demonstrate that they were not yet prepared for the "yoke of slavery" by sending the tea back to England. Hutchinson's refusal to grant the tea ships clearance papers to return to England with their cargoes finally led to dramatic action. Buoyed by resolutions from surrounding towns, 5,000 Bostonians packed Old South Church on December 16, 1773, noisily passing resolutions urging the governor to clear the ships. But Hutchinson was not swayed by the Bostonians' determination to resist what they regarded as another affront to their liberties. "This meeting," despaired Samuel Adams, "can do no more to save the country."

At nightfall, a band of Bostonians, dressed as Indians, boarded the tea ships, broke open the chests of tea, and flung £10,000 worth of the East India Company's property into Boston harbor. George Hewes, a 31-year-old shoemaker, recalled how he had garbed himself as a Mohawk, blackened "face and hands with coal dust in the shop of a blacksmith," and joined men of all ranks in marching stealthily to the wharves to do their work. In time, this would be remembered as The Boston Tea Party.

Now the die was cast. Lord North, the king's chief minister, called the Bostonians "fanatics" and argued that the dispute was no longer about taxes but about whether England had any authority over the colonies. George III put it succinctly: "We must master them or totally leave them to themselves and treat them as aliens."

Thoroughly aroused, Parliament passed the Coercive Acts, stern laws that Bostonians promptly labeled the "Intolerable Acts." The acts closed the port of Boston to all shipping until the colony paid for the destroyed tea. They barred local courts from trying British soldiers and officials for acts committed while suppressing civil disturbances. To hamstring the colony's truculent political assemblies, Parliament amended the Massachusetts charter to transform the council from an upper legislative chamber, elected by the lower house, to a body appointed by the governor. This stripped the council of its veto power over the governor's decisions.

The act also struck at local government by authorizing the governor to prohibit all town meetings except for one annual meeting to elect local officers of government. Finally, General Thomas Gage, commander in chief of British forces in America, replaced Thomas Hutchinson as governor. "This is the day, then," declared Edmund Burke in the House of Commons, "that you wish to go to war with all America, in order to conciliate that country to this."

Royal Governor Thomas Hutchinson called Sam Adams "[the greatest] incendiary in the King's dominion" whereas his cousin, John Adams, called him "a plain, simple, decent citizen of middling stature, dress, and manners." Boston's premier painter, John Singleton Copley, painted Adams in just this way—in a simple wool suit with no embroidery and a partially unbuttoned waistcoat suggesting the patriot leader's disdain for proper appearances. *(Samuel Adams, about 1772; John Singleton Copley, American (1738–1815), Oil on canvas; 49½ x 39½ in. (125.7 x 100.3 cm), Deposited by the city of Boston, 30.76c. Courtesy of the Museum of Fine Arts, Boston. Reproduced with permission. © 1999 The Museum of Fine Arts, Boston. All Rights Reserved.)*

Lord North's plan to strangle Massachusetts into submission and hope for acquiescence elsewhere in the colonies proved popular in England. Earlier, the colonies had gained supporters in Parliament for their resistance to what many regarded as attacks on their fundamental privileges. Now this support evaporated. After a decade of debating constitutional rights and mobilizing sentiment against what many believed was a systematic plot to enslave freeborn citizens, the Americans found their maneuvering room severely narrowed.

When the Intolerable Acts arrived in May 1774 aboard the *Harmony,* Boston's town meeting reacted belligerently. It dispatched a circular letter to all the colonies urging an end to trade with England. This met with faint support. But a second call, for a meeting in Philadelphia of delegates from all colonies, received a better response. The Continental Congress, as it was called, now began to transform a ten-year debate conducted by separate colonies into a unified American cause.

Fifty-five delegates from all the colonies except Georgia converged on Carpenter's Hall in Philadelphia in September 1774. The discussions centered not on how to prepare for a war that many sensed was inevitable but on how to resolve sectional differences that most delegates feared were irreconcilable. Overcoming prejudices and hostilities was as important as the formal debates. New Englanders were especially eyed with suspicion for their reputed intolerance and self-interest. "We have numberless prejudices to remove here," wrote John Adams from Philadelphia. "We have been obliged to keep ourselves out of sight, and to feel pulses, and to sound the depths; to insinuate our sentiments, designs, and desires by means of other persons, sometimes of one province, and sometimes of another."

The Continental Congress was by no means a unified body. Some delegates, led by cousins Samuel and John Adams from Massachusetts and Richard Henry Lee and Patrick Henry of Virginia, argued for outright resistance to Parliament's Coercive Acts. Moderate delegates from the middle colonies, led by Joseph Galloway of Pennsylvania and James Duane of New York, urged restraint and further attempts at reconciliation. After weeks of debate, the delegates agreed to a restrained Declaration of Rights and Resolves. It attempted to define American grievances and justify the colonists' defiance of English policies and laws by appealing to the "immutable laws of nature, the principles of the English constitution, and the several [colonial] charters and compacts" under which they lived. More concrete was the Congress's agreement on a plan of resistance. If England did not rescind the Intolerable Acts by December 1, 1774, a ban would take effect on all imports and exports between the colonies and Great Britain, Ireland, and the British West Indies. Some exceptions were made for the export of southern staple commodities to keep reluctant southern colonies in the fold.

By the time the Congress adjourned in late October, leaders from different colonies had transformed what had been primarily Boston's cause into a national movement. "Government is dissolved [and] we are in a state of nature," Patrick Henry argued dramatically. "The distinctions between Virginians, Pennsylvanians, New Yorkers, and New Englanders are no more. I am not a Virginian, but an American." Many other delegates were a long way from feeling this way, but still the Congress agreed to reconvene in May 1775.

Even before the Second Continental Congress met, the fabric of government had been badly torn in most colonies. Revolutionary committees, conventions, and congresses, entirely unauthorized by law, were replacing legal governing bodies. Assuming authority in defiance of royal governors, who suspended truculent legislatures in many colonies, they often operated on instructions from mass meetings where the legal franchise was ignored. These extralegal bodies created and armed militia units, bullied merchants and shopkeepers refusing to conform to popularly authorized boycotts, levied taxes, operated the courts, and obstructed the work of English customs officials. By the end of 1774, all but three colonies defied their own charters by appointing provincial assemblies without royal authority. In the next year, this independently created power became evident in the nearly complete cessation of trade with England.

The Quebec Act of 1774

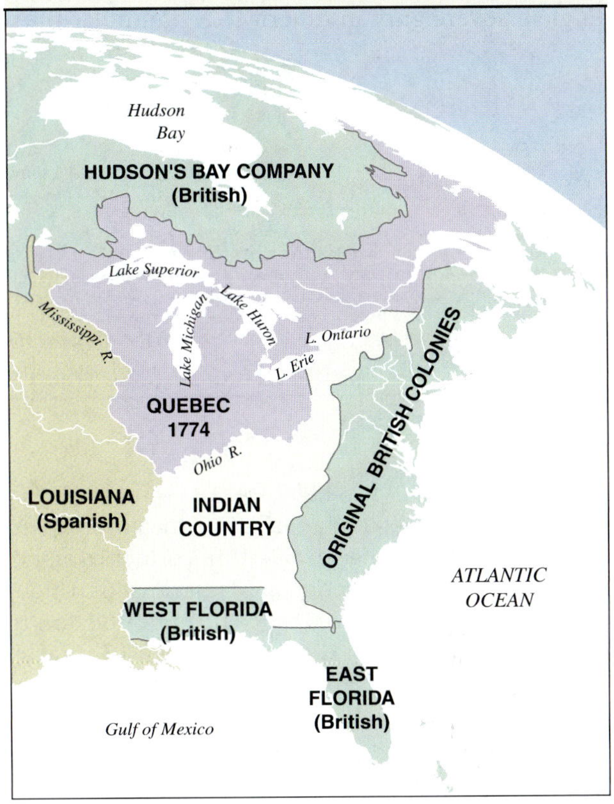

Most colonists hated the Quebec Act, which attached the trans-Appalachian interior north of the Ohio River to the British government in Quebec, because they believed this act passed by Parliament, like others during the prewar years, was aimed at the heart of colonial liberty. It not only sealed off the western lands from colonial speculators but guaranteed the right of French Catholics to practice their religion freely—an offense, especially, to New England Puritans.

The Final Rupture

The final spark to the revolutionary powder keg was struck in early 1775. General Gage had assumed the governorship of Massachusetts 11 months earlier and

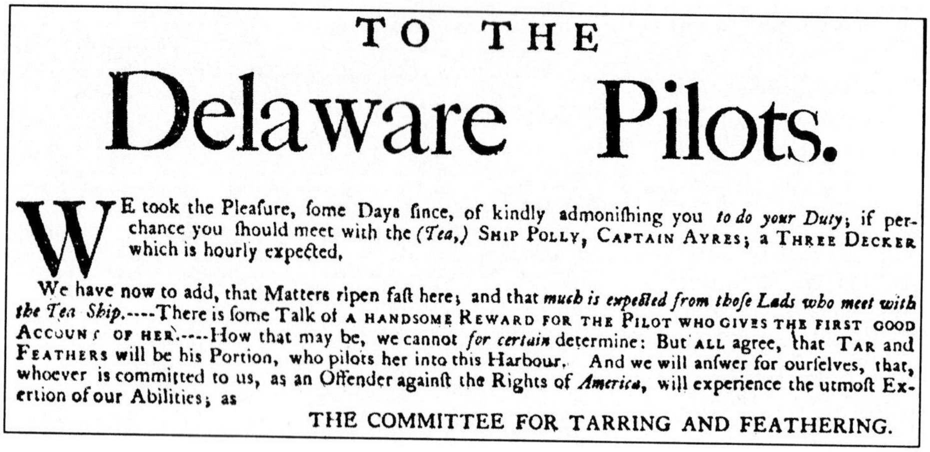

TO THE

Delaware Pilots.

WE took the Pleaſure, ſome Days ſince, of kindly admoniſhing you *to do your Duty*; if perchance you ſhould meet with the *(Tea,)* SHIP POLLY, CAPTAIN AYRES; a THREE DECKER which is hourly expected.

We have now to add, that Matters ripen faſt here; and that *much is expected from thoſe Lads who meet with the Tea Ship.*----There is ſome Talk of A HANDSOME REWARD FOR THE PILOT WHO GIVES THE FIRST GOOD ACCOUNT OF HER.----How that may be, we cannot *for certain* determine: But ALL agree, that TAR and FEATHERS will be his Portion, who pilots her into this Harbour. And we will anſwer for ourſelves, that, whoever is committed to us, as an Offender againſt the Rights of *America*, will experience the utmoſt Exertion of our Abilities; as

THE COMMITTEE FOR TARRING AND FEATHERING.

Not only Bostonians took action against the Tea Act. This Philadelphia broadside from "The Committee for Tarring and Feathering," issued several weeks before the Boston Tea Party, exhorts pilots on the Delaware River to watch for an arriving tea ship. *(Rare Book Collection, New York Public Library, Astor, Lenox and Tilden Foundations)*

occupied Boston with 4,000 troops—one for every adult male in the town. In April 1775, the government in London ordered Gage to arrest "the principal actors and abettors" of insurrection in Massachusetts. Under cover of night, he sent 700 redcoats out of Boston to seize colonial arms and ammunition in nearby Concord. But Americans learned of the plan. When the troops reached Lexington at dawn, 70 "Minutemen"—townsmen available on a minute's notice—were waiting. In the skirmish that ensued, 18 Massachusetts farmers fell, 8 of them mortally wounded.

Marching six miles west, the British entered Concord, where another firefight broke out. Withdrawing, the redcoats made their way back to Boston, harassed by militiamen firing from farmhouses and barns and from behind stone walls. Before the bloody day ended, 273 British and 95 Americans lay dead or wounded. News of the bloodshed swept through the colonies. Within weeks, thousands of men besieged the British troops in Boston. One colonist reported that wherever one traveled, "you see the inhabitants training, making firelocks, casting mortars, shells, and shot."

The outbreak of fighting vastly altered the debates of the Second Continental Congress, which assembled in Philadelphia in May 1775. The Congress had the same slim powers as its predecessor, but it acquired awesome new responsibilities. Many delegates knew one another from the earlier Congress. But fresh faces appeared, including Boston's wealthy merchant, John Hancock; a tall, young planter-lawyer from Virginia, Thomas Jefferson; and the much-applauded Benjamin Franklin, who had arrived from London only four days before the Congress convened.

The Congress had no power to legislate or command; it could only request and recommend. Delegate John Adams worried that such a body could form a constitution "for a great empire," and "at the same time they have a country of 1,500 miles to fortify, millions to arm and train, a naval power to begin, an extensive commerce to regulate, numerous tribes of Indians to negotiate with, a standing army of 27,000 men to raise pay, victual, and officer."

Another 14 months elapsed before the Congress issued a formal declaration of independence, but the war with England—and a civil war in America—had already begun. Meeting in the statehouse in Philadelphia, where the king's arms hung over the entrance and the inscription on the tower bell read "Proclaim liberty throughout the land unto all the inhabitants thereof," the Second Congress set to work. It authorized a continental army of 20,000 and, partly to cement Virginia to the cause, chose George Washington as commander in chief. It issued a "Declaration of Causes of Taking-up Arms," sent the king an "Olive Branch Petition" humbly begging him to remove the obstacles to reconciliation, made moves to secure the neutrality of the interior Indian tribes, issued paper money, erected a postal system, and approved plans for a military hospital.

While debate continued over whether the colonies ought to declare themselves independent, military action grew hotter. Hotheaded Ethan Allen and his Green Mountain Boys from eastern New York captured Fort Ticonderoga, controlling the Champlain valley, in May 1775. On New Year's Day in 1776, the British shelled Norfolk, Virginia. In March 1776, Washington's army forced the British to evacuate Boston. In spite of these acts of aggression, many members of the Congress dreaded a final rupture and still hoped for reconciliation with England. Such hopes crumbled at the end of 1775 when news arrived that the king, rejecting the Olive Branch Petition, had dispatched 20,000 additional British troops to quell the American insurrection and had proclaimed the colonies in "open and avowed rebellion." Those fatal

STEPS ON THE ROAD TO REVOLUTION

1763	Treaty of Paris ends Seven Years' War between England and France; France cedes Canada to England.
	Proclamation of 1763 forbids white settlement west of Appalachian Mountains.
1764	Sugar Act sets higher duties on imported sugar and lower duties on molasses and enlarges the power of vice-admiralty courts.
	Currency Act prohibits issuance of paper money by colonies.
1765	Stamp Act requires revenue-raising stamps purchased from British-appointed stamp distributors on printed documents.
	Stamp Act Congress meets in New York.
	Quartering Act requires colonies to furnish British troops with housing and certain provisions.
	Sons of Liberty formed in New York City and thereafter in many towns.
1766	Declaratory Act asserts Parliament's sovereignty over the colonies after repealing Stamp Act.
	Rent riots by New York tenant farmers.
1767	Townshend Revenue Acts impose duties on tea, glass, paper, paints, and other items.
	South Carolina Regulators organize in backcountry.
1768	British troops sent to Boston.
1770	British troops kill four and wound eight American civilians in Boston Massacre.
1771	Battle of Alamance pits frontier North Carolina Regulators against eastern militia led by royal governor.
1772	British schooner *Gaspee* burned in Rhode Island.
	Committee of Correspondence formed in Boston and thereafter in other cities.
1773	Tea Act reduces duty on tea but gives East India Company right to sell directly to Americans.
	Boston Tea Party dumps £10,000 of East India Company tea into Boston harbor.
1774	Coercive Acts close port of Boston, restrict provincial and town governments in Massachusetts, and send additional troops to Boston.
	Quebec Act attaches trans-Appalachian interior north of Ohio River to government of Quebec.
	First Continental Congress meets and forms Continental Association to boycott British imports.
1775	Battles of Lexington and Concord cause 95 American and 273 British casualties; Americans take Fort Ticonderoga.
	Second Continental Congress meets and assumes many powers of an independent government.
	Dunmore's Proclamation in Virginia promises freedom to slaves and indentured servants fleeing to British ranks.
	Prohibitory Act embargoes American goods.
	George III proclaims Americans in open rebellion.
1776	Thomas Paine publishes *Common Sense.*
	British troops evacuate Boston.
	Declaration of Independence.

words made all the Congress's actions treasonable and turned all who obeyed them into traitors.

By the time Thomas Paine's hard-hitting pamphlet *Common Sense* appeared in Philadelphia on January 9, 1776, members of the Congress were talking less gingerly about independence. Paine's blunt words and compelling rhetoric smashed through the remaining reserve. "O ye that love mankind! Ye that dare oppose not only the tyranny, but also the tyrant, stand forth!" wrote Paine. Within weeks, the pamphlet was in bookstalls all over the colonies. "The public sentiment which a few weeks before had shuddered at the tremendous obstacles, with which independence was envisioned," declared Edmund Randolph of Virginia, now "overleaped every barrier."

The Continental Congress continued to debate independence during the spring of 1776, even as the war became bloodier. While the delegates talked, men under arms acted. Washington's army forced the British to withdraw from Boston, but an American assault on Quebec failed in May 1776. England embargoed all trade to the colonies and ordered the seizure of American ships. That convinced the Congress to declare its ports open to all countries. "Nothing is left now," Joseph Hewes of North Carolina admitted, "but to fight it out." It was almost anticlimactic when Richard Henry Lee introduced his congressional resolution on June 7 calling for a declaration of independence. After two days of debate, the Congress ordered a committee chaired by Jefferson to begin drafting the document.

Though it would become revered as the new nation's birth certificate, the declaration was not a highly original statement. It drew heavily on the Congress's earlier justifications of American resistance, and its theory of government had already been set forth in scores of pamphlets over the previous decade. The ringing phrases that "all men are created equal, that they are endowed by their Creator with certain unalienable Rights, that among these are Life, Liberty and the pursuit of Happiness" were familiar in the writing of many pamphleteers, including John Adams, Thomas Paine, and James Wilson.

Jefferson's committee presented the declaration to the Congress on June 28. The proposals were read and ordered to "lie on the table" until the following Monday, July 1. "This morning is assigned for the greatest debate of all," noted John Adams, when the Congress reconvened. "May Heaven prosper the new-born republic, and make it more glorious than any former republics have been." At the end of the day, nine colonies voted to adopt the declaration, two voted against, one delegation split, and one abstained. The next day, July 2, twelve delegations voted yes, with New York's abstaining, thus allowing the Congress to say that the vote for independence was unanimous. Two days more were spent cutting and polishing the document. The major change was the elimination of a long argument blaming the king for slavery in America.

On July 4, Congress sent the Declaration of Independence to the printer. Four days later, Philadelphians thronged to the statehouse to hear it read aloud. They "huzzahed" the reading, tore the king's arms from above the statehouse door, and later that night, amid cheers, toasts, and clanging church bells, hurled this symbol of more than a century and a half of colonial dependency on England into a roaring bonfire.

THE IDEOLOGY OF REVOLUTIONARY REPUBLICANISM

Since 1763, the colonists responded to a variety of ideas that gave meaning to the events and conditions they were experiencing. Mostly these ideas took the form of newspaper articles and pamphlets written by educated lawyers, clergymen, merchants, and planters. But the middling and lower ranks of society had also expressed themselves in printed broadsides, appeals in the newspapers, and also street demonstrations where ordinary people carried out ideologically laden rituals of humiliation against their enemies such as tarring and feathering and burnings in effigy. Gradually, the colonists pieced together a political ideology, borrowed partly from English political thought, partly from the theories of the Enlightenment, and partly from their own experiences. Historians call this new ideology "revolutionary republicanism." But because the colonists varied widely in interests and experiences, no single coherent ideology united them all.

Liberty always had to struggle against power, as American colonists saw it. In this cartoon, England (power) forces Liberty (America in the form of a woman) to drink the "Bitter Draught" of tea. Uncompliant, America spits the tea into England's face while another corrupt Englishman peeks under her petticoat. (*Massachusetts Historical Society*)

A Plot Against Liberty

Many American colonists agreed with earlier English Whig writers who charged that corrupt and power-hungry men were slowly extinguishing the lamp of liberty in England. The so-called country party represented by these Whig pamphleteers proclaimed itself the guardian of the true principles of the English constitution and opposed the "court" party representing the king and his appointees.

When the king's ministers began a new program for disciplining the empire after 1763, American Whig writers were intellectually prepared to view the new laws and policies as attacks on such traditional English liberties as balanced government, representative rights, and disestablishment of standing armies in peacetime. Even Parliament, traditionally the preserver of the people's rights against tyrannical executive power, seemed to threaten a despotism of its own in its alliance with the monarchy. Every ministerial policy and parliamentary act in the decade after the Stamp Act appeared as a subversion of English liberties. Most Americans regarded resistance to such blows against liberty as wholly justified.

The belief that England was carrying out "a deep-laid and desperate plan of imperial despotism . . . for the extinction of all civil liberty," as the Boston town meeting expressed it in 1770, spread rapidly in the next few years. By 1774, John Adams was writing of the "conspiracy against the public liberty [that] was first regularly formed and begun to be executed in 1763 and 1764." From London, America's favorite writer, Benjamin Franklin, described the "extreme corruption prevalent among all orders of men in this old rotten state." Another pamphleteer reached the conclusion that England was no longer "in a condition at present to suckle us, being pregnant with vermin that corrupt her milk and convert her blood and juices into poison."

Among many Americans, especially merchants, the attack on constitutional rights blended closely with the threats to their economic interests contained in the tough new trade policies. Merchants saw a coordinated attack on their "lives, liberties, and property," as they frequently phrased it. If a man was not secure in his property, he could not be secure in his citizenship, for it was property that gave a man the independence to shape his identity.

Revitalizing American Society

The continuing crisis over the imperial relationship by itself inspired many colonists to resist impending tyranny. But for others, the revolutionary mentality was also fed by a belief that an opportunity was at hand to revitalize American society. They believed that the colonies had been undergoing a silent transformation and that the growing commercial connections with the decadent and corrupt mother country had injected poison into the American bloodstream. They worried about the luxury and vice they saw around them and came to believe that resistance to England would return American society to a state of civic virtue, spartan living, and godly purpose.

The fervent support of the patriot movement by much of the colonial clergy, especially in New England, and the clergy's importance in writing protest pamphlets helped give a high-toned moral character to colonial protest. Such appeals resonated most strongly in New England, where even so secular a man as John Adams groaned at the "universal spirit of debauchery, dissipation, luxury, effeminacy and gaming." As in most revolutionary movements, talk of moral regeneration, of a society-wide rebirth through battle against a corrupt enemy, ennobled the cause, inspiring people in areas that had been stirred a generation before by the Great Awakening.

The growth of a revolutionary spirit among ordinary people also owed much to the plain style of polemical writers such as Thomas Paine and Patrick Henry. Paine's *Common Sense* transformed the terms of the imperial argument by attacking monarchy itself. Its astounding popularity—it went through 25 editions in 1776 and sold more copies than any printed piece in colonial history—stemmed not only from its argument but also from its style. Paine wrote for the common people who knew nothing more than the Bible. Using biblical imagery and plain language, he appealed to their Calvinist heritage and their belief in their providential destiny. After savagely attacking the king, whom he called "a royal brute," Paine appealed to millennial yearnings: "We have it in our power to begin the world over again. The birthday of a new world is at hand," if only the Americans would stand up for liberty, the goddess whom "Europe regards . . . like a stranger, and England hath given . . . warning to depart."

Paine avoided the elaborate legalistic style of most of the pamphlets written by lawyers and clergymen in the preceding decade. His language could be understood on the docks, in the taverns, on the streets, and in the farmyards. Many Whig leaders found his pungent language and egalitarian call for ending hereditary privilege and concentrated power too strong. They denounced the disheveled immigrant with "genius in his eyes" as a "crack-brained zealot for democracy" and a dangerous man who appealed to "every silly clown and illiterate mechanic." But thousands who read or listened to *Common Sense* were radicalized by it and came to believe not only that independence could be wrested from England but also that a new social and political order could be created in North America.

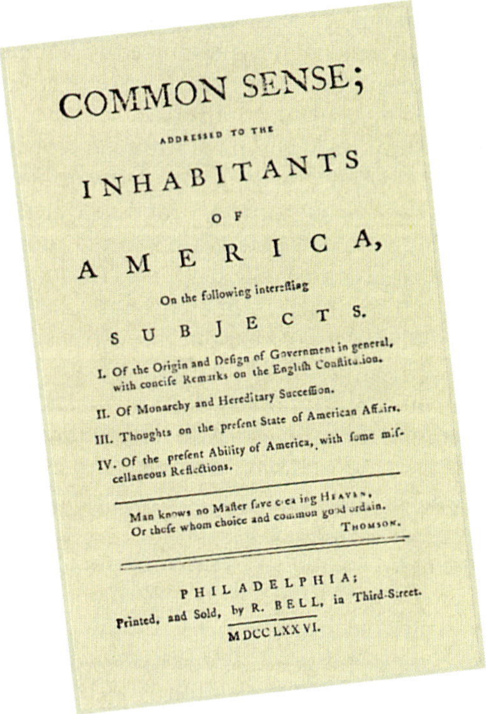

COMMON SENSE;

ADDRESSED TO THE

INHABITANTS

OF

AMERICA,

On the following intereſting

SUBJECTS.

I. Of the Origin and Deſign of Government in general, with conciſe Remarks on the Engliſh Conſtitution.

II. Of Monarchy and Hereditary Succeſſion.

III. Thoughts on the preſent State of American Affairs.

IV. Of the preſent Ability of America, with ſome miſcellaneous Reflections.

Man knows no Maſter ſave creating HEAVEN,
Or thoſe whom choice and common good ordain.
THOMSON.

PHILADELPHIA;
Printed, and Sold, by R. BELL, in Third-Street.
MDCCLXXVI.

In *Common Sense,* Thomas Paine dared to articulate, in plain but muscular language, the thoughts of rebellion and independence that others had only alluded to. Note that Paine did not put his name on the title page of Common Sense, though he was quickly identified as the author. *(Left, Library of Congress; Right, National Portrait Gallery, London)*

THE TURMOIL OF REVOLUTIONARY SOCIETY

The long struggle with England over colonial rights between 1764 and 1776 did not occur in a unified society. Social and economic change, which accelerated in the late colonial period, brought deep unrest and calls for reform from many quarters. By the end of the Seven Years' War, faith in the internal social systems of the colonies had waned among many colonists, just as allegiance to the mother country and to the British mercantile system had worn thin.

Many of the colonists who struggled for security in the aftermath of the Seven Years' War hoped that migration to frontier land would improve their fortunes. A flood of new immigrants from Ireland and Germany after the Treaty of Paris in 1763 added to the pressure to reach the trans-Appalachian river valleys. However, the western option involved much violence with Indian tribes unreceptive to encroaching settlers. So most colonists chose to work out their destinies at home or in other communities along the coastal plain to which they migrated in search of opportunity.

As agitation against English policy intensified, previously passive people took a more active interest in politics. In this charged atmosphere, the constitutional struggle with England spread quickly into uncharted territory. Groups emerged—slaves, urban laboring people, backcountry farmers, evangelicals, women—who enunciated goals of their own that were sometimes only loosely connected to the struggle with England. The stridency and potential power of these groups raised for many upper-class leaders the frightening specter of a radically changed society. Losing control of the protests they had initially led, many would abandon the resistance movement against England.

Urban People

Although the cities contained only about 5 percent of the colonial population, they formed the vital cores of revolutionary agitation. As centers of communications, government, and commerce, they led the way in protesting English policy, and they soon contained the most politicized citizens in America. Local politics could be rapidly transformed as the struggle against England became enmeshed with calls for internal reform.

Philadelphia offers a good example of popular empowerment. Before the Seven Years' War, craftsmen had usually acquiesced in politics to the merchant and lawyer politicos. But economic difficulties in the 1760s and 1770s led them to band together within their craft and community. Artisans played a central role in forging and—equally important—enforcing a nonimportation agreement in 1768, calling public meetings, publishing newspaper appeals, organizing secondary boycotts against foot-dragging merchants, and ferreting out and tarring and feathering opponents to their policies. Cautious merchants complained that mere artisans had "no right to give their sentiments respecting an importation" and called the craftsmen a "rabble." But artisans, casting off their customary deference, forged ahead.

By 1772, artisans were filling elected municipal positions and insisting on their right to participate equally with their social superiors in nominating assemblymen and other important officeholders. They also began lobbying for reform laws. The craftsmen called for elected representatives to be more accountable to their constituents. Genteel Philadelphians muttered, "It is time the tradesmen were checked—they ought not to intermeddle in state affairs—they will become too powerful."

By 1774, the Philadelphia working-class's meddling in state affairs reached a bold new stage—the de facto assumption of governmental powers by committees created by the people at large. Craftsmen had first assumed such extralegal authority in policing the nonimportation agreement in 1769. Five years later, responding to the Intolerable Acts, they proposed a radical slate of candidates for a committee to enforce a new economic boycott. Their ticket drubbed one nominated by conservative merchants.

As the impasse with England reached a climax in 1775, the political mobilization and heightened consciousness of laboring Philadelphians continued. By then, many pacifist Quaker leaders of the city had abandoned politics, and other conservative merchants had concluded that mob rule had triumphed. Into the leadership vacuum stepped a group of radicals from the middling ranks: the fiery Scots-Irish doctor Thomas Young, who had agitated in Boston and Albany before migrating to Philadelphia; Timothy Matlack, a hardware retailer who was popular with the lower class for matching his prize bantam cocks against those of New York's aristocratic James Delancy; James Cannon, a young schoolteacher; Benjamin Rush, whose new medical practice took him into the garrets and cramped rooms of the city's poor; and Thomas Paine, a recent immigrant seeking something better in America than he had found as an ill-paid excise officer in England.

The political support of the new radical leaders centered in the 31 companies of the Philadelphia militia, composed mostly of laboring men, and in the extralegal committees now controlling the city's economic life. Their leadership helped overcome the conservatism of the regularly elected Pennsylvania legislature, which was resisting the movement of the Continental Congress toward independence. In addition, the new radical leaders demanded internal reforms: curbing the accumulation of wealth by "our great merchants" who were "making immense fortunes at the expense of the people"; abolishing the property requirement for voting; allowing militiamen to elect their officers; and imposing stiff fines, to be used for the support of the families of poor militiamen, on men who refused militia service.

Benjamin Rush, a young Philadelphia doctor, was one of the revolutionary radicals who wanted to reform American society as well as win independence. Among the reforms Rush promoted were abolishing slavery and establishing free public schools that would teach women as well as men. (*Charles Willson Peale,* Portrait of Benjamin Rush, 1783/*The Henry Francis duPont Winterthur Museum*)

Philadelphia's radicals never controlled the city. They always jostled for position with prosperous artisans and shopkeepers of more moderate views and with cautious lawyers and merchants. But mobilization among artisans, laborers, and mariners, in other cities as well as Philadelphia, became part of the chain of events that led toward independence. Whereas most of the patriot elite fought only to change English colonial policy, the people of the cities also struggled for internal reforms and raised notions of how an independent American society might be reorganized.

Patriot Women

Women also played a vital role in the relentless movement toward revolution, and they drew upon

Technology Changes the American People

SMALLPOX INOCULATION

When thinking about the dangers early settlers in North America faced, Indian attacks and war with the French and Spanish capture the popular imagination. But the greatest threat by far was disease. Recurring epidemics swept through the colonies decade after decade. They ravaged the budding urban centers especially, where dense settlement made communicable diseases much more lethal than in rural areas, where people settled thinly.

The greatest killer of all was smallpox. In Boston alone, it struck with fury four times between 1640 and 1690 and four times again in 1702, 1721, 1730, and 1751. For half the population to contract smallpox and for half of those to die of it was not unusual. Smallpox claimed 848 Bostonians in 1721 (equivalent to 240,000 dying in Chicago today in a single year) and 569 in 1751.

For more than a century after settling Massachusetts in 1630 most Puritans thought of smallpox and other ravaging diseases such as influenza, diphtheria, and scarlet fever as visitations from an omnipotent and angry God. In view of this, prayer and fasting days were the Puritans' main defense against infection. Less religious persons, who thought contagion originated in a corruption of the air, believed that the chance of escaping a horrid disease, once an outbreak was discovered, depended on retreating from the city to the countryside.

In trying to combat disease, the colonists relied on medical knowledge imported from Europe and other places because the colonies had no schools of medicine or research capabilities. In Boston, the smallpox center of North America, such an attempt to use imported medical knowledge led to the first important experiment in America to use preventative medicine. Borrowing from experiments on "buying" the disease—introducing a mild case of smallpox that would give immunity to the patient—several doctors and ministers in Boston began to inoculate family members and friends in 1721. Learning of the success in greatly limiting the lethal character of smallpox in Turkey and Greece, Boston doctors also heard from the slave of Puritan minister Cotton Mather that he had been inoculated in Africa, where introducing the virus by placing pus from an infected patient under the skin of a healthy person had warded off lethal cases of the disease.

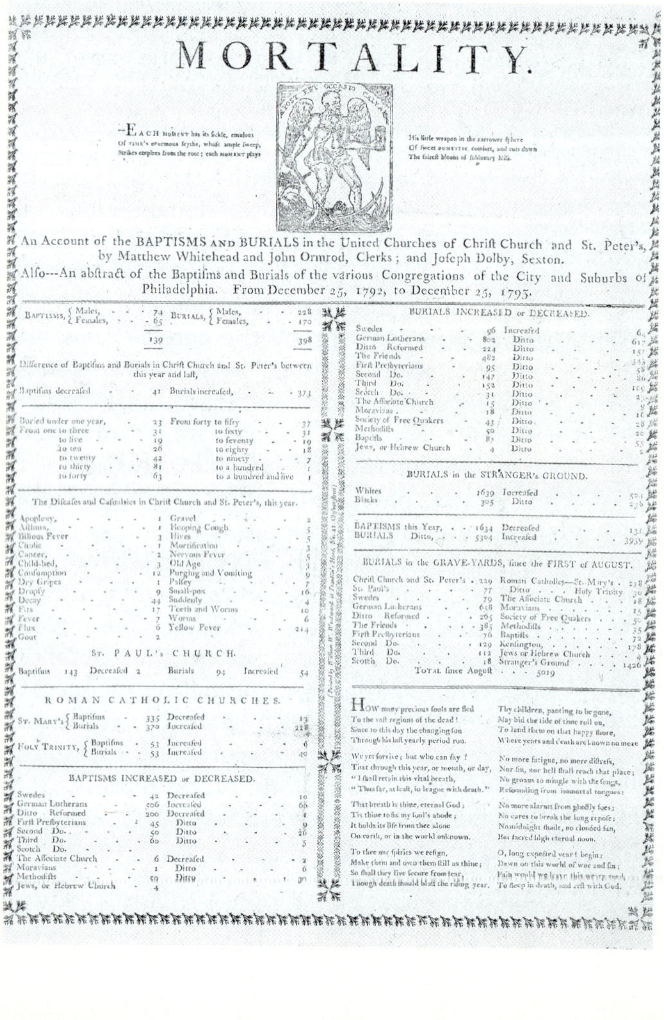

MORTALITY.

—Each moment has its sickle, emulous
Of time's enormous scythe, whose ample sweep,
Strikes empires from the root; each moment plays

His little weapon in the narrower sphere
Of sweet domestic comfort, and cuts down
The fairest bloom of sublunary bliss.

An Account of the BAPTISMS and BURIALS in the United Churches of Chriſt Church and St. Peter's, by Matthew Whitehead and John Ormrod, Clerks; and Joſeph Dolby, Sexton.
Alſo---An abſtract of the Baptiſms and Burials of the various Congregations of the City and Suburbs of Philadelphia. From December 25, 1792, to December 25, 1793.

Baptisms,	Males,	74	Burials, Males,	228
	Females,	65	Females,	170
		139		398

Difference of Baptiſms and Burials in Chriſt Church and St. Peter's between this year and laſt,

Baptiſms decreaſed	41	Burials increaſed,	373

Buried under one year,	23	From forty to fifty	37
From one to three	31	to ſixty	31
to five	19	to ſeventy	19
to ten	26	to eighty	18
to twenty	42	to ninety	7
to thirty	81	to a hundred	1
to forty	63	to a hundred and five	1

The Diſeaſes and Caſualties in Chriſt Church and St. Peter's, this year.

Apoplexy,	1	Gravel	2
Aſthma,	1	Hooping Cough	5
Bilious Fever	3	Hives	5
Cholic	1	Mortification	3
Cancer,	2	Nervous Fever	5
Child-bed,	3	Old Age	3
Conſumption	12	Purging and Vomiting	9
Dry Gripes	1	Palſey	7
Dropſy	9	Small-pox	16
Decay	44	Suddenly	4
Fits	17	Teeth and Worms	10
Fever	7	Worms	6
Flux	6	Yellow Fever	214
Gout	2		

St. PAUL's CHURCH.

Baptiſms	143	Decreaſed	2	Burials	94	Increaſed	54

ROMAN CATHOLIC CHURCHES.

St. Mary's	Baptiſms	335	Decreaſed	13
	Burials	370	Increaſed	228
Holy Trinity,	Baptiſms	53	Increaſed	6
	Burials	53	Increaſed	40

BAPTISMS INCREASED or DECREASED.

Swedes	42	Decreaſed	10
German Lutherans	506	Increaſed	66
Ditto Reformed	200	Decreaſed	1
Firſt Preſbyterians	45	Ditto	9
Second Do.	50	Ditto	26
Third Do.	60	Ditto	5
Scotch Do.			
The Aſſociate Church	6	Decreaſed	2
Moravians	1	Ditto	6
Methodiſts	59	Ditto	30
Jews, or Hebrew Church	4		

BURIALS INCREASED or DECREASED.

Swedes	96	Increaſed	64
German Lutherans	802	Ditto	617
Ditto Reformed	224	Ditto	[illegible]
The Friends	482	Ditto	343
Firſt Preſbyterians	95	Ditto	58
Second Do.	147	Ditto	86
Third Do.	152	Ditto	109
Scotch Do.	31	Ditto	[illegible]
The Aſſociate Church	15	Ditto	9
Moravians	18	Ditto	16
Society of Free Quakers	43	Ditto	28
Methodiſts	50	Ditto	20
Baptiſts	87	Ditto	55
Jews, or Hebrew Church	4	Ditto	2

BURIALS in the STRANGER's GROUND.

Whites	1639	Increaſed	[illegible]
Blacks	305	Ditto	235

BAPTISMS this Year,	1634	Decreaſed	[illegible]
BURIALS Ditto,	5304	Increaſed	3939

BURIALS in the GRAVE-YARDS, ſince the FIRST of AUGUST.

Chriſt Church and St. Peter's	229	Roman Catholics—St. Mary's	228
St. Paul's	77	Ditto . . . Holy Trinity	20
Swedes	79	The Aſſociate Church	18
German Lutherans	658	Moravians	15
Ditto Reformed	265	Society of Free Quakers	50
The Friends	385	Methodiſts	35
Firſt Preſbyterians	76	Baptiſts	72
Second Do.	129	Kenſington,	178
Third Do.	112	Jews or Hebrew Church	4
Scotch Do.	18	Stranger's Ground	1426
		Total ſince Auguſt	5019

How many precious ſouls are fled
To the vaſt regions of the dead!
Since to this day the changing ſun
Through his laſt yearly period run.

We yet ſurvive; but who can ſay?
That through this year, or month, or day,
"I ſhall retain this vital breath,
"Thus far, at leaſt, in league with death."

That breath is thine, eternal God;
'Tis thine to fix my ſoul's abode;
It holds its life from thee alone
On earth, or in the world unknown.

To thee our ſpirits we reſign,
Make them and own them ſtill as thine;
So ſhall they live ſecure from fear,
Though death ſhould blaſt the riſing year.

Thy children, panting to be gone,
May bid the tide of time roll on,
To land them on that happy ſhore,
Where years and death are known no more

No more fatigue, no more diſtreſs,
Nor ſin, nor hell ſhall reach that place;
No groans to mingle with the ſongs,
Reſounding from immortal tongues:

No more alarms from ghoſtly foes;
No cares to break the long repoſe;
No midnight ſhade, no clouded ſun,
But ſacred high eternal noon.

O, long expected year! begin;
Dawn on this world of woe and ſin;
Fain would we leave this weary road,
To ſleep in death, and reſt with God.

Philadelphia Mortality Bill, 1793 *(The Library Company of Philadelphia)*

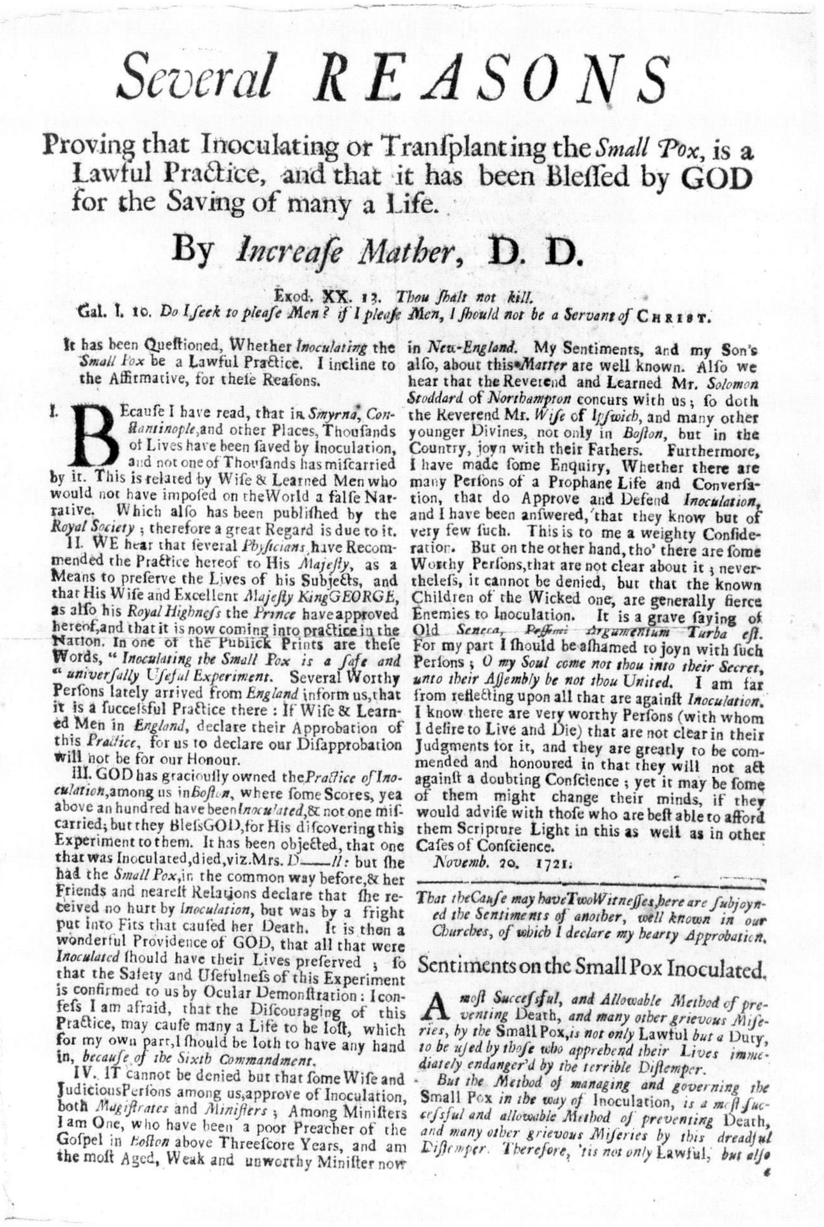

Several REASONS

Proving that Inoculating or Tranſplanting the *Small Pox*, is a Lawful Practice, and that it has been Bleſſed by GOD for the Saving of many a Life.

By *Increaſe Mather*, D. D.

Exod. XX. 13. *Thou ſhalt not kill.*
Gal. I. 10. *Do I ſeek to pleaſe Men? if I pleaſe Men, I ſhould not be a Servant of* CHRIST.

It has been Queſtioned, Whether *Inoculating* the *Small Pox* be a Lawful Practice. I incline to the Affirmative, for theſe Reaſons.

I. BEcauſe I have read, that in *Smyrna*, *Conſtantinople*, and other Places, Thouſands of Lives have been ſaved by Inoculation, and not one of Thouſands has miſcarried by it. This is related by Wiſe & Learned Men who would not have impoſed on the World a falſe Narrative. Which alſo has been publiſhed by the *Royal Society*; therefore a great Regard is due to it.

II. WE hear that ſeveral *Phyſicians* have Recommended the Practice hereof to His *Majeſty*, as a Means to preſerve the Lives of his Subjects, and that His Wiſe and Excellent *Majeſty* King GEORGE, as alſo his *Royal Highneſs* the *Prince* have approved hereof, and that it is now coming into practice in the Nation. In one of the Publick Prints are theſe Words, "*Inoculating the Small Pox is a ſafe and* "*univerſally Uſeful Experiment.* Several Worthy Perſons lately arrived from *England* inform us, that it is a ſucceſsful Practice there: If Wiſe & Learned Men in *England*, declare their Approbation of this *Practice*, for us to declare our Diſapprobation will not be for our Honour.

III. GOD has graciouſly owned the *Practice of Inoculation*, among us in *Boſton*, where ſome Scores, yea above an hundred have been *Inoculated*, & not one miſcarried; but they Bleſs GOD, for His diſcovering this Experiment to them. It has been objected, that one that was Inoculated, died, viz. Mrs. *D——ll*: but ſhe had the *Small Pox*, in the common way before, & her Friends and neareſt Relations declare that ſhe received no hurt by *Inoculation*, but was by a fright put into Fits that cauſed her Death. It is then a wonderful Providence of GOD, that all that were *Inoculated* ſhould have their Lives preſerved; ſo that the Safety and Uſefulneſs of this Experiment is confirmed to us by Ocular Demonſtration: I confeſs I am afraid, that the Diſcouraging of this Practice, may cauſe many a Life to be loſt, which for my own part, I ſhould be loth to have any hand in, *becauſe of the Sixth Commandment.*

IV. IT cannot be denied but that ſome Wiſe and Judicious Perſons among us, approve of Inoculation, both *Magiſtrates* and *Miniſters*; Among Miniſters I am One, who have been a poor Preacher of the Goſpel in *Boſton* above Threeſcore Years, and am the moſt Aged, Weak and unworthy Miniſter now in *New-England*. My Sentiments, and my Son's alſo, about this Matter are well known. Alſo we hear that the Reverend and Learned Mr. *Solomon Stoddard* of *Northampton* concurs with us; ſo doth the Reverend Mr. *Wiſe* of *Ipſwich*, and many other younger Divines, not only in *Boſton*, but in the Country, joyn with their Fathers. Furthermore, I have made ſome Enquiry, Whether there are many Perſons of a Prophane Life and Converſation, that do Approve and Defend *Inoculation*, and I have been anſwered, that they know but of very few ſuch. This is to me a weighty Conſideration. But on the other hand, tho' there are ſome Worthy Perſons, that are not clear about it; nevertheleſs, it cannot be denied, but that the known Children of the Wicked one, are generally fierce Enemies to Inoculation. It is a grave ſaying of Old *Seneca*, *Peſſimi Argumentum Turba eſt.* For my part I ſhould be aſhamed to joyn with ſuch Perſons; *O my Soul come not thou into their Secret, unto their Aſſembly be not thou United.* I am far from reflecting upon all that are againſt *Inoculation.* I know there are very worthy Perſons (with whom I deſire to Live and Die) that are not clear in their Judgments for it, and they are greatly to be commended and honoured in that they will not act againſt a doubting Conſcience; yet it may be ſome of them might change their minds, if they would adviſe with thoſe who are beſt able to afford them Scripture Light in this as well as in other Caſes of Conſcience.

Novemb. 20. 1721.

That the Cauſe may have Two Witneſſes, here are ſubjoyned the Sentiments of another, well known in our Churches, of which I declare my hearty Approbation.

Sentiments on the Small Pox Inoculated.

A *moſt Succeſsful, and Allowable Method of preventing* Death, *and many other grievous Miſeries, by the* Small Pox, *is not only* Lawful *but a* Duty, *to be uſed by thoſe who apprehend their* Lives *immediately endanger'd by the terrible Diſtemper.*

But the Method of managing and governing the Small Pox *in the way of* Inoculation, *is a moſt ſucceſsful and allowable Method of preventing* Death, *and many other grievous Miſeries by this dreadful Diſtemper. Therefore, 'tis not only* Lawful, *but alſo*

Pamphlet by Increase Mather in the debate over inoculation, 1721 *(The University of Virginia Library, Special Collection)*

A furious religious and scientific debate erupted in Boston over inoculation in 1721. Some thought that introducing mild cases of smallpox would spread the disease even further. Others, believing that God sent epidemics to chasten sinful people, argued that it was blasphemous to challenge providence. Yet the public was won over slowly as experiments in Philadelphia and Charleston showed that the inoculated rarely died of the disease while the uninoculated died in alarming numbers. By 1763, when smallpox broke out in Boston again, almost all the nonimmune stepped forward to receive inoculation (with only 46 deaths among 4,977 inoculated). Free inoculation for the poor at public dispensaries in several cities on the eve of the American Revolution sharply arrested the disease. Smallpox was all but eliminated as a killer disease after 1798 when an English doctor discovered that vaccination with cowpox gave almost foolproof immunity to the disease.

In conquering smallpox, Americans were only beginning to use science to win the war for public health. Repeated outbreaks of yellow fever, traveling from Africa to the West Indies to North America, caused terror in Philadelphia, New York, and other cities in the 1790s. The ghastly death tolls, reaching 5,000 in Philadelphia in 1793 and some 4,000 in New York in 1799, represented biological holocausts never experienced since. Almost all cities established boards of health in the early nineteenth century to improve sanitation, contain epidemic diseases, and urge vaccination against them when medical knowledge brought about effective procedures. But this did not prevent cholera epidemics that swept through American cities like a hurricane from the 1830s to the 1860s or stop a vicious wave of influenza in 1918 that moved like an avenging angel through military camps and civilian populations alike (killing ten times as many Americans as in World War I). As late as the 1940s, several million Americans were struck down or paralyzed by polio.

Before the twentieth century, few American families escaped untimely death through epidemic disease. As in the colonial period, terrifying epidemic diseases disrupted and disfigured family life and often brought local economies to their knees. Americans relied primarily on imported medical knowledge to combat epidemic diseases for a long time, but gradually after World War I, university schools of medicine, pharmaceutical company laboratories, and the National Institutes of Health (founded in 1930) put the United States in the forefront of disease control and research medicine.

How has religion remained a factor in medical intervention? What explains American preeminence in medical research after World War II?

Reading: Charles E. Rosenberg, *Explaining Epidemics and Other Studies in the History of Medicine* (Cambridge, Eng., 1992); J. H. Powell, *Bring Out Your Dead: The Great Plague of Yellow Fever in Philadelphia in 1793* (Philadelphia, 1949).

revolutionary arguments to define their own goals. They signed nonimportation agreements, harassed noncomplying merchants, and helped organize "fast days," on which communities prayed for deliverance from English oppression. But the women's most important role was to facilitate the boycott of English goods. The success of the nonconsumption pacts depended on substituting homespun cloth for English textiles on which colonists of all classes had always relied. From Georgia to Maine, women and children began spinning yarn and weaving cloth. "Was not every fireside, indeed a theatre of politics?" John Adams remembered after the war. Towns often vied patriotically in the manufacture of cotton, linen, and woolen cloth, the women staging open-air spinning contests to publicize their commitment. In 1769, the women of tiny Middletown, Massachusetts, set the standard by weaving 20,522 yards of cloth, about 160 yards each.

After the Tea Act in 1773, the interjection of politics into the household economy increased as patriotic women boycotted their favorite drink. Newspapers carried recipes for tea substitutes and recommendations for herbal teas. In Wilmington, North Carolina, women paraded solemnly through the town and then made a ritual display of their patriotism by burning their imported tea. Many women agreed with one Rachel Wells: "I have done as much to carry on the war as many that set now at the helm of government."

As marketgoers and consumers, urban women played a crucial role in applying economic pressure on England during the prerevolutionary decade. This British cartoon, published in 1775, derisively depicts a group of North Carolina women signing an anti-tea agreement. A slave woman looks on while a bewigged Whig focuses on something other than tea. (*Library of Congress*)

Women's perception of their role was also changed by colonial protests and petitions against England's arbitrary uses of power. The more male leaders talked about England's intentions to "enslave" the Americans and England's callous treatment of its colonial "subjects," the more American women began to rethink their own domestic situations. The language of protest against England reminded many American women that they too were badly treated "subjects" of their husbands, who often dealt with them cruelly and exercised power over them arbitrarily. If there was to be independence, new laws must be passed, Abigail Adams reminded her husband John in March 1776. As they did their work, the male lawmakers should think about the rights of women and their enslavement by men. Choosing words and phrases that had been used over and over in the protests against England, she wrote: "Do not put such unlimited power into the hand of the husbands. . . . Put it out of the power of the vicious and the lawless to use us with cruelty and indignity," she insisted. "Remember, all men would be tyrants if they could." Borrowing directly from the republican ideology used to protest Parliament's attempts to tax the Americans, Abigail Adams warned that American women "will not hold ourselves bound by any laws in which we have no voice, or representation" and even promised that women would "foment a rebellion" if men did not heed their rightful claims.

Many American women, still bound by the social conventions of the day, were not ready to occupy such new territory. But the protests against England had stirred up new thoughts about what seemed "arbitrary" or "despotic" in their own society. Hence, many agendas for change appeared and with them a new feeling that what had been endured in the past was no longer acceptable. "We have it in our power," warned Abigail Adams to her husband, "not only to free ourselves but to subdue our masters, and without violence throw both your natural and legal authority at our feet."

Protesting Farmers

In most of the agricultural areas of the colonies, where many settlers made their livelihoods, passions over English policies awakened only slowly. After about 1740, farmers had benefited from a sharp rise in the demand for foodstuffs in England, southern Europe, and the West Indies. Rising prices and brisk markets brought a higher standard of living to thousands of rural colonists, especially south of New England. Living far from harping English customs officers, impressment gangs, and occupying armies, the colonists of the interior had to be drawn gradually into the resistance movement by their urban cousins. Even in Concord, Massachusetts, only a dozen miles from the center of colonial agitation, townspeople found little to protest in English policies until England closed the port of Boston in 1774. They concerned themselves with local issues—roads, schools, the location of churches—but rarely with the frightful offenses to American liberty that Bostonians perceived.

Yet some parts of rural America seethed with social tension in the prewar era. The dynamics of conflict, shaped by the social development of particular regions, eventually became part of the momentum for revolution. In three western counties of North Carolina and in the Hudson River valley of New York, for example, widespread civil disorder marked the prerevolutionary decades. The militant rhetoric and tactics small farmers used to combat exploitation formed rivulets that fed the mainstream of revolutionary consciousness.

For years, the small farmers of western North Carolina had suffered exploitation by corrupt county court officials appointed by the governor and a legislature dominated by eastern planter interests. Sheriffs and justices, allied with land speculators and lawyers, seized property when farmers could not pay their taxes and sold it, often at a fraction of its worth, to their cronies. The legislature rejected western petitions for lower taxes, paper currency, and lower court fees. In the mid-1760s, frustrated at getting no satisfaction from legal forms of protest, the farmers formed associations of so-called Regulators that forcibly closed the courts, attacked the property of their enemies, and whipped and publicly humiliated judges and lawyers. When their leaders were arrested, the Regulators stormed the jails and released them.

In 1768 and again in 1771, Governor William Tryon led troops against the Regulators. Bloodshed was averted on the first occasion, but on the second, at the Battle of Alamance, two armies of more than 1,000 opened fire on each other. Nine men died on each side before the Regulators fled the field. Seven leaders were executed in the ensuing trials. Though the Regulators lost on the field of battle, their protests became part of the larger revolutionary struggle. They railed against the self-interested behavior of a wealthy elite and asserted the necessity for people of humble rank to throw off deference and assume political responsibilities.

Rural insurgency in New York flared up in the 1750s, subsided, and then erupted again in 1766. The conditions under which land was held precipitated the violence. The Hudson River valley had long been controlled by a few wealthy families with enormous landholdings, which they leased to small tenant farmers. The Van Rensselaer manor, for example, totaled a million acres, the Phillipses' manor nearly half as much. Hundreds of tenants with their families paid substantial annual rents for the right to farm on these lands, which had been acquired as virtually free gifts from royal governors. When tenants resisted rent increases or purchased land from Indians who swore that manor lords had extended the boundaries of their manors by fraud, the landlords began evicting them.

Timeline

1696	Parliament establishes Board of Trade
1701	Iroquois set policy of neutrality
1702–1713	Queen Anne's War
1713	Peace of Utrecht
1733	Molasses Act
1744–1748	King George's War
1754	Albany conference
1755	Braddock defeated by French and Indian allies
1756–1763	Seven Years' War
1759	Wolfe defeats the French at Quebec
1759–1761	Cherokee War against the English
1760s	Economic slump
1763	Treaty of Paris ends Seven Years' War
	Proclamation line limits westward expansion
1764	Sugar and Currency acts
	Pontiac's Rebellion in Ohio valley
1765	Colonists resist Stamp Act
	Virginia House of Burgesses issues Stamp Act resolutions
1766	Declaratory Act
	Tenant rent war in New York
	Slave insurrections in South Carolina
1767	Townshend duties imposed
1768	British troops occupy Boston
1770	"Boston Massacre"
	Townshend duties repealed (except on tea)
1771	North Carolina Regulators defeated
1772	*Gaspee* incident in Rhode Island
1773	Tea Act provokes Boston Tea Party
1774	"Intolerable Acts"
	First Continental Congress meets
1775	Second Continental Congress meets
	Battles of Lexington and Concord
1776	Thomas Paine publishes *Common Sense*
	Declaration of Independence

As the wealthiest men of the region, the landlords had the power of government, including control of the courts, on their side. Organizing themselves and going outside the law became the tenants' main strategy, as with the Carolina Regulators. By 1766, while New York City was absorbed in the Stamp Act furor, tenants led by William Prendergast began resisting sheriffs who tried to evict them from lands they claimed. The militant tenants threatened landlords with death and broke open jails to rescue their friends. British troops from New York were used to break the tenant rebellion. Prendergast was tried and sentenced to be hanged, beheaded, and quartered. Although he was pardoned, the bitterness of the Hudson River tenants endured through the Revolution. Most of them, unlike the Carolina Regulators, fought for the British because their landlords had joined the patriot cause

Conclusion

Forging a Revolution

The colonial Americans who lived in the third quarter of the eighteenth century participated in an era of political tension and conflict that changed the lives of nearly all of them. The Seven Years' War removed French and Spanish challengers and nurtured the colonists' sense of separate identity. Yet it left them with difficult economic adjustments, heavy debts, and growing social divisions. The colonists heralded the Treaty of Paris in 1763 as the dawning of a new era, but it led to a reorganization of England's triumphant yet debt-torn empire that had profound repercussions in America.

In the prerevolutionary decade, as England and the colonies moved from crisis to crisis, a dual disillusionment penetrated ever deeper into the colonial consciousness. Pervasive doubt arose concerning both the colonies' role, as assigned by England, in the economic life of the empire and the sensitivity of the government in London to the colonists' needs. At the same time, the colonists began to perceive British policies—instituted by Parliament, the king, and his advisors—as a systematic attack on the fundamental liberties and natural rights of British citizens in America.

The fluidity and diversity of colonial society and the differing experiences of Americans during and after the Seven Years' War evoked varying responses to the disruption that accompanied the English reorganization of the empire. In the course of resisting English policy, many previously inactive groups entered public life to challenge gentry control of political affairs. Often occupying the most radical ground in the opposition to England, they simultaneously challenged the growing concentration of economic and political power in their own communities.

When the Congress turned the 15-month undeclared war into a formally declared struggle for national liberation in July 1776, it steered its compatriots onto turbulent and unknown seas. Writing to his wife Abigail from his Philadelphia boardinghouse, the secularized Puritan John Adams caught some of the peculiar blend of excitement and dread that thousands shared. "You will think me transported with enthusiasm but I am not. I am well aware of the toil and blood and treasure that it will cost us to maintain this Declaration, and support and defend these States. Yet through all the gloom I can see the rays of ravishing light and glory. I can see that the end is more than worth all the means. And that posterity will triumph in that day's transactions, even though we should rue it, which I trust in God we shall not."

Recommended Reading

The Climactic Seven Years' War

Fred Anderson, *A People's Army: Massachusetts Soldiers and Society in the Seven Years' War* (1984); Gregory Dowd, *A Spirited Resistance: The North American Indian Struggle for Unity, 1745–1815* (1992); Tom Hatley, *The Dividing Paths: Cherokees and South Carolinians through the Era of Revolution* (1993); Francis Jennings, *Empire of Fortune: Crowns, Colonies, and Tribes in the Seven Years' War in America* (1988); Howard H. Peckham, *Pontiac and the Indian Uprising* (1947); Fred Anderson, *Crucible of War: The Seven Years' War and the Fate of Empire in British North America, 1754–1766* (2000).

The Crisis with England

John Brewer, *Party Ideology and Popular Politics at the Accession of George III* (1976); Ian R. Christie, *Crisis of Empire: Great Britain and the American Colonies, 1754–1783* (1966); Michael Kammen, *Empire and Interest* (1970); John Shy, *Toward Lexington: The Role of the British Army in the Coming of the American Revolution* (1965); Peter D. G. Thomas, *Tea Party to Independence: The Third Phase of the American Revolution* (1991).

The Ideology of Revolutionary Republicanism

Bernard Bailyn, *The Ideological Origins of the American Revolution* (1967); Ruth Bloch, *Visionary Republic: Millennial Themes in American Thought, 1750–1800* (1985); Richard Bushman, *King and People in Provincial Massachusetts* (1985); Jay Fliegelman, *Prodigals and Pilgrims: The American Revolution Against Patriarchal Authority, 1750–1800* (1982); Nathan O. Hatch, *The Sacred Cause of Liberty: Republican Thought and the Millennium in Revolutionary New England* (1977); Pauline

Maier, *From Resistance to Revolution: Colonial Radicals and the Development of American Opposition to Britain, 1765–1776* (1972); Edmund S. Morgan, *Inventing the People: The Rise of Popular Sovereignty in England and America* (1988); Gary B. Nash, *The Urban Crucible: Social Change, Political Consciousness, and the Origins of the American Revolution* (1979); Alfred F. Young, *The Shoemaker and the Tea Party: Memory and the American Revolution* (1999).

The Turmoil of Revolutionary Society

Edward Countryman, *A People in Revolution* (1981); David Hackett Fischer, *Paul Revere's Ride* (1994); Eric Foner, *Tom Paine and Revolutionary America* (1976); Robert Gross, *The Minutemen and Their World* (1976); Dirk Hoerder, *Crowd Action in Revolutionary Massachusetts, 1765–1780* (1977); Linda K. Kerber, *Women of the Republic: Intellect and Ideology in Revolutionary America* (1980); Henry Mayer, *A Son of Thunder: Patrick Henry and the American Republic* (1991); Mary Beth Norton, *Liberty's Daughters: The Revolutionary Experience of American Women, 1750–1800* (1980); Steven Rosswurm, *Arms, Country, and Class: The Philadelphia Militia and the "Lower Sort" During the American Revolution* (1987); Alfred E. Young, ed., *The American Revolution: Essays in the History of American Radicalism* (1976).

Fiction and Film

Americans have written novels about the American Revolution almost from the day the firing stopped. James Fenimore Cooper's *The Spy: A Tale of the Neutral Ground* (1822) is the best of the early ones. Historian Paul Leicester Ford's *Janice Meredith: A Story of the American Revolution* (1899) is absorbing a century after its publication. In the modern period, Kenneth Roberts's four novels on the Revolution have entertained American readers for two generations: *Arundel* (1933); *Oliver Wiswell* (1940); *Rabble in Arms* (1953); and *The Battle of Cowpens: The Great Morale-Builder* (1958). *Oliver Wiswell* is especially notable for its recreation of a Loyalist's view of the Revolution. *Mary Silliman's War* (Heritage Film and Citadel Film, 1993) shows the Revolution through the eyes of a Connecticut family where husband and wife must reconcile their differing views on the Patriots and Loyalists. The English film on George III, *The Madness of King George* (1994), brings alive the era of the American Revolution and turns the king into the deeply psychotic ruler that some at the time believed he was. *Liberty* (Middlemarch Films, 1997) is a docudrama produced for television that has many high moments but neglects the internal struggles within the Patriot ranks for reforming American society.

Suggested Web Sites

http://www.lib.virginia.edu/exhibits/lewis_clark/home.html

Exploring the West from Monticello: An Exhibition of Maps and Navigational Instruments. Maps and charts reveal knowledge and conceptions about the known and the unknown. This site includes a number of eighteenth-century maps.

http://scarlett.libs.uga.edu/darchive/hargrett/maps/colamer.html

http://scarlett.libs.uga.edu/darchive/hargrett/maps/revamer.html

Georgia's Rare Map Collection. These two sites contain maps of Colonial and Revolutionary America.

http://digitalhistory.org

The French and Indian War. Digital History LTD provides extensive archives in this site not intended for an exclusively academic audience.

http://web.syr.edu/~laroux/

The French and Indian War. This site is about French soldiers who came to New France between 1755 and 1760 to fight in the French and Indian War.

http://www.dpipc.com/cdadesign/paine/home.html

Thomas Paine National Historical Association. This official site contains a large archive of Paine's works and information about the association.

http://www.ushistoryplace.com

the history place

A richly detailed on-line learning environment complete with interactive maps, timelines, history activities, primary source documents, and links to related American history sites.

6

A PEOPLE *in* REVOLUTION

CHAPTER OUTLINE

Among the Americans wounded and captured at the Battle of Bunker Hill in the spring of 1775 was Lieutenant William Scott of Peterborough, New Hampshire. Asked by his captors how he had come to be a rebel, "Long Bill" Scott replied:

> The case was this Sir! I lived in a Country Town; I was a Shoemaker, & got [my] living by my labor. When this rebellion came on, I saw some of my neighbors get into commission, who were no better than myself. . . . I was asked to enlist, as a private soldier. My ambition was too great for so low a rank. I offered to enlist upon having a lieutenant's commission, which was granted. I imagined my self now in a way of promotion. If I was killed in battle, there would be an end of me, but if my Captain was killed, I should rise in rank, & should still have a chance to rise higher. These Sir! were the only motives of my entering into the service. For as to the dispute between Great Britain & the colonies, I know nothing of it; neither am I capable of judging whether it is right or wrong.

Scott may have been trying to gain the sympathy of his captors, but people fought in America's Revolutionary War for a variety of reasons—fear and ambition as well as principle among them. We have no way of knowing whether Long Bill Scott's motives were typical. Certainly many Americans knew more than he about the colonies' struggle with England, but many did not.

In the spring of 1775, the Revolutionary War had just begun. So had Long Bill's adventures. When the British evacuated Boston a year later, Scott was transported to Halifax, Nova Scotia. After several months' captivity, he managed to escape and make his way home to fight once more. He was recaptured in November 1776 near New York City, when its garrison fell to a surprise British assault. Again Scott escaped, this time by swimming the Hudson River at night with his sword tied around his neck and his watch pinned to his hat.

William Mercer, *Battle of Princeton*, c. 1786–1790. Because infantry weapons were inaccurate at long distances, lines formed in close proximity, where weapons were more deadly and combat was intensely personal. Here, General Washington directs the American force. (*Historical Society of Pennsylvania*)

During the winter of 1777, he returned to New Hampshire to recruit his own militia company. It included two of his eldest sons. In the fall, his unit helped defeat Burgoyne's army near Saratoga, New York, and later took part in the fighting around Newport, Rhode Island. When his light infantry company was ordered to Virginia in early 1778, Scott's health broke, and he was permitted to resign from the army. After only a few months' recuperation, however, he was at it again. During the last year of the war, he served as a volunteer on a navy frigate.

For seven years, the war held Scott in its harsh grasp. Scott's oldest son died of camp fever after six years of service. In 1777, Long Bill sold his New Hampshire farm to meet family expenses. He lost a second farm in Massachusetts shortly afterward. After his wife died, he turned their youngest children over to relatives and set off to beg a pension or job from the government.

Long Bill's saga was still not complete. In 1792, he rescued eight people when their boat capsized in New York harbor. Three years later, General Benjamin Lincoln took Scott with him to the Ohio country, where they surveyed land that was opening for white settlement. At last he had a respectable job and even a small government pension as compensation for his nine wounds. But trouble would still not let him go. While surveying on the Black River near Sandusky, Scott and his colleagues contracted "lake fever." Though ill, he guided part of the group back to Fort Stanwix in New York, then returned for the others. It was his last heroic act. A few days after his second trip, on September 16, 1796, he died.

American independence and the Revolutionary War that accompanied it were not as hard on everyone as they were on Long Bill Scott, yet together they transformed the lives of countless Americans. The war lasted seven years, longer than any other of America's wars until Vietnam, nearly two centuries later. And unlike the nation's twentieth-century contests, it was fought on American soil, among the American people. It called men by the thousands from shops and fields, disrupted families, destroyed communities, spread diseases, and made a shambles of the economy.

Amid this struggle for independence, the American people also mounted a political revolution of profound importance. Politics and government were transformed in keeping with republican principles and the rapidly changing circumstances of public life. What did republican liberty

entail? How should government power be organized? Who should be considered republican citizens? How democratic could American society safely be? These were among the questions with which the American people wrestled at the nation's beginning.

As the tempo of political activity increased under the pressures of war and revolution, people clashed repeatedly over new state constitutions and the shape of a national government. Seldom has America's political agenda been more troubled.

The American Revolution dominated the lives of all who lived through it. But it had different consequences for men than for women, for black slaves than for their white masters, for Native Americans than for frontier settlers, for overseas merchants than for urban workers, for northern businessmen than for southern planters. Our understanding of the experience out of which the American nation emerged must begin with the Revolutionary War, for liberty came at a high cost.

THE WAR FOR AMERICAN INDEPENDENCE

The war began in Massachusetts in 1775, but within a year its focus shifted to the middle states. After 1779, the South became the primary theater. Why did this geographic pattern develop, what was its significance, and why did the Americans win?

The War in the North

For a brief time following Lexington and Concord, British officials thought of launching forays out from Boston into the surrounding countryside. They soon reconsidered, however, for the growing size of the continental army and the absence of significant Loyalist strength in the New England region urged caution. Even more important, Boston became untenable after the Americans placed artillery on the strategic Dorchester Heights. On March 7, 1776, the British commander, General William Howe, decided to evacuate.

People worried that Howe would set fire to the city as he departed. Fearing retaliation against Loyalist property and wishing not to destroy any lingering hopes of reconciliation, Howe spared the city from the torch. The town, however, had been treated badly enough. British officers had taken over the homes of John Hancock, James Bowdoin, and others, while dragoons had used the Old South Meeting House as a riding school, after tearing out the pews, and the Old North Church had been demolished for firewood. All around lay trampled gardens, uprooted trees, and filth. "Almost everything here, appears Gloomy and Melancholy," lamented one returning resident.

For a half dozen years after Boston's evacuation, British ships prowled the New England coast, confiscating supplies and attacking coastal towns. Yet away from the coast, there was little fighting. Most New Englanders had reason to be thankful for their good fortune.

After evacuating Boston, British officials established their military headquarters in New York City. Their decision was strategically sound, for New York offered important strategic advantages. It was centrally located, and its spacious harbor lay at the mouth of the Hudson River, the major water route northward into the interior. Control of New York would, in addition, ensure access to the abundant grain and livestock of the Middle Atlantic states. Finally, Loyalist sentiment ran deep among the inhabitants of the city and its environs.

In the summer of 1776, Washington moved his troops south from Boston, determined to challenge the British for control of New York City. It proved a terrible mistake. Outmaneuvered and badly outnumbered, he suffered defeat at the Battle of Long Island and then in Manhattan itself. By late October, the city was firmly in British hands. It would remain so until the war's end.

In the fall of 1776, King George III instructed his two chief commanders in North America—General Howe and his brother, Admiral Richard Howe—to make a final effort at reconciliation with the colonists. They carried authority to pardon all Americans who acknowledged allegiance to the king and to negotiate with any colony that dissolved its revolutionary committees. In early September, the Howes met with three delegates from the Congress on Staten Island, in New York harbor. The outcome was not long in doubt, for when the Howes demanded revocation of the Declaration of Independence before negotiations could begin, all hope of reconciliation vanished.

For the next two years, the war swept back and forth across New Jersey and Pennsylvania. Reinforced by German mercenaries hired in Europe, the British moved virtually at will. Neither the state militias nor the continental army—weakened by losses, low morale, and inadequate supplies—offered serious opposition. At Trenton in December 1776 and again at Princeton the following month, Washington surprised the British and scored victories that prevented the

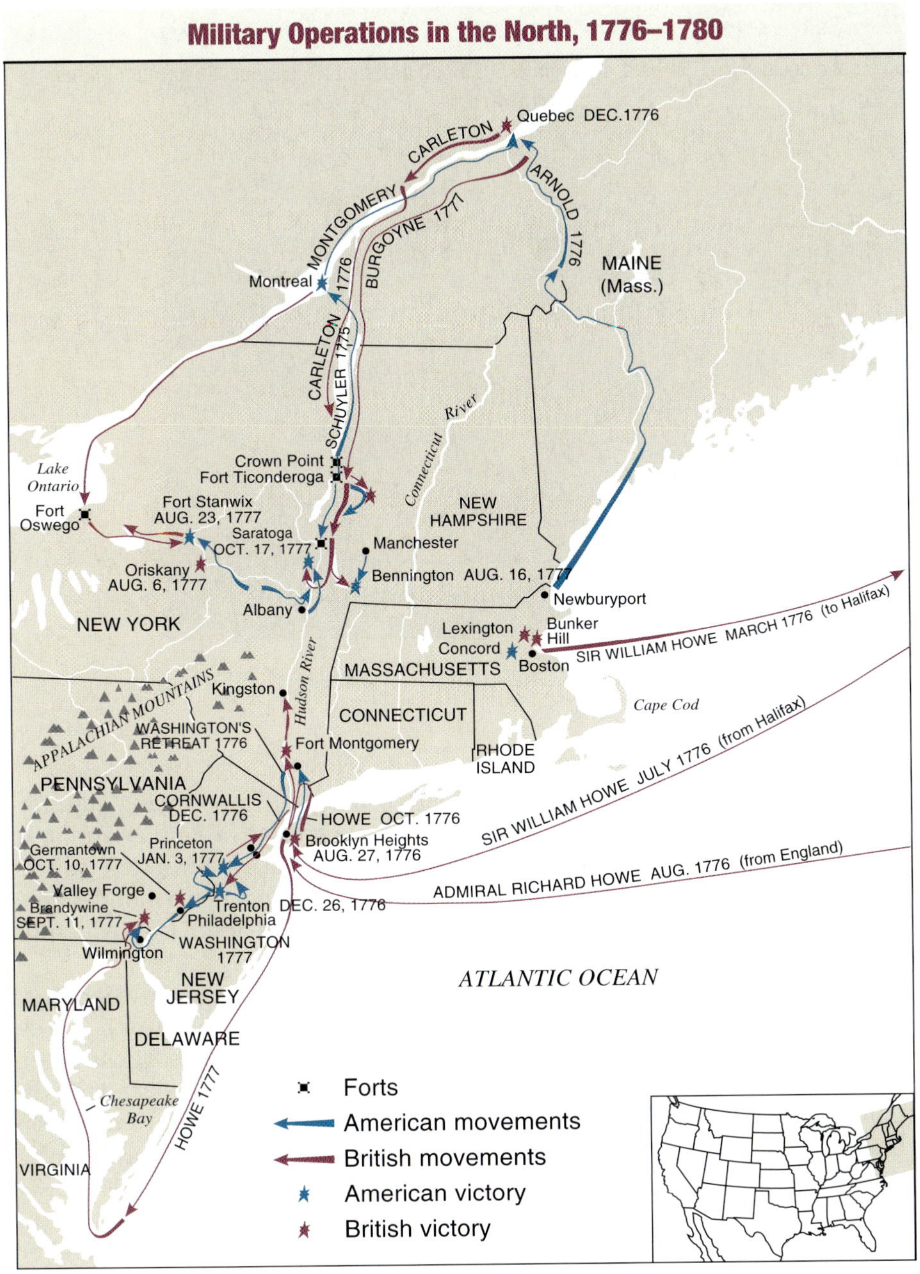

During the early years of the war, fighting was most intense in upper New York and the mid-Atlantic states. Note the importance of water routes to military strategies.

Americans' collapse. For the rebels, however, survival remained the primary goal.

American efforts during the first year of the war to invade Canada and bring that British colony into the rebellion also fared badly. In November 1775, American forces under General Richard Montgomery had taken Montreal. But the subsequent assault against Quebec ended with almost 100 Americans killed or wounded and more than 300 taken prisoner. The American cause could not survive many such losses.

Washington had learned the painful lesson at New York that his troops were no match for the British in frontal combat. He realized, moreover, that if the continental army was defeated, American independence would certainly be lost. Thus, he decided on a strategy of harassing the British, making the war as costly for them as possible, and protecting the civilian population as best he could while avoiding major battles. He would follow that strategy for the rest of the war.

As a consequence, the war's middle years turned into a deadly chase that neither side proved able to win. In September 1777, the British took Philadelphia, sending the Congress fleeing into the countryside, but then hesitated to press their advantage. On numerous occasions British commanders failed to act decisively, either reluctant to move through the hostile countryside or uncertain of their instructions. Offsetting

This watercolor painting offers a humorous, even mocking, depiction of the variety of uniforms worn by American troops. *(Anne S. K. Brown Military Collection, Brown University)*

British domination of the Middle Atlantic region was the American victory in October at Saratoga, New York, where General Burgoyne surrendered with 5,700 British soldiers. That victory prompted France to join the struggle against England.

Congress and the Articles of Confederation

As the war erupted, the Continental Congress turned to the task of creating a more permanent and effective national government. It was a daunting assignment, for prior to independence the colonies had quarreled repeatedly over colonial boundaries, control of the Indian trade, and commercial advantage within the empire. The crisis with England had forced them together, and the Congress was the initial embodiment of that tenuous union. The first Continental Congress had met for only seven weeks, limiting itself to protesting English policies and urging support for the Continental Association.

The Second Continental Congress, convening in May 1775, in the midst of the war crisis, began to exercise some of the most basic responsibilities of a sovereign government: raising an army and establishing diplomatic relations. Its powers, though, were unclear; its legitimacy, uncertain. As long as hopes of reconciliation with England lingered, these limitations posed no serious problems. But as independence and the prospects of an extended war loomed, pressure to establish a more durable central government increased. On June 20, 1776, shortly before independence was declared, Congress appointed a committee, chaired by John Dickinson of Pennsylvania, to draw up a plan of perpetual union. So urgent was the crisis that the committee responded in a month's time, and debate on its proposed Articles of Confederation quickly began.

The delegates promptly clashed over whether to form a strong, consolidated government or a loosely joined confederation of sovereign states. Those differences sharpened as the discussion proceeded. The Dickinson draft outlined a government of considerable power. Although each state was to retain "the . . . exclusive regulation . . . of its internal police," that was to be only in matters that did not interfere with the Articles of Confederation. The only unqualified restriction on the Congress was that it might never impose taxes or duties except in managing the post office. Dickinson's proposals met determined opposition. Experience with the "tyrannous" actions of the English king and Parliament had revealed how dangerous central governments, unmindful of the people's liberties, could be. Expressing fears widely held among congressional delegates, North Carolina's Thomas Burke warned that one oppressive government should not be substituted for another and insisted that Congress be subordinate to the states.

As finally approved, the Articles of Confederation represented a compromise. Article 9 gave the Congress sole authority to regulate foreign affairs, declare war, mediate boundary disputes between the states, manage the post office, and administer relations with Indians living outside state boundaries. The Articles also stipulated that the inhabitants of each state were to enjoy the "privileges and immunities" of the citizens of every other state. Embedded in that clause was the basis for national, as distinguished from state, citizenship.

At the same time, the Articles sharply limited what the Congress could do and reserved broad governing powers to the states. For example, the Congress could neither raise troops nor levy taxes but only ask the states for such support. Article 2 stipulated that each state was to "retain its sovereignty, freedom and independence," as well as "every power, jurisdiction, and right which is not by this confederation expressly delegated to the United States in Congress assembled." Nor could the Congress's limited powers be easily expanded, because the Articles could be amended only by the agreement of all 13 states.

Though the Congress sent the Articles to the states for approval in November 1777, they were not ratified until March 1781. For one thing, ratification required unanimous approval, and that was hard to obtain. The biggest impediment was a bitter dispute over control of the lands west of the Appalachian Mountains that pitted states such as Virginia, South Carolina, and New York, which had western claims tracing back to their colonial charters, against states such as Maryland and New Jersey, which had no such claims. In December 1778, the Maryland assembly announced that it would not ratify until all the western lands had been ceded to the Congress. For several years, ratification hung in the balance while politicians and land speculators jockeyed for advantage. In 1780 New York and Virginia finally agreed to transfer their western lands to the Congress. Those decisions paved the way for Maryland's ratification in early 1781. Approval of the Articles was now assured.

Meanwhile, Congress managed the war effort as best it could, using the unratified Articles as a guide. Events quickly proved its inadequacy, because Congress could do little more than pass resolutions and implore the states for support. If they refused, as they frequently did, the Congress could only protest and urge cooperation. Its ability to function was further limited by the stipulation that each state's delegation cast but one vote. On a number of occasions, disagreements within state delegations prevented them from voting at all. That could paralyze the Congress,

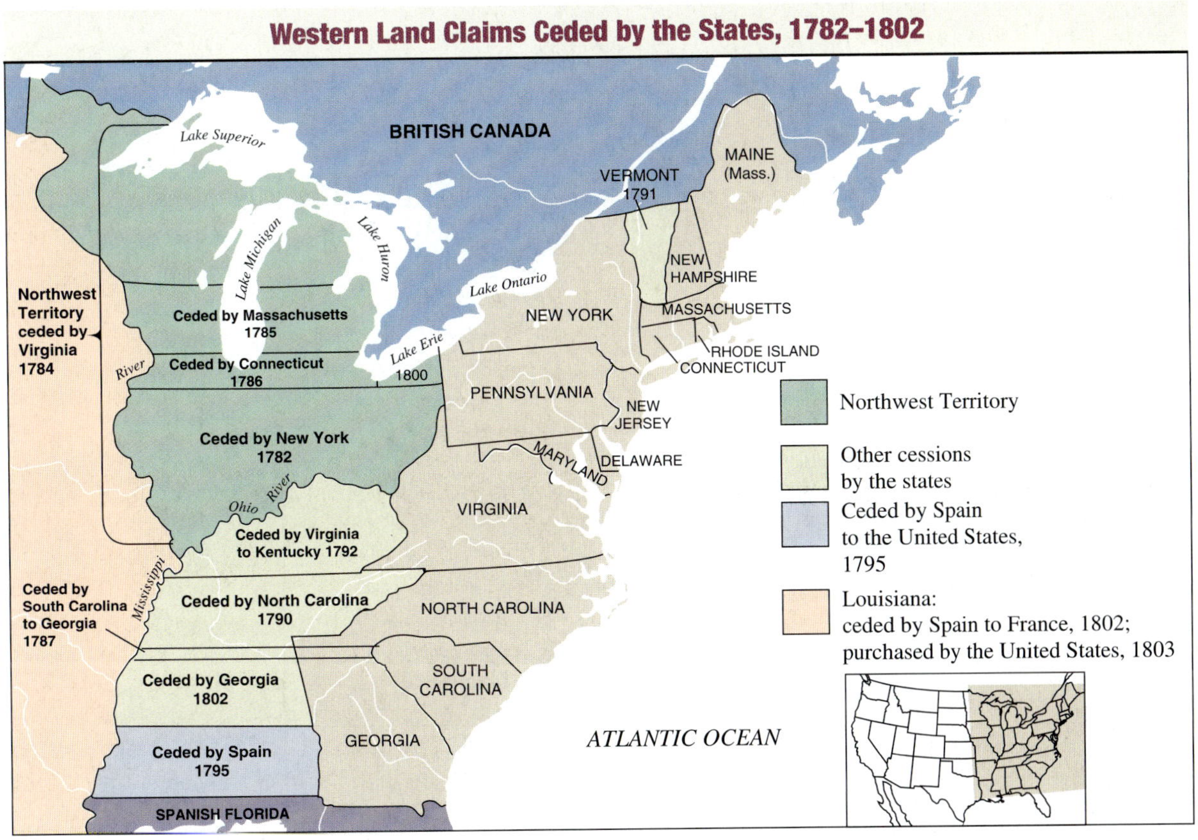

Based on their colonial charters, seven of the original states claimed land west of the Appalachian Mountains. Eventually those states ceded their western claims to the Congress, making ratification of the Articles of Confederation and the creation of new western states possible.

because most important decisions required a nine-state majority.

As the war dragged on, Washington repeatedly criticized the Congress for its failure to support the army. Acknowledging its own ineffectiveness, the Congress in 1778 temporarily granted Washington extraordinary powers and asked him to manage the war on his own. In the end, the Congress survived because enough of its members realized that disaster would follow its collapse.

The War Moves South

As the war in the North bogged down in a costly stalemate, British officials adopted an alternative strategy: invasion and pacification of the South. Royal officials in the South encouraged the idea with reports that thousands of Loyalists would rally to the British standard. The southern coastline with its numerous rivers, moreover, offered maximum advantage to British naval strength. Then there were the slaves, that vast but imponderable presence in southern society. If they could be lured to the British side, the balance might tip in Britain's favor. In any case, the threat of slave rebellion would weaken white southerners' will to resist. Persuaded by these arguments, British policymakers made the southern states the primary theater of military operations during the final years of the war.

Georgia—small, isolated, and largely defenseless—was the initial target. In December 1778, Savannah, the state's major port, fell before a seaborne attack of 3,500 men. For nearly two years, the Revolution in the state virtually ceased. Encouraged by their success, the British turned to the Carolinas, with equally impressive results. On May 12, 1780, Charleston surrendered after a month's siege. At a cost of only 225 casualties, the British captured the entire 5,400-man American garrison. It was the costliest American defeat of the war.

Military Operations in the South, 1778–1781

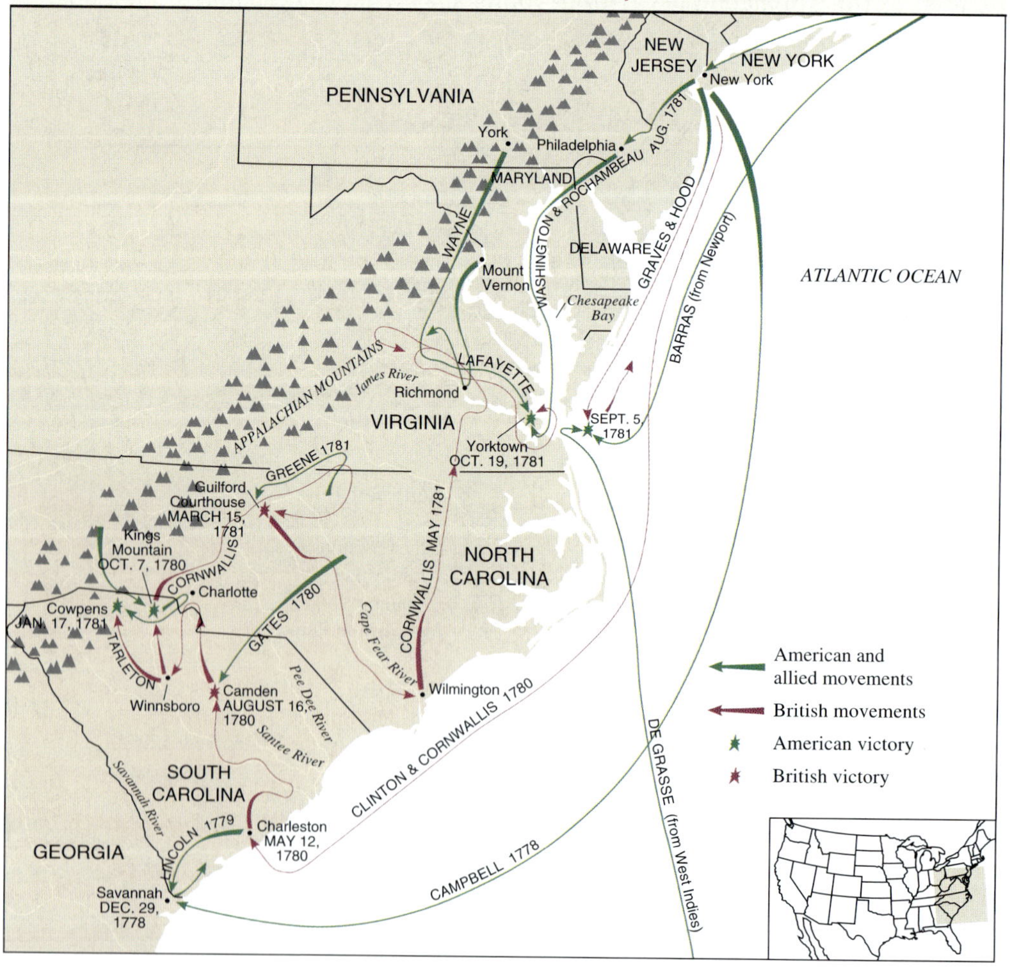

The war in the South was fought both along the coast and in the interior.

After securing Charleston, the British quickly extended their control north and south along the coast. At Camden, South Carolina, the British commander Cornwallis, aided by a corps of mounted dragoons, killed nearly 1,000 Americans and captured 1,000 more, temporarily destroying the southern continental army. With scarcely a pause, the British pushed on into North Carolina. There, however, British officers quickly learned the difficulty of extending their lines into the interior: distances were too large, problems of supply too great, the reliability of Loyalist troops too uncertain, and support among the people for the revolutionary cause too strong.

In October 1780, Washington sent Nathanael Greene south to lead the continental forces. It was a fortunate choice, for Greene knew the region and the kind of war that had to be fought. Determined, like Washington, to avoid large-scale encounters, Greene divided his army into small, mobile bands. Employing what today would be called guerrilla tactics, he harassed the British and their Loyalist allies at every opportunity, striking by surprise and then disappearing into the interior. Nowhere was the war more fiercely contested than through the Georgia and Carolina countryside. Neither British nor American authorities could restrain the violence. Bands of private marauders, roving the land and seizing advantage from the war's confusion, compounded the chaos.

In time, the tide began to turn. At Cowpens, South Carolina, in January 1781, American troops under General Daniel Morgan won a decisive victory, suffering fewer than 75 casualties to 329 British deaths, and taking 600 men prisoner. In March, at Guilford Court House in North Carolina, Cornwallis won, but at a cost that forced his retreat to Wilmington, near the sea.

In April 1781, convinced that British authority could not be restored in the Carolinas while the rebels continued to use Virginia as a supply and staging area, Cornwallis moved north. With a force of 7,500, he raided deep into Virginia, sending Governor Jefferson and the Virginia legislature fleeing from Charlottesville into the mountains. But again Cornwallis found the costs of victory high, and again he turned toward the coast for protection and resupply. On August 1, he reached Yorktown.

Cornwallis's position was secure as long as the British fleet controlled the waters of Chesapeake Bay. That advantage, however, did not last long. In 1778, the French government, still smarting from its defeat by England in the Seven Years' War and buoyed by the American victory at Saratoga in 1777, had signed an alliance with the American Congress, promising to send its naval forces into the war. Initially, the French concentrated their fleet in the West Indies, where they hoped to seize some of the British sugar islands. After repeated American urging, however, the French finally sailed north, and on August 30, 1781, the French admiral, Comte de Grasse, arrived off Yorktown. Reinforced by a second French squadron from the North, de Grasse established naval superiority in the region.

As Washington had foreseen, French entry turned the tide of war. Cut off from the sea and pinned down on a peninsula between the York and James Rivers by 17,000 French and American troops, Cornwallis's fate was sealed. On October 19, 1781, near the Virginia hamlet of Yorktown, he surrendered to General Washington. While a military band played "The World Turned Upside Down" and hundreds of civilians looked on, nearly 7,000 British troops laid down their arms.

Learning the news of Yorktown in London a month later, Lord North, the king's chief minister, exclaimed, "Oh, God! It is all over." On February 27, 1782, the House of Commons cut off further support of the war. The next month, Lord North resigned. In Philadelphia,

At Yorktown, Cornwallis asserted he was ill and sent a subordinate, Brigadier General Charles O'Hara, to yield the symbolic sword of surrender. (*Library of Congress*)

Indian Battles and the War in the West, 1775–1783

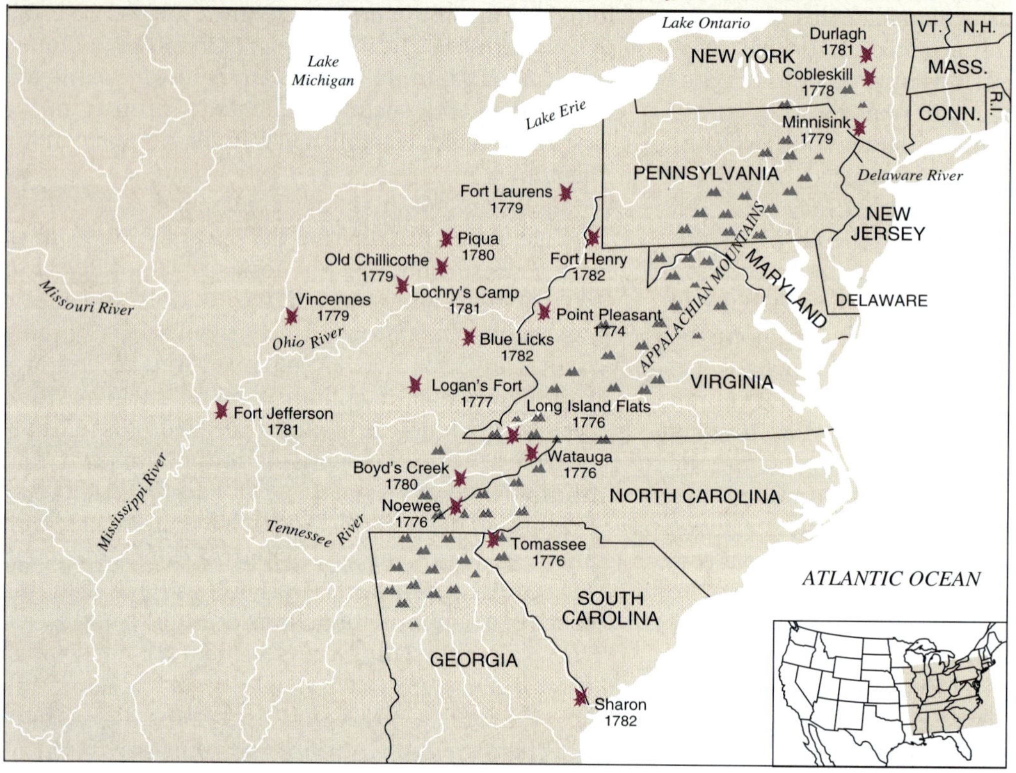

Though most battles were fought along the coastal plain, the British and their Indian allies opened a second front far to the west.

citizens poured into the streets to celebrate while the Congress assembled for a solemn ceremony of thanksgiving. Though the preliminary articles of peace were not signed until November 1782, everyone knew after Yorktown that the Americans had won their independence.

Native Americans in the Revolution

The Revolutionary War involved countless Native Americans as well as colonists and Englishmen. It could hardly have been otherwise, for the lives of all three peoples had been intertwined since the first English settlements more than a century and a half before.

Though small tribes still struggled to maintain their identities along the eastern seaboard and though Indians still roamed the streets of America's port cities, the coastal tribes—their villages displaced by white settlement and their numbers thinned by warfare and disease—no longer challenged white hegemony. Powerful tribes, however, still dominated the vast interior region between the Appalachian Mountains and the Mississippi River. The Iroquois Six Nations, a confederation numbering 15,000 people, controlled a huge area stretching westward from Albany, New York, and dominated the "western tribes" of the Ohio valley—the Shawnee, Delaware, Wyandotte, and Miami. In the Southeast, five tribes—the Choctaw, Chickasaw, Seminole, Creek, and Cherokee, 60,000 people in all—dominated the interior.

Though England's victory over France in the Seven Years' War had ended the Indians' "play-off game" and made them solely dependent on their Anglo-American trading partners, the interior tribes still retained their distinctive ways of life. Far outnumbering the few white settlers that had pushed across the Appalachians, they were more than a match, militarily and diplomatically, for the Anglo-Americans. As the imperial crisis between England and its colonies deepened, Native and European Americans eyed each other warily across this vast "middle ground."

When the Revolutionary War began, British and American officials urged neutrality on the Indians. The British, expecting the conflict to be short, wished to disrupt the interior as little as possible, while the Americans worried about Indian attacks from the west when confronting British power along the coast. The Native Americans, however, were too important militarily to ignore for long. By the spring of 1776, both sides were actively seeking Indian alliances.

Recognizing their immense stake in the imperial conflict, Native Americans up and down the interior debated their options. Alarmed by encroaching white settlement and eager to take advantage of the colonists' troubles with England, a band of Cherokee, led by the warrior Dragging Canoe, launched a series of raids in July 1776 in what is today eastern Tennessee. In a devastating response, the Virginia and Carolina militias laid waste a group of Cherokee towns. Thomas Jefferson expressed satisfaction at the outcome. "I hope that the Cherokees will now be driven beyond the Mississippi," he wrote. "Our contest with Britain is too serious, and too great to permit any possibility of [danger] . . . from the Indians." Though the Cherokee raided sporadically throughout the war, they never again mounted a sustained military effort against the rebels. Seeing what had befallen their neighbors, the Creek stayed aloof. Their time for resistance would come in the early nineteenth century, when white settlers began to push onto their lands.

In the Ohio country, the struggle lasted longer. For several decades before the Revolution, explorers such as Daniel Boone had contested with the Shawnee and others for control of the region bordering the Ohio River. The Revolutionary War intensified these conflicts. In February 1778, George Rogers Clark led a ragtag band of Kentuckians through icy rivers and across 180 miles of forbidding terrain to attack a British outpost at Vincennes, in present-day Indiana. Though outnumbered nearly four to one by the 500 British regulars and their Indian allies, Clark fooled the fort's defenders into believing that his force was much larger, and the British commander surrendered without a shot. Though skirmishes between Indians and marauding American forces continued for several years, Clark's victory tipped the balance in the war's western theater.

The Devastation of the Iroquois

To the northeast, a similar but even more deadly scenario unfolded. At a council in Albany, New York, in August 1775, representatives of the Iroquois Six Nations listened while American commissioners urged them to remain at home and keep the hatchet buried deep. "The determination of the Six Nations," replied Little Abraham, a Mohawk leader, "[is] not to take any part; but as it is a family affair, to sit still and see you fight it out." Iroquois neutrality, however, did not last long.

As the war spread throughout the Northeast in 1776, U.S. troops raided deep into Mohawk territory west of Albany. Alarmed, the British argued with words, rum, and trade goods that the Iroquois should join them against the rebels. At the Oswego Council in the summer of 1777, most of the Iroquois abandoned neutrality and took up arms against the Americans. They did so at the urging of Joseph Brant, a Mohawk warrior who had visited England several years before and argued England's value as an ally against American expansion.

It was a fateful decision for Indians and whites alike. Over the next several years, the Iroquois and their British allies devastated large areas in central New York and Pennsylvania, destroying property and terrorizing the inhabitants. An officer of the Pennsylvania militia reported somberly, "Our country is on the eve of breaking up. There is nothing to be seen but disolation, fire & smoak."

The Americans' revenge came swiftly. During the summer of 1779, General John Sullivan led a series of punishing raids into the Iroquois country, burning villages; killing men, women, and children; and destroying fields of corn. His motto for the campaign was blunt: "Civilization or death to all American savages." By war's end, the Iroquois had lost as many as a third of their people as well as countless towns. Their domination of the northeastern interior was permanently shattered.

Not all the Eastern Woodland tribes sided with England in the Revolutionary War. The Oneida and the Tuscarora, members of the Iroquois confederation, fought with the Americans, their decision driven by intertribal politics and effective diplomacy by emissaries of the Continental Congress. In New England, the Stockbridge, a small tribe surrounded by a sea of white settlement, contributed warriors and scouts, while farther to the south the Catawba, similarly dependent on the Americans for trade and diplomacy, also signed on. The Indians who fought for American independence, however, reaped little benefit from their efforts. Though General Sullivan spared the Oneida and Tuscarora villages, the British and their Iroquois allies destroyed them in turn. And although a number of Indian warriors were compensated by grateful state governments once the war was over, tribes allied with the victorious American cause enjoyed no protection from the accelerating spread of white settlement.

Most Indians had good reason for opposing American independence, because England provided them with trade goods, arms, and markets for their furs. England, moreover, had promised protection against colonial expansion, as the Proclamation Line of 1763 had demonstrated. At the peace talks that ended the Revolutionary War, however, the British ignored their Indian allies. They received neither

Mohawk chief Joseph Brant (Thayendanegea) played a major role in the Iroquois's decision to enter the war on the side of Britain. (*The National Gallery of Canada, Ottawa*)

compensation for their losses nor guarantees of their land, for the boundary of the United States was set far to the west, at the Mississippi River.

Though the Indians' struggle against white expansion would continue, their own anticolonial war of liberation had failed. The American Revolution, declared a gathering of Indian chiefs to the Spanish governor at Saint Louis in 1784, had been "the greatest blow that could have been dealt us."

Negotiating Peace

In September 1781, formal peace negotiations began in Paris between the British commissioner, Richard Oswald, and the American emissaries, Benjamin Franklin, John Adams, and John Jay. The negotiations were complicated by the involvement in the war of several European countries seeking to weaken Great Britain. The Americans' main ally, France, had entered the war in February 1778. Eight months later, Spain declared war on England, though it declined to recognize American independence. Between 1780 and 1782, Russia, the Netherlands, and six other European countries joined in a League of Armed Neutrality aimed at protecting their maritime trade against British efforts to control it. America's Revolutionary War had quickly become internationalized. It could hardly have been otherwise, given England's centrality to the European balance of power and the longstanding competition among European powers for colonial dominance in North America.

Dependent on French economic and military support, the Congress instructed the American commissioners to follow the advice of the French foreign minister, Charles Grannier de Vergennes. The American commissioners, however, soon learned that he was prepared to let the exhausting war continue in order to weaken England and tighten America's dependence on France. Even more alarming, Vergennes suggested that the new nation's western boundary should be set no farther west than the crest of the Appalachian Mountains and hinted that the British might retain areas they controlled at the war's end. That proposal threatened to leave New York City and other coastal enclaves in British hands.

In the end, the American commissioners ignored Congress's instructions and, without a word to Vergennes, arranged a provisional peace agreement with the British emissaries. It was fortunate that they did so, for the British were prepared to be generous. In the Treaty of Paris signed in September 1783, England recognized American independence and agreed to place the western boundary of the United States at the Mississippi River. Moreover, Britain promised that U.S. fishermen would have access to the waters off Newfoundland and that British forces would evacuate American territory "with all convenient speed" once hostilities had ended. In return, the Congress agreed to recommend that the states restore the civil rights and property of the Loyalists. Both sides agreed that prewar debts owed the citizens of one country by the citizens of the other would remain valid. Each of these issues would trouble Anglo-American relations in the years ahead, but for the moment it seemed a splendid outcome to a long and difficult struggle.

The Ingredients of Victory

How were the weak and disunited American states able to defeat Great Britain, the most powerful nation in the Atlantic world? Certainly Dutch and French loans, as well as French war supplies and military forces, were crucially important. More decisive, though, was the American people's determination not to submit. Often the Americans were disorganized and uncooperative. Repeatedly, it seemed that the war effort was about to collapse as continental troops drifted away, state militias refused to march, and military supplies failed to materialize. Neither the Congress nor the states proved capable of providing consistent direction to the struggle. Yet as the war progressed, the people's estrangement from England deepened and their commitment to the "glorious

John Jay, John Adams, and Benjamin Franklin (the three figures on the left in the unfinished painting by Benjamin West) meet with the British commissioners in Paris to negotiate preliminary conditions of peace in 1783. *(Benjamin West,* Commissioners of the Preliminary Peace Negotiations with Great Britain, *c. 1783/Courtesy, The Henry Francis du Pont Winterthur Museum)*

cause" grew stronger. To subdue the colonies, England would have had to occupy the entire eastern third of the continent, and that it could not do.

Even though state militias frequently refused to go beyond their own borders and, after the first months of the war, engaged in relatively few battles, they provided a vast reservoir of manpower capable of intimidating Loyalists, gathering intelligence, and harassing British forces that would otherwise have been free to engage the continental army. And though Washington frequently disparaged the militia's fighting qualities and complained that their independent maneuvers threatened to disrupt his own plans, he gradually learned to utilize their strengths in the war effort.

The American victory owed much as well to the administrative and organizational talents of Washington. Against massive odds, he held the continental army together, often by the sheer force of his will. Facing inadequate supplies, high rates of turnover among the troops, ineffective support from the Congress, and lack of cooperation from the states, he created a military force capable of winning selected encounters and, more important, of surviving over time. Had he failed, the Americans could not possibly have succeeded.

In the end, however, it is as accurate to say that Britain lost the war as that the United States won it. With vast economic and military resources, Britain enjoyed clear military superiority over the American states. Its troops were more numerous, better armed and supplied, and more professionally trained. Until the closing months of the contest, Britain enjoyed naval superiority as well. As a consequence, its forces moved up and down the coast virtually at will.

Britain, however, could not capitalize on its advantages. It had difficulty extending command structures and supply routes across several thousand miles of ocean. Because information flowed erratically across the water, strategic decisions made in London were often based on faulty or outdated intelligence. Given the difficulties of supply, British troops often had to live off the land, reducing their mobility and increasing the resentment of Americans whose crops and animals they commandeered.

Faced with these circumstances, British leaders were often overly cautious. Burgoyne's attempt in 1777 to isolate New England by invading from Canada failed because Sir William Howe decided to attack Philadelphia rather than move northward up the Hudson River to join him. Similarly, neither Howe nor Cornwallis pressed his advantage in the central states during the middle years of the war, when more aggressive action might have crushed the continental force.

Just as important, British commanders generally failed to adapt their battlefield tactics to the realities of the American war. They continued to fight in the

European style, during specified times of the year and using formal battlefield formations when the rough, wooded American terrain was better suited to the use of smaller units and irregular tactics.

Washington and Greene were more flexible, often employing a patient strategy of raiding, harassment, and strategic retreat. Behind this strategy lay a willingness, grounded in necessity, to allow England control of territory along the coast. But it was based as well on the conviction that popular support for the revolutionary cause would grow and that the costs of subduing the colonial rebellion would become greater than the British government could bear. As a much later American war, in Vietnam, would also reveal, a guerrilla force can win if it does not lose, while a regular army loses if it does not consistently win.

The American strategy proved sound. As the war dragged on and its costs escalated, Britain's will began to waver. After France and Spain entered the conflict, Britain had to worry about Europe and the Mediterranean as well as North America, while unrest in Ireland and food riots in London tied down additional English troops. As the cost in money and lives increased and prospects of victory dimmed, opposition to the war mounted. It was spearheaded by long-time critics of imperial policy such as Edmund Burke and given popular voice by the followers of John Wilkes and other English radicals who saw in America's rebellion the promise of political reform at home. With the defeat at Yorktown, support for the war collapsed. Britain's effort to hold onto its 13 North American colonies had failed.

THE EXPERIENCE OF WAR

In terms of loss of life and destruction of property, the Revolutionary War pales by comparison with America's more recent wars. Yet modern comparisons are misleading, for the War of American Independence proved terrifying to the people caught up in it.

Recruiting an Army

Estimates vary, but on the American side as many as 250,000 men may at one time or another have borne arms. That amounted to about one out of every two or three adult white males. Though a majority of recruits were native born, many who fought for American freedom came from the thousands of British and European immigrants who streamed into North America during the middle decades of the eighteenth century. Of the 27 men enrolled in Captain John Wendell's New York company, for example, over half had been born abroad, the majority in Ireland but others in Germany and the Netherlands as well. And while the motives of these laborers and farmers, carpenters and coppersmiths were as various as those of native born soldiers, many had come to America seeking to better their lives and eagerly embraced the Revolution's democratic promise. They were the vanguard of a transatlantic political network that, over the final quarter of the eighteenth century, would tie the new American republic to English reformers and French radicals during what historians have called the age of democratic revolution.

As the war began, most state militias were not effective fighting forces. This was especially true in the South, where Nathanael Greene complained that the men came "from home with all the tender feelings of domestic life" and were not "sufficiently fortified . . . to stand the shocking scenes of war, to march over dead men, [or] to hear without concern the groans of the wounded." The militia did, however, serve as a convenient recruiting system, for men were already enrolled, and arrangements were in place for calling them into the field on short notice. This was of special importance before the continental army took shape. Given its grounding in local community life, the militia also legitimated the war among the people and secured their commitment to the revolutionary cause. What better way, as well, to separate Patriots from Loyalists than by mustering the local company and seeing who turned out?

During the early years of the war, when enthusiasm ran high, men of all ranks—from the rich and middle classes as well as the poor—volunteered to fight the British. But as the war went on, casualties increased, enlistment terms grew longer, and military discipline became stiffer, so the army filled with conscripts. Eventually, the war was transformed, as wars so often are, into a poor man's fight as wealthier men hired substitutes and communities filled their quotas with strangers lured by enlistment bonuses or dragooned by laws that subjected "vagrants" and men with "no family . . . or visible means of support" to impressment. Convicts, out-of-work laborers, free and unfree blacks, even occasional British deserters filled the continental army with an array of "Tag, Rag, and Bobtail" soldiers.

For the poor and the jobless, whose ranks the war rapidly swelled, military bonuses and the promise of board and keep proved attractive. But often the bonuses failed to materialize, and pay was long overdue. Moreover, life in the camps was harsh, and soldiers' families at home were frequently in distress. As the war dragged on, desertion rose as high as 25 percent, while Washington imposed harsher discipline in an effort to hold his troops in line.

Occasionally, frustration spilled over into open revolt. In 1779, Sergeant Samuel Glover and a group of

As this painting suggests, military recruiting was a community affair in the eighteenth century. What do you suppose the man with upraised arms is doing? What role might the women be playing in the recruitment process? *(William T. Ranney & Charles F. Blauvelt,* Recruiting for the Continental Army, *c. 1857–59, oil on canvas, 53¾ x 82¼ in, Munson-Williams-Proctor Institute, Museum of Art, Utica, New York, Gift of T. Proctor Eldred)*

soldiers from the North Carolina line, who had been unpaid for 15 months, refused to obey the commands of their superior officer "until they had justice done them." Glover was executed for insubordination. His widow later apologized to the North Carolina assembly for her husband's conduct but asked sorrowfully, "What must the feeling of the man be who . . . with poverty staring him full in the face, was denied his pay?" Soldiers, she protested, possessed the same affection for their families as those in command.

Throughout the war, soldiers suffered from shortages of supplies. At Valley Forge during the terrible winter of 1777–1778, men went without shoes or coats. In the midst of that winter's gloom, Washington wrote, "There are now in this army 4,000 men wanting blankets, near 2,000 of which have never had one, altho' some of them have been 12 months in service." "I am sick, discontented, and out of humour," declared one despairing soul. "Poor food, hard lodging, cold weather, fatigue, nasty cloathes, nasty cookery, vomit half my time, smoaked out of my senses. The Devil's in't, I can't Endure it. Why are we sent here to starve and freeze?"

The states possessed food and clothing enough but were often reluctant to strip their own people of wagons and livestock, blankets and shoes for use elsewhere. Moreover, mismanagement often stood in the way. Neither the state governments nor the Congress could effectively administer a war of such magnitude. Wagon transport was slow and costly, and the British fleet made water travel along the coast perilous. Though many individuals served honorably as supply officers, others took advantage of the army's distress. Washington commented bitterly on the "speculators, various tribes of money makers, and stock-jobbers" whose "avarice and thirst for gain" threatened the country's ruin.

Swarms of camp followers further complicated army life. Wives and prostitutes, personal servants and slaves, con men and official sutlers swarmed around the continental army. While often providing essential services, they slowed its movement and threatened its discipline as well.

The Casualties of Combat

The death that soldiers dispensed to each other on the battlefield was intensely personal. Because the effective range of muskets was little more than 100 yards, soldiers came virtually face-to-face with the men they killed. According to eighteenth-century practice, armies formed on the battlefield in ranks and fired in unison. After massed volleys, the lines often closed for hand-to-hand combat with knives and bayonets. Such encounters were indelibly etched in the memory of individuals who survived them. Partisan warfare in the South, with its emphasis on ambush and cyclic patterns of revenge and counterrevenge, personalized combat even more. British officers expressed shock at the "implacable ardor" with which the Americans fought.

The Americans' ferocity is attributable to the fact that this was a civil war. Not only did Englishmen fight Americans, but American Loyalists and Patriots confronted each other as well. As many as 50,000 colonists fought for the king in some of the war's bitterest encounters. They figured importantly in Burgoyne's invasion from Canada and in the attacks on Savannah and Charleston. Benedict Arnold, the American traitor who was then fighting for the British, led a force of Loyalists on raids through the Connecticut and James River valleys, and Loyalist militia units joined Indian allies in destructive sweeps through central New York, Pennsylvania, and the backcountry of the Carolinas. The passion with which American Patriots fought derived as well from their belief that the very future of human liberty depended on their success. In such a historic crusade, nothing was to be spared that might bring victory.

Medical treatment, whether for wounds or the diseases that raged through military camps, frequently did little good and often did harm. Casualties poured into hospitals, overcrowding them beyond capacity. Dr. Jonathan Potts, the attending physician at Fort George in New York, reported that "we have at present upwards of one thousand sick crowded into sheds & labouring under the various and cruel disorders of dysentaries, bilious putrid fevers and the effects of a confluent smallpox. . . ." The entire medical staff consisted of "four seniors and four mates" in addition to Potts himself.

Surgeons, operating without anesthetics and with the crudest of instruments, threatened life as often as they preserved it. Few understood the causes or proper treatment of infection. Doctoring consisted of bleeding, blistering, and vomiting (which was "deemed of excellent use, by opening and squeezing all the glands of the body, & then shaking from the nervous system, the contaminating poison"). One doctor reported that "we lost no less than from 10 to 20 of camp diseases, for one by weapons of the enemy."

How many soldiers actually died we do not know, for no one kept accurate records. But the most conservative estimate runs to over 25,000, a higher percentage of the total population than for any other American conflict except the Civil War. For Revolutionary War soldiers, death was an imminent reality.

Civilians and the War

While the experience of war varied from place to place depending on people's proximity to battle, vulnerability to economic disruption, and racial and ethnic makeup, it touched the lives of virtually every American in one way or another. Noncombatants experienced the realities of war with greatest immediacy in densely settled areas along the coast. The British concentrated most of their military efforts there because the coastal communities were the political and economic centers of American life and were vulnerable to England's naval power. At one time or another, British troops occupied every major port city: Boston for a year at the war's start, New York from 1777 to 1783, Philadelphia over the winter and spring of 1777–1778, Charleston in 1780–1781, and Savannah two years earlier.

The disruptions of urban life were profound. In September 1776, a fire consumed 500 houses, nearly a quarter of the dwellings, in New York City. About half the town's inhabitants fled when the British occupation began and were replaced by an equal number of Loyalists who streamed in from the surrounding countryside. Ten thousand British and German troops added to the crowding. Makeshift shelters of sailcloth and timber, patched together by the growing number of the poor, stretched along Broadway. An American officer somberly reported what he found as his troops entered New York at the war's end: "Close on the eve of an approaching winter, with an heterogeneous set of inhabitants, composed of almost ruined exiles, disbanded soldiery, mixed foreigners, disaffected Tories, and the refuse of the British army, we took possession of a ruined city."

In Philadelphia, the occupation was shorter and the disruptions less severe, but the shock of invasion was no less real. Elizabeth Drinker, living alone after local Patriots had exiled her Quaker husband, found herself the unwilling landlady of a British officer and his friends. Though the major's presence may have protected her from the plundering that went on all around, she was constantly anxious, confiding to her journal that "I often feel afraid to go to Bed." During the occupation, British soldiers frequently tore down fences for their campfires and confiscated food to supplement their own tedious fare. Even the Loyalists commented on the "dreadful consequences" of British occupation.

Along the entire coastal plain, British landing parties descended without warning, seizing supplies and terrorizing the inhabitants. In 1780 and 1781, the British mounted a punishing attack along the Connecticut coast. Over 200 buildings in Fairfield were burned, and much of nearby Norwalk was destroyed. The southern coast, with its broad, navigable rivers, was even more vulnerable. In December 1780, Benedict Arnold ravaged Virginia's James River valley, uprooting tobacco, confiscating slaves, and creating panic among whites. Similar devastation befell the coasts of Georgia and the Carolinas.

Such punishing attacks sent civilians fleeing into the interior. During the first years of the war, the port cities lost nearly half their population, and inland communities struggled to cope with the thousands of refugees who streamed into them. At one point, so many Bostonians had crowded into Concord, Massachusetts, that they decided to hold a town

In September 1776, as American troops fought unsuccessfully for control of New York, nearly a quarter of the city was destroyed by a fire apparently set by a defiant Patriot woman. Not until the war ended did cleanup of the ruins and reconstruction of the city begin. *(Library of Congress)*

meeting there! By March 1776, Concord's population had grown by 25 percent, creating problems of housing, social order, and public health.

Not all the refugee traffic moved inland, away from the coast. In western New York, Pennsylvania, Virginia, and the Carolinas, frontier settlements collapsed under British and Indian assaults. By 1783, the white population along the Mohawk River west of Albany, New York, had declined from 10,000 to 3,500. According to one observer, after nearly five years of warfare in Tryon County, 12,000 farms had been abandoned, 700 buildings burned, thousands of bushels of grain destroyed, nearly 400 women widowed, and perhaps 2,000 children orphaned. The destruction in western New York was duplicated up and down the backcountry from Maine to Georgia as Loyalist rangers, their Indian allies, and Patriot militias joined in a violent, often chaotic struggle.

Wherever the armies went, they generated a swirl of refugees, who spread vivid tales of the war's devastation. This refugee traffic, together with the constant movement of soldiers back and forth between army and civilian life, brought the war home to countless people who did not experience it at first hand. Moreover, disease followed the armies like an avenging angel, ravaging soldiers and civilians alike.

As they moved across the countryside, the armies lived off the land, impressing the supplies they needed. In an effort to protect the surrounding population during the desperate winter of 1777–1778, Washington prohibited his troops from roaming more than a half mile from camp. In New Jersey, Britain's German mercenaries raised additional fears, particularly among women. In April 1777, a committee of the Congress, taking affidavits from women who had been raped, reported that it had "authentic information of many instances of the most indecent treatment, and actual ravishment of married and single women." Such was the nature of that "most irreparable injury," however, that the persons suffering it, "though perfectly innocent, look upon it as a kind of reproach to have the facts related and their names known." Whether the report had any effect is unknown.

The Loyalists

No Americans suffered greater personal losses during the revolution than those who remained loyal to the crown. Although we do not know how many Loyalists there actually were, we do know that tens of thousands evacuated with British troops from New York, Charleston, and Savannah at the end of the war. At least as many slipped away to

Loyalists, or "Tories," as the Patriots called them, often suffered the indignities of tarring, feathering, and public humiliation for their loyalty to England. *(Corbis-Bettmann)*

England, Canada, or the West Indies while fighting was still under way. Additional thousands who wished that the Revolution had never occurred stayed on in the new nation, trying to keep out of trouble and struggling to rebuild their lives. The incidence of loyalism differed from region to region. There were fewest Loyalists in New England and most in and around New York City, the center of British authority throughout the war.

Emotions ran high between Patriots and Loyalists. "The rage of civil discord," lamented one individual, "hath advanced among us with an astonishing rapidity. The son is armed against the father, the brother against the brother, family against family." Many Patriots were determined to exact revenge against those who had rejected the revolutionary cause.

In each state, revolutionary assemblies enacted laws depriving Loyalists of the vote, confiscating their property, and banishing them from their homes. In 1778, the Georgia assembly declared 117 persons guilty of treason, expelled them from the state on pain of death, and declared their possessions forfeit. Two years earlier, the Connecticut assembly had passed a remarkably punitive law threatening anyone who criticized either the assembly or the Continental Congress with immediate fine and imprisonment. Probably not more than a few dozen Loyalists actually died at the hands of the revolutionary regimes, but thousands found their livelihoods destroyed, their families ostracized, and themselves subject to physical attack.

Punishing Loyalists—or people accused of loyalism, a distinction that was often unclear in the confusion of the times—was politically popular. Most Patriots argued that such "traitors" had put themselves outside the protection of American law. Others, however, argued that republics were intended to be "governments of law and not of men" and worried that no one's rights would be safe when the rights of any were disregarded. No other war-time issue raised so starkly the nettlesome question of balancing individual liberty against the requirements of public security. That issue would return to trouble the nation in the years ahead.

Though many Loyalist émigrés established successful lives in England, the Maritime Provinces of Canada, and the British West Indies, others found the uprooting an ordeal from which they never recovered. On September 8, 1783, Thomas Danforth, formerly a prosperous lawyer from Cambridge, Massachusetts, appeared in London before the King's Commission of Enquiry into the Losses and Services of the American Loyalists. Like others who appealed to the commission, Danforth began by explaining the consequences of his loyalty to the crown. Having devoted his whole life to "preparing himself for future usefulness," he now found himself "near his fortieth year, banished under pain of death, to a distant country, where he has not the most remote family connection . . . cut off from his profession, from every hope of importance in life, and in a great degree from social enjoyments." Without assistance he would sink to "a station much inferior to that of a menial servant."

The commission's response to Danforth's plea is unknown, but many of the several thousand Loyalists who appeared before the commission recovered no more than a third of their losses, meager compensation for the loss of house and property, expulsion from their communities, and relocation in an unfamiliar land. Along with countless others, Danforth found himself relegated to the fringes of English society, his financial affairs in disarray, his future uncertain.

Why did so many Americans remain loyal, often at the cost of personal danger and loss? Customs officers, members of the governors' councils, and Anglican clergy—all appointed to office in the king's name—often sided with England. Loyalism was common as well among groups dependent on British authority—for example, settlers on the Carolina frontier who believed themselves mistreated by the planter elite along the coast; ethnic minorities, such as Germans in the middle states who feared domination by the Anglo-American majority; and tenants on large estates along the Hudson River, who had struggled for years with Patriot landlords over the terms of their leaseholds. Many Loyalists made their choice because they believed it futile to oppose English military power or doubted the ability of a new nation to survive in an Atlantic world dominated by competing empires, even if independence could be won.

Loyalism often had a principled grounding as well, as Samuel Seabury made clear. "Every person owes obedience to the laws of the government," Seabury insisted, "and is obliged in honour and duty to support them. Because if one has a right to disregard the laws of the society to which he belongs, all have the same right; and then government is at an end." William Eddis wondered what kind of society independence would bring when revolutionary crowds showed no respect for the rights of Loyalist dissenters such as he. "If I differ in opinion from the multitude," he asked, "must I therefore be deprived of my character, and the confidence of my fellow-citizens; when in every station of life I discharge my duty with fidelity and honour?" Loyalists such as Eddis and Seabury claimed to be upholding reason and the rule of law against revolutionary disorder.

After the war ended and passions had cooled, most states repealed their anti-Loyalist legislation. In 1786, the Connecticut assembly went so far as to invite its émigrés to return, hoping that their skills and experience would contribute to postwar recovery. In a number of instances, former Loyalists even reentered public life. Still, the permanent departure of so many colonists committed to monarchy, with its values of social and political hierarchy, weakened the forces of conservatism in America and facilitated revolutionary change.

African Americans and the Revolutionary War

The American Revolution was more than a struggle between white belligerents, for it caught up American blacks in its toils as well. In the northern states, both free and enslaved blacks were enlisted in support of the revolutionary cause. In the South nearly 400,000 slaves constituted a vast and uncertain force, viewed by the British as a resource to be exploited and by southern whites as a source of great vulnerability and danger. Sizing up the opportunities provided by the war's confusion, southern blacks struck out for their own freedom by seeking liberty behind English lines or fleeing to mixed-race, maroon settlements in the interior. Before the war was over, the conflict provoked the largest slave rebellion in American history prior to the Civil War.

Hearing their masters talk excitedly about liberty, increasing numbers of black Americans questioned their own oppression. In the North, slaves petitioned state legislatures for their freedom, while in the South pockets of insurrection appeared. In 1765, more than 100 South Carolina slaves, most of them young men in their 20s and 30s, fled their plantations. The next year, slaves paraded through the streets of Charleston chanting, "Liberty, liberty!"

In November 1775, the royal governor of Virginia, Lord Dunmore, issued a proclamation offering freedom to all slaves and servants, able and willing to bear arms, who would leave their masters and join the British forces at Norfolk. Within weeks, 500 to 600 slaves had responded. Among them was Thomas Peters, of Wilmington, North Carolina.

Kidnapped from the Yoruba tribe in what is now Nigeria and brought to North America by a French slave trader, Peters had been purchased in Louisiana about 1760. He resisted enslavement so fiercely that his master sold him into the English colonies. By 1770, Peters belonged to William Campbell, an immigrant Scots planter on North Carolina's Cape Fear River. Here Peters toiled while the storm brewed between England and the colonies.

Peters's plans for his own declaration of independence may have ripened as a result of the rhetoric of liberty he heard around his master's house, for William Campbell was a leading member of Wilmington's Sons of Liberty and talked excitedly about inalienable rights. By mid-1775, the Cape Fear region, like many areas from Maryland to Georgia, buzzed with rumors of slave uprisings. The importation of new slaves was banned, and patrols were dispatched to disarm all blacks in the area. In July, the state's revolutionary government imposed martial law when the British commander of Fort Johnston, near Wilmington, encouraged Negroes to "elope from their masters." When 20 British ships entered the Cape Fear River in March 1776 and disembarked royal troops, Peters seized the moment to redefine himself as a man, instead of William Campbell's property, and escaped. Before long, he would fight with the British-officered Black Pioneers.

How many African Americans sought liberty behind British lines is unknown, but as many as 20 percent may have done so. Unlike their white masters, blacks saw in England the promise of freedom, not tyranny. As the war dragged on, English commanders pressed blacks into service. A regiment of black soldiers, formed from Virginia slaves who responded to

James Armistead Lafayette, a Virginia slave, served as a spy against the British for the French general Lafayette. In recognition of his service, the Virginia General Assembly granted him his freedom in 1786. *(Valentine Museum, Richmond, VA)*

Dunmore's proclamation, marched into battle, their chests covered by sashes emblazoned with the slogan "Liberty to Slaves."

Some of the blacks who joined England achieved their freedom. At the war's end, several thousand were evacuated with the British to Nova Scotia. Their reception by the white inhabitants, however, was generally hostile. By 1800, most had left Canada to settle in the free black colony of Sierra Leone on the west coast of Africa. Thomas Peters was a leader among them.

Many of the slaves who fled behind British lines, however, never won their freedom. Under the terms of the peace treaty, hundreds were returned to their American owners. Several thousand others, their value as field hands too great to be ignored, were transported to the harsher slavery of the sugar plantations in the British West Indies. England had not entered the war to abolish slavery.

Other blacks took advantage of the war's confusion to slip away from their masters in pursuit of a new life. Some made their way north, following rumors that slavery had been abolished there, while others sought refuge among the Indians in the southern interior. The Seminole of Georgia and Florida generally welcomed black runaways and through intermarriage absorbed them into tribal society. Blacks met a more uncertain reception, however, among the Cherokee and Creek. While some were taken in, others were returned to their white owners in return for bounties, and still others were held in slavelike conditions by new Indian masters. Whatever their destination, thousands of African Americans acted to throw off the bonds of slavery.

Fewer blacks fought on the American side than on England's, in part because neither the Congress nor the states were eager to see them armed. Faced with the increasing need for troops, however, the Congress and each of the states except Georgia and South Carolina eventually relented and pressed blacks into service. Of those who served the Patriot cause, many received the freedom they were promised. The patriotism of countless others, however, went unrewarded.

THE FERMENT OF REVOLUTIONARY POLITICS

The Revolution altered people's lives in countless ways that reached beyond the sights and sounds of battle. No areas of American life were more powerfully changed than politics and government. Who would have a voice in revolutionary politics, and who would be excluded? How vigorously would notions of political equality be pursued, or how tenaciously would people cling to the more traditional belief that ordinary citizens should defer to their political betters? And how would the new state governments balance the need for order and the security of property against demands for democratic openness and accountability? These were some of the explosive questions that had to be addressed. Seldom has American politics been more heated; seldom has it struggled with more fundamental or more daunting problems than during the years of the nation's founding.

Mobilizing the People

Under the pressure of revolutionary events, politics absorbed people's energies as never before. The politicization of American society was evident in the flood of printed material that streamed from American presses. While newspapers multiplied in number, pamphlets by the thousands fanned the political debate. Declared one contemporary in amazement, it was

> a spectacle . . . without a parallel on earth. . . . Even a large portion of that class of the community which is destined to daily labor have free and constant access to public prints, receive regular information of every occurrence, [and] attend to the course of political affairs. [Never were political writings] so cheap, so universally diffused, so easy of access.

Ordinary men and women took to the streets in political rallies, such as this mock parade of 1780 in Philadelphia, in which Benedict Arnold, an American general who deserted to the British, was burned in effigy. Such rallies were filled with powerful symbols. *(American Antiquarian Society)*

Pulpits rocked with political exhortations as well. Religion and politics had never been sharply separated in colonial America, but the Revolution drew them more tightly together. Some believed that God had designated revolutionary America as the place of Christ's Second Coming and that independence foretold that glorious day. Others of a less millennial persuasion thought of America as a "New Israel," a covenanted people specially chosen by God to preserve liberty in a threatening world. Giving the metaphor a classical twist, Samuel Adams called on Bostonians to join in creating a "Christian Sparta."

In countless sermons, Congregational, Presbyterian, and Baptist clergy exhorted the American people to repent the sins that had brought English tyranny upon them and urged them to rededicate themselves to God's purposes by fighting for American freedom. It was language that people nurtured in Puritan piety and the Great Awakening instinctively understood.

The belief that God sanctioned their revolution strengthened Americans' resolve. It also encouraged them to identify their own political interests with divine intent and thus offered convenient justification for whatever they believed necessary to do. This was not the last time Americans would make that dangerous equation.

By contrast, Loyalist clergy, such as Maryland's Jonathan Boucher, urged their parishioners to support the king as head of the Anglican Church. During the months preceding independence, as the local Committee of Safety interrupted worship to harass him, Boucher carried a loaded pistol into the pulpit while he preached submission to royal authority.

Belief in the momentous importance of what they were doing increased the intensity of revolutionary politics. John Adams, writing to his wife, Abigail, as the Congress moved toward its fateful declaration, exalted independence as "the greatest question . . . which ever was debated in America." This moment, he continued,

> ought to be solemnized with pomp and parade, with shows, games, sports, guns, bells, bonfires, and illuminations, from one end of this continent to the other, from this time forward forevermore.

As independence was declared, people in towns and hamlets throughout the land raised toasts to the great event: "Liberty to those who have the spirit to preserve it," and "May Liberty expand sacred wings, and, in glorious effort, diffuse her influence o'er and o'er the globe." Inspired by the searing experience of rebellion, war, and nation building, they believed they held the future of human liberty in their hands. Small wonder that they took their politics so seriously.

The expanding array of extralegal committees and spontaneous public gatherings that erupted during the 1770s and 1780s provided the most dramatic evidence of the people's newly awakened political commitment. Prior to independence, crowds had taken to the streets to protest measures like the Stamp Act (see Chapter 5). After 1776, direct political action accelerated as people gathered to intimidate Loyalists, enforce price and wage controls, administer rough-hewn justice, and, as one individual protested, even direct "what we shall eat, drink, wear, speak, and think"—all on behalf of the Revolution.

Patriots of more radical temperament defended these activities as essential expressions of the popular will. More conservative republicans, however, worried that such behavior threatened political stability. Direct

Recovering the Past

PATRIOTIC PAINTINGS

The work that historians do is limited only by their own curiosity and the evidence left behind for them to study. In addition to written evidence such as household inventories and Indian treaties and material artifacts like tombstones and the archaeological residue of burial mounds, historians also examine paintings and other forms of visual evidence for information about the past.

While revealing the development of artistic styles and techniques, paintings also provide important windows into past eras for social and cultural historians by revealing how people looked and did their work, as well as what the landscape and built environment were like. Paintings offer insights additionally into the values and attitudes of past times, for they are often intended to enlighten and instruct, as well as please the viewer's eye.

So it was with Charles Willson Peale, who, as a member of the Pennsylvania militia, carried paint kits and canvas along with his musket as he followed George Washington during the Revolutionary War. Before it was over, he had completed four portraits of the general.

And so it was, even more spectacularly, with the artist John Trumbull, who recorded on canvas some of the most dramatic events of the nation's founding. Slighted for promotion during the Rhode Island campaign early in the war, Trumbull resigned his commission to become a painter. After a frustrating start, he sailed for London, where he studied with the artist Benjamin West, another transplanted American. Imprisoned briefly at the urging of angry American Loyalists, Trumbull was deported to the United States. Returning to England at the war's end, he was urged by West and Thomas Jefferson to paint an ambitious series of "national history" canvases. Over the next four decades, in addition to numerous portraits, religious subjects, and landscapes, Trumbull fashioned the most famous sequence of patriotic paintings ever undertaken by an American artist.

Included were four canvases, depicting crucial military and civil turning points in the struggle for American independence, commissioned by Congress in the early nineteenth century and now hanging in the capitol rotunda in Washington, D.C.—*The Surrender of General Burgoyne at Saratoga, The Surrender of Lord Cornwallis at Yorktown, The Declaration of Independence,* and *The Resignation of General Washington* as commander of the continental army. In addition to those monumental works, Trumbull fashioned a number of heroic battle scenes, including *The Death of General Warren at the Battle of Bunker Hill,* shown opposite.

Though Trumbull knew Warren and others who fought at Bunker Hill, had witnessed the battle from a distance, and was familiar with the techniques of military combat from his own months in the army, he was not primarily concerned with literal accuracy as he composed his painting. Guided by the canons of classical aesthetics popular at the time, he was more interested in the power of artistic "invention" to impart "ideal" truths through the use of brush and pigment.

Examine the painting carefully. How has the artist arranged the figures in relationship to each other? What facial expressions and postures has he given to the people depicted? In what ways do the banners, clouds, and uses of light and color contribute to the painting's overall effect? What messages about the Revolutionary War did Trumbull want viewers to carry away from the canvas?

In all his historical canvases, Trumbull was intent on promoting national pride and constructing a usable public memory. How does this painting serve those purposes? Why was the creation of a shared public memory so important during the early years of the new republic? Might Trumbull have had future generations of Americans as well as his own contemporaries in mind as he did his work?

Art and politics have been intimately related throughout our history, for painting and theater, music, and other forms of performance art have been employed to challenge as well as celebrate political leaders and their policies. Think for a moment about the connections between art and politics in our own time. Why have controversies recently swirled around the National Endowments for the Arts and the Humanities? Should the government provide financial assistance for the arts? If so, should such assistance be accompanied by restrictions on the political messages such art might convey? Is art ever nonpolitical?

John Trumbull, *The Death of General Warren at the Battle of Bunker Hill. (Yale University Art Gallery, Trumbull Collection)*

In celebration of American independence, Patriots and their slaves toppled the statue of King George III that stood at Bowling Green in New York City. *(Library of Congress)*

action by the people had been necessary in the struggle against England, but why such restlessness now, after the yoke of English tyranny had been cast aside? Even Thomas Paine expressed concern. "It is time to have done with tarring and feathering," he wrote in 1777. "I never did and never would encourage what may properly be called a mob, when any legal mode of redress can be had."

This dramatic expansion of popular politics resulted from an explosive combination of circumstances: the momentous events of revolution and war; the efforts of Patriot leaders to mobilize popular support for the desperate struggle against England; and the determination of artisans, workingmen, farmers, and other common folk to apply the principles of liberty to the conditions of their own lives.

A Republican Ideology

Throughout history, as people have moved from colonial subordination to independence, they have struggled to define their identities as free and separate nations. It was no different with the American Revolutionary generation. No longer English, they struggled to understand what it meant to be American. "Our style and manner of thinking," observed Thomas Paine in amazement, "have undergone a revolution. . . . We see with other eyes, we hear with other ears, and think with other thoughts than those we formerly used." The ideology of revolutionary republicanism, pieced together from English political thought, Enlightenment doctrine, and assorted religious beliefs, constituted that revolution in thought. Many of its tenets were broadly shared among the American people, but its larger meanings were sharply contested throughout the revolutionary era.

The rejection of monarchy was one basic component of America's new republican faith. "The word *republic,*" explained Paine, "means the public good of the whole, in contradistinction to the despotic form which makes the good of the sovereign, or of one man, the only object of government." It was Paine's unsparing rejection of monarchy that made his pamphlet *Common Sense* seem so radical. "Of more worth is one honest man to society, and in the sight of God," he scoffed, "than all the crowned ruffians that ever lived."

In rejecting monarchy, the American people also rejected the system of hierarchical authority on which monarchy rested, a system that promised protection by the crown in return for obedience by the people. Under a republican system, by contrast, public authority was created by the people contracting together for their mutual good. In that fundamental change lay much of the American Revolution's radical promise.

No doctrine was more basic to republican belief than the notion that government power, when removed from the people's close oversight and control, threatened to expand at the expense of liberty. The recent experience with England had burned that lesson indelibly into people's consciousness. Although too much liberty might degenerate into political chaos, history seemed to demonstrate that trouble arose most often from too much government, not too little. "It is much easier to restrain the people from running into licentiousness," went a typical refrain, "than power from swelling into tyranny and oppression."

Given the need to limit government power, how could political order be maintained? The revolutionary generation offered an extraordinary answer to that question. Order was not to be imposed from above through traditional agencies of central control such as monarchies, standing armies, and state churches. In a republic, political discipline had to flow upward from the self-regulated behavior of citizens, especially from their willingness, whenever necessary, to put the public good ahead of their own interests. In a republic, explained one pamphleteer, "each individual gives up all private interest that is not consistent with the general good." This radical principle of "public virtue" was an essential ingredient of the republican ideology.

By contrast, political "faction," or organized self-interest, constituted the "mortal disease" to which popular governments throughout history had succumbed. Given the absence in republics of a strong central government capable of imposing political order, factional conflict could easily spin out of control. This fear of "party faction" added to the intensity of political conflict in revolutionary America by inclining people to attribute the most selfish motives to their political opponents.

The idea of placing responsibility for political order with the people and counting on them to act selflessly for the good of the whole, alarmed countless Americans, for what if the people proved unworthy? If the attempt was made, warned one individual darkly, "the bands of society would be dissolved, the harmony of the world confused, and the order of nature subverted." A strong incentive toward loyalism lurked in such concerns.

Few Patriots were so naive as to believe that the American people were altogether virtuous. During the first years of independence, when revolutionary enthusiasm ran high, however, many believed that public virtue was sufficiently widespread to support republican government, while others argued that the American people would learn public virtue by its necessary practice. The revolutionary struggle would serve as a "furnace of affliction," refining the American character as it strengthened people's capacity for virtuous behavior. It was an extraordinarily hopeful but risk-filled undertaking.

The principle of political equality was another controversial touchstone of republicanism. It was broadly assumed that republican governments must be grounded in popular consent, that elections should be frequent, and that citizens must be vigilant in defense of their liberties. There, however, agreement often ended.

Some Americans took literally the principle of political equality by arguing that every citizen should have an equal voice and that public office should be open to all. This position was most forcefully articulated by tenants and small farmers in the interior, as well as workers and artisans in the coastal cities who had long struggled to claim a political voice. More cautious citizens emphasized the need for order as well as liberty, arguing that stable republics required leadership by men of ability and experience, an "aristocracy of talent" that could give the people clear direction. Merchants, planters, and large commercial farmers who were used to providing such leadership saw no need for radical changes in the existing distribution of political power.

Creating Republican Governments

These competing differences of ideology and self-interest burst through the surface of American political life during the debates over new state constitutions that occurred immediately following independence. Fashioning new, republican governments would not be easy, for the American people had no experience with government making on such a scale and had to make the attempt in the midst of a disruptive war. In addition, there were sharp divisions over the kinds of "new modelled" governments they wished to create. One person thought it the "most difficult and dangerous business" that was to be done. Events proved those words prophetic.

Connecticut and Rhode Island continued under their colonial charters, simply deleting all reference to the British crown. The other 11 states set their charters aside and started anew. Within two years following independence, all but Massachusetts had completed the task. By 1780, it had done so as well.

Given their recent experience with England and the prompting of republican theory, constitution makers began with two overriding concerns: to limit the powers of government and to make public officials accountable. The only certain way of accomplishing these goals was by establishing a fundamental law, in the form of a written constitution, that could serve as a standard for regulating government behavior.

In most states, the provincial congresses, extralegal successors to the defunct colonial assemblies, wrote the first constitutions. But this made people increasingly uneasy. If government bodies wrote the documents, they could change them as well, and what would then protect liberty against the abuse of government power? Some way had to be found of grounding the fundamental law, not in the actions of government but directly in the people's sovereign will.

Massachusetts was the first state to solve the problem. In 1779, its citizens elected a special convention

Massachusetts was the first state to elect a special convention to draw up a new constitution and then return that constitution to the people for approval. The new government—along with Boston's officials, courts, and the Merchants' Exchange—met in the old colonial statehouse. *(Stokes Collection, The New York Public Library, Astor, Lenox and Tilden Foundations)*

for the sole purpose of preparing a new constitution. The convention did its work, and the resulting document was returned to the people for ratification.

Through trial and argumentation, the revolutionary generation gradually worked out a clear understanding of what a constitution was and how it should be developed. In the process, it established some of the most basic doctrines of American constitutionalism: that sovereignty resides in the people; that written constitutions, produced by specially elected conventions and then ratified by the people, embody their sovereign will; and that governments must function within clear constitutional limits. No principles have been more important to the preservation of American liberty.

The new constitutions redefined American government in fundamental and lasting ways. For one thing, the new governments were considerably more democratic than the colonial regimes had been. Most state officials were now elected, many of them annually rather than every two or three years as before. The assemblies, moreover, were now larger and more representative than they had been prior to 1776, and many of the powers formerly held by colonial governors—such as control over the budget, veto power over legislation, and the right to appoint various state officials—were either stripped away or reallocated to the assemblies.

Different Paths to the Republican Goal

At the same time, constitution making generated considerable controversy, especially over how democratic the new governments should be. In Pennsylvania, a coalition of western farmers, Philadelphia artisans, and radical leaders such as Thomas Paine, Timothy Matlack, and Thomas Young pushed through the most democratic state constitution of all. Drafted less than three months after independence, during the most intense period of political reform, it rejected the familiar English model of two legislative houses and an independent executive. Republican governments, the radicals insisted, should be simple and easily understood. The constitution thus provided for a single, all-powerful legislative house, its members annually elected and its debates open to the public. There was to be no governor; legislative committees would handle executive duties. A truly radical assumption underlay this unitary design: that only the "common interest of society" and not "separate and jarring private interests" should be represented in public affairs. Property-holding requirements for public office were abolished, and the franchise was opened to every taxpaying, white male over 21. A bill of rights guaranteed every citizen religious freedom, trial by jury, and freedom of speech.

The most radical proposal of all called for the redistribution of property. "An enormous proportion of property vested in a few individuals," declared the proposed constitution, "is dangerous to the rights, and destructive of the common happiness of mankind." Alarmed conservatives just managed to have the offending language removed.

Debate over the constitution divided the state deeply. Men of wealth condemned the document's

Occupational Composition of Several State Assemblies in the 1780s

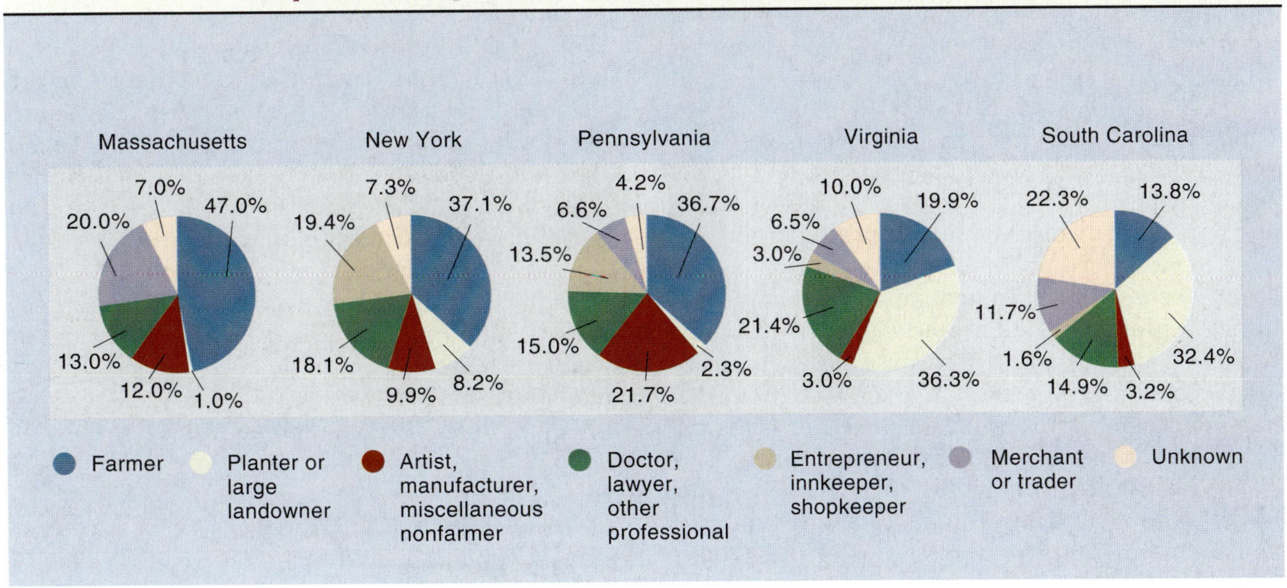

Membership in the revolutionary assemblies reflected differences in the economies and societies of the various states. Those differences often generated political conflict throughout the revolutionary era. What are the major differences between northern and southern state assemblies, and how do you explain them? Source: Jackson T. Main, *Political Parties Before the Constitution,* 1973.

supporters as "coffee-house demagogues" seeking to introduce a "tyranny of the people." The constitution's proponents—tradesmen, farmers, and other small producers—shot back that their critics were "the rich and great men" who had no "common interest with the body of the people."

In 1776, the radicals had their way, and the document was approved. The Pennsylvania constitution, together with its counterparts in Vermont and Georgia, represented the most radical thrust of revolutionary republicanism. Its guiding principle, declared Thomas Young, was that "the people at large [are] the true proprietors of governmental power." As later events would reveal, the struggle for political control in Pennsylvania was not over, for in 1790 a new and more conservative constitution would be approved. For the moment, however, the lines of political power in Pennsylvania had been decisively redrawn.

In Massachusetts, constitution making followed a different and more cautious course. There the disruptions of war were less severe and the continuity of political leadership was greater. John Adams, the main architect of the constitution, readily admitted that the new government had to be firmly grounded in the people. Yet he warned against "reckless experimentation" and regarded the Pennsylvania constitution as far too democratic. He thought a balance between two legislative houses and an independent executive was essential to preserving liberty.

Believing that society was inescapably divided between "democratic" and "aristocratic" forces, Adams sought to isolate them in separate legislative houses where they could guard against each other. The lower house or assembly, he explained, should be "an exact portrait, in miniature," of the people; it should "think, feel, act, and reason" like them. The senate, by contrast, should constitute a "natural aristocracy" of wealth, talent, and good sense. Following Adams's advice, the Massachusetts convention provided for a popular, annually elected assembly and a senate based on wealth, its members apportioned according to the amount of taxes paid in special senatorial districts. The constitution also provided for an independent governor with the power to veto legislation, make appointments, serve as commander in chief of the militia, and oversee state expenditures. The convention endorsed as well an escalating scale of property requirements for assemblymen, senators, and the governor as a way of ensuring that only the better sort would qualify for public office.

When the convention sent the document to the town meetings for approval on March 2, 1780, farmers and Boston artisans attacked it as "aristocratic." The citizens of Dorchester warned that the property requirement for the franchise would exclude "half the people of this commonwealth" from participation in the choice of their elected officials, while thc inhabitants of Petersham feared that "rich and powerful men" would control the proposed government. Despite these and other objections, the convention reconvened in June, declared the document approved, and the constitution went into effect four months later.

Women and the Limits of Republican Citizenship

While men of the revolutionary generation battled among themselves over the degree of political equality appropriate for themselves, they were virtually unanimous in the belief that women could not be full republican citizens. Though women participated in revolutionary crowds and other political activities, they continued to be denied the franchise. Except on scattered occasions, women had neither voted nor held public office during the colonial period. Nor, with rare exceptions, did they do so in revolutionary America.

The New Jersey constitution of 1776 opened the franchise to "all free inhabitants" meeting property and residency requirements. During the 1780s, numerous women took advantage of that opening and cast their votes, leading one disgruntled male to protest, "It is evident that women, generally, are neither by nature, nor habit, nor education . . . fitted to perform this duty with credit to themselves, or advantage to the public." Reflecting that widely held, male sentiment, the New Jersey assembly passed a bill in 1807 specifically disenfranchising women. Its author, John Condict, had narrowly escaped defeat several years earlier when women voted in conspicuous numbers for his opponent. In no other state did women even temporarily secure the vote. Not until the twentieth century would women secure the franchise, the most fundamental attribute of citizenship.

Prior to independence, most women had accepted the principle that political debate fell outside the feminine sphere. The Revolution altered that attitude, for women felt the urgency of the revolutionary crisis as intensely as men. "How shall I impose a silence upon myself," wondered Anne Emlen in 1777, "when the

Though women were discouraged from public writing, Mercy Otis Warren, related by both birth and marriage to leading Massachusetts Patriots, published pamphlets and plays dealing with revolutionary politics. *(Courtesy, Museum of Fine Arts, Boston. Reproduced with permission ©1999 The Museum of Fine Arts, Boston. All Rights Reserved.)*

Timeline

1775	Lord Dunmore's proclamation to slaves and servants in Virginia
	Iroquois Six Nations pledge neutrality
	Continental Congress urges "states" to establish new governments
1776	British evacuate Boston and seize New York City
	Declaration of Independence
	Eight states draft constitutions
	Cherokee raids and American retaliation
1777	British occupy Philadelphia
	Most Iroquois join the British
	Americans win victory at Saratoga
	Washington's army winters at Valley Forge
1778	War shifts to the South
	Savannah falls to the British
	French treaty of alliance and commerce
1779	Massachusetts state constitutional convention
	Sullivan destroys Iroquois villages in New York
1780	Massachusetts constitution ratified
	Charleston surrenders to the British
	Pennsylvania begins gradual abolition of slavery
1780s	Virginia and Maryland debate abolition of slavery
	Destruction of Iroquois Confederacy
1781	Cornwallis surrenders at Yorktown
	Articles of Confederation ratified by states
1783	Peace treaty with England signed in Paris
	Massachusetts Supreme Court abolishes slavery
	King's Commission on American Loyalists begins work

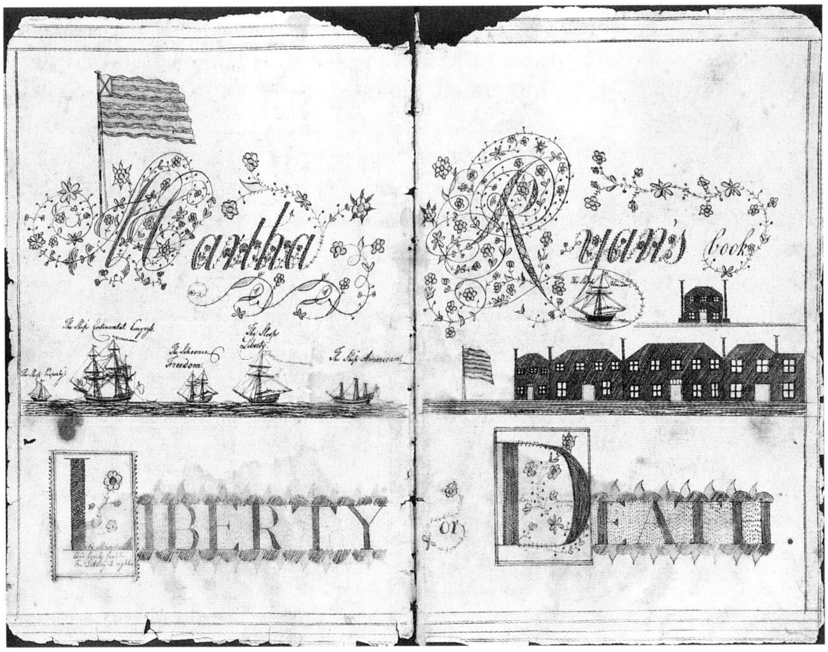

Martha Ryan, a young North Carolina girl, decorated the cover of her copybook with political themes. *(from the Ryan Cipher Book, #1940, Southern Historical Collection, The Library of the University of North Carolina at Chapel Hill)*

subject is so very interesting, so much engrossing conversation & what every member of the community is more or less concerned in?" With increasing frequency, women wrote and spoke to each other about public events, especially as they affected their own lives. Declared Eliza Wilkerson of South Carolina during the British invasion of 1780, "None were greater politicians than the several knots of ladies, who met together. All trifling discourses of fashions, and such low chat were thrown by, and we commenced perfect statesmen."

As the war progressed, increasing numbers of women spoke out publicly. A few, such as Esther DeBerdt Reed of Philadelphia, published essays explaining women's urgent desire to contribute to the Patriot cause. In her 1780 broadside "The Sentiments of an American Woman," she declared that women wanted to serve like "those heroines of antiquity, who have rendered their sex illustrious," and she called on women to renounce "vain ornament" as they had earlier renounced English tea. The money thus saved would be the "offering of the Ladies" to Washington's army. In Philadelphia, women responded by collecting \$300,000 in continental currency from over 1,600 individuals. Refusing Washington's proposal that the money be mixed with general funds in the national treasury, they insisted on using it to purchase materials for shirts so that each soldier might know he had received a contribution directly from the women.

Even women's traditional roles took on new political meaning. With English imports cut off and the army badly in need of clothing, spinning and weaving assumed patriotic significance. Coming together as Daughters of Liberty, women made shirts and other items of clothing. Charity Clarke, a New York teenager, acknowledged that she "felt Nationaly" as she knitted stockings for the soldiers. Though "heroines may not distinguish themselves at the head of an army," she informed an English cousin, a "fighting army of amazons . . . armed with spinning wheels" would emerge in America.

The most traditional of all female roles, the care and nurture of children, took on special political resonance during the revolutionary era. How could the republic be sustained once independence had been won? Only by a rising generation of republican citizens schooled in the principles of public virtue and ready to assume the task. How would they be prepared? During their formative years by their "Republican Mothers," the women of the Revolution.

Most women did not press for full political equality, since the idea flew in the face of long-standing social convention and its advocacy exposed a person to public ridicule. Some women did make the case to each other or their husbands. "I cannot say, that I think you are very generous to the ladies," Abigail Adams chided her husband, John. "For whilst you are proclaiming peace and good will to men, emancipating all nations, you insist upon retaining an absolute power over all wives." John consulted Abigail on many things but turned this admonition quickly aside.

While women developed new ties to the public realm during the revolutionary years, the assumption that politics and government were an exclusively male domain did not easily die. Indeed, the republican ideology, so effectively invoked in support of American liberty against the English king and

Parliament, actually sharpened political distinctions between women and men. The independence of judgment required of republican citizens assumed a level of economic self-sufficiency denied married women by the long-established principle of *coverture*, a legal doctrine that transferred women's property to their husbands and designated them as political dependents as well.

Republican virtue, moreover, was understood to encompass such "manly" qualities as rationality, self-discipline, and public sacrifice, qualities believed inconsistent with "feminine" attributes of passion and self-indulgence. Finally, the desperate struggle against England emphasized the patriarchal values of the military hero and classic lawgiver.

In time, further challenges to male political hegemony would emerge. When they did, women would find guidance in the principles enshrined in the Declaration of Independence that the women of the Revolution had helped to defend.

Conclusion

The Crucible of Revolution

Independence and war redrew the contours of American life and changed the destinies of the American people. Though the Revolutionary War ended in victory, liberty had its costs. Lives were lost, property was destroyed, and local economies were deranged. The war altered relationships between Indians and whites, for it left the Iroquois and Cherokee severely weakened and opened the floodgates of western expansion. For African Americans, the revolution had paradoxical results. It produced an ideology that decried slavery, generated efforts to end the slave trade, and marked the first general debate over abolishing the oppressive institution. Yet slavery was eradicated only where it was least important, in the North, while in the South, where slavery had the strongest hold, its future was guaranteed. In spite of the political ferment generated by the Revolution, women reaped few clear advantages. Though they participated in many revolutionary activities and achieved enhanced status as "Republican Mothers," they were still denied the franchise, the critical right of full republican citizenship.

By 1783, a new nation had come into being where none had existed before, a nation based not on age-encrusted principles of monarchy and aristocratic privilege but on the doctrines of republican liberty. That was the greatest change of all. The political transformations set in motion, however, generated angry disputes whose outcomes could be only dimly foreseen. Thomas Paine put the matter succinctly: "The answer to the question, can America be happy under a government of her own, is short and simple—as happy as she pleases; she hath a blank sheet to write upon." The years immediately ahead would determine whether America's republican experiment, launched with such hopefulness in 1776, would succeed.

Recommended Reading

The War for American Independence

John Ferling, ed., *The World Turned Upside Down: The American Victory in the War of Independence* (1988); Don Higginbotham, *The War of Independence* (1983); Ronald Hoffman and Peter Albert, eds., *Arms and Independence: The Military Character of the American Revolution* (1984); Mark Kwasney, *Washington's Partisan War, 1775–1783* (1996); Holly Mayer, *Belonging to the Army: Camp Followers and Community During the American Revolution* (1996); Robert Middlekauff, *The Glorious Cause* (1982).

Colin Calloway, *The American Revolution in Indian Country* (1995); Tom Hatley, *The Dividing Paths: Cherokees and South Carolinians Through the Revolutionary Era* (1993); Isabel Kelsey, *Joseph Brant, 1743–1807: Man of Two Worlds* (1984); Max Mintz, *Seeds of Empire: The American Revolutionary Conquest of the Iroquois* (1999); Anthony Wallace, *The Death and Rebirth of the Seneca* (1969).

Jonathan Dull, *A Diplomatic History of the American Revolution* (1985); Ronald Hoffman and Peter Albert, eds., *Peace and the Peacemakers: The Treaty of 1783* (1986); Reginald Horsman, *Diplomacy of the New Republic, 1775–1815* (1985).

The Experience of War

E. Wayne Carp, *To Starve the Army at Pleasure: Continental Army Administration and American Political Culture, 1775–1783* (1984); Lawrence Cress, *Citizens in Arms: The Army and the Militia in American Society to the War of 1812* (1982); Sylvia Frey, *The British Soldier in America: A Social History of Military Life in the Revolutionary Period* (1981); Charles Neimeyer, *America Goes to War: A Social History of the Continental Army* (1996); Charles Royster, *A Revolutionary People at War: The Continental Army and American Character, 1775–1783* (1979).

John Buchanan, *The Road to Guilford Courthouse: The American Revolution in the Carolinas* (1997); John Franz and William Pencak, eds., *Beyond Philadelphia: The American Revolution in the Pennsylvania Hinterland* (1998); James Leamon, *Revolution Downeast: The War for American Independence in Maine* (1993); John Pancake, *This Destructive War: The British Campaign in the Carolinas, 1780–1782* (1985).

Bernard Bailyn, *The Ordeal of Thomas Hutchinson* (1974); Robert Calhoon, *The Loyalists in Revolutionary America, 1760–1781* (1973); Mary Beth Norton, *The British Americans: The*

Loyalist Exiles in England, 1774–1789 (1972); Janice Potter, *Liberty We Seek: Loyalist Ideology in Colonial New York and Massachusetts* (1983).

Ira Berlin and Ronald Hoffman, eds., *Slavery and Freedom in the Age of the American Revolution* (1983); David B. Davis, *The Problem of Slavery in the Age of the Democratic Revolution* (1975); Sylvia Frey, *Water from the Rock: Black Resistance in a Revolutionary Age* (1991); Sidney Kaplan, *The Black Presence in the Era of the American Revolution, 1770–1800* (1973); Gary B. Nash, *Race and Revolution* (1990).

The Ferment of Revolutionary Politics

Bernard Bailyn, *Faces of Revolution* (1991); Edward Countryman, *A People in Revolution: The American Revolution and Political Society in New York, 1760–1790* (1981); Eric Foner, *Tom Paine and Revolutionary America* (1976); Ronald Hoffman, *A Spirit of Dissension: Economics, Politics, and the Revolution in Maryland* (1973); Norman Risjord, *Representative Americans: The Revolutionary Generation* (1980); John Selby, *The Revolution in Virginia, 1775–1783* (1988); Robert Shalhope, *Bennington and the Green Mountain Boys: The Emergence of Liberal Democracy in Vermont, 1760–1850* (1996); Alan Taylor, *Liberty Men and Great Proprietors: The Revolutionary Settlement on the Maine Frontier, 1760–1820* (1990); Peter Thompson, *Rum, Punch, and Revolution: Taverngoing and Public Life in Eighteenth Century Philadelphia* (1999); Gordon Wood, *The Creation of the American Republic, 1776–1787* (1969) and *The Radicalism of the American Revolution* (1992); Al Young, ed., *Beyond the American Revolution: Explorations in the History of American Radicalism* (1993).

Willi Paul Adams, *The First American Constitutions: Republican Ideology and the Making of the State Constitutions in the Revolutionary Era* (1980); Mark Kruman, *Between Authority and Liberty: State Constitution Making in Revolutionary America* (1997); Donald Lutz, *Popular Consent and Popular Control: Whig Political Thought in the Early State Constitutions* (1980); Edmund Morgan, *Inventing the People: The Rise of Popular Sovereignty in England and America* (1988); John Phillip Reid, *Constitutional History of the American Revolution* (1995).

Joy Day Buel and Richard Buel, Jr., *The Way of Duty: A Woman and Her Family in Revolutionary America* (1995); Edith Gelles, *Portia: The World of Abigail Adams* (1992); Joan Gunderson, *To Be Useful to the World: Women in Revolutionary America* (1996); Ronald Hoffman and Peter Albert, eds., *Women in the Age of the American Revolution* (1989); Mark Kann, *A Republic of Men: The American Founders, Gendered Language, and Patriotic Politics* (1998); Linda Kerber, *Women of the Republic* (1980); Cynthia Kerner, *Southern Women in Revolution, 1776–1800* (1998); Mary Beth Norton, *Liberty's Daughters* (1980); Jeffrey Richards, *Mercy Otis Warren* (1995).

Fiction and Film

The Broken Chain, a made-for-television historical drama produced and aired in 1994, tells the story of the Mohawk war chief Joseph Brant, who fought with England during the Revolutionary War and then led many of his people to Canada following the peace of 1783.

The Way of Duty, a PBS documentary drama based on a book by the historians Richard and Joy Buel, traces the challenging experiences of a Connecticut woman and her family during the American Revolution.

James Fenimore Cooper's dramatic novel *The Pilot* (1824) offers an imaginative account of naval warfare and seafaring life during the Revolution. In the more recently published novel *Oliver Wiswell* (1940), Kenneth Roberts depicts the Revolution as seen through the eyes of an American Loyalist.

Suggested Web Sites

http://nwta.com/main.html

Northwest Territory Alliance. This Revolutionary era reenactment organization site contains several links and offers an interesting look at historical reenactment.

http://users.erols.com/candidus/index.htm

Maryland Loyalism and the American Revolution. This look at Maryland's Loyalists promotes the book Maryland Loyalists in the American Revolution, but it also has good information about an underappreciated phenomenon, including Loyalist songs and poems.

http://www.geocities.com/Athens/Forum/9061/USA/revolution/rev.html

Revolution Era Documents. The Historical Text Archive has numerous useful documents for the period of the revolution.

http://revolution.h-net.msu.edu/

The American Revolution. This site accompanies the PBS series Liberty! with essays and resource links to a rich array of sites containing information on the American Revolution. Included are the Bill of Rights, slave documents, and maps of the era.

http://earlyamerica.com/

Archiving Early America. Via this site students can access writings, maps, and images of leading men and women reproduced from newspapers and magazines of the revolutionary era.

http://www.colonialhall.com/index.asp

Colonial Hall: Biographies of America's Founding Fathers. This site provides interesting information about the men who signed the Declaration of Independence and includes a trivia section.

http://www.ushistoryplace.com

the History place

A richly detailed on-line learning environment complete with interactive maps, timelines, history activities, primary source documents, and links to related American history sites.

7

CONSOLIDATING *the* REVOLUTION

CHAPTER OUTLINE

Timothy Bloodworth of New Hanover County, North Carolina, knew what the American Revolution was all about, for he had experienced it firsthand. A man of humble origins, Bloodworth had known poverty as a child. Lacking any formal education, he had worked hard during the middle decades of the eighteenth century as an innkeeper and ferry pilot, self-styled preacher and physician, blacksmith and farmer. By the mid-1770s, he owned nine slaves and 4,200 acres of land, considerably more than most of his neighbors.

His unpretentious manner and commitment to political equality earned Bloodworth the confidence of his community. In 1758, at the age of 22, he was elected to the North Carolina colonial assembly. Over the next three decades, he was deeply involved in the political life of his home state.

When the colonies' troubles with England drew toward a crisis, Bloodworth spoke ardently of American rights and mobilized support for independence. In 1775, he helped form the Wilmington Committee of Safety. Filled with revolutionary fervor, he urged forward the process of republican political reform and, as commissioner of confiscated property for the district of Wilmington, pressed the attack on local Loyalists.

In 1784, shortly after the war ended, the North Carolina assembly named Bloodworth one of the state's delegates to the Confederation Congress. There he learned for the first time about the problems of governing a new nation. As the Congress struggled through the middle years of the 1780s with the intractable problems of foreign trade, war debt, and control of the trans-Appalachian interior, Bloodworth shared the growing conviction that the Articles of Confederation were too weak. He supported the Congress's call for a special convention to meet in Philadelphia in May 1787 for the purpose of taking action necessary "to render the constitution of the federal government adequate to the exigencies of the Union."

Like thousands of other Americans, Bloodworth eagerly awaited the convention's work. And like countless Americans, he was stunned by the result, for the proposed constitution described a government that seemed to him certain not to preserve republican liberty but to endanger it.

Once again sniffing political tyranny on the breeze, Bloodworth resigned his congressional seat and in August 1787 hurried back to North Carolina to help organize opposition to the proposed constitution. Over the next several years, he worked tirelessly for its defeat.

Alarmed by the prospect of such a powerful central government, Bloodworth protested that "we cannot consent to the adoption of a Constitution whose revenues lead to aristocratic tyranny, or monarchical despotism, and open a door wide as fancy can point, for the introduction of dissipation, bribery and corruption to the exclusion of public virtue." Had Americans so quickly forgotten the dangers of consolidated power? Were they already prepared to turn away from their brief experiment in republicanism?

Alarmed by a variety of provisions in the document, Bloodworth demanded the addition of a federal bill of rights to protect individual liberties. Echoing the language of revolutionary republicanism, he warned the North Carolina ratifying convention that "without the most express restrictions, Congress may trample on your rights. Every possible precaution should be taken when we grant powers," he continued, for "Rulers are always disposed to abuse them."

Bloodworth also feared the sweeping authority Congress would have to make "all laws which shall be necessary and proper" for carrying into execution "all other powers vested . . . in the government of the United States." That language, he insisted, "would result in the abolition of the state governments. Its sovereignty absolutely annihilates them."

In North Carolina, the arguments of Bloodworth and his Anti-Federalist colleagues carried the day. By a vote of 184 to 84, the ratifying convention declared that a bill of rights "asserting and securing from encroachment the great Principles of civil and religious Liberty, and the unalienable rights of the People" must be approved before North Carolina would concur. The convention was true to its word. Not until November 1789, well after the new government had gotten under way and Congress had forwarded a national bill of rights to the states for approval, did North Carolina, with Timothy Bloodworth's cautious endorsement, finally enter the new union.

Ratification of the U.S. Constitution by the states in 1788 brought an end to the revolutionary years and ushered in a dramatically new era in the nation's history. *(John Feingersh/Stock Boston)*

Just as Timothy Bloodworth knew the difficulties of achieving American independence, so he learned the problems of preserving American liberty once independence had been won. As a member of the Confederation

Congress, Bloodworth confronted the continuing vestiges of colonialism: the patronizing attitudes of England and France, their continuing imperial ambitions in North America, and the republic's ongoing economic dependence on Europe. He also observed the Congress's inability to pay off the war debt, pry open foreign ports to American commerce, and persuade the states to join in a common tariff policy against England. As a southerner, Bloodworth was equally alarmed by the willingness of a congressional majority to forgo free navigation of the Mississippi River, deemed essential for development of the southern backcountry, in exchange for northern commercial advantages in Europe. Finally, he worried about political turmoil in the states as issues of taxation, debt, and paper money led discontented citizens openly to challenge public authority.

By 1786, Bloodworth, like countless other Americans, was caught up in an escalating debate between the Federalists, who believed that the Articles of Confederation were fatally deficient and must be replaced by a stronger national government, and the Anti-Federalists, who were deeply troubled by the dangers consolidated power posed to individual liberties.

That debate over the future of America's republican experiment came to a head in the momentous Philadelphia convention of 1787, which produced not reform but revolutionary change in the national government. With ratification of the new Constitution, the revolutionary era came to an end, and the American people opened a portentous new chapter in their history.

STRUGGLING WITH THE PEACETIME AGENDA

As the war ended, problems of demobilization and adjustment to the conditions of independence troubled the new nation. Whether the Confederation Congress could effectively deal with the problems of the postwar era remained unclear.

Demobilizing the Army

Demobilizing the army presented the Confederation government with some difficult moments, for when the fighting stopped, many of the troops refused to go home until the Congress redressed their grievances. Trouble first arose in early 1783 when officers at the continental army camp in Newburgh, New York, sent a delegation to the Congress to complain about arrears in pay and other benefits that had been promised them during the dark days of the war. When Congress called on the army to disband, an anonymous address circulated among the officers, attacking the "coldness and severity" of the Congress, calling for "a last remonstrance," and hinting darkly at more direct action if their grievances were not met.

Several Congressmen encouraged the officers' muttering, hoping the crisis would add urgency to their own calls for a stronger central government. Most, however, found the challenge to Congress's authority alarming. Washington moved quickly to calm the situation. Promising that Congress would treat the officers justly, he counseled patience and urged his comrades not to tarnish the victory they had so recently won. His efforts succeeded, for the officers reaffirmed their confidence in the Congress and agreed to disband.

Military officers were not the only ones to take action. In June, several hundred disgruntled continental soldiers and Pennsylvania militiamen gathered in front of Philadelphia's Independence Hall, where both Congress and Pennsylvania's executive council were meeting. When the state authorities would not guarantee the Congress's safety, it fled to Princeton, New Jersey. Once there, tension eased when Congress issued the soldiers three months' pay and furloughed them until they could be fully discharged. By early November, the crisis was over, but congressional authority had been seriously damaged.

Over the next several years, the country's governing body shuffled between Princeton and Annapolis, Trenton and New York City, its transience visible evidence of its steadily eroding authority. A hot-air balloon, scoffed the *Boston Evening Herald,* would "exactly accommodate the itinerant genius of Congress," because it could then "float along from one end of the continent to the other . . . and when occasion requires . . . suddenly pop down into any of the states they please." Never had the Congress been so openly mocked.

Opening the West

The Congress was not without important accomplishments during the postwar years. Most notable were the two great land ordinances of 1785 and 1787. The first provided for the systematic survey and sale of the region west of New York and Pennsylvania and north of the Ohio River. The area was to be laid out in townships 6 miles square, which were in turn to be subdivided into lots of 640 acres each. Thus began the rectangular grid pattern of land survey and settlement that to this day characterizes the Midwest and distin-

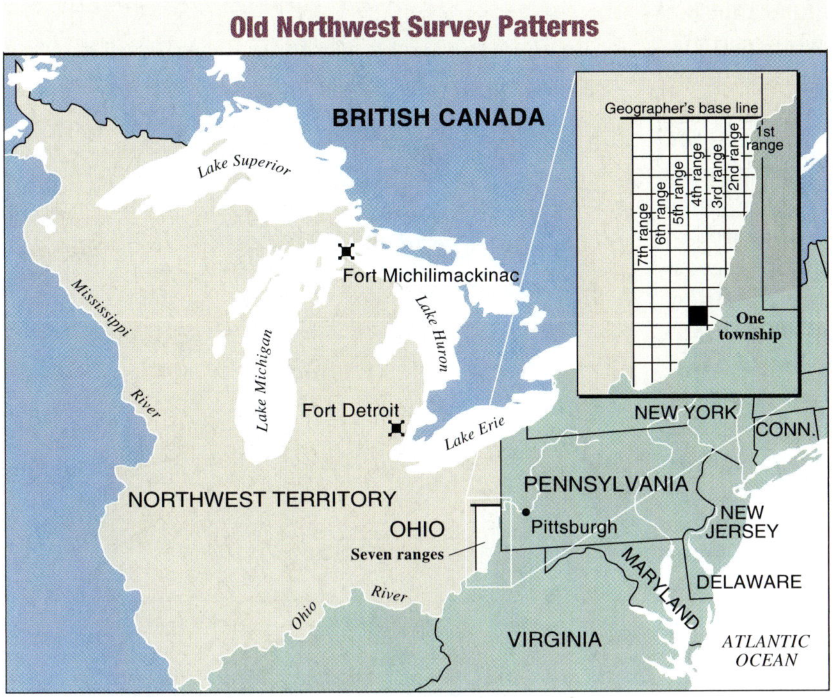

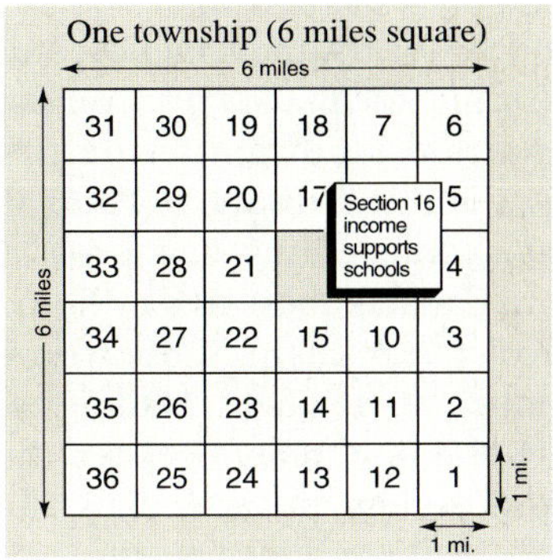

The Land Ordinance passed by Congress in 1785 provided for townships divided into lots of 640 acres. Its purpose was to promote the rapid and orderly settlement of the Old Northwest.

guishes it so markedly from the irregular settlement patterns of the older, colonial areas to the east.

Two years later, Congress passed the Northwest Ordinance. It provided for the political organization of the same interior region, first under congressionally appointed officials, then under popularly elected territorial assemblies, and ultimately as new states to be incorporated into the Union "on an equal footing with the original states in all respects whatsoever." Together these laws represented a conception of empire dramatically different from the one that had guided England's colonial domain. Rather than seeking to restrain white settlement on behalf of England's national interest as Parliament had attempted to do in the Proclamation Line of 1763, the central government in America's "empire of liberty" would actively promote its citizens' well-being by making land available via land laws and Indian policies. In addition, settlements established in the American West would not remain permanent colonies but would be fully incorporated into the expanding American nation. These changes carried profound importance for the future.

Both bills enjoyed broad political support, for they opened land to settlers and profits to speculators. The income from land sales, moreover, promised to help reduce the Revolutionary War debt. While permitting slave owners already living north of the Ohio River to retain their chattels, the Ordinance of 1787 prohibited the importation of new slaves into the region. This made the area more attractive to white farmers who worried about competing with slave labor and living among blacks. Southern delegates in the Congress accepted the restriction because they could look forward to slavery's expansion south of the Ohio. During the 1780s, the country's interior seemed large enough to accommodate everyone's needs.

Despite these accomplishments, however, the Congress could neither get British troops out of the western posts south of the Great Lakes nor guarantee free navigation of the Mississippi. Nor was it able to clear the tribes of the Ohio region out of the white settlers' way. These failings led growing numbers of Americans to question whether the Confederation government was capable of promoting the nation's westward expansion.

During the immediate postwar years, the Congress operated as if the Native Americans of the interior were "conquered" peoples—allies of England who had lost the war and had thus come under U.S. control. Since the Treaty of Paris gave the United States ownership of all land east of the Mississippi River, Americans insisted that it gave the U.S. political sovereignty over the tribes living there.

Such claims were grounded as well in notions of Indian inferiority. Even the most sympathetic whites believed that Native Americans would have to become "civilized" and "Christianized" before they could coexist with white society. Many whites doubted that such "improvements" were possible, and argued that the Indians must simply be driven out of white settlers' way. George Washington gave blunt expression to the prevailing view. "The gradual extension of our settlements," he explained, "will as certainly cause the savage as the wolf to retire; both being beasts of prey though they differ in shape."

For a few years, the conquest strategy appeared to work. During the mid-1780s, Congress imposed several important land treaties on the interior tribes, among them the Iroquois. Their numbers reduced and their confederation shattered, many Iroquois had fled into Canada. Pressured by both Congress and the New York government, those who remained deeded away much of their land. At the Treaty of Fort Stanwix in 1784, the first treaty between the newly independent government and an Indian tribe, the Six Nations officially made peace, ceded most of their lands to the United States, and retreated to small reservations. By the 1790s, little remained of the once imposing Iroquois domain but a few islands in a spreading sea of white settlement. On those islands—"slums in the wilderness" they have been called—the Iroquois struggled for survival against disease and poverty, their traditional lifeways gone, their self-confidence broken. The Iroquois were not the only tribe to lose their land. In January 1785, representatives of the Wyandotte, Chippewa, Delaware, and Ottawa tribes relinquished claim to most of present-day Ohio.

Often exacted under the threat of force, many of the treaties generated resentment. At Fort Stanwix negotiations were held at gunpoint, and hostages were taken to coerce the Indian delegates. Two years later the Iroquois openly repudiated the treaty, asserting that they were still sovereigns of their own soil and "equally free as . . . any nation under the sun." The Revolution, moreover, left behind a legacy of bitterness: among Indians because they had suffered betrayal and defeat, among white Americans because the Indians had sided with England and thus threatened the Revolution's success. Such bitterness would trouble Indian–white relations for years to come.

By the mid-1780s, tribal groups in the Ohio Valley were actively resisting white expansion. North of the river, the Shawnee, Delaware, and Miami moved to strengthen their Western Confederacy and prepare for the defense of their homeland. In the fall of 1786, the confederacy rejected congressional claims of conquest and asserted that the Ohio River was the proper boundary between them and the United States. When white settlers continued to press into the region, Native Americans launched a series of devastating raids, bringing white settlement to a virtual halt. By the end of 1786, the entire region from the Great Lakes

The symbolic figure of Columbia, often presented in the form of an Indian maiden embodying the innocence and freedom of the new republic, first became popular during the Revolution. This began to change as Americans moved west across the Appalachians. By the time this French engraving appeared in the early nineteenth century, Columbia was usually garbed in classical attire and had lost her Indian headdress. *(Library of Congress)*

"Utmost Good Faith" Clause from the Northwest Ordinance (1787)

The following articles shall be considered as articles of compact between the original States and the people and States in the said territory and forever remain unalterable, unless by common consent, to wit:

> The utmost good faith shall always be observed towards the Indians; their land and property shall never be taken from them without their consent; and, in their property, rights, and liberty, they shall never be invaded or disturbed, unless in just and lawful wars authorized by Congress, but laws founded in justice and humanity, shall from time to time be made for preventing wrongs being done to them, and for preserving peace and friendship with them.

Though victorious in its struggle for independence, the United States remained surrounded on three sides by British and Spanish possessions. North America continued to be a focus of European colonial ambitions after 1783.

to the Gulf of Mexico was embroiled in warfare. With the continental army disbanded, there was little that the Congress could do.

Congress's inability to open the interior to white settlement alarmed countless Americans: speculators facing the loss of their investments; farmers wanting to leave the crowded lands of the East; revolutionary soldiers eager to start afresh on the rich soil of Kentucky and Ohio that they had been promised as payment for military service; and leaders such as Thomas Jefferson who believed that republican liberty depended on an ever expanding frontier. With the Confederation Congress unable to implement the promised "empire of liberty," there was growing reason to question its adequacy.

Settling the interior, the indispensable land reserve for the fast-growing nation, involved delicate negotiations with European nations as well. Here, too, the Congress proved ineffective. In June 1784, Spain—still in possession of Florida, the Gulf Coast, and the trans-Mississippi West—closed the mouth of the Mississippi River at New Orleans to American shipping. Spain's action raised a storm of protest among western settlers who counted on floating their produce downstream to New Orleans for transshipment to markets along the East Coast and in Europe. Land speculators were angered as well, for closure of the Mississippi would discourage development of the southern backcountry and reduce their profits. Rumors spread, moreover, that Spanish agents were urging American frontiersmen to break away from the new nation and seek affiliation with Spain. Washington commented uneasily that settlers were "on a pivot" throughout the West. "The touch of a feather," he feared, "would turn them away."

For more than a year, Foreign Secretary John Jay negotiated with the Spanish ambassador to the United States, Don Diego de Gardoqui, in an effort to reopen the vital Mississippi River outlet. When Gardoqui held firm, Jay offered to relinquish American claims to free transit of the Mississippi in return for a commercial treaty opening Spanish ports to American shipping. Excited by the prospect of Spanish trade, northern merchants supported the bargain, but the southern delegates in Congress, angry at Jay's betrayal of their interests, refused to go along. Stalemated, the Congress took no action at all.

Wrestling with the National Debt

The Congress's inability to deal effectively with the nation's war debt, estimated at $35 million, offered further evidence of the Confederation government's weakness. Much of the debt was held by French and Dutch bankers. Unable to make regular payment against the loan's principal, the Congress had to borrow additional money abroad simply to pay the accumulating interest. At home, things were no better. In response to the incessant demands of its creditors, the government could only delay and try to borrow more.

In 1781, the Congress appointed Robert Morris, a wealthy Philadelphia merchant, superintendent of finance and gave him broad authority to deal with the nation's troubled affairs. Morris urged the states to stop issuing paper money and persuaded the Congress to demand that the states pay their requisitions in specie. In addition, he secured a Congressional charter for the Bank of North America and took steps to make federal bonds more attractive to investors.

Though Morris made considerable progress, the government's finances remained shaky. Lacking the power to tax, the Congress continued to depend on the states' willingness to meet their financial obligations. This arrangement, however, proved unworkable. Desperate for resources, the Congress, in October 1781, requested $8 million from the states. Two and a half years later, less than $1.5 million of that amount had come in. In January 1784, Morris resigned, partly in despair over the government's financial situation and partly to recoup his personal fortunes.

By 1786, total federal revenue amounted to no more than $370,000 a year, not enough, as one official lamented, to provide for "the bare maintenance of the federal government [even] on the most economical establishment." Declared a congressional committee, Americans "must decide whether they will support their rank as a nation, by maintaining the public faith at home and abroad; or whether, for want of . . . a general revenue . . . they will hazard . . . the great and invaluable privileges for which they have so arduously and so honorably contended."

Not all Americans were alarmed. Some pointed out approvingly that several state governments, having brought their own financial affairs under control, were beginning to assume responsibility for portions of the national debt. Others, however, saw that as additional evidence of the Congress's weakening condition and wondered how a government unable to maintain its credit could long endure.

Surviving in a Hostile Atlantic World

The Congress's difficulties in dealing with its creditors abroad and countering Spain's closure of the Mississippi River at home pointed to a broader problem in American foreign relations. Even after the United States had formally won independence, England, France, and Spain continued to threaten the new republic.

The Revolutionary War had dramatically transformed America's relationships with other nations. England, once the nurturing "mother country," had become the enemy, while France, long the mortal foe of England and the colonies alike, had proved a vital ally. Yet France was at best an uncertain friend. With an empire of its own, it feared colonial rebellions. In addition, the French king and aristocracy regarded republicanism as deeply subversive, and France's efforts to manipulate the peace process for its own advantage had taught the Americans a hard lesson in the realities of power diplomacy.

Independence, moreover, did not end European ambitions in North America. Though France had lost its North American possessions in the Seven Years' War (see Chapter 5), it would gain title to most of the trans-Mississippi west by 1800. Meanwhile, Great Britain's Union Jack continued to fly over eastern Canada, while British troops retained possession of strategic outposts on American soil at Detroit, Michilimackinac, and Niagara. And as alarmed reaction to the Jay–Gardoqui affair made evident, Spain still conjured up grim memories of past New World conquests. The reason for America's diplomatic troubles was clear: the country was new, weak, and republican in an Atlantic world dominated by strong, monarchical governments and divided into warring empires.

Nothing revealed the difficulties of national survival more starkly than the Congress's futile efforts to rebuild America's crucially important overseas commerce. As we have seen, the Revolutionary War brought American trade virtually to a halt. Once the war was over, American merchants eagerly sought to reopen commerce with England. While highly desired English goods once again flooded American markets, few American goods flowed the other way. John Adams learned why. In 1785, he arrived in London as the first American minister to England. The Congress had assigned him the task of negotiating a commercial treaty, but he soon discovered how difficult that would be. After endless rebuffs, he reported in frustration that England had no intention of reopening the empire's ports to American shipping. English officials testily reminded him that Americans had desired independence and must now live with its consequences. Moreover, British goods could command the American market, they pointed out, without England's needing to grant trade concessions in return.

Progress was slow as American merchants searched for new commercial arrangements during the 1780s. Not only did England remain intractable, but France and Spain also withdrew wartime trading privileges and returned to a policy of maritime restrictions. In an effort to rebuild American commerce, the Congress tried to secure the states' cooperation in a program of economic recovery. Its efforts, however, were unavailing. In 1784, it failed to obtain authorization from the states to regulate the nation's foreign trade because each state was preoccupied with its own commercial advantage. As a consequence, American overseas trade continued to languish.

The result was deepening economic hardship. In Philadelphia, only 13 ships were built in 1786, one-third as many as just two years before. By the late 1780s, the per capita value of American exports had fallen a startling 30 percent from the 1760s. No wonder that merchants and artisans, carpenters and shopkeepers, sailors and dock workers—all directly dependent on shipbuilding and overseas commerce—suffered. In an Atlantic world divided into exclusive, imperial trading spheres, the United States lacked both the political unity and the economic muscle to protect its interests.

REVOLUTIONARY POLITICS IN THE STATES

Revolutionary politics took different forms in each state, depending on the impact of the war, the extent of

Loyalism, patterns of social conflict, and the disruptions of economic life. Throughout the nation, though, citizens struggled with an often intractable array of issues that arose during the war years but continued to trouble American politics well into the 1780s.

Separating Church and State

Among the most explosive issues was determining the proper relationship between church and state. Prior to independence, only Rhode Island, New Jersey, Pennsylvania, and Delaware had allowed full religious liberty. In the other colonies one or another religious group benefited from endorsement by the government and public tax support for its clergy. There civil authorities grudgingly tolerated "dissenters" such as the Methodists and Baptists, whose numbers were growing among the lower classes of the city and countryside and who were noisily pressing their case for full religious liberty.

With independence, pressure built for severing all ties between church and state. Such arguments were strengthened by the belief that alliances between government and church authorities had resulted in religious oppression throughout history and that voluntary choice was the only safe principle of religious association.

In Massachusetts, Connecticut, and New Hampshire, Congregationalists fought to retain their long-established privileges. Separating church and state, they argued, risked the growth of infidelity and disorder. Isaac Backus, the most outspoken of New England's Baptists, protested that "many, who are filling the nation with the cry of *liberty* and against *oppressors* are at the same time themselves violating that dearest of all rights, *liberty of conscience.*"

Massachusetts's new constitution guaranteed everyone the right to worship God "in the manner and season most agreeable to the dictates of his own conscience." But as Backus pointed out, it also empowered the legislature to require that towns tax their residents to support the public worship of God. Such support, Backus argued, should be ended completely, since religious toleration fell far short of true religious freedom. Not until the early nineteenth century—in Massachusetts not until 1833—were the laws linking church and state finally repealed.

In Virginia, the Baptists pressed their cause against the Protestant Episcopal Church, successor to the Church of England. The adoption in 1786 of Thomas Jefferson's Bill for Establishing Religious Freedom, rejecting all connections between church and state and removing all religious tests for public office, decisively settled the issue. Three years later, that statute served as a model for the First Amendment to the new federal Constitution.

Even most supporters of religious freedom, however, were not prepared to extend it universally. While the wartime alliance with Catholic France together with congressional efforts to entice Catholic settlers in Quebec to join the resistance against England had weakened long-established prejudices, anti-Catholic biases remained strong, especially in New England.

This nineteenth-century print says it gives "A Correct View of the Old Methodist Church in John Street, New York. The first erected in America. Founded A.D. 1768." Methodists and Baptists were among the "dissenting" groups pressing for full religious freedom during the revolutionary era. *(The Metropolitan Museum of Art, Bequest of Edward W. C. Arnold, 1954. The Edward W. C. Arnold Collection of New York Prints, Maps and Pictures. (54.90.168))*

Recovering the Past

INDIAN TREATIES

During the 1780s, the new American government contracted its first treaties with Native Americans of the trans-Appalachian interior, including the Wyandotte, the Delaware, and the Cherokee. The treaties were necessary to complete the peacemaking process at the end of the Revolutionary War, because most of the interior tribes had sided with England. The treaties were also intended to open trans-Appalachia to white settlement.

The treaty texts, like the agreement between the Congress and the Cherokee signed at Hopewell in November 1785, presented here, tell us a great deal about the issues that lay at the center of Indian–white relations during the 1780s. What major issues did the treaty of 1785 attempt to resolve? Why were these issues important to the Congress and the Native Americans?

A careful reading of the treaty language can also tell us much about the attitudes and values that white negotiators brought to the treaty-making process and provide hints of how that process functioned. Which phrases in the treaty reveal how the Congress's negotiators viewed their Cherokee counterparts? From the evidence of the treaty text, how would you characterize the treaty negotiations?

Most of the treaties arranged during the 1780s failed to last, and by the end of the decade trans-Appalachia, both north and south of the Ohio River, was embroiled in Indian–white warfare. Why did these agreements prove so fragile?

Treaty with the Cherokee, 1785

Articles concluded at Hopewell, on the Keowee, between Benjamin Hawkins, Andrew Pickens, Joseph Martin, and Lachlan M'Intosh, Commissioners Plenipotentiary of the United States of America, of the one Part, and the Head-Men and Warriors of all the Cherokees of the other.

The Commissioners Plenipotentiary of the United States, in Congress assembled, give peace to all the Cherokees, and receive them into the favor and protection of the United States of America, on the following conditions:

Article I

The Head-Men and Warriors of all the Cherokees shall restore all the prisoners, citizens of the United States, or subjects of their allies, to their entire liberty: They shall also restore all the Negroes, and all other property taken during the late war from the citizens, to such person, and at such time and place, as the Commissioners shall appoint.

Article II

The Commissioners of the United States in Congress assembled, shall restore all prisoners taken from the Indians, during the late war, to the Head-Men and Warriors of the Cherokees, as early as is practicable.

Article III

The said Indians for themselves and their respective tribes and towns do acknowledge all the Cherokees to be under the protection of the United States of America, and of no other sovereign whosoever.

Article IV

The boundary allotted to the Cherokees for their hunting grounds, between the said Indians and the citizens of the United States, within the limits of the United States of America, is, and shall be the following. . . .

Article V

If any citizen of the United States, or other person not being an Indian, shall attempt to settle on any of the lands westward or southward of the said boundary which are hereby allotted to the Indians for their hunting grounds, or having already settled and will not remove from the same within six months after the ratification of this treaty, such person shall forfeit the protection of the United States, and the Indians may punish him or not as they please. . . .

Article VI
If any Indian or Indians, or person residing among them, or who shall take refuge in their nation, shall commit a robbery, or murder, or other capital crime, on any citizen of the United States, or person under their protection, the nation, or the tribe to which such offender or offenders may belong, shall be bound to deliver him or them up to be punished according to the ordinances of the United States; Provided, that the punishment shall not be greater than if the robbery or murder, or other capital crime had been committed by a citizen on a citizen.

Article VII
If any citizen of the United States, or person under their protection, shall commit a robbery or murder, or other capital crime, on any Indian, such offender or offenders shall be punished in the same manner as if the murder or robbery, or other capital crime, had been committed on a citizen of the United States; and the punishment shall be in presence of some of the Cherokees, if any shall attend at the time and place. . . .

Article VIII
It is understood that the punishment of the innocent under the idea of retaliation, is unjust, and shall not be practiced on either side, except where there is a manifest violation of this treaty; and then it shall be preceded first by a demand of justice, and if refused, then by a declaration of hostilities.

Article IX
For the benefit and comfort of the Indians, and for the prevention of injuries or oppressions on the part of the citizens or Indians, the United States in Congress assembled shall have the sole and exclusive right of regulating the trade with the Indians, and managing all their affairs in such manner as they think proper. . . .

Article XI
The said Indians shall give notice to the citizens of the United States, of any designs which they may know or suspect to be formed in any neighboring tribe, or by any person whosoever, against the peace, trade or interest of the United States.

Article XII
That the Indians may have full confidence in the justice of the United States, respecting their interests, they shall have the right to send a deputy of their choice, whenever they think fit, to Congress.

Article XIII
The hatchet shall be forever buried, and the peace given by the United States, and friendship re-established between the said states on the one part, and all the Cherokees on the other, shall be universal; and the contracting parties shall use their utmost endeavors to maintain the peace given as aforesaid, and friendship re-established.

In witness of all and every thing herein determined, between the United States of America and all the Cherokees, we, their underwritten Commissioners, by virtue of our full powers, have signed this definitive treaty, and have caused our seals to be hereunto affixed.

Done at Hopewell, on the Keowee, this twenty-eighth of November, in the year of our Lord one thousand seven hundred and eighty-five.

Benjamin Hawkins,
And'w Pickens,
Jos. Martin,
Lach'n McIntosh,
Koatohee, or Corn Tassel of Toquo, his x mark,
Scholauetta, or Hanging Man of Chota, his x mark,
Tuskegatahu, or Long Fellow of Chistohoe, his x mark,
Ooskwha, or Abraham of Chilkowa, his x mark,
Kolakusta, or Prince of Noth, his x mark,
Newota, or the Gritzs of Chicamaga, his x mark,
Konatota, or the Rising Fawn of Highwassay, his x mark,
Tuckasee, or Young Terrapin of Allajoy, his x mark,
Toostaka, or the Waker of Oostanawa, his x mark,
Untoola, or Gun Rod of Seteco, his x mark,
Unsuokanail, Buffalo White Calf New Cussee, his x mark,
Kostayeak, or Sharp Fellow Wataga, his x mark,
Chonosta, of Cowe, his x mark,
Chescoonwho, Bird in Close of Tomotlug, his x mark,
Tuckasee, or Terrapin of Hightowa, his x mark,
Chesetoa, or the Rabbit of Tlacoa, his x mark. . . .
Witness:
Wm. Blount,
Sam'l Taylor, Major.,
John Owen,
Jess. Walton,
Jno. Cowan, capt. comm'd't,
Thos. Gregg, 4
W. Hazzard,
James Madison,
Arthur Cooley, Sworn interpreters.

Source: Charles Kapple, ed., *Indian Affairs: Laws and Treaties* (Washington, D.C.: U.S. Government Printing Office, 1904–1941), vol. 2, pp. 8–11.

The people of Northbridge, Massachusetts, wanted to exclude "Roman Catholics, pagons, or Mahomitents" from public office. Disestablishment did not end religious discrimination. But it implanted the principle of religious freedom firmly in American law.

Slavery under Attack

Whether human slavery was tolerable in a republican society committed to the inalienable right to life, liberty, and the pursuit of happiness also vexed the revolutionary generation. During the several decades preceding independence, the trade in human chattels had flourished. While the 1760s had witnessed the largest importation of slaves in colonial history, the Revolutionary War halted the slave trade almost completely. Though southern planters talked of replacing their lost chattels once the war ended, a combination of revolutionary principles, a reduced need for field hands in the depressed Chesapeake tobacco economy, the continuing natural increase among the slave population, and anxiety over black rebelliousness argued for the slave trade's permanent extinction. By 1790, every state except South Carolina and Georgia had outlawed slave importations.

Ending the slave trade had powerful implications, for it reduced the infusion of new Africans into the black population. As a result, an ever higher proportion of blacks was American born, thus speeding the cultural transformation by which Africans became African Americans.

Slavery itself came under attack during the revolutionary era, with immense consequences for blacks and for the nation's future. As the crisis with England heated up, catchwords such as *liberty* and *tyranny,* mobilized by colonists against British policies, reminded citizens that one-fifth of the colonial population was in chains. Samuel Hopkins, a New England clergyman, accosted his compatriots for "making a vain parade of being advocates for the liberties of mankind, while . . . continuing this lawless, cruel, inhuman, and abominable practice of enslaving your fellow creatures." Following independence, the antislavery attacks intensified.

In Georgia and South Carolina, where blacks outnumbered whites more than two to one, slavery escaped significant challenge. Committed to the doctrine of racial superiority and fearing the black majority, whites shuddered at the prospect of black freedom. Moreover, slave labor remained essential to the still prosperous rice economy. In response to the dangers generated by the war, whites wound the local slave codes even tighter.

In Virginia and Maryland, by contrast, whites openly argued whether slavery was compatible with republicanism, and in these states significant change did occur. The weakened demand for slave labor posed by the depressed tobacco economy facilitated the debate. Though neither state abolished slavery, both passed laws making it easier for owners to manumit (that is, to free) their slaves without continuing to be responsible for their behavior. Moreover, increasing numbers of blacks purchased freedom for themselves and their families or simply ran away. By 1800, more than one of every ten blacks in the Chesapeake region was no longer enslaved, a dramatic increase from 30 years before. Not all were genuinely free, since many found their lives constrained as indentured servants obligated to work for others. For them, true freedom was postponed.

The majority of free blacks lived and worked in Baltimore, Richmond, and other towns, where they formed communities that served as centers of an expanding African American society as well as havens for slaves escaping from the countryside. In the Chesapeake region, the conditions of life for black Americans slowly changed for the better.

The most dramatic breakthrough occurred in the North. There slavery was either abolished or put on the road to gradual extinction. Abolition was possible in the North because blacks were a numerical minority—in most areas, blacks constituted no more than 4 percent of the population—and slavery had neither the economic nor social importance that it did in the South.

Northern blacks joined in the attacks on slavery. Following independence, they eagerly petitioned state assemblies for their freedom. "Every Principle from which America has acted in the course of their unhappy difficulties with Great Britain," declared one group of Philadelphia blacks, "pleads stronger than a thousand arguments in favor of our petition." In 1780, the Pennsylvania assembly passed a law stipulating that all newborn blacks were to be free when they reached age 21. It was a cautious but decisive step. Other northern states adopted similar policies of gradual emancipation.

In scattered instances, free blacks participated actively in revolutionary politics. When the first draft of the Massachusetts constitution, explicitly excluding blacks and mulattoes from the franchise, was made public, William Gordon, a white clergyman, voiced his protest. "Would it not be ridiculous . . . and unjust to exclude freemen from voting . . . though otherwise qualified, because their skins are black?" he questioned. "Why not . . . for being long-nosed, short-faced, or . . . lower than five feet nine?" In the end, Massachusetts's constitution made no mention of race, and there, as well as in Pennsylvania and New York, African Americans occasionally cast their ballots.

If civic participation by blacks was scattered and temporary in the North, it was almost totally absent in the South. With the brief exception of North Carolina, African Americans in the South could neither vote nor enjoy such basic rights of citizenship as protection of their persons and property under the law. Here, blacks remained almost entirely without political voice, except in the petitions against slavery and mistreatment that they pressed upon the state regimes. Even as freemen, blacks continued to encounter pervasive discrimination.

Still, remarkable progress had been made. Prior to the Revolution, slavery had been an accepted fact of northern life. After the Revolution, it no longer was. That change made a vast difference in the lives of countless black Americans. The abolition of slavery in the North, moreover, widened the sectional divergence between North and South, with enormous consequences for the years ahead. In addition, there now existed a coherent, publicly proclaimed antislavery ideology that was closely linked in Americans' minds to the nation's founding. The first antislavery organizations had been created as well. Although another half century would pass before antislavery became a significant force in American politics, the groundwork for slavery's final abolition had been laid.

Politics and the Economy

The devastating economic effects of independence and the Revolutionary War continued to plague the American people throughout the 1780s. The cutoff of long-established patterns of overseas trade with England sent American commerce into a tailspin from which it did not recover for nearly 20 years. While English men-of-war prowled the coast, American ships rocked idly at empty wharves, New England's once booming shipyards grew quiet, and communities whose livelihood depended on the sea sank into depression. Virginia tobacco planters, their English markets gone and their plantations open to seaborne attack, struggled to survive. Farmers in the middle and New England states often prospered while hungry armies were nearby but saw their profits plummet when the armies moved on.

Not everyone suffered equally. With British goods excluded from American markets and wearing homespun clothes deemed patriotic, American artisans often prospered. (The familiar slogan "Buy American" has a long tradition.) Handsome profits from government contracts, moreover, were enjoyed by people with the right political connections. Henry Knox, sometime merchant and commander of the continental artillery, observed that he was "exceedingly anxious to effect something in these fluctuating times, which may make . . . [me] easy for life." In the eight-

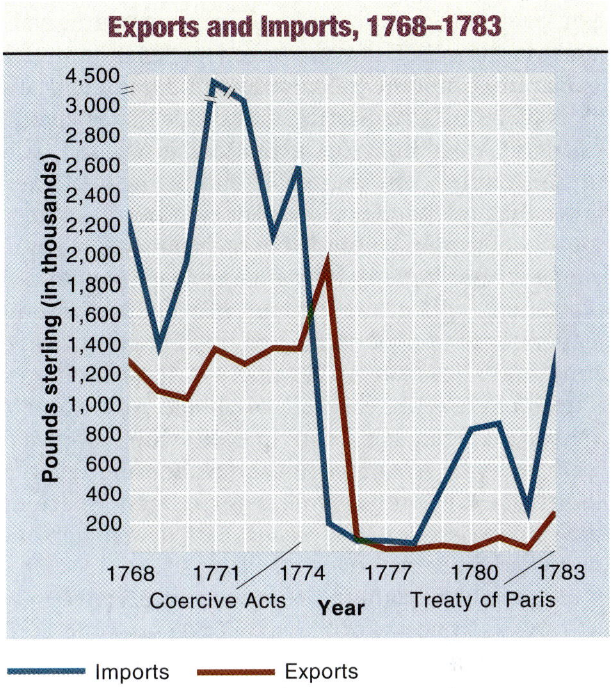

Nonimportation affected colonial commerce during the late 1760s and early 1770s, but exports as well as imports plummeted with the Coercive Acts and the outbreak of war. Source: U.S. Bureau of the Census.

As this Massachusetts broadside suggests, the lure of adventure and hope for quick profits enticed countless young men into dangerous but exciting service aboard American privateers. *(American Antiquarian Society)*

eenth century, as now, the boundary between private interest and public duty was often unclear.

But even as some prospered, countless others saw their affairs fall into disarray. Intractable issues such as price and wage inflation, skyrocketing taxation, and mushrooming debt set people sharply against each other. Heated debates arose over whether the states' war debts should be funded at face value or at some reduced rate. Arguing for full value were creditors—merchants and other persons of wealth who had loaned money to the states and had bought up large amounts of government securities at deep discounts. These people spoke earnestly of upholding the public honor and giving fair return to those who had risked their personal resources in the revolutionary cause. Opposed were common folk angered by the speculators' profits. No one, they argued, should reap personal advantage from public distress.

The issue of taxation, seared into Americans' consciousness by their troubles with England, generated similarly heated controversy. As the costs of the war mounted, so did taxes. Between 1774 and 1778, Massachusetts levied more than £400,000 in taxes, a stunning increase over colonial days. Complained one anguished soul, taxes siphoned off nearly one-third of the inhabitants' incomes. Massachusetts was not unique.

As taxes skyrocketed, farmers, artisans, and others of modest means argued that taxes should be payable in depreciated paper money or government securities rather than only in specie (gold or silver coin), as some state laws required. Lacking specie, they faced foreclosure of their property when they could not meet their obligations. Government officials responded that allowing payment in depreciated paper would deprive the government of critically needed revenue.

Controversy swirled as well around efforts to control soaring prices. Every state experimented with price controls at one time or another. Seldom were such efforts effective; frequently, they generated political firestorms. In general, the poor and those not yet integrated into the market economy supported controls. Faced with escalating prices, they had difficulty making ends meet. They also believed that goods should carry a "just price" that was fair to buyer and seller alike. In keeping with these principles, a crowd in New Windsor, New York, seized a shipment of tea bound for Albany in 1777 and sold it for what they deemed a fair offering.

Merchants, shopkeepers, and others accustomed to a commercial economy, however, believed that the laws of supply and demand should regulate economic transactions. "It is contrary to the nature of commerce," observed Benjamin Franklin, "for government to interfere in the prices of commodities." Attempts to regulate prices only created a disincentive to labor, which was "the principal part of the wealth of every country."

Disputes over paper money divided the American people as well. Faced with the uncontrollable escalation of wartime expenses, Congress and the states did what colonial governments had done before and American governments have done ever since: they printed money. In the first year of the war alone, they issued more than $400 million in various kinds of paper, and that was just the beginning. Only the citizens' willingness to accept such paper supported its value. That willingness rapidly disappeared as the flood of paper increased. Congressional bills of credit that in 1776 were pegged against gold at the ratio of 1.5 to 1 had slipped five years later to 147 to 1. State currencies depreciated just as alarmingly. In 1780, New York exchanged its old currency for new at the rate of 128 to 1.

Immense quantities of counterfeit currency produced by unscrupulous Americans out to make a profit as well as by British agents intent on disrupting the American war effort added to the monetary confusion. So worthless did American currency become that a crowd paraded the streets of Philadelphia in 1781 with paper money stuck in their hats as cockades and leading a dog plastered with congressional dollars.

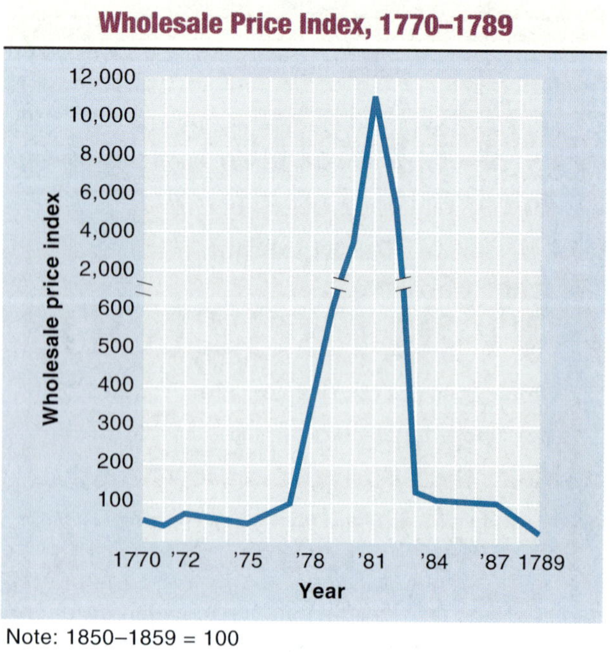

Prices skyrocketed as Congress and the state governments printed huge amounts of paper money in a desperate effort to cover the costs of the war. Source: U.S. Bureau of the Census.

Lacking sufficient gold and silver to cover the escalating costs of war, Congress printed massive amounts of paper money, which, in spite of the printed pledge, rapidly depreciated in value. *(Smithsonian Institution)*

The upward spiral of prices was staggering. In Massachusetts, a bushel of corn that sold for less than a dollar in 1777 went for nearly $80 two years later, and in Maryland the price of wheat increased several thousandfold. In Boston, a crowd of women, angered by the escalating costs of food, tossed a merchant suspected of monopolizing commodities into a cart and dragged him through the city's streets while "a large concourse of men stood amazed."

The disastrous monetary depreciation threatened to disrupt long-established social arrangements. James Lovell reported nervously that "sailors with clubs" were parading the streets of Boston "instead of working for paper." With property values in disarray, it seemed at times as if the very foundations of society were coming unhinged. "The war," wrote Thomas Paine,

> has thrown property into channels where before it never was. . . . Monies in large sums . . . enable . . . [profiteers] to roll the snow ball of monopoly and forestalling . . . [and] while these people are heaping up wealth . . . the remaining part are jogging on in their old way, with few or no advantages.

The poor suffered most severely, for they were most vulnerable to losses in the purchasing power of wages and military pay. They, however, were not alone. Farmers and merchants, planters and artisans also faced the burden of growing debt and uncertainty.

Rarely has the American economy been in such disarray as at the nation's founding. There were no ready solutions to the problems of debt, taxation, price control, and paper money for such issues often exceeded the capacity of politics for compromise and resolution. Divisive and intractable, they continued to heighten political tensions during the postwar years.

POLITICAL TUMULT IN THE STATES

Among the many issues embroiling state politics, debt relief, paper money, and arguments over equality came together with particularly explosive force in the mid-1780s. The political crisis that resulted spurred demands for a new and more powerful national government.

The Limits of Republican Experimentation

In a pattern that would frequently recur in American history, the postwar era witnessed growing social and political conservatism. Exhausted by the war's ordeal, many Americans turned their energies toward solving the problems troubling their personal lives. With the patriotic crusade against England successfully concluded, the initial surge of republican reform subsided. As a consequence, political leadership fell increasingly to men convinced that republican experimentation had gone too far, that the balance between order and liberty had to be reestablished, and that the "better sort" of men, not democratic newcomers, should occupy public office.

The most dramatic change occurred in Pennsylvania, where the democratic constitution of

1776 was replaced by a far more conservative document in 1790. The new constitution provided for a strong governor who could veto legislation and control the militia and a conservative senate designed to balance the more democratic assembly. Gaining a legislative majority by the mid-1780s, the conservatives dismantled much of the radicals' program by repealing revolutionary test oaths, stopping the issuance of paper money, and rechartering the Bank of North America. Pennsylvania's experiment in radical republicanism was over.

Shays's Rebellion

The conservative resurgence generated surprisingly little controversy in Pennsylvania. Elsewhere, however, popular opposition to hard money and high-tax policies produced vigorous protest. Nowhere was the situation more volatile than in Massachusetts. The controversy that erupted there in 1786 echoed strongly of equal rights and popular consent, staples of the rhetoric of 1776.

Given the war's disruption of economic affairs, increasing numbers of Massachusetts citizens found that they had to borrow money just to pay their taxes and support their families. Others who were more fortunate borrowed in order to speculate in western land or government securities. Because there were no commercial banks, people borrowed from each other in a complicated and highly unstable pyramid of credit and debt that reached from wealthy merchants along the coast to shopkeepers and farmers in the interior.

Trouble began when English goods glutted the American market, forcing down prices. In 1785, a number of English banking houses, heavily overcommitted in the American trade, began calling in loans they had extended to American importers. In a desperate effort to survive, these wholesalers demanded payment of the debts due them from retail storekeepers, sending a credit crisis surging through the state's economy.

Hardest hit were laboring people and farmers in town and countryside. Caught in a tightening financial bind, they turned to the state government for "stay laws" suspending the collection of private debts and thus easing the threat of foreclosure against their farms and shops. They also demanded new issues of paper money with which to pay both private debts and public taxes. The largest creditors, most of whom lived in commercial areas along the coast, fought such proposals because they wanted to collect the sums owed them promptly and in hard money. They also feared that paper money would quickly depreciate and further confound economic affairs.

By 1786, Massachusetts farmers, desperate in the face of mounting debt and a lingering agricultural depression, were petitioning the Massachusetts assembly for relief in words that echoed the colonial protests of the 1760s. Their appeals, however, fell on deaf ears, for commercial and creditor interests now controlled the government. Turning aside appeals for tax relief, the government passed a law calling for full repayment of the state debt and levied a heavy new round of taxes that would make such payment possible. No matter that, as one angry citizen reported, "there was not . . . the money in possession or at command among the people . . . to discharge their taxes." Between 1784 and 1786, 29 towns defaulted on their tax obligations.

This woodcut from *Bickerstaff's Genuine Boston Almanack* of 1787 depicts a county convention framing a petition for redress of grievances to the Massachusetts government. *(Library of Congress)*

Shays's Rebellion generated considerable alarm throughout Massachusetts. Grateful citizens of Springfield commissioned Paul Revere to make this silver punch bowl for General William Shepard, who was credited with defeating the insurgents. *(Yale University Art Gallery, The Mabel Brady Garvan Collection)*

As frustrated citizens had done before and would do again when the law proved unresponsive to their needs, Massachusetts farmers took matters into their own hands. A Hampshire County convention of delegates from 50 towns condemned the state senate, court fees, and the tax system. It advised against violence, but mobs soon began to form.

The county courts drew much of the farmers' wrath because they issued the writs of foreclosure that state and private creditors demanded. On August 31, 1786, armed men prevented the county court from sitting at Northampton, and on September 5 angry citizens closed down the court at Worcester. When farmers threatened similar actions elsewhere, an alarmed Governor James Bowdoin dispatched 600 militiamen to protect the state Supreme Court, then on circuit at Springfield.

About 500 insurgents had gathered nearby under the leadership of Daniel Shays, a popular Revolutionary War captain recently fallen on hard times. A "brave and good soldier," Shays had returned home in 1780, tired and frustrated, to await payment for his military service. Like thousands of others, he had a long wait. Meanwhile, his farming went badly, his debts accumulated, and, as he later recalled, "the spector of debtor's jail . . . hovered close by." Most of the men who gathered around Shays were also debtors and veterans.

The Continental Congress, urged by the Massachusetts delegates to take action and worried about a possible raid on the federal arsenal at Springfield, authorized 1,300 troops, ostensibly for service against the Indians but actually to be ready for use against Shays and his supporters. For a few weeks, Massachusetts teetered on the brink of civil conflict.

The insurrection collapsed in eastern Massachusetts in late November but was far from over in the west. When several insurgent groups refused Governor Bowdoin's order to disperse, he called out a force of 4,400 men, financed and led by worried eastern merchants. On January 26, 1787, Shays led 1,200 men toward the federal arsenal at Springfield. Its frightened defenders opened fire, killing four of the attackers and sending the Shaysites into retreat.

Over the next several weeks, the militia chased the remnants of Shays's followers across the state and sent Shays himself fleeing into Vermont for safety. By the end of February, the rebellion was over. In March, the legislature pardoned all but Shays and three other leaders; in another year, they too were forgiven.

Similar challenges to public authority, fired by personal troubles and frustration over unresponsive government, erupted in six other states. In Charles County, Maryland, a "tumultuary assemblage of the people" rushed into the courthouse in June 1786 and closed it down. Like the Massachusetts rebels, they demanded paper money and the suspension of debt proceedings. In Cecil County, farmers circulated

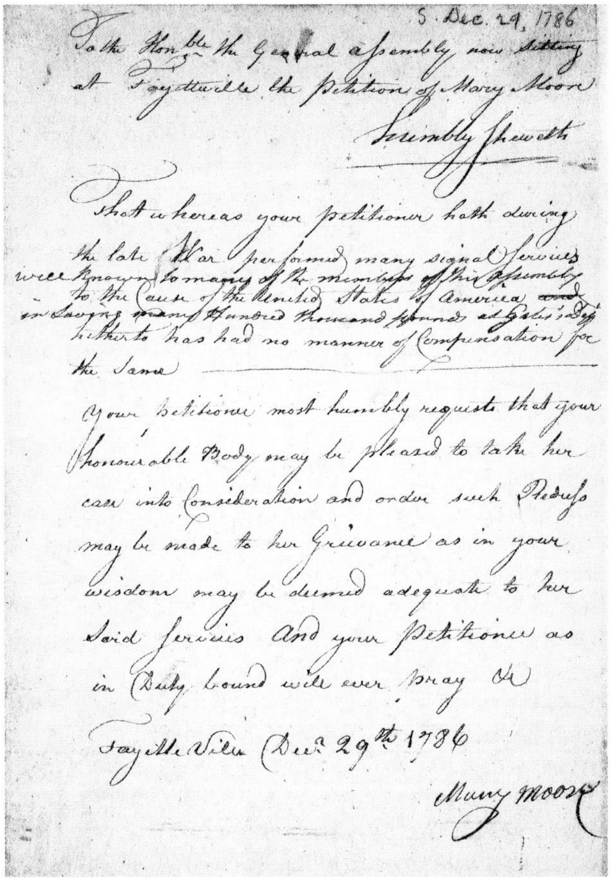
5. Dec. 29, 1786

To the Hon.ble the General assembly now sitting at Fayetteville the Petition of Mary Moore

Humbly Sheweth

That whereas your petitioner hath during the late War performed many signal Services well known to many of the members of this Assembly to the Cause of the United States of America and in saving many Hundred thousand pounds at Gates's Defeat hitherto has had no manner of Compensation for the Same

Your petitioner most humbly requests that your Honourable Body may be pleased to take her case into Consideration and order such Redress may be made to her Grievance as in your wisdom may be deemed adequate to her said Services And your petitioner as in Duty bound will ever pray &c

Fayetteville Decr 29th 1786

Mary Moore

Following the war, hundreds of women petitioned state legislatures to recover property and seek redress for other war related grievances. In this petition, Mary Moore seeks compensation from the North Carolina Assembly. *(Courtesy of the North Carolina Division of Archives and History)*

unsigned handbills threatening state officers if they seized people's property for unpaid taxes. The governor condemned the "riotous and tumultuous" proceedings and warned against further "violence and outrages." In South Carolina in May 1785, an incensed Hezekiah Mayham, "being served by the sheriff with a writ [of foreclosure], obliged him to eat it on the spot." Warned Judge Aedanus Burke, not even "5,000 troops, the best in America or Europe, could enforce obedience" to the court under such conditions.

Across the states, politics was in turmoil. While some felt betrayed by the Revolution's promise of equal rights and were angered by the "arrogant unresponsiveness" of government leaders, others were alarmed by the "democratic excesses" that the revolution appeared to have unleashed. What the immediate future might hold seemed exceedingly uncertain.

TOWARD A NEW NATIONAL GOVERNMENT

By 1786, belief was spreading among members of Congress and other political leaders that the nation was in crisis and that the experiment in republicanism was in danger of foundering. Explanations for the crisis and prescriptions for its resolution varied, but attention focused on the inadequacies of the Articles of Confederation. Within two years, following a raucous and deeply divisive political struggle, a new constitution had replaced the Articles, altering forever the course of American history.

The Rise of Federalism

The supporters of a stronger national government called themselves Federalists (leading their opponents to adopt the name Anti-Federalists). Led by men such as Washington, Hamilton, Madison, and Jay, whose experiences in the continental army and Congress had strengthened their national vision, the Federalists believed that the nation was in the midst of a political crisis that threatened its survival. Such men had never been comfortable with the democratic impulses of the Revolution. While committed to moderate republicanism, they believed that democratic change had been carried too far, property rights needed to be secured, and an aristocracy of talent should lead the country.

The Revolution, lamented John Jay, "laid open a wide field for the operation of ambition," especially for "men raised from low degrees to high stations and rendered giddy by elevation." It was time, he insisted, to find better ways of protecting "the worthy against the licentious."

Federalist leaders feared the loss of their own social and political power, but they were concerned as well about the collapse of the orderly world they believed essential to the preservation of republican liberty. In 1776, American liberty had required protection from overweening British power. Now, however, danger arose from an excess of liberty that threatened to degenerate into license. "We have probably had too good an opinion of human nature," concluded Washington somberly. "Experience has taught us, that men will not adopt and carry into execution measures the best calculated for their own good, without the intervention of a coercive power." What America now needed was a "strong government, ably administered."

The Federalists regarded outbursts such as Shays's uprising in Massachusetts not as evidence of genuine social distress but as threats to social and political order. Although they were reassured by the speed with which the Shaysites had been dispatched, the episode persuaded them of the need for a stronger national government managed by the "better sort."

Congress's inability to handle the national debt, establish public credit, and restore overseas trade also troubled the Federalists. Sensitive to America's economic and military weakness, smarting from French and English arrogance, and aware of continuing Anglo-European designs on North America, the Federalists called for a new national government capable of extending American trade, spurring economic recovery, and protecting national interests.

Beyond that, the Federalists shared a vision of an expanding commercial republic, its people spreading across the rich lands of the interior, its merchant ships connecting America with the markets of Europe and beyond. That vision, so rich in national promise, seemed also at risk.

The Grand Convention

The first step toward government reform came in September 1786, when delegates of five states who had gathered in Annapolis, Maryland, to discuss interstate commerce issued a call for a larger, more ambitious convention to convene in Philadelphia in May 1787. In February, the Confederation Congress cautiously endorsed the idea of a convention to revise the Articles of Confederation. Before long, it became clear that substantially more than a revision of the Articles was afoot.

During May, delegates representing every state except Rhode Island began assembling in Philadelphia. Eventually, 55 delegates would participate in the convention's work, though daily attendance hovered between 30 and 40. The city bustled with excitement as they gathered, for the Grand Convention's roster read like an honor roll of the Revolution. From Virginia came the distinguished lawyer George Mason, chief author of Virginia's trailblazing bill of rights, and the already legendary George Washington. Proponents of the convention had held their breath while Washington considered whether to attend. His presence vastly increased the prospect of success. James Madison was there as well. No one, with perhaps the single exception of Alexander Hamilton, was more committed to nationalist reform. Certainly, no one had worked harder to prepare for the convention than he. Poring over treatises on republican government and natural law that his friend Thomas Jefferson sent from France, Madison brought to Philadelphia his own design for a new national government. That design, presented to the convention as the Virginia Plan, would serve as the basis for the new constitution. Nor did anyone rival the diminutive Madison's contributions to the convention's work. Tirelessly, he took the convention floor to argue the nationalist cause or buttonhole wavering delegates to strengthen their resolve. Somehow, he also found the energy to keep extensive notes in his personal shorthand. Those notes constitute our essential record of the convention's proceedings.

Two distinguished Virginians were conspicuously absent. Thomas Jefferson was abroad serving as minister to France, and the old patriot Patrick Henry, an ardent champion of state supremacy, feared what the convention might do and wanted no part of it.

From Pennsylvania came the venerable Franklin, too old to contribute significantly to the debates but still able to call quarreling members to account and reinspire them in their work. His colleagues from Pennsylvania included the erudite Scots lawyer James Wilson, whose nationalist sympathies had been inflamed when a democratic mob, resentful of privileged lawyers and merchants, attacked his elegant Philadelphia townhouse in 1779. Robert Morris, probably the richest man in America, was there as well. Massachusetts was ably represented by Elbridge Gerry and Rufus King, while South Carolina sent John Rutledge and Charles Pinckney. Roger Sherman led Connecticut's contingent.

The New York assembly sent a deeply divided delegation. Governor George Clinton, long a personal enemy of Alexander Hamilton and determined to protect New York's autonomy as well as his own political power, saw to it that several Anti-Federalist skeptics made the trip to Philadelphia. They were no match for Hamilton, however.

Born in the Leeward Islands, the "bastard brat of a Scots-peddlar" and a strong-willed woman with a troubled marriage, Hamilton used his immense intelligence and ingratiating charm to rise rapidly in the world. Sent to New York by wealthy sponsors, he quickly established himself as a favorite of the city's mercantile community. While still in his early twenties, he became Washington's wartime aide-de-camp.

James Madison of Virginia, only 36 years old when the Philadelphia convention met, worked tirelessly between 1786 and 1788 to replace the Articles of Confederation with a new and more effective national constitution. *(Mead Art Museum, Amherst Collection, Bequest of Herbert L. Pratt, 1895, 1945.82)*

That relationship served Hamilton well for the next 20 years. Returning from the war, he married the wealthy Elizabeth Schuyler, thereby securing his personal fortune and strengthening his political connections. Together with Madison, Hamilton had promoted the abortive Annapolis convention. At Philadelphia, he was determined to drive his nationalist vision ahead.

Meeting in Independence Hall, where the Declaration of Independence had been proclaimed little more than a decade earlier, the convention elected Washington as its presiding officer, adopted rules of procedure, and, after spirited debate, voted to close the doors and conduct its business in secret.

Debate focused first on the Virginia Plan, introduced on May 29 by Edmund Randolph. It outlined a potentially powerful national government and effectively set the convention's agenda. According to its provisions, there would be a bicameral Congress, with the lower house elected by the people and the upper house, or senate, chosen by the lower house from nominees proposed by the state legislatures. The plan also called for a president who would be named by the Congress, a national judiciary, and a Council of Revision, whose task was to review the constitutionality of federal laws.

The smaller states quickly objected to the Virginia Plan's call for proportional rather than equal representation of the states. On June 15, William Paterson introduced a counterproposal, the New Jersey Plan. It urged retention of the Articles of Confederation as the basic structure of government while conferring on Congress the long-sought powers to tax and regulate foreign and interstate commerce. After three days of heated debate, by a vote of seven states to three, the delegates adopted the Virginia Plan as the basis for further discussions. It was now clear that the convention would set aside the Articles for a much stronger national government. The only question was how powerful the new government would be.

At times over the next four months, it seemed that the Grand Convention would collapse under the weight of its own disagreements and the oppressive summer heat. How were the sharply conflicting interests of large and small states to be reconciled? How should the balance of power between the national and state governments be struck? Could an executive branch be created that was strong enough to govern but not so strong as to endanger republican liberty? And what, if anything, would the convention say about slavery and the slave trade, issues on which northerners and southerners, antislavery and proslavery advocates so passionately disagreed?

At one extreme was Hamilton's audaciously conservative proposal, made early in the convention's deliberations, for a Congress and president elected for life and a national government so powerful that the states would survive as little more than administrative agencies. Finding his plan under attack and his influence rapidly eroding, Hamilton withdrew from the convention in late June. He would return a month later but make few additional contributions to the convention's work.

At the other extreme stood the ardent Anti-Federalist Luther Martin of Maryland. Rude and unkempt, Martin voiced his uncompromising opposition to anything that threatened state sovereignty or smacked of aristocracy. Increasingly isolated by the convention's nationalist inclinations, Martin also returned home, in his case to spread the alarm.

By early July, with tempers frayed and frustration growing over the apparent deadlock, the delegates agreed to recess, ostensibly for Independence Day but actually to let Franklin, Roger Sherman of Connecticut, and others make a final effort at compromise. All agreed that only a bold stroke could prevent a collapse.

That stroke came on July 12, as part of what has become known as the Great Compromise. The reassembled delegates settled one major point of controversy by agreeing that representation in the lower house should be based on the total of each state's white population plus three-fifths of its blacks. Though African Americans were not accorded citizenship and

This painting by Thomas Rossiter, done in the early nineteenth century, provides an imaginative portrayal of the Philadelphia convention, with George Washington presiding and a rising sun, symbolic of the new nation, shining behind him. *(Independence National Historical Park Collection)*

could not vote, the southern delegates argued that they should be fully counted for this purpose. Delegates from the northern states, where relatively few blacks lived, did not want them counted at all, but the bargain was struck. As part of this compromise, the convention agreed that direct taxes would also be apportioned on the basis of population and that blacks would be counted similarly in that calculation. On July 16, the convention accepted the principle that each state should have an equal vote in the senate. Thus the interests of both large states and small were effectively accommodated.

The convention then submitted its work to a committee of detail for drafting in proper constitutional form. That group reported on August 6, and for the next month the delegates hammered out the exact language of the document's seven articles. On several occasions, differences seemed so great that it was uncertain whether the convention could proceed. In each instance, however, agreement was reached, and the discussion continued.

Determined to give the new government the stability that state governments lacked, the delegates created an electoral process designed to bring only persons of experience and reputation into national office. An Electoral College of wise and experienced leaders would meet to choose the president. The process functioned exactly that way during the first several presidential elections.

Selection of the Senate would be similarly indirect, for its members were to be named by the state legislatures. (Not until 1913, with ratification of the Seventeenth Amendment, would the American people begin electing their senators.) Even the House of Representatives, the only popularly elected branch of the new government, was to be filled with people of standing and wealth, for the Federalists were confident that only well-established leaders would be able to attract the necessary votes.

The delegates' final set of compromises touched the fate of black Americans. At the insistence of southerners, the convention agreed that the slave trade would not formally end for another 20 years. The delegates never used the words *slavery* or *slave trade,* but spoke more vaguely about not prohibiting the "migration or importation of such persons as any of the states now existing shall think proper to admit." Their meaning, however, was entirely clear.

Despite an impassioned charge by Gouverneur Morris of New York that slavery was a "nefarious institution" that would bring "the curse of Heaven on the states where it prevails," the delegates firmly rejected a proposal to abolish slavery, thereby acknowledging its legitimacy. More than that, they guaranteed slavery's protection, by writing in Section 2 of Article 4 that "No person held to service or labour in one state, . . . [and] escaping into another, shall, in consequence of any law . . . therein, be discharged from such service, but shall be delivered up on claim of the party to whom such service or labour may be due." The delegates thus provided federal sanction for the capture and return of runaway slaves. This fugitive slave clause would return to haunt northern consciences in the years ahead. At the time, however, it seemed a small price to pay for sectional harmony and a new government. Northern accommodation to the demands of the southern delegates was eased, moreover, by knowledge that southerners in the Confederation Congress had just agreed to prohibit new slaves from entering the Northwest Territory.

Although the Constitution's unique federal system of governance called for shared responsibilities between the nation and the states, it decisively strengthened the national government. Among the extensive list of powers granted to Congress were the authority to levy and collect taxes, regulate commerce with foreign nations and between the states, devise uniform rules for naturalization, administer national patents and copyrights, and control the federal district in which it would eventually be located. Conspicuously missing was any statement reserving to the states all powers not explicitly conferred on the central government. Such language had proved crippling in the Articles of Confederation. On the contrary, the Constitution contained a number of clauses bestowing vaguely defined grants of power on the new government. Section 8 of Article 1, for example, granted Congress the authority to "provide for the . . . general welfare of the United States" as well as to "make all laws . . . necessary and proper for carrying into execution . . . all . . . powers vested by this Constitution in the government of the United States." Later generations would call these phrases "elastic clauses" and would use them to expand the federal government's activities.

In addition, Section 10 of Article 1 contained a litany of powers now denied the states, among them issuing paper money, passing laws impairing the obligation of contracts, and entering into agreements with foreign powers other than by the consent of Congress. A final measure of the Federalists' determination to make the new government supreme over the states was the assertion in Article 6 that the Constitution and all laws passed under it were to be regarded as the "supreme Law of the Land."

When the convention had finished its business, 3 of the 42 remaining delegates refused to sign the document. The other 39 affixed their names and forwarded it to the Confederation Congress along with the request that it be sent on to the states for approval. On September 17, the Grand Convention adjourned.

Federalists versus Anti-Federalists

Ratification presented the Federalists with a more difficult problem than they had faced at Philadelphia, for the debate now shifted to the states, where sentiment was sharply divided and the political situation was more difficult to control. Recognizing the unlikelihood of gaining quick agreement from all 13 states, the Federalists stipulated that the Constitution should go into effect when any 9 agreed to it. Other states could then enter the Union as they were ready. Ratification was to be decided by specially elected conventions rather than by the state assemblies, because under the Constitution the assemblies would lose substantial amounts of power. Ratification by such conventions would also give the Constitution greater legitimacy by grounding it directly in the people.

In the Confederation Congress, opponents of the new Constitution charged that the Philadelphia Convention had exceeded its authority. But after a few days' debate, the Congress dutifully forwarded the document to the states for consideration. Word of the dramatic changes being proposed spread rapidly. In each state, Federalists and Anti-Federalists, the latter now actively opposing the Constitution, prepared to debate the new articles of government.

Although levels of Federalist and Anti-Federalist strength differed from state to state, opposition to the Constitution was widespread and vocal. Some critics feared that a stronger central government would threaten state interests or their own political power. Others, like Timothy Bloodworth, charged the Federalists with betraying revolutionary republicanism. Like all "energetic" governments, they warned, the new one would be corrupted by its own power. Far from the watchful eyes of the citizenry, its officials would behave as power wielders always had, and American liberty, so recently preserved at such high cost, would once again come under attack.

The Anti-Federalists were aghast at the Federalists' vision of an expanding "republican empire." "The idea of . . . [a] republic, on an average of 1,000 miles in length, and 800 in breadth, and containing 6 millions of white inhabitants all reduced to the same standards of morals, . . . habits . . . [and] laws," exclaimed one critic incredulously, "is itself an absurdity, and contrary to the whole experience of mankind." Such an extended republic would quickly fall prey to factional conflict and internal disorder. The Anti-Federalists continued to believe that republican liberty could be preserved only in small, homogeneous societies, where the seeds of faction were few and public virtue guided citizens' behavior.

Nor did the Anti-Federalists believe that either the proposed separation of executive, legislative, and judicial branches or the balancing of state and national governments would prevent power's abuse.

Gradually, a white woman clothed in the flowing robes of classical attire replaced the Indian Columbia. In this painting by Samuel Jennings, Columbia offers the promise of education to a group of black Americans. *(The Library Company of Philadelphia)*

Government, they insisted, must be kept simple, for complexity only confused the people and cloaked selfish ambition.

Not all the Anti-Federalists were democrats. In the South, many held slaves, and their appeals to local authority did not always mean support for political equality, even among whites. Yet along with their warnings against centralized power, they often spoke fervently of democratic principles. Certainly, they believed more firmly than their Federalist opponents that if government was to be safe, it must be tied closely to the people.

Federalist spokesmen moved quickly to counter the Anti-Federalists' attack, for many of those criticisms carried the sanction of the revolutionary past. Their most important effort was a series of essays penned by James Madison, Alexander Hamilton, and John Jay and published in New York under the pseudonym Publius. *The Federalist* essays, as they were called, were written to promote ratification in New York but were quickly reprinted by Federalists elsewhere.

Madison, Hamilton, and Jay moved systematically through the Constitution, explaining its virtues and responding to the Anti-Federalists' attacks. In the process, they described a political vision fundamentally at odds with that of their Anti-Federalist opponents.

No difference was more dramatic than the Federalists' treatment of government power. Power, the Federalists now argued, was not the enemy of liberty but its guarantor. Where government was not sufficiently "energetic" and "efficient" (these were favorite Federalist words), demagogues and disorganizers would find space to do their nefarious work. It is far better, Hamilton wrote in *Federalist No. 26,* "to hazard the abuse of . . . confidence than to embarrass the government and endanger the public safety by impolitic restrictions of . . . authority."

The authors of the *Federalist* also countered the Anti-Federalists' warning that a single, extended republic encompassing the country's economic and social diversity would lead inevitably to factional conflict that would destroy republican liberty. Turning the Anti-Federalists' classic, republican argument on its head, they explained that factional divisions were the inevitable accompaniment of human liberty. Wrote Madison in *Federalist No. 10:* "Liberty is to faction what air is to fire, an aliment without which it instantly expires." To suppress faction would require the destruction of liberty itself.

Earlier emphasis on public virtue as the guarantor of political order, the Federalists explained, had been naive, for few people would consistently put the public good ahead of their own interests. Politics had to heed this harsh fact of human nature and provide for peaceful compromise among conflicting groups. That could be best accomplished by expanding the nation so that it included innumerable factions. Out of the clash and accommodation of multiple social and economic interests would emerge compromise and the best possible approximation of the public good.

The Federalists' argument established the basic rationale for modern democratic politics, but it left the Anti-Federalists sputtering in frustration. Where in the

The eagle, an important symbol of the new nation, appeared on water pitchers, whiskey bottles, flags, newspaper mastheads, and fabrics of all kinds. The flag also became an important icon. While its red and white stripes represented the 13 original states, its blue field of stars was modified as new states entered the Union. (quilt: *Magnette, Edith,* Quilt, *Index of American Design, ©2000 Board of Trustees, National Gallery of Art, Washington, c. 1941, watercolor and graphite on paperboard, .759 x .506 [$29\frac{7}{8}$ x $19\frac{15}{16}$];* pine chest: *formerly in the Collection of The Henry Ford Museum and Greenfield Village*)

Federalists' scheme was there a place for that familiar abstraction, the public good? What would become of public virtue in a system built on the notion of competing interests? In such a free market of competition, the Anti-Federalists warned, the wealthy and powerful would thrive while ordinary folk would suffer.

As the ratification debate revealed, the Federalists and Anti-Federalists held sharply contrasting visions of the new republic. The Anti-Federalist vision remained much closer to the original republicanism of 1776, with its suspicion of power and wealth, its emphasis on the primacy of local government, and its fears of national development. The Anti-Federalists envisioned a decentralized republic filled with self-reliant citizens, limited in personal ambition and guided by public virtue, whose destiny was determined primarily by what happened in the states rather than the nation. Anxious about the future, they longed to preserve the political world much as it had been.

The Federalists, on the other hand, persuaded that America's situation had changed dramatically since 1776, embraced the idea of nationhood and looked forward with anticipation to the development of a rising "republican empire," based on commercial development and led by men of wealth and talent. Both Federalists and Anti-Federalists claimed to be heirs of the Revolution, yet they differed fundamentally in what they understood that heritage to be.

The Struggle over Ratification

No one knows what most Americans thought of the proposed Constitution, for no national plebiscite on it was ever taken. Probably no more than several hundred thousand people participated in the elections for the state ratifying conventions, and many of the delegates carried no binding instructions from their constituents on how they should vote. A majority of the people probably opposed the document, either out of indifference or alarm. Fortunately for the Federalists, they did not have to persuade most Americans but needed only to secure majorities in nine of the state ratifying conventions, a much less formidable task.

They set about it with determination. As soon as the Philadelphia Convention adjourned, its members hurried home to organize the ratification movement in their states. In Delaware and Georgia, New Jersey and Connecticut, where the Federalists were confident of their strength, they pressed quickly for a vote. Where the outcome was uncertain, as in New York, Massachusetts, and Virginia, they delayed, hoping that word of ratification elsewhere would work to their benefit.

It took less than a year to secure approval of the necessary nine states. Delaware, Pennsylvania, and New Jersey ratified first, in December 1787. Approval came a month later in Georgia and Connecticut. Massachusetts ratified in February 1788, but only after considerable political maneuvering. In an effort to woo Anti-Federalist delegates and persuade the uncommitted, Federalist leaders there agreed to forward a set of amendments outlining a federal "bill of rights" along with notice of ratification. The strategy worked, for it brought Samuel Adams and John Hancock into line. They brought with them the crucial convention votes that were needed.

Maryland and South Carolina were the seventh and eighth states to approve. That left New Hampshire and Virginia as the most likely candidates for the honor of being ninth and putting the Constitution over the top. There was staunch opposition in both states. The New Hampshire convention met on February 13. Sensing that they lacked the necessary votes, the Federalists adjourned the convention until mid-June and worked feverishly to build support. When the convention reconvened, it took but three days to secure a Federalist majority. New Hampshire ratified on June 21.

Two massive gaps in the new Union remained—Virginia and New York. The nation clearly could not endure without them. In Virginia, Madison gathered support by promising that the new Congress would immediately consider a federal bill of rights. Other Federalists spread the rumor that Patrick Henry, one of the most ardent Anti-Federalist leaders, had changed sides, a charge that Henry angrily denied. His eloquence, however, proved no match for the careful politicking of Madison and others. On June 25, the Virginia convention voted to ratify by the narrow margin of ten votes.

The New York convention gathered on June 17 at Poughkeepsie, with the Anti-Federalist followers of

RATIFICATION OF THE CONSTITUTION

Votes of State Ratifying Conventions

State	Date	For	Against
Delaware	December 1787	30	0
Pennsylvania	December 1787	46	23
New Jersey	December 1787	38	0
Georgia	January 1788	26	0
Connecticut	January 1788	128	40
Massachusetts	February 1788	187	168
Maryland	April 1788	63	11
South Carolina	May 1788	149	73
New Hampshire	June 1788	57	47
Virginia	June 1788	89	79
New York	July 1788	30	27
North Carolina	November 1789	194	77
Rhode Island	May 1790	34	32

Governor Clinton firmly in command. Hamilton worked for delay, hoping that news of the results in New Hampshire and Virginia would turn the tide. For several weeks, approval hung in the balance while the two sides maneuvered for support. On July 27, approval squeaked through, 30 to 27. That left two states still uncommitted. North Carolina (with Timothy Bloodworth's skeptical approval) finally ratified in November 1789. Rhode Island did not enter the Union until May 1790, more than a year after the new government had gotten under way.

The Social Geography of Ratification

A glance at the geographic pattern of Federalist and Anti-Federalist strength reveals their very different sources of political support. Federalist strength was concentrated in areas along the coast and navigable rivers and was strongest in cities and towns. Merchants and businessmen supported the Constitution most ardently. Enthusiasm also ran high among urban laborers, artisans, and shopkeepers—surprisingly so, given the Anti-Federalists' criticism of wealth and power and their emphasis on democratic equality. While city artisans and workers had been in the vanguard of democratic reform during the Revolution, in the troubled circumstances of the late 1780s they worried primarily about their livelihoods and believed that a stronger government could promote overseas trade and better protect American artisans from foreign competition.

Federalist and Anti-Federalist Areas, 1787–1788

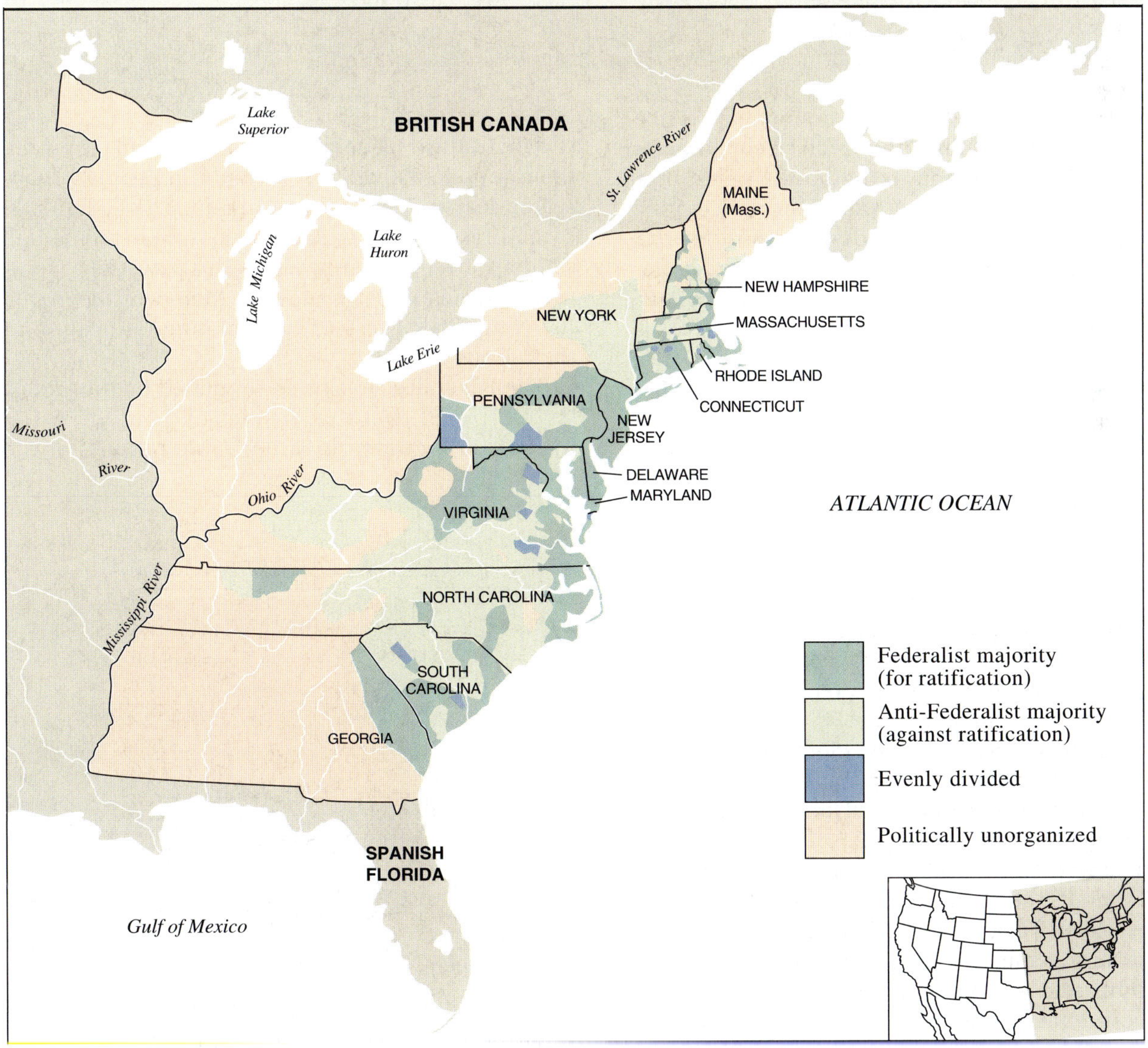

Distinct geographic patterns of Federalist and Anti-Federalist strength developed during the ratification debate. This map shows areas whose delegates to the state ratifying conventions voted for and against the Constitution.

The federal ship *Hamilton* formed the centerpiece of a grand procession in New York City celebrating the successful ratification of the new Constitution.

On July 4, 1788, a grand procession celebrating the Constitution's ratification wound through the streets of Philadelphia. Seventeen thousand strong, it graphically demonstrated the breadth of support for the Constitution. At the head of the line marched lawyers, merchants, and others of the city's elite. Close behind them came representatives of virtually every trade in the city, from ship's carpenters to shoemakers, each with its own floats, flags, and mottoed banners. "May commerce flourish and industry be rewarded," declared the mariners and shipbuilders. "May the federal government revive our trade," exclaimed the bakers. "Home-brewed is best," insisted the maltsters. For the moment, declared Benjamin Rush in amazement, "rank . . . forgot all its claims. Hand in hand marched merchants and sea-men, lawyers and artisans." Within a few years, political disputes would divide them once again. For the moment, however, people of all ranks joined in celebrating the new Constitution.

Elsewhere class differences and geographic location separated people more clearly. The Constitution found support among commercial farmers and southern planters eager for profit and anxious about overseas markets, but Federalist enthusiasm waned and Anti-Federalist sentiment grew in the interior. The centers of Anti-Federalism lay away from the coast in central New England, upstate New York, the Virginia Piedmont and southside, and western Carolina. Among ordinary farmers living outside the market economy, local loyalties outweighed their interest in national affairs. Federalist visions of a growing "American empire" they found strange and alarming.

Why did the Federalists finally prevail? After all, their opponents had only to tap into people's deep-seated fears of central government. The Federalists, by contrast, had to explain how republicanism had suddenly become compatible with a powerful government and an expanding empire. Moreover, they faced the complicated task of coordinating ratification in the various states.

The Federalists' task was simplified by the widely shared belief that the Articles of Confederation needed strengthening. The troubled events of the

Timeline

1784	Treaty of Fort Stanwix with the Iroquois
	Spain closes the Mississippi River to American navigation
1785	Treaty of Hopewell with the Cherokee
	Land Ordinance for the Northwest Territory
	Jay–Gardoqui negotiations
1786	Virginia adopts "Bill for Establishing Religious Freedom"
	Annapolis Convention calls for revision of the Articles of Confederation
1786–1787	Shays's Rebellion
1787	Northwest Ordinance
	Constitutional Convention
	Federalist Papers published by Hamilton, Jay, and Madison
1788	Constitution ratified

1780s supported Federalist arguments that America's experiment in republican independence was doomed unless decisive action was taken. More than anything, however, the Federalists succeeded because of their determination and political skill. Most of the Revolution's major leaders were Federalists. Time and again these worthies spoke out for the Constitution, and time and again their support proved decisive. Their experience as army officers and as members of the Continental and Confederation Congresses caused them to identify with the nation and imagine what it might become. They brought their vision to the ratification process and asked others to share it. Altogether, it was an impressive political performance. With their success, the Federalists turned the American republic in a new and fateful direction.

Conclusion

Completing the Revolution

Only five years had passed between England's acknowledgment of American independence in 1783 and ratification of the new national Constitution, yet to many Americans it seemed far longer. At war's end, the difficulties of sustaining American liberty were evident. The experience of the next half decade added to them. While struggling to survive in a hostile Atlantic environment and coping with economic distress and political turmoil at home, Americans continued to argue about their experiment in republicanism. Above all, they wondered how democratic it could safely be, and even whether it would survive.

At the same time, the American people retained an immense reservoir of optimism about the future. Had they not defeated mighty England? Was not their Revolution destined to change the course of history and provide a model for all mankind? Did not America's wonderfully rich interior contain a limitless promise of economic and social opportunity? Most Americans, still filled with the enthusiasm of their new beginning, answered with a resounding "Yes." Much would depend, of course, on their new Constitution and the government soon to be created under it. As the ratification debate subsided and the Confederation Congress prepared for the transition, the American people looked eagerly and anxiously ahead.

Recommended Reading

Struggling with the Peacetime Agenda

Ira Berlin and Ronald Hoffman, eds., *Slavery and Freedom in the Age of the American Revolution* (1983); Richard Buel, Jr., *In Irons: Britain's Naval Supremacy and the American Revolutionary Economy* (1998); Thomas Curry, *The First Freedoms: Church and State in America to the Passage of the First Amendment* (1986); Eric Hinderaker, *Elusive Empires: Constructing Colonialism in the Ohio Valley, 1673–1800* (1997).

Ronald Hoffman and Peter Albert, eds., *Religion in a New Age* (1994) and *Sovereign States in an Age of Uncertainty* (1778); James Hutson, *Religion in a Revolutionary Age* (1994); Merrill Jensen, *The New Nation: A History of the United States During the Confederation, 1781–1789* (1950); Susan Juster, *Disorderly Women: Sexual Politics and Evangelicalism in Revolutionary New England* (1994); Jackson T. Main, *Political Parties Before the Constitution* (1973); Frederick Marks, *Independence on Trial: Foreign Affairs and the Making of the Constitution* (1973); Cathy Matson and Peter Onuf, *A Union of Interests: Political and Economic Thought in Revolutionary America* (1990); William McLaughlin, *Soul Liberty: The Baptists' Struggle in New England, 1630–1833* (1991); Gary B. Nash and Jean Soderlund, *Freedom By Degrees: Emancipation in Pennsylvania and Its Aftermath* (1991); Robert Olwell, *Masters, Slaves, and Subjects: The Culture of Power in the South Carolina Low Country, 1740–1790* (1998).

Peter Onuf, *The Origins of the Federal Republic: Jurisdictional Controversies in the United States, 1775–1787* (1983) and *Statehood and Union: A History of the Northwest Ordinance* (1987); Merrill Peterson and Robert Vaughan, eds., *The Virginia Statute for Religious Freedom* (1988); Jack Rakove, *The Beginnings of National Politics: An Interpretive History of the Continental Congress* (1979); T. Stephen Whitman, *The Price of Freedom: Slavery and Manumission in Baltimore and Early National Maryland* (1997).

Political Tumult in the States

Robert Gross, ed., *In Debt to Shays: The Bicentennial of an Agrarian Rebellion* (1993); Ronald Hoffman et al., *An Uncivil War: The Southern Backcountry During the American Revolution* (1985); David Szatmary, *Shays's Rebellion: The Making of an Agrarian Rebellion* (1988); Robert Taylor, *Western Massachusetts in the Revolution* (1954); Albert Tillson, Jr., *Gentry and Commonfolk: Political Culture on a Virginia Frontier, 1740–1789* (1991).

Toward a New National Government

Lance Banning, *The Sacred Fire of Liberty: James Madison and the Founding of the Federal Republic* (1995); Richard Beeman et al., *Beyond Confederation: Origins of the Constitution and American National Identity* (1987); Stephen Boyd, *The Politics of Opposition: Antifederalists and the Acceptance of the Constitution* (1979); Patrick Conley and John Kaminsky, eds., *The Constitution and the States* (1988); Jack Greene, *Peripheries and Center: Constitutional Development in the Extended Polities of the British Empire and the United States, 1687–1788* (1986); Jackson T. Main, *The Antifederalists: Critics of the Constitution, 1781–1788* (1961); Frederick Marks III, *Independence on Trial: Foreign Affairs and the Making of the Constitution* (1973); Forrest McDonald, *Novus Ordo Seclorum: The Intellectual Origins of the Constitution* (1985); Richard Morris, *Witnesses at the Creation: Hamilton, Madison, Jay, and the Constitution* (1985); Jack Rakove, *Original Meanings: Politics and Ideas in the Making of the Constitution* (1996); Gary Wills, *Explaining America: The*

"Federalist" (1981); Gordon Wood, *The Creation of the American Republic, 1776–1787* (1969).

Fiction and Film

The visually lush commercial film *Jefferson in Paris* (1995) combines a depiction of Jefferson's years as U.S. minister to France (1785–1789) with commentaries on themes of liberty and slavery involving events leading to the French Revolution and Jefferson's controversial liaison with his slave girl Sally Hemmings.

The documentary film *Unearthing the Slave Trade* (1994) uses the recent discovery and excavation of an old black burying ground near Wall Street in New York City, where deceased slaves were interred from about 1712 to 1790, to depict the life of urban slaves in eighteenth-century America.

Herman Melville's novel *Israel Potter* (1855) tells the story of a fictitious Revolutionary War sailor who encounters Benjamin Franklin, Ethan Allen, and John Paul Jones during his adventures and ends up in England as a gardener to King George III.

In *Those Who Love: A Biographical Novel of Abigail and John Adams* (1965), Irving Stone traces the life story of this remarkable couple, largely through Abigail's eyes, as they move from early courtship through the end of John's presidency in 1800.

Suggested Web Sites

http://lcweb.loc.gov/exhibits/religion/religion.html

Religion and the Founding of the American Republic. This Library of Congress site is an on-line exhibit about religion and the creation of the United States.

http://www.nara.gov/fedreg/ec-hmpge.html

The Electoral College. This National Archives and Records Administration site explains how the Electoral College works.

http://www.taxhistory.org/federalists/

Taxing Federalism. This site, provided by the Tax History Project, offers information on the history of U.S. federal taxation by describing several of the *Federalist Papers* related to federal taxing power.

http://www.law.emory.edu/FEDERAL/federalist/

The Federalist. This site is a collection of the most important *Federalist Papers,* a series of documents designed to convince people to support the new Constitution and the Federalist party.

http://www.pbs.org/jefferson/

Thomas Jefferson Online. This companion site to the PBS series on Jefferson is especially important because it contains a fine collection of other people's views of Jefferson.

http://www.law.emory.edu/FEDERAL/usconst.html

The Constitution of the United States. This is a searchable site to the Constitution, especially useful for its information about the Bill of Rights and other constitutional amendments.

http://rs6.loc.gov/ammem/bdsds/bdsdhome.html

Continental Congress and the Constitutional Convention Home Page. This site, presented by the Library of Congress, allows access to the Continental Congress Broadside Collection (253 titles) and the Constitutional Convention Broadside Collection (21 titles), containing documents relating to the work of Congress and the drafting and ratification of the Constitution. Items include extracts of the journals of Congress, resolutions, proclamations, committee reports, treaties, and early printed versions of the U.S. Constitution and the Declaration of Independence.

http://www.americanhistory.si.edu/hohr/springer

Smithsonian Institution. Part of the Smithsonian's on-line museum, this exhibit enables students to examine artifacts from the home of New Castle, Delaware, residents Thomas and Elizabeth Springer and interpret the lives of a late eighteenth-century American family.

http://www.ushistoryplace.com

the History place A richly detailed on-line learning environment complete with interactive maps, timelines, history activities, primary source documents, and links to related American history sites.

8

CREATING *a* NATION

CHAPTER OUTLINE

In October 1789, David Brown arrived in Dedham, Massachusetts. Born about 50 years earlier in Bethlehem, Connecticut, Brown served in the revolutionary army. After the war was over, he shipped out on an American merchantman to see the world. His travels, as he later reported, took him to "nineteen different . . . Kingdoms in Europe, and nearly all the United States." For two years before settling in Dedham, he visited scores of Massachusetts towns, supporting himself as a day laborer while discussing the troubled state of public affairs with local townspeople.

Initially, the people of Dedham took little notice of Brown, but he soon made his presence felt. Though he had little formal schooling, he was a man of powerful opinions and considerable natural ability. His reading and personal experience had persuaded him that government was a conspiracy of the rich to exploit farmers, artisans, and other common folk, and he was quick to make his opinions known.

The object of his wrath was the central government recently established under the new national constitution. Though he could cite no evidence, he accused government leaders of engrossing the nation's western lands for themselves. "Five hundred [people] out of the union of five millions receive all the benefit of public property and live upon the ruins of the rest of the community," he wrote in one of his numerous pamphlets. Brown warned that no government could survive "after the confidence of the people was lost."

In the highly charged political climate of the 1790s, Brown's radical language and exaggerated attacks on the new government's leaders brought a sharp response. In 1798, John Davis, the federal district attorney in Boston, issued a warrant for Brown's arrest on charges of sedition, while government-supported newspapers attacked him as a "rallying point of insurrection and disorder." Fearing arrest, Brown fled to Salem on the Massachusetts coast, but there he was caught and charged with intent to defame the government and aid the country's enemies. For want of $400 bail, he was clapped in prison.

In June 1799, Brown came before the U.S. Circuit Court, Justice Samuel Chase presiding. Chase's behavior was anything but judicious. Persuaded that critics of the administration were also enemies of the republic, Chase was determined to make Brown an example. Confused and hoping for leniency, Brown pleaded guilty to the charges against him.

Ignoring Brown's plea, Chase directed the federal prosecutor to "examine the witness . . . that the degree of his guilt might be duly ascertained." Before sentencing him, Chase demanded that Brown provide the names of his accomplices and a list of subscribers to his writings. When Brown refused, protesting that he would "lose all my friends," Chase sentenced him to a fine of $480 and 18 months in jail. That Brown could not pay the fine and faced the prospect of indefinite imprisonment did not matter.

In rendering judgment, Chase castigated Brown for his "disorganizing doctrines and . . . falsehoods, and the very alarming and dangerous excesses to which he attempted to incite the uninformed part of the community." Not all citizens, Chase thought, should be allowed to comment so brashly on public affairs. For nearly two years, Brown languished in prison. Not until the Federalist party was defeated in the election of 1800 and the Jeffersonian Republicans had taken office was he freed.

David Brown discovered how easy it was for critics of the government to get into trouble during the 1790s, one of the most tumultuous decades in American political history. Though independence had been won, the struggle over control of the revolutionary heritage continued. As Benjamin Rush, Philadelphia physician and revolutionary patriot, explained: "The American War is over, but this is far from being the case with the American Revolution. On the contrary, nothing but the first act of the great drama is closed. It remains [for us] . . . to establish and perfect our new forms of government."

Those efforts proceeded differently in the states than at the center of the new, national government in Philadelphia. In the states, government and politics remained close to the people. There the fires of political controversy, fanned to a white heat over taxes and paper money, slavery and the separation of church and state, as well as issues of political democracy continued to burn.

In the new Congress, the Senate and House of Representatives were filled with men of distinction, heroes of the Revolution, exactly as the Constitution's Federalist

Prior to 1799, when the national government moved to the new capital in the District of Columbia, it shared the State House in Philadelphia with the Pennsylvania assembly. In this image, a variety of people, including several Indians, mingle informally in the State House yard. *(William Birch,* The State House, *Philadelphia, 1800, Historical Society of Pennsylvania)* architects had intended. Though they would soon divide into competing Federalist and Jeffersonian coalitions over an array of foreign and domestic policies, they were united in the belief that the nation's well-being depended on the leadership of gentlemen such as themselves, men of wisdom and accomplishment who were ultimately responsible to the people but who were at the same time obligated to govern according to their own, independent judgment.

At first, the gentry-led politics of congressional elites and the more rapidly evolving, democratic politics of the states proceeded along parallel trajectories. Before long, however, the decade's events began to force them together. As a result, by 1800 a distinctly new form of American politics was becoming visible.

Controversy first erupted in the Congress over a series of economic policies designed to stabilize the new government's finances. Within a few years, foreign policy issues generated by the French Revolution and the accompanying European war further inflamed congressional politics and began to rouse the people at large. By the last years of the decade, accumulating political divisions, intensified by the Alien and Sedition Acts and other Federalist measures, brought the nation to the brink of political upheaval, a prospect narrowly avoided by the Federalists' defeat and Thomas Jefferson's election to the presidency in 1800.

A number of additional circumstances added to the political volatility of the 1790s: the still unproven nature of America's unprecedented "experiment" in an extended republican empire; fundamental disagreements over the proper course of the nation's development; threats to the nation's security posed by a hostile international environment; and the absence of political parties capable of forging political compromise.

As political controversy grew, it caught up countless people like David Brown in its toils. By decade's end, it was apparent how fragile, and yet how resilient, America's new government had proven to be.

LAUNCHING THE NATIONAL REPUBLIC

Once the Constitution had been ratified, its Anti-Federalist critics seemed ready to give the new experiment a chance. They were determined, however, to watch it closely for the first signs of danger. It was not many months before they sounded the alarm.

Beginning the New Government

On April 16, 1789, George Washington started north from Virginia toward New York City to be inaugurated as the first president of the United States. The Electoral College had unanimously elected him to the nation's highest office. Washington's feelings were mixed as he set forth. "I bade adieu to Mount Vernon, to private life, and to domestic felicity," he confided to his diary, "and with a mind oppressed with more anxious and painful sensations than I have words to express, set out for New York . . . with the best disposition to render service to my country in obedience to its call, but with less hope of answering its expectations." Events would soon show that he had good reason for such foreboding.

Washington's journey resembled a royal procession, for he was the object of constant adulation along the way. In villages and towns, guns boomed their salutes, children danced in the streets, church bells pealed, and dignitaries toasted his arrival. On April 23, the president-elect and his entourage reached the New Jersey shore, where he climbed aboard an elegant barge festooned with flowers. Accompanied by a flotilla of boats, he was rowed across the harbor to New York City, where throngs of citizens and newly elected members of Congress greeted the weary traveler. Over the streets of the city stretched gaily decorated arches. During the parade uptown to the governor's mansion, young women in white, flowing robes strewed flowers in his path. That night, bonfires illuminated the city.

On October 10, the old Confederation Congress had transacted its last official business and adjourned *sine die* after setting March 4, 1789, as the day for the new government to assemble. Inaugural day was April 30. Shortly after noon on that day, on a small balcony overlooking Wall Street thronged with people, Washington took the oath of office. "It is done," exulted New York's chancellor, Robert Livingston. "Long live George Washington, President of the United States!" With the crowd roaring its approval and 13 guns booming in the harbor, the president bowed his way off the balcony and into Federal Hall. Late into the night, celebrations filled the air.

Though hopefulness and excitement attended those first weeks, it was important that the new government begin properly. "Things which appear of

This imaginative scene of President-elect Washington's reception in Trenton, New Jersey, during his trip from Virginia to New York City for his first inauguration depicts the popular adulation that surrounded him, as well as the sharply different political roles of men and women. *(Library of Congress)*

little importance in themselves and at the beginning," the president warned, "may have great and durable consequences" from having been established at the commencement of the new government.

When Washington addressed the first Congress, it prompted republican purists to complain that the ceremony smacked too much of the English monarch's speech from the throne at the opening of Parliament. The occasion also raised the question of how the president should be addressed. Several congressmen pointed out that state governors and foreign ambassadors carried the title of "Excellency" and argued that the American president should be more exalted than that. Vice President Adams proposed "His Most Benign Highness," while others offered the even gaudier suggestion: "His Highness, the President of the United States, and Protector of the Rights of the Same." Both proposals elicited howls of outrage from those who thought titles had no place in a republican government. Good sense finally prevailed, and Congress settled on the simple and now familiar "Mr. President." Every decision seemed filled with significance, for people believed they were setting the new government's direction for years to come. That belief gave special intensity to the politics of the time.

President Washington took the oath of office on the balcony of Federal Hall in New York City, where the new national government first met. The shield of the United Sates and thirteen stars emblazoned its cornice, while arrows (symbolizing war) and olive branches (symbolizing peace) appeared above the windows. *(Museum of the City of New York)*

The Bill of Rights

Among the Congress's first tasks was consideration of the constitutional amendments that several states had made conditions of their ratification. Although Madison, Hamilton, and other Federalists had argued that a national bill of rights was unnecessary, they were prepared to keep their promise that such amendments would be considered. That would reassure the fearful, head off calls for a second constitutional convention, and build support for the new regime. "We have in this way something to gain," Madison observed, "and if we proceed with caution, nothing to lose."

From the variety of proposals offered by the states, Madison culled a set of specific propositions for Congress to consider. After extensive debate, Congress reached agreement in September 1789 on twelve amendments and sent them to the states for approval. By December 1791, ten had been ratified and became the national Bill of Rights. Among other things, they guaranteed freedom of speech, press, and religion; pledged the right of trial by jury and due process of law; forbade "unreasonable searches and seizures"; and protected individuals against self-incrimination in criminal cases. The Bill of Rights was the most important achievement of these early years, for it has protected individuals' democratic rights throughout the nation's history.

The People Divide

During its first months in office, Washington's administration enjoyed almost universal support. The honeymoon did not last long, however, for criticism of the administration's policies soon appeared. First in Congress and then increasingly among the people, the growing opposition coalesced in a political party known as the Jeffersonian Republicans. As that occurred, the administration's supporters rallied under the name of Federalists.

Disagreement began in January 1790, when Secretary of the Treasury Alexander Hamilton submitted to Congress the first of several major policy statements on the country's economic future. Seldom in the nation's history has a single official so dominated public affairs as Hamilton did during these early years. A man of extraordinary intelligence and ambition, Hamilton preferred to act behind the scenes, where he could shape events beyond the public eye. His instincts for locating and seizing the levers of political power were unerring.

An ardent proponent of America's economic development, Hamilton foresaw the country's future strength and was determined to promote its growth through government efforts to foster domestic manufacturing and overseas trade. The United States, he was fond of saying, was a "Hercules in the cradle." The people he most admired were men of wealth and ambition, entrepreneurs eager to tie their fortunes to America's rising empire. A close alliance between such people and government officials he regarded as essential to achieving American greatness.

Alexander Hamilton used the office of secretary of the treasury and his personal relationship with President Washington to shape national policy during the early 1790s. (*White House Collection*)

If Hamilton's economic policies were liberal in looking forward to enhanced economic opportunity, his politics were profoundly conservative. Deeply impressed by the stability of the British monarchy and the confident governing style of the British upper class, Hamilton distrusted the people's wisdom and feared their purposes. "The people," he asserted, "are turbulent and changing; they seldom judge or determine right." That stark belief guided his public career.

While Hamilton thought the Constitution not "high-toned" enough, he was anxious to give it proper direction. His opportunity came when Washington named him secretary of the treasury. Recognizing the potential importance of his office, he determined to use it to build the kind of nation he envisioned.

In his first "Report on the Public Credit," Hamilton recommended funding the remaining Revolutionary War debt by allowing the government's creditors to exchange their depreciated public securities at face value for new, interest-bearing bonds. The foreign-held debt Hamilton set at $11.7 million; the domestic debt, including back interest, he fixed at $40.4 million. Second, he proposed that the federal government assume responsibility for the $21.5 million in remaining state war debts. These actions were intended to stabilize the government's finances, establish its credit, build confidence in the new nation at home and abroad, and tie business and commercial interests firmly to the new administration.

The proposal to fund the foreign debt aroused little controversy, but Hamilton's plans for handling the government's domestic obligations generated immediate opposition. In the House of Representatives, James Madison, Hamilton's recent ally in the ratification process, protested the unfairness of funding depreciated securities at face value because speculators, some anticipating Hamilton's proposals, had acquired many of them at a fraction of their initial worth. In addition, Madison and his southern colleagues knew that northern businessmen held most of the securities and that funding would bring little benefit to the South.

Hamilton was not impressed. Speculators, he observed, "paid what the commodity was worth in the market, and took the risks"—they should therefore "reap the benefit." If his plan served the interests of the wealthy, that was exactly as he intended, for it would further strengthen the ties between personal wealth and national power. After a bit of grumbling, Congress endorsed the funding plan.

Federal assumption of the remaining state debts, another important part of Hamilton's program, aroused greater criticism. States with the largest unpaid obligations, such as Massachusetts, thought assumption a splendid idea. But others, such as Virginia and Pennsylvania, which had already retired much of their debt, were adamantly opposed. Critics also warned that assumption would strengthen the central government at the expense of the states, since wealthy individuals would look to it rather than the states for a return on their investments. Moreover, with its increased need for revenue to pay off the accumulated debt, the federal government would have additional reason to exercise its newly acquired power of taxation. That was exactly what Hamilton intended.

Once again, Congress supported Hamilton's bill, in good measure because Madison and Jefferson approved it as part of an agreement to relocate the seat of government from New York to Philadelphia and then finally to a permanent federal district on the Potomac River. Southerners hoped that moving the government away from northern commercial centers would enable them to control its development and keep it more closely aligned with their own agrarian interests.

Opposition to the funding and assumption scheme, however, did not die. In December 1790, the Virginia assembly passed a series of resolutions, framed by that old Anti-Federalist Patrick Henry, warning that southern agriculture was being subordinated to the interests of northern commerce, and that the government's powers were expanding in dangerous fashion. Hearing of the Virginia resolutions, Hamilton wrote privately that "This is the first symptom of a spirit which must either be killed, or will kill the Constitution." The contest for control of the new government was now vigorously joined.

As controversy grew, Hamilton introduced the second phase of his financial program in December 1790—establishment of a national bank capable of handling the government's financial affairs and pooling private investment capital for economic development. Though he was careful not to mention it publicly, he considered the Bank of England and its mutually beneficial ties to the royal government as a model.

Congressional opposition to the bank came almost entirely from the South (only one northern delegate voted against it), since it seemed clear that the bank would serve the needs of northern merchants and manufacturers far better than of southern agrarians. Still, in February 1791, Congress approved the bank bill.

Before signing it, Washington asked his cabinet for advice. Hamilton urged him to sign the legislation, following the constitutional doctrine of "implied powers," the principle that the government possessed the authority to make any laws "necessary and proper" for exercising the powers specifically granted it by the Constitution. He argued that the authority to charter such a bank followed from Congress's power to collect taxes and regulate trade. Secretary of State Jefferson, however, advised a presidential veto. He saw in Hamilton's argument a blueprint for the indefinite expansion of federal authority and insisted that the government possessed only those powers specifically itemized in the Constitution. Because the Constitution said nothing about chartering banks, the bill was unconstitutional and should be rejected. Jefferson also feared the rapid development of commerce and domestic manufacturing that the bank was intended to promote. To Jefferson's distress, Washington followed Hamilton's advice and signed the bank bill into law.

In December 1790, in his second "Report on the Public Credit," Hamilton proposed a series of excise taxes, including one on the manufacture of distilled liquor. By this so-called Whiskey Tax, he intended to signal the government's intention to use its taxing authority to increase federal revenue. The power to tax and spend, Hamilton knew, was the power to govern. The Whiskey Tax became law in March 1791.

Finally, in a "Report on Manufactures" issued in December 1791, Hamilton called for a schedule of tariffs (i.e., taxes) on imported European goods as a way of protecting American industries; bounties to encourage the expansion of commercial agriculture; and a network of federally sponsored internal

The revolutionary generation found inspiration in the republican eras of ancient Greece and Rome. This bust of Thomas Jefferson, cast in the classical style, was completed in 1789 by the French sculptor Jean-Antoine Houdon. *(Collection of the New-York Historical Society)*

improvements such as roadways and lighthouses, intended to stimulate commerce and bind the nation more tightly together. Because of opposition from southern agrarians and northern merchants who feared that such tariffs would reduce overseas trade and raise the cost of living, Congress never endorsed this report.

All the while, criticism of Hamilton's ambitious program continued to mount. In October 1791, opposition leaders in Congress established a newspaper, the *National Gazette,* that vigorously attacked the administration's policies. Hamilton responded with a series of anonymous articles in the administration's paper, *The Gazette of the United States,* accusing Jefferson (inaccurately) of having opposed the Constitution and charging him (also inaccurately) of fomenting opposition to the government. Alarmed at the division within his administration, Washington pleaded for restraint.

Congressional criticism of Hamilton's policies reached a climax in January 1793, when Representative William Branch Giles of Virginia introduced a series of resolutions calling for an inquiry into the condition of the Treasury, accusing Hamilton of using the office for his own benefit, and urging censure of the secretary's conduct. Hamilton vigorously defended both his policies and his behavior and none of Giles's accusations passed the House. The month-long debate, however, showed just how acrimonious politics at the nation's capital had already become.

Political conflict was now spreading beyond the circle of governing officials in Philadelphia. Among ordinary Americans, Hamilton's financial program drew a mixed response. In northern towns and cities, artisans and other working people generally approved his efforts to improve credit and stimulate economic development. With their own economic circumstances now improving, they seemed undisturbed by the special benefits that funding, assumption, and the bank brought to a few. Within several years, many of them would move into the Jeffersonian opposition, but for the moment, their support of the government was secure.

The Whiskey Rebellion

The farmers of western Pennsylvania provided the most dramatic expression of popular discontent over government policies. Their anger focused on the Whiskey Tax. Ever since the trouble with England 30 years before, Americans had been sensitive to taxation and suspicious of its connections with government power. The farmers of western Pennsylvania had special reason to dislike this particular tax. Their livelihood depended on transporting surplus grain eastward across the mountains to market. Shipping it in bulk was prohibitively expensive, so they distilled the grain and moved it far more efficiently as whiskey. Hamilton's tax threatened to make this unprofitable. They also objected that people charged with tax evasion had to stand trial in federal court hundreds of miles away in Philadelphia.

The farmers' frustration, however, went deeper than that. Although they frequently turned to state authorities for help against Indians and depended on eastern markets for their grain, they resented the loss of control over their own lives as their communities were absorbed in the expanding market economy and fell under the control of a political system dominated by more populous areas to the east. In southern states like South Carolina, the integration of coastal and interior regions occurred more smoothly because of their similar agricultural interests and a white racial alliance against blacks. In the more economically diverse and racially homogenous states of the north, however, conflicts between coastal and backcountry regions sharpened.

Hamilton cared little what the farmers thought either about the Whiskey Tax or local self-reliance. The government needed revenue, and the farmers would have to bear the cost. George Clymer, federal supervisor of revenue for Pennsylvania, was equally unsympathetic. Referring to the "moral and personal weakness" of "lesser folk," Clymer publicly castigated the "sordid shopkeepers" who retailed Pennsylvania whiskey and the "depraved" farmers who produced it. Westerners resented such official arrogance as much as the tax and quickly made their resentment known.

Trouble was brewing by the summer of 1792 as angry farmers gathered in mass meetings across western Pennsylvania. In August, a convention at Pittsburgh denounced the Whiskey Tax and declared that the people would prevent its collection. Like opponents of the Stamp Act in 1765, they concluded that liberties would be lost if resistance did not soon begin.

Alarmed, Washington issued a proclamation warning against such "unlawful" gatherings and insisting that the Excise Tax would be enforced. As tax collections began, the farmers took matters into their own hands.

In July 1794, when federal marshal David Lennox, in company with John Neville, a local excise inspector, attempted to serve papers on several recalcitrant farmers near Pittsburgh, an angry crowd gathered and stood in the way. Soon 500 armed men surrounded Neville's home demanding his resignation. Learning that Neville had fled, they ordered the dozen soldiers trapped in the house to lay down their arms and come out. Fearing for their safety, the soldiers refused, and for several hours the two sides exchanged gunfire. After several men had been wounded, the soldiers finally surrendered, whereupon Neville's house was put to the torch. Similar episodes involving angry crowds, the erection of liberty poles reminiscent of the Revolution, and the hoisting of banners bearing slogans such as "Liberty and No Excise. O Whiskey!" erupted across the state. At Parkinson's Ferry, a convention of over 200 delegates debated armed resistance and talked ominously about secession from the state.

Alarmed that the protests might spread through the entire backcountry region from Maine to Georgia, Washington ordered the insurgents home and called out troops from eastern Pennsylvania and surrounding states to restore order. For more than a year, Hamilton had been urging the use of force against the protesters. He viewed the insurrection not as indication of an unjust policy needing change but as a test of the administration's ability to govern. Suppressing the rebellion, Hamilton explained, "will . . . add to the solidity of everything in this country." He eagerly volunteered to accompany the federal army west.

In late August, a force of nearly 13,000 men, larger than the average strength of the continental army during the Revolutionary War, moved into western Pennsylvania. At its center was Colonel William McPherson's "Pennsylvania Blues," an upper-class, strongly Federalist cavalry regiment. At its head rode the president of the United States and the secretary of the treasury. Washington soon returned to Philadelphia, persuaded by his aides of the danger to his safety, but Hamilton pressed ahead. When later criticized for accompanying the army to Pittsburgh,

President Washington and Treasury Secretary Hamilton led a federal army of nearly 13,000 troops into western Pennsylvania in 1794. Rebellious farmers, protesting the government's excise tax on whiskey, dispersed as the army approached. *(The Metropolitan Museum of Art, Gift of Edgar William and Bernice Chrysler Garbisch, 1963)*

he replied that he had "long since . . . learned to hold public opinion of no value." The battle that Hamilton had anticipated, however, never materialized, for as the federal army approached, the "Whiskey Rebels" dispersed, two of their leaders fleeing across the Ohio River. Of the 20 men taken prisoner, two were convicted of treason and sentenced to death. Later, in a calmer mood, Washington pardoned them both.

As people quickly realized, the "Whiskey Rebellion" had never threatened the government's safety. "An insurrection was . . . proclaimed," Jefferson scoffed, "but could never be found." Hamilton was merely pursuing his "favorite purpose of strengthening government" under the sanction of Washington's name. Even such an ardent Federalist as Fisher Ames was uneasy at the sight of federal troops marching against American citizens. Though a government "by overcoming an unsuccessful insurrection becomes stronger," he warned, "elective rulers can scarcely ever employ the physical force of a democracy without turning the moral force, or the power of public opinion, against the government." Americans would soon have additional reason to ponder Ames's warning.

Although the Pennsylvania rebels were promptly dispersed, their outburst pointed toward broader patterns of disaffection within the extended backcountry, revealed in rumors that Spanish emissaries and American adventurers were plotting secession among settlers in Kentucky and the western Carolinas. The whiskey affray gave indication as well that the gentry-led politics of Congress and the locally based politics of the people were becoming more closely joined.

THE REPUBLIC IN A THREATENING WORLD

Because the nation was so new and the outside world so threatening, foreign policy issues generated extraordinary excitement during the 1790s. This was especially so after the tumultuous events of the French Revolution and the accompanying European war burst on the international scene. In their disputes over the revolution in France and its implications for the United States, the American people revealed once again how sharply they differed and how deeply engaged in national politics they were becoming.

The Promise and Peril of the French Revolution

France's revolution began in 1789 as an effort to reform a monarchy weakened by debt and administrative decay. Pent-up demands for social justice, however, quickly outran initial attempts at moderate, constitutional reform, and by 1793 France was embroiled in a genuinely radical revolution. In January the monarch, Louis XVI, was beheaded. While the rest of Europe watched in horrified fascination, the forces of revolution and reaction struggled for the nation's soul.

As the revolution extended its attack on the aristocracy, the monarchy, and the Catholic Church, conservatives across the European Continent gathered in opposition, their fears fueled by the frantic accounts of fleeing French aristocrats. Finding itself surrounded and facing assault by Austria and Prussia, France's revolutionary government launched a series of military thrusts triggering a general declaration of war. By the end of 1793, Europe was locked in a deadly struggle between revolutionary France and a counterrevolutionary coalition led by Prussia and Great Britain.

For more than a decade, the French Revolution dominated European affairs. Before it was finished, it would transform the course of Western history. The revolution also cut like a plowshare through the surface of American politics, not only threatening the nation's security but also capturing people's imaginations and setting them against each other.

The outbreak of European war posed thorny diplomatic problems for Washington's administration. Under international law, neutral nations could continue to trade with warring powers as long as such trade did not include goods directly related to the war effort. American merchants eagerly took advantage of that opportunity because it promised handsome profits. Within a few years, American commerce was booming. For the first time since the Revolutionary War, prosperity returned to the nation's coastal cities. By 1800, American exports had more than doubled, and American ships were carrying an astonishing 92 percent of all commerce between America and Europe. Though the benefits were most evident in coastal cities, they radiated as well into the surrounding countryside, where cargoes of agricultural and forest goods as well as the provisions required by ships' crews were produced.

America's expanding commerce, however, quickly encountered problems, for while both England and France sought access to American goods, each was determined to keep those goods from reaching the other, if necessary by stopping American ships and confiscating their cargoes. Neither belligerent was willing to tie itself down with legal formalities when locked in such a deadly struggle.

America's relations with England were further complicated by the Royal navy's practice of impressing American sailors into service aboard its warships to meet its growing demand for seamen. Washington faced the dilemma of upholding the country's neutral rights and protecting its citizens without getting drawn into the European conflict.

This scene of bustling commercial activity in New York City in 1797 reveals the benefits that expanded neutral trade brought to the nation's major seaports. *(The New-York Historical Society)*

The French alliance of 1778 compounded the government's troubles because it seemed to require the United States to come to France's aid, much as France had assisted the American states a decade and a half before. Those sympathetic to the French cause argued that America's commitment still held. Others, fearing the consequences of American involvement and the political infection that closer ties with revolutionary France might bring, insisted that the treaty had lapsed when the French monarchy was overthrown.

The American reaction to the European drama further complicated the situation. At first the revolution in France had seemed an extension of America's own struggle for liberty and thus was to be celebrated as an event linking France and America in a universal struggle for liberty. Even the swing toward genuine social revolution did not immediately dampen American enthusiasm.

By the mid-1790s, however, especially after France's revolutionary regime launched an attack on organized Christianity, many Americans pulled back in alarm. What connection could there possibly be between the principles of 1776 and the chaos of revolutionary France? Insisted the *Gazette of the United States,* a staunchly Federalist newspaper, "In America no barbarities were perpetrated—no men's heads were stuck upon poles—no mangled ladies' bodies were carried thro' the streets in triumph. . . . Whatever blood was shed, flowed gallantly in the field." The writer conveniently ignored the violence meted out by supporters of the French monarchy and betrayed a selective memory of America's own revolution. Even so, the differences were indeed profound.

For the Federalists, revolutionary France now symbolized social anarchy and threatened the European order on which America's commercial and diplomatic security depended. With increasing vehemence, they castigated the revolution, championed England as the defender of European civilization, and sought ways of linking England and the United States more closely together.

Other Americans, however, continued to support France. While decrying the revolution's excesses, they noted how difficult it was to uproot deeply entrenched forces of reaction. Though Jefferson regretted the shedding of innocent blood, he thought it necessary if true liberty was to be achieved. John Bradford, editor of the *Kentucky Gazette,* agreed. "Instead of reviling the French republicans as monsters," he wrote, "the friends of royalty in this country should rather admire their patience in so long deferring the fate of their perjured monarch." In Bradford's judgment, England was not a bastion of civilization and order but of privilege and political oppression.

Citizen Genêt and the Democratic-Republican Societies

Popular associations known as Democratic-Republican societies—political and philosophical heirs of the Sons of Liberty and Committees of Correspondence (see Chapter 5) that had mobilized patriots against England twenty years earlier—provided the most vocal support for the revolution in France, as well as for political democracy at home. As early as 1792, ordinary citizens began to form "constitutional societies" dedicated to "watching over the rights of the people, and giving an early alarm in case of governmental encroachments." During the government's first years, several dozen societies had formed in opposition to Hamilton's financial program. The French Revolution stoked the fires of democratic enthusiasm and stimulated the societies' growth.

The arrival in April 1793 of Citizen Edmund Genêt, minister from the French republic to the United States, sparked a firestorm of democratic enthusiasm. Genêt landed at Charleston, South Carolina, to a tumultuous reception. His instructions were to court popular support and negotiate a commercial treaty. Shortly after his arrival, however, he began commissioning American privateers to prey on British shipping in the Caribbean and enlisting American seamen for expeditions against Spanish Florida. Both were clear violations of American neutrality.

The enthusiastic receptions he encountered as he traveled north toward Philadelphia soon led him astray. Despite a warning from Secretary of State Jefferson and in open defiance of diplomatic protocol, he urged Congress to reject Washington's recently issued neutrality proclamation and side with revolutionary France. That was the final straw. On August 2, the president demanded Genêt's recall, charging that his conduct threatened "war abroad and anarchy at home." Washington's decision drew sharp cries of protest.

As the Genêt controversy escalated, other circumstances added to the sense of anxiety gripping politicians at the Philadelphia capital. Through the summer of 1793 an unrelenting heat wave descended on southeastern Pennsylvania, searing trees and gardens, threatening supplies of potable water, and raising a stench in the refuse-filled streets. Even more alarming, from early August to mid-October a deadly epidemic of yellow fever gripped the city, sending those able to escape fleeing to the countryside for safety and taking a terrible toll on those forced to stay behind. Before early frosts finally destroyed the swarms of mosquitoes that carried the deadly pestilence through the city's crowded streets, well over 4,000 black and white Philadelphians had died, a full 10 percent of the city's 35,000 people. Yellow fever was not new to Philadelphia, and it would return again before the decade was out. But never did it reap such a destructive harvest as in 1793.

If Genêt failed as a diplomat, he succeeded in fanning popular enthusiasm for revolutionary France. In June 1793, with his open encouragement, the largest and most influential of the new societies, the Democratic Society of Pennsylvania, was founded in Philadelphia. It immediately called for the formation of similar societies elsewhere to join in supporting France and promoting the "spirit of freedom and equality" at home. People across the land, it declared, should join in "erecting the temple of liberty on the ruins of palaces and thrones." Washington and his Federalist colleagues had reason to wonder if that challenge was aimed at them.

Although a full network of popular societies never developed, about 40 organizations scattered from Maine to Georgia sprang up during the next several years. Working people—artisans and laborers in the cities, small farmers and tenants in the countryside—provided the bulk of membership. Federalist critics derided them as "the lowest orders of . . . draymen . . . broken hucksters, and trans-Atlantic traitors." That final canard was in reference to a growing tide of Irish immigrants, fleeing hard times and English oppression at home, who voiced not only demands for Irish independence but a commitment to political equality as well, together with a relish for an in-your-face, rough-and-tumble style of politics. Many of them soon enlisted as foot soldiers in the growing opposition to Federalist rule.

The societies' leaders were generally individuals of acknowledged respectability, such as doctors, lawyers, and tradesmen. But leaders and followers were united by a dedication to the "principles of '76" and a determination to preserve those principles against the "royalizing" tendencies of Washington's administration.

Lamenting the threats to egalitarianism at home, the societies urged citizens to be vigilant in the face of Federalist behavior. Asserted the Newark, New Jersey, society, "members of the government are nothing more than the agents of the people," and "have no right to prevent their employers from inspecting into their conduct." Committed to an awakened citizenry, the societies organized public celebrations, issued ringing addresses filled with democratic principles, and sent petitions sharply critical of administration policies to the president and Congress. Washington's proclamation of neutrality they labeled a "pusillanimous truckling to Britain, despotically conceived and unconstitutionally promulgated." Several of the societies openly urged the United States to enter the war on France's behalf. Declared the New York society: "We firmly believe that he who is an enemy to the French revolution cannot be a firm republican; and therefore . . . ought not to be entrusted with the guidance of any part of the machine of government."

West of the Appalachians, local societies agitated against England's continuing occupation of the frontier posts around the Great Lakes and berated Spain for closing the Mississippi River. In the Northeast, they castigated England for its "piracy" against American shipping. In the Carolinas, they demanded greater representation for the growing backcountry in the state's assembly. And everywhere they protested the

Excise Tax, opposed the administration's overtures to England, and demanded that public officials attend to the people's wishes.

Finally, they campaigned for a press free from control by Federalist "aristocrats." Declared William Manning, a Massachusetts farmer who had marched to the "Concord fight" in 1775 and who continued to praise the principles for which he had fought: "A labouring man may as well hunt for pins in a haymow as to try to collect the knowledge necessary for him to have from such promiscuous piles of contradictions" as appeared in the Federalist press.

President Washington and other Federalists were incensed by the societies' support of Genêt and criticism of the government. The "real design" of these "nurseries of sedition," thundered Fisher Ames, was to revolutionize America as the Jacobins had revolutionized France. Writing in the *Virginia Chronicle* of January 17, 1794, a Federalist author berated Kentucky's Democratic Society as "that horrible sink of treason, that hateful synagogue of anarchy, that odious conclave of tumult, that frightful cathedral of discord, that poisonous garden of conspiracy, that hellish school of rebellion and opposition to all regular and well-balanced authority!" Such breathless expressions of alarm gave evidence of how inflamed public discourse had become.

Jay's Controversial Treaty

The uproar over Jay's Treaty with England further heightened tensions at mid-decade. Alarmed by the deteriorating relations with England, Washington sent Chief Justice John Jay to London in the spring of 1794 with instructions to negotiate a wide range of troublesome issues carried over from the Revolutionary War. Notable among them were continued British occupation of the western posts, interference with American neutral shipping, and impressment of American seamen.

Early in 1795, Jay returned home with a treaty that resolved almost none of these grievances. England finally agreed to vacate the western posts, but not for

Cartoons became powerful weapons in the superheated politics of the 1790s. This Jeffersonian cartoon lampoons William Cobbett, one of the Federalists' most acid-penned pamphleteers who wrote under the pseudonym Peter Porcupine. While Columbia swoons over the political division, the English Lion urges Cobbett to "sow the seeds of discord." *(The Historical Society of Pennsylvania (HSP),* "Caricature against William Cobbett, editor of the Porcupine Gazette," *1796, [Accession #Bb612Se31])*

Recovering the Past

FOREIGN TRAVEL JOURNALS

Historians utilize many different kinds of sources in their quest to recover the American past. Among the most revealing are travel accounts penned by foreign visitors eager to learn about the United States and record their impressions of it. From the days of earliest explorations to our own time, travelers have been fascinated by the people, customs, institutions, and physical setting of North America. Out of this continuing interaction between America and its foreign visitors has emerged a rich and fascinating travel literature that reveals much not only about America but about the travelers who have visited it as well.

During the second quarter of the nineteenth century, a stream of perceptive European visitors—Alexis de Tocqueville, Harriet Martineau, and Francis Grund among them—toured the United States, eager to record their impressions of what Jacksonian America was like. Fifty years earlier, the American Revolution fanned similar interest in the minds of Europeans fascinated by the newly independent nation and anxious to discern its implications for them. Among the most opinionated and engaging of these earlier commentators was the Frenchman Moreau de Saint Méry.

Born on the French island of Martinque in January 1750, de Saint Méry established a successful legal practice before moving to France, where relatives introduced him to polite, Parisian society. In the late 1780s, he became an ardent champion of political reform during the early days of the French Revolution. As the revolution entered its radical phase, however, he was forced to flee to the United States for safety. Arriving at Norfolk, Virginia, with his wife and two children, de Saint Méry settled in Philadelphia, where he remained from October 1794 to August 1798. While there, he mingled with civic and cultural leaders, opened a bookstore that served as a rendezvous for French émigrés who also had fled the revolution's turmoil, and published a French-language paper that reported the latest news from home. In the late summer of 1798, de Saint Méry returned safely to France.

As with all such travel accounts, de Saint Méry's commentary must be read with a critical eye, for travelers disagreed over what they thought important and worth reporting, and interpreted what they saw in very different ways. In nearly 400 pages of commentary, de Saint Méry touched on numerous aspects of American life, but none in more frank and compelling fashion than relations between the sexes. The selections that follow (somewhat rearranged for greater continuity) provide tantalizing insights into the behavior and sexual mores of American men and women in the early years of the republic.

What did de Saint Méry find most interesting about gender relations in Philadelphia? How did religion, class, and ethnicity shape men's and women's behavior? What forms of behavior did he approve and disapprove?

de Saint Méry's explicit commentary is virtually unique among the numerous accounts left by foreign travelers in the early republic, most of whom showed far more interest in America's racial makeup, political practices, and physical environment. de Saint Méry's observations may thus be idiosyncratic and should be approached with caution.

What other kinds of sources might enable us to evaluate the accuracy of such travel accounts? In what ways is a traveler's own nationality, gender, religion, or class likely to shape his or her impressions of the United States? Similarly, how important is it to know travelers' motives for coming, how long they stayed, which parts of the country they visited, and with whom they associated while here?

Does the gendered world of late eighteenth-century Philadelphia, as described by de Saint Méry, seem strange or familiar, attractive or distasteful to your own sensibilities? If you were to visit another country today, how accurate do you think you could be in assessing the social behavior and cultural values of its people? To what extent would your values, perhaps like those of Moreau de Saint Méry, color your impressions? Might it be more difficult to understand some foreign cultures than others? Why?

Moreau de Saint Méry's American Journal

American men, generally speaking, are tall and thin . . . [and] seem to have no strength. . . . They are brave, but they lack drive. Indifferent toward almost everything, they sometimes behave in a manner that suggests real energy; then follow it with a "Oh-to-hell-with-it" attitude which shows that they seldom feel genuine enthusiasm.

Their dinner consists of . . . English roast surrounded by potatoes. Following that are boiled green peas . . . baked or fried eggs, boiled or fried fish, salad which may be thinly sliced cabbage . . . [and] sweets to which they are excessively partial. . . . For dessert, they have a little fruit, some cheese, and a pudding. The entire meal is washed down with cider, weak or strong beer . . . [and] wine . . . which they keep drinking right through dessert, toward the end of which any ladies who are at the dinner leave the table and withdraw by themselves, leaving the men free to drink as much as they please. . . . Toasts are drunk, cigars are lighted, diners run to the corners of the room hunting night tables and vases which will enable them to hold a greater amount of liquor. . . . Finally the dinner table is deserted because of boredom, fatigue or drunkenness. . . .

American women are pretty, and those of Philadelphia are prettiest of all. . . .. Girls ordinarily mature in Philadelphia at the age of fourteen, and reach that period without unusual symptoms. . . . But they soon grow pale. . . . After eighteen years old they lose their charms. . . . Their hair is scanty, their teeth bad. . . . In short, while charming and adorable at fifteen, they are faded at twenty-three, old at thirty-five, decrepit at forty or forty-five. . . .

American women carefully wash their faces and hands, but not their mouths, seldom their feet and even more seldom their bodies. . . .. They are greatly addicted to finery and have a strong desire to display themselves—a desire . . . inflamed by their love of adornment. They cannot, however, imitate that elegance of style possessed by Frenchwomen. . . .

One is struck by the tall and pretty young girls one sees in the streets, going and coming from school. They wear their hair long, and skirts with closed seams. But when nubility has arrived they put up their hair with a comb, and the back of the skirt has a placket. At this time, they . . . become their own mistresses, and can go walking alone and have suitors. . . .

They invariably make their own choice of a suitor, and the parents raise no objection because that's the custom of the country. The suitor comes into the house when he wishes; goes on walks with his loved one whenever he desires. On Sunday he often takes her out in a cabriolet, and brings her back in the evening without anyone wanting to know where they went. . . . Although in general one is conscious of widespread modesty in Philadelphia, the customs are not particularly pure, and the disregard . . . of some parents for the manner in which their daughters form relationships to which they . . . have not given their approval is an encouragement to indiscretions . . .

A young woman trusts in her suitor's delicacy and charges him with maintaining for her a respect which she is not always able to command. Each day both of them are entrusted to no one but each other. . . . Her servant . . . leaves the house as soon as night as arrived. . . . Her father, her mother, her entire family have gone to bed. The suitor and his mistress remain alone; and sometimes, when the servant returns, she finds them asleep and the candle out, such is the frigidity of love in this country. . . . [American women] endure the company of their lovers for whole hours without being sufficiently moved to change their expression.

When one considers the unlimited liberty which young ladies enjoy, one is astonished by their universal eagerness to be married. . . . When a young woman marries, she enters a wholly different existence. She is no longer a . . . butterfly who denies herself nothing and whose only laws are her whims and her suitor's wish. She now lives only for her husband, and to devote herself without surcease to the care of her household and her home. . . . The more her husband is capable of multiplying . . . the pleasures of matrimony . . . the more her health may suffer, most of all when she has a child; for sometimes while nursing it, or as soon as it is weaned, she has already conceived another. . . .

One very remarkable and important thing is the respect in which married women are held, and the virtuous conduct of almost all. . . . In spite of conjugal customs which would seem to indicate a state of happiness, they do not produce the happiness which would be expected to result. . . . This is evidenced by the multiplicity of second marriages. . . . The men in particular remarry oftenest. . . . Divorce is obtained with scandalous ease. From this alone one can judge the extent of loose habits. . . .

Bastards are extremely common in Philadelphia. There are two principal reasons for this. In the first place, the city is full of religious sects, but none of them give their clergymen any authority to enforce obedience. Consequently there is no way of inspiring shame in women who become mothers for no reason except the pleasure they get out of it. In the second place, once an illegitimate child is twelve months old, a mother can disembarrass herself of him by farming him out for twenty-one years. This makes it possible for her to commit the same sin for a second time. It never occurs to her that her child can never know her, and that the whole business is shameful. . . .

There are streetwalkers . . . in Philadelphia. These are very young and very pretty girls, elegantly dressed, who promenade two by two, arm in arm and walking very rapidly, at an hour which indicates that they aren't just out for a stroll. . . . Anyone who accosts them is taken to their home . . . [where] they fulfill every desire for two dollars, half of which is supposed to pay for the use of the room. Quaker youths are frequent visitors in the houses of ill fame, which have multiplied in Philadelphia and are frequented at all hours. There is even a well-known gentleman who leaves his horse tied to the post outside one of these houses, so that everyone knows when he is there and exactly how long he stays. . . .

Source: Moreau de St. Mery's American Journey, 1793–1798, trans. and ed., Kenneth Roberts and Anna M. Roberts. (New York: Doubleday & Co., 1947), pp. 265, 281–283, 312–313.

another year and then only if it was guaranteed continued access to the fur trade on American soil south of the Great Lakes. Jay failed as well to secure compensation for American slaves carried off by the British at the end of the Revolutionary War. Nor would the British foreign minister offer assurances against the future impressment of American seamen, compromise on the issue of neutral rights, or agree to open the British West Indies to American shipping.

When the terms of Jay's treaty were made public, they triggered an explosion of protest. The administration's pleas that the agreement headed off an open breach with England and was the best that could be obtained failed to pacify its critics. In New York City, Hamilton was stoned when he defended the treaty at a noonday mass meeting. The "rabble," sniffed one disgusted Federalist, attempted "to knock out Hamilton's brains to reduce him to an equality with themselves." Southern planters were angry because the agreement brought no compensation for their lost slaves. Westerners complained that the British were not evacuating the posts, while merchants and sailors railed against Jay's failure to open the West Indies trade or stop impressment. After a long and acrimonious debate, the Senate ratified the treaty by the narrowest of margins.

The administration made better progress on the still volatile issue of free transit of the Mississippi River at New Orleans. In the Treaty of San Lorenzo, negotiated by Thomas Pinckney in 1795, Spain for the first time recognized the United States' boundaries under the peace treaty of 1783 (the Mississippi River to the west and the 31st parallel to the south) and thus gave up all claim to U.S. territory. Spain also granted American shippers free navigation of the Mississippi and the right to unload goods for transshipment at New Orleans, though only for three years.

By mid-decade, political harmony had disappeared both in Congress and the country more generally, as divisions deepened on virtually every important issue of foreign and domestic policy. Increasingly estranged from Washington's administration, Jefferson resigned as secretary of state in July 1793. He soon joined politicians such as Madison and Albert Gallatin of Pennsylvania in open opposition.

In September 1796, in what came to be called his Farewell Address, Washington announced that he would not accept a third term as president. He had long been contemplating retirement, for he was now 64 and was exhausted by the controversies swirling around him. Even the Great Patriot was no longer immune to personal attack. "As to you, sir," fumed Thomas Paine in an open letter to the Philadelphia *Aurora*, "treacherous in private friendship . . . and a hypocrite in public life, the world will be puzzled to decide, whether you are an apostate or an impostor; whether you have abandoned good principles, or whether you ever had any." Seldom has an American president been subjected to such public abuse as was Washington during his final year in office.

THE POLITICAL CRISIS DEEPENS

By 1796, bitter controversy surrounded the national government. That controversy intensified during the last half of the 1790s until the very stability of the country seemed threatened.

The Election of 1796

The presidential election of 1796 reflected the political storms buffeting the nation. Four years earlier, Washington and Adams had been reelected without significant opposition. The situation now was vastly different.

With Washington out of the picture, the contest quickly narrowed to Adams and Jefferson. Both were elder statesmen; Adams was 61 years old, while

John Adams, Washington's vice president, won a narrow victory over Jefferson for the presidency in 1796. His administration foundered on conflicts over foreign policy abroad and the suppression of political dissent at home. *(Adams National Historic Site/U.S. Department of the Interior, National Park Service)*

PRESIDENTIAL ELECTIONS, 1788–1800

Year	Candidate	Party	Electoral Votes
1788	GEORGE WASHINGTON	None	69
1792	GEORGE WASHINGTON	Federalist	132
1796	JOHN ADAMS	Federalist	71
	Thomas Jefferson	Democratic-Republican	68
	Thomas Pinckney	Federalist	59
	Aaron Burr	Democratic-Republican	30
	Minor Candidates	—	48
1800	THOMAS JEFFERSON	Democratic-Republican	73
	Aaron Burr	Democratic-Republican	73
	John Adams	Federalist	65
	Charles C. Pinckney	Federalist	64
	John Jay	Federalist	1

Note: Winners' names are in capital letters.

Jefferson was eight years his junior. They had become friends and earned each other's respect years earlier, during the Revolution. Sharing first in the electrifying task of drafting the Declaration of Independence, they joined forces abroad during the 1780s when Adams served as first U.S. minister to Great Britain while Jefferson was minister to France. They came together a third time in the early 1790s, Adams as vice president (a position he regarded as "wholly insignificant") and Jefferson as secretary of state.

Though they had worked closely together, they differed in many ways. Short, rotund, and fastidiously neat, Adams contrasted sharply in physical appearance with the tall, frequently disheveled Jefferson. At once intensely ambitious and deeply insecure about the judgments of both his contemporaries and history, Adams struggled self-consciously to construct his public career. Jefferson, by contrast, charted his course more quietly and repeatedly sought the solace of private life. They differed in intellect and vision as well. Jefferson's mind was more expansive and his interests more encompassing. Politician and political theorist, he was also an avid naturalist, architect, and philosopher. Adams's interests were more tightly focused on legal and constitutional affairs.

By the mid-1790s, the two statesmen differed also in their visions of the nation's future. Though fearing Hamilton's ambition and distrusting his infatuation with England, Adams was a committed Federalist. He believed in a vigorous national government, was appalled by the French Revolution, and was persuaded that the impulses of popular democracy must be counterbalanced by a stable and propertied elite. Jefferson, while firmly supporting the Constitution, was alarmed by Hamilton's financial program, viewed France's revolution as a logical if chaotic extension of America's struggle for freedom, and sought the expansion of political democracy. By 1796, he had become the vocal leader of an increasingly articulate political opposition, the Jeffersonian Republicans.

The election that year bound Jefferson and Adams together in a deeply strained and ill-fated alliance. With Washington gone, Adams became the Federalists' candidate for president. Though Jefferson did not openly oppose Adams, he sanctioned a vigorous campaign on his own behalf. In the election, Adams received 71 electoral votes and won the presidency. Jefferson came in second with 68 and, as the Constitution then specified, assumed the vice presidency. The narrowness of Adams's majority—his enemies gleefully reminded him that he was only a "President of three votes"—foreshadowed the troubles that lay ahead.

Adams later recalled his inaugural day. "A solemn scene it was indeed, and it was made more affecting by the presence of the General [Washington], whose countenance was as serene and unclouded as the day. He seemed to enjoy a triumph over me. Methought I heard him say, 'Ay! I am fairly out and you fairly in! See which of us will be the happiest.'" The answer was not long in coming.

The War Crisis with France

Adams had no sooner taken office than he confronted a deepening crisis with France that would push the nation to the brink of civil conflict. Hoping to ease relations between the two countries, he sent three commissioners to Paris to negotiate an accord. When they arrived, agents (identified only as "X," "Y," and "Z") of the French foreign minister, Talleyrand, made it clear that the success of their mission depended on a substantial loan to the French government and a

$240,000 gratuity for themselves. The two staunchly Federalist commissioners, John Marshall and Charles Pinckney, indignantly rejected the demands and sailed for home. The third commissioner, Elbridge Gerry, stayed behind, hoping for an accommodation and alarmed by Talleyrand's intimation that if all three Americans left, France would declare war.

When Adams reported to Congress on the so-called XYZ Affair, American opinion was outraged. The Federalists quickly exploited the French blunder. Secretary of State Pickering urged an immediate declaration of war, while Federalist congressmen thundered against the insult to American honor and promised "millions for defense, but not one cent for tribute." Adams now found himself an unexpected hero. When he attended the theater in Philadelphia, audiences cheered themselves hoarse with shouts of "Adams and Liberty!" Caught up in the anti-French furor and emboldened by the petitions of support that flooded in from around the country, the president lashed out at "enemies" at home and abroad. The nation, he warned ominously, had never been in greater danger from "traitors" ready to "unite with the invading enemy and fly within their lines." Emotions were further inflamed by the so-called Quasi War, a series of naval encounters between American and French ships on the high seas.

As tensions with France increased, the government built men-of-war to defend American commerce on the high seas and in anticipation of a French invasion that never materialized. (*William Russell Birch,* Preparation for War to Defend Commerce, *1800, Free Library of Philadelphia)*

For the moment, the Republicans were in disarray. Publicly, they deplored the French government's behavior and pledged to uphold the nation's honor. But among themselves, they talked with alarm about the Federalists' intentions. They had good reason for concern, because the Federalists soon mounted a crash program to repel foreign invaders and roust out traitors in the country's midst.

The Alien and Sedition Acts

In May 1798, Congress created a Navy Department and called for the development of a naval force capable of defending the American coast against French attack. In July, Congress moved closer to an open breach with France by unilaterally repealing the treaty of 1778 and calling for the formation of a 10,000-man army. (The Federalists' original goal had been 50,000 men.) The army's stated mission was to repel an anticipated French invasion. Given France's desperate struggle in Europe, however, such an attack seemed exceedingly unlikely. The Jeffersonians, remembering the speed with which Federalist troops had been deployed against the Whiskey Rebels only a few years earlier, feared the army would be used against them.

As criticism of the army bill mounted, Adams had second thoughts. He was still enough of an old revolutionary to worry about the domestic dangers of a standing army. "This damned army," he burst out, "will be the ruin of the country." The navy, he believed, should be America's first line of defense. He was further angered when members of his party sought to put Hamilton in command of the army. To the dismay of hard-line Federalists, Adams issued only a few of the officers' commissions that Congress had authorized. Without officers, the troops could not be mobilized.

Fearful of foreign subversion and aware that French as well as Irish immigrants were active in the Jeffersonian opposition, the Federalist-dominated Congress moved in the summer of 1798 to curb the flow of aliens into the country. The Naturalization Act raised the residence requirement for citizenship from 5 to 14 years, while the Alien Act authorized the president to expel aliens whom he judged "dangerous to the peace and safety of the United States." Imprisonment and permanent exclusion from citizenship awaited individuals who were warned to leave but refused to go. Another bill, the Alien Enemies Act, empowered the president in time of war to arrest, imprison, or banish the subjects of any hostile nation without specifying charges against them or providing opportunity for appeal. The Federalist Congressman Harrison Gray Otis explained that there was no need "to invite hordes of Wild Irishmen, nor the turbulent and disorderly of all

A fight erupted in the House of Representatives in 1798 when Matthew Lyon, a Jeffersonian from Vermont, spat on the Federalist Roger Griswold. As the two congressmen battle, other representatives and a dog look on. *(Print Collection, Miriam and Ira D. Wallach Division of Art, Prints and Photographs, The New York Public Library, Astor, Lenox and Tilden Foundations)*

parts of the world, to come here with a view to distract our tranquility."

The implications of these acts for basic political liberties were ominous enough, but the Federalists were not yet finished. In July 1798, Congress passed the Sedition Act, aimed directly at the Jeffersonian opposition. The bill made it punishable by fine and imprisonment for anyone to conspire in opposition to "any measure or measures of the government" or to aid "any insurrection, riot, unlawful assembly, or combination." Fines and imprisonment also awaited those who dared "write, print, utter, or publish . . . any false, scandalous and malicious writing" bringing the government, Congress, or the president into disrepute.

The Federalist moves stunned the Jeffersonians, for they threatened to smother all political opposition. The Federalists left no room for doubts on the matter. With an open declaration of war, predicted Congressman James Lloyd of Delaware, "traitors and sedition mongers who are now protected and tolerated, would . . . be easily restrained or punished." The Federalists had come to equate their own political control with the nation's survival.

Under the terms of the Alien Act, Secretary of State Pickering launched investigations intended to force all foreigners to register with the government. The act's chilling effects were immediate and widespread. In July, Pickering noted approvingly that large numbers of aliens, especially people of French ancestry, were leaving the country. As prosecutions under the Sedition Act went forward, 25 people, among them David Brown of Dedham, were arrested. Fifteen were indicted, and 10 were ultimately convicted, the majority of them Jeffersonian printers and editors.

Representative Matthew Lyon, a cantankerous, acid-tongued Jeffersonian from Vermont, learned the consequences of political indiscretion, even for members of Congress. Born in Ireland, Lyon had come to America as a young indentured servant harboring undying enmity toward England and disrespect for privilege of every sort. A veteran of the War for Independence, he took his revolutionary principles seriously.

During a particularly heated debate over the Sedition Act, Lyon spat in the face of a Federalist opponent, Roger Griswold of Connecticut, thus earning the derisive sobriquet of the "Spitting Lion." Two weeks later, Griswold exacted revenge by caning Lyon on the House floor. Later that year, Lyon was hauled into court, fined $1,000, and sentenced to four months in prison. His crime? Making reference in a personal letter to President Adams's "unbounded thirst for ridiculous pomp, foolish adulation, and selfish avarice."

Local Reverberations

David Brown was not the only ordinary citizen to experience the enmity of Federalist authorities, for the political conflict that was brewing penetrated deeply into American communities. Luther Baldwin of Newark, New Jersey, discovered how little it took to get into trouble. On July 27, 1798, President and Mrs.

Adams passed through Newark on their way from Philadelphia to their home in Quincy, Massachusetts. As the nation's first couple moved along Broad Street around 11 o'clock that morning, they were greeted by firing cannon, ringing church bells, and the cheers of the citizenry.

Not all Newark's residents shared in the moment's enthusiasm. Luther Baldwin happened to be coming toward John Burnett's dram shop when one of the tavern's customers, noting that the cannon continued to fire after the president had passed by, commented acidly, "There goes the President and they are firing at his a — —." Already "a little merry with drink," Baldwin replied that "he did not care if they fired thro' his a — —." Whereupon, the Federalist tavern keeper cried out that Baldwin had spoken sedition and must be punished. Within two months, a local grand jury indicted him, and the following year he was hauled before the federal Circuit Court, where he was convicted of speaking "seditious words tending to defame the President and Government of the United States," fined, and committed to jail until both fine and court fees were paid.

Local Jeffersonians made a field day of Baldwin's trial. The New York *Argus* wondered in mock astonishment whether the "most enthusiastic Federalists and Tories" supposed that anyone "would feel . . . justification in firing at such a disgusting target as the a— — of J. A.?" The Jeffersonians, however, saw danger as well as humor in the Federalists' zealous overreaction. When so much is made of such a "ridiculous expression" as Baldwin's, the *Argus* warned, the "malignancy of the federal faction" was evident.

With little prospect of reversing the actions of the Federalist-dominated Congress, the Jeffersonians turned to the states for support. Building on the firestorm of protest that greeted the Alien and Sedition Acts, the Virginia and Kentucky assemblies mounted a direct challenge to the Federalist laws. The Kentucky Resolutions, drafted by Jefferson and passed on November 16, 1798, declared that the national government had violated the Bill of Rights. Faced with the arbitrary exercise of federal power, the resolutions continued, each state "has an equal right to judge [of infractions] by itself . . . [and] the mode and measure of redress." Nullification (declaring a federal law invalid within a state's borders) was the "rightful remedy" for such unconstitutional laws. The Virginia Resolutions, written by Madison and passed the following month, asserted that when the central government threatened the people's liberties, the states "have the right and are in duty bound to interpose for arresting the progress of the evil." It would not be the last time in American history that state leaders would claim authority to set aside a federal law.

The Kentucky and Virginia resolutions received little support in either the North or South, and neither state actually attempted to obstruct enforcement of the Alien and Sedition Acts. Still, the resolutions indicated the depth of opposition to the Federalists' program.

As Federalists pressed ahead, some Jeffersonians prepared for open conflict. The Virginia assembly called for the formation of a state arsenal at Harpers Ferry, reorganization of the militia, and a special tax to pay for these preparations. In Philadelphia, Federalist patrols walked the streets to protect government officials from angry crowds. As a precaution, President Adams smuggled arms into his residence. As 1799 began, the country seemed on the brink of upheaval.

Within a year, however, the political cycle turned again, this time decisively against the Federalists. The break came with Adams's dramatic decision to send a new emissary to France. From Europe, the president's son, John Quincy Adams, sent assurances that Talleyrand was now ready to negotiate an honorable accord. Alarmed at the political furor consuming the nation and fearful that war with France "would convulse the attachments of the country," Adams eagerly seized the opening. "The end of war is peace," he explained, "and peace was offered me." Moreover, he had concluded that his only chance of reelection lay in fashioning a peace coalition out of both parties.

Adams's cabinet was enraged when they learned of the new mission, for the legitimacy of the Federalist war program depended on the continuation of the French crisis. After Secretary of State Pickering repeatedly ignored the president's orders to send the new commissioners on their way, Adams dismissed him and personally ordered the commissioners to depart. By year's end, the envoys had secured an agreement releasing the United States from the 1778 alliance and restoring peaceful relations between the two nations.

The "Revolution of 1800"

As the election of 1800 approached, the Federalists were in disarray, having squandered the political advantage handed them by the XYZ Affair in 1798. With peace now a reality, they stood before the nation charged with the unconstitutional exercise of federal power, the suppression of political dissent, and the intention of using the federal army against American citizens. The Federalists, moreover, were bitterly divided. Followers of Hamilton were furious at Adams's "betrayal." When the president announced his intention of standing for reelection, they plotted his defeat.

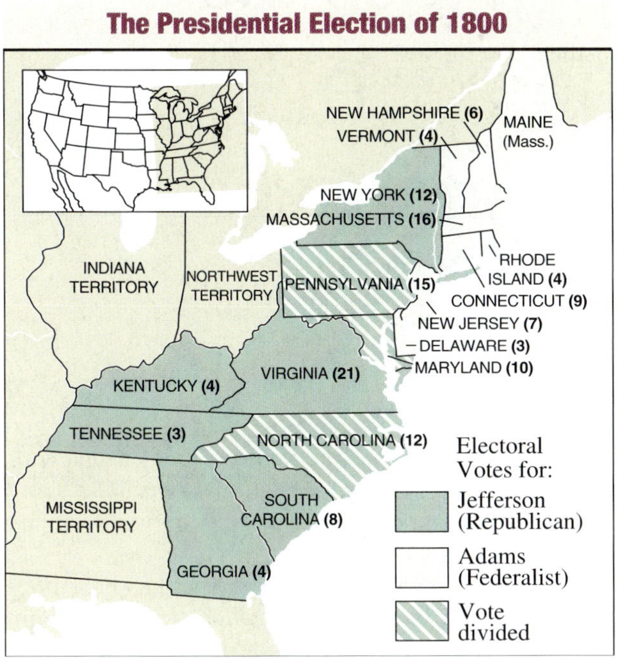

Though the federal government was little more than a decade old, the electoral vote in 1800 revealed the sectional divisions that already troubled national politics.

Emotions were running high as the election approached. In Philadelphia a group of young men showing their sympathy with England by wearing black cockades in their caps confronted another group sporting the tricolored cockade of France. "A fray ensued," Jefferson reported, "the light horse were called in, and the city was so filled with confusion from about 6 to 10 o'clock . . . that it was dangerous going out."

The arch-Federalist Fisher Ames berated the Jeffersonians as "fire-eating salamanders" and "poison-sucking toads," while the Jeffersonians returned the abuse in kind. Both sides believed that the republic's survival depended on their own political triumph and the destruction of their political enemies. In the heat of the moment, no compromise seemed possible. This election, Jefferson declared, will "fix our national character" and "determine whether republicanism or aristocracy" will prevail. In Virginia, rumors of a slave insurrection briefly interrupted the feuding, but the scare passed and soon Federalists and Jeffersonians were at each others' throats once again.

Election day was tense throughout the nation but passed without serious interruption. As the results were tallied, it became clear that the Jeffersonians had handed the Federalists a decisive defeat. The two Republican candidates for president, Jefferson, the Republicans' first choice, and Aaron Burr, their other nominee, each had 73 electoral votes while Adams followed with 65.

Because of the tie vote, the election was thrown into the House of Representatives, as provided in the Constitution. There a deadlock quickly developed. In spite of pressure from Jefferson's supporters, Burr refused to give way. The Federalist caucus decided to back Burr, believing him less dangerous than Jefferson. After a bitter struggle, the House finally elected Jefferson, 10 states to 4, on the thirty-sixth ballot. (Seeking to prevent a recurrence of such a crisis, the next Congress passed and the states ratified the Twelfth Amendment, providing for separate Electoral College ballots for president and vice president.) The magnitude of the Federalists' defeat was even more evident in the congressional elections, where they lost their majority in both House and Senate.

The election's outcome revealed the strong sectional divisions now evident in the country's politics. The Federalists dominated New England because of regional loyalty to Adams, the area's commercial ties with England, and fears, fed by local ministers and politicians alike, that the Jeffersonians intended to import social revolution from France. From Maryland south, Jeffersonian control was almost as complete. In the middle states, where issues of foreign and domestic policy cut across society in more complicated ways, the election was more closely contested. In the years ahead, sectional differences would continue to shape American politics.

The conflict between Federalists and Jeffersonians was deeply rooted as well in socioeconomic divisions among the American people. Federalist strength was strongest among merchants, manufacturers, and commercial farmers situated within easy reach of the coast—groups that had supported the Constitution in 1787 and 1788. Connecticut Federalists claimed the support of "men of talents, information, and property." In New York City and Philadelphia, Federalists were most numerous in wards where assessments were highest, houses largest, and addresses most fashionable.

By contrast, the Jeffersonian opposition included most of the old Anti-Federalists as well as agriculturalists in both North and South. They marshaled significant support as well among urban workers and artisans, many of whom had once been staunch Federalists. An important reason for their shift in political allegiance was illustrated by an episode that occurred in New York City in 1795.

Thomas Burke and Timothy Crady, two recent Irish immigrants, operated a ferry across the East River between lower Manhattan and Brooklyn. One day in

Technology Changes the American People

INDUSTRIAL TECHNOLOGY IN THE WOODEN AGE

The decades between 1790 and 1830 witnessed the first stirring of a revolution in industrial technology that would eventually transform the American economy and shape the working lives of millions of Americans. The nation's earliest experiments in industrial technology were fashioned out of wood, not iron. Though wooden machinery often broke down, required continuous maintenance, and frequently caught fire from friction, it was cheap to construct, easily repaired, and readily fabricated by experienced craftsmen. Wooden machinery, moreover, was especially well suited to the small scale of American manufacturing. The early republic was still part of the "wooden age," when, in addition to tools and machines, wood was the major source of fuel, construction material for ships and wagons, fences and houses, and important chemicals such as potash and turpentine.

Within a few years, young women joined children as workers in many of the nations' textile mills. *(The Slater Mill Historic Site)*

Many Americans in the young republic were enthusiastic about technology's promise for the nation's future. Robert Fulton, inventor of one of the earliest steamboats, explained how technological progress would strengthen American republicanism. "Every order of things which has a tendency to remove oppression and meliorate the condition of man, by directing his ambition to useful industry," he proclaimed in a speech before Congress in 1810, "is, in effect, republican." Fulton's comments reflected a widely held belief that technology, representing the application of reason and science to practical, everyday needs, would foster the betterment of mankind.

In 1789, an enterprising English mechanic named Samuel Slater arrived in New York. Familiar with British textile technology, he brought with him detailed knowledge of mechanical carding machines that combed cotton fibers into alignment suitable for spinning, as well as the Arkwright spinning frame, capable of fashioning 48 uniform cotton threads at a time. Slater wasn't the only immigrant who made valuable contributions to technological development in the early republic, for much American technical know-how was borrowed from Europe. Powered by waterwheels and placed in the fledgling textile factories that sprung up in increasing numbers along New England's fast-flowing rivers from the 1790s on, the new wooden machines spurred a startling growth in the American textile industry. In 1800, an estimated 1,000 wage earners labored in the nation's textile factories. By 1830, the number had climbed to 55,000.

Thought they vastly increased the output of cotton cloth, the new machines also created a dangerous environment for the workers who tended them. Not only were the early textile factories deafeningly noisy because of the pounding motion and clacking wooden gears, but also cotton dust filled the air, and the

Samuel Slater's textile mill at Pawtucket Falls in Rhode Island was among the first to employ new wooden machinery. *(Courtesy The Rhode Island Historical Society)*

leather belts that transmitted power from the factories' waterwheels frequently snared workers' hair or clothing, with awful results. Tending the machines, moreover, required repetitious, deadening labor far different from the traditionally slower-paced and more varied work of artisan shops.

Enterprising factory managers quickly learned to fill their workforce with children whose nimble fingers, greater docility, and lower wages promised high profits. Samuel Slater staffed his first factory entirely with youngsters between the ages of 7 and 12. By 1820, children comprised an estimated 47 percent of the labor force in Connecticut and 55 percent in Rhode Island. The children's workweek in the Connecticut mills ranged from 72 to 84 hours. In response to such obvious exploitation, the Connecticut legislature passed a law requiring instruction in reading, writing, and arithmetic for all children working in factories. The law, however, simply made child labor more productive and thus acceptable.

Not until the middle of the nineteenth century would factories replace homes and shops as producers of most American textiles. The awesome transformation of manufacturing technology and the conditions of American industrial labor, however, had its beginning many years earlier, in the primitive wooden machinery of early America.

Many of the goods sold today in American stores are manufactured by children and other laborers in underdeveloped countries. Defenders of such practices argue that child labor provides desperately needed income for poor families and enables American manufacturers to compete with foreign producers. Similar arguments were made in the early nineteenth century. What do you think of the nineteenth-century arguments? What do you think of similar arguments today?

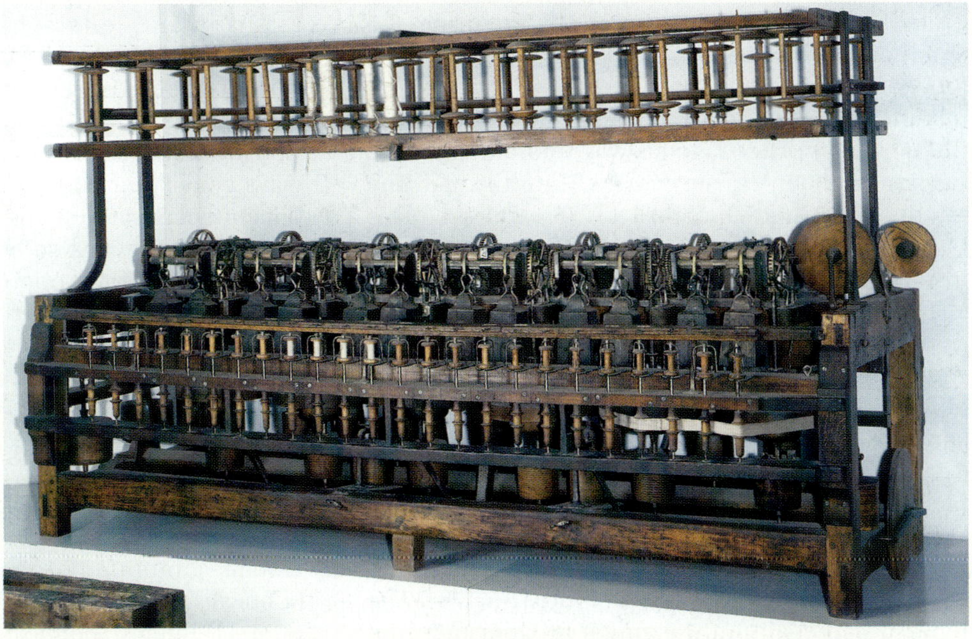

A 48-spindle frame built by Samuel Slater in Pawtucket, 1790. *(Courtesy National Museum of History and Technology, Smithsonian Institution, Washington, D.C.)*

early November, Gabriel Furman, a merchant and Federalist alderman, arrived on the Brooklyn shore a bit before the scheduled departure time. Impatient to get across, Furman instructed the ferrymen to leave early. When they refused, he upbraided the "rascals" for their disrespect and threatened to have them arrested. Crady was especially angered by the alderman's arrogance. He and Burke, Crady exploded, "were as good as any buggers," and he threatened to use his boathook on anyone who tried to arrest him.

When the ferry landed on the Manhattan shore, Furman had the two arrested, brandishing his cane at them as they were taken off to jail, where they were charged with vagrancy. Their employer offered bail, but Furman refused to allow it, and so the boatmen remained 12 days in Bridewell prison awaiting trial.

Crady and Burke were eventually hauled before Mayor Varick and three other Federalist aldermen, sitting as the Court of General Sessions. The judges quickly decided to make examples of the two insolent Irishmen. "You rascals, we'll trim you," Varick allegedly said; "we'll learn you to insult men in office." The two ferrymen were not allowed to speak on their own behalf, nor were friendly witnesses permitted to testify. The magistrates found the two guilty on charges of insulting an alderman and threatening the constable, sentenced them to two months at hard labor, and ordered that 25 lashes be laid on Crady for good measure.

Within a month, the two ferrymen bolted from jail and disappeared into the woods of Pennsylvania, never to be heard from again. The episode, however, was not yet over, for a young Jeffersonian lawyer named William Keteltas publicly castigated the "tyranny and partiality of the court," arguing that Burke and Crady had been punished to "gratify the pride, the ambition and insolence of men in office." The authorities had supposedly acted to protect the mayor's reputation. But what, he asked, about the reputation of the ferrymen? After Keteltas was upbraided for his insolence, 2,000 citizens carried him through the streets chanting "The Spirit of '76" and waving a banner sardonically inscribed "What, you rascal, insult your superiors?"

In the politically charged setting of the 1790s, tensions between social privilege and democratic equality suffused American political life. As things turned out, the Jeffersonians' opposition to Federalist arrogance, support for revolutionary France, and challenge to the Alien and Sedition Acts worked steadily to their political advantage.

The political alignment evident in the election of 1800 resembled but did not duplicate the Federalist/Anti-Federalist division of 1787–1788. The Jeffersonian coalition was much broader than the Anti-Federalists' had been, for it included countless individuals, from urban workers to leaders such as Madison and Jefferson, who had supported the Constitution and had helped set the new government on its feet. Unlike the Anti-Federalists, the Jeffersonians were ardent supporters of the Constitution but insisted that it be implemented in ways consistent with political liberty and a strong dependence on the states.

The Jeffersonians differed even more dramatically from their Federalist opponents. Suspicious of central government, they placed their political faith in the states. And far more than the Federalists, they believed that government should be closely accountable to the people. While some Jeffersonian leaders continued to argue the importance of leadership by a "natural aristocracy of talent," and while southern Jeffersonians continued to reconcile black slavery and white liberty, the Jeffersonian coalition numbered countless individuals committed to the creation of a democratic political society. Motivated by a combination of electoral self-interest, political principle, and the determi-

Timeline

1789	George Washington inaugurated as first president
	Outbreak of the French Revolution
1790	Slave trade outlawed in all states except Georgia and South Carolina
	Hamilton's "Reports on the Public Credit"
1791	Bill of Rights ratified
	Whiskey Tax and national bank established
	Hamilton's "Report on Manufactures"
1792	Washington reelected
1793	Outbreak of war in Europe
	Washington's Neutrality Proclamation
	Jefferson resigns from cabinet
	Controversy over Citizen Genêt's visit
1794	Whiskey Rebellion in Pennsylvania
1795	Controversy over Jay's Treaty with England
1796	Washington's Farewell Address
	John Adams elected president
1797	XYZ Affair in France
1798	Naturalization Act
	Alien and Sedition Acts
	Virginia and Kentucky Resolutions
1798–1800	Undeclared naval war with France
1799	Trials of David Brown and Luther Baldwin
1801	Jefferson elected president by House of Representatives

nation of ordinary men to claim their rights as republican citizens, the Jeffersonians mounted elaborate parades, organized voters, and exploited the popular press to mobilize the people. And when Jeffersonian leaders hesitated, they found themselves pushed ahead by the growing tide of popular politics.

Conclusion

Toward the Nineteenth Century

The election of 1800 proved a remarkable outcome to more than a decade of political crisis. It had begun in the late 1780s with the intensifying debate over the Articles of Confederation and the movement toward a stronger central government. Then had come the heated contest over ratification of the new Constitution. Scarcely had the new government gotten under way than divisions began to form, first among political leaders in Congress but increasingly among the American people as well. Hamilton's domestic policies generated the first outburst of political conflict, but it was the French Revolution, the European war, Jay's Treaty, and the Federalist war program that galvanized political energies and set Federalists and Jeffersonians so adamantly against each other.

By 1800, the system of gentry-led politics centered in Congress and the more popular, democratic politics brewing in the states had drawn more closely together. The years ahead would bring them into even closer alignment, with dramatic consequences for the nation's political future.

In the election of 1800, control of the federal government passed for the first time from one political party to another, not easily but peacefully and legally. "The Revolution of 1800," the Jeffersonians claimed, was "as real a revolution in the principles of our government as that of 1776 was in its form." The future would show whether they were correct. But for the moment, the crisis had passed, the Federalists had been defeated, and the government was securely in the hands of the Jeffersonians.

Recommended Reading

Launching the National Republic

Richard Beeman, *Evolution of the Southern Backcountry* (1988); David Currie, *The Constitution in Congress: The Federal Period, 1789–1801* (1997); Stanley Elkins and Eric McKitrick, *The Age of Federalism* (1993); Ronald Hoffman and Peter Albert, eds., *Launching the "Extended Republic"* (1996); Rachel Klein, *The Unification of a Slave State* (1990); Norman Risjord, *Chesapeake Politics, 1781–1800* (1978); Robert Rutland, *The Birth of the Bill of Rights, 1776–1791* (1983); Stephen Schechter and Richard Bernstein, eds., *Contexts of the Bill of Rights* (1990); Bernard Schwartz, *The Great Rights of Mankind* (1977); Thomas Slaughter, *The Whiskey Rebellion* (1986); Alan Taylor, *Liberty Men and Great Proprietors: The Revolutionary Settlement of the Maine Frontier* (1990); Patricia Watlington, *The Partisan Spirit: Kentucky Politics, 1779–1792* (1972).

The Republic in a Threatening World

Albert Bowman, *The Struggle for Neutrality: Franco-American Diplomacy During the Federalist Era* (1974); Jerald Combs, *The Jay Treaty* (1970); Michael Durey, *Transatlantic Radicals and the Early American Republic* (1997); J. Worth Estes and Billy G. Smith, eds., *A Melancholy Scene of Devastation: The Public Response to the 1793 Yellow Fever Epidemic* (1997); Daniel Lang, *Foreign Policy in the Early Republic* (1985); David Wilson, *United Irishmen, United States: Immigrant Radicals in the Early Republic* (1998).

The Political Crisis Deepens

Stuart Andrews, *The Rediscovery of America: Transatlantic Crosscurrents in an Age of Revolution* (1998); Joyce Appleby, *Capitalism and the New Social Order: The Republican Vision of the 1790s* (1984); Aliene Austin, *Matthew Lyon: "New Man" of the Democratic Revolution, 1749–1800* (1981); Doron Ben-Atar and Barbara Oberg, eds., *Federalists Reconsidered* (1998); Joseph Ellis, *Passionate Sage: The Character and Legacy of John Adams* (1993); John Hoadley, *Origins of American Political Parties, 1789–1803* (1986); John Howe, *The Changing Political Thought of John Adams* (1966); Richard Kohn, *Eagle and Sword: The Federalists and the Creation of a Military Establishment in America, 1783–1802* (1975); Leonard Levy, *Freedom of the Press from Zenger to Jefferson* (1966); Simon Newman, *Parades and the Politics of the Street* (1997); James Roger Sharp, *American Politics in the Early Republic* (1998); James Morton Smith, *Freedoms's Fetters: The Alien and Sedition Laws and American Civil Liberties* (1956); Charles Steffen, *The Mechanics of Baltimore: Workers and Politics in the Age of Revolution, 1763–1812* (1984); William Stinchcomb, *The XYZ Affair* (1981).

Fiction and Film

Adapted from Laurel Thatcher Ulrich's prize-winning book, the docudrama *A Midwife's Tale* (1997) depicts the daily life of nurse-midwife Martha Ballard, who delivered a thousand babies and served her New England community during the closing years of the eighteenth century.

The initial installment of C-SPAN's *American Presidents: Life Portraits* series (1999) effectively portrays the challenges and accomplishments of the nation's first president, George Washington.

In the novel *Fever* (1996), John Weidman offers a vivid account of the yellow fever plague that killed hundreds of people and threatened social chaos in Philadelphia in 1793.

The essayist and novelist Gore Vidal explores the tangled politics and personalities of the early republic via a largely sympathetic portrayal of Aaron Burr (who killed Alexander Hamilton in a duel in 1804), in *Burr: A Novel* (1973).

Suggested Web Sites

http://www.virginia.edu/~gwpapers/

The Papers of George Washington Papers Homepage. This site is a wealth of information on a project that aims to publish a complete edition of Washington's correspondence. You can view selected documents, essays, and an index of the published volumes.

http://www.mountvernon.org/

Historic Mount Vernon. This is a vast site about Mount Vernon, the home of George Washington. Take a tour, visit the library, even see a reenactment of Washington's funeral.

http://www.nps.gov/inde/visit.html

Independence Hall National Historical Park. This site includes images and historical accounts of Independence Hall and other Philadelphia buildings closely associated with the nation's founding.

http://www.whitehousehistory.org/whha/default.asp

White House Historical Association. This interactive site contains a timeline of the history of the White House and several interesting photos and links.

http://www.whitehouse.gov/WH/glimpse/presidents/html/ja2.html

John Adams. This site contains biographical information about the second president and links to his inaugural address, his more quotable phrases, and information about his wife, Abigail.

http://www.DoHistory.org/

DoHistory, Harvard University Film Study Center. Focusing on the life of Martha Ballard, a late eighteenth-century New England woman, this site employs selections from her diary, excerpts from a book and film of her life, and other primary documents to enable students to conduct their own historical investigation.

http://www.ushistoryplace.com

the history place A richly detailed on-line learning environment complete with interactive maps, timelines, history activities, primary source documents, and links to related American history sites.

9

SOCIETY *and* POLITICS *in the* EARLY REPUBLIC

CHAPTER OUTLINE

Restoring American Liberty
- *The Jeffersonians Take Control*
- *Politics and the Federal Courts*
- *Dismantling the Federalist War Program*

Building an Agrarian Nation
- *The Jeffersonian Vision*
- *The Windfall Louisiana Purchase*
- *Opening the Trans-Mississippi West*

A Nation of Regions
- *The Northeast*
- *The Nation's Cities*
- *The South*
- *Trans-Appalachia*

Indian–White Relations in the Early Republic
- *The Initial Goals of Indian Policy*
- *Strategies of Survival: The Iroquois and the Cherokee*
- *Patterns of Armed Resistance: The Shawnee and the Creek*

Perfecting a Democratic Society
- *The Revolutionary Heritage*
- *The Evangelical Impulse*
- *Alleviating Poverty and Distress*
- *Women's Lives*
- *Race, Slavery, and the Limits of Reform*
- *Forming Free Black Communities*

A Foreign Policy for the New Nation
- *Jeffersonian Principles*
- *Struggling for Neutral Rights*
- *The War of 1812*
- *The United States and the Americas*

Politics in Transition
- *Division Among the Jeffersonians*
- *American Nationality and the Specter of Sectionalism*
- *Collapse of the Federalist-Jeffersonian Party System*
- *A New Style of Politics*

Conclusion: The Passing of an Era

In May 1809, Mary and James Harrod gathered their five children, loaded a few belongings (tools, seeds for the summer planting, and several prized pieces of furniture) on a wagon, closed the door on their four-room cabin, fell in line with a dozen other families, and headed west from Spotsylvania County, Virginia, toward a new life in Kentucky. They left behind 15 years of wearying effort trying to wring a modest living from 10 acres of marginal upland, and a family cemetery that held two of their other children and Mary's parents.

Beyond the Appalachian Mountains, 450 difficult miles ahead, lay additional hard work and uncertainty. Though central Kentucky where the Harrods would settle contained few Indian villages, powerful tribes from north and south of the Ohio River hunted there and fought over its control. They also fought the growing tide of white settlers. The first years would be especially hard for James and Mary as they "opened up" the land, planted the first crops, and erected a cabin. They would be lonesome as well, for the Harrods would be unlikely to see even the chimney smoke of their nearest neighbors.

James and Mary were hopeful, though, as they trudged west. The land agent who had sold them their claim had promised rich, fertile soil that in time would support a good life. And they had been excited at the prospect of joining the swelling stream of migrants seeking new lives in the trans-Appalachian West. They looked forward as well to escaping Virginia's slave society with its arrogant planters and oppressed slaves. That was no place for poor whites to live. Once in Kentucky, they settled on their own plot of land, joined with others in fashioning a new community, and took responsibility for their own lives.

In April 1795, Ben Thompson started north from Queen Anne's County, Maryland, for New York City. Ben knew little beyond farming, but he was ambitious and when he arrived in New York he listened carefully to the ship's captains who talked about life at sea while they recruited men for their crews. Ben was lucky, for he arrived just as American overseas commerce, stimulated by renewed war in Europe, was entering a decade of unprecedented prosperity. Sailors were in demand, pay was good, and few questions were asked. For five years, Ben sailed the seas. Having enough of travel, he returned to New York and hired out as an apprentice to a ship's carpenter.

About the same time, Phyllis Sherman left her home in Norwalk, Connecticut. She also headed for New York, where she took a job as a maid in the household of one of the city's wealthy merchants. As fate would have it, Phyllis and Ben met, fell in love, and in the spring of 1802 were married.

There is little of note in this except that Ben and Phyllis were former slaves and were married in the African Methodist Episcopal Zion Church. Ben had cast off his slave name, Cato, as a sign of liberation, while Phyllis kept the name her master had given her. Ben was doubly fortunate, for he had purchased his freedom just as cotton production began to expand through the Chesapeake region. In another decade, he would have faced greater difficulty securing his independence. Phyllis had been freed as a child when slavery ended in Connecticut. As she grew up, she tired of living as a servant with her former owner's family and longed for the companionship of other blacks. She had heard that there were people of color in New York City, and she was correct. In 1800, it contained 6,300 African Americans, more than half of them free.

Though life in New York was better than either Ben or Phyllis had known before, it was hardly easy. They shared only marginally in the city's commercial prosperity. In 1804, they watched helplessly as yellow fever carried off their daughter and many of their friends. And while they found support in newly established African American churches and the expanding black community, they had to be constantly on guard because slave ships still moved in and out of the port and slave catchers pursued southern runaways in the city's streets.

During the early years of the nineteenth century, thousands of people like Mary and James and Ben and Phyllis seized whatever opportunities they could find to improve their lives. In doing so, they helped strengthen America's commitment to social equality, individual opportunity, political democracy, and personal autonomy—doctrines that would gradually transform the nation.

This transformation—some have called it the "opening" of American society—was driven in part by the accelerating expansion of white settlement out of long-settled areas along the Atlantic coast onto new lands in the trans-Appalachian interior. That expansion disrupted families and disorganized older communities even as it

Detail from Thomas Coke Ruckle, *Fairview Inn or Three Mile House on Old Frederick Road* (near Baltimore), 1829. At country inns, people on the move bought supplies, exchanged goods, and secured information about the routes that lay ahead. *(Maryland Historical Society, Baltimore, Maryland)* generated new settlements and social relationships. At work as well was an increasingly dynamic market economy with its relentless discipline of supply and demand, individual profit, and impersonal, contractual relationships. As the market economy expanded, long-standing commitments to notions of a "just price" and the social good, staples of an earlier, "moral economy," weakened.

Contributing also to the promotion of individualism and equality was the wave of religious revivalism known as the Second Great Awakening that swept through American society beginning about 1800. The Gospel message, carried by swarms of untutored, itinerant Methodist and Baptist preachers, stressed universal salvation, the equality of all believers before God, and the individual's responsibility for her or his own soul.

The transformation of American society was spurred finally by the accelerating challenge of locally based democratic forces to a more conservative, gentry-led politics centered in the national Congress. Those democratic forces, energized initially during the revolutionary struggle against England and strengthened during the tumultuous politics of the 1790s, were promoted as well by younger political leaders eager to supplant the revolutionary generation and claim their place in shaping the nation's future.

Not all Americans benefited equally from the changes of these early nineteenth-century years. Doctrines of equality, opportunity, and individual autonomy resonated far more powerfully in the lives of white men than of white women, while numerous Americans were actually disadvantaged by the changes that were under way. In the South, African Americans found their lives more harshly constrained by a revitalized system of slavery, while in the North free blacks faced an increasingly racialized society. West of the Appalachians, Native Americans confronted a swelling tide of white settlement sweeping across their homeland.

As the nineteenth century progressed, these processes of social, economic, and political change would radically transform the American nation. The beginnings of that transformation were clearly evident by the 1820s.

The years of the early republic witnessed as well a diplomatic revolution of major importance as the American people broke free from their centuries-old dependence on Europe and focused their energies on exploiting the vast North American continent. At the same time, the United States asserted a bold, new role among the emerging nations of Latin America as they also threw off the yoke of colonialism.

RESTORING AMERICAN LIBERTY

The Jeffersonians took office in 1801 determined to rescue the national government from Federalist mismanagement. They had several objectives in mind: calming the political storms that had threatened to tear the country apart, purging the government of Federalist influences, and consolidating their recent political victory.

The Jeffersonians Take Control

In November 1800, while John Adams was still president, the government had moved from Philadelphia to the new capital in the District of Columbia. When the politicians arrived there, they were stunned by its primitiveness and isolation. New York and Philadelphia, seats of the national government since 1789, had offered comfortable accommodations, sophisticated surroundings, and direct contact with the Atlantic world. By contrast, the new capital was little more than a swampy village of 5,000 inhabitants on the banks of the Potomac River.

Boasting that Washington would become the "Rome of the New World," Congress had commissioned a Frenchman, Pierre L'Enfant, to develop a plan for the capital city's development. Aided by a black American mathematician and surveyor, Benjamin Banneker, L'Enfant produced a magnificent design, replete with central plazas and broad boulevards radiating outward from a government center anchored by the Capitol and the presidential mansion. Little of that grand design, however, had materialized by 1800. The Capitol wing containing the House chamber had been completed, but the Senate chamber was still under construction, and the president's mansion remained unfinished.

As a symbolic gesture intended to rid the government of Federalist pomp, Jefferson planned a simple inauguration. Shortly before noon on March 4, he walked to the Capitol from his nearby boardinghouse. "His dress," noted one observer, "was . . . that of a plain citizen, without any distinctive badge of office." The president-elect read his short inaugural address, Chief Justice John Marshall (a fellow Virginian but a staunch Federalist) administered the oath of office, and a militia company fired a 16-gun salute. That was it.

Unlike highly commercial, cosmopolitan centers such as New York and Philadelphia that had served as earlier capitals, Washington seemed lost in the woods of southern Maryland and northern Virginia. *(Library of Congress)*

Though fleeting, the moment was filled with significance. For the first time in the nation's brief history, control of the government had shifted from one political party to another. Mrs. Samuel Harrison Smith, Washington resident and political observer, described the occasion's drama. "I have this morning witnessed one of the most interesting scenes a free people can ever witness," she wrote to a friend. "The changes of administration, which in every . . . age have most generally been epochs of confusion, villainy, and bloodshed, in this our happy country take place without any species of distraction or disorder." Many Americans shared her sense of pride and relief.

In his inaugural speech, Jefferson enumerated the "essential principles" that would guide his administration: "equal and exact justice to all," support of the states as "the surest bulwarks against antirepublican tendencies," "absolute acquiescence" in majority rule, supremacy of civil over military authority, reduction of government spending, "honest payment" of the public debt, freedom of the press, and "freedom of the person under the protection of the habeas corpus." Though Jefferson never mentioned the Federalists by name, his litany of principles reverberated with the dark experience of the 1790s.

The president spoke also of political reconciliation. "Every difference of opinion," he declared, "is not a difference of principle. We have called by different names brethren of the same principles. We are all republicans—we are all federalists." Not all his followers welcomed that final flourish, for many were eager to scatter the Federalists to the political winds. Jefferson eventually agreed that a "general sweep" of Federalist officeholders was necessary. By 1808, virtually all government offices were in Republican hands.

Politics and the Federal Courts

Having lost Congress and the presidency, the Federalists turned to the judiciary for protection against the expected Jeffersonian onslaught. In the last months of the Adams administration, the lame duck Congress had passed a new Judiciary Act increasing the number of circuit courts, complete with judges, marshals, and clerks. Before leaving office, Adams filled many of those offices with staunch Federalists. Our opponents, observed Jefferson bitterly, "defeated at the polls, have retired into the Judiciary, and from that barricade . . . hope to batter down all the bulwarks of Republicanism." Something had to be done. In January 1802, the new Congress repealed the Federalist Judiciary Act by a strict party vote.

As Federalists spluttered in anger, the Jeffersonians prepared to purge several highly partisan Federalist judges from the bench. In March 1803, the House of Representatives impeached District Judge John Pickering of New Hampshire. The grounds were not "high crimes and misdemeanors," as the Constitution required, but the Federalist diatribes with which Pickering regularly assaulted both juries and defendants. Impeachment, declared Representative William Branch Giles of Virginia, is nothing more than a decla-

Only the wing housing the House of Representatives had been completed when Congress first met in the new capitol in 1800. *(Library of Congress)*

ration by Congress that an individual holds "dangerous opinions," which appear to threaten the union. Although Giles's speech echoed the language of repression used by Federalists only a few years earlier, the Jeffersonian-controlled Senate convicted Pickering handily.

Spurred on by their success, the Jeffersonians next brought impeachment charges against Supreme Court Justice Samuel Chase, one of the most notorious Republican baiters. The indictment charged Chase with "intemperate and inflammatory political harangues," delivered "with intent to excite the fears and resentment of the . . . people . . . against the Government of the United States." When the trial revealed that Chase had committed no impeachable offense, he was acquitted and returned triumphantly to the bench.

Chase was a sorry hero, but constitutional principles are often established in the defense of less than heroic people. Had Chase's impeachment succeeded, Chief Justice Marshall would almost certainly have been next, and that would surely have precipitated a serious constitutional crisis. Sensing the danger, the Jeffersonians pulled back, content to allow time and the regular turnover of personnel to cleanse the courts of Federalist control. The vital principle of judicial independence had been narrowly preserved.

In two trailblazing decisions, the Supreme Court shortly laid down some of the most fundamental doctrines of American constitutional law. The first, *Marbury* v. *Madison* (1803), established the principle of judicial review, the notion that it was the court's responsibility to judge the constitutionality of congressional laws and executive

John Marshall, appointed chief justice of the United States by President Adams in 1801, served in that position for 34 years. Under his leadership, the Supreme Court established some of the most basic principles of American constitutional law. *(Boston Atheneum)*

behavior. In the majority opinion, Chief Justice Marshall declared that "It is emphatically the province and duty of the judicial department to say what the law is." Sixteen years later, in another landmark decision, *McCulloch* v. *Maryland,* the court struck down a Maryland law taxing the Baltimore branch of the Second Bank of the United States. No state, Marshall ruled, possessed the right to tax a nationally chartered bank, for "the power to tax involves the power to destroy." In the McCulloch decision, Marshall also established the constitutional basis for broad congressional authority. Let congressional intent "be within the scope of the Constitution," he wrote, "and all means which are appropriate . . . which are not prohibited, but consist with the letter and spirit of the Constitution, are constitutional."

Dismantling the Federalist War Program

The Jeffersonians had regarded the Federalists' war program as a threat to public liberty, so they moved quickly to dismantle it. Jefferson ended prosecutions under the Sedition Act, freed its victims, and silently let it lapse in 1802. Neither Jefferson nor most of his followers were consistent civil libertarians, for a number of opposition editors felt the sting of government displeasure. Still, Jefferson never duplicated the Federalists' attempts to stifle dissent.

The president undercut the Alien Acts by dismantling the hated inspection system. In 1802, Congress passed a new naturalization law, restoring the requirement of 5 rather than 14 years before a foreigner could be naturalized. The Federalists' provisional army also fell victim to the Jeffersonian assault and was quickly disbanded. Federal troops would no longer intimidate American citizens.

Finally, Jefferson acted to reduce the size of the federal government. Tiny by modern standards, the government had fewer than 3,000 civilian employees, only 300 of them, including the cabinet and members of Congress, located in Washington. That amounted to one federal public official for every 1,914 citizens, compared with one for approximately every 68 citizens today. Even so, Jefferson wrote that he was "hunting out and abolishing multitudes of useless offices, striking off jobs, etc., etc." The "principal care of our persons and property," he declared, should be left to the states because they were more closely attuned to the people's needs and could be held more closely accountable. Under Jefferson's administration, the federal government did little

FEDERAL REVENUES AND EXPENDITURES, 1790–1820 (IN THOUSANDS OF DOLLARS)

Year	Revenues		Expenditures	
1790	Customs	4,399	Military	634
	Other	19	Interest on public debt	2,349
		4,418	Other	1,426
				4,409
1800	Customs	9,081	Military	6,010
	Internal revenue	809	Interest on public debt	3,375
	Other	793	Other	1,466
		10,683		10,851
1810	Customs	8,583	Military	3,948
	Internal revenue	7	Interest on public debt	2,845
	Sale of public lands	697	Other	1,447
	Other	793		8,240
		10,080		
1820	Customs	15,006	Military	7,018
	Internal revenue	106	Interest on public debt	5,126
	Sale of public lands	1,636	Other	9,324
	Other	2,769		21,468
		19,517		

Note: In constant dollars, the revenue of the federal government in 1998 was $1,658 trillion and its expenditures were $1,668 trillion.

Source: U.S. Bureau of the Census

more than deliver the mail, deal with Indians on federal land, and administer the public domain. In addition to cutting jobs, the Jeffersonians reduced the national debt from $83 million in 1801 to $57 million a decade later.

Not everything the Jeffersonians did was consistent with limited government. As the nation grew, so did pressures for a federal program of internal improvements, especially from the new states forming beyond the Appalachians that sought closer ties with the East. Before many years, the government responded by constructing several western routes, including the National Road (1811) connecting Cumberland, Maryland, with Wheeling on the Ohio River. The states, however, continued to carry the major responsibility for internal improvements. Though the Jeffersonians may not have "revolutionized" the government as they claimed, they reduced its size and pointed it in a new direction.

BUILDING AN AGRARIAN NATION

The Jeffersonians did far more than reverse Federalist initiatives, for they were committed to implementing their own vision of an expanding, agrarian nation. That vision was mixed and inconsistent, because the Jeffersonian party embraced an array of often conflicting groups: southern patricians like Jefferson himself, determined to maintain a gentry-led, slavery-based agrarian order; lower- and middle-class southern whites committed to black servitude but ardent proponents of political equality among whites; northern artisans who brought to the Jeffersonian party an aversion to slavery (though rarely a commitment to racial equality) together with a fierce dedication to honest toil and their own economic interests; western farmers devoted to personal self-sufficiency on the land; and northern intellectuals ideologically committed to political democracy. In time, such diversity would splinter the Jeffersonian coalition. For the moment, however, these groups found unity not only in opposing their Federalist enemies but also in a set of broadly shared principles that guided Jeffersonian policies through the presidential administrations of Jefferson (1801–1808), James Madison (1809–1816), and James Monroe (1817–1824).

The Jeffersonian Vision

Political liberty, the Jeffersonians believed, could survive only under conditions of broad economic and social equality. They placed their faith in a nation filled with independent, yeoman farmers who were self-reliant, industrious, and filled with concern for the public good. Such people exemplified the qualities essential to democratic citizenship.

The Jeffersonian vision was clouded, however, by the realization that industriousness and self-discipline generated personal wealth, that wealth bred social inequality, and that inequality threatened to destroy the very foundation of a democratic society. The solution to that dilemma, they believed, was to be found in rapid territorial expansion that would provide land for the nation's yeoman citizens, draw restless people out of the cities and off the crowded lands of the East, and preserve the social equality that democratic liberty required. The expansion of white settlement across the North American continent would delay, perhaps even prevent, the cyclical process of growth, maturity, and decay that had been the fate of all past societies.

Calls for expanding white settlement were strengthened by the somber writings of an English clergyman and political economist named Thomas Malthus. In 1798, Malthus published an essay that jolted Europeans and Americans alike. Observing the increasingly crowded conditions of his native England, Malthus argued that "the power of population" was "greater than the power in the earth to produce subsistence for man." Enlightenment hopes for a steadily improving quality of life, he warned, were a delusion, for the future would be filled with increasing misery as population outran the supply of food.

Jefferson took Malthus's warnings seriously but believed that the Englishman failed to understand that America's vast reservoir of land would enable its people to escape Europe's fate. Differences of circumstance, Jefferson explained, would produce a different result. "There . . . the quantity of food is fixed . . . [while] supernumerary births add only to mortality. Here the immense extent of uncultivated and fertile lands enables every one who will labor, to marry young, and to raise a family of any size. Our food, then, may increase geometrically with our laborers, and our births, however multiplied, become effective." Rapid and continuing territorial expansion was thus indispensable to the Jeffersonian vision of the nation's future.

There were more immediate reasons for promoting American expansion, too, for occupation of the West would secure America's borders against continuing threats from England, France, and Spain. Finally, the Jeffersonians calculated that the creation of new, western states, committed to democratic forms of politics, would strengthen their own political control and assure the Federalists' permanent demise.

Time would reveal that American exceptionalism—the idea that America could avoid Europe's woes by continental expansion—was more limited than Jefferson imagined. Yet from the perspective of the early nineteenth century, the Jeffersonians offered a hopeful, indeed compelling, vision of the nation's future.

The Windfall Louisiana Purchase

Efforts to ensure agrarian democracy through territorial expansion lay behind Jefferson's most dramatic accomplishment, buying the Louisiana Territory in 1803. The purchase nearly doubled the nation's size.

In 1800, Spain ceded the vast trans-Mississippi region called Louisiana to France. Jefferson was profoundly disturbed by such clear evidence that European nations still coveted North American territory. His fears were well grounded, for in October 1802, the Spanish commander at New Orleans, which Spain had retained, once again closed the Mississippi River to American commerce.

In January 1803, the president sent his young associate James Monroe to Paris with instructions to purchase New Orleans and West Florida (which contained Mobile, the only good harbor on the Gulf Coast). When Monroe arrived, he was surprised to find French officials prepared to sell all of Louisiana (though not West Florida). The successful black rebellion against French rule in Haiti and the renewed threat of war with England made the French ruler, Napoleon Bonaparte, eager to concentrate French troops in Europe. In addition, he feared American designs on Louisiana and knew that he would not be able to defend it. In April, the deal was struck. For $15 million, the United States obtained all of Louisiana, nearly 830,000 square miles of land.

Federalists reacted with alarm to news of the acquisition, fearing with good reason that the states to be carved from Louisiana would be staunchly Jeffersonian. In addition, they worried that a rapidly expanding frontier would "decivilize" the entire nation.

Expansion did not stop with Louisiana. In 1810, American adventurers fomented a revolt in Spanish West Florida, proclaimed an independent republic, and sought annexation by the United States. Two years later, over vigorous Spanish objections, Congress annexed the region. In 1819, Spain ceded East Florida as well. As part of that agreement, the United States extended its territorial claims beyond Louisiana to include the Pacific Northwest. These impressive accomplishments set the stage for the final surge of continental expansion that would come during the 1840s.

Opening the Trans-Mississippi West

If America's vast domain was to serve the needs of the agrarian nation, it would have to be explored and prepared for white settlement. In the summer of 1803, Jefferson dispatched an expedition led by his secretary, Meriwether Lewis, and a young army officer named William Clark to explore the Far Northwest, make contact with Native Americans there, open the fur trade, and bring back scientific information about the area. For nearly two and a half years, the intrepid band of explorers, assisted by the Shoshoni woman Sacajawea, made its way across thousands of miles of unmapped and hostile terrain—up the Missouri River, through the

In this panorama by Boqueto de Woiserie, the American eagle flies over the French colonial city of New Orleans following the Louisiana Purchase of 1803. *(Chicago Historical Society)*

Recovering the Past

MAPS

Of the several exploring ventures President Jefferson sent into the trans-Mississippi West, the Lewis and Clark expedition (1803–1806) was the most important. It proved the feasibility of an overland route to the Pacific, produced scientific information about the fauna and flora of the Far Northwest, established contact with the Native Americans of the area, and helped stimulate westward expansion. Many of the place names the explorers gave to rivers and other natural features are still in use today.

During their travels, Meriwether Lewis, William Clark, and others in their party kept extensive journals in which they recorded their experiences and observations. These journals provide a vivid account of the expedition, including information on the landscape through which the explorers passed and the people they encountered. The journals also reveal a great deal about the attitudes and expectations of the explorers themselves. As they moved across the continent, the explorers produced detailed trail maps as well. These cartographic records also tell us a great deal about the experience and perceptions of the explorers, as well as about the regions through which they passed.

Examine the map shown here. It is an example of the sketch maps that William Clark drew as the expedition made its way across the land. The map represents about a 30-mile stretch along the Missouri River in what is today west-central North Dakota. After the expedition was over, these detailed studies were used to prepare large, composite maps of the entire region that were far more accurate than any that had been made before.

Mapmaking has changed dramatically since Clark's early efforts. Over the years, as surveying technology and map design have changed, we have vastly improved our knowledge of the earth's topography, as well as our ability to represent the earth's rounded surface on a map's flat plane. Today, the most detailed and accurate maps are drawn from high-resolution photos taken by satellites.

To imagine Clark's mapmaking difficulties, as well as to appreciate his accomplishment, try this experiment. Without consulting anything but your own memory, try to draw a map of the region you passed through on your way to college. Include the major topographical and other interesting features on the route. Also indicate the groups of people you met or passed near. Alternatively, draw a map of the area around your hometown, including the major features, inhabitants, and travel routes. Make your map as accurate as possible to aid others who might depend on it for their own travels.

Now consider Clark's map carefully. How accurate do you suppose it is? How accurate would it have had to be to be useful? What does the map reveal about the explorers' rate of travel through this region? Why do you suppose they traveled along the winding course of the Missouri River rather than overland?

Cartographers, or mapmakers, have to decide what to include and what to omit from their maps. Those decisions depend on the purposes the map is intended to serve. Under what circumstances and for what purposes was Clark's map created? How many different kinds of information does it contain? What are its dominant features, and why are they emphasized? Imagine yourself in the role of Clark. As you observe your surroundings, what do you see but decide not to record on the map? How would a modern map of the same region differ?

Finally, think about the significance of the maps, written journals, and oral accounts generated by the Lewis and Clark expedition. How did they help change the map of the United States?

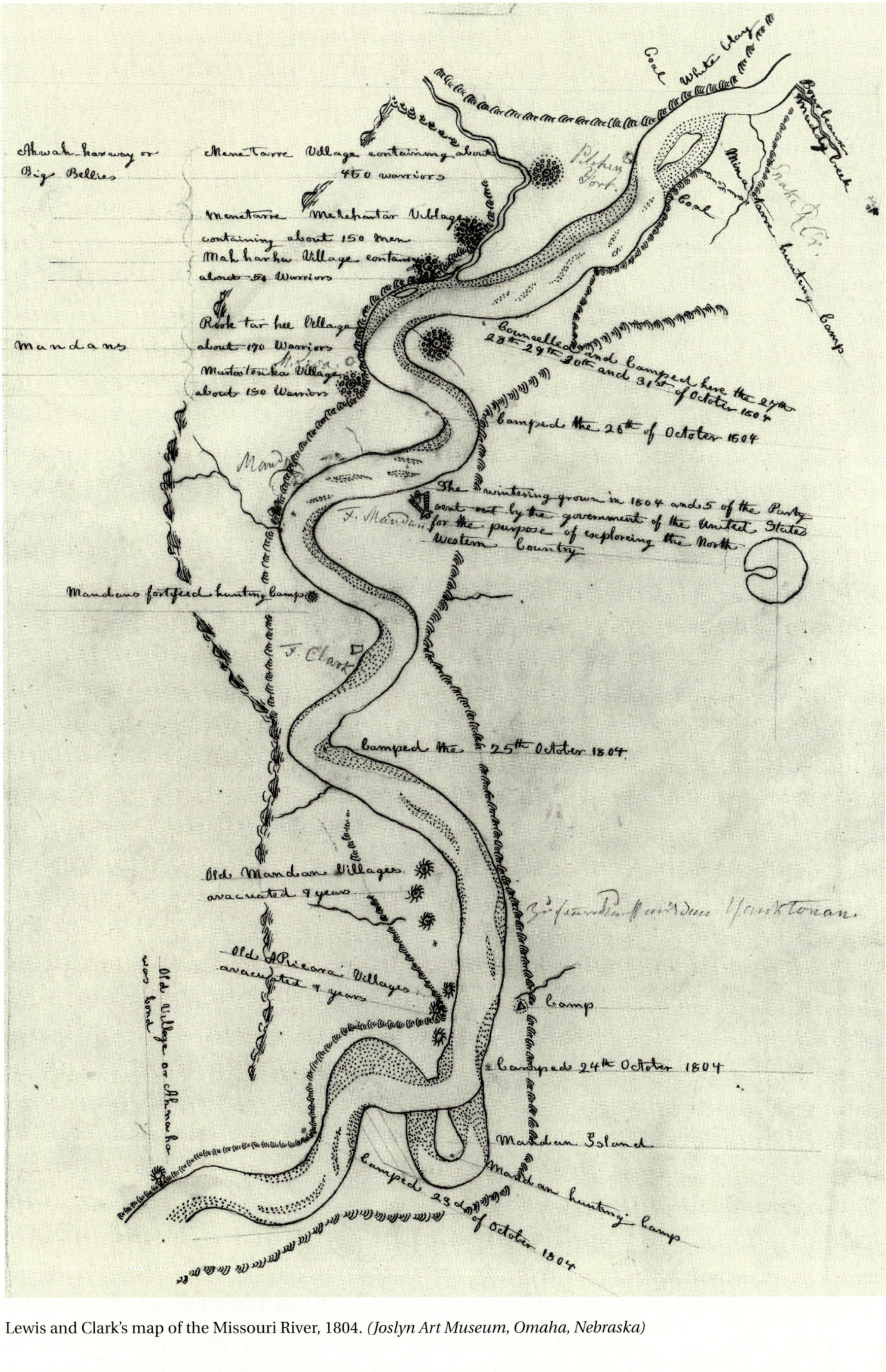

Lewis and Clark's map of the Missouri River, 1804. *(Joslyn Art Museum, Omaha, Nebraska)*

Exploring the Trans-Mississippi West, 1804–1807

With the nation nearly doubled in size following the Louisiana Purchase, President Jefferson sent out exploring expeditions to map the region and establish an American presence there.

Rockies via the Bitterroot Valley and Lolo Pass, down the Columbia to the Pacific coast, and back again, finally reemerging at St. Louis in September 1806. Lewis and Clark's journey fanned American interest in the trans-Mississippi West and demonstrated the feasibility of an overland route to the Pacific.

In 1805 and 1806, Lieutenant Zebulon Pike explored the sources of the Mississippi River in northern Minnesota, then followed that trek with an equally bold venture into the southern Rocky Mountains, where he explored the peak that still bears his name. In the following decade, the government established a string of military posts from Fort Snelling, at the confluence of the Minnesota and Mississippi Rivers, to Fort Smith on the Arkansas. They were intended to secure the American frontier, promote the fur trade, and support white settlement.

The Jeffersonians' blueprint for an agrarian democracy also guided changes in federal land policy. While Federalists had viewed the sale of public land as a source of government revenue, the Jeffersonians were primarily concerned to speed white settlement. Accordingly, the Land Act of 1801 reduced the minimum purchase from 640 to 320 acres, established a generous credit system, and offered 8 percent discounts for cash sales. Over the next year and a half, settlers, speculators, and land companies bought nearly four times as much land as during the entire 1790s. In the years ahead, principles of preemption (which enabled squatters to secure title to land simply by occupying it) and pricing graduation (whereby lands that did not readily sell were offered at discounted prices or given away) were added. Though Jeffersonian land policy fostered widespread speculation and contributed to the Panic of 1819, it speeded the transfer of public land into private hands.

A NATION OF REGIONS

During the early years of the republic, the vast majority of Americans drew their living from the land. In 1800, fully 83 percent of the labor force was engaged in agriculture; that figure had hardly changed 25 years later. Yet people occupied the land differently in various regions of the country. While long-standing differences between the Northeast and the South persisted, a new region of white settlement took shape in the nation's interior.

AGRICULTURAL PRODUCTIVITY IN 1800 AND 1997

	Wheat		Cotton	
	Worker-Hours per Acre	Yield per Acre	Worker-Hours per Acre	Yield per Acre
1800	56.0	15 bushels	185	147 pounds
1997	2.4	40 bushels	4.6	686 pounds

Source: U.S. Bureau of the Census.

The Northeast

In the region stretching from eastern Pennsylvania and New Jersey through New England, family farms dominated the landscape. Because much of New England's land was poor, farmers there often abandoned crop agriculture for the greater profits to be made from dairying and livestock. By contrast, on the richer agricultural lands of New York and Pennsylvania, farmers cultivated the land intensively, planting crops year after year rather than following the customary practice of allowing worn-out fields to lie fallow and recover their fertility. Before 1776, much of the mid-Atlantic landscape had looked cluttered and unkempt, with wide areas still covered by timber and fallow lands lapsing back into brush. Fifty years later, the countryside appeared clean and orderly, its cultivated fields clearly marked by hedges and stone walls.

Farmers in New York's Hudson River valley and southeastern Pennsylvania produced an agricultural surplus, which they exchanged in nearby towns for commodities such as tea, sugar, window glass, and tools. Even there, however, most farmers marketed only what was left over after they had met their own family's needs. "The great effort," reported a European visitor, "was for every farmer to produce anything he required within his own family; and he was esteemed the best farmer, to use a phrase of the day, 'who did everything within himself.'"

Across large areas of the rural Northeast, cash played a small part in economic exchanges. Declared an observant Frenchman, people "supply their needs in the countryside by direct reciprocal exchanges. The tailor and the bootmaker go and do the work of their calling at the home of the farmer . . . who . . . provides the raw material for it and pays for the work in goods. . . . They write down what they give and receive on both sides, and at the end of the year they settle a large variety of exchanges with a very small quantity of coin."

Most farms were not large. By 1800, the average farm in the longer settled areas of New England and the mid-Atlantic states was no more than 100 to 150 acres, down substantially from half a century before, as a result of the continued division of farm property across generations of fathers and sons. Even in southeastern Pennsylvania, probably the most productive agricultural region in the entire Northeast, economic opportunity was declining. Long and continuous cropping had robbed the soil of its fertility, forcing farmers to bring more marginal land under cultivation. By 1800, nearly 20 percent of the area's male taxpayers were single, clear evidence that young men were finding it harder to establish themselves on the land before taking a wife.

Frustrated at the backwardness of much American agriculture, some individuals called for more "scientific" practices. Leading citizens like John Adams joined in creating agricultural associations such as the Massachusetts Society for Promoting Agriculture that established agricultural libraries and issued publications. Others, such as Elkanah Watson, a prosperous businessman turned gentleman farmer, urged farmers to turn their attention to raising the fine-fleeced merino sheep that agricultural reformers promised would bring newfound prosperity.

Watson was instrumental as well in creating the nation's first agricultural fairs in western Massachusetts. Part visionary, part huckster, and part enthusiast for scientifically based farming, Watson intended the fairs' displays of equipment, animals, and produce not only to educate farmers but to "excite a lively spirit of competition" and thus energize them as well. His efforts succeeded beyond his fondest hopes, for within a few years rural folk by the thousands were converging on the annual Berkshire gatherings. In a short while, these precursors to the county fairs that have remained a staple of rural and small town American life had spread from Maine to Virginia and as far west as Illinois. In addition to farming, growing numbers of rural folk also worked as artisans or day laborers in surrounding towns or toiled in the small-scale manufactories—grain and saw mills, potash works, and iron forges—that dotted the rural landscape. It would be another generation, however, before urban factories began luring large numbers of young men off the land.

Though this Pennsylvania scene features cattle rather than merino sheep, it reveals the interests of farmers and more elegantly attired gentlemen in the commercial benefits of "scientific" livestock breeding. Note what appear to be plowing contests in the background. *(John A. Woodside,* A Country Fair in Pennsylvania, *1824, from the Collection of Harry T. Peters, Jr.)*

By 1830, the relentless demands of the Northeast's expanding population for land and a wide variety of wood products had significantly transformed the region's once heavily forested landscape. Iron furnaces dotting the countryside consumed firewood voraciously. The Union Furnace in New Jersey exhausted a forest of nearly 20,000 acres in less than 15 years and had to be abandoned, a fate duplicated at the Sterling Ironworks in southern New York, as well as at Stockbridge and Pittsfield in Massachusetts. The production of pot and pearl ash, turpentine, and planking for wooden houses and fencing further depleted forest ranges.

More than anything, though, it was the demand for heating fuel during the long winter months that made the woodcutter's axe ring. "So much of the comfort and convenience of our life," observed Benjamin Franklin, "depends on the article of *fire*." Rural households consumed from 20 to 30 cords of firewood annually in the highly inefficient open fireplaces that warmed their homes. As the region's coastal cities grew and nearby woodlots were exhausted, wood had to be fetched from as far away as 100 miles. By 1800, Bostonians were dependent on wood shipped in from Maine and New Hampshire. Although deserted farmlands here and there lapsed into new growth, thus contributing a bit of ecological renewal, the northeastern coastal plain had been largely denuded of forest.

The Nation's Cities

Though most Northeasterners lived on the land or in the small towns dotting the countryside, increasing numbers of people dwelt in the region's cities. Between 1790 and 1830, the nation's population increased by nearly 230 percent. During those same years, urban places of more than 2,500 residents grew almost twice as fast. In 1790, there were only five cities holding more than 10,000 inhabitants. By 1810 there were 23 such places, including four cities of over 50,000 and one, New York, with well over 100,000 people. Though fledgling cities such as Pittsburgh, Cincinnati, and Saint Louis dotted river valleys of the western interior, the majority of the nation's burgeoning urban centers were located along the northeastern coast.

Though increasing rapidly in population, these urban places were small in area, "walking cities" in which residents could easily stroll from one side of town to the other. The result was increasing crowding and congestion. Asa Greene, a New York physician, observed ruefully that to cross Broadway "you must button your coat tightly about you . . . settle your hat firmly on your head, look up street and down street . . . to see what carts and carriages are upon you, and then run for your life."

Along with crowding came serious problems of public health and safety. While Philadelphia led the way in street paving, dust in dry weather and mud when it rained were constant sources of complaint. One alarmed citizen, finding a man embedded up to his neck in a mud hole following a violent downpour, offered to help pull him out. "No need to worry," replied the man, "I have a horse underneath me." So, at least, went a popular fable.

More than dirt clogged urban streets in the early nineteenth century, for residents dumped their garbage there, privies leached into open drains, and kitchen waste was tossed out the door. Untethered cows, goats, and sheep left their droppings as well.

Francis Guy, *Winter Scene in Brooklyn,* c. 1817–1820. Many areas of early nineteenth-century cities retained a small-town, neighborhood atmosphere, as this Brooklyn scene reveals. *(The Brooklyn Museum, 97.13, Gift of the Brooklyn Institute of Arts and Sciences)*

Though one urban dweller regarded the hogs that scavenged off such refuse as "disgusting," she acknowledged that without them the streets would soon be choked with filth.

Under such conditions, diseases like typhoid and dysentery, which spread via contaminated water supplies, took a continuous human toll. The aristocratic John Pintard attributed the 1832 cholera epidemic in New York City to "the lower classes of intemperate dissolute & filthy people huddled together like swine in their polluted habitations." Nothing, he concluded, could be done to help them. "The . . . quicker . . . [their] dispatch," he concluded, "the sooner the malady will cease." Such attitudes, combined with ignorance about the causes and etiology of disease, put urban populations continuously at risk.

Though buildings and streets were virtually devoid of the commercial signage that would emblazon American cities by the middle of the nineteenth century, the urban economies of these northeastern cities hummed with activity. As during the colonial era, economic life continued to center on the wharves where sailing ships from around the world tied up and the warehouses where overseas cargoes were unloaded. Sailors and ships' captains, often speaking unfamiliar tongues, filled the harbor-front taverns with colorful stories of far-off lands, adding raucous behavior and at times an edge of danger to urban life.

Though true industrialization would not become evident in the cities of the northeast until the second half of the nineteenth century, large-scale manufacturing was beginning to transform their economies by 1830. The expansion of southern cotton production was turning Philadelphia into a textile manufacturing center, while places like New York City and Newark, New Jersey, were producing shoes and other manufactured products. As these enterprises expanded, artisanal production began to give way to factory-based wage labor.

As these urban places evolved, the gap between richer and poorer inhabitants widened. Prosperous merchants, reaping the rewards of overseas trade and investing much of their profit in budding manufacturing enterprises, rested securely at the top. Below them came an aspiring middle class of shopkeepers and professional men whose families shared modestly in the general prosperity. At the bottom of the human pyramid lay a spreading underclass of common laborers, dock workers, and the unemployed, their lives taken up with a continuing struggle for survival. Though rich and poor had often lived close together in colonial cities, rising land values now forced the lower classes into crowded alleys and tenements, while more prosperous urban dwellers congregated in separate, fashionable neighborhoods.

By 1830, the living standard of many middle- and upper-class families had significantly improved. As wills and estate inventories show, such households were now more likely to possess table linens and china bowls, store-bought furniture, and tailor-made clothes, the artifacts of an expanding consumer economy. Material prosperity, however, passed most urban folk by.

The South

Life was very different in the American South, a region stretching from Maryland to Georgia, and west across the southern interior. As the nineteenth century began, much of southern agriculture was in disarray. Falling prices, worn-out land, and the destruction wrought by the Revolutionary War had left the Chesapeake's tobacco economy in shambles. One English traveler reported that throughout much of the upper Shenandoah Valley crops were "so intermixed with extensive tracts of waste land, worn out by the culture of tobacco . . . that on the whole the country had the appearance of barrenness." The extensive loss of slaves added to the region's economic woes.

Southern planters experimented with wheat and other grains in an effort to bolster their sagging fortunes, but regional recovery began in earnest when they turned to a new staple crop—cotton. Especially valuable was the hardier short-staple variety that could be successfully cultivated across large areas of the southern interior. While its fibers could be separated from the plant's sticky, green seeds only with great difficulty, Eli Whitney's cotton gin effectively solved that problem.

In 1790, the South had produced only 3,135 bales of cotton. By 1820, output had mushroomed to 334,378 bales. In 1805, cotton accounted for 30 percent of the nation's agricultural exports; by 1820, it exceeded half. Across both the old coastal South and the newly developing states of Alabama, Mississippi, and Tennessee, cotton was becoming king. The growing demand of textile mills in England and the American Northeast provided the essential stimulus, but a portentous combination of other factors made possible the South's dramatic response: wonderfully productive virgin soil; a long, steamy growing season; an ample supply of slave labor; and southern planters with long experience in the production and marketing of staple crops.

As we shall see in later chapters, the swing to cotton marked a momentous turning point for both the South and the nation. Not only did it raise the value of prime southern land and open economic opportunity for countless southern whites, but it also increased the demand for black field hands and breathed new life into the institution of slavery. Some of the escalating demand for slave labor was met from overseas. In 1803 alone, Georgia and South Carolina imported 20,000 new slaves, as southern planters and northern suppliers rushed to fill the need before the slave trade ended in 1807. Much of the demand for agricultural labor, however, would be met by the internal slave trade that moved African Americans from the worn-

Slave labor, provided by women as well as men, followed the spread of cotton cultivation into new lands of the southern interior. This Benjamin Latrobe sketch is of *An Overseer Doing His Duty.* *(Maryland Historical Society, Baltimore, Maryland)*

out lands of the Chesapeake to the lush cotton fields of the Deep South.

Trans-Appalachia

West of the Appalachian Mountains a third, distinctive region of settlement was forming as the nineteenth century began. In the eighteenth century, European Americans had called the interior beyond the area of white settlement the "backcountry," because their lives were still dominated by the centers of economic and political activity along the coast. As attention began to shift toward settlement of the trans-Appalachian West, however, people spoke increasingly of an ever expanding "frontier."

Trans-Appalachia extended west from the Appalachian Mountains to the Mississippi River and south from the Great Lakes to the Gulf of Mexico. In 1790, scarcely 100,000 white settlers lived there. By 1810, their number had swollen to nearly a million. A decade later, augmented by people like Mary and

The Movement of White and Black Population into Trans-Appalachia, 1790–1830

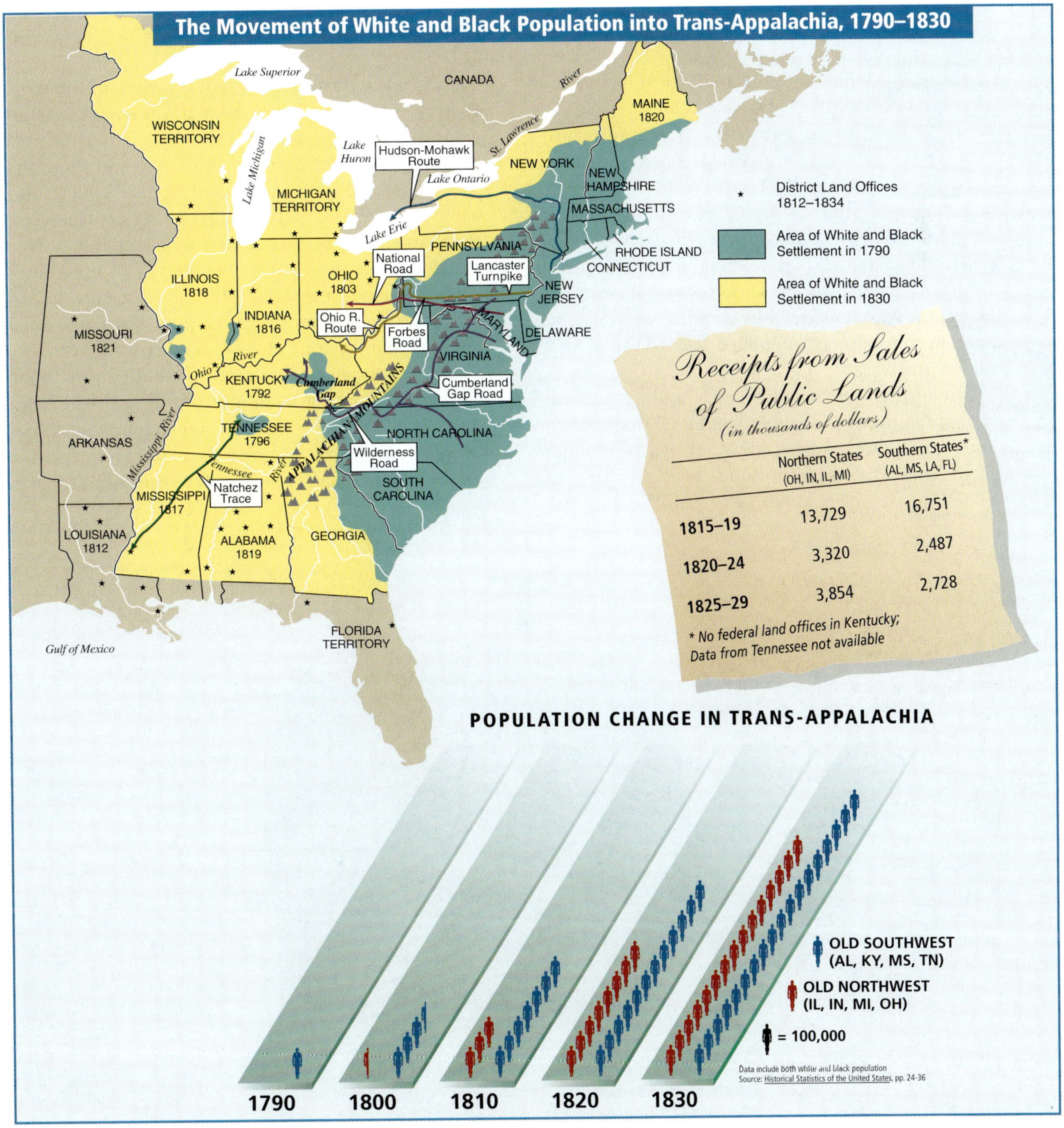

Receipts from Sales of Public Lands (in thousands of dollars)

	Northern States (OH, IN, IL, MI)	Southern States* (AL, MS, LA, FL)
1815–19	13,729	16,751
1820–24	3,320	2,487
1825–29	3,854	2,728

* No federal land offices in Kentucky; Data from Tennessee not available

Technology Changes the American People

ELI WHITNEY AND THE COTTON GIN

Though the technological innovations of the early American republic may seem primitive, they generated intense enthusiasm at the time. Observed Tench Coxe, an ardent promoter of American economic development, "Machines, ingeniously constructed, will give . . . immense assistance" in developing the nation. Coxe's comment echoed the widely held belief that technological genius was embedded in the American character and that commitment to applied science would foster human progress.

One of the most significant technological breakthroughs in the early republic was Eli Whitney's cotton gin. By the 1790s, cotton cultivation was beginning to expand across the American South, as planters began to experiment with the short-staple variety of the crop. Though its fibers were less luxuriant than the long-staple cotton that flourished in the hot coastal lowlands and sea islands of Georgia and South Carolina, the hardier short-staple variety could be successfully cultivated in large areas of the southern interior. In contrast to the long, silky fibers of long-staple cotton, however, short-staple cotton clung tenaciously to the plant's sticky, green seeds, making it difficult to prepare the raw cotton for manufacturing into cloth. A slave could clean no more than a pound of short-staple cotton a day.

During these same years, demand for cotton of all sorts was growing in England and the American Northeast, where the weaving and spinning machines of new textile factories created an insatiable appetite for the crop. Demand and supply began to converge in

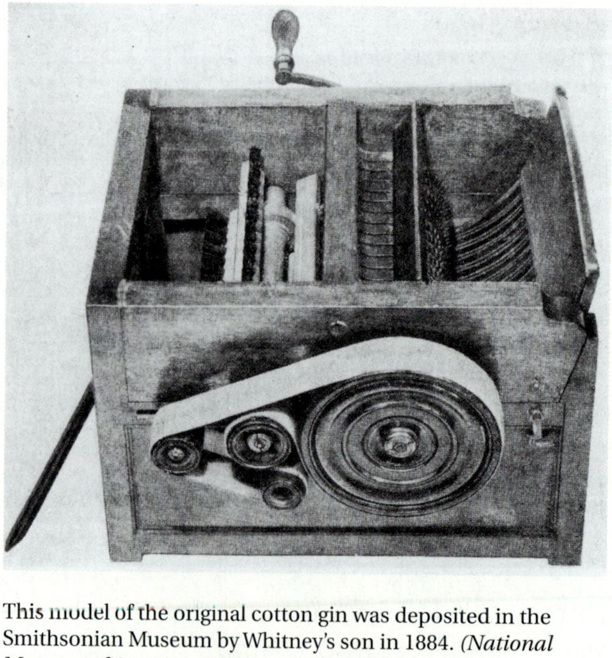

This model of the original cotton gin was deposited in the Smithsonian Museum by Whitney's son in 1884. *(National Museum of American History, Smithsonian Institution)*

Though others had tinkered with mechanical devices for stripping cotton fibers from their seeds, Whitney was the first to develop a successful gin. *(Library of Congress)*

1793 when Eli Whitney, a Yale graduate then supporting himself as a teacher on a Georgia plantation, turned his mind to the problem of short-staple cotton and its seeds. Within a short time he had designed a functioning model of a machine he called a "cotton gin." In conception it was disarmingly simple, nothing more than a wooden box containing a roller, equipped with wire teeth, designed to pull the fibers through a comblike barrier, thus stripping them from the seeds. A hand crank activated the mechanism. The implications of Whitney's invention were immediately apparent, for with this crude device a slave could clean up to 50 pounds of short-staple cotton in a day.

As Chapter 9 explains, a variety of circumstances combined to produce the cotton boom that exploded across the American South during the first half of the nineteenth century, a boom that held profound implications for black and white Americans (and in the Civil War crisis, for the nation at large). The cotton gin, fashioned by hand in a plantation shed and then improved by other craftsmen in succeeding decades, played a major role in that fateful development.

Whitney patented his device under the first federal Patent Law of 1794 but exhausted most of the profit it produced protecting his patent rights against infringement. Better times, however, lay ahead. Though he reaped little financial advantage from his invention, he opened a factory in Connecticut manufacturing firearms by an ingenious system of interchangeable parts. A government contract finally brought him financial success.

By the late nineteenth and twentieth centuries, successful technological innovations would require large amounts of venture capital, sophisticated engineering know-how, and large-scale organizational support. In the early years of the republic, however, the tinkering of lone inventors could produce dramatic results.

Historians frequently disagree over the extent to which heroic inventors are able to alter the course of history. Some assert that men and women capable of thinking beyond the conventional wisdom of their time and envisioning solutions to complicated technological problems can move history decisively in new directions. Others argue that broad economic and social forces determine the basic path that technology takes and that most inventions are as much the result of chance or simple trial and error as of individual genius.

How do you think Eli Whitney should be regarded? Did his cotton gin transform the nation's history, or did it represent little more than the work of a clever craftsman with the patience to solve a bothersome problem? Was his work pivotal, or is it likely that someone else would have come along to solve the problem of short-staple cotton if Whitney had never traveled into the South? Think about comparable technological breakthroughs in your own time.

Sources: Constance Green, *Eli Whitney and the Birth of American Technology* (1956); Brooke Hindle, ed., *Material Culture in the Wooden Age* (1981).

As settlers moved west, they cleared the land of trees for agriculture and produced lumber for houses and fences, as this sketch of a sawmill in upstate New York suggests. *(Library of Congress)*

James Harrod, there were over a million more. There, in a broad and constantly shifting "middle ground," resident Indians and white intruders engaged in intricate patterns of cultural, economic, sexual, and military exchange.

White settlers entered the region by wagon along Zane's Trace and other tortuous, overland routes into Kentucky and Tennessee and clambered aboard flatboats at Pittsburgh every spring when the water was high enough to float down the Ohio River to destinations at Wheeling, Cincinnati, and Louisville. The human tide appeared to grow with each passing year. "Genessee fever" brought thousands of settlers surging into the river country of western New York. "The woods are full of new settlers," wrote an amazed observer near Batavia, New York, in 1805. "Axes are resounding, and the trees literally falling around us as we passed." By 1812, 200,000 souls lived in the western part of the state, where scarcely 30,000 whites had resided only 20 years before. "America is breaking up and going west!" exclaimed the British traveler Morris Birkbeck in wonder. At the time, it seemed literally true.

Settlers were drawn by the promotions of speculators seeking their fortunes in the sale of western land. Between 1790 and 1820, land companies hawked vast areas of New York, Ohio, and Kentucky to prospective settlers like James and Mary Harrod. The most extravagant ventures often failed, but countless others succeeded, returning handsome profits to their investors. Individual settlers shared in the speculative fever, often going deeply into debt to buy extra land for resale when population increased and land prices rose.

North of the Ohio River, settlement followed the grid pattern prescribed in the Land Ordinance of 1785. There mixed, free-labor agriculture took hold and towns such as Columbus and Cincinnati emerged to provide services and cultural amenities for the surrounding population. South of the Ohio, people distributed themselves more randomly across the land, much as their ancestors had done back east. In Kentucky and Tennessee, free-labor agriculture was soon challenged by the spread of slavery-based cotton.

As people poured into the region, they established churches, schools, and colleges. Transylvania University, founded in Lexington, Kentucky, in 1780, was the first college west of the Appalachians. Even so, trans-Appalachia retained a reputation for its rough and colorful ways. While life could be depressingly lonesome for families lost in the hollows of the Cumberland Mountains of eastern Tennessee, in towns along the Ohio River boatmen and gamblers, con men and speculators gave civic life a raucous quality. And everywhere the transience, youthfulness, and predominant maleness of the population kept society unsettled.

The constant drama of migration together with the grandeur of the natural surroundings stoked people's imaginations. No characters were more famous in popular folklore than western adventurers such as Daniel Boone. None was more colorful than the mythical riverman Mike Fink, "half man, half alligator," who could "whip his weight in grizzly bears." And nothing revealed more graphically the West's rawness than the eye-gouging, ear-biting, no-holds-barred, "rough and tumble" brawls that regularly erupted.

As settlers arrived, they began the long process of transforming the region's heavily forested land. In the mountainous areas of western Pennsylvania, entire hillsides were denuded of trees that anxious travelers dragged behind their wagons as makeshift brakes during the jolting rides downhill. Believing, erroneously, that the unforested "oak openings" scattered through the woods of Ohio and southern Michigan were infertile, many farmers staked their claims where the trees grew thickest and set about the arduous task of clearing the land. They followed the time-honored practice of cutting a girdle of bark off the trees and then setting them on fire or leaving them to die in place while planting crops around the decaying hulks. "The scene is truly savage," observed an English traveler used to the orderly landscape of his own country. "Immense trees stripped of their foliage, and half consumed by fire extend their sprawling limbs . . . now bleached by the weather." By this method, a family could clear 3 to 5 acres a year for cultivation.

The relentless demands for wood generated by the growing white population added to the assault on the region's forests. As expanding areas of trans-Appalachia came under the farmers' plows, forests and wildlife gave way.

INDIAN–WHITE RELATIONS IN THE EARLY REPUBLIC

The years from 1790 to the end of the 1820s witnessed a dramatic turning point in Indian–white relations. As the era began, Native American tribes still controlled vast areas of the trans-Appalachian interior. North of the Ohio River, the Shawnee, Delaware, and Miami formed a western confederacy capable of mustering several thousand warriors. South of the river lived five major tribal groups: the Cherokee, Creek, Choctaw, Chickasaw, and Seminole. Together, these southern tribes totaled nearly 60,000 people. By 1830, however, the balance of power between Indians and European Americans had shifted decisively as white settlers streamed into the region (bringing black slaves with them south of the Ohio River) to occupy the land.

As white expansion increased, Indian tribes devised various strategies of resistance and survival. Among the Cherokee, many followed a path of peaceful accommodation, while others like the Shawnee and the Creek rose in armed resistance. Neither strategy was altogether successful, for by 1830 the Indians faced a future of continued acculturation, military defeat, and forced migration to lands west of the Mississippi River.

Less dramatic but no less important, during these years the social and cultural separation of Indians and white Americans increased sharply. As late as the 1780s, Native Americans still walked the streets of Boston and Philadelphia, while Indians and white Americans interacted regularly as allies and antagonists, traders and marriage partners. By 1830, such contacts were much less common. East of the Appalachians, whites now regarded Indians as exotic curiosities, while west of the mountains the Indians' increasing confinement on reservations, together with the forced removal of northern tribes to areas west of the Mississippi River, began a similar process of racial separation.

The Initial Goals of Indian Policy

During the years from 1790 to 1830, the federal government established a set of Indian policies that would govern Indian–white relations through much of the nineteenth century. Intended initially to promote the eventual assimilation of Native Americans into white society, those policies speeded the transfer of Indian land to white settlers and helped set the stage for a later, more dramatic program of Indian removal.

With the government's initial "conquest" theory rendered ineffective by the Indians' refusal to regard themselves as a conquered people (see Chapter 7), government officials shifted course by recognizing Indian rights to the land they inhabited and declaring that future land transfers be accomplished by treaty agreements.

Henry Knox, Washington's first secretary of war, laid out the government's new position in 1789. The Indians, he explained, "being the prior occupants of the soil, possess the right of the soil." It should not be taken from them "unless by their free consent, or by the right of conquest in case of just war." To dispossess them for other reasons "would violate the fundamental laws of nature and . . . justice." Though Knox helped establish a more humane Indian policy, the acquisition of Indian land for white settlement remained the overarching goal.

The new treaty-based strategy proved effective, as Native American leaders agreed to cede land in return for trade goods, yearly annuity payments, and assurances that no further demands would be made on them. Reluctant tribal leaders could often be persuaded to cooperate by warnings about the inevitable spread of white settlement, or more tractable chieftains could be found. In these ways, vast areas of trans-Appalachia passed into the possession of white settlers.

As white settlers streamed across the nation's interior, state and federal governments wrung land cessions from the Indians. By 1830, only the southeastern tribes still controlled significant areas of their ancestral land east of the Mississippi River. Labels in red indicate the major Native American tribes.

Federal policy also attempted to regulate the fur trade. Both Native Americans and whites found benefit in the trade. The Indians, in return for their abundant furs, secured goods such as blankets, guns, rum, and ironware that they valued highly. White traders, by contrast, acquired highly desired furs in exchange for inexpensive trade goods.

While the fur trade brought handsome profits to private companies such as John Jacob Astor's American Fur Company (1808), it often worked to the Indians' disadvantage. Trade goods frequently transmitted diseases such as measles and smallpox. Indians, moreover, became dependent on the trade because it provided the only certain supplies of coveted goods such as rum and firearms. As the demand for furs and pelts increased, moreover, Native Americans overtrapped their hunting grounds, forcing them to compete with other tribes for access to fresh sources of furs farther to the west.

In 1796, in an effort to reduce fraud and its attendant conflict, Congress created government trading posts, or "factories," where Indians could come for fair treatment. The system lasted until 1822 but never supplanted private traders as Congress had intended.

A third objective of federal Indian policy was to civilize and Christianize the Native Americans, then assimilate them into white society. In the trans-Appalachian West, most settlers regarded Indians as savages to be moved out of white settlement's way. In the East, however, clergymen and government officials displayed greater concern over the Native Americans' well-being. While uneasy over Indian "savagery," easterners admired the Native Americans' "bravery," "independence," and "simplicity of life," qualities resembling highly valued democratic virtues.

Following the revolution, Moravians, Quakers, and Baptists sent scores of missionaries to live among the Indians, preach the Gospel, and teach the benefits of white civilization. John Stewart, a freeborn, part-Indian mulatto, was one such missionary. From 1815 to his death in 1821, he preached to the Wyandotte near Sandusky, Ohio. Among the most selfless were Quaker missionaries who labored with the Iroquois in New York, attempting to inspire conversion and improve the conditions of Iroquois life. In spite of the missionaries' best efforts, however, most Native Americans remained aloof, because the chasm between Christianity and their own religion was wide (see Chapter 1), and the missionaries' denigration of Indian culture was clearly apparent.

Education was another weapon of the assimilationists. In 1793, Congress appropriated $20,000 to promote literacy, agriculture, and vocational instruction. With government encouragement, missionaries established schools in which Indian children were taught reading, writing, and vocational skills. The vast majority of Indian children never attended the mission schools. Among those who did, many stayed but a short while, they and their parents preferring the education offered by family and tribe over the culturally threatening environment of the white-run schools.

Although the assimilationists cared deeply about the physical and spiritual fate of Native American people, they showed little sympathy for Indian culture, for they demanded that Native Americans give up their language, religion, dress, and extended family arrangements—that is, cease being Indian and adopt the ways of white society. Assimilation or removal were the alternatives posed by even the most benevolent whites.

Strategies of Survival: The Iroquois and the Cherokee

Faced with the steady loss of land and tribal autonomy, Native Americans devised various strategies of resistance and survival. Among the Iroquois, a prophet named Handsome Lake, who had fought with England during the Revolutionary War and then succumbed to the despair of military defeat and reservation life, led his people through a process of cultural revitalization. In 1799, following a series of trancelike visions, he preached a combination of Indian and white ways that included temperance, peace, land retention, and the rituals of *Gaiwiio,* a new religion combining elements of Christianity and traditional Iroquois belief. His vision, providing a new definition of what it meant to be an Indian, offered hope and renewed pride for the Iroquois in the midst of their radically transformed lives.

Far to the south, the Cherokee followed a different path of accommodation. As the nineteenth century began, the Cherokee still controlled millions of acres in Tennessee, Georgia, and the western Carolinas. Their land base, however, was shrinking. By 1800, more than 40 Cherokee towns had disappeared.

Southern state governments, responding to white demands for Indian land, sought ways to undercut tribal autonomy. In 1801, Tennessee unilaterally brought Cherokee territory under state authority. As violence escalated along the borders between white and Indian settlements, state officials demanded that Native Americans accused of horse stealing and other crimes stand trial in state courts. The Cherokee, who had their own system of justice and distrusted the state courts with their all-white juries and exclusion of Indian testimony, rejected Tennessee's demands.

In Cherokee councils, a group of full-blood leaders called for armed resistance. Better to stand and fight, they argued, than follow the false path of accommodation. Others, however, including mixed-bloods such as John Ross, insisted that accommodation offered the best hope for survival. After a bitter struggle, the accommodationists won out. Soon they began to bring the tribe's scattered villages under a common government, the better to defend their freedom and prevent the further loss of land. In 1808, the Cherokee National Council adopted a written code combining elements of American and Indian law, and in 1827 it devised a written constitution patterned after those of nearby states. Members of the council accompanied it with a bold declaration that the Cherokee constituted an independent nation with full sovereignty over their lands. In 1829, the Cherokee government made it an offense punishable by death for any member of the tribe to transfer land to white ownership without the consent of tribal authorities.

Meanwhile, the process of social and cultural accommodation, encouraged by Cherokee leaders such as Ross and promoted by white missionaries and

Sequoyah, who sat for this portrait in 1838, devised the Cherokee alphabet, which formed the basis for the first written Indian language in North America. *(The Newberry Library, Chicago)*

government agents, went forward. Missionaries opened a school for Cherokee youth in 1804 on the Hiwasee River on the Tennessee–Georgia boundary and established a boarding school near present-day Chattanooga 12 years later. They stepped up their religious activities as well, baptizing Cherokee into the Christian faith.

As the Cherokee turned from their traditional hunting, gathering, and farming economy to settled agriculture, many moved from town settlements onto individual farmsteads, while others established sawmills, country stores, and blacksmith shops. In contrast to traditional Cherokee practices of sharing and the communal ownership of property, notions of private property took hold.

The majority of Cherokee people continued to inhabit crude log cabins and live a hand-to-mouth existence. Some mixed-bloods, however, like Joseph Vann who learned English and understood how to deal with white authorities, accumulated hundreds of acres of fertile land and scores of black slaves. Since the mid-eighteenth century, the Cherokee had held a few runaway blacks in slavelike conditions. During the early nineteenth century, Cherokee slavery expanded and became more harsh. By 1820, there were nearly 1,300 black slaves in the Cherokee nation. A Cherokee law of 1824 forbade intermarriage with blacks. The accelerating spread of cotton cultivation increased demand for slave labor among Cherokee as well as southern whites. As accommodation increased, slave ownership became a mark of social standing.

By 1820, the strategy of peaceful accommodation had brought clear rewards. Tribal government was stronger, and the sense of Cherokee identity was reasonably secure. Before long, however, the Cherokee's success would prove their undoing, for as their self-confidence grew, so did the hostility of neighboring whites impatient to gain possession of their land. That hostility would erupt in a final campaign to remove the Cherokee from their land forever (see Chapter 12).

Patterns of Armed Resistance: The Shawnee and the Creek

Not all tribes proved so accommodating to white expansion. Faced with growing threats to their political and cultural survival, the Shawnee and Creek nations rose in armed resistance. Conflict was smoldering as the nineteenth century began; it burst into open flame during the War of 1812.

In the late 1780s, chieftains such as Little Turtle of the Miami and Blue Jacket of the Shawnee had led a series of devastating raids across Indiana, Ohio, and western Pennsylvania, creating panic among white settlers and challenging the federal government's control of the Old Northwest. After two efforts to quell the uprising had failed, President Washington determined to smash the Indians' resistance once and for all. In 1794, a federal army led by the old Revolutionary War general Anthony Wayne defeated 2,000 Indian warriors in the Battle of Fallen Timbers. Shortly after, in the Treaty of Greenville, the assembled chiefs ceded the southern two-thirds of Ohio. That cession opened the heart of the Old Northwest to white control. In subsequent years, additional treaties further reduced the Indians' land base, driving the tribes more tightly in upon each other.

By 1809, two Shawnee leaders, the brothers Tecumseh and Elskwatawa, the latter known to whites as "the Prophet," were traveling among the region's tribes attempting to forge an alliance against the invading whites. They established headquarters at an ancient Indian town named Kithtippecanoe in northern Indiana. Soon it became a gathering point for Native Americans from across the region responding to the messages of cultural pride, land retention, and pan-Indian resistance presented by the Shawnee brothers.

Between 1809 and 1811, Tecumseh carried his message of Indian nationalism and military resistance south to the Creek and Cherokee. His speeches rang with bitterness. "The white race is a wicked race," he told his listeners. "Since the days when the white race first came in contact with the red men, there has been a continual series of aggressions. The hunting grounds are fast disappearing, and they are driving the red men farther and farther to the west. . . . The only hope . . . is a war of extermination against the paleface." Though the southern tribes refused to join, by 1811 over 1,000 fighting men had gathered at Kithtippecanoe.

Alarmed, the governor of the Indiana Territory, William Henry Harrison, surrounded the Indian stronghold with a force of 1,000 soldiers. At dawn on November 7, 1811, 400 Indian warriors assaulted Harrison's lines. After a furious encounter, the victorious Harrison counted over 150 warriors dead. Before retiring to the territorial capital at Vincennes, he burned Kithtippecanoe to the ground.

Over the next several months, Tecumseh's followers, taking advantage of the recent outbreak of the War of 1812 and aided by British troops from Canada, carried out devastating raids across Indiana and southern Michigan. Together, they crushed American armies at Detroit and Fort Nelson and followed up with forays against Fort Wayne. The tide turned, however, at the Battle of the Thames near Detroit, where Harrison inflicted a grievous defeat on a combined British and Indian force. Among those slain was Tecumseh.

The American victory at the Thames signaled an end to Indian resistance in the Old Northwest.

Beginning in 1815, American settlers surged once more across Ohio and Indiana and pressed on into Illinois and Michigan.

To the south, the Creek challenged white intruders with similar militancy. By 1800, white settlers were pushing onto Creek lands in northwestern Georgia and central Alabama. Although some Creek leaders urged accommodation, others, called Red Sticks, prepared to fight. The embers of this smoldering conflict were fanned into flame by an aggressive Tennessee militia commander named Andrew Jackson. Citing Creek atrocities against "defenseless women and children," Jackson in 1808 urged President Jefferson to endorse a campaign against the "ruthless foe."

He got his chance in the summer of 1813, when the Red Sticks carried out a series of frontier raids, killing and scalping two white families and capping their campaign with an assault on Fort Mims on the Alabama River where they killed as many as 500 people, women and children among them. News of the tragedy raised bitter cries for revenge. "When the tomahawk and the scalping knife are drawn in the cabins of our peaceful and unsuspecting citizens," declared the Tennessee legislature, "it is time, high time to prepare . . . for defense."

At the head of 5,000 Tennessee and Kentucky militia, augmented by Cherokee, Choctaw, and Chickasaw warriors eager to punish their traditional Creek enemies, Jackson launched his long-awaited attack. As he moved south, the ferocity of the fighting increased. Davey Crockett later reported that the militia volunteers shot the Red Sticks down "like dogs." The Indians gave like measure in return.

The climactic battle of the Creek War came in March 1814 at Horseshoe Bend, on the Tallapoosa River in central Alabama. There, in the fortified town of Tohopeka, 1,000 Creek warriors made their stand against fourteen hundred state troops and 600 Cherokee allies. While American cannon fire raked the Creek defenses, the allied Cherokee crossed the river to cut off retreat. In the battle that followed, over 800 Native Americans died, more than in any other Indian–white battle in American history.

Jackson followed up his victory with a scorched-earth sweep through the remaining Red Stick towns. With no hope left, Red Eagle, one of the few remaining Red Stick leaders, walked alone into Jackson's camp and addressed the American commander: "General Jackson, I am not afraid of you. I fear no man, for I am a Creek warrior. I have nothing to request in behalf of myself; you can kill me if you desire. But I come to beg you to send for the women and children of the war party, who are now starving in the woods. . . . I am now done fighting."

Jackson allowed Red Eagle and his followers to return home, but in August 1814 he exacted his final revenge by constructing Fort Jackson on the Hickory Ground, the most sacred spot of the Creek nation. Over the following months, he seized 22 million acres, nearly two-thirds of the Creek domain. Before his Indian-fighting days were over, Jackson would acquire for the United States, through treaty or military conquest, nearly three-fourths of Alabama and Florida, a third of Tennessee, and a fifth of Georgia and Mississippi.

Just as Tecumseh's death had signaled the end of Indian resistance in the North, so Jackson's defeat of the Creek at Horseshoe Bend broke the back of Indian defenses in the South. With all possibility of armed resistance gone, Native Americans gave way before the swelling tide of white settlement.

PERFECTING A DEMOCRATIC SOCIETY

Throughout our nation's history, the American people have launched a variety of reform movements aimed at achieving social justice and bringing the conditions of daily life into conformity with the nation's democratic ideals. The first of those reform eras occurred in the early nineteenth century.

The Revolutionary Heritage

Reform was inspired in part by democratic ideals fostered during the Revolution and still fresh in Americans' minds. Preeminent among them was the principle of social equality. In part, this meant equality of opportunity, the notion that people should have a chance to rise as far as ability and ambition would carry them. Such an idea appealed to social democrats, for it spoke of setting privilege aside and giving everyone an equal chance. Social conservatives could embrace it as well, for it could be used to justify the social inequalities that individual effort often produced. The doctrine of social equality had a powerful moral dimension as well, because it implied an equality of worth among individuals, no matter their social standing. Though Americans generally accepted differences of wealth and social position, they were less willing to tolerate social pretension or the assumption that such differences made some people better than others.

The Evangelical Impulse

More than revolutionary idealism lay behind the concern over social justice, for a surge of evangelical religion inspired the reform impulse also. Throughout our history, religion has been a major force in American public life. This was true during the years of the early republic, when a wave of religious revivalism known as the Second Great Awakening swept across the American nation. From its beginnings in the 1790s through much of the nineteenth century, and in settings as different as the Cane Ridge district of backwoods Kentucky and the sophisticated cities of the Northeast, Americans by the tens of thousands sought personal salvation and found a sense of social belonging in the shared experience of religious enthusiasm.

Displayed most spectacularly among ordinary folk gathered in Methodist and Baptist camp meetings, the revivals reached across boundaries of class and race. Rough-hewn itinerant preachers, black as well as white, many of them theologically untrained but all of them afire with religious conviction, carried the Gospel message from place to place, in the process knitting networks of believers closely together.

In 1809, Benjamin Latrobe, principal architect of the new Capitol building in Washington, D.C., and shrewd observer of the American scene, visited a Methodist camp meeting on the Leesburg Road in northern Virginia, just outside the nation's capital. "As we approached the meeting ground. . . ," Latrobe reported, "we could distinguish among the trees, half concealed by the underwood, houses, chaises, light wagons, hacks, & a crowd of men and women, in the midst of whom we presently arrived. . . . Crowds of negroes & mullatoes tastily dressed stood among the trees, & the groups looked as if any motives but religious ones had assembled them."

Positioning himself at the head of the clearing, Latrobe watched in fascination as "Mr. Bunn, a blacksmith of G[eorge] Town . . . spoke [with] immense rapidity & exertion . . . of the judgement to come." As Bunn exhorted the assembled throng, "a general groaning & shrieking was . . . heard from all Quarters" while the preacher "threw out both his arms sideways at full length, & shook himself violently." Every time Bunn pronounced "the stroke of grace," Latrobe continued, he brought his hands together so as to produce an astonishing clap. "The stroke again," Bunn shouted, "and another stroke, and another . . . and now it works, it works. . . . There it is, now she has it, glory! glory! glory!"

Though the salvation of souls was the camp meeting's central purpose, Latrobe perceived that it ministered to a variety of other human needs as well. "The illumination of the woods, the novelty of a camp especially to the women and children, the dancing and singing, & the pleasure of a crowd, so tempting to the most fashionable," generated a powerful sense of social belonging at such gatherings.

Offering a simple message that ordinary folks could readily grasp, itinerant preachers such as Bunn emphasized the equality of all believers before God and declared each individual responsible for his or her own soul. The power and inclusiveness of that message was revealed in the explosive growth of Methodist and Baptist churches. By mid-century, they would constitute the nation's largest religious denominations.

The Awakening had additional implications, for it called on believers to demonstrate their faith by going into the world to lift up the downtrodden and do good works. That religious impulse would provide much of the energy for later antebellum reforms such as temperance and abolition (see Chapter 12). Its influence was evident as well in earlier efforts at perfecting American society.

Alleviating Poverty and Distress

In the early republic, as at other times in the nation's history, ideals jarred awkwardly against social reality. One source of tension was the contrast between the doctrine of democratic equality and the reality of deepening class distinctions.

As the nineteenth century began, women still held far less property than men. For black slaves, ownership of more than the most basic personal possessions

Women as well as men among the urban poor peddled food and other commodities on the streets in an effort to make ends meet. *(Niccolino Calyo,* The Hot Corn Seller, *c. 1840. Museum of the City of New York)*

The American Revolution together with broader humanitarian impulses prompted various efforts at social reform in early America. Pictured here, from left to right, are the Philadelphia Almshouse, House of Employment, and Prison. *(Will Brown, Philadelphia, PA/The Dietrich American Foundation)*

was beyond reach. Though the condition of free blacks such as Ben Thompson and Phyllis Sherman was considerably better, they, too, enjoyed little of the country's bounty.

Among white males, property was most broadly shared in rural areas of the North, where free labor and family-farm agriculture predominated, and least so in the South, where the planters' control of slave labor and the best land permitted them to monopolize the region's wealth. The most even distribution of wealth existed on the edges of white settlement in trans-Appalachia, but it was little more than an equality of want. As the frontier developed, differences in wealth appeared there as well.

Though America, unlike Europe, contained no permanent, destitute underclass (at least among its white citizens), poverty was real and increasing. In the South, it was most evident among poor whites living on the sandy pine barrens of the backcountry. In the North, the port cities held growing numbers of poor. Boston artisans and shopkeepers who together had owned 20 percent of the city's wealth in 1700, for example, held scarcely half as much a century later.

Recurring recessions hit the urban poor with particular force, while winter added to hard times as shipping slowed and jobs disappeared. During the winter of 1805, New York's Mayor DeWitt Clinton worried publicly about the disruptive behavior of 10,000 impoverished New Yorkers and asked the state legislature for help. During the winter of 1814–1815, relief agencies assisted nearly one-fifth of the city's population.

In rural New England and southeastern Pennsylvania, a transient, propertyless underclass was growing. The "strolling poor," they were called—men, and sometimes women, unable to secure land of their own, and thus forced to roam the countryside searching for work.

Three other groups were conspicuous among the nation's poor. One consisted of old Revolutionary War veterans like Long Bill Scott, who had found poverty as well as adventure in the war. State and federal governments were peppered with petitions from grizzled veterans and their widows, detailing their misery and seeking relief. Women and children also suffered disproportionately from poverty. Annual censuses of almshouse residents in New York City from 1816 to 1821 consistently listed more women and children than men.

For every American who actually suffered poverty's effects, several others struggled to get by, living just beyond its reach. The thinness of their margin of safety became clear during the depression of 1819–1822. Triggered by a financial panic created by the unsound practices of hundreds of newly chartered state banks, a deep depression settled over the land, causing bankruptcies and sending unemployment soaring. In upstate New York, the pay of turnpike workers sank from 75 to 12 cents a day. In Ohio, the governor reported that "the greater part of our mercantile citizens are in a state of bankruptcy," while "the citizens of every class are . . . delinquent in discharging even the most trifling of debts." In the South, farms and plantations were abandoned as cotton and tobacco exports fell. By the early 1820s, the depression was lifting, but it left behind broken fortunes and shattered dreams.

Alleviating poverty was a central goal of the early reformers. In New York City, private and public authorities established over 100 charitable and relief agencies to aid orphans and widows, aged women and young prostitutes, imprisoned debtors and poverty-stricken seamen. Across the nation, a "charitable revolution" increased benevolent institutions from 50 in 1790 to nearly 2,000 by 1820. Most of these ventures drew a distinction between the "worthy poor," respectable folk who were victims of circumstance and merited assistance, and the "idle" or "vicious poor," who were deemed to lack character and thus deserved their fate. Many Americans believed such distinctions were clearly discoverable. No matter that a New York commission in 1823 found only 46 able-bodied adults (37 women and 9 men) among the 851 inmates of the city's almshouses or that a similar listing of supposed ne'er-do-wells included disabled Revolutionary War veterans, abandoned infants, and indigent immigrants recently arrived from Europe. New Yorkers had not yet made the connection between pauperism and the changing conditions of urban life.

Poverty was not the only target of public and private reform. Municipal authorities and private charities also established orphanages for children, asylums for the insane, and hospitals for the sick. Many such efforts were limited and shortlived, but they attested to the continuing strength of both revolutionary and religious ideals. Moreover, they provided a foundation for more ambitious reform efforts several decades later.

Women's Lives

Women's lives were not markedly altered during these early nineteenth-century years. Changes, however, did occur that helped set the stage for later, more dramatic breakthroughs.

Divorce was one area where women achieved greater equality. When a neighbor asked John Backus, a silversmith in Great Barrington, Massachusetts, why he kicked and struck his wife, John replied that it was partly because his father had treated his mother in the same way. We do not know whether John's mother tolerated such abuse, but his wife did not. She complained of cruelty and secured a divorce. More and more women followed her example.

Divorce was not easy to come by for women, since most states allowed it only on grounds of their husband's adultery. South Carolina did not permit it at all. Moreover, women typically faced the discomfort of presenting detailed evidence of their husbands' infidelities to an all-male court. Accusations of a wife's transgressions, by contrast, were more easily proven.

Still, divorce was becoming more available to women. In Massachusetts during the decade after independence, 50 percent more women than men filed for divorce, with almost identical rates of success. Part of the explanation for the increase lay in the war's disruptions, which led large numbers of men to desert their families and thus encouraged their wives to take action. It seems just as certain, however, that women's firmer commitment to individualism and equality led them to expect more of marriage.

Changes also occurred in women's education. Given their special role as Republican Mothers, women would have to prepare for their responsibilities as keepers of public morality and nurturers of republican citizens. Judith Sargeant Murray, along with other women, however, demanded even more of women's education. In a series of essays published in the 1790s, Murray criticized parents who "pointed their daughters" exclusively toward marriage and dependence. "They should be enabled to procure for themselves the necessaries of life; independence should be placed within their grasp," she wrote. "A woman should reverence herself."

Between 1790 and 1820, a number of female academies were established. Most, such as Susanna Rowson's Young Ladies Academy in Philadelphia, were located in northeastern cities. Timothy Dwight, the future president of Yale, opened his academy at Greenfield Hill in Connecticut to girls and taught them the same subjects he taught boys. Dwight, however, was the exception. Most proposals for female education assumed that girls should be taught separately from boys and that the curriculum should be less demanding. Though Benjamin Rush prescribed bookkeeping, reading, geography, music ("because it soothes cares and is good for the lungs"), and history as proper elements of a girl's education, traditionalists such as the Boston minister John Gardiner were more conservative. Warning that intellectual activity would unsex women, he declared that "Women of masculine minds have generally masculine manners, and a robustness of person ill calculated to inspire the tender passions." Even the most ardent supporters of female learning, like Murray, insisted that education was primarily important so that women might function more effectively within the domestic sphere. The happiness of the nation, she explained, was based on the happiness of families, and that depended in turn on "daughters of Columbia," educated women who would "fill with honor the parts allotted to them."

The evangelical impulse to which so many women were drawn actually reduced women's place in the churches. Whereas women had previously served as religious exhorters and participated in Baptist and Methodist church governance, they found themselves

Female academies in the early republic provided young middle- and upper-class women with the knowledge and skills necessary for their roles as Republican Mothers. (*Jacob Marling,* The Crowning of Flora, *1816/The Chrysler Museum of Art, Norfolk, VA, Gift of Edgar William and Bernice Chrysler Garbisch 80.118.20*)

increasingly marginalized as evangelical churches strove for social acceptance and adopted the rigidly gendered rules that Presbyterians and Congregationalists had always followed. In matters of church discipline, women were more frequently charged with "disorderliness" and condemned by their male brethren for "disobedience", thus calling into question a once robust tradition of piety in which men and women shared spiritual truth and ministered to each other's souls.

Race, Slavery, and the Limits of Reform

As we have seen (Chapter 7), the Revolution initiated the end of slavery in the northern states and challenged its continued existence in the Upper South. As the new century began, however, private manumissions were declining across Maryland and Virginia, while antislavery sentiment was weakening and more rigid categories of racial exclusiveness were appearing in the North.

In the southern states, the accelerating spread of cotton increased the value of slave labor, while revolutionary idealism faded with the passage of time. Equally important were two slave rebellions that generated intense alarm among southern whites. Panic-stricken refugees fleeing the Caribbean island of Saint Domingue beginning in 1791 carried word to the North American mainland of the black Haitians' rebellion against French colonial authority. Inspired by Toussaint L'Ouverture and other black leaders, the island's slaves struggled for 13 years against a French army of 25,000 before finally throwing off their French oppressors. By the time that struggle was finished, it achieved the first mass emancipation of a slave society and establishment of the first black republic in the Americas.

While Thomas Jefferson, as secretary of state, initially applauded the Haitian independence movement, he refused as president to extend diplomatic recognition to the new Haitian republic and sought to quarantine it within the Americas. He had solid political reasons for doing so, for news of the revolution spread terror through the South, where rumors abounded that Haitian incendiaries would soon be landing. In response, southern whites tightened their "black codes," cut the importation of new slaves from the Caribbean, and sought out malcontents among their own chattels. Colonial rebellions were admirable, but not when they set blacks against their white masters.

A second shock occurred in the summer of 1800, when a rebellion just outside Richmond, Virginia, was nipped in the bud. A 24-year-old slave named Gabriel had devised a plan to arm 1,000 slaves for an assault on the city. Gabriel and his accomplices were American-born blacks who spoke English, worked at skilled jobs that allowed them considerable personal freedom (and thus opportunity to lay their plans), and had fashioned their own ideology of liberation and racial justice by appropriating Virginia's revolutionary tradition and applying it to the circumstances of their own lives. A drenching downpour delayed the attack, providing time for several house servants (subsequently granted their freedom by the Virginia Assembly) to sound the alarm before the conspirators could act. No white lives were lost, but authorities arrested scores of slaves and free blacks, while 25 suspects, including Gabriel, were hanged at the order of Governor James Monroe. The carnage both alarmed and saddened Jefferson. "There is strong sentiment that there has been hanging enough," he confided to Monroe. "The other states and the world at large will forever condemn us if we . . . go one step beyond absolute necessity." In the midst of panic, however, the line between necessity and revenge was hard to find.

In the early nineteenth century, antislavery appeals all but disappeared from the South. Even religious groups that had once denounced slavery now grew quiet. "A majority of the people of the southern states," declared Congressman Peter Early of Georgia in 1806, "do not consider . . . it immoral to hold human flesh in bondage. Many deprecate slavery as an evil, as a political evil," he continued, "but not as a crime." At the time of the American Civil War, Confederate spokesmen would be saying much the same thing.

In the North, where the gradual abolition of slavery soothed white consciences, sentiment was increasingly conciliatory toward southern slave owners. At the same time, the conviction grew that immutable racial differences, grounded in nature, differentiated whites from blacks and that the two races existed in a hierarchical relationship to each other.

In the eighteenth century, ideas of racial exclusiveness had competed with Enlightenment beliefs in the common humanity of all mankind. American independence, however, dramatized for white Americans the contrast between their own successful struggle to throw off the threatened yoke of English "slavery" and the perpetual slavery of black Americans in their midst. That contrast seemed explainable by racial differences. The Revolution, moreover, focused the attention of white Americans on the essential attributes of republican citizenship—civic responsibility, economic self-sufficiency, and independence of judgment—qualities clearly lacking among the slave population. Even the gains achieved by free blacks as slavery was abolished appeared to harden white racial attitudes in the North. With racial domination no longer enforced by law, northern whites more readily invoked doctrines of black racial inferiority to assure their own continued predominance.

The hardening of white racial attitudes was clearly evident in the strengthening calls for colonizing free

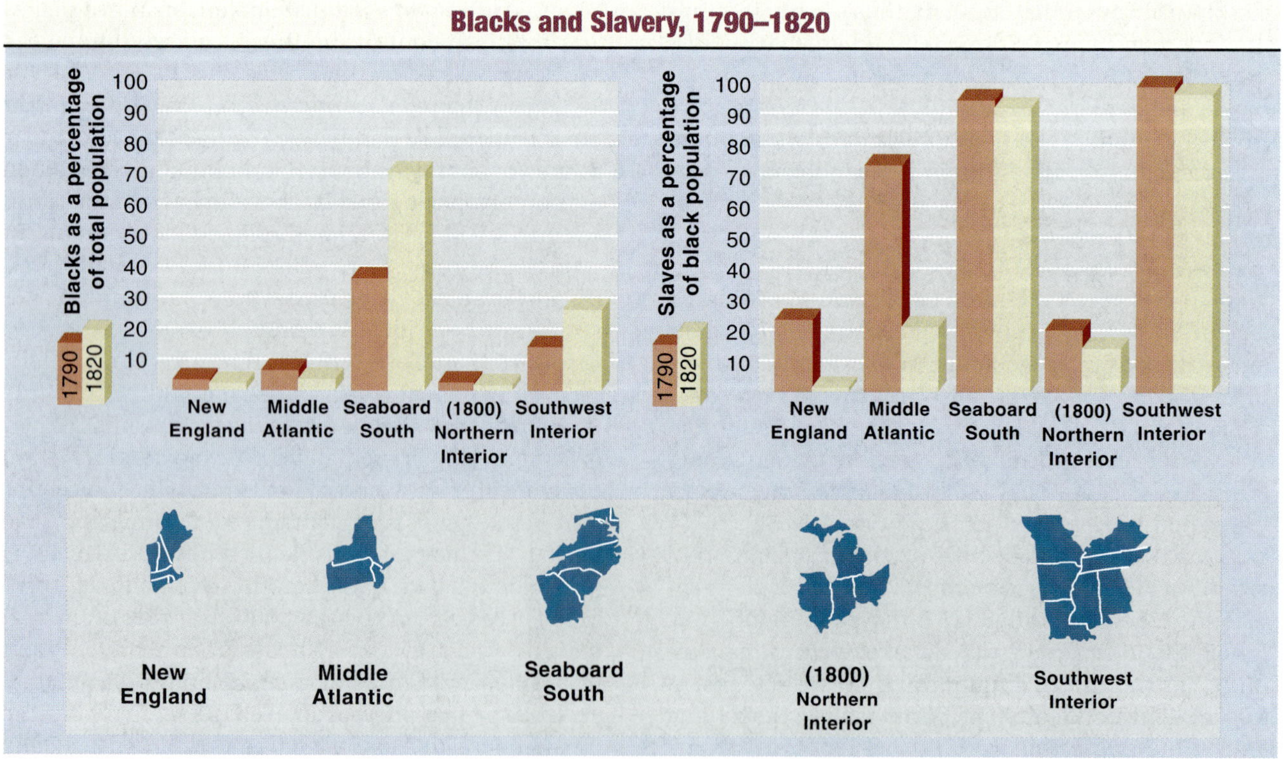

Though regions had differed in the importance of slavery and the number of blacks in their population as the Revolutionary War ended, those differences increased significantly over the next 30 years. Source: U.S. Bureau of the Census.

blacks outside the United States, in areas of western Africa that would become Liberia and Sierre Leone. The American Colonization Society, founded in 1816, typified these attitudes. Its supporters, while detesting slavery, believed that the two races could not peacefully coexist. That position was affirmed by many southern slaveholders who saw in colonization a convenient way of reducing the free black population and eliminating troublesome bondsmen. In the end, the Colonization Society never sent many freedmen and women abroad, but it did help to allay white anxieties.

Although some blacks were sympathetic to colonization, believing it offered the best promise of true freedom, most black spokesmen vigorously opposed it, condemning the ideology of black racial inferiority upon which colonization was based and demanding their full rights as Americans. In joining together in active opposition to colonization, American blacks gained experience in forging a more effective political voice. That experience would prove valuable training for the abolitionist crusade that lay ahead.

Not all northern whites succumbed to the new racism, for the states of Massachusetts, Rhode Island, and Pennsylvania would soon become hotbeds of a resurgent, multiracial abolition movement. Blacks, moreover, enjoyed greater liberty in the cities of the Northeast than elsewhere in the nation. Nonetheless, during the early years of the republic the revolutionary promise of equality rang hollow for most black Americans.

Forming Free Black Communities

During the half century following independence, vibrant black communities appeared in the port cities. As the lives of Ben Thompson and Phyllis Sherman revealed, emancipation in the North and the increase of freedmen in the Upper South enabled growing numbers of African Americans to seek the companionship of people of color in places such as Boston, New York, Philadelphia, and Baltimore. On the eve of independence, 4,000 slaves and a few hundred free blacks had called these four port cities home; 50 years later, more than 30,000 African Americans did so.

The men sought employment as laborers or sailors, the women as domestics. There were hundreds like Alexander Giles, a free black Philadelphia seaman who had been born in 1777 in nearby Kent County, Delaware, and Randall Shepherd, who had made his way north from Nansemond County, Virginia, in 1798. In rural areas, free blacks such as Phyllis Sherman had lived in isolation. In the port cities, black communities provided a higher measure of security and better chances of finding a marriage partner, establishing a family, and participating in community organizations.

Family formation was eased because many of the migrants were women, thus correcting a long-standing urban imbalance in the black population. Former slaves often created extended households that included relatives, friends, and boarders. As circumstances allowed, single-family units were formed. By 1820, most blacks in the northern cities lived in autonomous households.

As their numbers grew, African Americans created institutions independent of white control and capable of serving the needs of the black community. Schools educated children excluded from white academies, while mutual-aid societies offered help to the down and out and fraternal associations, such as the first African American Masonic Lodge established in Boston in 1797, provided fellowship and mutual support. It was black churches, however, that emerged as the institutional cornerstones of black community life, a position they would occupy throughout the nation's history.

In the years following the Revolution, free blacks joined integrated Methodist and Baptist congregations in cities such as Philadelphia and New York, drawn by their strongly biblical theology, enthusiastic forms of worship, and opposition to slavery. By 1790, 20 percent of Methodist church members were black. As the numbers of black communicants grew, however, they found themselves increasingly segregated in church galleries, excluded from leadership roles, and even denied communion. Whereas Christianity often comforted blacks by promising equality in the eyes of God, empowering them to adapt Christian beliefs to their own cultural and religious needs, and at times inspiring them to rebellion, the Christianity of white churches served increasingly to legitimize white supremacy and racial separation. Although many black Christians were reluctant to withdraw from biracial congregations, others sought opportunity to control their religious lives by breaking away.

In 1794, a small group of black Methodists led by Richard Allen, a slave-born, itinerant preacher, organized the Bethel African American Methodist Church in Philadelphia. Originally established as an integral part of American Methodism, Allen's congregation moved toward separatism by requiring that only "Africans and descendants of the African race" be admitted to membership. In 1816, it joined with a similar congregation in Baltimore to form the African Methodist Episcopal Church—the first independent black denomination in the United States. Though never as numerous as black Methodists, black Baptists established their own separate churches during the early nineteenth century in places such as Boston (1805), Philadelphia (1810), New Orleans (1826), and St. Louis (1827).

In his watercolor of a black Methodist church meeting, Paul Svinin, a traveler from Russia, reveals his amazement at the physical emotion displayed by the worshippers. "African" churches and other organizations were rare before 1800 but grew steadily in the ensuing decades. *(The Metropolitan Museum of Art, Rogers Fund, 1942 (42.95.19))*

Located in the heart of black communities, these churches not only nurtured distinctive, African American forms of worship but also provided education for black children and burial sites for families excluded from white cemeteries. Equally important, black churches offered secure sites where the basic rituals of family and community life—marriages and birth announcements, funerals and anniversaries—could be celebrated and where community norms could be enforced. By the 1830s, a rich cultural and institutional life had taken root in the black neighborhoods of American cities.

White hostility, however, remained a reality of black urban life, especially during hard times when free blacks competed with white laborers for scarce jobs. Working-class whites were unnerved as well by the growing competition for cheap housing. Overt violence against free blacks was infrequent during the early decades of the century, but even so, blacks found themselves increasingly segregated in residence, employment, and social life.

In response, leaders such as Richard Allen, Prince Hall, and Absolom Jones, through speeches, pamphlets, and public meetings, explored the meaning of black "freedom" in a white republic. In the process, they struggled to create a sense of civic identity for Americans of African descent.

A FOREIGN POLICY FOR THE NEW NATION

During the early decades of the nineteenth century, the Jeffersonians struggled to fashion a foreign policy appropriate for the expanding agrarian nation. Several goals guided their efforts: protecting American interests on the high seas, clearing the West of foreign troops, and breaking free from the country's historic dependence on Europe. The goals were not easily accomplished, yet by the 1820s the Jeffersonians had fashioned a new relationship with Europe. In the Monroe Doctrine of 1823, they projected a momentous new role for the United States within the Americas as well.

Jeffersonian Principles

Jeffersonian foreign policy was based on the doctrine of "no entangling alliances" with Europe that Washington had articulated in his Farewell Address of 1796. In the Jeffersonians' minds, England was still the principal enemy, but France was now suspect as well. By the time the Jeffersonians took office, the French Revolution had run its course. Although some Jeffersonians continued to harbor hopes for French liberty, most were sobered by Napoleon's dictatorial rule.

Second, the Jeffersonians emphasized the importance of overseas commerce for the nation's well-being. Foreign trade would provide markets for America's agricultural produce and fetch manufactured goods in return. The Federalists had nurtured domestic manufacturing by offering tariff protection against European competition. The Jeffersonians hoped to keep large-scale manufacturing in Europe, because they feared the concentrations of wealth and dependent working classes that domestic manufacturing would bring.

The Jeffersonians' third goal was maintaining peace. They feared war's effects on democratic liberty because it stifled free speech, increased the public debt, and expanded government power. Although seeking peace, the Jeffersonians understood the dangers lurking throughout the Atlantic world and knew that protecting the nation's interests might require force. Between 1801 and 1805, Jefferson dispatched naval vessels to the Mediterranean to defend American commerce against the Barbary States (Algiers, Morocco, Tripoli, and Tunis) of North Africa. War, however, was to be a policy of last resort. The Jeffersonians' handling of the crisis leading into the War of 1812 against Great Britain illustrates how eagerly, and in this case how futilely, they sought to avoid conflict.

Struggling for Neutral Rights

After a brief interlude of peace, European war resumed in 1803. Once again Britain and France seized American shipping. Britain's overwhelming naval superiority made its attacks especially serious, while its continuing refusal to negotiate on issues of impressment, occupation of the fur-trading posts, and reopening the West Indian trade increased Anglo-American tension.

In response to British seizures of American shipping, Congress passed the Non-Importation Act in April 1806, banning British imports that could be produced domestically or acquired elsewhere. A month later, Britain blockaded the European coast. Threatened by Britain's action, Napoleon answered by forbidding all commerce with the British Isles.

Tension between Britain and the United States reached the breaking point in June 1807, when the British warship *Leopard* stopped the American frigate *Chesapeake* off the Virginia coast and demanded that four crew members be handed over as British deserters. When the American commander refused, protesting that the sailors were Americans, the *Leopard* opened fire, killing 3 and wounding 18. After the *Chesapeake* limped back into port with the story, cries of outrage rang across the land.

Knowing that the United States was not prepared to confront Britain, Jefferson withdrew American ships from the Atlantic. In December 1807, Congress passed the Embargo Act, forbidding all American vessels from sailing for foreign ports. Urging the embargo was one of Jefferson's most ill-fated decisions.

The embargo had relatively little effect. British shipping actually profited from the withdrawal of American competition, and British importers effectively supplied the country's agricultural needs from Latin America. The measure's domestic impact, however, was immediate and far-reaching. American exports plummeted 80 percent in a year, while imports dropped by more than half. New England was hardest hit. In ports such as Salem, Boston, and Providence, ships rocked idly at the wharves and thousands of workers were unemployed as depression settled in.

American Foreign Trade, 1790–1825

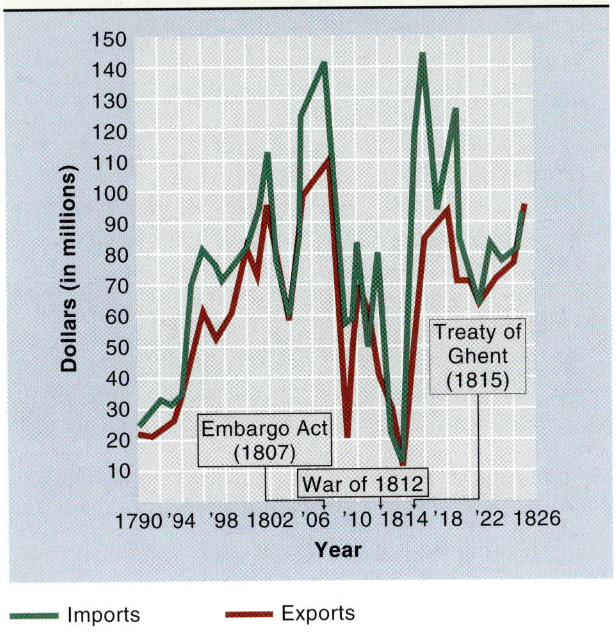

American overseas trade fluctuated dramatically as tensions with England and France ebbed and flowed. Source: U.S. Bureau of the Census.

Up and down the coast, communities dependent on overseas commerce openly ignored the embargo's restrictions. Attempts to police it proved futile, for the government could not close off either the Atlantic coast or the northern border across which large quantities of American goods were smuggled into Canada. In the area of Lake Champlain, federal officials declared martial law and sent in troops in an effort to control the situation. Guerrilla skirmishing resulted as local citizens fired on U.S. revenue boats and recaptured confiscated goods.

Throughout the Federalist Northeast, bitterness threatened to escalate into open rebellion. Connecticut's governor, in words reminiscent of the Virginia and Kentucky Resolutions, warned that if Congress exceeded its authority, the states were duty-bound "to interpose their protecting shield between the rights and liberties of the people and the assumed power of the general government."

In the election of 1808, the Federalists rebounded after nearly a decade's decline. James Madison handily succeeded Jefferson in the presidency, but the Federalist candidate, C. C. Pinckney, garnered 47

The tranquillity of Crowninshield wharf in Salem, Massachusetts, reveals ships idled and docks emptied by Jefferson's embargo. *(George Ropes, Crowninshield Wharf/The Essex Institute, Salem, Massachusetts)*

electoral votes. The Federalists made gains in Congress and recaptured several state legislatures as well.

Faced with the embargo's ineffectiveness abroad and disastrous consequences at home, Congress repealed the measure in 1809. Over the next several years, Congress tried more limited trade restrictions aimed at reducing British and French attacks on American shipping. When these failed as well, war fever continued to mount.

The War of 1812

The loudest calls for war came from the West and South. The election of 1810 brought to Congress a new group of western and southern leaders, firmly Republican in party loyalty but impatient with the administration's bumbling policy and insistent that tougher measures were needed. These "War Hawks"—including Henry Clay and Richard Johnson of Kentucky, John Calhoun and Langdon Cheves of South Carolina, Felix Grundy of Tennessee, and Peter Porter from western New York—were an impressive group.

For too long, the War Hawks cried, the United States had tolerated Britain's presence on American soil, encouragement of Indian raids, and attacks on American commerce. They talked openly of expanding the nation north into Canada and south into Spanish Florida. Most of all, these young nationalists resented British arrogance and America's continuing humiliation. No government and no political party, they warned, could survive unless it protected its people's interests and upheld the nation's honor.

Responding to the growing pressure, President Madison finally asked Congress for a declaration of war on June 1, 1812. Opposition came entirely from the New England and Middle Atlantic states—ironically, the regions British policies affected most adversely—whereas the South and West voted solidly for war. Rarely had sectional alignments been more sharply drawn.

Rarely also had American foreign policy proven less effective. Madison decided to abandon economic coercion just as the British government suspended its European blockade. Three days later, unaware of Britain's action, the Congress declared war.

The war itself was a curious affair. Britain beat back several American forays into Canada and launched a series of attacks along the Gulf Coast. As it had done during the Revolutionary War, the British navy blockaded American coastal waters, while landing parties launched punishing attacks up and down the Atlantic Coast. On August 14, a British force occupied Washington, torched the Capitol and the president's mansion (which became known as the White House after being repaired and whitewashed), and sent the president and Congress fleeing into Virginia. Britain, however, did not press its advantage, for it was preoccupied with Napoleon's armies in Europe and wanted to end the American quarrel.

On the American side, emotions ran high among the war's Federalist critics and Republican supporters. On the night of June 22, 1812, a Republican crowd in Baltimore demolished the printing office of a local Federalist newspaper. The attack was inspired by partisan politics, but even more by working-class animosity toward Federalist "aristocrats" and the eagerness of working people to support the job-creating war. In late July, after copies of the *Federal-Republican* again appeared on Baltimore's streets, a crowd of 1,000 men and women once more surrounded the paper's office. When Federalist defenders opened fire, the crowd rolled up a cannon and sent a round of

A British cartoon shows President Madison spilling official papers as he flees the burning capital, while citizens react with sarcastic comments during the British attack on Washington in 1814. *(Anne S. K. Brown Military Collection, Brown University Library)*

grapeshot into the building. Several people lay dead on both sides before the militia finally carted the Federalists off to the safety of jail.

The bloody encounter was not over yet, for the following night, a crowd assembled in front of the city jail, brushed aside the mayor's pleas to disperse, and seized ten prisoners, including James Lingan, an old Revolutionary War general. The enraged mob beat Lingan and several others to death and left the bodies, stripped of their fine clothing, sprawling in the street.

Though fortunately the Baltimore riots were not duplicated elsewhere, emotions continued to run high throughout the country. In Federalist New England, opposition to the war veered toward outright disloyalty. In December 1814, delegates from the five New England states met at Hartford, Connecticut, to debate proposals for secession. Cooler heads prevailed, but before adjourning, the Hartford Convention asserted the right of a state "to interpose its authority" against "unconstitutional" acts of the government. Now it was New England's turn to play with the nullification fire. As the war dragged on, Federalist fortunes soared in the Northeast, while elsewhere bitterness grew over New England's disloyalty.

Before the war ended, American forces won several impressive victories, among them Commander Oliver Hazard Perry's defeat of the British fleet on Lake Erie in 1813. That victory proved a turning point of the war in the Old Northwest, for it secured American dominance on the Great Lakes, ended the threat of a British invasion of Michigan, and weakened the British–Indian alliance that had menaced American interests in the region. The most dramatic American triumph was Andrew Jackson's smashing victory in 1815 over an attacking British force at New Orleans. It had little to do with the war's outcome, however, for it occurred after preliminary terms of peace had already been signed.

Increasingly concerned about the balance of power in Europe, Britain's foreign secretary, Lord Castlereagh, offered to negotiate peace. Madison eagerly accepted, and on Christmas Eve in 1814, at Ghent, Belgium, the two sides reached agreement. The treaty resolved almost nothing, for it ignored impressment, blockades, neutral rights, and American access to Canadian fisheries. Britain did agree to evacuate the western posts, but other than that, the agreement did little more than declare the conflict over, provide for an

The War of 1812

The War of 1812 scarcely touched the lives of most Americans, but areas around the Great Lakes, Lake Champlain, Chesapeake Bay, and the Gulf Coast witnessed significant fighting.

exchange of prisoners and the restoration of conquered territory, and call for the appointment of joint commissions to resolve lingering disputes.

Still, the war left its mark on the American nation. Nearly 20 percent of American seamen during the war were black, seafaring offering one of the few occupations commonly available to black men. Altogether, 4,000 African Americans served in the struggle against England, further strengthening black claims for full American citizenship. In addition, the war made Andrew Jackson a national hero and established him as a political figure of major importance. The American people, moreover, regarded the contest as a "Second War of American Independence," another twisting of the English lion's tail that finally secured the country against outside interference. In the years following 1815, the nation turned its primary energies toward the task of internal development—occupying the continent, strengthening the economy, and perfecting American society.

Perry's victory at the Battle of Lake Erie turned the tide of naval warfare on the Great Lakes. *(U.S. Capitol Historical Society)*

At the same time, European nations, increasingly occupied with their own problems of unification and economic development, began what would prove to be nearly a century free of general war. In the past, European wars had drawn in the American people; in the twentieth century, they would do so again. For the remainder of the nineteenth century, however, that fateful link was broken. In addition, the focus of European colonial competition was shifting to Africa and Asia, and that diverted European attention from the Americas as well.

The United States and the Americas

While disengaging from Europe, the president and Congress fashioned new policies for Latin America that would guide the nation's hemispheric relations for years to come. Americans cheered when Spain and Portugal's Latin American colonies began their struggles for independence in 1808. Though some were skeptical that the racially mixed populations of Latin America, with their history of brutal colonialism, were capable of orderly self-government, it was flattering to have leaders such as Simón Bolívar hold the United States up as a model for Latin American liberation. North Americans, moreover, were happy to see European colonialism weakened and believed that independent nations in Latin America offered the promise of increased trade.

Both the president and Congress were initially reluctant to recognize the governments of Colombia, Mexico, Chile, and Argentina. In part, that reflected a fear of disrupting delicate efforts then under way to secure Florida from Spain. There was concern as well that the newly independent countries might attempt to form their own united confederacy. "In a single mass," the aged Jefferson mused, "they would be a very formidable neighbor." Far better if they remained separate nations, enabling the United States to act as a dominant, "balancing" power.

Eventually, President Monroe sent Congress a message proposing formal recognition of the new republics. Congress quickly agreed, and over the next several years the United States established diplomatic relations with seven Latin American nations.

Trouble arose, however, in November 1822, when the major European powers talked of helping Spain regain its American possessions. Such prospects alarmed Great Britain as well as the United States, and in August 1823, British Foreign Secretary George Canning broached the idea of Anglo-American cooperation to thwart Spain's intentions.

Secretary of State John Quincy Adams opposed the idea. Son of the former president, Adams had joined the Jeffersonian camp some years before as part of the continuing exodus from the Federalist party. Filled with nationalist fervor generated by the War of 1812 and suspicious, like his father, of British intentions, Adams declared that the United States would not "come in as a cockboat in the wake of the British man-of-war." He called instead for independent action based on two principles: a sharp separation between the Old World and the New, and U.S. dominance in the Western Hemisphere.

Monroe agreed that the United States should issue its own policy statement. In his annual message of December 1823, he outlined a new Latin American policy. Though known as the Monroe Doctrine, it was of Adams's devising.

The doctrine asserted four basic principles: (1) the American continents were closed to new European colonization, (2) the political systems of the Americas were separate from those of Europe, (3) the United States would consider as dangerous to its peace and safety any attempts to extend Europe's political influence into the Western Hemisphere, and (4) the United States would neither interfere with existing colonies in the New World nor meddle in European affairs.

Monroe's declaration had little immediate effect, for the United States possessed neither the economic nor the military power to enforce it. By the end of the nineteenth century, when the nation's might had increased, however, it would become clear what a fateful moment in the history of the Americas Monroe's declaration had been.

POLITICS IN TRANSITION

For two decades following the election of 1800, the Jeffersonian Republicans monopolized the presidency and dominated Congress. Though Federalists for a while kept up a drumfire of attack on their political opponents, including the charge published by a Federalist editor in 1803 that Jefferson had sired several children by his slave girl Sally Hemmings, the Federalist party gradually collapsed, its reputation soiled by charges of disloyalty during the War of 1812 and its "aristocratic" image. Even so, by the late 1820s the Jeffersonian ascendancy was at an end and the Federalist-Jeffersonian party system was in disarray.

As the old, gentry-based politics declined, a new, more democratic system emerged to take its place. The new politics appeared first in the states, for it was there that government acted decisively on people's lives, claimed their attention, and lured them in extraordinary numbers to the polls. It was there as well that vestiges of gentry elitism came under sharpest attack and assertions of political equality were most forcefully put forward. And it was in the states that a younger generation of political leaders, uninhibited by their elders' fears of "party faction," first learned how to create political parties capable of managing democratic electoral politics. By the end of the 1820s, America stood poised on the threshold of an entirely new political era.

Division Among the Jeffersonians

With the Federalists in disarray following the War of 1812, the Jeffersonian Republicans stood triumphant, their ranks swollen by fresh recruits in the East and the admission of new states in the West. The Jeffersonians' success, however, proved their undoing, for no single party could contain the nation's swelling diversity of economic and social interests, its increasing sectional differences, or the personal ambitions of a new generation of political leaders.

In response to growing pressures from both West and Northeast, as well as to nationalist sentiment stimulated by the War of 1812, Madison's administration launched a Federalist-like program of national development. In March 1816, President Madison signed a bill creating a second Bank of the United States (the first bank's charter had expired in 1811), intended to stimulate economic expansion and regulate the loose currency-issuing practices of the country's countless state-chartered banks. At Madison's urging, the Congress also passed America's first protective tariff, a set of duties on imported woolen and cotton goods, iron, hats, and sugar.

The administration's program of national development drew sharp criticism from so-called Old Republicans, southern politicians who regarded themselves as guardians of the Jeffersonian conscience. Speaking in opposition to the bank bill in 1816, Congressman John Randolph of Virginia warned that "the question is whether . . . the state governments are to be swept away; or whether we . . . still . . . regard their integrity and preservation as part of our policy." Over the following decade, the Old Republicans continued to sound the alarm, even as their numbers dwindled.

Madison also recommended construction of a federally subsidized network of roads and canals to speed economic development and enhance national security. He counseled that a constitutional amendment authorizing such action should first be passed, but Representatives John Calhoun and Henry Clay, unwilling to delay, pushed an internal improvements bill through Congress. True to his principles, Madison vetoed the bill, temporarily stopping the project. Schemes for federal programs of national development, however, would not die. By the early 1820s, Clay and others, calling themselves National Republicans, were proposing an even more ambitious program of tariffs and internal improvements under the name the American System.

American Nationality and the Specter of Sectionalism

During the years of the early republic, sectional identities, deeply rooted in the long colonial experience, competed with an emerging sense of national identity for the loyalty of the American people. Among the circumstances strengthening American nationalism were the second War of Independence against England; the constitution uniting the 13 original states and promising to embrace America's expanding western empire; a shared English language and system of laws; the galvanizing experience of the Second Great Awakening that strengthened belief in America as God's chosen nation; and a rapidly expanding postal service that by 1830 was carrying nearly 14 million letters annually, a 136 percent increase since the new government began.

Shared rituals of patriotic celebration on occasions such as Washington's birthday and the Fourth of July helped unify the nation as well. Although Federalists and Jeffersonian-Republicans, northerners and southerners, black and white Americans competed to fill these celebratory occasions with political meaning, those very clashes revealed the sense of urgency with which all Americans sought to stake their claim to a common heritage. Moreover, the printed reports of local celebrations, carried throughout the land via the expanding circulation of newspapers, knitted communities together in a national conversation of patriotism.

Even as the construction of a shared national identity went forward, however, the Virginia and Kentucky Resolutions of the 1790s and Federalist talk of disunion during the War of 1812 revealed how fragile national unity continued to be. Though congressional debates over the tariff, internal improvements, and the national bank echoed with sectional tensions, it was the Missouri crisis of 1819–1820 that jolted the nation's consciousness.

Ever since 1789, politicians had labored to keep the explosive issue of slavery tucked safely beneath the surface of political life, for they recognized how quickly it could jeopardize national unity. Their fears were borne out in 1819 when Missouri's application for admission to the Union raised anew the question of slavery's expansion. The Northwest Ordinance of 1787 had limited slavery north of the Ohio River while allowing its expansion to the south. But Congress had said nothing about slavery's place in the vast new territory west of the Mississippi River.

Seizing the opportunity to deal with that question, Senator Rufus King of New York demanded that Missouri prohibit slavery before entering the Union. His proposal triggered a fierce debate over Congress's authority to regulate the spread of slavery. Southerners were adamant that the trans-Mississippi West remain open to their slave property and were determined to maintain the Senate's equal balance between slave and free states. Already by 1819, the North's more rapidly growing population had given it a 105-to-81 advantage in the House of Representatives. Equality in the Senate

In the early republic, celebrations of Independence Day mingled military processions with patriotic displays and neighborhood conviviality. *(The Historical Society of Pennsylvania (HSP),* "Fourth of July Celebration," *India ink and watercolors on paper by Lewis Krimmel, Accession #Bc882K897)*

The House of Representatives, depicted in this 1821 painting by Samuel F. B. Morse, later inventor of the telegraph, rang with debate over the Missouri Compromise and other explosive issues. *(Samuel F. B. Morse,* The Old House of Representatives, *1882, 86½ x 130¾ in, oil on canvas. In the Collection of the Corcoran Gallery of Art, Washington, D.C., Museum Purchase, Gallery Fund 11.14)*

offered the only sure protection of southern interests. Northerners, however, vowed to keep the trans-Mississippi West open to free labor, which meant closing it to slavery.

For nearly three months, Congress debated the issue. During much of the time, free blacks, listening intently to northern antislavery speeches, filled the House gallery. "This momentous question," worried the aged Jefferson, "like a fire-bell in the night, [has] awakened and filled me with terror." Northerners were similarly alarmed. The Missouri question, declared the editor of the New York *Daily Advertiser,* "involves not only the future character of our nation, but the future weight and influence of the free states. If now lost—it is lost forever."

In the end, compromise prevailed. Missouri gained admission as a slave state, while Maine came in as a counterbalancing free state, and a line was drawn west from Missouri at latitude 36° 30' to the Rocky Mountains, dividing the lands that would be open to slavery from those that would not. For the moment, the issue had been put to rest. It would not be long, however, before the problem of slavery's expansion would set North and South even more violently against each other.

Collapse of the Federalist-Jeffersonian Party System

The final collapse of the Federalist-Jeffersonian system of politics was triggered by the presidential election of 1824. For the first time since 1800, when the "Virginia dynasty" of Jefferson, Madison, and Monroe began, there was competition for the presidency from every major wing of the Jeffersonian party. Of the five candidates, John Quincy Adams of Massachusetts and Henry Clay of Kentucky advocated active federal programs of economic development. William Crawford of Georgia and Andrew Jackson of Tennessee clung to traditional Jeffersonian principles of limited government, agrarianism, and states' rights. In between stood John Calhoun of South Carolina, just beginning his fateful passage from nationalism to southern nullification.

Attracting limited support, Calhoun withdrew to become the vice-presidential partner of both Adams and Jackson. When none of the remaining candidates received an electoral majority, the election, as in 1800, moved into the House of Representatives. There, an alliance of Adams and Clay supporters gave the New Englander the election, even though he trailed Jackson in electoral votes, 84 to 99. The Jacksonians' charges of a "corrupt bargain" gained credence when Adams appointed Clay secretary of state.

Adams's ill-fated administration revealed the disarray in American politics. His stirring calls for federal road and canal building, standardization of weights and measures, establishment of a national university, and government support for science and the arts quickly fell victim to sectional conflicts, political factionalism, and his own open scorn for the increasingly democratic politics of the day. Against the urging of his political advisers, Adams declined an invitation from the Maryland Agricultural Society to attend its annual cattle show, explaining that the president

Missouri Compromise of 1820

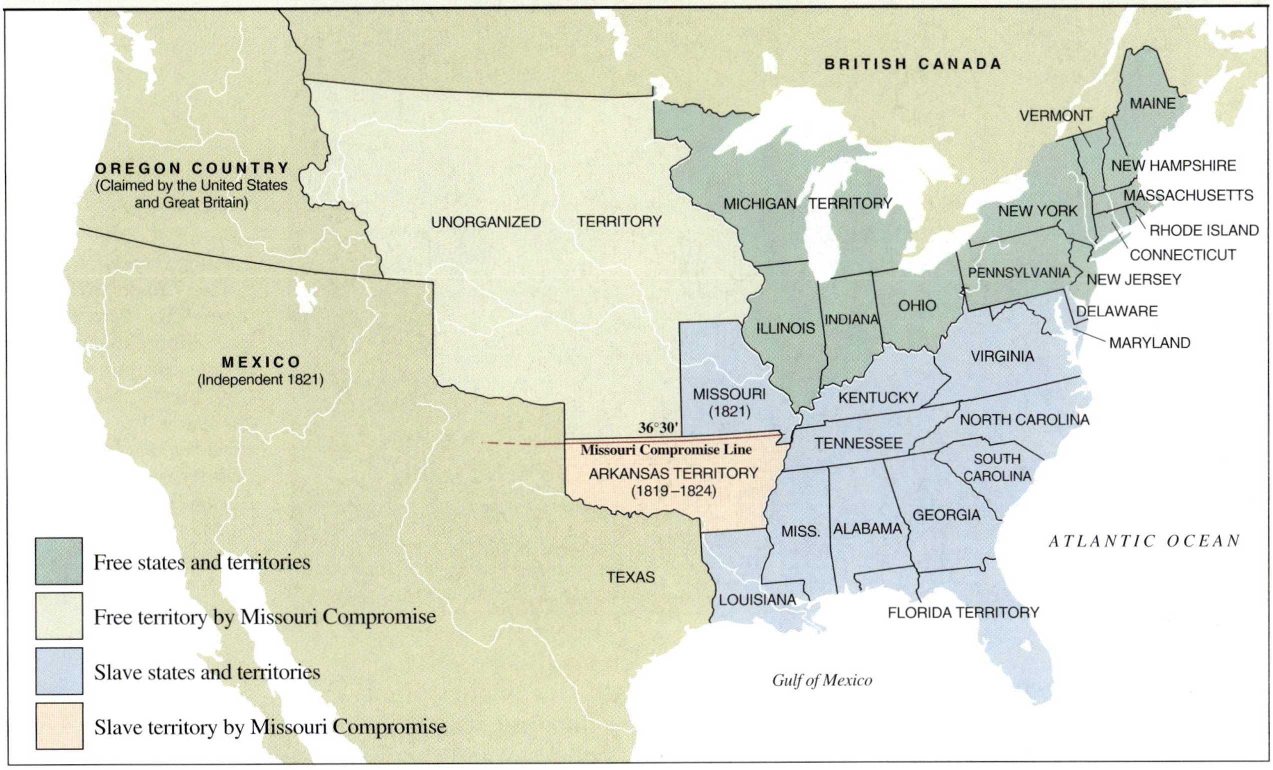

In the early nineteenth century, politicians struggled to contain the explosive issue of slavery's expansion. In 1820, they did so by balancing Missouri's admission as a slave state with Maine's as a free state and drawing the Missouri Compromise line, separating free territories from slave territories.

should stand above such efforts to court popular favor. In the increasingly raucous, democratic political climate of the 1820s, such an attitude amounted to political suicide. Within a year of his inauguration, Adams's administration had foundered. For the rest of his term, politicians jockeyed for position in the political realignment that was under way.

A New Style of Politics

At the same time, political energies continued to stir in the states, most dramatically in the surge of voter participation in state elections. Women, blacks, and Native Americans were still excluded, but white men flocked to the polls in unprecedented numbers. In the New Hampshire gubernatorial election of 1814, participation soared as high as 81 percent of eligible voters. On one occasion in Alabama, voter turnout topped 90 percent.

The flood of voters resulted in part from the removal of long-established, property-holding restrictions on the franchise. The constitutions of new states such as Indiana (1816), Illinois (1818), and Alabama (1819) provided for universal white, male suffrage. Older states such as Connecticut and New York abolished property requirements as well.

Voters' intensifying interest in politics was stimulated as well by the active role of state governments in their daily lives. While the domestic policies of the national government remained limited, state legislatures buzzed with activity over building highways, bridges, and ferries; regulating banks, lotteries, stray cattle, and insane asylums; enforcing Sunday blue laws and temperance; passing regulations providing consumer protection; and regulating relief for the poor. Electoral politics provided the essential connections between public demands and legislative behavior in the spirited civic arenas of the states.

Just as important was the emergence of a post-Revolutionary generation of political leaders—men such as Martin Van Buren of New York, Levi Woodbury of New Hampshire, and Lewis Cass of Ohio—ready to set aside old worries about "party faction" and eager to experiment with the techniques of mass, democratic politics. Even some of the younger Federalists, learning from the disastrous consequences of their elders' elitist behavior, changed their political ways. By the 1820s, successful politicians of every persuasion vied for voters' support through registration drives, party conventions, and popular campaigning.

Election days were often raucous affairs in the increasingly democratic, male-dominated politics of the early republic, as this Philadelphia scene (c. 1815) amply testifies. *(The Historical Society of Pennsylvania (HSP), India ink and watercolors on paper of* "Election Day at the State House, 1816" *by John Lewis Krimmel, Accession #Bc47K897)*

While the conduct of mass, democratic politics was first evident in the states where the new party machinery could be most easily developed, the election of Andrew Jackson to the presidency in 1828 would bring the techniques of mass politics to presidential electioneering as well. When that happened, American politics would change forever.

Timeline

1789	Knox's report on Indian affairs
1790s	Second Great Awakening begins
1794	Battle of Fallen Timbers
1795	Treaty of Greenville
1796	Congress establishes Indian Factory System
1800	Capital moves to Washington
1801	Thomas Jefferson elected president
	Judiciary Act
	New Land Act
1802	Judiciary Act repealed
1803	*Marbury* v. *Madison*
	Louisiana Purchase
1803–1806	Lewis and Clark expedition
1803–1812	Napoleonic wars resume
	British impress American sailors
1804	Jefferson reelected
1805–1807	Pike explores the West
1806	Non-Importation Act
1807	Embargo Act
	Chesapeake–Leopard affair
	Congress prohibits slave trade
1808	James Madison elected president
	Cherokee legal code established
1809	Tecumseh's confederacy formed
1811	Battle of Kithtippecanoe
1812	Madison reelected
	West Florida annexed
	War declared against Great Britain
1813	Battle of the Thames
1813–1814	Creek War
1814	Treaty of Ghent
	Battle of Horseshoe Bend
1814–1815	Hartford Convention
1815	Battle of New Orleans
	U.S. establishes military posts in trans-Mississippi West
1816	James Monroe elected president
	Second Bank of the United States chartered
1819	Adams–Onis Treaty with Spain
	Spain cedes East Florida to United States
	McCulloch v. *Maryland*
1819–1822	Bank panic and depression
1820	Missouri Compromise
1822	Diplomatic recognition of Latin American republics
1823	Monroe Doctrine proclaimed
1824	John Quincy Adams elected president
1827	Cherokee adopt written constitution

Conclusion

The Passing of an Era

During the first quarter of the nineteenth century, Americans reshaped the social, territorial, and political dimensions of their republic. Safely in control of the federal government, the Jeffersonians labored to set it on a new, more democratic course. In the process, they fashioned domestic policies designed to promote the country's agrarian expansion and foreign policies that transformed the nation's relations with Europe and the Americas. They also sought, less successfully, to reconcile Native American rights with national growth. By the end of the 1820s, an earlier system of politics divided between gentry domination in the Congress and popular politics in the states was in its final throes. In the years immediately ahead, its place would be taken by a new and dramatically different national system of democratic politics.

The events of the early republic testified to the strength, as well as limitations, of America's democratic faith. The nation's continuing task was to bring that faith into closer alignment with the lives of the American people.

During the decade of the 1820s, the American people turned from an earlier era of founding, when the national government was new and the outcome of the republican experiment uncertain, to a new era of national expansion. That transition was dramatized on July 4, 1826, the fiftieth anniversary of American independence, when two of the remaining revolutionary patriarchs, John Adams and Thomas Jefferson, died within a few hours of each other. "The sterling virtues of the Revolution are silently passing away," mused George McDuffie of South Carolina, "and the period is not distant when there will be no living monument to remind us of those glorious days of trial." As the anniversary celebrations ended and memories of the revolutionary founders died away, the American people had reason to ponder what the future would bring.

Recommended Reading

Restoring American Liberty

Noble Cunningham, *The Process of Government Under Jefferson* (1978); Joseph Ellis, *American Sphinx: The Character of Thomas Jefferson* (1997); Richard Ellis, *The Jeffersonian Crisis: Courts and Politics in the Young Republic* (1971); Annette Gordon-Reed, *Thomas Jefferson and Sally Hemmings: An American Controversy* (1997); Herbert Johnson, *The Chief Justiceship of John Marshall, 1801–1835* (1997); Merrill Peterson, *Thomas Jefferson and the New Nation* (1970); Francis Stites, *James Madison, Defender of the Constitution* (1981).

Building an Agrarian Nation

Lance Banning, *The Jeffersonian Persuasion: The Evolution of a Party Ideology* (1978); Donald Jackson, *Thomas Jefferson and the Stony Mountains: Exploring the American West from Monticello* (1981); Drew McCoy, *The Elusive Republic* (1980); James Ronda, *Lewis and Clark Among the Indians* (1984).

A Nation of Regions

Jeremy Atack and Fred Bateman, *To Their Own Soil: Agriculture in the Antebellum North* (1987); Jeanne Boydston, *Home and Work: Housework, Wages, and the Ideology of Labor in the Early Republic* (1990); Stephen Hahn and Jonathan Prude, *The Countryside in the Age of Capitalist Transformation* (1985); James Lemon, *The Best Poor Man's Country* (1972); Howard Rock et al., *American Artisans: Crafting Social Identity* (1995); Daniel Vickers, *Farmers and Fishermen: Two Centuries of Work in Essex County, Massachusetts, 1630–1850* (1994).

Robert Doherty, *Society and Power: Five New England Towns, 1800–1860* (1977); Richard Wade, *The Urban Frontier: The Rise of Western Cities, 1790–1830* (1959).

Daniel Dupre, *Transforming the Cotton Frontier: Madison County, Alabama, 1800–1840* (1997); Allan Kulikoff, *The Agrarian Origins of American Capitalism* (1992).

Michael Allen, *Western Rivermen, 1763–1861* (1990); Andrew R. L. Cayton and Fredrika Teute, eds., *Contact Points: American Frontiers from the Mohawk Valley to the Mississippi, 1750–1830* (1998); William C. David, *A Way Through the Wilderness: The Natchez Trace and the Civilizing of the Southern Frontier* (1995); John Mack Farragher, *Daniel Boone: The Life and Legend of an American Pioneer* (1992); Robert Mitchell, ed., *Appalachian Frontiers: Settlement, Society, and Development in the Preindustrial Era* (1991); Malcolm Rohrbough, *The Trans-Appalachian Frontier* (1978).

Indian–White Relations in the Early Republic

Gregory Dowd, *Spirited Resistance: The North American Indian Struggle for Unity, 1745–1815* (1992); R. David Edmunds, *Tecumseh and the Quest for Indian Leadership* (1984); William McLaughlin, *Cherokee Renascence in the New Republic* (1986); Theda Perdue, *Cherokee Women: Gender and Culture Change, 1700–1835* (1998); Francis Paul Prucha, *American Indian Policy in the Formative Years* (1970); Bernard Sheehan, *Seeds of Extinction: Jeffersonian Philanthropy and the American Indian* (1973); Wiley Sword, *President Washington's Indian War, 1790–1795* (1985); Richard White, *The Middle Ground: Indians, Empires, and Republics in the Great Lakes Region, 1650–1815* (1991).

Perfecting a Democratic Society

Paul Conkin, *Cane Ridge: American Pentacost* (1990); Nathan Hatch, *The Democratization of American Christianity* (1989); Jean Mathews, *Toward a New Society: American Thought and Culture, 1800–1830* (1990); Randolph Roth, *The Democratic Dilemma: Religion, Reform, and the Social Order in the Connecticut River Valley of Vermont, 1791–1850* (1987); John Wigger, *Taking Heaven by Storm: Methodism and the Rise of Popular Christianity in America* (1998).

Robert Cray, Jr., *Paupers and Poor Relief in New York City and Its Rural Environs, 1700–1830* (1988); Michael Meranze, *Laboratories of Virtue: Punishment, Revolution, and Authority in Philadelphia, 1760–1835* (1996); Conrad Wright, *The*

Transformation of Charity in Post-Revolutionary New England (1992).

Norma Basch, *Framing American Divorce: From the Revolutionary Generation to the Victorians* (1999); Lee Chambers-Schiller, *Liberty, A Better Husband* (1984); Nancy Cott, *The Bonds of Womanhood: "Women's Sphere" in New England, 1780–1835* (1977); Cathy Davidson, *Revolution and the Word: The Rise of the Novel in America* (1986); Joan Jensen, *Loosening the Bonds: Mid-Atlantic Farm Women, 1750–1850* (1986); Susan Juster, *Disorderly Women: Sexual Politics and Evangelicalism in Revolutionary New England* (1994); Mark Kann, *A Republic of Men: The American Founders, Gendered Language, and Patriotic Politics* (1998); Cynthia Kierner, *Beyond the Household: Women's Place in the Early South, 1700–1835* (1998).

Sylvia Frey and Betty Wood, *Come Shouting to Zion: African-American Protestantism in the American South and British Caribbean to 1830* (1998); Kimberly Hanger, *Bounded Lives, Bounded Places: Free Black Society in New Orleans, 1769–1803* (1997); Joanne Pope Melish, *Disowning Slavery: Gradual Emancipation and "Race" in New England, 1780–1860* (1998); Gary B. Nash, *Forging Freedom: The Formation of Philadelphia's Black Community, 1720–1840* (1988); James Sidbury, *Plowshares into Swords: Race, Rebellion, and Identity in Gabriel's Virginia, 1730–1810* (1997); T. Stephen Whitman, *The Price of Freedom: Slavery and Manumission in Baltimore and Early National Maryland* (1997).

A Foreign Policy for the New Nation

Lawrence Kaplan, *"Entangling Alliances With None": American Foreign Policy in the Age of Jefferson* (1987); James Lewis, Jr., *The American Union and the Problem of Neighborhood: The United States and the Collapse of the Spanish Empire, 1783–1829* (1998); Ernest May, *The Making of the Monroe Doctrine* (1975); Robert Rutland, *The Presidency of James Madison* (1990); David C. Skaggs and Gerard Altoff, *A Signal Victory: The Lake Erie Campaign, 1812–1813* (1997); Burton Spivak, *Jefferson's English Crisis: Commerce, Embargo, and the Republican Revolution* (1974); J. C. A. Stagg, *Mr. Madison's War* (1983).

Politics in Transition

Andrew Cayton, *The Frontier Republic: Ideology and Politics in the Ohio Country, 1780–1825* (1986); Donald Cole, *Martin Van Buren and the American Political System* (1984); Evan Cornog, *The Birth of Empire: DeWitt Clinton and the American Experience, 1769–1828* (1998); Richard John, *Spreading the News: The American Postal System from Franklin to Morse* (1995); David Konig, ed., *Devising Liberty: Preserving and Creating Freedom in the New American Republic* (1995); Drew McCoy, *The Last of the Fathers: James Madison and the Republican Legacy* (1989); Paul Nagel, *John Quincy Adams: A Public Life, A Private Life* (1997); Ronald Schultz, *The Republic of Labor: Philadelphia Artisans and the Politics of Class, 1720–1830* (1993); Alan Taylor, *William Cooper's Town: Power and Persuasion on the Frontier in the Early American Republic* (1995); Len Travers, *Celebrating the Fourth: Independence Day and the Rites of Nationalism in the Early Republic* (1997); David Waldstreicher, *In the Midst of Perpetual Fetes: The Making of American Nationalism, 1776–1820* (1997); Steven Watts, *The Republic Reborn: War and the Making of Liberal America, 1790–1820* (1987).

Fiction and Film

Scandalmonger (2000), a novel by the *New York Times* columnist William Safire, describes personal intrigue within high political circles in the early republic. *Tecumseh: The Last Warrior* (1995), a made-for-television historical drama, offers an imaginative rendering of the Shawnee leader who sought to unite tribes north and south of the Ohio River against invading white settlers in the early nineteenth century. *Lewis and Clark: The Journey of the Corps of Discovery* (1997), a PBS documentary by Ken Burns, tells the story of this path-breaking expedition and reveals the dramatic landscape through which it passed.

In the classic American novel *Rip Van Winkle* (1829), Washington Irving explores the transiency of historical memory via the story of an eighteenth-century New Yorker who mysteriously falls asleep during the American Revolution and awakes decades later to find his community radically changed and himself the object of intense curiosity.

Suggested Web Sites

http://www.lcweb.loc.gov/exhibits/us.capitol/s0.html

Temple of Liberty—Building the Capitol for a New Nation. Compiled from holdings in the Library of Congress, this site contains detailed information on the design and early construction of the capitol building in Washington, D.C.

http://etext.virginia.edu/jefferson/

Thomas Jefferson Online Resources at the University of Virginia. Mr. Jefferson's University—the University of Virginia—houses this site, with numerous resources about Jefferson and his times.

http://www.syracuse.com/features/eriecanal

Erie Canal Online. This site, built around the diary of a fourteen-year-old girl who travelled from Amsterdam to Syracuse, New York, in the early nineteenth century, explores the construction and importance of the Erie Canal.

http://www.pbs.org/lewisandclark/

PBS Online—Lewis and Clark. This is a companion site to Ken Burns's site, containing a timeline of the expedition, a collection of related links, a bibliography, and over eight hundred minutes of unedited, full-length RealPlayer interviews with seven experts featured in the film.

http://www.indianapolis.in.us/cp/stories.html

Prairietown Stories. This fictional model of a town (Prairietown, Indiana) and its inhabitants on the early frontier says much about America's movement westward and the everyday lives of Americans.

http://members.tripod.com/~war1812/index.html

War of 1812–1814. This site offers in-depth and varied information about the War of 1812.

http://www.seminoletribe.com/

Indians—Seminole Tribe of Florida. This site is dedicated to the rich history and culture of the Seminole, a tribe against which Andrew Jackson began a war before he was president.

http://www.ushistoryplace.com

A richly detailed on-line learning environment complete with interactive maps, timelines, history activities, primary source documents, and links to related American history sites.

CURRENTS *of* CHANGE *in the* NORTHEAST *and the* OLD NORTHWEST

CHAPTER OUTLINE

For her first 18 years, Susan Warner was little touched by the far-reaching economic and social changes that were transforming the character of the country and her own city of New York. Whereas some New Yorkers toiled to make a living by taking in piecework and others responded to unsettling new means of producing goods by joining trade unions to agitate for wages that would enable them to "live as comfortable as others," Susan was surrounded by luxuries and privilege. Much of the year was spent in the family's townhouse in St. Mark's Place, not far from the home of the enormously rich real estate investor and fur trader John Jacob Astor. There Susan acquired the social graces and skills appropriate for a girl of her position and background. She had dancing and singing lessons, studied Italian and French, and learned the etiquette involved in receiving visitors and making calls. When hot weather made life in New York unpleasant, the Warners escaped to the cooler airs of Canaan, where they had a summer house. Like any girl of her social class, Susan realized that her carefree existence could not last forever. With her marriage, which she confidently expected some time in the future, would come significant new responsibilities as a wife and mother but not the end of the comfortable life to which she was accustomed.

It was not marriage and motherhood that disrupted the pattern of Susan's life but financial disaster. Sheltered as she had been from the unsettling economic and social changes of the early nineteenth century, Susan discovered that she, too, was at the mercy of forces beyond her control. Her father, heretofore so successful a provider and parent, lost most of his fortune during the financial Panic of 1837. Like others experiencing a sharp economic reversal, the Warners had to make radical adjustments. The fashionable home in St. Mark's Place and the pleasures of New York were exchanged for a more modest existence on an island in the Hudson River. Susan turned "housekeeper" and learned how to do tasks once relegated to others: sewing and making butter, pudding sauces, and johnny cake.

The change of residence and Susan's attempt to master domestic skills did not halt the family's financial decline. Prized possessions, including the piano and engravings, all symbols of the life the Warners had once taken for granted, eventually went up for auction. "When at last the men and the confusion were gone," Susan's younger sister, Anna, recalled, "then we woke up to life."

Waking up to life meant facing the necessity of making money. But what could Susan do to reverse sliding family fortunes? True, some women labored as factory operatives, domestics, seamstresses, or schoolteachers, but it was doubtful Susan could even imagine herself in any of these occupations. Her Aunt Fanny, however, had a suggestion that was more congenial to the genteel young woman. Knowing that the steam-powered printing press had revolutionized the publishing world and created a mass readership, much of it female, Aunt Fanny told her niece, "Sue, I believe if you would try, you could write a story." "Whether she added 'that . . . would sell,' I am not sure," recalled Anna later, "but of course that was what she meant."

Taking Aunt Fanny's advice to heart, Susan started to write a novel that would sell. She constructed her story around the trials of a young orphan girl, Ellen Montgomery. As Ellen suffered one reverse after another, she learned the lessons that allowed her to survive and eventually triumph over adversity: piety, self-denial, discipline, and the power of a mother's love. Entitled *The Wide, Wide World,* the novel was accepted for publication only after the mother of the publisher, George Putnam, read it and told her son, "If you never publish another book, you must make *The Wide, Wide World* available for your fellow men." A modest 750 copies were printed. Much to the surprise of the cautious Putnam, if not to his mother, 13 editions were published within two years. *The Wide, Wide World* became the first American novel to sell more than a million copies. It was one of the best-sellers of the century.

Long before she realized the book's success, Susan, now much aware of the need to make money, was working on a new story. Drawing on her own experience of economic and social reversal, Susan described the spiritual and intellectual life of a young girl thrust into poverty after an early life of luxury in New York. Entitled *Queechy,* this novel was also a great success.

Though her fame as a writer made Susan Warner unusual, her books' popularity suggested how well they spoke to the concerns and interests of a broad readership. The background of social and financial uncertainty, with its sudden changes of fortune, so prominent in several of the novels, captured the reality and fears of a fluid society in the process of transformation. While one French writer was amazed that "in America a three-volume novel is devoted to the

This picture of an 1845 fair suggests the cornucopia of goods made available in the early stages of industrialization. *(B. J. Harrison,* Fair of the American Institute at Niblo's Garden, *1845/Museum of the City of New York)*

history of the moral progress of a girl of thirteen," pious heroines like Ellen Montgomery, who struggled to master their passions and urges toward independence, were shining exemplars of the new norms for middle-class women. Their successful efforts to mold themselves heartened readers who believed that the future of the nation depended on virtuous mothers and who struggled to live up to new ideals. Susan's novels validated their efforts and spoke to the importance of the domestic sphere. "I feel strongly impelled to pour out to you my most heartful thanks," wrote one woman. None of the other leading writers of the day had been able to minister "to the highest and noblest feelings of my nature *so much as yourself.*"

Susan Warner's life and her novels serve as an introduction to the far-reaching changes that this chapter explores. Between 1820 and 1860, as Susan Warner discovered, economic transformations in the Northeast and the Old Northwest reshaped economic, social, cultural, and political life. Though most Americans still lived in rural settings rather than in factory towns or cities, economic growth and the new industrial mode of production affected them through the creation of new goods, opportunities, and markets. In urban communities and factory towns, the new economic order ushered in new forms of work, new class arrangements, and new forms of social strife.

After discussing the factors that fueled antebellum growth, the chapter turns to the industrial world, where so many of the new patterns of work and life appeared. An investigation of urbanization reveals shifting class arrangements and values as well as rising social and racial tensions. Finally, an examination of rural communities in the East and on the frontier in the Old Northwest highlights the transformation of these two sections of the country. Between 1840 and 1860, industrialization and economic growth increasingly knit them together.

ECONOMIC GROWTH

Between 1820 and 1860, the American economy entered a new and more complex stage of development as it moved away from its reliance on agriculture as the major source of growth toward an industrial and technological future. In this period of general national expansion, real per capita output grew an average of 2 percent annually between 1820 and 1840 and slightly less between 1840 and 1860. This doubling of per capita income over a 40-year period suggests that many Americans were enjoying a rising standard of living.

Though expanding, the economy was also unstable, as the Warners discovered so dramatically. Periods of boom (1822–1834, mid-1840s–1850s) alternated with periods of bust (1816–1821, 1837–1843). As never before, Americans faced dramatic and recurrent shifts in the availability of jobs and goods and in prices and wages. Particularly at risk were working-class Americans, a third of whom lost their jobs during years of depression. Moreover, because regional economies were increasingly linked, problems in one area tended to affect conditions in others.

Factors Fueling Economic Development

What accounted for this new phase of growth and economic development? As the table nearby suggests, the abundance of natural resources and an expanding population provided the raw materials and the human brawn and brains that supported growth and transformation. Because the size of American families gradually shrank—in 1800, the average white woman bore seven children; by 1860, the number had declined to five—immigration from Europe (discussed in detail later in the chapter) played an important part in providing the new workers, new households, and new consumers so essential to economic development as well as the capital and technological ideas that helped to shape American growth.

Improved transportation played a key role in bringing about economic and geographic expansion. Early in the century, high freight rates discouraged production for distant markets and the exploitation of resources, and primitive transportation hindered western settlement. As one disgruntled Senate committee pointed out, "A coal mine may exist in the United States not more than ten miles from valuable ores of iron and other materials, and both of them be useless . . . as the price of land carriage is too great to be borne by either." During the 1820s and 1830s, however, canal-building projects dramatically transformed this situation. The 363-mile-long Erie Canal, the last link in a chain of waterways binding New York City to the Great Lakes and the Northwest, was the most impressive of these new canals. The volume of goods and people it carried at low cost, the economic advantages it conferred on those within its reach (suggested by both the figure on inland freight rates and the table on economic growth) prompted the construction of over 3,000 miles of canals by 1840, primarily in eastern and midwestern states.

SIGNIFICANT FACTORS PROMOTING ECONOMIC GROWTH, 1820–1860

Factor	Important Features	Contribution to Growth
Abundant natural resources	Acquisition of new territories (Louisiana Purchase, Florida, trans-Mississippi West); exploitation and discovery of eastern resources	Provided raw materials and energy vital to economic transformation
Substantial population growth	Increase from 9 million in 1820 to over 30 million in 1860—due to natural increase of population and, especially after 1840, to rising immigration; importance of immigration from Ireland, Germany	Provided workers and consumers necessary for economic growth; immigration increased diversity of workforce with complex results, among them supply of capital and technological know-how
Transportation revolution	Improvement of roads; extensive canal building, 1817–1837; increasing importance of railroad construction thereafter; by 1860, 30,000 miles of tracks; steamboats facilitate travel on water	Facilitated movement of peoples, goods, and information; drew people into national economy market; stimulated agricultural expansion, regional crop specialization; decreased costs of shipping goods; strengthened ties between Northeast and Midwest
Capital investment	Investments by European investors and U.S. interests; importance of mercantile capital and banks, insurance companies in funneling capital to economic enterprises	Provided capital to support variety of new economic enterprises, improvements in transportation
Government support	Local, state, and national legislation; loans favoring enterprise; judicial decisions	Provided capital, privileges, and supportive climate for economic enterprises
Industrialization	New methods of producing goods, with and without involvement of machinery	Produced more numerous, cheaper goods for mass market; transformed classes and nature of work; affected distribution of wealth and individual opportunity

Even at the height of the canal boom, politicians, promoters, and others, impressed with Britain's success with railways, also supported the construction of railroads. Railroads, unlike canals that might freeze during the winter, were capable of operating year-round. Nor did they need large amounts of water to operate, as canals did. They could be built almost anywhere, an advantage that encouraged Baltimore merchants, envious of New York's water link to the Northwest, to begin the Baltimore & Ohio Railroad in 1828.

Despite the interest in and advantages of railroads, there were technical problems to resolve; for example, the first trains jumped their tracks and spewed sparks, setting nearby fields ablaze. But such difficulties were quickly overcome. By 1840, there were 3,000 miles of track, most in the Northeast. Another 5,000 miles were laid during the 1840s, and by the end of the 1850s, total mileage soared to 30,000. Like the canals, the new railroads strengthened the links between the Old Northwest and the East.

Improved transportation had such a profound influence on American life that some historians use the term *transportation revolution* to refer to its impact. Canals and railroads bound the country together in a new way. They provided farmers, merchants, and manufacturers with cheap and reliable access to distant markets and goods and encouraged Americans to settle the frontier and cultivate virgin lands. The economic opportunities they opened fostered technological innovations that might increase production. Eventually, the strong economic and social ties the waterways and then the railways fostered between the Northwest and the East led people living in the two regions to share political outlooks.

Especially in terms of the pattern of western settlement, railroads exerted enormous influence. As the railroads followed—or led—settlers westward, their routes could determine whether a city, town, or even homestead survived. The railroad transformed Chicago from a small settlement into a bustling commercial and transportation center. In 1850, the city contained not one mile of track, but within five years, 2,200 miles of track serving 150,000 square miles terminated in Chicago.

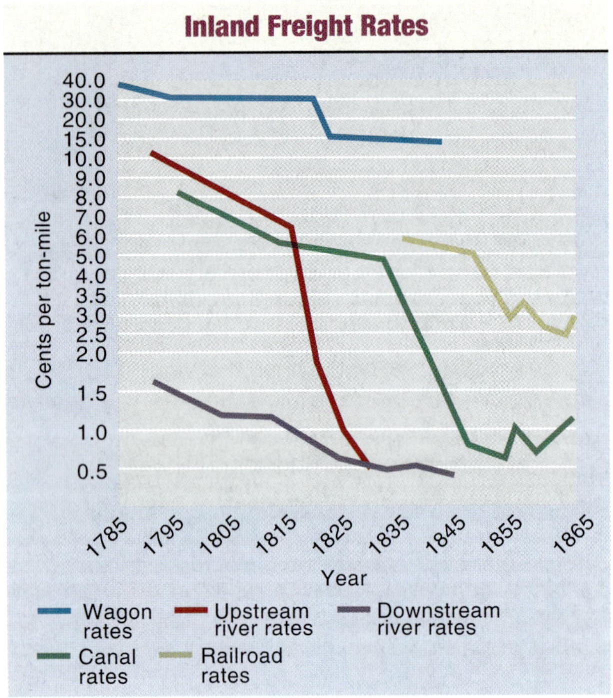

As this chart makes dramatically clear, the transportation revolution had a tremendous impact on the cost of shipping goods and materials to markets and factories.

The dramatic rise in railroad construction in the two decades before the Civil War contributed to faster economic growth after 1839. Goods, people, commercial information, and mail flowed ever more predictably, rapidly, and cheaply. In 1790, an order from Boston took two weeks to reach Philadelphia; in 1836, it took only 36 hours.

Improved transportation stimulated agricultural expansion and regional specialization. Farmers began to plant larger crops for the market, concentrating on those most suited to their soil and climate. By the late 1830s, the Old Northwest had become the country's granary, and New England farmers turned to dairy or produce farming. By 1860, American farmers were producing four to five times as much wheat, corn, cattle, and hogs as they had in 1810. Their achievements meant plentiful, cheap food for American workers and more income for farmers to spend on the new consumer goods.

Capital and Government Support

Internal improvements, the exploitation of natural resources, and the cultivation of new lands all demanded capital. Much of it came from European investors. Between 1790 and 1861, over $500 million

This view of the junction of the Erie and Champlain Canals around 1830 suggests the ambitious construction efforts that lay behind the improvement of transportation. The Erie Canal stretched for 363 miles and was the last link in a chain of waterways connecting New York to the Great Lakes and the Northwest. Irish immigrants who flooded into the country during the antebellum period provided the muscle power for building the Erie Canal and worked on many other transportation projects. One of the laborers' songs captures the pride and magnitude of "such a great undertaking. . . . To dig through the vallies so level, through rocks for to cut a canal." *(© Collection of the New-York Historical Society)*

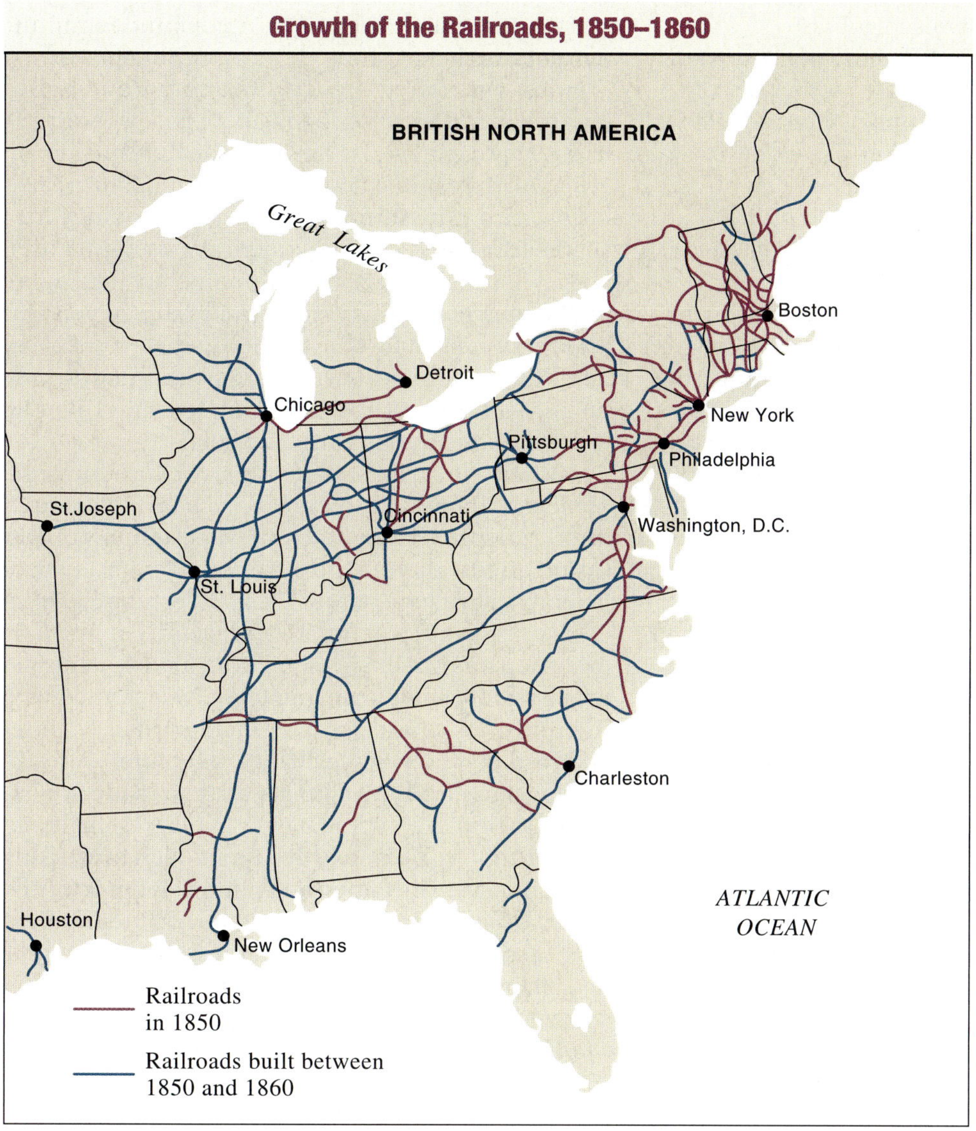

This map shows the tremendous surge of railroad building between 1850 and 1860 and the ways the railroad strengthened the ties between the Northeast and the Midwest. Notice that the railroad has crossed the Mississippi River. Because of the transportation revolution, almost the entire area east of the Mississippi was within a week's journey of New York City by 1860.

flowed into the United States from Europe. Foreign investors from Europe, adding to funds brought by immigrant families, financed as much as a third of all canal construction and bought about a quarter of all railroad bonds.

American mercantile capital fueled growth as well. As Chapter 9 suggested, the merchant class prospered in the half century after the Revolution. Now merchants invested in schemes ranging from canals to textile factories. Many ventured into the production of goods and became manufacturers themselves.

Prosperous Americans, like Arthur Bronson and Charles Butler, eagerly sought opportunities to put their capital to work. Intrigued by the Northwest's investment possibilities, the two New Yorkers toured the region in 1833. Despite primitive conditions, both men saw wonderful opportunities. Detroit, Butler concluded, "is destined to be a very great city," and Chicago "presents one of the finest fields in America for industry & enterprise." Each man channeled funds into western projects. Bronson's investments included Ohio banks; farmland in Wisconsin territory, Illinois, Michigan, Ohio, and Indiana; and real estate in Chicago and Detroit, all in addition to his holdings in New York ironworks and banks.

Bronson's investment in banks indicated his understanding of their role in stimulating economic growth. He also actively promoted life insurance companies, which, unlike commercial banks, lent money on a long-term basis. These financial institutions, he realized, served as intermediaries, funneling into economic enterprises the capital of people with neither the time nor the expertise to invest their money themselves.

Local and state government played their part by enthusiastically supporting economic growth. States often helped new ventures raise capital by passing laws of incorporation, by awarding entrepreneurs special privileges such as tax breaks or monopolistic control, by underwriting bonds for improvement projects, which increased their investment appeal, and by providing loans for internal improvements. New York, Pennsylvania, Ohio, Indiana, Illinois, and Virginia publicly financed almost 75 percent of the canal systems in their states between 1815 and 1860.

The national government also encouraged economic expansion by cooperating with states on some internal improvements, such as the National Road linking Maryland and Illinois. Federal tariff policy shielded American products, and the second U.S. Bank provided the financial stability investors required. So widespread was the enthusiasm for growth that the line separating the public sector from the private often became unclear.

The law also helped promote aggressive economic growth. Judicial decisions created a new understanding of property rights. The case of *Palmer* v. *Mulligan,* decided by the New York State Supreme Court in 1805, laid down the principle that property ownership included the right to develop property for business purposes. Land was increasingly defined as a productive asset for exploitation, not merely subsistence, as earlier judicial rulings had suggested.

Investors and business operators alike wanted to increase predictability in the conduct of business. Contracts lay at the heart of commercial relationships, but contract law hardly existed in 1800. A period of rapid development ensued. A series of important Supreme Court decisions between 1819 and 1824 established the basic principle that contracts were binding. In *Dartmouth College* v. *Woodward,* the Court held that a state charter could not be modified unless both parties agreed, and it declared in *Sturges* v. *Crowninshield* that a New York law allowing debtors to repudiate their debts was unconstitutional.

A New Mentality

As the discussion of the links between law and economic growth suggests, economic expansion depends on intangible factors as well as more obvious ones such as improved transportation. When a farmer decided to specialize in apples for the New York market rather than to concentrate on raising food for his family, he was thinking in a new way just as was Arthur Bronson when he invested in banks that would, in turn, finance a variety of economic enterprises. The entrepreneurial outlook, the *"universal desire,"* as one newspaper editor put it, *"to get forward,"* was shared by millions of Americans. By encouraging investment, new business and agricultural ventures, and land speculation, entrepreneurialism played a vital role in antebellum economic development.

Europeans often recognized another intangible factor when they described Americans as energetic and open to change. As one Frenchman explained in 1834, "All here is circulation, motion, and boiling agitation. Experiment follows experiment; enterprise succeeds to enterprise." An American observer agreed. "Every man seems born with some steam engine within him, driving him into an incessant and restless activity of body and mind . . . every head and every hand busy, with a thousand projects, and only one holiday—the 4th of July—working from morning till night with the most intense industry."

Others described an American mechanical "genius." The American was "a mechanic by nature," one Frenchman insisted. "In Massachusetts and Connecticut, there is not a labourer who had not invented a machine or tool." This observer exaggerated the uniqueness of American inventiveness. Many American innovations drew on British precedents and were introduced by immigrants well acquainted with the British originals. Nor was every ordinary laborer an inventor. Many of the changes that improved efficiency came from machinists as they made adjustments to British equipment or tinkered with malfunctioning mill machines to get them back in working order. But every invention and improvement attracted scores of imitators. In 1854, the government patent office issued 56 patents for harvesting implements and 39 for seed planters; the next year, it issued 40 for sewing machines.

Mechanically minded Americans prided themselves on developing efficient and productive tools and machines. The McCormick harvester was the product of two generations of the McCormick family who dreamed of replacing scythes and sickles with a horsedrawn reaping machine and worked for years to realize that dream. Like the McCormicks, John Jervis experimented for years to modify the heavy rigid English railroad engine into a lighter, more flexible engine suited to American conditions. The Colt revolver, Goodyear vulcanized rubber products, and the sewing machine were developed, refined, and developed further. Such improvements cut labor costs and increased efficiency. By 1840, the average American cotton textile mill was about 10 percent more efficient and 3 percent more profitable than its British counterpart.

Although the shortage of labor in the United States stimulated technological innovations that replaced humans with machines, the rapid spread of education after 1800 also contributed to innovation and increased productivity. By 1840, most whites were literate. In that year, public schools nationwide were

White Secondary School Enrollment, 1840–1860*

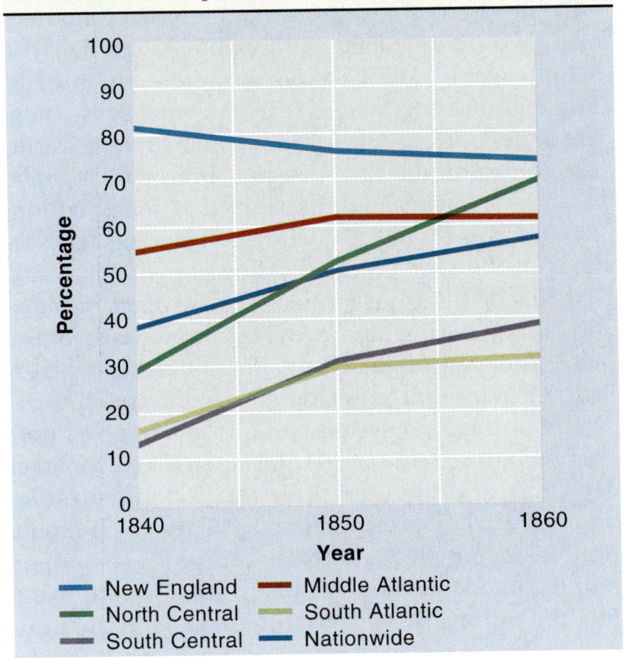

*Note the regional difference in school enrollment and changes over time. Source: Albert W. Niemi, *U.S. Economic History* (1975).

educating 38.4 percent of white children between the ages of five and nineteen. The belief that education spurred economic growth helped foster enthusiasm for public education, particularly in the Northeast. The development of the Massachusetts common school illustrates the connections many saw between education and progress.

Although several states had decided to use tax monies for education by 1800, Massachusetts moved first toward mass education by mandating in 1827 that taxes pay the whole cost of the state's public schools. Several years later, the state set up a permanent elementary education fund and in 1836 forbade factory managers to hire children who had not spent three of the previous twelve months in school. Despite the legislation, the Massachusetts school system limped along. School buildings were often run-down, even unheated. Because school curricula were virtually nonexistent, students often lounged idly at their desks.

Under the leadership of Horace Mann, the reform of state education for white children began in earnest in 1837. Mann intended to regularize the operation of schools and attract more students to them. He and others pressed for graded schools, uniform curricula, and teacher training. Believing that the power of local districts over their schools presented a barrier against improvement, he sought to reduce local control. Mann's success inspired reformers everywhere. For the first time in American history, primary education became the rule for most children outside the South between five and nineteen. The expansion of education created a whole new career of schoolteaching, a career that attracted mostly young women.

Mann believed that education promoted inventiveness. It "had a market value." Businessmen often agreed. Prominent industrialists in the 1840s were convinced that education produced workers who could handle complex machinery without undue supervision and were superior employees—reliable, punctual, industrious, and sober. Manufacturers valued education not merely because of its intellectual content but also because it encouraged habits essential to a disciplined and productive workforce.

Ambivalence Toward Change

While supporting education as a means to economic growth, many Americans also firmly believed in its social value. They expected the public schools to mold student character and promote "virtuous habits" and "rational self-governing" behavior. Many school activities sought to instill good habits. Students learned facts by rote because memory work and recitation taught them discipline and concentration. Nineteenth-century schoolbooks reinforced classroom goals. "It is a great sin to be idle," children read in one 1830 text, and another encouragingly pointed out, "He who rises early and is industrious and temperate will acquire health and riches." A third warned of the consequences of ignoring the message: "Poverty is the fruit of idleness."

The concern with education and character indicates that as much as Americans welcomed economic progress, they also feared its results. The much-heralded improvements in transportation that encouraged trade and emigration, for example, created anxieties that civilization might disintegrate as people moved far from their place of birth and from familiar institutions. Others worried that rapid change undermined the American family and would turn children into barbarians. Schools, which taught students to be deferential, obedient, and punctual, could counter the worst by-products of change. The schools served as much as a defense against change as they did its agent. Fear and confidence were two sides of the coin of economic transformation.

Other signs of cultural uneasiness appeared. In the eighteenth century, Benjamin Franklin emphasized the importance of hard work in his celebrated *Poor Richard's Almanack*. In the 1830s, popularizers restated Franklin's message. As the publishing revolution lowered costs and speeded the production of printed material, these authors poured out tracts, stories, and

This photograph of the Emerson School for Young Ladies was taken sometime between 1840 and 1862. An examination of the way the classroom was organized—the relative position of students and teacher and the prominent role of the clock—begins to suggest the emphasis schools placed on obedience, deference, order, and punctuality. The varied clothing of the students also highlights the impact of the manufacturing revolution on everyday life. *(The Metropolitan Museum of Art, Gift of I. N. Phelps Stokes, Edward S. Hawes, Alice Mary Hawes, Marion Augusta Hawes, 1937)*

manuals on how to get ahead. Claiming that hard work and good character led to success, they touted the virtues of diligence, punctuality, temperance, and thrift. These habits probably did assist economic growth. Slothful workers are seldom productive. Industry and perseverance often pay off. But the success of early nineteenth-century economic ventures frequently depended on the ability to take risks, to think daringly. The emphasis these publicists gave to the safe but stolid virtues and to responsible behavior suggests their fear of social disintegration. Their books and tracts aimed to counter unsettling effects of change and ensure the dominance of middle-class values.

The Advance of Industrialization

Significant economic growth between 1820 and 1860 resulted from the reorganization of production. Before industrialization, individual artisans fashioned goods with hand tools. Many American families also fabricated necessary articles; as late as 1820, Americans made two-thirds of all their clothes at home.

Factory production moved away from this decentralized system of artisan or family-based manufacturing and reorganized work by breaking down the manufacture of an article into discrete steps. Initially, early manufacturers often relied on what came to be called the "putting-out" system. Their strategy was to gain control of the raw materials from which goods were fashioned—leather in the case of shoes; cotton, flax, and wool for textiles—and arrangements for marketing the finished products. Some steps in the manufacturing process they farmed out to workers in shops and homes, paying them on a piecework basis, for the pieces they were able to "put out." Other steps manufacturers consolidated in their own central shops.

The putting-out system not only reorganized production but also entangled rural families in the market economy and affected their relationships to one another. Early pieceworkers might labor as a family unit, leaving men to exercise their power as fathers and husbands. But by the 1830s, men were moving into the workplace while wives and daughters continued to take in piecework. Unless they were driven by poverty, the women usually worked only intermittently. They took in shoes or made palm-leaf hats to pay off a family debt or to earn some cash for a desirable new good like cotton cloth or an iron cook stove. While most outworkers were not highly paid, they enjoyed earning their own cash and store credit. Piecework provided them with a new kind of independence even as they continued to stay at home.

The putting-out system persisted even as some manufacturers moved to consolidate all the steps of production under one roof. Hand labor gradually gave way to power-driven machinery such as wooden "spinning jennies." Often manufacturers sought the help of British immigrants who had the practical experience and technical know-how that few Americans possessed.

In 1789, William Ashley and Moses Brown, Rhode Island merchants, hired 21-year-old Samuel Slater, a former apprentice with an English cotton textile firm, to devise a water-powered, yarn-spinning machine. Slater did that, but he also developed a machine capable of carding, or straightening, the cotton fibers. Within a year, Ashley and Brown's spinning mill had begun operations in Pawtucket, Rhode Island. Its initial workforce consisted of nine children, ranging in age from seven to twelve. Ten years later, their number had grown to over 100. As factory workers replaced artisans and home manufacturers, the volume of goods rose, and prices dropped dramatically. The price of a yard of cotton cloth fell from 18 to 2 cents over the 45 years preceding the Civil War.

The transportation improvements that provided the opportunity to reach large markets after 1820

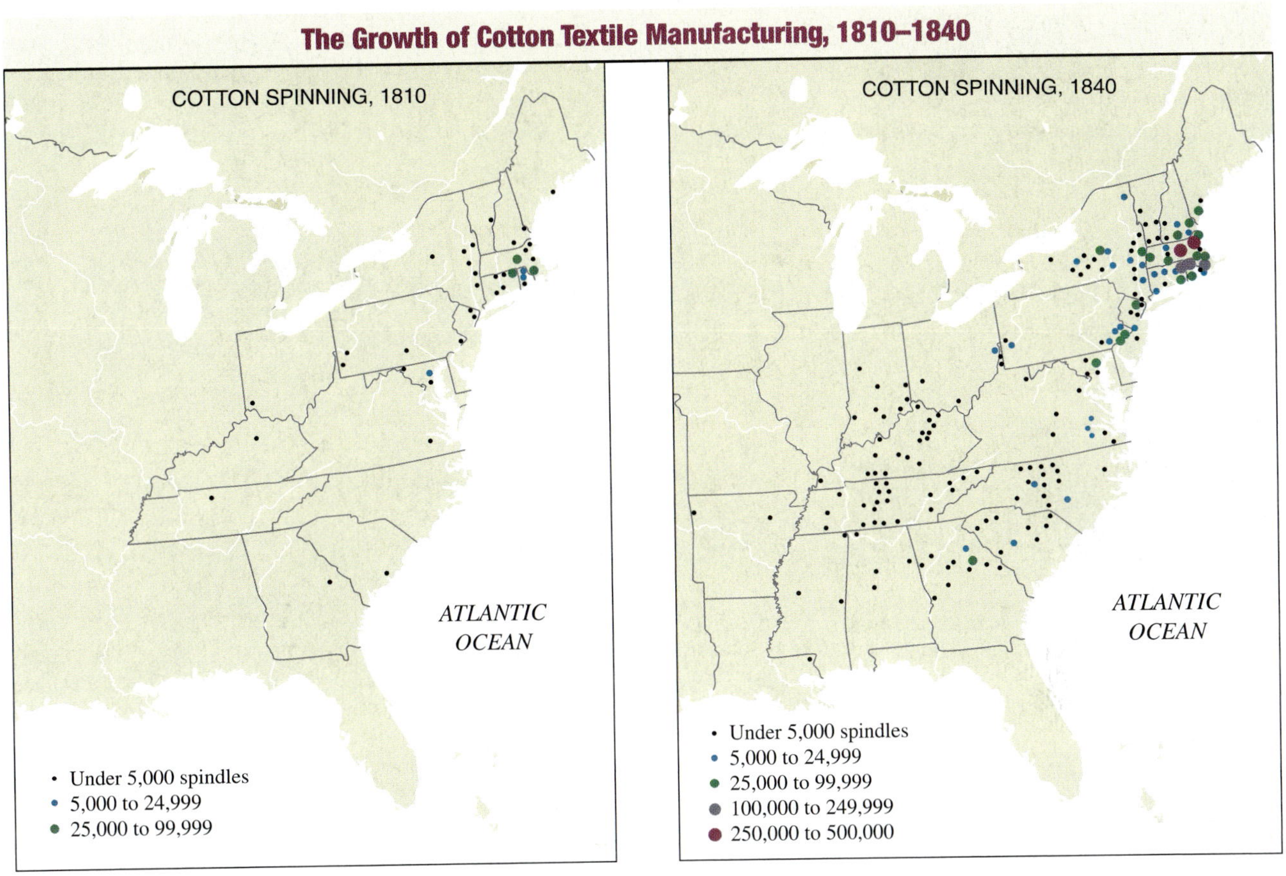

The concentration of textile manufacturing in New England suggests the changing economic and social trends in that region.

encouraged the reorganization of the production process and the use of machinery. The simple tastes and rural character of the American people suggested the wisdom of manufacturing inexpensive everyday goods like cloth and shoes rather than luxuries for the rich.

Between 1820 and 1860, textile manufacturing became the country's leading industry. Textile mills sprang up across the New England and Middle Atlantic states, regions that contained swift-flowing streams to power the mills, capitalists eager to finance the ventures, children and women to tend the machines, and numerous cities and towns with ready markets for cheap textiles. Early mills were small affairs, containing only the machines for carding and spinning. The thread was then put out to home workers to be woven into cloth. The early mechanization of cloth production did not replace home manufacture but supplemented it.

Already under way, however, were experiments that would further transform the industry. Closeted in the attic of a Boston house in 1813, Francis Cabot Lowell, a merchant, and Paul Moody, a mechanic, worked to devise a power loom capable of weaving cloth. Lowell's study of mechanical looms during his earlier tour of English and Scottish cotton factories guided their work. Eventually, they succeeded, and the loom they devised was soon installed in a mill at Waltham, Massachusetts, capitalized at $300,000 by Lowell and his Boston Associates.

The most important innovation of the Waltham operation was Lowell's decision to bring all the steps of cotton cloth production together under one roof. The Waltham mill thus differed from mills in Rhode Island and Great Britain, where spinning and weaving were separate operations. Through this centralizing of the entire manufacturing process and workforce in one factory, cloth for the mass market could be produced more cheaply and more profitably. The work of maintaining the equipment in good order encouraged machinists to improve upon existing machines. Constant innovation thus helped mills to make cloth ever more cheaply and quickly. In 1823, the Boston Associates expanded their operations to East Chelmsford on the Merrimack River, a town they renamed Lowell.

Most New England mills followed the Lowell system. In the Middle Atlantic states, the textile industry was more varied. Philadelphia became a center for fine textiles, and Rhode Island factories produced less

Gleason's Pictorial, one of the many modestly priced publications that the introduction of steam-powered printing presses put within reach of the reading public, pictures the Manchester Print Works in New Hampshire in 1854. Although the smokestacks spewing forth black clouds of smoke hint at the pollution that accompanied the Industrial Revolution, nineteenth-century viewers most likely were impressed by the dignified mill building and the seemingly spacious surroundings. Men appear in the foreground, but over half the workers in this calico factory were female. *(Library of Congress)*

expensive materials. Maryland manufacturers, like those in Philadelphia, focused on quality goods. The cumulative impact of the rise of the textile industry was to supplant the home production of cloth, even though some women would continue to spin and weave for their families for some years to come, and hand-loom weavers would survive for another generation. In the process, Americans were transformed from a people clad in earth-colored homespun into a nation decked out in gayer, more colorful clothing.

Textile mills were an important component of the increasingly industrial character of the Northeast. The majority of the South's cotton still went to England, but an increasing share flowed to northeastern mills. Other manufacturing concerns, such as shoemaking, also contributed to the Northeast's economy. By 1860, fully 71 percent of all manufacturing workers lived in this region of the country. Still other important manufacturing operations reached west and south from New England. The processing of wheat, timber, and hides using power-driven machinery was common in most communities of 200 families or more. Although a third of them were clustered in Philadelphia, paper mills were widespread. The ironworking and metalworking industry stretched from Albany, New York, south to Maryland and west to Cincinnati.

Environmental Consequences

Although canals, railroads, steamboats, and the growth of industry undergirded economic growth, their impact on the environment was far-reaching and often harmful. Steamboats and early railroads, for example, depended on wood for fuel. So, too, did the heating stoves that were keeping American families warm. Armed with new steel axes, lumbermen and farmers kept up with the increased demand for wood, and the eastern forest and the wildlife that lived there rapidly disappeared. Better transportation, which encouraged western settlement, also promoted forest clearance as individual settlers cleared land for crops and cut wood for housing. Sawmills and milldams interfered with spawning habits of fish, clogged their gills with sawdust, and even changed the flow of rivers. The process of ecological change, spurred by the desire for wood, recurred as lumber companies and entrepreneurs moved from the East to exploit the forests of the Great Lakes and of the Gulf states.

As late as 1840, wood was the main source for the country's energy needs. But the high price of wood and the discovery of anthracite coal in Pennsylvania signaled the beginning of a shift to coal as the major source of power. While the East gradually regained some of its forest cover, the heavy use of coal resulted in air pollution. Steam engines and heating stoves poured out dirty fumes into the air. In New York City, one could see the evidence of pollution everywhere—in the gray cloud hanging over the city; in the smoke rising from its machine shops, refineries, and private houses; in the acrid smells and black soot that were a part of daily life. Pittsburgh, considered by some the dirtiest city in the United States, was surrounded by "a dense black smoke" and rained down "flakes of soot" on houses and people alike.

Textile mills located along rivers and streams might present a prettier picture than the shops and refineries of New York because they used water as the source of power. But mills also adversely affected the environment. Dams and canals supporting industrial activities contributed to soil erosion. "Industrial operations," declared the Vermont fish commissioner in 1857, are "destructive to fish that live or spawn in fresh water. . . . The thousand deleterious mineral substances, discharged into rivers from metallurgical, chemical, and manufacturing establishments, poison them by shoals."

Some Americans were aware of the environmental consequences of rapid growth and change. Author James Fenimore Cooper had one of his characters in his novel *The Pioneers* condemn those who destroyed nature "without remorse and without shame." The popularity in the 1820s of a song with the lines "Woodman, / Spare that Tree / Touch not a single bough" suggested sympathy for that point of view. Yet most Americans accepted the changing environment as an inevitable part of progress.

EARLY MANUFACTURING

Industrialization created a more efficient means of producing more goods at much lower cost than had been possible in the homes and small shops of an earlier day. Philadelphian Samuel Breck's diary reveals some of the new profusion and range of goods. "Went to town principally to see the Exhibition of American Manufactures at the Masonic Hall," he noted in 1833. "More than 700 articles have been sent. Among this great variety, I distinguished the Philadelphia porcelains, beautiful Canton cotton, made at York in this state, soft and capacious blankets, silver plate, cabinet ware, marble mantels, splendid pianos and centre tables, chymical drugs, hardware, saddlery, and the most beautiful black broadcloth I ever saw."

The Impact of Industrialization

Two examples illustrate how industrialization transformed American life in both simple and complex ways. Before the nineteenth century, local printing shops depended on manual labor to produce books, newspapers, and journals. The cost of reading material was high enough to make a library a sign of wealth. Many literate families of moderate means had little in their homes to read other than a family Bible and an almanac.

Between 1830 and 1850, however, adoption and improvement of British inventions revolutionized the printing and publishing industries. Like other changes in production, the transformation of publishing involved not only technological but also managerial and marketing innovations. A $2.5 million market in 1830, the book business quintupled by 1850.

As books and magazines dropped in cost and grew in number, far more people could afford them. Without this new mass market of readers, Susan Warner's literary success would hardly have been possible. But the implications of the changes in publishing went beyond best-sellers. The presence of inexpensive reading material inspired and nourished literacy. Easy access to reading material also encouraged a new sort of independence. No longer needing to rely solely on the words of the "better sort" for information, people could form their own views on the basis of what they read. At the same time, however, readers everywhere were exposed repeatedly to the mainstream norms, values, and ideas expressed in magazines and books. Even on the frontier, pioneer women could study inexpensive ladies' magazines and books of domestic advice or be inspired by the pious example of Ellen Montgomery in *The Wide, Wide World.* Their husbands could follow the latest political news, market prices, or theories about scientific farming while the children learned their letters and the moral lesson in McGuffey readers. The proliferation of printed matter had an enormous impact on people's stock of information, values, tastes, and use of leisure time.

Just as printed materials wrought great changes in American life, the making of inexpensive timepieces affected its pace and rhythms. Before the 1830s, when few Americans could afford a clock, it was difficult to make exact plans or to establish rigid schedules. But the production of timepieces soared in the 1830s, and by mid-century, peddlers had carried inexpensive mass-produced wooden clocks everywhere. Even on the frontier, "in Kentucky, in Indiana, in Illinois, in Missouri, and here in every dell in Arkansas, and in cabins where there was not a chair to sit on," according to one observer, "there was sure to be a Connecticut clock." Free of nature's irregular divisions of the day, Americans could decide how to use their time and coordinate their activities. Clocks encouraged a more disciplined use of time and undergirded the economic changes taking place. Timepieces, for example, were essential for the successful operation of steamboats and railroads, which ran on schedules.

Clocks also imposed a new rhythm in many workplaces. For some Americans, the clock represented a form of oppression rather than liberation. An early mill song put it directly: "The factory bell begins to

This simple thirty-hour clock was the result of successful technological innovations by Eli Terry. As a boy, when Terry learned the trade, each clock was made by hand and was far too expensive for ordinary people to purchase. Terry experimented with replacing brass parts with wooden ones and developed machinery capable of mass producing clocks with the assistance of unskilled workers. His modestly priced timepieces, carried by peddlers into the countryside, helped to transform the ways Americans contemplated and used their time. *(National Museum of American History, Smithsonian Institution)*

ring / And we must all obey, / And to our old employment go / Or else be turned away."

A NEW ENGLAND TEXTILE TOWN

The process of industrialization and its impact on work and the workforce are ably illustrated by Lowell, the "model" Massachusetts textile town, and Cincinnati, a bustling midwestern industrial center. Though there were similarities between the process of industrialization in these two communities, significant differences also existed. The example of Lowell points out the importance of women in the early manufacturing workforce, whereas Cincinnati shows that industrialization was often an uneven and complex process.

Lowell was a new town, planned and built expressly for industrial purposes in the 1820s. Planners gave most attention to the shops, mills, and workers' housing, but the bustling town had a charm that prompted visitors to see it as a model factory community. In 1836, Lowell, with 17,000 inhabitants, aspired to become the "Manchester of America." It was the country's most important textile center.

By 1830, women composed nearly 70 percent of the Lowell textile workforce, with men and children filling the remaining positions. The women who came to Lowell for jobs were the first women to labor outside their homes in large numbers. Some had already labored for wages by taking in piecework. Now they became some of the first Americans to experience the full impact of the factory system.

Lowell's planners realized the difficulty of persuading men to leave farming for millwork, but saw that they might recruit unmarried women relatively cheaply for a stint. Unlike mill owners farther south, they decided not to depend on child labor. By hiring women who would work only until marriage, they hoped to avoid the depraved and depressed workforce so evident in Great Britain. New England factory communities, they hoped, because of their special arrangements, would become models for the world.

Working and Living in a Mill Town

At the age of 15, Mary Paul wrote to her father asking him "to consent to let me go to Lowell if you can." This young woman from Vermont was typical of those drawn to work in Lowell and other New England textile towns. As the planners had anticipated, the bulk of the workforce was made up of young unmarried women. In 1830, more than 63 percent of Lowell's population was female, and most were between the ages of 15 and 29.

These women, from New England's middling rural families, came to the mills for a variety of reasons, but desperate poverty was not one of them. The decline of home manufacture deprived many women, especially daughters in farming families, of their traditional productive role. Some rural young women took in piecework to replace or supplement regular chores. Millwork offered them more money than piecework and the possibility of independence. As Sally Rice from Vermont explained, "I am almost nineteen years old. I must of course have something of my own before many more years have passed over my head.

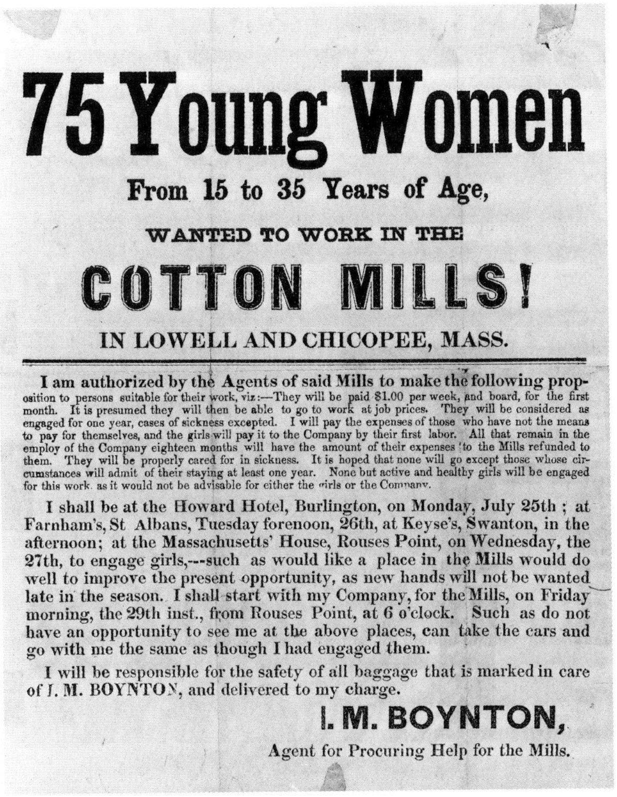

75 Young Women

From 15 to 35 Years of Age,

WANTED TO WORK IN THE

COTTON MILLS!

IN LOWELL AND CHICOPEE, MASS.

I am authorized by the Agents of said Mills to make the following proposition to persons suitable for their work, viz:—They will be paid $1.00 per week, and board, for the first month. It is presumed they will then be able to go to work at job prices. They will be considered as engaged for one year, cases of sickness excepted. I will pay the expenses of those who have not the means to pay for themselves, and the girls will pay it to the Company by their first labor. All that remain in the employ of the Company eighteen months will have the amount of their expenses to the Mills refunded to them. They will be properly cared for in sickness. It is hoped that none will go except those whose circumstances will admit of their staying at least one year. None but active and healthy girls will be engaged for this work, as it would not be advisable for either the girls or the Company.

I shall be at the Howard Hotel, Burlington, on Monday, July 25th; at Farnham's, St Albans, Tuesday forenoon, 26th, at Keyse's, Swanton, in the afternoon; at the Massachusetts' House, Rouses Point, on Wednesday, the 27th, to engage girls,---such as would like a place in the Mills would do well to improve the present opportunity, as new hands will not be wanted late in the season. I shall start with my Company, for the Mills, on Friday morning, the 29th inst., from Rouses Point, at 6 o'clock. Such as do not have an opportunity to see me at the above places, can take the cars and go with me the same as though I had engaged them.

I will be responsible for the safety of all baggage that is marked in care of I. M. BOYNTON, and delivered to my charge.

I. M. BOYNTON,

Agent for Procuring Help for the Mills.

This recruiting poster, if read carefully, reveals the ways young women were brought to the mills and the conditions of their employment. What might a young woman find attractive about millwork if she read this poster? Are there any statements that might make her reluctant to work in the mills? *(Courtesy of Baker Library, Harvard Graduate School of Business Administration, Boston, Mass.)*

And where is that something coming from if I go home and earn nothing." Millwork paid women relatively well in the 1820s and 1830s. Domestic servants' weekly wages hovered around 75¢, and seamstresses' 90¢, whereas in the mid-1830s women could make between $2.40 and $3.20 a week in the mill. The lure of the "privileges" of the new environment also drew young women to Lowell.

Few considered their decision to come to Lowell a permanent commitment. Most young women were like Mary Paul and Sally Rice. They came to work for a few years, felt free to go home or to school for a few months, and then returned to millwork. Once married—and the majority of women did marry—they left the millwork force forever.

New manufacturing work was regimented and exhausting. The day began at dawn or even earlier and ended about 7 in the evening. The standard schedule was 12 hours a day, six days a week, with only a half-hour for breakfast and lunch. The clock tower atop the attractive four- to six-story brick mills symbolized the new control of work.

Within the factory, the organization of space facilitated production. In the basement was the waterwheel, the source of power. Above, successive floors were completely open, each containing the machines necessary for the different steps of cloth making: carding, spinning, weaving, and dressing. Elevators moved materials from one floor to another. On a typical floor, rows of machines stretched the length of the low room, tended by operatives who might watch over several machines at the same time. From his elevated

This depiction of Lowell workers, engraved in the 1850s by the American Banknote company, shows neatly dressed young women carefully tending to their machines. Their concentration on their task suggests that they had to pay close attention to their repetitive work. The engraving gives little idea of the tedium, noise, and other difficulties of millwork that the young women often mentioned in their letters. *(Print Collection, Miriam and Ira D. Wallach Division of Art, Prints and Photographs, The New York Public Library, Astor, Lenox and Tilden Foundations)*

desk at the end of the room, the overseer watched the workers. The male supervisor and two or three children roamed the aisles to survey the work and to help out. The rooms were noisy, poorly lit, and badly ventilated. Overseers, believing that humidity would prevent threads from breaking, often nailed the windows shut.

Although machines, not operatives, did the basic work of production, workers had to ensure that their machines worked properly. The lowest-paid women workers who watched over the spinning frames and drawing frames were responsible for piecing together broken yarn once the machines had automatically halted. The better-paid weavers made skillful interventions in the production process, repairing warp yarns and rapidly replacing shuttle bobbins when they ran out of yarn so that production would slow down for only a moment. "I can see myself now," recalled Harriet Robbins, "racing down the alley, between the spinning frames, carrying in front of me a bobbin-box bigger than I was . . . so as not to keep the spinning-frames stopped long."

Involving an adaptation to a new work situation, millwork also entailed a new living situation for women operatives. The companies provided substantial quarters for their overseers and housing for male workers and their families. Hoping to attract respectable females to Lowell and to avoid the kind of slums found in English industrial cities, the mill owners constructed company boardinghouses for women workers. Headed by female housekeepers, the boardinghouse maintained strict rules, including a 10 o'clock curfew. Owners wanted a respectable and well-rested work force. Little personal privacy was possible. Normally, four or six women shared a small room, which contained little more than the double beds in which they slept together.

Amid such intimate working and living conditions, young women formed close ties with one another and developed a strong sense of community. Strong group norms dictated acceptable behavior, clothing, and speech and shared leisure activities at lectures, night classes, sewing and literary circles, and church. At work, experienced operatives initiated newcomers into the mysteries of tending machines, stood in for each other, and shared work assignments.

Female Responses to Work

Although millwork offered better wages than other occupations open to women, all female workers had limited job mobility. The small number staying in the mills for more than a few years did receive increases in pay and promotions to more responsible positions. A top female wage earner took home 40 percent more than a newcomer. But she never could earn as much as male employees, who at the top of the job ladder earned 200 percent more than men at the bottom. Because only men could hold supervisory positions, economic and job discrimination were an integral part of the early American industrial system.

Job discrimination generally went unquestioned, for most female operatives accepted sexual differences as part of life. But the sense of sisterhood, so much a part of the Lowell work experience, supported open protest, most of it focused against a system that workers feared was turning them into a class of dependent wage earners. Lowell women's critique of the new industrial order drew on both the sense of female community and the revolutionary tradition.

Trouble broke out when hard times hit Lowell in February 1834. Falling prices, poor sales, and rising inventories prompted managers to announce a 15 percent wage cut. This was their way of protecting profits—at the expense of their employees. The millworkers sprang into action. Petitions circulated, threatening a strike. Meetings followed. At one lunchtime gathering, the company agent, hoping to end the protests, fired an apparent ringleader. But, as the agent reported, "she declared that every girl in the room should leave with her," then "made a signal, and . . . they all marched out & few returned the ensuing morning." The strikers roamed the streets appealing to other workers and visited other mills. In all, about a sixth of the town's workforce turned out.

Though this work stoppage was brief and failed to prevent the wage reduction, it demonstrated women workers' concern about the impact of industrialization on the labor force. Strikers, taunted as unfeminine for their "amazonian display," refused to agree that workers were inferior to bosses. Pointing out that they were daughters of free men, strikers, as the words of their song suggest, sought to link their protest to their fathers' and grandfathers' efforts to throw off the bonds of British oppression during the Revolution.

Let oppression shrug her shoulders,
And a haughty tyrant frown,
And little upstart Ignorance,
In mockery look down.
Yet I value not the feeble threats
Of Tories in disguise,
While the flag of Independence
O'er our noble nation flies.

The women viewed threatened wage reductions as an unjust attack on their economic independence and also on their claim to equal status with their employers. Revolutionary rhetoric that once held only political meaning took on economic overtones as Lowell women confronted industrial work.

During the 1830s, wage cuts, long hours, increased workloads, and production speedups, mandated by owners' desires to protect profits, constantly reminded Lowell women and other textile workers of the possibility of "wage slavery." In Dover, New Hampshire, 800 women turned out and formed a union in 1834 to protest wage cuts. In the 1840s, women in several New England states agitated for the ten-hour day, and petitions from Lowell prompted the Massachusetts legislature to hold the first government hearing on industrial working conditions.

The Changing Character of the Workforce

Most protest efforts met with limited success. The short tenure of most women millworkers prevented permanent labor organizations. Protests mounted in hard times often failed because mill owners could easily replace striking workers. Increasingly, owners found that they could do without the Yankee women altogether. The waves of immigration that deposited so many penniless foreigners in northeastern cities in the 1840s and 1850s created a new pool of labor. The newcomers were desperate for jobs and would accept lower wages than New England farm girls. Gradually, the Irish began to replace Yankee women in the mills. Representing only 8 percent of the Lowell workforce in 1845, the Irish composed nearly half the workers by 1860.

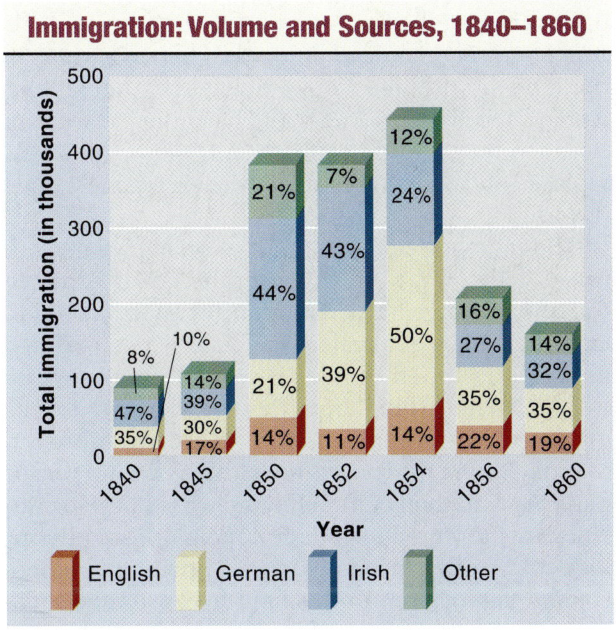

This chart captures the growing ethnic diversity of the country in the years before the Civil War. What is only implied is the element of religious diversity that immigration also introduced. Most of the Irish immigrants and half of the Germans were Roman Catholics. The presence of immigrants who differed so dramatically from Protestant Americans in background and culture contributed to the tensions of the period.

As the example of Lowell suggests, the reality of massive immigration had a far-reaching effect on American life in the antebellum period. Immigration, of course, had been a constant part of the country's experience from the early seventeenth century. But it occurred on an unprecedented scale after 1845, the nearby figure makes clear. What had been a trickle in the 1820s—some 128,502 foreigners came to U.S. shores during that decade—became a torrent in the 1850s, with more than 2.8 million migrants to the United States. Although families and single women emigrated, the majority of the newcomers were young European men of working age.

This vast movement of people, which began in the 1840s and continued throughout the nineteenth century, resulted from dramatic changes in European life: a population explosion between 1750 and 1845 and the introduction of new farming and industrial practices that undermined or ended traditional means of livelihood. Agricultural disaster also played a major role in uprooting the Irish from their homeland. Potatoes were the staple of the Irish diet. In 1845, a terrible blight attacked and destroyed the potato crop. Years of devastating famine followed. One million Irish starved to death between 1841 and 1851; another million and a half emigrated. Although not all chose the United States as their destination, the Irish were the most numerous of all newcomers to America in the two decades preceding the Civil War. They usually arrived almost penniless in eastern port cities without the skills needed for good jobs. With only their raw labor to sell, employers, as one observer noted, "will engage Paddy as they would a dray horse."

German immigrants, who made up the second largest group of newcomers during this period (1,361,506 arrived between 1840 and 1859), were not driven to the United States by the kind of desperate circumstances forcing the Irish to leave their homeland. Some even arrived with sufficient resources to go west and buy land. (The significance of this German midwestern presence is suggested by the fact that as late as 1940, German was one of the most common "street" languages in Minnesota.) Others had the training to join the urban working class as shoemakers, cabinetmakers, and tailors.

The arrival of so many non-British newcomers made American society more diverse than it had ever been. The consequences of this diversity were complex, as discussions in this and subsequent chapters will make clear. Because over half of the Irish and German immigrants were Roman Catholics, a religion long feared and disliked by Protestants, religious differences acerbated economic and ethnic tensions.

The impact of the Irish presence in Lowell was far-reaching. As the ethnic makeup of the workforce changed in the city, so did its gender composition. More men came to work in the mills. By 1860, some 30 percent of the Lowell workers were male. All these changes made the Yankee women expendable and increased the costs of going "against the mill."

It was easy for New England women to blame the Irish for declining pay and deteriorating conditions. Gender no longer unified women workers, not only because there were more men in the mills but also because Irish women and New England women had little in common. The Irish mill girl who started working as early as age 13 to earn money for her family's survival had a different perspective on work than the older Yankee woman who was earning money for herself. Segregated living conditions further divided the workforce and undermined the likelihood of united worker actions in the 1850s.

Lowell itself changed as the Irish crowded into the city and New England women gradually left the mills. With owners no longer feeling the need to continue paternalistic practices, boardinghouses disappeared. A permanent workforce, once a nightmare to owners, had become a reality by 1860, and Lowell's reputation as a model factory town faded away.

Factories on the Frontier

Cincinnati, a small Ohio River settlement of 2,540 in 1810, grew to be the country's third-largest industrial center by 1840. With a population of 40,382, it contained a variety of industries at different stages of development. Cincinnati manufacturers who turned out machines, machine parts, hardware, and furniture were quick to mechanize for increased volume and profits. Other trades like carriage making and cigar making moved far more slowly toward mechanization before 1860. Alongside these concerns, artisans like coopers, blacksmiths, and riverboat builders still labored in small shops, using traditional hand tools. The new and the old ways coexisted in Cincinnati, as they did in most manufacturing communities.

No uniform work experience prevailed in Cincinnati. The size of the shop, the nature of work, the skills required, and the rewards all varied widely. In 1850, most Cincinnati workers worked in small or medium-sized shops, but almost 20 percent labored in factories with over 100 employees. Some craftsmen continued to use a wide array of skills as they produced goods in time-honored ways. Others used their skills in new factories, but they tended to focus on more specialized and limited tasks. In furniture factories, for example, machines did the rough work of cutting, boring, and planing, while some artisans worked exclusively as varnishers, others as carpenters, and still others as finishers. No single worker made a chair from start to finish. But all used some of their skills and earned steady wages. Though in the long run, machines threatened to replace them, these skilled factory workers often had reason in the short run to praise the factory's opportunities.

Less fortunate was the new class of unskilled factory laborers who performed limited operations at their jobs either with or without the assistance of machinery. In the meatpacking industry, for example, workers sat at long tables. Some cleaned the ears of the hogs, others scraped the bristles, others had the unenviable task of gutting the dead animals. Whereas owners in the industry profited from efficient new operations, workers received low wages and had little job security. Because they had no skills to sell, they were easily replaced and casually dismissed during business slowdowns.

The experience of Cincinnati's working women differed from that of their male counterparts. Cincinnati's large black community was so economically marginal that a majority of black women labored as washerwomen, cooks, or maids. Many white women were earning money as "outworkers" for the city's growing ready-to-wear clothing industry. Manufacturers purchased the cloth, cut it into basic patterns, and then contracted the work out to be finished by the women in small workshops or at home. Like many other urban women, Cincinnati women sought employment of this kind because they could not count on their husbands or fathers earning enough to support the family and because outwork allowed them to labor at home. Middle-class domestic ideology prescribed that home was the proper sphere for women, not the workplace. Many working men supported these views because they feared female labor would undercut their wages and destroy order in

CHANGING OCCUPATIONAL DISTRIBUTION, 1820–1860*

	1820	1840	1860
Agriculture	78.8%	63.1%	52.9%
Mining	0.4	0.6	1.6
Construction	—	5.1	4.7
Manufacturing	2.7	8.8	13.8
Trade	—	6.2	8.0
Transport	1.6	1.8	2.0
Service	4.1	5.0	6.4
Other	12.4	9.4	10.6

*The decline of agriculture and the increased involvement in industrial pursuits are represented in this table.

Source: U.S. Bureau of the Census.

In 1848, an unknown photographer took this picture of Cincinnati. The prominence of steamboats in the picture suggests the role that location and improvements in transportation played in the city's growth. Although the countryside is visible in the background, the rows of substantial commercial and industrial buildings make Cincinnati's status as a bustling urban center clear. *(Public Library of Cincinnati and Hamilton County, Ohio)*

the family. Outwork, then, allowed poor married women to supplement their family income while honoring social norms.

Paid by the piece, female outworkers were among the most exploited of Cincinnati's workers. Long days spent sewing in darkened rooms not only often failed to bring an adequate financial reward but also led to health problems—ruined eyes and curved spines.

The successful marketing of sewing machines in the 1850s contributed to worsening working conditions and lower pay. The sewing machine made stitching easier, so the pool of potential workers increased and the volume of work that bosses expected grew. As tasks were further subdivided, work also became more monotonous. As one Cincinnati citizen observed, "As many as 17 hands" were employed on a single pair of pants.

Cincinnati employers claimed that the new industrial order offered great opportunities to most of the city's male citizens. Manufacturing work encouraged the "manly virtues" so necessary to the "republican citizen." Not all Cincinnati workers agreed. Like workers in Lowell and other manufacturing communities, Cincinnati's laborers rose up against their bosses in the decades before the Civil War.

The workingman's plight, as Cincinnati labor leaders analyzed it, stemmed from his loss of independence. Even though a manufacturing job provided a decent livelihood for some people, the new industrial order was changing the nature of the laboring class itself. A new kind of worker had emerged. Rather than selling the products of his skills, he had only his raw labor to sell. His "wage slavery," or dependence on wages, promised to be lifelong. The reorganization of work signaled the end of the progression from apprentice to journeyman to master and undermined traditional skills. Few workers could expect to rise to the position of independent craftsman. Most would labor only for others, just as slaves labored for their masters. Nor would wages bring to most that other form of independence, the ownership of shop and home. The expression "wage slavery" contained a deep truth about the changed conditions of many American workingmen.

Workers also resented the masters' attempts to control their lives. In the new factories, owners insisted on a steady pace of work and uninterrupted production. Artisans who were used to working in spurts, stopping for a few moments of conversation or a drink, disliked the new routines. Those who took a dram or two at work found themselves discharged. Even outside the workplace, manufacturers attacked Cincinnati's working-class culture. Crusades to abolish volunteer fire companies and to close down saloons, both attacked as nonproductive activities, suggested how little equality the Cincinnati worker enjoyed in an industrializing society.

The fact that workers' wages in Cincinnati, as in other cities, rose more slowly than food and housing costs compounded discontent over changing working conditions. The working class sensed it was losing ground at the very time the city's rich were visibly growing richer. In 1817, the top tenth of the city's taxpayers owned over half the wealth, whereas the bottom half possessed only 10 percent. In 1860, the share of the top tenth had increased to two-thirds, while the bottom half's share had shrunk to 2.4 percent. Cincinnati workers may not have known these exact percentages, but they could see growing social and economic inequality in the luxurious mansions the city's rich were building and in the spreading blight of slums.

In the decades before the Civil War, Cincinnati workers formed unions, turned out for fair wages, and rallied in favor of the ten-hour day. Like the Lowell mill girls, they cloaked their protest with the mantle of the Revolution. Striking workers staged parades with fifes and drums and appropriated patriotic symbols to bolster their demands for justice and independence. Although they did not see their bosses as a separate or hostile class, labor activists insisted that masters were denying workers a fair share of profits. This unjust distribution doomed them to economic dependency. Because the republic depended on a free and independent citizenry, the male workers warned that their bosses' policies threatened to undermine the republic itself.

Only in the early 1850s did Cincinnati workers begin to suspect that their employers formed a distinct class of parasitic "nonproducers." Although most strikes still revolved around familiar issues of better hours and wages, signs appeared of the more hostile labor relations that would emerge after the Civil War.

As elsewhere, skilled workers were in the forefront of Cincinnati's labor protest and union activities. But their victories proved temporary. Depression and bad times always harmed labor organizations and canceled out employers' concessions. Furthermore, Cincinnati workers did not readily unite to protest new conditions. The uneven pace of industrialization meant that these workers, unlike the Lowell mill women, had no common working experience. Moreover, growing cultural, religious, and ethnic diversity compounded differences in the workplace. By 1850, almost half the people in the city were foreign-born, most of them German, whereas only 22 percent had been in 1825.

As the heterogeneity of the American people increased, ethnic and religious tensions simmered. Immigrants, near the bottom of the occupational ladder, faced limited job choices and suspicion of their faith, habits, and culture. Protestant workers frequently felt that they had more in common with their Protestant bosses than with Catholic Irish or German fellow workers. These tensions exploded in Cincinnati in the spring of 1855. Americans attacked barricades erected in German neighborhoods, crying out death threats. Their wrath visited the Irish as well. Ethnic, cultural, and social differences often drove workers apart and concealed their common grievances. In many cases, disunity served economic progress by undermining workers' efforts for higher pay, shorter hours, and better working conditions, thus enabling businesses to maximize productivity and profits while minimizing the cost of labor.

URBAN LIFE

Americans experienced the impact of economic growth most dramatically in the cities. In the four decades before the Civil War, the rate of urbanization in the United States was faster than ever before or since. In 1820, about 9 percent of the American people lived in cities (defined as areas containing a population of 2,500 or more). Forty years later, almost 20 percent of them did. Older cities like Philadelphia and New York mushroomed, while new cities like Cincinnati, Columbus, and Chicago sprang up "as if by enchantment." Although urban growth was not confined to the East, it was most dramatic there. By 1860, more than a third of the people living in the Northeast were urban residents, compared with only 14 percent of westerners and 7 percent of southerners. Although the majority of northerners still lived on farms or in small farm towns, the region was clearly urbanizing.

The Process of Urbanization

Three distinct types of cities—commercial centers, mill towns, and transportation hubs—emerged during these years of rapid economic growth. Although the lack of water power limited industrial development, commercial seaports like Boston, Philadelphia, and Baltimore expanded steadily and developed diversified manufacturing to supplement the older functions of importing, exporting, and providing services and credit. New York replaced Philadelphia as the country's largest and most important city. The completion of the Erie Canal allowed New York merchants to gain control of much of the trade with the West. By 1840, they had also seized the largest share of the country's import and export trade.

Access to water power fueled the development of a second kind of city, exemplified by Lowell,

The balloon frame, the most important technological improvement in building in the years before the Civil War, allowed the rapid construction of housing in new and old sections of the country. First introduced in 1839 in Chicago, the balloon frame was made of small, light, mill-cut pieces of lumber joined by factory-produced nails. Unlike the older forms of building construction that had used heavy timbers joined by hand-made pegs and mortise-and-tenon joints, balloon frames were easy to put together and demanded only a few workers. Since this construction is still used today, you have probably seen examples of the balloon frame. *(Engraving by W. W. Wilson, From Edward Shaw,* The Modern Architect, *1855, Constructing a Balloon Frame House, The Metropolitan Museum of Art, Harris Brisbane Dick Fund, 1934. [34.46.9])*

Massachusetts; Trenton, New Jersey; and Wilmington, Delaware. Situated inland along the waterfalls and rapids that provided the power to run their mills, these cities burgeoned, as American industry, especially the production of textiles, expanded in the decades before the Civil War.

Between 1820 and 1840, one-quarter of the increase in urban population occurred west of the Appalachian Mountains, where a third type of city arose. Louisville, Cleveland, and St. Louis were typical of cities that had served as transportation service and distribution centers from the earliest days of frontier settlement. Chicago acted as "grand depot, exchange, counting-house, and metropolis" for its hinterlands. Like most of these western cities, Chicago was a commercial rather than an industrial center. In the 1850s, selling lumber to prairie farmers who needed it for fences and housing was one of Chicago's most significant commercial activities.

As the number of urban dwellers grew, their needs helped generate economic growth. City dwellers rarely had gardens or animals, so they had to purchase their food. This encouraged farmers to turn to commercial farming. Cities also provided a growing market for other products, including shoes, clothing, furniture, and carriages. The iron industry sold more than a half million cast-iron stoves yearly, mainly to city dwellers, and city governments purchased cast-iron pipes for sewers and the water supply and city merchants erected cast-iron buildings.

Until 1840, the people eagerly crowding into cities came mostly from the American countryside. Then ships began to spill their human cargoes into seaboard cities, and a growing number of immigrants began their lives anew in the United States. Immigrants who could afford to leave the crowded port cities for the interior, many of them Germans and Scandinavians, did so. But the penniless had little choice but to remain in eastern cities and search for work there. By 1860, fully 20 percent of the people living in the Northeast were immigrants; in some of the largest cities, they and their children made up more than half the population. The Irish, fleeing famine and poverty at home, were the largest foreign group in the Northeast.

A look at Philadelphia reveals the character, rhythms, rewards, and tensions of urban life during the antebellum period. The city was one of the giants of the age. An inland port, a bustling mercantile city, a center of shops producing textiles, metals, and a host of other products, Philadelphia stood second only to New York. Though William Penn's "green country town" boasted an attractive appearance and an orderly plan, the expanding nineteenth-century city merited little praise. Speculators interested only in profit relied on the grid pattern as the cheapest and most efficient way to divide land for development. They built monotonous miles of new streets, new houses, new alleys, with "not a single acre left for public use, either for pleasure or health," as merchant Samuel Breck observed.

A few cities, like New York and Boston, did lay aside areas where residents could escape from the noises, sights, and smells of urban life. Frederick Law Olmsted and Calvert Vaux designed New York's picturesque Central Park, adorning it with grass, trees, and tranquil lakes. Olmsted envisioned the park as a place where all classes of New Yorkers could come together to enjoy themselves in a "quiet and orderly" manner. As with so much else of urban life, however, it was mainly the middle and upper classes who had the time to spend in the park and the money to pay for transportation to it.

As the example of Central Park suggests, not all citizens enjoyed the benefits of urban life. Overwhelmed by rapid growth, city governments provided few of the

Although this panoramic view of Philadelphia in about 1855 shows individual buildings and empty lots, it is the grid street pattern that stands out as the main feature of the city. By imposing the grid pattern on varied landscapes, Americans created similar types of urban spaces all over the country. This picture does not hint at the underside of Philadelphia life; its purpose seems to be to highlight the importance of the nation's second-largest city. *(The Historical Society of Pennsylvania)*

services we consider essential today, and usually only to those who paid for them. Poor families devoted many hours to securing necessities that affluent citizens had at their fingertips. Water is a case in point. By 1801, Philadelphia had constructed a system of waterworks that drew water from the Schuylkill River and then pumped it through wooden pipes to street hydrants. Only by paying a special fee could Philadelphians have water brought into their homes, so most of the city's residents went without. In the 1820s, the city expanded the water system by constructing the Fairmount waterworks, but the more abundant supply of water again benefited those who could afford to pipe it into their homes.

In 1849, Isaac Parrish's report on the sanitary conditions in Philadelphia lamented some of the consequences. "There is . . . a general absence of bathing apparatus, and even of hydrants," he wrote, "in the houses of the poorer classes, and especially in confined courts and alleys of the populous districts of the city." An earlier inspection, carried out by Mathew Carey in 1837, had pointed to an even more basic problem: 253 persons crowded into 30 tenements without even one privy. The ability to pay for services determined not only comfort but health.

Class Structure in the Cities

The drastic differences in the quality of urban life reflected social fluidity and the growing economic inequality that characterized Philadelphia and other American cities. In sharp contrast to the colonial period, the first half of the nineteenth century witnessed a dramatic rise in the concentration of wealth in the United States. The pattern was most extreme in cities.

Because Americans believed that capitalists deserved most of their profits, the well-to-do profited handsomely from this period of growth, whereas workers lost ground. The merchants, brokers, lawyers, bankers, and manufacturers of Philadelphia's upper class gained control of more and more of the city's wealth. By the late 1840s, the wealthiest 4 percent of the population held about two-thirds of the wealth. The economic pattern was similar in other American cities, as the nearby table on wealth distribution indicates. The houses of the city's elite were spacious and filled with new conveniences. Samuel Breck's house in 1839 was elegant and luxurious, with "parlours 14 feet high, . . . furnaces, water closet and shower and common bath up stairs, marble mantels and fireplaces in dressing rooms." Costing $22,500, Breck's "splendid house" represented the sum an ordinary Philadelphia textile factory operative might expect to earn in 75 years of work.

The widening gap between the upper class and the working class did not translate into mass suffering, because more wealth was being generated. But the growing inequality hardened class lines, nourished social tensions, and contributed to the labor protests of the antebellum period.

Between 1820 and 1860, a new working and middle class were in the process of formation in Philadelphia

WEALTH DISTRIBUTION IN THREE EASTERN CITIES IN THE 1840S*

Level of Wealth	Percentage of Population	Approximate Noncorporate Wealth Owned	Percentage Noncorporate Wealth
Brooklyn in 1841			
$50,000 or more	1	$10,087,000	42
$15,000 to $50,000	2	$14,000,000	17
$4,500 to $15,000	9	$15,730,000	24
$1,000 to $4,500	15	$12,804,000	12
$100 to $1,000	7	$11,000,000	4
Under $100	66	—	—
New York City in 1845			
$50,000 or more	1	$85,804,000	40
$20,000 to $50,000	3	$55,000,000	26
Boston in 1848			
$90,000 or more	1	$47,778,500	37
$35,000 to $90,000	3	$34,781,800	27
$4,000 to $35,000	15	$40,636,400	32
Under $4,000	81	$16,000,000	4

*Americans and foreign visitors often commented on the rough equality they believed characterized American life. Wealth distribution figures, although incomplete, suggest a different picture of American society.

Source: Edward Pessen, *Riches, Class, and Power Before the Civil War* (1973).

and elsewhere. As preindustrial ways of producing goods yielded to factory production and as the pace of economic activity quickened, some former artisans and skilled workers took advantage of newly created opportunities. Perhaps 10 to 15 percent of Philadelphians in each decade before the Civil War were able to improve their occupations and places of residence. They became businessmen, factory owners, mill supervisors, clerks, bookkeepers, engineers, or shopkeepers. Increasingly, membership in this middle class meant having a nonmanual occupation and a special place of work suited to activities that demanded brainpower rather than brawn. But as new opportunities opened up for some, downward occupational mobility increased. Former artisans or journeymen became part of a new class of permanent manual workers, dependent on wages for their livelihood. Fed by waves of immigrants, the lower class was growing at an accelerating rate. Moreover, within the working class itself, the percentage of unskilled wage earners living in poverty or on its brink increased from 17 to 24 percent between 1820 and 1860. At the same time, the proportion of craftsmen, once the heart of the laboring class, shrank from 56 to 47 percent.

The Urban Working Class

As with so much else in urban life, housing patterns reflected social and economic divisions. The poorest rented quarters in crowded, flimsily constructed shacks, shanties, and two-room houses. Because renters moved often, from one cramped lodging to another, it was difficult for them to create close-knit neighborhoods that might offer the fellowship and assistance to offset the harsh conditions of daily life.

Substantial houses fronting the main streets concealed the worst urban housing, which was in back alleys or even in backyards. Many visitors did not even realize slums lay behind the rows of brick housing, nor did they know of the uncollected garbage, privy runoffs, and fetid decay in the dark, unpaved alleys. In his diary, Philadelphia shopkeeper Joseph Sill left a description of living conditions at the bottom. "In the afternoon," he wrote, "Mrs. S & I went to the lowest part of the City to see some poor persons who had call'd upon us for Charity. We found one woman, with two children, & expecting soon to be confined, living in a cellar, part of which was unfloored, & exhibited much wretchedness; but it was tolerably clean. Her husband is a Weaver, & had his loom in the Cellar, but has only occasional work."

What the Sills witnessed during their visit to the weaver's family was not just poverty but the transformation of working-class family life. Men could no longer be sure of supporting their wives and children, even when they were employed. Women, who had once been able to feed their families by raising food on small garden plots and by keeping pigs and chickens, were forced to use scarce cash to buy food at urban markets now that overcrowding and city regulations made keeping gardens and animals impossible. Making ends meet was a struggle that colored family relations. Men felt they had lost much of their authority and power, and some thought their wives no longer subservient or seemingly careless with their hard-earned money. When one woman failed to explain clearly what she had done with the grocery money, her angry husband "said if she did not give him a full account . . . he would kill her or something like that." The squabble ended in murder. This family was an extreme case, but family violence that spilled out onto the streets was not uncommon in working-class quarters.

Middle-Class Life and Ideals

Although the Sills ventured into the world of the working class, their life could not have been more different. Members of the new middle class like the Sills profited from the dramatic increase in wealth in antebellum America. They lived in pleasantly furnished houses, enjoying more peace, more privacy, and more comfort than the less affluent. Franklin stoves gave warmth in winter, and iron cookstoves made cooking easier. Conveniences like Astral lamps made it possible to read after dark. Bathing stands and bowls ensured higher standards of cleanliness. Rugs muffled sounds and kept in the heat.

Material circumstances were one badge of middle-class status, but there were others as well. The acceptance of certain norms and values also identified a person as a member of the new middle class. Genteel behavior and the careful observance of elaborate rules of etiquette (a gentleman was expected to back out of a parlor after making a call upon a lady), the appropriate clothes and conversation, an elegantly furnished parlor for the entertainment of visitors—all served to establish the standing of the members of a middle-class family.

New expectations about the roles of men and women, prompted partly by economic change, also shaped middle-class life. In the seventeenth and eighteenth centuries, the labor of men and women, adults and children, all contributed to the family's economic welfare. But improved transportation, new products, and the rise of factory production and large businesses changed the family economy. Falling prices for processed and manufactured goods like soap, candles, clothing, and even bread made it unnecessary for women, except on the frontier, to continue making these items at home.

As men increasingly involved themselves in a money economy, whether through commerce or market farming, women's and children's contributions to the family welfare became relatively less significant. Although middle-class women and children still worked in their homes as their husbands left to "bring home the bacon," they often neither produced vital goods nor earned money. Even the rhythm of their lives, oriented to housework rather than the demands of the clock, separated them from the bustling commercial world where their husbands now labored. By 1820, the notion that the sexes occupied separate spheres emerged to express the new reality. Men's sphere was the public world, whereas women's was the domestic.

Men were charged with the task of financial support, a responsibility that, as Susan Warner's family experience suggested, was a heavy one in a changing economy. Women's duties included working at home—not as producer but as housekeeper. As a popular book, *Whisper to a Bride,* counseled readers, "For his sake . . . acquaint thyself with the knowledge that appertaineth unto a wife and housekeeper. If thou art deficient in this knowledge, rest not, till thou hast acquired it. It cometh readily to an attentive mind, and groweth with experience."

The role of housekeeper had both pleasure and frustration built into it. Susan Warner's celebration of domestic life in her novels suggested the satisfactions derived from a cozy household. Yet it was sometimes impossible to achieve the new standards of cleanliness, order, and beauty. Catharine Beecher's "Words of Comfort for a Discouraged Housekeeper" listed just a few of the problems—an inconvenient house, sick children, poor domestics—that undermined efforts to create a perfect harmonious home.

Although women were expected to become "systematic, neat and thorough" housekeepers, whatever the personal costs might be, they were also given more elevated responsibilities as moral and cultural guardians of their own families and, by extension, of society as a whole. Believing that women were innately pious, virtuous, unselfish, and modest (all characteristics that men lacked), publicists built on the argument developed during the revolutionary era. By training future citizens and workers to be obedient, moral, patriotic, and hardworking, mothers ensured the welfare of the republic. Just as important, they preserved important values in a time of rapid change. Because men had none of women's virtues and were daily caught up in the fast-paced world of business, wives were responsible for helping husbands cope with temptations and tensions. A wife was, in the words of one preacher, the "guardian angel" who "watches over" her husband's interests, "warns him against dangers, comforts him under trial; and by . . . pious, assiduous, and attractive deportment, constantly endeavors to render him more virtuous, more useful, more honourable, and more happy."

This view, characterizing women as morally superior to and different from men, had important conse-

This illustration, entitled "Maternal Instruction," from an 1845 issue of *Godey's Lady's Book and Magazine* not only suggests the importance of the printing revolution in spreading the new middle-class norms but also emphasizes the importance attached to women's role as guides for their children. *(The Newberry Library, Chicago)*

quences for female life. Because women thought they had a unique nature and because their husbands spent much of their time away from home working, friendship with other women often became central. Women felt that they shared more with one another than with men, even their husbands. Similar social experiences and perspectives made female friendships a source of comfort, security, and happiness.

Although the concept of domesticity seemed to confine women to their homes and to emphasize the private nature of family life, it actually prompted women to take on activities in the outside world. If women were the guardians of morality, why should they not carry out their tasks in the public sphere? "Woman," said Sarah Hale, editor of the popular magazine *Godey's Lady's Book,* was "God's appointed agent of *morality.*" Such reasoning lay behind the tremendous growth of voluntary female associations in the early decades of the nineteenth century. Initially, most involved religious and charitable activities. Women supported orphanages, paid for and distributed religious tracts and Bibles, established Sunday schools, and ministered to the poor. The associations provided women with congenial companions and suitable tasks for their "moral character." Sometimes the women recognized special interests that men did not share. In the 1830s, as we shall see in Chapter 12, women added specific moral concerns like the abolition of slavery to their missionary and benevolent efforts. As these women took on more active and controversial tasks, they often clashed with men and with social conventions about "woman's place."

Domesticity described norms, not the actual conduct of middle-class women. Obviously, not all women were pious, disinterested, selfless, virtuous, cheerful, and loving. But these ideas, expressed so movingly by novelists like Susan Warner, influenced how women thought of themselves, promoted "female" behavior by encouraging particular choices, and helped many women make psychological sense of their lives. New norms, effectively spread by the publishing industry, also influenced rural and urban working women. The insistence on marriage and service to family discouraged married women from entering the workforce. Many took in poorly paid piecework so that they could remain at home. Those who had to work often bore a burden of guilt. Though the new feminine ideal may have suited urban middle-class women, it created difficult tensions in the lives of working-class women.

As family roles were reformulated, a new view of childhood emerged. Working-class children still worked or scavenged for goods to sell or use at home, but middle-class children were no longer expected to contribute economically to the family. Middle-class parents now came to see childhood as a special stage of life, a period of preparation for adulthood. In a child's early years, mothers were to impart important values, including the necessity of behaving in accordance with gender prescriptions. Harsh punishments lost favor. As Catharine Beecher explained, "Affection can govern the human with a sway more powerful than the authority of reason or [even] the voices of conscience." Schooling also prepared a child for the future, and urban middle-class parents supported the public school movement.

Children's fiction, which poured off the printing presses, also socialized children. Stories pictured modest youngsters happily making the correct choices of playmates and activities, obeying their parents, and being dutiful, religious, loving, and industrious. Occasionally, as in *The Child at Home* (1833), the reader could discover the horrible consequences of wrongdoing. The young girl who refused to bring her sick mother a glass of water saw her promptly die. Heavy-handed moralizing made sure that children got the proper message.

The growing publishing industry helped spread new ideas about family roles and appropriate family

Recovering the Past

FAMILY PAINTINGS

Although paintings are often admired and studied for artistic reasons alone, their value as historical documents should not be overlooked. In an age before the camera, paintings, sketches, and even pictures done in needlework captured Americans at different moments of life and memorialized their significant rituals. Paintings of American families in their homes, for example, reveal both an idealized conception of family life and the details of its reality. In addition, the paintings provide us with a sense of what the houses of the middle and upper classes (who could afford to commission art) were like.

Artists trained in the European tradition of realism painted family scenes and portraits, but so did many painters who lacked formal academic training, the so-called primitive artists. Their art was abstract in the sense that the artists tended to emphasize what they knew or felt rather than what they actually saw.

Some primitive artists were women who had received some drawing instruction at school. They often worked primarily for their own pleasure. Other artists were craftsmen, perhaps house or sign painters, who painted pictures in their leisure time. Some traveling house decorators made a living by making paintings and wall decorations. Many primitive paintings are unsigned, and even when we know the painter's identity, we rarely know more than a name and perhaps a date. Primitive artists flourished in the first three-quarters of the nineteenth century, eventually supplanted by the camera and inexpensive prints.

We see here a painting of the Sargent family done by an unknown artist around 1800. Though not an exact representation of reality, it does convey what the artist and the buyer considered important. Like any piece of historical evidence, this painting must be approached critically and carefully. Our questions focus on four areas: (1) the individual family members and their treatment, (2) the objects associated with each, (3) the implied or apparent relationship between family members, and (4) the domestic environment. The painting gives us an idealized version of what both the painter and the subjects felt ought to be as well as what actually was. First, study the family itself. Describe what you see. How many family members are there, and what is each one doing? What seems to be the relationship between husband and wife? Why do you think Mr. Sargent is painted with his hat on? Who seems to dominate the painting, and how is this dominance conveyed (positioning, attitude or facial expression, eye contact, clothing)? What can you conclude about different "spheres" and roles for men and women?

Why do you think the artist painted two empty chairs and included a ball and a dog in this scene of family life? What do these choices suggest about attitudes toward children and their upbringing? What seems to be the role of the children in the family? What does the painting suggest about how this family wished to be viewed? How do your conclusions relate to information discussed in this chapter?

Take a look at the room in which the Sargents are gathered. Make an inventory of the objects and furnishings in it. The room seems quite barren in comparison with present-day interiors. Why? Why do you think the chairs are placed near the window and door? What kind of scene does the window frame?

The *Family at Home*, painted by H. Knight in 1836, is a more detailed painting showing a larger family gathering almost 40 years later. Similar questions can be asked about this painting, particularly in relationship to the different treatment of boys and girls and the positioning and objects associated with each sex. There are many clues about the different socialization of male and female children. The family's living room can be contrasted with the Sargent family's room to reveal some of the changes brought about by industrialization.

Finally, how do these nineteenth-century homes and sex roles differ from those in colonial New England and the Chesapeake?

Anonymous, *The Sargent Family*, 1800. *(National Gallery of Art)*

H. Knight, *The Family at Home*, 1836. *(Private collection)*

behavior. Novels, magazines, etiquette and child-rearing manuals, and schoolbooks all carried the message from northern and midwestern centers of publishing to the South, to the West, and to the frontier. Probably few Americans lived up to the new standards established for the model parent or child, but the standards increasingly influenced them.

New notions of family life supported the widespread use of contraception for the first time in American history. Because children required so much loving attention and needed careful preparation for adulthood, many parents desired smaller families. The declining birthrate was evident first in the Northeast, particularly in cities and among the middle class. Contraceptive methods included abortion, which was legal in many states until 1860. This medical procedure terminated perhaps as many as a third of all pregnancies. Other birth control methods included coitus interruptus and abstinence. The success of these methods for family limitation suggests that many men and women adopted the new definitions of the female sex as naturally affectionate but passionless and sexually restrained.

Mounting Urban Tensions

The social and economic changes transforming U.S. cities in the half century before the Civil War produced urban violence on a scale never before witnessed in the United States, not even during the Revolution. Festering ethnic and racial tensions often triggered mob actions that lasted for days. American cities were slow to establish a modern police force (London had organized one in 1829). Most still had the traditional constable-and-watch system. The night watch lit city streetlights and patrolled the streets to preserve order and arrest suspicious characters. During the day, constables investigated health hazards, carried out court orders, and apprehended criminals against whom complaints had been lodged. Neither group tried to prevent crimes or discover offenses. Neither wore uniforms. Certainly, neither was able to "prevent a tumult." Each chaotic event made the London model more attractive.

Racial tensions contributed to Philadelphia's disorders. An unsavory riot in August 1834 revealed other important sources of social antagonism as well as the inability of its police force to control disorder.

One hot August evening, several hundred white Philadelphians wrecked a building on South Street that contained a merry-go-round patronized by both blacks and whites. A general melee followed. As the *Philadelphia Gazette* reported, "At one time it is supposed that four or five hundred persons were engaged in the conflict, with clubs, brickbats, paving stones, and the materials of the shed in which the flying horses were kept." Spurred by the taste of blood, the white mob moved into the center of the crowded, racially mixed neighborhood, where they continued their orgy of destruction, looting, and intimidation of black residents. Similar mayhem followed on the next two nights. Intermittent rioting broke out the succeeding night as well, but the presence of 300 special constables, a troop of mounted militia, and a company of infantry prevented the violence from reaching the pitch of the previous nights.

An investigation following the riots revealed at least $4,000 of damage to two black churches and more than 36 private homes. At least one black had been killed, and numerous others were injured. As one shocked eyewitness reported, "The mob exhibited more than fiendish brutality, beating and mutilating some of the old, confiding and unoffending blacks with a savageness surpassing anything we could have believed men capable of."

Many rioters bragged that they were "hunting the nigs." Riots, however, are complicated events, and this racial explanation does not reveal the range of causes underlying the rampage of violence and destruction. The rioters were young and generally of low social standing. Many were Irish. Some had criminal records. A number of those arrested, however, were from a "class of mechanics of whom better things are expected": weavers, house painters, a cabinetmaker, a carpenter, a blacksmith, and a plasterer. No professional people or businessmen seem to have been involved. Accompanying the rioters, however, were onlookers who egged the mob on. As one paper reported, these onlookers "countenanced" the operations of the mob "and in one or two instances coincided with their conduct by clapping." The rioters revealed that in the event of an "attack by the city police, they confidently counted" on the assistance of these bystanders.

The mob's composition hints at some of the reasons for participation. Many of the rioters were at the bottom of the occupational and economic ladder and competed with blacks for jobs. This was particularly true of the newly arrived Irish immigrants, who were attempting to replace blacks in low-status jobs. Subsequent violence against blacks suggested that economic rivalry was an important component of the riot. "Colored persons, when engaged in their usual vocations," the *Niles Register* observed, "were repeatedly assailed and maltreated. . . . Parties of white men have insisted that no blacks shall be employed in certain departments of labor."

If blacks threatened the dream of advancement of some whites, this was not quite the complaint of the skilled workers. These men were more likely to have experienced the negative impact of a changing economic system that was undermining the small-scale mode of production. The dream of a better life seemed increasingly illusory as their declining wages drew them closer to unskilled workers than to the middle class. Like other rioters, they were living in one of the poorest and most crowded parts of the city. Their immediate scapegoats were blacks, but for them, the real but intangible villain was the economic system itself. Trade union organizing and a general strike a year later would highlight the grievances of this group.

Urban expansion also contributed to the racial violence. Most of the rioters lived either in the riot area or nearby. All had experienced the overcrowded and inadequate living conditions caused by the city's rapid growth. The racial tensions generated by squalid surroundings and social proximity go far to explain the outbreak of violence. The same area would later become the scene of race riots and election trouble and became infamous for harboring criminals and juvenile gangs. The absence of middle- and upper-class participants did not mean that these groups were untroubled during times of growth and change, but their material circumstances cushioned them from some of the more unsettling forces.

The city's police proved unable to control the mob, thus prolonging the violence. Philadelphia, like other eastern cities, was in the midst of creating its police force. In 1833, a small force had been added to the constable-and-watch system. Its task was to deter crime by walking the city streets. But the police were too few to cope with the angry mob. Only continued rowdiness, violence, and riots would convince residents and city officials in Philadelphia (and in other large cities) to support an expanded, quasi-military, preventive, and uniformed police force. By 1855, most sizable eastern cities had established such forces.

Finally, the character of the free black community itself was a factor in producing those gruesome August events. Not only was the community large and visible, but it also had created its own institutions and its own elite. Whites resented "dressy blacks and dandy coloured beaux and belles" returning from "their proper churches." The mob vented its rage against black affluence by targeting the solid brick houses of middle-class blacks and robbing them of silver and watches. Black wealth threatened the notion of the proper social order held by many white Philadelphians and seemed unspeakable when whites could not afford life's basic necessities or lacked jobs.

The Black Underclass

Events in Philadelphia showed how hazardous life for free blacks could be. Although a small elite group of blacks emerged in Philadelphia and in other cities as well, most African Americans did not enjoy the rewards of economic expansion and industrial progress. Black men, often with little or no education, held transient and frequently dangerous jobs. Black women, many of whom headed their households because men were away working or had died, held jobs before and after marriage. In Philadelphia in 1849, almost half of the black women washed clothes for a living. Others took boarders into their homes and thereby added to their domestic chores.

Northern whites, like southerners, believed in black inferiority and depravity and feared black competition for jobs and resources. Although northern states had passed gradual abolition acts between 1780 and 1803 and the national government had banned slaves from entering new states to be formed out of the Northwest Territory, nowhere did any government extend equal rights and citizenship or economic opportunities to free blacks in their midst.

For a time in the early nineteenth century, some blacks living in the North were permitted to vote, but they soon lost that right. Beginning in the 1830s, in part because of the influx of fugitive slaves and manumitted blacks without property or jobs, Pennsylvania, Connecticut, and New Jersey disenfranchised blacks. New York allowed only those with three years' residence and property valued at $250 or more to vote. Only the New England states (with the exception of Connecticut), which had tiny black populations, preserved the right to vote regardless of color. By 1840, fully 93 percent of the northern free black population lived in states where law or custom prevented them from voting.

Other black civil rights were also restricted. In five northern states, blacks could not testify against whites or serve on juries. In most states, the two races were thoroughly segregated. Blacks increasingly endured separate and inferior facilities in railway cars, steamboats, hospitals, prisons, and other asylums. In some states, they could enter public buildings only as personal servants of white men. They sat in "Negro pews" in churches and took communion only after whites had left the church. Although most Protestant religious denominations in the antebellum period split into northern and southern branches over the issue of slavery, most northern churches were not disposed to welcome blacks as full members.

As the Philadelphia riot revealed, whites were driving blacks from their jobs. In 1839, *The Colored American* blamed the Irish. "These impoverished and destitute beings . . . are crowding themselves into every place of business . . . and driving the poor colored American citizen out." Increasingly after 1837, these "white niggers" became coachmen, stevedores, barbers, cooks, house servants—all occupations blacks had once held.

Educational opportunities for blacks were also severely limited. Only a few school systems admitted blacks, in separate facilities. The case of Prudence Crandall illustrates the lengths to which northern whites would go to maintain racial segregation. In 1833, Crandall, a Quaker schoolmistress in Canterbury, Connecticut, announced that she would admit "young colored ladies and Misses" to her school. The outraged townspeople, fearful that New England would become the "Liberia of America," tried all sorts of persuasion and intimidation to induce Crandall to abandon her project.

Nonetheless, Crandall opened the school. Hostile citizens harassed and insulted students and teachers, refused to sell them provisions, and denied them medical care and admission to churches. Ministers preached against Crandall's efforts, and local residents poured manure in the school's well, set the school on fire, and knocked in walls with a battering ram. Crandall was arrested, and after two trials—in which free blacks were declared to have no citizenship rights—she finally gave up and moved to Illinois.

Crandall likely did not find the Old Northwest much more hospitable. The fast-growing western states were intensely committed to white supremacy and black exclusion. In Ohio, the response to talk of freeing the slaves was to pass "black laws" excluding them from the state. Said one Ohioan, "The banks of the Ohio would be lined with men with muskets to keep off the emancipated slaves." In 1829 in Cincinnati, where evidence of freedom papers and $500 bond were demanded of blacks who wished to live in the city, white rioters ran nearly 2,000 blacks out of town.

As an Indiana newspaper editor observed in 1854, informal customs made life dangerous for blacks. They were "constantly subject to insults and annoyance in traveling and the daily avocations of life; [and] are practically excluded from all social privileges, and even from the Christian communion." An Indiana senator proclaimed in 1850 that a black could "never live together equally" with whites because "the same power that has given him a black skin, with less weight or volume of brain, has given us a white skin with greater volume of brain and intellect." A neighboring politician, Abraham Lincoln of Illinois, would not have disagreed with this assessment.

RURAL COMMUNITIES

Although the percentage of families involved in farming fell from 72 to 60 percent between 1820 and 1860, Americans remained a rural people. Agriculture persisted as the country's most significant economic activity, and farm products still made up most of the nation's exports. The small family farm still characterized eastern and western agriculture.

Even though farming remained the dominant way of life, agriculture changed in the antebellum period. Vast new tracts of land came under cultivation in the West. Railroads, canals, and better roads pulled rural Americans into the orbit of the wider world. Some crops were shipped to regional markets; others, like grain, hides, and pork, stimulated industrial processing. Manufactured goods, ranging from cloth to better tools, flowed in return to farm families. Like city dwellers, farmers and their families read books, magazines, and papers that exposed them to new ideas. Commercial farming encouraged different ways of thinking and acting and lessened the isolation so typical before 1820.

Farming in the East

During the antebellum period, economic changes created new rural patterns in the Northeast. Marginal lands in New England, New York, and Pennsylvania, cultivated as more fertile lands ran out, yielded discouraging returns. Gradually, after 1830, farmers abandoned these farms, forest reclaimed farmland, and the New England hill country began a slow decline. By 1860, almost 40 percent of people who had been born in Vermont had left their native state. A popular song of the 1840s captured the pattern of flight: "Come, all ye Yankee farmers who wish to change your lot, / Who've spunk enough to travel beyond your native spot. / And leave behind the village where Pa and Ma do stay, / Come follow me, and settle in Michigan, yea, yea."

Farmers who did not migrate west had to transform their production. By the 1830s, eastern farmers, realizing that they could not compete with western grain, sought new agricultural opportunities created by better transportation and growing urban markets. One demand was for fresh milk. By the 1830s, some eastern cities had grown so large that milk was turning sour before it reached central marketplaces. As a result, several cities, including New York, started urban dairies, where cows often fed on garbage and slop from distilleries and breweries. When railroad lines extended into rural areas, however, farmers living as far away as Vermont and upper New York State discovered that they could ship cooled milk to urban centers. In 1842 and 1843, the Erie Railroad carried 750,000 gallons of milk to New York City. New dairy farmers eventually drove the unsavory city dairies out of business. City residents had fresher and cheaper milk and drank more of it as a result.

Urban appetites encouraged other farmers to cultivate fruit and vegetables. Every city was surrounded by farmers growing produce for urban consumption.

National Expansion and the Movement West to 1830

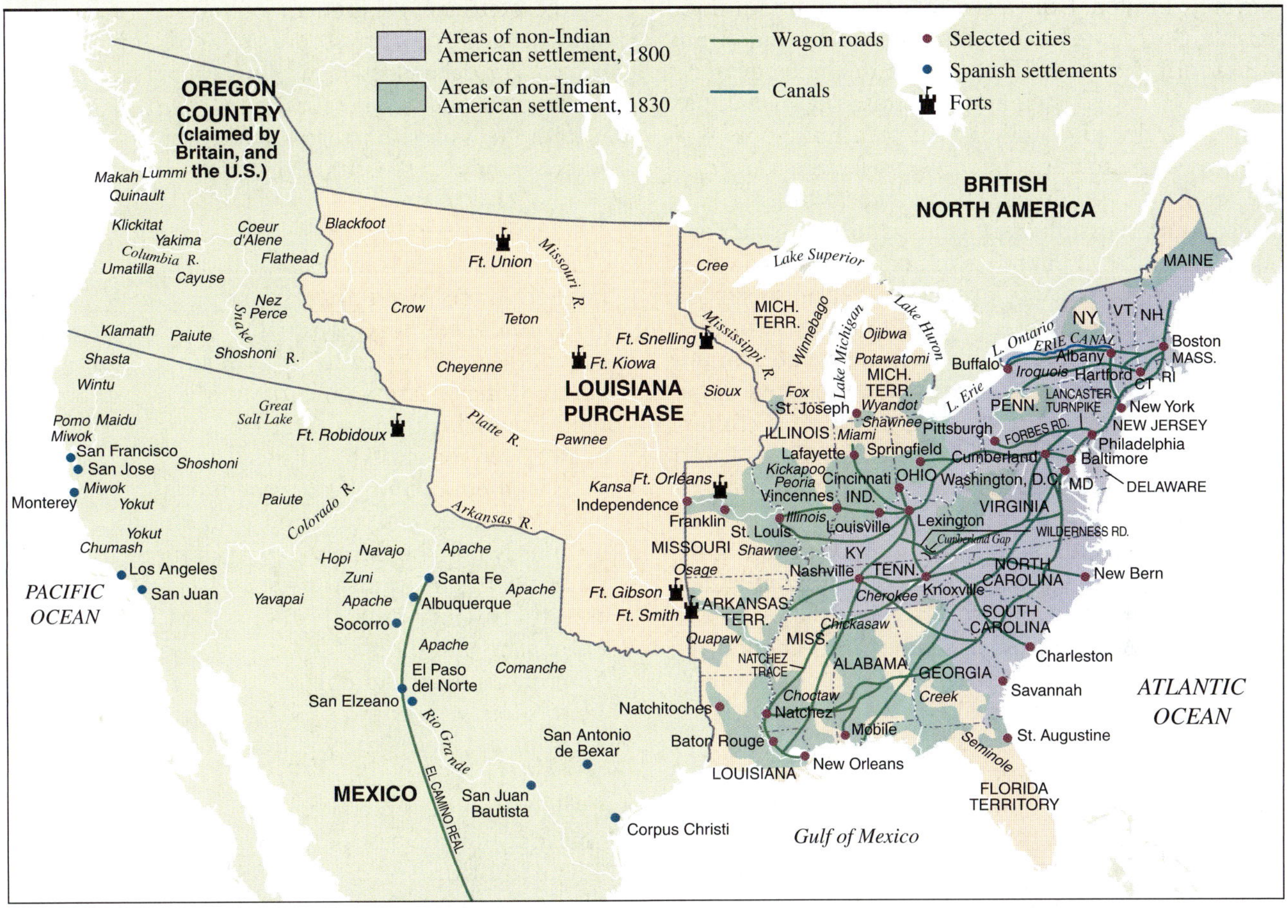

This map shows the expansion of American settlement in the first decades of the nineteenth century as well as the expanding transportation network that facilitated the movement of people and goods.

Railroads also prompted farmers miles away to turn to specialized farming. Upper New York State farmers began to raise and ship apples, while New Jersey and Delaware farmers became famous for their peaches. Thus, in July 1837, a Boston housewife could buy at the central market a wide variety of fresh vegetables and fruits, ranging from peas, summer squash, and cauliflower to grapes, cherries, and raspberries. Cookbooks began to include recipes calling for fresh ingredients.

As northern farmers adopted new crops, they began to consider farming as a scientific endeavor. After 1800, northern farmers started using manure as fertilizer rather than disposing of it as a smelly nuisance. By the 1820s, some farmers were rotating their crops and planting new grasses and clover to restore fertility to the soil. These techniques recovered worn-out wheat and tobacco lands in Maryland and Delaware for livestock farming. Calculation began to replace "habit and prejudice . . . the powerful opponents of improvement."

Farmers in the Delaware River valley were leaders in adopting new methods, but interest in scientific farming was widespread. By 1860, American farmers had developed thousands of special varieties of plants for local conditions. Many improvements resulted from experimentation, but farmers also enjoyed more and better information. New journals like the *New England Farmer*, the *Farmers' Register*, and the *Cultivator* informed readers of modern farming practices, fertilizers, scientific breeding, and methods for treating fruits and vegetables. Following New York's lead in 1819, many states established agricultural agencies to propagate new ideas. Although wasteful farming practices did not disappear, they became less characteristic of the Northeast. Improved farming methods contributed to increased agricultural output and helped reverse a two-hundred-year decline in farm productivity in some of the oldest areas of settlement. The increased use of a tool called the cradle increased farmers' ability to harvest grain and made it possible to cultivate more acres than before. A "scientific" farmer in 1850 could often produce two to four times as much per acre as in 1820.

Farmers in the fertile area around Northampton, Massachusetts, illustrate the American farmer's adjustment to new economic conditions. As early as 1800, better roads, a turnpike, and stage routes reduced rural isolation. Canal improvements and then railroads strengthened new contacts. With markets ever more accessible, farmers began to change agricultural patterns. Rather than raising crops and animals for home use or for local barter, farmers started to cultivate crops "scientifically" to increase profits. Farming was becoming a business. At home, women found themselves freed from many of their traditional tasks. Peddlers brought goods to the door. The onerous duty of making cloth and clothing disappeared with the coming of inexpensive ready-made cloth and even ready-made clothes in the 1820s. Daughters liberated from the chores of home manufacturing went off to the mills or earned money by taking in piecework from local merchants.

As the rhythms of rural life in the Connecticut River valley quickened, attitudes also changed. Cash transactions replaced the exchange of goods. Country stores became more reluctant to accept wood, rye, corn, oats, and butter as payment for goods instead of cash. Some farmers adopted the ethic of getting ahead, although their motive was not entrepreneurship but rather a desire to provide for family material comfort.

Traditional attitudes did not disappear completely, however. Some farmers contented themselves with making a living rather than chasing a profit. "Reason's whole pleasure, all the joys of sense / Lie in three words, health, peace and competence" remained their motto. The desire to just get along rather than becoming involved in the market economy helps explain why wealth inequality increased near Northampton, as it did elsewhere in the rural Northeast.

Frontier Families

Many people who left the North during these years headed for the expanding frontier. After the War of 1812, Americans flooded into the Old Northwest. Early communities dotted the Ohio River, the link to the South. Concentrating on corn and pork, settlers sent their products down the Ohio and Mississippi Rivers to southern buyers. In 1820, less than one-fifth of the American population lived west of the Appalachians; by 1860, almost half did, and Ohio and Illinois had become two of the nation's most populous states.

By 1830, Ohio, Indiana, and southern Illinois were heavily settled, but Michigan, northern Illinois, Wisconsin, and parts of Iowa and Missouri were still frontier. Chicago had only 250 residents. Conditions were often primitive, as Charles Butler and Arthur Bronson discovered during their 1833 trip. Their hotel in Michigan City, Indiana, was "a small log house, a single room . . . [where] some eleven or twelve persons lodged in beds & on the floor."

During the 1830s, land sales and settlement boomed in the Old Northwest. Changes in federal land policy, which reduced both prices and the minimum acreage a settler had to buy, helped stimulate migra-

This 1856 print titled "Preparing for Market" shows the farm as a center of human and animal activity and suggests the shifts in eastern agriculture that took place in the East as competition from the Midwest stimulated farmers to raise new crops for the market. The rise of commercial farming also encouraged technological innovation—The McCormick reaper was patented in 1834. *(Yale University Art Gallery, New Haven. CT/Mabel Brady Garvan Collection)*

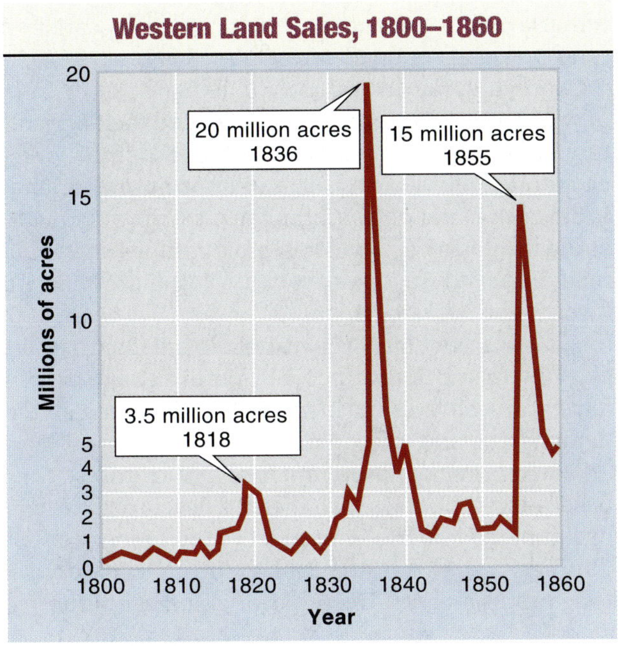

Changing prices for federal lands and the reduction in the number of acres a settler had to buy stimulated migration and land purchases.

tion, as the nearby figure on western land sales shows. Eastern capital also contributed to the boom with loans, mortgages, and speculative buying. Speculators frequently bought up large tracts of land from the government and then subdivided them and sold parcels off to settlers.

Internal improvement schemes after 1830 also contributed to new settlement patterns and tied the Old Northwest firmly to the East. Erasmus Gest, who as a 17-year-old had worked on canal projects in Indiana, recalled the settlers' enthusiasm for improvements: "We Engineers were favorites with the People wherever we went."

Wheat for the eastern market rather than corn and hogs for the southern market became increasingly important with the transportation links eastward. Between 1840 and 1860, Illinois, southern Wisconsin, and eastern Iowa turned into the country's most rapidly growing grain regions. In the 1850s, these three states accounted for 70 percent of the increase in national wheat production.

Although the Old Northwest passed rapidly through the frontier stage between 1830 and 1860, its farming families faced severe challenges. Catharine Skinner, who moved from New York to Indiana with her husband when she was 24, described her rigorous existence. "We are poor and live in the woods where deers roam plentifully and the wolf is occasionally heard," she wrote to her sister in 1849. "We are employed in honest business and trying to do the best we can; we have got 80 acres of land in the woods of Indiana, a very level country; we have got two acres cleared and fenced and four more pirty well under way; we have got about five acres of wheat in the ground; we raised corn enough for our use and to fat our pork . . . we have a cow so that we have milk and butter and plenty of corn bread but wheat is hard to be got in account of our not having mony."

The Skinners were typical. Western farms were small, for there were limits to what a family with hand tools could manage. A family with two healthy men could care for about 50 acres. In wooded areas, it took several years to get even that much land under cultivation, for only a few acres could be cleared in a year. The Skinners' target was to clear 10 acres during the first 12 months, if, as Catharine said, "health permit." At this rate, it could take ten years for settlers in forested areas to get a farm in full operation. On the prairies, the typical settler would need only half that time.

Catharine Skinner mentioned the shortage of money and described her family as "poor." Although money was in short supply in the Northwest, she probably overstated her family's poverty. It took capital to begin farming—a minimum initial investment of perhaps $100 for 80 acres of government land, $300 for basic farming equipment, and another $100 or $150 for livestock. To buy an already "improved" farm cost more, and free bidding at government auctions could drive the price of unimproved federal land far above the minimum price. Once farmers moved onto the prairies of Indiana and Illinois, they needed an initial investment of about $1,000 because they had to buy materials for fencing, housing, and expensive steel plows. If farmers invested in the new horse-drawn reapers, they could cultivate more land, but all their costs also increased.

Opportunities in the Old Northwest

It was possible to begin farming with less, however. Some farmers borrowed from relatives, banks, or insurance companies like the Ohio Life Insurance and Trust Company. Others rented land from farmers who had bought more acres than they could manage. Tenants who furnished their own seeds and animals could expect to keep about a third of the yield. Within a few years, some saved enough to buy their own farms. Even those without any capital could work as hired hands. Labor was scarce, so they earned good wages. In Indiana, German settler Jacob Schramm hired men "to help with heavy labors of lumbering and field work, ditch-digging, and so on." Five to ten years of frugal living and steady work for men like Schramm would bring the sum needed to get started.

Probably about a quarter of the western farm population consisted of young men laboring as tenants or hired hands. Although they stood on the bottom rung of the agricultural ladder, their chances of moving up and joining the rural middle class were favorable. Widespread ownership of land characterized western rural communities. Lucinda Easteen knew as much when she told her younger sister to come to Illinois, where "you can have a home of your own, but never give your hand or heart to a lazy man."

Rural communities, unlike the cities, had no growing class of propertyless wage earners, but inequalities nevertheless existed in the Old Northwest. In Butler County, Ohio, for example, 16 percent of people leaving wills in the 1830s held half the wealth. By 1860, the wealthiest 8 percent held half the wealth. In a Wisconsin frontier county in 1860, the richest tenth owned 40 percent of all property. Although wealth was not as concentrated in rural areas as in the cities, a few residents benefited more from rapid economic development than others.

Nevertheless, the Northwest offered many American families the chance to become independent producers and to enjoy a "pleasing competence." The rigors of frontier life faded with time. As Catharine Skinner wrote to her sister from her new Illinois home in 1850, "We here have meetings instead of hearing the hunters gun and the woo[d]man's ax on the sabbath."

Commercial farming brought new patterns of family life. As one Illinois farmer told his wife and daughter, "Store away your looms, wheels, [and] warping bars . . . all of your utensils for weaving cloth up in the loft. The boys and I can make enough by increasing our herds." Many farm families had money to spend on new goods. As early as 1836, the *Dubuque Visitor* was advertising the availability of ready-made clothing and "Calicoes, Ginghams, Muslins, Cambricks, Laces and Ribbands." The next year the *Iowa News* told of the arrival of "Ready Made Clothing from New York."

Agriculture and the Environment

Shifting agricultural patterns in the East and expanding settlement into the Old Northwest contributed to the changing character of the American landscape. As naturalist John Audubon mused in 1826, "A century hence," the rivers, swamps, and mountains "will not be here as I see them. Nature will have been robbed of many brilliant charms, the rivers will be tormented and turned astray from their primitive course, the hills will be levelled with the swamps, and perhaps the swamps will have become a mount surmounted by a fortress of a thousand guns." His sense of the consequences of the movement of peoples and the exploitation of land was shared by one French visitor who remarked that Americans would never be satisfied until they had subdued nature.

More than the subjugation of nature was involved, however. When eastern farmers changed their agricultural practices as they became involved in the market economy, their decisions left an imprint on the land. Selling wood and potash stimulated clearing of forests, as did the desire for new tools, plow castings, threshing machines, and wagon boxes, which were produced in furnaces fueled by charcoal. As forests disappeared, so, too, did their wildlife. Even using mineral manures like gypsum or lime or organic fertilizers like guano to revitalize worn-out soil and increase crop yields meant the depletion of land elsewhere.

When farmers moved into the Old Northwest, they used new steel plows, like the one developed in 1837 by Illinois blacksmith John Deere. Unlike older eastern plows, the new ones could cut through the dense, tough prairie cover. Deep plowing and the intensive

Timeline

1805	*Palmer* v. *Mulligan*
1816	Second U.S. Bank chartered
1817	New York Stock Exchange established
1819	*Dartmouth College* v. *Woodward*
1820	City of Lowell, Massachusetts, founded by Boston Associates
	Land Act of 1820
	The expression "woman's sphere" becomes current
1824	*Sturges* v. *Crowninshield*
1824–1850	Construction of canals in the Northeast
1825–1856	Construction of canals linking the Ohio, the Mississippi, and the Great Lakes
1828	Baltimore & Ohio Railroad begins operation
1830	Preemption Act
1830s	Boom in the Old Northwest
	Increasing discrimination against free blacks
	Public education movement spreads
1833	Philadelphia establishes small police force
1834	Philadelphia race riots
	Lowell work stoppage
	Cyrus McCormick patents his reaper
1837	Horace Mann becomes secretary of Massachusetts Board of Education
1837–1844	Financial panic and depression
1840	Agitation for ten-hour day
1840s–1850s	Rising tide of immigration
1841	Distributive Preemption Act

cultivation of large cash crops had immediate benefits. But these practices could result in robbing the soil of necessary minerals like phosphorous, carbon, and nitrogen. When farmers built new timber houses as frontier conditions receded, they helped fuel the destruction of the country's forests.

Conclusion

The Character of Progress

Between 1820 and 1860, the United States experienced tremendous growth and economic development. Transportation improvements facilitated the movement of people, goods, and ideas. Larger markets stimulated both agricultural and industrial production. There were more goods and ample food for the American people. Cities and towns were established and thrived. Visitors constantly remarked on the amazing bustle and rapid pace of American life. The United States was, in the words of one Frenchman, "one gigantic workshop, over the entrance of which there is the blazing inscription 'NO ADMISSION HERE, EXCEPT ON BUSINESS.'"

Although the wonders of American development dazzled foreigners and Americans alike, economic growth had its costs. Expansion was cyclic, and financial panics and depression punctuated the era. Industrial profits were based partly on low wages to workers. Time-honored routes to economic independence disappeared, and a large class of unskilled, impoverished workers appeared in U.S. cities. Growing inequality characterized urban and rural life, prompting some labor activists to criticize new economic and social arrangements. But workers, still largely unorganized, did not speak with one voice. Ethnic, racial, and religious diversity divided Americans in new and troubling ways.

Yet a basic optimism and sense of pride also characterized the age. To observers, however, it frequently seemed as if the East and the Old Northwest were responsible for the country's achievements. During these decades, many noted that the paths between the East, Northwest, and South seemed to diverge. The rise of King Cotton in the South, where slave rather than free labor formed the foundation of the economy, created a new kind of tension in American life, as the next chapter will show.

Recommended Reading

Economic Growth

Thomas C. Cochran, *Frontiers of Change: Early Industrialism in America* (1981); Robert F. Dalzell Jr., *Enterprising Elite: The Boston Associates and the World They Made* (1987); David Freeman Hawke, *Nuts and Bolts of the Past: A History of American Technology, 1776–1860* (1988); David A. Hounshell, *From the American System to Mass Production, 1800–1832: The Development of Manufacturing Technology in the United States* (1984); David J. Jeremy, *Transatlantic Industrial Revolution: The Diffusion of Textile Technology Between Britain and America, 1790–1830* (1981); Nathan Rosenberg, *Technology and American Economic Growth* (1972); Charles G. Sellers, *The Market Revolution: Jacksonian America, 1815–1848* (1991); Carol Sheriff, *The Artificial River: the Erie Canal and the Paradox of Progress, 1817–1862* (1996).

Early Manufacturing

Mary H. Blewett, *Men, Women, and Work: Class, Gender, and Protest in the New England Shoe Industry, 1780–1910* (1988); Alan Dawley, *Class and Community: The Industrial Revolution in Lynn* (1976); Thomas Dublin, *Women at Work: The Transformation of Work and Community in Lowell, Massachusetts, 1826–1860* (1979), and ed., *Farm to Factory: Women's Letters, 1830–1860* (1981); Bruce Laurie, *Artisans into Workers: Labor in Nineteenth-Century America* (1989); Steven J. Ross, *Workers on the Edge: Work, Leisure, and Politics in Industrializing Cincinnati, 1788–1890* (1985); Richard B. Stott, *Workers in the Metropolis: Class, Ethnicity, and Youth in Antebellum New York City* (1990); Sean Wilentz, *Chants Democratic: New York City & The Rise of the American Working Class, 1788–1850* (1984).

Urban Life

Stuart M. Blumin, *The Emergence of the Middle Class: Social Experience in the American City, 1760–1900* (1989); Tamara K. Hareven, ed., *Family and Kin in Urban Communities, 1700–1930* (1977); John F. Kasson, *Rudeness and Civility: Manners in Nineteenth-Century America* (1990); Gary B. Nash, *Forging Freedom: The Formation of Philadelphia's Black Community, 1720–1840* (1988); Edward Pessen, *Riches, Class, and Power Before the Civil War* (1973); Christopher Phillips, *Freedom's Port: The African-American Community of Baltimore, 1780–1860* (1997); Mary P. Ryan, *Cradle of the Middle Class: The Family in Oneida County, New York, 1790–1865* (1981); Christine Stansell, *City of Women: Sex and Class in New York, 1789–1860* (1986).

Rural Communities

Jeremy Atack and Fred Bateman, *To Their Own Soil: Agriculture in the Antebellum North* (1987); Christopher Clark, *The Roots of Rural Capitalism: Western Massachusetts, 1780–1860* (1992); Don H. Doyle, *The Social Order of a Frontier Community: Jacksonville, Illinois, 1825–1870* (1978); John Mack Faragher, *Sugar Creek: Life on the Illinois Prairies* (1986); Susan E. Gray, *The Yankee West: Community Life on the Michigan Frontier* (1996); John Denis Haeger, *The Investment Frontier: New York Businessmen and the Economic Development of the Old Northwest* (1981); Joan M. Jensen, *Loosening the Bonds: Mid-Atlantic Farm Women, 1750–1850* (1986); Robert Leslie Jones, *History of Agriculture in Ohio to 1880* (1983); Donald H. Parkerson, *The Agricultural Transition in New York State: Markets and Migration in Mid-Nineteenth Century America* (1995).

Fiction and Film

Nathaniel Hawthorne's novel *The Scarlet Letter* (1850, but use any edition), although set in the Puritan period, reveals more about the attitudes and controversies of the antebellum period than it does about the seventeenth century. The novels of James Fenimore Cooper provide a picture of the impact of social and economic change on the frontier. Susan Warner's *The Wide, Wide World* (any edition) as well as her other popular novels provide an excellent picture of female interests and concerns in this period (although certainly not all her readers were women).

Little Women (1994) is a feature film presenting a moving picture of the domestic and family life so idealized by the middle class. It also suggests the struggle of the middle class to maintain its status in difficult times. Some critics have pointed out that this adaptation of Louisa May Alcott's novel has strong overtones of contemporary feminism. *Out of Ireland: The Story of Irish Emigration to America,* (1994) gives a vivid picture of Irish emigration between 1840 and 1920.

Suggested Web Sites

http://www.si.edu/lemelson/centerpieces/whole_cloth/

Whole Cloth: Discovering Science and Technology Through American History. The Jerome and Dorothy Lemelson Center for the Study of Invention and Innovation/Society for the History of Technology put together this site, which includes excellent activities and sources concerning early American manufacturing and industry.

http://www.connerprairie.org/ntlroad.html

Road Through the Wilderness. The National Road was a hot political topic in the early republic and was part of the beginning of the development of America's infrastructure. This site tells the history of the building of the National Road.

http://www.history.rochester.edu/Scientific_American/

19th Century Scientific American Online. Magazines and journals are windows through which we can view society. This site provides on-line editions of one of the more interesting nineteenth-century journals.

http://www.indianapolis.in.us/cp/jmed.html

Jacksonian Medicine. Survival was far from certain in the Jacksonian era. This site discusses some of the reasons and some of the possible cures of the times.

http://www.upenn.edu/AR/1830/

Penn 1830: A Virtual Tour. This "virtual tour" shows what a fairly typical campus looked like and what student life was like at one of the larger universities in the antebellum era.

http://www.connerprairie.org/clothing.html

Clothing of the 1830s. Visit this site to see how clothing worn in the early republic was quite different from what you are wearing now.

http://www.ushistory

the History place

A richly detailed on-line learning environment complete with interactive maps, timelines, history activities, primary source documents, and links to related American history sites.

11

SLAVERY *and the* OLD SOUTH

CHAPTER OUTLINE

As a young slave boy, Frederick Douglass was sent by his master to live in Baltimore. When he first met his mistress, Sophia Auld, she appeared to be a "woman of the kindest heart and finest feelings." He was "astonished at her goodness" as she began to teach him to read. Her husband, however, ordered her to stop because Maryland law forbade teaching slaves to read. A literate slave was "unmanageable," utterly "unfit . . . to be a slave." From this episode Douglass learned to set inverse goals from Master Auld's wishes. "What he most dreaded, that I most desired . . . and the argument which he so warmly urged, against my learning to read, only served to inspire me with a desire and determination to learn."

In the seven years he lived with the Aulds, young Frederick used "various stratagems" to teach himself to read and write. In the narrative of his early life, written after his dramatic escape to the North, Douglass acknowledged that his master's "bitter opposition" had been as beneficial to him as Mrs. Auld's "kindly aid" in achieving his eventual freedom.

Most slaves did not, like Douglass, escape to freedom. But all were as inextricably tied to their masters as Douglass was to the Aulds. Nor could whites in antebellum America escape the pervasive influence of slavery. Otherwise decent people were often compelled by the "peculiar institution" to act inhumanely. After her husband's interference, Sophia Auld, Douglass observed, was transformed from an angel into a demon by the "fatal poison of irresponsible power." Her formerly tender heart turned to "stone" when she ceased teaching him. "Slavery proved as injurious to her," Douglass wrote, "as it did to me."

Such was also the case in Douglass's relationship with Mr. Covey, a slavebreaker to whom he was sent in 1833 to have his will broken. Covey succeeded for a time, Douglass reported, in breaking his "body, soul, and spirit" by brutal hard work and discipline. But one hot August day in 1833, the two men fought a long, grueling battle, which Douglass won. His victory, he said, "rekindled the few expiring embers of freedom, and revived within me a sense of my own manhood." Although it would be four more years before his escape to the North, the young man never again felt like a slave. The key to Douglass's successful resistance to Covey's power was not just his strong will, or even the magical root he carried in his pocket, but rather his knowledge of how to jeopardize Covey's reputation and livelihood as a slavebreaker. The oppressed survive by knowing their oppressors.

As Mrs. Auld and Covey discovered, as long as some people were not free, no one was free. Douglass observed, "You cannot outlaw one part of the people without endangering the rights and liberties of all people. You cannot put a chain on the ankle of the bondsman without finding the other end of it about your own necks." After quarreling with a house servant, one plantation mistress complained that she "exercises dominion over me—or tries to do it. One would have thought . . . that I was the Servant, she the mistress." Many whites lived in constant fear of a slave revolt. A Louisiana planter recalled that he had "known times here when there was not a single planter who had a calm night's rest; they then never lay down to sleep without a brace of loaded pistols at their sides." In slave folktales, the clever Brer Rabbit usually outwitted the more powerful Brer Fox or Brer Wolf, thus reversing the roles of oppressed and oppressor.

Slavery, then, was an intricate web of human relationships as well as a labor system. After showing the economic growth and development of the Old South, in which slavery and cotton played vital roles, this chapter will emphasize the daily lives and relationships of masters and slaves who, like Douglass and the Aulds, lived, loved, learned, worked, and struggled with one another in the years before the Civil War.

The young Frederick Douglass, shown here in a photograph from about 1855, understood as well as any American the profound human, social, and political complexities and consequences of slavery. *(New York Public Library, Schomburg Center for Research in Black Culture)*

Perhaps no issue in American history has generated quite as many interpretations or as much emotional controversy as that of slavery. As American attitudes toward that institution have changed over the years, three interpretive schools have developed, each adding to our knowledge of the peculiar institution. The first saw slavery as a relatively humane and reasonable institution in which plantation owners took care of helpless, childlike slaves. The second depicted slavery as a harsh and cruel system of oppressive exploitation. The third, and most recent, interpretation described the slavery experience from the perspective of the slaves, who did indeed suffer brutal

treatment in slavery yet nevertheless survived with integrity, self-esteem, and a sense of community and culture.

The first and second interpretive schools emphasized workaday interactions among masters and mostly passive, victimized slaves, while the third focused on the creative energies and survival of life in the slave quarters from sundown to sunup. In a unique structure, this chapter follows these masters and slaves through their day, from morning in the Big House through hot afternoon in the fields to the slave cabins at night. Although slavery was the crucial institution in defining the Old South, many other social groups and patterns contributed to the tremendous economic growth of the South from 1820 to 1860. We will look first at these diverse aspects of antebellum southern life.

BUILDING THE COTTON KINGDOM

Many myths obscure our understanding of the vast region of the antebellum South. It was not a monolithic society filled only with large cotton plantations worked by hundreds of slaves. The realities of the South and slavery were much more complex. Large-plantation agriculture was dominant in the antebellum South, but most southern whites were not even slaveholders, much less large planters. Most southern farmers lived not in mansions but in dark, cramped, two-room cabins. Cotton was a key cash crop in the South, but it was not the only crop grown there. Some masters were kindly, but many were not; some slaves were contented, but most were not.

There were many Souths, encompassing several geographic regions, each with different economic bases and social structures and each reflecting its own cultural and political values. The older Upper South of Virginia, Maryland, North Carolina, and Kentucky grew different staple crops from those grown in the newer, Lower or "Black Belt" South that stretched from South Carolina to eastern Texas. Within each state, moreover, the economies of flat coastal areas, inland upcountry forests, and pine barrens all differed. A still further diversity existed between these areas and the Appalachian highlands of northern Alabama and Georgia, eastern Tennessee and Kentucky, and western Virginia and North Carolina. Finally, the cultural and economic life of New Orleans, Savannah, Charleston, and Richmond differed dramatically from rural areas of the South.

Although the South was diverse, agriculture dominated its industry and commerce. In 1859, a Virginia planter complained about a neighbor who was considering abandoning his farm to become a merchant. "To me it seems to be a wild idea," the planter wrote in his diary, hoping that his friend would "give it up and be satisfied to farm." Southerners placed a high value on agricultural labor. Slavery was primarily a labor system intended to produce wealth for landowners. Although slavery in older areas was paternalistic, with masters and slaves owing mutual obligations to each other, increasingly it became a capitalistic enterprise intended to maximize productivity and profits.

Economic Expansion

In the 20 years preceding the Civil War, the South's economy grew slightly faster than the North's. Personal income in 1860 was 15 percent higher in the South than in the prosperous states of the Old Northwest. If the South had become an independent nation in 1860, it would have ranked as one of the wealthiest countries in the world in per capita income. One dramatic technological breakthrough, the cotton gin, was fundamental to this economic growth. The cotton gin had two momentous effects: first, it tied the southern economy to cotton production for a century; second, it allowed the expansion of slavery into vast new territories.

As we learned in Chapter 9, most cotton farmers planted "long-staple" cotton before the invention of Eli Whitney's cotton gin in 1793. After the cotton gin, the "short-staple" variety, which could grow anywhere in the South, predominated. But only large-plantation owners could afford to buy gins and purchase the fertile bottomlands of the Gulf states. Thus, the plantation system spread with the rise of cotton.

Because cotton could be grown all over the South after the perfection of the cotton gin, men rushed westward to fresh, fertile lands. Large-scale farming increased, demanding more and more slave labor. As a valuable capital resource, slaves received a degree of care and protection. But despite the abolition of slavery in the North and occasional talk of emancipation in the South, slavery became more deeply entrenched, seemingly a permanent part of southern life. Any doubts whispered about ending it could be dispelled by one word: cotton.

Although corn was a larger crop than cotton in total acreage, cotton was the largest cash crop and for that reason was called "king." In 1820, the South became the world's largest producer of cotton, and from 1815 to

The Varied Economic Life in the South

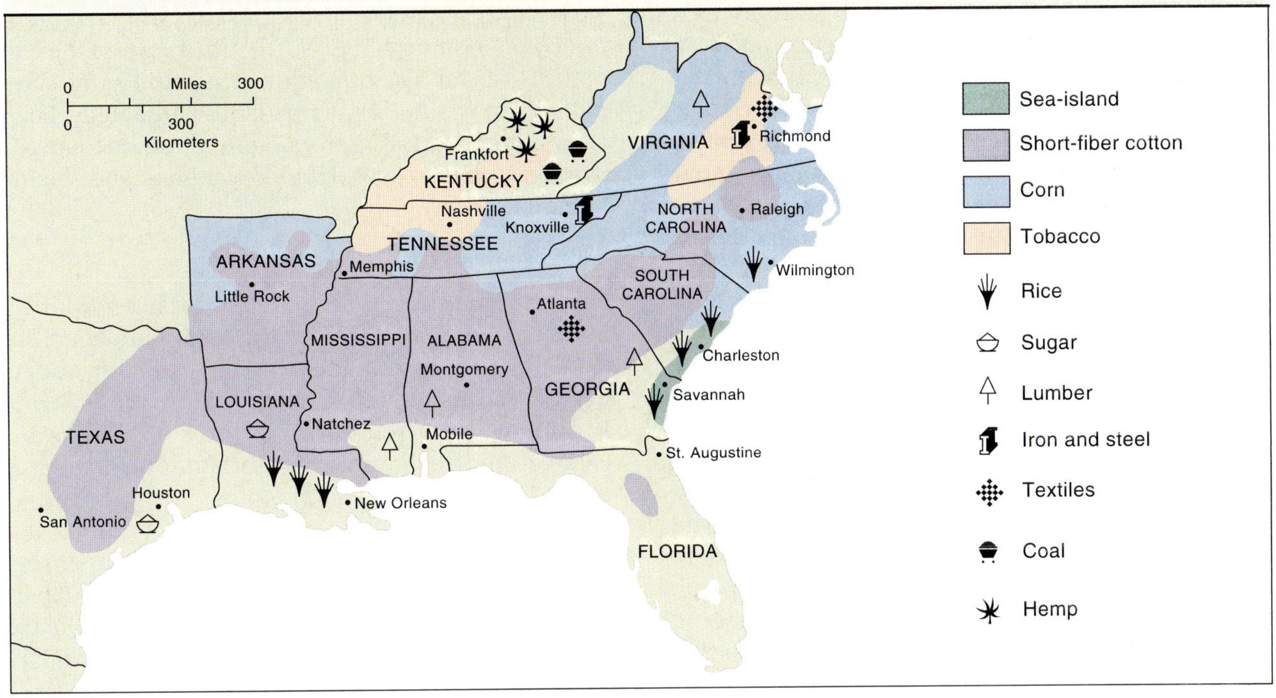

Note the short-fiber, cotton-growing "black belt" running from southern Virginia to eastern Texas. Despite the economically varied South, cotton was "king."

1860, cotton represented more than half of all American exports. The economic growth spurred by cotton helped not only the South but also the North and the Midwest. Northern merchants gained by shipping, insuring, and marketing southern cotton. Western farmers found a major market for their foodstuffs. Cotton was the mainstay of the southern economy, but it was also a crucial link in the national economy.

The supply of cotton from the South grew at an astonishing rate. Cotton production soared from 461,000 bales in 1817 to 1.35 million bales in 1840. A cotton "boom" started in 1849 when output reached 2.85 million bales and continued until 1860, when production peaked at 4.8 million bales. In the period from 1817 to 1860, cotton production jumped over tenfold. This rapid growth was stimulated by world demand, especially from English textile mills. The availability of new lands, a self-reproducing supply of cheap slave labor, and low-cost steamboat transportation down the Mississippi River to New Orleans helped keep cotton king.

White and Black Migrations

Southerners migrated southwestward in huge numbers between 1830 and 1860 to grow more and more cotton. Seeking profits from the worldwide demand for cotton, they pushed the southeastern Indians and the Mexicans in Texas out of the way and were still moving into Texas as the Civil War began.

Southern cotton growers, like northern grain farmers, followed parallel migration paths westward. Whereas New Englanders moved into the upper Midwest, southerners migrated from the coastal states westward into the lower Midwest and the Lower South. By the 1830s, the center of cotton production had shifted from South Carolina and Georgia to Alabama and Mississippi. This process continued in the 1850s as southerners forged into Arkansas, Louisiana, and eastern Texas. As they moved, they carried their values and institutions, including slavery, with them. Usually, a father and his sons would go west first, find land and clear it, plant some corn, and begin to raise a cabin. Leaving the sons to finish, the father would return east, where his wife and daughters had been managing the farm, pack up the household, and bring it to the new home. Thus, in November 1835, one extended family of nearly 50 people left South Carolina for Alabama. "We bade adieu to friends," a daughter wrote, "and left the old homestead never to look upon it again."

Not only were these migrating southern families attracted by the pull of fresh land and cheap labor, but they also were pushed westward by deteriorating economic conditions and other pressures in the older Atlantic states. Beginning in the 1820s, the states of the Upper South underwent a long depression affecting tobacco and cotton prices. Moreover, years of constant use had exhausted their lands, and families with numerous children struggled to give each child an inheritance or financial help to start a family or a career. In a society that valued land ownership, farm families had several choices. One was to move west. Another was to stay and diversify. Therefore, the older states of the Upper South continued to shift to grains, mainly corn and wheat. Because these crops required less labor than tobacco, slave owners, especially those with pressing debts, began to sell some of their slaves.

The internal slave trade from Virginia "down the river" to the Old Southwest thus became a multimillion-dollar "industry" in the 1830s. Between 1830 and 1860, an estimated 300,000 Virginia slaves were transported south for sale. One of the busiest routes was from Alexandria, Virginia, almost within view of the nation's capital, to a huge depot near Natchez, Mississippi. Although most southern states attempted occasionally to outlaw or control the traffic in slaves, these efforts were poorly enforced and usually short-lived. Besides, the reason for outlawing the slave trade was generally not humanitarian but rather originated in a fear of a rapid increase in the slave population, especially of "wicked" slaves sent south because they were considered unmanageable. Alabama, Mississippi, and Louisiana all banned the importation of slaves after the Nat Turner revolt in Virginia in 1831 (described later in this chapter). But all three states permitted the slave trade again during the profitable 1850s.

Congress formally ended the external slave trade on January 1, 1808, the earliest time permitted by the Constitution. Enforcement by the United States was weak, however, and many thousands of blacks continued to be smuggled to North America until the end of the Civil War. The tremendous increase in the slave population was the result not of this illegal trade, however, but of natural reproduction, often encouraged by slave owners eager for more laborers and salable human property.

The Dependence on Slavery

The rapid increase in the number of slaves, from 1.5 million in 1820 to 4 million in 1860, paralleled the growth of the southern economy and its dependence on the slave labor system. Economic growth and migration southwestward changed the geographic distribution of slaves, thus hindering the cause of abolition.

Although most slaves worked on plantations and medium-size farms, they could be found in all segments of the southern economy. In 1850, some 75 percent of all slaves were engaged in agricultural labor: 55 percent growing cotton, 10 percent tobacco, and 10 percent rice, sugar, and hemp. Of the remaining one-fourth, about 15 percent were domestic servants, and the remainder were in mining, lumbering, construction, and industry.

The 300,000 slaves in 1850 who were not domestics or agricultural laborers worked as lumberjacks and turpentine producers in Carolina and Georgia forests; gold, coal, and salt miners in Virginia and Kentucky; boiler stokers and deckhands on

Slaves were found not just on plantations doing agricultural labor but in nearly every kind of labor in the South. These Virginia dockworkers were photographed about 1860 in Alexandria, Virginia, by Mathew Brady. *(National Archives)*

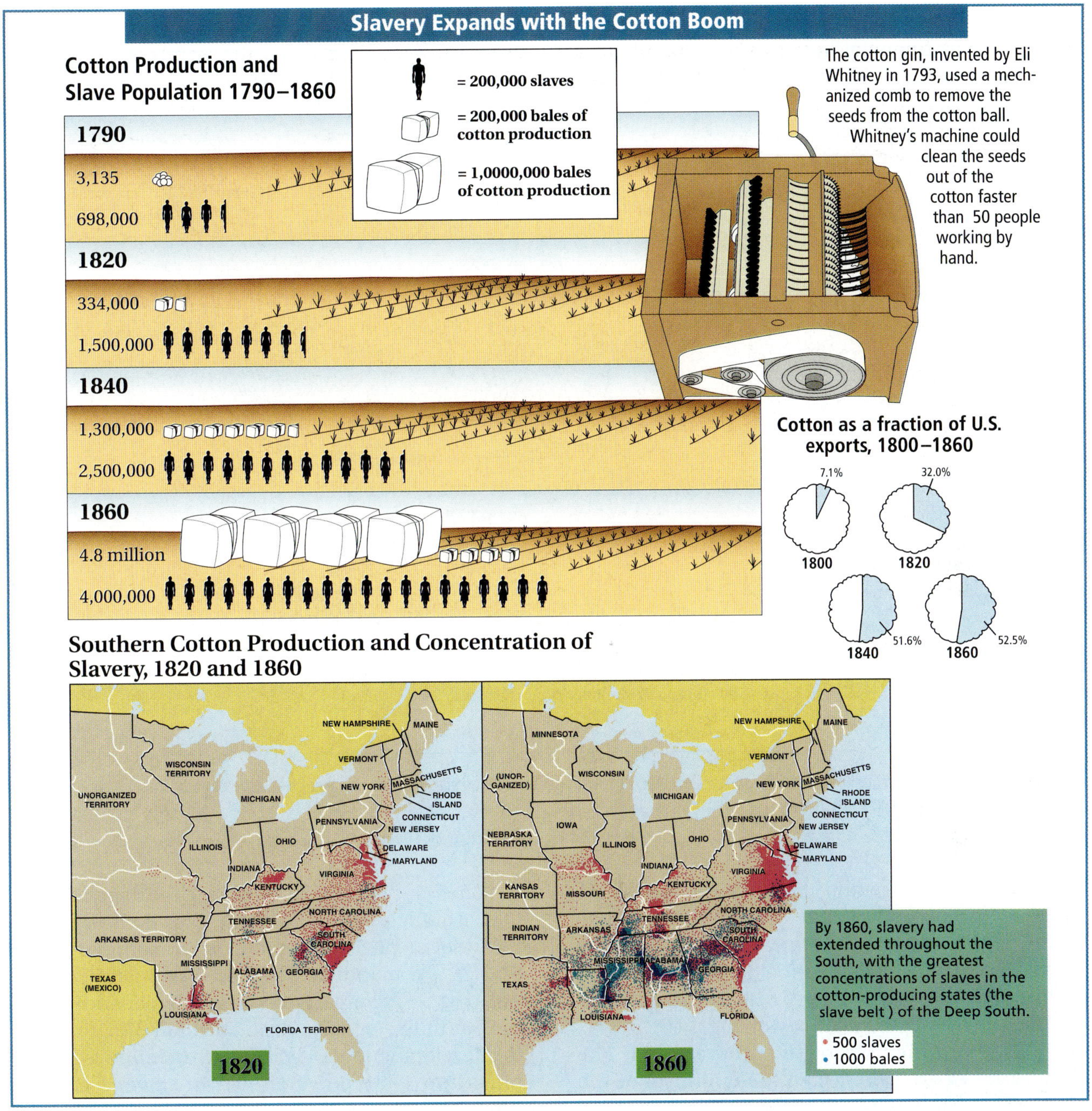

Mississippi River steamships; toilers on road and railroad construction gangs in Georgia and Louisiana; textile laborers in Alabama cotton mills; dockworkers in Savannah and Charleston; and tobacco and iron workers in Richmond factories. A visitor to Natchez in 1835 observed slaves working as "mechanics, draymen, hostelers, labourers, hucksters, and washwomen, and the heterogeneous multitude of every other occupation, who fill the streets of a busy city—for slaves are trained to every kind of manual labour."

Masters also used slaves in industry. The Tredegar Iron Company of Richmond decided in 1847 to shift from white labor "almost exclusively" to slave labor to destroy the potential power of organized white workers to strike. Tredegar's decision foreshadowed the similar strategy of many future employers to exploit black laborers as a means of eliminating or putting an economic squeeze on organized white laborers.

Whether in iron factories, coal mines, or cotton fields, slavery was profitable as a source of labor and as a capital investment. In 1859, the average plantation slave produced $78 in cotton earnings for his master annually while costing only about $32 to be fed, clothed, and housed. Despite maintenance costs, debts from the purchase of land and more slaves, and

Population Patterns in the South: Whites, Slaves, and Free Blacks, by State, 1860

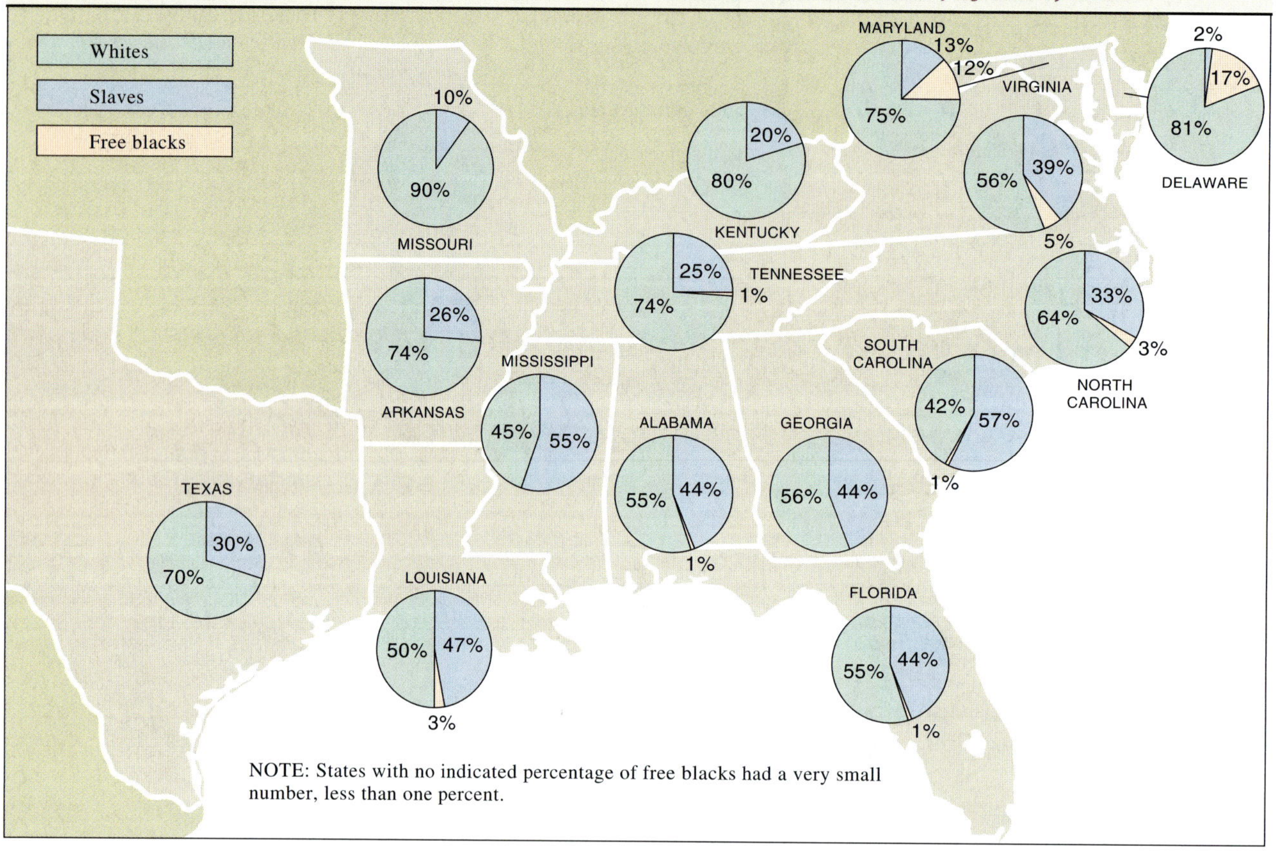

Note how the largest proportions of free blacks were in the older Upper South and in Louisiana (mostly in New Orleans). Note also the two states with more slaves than whites.

the unstable price of cotton, the "crop value per slave" increased from about $15 in 1800 to $125 in 1860. Slaves were also a good investment. In 1844, a "prime field hand" sold for $600. A cotton boom beginning in 1849 raised this price by 1860 to $1800. A slave owner could prosper by buying slaves, working them for several years, and then selling them for a profit. The rising price of slaves reflected the optimism of the planter class.

The economic growth of the slaveholding South was impressive, but slavery still limited it. Generally, agricultural growth leads to the rise of cities and industry, facilitating sustained economic growth. In the planter-dominated antebellum South, however, agricultural improvements did not lead to industrialization and urbanization. In 1860, the South had 35 percent of the country's population and only 15 percent of its manufacturing establishments. On the eve of the Civil War, 1 southerner in 14 was a city dweller, compared with 1 of every 3 people in the North. The South would continue its economic backwardness as long as whites with capital insisted on putting all their business energies toward cotton production.

Some southerners were aware of the dangers of following a single path to wealth. J. D. B. De Bow created a journal in 1846 dedicated to trade, commerce, and manufacturing. De Bow's *Review* called for greater economic independence in the South through the diversification of agriculture, the development of industry, and an improved transportation system. A believer in slavery, De Bow thought that slave labor could fuel the Industrial Revolution in the South. But the planter class had little enthusiasm for such plans. As long as money could be made through an agricultural slave system, plantation owners saw no reason to risk capital in new areas.

Slavery and Class in the South

Slavery also served social purposes. Although the proportion of southern white families that owned slaves slowly declined from 40 to 25 percent as some families sold off their slaves to cotton planters, the ideal of slave ownership still permeated all classes and determined the hierarchical character of the southern social structure. At the top stood the planter aristocracy, much of it new wealth, elbowing its way among

White Class Structure in the South, 1860

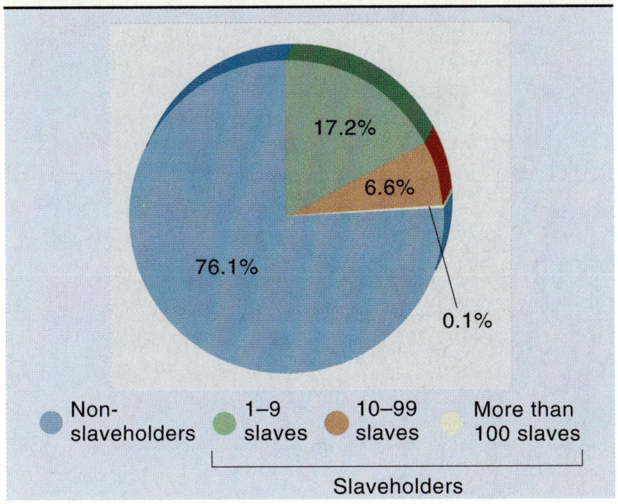

In a pyramidal class structure, the richest southerners were those few with the largest number of slaves. As the chart shows, three-fourths of antebellum southerners held no slaves at all.

the old established families like the Byrds and Carters of Virginia. Some 10,000 rich families owned 50 or more slaves in 1860; about 3,000 of these owned over 100. Below them was a slightly larger group of small planters who held from 10 to 50 slaves. But the largest group, 70 percent of all slaveholders in 1860, comprised 270,000 middle-level farm families with fewer than 10 slaves. The typical slaveholder worked a small family farm of about 100 acres with 8 or 9 slaves, perhaps members of the same family. The typical slave, however, was more likely to be in a group of 20 or more other slaves on a large farm or small plantation.

In 1841, a young white North Carolinian, John Flintoff, went to Mississippi to fulfill his dream of wealth and prestige. Beginning as an overseer managing an uncle's farm, he bought a "negro boy 7 years old" even before he owned any land. After several years of unrewarding struggle, Flintoff married and returned to North Carolina. There he finally bought 124 acres and a few more cheap, young blacks, and by 1860, he had a modest farm with several slaves growing corn, wheat, and tobacco. Although he never became as prosperous as he had dreamed, his son went to college, and his wife, he reported proudly, "has lived a Lady."

Slavery was a powerful force in the lives of middle-level farmers like John Flintoff, who had only a few slaves, and even for those who owned none. Economic, social, and political standing depended on owning slaves. Whites like John Flintoff hoped to purchase one slave, perhaps a female who would bear children, and then climb the economic and social ladder of southern society. White southerners therefore supported slavery whether they owned slaves or not.

They also defended the institution because it gave them a sense of superiority over at least one group and a sense of kinship, if not quite equality, with other whites. Although there was always a small element of southern society that believed in emancipation, most southerners did not. A small Alabama farmer told a northern visitor in the 1850s that if the slaves were given their freedom, "they'd all think themselves just as good as we. . . . How would you like to hev a nigger feelin' just as good as a white man?" Another said that he wished "there warn't no niggers here" and did not know anybody who favored freeing them.

The Nonslaveholding South

Below Flintoff and other middling farmers lived the majority of white southerners, who owned no slaves but were equally, or even more, antiblack. Newton Knight, for example, worked a harsh piece of land cut out of the pines of southern Mississippi. He and his wife lived in a crude log cabin, scratching out their livelihood by growing corn and sweet potatoes and raising chickens and hogs. A staunch Baptist given to fits of violence, Knight had once killed a black.

The 75 percent of southern whites who, like Newton Knight and his family, owned no slaves were scattered throughout the South. Many were Scots-Irish. Most lived in the foothills of the mountains and worked generally poorer land than the large planters. They did not need to be near commercial centers because they were largely self-sufficient. Working together as a family, they raised mostly corn and wheat, hogs, enough cotton for their own clothes and a little cash, and subsistence vegetable crops. These farmers maintained a household economy, making soap, shoes, candles, whiskey, coarse textiles, and ax handles and trading hogs, eggs, small game, or homemade items for cash and other goods. They lived in two-room log houses separated by a "dog run." Cooperation with neighbors brightened the yeoman farmer's drab and isolated life. Families gathered at corn huskings and quilting parties, logrolling and wrestling matches, and political stump and revivalist camp meetings.

In many ways, the yeoman farmers were the solid backbone of the South. In 1860 in North Carolina, 70 percent of the farmers held fewer than 100 acres; in Mississippi and Louisiana, reputedly large plantation states, more than 60 percent of the farms were under 100 acres. Fiercely proud of their independence, the yeoman farmers had a share of political power, voting overwhelmingly for Andrew Jackson. Although some resented the tradition of political deference to "betters,"

Southern yeoman farm families lived self-sufficient lives in cabins such as this one on the edge of a clearing. The isolation of the woman drawing water from a well was partly relieved by gatherings such as quilting parties, which created not only social contact but also a uniquely female American work of useful art. Note that men were also at the party, talking (politics, perhaps) by the stove, bouncing a baby, carrying food, and courting a young woman by the quilt. *(Above, Abby Aldrich Rockefeller Folk Art Center; right, North Wind Picture Archives)*

these farmers were not yet ready to challenge planters for political power. Yeoman farmers fought with the Confederacy during the Civil War; but some, like Newton Knight, refused to fight against the Union and ended up organizing a guerrilla band of Unionists in southern Mississippi.

Another little-known group of southern whites included the herdsmen who raised hogs and other livestock. Living among the plantations and small farms, they supplied bacon and pork to local slaveholders (who often thought hog growing was beneath their dignity) and drove herds of hogs to stockyards in Nashville, Louisville, and Savannah. The South raised two-thirds of the nation's hogs. In 1860, the value of southern livestock was $500 million, twice that of cotton. Although much of the corn crop fed the hogs, many herdsmen preferred to let their stock roam loose in the woods. As one South Carolinian explained, "We raise our hogs by allowing them to range in our woods, where they get fat . . . on acorns," which he and others considered a better diet for bacon and pork than corn. However valuable the total size of the hog business, individual hog herdsmen did not stand very high on the southern social ladder.

Below them were the poor whites of the South, about 10 percent of the population. Often sneeringly called "hillbillies," "dirt eaters," "crackers," or "poor white trash," they eked out a living in isolated, inhospitable areas. Although they grew a little corn and vegetables, their livelihood came mostly from fishing, hunting small game, and raising a few pigs. Some made corn whiskey, and many hired themselves out as farmhands for an average wage, with board, of about $14 per month. Because of poor diet and bad living conditions, these poor whites often suffered from hookworm and malaria. This, and the natural debilitation of heat and poverty, gave them a reputation as lazy, shiftless, and illiterate. An English visitor, Fanny Kemble, described them as "the most degraded race of human beings claiming an Anglo-Saxon origin that can be found on the face of the earth."

The poor whites stayed poor partly because the slave system allowed the planter class to accumulate a disproportionate amount of land and political power. High slave prices made entry into the planter class increasingly difficult, increasing class tensions within the South. Because the larger planters dominated southern life and owned the most slaves, an understanding of the character of slavery and the relationships between masters and slaves is best accomplished by looking at plantation life during a typical day from morning to night.

MORNING: MASTER IN THE BIG HOUSE

It is early morning in the South. Imagine four scenes. In the first, William Waller of Virginia and a neighbor are preparing to leave with 20 choice slaves on a long trip to the slave market in Natchez, Mississippi. Waller is making this "intolerable" journey, as he calls it, to sell some of his slaves to ease his heavy debts. Although he "loaths the vocation of slave trading," he must recover some money out of a "sense of duty" to see his family "freed from my bondage" of indebtedness. To ease his conscience, he intends to supervise the sale personally, thus securing the best possible deal not only for himself but also for his departing slaves.

On another plantation, owned by James Hammond of South Carolina, the horn blows an hour before daylight to awaken the slaves for work in the fields. Hammond rises soon after, ever aware that "to continue" as a wealthy master, he must "draw the rein tighter and tighter" to hold his slaves "in complete check." He is as good as his word, recommending that "in general 15 to 20 lashes will be sufficient flogging" for most offenses but that "in extreme cases," the punishment "must not exceed 100 lashes in one day."

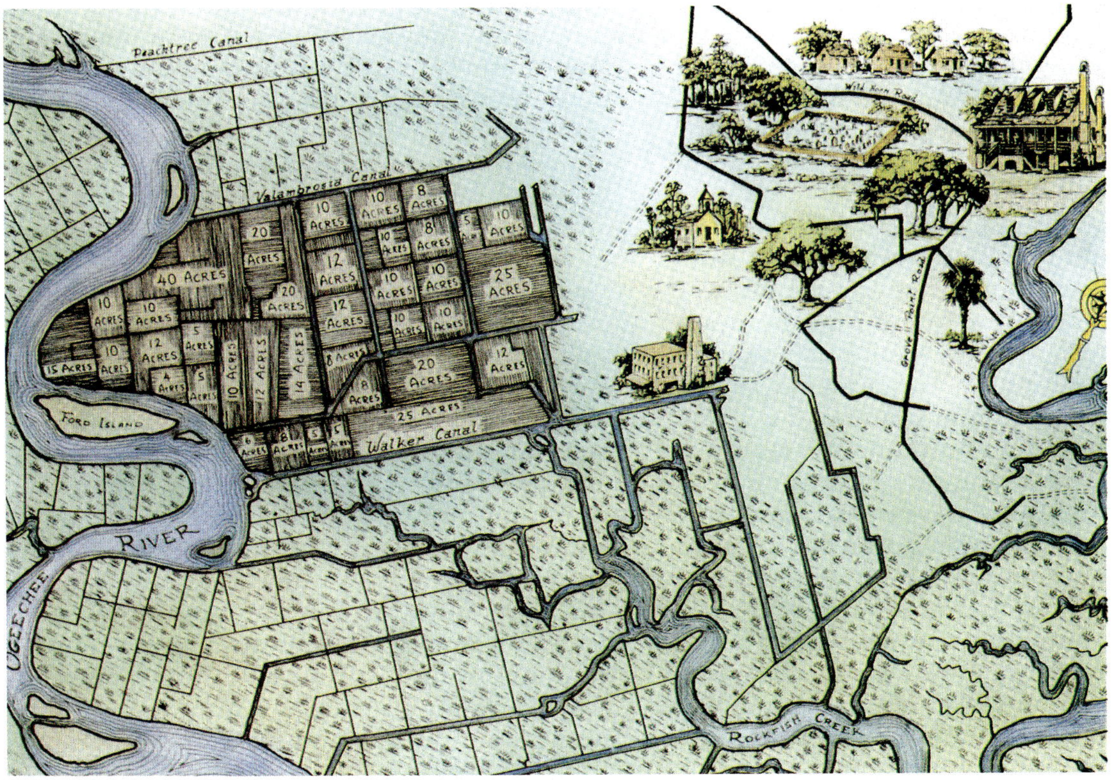

This modern map shows Wild Heron, a rice plantation near Savannah similar to the Allston's. Note the elaborate system of canals, roads, and paths connecting the rice fields with the mill, plantation house, slave quarters, cemetery, and chapel. *(Danzer Map Collection/University of Tennessee Press)*

On an Alabama plantation, Hugh Lawson is up early, writing a sorrowful letter to Susanna Clay, telling her of the death of a "devotedly attached and faithful" slave, Jim. "I feel desolate," Hugh writes, "my most devoted friend is gone and his place can never be supplied by another." As Lawson pens his letter, a female slave has already awakened and "walked across a frosty field in the early morning and gone to the big house to build a fire" for her mistress. As the mistress wakes up to a warming house, she says to the slave, a grown woman responsible for the welfare of two families, "Well, how's my little nigger today?"

In a fourth household, this one a medium-size farm in upcountry Georgia, not far from Hammond's huge plantation, Charles Brock wakes up at dawn and joins his two sons and four slaves to work his modest acreage of grains and sweet potatoes, while Brock's wife and a female slave tend the cows that provide milk and butter. On small and medium-size family farms with five or fewer slaves, blacks and whites commonly worked together, as one observer noted, with the "axe of master and man [slave] falling with alternate strokes . . . [and] ploughing side by side."

As these diverse scenes suggest, slavery thoroughly permeated the lives of southern slaveholders. For the slaves, morning was a time for getting up and going to work. But for white slaveholders, morning involved contact with slaves in many ways: as burdens of figuring profit and loss, as objects to be kept obedient and orderly, as intimates and fellow workers, and as ever-present reminders of fear, hate, and uncertainty.

The Burdens of Slaveholding

Robert Francis Withers Allston (1801–1864) was a major rice planter in the Georgetown district of South Carolina, a low, swampy, mosquito-infested tidal area where four rivers empty into Winyah Bay. It was a perfect spot for growing rice, but so unhealthy that few whites wanted to live there. The death rate among slaves was appallingly high. In 1840, a total of 18,274 slaves toiled in the Georgetown district, but only 2,193 whites, many for only part of the year. Robert was the fifth generation of Allstons to live in this inhospitable land. By 1860, he owned seven plantations along the Peedee River, totaling some 4,000 acres, in addition to another 9,500 acres of pasture and timberland. He held nearly 600 slaves, 236 of whom worked at the home plantation, Chicora Wood. The total value of his land and slaves in the 1850s was approximately $300,000. Rich in land and labor, he nevertheless had large mortgages and outstanding debts.

Allston was an enlightened, talented, public-spirited man. Educated at West Point but also trained in the law, he did far more than practice agriculture. He served as a state senator in South Carolina for 24 years and as governor from 1856 to 1858. His political creed, he wrote in 1838, was one of "virtue and purity" based on "the principles of Thomas Jefferson." The core of his conviction was a "plain, honest, commonsense reading of the Constitution," which for Allston clearly meant the constitutionality of slavery and nullification and the illegitimacy of abolitionism and the United States Bank.

Allston also reflected Jefferson's humane side. He was an ardent reformer, advocating liberalization of South Carolina's poor laws; an improved system of public education open to rich and poor alike; humanitarian care of the deaf, blind, insane, and other disabled people; and the improvement of conditions on the reservations of the Catawba Indians. He was active in the Episcopal Church and gave money generously to support ministerial students.

In 1832, Allston married Adele Petigru, an equally enlightened and hardworking person. She participated fully in the management of the plantation and ran it while Robert was away on politics. In a letter to her husband, written in 1850, Adele demonstrated her diverse interests by reporting on family affairs and the children's learning, sickness among the slaves, the status of spring plowing, the building of a canal and causeway, her supervision of the bottling of some wine, and current politics. After Robert's death during the Civil War, she assumed control of the Allston plantations, which had been abandoned when Union troops moved through the area. Eventually, she had to sell most of the estate at auction, holding on only to Chicora Wood, which she managed with a daughter until her death in 1896.

State politics lured Robert from his land for part of each year, but he was by no means an absentee owner. Except when away to escape the worst periods of mosquitoes and heat, the Allstons were fully engaged in the operation of their plantations. Managing thousands of acres of rice required not only an enormous investment in labor and equipment but also careful supervision of both the slaves and an elaborate irrigation system. Although Robert Allston's acreage and slave population were larger than those of most big planters and he grew rice rather than cotton, his concerns were typical.

Allston's letters frequently expressed the serious burdens of owning slaves. Although he was careful to distribute enough cloth, blankets, and shoes to his slaves and to give them sufficient rest, the sickness and death of slaves, especially young field workers, headed his list of concerns. "I lost in one year 28 negroes," Allston complained, "22 of whom were task hands." He tried to keep slave families together but sold slaves when necessary. In a letter to his son, Benjamin, he

Agreement To Purchase Slaves, January 25, 1859

Robert Allston bought these slaves for his son, Benjamin, who was then 25 years old and taking charge of one of his father's many plantations, Guendalos. Note that in this (not unusual) case, slave families were kept together in the transaction.

Agreed to purchase from Dr. Forster Forty one Negroes of Mrs. Withers of the "remainder" from the Estate of the late Francis Withers, to be deliver'd in all this week at $500. Titles to Ben Allston his Bond and mine payable in 8, 10, 12 yrs. secured by mortgage of the property, viz

$1,000	1	Andrew	38	yrs.
800	2	Serena	36	
400	3	Jos.	10	
300	4	Judy	8	
200	5	Henry	5	
1,000	6	Jack	30	
800	7	Patience	27	pregnant
400	8	Daniel	11	
300	9	Prince	9	
250	10	Phyllis	5	
200	11	Bess	3½	
800	12	James*	28	carpenter, Drinks, delicate
800	13	Hagar	24	pregnant, near time of delivery
200	14	Joe	39	carpenter and cooper
800	15	Levi	50	
500	16	Betsey†	40	delicate
400	17	Murria‡	18	
400	18	Toby	14	
$1,000	19	Paris	35	
800	20	Hannah	33	
800	21	Frank	16½	
500	22	William	14	
350	23	Caty	9	
300	24	Michael	6	
150	25	Eleanor	3½	
50	26	Dandy	1	
800	27	Strophon	50	
700	28	Lucy	18	
500	29	Judy	14	
1,000	30	Toney	38	an indifferent carpenter
800	31	Betty	35	
800	32	Daniel	16½	3 years with Bricklayers to mix mortar
200	33	Francis	4½	
100	34	Caesar	1½	
500	35	O Sary	50	cook and washer
1,000	36	Israel	31	
800	37	Esther	28	
100	38	William	1½	
800	39	Dinah	18½	
500	40	Quash	14½	
300	41	William	9	

*Has Epileptic attacks produced by drink, would be valuable if kept from drink.
†With this family there is the incumbrance of an old man of 80 years, father of Betsey.
‡Murria is half witted.
Note: Prices are from a second list, as are some of the remarks concerning individuals. The horizontal lines probably separate family groups.

Source: This and other material on the Allstons is from *The South Carolina Rice Plantation as Revealed in the Papers of Robert F. W. Allston,* ed., J. H. Easterby (1945).

Adele and Robert F. W. Allston shared the work and burdens of managing their rice plantations, while their slaves, many of them women, as seen in these drawings, planted rice seeds by covering them with their feet (as was done in Africa), and later carried the harvested rice to flatboats, where it was taken to the threshing yard. *(Portraits, South Carolina Library, Columbia; Drawings,* From Down by the Riverside, *Charles Joyner, 1984, sketch by Alice R. Huger Smith, c. 1914; photograph from Photographs and Prints Division, Schomburg Center for Research in Black Culture, The New York Public Library, Astor, Lenox and Tilden Foundations)*

expressed concern over the bad example set by a slave driver who was "abandon'd by his hands" because he had not worked with them the previous Sunday. In the same letter, Allston urged Benjamin to keep up the "patrol duty," less to guard against runaway slaves, he said, than to restrain the excesses of "vagabond whites." Clearly, the planter class felt a duty to control lower-class whites as well as black slaves.

Other planters shared Allston's concerns, seeing slavery as both a duty and a burden. A Louisiana planter, in financial difficulty, wrote how much he dreaded the "miserable occupation of seeing to negroes, and attending to their wants and sickness and to making them do their duty—and after all have no prospect of being paid for my trouble." Many planters insisted that they worked harder than their slaves to feed and clothe them and to make their lives "as comfortable as possible." Some accepted this as part of their responsibility, and others complained loudly. R. L. Dabney of Virginia exclaimed: "There could be no greater curse inflicted on us than to be compelled to manage a parcel of Negroes." Curse or not, Dabney and other planters profited from their burdens, a point they seldom admitted.

Their wives experienced other kinds of burdens. "The mistress of a plantation," wrote Susan Dabney Smedes, "was the most complete slave on it." Southern women were expected to adhere to the cult of domesticity both by improving their husbands' morals, which often meant restraining them from excessive cruelty toward slaves, and by beautifying their parlors. Moreover, plantation mistresses suffered under a double standard of morality. They were expected to act as chaste ladies, whereas their husbands had virtually unrestricted sexual access to slave women. "God forgive us, but ours is a monstrous system," Mary Boykin Chesnut wrote in her diary. "Like the patriarchs of old, our men live all in one house with their wives and their concubines; and the mulattoes one sees in every family partly resemble the white children. Any lady is ready to tell you who is the father of all the mulatto children in everybody's household but her own. Those, she seems to think, drop from the clouds."

Chesnut called the sexual dynamics of slavery "the sorest spot." There were others. Together with female slaves, plantation mistresses had to tend to the food, clothing, health, and welfare of not just their husbands and children, but the plantation slave population as well. Adele Allston, we saw, added plantation management to these duties. The son of a Tennessee slaveholder remembered his mother and grandmother as "the busiest women I ever saw." One woman, who spent the night sitting up to attend a slave birth, complained to a northern visitor: "It is the slaves who own me. Morning, noon, and night, I'm obliged to look after them, to doctor them, and attend to them in every way." The plantation mistress, then, served many roles: as a potential humanizing influence on men; as a tough, resourceful, responsible manager of numerous plantation affairs; as a coercer of slaves and perpetuator of the system; and sometimes as a victim herself.

Justifying Slavery

The behavior of Douglass's mistress suggests that the institution of slavery pressured well-intentioned people, women and men alike, to act inhumanely. Increasingly attacked as immoral, slaveholders felt compelled to justify their institution. Until the 1830s, they explained slavery as a "necessary evil." After abolitionists stepped up their attack in that decade, however, they shifted to justifying slavery, in John C. Calhoun's words, as a "positive good." Various arguments were used: biblical, historical, constitutional, scientific, and sociological.

The biblical justification was based in part on the curse that had fallen upon the son of Ham, one of Noah's children, and in part on Old and New Testament admonishments to servants to obey their masters. As a historical justification, southerners claimed that slavery had always existed and that great ancient civilizations—Egypt, Greece, and Rome—had built their grandeur in part on slave labor.

The legal justification rested on the U.S. Constitution's acceptance of slavery. In fact, although slavery was not mentioned specifically, three passages in the original document clearly implied its constitutionality. First, slaves, called "all other Persons," were counted as three-fifths of a person for purposes of representation. Second, the overseas slave trade was protected from congressional abolition for 20 years. Third, the Constitution mandated the return of runaway slaves from one state to another.

A fourth justification was scientific. Until the 1830s, most white southerners believed that blacks were degraded not by nature but by African climate and their slave condition. As a result of books on cranial shapes and sizes written by northern writers (or scholars), scientists maintained that in the black "the animal parts of the brain preponderate over the moral and intellectual, which explains why he is deficient in reason, judgement and forecast." Southerners bought the argument, increasingly insisting that blacks had been created separately as an inherently inferior race, which justified their argument that they were destined to labor for the superior Caucasians. This led to the "positive good" defense of slavery in which the patriarchal slave system would tame and domesticate the uncivilized Africans. As Allston put it, "The educated master is the negro's best friend upon earth."

Allston's point suggested a paternalistic sociological defense of slavery. George Fitzhugh, a leading advocate of this view, argued that "the Negro is but a grown child and must be governed as a child." Therefore, he needed the paternal guidance, restraint, and protection of his white masters. Many southerners believed that chaos and race mixing would ensue if slaves were freed. Allston wrote that emancipation "cannot be contemplated," for it would lead to "giving up our beautiful country to the ravages of the black race and amalgamation with savages." Fitzhugh was a little less direct. He compared the treatment of southern slaves favorably with that of free blacks and of free laborers working in northern factories. These "wage slaves," he argued, worked as hard as slaves, yet with their paltry wages they had to feed, clothe, and shelter themselves. Southern masters took care of all these necessities. Emancipation, therefore, would be heartless and unthinkable, a burden to both blacks and whites.

Southern apologists for slavery faced the difficult intellectual task of justifying a system that ran counter to the main ideological directions of nineteenth-century American society: the expansion of individual liberty, mobility, economic opportunity, and democratic political participation. Moreover, the southern defense of slavery had to take into account the 75 percent of white families who owned no slaves and who envied those who did. Because of the potential for class antagonisms among whites, wealthy planters developed a justification of slavery that deflected class differences by maintaining that all whites were superior to all blacks but equal to one another. The theory of democratic equality among whites, therefore, was made consistent with racism and the holding of slaves.

However couched in the language of science, law, history, or religion, the underlying motive of these various justifications, though rarely admitted, was that slavery was profitable. As the southern defense of slavery intensified in the 1840s and 1850s, it aroused greater opposition from northerners and from slaves themselves. Although slavery was cruel in many ways, perhaps its worst feature was not physical but psychological: to be enslaved at all and barred from participation in a nation that put a high value on freedom and equality of opportunity. "One of the grossest frauds committed upon the down-trodden slave," Douglass wrote, was to encourage drunkenness during holidays so that the slaves would be disgusted with freedom and would look forward to marching back to the fields.

NOON: SLAVES IN HOUSE AND FIELDS

It is two o'clock on a hot July afternoon on the plantation. The midday lunch break is over, and the slaves are returning to their work in the fields. Lunch was the usual fare of cornmeal and pork. The slaves return to work slowly and listlessly, not because of innate laziness but because of a lack of stamina resulting from deficient diet and the suffocating heat and humidity. Douglass remembered that "we worked all weathers. . . . It was never too hot, or too cold" for toiling in the fields. Mary Reynolds of Louisiana recalled that she hated most having to pick cotton "when the frost was on the bolls," which made her hands "git sore and crack open and bleed."

Daily Toil

The daily work schedule for most slaves, whether in the fields or the Big House, was long and demanding. Aroused by a bell or horn before daybreak, they worked on an average day 14 hours in the summer and 10 hours in the winter. During harvest time, it was not uncommon to work for 18 hours. Depending on the size of the workforce and the crop, the slaves were organized either in gangs or according to tasks. The gangs, usually of 20 to 25, worked their way along the cotton rows under the watchful eye and quick whip of a driver. Ben Simpson, a Georgia slave, remembered vividly how his master would use a "great, long whip platted out of rawhide" to hit a slave in the gang who would "fall behind or give out."

Under the task system, each slave had a specific task to complete daily. This system gave slaves the incentive to work hard enough to finish early, but it meant that the quality of their work was scrutinized constantly. An overseer's weekly report to Robert Allston in 1860 noted that he had "flogged for hoeing corn bad Fanny 12 lashes, Sylvia 12, Monday 12, Phoebee 12, Susanna 12, Salina 12, Celia 12, Iris 12." The black slave driver, George Skipwith, was no less rigorous in his expectations of work from fellow slaves. In 1847, he reported to his master that several slaves working under him "at a reasonable days work" should have plowed 7 acres apiece but had done only 1½. Therefore, George proudly reported, "I gave them ten licks a peace upon their skins [and] I gave Julyann eight or ten licks for misplacing her hoe."

An average slave was expected to pick 130 to 150 pounds of cotton per day. The work on sugar and rice plantations was even harder. Sugar demanded constant cultivation and the digging of drainage ditches in snake-infested fields. At harvest time, cutting, stripping, and carrying the cane to the sugar house for boiling was exhausting. In addition, huge quantities

An Overseer's Report

W. Sweet to Adele Petigru Allston N[ightin]gale hall, 14th September, 1864.

Dear madam I comence my harvest on last saterday on Boath Plantations the weather is very fin for harvest so far I will Bring some Rice in to the Barn yard at N[ightin]gale hall to Day and at ganderloss to morrow. I think that I will make about 2 Barrels of Syrrup on Each Place I finish grinding at ganderloss to Day I will not finish at Nightingale hall until the last of next weeak. litle Dianah was confined with a boy child on the 9 I am very sorry to say to you that one of Prisilia children a boy name July Dide on 12th with fits a[nd] fever I have had a grea[t] deal of fever among the children But not much among the grone negroes. old Rose is Stil quite sick mr Belflowers sent toney to mee on friday last I have concluded to let toney wife stay whare she is for a while as I understand that she is Pregnant and will not Be much survice in the harvest if I am Rong for soe Doing Pleas let mee know. the negroes all sends thare love to you an family my self and family is very un well.

N[ightin]gale hall

8th September	all hands hoing Bancks and grinding shugar cain no sick
9th September	all hands hoing Bancks grind shugar cain no sick
10th September	all hands cu[tt]ing Rice grinding shugar cain no sick
12th September	all hands harvesting grinding shugar cain 3 women with sick children
13th September	all hands harvesting grinding shugar cain 3 women with sick children
14th September	all hands harvesting grinding shugar cain 1 woman with sick child

Source: *The South Carolina Rice Plantation as Revealed in the Papers of Robert F. W. Allston*, ed., J. H. Easterby (1945).

of firewood had to be cut and carried. Working in the low-country rice fields was worse: slaves spent long hours standing in water up to their knees.

House slaves, most of them women, had relatively easier assignments than the field slaves, though they were usually called on to help with the harvest. Their usual work was in or near the Big House as house-maids, cooks, seamstresses, laundresses, coachmen, drivers, gardeners, and mammies. Slaves did most of the artisanal work on the plantation; many became skilled carpenters, blacksmiths, stonemasons, weavers, mechanics, and millers. More intimacy between whites and blacks occurred near the house. House slaves ate and dressed better than their fellow slaves in the fields.

But there were also disadvantages. House slaves were watched more closely, were on call at all hours of the day and night, and were more often involved in personality conflicts in the white household. As one house servant put it, "We were constantly exposed to the whims and passions of every member of the family." This meant everything from assignment to petty jobs to insults, spontaneous angry whippings, and sexual assault. The most feared punishment for a house slave, however, other than sale to the Deep South, was to be sent to the fields.

Slave Health

Although slave owners had an interest in keeping their slaves healthy, slaves led sickly lives. Home was a crude one-room log cabin with a dirt floor and a fire-place; some such houses were well made, others were not. Cracks and holes allowed mosquitoes easy entry, disturbing sleep. Typical furnishings included a table, some stools or boxes to sit on, an iron pot and wooden dishes, and perhaps a bed. Some slaves slept on the ground on mattresses of corn shucks, using burlap bags for blankets. Cabins were crowded, with usually more than one family. Clothing was shabby and uncomfortable. Usually, each man was issued two cotton shirts and two pairs of cotton or woolen pants each fall and spring and a pair of stout shoes once a year. Women were given cotton and woolen cloth twice a year with which to make their own and their children's clothes.

Studies disagree on the adequacy of slave diet, some showing that the food most slaves ate was deficient in calories and vitamins, others claiming that the energy value of the slave diet exceeded that of free whites in the general population. Compared with Latin American slavery, where the ratio of male slaves to white residents was much higher than in the United States, American slaves were well fed. Once a week,

Slaves survived nobly despite hard work, ill health, a deficient diet, and poor living conditions. Female slaves had a double burden of work and caring for their families, as seen in the photograph of the woman picking cotton with her child and of the woman cooking in her cabin while her children look out from the doorway. But female slaves also managed to develop networks of support while working, as seen to the left in the drawing of the three women winnowing rice. *(top left,* From Down by the Riverside, *Charles Joyner, 1984, sketch by Alice R. Huger Smith, c. 1914; top right, photograph from Photographs and Prints Division, Schomburg Center for Research in Black Culture, The New York Public Library, Astor, Lenox and Tilden Foundations; directly above, Private Collection)*

each slave was issued an average ration of a peck of cornmeal, three to four pounds of salt pork or bacon, some molasses, and perhaps some sweet potatoes. The mainstay was corn. This bland fare was supplemented for some slaves, with the master's permission, by growing vegetables in a small garden and by fishing or hunting small game.

Most slaves, however, rarely enjoyed fresh meat, dairy products, fruits, or vegetables. The limitations of their diet led to theft from the master's kitchen, gardens, and barnyard. Such offenses were frequent, and just as frequently punished. A Louisiana planter told a neighbor, "I beg to regrets that two of my men have been found guilty of killing one of your calves," and another complained of many acts of theft committed by "famished negroes." Inadequate diet, moreover, led some slaves to become dirt eaters, which gave them worms and "swollen shiny skin, puffy eyelids, pale palms and soles." Others suffered regularly from skin disorders, cracked lips, and sore eyes. Many children were malnourished, and, like poor whites, slaves came down with vitamin deficiency diseases and even mental illness.

Women slaves especially suffered weaknesses caused by vitamin deficiency, hard work, and disease, as well as those associated with the menstrual cycle and childbirth. Women were expected to do the same tasks in the fields as the men, in addition to cooking, sewing, child care, and traditional female jobs in the quarters when the fieldwork was finished. "Pregnant women," the usual rule stated, "should not plough or lift but must be kept at moderate work until the last hour" and were given a three-week recovery period after giving birth. But these guidelines were more often violated than honored. Infant mortality of slave children under five years of age was twice as high as for white children.

Life expectancy for American slaves was longer than for those in Latin America and the Caribbean, but not very high for either blacks or whites in the antebellum South (21.4 for blacks and 25.5 for whites in 1850). In part because of poor diet and climate, slaves were highly susceptible to epidemic diseases. Despite some resistance as a result of the sickle-cell trait, many slaves still contracted and died from malaria, yellow fever, cholera, and other diseases caused by mosquitoes or bad water, especially in the dangerous low-lying rice fields of the Georgia coast and the sugar fields of Louisiana. Slaves everywhere suffered and died from intestinal ailments in the summer and respiratory diseases in the winter. An average of 20 percent (and sometimes 50 to 60 percent) of the slaves on a given plantation would be sick at one time, and no overseer's report was complete without an account of sickness and the number of days of lost labor.

The relatively frequent incidence of whippings and other physical punishments aggravated the poor physical condition of the slaves. Many slaveholders offered rewards—a garden plot, an extra holiday, hiring oneself out, or passes—as inducements for faithful labor, which helped some slaves to build a supplemental livelihood for themselves and their family. For punishments, some whites would withhold these privileges rather than resort to the lash. Southern court records, plantation diaries, and slave memoirs, however, also reveal that sadistic slave punishments were frequent and harsh.

The slave William Wells Brown reported that on his plantation, the whip was used "very frequently and freely" for inadequate or uncompleted work, stealing, running away, and even insolence and lying. Whippings ranged from 10 to 100 strokes of the lash, occasionally even more. Former slaves described a good owner as one who did not "whip too much" and a bad owner as one who "whipped till he'd bloodied you and blistered you." Slaveholders had many theories on the appropriate kind of lash to inflict sufficient pain and punishment without damaging a valuable laborer. Other forms of punishment included isolation and confinement in stocks and jails during leisure hours, chains, muzzles, salt on lash wounds, brands, burns, and castration.

Nothing testifies better to the physical brutality of slavery than the advertisements for runaways that slaveholders printed in antebellum newspapers. In searching for the best way to describe the physical characteristics of a missing slave, slave owners unwittingly condemned their own behavior. One Mississippi slave had "large raised scars . . . in the small of his back and on his abdomen nearly as large as a person's finger." Another, a Georgia female, was "considerably marked by the whip." Still another, who according to his North Carolina master had a "remarkably bad temper," was described by the "marks of the lash upon his back." Slaves who were branded were even easier to identify in these advertisements. One fugitive, Betty, was described as recently "burnt . . . with a hot iron on the left side of her face." "I tried to make the letter M," her master admitted in his diary. One can almost imagine Betty's master agonizingly applying his brand.

Slave Law and the Family

Complicating master–slave relationships was the status of slaves as both human beings and property, a legal and psychological ambiguity the South never resolved. On the one hand, the slaves had names, personalities, families, and wills of their own. This required dealing with them as fellow humans. On the other hand, they were items of property, purchased and maintained to perform specific profit-making tasks. As a Kentucky court put the problem in 1836, "Although the law of this state considers slaves as property, . . . it recognizes their personal existence, and, to a qualified extent, their natural right."

This ambiguity led to confusion in the laws governing treatment of slaves. Until the early 1830s, some southern abolitionist activity persisted, primarily in the Upper South, and slaves had slight expectations that they might be freed, if not by state action then by individual manumission. But along with this ray of hope, they suffered careless and often brutal treatment in matters of food, housing, work load, and punishments. This confusion changed with

The breakup of families and friendships was an ever-present fear for slaves, who might be sold for purely economic reasons as well as in retribution for uncooperative behavior. In this painting of a slave market by an unidentified artist in the 1850s, note the varied colors of the African Americans (a sad light-skinned young woman in the center, a mulatto male in the left foreground staring longingly at her, and dark-skinned women clutching their children to the right) and the diverse social class of the whites (the suave merchant leaning back in a chair on the porch, nattily attired slave auctioneers and buyers, and a gaudily dressed lower-class overseer cracking the whip over the separation of child from mother). All southern social classes perpetuated slavery, and African Americans of all hues were victimized by it. *(Anonymous American,* Slave Market, *c. 1860/The Carnegie Museum of Art, Gift of Mrs. W. Fitch Ingersoll)*

the threatening convergence in 1831 of Nat Turner's revolt and William Lloyd Garrison's publication of the abolitionist *Liberator.* After 1831, the South tightened up the slave system. Laws prohibiting manumission were passed, and the slaves' expectation of freedom other than by revolt or escape vanished. At the same time, laws protecting them from overly severe treatment were strengthened, and material conditions generally improved.

But whatever the law said, the practice was always more telling. Treatment varied with individual slaveholders and depended on their mood and other circumstances. This was especially true with regard to the slave family. Most planters, like Robert Allston, generally encouraged their slaves to marry and did all they could to keep families intact. They believed that families made black males more docile and less inclined to revolt or run away. But some masters failed to respect slave marriages or broke them up because of financial problems. This tendency was supported by southern courts and legislatures, which did not legally recognize slave marriages or the right to family unity. As a North Carolina Supreme Court justice said in 1853, "Our law required no solemnity or form in regard to the marriage of slaves."

Adding to the pain of forced breakup of the slave family was the sexual abuse of black women. Although the frequency of such abuse is unknown, the presence of thousands of mulattoes in the antebellum era is testimony to this practice. White men in the South abused black slave women in several ways: by offering gifts for sexual "favors," by threatening those who refused sex with physical punishment or the sale of a child or loved one, by purchasing concubines, and by outright rape. As Frederick Douglass put it, "The slave woman is at the mercy of the fathers, sons or brothers of her master."

Because of the need to obtain cheap additional slaves for the workforce, slaveholders encouraged young slave women to bear children, whether married or not. If verbal prodding and inducements such as less work and more rations did not work, masters would choose mates and foist them on slave women. Massa Hawkins, for example, selected Rufus to live

Administrator's Sale, by Order of the Ordinary.

A PRIME AND ORDERLY GANG OF

68 Long Cotton Field Negroes,

Belonging to the Estate of the late Christopher J. Whaley.

WILBUR & SON

Will sell at PUBLIC AUCTION in Charleston,

At the Mart in Chalmers Street,

On Thursday, Feb. 2d, 1860,

COMMENCING AT ELEVEN O'CLOCK,

THE FOLLOWING GANG OF LONG COTTON NEGROES,

Who are said to be remarkably prime, and will be sold as per Catalogue.

NAMES.		AGES.	NAMES.		AGES.
Jimmy,	driver,	30	Carter,		36
Flora,	seamstress,	24	Taffy,		13
James,		5	Rachel,	($ 720,)	8
Charles,	($ 125,)	1	Jannett,		18
August,		52	Phebe,	($ 860,)	40
Mathias,	($ 1,220,)	18	Judy,		8
Sandy,		16	Major,		40
John,		13	Lavinia,		30
Tom,		70	Billy,	($ 550,)	10
Jack,		38	Tamor,		6
James,		6	Jimmy,		52
Leah,		5	Kate,		46
Flora,		2	Susan,		25
Andrew,		42	Thomas,	($ 380,)	6
Binah,		40	Kate,		1
Phillis,		20	Edward,	coachman,	49
Mary,		15	Amey,		22
Lymus,		10	Teneb,	washer,	30
Abram,	($ 275,)	2	Josephine,		9
Binah, ·		2 mos.	Sam,		11
Andrew,		29	Isaac,		5
Hagar,		25	William,		1
Dayman,		4	Amey,		27
Cuffy,		21	Louisa,	($ 750,)	8
Hagar,	($ 1,320,)	20	Joe,		3
Margaret,		85	Sam,	ruptured,	65
Lucy,	cripple,	60	Andrew,	dropsical,	61
John,		22	Daniel,		70
Ellick,	($ 1,160,)	18	Lymus,		30
Libby,		19	Lucy,	nurse,	58

TERMS.

One-third Cash; balance in one and two years, secured by bond, and mortgage of the negroes, with approved personal security. Purchasers to pay us for papers.

29

Announcement of slave sale in Charleston, 1860.
(Public Domain)

with 16-year-old Rose Williams, as she recalled many years later. She resisted the attempted liaison with unmistakable clarity: "I puts de feet 'gainst him and give him a shove and out he go on de floor 'fore he knew what I's doin'." When Rufus persisted, Rose took a poker and "lets him have it over de head." Hawkins then threatened Rose with a "whippin' at de stake" or sale away "from my folks." This was too much for her. "What am I's to do? So I 'cides to do as de massa wish and so I yields."

Unlike the case of Rose and Rufus, however, slaves usually chose their own mates on the basis of mutual attraction during an uneasy courtship complicated by the threat of white interference. As among poor whites, premarital intercourse was frequent, but promiscuous behavior was rare. Most couples maintained affectionate, lasting relationships. This, too, led to numerous sorrows in slavery. Members of slave families had to witness the flogging or physical abuse of loved ones and were powerless to intervene. William Wells Brown remembered that "cold chills ran over me and I wept aloud" when he saw his mother whipped for being late into the fields for work. For this reason, some slaves preferred to marry a spouse from a plantation other than their own.

Although motherhood was the key event in a slave woman's life, bearing children and the double burden of work and family responsibilities challenged her resourcefulness. New mothers often had to choose between taking their babies into the fields to be fed or leaving them to the care of others. Some masters would provide time off for nursing mothers, but the more common practice was for them to work in the fields with their newborn infants lying nearby, wrapped in cloth to protect them from the sun. Although children were sometimes denied proper physical care and emotional support by the absence of their parents during the working day, the slaves adapted. Women developed networks of mutual support, looking after one another's children; meeting together to sew, quilt, cook, or do laundry; and attending births, caring for the sick and dying, and praying together.

The most traumatic problem for slaves was the separation of families, a haunting fear rarely absent from slave consciousness. Although many slaveholders had both moral and economic reasons to maintain families, inevitably they found themselves destroying them. One study, compiling 30 years of data from three Deep South states, shows that masters dissolved one-third of all slave marriages. Even then, the slaves tried to maintain contact. When Abream Scriven informed his wife, Dinah, of his sale to a trader in New Orleans, he had no idea where he would be sold but promised to "write and let you know where I am. . . . My Dear Wife for you and my Children my pen cannot Express the griffe I feel to be parted from you all." Two Missouri slave women, when told they might be sent to Texas, begged their master to reconsider, pleading that "to be separated from our husbands forever in this world would make us unhappy for life."

There was a sound basis in fact for the abolitionists' contention that slavery was a harsh, brutal system. However, two points need to be emphasized. First, although slavery was a barbarous institution that led otherwise decent human beings to commit inhumane acts, many slaveholders throughout the South were neither sadistic nor cruel; they did what they could for their slaves, out of both economic self-interest and Christian morality. Second, whether under kind or cruel masters, the slaves endured with dignity, communal sensitivity, and even some joy. If daytime in the fields describes a view of slavery at its worst, nighttime in the quarters, examined from the black perspective, reveals the slaves' survival powers and their capacity to mold an African American culture even under slavery.

NIGHT: SLAVES IN THEIR QUARTERS

It is near sundown, and the workday is almost over. Some of the slaves begin singing the gentle spiritual "Steal Away to Jesus," and others join in. Or perhaps they sing "Dere's a Meeting Here Tonight." To the unwary overseer or master, the humming, soothing sound of the song suggests happy slaves, content with their earthly lot and looking forward to deliverance in heaven, "in the sweet bosom of Jesus." To the slaves, however, the songs are a signal that, as a former slave, Wash Wilson, put it, they are to "steal away to Jesus" because "dere gwine be a 'ligious meetin' dat night." When evening arrived on the plantation, after a hard day of work in the hot sun or in the Big House, the slaves returned to their own quarters. There, as Wilson said, "sometimes us sing and pray all night."

In the slave quarters, away from white masters, overseers, and the burdens of daily work, an elaborate black community helped the slaves make sense out of their lives. In family life, religion, song, dance, the playing of musical instruments, and the telling of stories, the slaves both described their experiences and sought release from hardship and suffering. However burdensome their lives from sunup to sundown, after work the slaves experienced enjoyment and a sense of self-worth, hope, and group identity in their quarters.

Black Christianity

As suggested by the scene described by Wash Wilson, Christian worship was an indispensable part of slave life in the quarters. The revivals of the early nineteenth century led to an enormous growth of Christianity among black Americans. Some independent black Baptist and Methodist churches, especially in border states and cities, served both slaves and free blacks and occasionally even whites. These separate churches had to steer a careful path to maintain their freedom and avoid white interference. But the vast majority of southern blacks were slaves, attending plantation missions set up by their masters.

Robert Allston built a prayer house for his slaves, reporting with pride that they were "attentive to religious instruction, and greatly improved in intelligence and morals." For the slaveholders, religion often represented a form of social control. Despite the presence of illiterate but eloquent slave preachers on the plantation, who frequently played a prominent role in administering baptisms, weddings, and funerals, white masters sought to direct the purposes of religion to their own ends. Black religious gatherings were usually forbidden unless white observers were present or white preachers led them. Whether in slave or white churches (where blacks sat in the back), preachers often delivered sermons from the text "Servants, obey your masters." These sermons emphasized the importance of work, obedience, honesty, and respect for the master's property. One former slave complained that "all that preacher talked about was for us slaves to obey our masters and not to lie and steal."

There were limits, however, to the effectiveness of white control. Although some slaves accommodated themselves to the master's brand of Christianity and patiently waited for heavenly deliverance, others rebelled and sought earthly liberty. Not far from Allston's plantation, several slaves were discovered (and imprisoned) for singing "We'll soon be free / We'll fight for liberty / When de Lord will call us home." Douglass had an illegal Sabbath school on one plantation, where he and others risked being whipped while learning about Christianity and how to read. "The work of instructing my dear fellow-slaves," he wrote, "was the sweetest engagement with which I was ever blessed."

In religious schools and meetings like these, the slaves created an "invisible" church. On Sunday morning, they sat dutifully through the master's service and waited for the "real meetin'" and "real preachin'" later that night. Sarah Fitzpatrick, an Alabama slave, recalled that the slaves wanted so much to "go to church by de'selves" that they were willing to sit through the "white fo'ks' . . . service in de mornin'." But when evening came, "a'ter dey clean up, wash de dishes, an' look a'ter ever'thing," the slaves would "steal away" to the nearby woods for their own service.

Long into the night, they would sing, dance, shout, and pray. "Ya' see," Sarah explained, "niggers lack ta shout a whole lot an' wid de white fo'ks al'round 'em, dey couldn't shout jes' lack dey want to." But at night they could, taking care to deaden the sound to keep the whites away. One method was to hang a curtain from the trees. Another, an African custom, was to turn over a pot to "catch the sound." Another African practice, the frenetic dancing of the ring shout, survived in adapted form. Dance, forbidden by Methodists, was transformed into the "ecstatic shout," praising the Lord. The religious ceremony itself, with its camp meeting features, relieved the day's burdens and expressed communal religious values. "At night," another former slave recalled with pride, "was when the darkies really did have they freedom of spirit."

Although many of the expressive forms were African, the message reiterated over and over in the invisible slave church was the Christian theme of suffering and deliverance from bondage. Slaves identified with the children of Israel and with the Exodus story, as well as with the suffering of Jesus and the inner turmoil of an unconverted "trebbled spirit." "We prayed a lot to be free," Anderson Edwards recalled, but the freedom the slaves sought was a complex blend of a peaceful soul and escape from slavery. Nothing illustrated both the communal religious experience and these mixed Christian themes of suffering and redemption better than slave spirituals.

The Power of Song

A group of slaves gathers in the dark of night in the woods behind their quarters to sing and shout together:

O brothers, don't get weary
O brothers, don't get weary
O brothers, don't get weary
We're waiting for the Lord.
We'll land on Canaan's shore
We'll land on Canaan's shore
When we land on Canaan's shore
We'll meet forever more.

Then, after moaning of being stolen from Africa and sold in Georgia, with families "sold apart," they sing:

There's a better day a-coming,
Will you go along with me?
There's a better day a-coming,
Go sound the jubilee!

Music was a crucial form of expression in the slave quarters on both secular and religious occasions. The slaves were adept at creating a song, as one slave woman recalled, "on de spurn of de moment." Jeanette Robinson Murphy described a process of spontaneous creation that, whether in rural church music or urban jazz, describes black music to this day. "We'd all be at the 'prayer house' de Lord's day," she said, when all of a sudden, perhaps even in the midst of a white preacher's sermon, "de Lord would come a-shinin' thoo dem pages and revive dis ole nigger's heart, and I'd jump up dar and den and holler and shout and sing and pat, and dey would all cotch de words and I'd sing it to some ole shout song I'd heard 'em sing from Africa, and dey'd all take it up and keep at it, and keep a-addin' to it, and den it would be a spiritual."

Although the spirituals were composed for many purposes, they reiterated one basic Judeo-Christian theme: a chosen people, the children of God, were held captive in bondage but would be delivered. The titles and lyrics reveal the message: "We Are de People of de Lord," "To the Promised Land I'm Bound to Go," "Go Down, Moses," "Who Will Deliver Po' Me?" What they meant by deliverance was not always clear and

After sundown, when the work was done, slaves often gathered in "hush arbors" deep in the woods away from the overseer's and master's interference. There they danced the "ring shout" and "praised de Lord" in ways that combined African and Christian forms of spiritual expression. This painting by John Antrobus shows a "Negro Burial." *(The Historic New Orleans Collection)*

often had a double meaning: freedom in heaven and freedom in the North. Where, exactly, was the desired destination of "Oh Canaan, sweet Canaan / I am bound for the land of Canaan"? Was it heaven? A vague symbol for freedom "anyplace else but here"? A literal reference to the terminus of the underground railroad? For different slaves, and at different times for the same person, it meant all of these.

"The songs of the slave," Douglass wrote, "represent the sorrows of his heart." Indeed, they often expressed the sadness of broken families and the burdens of work and were filled with images of trouble, toil, and homelessness. But they also expressed joy, triumph, and deliverance. Each expression of sorrow usually ended in an outburst of eventual affirmation and justice. "O nobody knows a who I am" resolved itself on "judgment morning" when one heard the "bells a-ringing in my soul." The sadness of "Nobody knows the trouble I've seen" was lightened by happening upon some juicy berries hanging down "just as sweet as de honey in de comb." And the deep sorrow of "Sometimes I feel like a motherless chile," as terrible a situation as any person could endure, was transformed later in the song into "Sometimes I feel like / A eagle in de air. . . . / Gonna spread my wings an' / Fly, fly, fly."

Slave songs did not always contain hidden meanings. Sometimes slaves gathered simply for music, to play fiddles, drums, and other instruments fashioned by local artists in imitation of West African models.

In the quarters at night, slave men, women, and children created a vibrant black community, socializing outdoors amid the physical objects typical of their daily life. *(© Collection of the New-York Historical Society)*

Some musicians were so talented that whites invited them to perform at ceremonies and parties. Most, however, played for the slave community. Sacred and secular events such as weddings, funerals, holiday celebrations, family reunions, and a successful harvest were all occasions for a communal gathering, usually with music. So, too, was news of external events that affected their lives—a crisis in the master's situation, a change in the slave code, the outcome of a battle during the Civil War, or emancipation itself.

The Enduring Family

The role of music in milestones of family life suggests that the family was central to life in the slave quarters. Although sexual abuse and family separation happened all too often during slavery, many families maintained remarkable continuity. Naming practices, for example, show that children were connected to large extended families. In the records of one plantation for the century from 1760 to the eve of the Civil War, some 175 men, women, and children were linked by blood and marital ties, respecting taboos against marrying first cousins.

The benefits of family cohesion were those of any group: love, protection, education, moral guidance, the transmission of culture, and the providing of status, role models, and basic support. All of these existed in the slave quarters. As the slaves gathered together at the end of the working day, parents passed on to their children the family story, language patterns and words, recipes, folktales, religious and musical traditions, and strong impressions of strength and beauty. In this way, they preserved cultural traditions, which enhanced the identity and self-esteem of parents and children alike. Parents taught their children how to survive in the world and how to cope with life under slavery. As the young ones neared the age when they would work full time in the fields, their parents instructed them in the best ways to pick cotton or corn, how to avoid the overseer's whip, whom to trust and learn from, and ways of fooling the master.

Opportunities existed on many plantations for slave parents to improve the welfare of the family by working extra to earn money to buy scarce items like sugar or clothing, by hunting and fishing to add protein to the diet, or by working a small garden to grow vegetables. J. W. C. Pennington proudly recalled helping his "father at night in making straw hats and willow-baskets, by which means we supplied our family with little articles of food, clothing and luxury."

Slaves were not always totally at the mercy of abusive masters and overseers. Occasionally, one family member could intervene to prevent the abuse of another. Harriet Jacobs successfully fended off her master's lustful advances partly by her own cleverness

Despite separation, sale, and sexual abuse by white masters, many slave families endured and provided love, support, and self-esteem to their members. This 1862 photograph shows five generations of a slave family, all born on the plantation of J. J. Smith of Beaufort, South Carolina. *(Library of Congress)*

and sass: "I . . . openly expressed my contempt for him." She also threatened to use her free black grandmother's considerable influence in the community against him: "I told him that I must and would apply to my grandmother for protection." That enraged but always stopped him.

When family intervention, emotional appeals for mercy, or the magic effects of the conjurer's bag of herbs hung around the neck did not work, some slaves resorted to physical force. In 1800, a slave called Ben shot and killed a white man for living with Ben's wife, and another slave killed an overseer in 1859 for raping his wife. Female slaves, too, risked the consequences of resistance to protect themselves or family members from harm. When Cherry Loguen was attacked by a knife-wielding rapist, she knocked him out with a large branch. When an Arkansas overseer tried to make an example of a slave woman named Lucy, according to her son, "she jumped on him and like to tore him up."

Despite numerous incidents of mutual support, the love and affection that slaves had for each other was sometimes a liability. Many slaves, women especially, were reluctant to run away because they did not want to leave their families. Others were reluctant to give up a private means of modest income and supplemental diet from hiring out and growing food for trade. Those who fled were easily caught because, as an overseer near Natchez, Mississippi, told a northern visitor, they "almost always kept in the neighborhood, because they did not like to go where they could not sometimes get back and see their families."

As these episodes suggest, violence, sexual abuse, and separation constantly threatened slave families. Despite these serious obstacles, slave parents served as protectors, providers, comforters, transmitters of culture, and role models for their children. The slave family, though constantly endangered, played a crucial role in helping blacks adapt to slavery and achieve a sense of self-esteem.

RESISTANCE AND FREEDOM

Songs, folktales, and other forms of cultural expression enabled slaves to articulate their resistance to slavery. For example, Old Jim was going on a "journey" to the "kingdom," and, as he invited others to "go 'long" with him, he taunted his owner: "O blow, blow, Ole Massa, blow de cotton horn / Ole Jim'll neber wuck no mo' in de cotton an' de corn." From refusal to work, it was a short step to outright revolt. In another song, "Samson," the slaves clearly stated their determination to abolish the house of bondage: "An' if I had-'n my way / I'd tear the buildin' down! / . . . And now I got my way / And I'll tear this buildin' down." Every hostile song, story, or event, like Douglass's victory over Covey, was an act of resistance by which the slaves asserted their dignity and gained a measure of freedom. Some escaped slavery altogether to achieve such autonomy as was possible for free blacks in the antebellum South.

Forms of Black Protest

One way slaves protested the burdensome demands of continuous forced labor was in various "day-to-day" acts of resistance. These ranged from breaking tools to burning crops, barns, and houses, from stealing or destroying animals and food to defending fellow slaves from punishment, from self-mutilation to deliberate work slowdowns, and from poisoning masters to feigning illness. Two favorite techniques were to pretend sickness during periods when the overseers were driving the hardest and to misplace tools or deliberately leave them in the fields so that they would have to be "hunted all over the place when wanted."

Slave women, aware of their childbearing value, were adept at missing work on account of "disorders and irregularities," as a frustrated Virginia planter put it, "which cannot be detected by exterior symptoms." He went on to complain that "you dare not set her to work, and so she will lay up till she feels like taking the air again; and plays the lady at your expense." They established networks of support while winnowing and pounding rice or shucking corn, sharing miseries but also encouraging each other in private acts of subtle defiance and resistance such as ruining the master's meals and faking sickness.

Overseers also suffered from these acts of disobedience, for their job depended on productivity, which in turn depended on the goodwill of the slave workers. No one knew this better than the slaves themselves, who cleverly played on the frequent struggle between overseer and master. Often, conflicts were ended by firing a bad overseer and hiring a more suitable replacement. Many slaveholders eventually resorted to using black drivers rather than overseers, but this created other problems.

The black slave drivers were "men between," charged with the tricky job of getting the master's work done without alienating fellow slaves or compromising their own values. Although some drivers were as brutal as white overseers, many became leaders and role models for other slaves. A common practice of the drivers was to appear to punish without really doing so. Solomon Northrup reported that he "learned to handle the whip with marvellous dexterity and precision, throwing the lash within a hair's breadth of the back, the ear, the nose, without, however, touching either of them." As he did this, the "punished" slave would howl in pretended pain and complain loudly to his master about his harsh treatment.

Another form of resistance was to run away. So many blacks ran off that a southern doctor coined a new word, *drapetomania,* which meant "the disease causing negroes to run away." The typical runaway was a young male, who ran off alone and hid out in a nearby wood or swamp. He left to avoid a whipping or because he had just been whipped, to protest excessive work demands, or, as one master put it, for "no cause" at all. But there was a cause—the need to experience a period of freedom away from the restraints and discipline of the plantation. Many runaways would sneak back to the quarters at night for food, and after a few days, if not tracked down by hounds, they would return, perhaps to be whipped, but also perhaps with some concessions for better treatment in the future.

Some slaves left again and again. Remus and his wife, Patty, ran away from their master, James Battle, in Alabama. They were caught and jailed three times, but each time they escaped again. Battle urged the next jailer to "secure Remus well." Some runaways, called "Maroons," hid out for months and years at a time in communities of runaway slaves. Several Maroon colonies were located in the swamps and mountains of the South, especially in Florida, where Seminole and other Indians befriended them. In these areas, blacks and Indians, sharing a common hostility to local whites, frequently intermarried, though sometimes southeastern Indians were hired to track down runaway slaves.

The means of escape were manifold: forging passes, posing as master and servant, disguising one's sex, sneaking aboard ships, and pretending loyalty until taken by the master on a trip to the North. One slave even hid in a large box and had himself mailed to the North. The Underground Railroad, organized by abolitionists, was a series of safe houses and stations where runaway slaves could rest, eat, and spend the night before continuing. Harriet Tubman, who led some 300 slaves out of the South on 19 separate trips, was the railroad's most famous "conductor." It is difficult to know exactly how many slaves actually escaped to the North and Canada, but the numbers were not large. One estimate suggests that in 1850, about 1,000 slaves (out of over 3 million) attempted to run away, and most of them were returned. Nightly patrols by white militiamen, an important aspect of southern life, reduced the chances for any slave to escape and probably deterred many slaves from even trying to run away.

Slaves also sought their freedom by petitioning Congress and state legislatures, bringing suit against their masters that they were being held in bondage illegally, persuading masters to provide for emancipation in their wills, and purchasing their own freedom by hiring out to do extra work at night and on holidays.

Slave Revolts

The ultimate act of resistance, of course, was rebellion. Countless slaves committed individual acts of revolt. In addition, there were hundreds of conspiracies whereby slaves met to plan a group escape and often the massacre of whites. Most of these conspiracies never led to action, either because circumstances changed or the slaves lost the will to follow through or, more often, because some fellow slave—perhaps planted by the master—betrayed the plot. Such spies thwarted the elaborate conspiracies of Gabriel in Virginia in 1800 and Denmark Vesey in South Carolina in 1822. Gabriel and Vesey were both skilled, knowledgeable blacks who planned their revolts in hopes that larger events (a possible war with France in 1800 and the Missouri debates in 1820) would support their efforts. They planned to seize, respectively, Richmond and Charleston, but both were discovered and put down before the revolts could begin. Both resulted in severe reprisals by whites, including mass executions of leaders and the random killing of innocent blacks. The severity and intensity of the white response indicated the enormous fear southern whites had of a slave revolt.

Only a few organized revolts, in which slaves threatened white lives and property, ever actually took place. Latin American slaves challenged their masters more often than their North American counterparts. Weaker military control, easier escape to rugged interior areas, the greater imbalance of blacks to whites, and the continued dependence of Latin American slaveholders on the African slave trade for their supply of mostly male workers explain this pattern. Nearly 80 percent of the Africans imported into Brazil in the 1830s and 1840s were male, and as late as 1875, only one in six Brazilian slaves was recorded as married. The imbalance of males to females (156 to 100 in Cuba in 1860, for example, compared with a near one-to-one ratio in the United States) weakened family restraints on violent revolts.

The most famous slave revolt in North America, led by Nat Turner, occurred in Southampton County, Virginia, in 1831. Turner was an intelligent, skilled, unmarried, religious slave who had experienced many visions of "white spirits and black spirits engaged in battle." He believed that he was "ordained for some great purpose in the hands of the Almighty."

On a hot August night, Turner and a small band of fellow slaves launched their revolt. They intended, as Turner said, "to carry terror and devastation" throughout the country. They crept into the home of Turner's

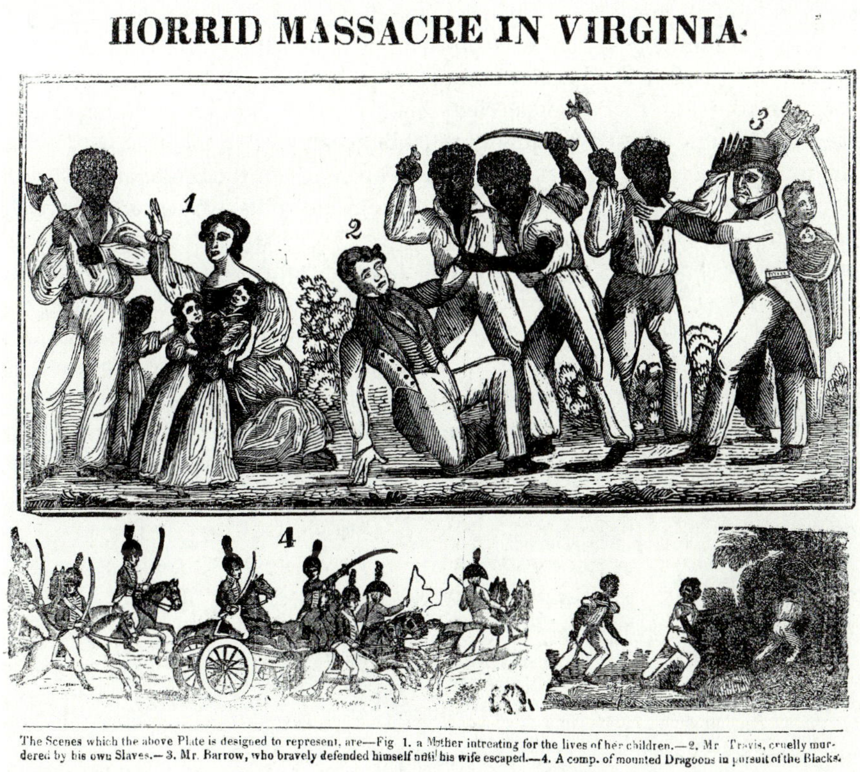

Nat Turner's revolt, in 1831, the most famous American slave uprising, killed 55 whites in Southampton County, Virginia, before overwhelming white forces drove Turner to a hiding place in the woods. *(Library of Congress)*

Recovering the Past

FOLKTALES

A frequent activity of family life in the slave quarters was telling stories. The folktale was an especially useful and indirect way in which older slaves could express hostility toward their masters, impart wisdom to the young, teach them how to survive, portray and mock their own weaknesses, and entertain themselves. Thus, folktales reveal to historians a great deal about the slaves' view of their experience.

Although the tales took many forms, perhaps the best known were the "Brer Rabbit" animal stories. The trickster rabbit, who existed originally in African folklore, was weak and careless, and was looked down on by the other animals. Like the slaves, he was a victim. But he was also clever, boastful, and full of mischief, and he knew how to use his cunning to outwit stronger foes, usually by knowing them better than they knew him, a psychological necessity for all who are oppressed.

In one story, the powerful Brer Tiger took all the water and food for himself during a time of famine, leaving the weaker animals miserable. Brer Rabbit, however, turned things around. He played on Brer Tiger's fears that he would be blown away by a "big wind," secretly manufactured by the rabbit. The tiger was so afraid of the wind (perhaps the winds of revolt?) that he begged Brer Rabbit to tie him "tightly" to a tree to keep from being blown away. Brer Rabbit was happy to oblige, after which all the creatures of the forest were able to share the cool water and juicy pears.

In another folktale, Brer Rabbit fell into a well, but then got out by tricking Brer Wolf into thinking it was better to be in the cool bottom of the well than outside where it was hot. As the wolf lowered himself down in one bucket, Brer Rabbit rose up in the other, laughingly saying as he passed Brer Wolf, "Dis am life; some go up and some go down." In these stories, the slaves vicariously outwitted their more powerful masters and even reversed roles, thus revealing much about their experience under slavery and their aspirations for freedom.

The accompanying excerpt is from perhaps the most famous animal tale, "The Tar Baby Tricks Brer Rabbit." This version is by William J. Faulkner, who, after he retired as minister and dean of men at Fisk University, gathered and recorded the folktales he had heard in his youth in South Carolina as told by a former slave, Simon Brown. Rev. Faulkner opposed telling the stories in dialect because he believed readers formed stereotyped judgments from the dialect and missed the significance of the tale itself. We enter the story as an angry Brer Wolf has decided on a plan to catch the lazy Brer Rabbit, who refused to help the wolf build a well and has been fooling him by drinking from the well while Brer Wolf was asleep.

When you have finished reading the story, ask yourself what you learned about slavery from this story. Did violence work for Brer Rabbit or did it only make things worse? What finally worked? How do you interpret the ending? Brer Rabbit is returned to the briar patch, "the place where I was born." But is the briar patch, with all its thorns, scratches, and roots, Africa or slavery? Or what?

Finally, reflect on the stories you heard as a child or now find yourself telling others. How do they express the realities, flaws, values, and dreams of the American people? The same question applies to the songs we sing, the art we make, the rhythms we move to, and the jokes we tell: What do they tell us about ourselves and our values? In answering these questions, we deepen the knowledge of our own history.

Tar Baby

*Brer Wolf studied and studied to find a way to catch Brer Rabbit. He scratched his head, and he pulled his chin whiskers until by and by he said, "I know what I'll do. I'll make me a tar baby, and I'll catch that good-for-nothing rabbit."**

And so Brer Wolf worked and worked until he had made a pretty little girl out of tar. He dressed the tar baby in a calico apron and carried her up to the well, where he stood her up and fastened her to a post in the ground so that nobody could move her. Then Brer Wolf hid in the bushes and waited for Brer Rabbit to come for some water. But three days passed before Brer Rabbit visited the well again. On the fourth day, he came with a bucket in his hand. When he saw the little girl, he stopped and looked at her. Then he said, "Hello. What's your name? What are you doing here, little girl?"

The little girl said nothing.

This made Brer Rabbit angry, and he shouted at her, "You no-mannered little snip, you! How come you don't speak to your elders?"

The little girl still said nothing.

"I know what to do with little children like you. I'll slap your face and teach you some manners if you don't speak to me," said Brer Rabbit.

Still the little girl said nothing.

And then Brer Rabbit lost his head and said, "Speak to me, I say. I'm going to slap you." With that, Brer Rabbit slapped the tar baby in the face, and his right hand stuck.

"A-ha, you hold my hand, do you? Turn me loose, I say. Turn me loose. If you don't, I'm going to slap you with my left hand. And if I hit you with my left hand, I'll knock the day-lights out of you."

But the little girl said nothing. So Brer Rabbit drew back his left hand and slapped the little girl in her face, bim, and his left hand stuck.

"Oh, I see. You're going to hold both my hands, are you? You better turn me loose. If you don't, I'm going to kick you. And if I kick you, it's going to be like thunder and lightning!" With that, Brer Rabbit drew back his right foot and kicked the little girl in the shins with all his might, blap! Then his right foot stuck.

"Well, sir, isn't this something? You better turn my foot loose. If you don't, I've got another foot left, and I'm going to kick you with it, and you'll think a cyclone hit you." Then Brer Rabbit gave that little girl a powerful kick in the shins with his left foot, blip! With that, his left foot stuck, and there he hung off the ground, between the heavens and the earth. He was in an awful fix. But he still thought he could get loose.

So he said to the little girl, "You've got my feet and my hands all stuck up, but I've got one more weapon, and that's my head. If you don't turn me loose, I'm going to butt you! And if I butt you, I'll knock your brains out." Finally then, Brer Rabbit struck the little girl a powerful knock on the forehead with his head, and it stuck, and there he hung. Smart old Brer Rabbit, he couldn't move. He was held fast by the little tar baby.

Now, Brer Wolf was hiding under the bushes, watching all that was going on. And as soon as he was certain that Brer Rabbit was caught good by his little tar baby, he walked over to Brer Rabbit and said, "A-ha, you're the one who wouldn't dig a well. And you're the one who's going to catch his drinking water from the dew off the grass. A-ha, I caught the fellow who's been stealing my water. And he isn't anybody but you, Brer Rabbit. I'm going to fix you good."

"No, sir, Brer Wolf, I haven't been bothering your water. I was just going over to Brer Bear's house, and I stopped by here long enough to speak to this little no-manners girl," said Brer Rabbit.

"Yes, you're the one," said Brer Wolf. "You're the very one who's been stealing my drinking water all this time. And I'm going to kill you."

"Please, sir, Brer Wolf, don't kill me," begged Brer Rabbit. "I haven't done anything wrong."

"Yes, I'm going to kill you, but I don't know how I'm going to do it yet," growled Brer Wolf. "Oh, I know what I'll do. I'll throw you in the fire and burn you up."

"All right, Brer Wolf," said Brer Rabbit. "Throw me in the fire. That's a good way to die. That's the way my grandmother died, and she said it's a quick way to go. You can do anything with me, anything you want, but please, sir, don't throw me in the briar patch."

"No, I'm not going to throw you in the fire, and I'm not going to throw you in the briar patch. I'm going to throw you down the well and drown you," said Brer Wolf.

"All right, Brer Wolf, throw me down the well," said Brer Rabbit. "That's an easy way to die, but I'm surely going to smell up your drinking water, sir."

"No, I'm not going to drown you," said Brer Wolf. "Drowning is too good for you." Then Brer Wolf thought and thought and scratched his head and pulled his chin whiskers. Finally he said, "I know what I'm going to do with you. I'll throw you in the briar patch."

"Oh, no, Brer Wolf," cried Brer Rabbit. "Please, sir, don't throw me in the briar patch. Those briars will tear up my hide, pull out my hair, and scratch out my eyes. That'll be an awful way to die, Brer Wolf. Please, sir, don't do that to me."

"That's exactly what I'll do with you," said Brer Wolf all happy-like. Then he caught Brer Rabbit by his hind legs, whirled him around and around over his head, and threw him way over into the middle of the briar patch.

After a minute or two, Brer Rabbit stood up on his hind legs and laughed at Brer Wolf and said to him, "Thank you, Brer Wolf, thank you. This is the place where I was born. My grandmother and grandfather and all my family were born right here in the briar patch."

And that's the end of the story.

**Tar was often spread on fences by masters to catch slaves who, out of hunger or mischief, would sneak into field and orchards to steal food. Tar stuck on the hands would betray the "guilty" slave.*

master, Joseph Travis, who Nat said was a "kind master" with "the greatest confidence in me," and killed the entire family. Before the revolt was finally put down, 55 white men, women, and children had been murdered and as many blacks killed in the aftermath. Turner hid in the woods for two weeks before he was apprehended and executed, but not before dictating a chilling confession to a white lawyer who may have exaggerated his role. The Turner revolt was a crucial moment for southern whites. A Virginia legislator said that he suspected there was "a Nat Turner . . . in every family." Rarely thereafter would slaveholders go to sleep without the Southampton revolt in mind.

The fact that Turner was an intelligent and trusted slave, with "no cause to complain" of his master's treatment, yet led such a terrible revolt suggests again how difficult it is to generalize about slavery and slave behavior. Slaves, like masters, had diverse personalities and changeable moods, and their behavior could not be easily predicted. Sometimes humble and deferential, at other times obstinate and rebellious, the slaves made the best of a bad situation and did what they needed to do to survive and achieve a measure of self-worth.

Free Blacks: Becoming One's Own Master

No matter how well they coped with their bondage, the slaves obviously preferred freedom. As Frederick Douglass said of the slave, "Give him a bad master, and he aspires to a good master; give him a good master, and he wishes to become his own master." When Douglass himself had successfully forged a free black's papers as a seaman and sailed from Baltimore to become his own master in the North, he found "great insecurity and loneliness." Apart from the immediate difficulties of finding food, shelter, and work, he realized that he was a fugitive in a land "whose inhabitants are legalized kidnappers" who could at any moment seize and return him to the South. Apart from this fear, which haunted blacks in the North, what was life like for the 11 percent of the total African American population who in 1860 were not slaves?

Between 1820 and 1860, the number of free blacks in the United States doubled, from 233,500 to 488,000. This rise resulted from natural increase, successful escapes, "passing" as whites, purchasing of freedom, and a continuation of occasional manumissions despite legal restriction in most states after the 1830s. Some free blacks passed into the white population, and others migrated to Canada or the West Indies. The free African American population actually decreased from 13.2 percent in 1820 to a little more than 11 percent in 1860. Thus, the percentage of American blacks who were slaves grew faster than those who were free.

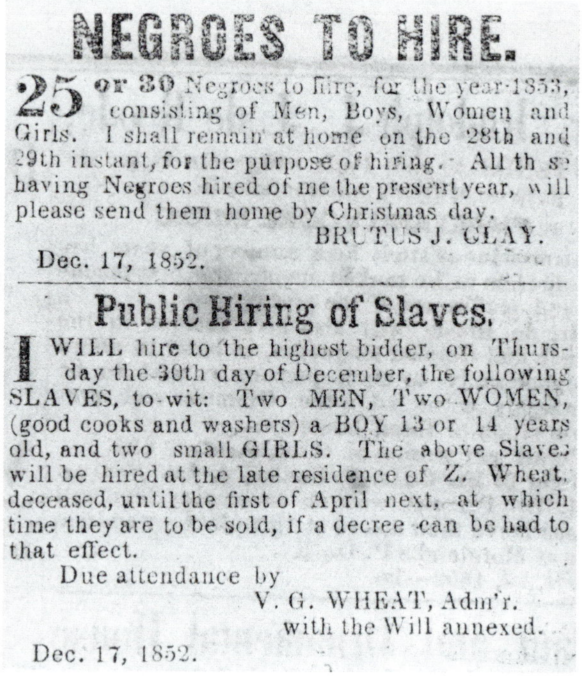
NEGROES TO HIRE.

25 or 30 Negroes to hire, for the year 1853, consisting of Men, Boys, Women and Girls. I shall remain at home on the 28th and 29th instant, for the purpose of hiring. All th s having Negroes hired of me the present year, will please send them home by Christmas day.

BRUTUS J. CLAY.

Dec. 17, 1852.

Public Hiring of Slaves.

I WILL hire to the highest bidder, on Thursday the 30th day of December, the following SLAVES, to-wit: Two MEN, Two WOMEN, (good cooks and washers) a BOY 13 or 14 years old, and two small GIRLS. The above Slaves will be hired at the late residence of Z. Wheat, deceased, until the first of April next, at which time they are to be sold, if a decree can be had to that effect.

Due attendance by

V. G. WHEAT, Adm'r.

with the Will annexed.

Dec. 17, 1852.

Many slaves were able to acquire a degree of autonomy and self-esteem, and occasionally new skills and some money of their own, by hiring out, as seen in these two advertisements in the *Paris Western Citizen* in 1852. *(Audio-Visual Archives, Special Collections and Archives, University of Kentucky Libraries)*

More than half the free blacks lived in the South, most (85 percent in 1860) in the Upper South, where the total number of slaves had declined slightly.

Because free African Americans represented a constant reminder of freedom to slaves and feared reenslavement themselves, they were found least frequently in the Black Belt of the Lower South. They lived, rather, away from the dense plantation centers, scattered on impoverished rural farmlands and in small towns and cities. Still, fully one-third of the southern free African American population lived in cities or towns (compared with only 15 percent of whites and 5 percent of slaves). In part, because it took a long time to buy their freedom, they tended to be older, more literate, and lighter-skinned than other African Americans. In 1860, over 40 percent of free blacks were mulattoes (compared with 10 percent of the slaves). With strong leadership, Baltimore, Richmond, Charleston, New Orleans, and other southern cities developed vibrant African American communities, as free blacks formed churches, schools, and benevolent societies in the midst of white hostility and restrictions.

Most African Americans in the antebellum South were poor, laboring as farmhands, day laborers, or woodcutters. In the cities, they worked in factories and lived in appalling poverty. A few skilled jobs,

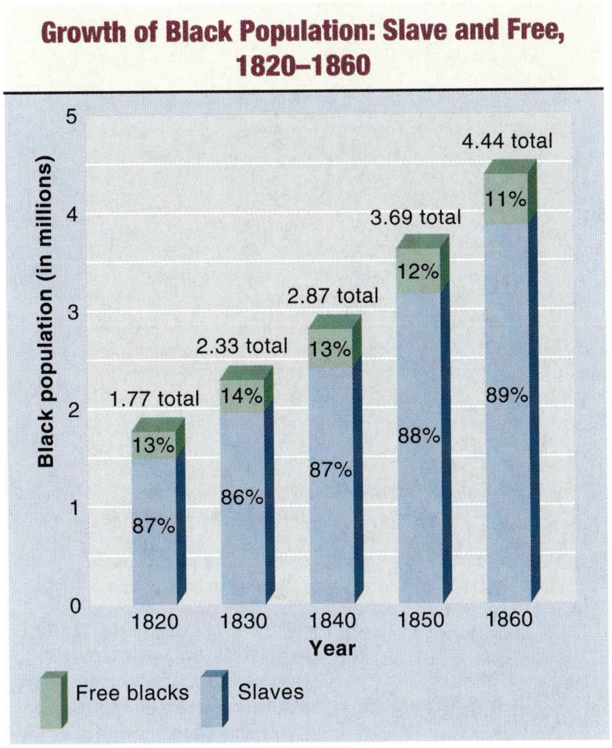

Although the number of free African Americans doubled in size between 1820 and 1860, their proportion relative to the total black population actually decreased. This indicates that the institution of slavery seemed unlikely to be ended voluntarily by southerners.

such as barbering, shoemaking, and plastering, were reserved for black men; they were barred from more than 50 other trades. Women worked as cooks, laundresses, and domestics. The 15 percent of free African Americans who lived in the Lower South were divided into two distinct castes. Most were poor. But in New Orleans, Charleston, and other southern cities, a small, mixed-blood class of free blacks emerged as an elite group, closely connected to white society and removed from the mass of poor blacks. A handful even owned land and slaves. One white observed that these blacks were "respectable" and enjoyed "their rights."

Most free blacks, however, had no such privileges. "We reside among you . . . surrounded by the freest people and most republican institutions in the world," a Baltimore black paper said in 1826, pointing out that African Americans were not yet citizens: "Though we are not slaves, we are not free." Southern state laws seriously limited the mobility, rights, and opportunities of free blacks. In most states, they could not vote, bear arms, buy liquor, assemble, speak in public, form societies, or testify against whites in court. Nevertheless, the African American persistence to gather together and support each other in prayer meetings, back alleys, burial societies, and grocery stores was stronger than white efforts to impede it.

One reason urban whites sought to restrain African American contact was their fear of free black influence as they mixed with whites in working-class grogshops, gambling halls, and brothels. Richmond police closed one house of ill fame where "men and women of diverse colors . . . congregate for most unhallowed purposes." Efforts were made to confine the free blacks to certain sections of the city or, increasingly by the 1850s, to compel them to leave the city, county, or state altogether. Those who stayed had trouble finding work, were required to carry licenses and freedom papers to be surrendered on demand, and often needed a white guardian to approve their actions. Southern whites were especially afraid of contact between free blacks and slaves, who often worked together, attended the same churches and places of entertainment in the city, occasionally got married, and developed strong bonds of mutual protection and identity.

The key institution in these developments was the African American Church. "As among our people generally," Martin Delaney wrote to Douglass in 1849, "the church is the Alpha and Omega of all things." Welcoming the freedom from white control, independent urban black churches grew enormously in the two decades before the Civil War. The African Methodist Episcopal (AME) Church in Baltimore doubled its membership between 1836 and 1856, with the overflow from the first congregation creating a second. By 1860, Baltimore had 15 African churches representing five different denominations. In Richmond the First African Church opened in 1841, soon followed by another; 20 years later, there were four! In the same period, 14 new black Baptist churches were founded in Virginia. These institutions not only performed the usual ritual functions and guarded moral discipline and community values but also provided and promoted education, social insurance, self-help benevolent societies, picnics, concerts, and other forms of recreation.

The growth of African American churches resulted from the overflow of successful institutions, doctrinal differences, the vital role the urban church played in black community life, and conversions. White southerners were trapped by their need to convert Africans to Christianity and then not wanting them in their own churches. Besides, blacks were unwilling parishioners. As one Baptist observed about those forced to attend white churches: "The usual African resort is a loud, comfortable snoring nap."

Nor were African American Catholics left out. Baltimore and New Orleans had strong black Catholic adherents made up of Creoles, converts, former

Churches for free blacks, rare before 1800, became a major source of social as well as religious activity by the 1840s. *(Library of Congress)*

slaves, and refugees from Haiti. The first ordained African American priests were three Georgia sons, born of a mulatto slave mother and an Irish immigrant father and educated at Holy Cross in the 1850s. The next black priest, however, was ordained three decades later. In the absence of African American priests, black sisterhoods took on special importance. The Sisters of the Holy Family and other communities of Catholic black women, begun in eastern cities, started schools and ministered to the aged and infirm as they spread with black Catholic communities westward to Louisville and St. Louis.

The African American churches not only were centers of vital urban black community activities but also were springboards for activist black preachers seeking larger changes in American society. The Reverend James W. C. Pennington, an escaped slave (see Chapter 12, "Recovering the Past: Slave Narratives,"), attended lectures at Yale Divinity School, though he was denied the right to enroll or borrow books. Licensed to preach in 1838, he headed prominent black churches in New Haven, Hartford, and finally New York City. Pennington started several schools, was an abolitionist leader of the National Negro Convention movement (see Chapter 12), and founded the Union Missionary Society in 1841, a black organization that focused on African missions and eventually merged with the American Missionary Society in 1846.

Charles Bennett Ray was educated at Wesleyan University in Connecticut and, as minister of Bethesda Church in New York City for 20 years, was involved

Timeline

1787	Constitution adopted with proslavery provisions
1793	Eli Whitney invents cotton gin
1800	Gabriel conspiracy in Virginia
1808	External slave trade prohibited by Congress
1820	South becomes world's largest cotton producer
1822	Denmark Vesey's conspiracy in Charleston
1830s	Southern justification of slavery changes from a necessary evil to a positive good
1831	Nat Turner's slave revolt in Virginia
1845	*Narrative of the Life of Frederick Douglass* published
1850s	Cotton boom
1851	Indiana state constitution excludes free blacks
1852	Harriet Beecher Stowe publishes best-selling *Uncle Tom's Cabin*
1860	Cotton production and prices peak

with the Underground Railroad and for four years was the editor of *The Colored American.* These and other black religious leaders prepared the way not only for Civil War but also for an unprecedented further growth of African American churches in the postwar years.

A young minister, Henry M. Turner, later an AME bishop, proudly proclaimed in the 1850s, "We, as a race, have a chance to be Somebody, and if we are ever going to be a people, now is the time." Turner's exhortations were heralded 20 years earlier by Maria Stewart, the first African American woman to give published public speeches. Stewart's religious conversion gave her the confidence to brave censure and ridicule in speaking out not only against slavery and northern racism but also in opposition to those who cited St. Paul in defending the established order. "Did Saint Paul but know of our wrongs and deprivations," Stewart said, "I presume he would make no objections to our pleading in public for our rights."

In part because free blacks were becoming more of a "people," they faced a crisis of extinction in the 1850s. Growing prosperity and the worsening conflict between North and South over slavery in the territories caused many white southerners to be even more concerned than usual with the presence of free blacks in their midst. North Carolina whites complained in 1852 that free blacks were "a perfect nuisance" because they attempted "in divers ways to equalize themselves with [the] white population." Pressures increased in the late 1850s, either to deport the free blacks or to enslave them. In the wake of increasing threats to their already precarious free status, some black leaders not surprisingly began to look more favorably on migration to Africa. That quest was interrupted, however, by the outbreak of the Civil War, rekindling in Douglass and others the "expiring embers of freedom."

Conclusion

Douglass's Dream of Freedom

Frederick Douglass eventually won his freedom by forging a free black sailor's pass and escaping through Chesapeake Bay to New York. In a real sense, he wrote himself into freedom. *The Narrative of the Life of Frederick Douglass,* "written by himself" in 1845, was a way both of exposing the many evils of slavery and of creating his own identity, even to the point of choosing his own name. Ironically, Douglass had learned to value reading and writing, we recall, from his Baltimore masters, the Aulds. This reminds us again of the intricate and subtle ways in which the lives of slaves and masters were tied together in the antebellum South. Our understanding of the complexities of this relationship is enhanced as we consider the variations of life in the Big House in the morning, in the fields during the afternoons, in the slave quarters at night, and in the degrees of freedom blacks achieved through resistance, revolt, and free status.

In a poignant moment in his *Narrative,* Douglass described his dreams of freedom as he looked out at the boats on the waters of Chesapeake Bay as a boy. Contrasting his own enslavement with the boats he saw as "freedom's swift-winged angels," Douglass vowed to escape: "This very bay shall yet bear me into freedom. . . . There is a better day coming." As we will see later, southern white planters also bemoaned their lack of freedom relative to the North and made their own plans to achieve independent status through secession. Meanwhile, as that struggle brewed beneath the surface of antebellum life, many other Americans were dismayed by various evil aspects in their society, slavery among them, and sought ways of shaping a better America. We turn to these other dreams in the next chapter.

Recommended Reading

Building the Cotton Kingdom

Charles Bolton, *Poor Whites of the Antebellum South: Tenants and Laborers in Central North Carolina and Northeast Mississippi* (1994); Bruce Collins, *White Society in the Antebellum South* (1985); Charles Dew, *Bond of Iron: Master and Slave at Buffalo Forge* (1994); Clement Eaton, *The Growth of Southern Civilization* (1961); Robert Fogel, *Without Consent or Contract: The Rise and Fall of American Slavery* (1989); John Hope Franklin, *The Militant South* (1966); Peter Kolchin, *American Slavery, 1619–1877* (1993); Grady McWhiney, *Cracker Culture: Celtic Folkways in the Old South* (1988); James Oakes, *Slavery and Freedom: An Interpretation of the Old South* (1990); Frank Owsley, *Plain Folk in the Old South* (1949); Harold Woodman, *Slavery and the Southern Economy* (1966); Gavin Wright, *The Political Economy of the Cotton South: Households, Markets, and Wealth in the Nineteenth Century* (1978).

Morning: Master in the Big House

Victoria E. Bynum, *Unruly Women: The Politics of Social and Sexual Control in the Old South* (1990); Catharine Clinton, *Plantation Mistress* (1983); J. H. Easterby, ed., *The South Carolina Rice Plantation as Revealed in the Papers of Robert F. W. Allston*

(1945); Drew Faust, *James Henry Hammond and the Old South: A Design for Mastery* (1982); Elizabeth Fox-Genovese, *Within the Plantation Household: Black and White Women of the Old South* (1988); George Fredrickson, *The Black Image in the White Mind: The Debate on Afro-American Character and Destiny, 1817–1914* (1971); Eugene Genovese, *The Slaveholder's Dilemma: Freedom and Progress in Southern Conservative Thought, 1820–1860* (1992); Suzanne Lebsock, *The Free Women of Petersburg: Status and Culture in a Southern Town, 1784–1860* (1984); Stephanie McCurry, *Masters of Small Worlds: Yeoman Households, Gender Relations & the Political Culture of the Antebellum South Carolina Lowcountry, 1850–1890* (1995); James Oakes, *The Ruling Race: A History of American Slaveholders* (1982); Steven Stowe, *Intimacy and Power in the Old South: Rituals in the Lives of the Planters* (1987).

Noon: Slaves in House and Fields

Edward Ball, *Slaves in the Family* (1998); John Blassingame, ed., *Slave Testimony* (1977); Paul David et al., *Reckoning with Slavery: A Critical Study of the Quantitative History of American Negro Slavery* (1976); Carl Degler, *Neither Black Nor White: Slavery and Race Relations in Brazil and the United States* (1971); Eugene Genovese, *Roll, Jordan, Roll: The World the Slaves Made* (1974); Larry E. Hudson Jr., *To Have and to Hold: Slave Work and Family Life in Antebellum South Carolina* (1997); Peter Kolchin, *American Slavery, 1619–1877* (1993); Ulrich B. Phillips, *American Negro Slavery* (1919) and *Life and Labor in the Old South* (1929); Kenneth Stampp, *The Peculiar Institution* (1956).

Night: Slaves in Their Quarters

William L. Andrews, *To Tell a Free Story: The First Century of Afro-American Autobiography, 1760–1865* (1986); John Blassingame, *The Slave Community*, rev. ed. (1979); Jacqueline Jones, *Labor of Love, Labor of Sorrow: Black Women, Work, and the Family from Slavery to the Present* (1985); Herbert Gutman, *The Black Family in Slavery and Freedom, 1750–1925* (1976); James Oliver Horton, *Free People of Color: Inside the African-American Community* (1993); Charles Joyner, *Down by the Riverside: A South Carolina Slave Community* (1984); Lawrence Levine, *Black Culture and Black Consciousness: Afro-American Folk Thought from Slavery to Freedom* (1977); Anne Patton Malone, *Sweet Chariot: Slave Family and Household Structure in Nineteenth Century Louisiana* (1992); George Rawick, *From Sundown to Sunup: The Making of a Black Community* (1972); Albert Roboteau, *Slave Religion: The "Invisible Institution" in the Ante-bellum South* (1978); Sterling Stuckey, *Slave Culture: Nationalist Theory and the Foundation of Black America* (1987); Thomas L. Webber, *Deep Like Rivers: Education in the Slave Quarters, 1831–1865* (1978); Deborah Gray White, *Arn't I a Woman?* (1985).

Resistance and Freedom

William L. Andrews, ed., *The Oxford Frederick Douglass Reader* (1996); Herbert Aptheker, *Nat Turner's Slave Rebellion* (1966); Ira Berlin, *Slaves Without Masters: The Free Negro in the Antebellum South* (1976); Leonard Curry, *The Free Black in Urban America, 1800–1850: The Shadow of the Dream* (1981); Merton L. Dillon, *Slavery Attacked: Southern Slaves and Their Allies, 1619–1865* (1990); Douglass R. Egerton, *He Shall Go Out Free: The Lives of Denmark Vesey* (1999); John Hope Franklin, *Runaway Slaves: Rebels on the Plantation* (1999); Michael P. Johnson and James L. Roark, *No Chariot Down: Charleston's Free People of Color on the Eve of the Civil War* (1984) and *Black Masters: A Free Family of Color in the Old South* (1984); Norrece R. Jones Jr., *Born a Child of Freedom, Yet a Slave: Mechanisms of Control and Strategies of Resistance in Antebellum South Carolina* (1990); Robert S. Levine, *Martin Delany, Frederick Douglass, and the Politics of Representative Identity* (1997); Waldo Martin Jr., *The Mind of Frederick Douglass* (1984); William S. McFeely, *Frederick Douglass* (1991).

Fiction and Film

Charles Johnson's *Middle Passage* (1990) is a novel about antebellum life in New Orleans and on slave trade ships between West Africa and the Caribbean. Toni Morrison's novel *Beloved* (1988), a powerful and challenging account of African American life both during and after slavery, is based on the historical case of infanticide by a runaway slave mother near Cincinnati who killed her baby girl, Beloved, rather than allow her to be taken back to the South. Harriet Beecher Stowe's *Uncle Tom's Cabin* (1852), the novel that captivated northern readers in the 1850s, follows various black and white lives in antebellum Kentucky and the deep South. Harriet Wilson's novel *Our Nig; or, Sketches from the Life of a Free Black* (1859), the first known novel written by an African American woman, combines Victorian sentimentalism in the tradition of *Uncle Tom's Cabin* with conventions of the slave narrative.

Amistad, is a 1997 Hollywood film based on a successful mutiny on a slave ship in 1839 near Cuba and the subsequent capture and trial of the mutineers in Connecticut, where they were defended by ex-President John Quincy Adams. The film contains gripping scenes aboard slave ships. *Beloved* is a 1998 film version of Toni Morrison's 1988 novel of the same name.

Suggested Web Sites

http://newdeal.feri.org/asn/index.htm

"Been Here So Long." This site offers selections from the Works Progress Administration (WPA) slave narratives, some of the more interesting primary sources about slavery.

http://amistad.mysticseaport.org/main/welcome.html

Exploring Amistad: Race and the Boundaries of Freedom in Antebellum Maritime America. Mystic Seaport, a maritime museum in Mystic, Connecticut, runs this site, which includes extensive collections of historical resources relating to the Amistad Revolt and the subsequent trial of enslaved Africans.

http://www.pbs.org/wgbh/aia/home.html

Africans in America. This PBS site contains images and documents recounting slavery in America.

http://www.law.umkc.edu/faculty/projects/ftrials/amistad/AMISTD.HTM

Amistad Trial Home Page. Images, chronology, and court and official documents make up this site by Dr. Douglas Linder at University of Missouri—Kansas City Law School.

http://metalab.unc.edu/docsouth/neh/neh.html

North American Slave Narratives, Beginnings to 1920. This site, part of *Documenting the American South*, presents the telling narratives of the African American struggle for freedom.

http://www.loc.gov/exhibits/african/perstor.html

Personal Stories and ACS New Directions. This site contains images and text relating to the colonization movement to return African Americans to Africa.

http://www.cr.nps.gov/delta/under.htm

The Underground Railroad. This is perhaps the best and most extensive National Park Service site, telling the story of the Underground Railroad, with special reference to the Lower Mississippi river valley.

http://www.ushistoryplace.com

A richly detailed on-line learning environment complete with interactive maps, timelines, history activities, primary source documents, and links to related American history sites.

12

SHAPING AMERICA *in the* ANTEBELLUM AGE

CHAPTER OUTLINE

On November 19, 1836, as the second term of President Andrew Jackson neared its end, 30-year-old Marius Robinson and Emily Rakestraw were married near Cincinnati, Ohio. Two months after their wedding, he went on the road to speak against slavery and to organize abolitionist societies throughout Ohio. Emily stayed in Cincinnati to teach in a school for free blacks. During their ten-month separation, they exchanged affectionate letters that reflected their love and work.

Writing after midnight from Concord, Ohio, Marius complained of the "desolation of loneliness" he felt without her. Emily responded that she felt "about our separation just as you do" and confessed that her "womanish nature" did not much enjoy self-denial. In their letters, each imagined the "form and features" of the other and chided the other for not writing more often. Each voiced concern for the responsibilities and burdens of the other's work. Each expressed comfort and support, doubted his or her own abilities ("a miserable comforter I am"), and agreed that in their separation, as Marius put it, "we must look alone to God."

With such love for each other, what prompted this painful separation so early in their marriage? Emily wrote of their duty "to labor long in this cause so near and dear to us both," together if they could, but apart if so decreed by God. Marius, who had experienced a series of conversions inspired by the revivalist Charles G. Finney and his abolitionist disciple Theodore Dwight Weld, described the reason for their separation: "God and humanity bleeding and suffering demand our services apart." Thus motivated by a strong religious commitment to serve others, these two young reformers dedicated themselves to several social causes: the abolition of slavery, equal rights and education for free blacks, temperance, and women's rights.

Their commitments cost more than separation. When Emily went to Cincinnati to work with other young reformers, her parents disapproved. When she married Marius, who already had a reputation as a "rebel," her parents disowned her altogether. Emily wrote with sadness that her sisters and friends also "love me less . . . than they did in by-gone days." Marius responded that he wished he could dry her tears and sought to heal the rift. Although Emily's family eventually accepted their marriage, there were other griefs. Teaching at the school in Cincinnati was demanding, and Emily could not get rid of a persistent cough. Furthermore, the white citizens of the city resented the school and the young abolitionists in their midst, treating them with contempt. Earlier in the year, Marius had escaped an angry mob by disguising himself and mingling with the crowd that came to sack the offices of a reformist journal edited by James G. Birney. Emily, meanwhile, tirelessly persisted in the work of "our school" while worrying about the health and safety of her husband on the road.

She had good reason for concern, for Marius's letters were full of reports of mob attacks, disrupted meetings, stonings, and narrow escapes. At two lectures near Granville, Ohio, he was "mobbed thrice, once most rousingly," as he faced crowds of "the veriest savages I ever saw," armed with clubs, cudgels, and intense hatred for those speaking against slavery. In June, he was dragged from the home of his Quaker host and beaten, tarred, and feathered. Never quite recovering his health, Marius spent half a year in bed, weak and dispirited. For nearly ten years after that, the Robinsons lived quietly on an Ohio farm, only slightly involved in the abolitionist movement. Despite the joyous birth of two daughters, they felt lonely, restless, and guilt-ridden, "tired of days blank of benevolent effort and almost of benevolent desires."

Marius and Emily Robinson, like other Americans, sought to find goodness and order in a society that seemed "everywhere unhinged." *(Anonymous,* Moving Day in the City, *c. 1829, Photo by Eric Schaal/LIFE Magazine © Time Inc.)*

The work of Emily and Marius Robinson represents one response by the American people to the rapid social and economic changes of the antebellum era described in chapters 10 and 11. In September 1835, a year before the Robinsons' marriage, the *Niles Register* commented on some 500 recent incidents of mob violence and social upheaval. "Society seems everywhere unhinged, and the demon of 'blood and slaughter' has been let loose upon us. . . . [The] character of our countrymen seems suddenly changed." How did Americans adapt to these changes? In a world that seemed everywhere "unhinged" and out of control, in which old rules and patterns no longer provided guidance, how did people maintain some sense of control over their lives? How did they seek to shape their altered

world? How could they both adopt the benefits of change and reduce the accompanying disruptions?

One way was to embrace the changes fully. Thus, some Americans became entrepreneurs in new industries; invested in banks, canals, and railroads; bought more land and slaves; and invented new machines. Others went west or to the new textile mills, enrolled in common schools, joined trade unions, specialized their labor in both the workplace and the home, and celebrated the practical benefits that resulted from modernization. Marius Robinson eventually went into life insurance, though he and Emily never fully abandoned their reformist efforts and idealism.

But many Americans were uncomfortable with the character of the new era. Some worried about the unrestrained power and selfish materialism symbolized by the slavemaster's control over his slaves. Others feared that institutions like the U.S. Bank represented a "monied aristocracy" capable of undermining the country's honest producers. Seeking positions of leadership and authority, these critics of the new order tried to shape a nation that retained the benefits of economic change without sacrificing humane principles of liberty, equality of opportunity, and community virtue. This chapter examines four ways the American people responded to change by attempting to influence their country's development: religious revivalism, party politics, utopian communitarianism, and social reform.

RELIGIOUS REVIVAL AND REFORM PHILOSOPHY

When the Frenchman Alexis de Tocqueville visited the United States in 1831 and 1832, he observed that he could find "no country in the whole world in which the Christian religion retains a greater influence over the souls of men than in America." What de Tocqueville was describing was a new and powerful religious enthusiasm among American Protestants. Fired by the power of religious rebirth, some discovered that religion provided them with moorings in a fast-changing world. Others were inspired by revivalism to refashion American society, working through new political parties to shape an agenda for the nation or through reform associations organized to eliminate a particular social evil. Although not all evangelicals agreed about politics or even about what aspects of American society needed to be reformed, religion was the lens through which they viewed contemporary events and through which they sought to effect change.

Finney and the Second Great Awakening

From the late 1790s until the late 1830s, a wave of religious revivals that matched the intensity of the Great Awakening in the 1730s and 1740s swept through the United States. The camp meeting revivals of the frontier at the turn of the century and the New England revivals sparked by Lyman Beecher took on a new emphasis and location after 1830. Led by the spellbinding Charles G. Finney, under whose influence Marius Robinson had been converted, revivalism shifted to upstate New York and the Old Northwest. Both areas had been experiencing profound economic and social changes, as the example of Rochester, New York, suggests.

By the 1830s, Rochester, like Lowell and Cincinnati, was a rapidly growing American city. Located on the recently completed Erie Canal, it was a flour-milling center for the rich wheatlands of western New York. The canal changed Rochester from a sleepy little village of 300 in 1815 to a bustling commercial and milling city of nearly 20,000 inhabitants by 1830. As in other cities, economic growth affected relationships between masters and workers, distancing them both physically and psychologically. As the gulf widened, the masters' control over their laborers weakened. Saloons and unions sprang up in workingmen's neighborhoods, and workers became more transient, following the canal and other opportunities westward.

Prominent Rochester citizens therefore invited Charles Finney to come to town in 1830 to deliver some sermons. What followed was one of the most successful revivals of the Second Great Awakening. "You could not go upon the streets," a convert recalled, "and hear any conversation, except upon religion." Finney preached nearly every night and three times on Sundays, converting first the city's business elite, often through their wives, and then many workers. For six months, Rochester went through a citywide prayer meeting in which one conversion led to another.

The Rochester revival was part of the wave of religious enthusiasm in America that contributed to the tremendous growth of Methodists, Baptists, and other evangelical denominations in the first half of the nineteenth century. By 1844, for example, the

This 1839 painting of a camp meeting captures the religious fervor that many Americans turned to in the face of social and economic upheavals. These mass conversions led some believers to individual salvation and others to social reform. *(Old Dartmouth Historical Society-New Bedford Whaling Museum)*

Methodist church had become the largest denomination in America, with over a million members. To bring large masses of people to accept Christ as their savior, revivalist preachers deemphasized doctrine in favor of emotion, softening strict Calvinist tenets such as predestination, original sin, and limited atonement.

Unlike Jonathan Edwards, who believed that revivals were God's miracles, Finney understood that the human "agency" of the minister was crucial in causing a revival. He even published a do-it-yourself manual for other revivalists. Few, however, could match Finney's powerful preaching style. The hypnotic effect of his eyes and voice carried such power that he could dissolve an audience into tears. When he threw an imaginary brick at the Devil, people ducked. When his finger pointed the descent of a sinner into hell, people in the back row stood up to see the final disappearance. A former lawyer, Finney used logic as well as emotion to bring about conversions.

Many revivalists, especially in the South, sought individual salvation. American Catholics also caught the revival fervor in the 1830s. Scattered in small but growing numbers in eastern cities like Baltimore, Philadelphia, and New York and in western cities such as Cincinnati, St. Louis, Louisville, and New Orleans, Catholic leaders recognized that survival as a small and often despised religion depended on constant reinvigoration and evangelism. Focusing on the parish mission, energetic retreats and revivals gathered Catholics from miles around to preserve a religious heritage seriously threatened by life in Protestant America.

The Finney revivals differed from Catholic and southern revivalism because they insisted that conversion and salvation were not the end of religious experience but the beginning. Finney believed that humans were not passive objects of God's predestined plan but moral free agents who could choose good over evil, convince others to do the same, and thereby eradicate sin from the world. Finney's idea of the "utility of benevolence" meant not only individual reformation but also the commitment to do one's sacred duty in reforming one's society.

The Transcendentalists

No one knew this better than Ralph Waldo Emerson, a Concord, Massachusetts, essayist who was the era's foremost intellectual figure. Emerson's essays of the 1830s—"Nature," "American Scholar," and "Divinity School Address," among others—influenced the generation of reformist American intellectuals coming of age in mid-century and helped inspire artists and writers. The small but influential group of New England intellectuals who lived near Emerson were called Transcendentalists because of their belief that truth was found in intuition beyond sense experience. Casting off the European intellectual tradition, Emerson urged Americans to look inward and to nature for self-knowledge, self-reliance, and the spark of divinity burning within all people. "To acquaint a man with himself," he wrote, would inspire a "reverence" for self and others, which would then lead outward to social reform. "What is man born for," Emerson wrote, "but to be a Reformer?"

Inspired by self-reflection, the Transcendentalists asked troublesome questions about the quality of American life. They questioned not only slavery, an obvious evil, but also the obsessive competitive pace of economic life, the overriding concern for materialism, and the restrictive conformity of social life.

Although not considered Transcendentalists, Nathaniel Hawthorne and Herman Melville, two giants of mid-century American literature, also reflected these concerns in their fiction. Like Emerson, they were romantic in spirit, celebrating emotion over reason, nature over civilization, and virtue over self-interest. Hawthorne's great subject was the "truth of the human heart," which he portrayed as more authentic than the calculating minds of scientists and their schemes. In his greatest novel, *The Scarlet Letter* (1850), Hawthorne sympathetically told the story of a courageous Puritan woman's adultery and her eventual loving triumph over the narrowness of both cold intellect and intolerant social conformity.

Herman Melville dedicated his epic novel *Moby Dick* (1851) to Hawthorne. At one level, a rousing story of whaling on the high seas in pursuit of the great white whale, *Moby Dick* was actually an immense allegory of good and evil, bravery and weakness, innocence and experience. In Melville's other novels, he continued this sea voyage setting to make a powerful statement on behalf of the lowly seaman's claims for freedom and just social relations against the tyranny of the ship captain. Like Emerson, Hawthorne and Melville mirrored the tensions of the age as they explored issues of freedom and control.

When Emerson wrote, "Whoso would be a man, must be a nonconformist," he described his friend Henry David Thoreau. No one thought more deeply about the virtuous natural life than Thoreau. On July 4, 1845, he went to live in a small hut by Walden Pond, near Concord. There he planned to confront the "essential facts of life"—to discover who he was and how to live well. When Thoreau left Walden two years later, he protested against slavery and the Mexican War by refusing to pay his taxes. He went to jail briefly and wrote an essay, "On Civil Disobedience" (1849), and a book, *Walden* (1854), which are still considered classic statements of what one person can do to protest unjust laws and wars and live a life of principle.

THE POLITICAL RESPONSE TO CHANGE

Transcendentalism touched only a few elite New Englanders, but perhaps as many as 40 percent of the American people were affected by the winds of evangelical Protestantism. Although economic, ethnic, and even regional factors played a part in shaping political loyalties, evangelical values and religious loyalties colored many people's understanding of the appropriate role of government and influenced their involvement in political activities. As politics became more of a popular than elite interest, it was not surprising that religious commitments spilled over into the political sphere.

At the heart of American politics was the concern for the continued health of the republican experiment. As American society changed, so, too, did the understanding of what was needed to maintain that health. In the late 1850s, a Maine newspaper warned that the preservation of the nation's freedom depended on the willingness of its citizens to go to the polls. It was, in fact, the "positive duty of every citizen of a Republic to vote." This insistence on voting as crucial to the well-being of the country was new. Before the 1820s, politics was primarily for the social and economic elite. Even though many states were removing voting restrictions in the early nineteenth century, the majority of white men did not trouble themselves with political matters. But the trauma of the Panic of 1819 and the spirited presidential campaigns for Andrew Jackson helped create widespread interest in politics. For many Americans, political participation became an important way of asserting and supporting important values and promoting their vision of the republic.

Changing Political Culture

Jackson's presidency was crucial in bringing politics to the center of many Americans' lives. Styling himself as the people's candidate in 1828, Andrew Jackson derided the Adams administration as corrupt and aristocratic and promised a more democratic political system. He told voters that he intended to "purify" and "reform the Government," purging all "who have been appointed from political considerations or against the will of the people." Unlike in our own age, most Americans then believed the campaign rhetoric. Four times more men turned out to vote in the election of 1828 than had four years earlier. They gave Jackson a resounding 56 percent of their ballots. No other president in the century would equal that percentage of popular support.

Despite campaign rhetoric and his image as a democratic hero, Jackson was not personally very democratic, nor did the era he symbolized involve any significant redistribution of wealth. Jackson himself owned slaves, defended slavery, and condoned mob attacks on abolitionists like Marius Robinson. He disliked Indians and ordered the forcible removal of the southeastern Indian nations to west of the Mississippi River in blatant disregard of the treaty rights and a Supreme Court decision. Belying promises of widening opportunity, the rich got richer during the Jacksonian era, and most farming and urban laboring families did not prosper.

But the nation's political life had changed in important ways. The old system of politics, based on elite coalitions bound together by ties of family and friendship and dependent on the deference of voters to their "betters," largely disappeared. In its place emerged a competitive party system, begun early in the republic but now oriented toward widespread voter participation. The major parties grew adept at raising money, selecting and promoting candidates, and bringing voters to the polls. A new "democratic" style of political life emerged as parties sponsored conventions, rallies (much like evangelical revivals in their flavor and fervor), and parades to encourage political participation and identification. Party politics became a central preoccupation for many adult white males. In the North, even women turned out for political hoopla, riding on floats at party parades.

Parties appealed to popular emotions, religious views, and ethnic prejudices. Party-subsidized newspapers regularly indulged in scurrilous attacks on political candidates. The language of politics became contentious and militaristic. Jackson's rhetoric exemplified the new trends. He described an opponent as an "enemy" who waged "war against the cause of the people." He reminded Americans that "those who are not for us are against us." Politicians talked of elections as battles and party members as their disciplined "rank and file." Strong party identification was part of the new national political culture. James Buchanan complained in 1839 about a colleague who urged politicians "to rise above mere party, and to go for our country." Instead, Buchanan said, "in supporting my party, I honestly believe I am . . . promoting the interest of my country."

More Americans Vote for President, 1824–1840

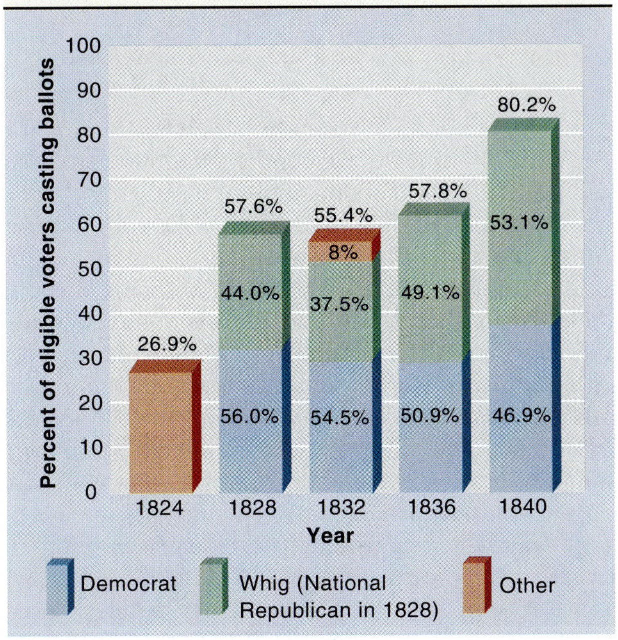

The single-party system (Jeffersonian Democratic Republican) that existed in 1824 collapsed with the intense personal rivalries and ideological differences of the 1820s and 1830s. The emergence of a two-party system in the Jacksonian era dramatically increased (white male) voter participation to percentages far exceeding those of modern U.S. presidential elections.

Jackson's Path to the White House

The early career of Andrew Jackson gave few hints of his future political importance. Orphaned at 14, young Jackson was rowdy, indecisive, and often in trouble. As a law student, he was "a most roaring, rollicking, game-cocking, horse-racing, card-playing, mischievous fellow." Despite these preoccupations, which included dueling, Jackson passed the bar and set out at the age of 21 to seek his fortune in the West. Settling in frontier Nashville, the tall, red-headed young man built up a successful law practice in Tennessee and went on to become state attorney general, a substantial landowner, and a prominent citizen of Nashville.

Jackson's national reputation stemmed mainly from his military exploits, primarily against American Indians. As major general of the Tennessee militia, he proved able and popular. Jackson's troops admired his toughness and nicknamed him "Old Hickory." His savage victory over the Creek nation in the South in 1813 and 1814 brought notoriety and an appointment as major general in the U.S. Army. His victory at New Orleans in 1815 made him a national hero. His tour of the country after the war suggested political ambitions. As early as 1817, resolutions supporting a Jackson bid for the presidency began to appear in several states.

Although Jackson's aggressive military forays into Spanish Florida in 1818 bothered rival politicians and added to his reputation for scandal, they increased his popularity and his interest in the presidency. Jackson recognized that his greatest appeal lay with ordinary people, whom he cultivated. But he also secured effective political backing. Careful political maneuvering in Tennessee in the early 1820s brought him election as U.S. senator and nomination for the presidency in 1824.

In the 1824 election, Jackson won both the popular and the electoral votes but lost in the House of Representatives to John Quincy Adams. When Henry Clay threw his support to Adams and was named secretary of state, Jackson condemned this deal as a "corrupt bargain." Jackson's loss convinced him of the importance of having an effective political organization. He felt confident of his strength in the West, and support by Adams's vice president, John C. Calhoun, helped him in the South. Jackson organized his campaign by setting up loyal committees and newspapers in many states and by encouraging efforts to undermine Adams and Clay.

A loose coalition promoting Jackson's candidacy began to call itself the Democratic party. Politicians of diverse views from all sections of the country were drawn to it, including Martin Van Buren of New York. Jackson masterfully waffled on controversial issues. He concealed his dislike of banks and paper money and vaguely advocated a "middle and just course" on the tariff. And he promised to cleanse government of corruption and privileged interests.

The Jackson–Adams campaign in 1828 degenerated into a nasty but entertaining contest. The Democrats whipped up enthusiasm with barbecues, mass rallies, and parades and gave out buttons and hats with hickory leaves attached. Amid the hoopla, few people discussed issues. Both sides made slanderous personal attacks. Supporters of Adams and Clay, who called themselves National Republicans, branded Jackson "an adulterer, a gambler, a cockfighter, a brawler, a drunkard, and a murderer." His wife, Rachel, was maligned as common and immoral.

The Jacksonians in turn charged Adams with bribing Clay for his support in 1824. They described him as a "stingy, undemocratic" aristocrat determined to destroy the people's liberties. Worse yet, Adams was an intellectual. Campaign slogans emphasized the differences between the hero of New Orleans, "a man who can fight," and the wimpy Adams, "a man who can write." "Who do you want," one slogan asked, "John Quincy Adams, who quotes law, or Andy Jackson, who makes law?" The question left little doubt as to how proud Americans would vote.

Jackson's supporters in Washington worked to ensure his election by devising a tariff bill to win necessary support in key states. Under the leadership of Van Buren, who hoped to replace Calhoun as Jackson's heir apparent, the Democrats in Congress put together enough votes to pass what opponents called the "Tariff of Abominations." It arbitrarily raised rates to protect New England textiles, Pennsylvania iron, and some agricultural goods, winning voters in those states where the Democrats needed more support. John Randolph of Virginia sneered that the tariff "referred to manufactures of no sort or kind but the manufacture of a President of the United States."

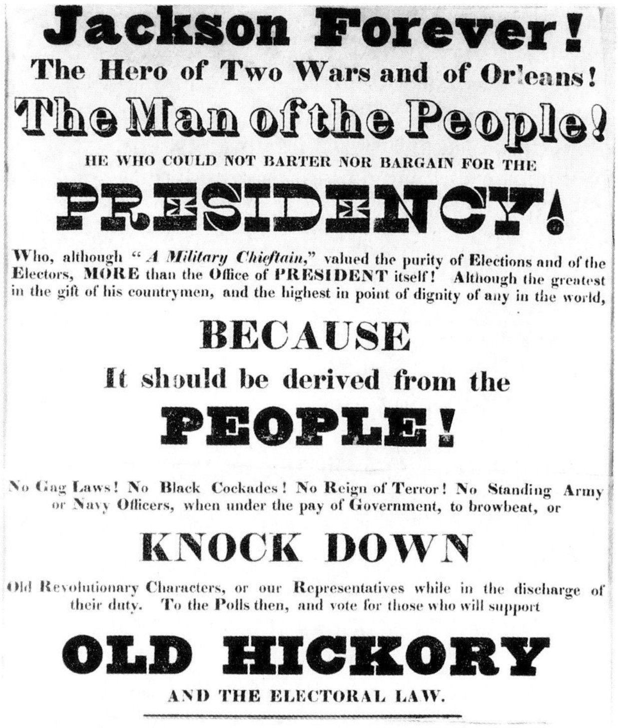

Unlike his rivals, J. Q. Adams and Henry Clay, who deprived Jackson of the presidency in 1824, Jackson, nicknamed "old Hickory" after America's toughest hardwood, claimed to honor the constitutional electoral system and the will of the people. *(© Collection of the New-York Historical Society)*

The efforts of Jackson and his party paid off as he won an astonishing 647,286 ballots, about 56 percent of the total. Organization, money, effective publicity, and a popular style of campaigning had brought the 60-year-old Jackson to the presidency. His inauguration, however, horrified many Americans. Washington was packed for the ceremonies. Daniel Webster noted that "persons have come five hundred miles to see General Jackson, and they really seem to think that the country is to be rescued from some dreadful danger." When Jackson stood to take the oath of office, wild cheering broke out. Few in the crowd heard him, but many hoped to shake the new president's hand, and Jackson was all but mobbed as he tried to make his way to his horse.

As depicted in the Robert Cruikshank lithograph, *All Creation Going to the White House,* the first inauguration of Andrew Jackson in 1829 was the scene of wild festivities, a harbinger of the excesses in American life and politics in the ensuing years. *(Library of Congress)*

The White House reception soon got completely out of hand. A throng of people, "from the highest and most polished, down to the most vulgar and gross," Justice Joseph Story observed, poured into the White House with muddy boots to overturn furniture in a rush for food and punch. Jackson was forced to leave by a side door. When wine and ice cream were carried out to the lawn, many guests followed by diving through the windows. The inauguration, Story concluded, meant the "reign of King Mob." Another observer called it a "proud day for the people." These contrasting views on the events of the inauguration captured the essence of the Jackson era. For some, they symbolized the excesses of democracy; for others, they represented democratic fulfillment.

Old Hickory's Vigorous Presidency

Although Jackson had taken vague positions on important issues during the campaign, as president he needed to confront many of them. His decisions, often controversial, helped sharpen what it meant to be a Democrat and what it meant to be Democracy's opponent.

A few key convictions—the principle of majority rule, the limited power of the national government, the obligation of the national government to defend the interests of the nation's average people against the "monied aristocracy"—guided Jackson's actions as president. Seeing himself as the people's most authentic representative (only the president was elected by all the people), Jackson intended to be a vigorous executive. More than any previous president, Jackson used presidential power in the name of the people and justified his actions by appeals to the people.

Jackson asserted his power most dramatically through the veto. His six predecessors had cast only nine vetoes, mostly against measures that they had believed unconstitutional. Jackson, however, argued that he had "undoubted right . . . to withhold . . . assent from bills on other grounds than their constitutionality." Jackson vetoed 12 bills during his two terms, often because they conflicted with his political agenda.

One of the abuses Jackson had promised to correct was what he described as an undemocratic and corrupt system of government officeholding. Too often "unfaithful or incompetent" men clung to government jobs for years. Jackson proposed to throw these scoundrels out and establish a system of rotation of office. The duties of public office were so "plain and simple," he said, that ordinary men could fulfill them.

Jackson's rhetoric was more extreme than his actions. He did not replace officeholders wholesale. In the first year and a half of his presidency, he removed 919 officeholders of a total of 10,093, fewer than one in ten. Most of these were for good reason—corruption or incompetence. Nor were the new Democratic appointees especially plain, untutored, or honest; they were in fact much like their predecessors. Still, Jackson's rhetoric helped create a new kind of democratic political culture that would prevail for most of the nineteenth century.

His policy on internal improvements—roads, canals, and other forms of transportation—was less far-seeing. Like most Americans, Jackson recognized their economic importance and as president wished "to see them extended to every part of the country." But Jackson was against infringement on states' rights. When proposals for federal support for internal improvements seemed to rob local and state authorities of their proper function, he opposed them. In 1830, he vetoed the Maysville Road bill, which proposed federal funding for a road in Henry Clay's Kentucky. But projects of national significance, like river improvements or lighthouses, were different. During his presidency Jackson supported an annual average of $1.3 million in internal improvements.

In a period of rapid economic change, tariffs stirred heated debate. New England and the Middle Atlantic states, the center of manufacturing operations, favored protective tariffs. The South had long opposed them because they made it more expensive to buy manufactured goods from the North or abroad and threatened to provoke foreign retaliation against southern cotton and tobacco exports. Feelings against the "Tariff of Abominations" ran particularly high in South Carolina. Some of that state's leaders mistakenly believed the tariff was the prime reason for the economic depression that hung over their state. In addition, some worried that the federal government might eventually interfere with slavery, a frightening prospect in a state where slaves outnumbered whites.

Vice President Calhoun, a brilliant political thinker and opponent of the tariff, provided the appropriate theory to check federal power and to protect minority rights. "We are not a nation," he once remarked, "but a Union, a confederacy of equal and sovereign states." In 1828, the same year as the hateful tariff, Calhoun anonymously published *Exposition and Protest*, presenting the doctrine of nullification as a means by which southern states could protect themselves from harmful national action. He argued that when federal laws overstepped the limits of constitutional authority, a state had the right to declare that legislation null and void and to refuse to enforce it.

Two years later, Calhoun's doctrine was aired in a Senate debate over public land policy. South Carolina's Robert Hayne defined nullification and, in the name of liberty, urged western states to adopt the doctrine. Daniel Webster responded. The federal government, he said, was no mere agent of the state legislatures. It was "made for the people, made by the people, and answerable to the people." No state legislature, therefore, could ever be sovereign over the people. Aware that nullification raised the specter of a "once glorious Union . . . drenched . . . in fraternal blood," Webster cried out in his powerful closing words that the appropriate motto for the nation was not "Liberty first and Union afterwards, but Liberty and Union, now and forever, one and inseparable!"

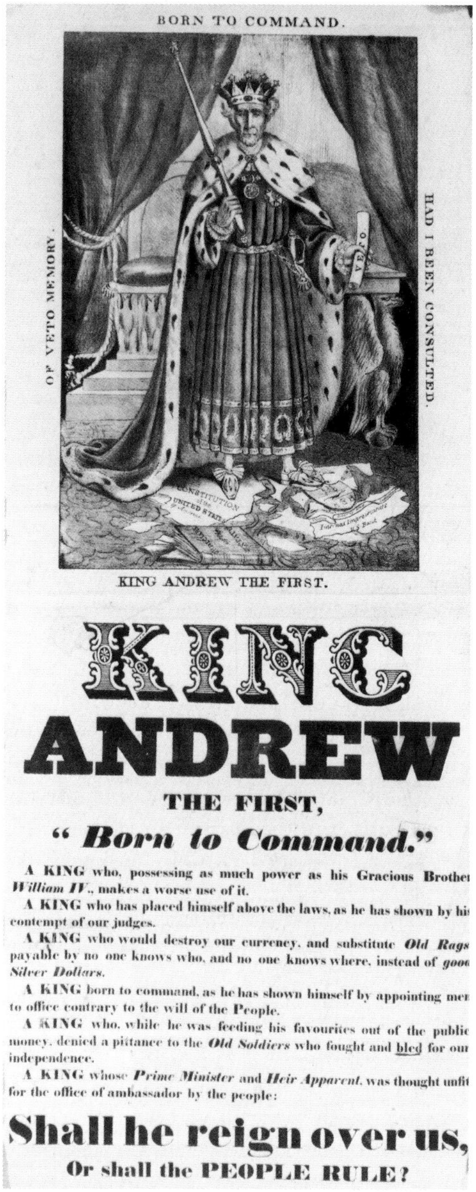

With references to the still-hated British royalty, this cartoon, widely distributed by Whigs (a name chosen with antimonarchical British politics in mind), shows President Jackson, with a vetoed bill in one hand and kingly scepter in the other, trampling on the Constitution, the U.S. Bank, and internal improvements. *(Collection of The New-York Historical Society)*

The drama was repeated a month later at a birthday dinner in memory of Thomas Jefferson, when President Jackson declared himself on the issue. Despite his support of states' rights, Jackson did not believe that any state had the right to reject the will of the majority or to destroy the Union. Knowing that the supporters of nullification hoped to use the gathering to win adherents, Jackson rose for a toast, held high his glass, and said, "Our Union—it must be preserved." Thus challenged, Calhoun followed: "The Union—next to our liberty most dear." The split between them widened over personal as well as ideological issues, and in 1832 Calhoun resigned as vice president. Final rupture came in a collision over the tariff and nullification.

In 1832, hewing to Jackson's "middle course," Congress modified the tariff of 1828 by retaining high duties on goods such as wool, woolens, iron, and hemp but lowering other rates to an earlier level. Many southerners felt injured. A South Carolina convention later that year adopted an Ordinance of Nullification, voiding the tariffs of 1828 and 1832 in that state. The South Carolina legislature funded a volunteer army and threatened secession if the federal government tried to force the state to comply.

South Carolina's actions represented a direct attack on the concepts of federal union and majority rule. Jackson responded forcefully. To the "ambitious malcontents" in South Carolina, as he called the nullifiers, he proclaimed emphatically that "the laws of the United States must be executed. . . . Disunion by armed force is treason. . . . The Union will be preserved and treason and rebellion promptly put down."

Jackson's proclamation stimulated an outburst of patriotism all over the country. South Carolina stood alone, abandoned even by other southern states. Jackson asked Congress for legislation to enforce tariff duties (the Force Bill of 1833), and new tariff revisions, engineered by Henry Clay and supported by Calhoun, called for reductions over a ten-year period. South Carolina quickly repealed its nullification of the tariff laws but saved face by nullifying the Force Bill, which Jackson ignored. The crisis was over, but left unresolved were the constitutional issues it raised. Was the Union permanent? Was secession a valid way to protect minority rights? Such questions would trouble Americans for three decades.

Jackson's Indian Policy

Although Jackson only threatened force on South Carolina, he used it on the southeastern Indians. His policy of forcible removal and relocation westward and on reservations defined white American practice toward the Native American Indians for the rest of the century. In the opening decades of the nineteenth century, the vast landholdings of the five "civilized nations" of the Southeast (the Cherokee, Choctaw, Chickasaw, Seminole, and Creek) had been seriously eroded by the pressures of land-hungry whites supported by successful military campaigns led by professional Indian fighters like Jackson. The Creek lost 22 million acres in southern Georgia and central Alabama after Jackson defeated them at Horseshoe Bend in 1814. Land cessions to the government and private sales accounted for even bigger losses: Cherokee tribal holdings, for example, of more than 50 million acres in 1802 had dwindled to only 9 million 20 years later.

The trend was bolstered by a Supreme Court decision in 1823 declaring that Indians could occupy but not hold title to land in the United States. Recognizing that their survival was threatened, Indian nations acted to end the pattern. By 1825, the Creek, Cherokee, and Chickasaw had each resolved to restrict land sales to government agents. The Cherokee, who had already assimilated many elements of white culture including clothing, agricultural practices, and slaveholding (see Chapter 9), established a police force to prevent local leaders from selling off tribal lands. Indian determination to resist pressure confronted white resolve to gain these southern lands for cotton planting and mining. Jackson's election in 1828 boosted efforts to relocate the Indians west of the Mississippi.

In his first annual message to Congress in 1829, Jackson recommended removal of the southeastern tribes. Appealing at first more to sympathy than to force, Jackson argued that because the Indians were "surrounded by the whites with their arts of civilization," it was inevitable that the "resources of the savage" would be destroyed, dooming the Indians to "weakness and decay." Removal was justified, Jackson claimed, by both "humanity and national honor." He also endorsed the paramount right of state laws over the claims of either Indians or the federal government (thus contradicting his tariff policy).

The crisis soon came to a head in Georgia. In 1829, the Georgia legislature declared the Cherokee tribal council illegal and its laws null and void in Cherokee territories and announced that the state had jurisdiction over both the tribe and its lands. In the following year, the Cherokee were forbidden to defend their interests by bringing suits against whites into the Georgia courts or even by testifying in such cases. Without legal recourse on the state level, the Cherokee carried their protests to the Supreme Court. In 1832, Chief Justice Marshall supported their position in *Worcester* v. *Georgia,* holding that the Georgia law was "repugnant to the Constitution" and did not apply to the Cherokee nation.

Legal victory could not, however, suppress white land hunger. With Jackson's blessing, Georgians defied the Court ruling. By 1835, harassment, intimidation, and bribery had persuaded a minority of chiefs to sign a removal treaty. That year, Jackson informed the

This map shows the westward routes of Indians removed from the Southeast to the new Indian territory in Oklahoma and from the Midwest (Old Northwest Territory) to present day Kansas. See the painting on the next page.

Cherokee, "You cannot remain where you are. Circumstances . . . render it impossible that you can flourish in the midst of a civilized community." Despite the president's pronouncement and the treaty, many Cherokee refused to leave their lands, and the Cherokee people divided into two factions over what to do. In 1837 and 1838, the U.S. Army searched out and seized those opposed to migration westward and gathered them in stockades before herding them west to the "Indian Territory" in Oklahoma. An eyewitness described how the Cherokee trek began:

> Families at dinner were startled by the sudden gleam of bayonets in the doorway and rose to be driven with blows and oaths along the weary miles of trail that led to the stockade. Men were seized in their fields, or going along the road, women were taken from their [spinning] wheels and children from their play. In many cases, on turning for one last look as they crossed the ridge they saw their homes in flames, fired by the lawless rabble that followed on the heels of the soldiers to loot and pillage.

The removal, whose $6 million cost was deducted from the $9 million awarded the Cherokee for its eastern lands, killed perhaps a quarter of the 15,000 who set out. The Cherokee "Trail of Tears" followed those of other southeastern Indian nations. Tribal communities in the Old Northwest between 1821 and 1840 were also forced westward to Kansas and Oklahoma. The Chickasaw suffered as high a death rate as the Cherokee during their removal, while the Seminole and the Sac and Fox fought back. Although Jackson and the Removal Act of 1830 had promised to protect and forever guarantee the Indian lands in the West, within a generation those promises, like others before and since, would be broken. Indian removal left the eastern United States open for the enormous economic expansion described in Chapter 10.

Jackson's Bank War and "Van Ruin's" Depression

As the (white) people's advocate, Jackson could not ignore the Second Bank of the United States, which in 1816 had received a charter for 20 years. The bank generated intense feelings. Jackson called it a "monster" that threatened the people's liberties. But it was not as irresponsible as Jacksonians imagined.

Guided since 1823 by the aristocratic Nicholas Biddle, the Philadelphia bank and its 29 branches gen-

Their attempts at assimilating into white society having failed, the Cherokee finally succumbed to white pressures and their own internal divisions and were forced to travel along the "Trail of Tears" to Oklahoma in 1838. About 4,000 died along the way. The Cherokee removal was actually the last major Indian group east of the Mississippi forced west. Upper midwestern Indian nations such as the Shawnee, Potawatomi, Miami, Kickapoo, and Peoria had been removed to Missouri, Kansas, and Oklahoma in the 1810s and 1820s; the migration of southeastern nations began with the Choctaw in 1830. *(Woolaroc Museum, Bartlesville, Oklahoma)*

erally played a responsible economic role in an expansionary period. As the nation's largest commercial bank, the U.S. Bank could shift funds around the country as necessary and could influence state banking activity. It restrained state banks from making unwise loans by insisting that they back their notes with specie (gold or silver coin) and by calling in its own loans to these institutions. The bank accepted federal deposits, made commercial loans, and bought and sold government bonds. Businessmen, state bankers needing credit, and nationalist politicians such as Webster and Clay, who were on the bank's payroll, all favored it.

Other Americans, however, led by the president, distrusted the bank. Businessmen and speculators in western lands resented its careful control over state banking and wanted cheap, inflated money. Some state bankers resented its power. Southern and western farmers regarded it as immoral because it dealt with paper, not landed property. Others simply thought it was unconstitutional and should be abolished.

Jackson had long opposed the Bank of the United States. He hated banks in general because of a near financial disaster in his own past and also because he and his advisers considered the bank the chief example of a special privilege monopoly that hurt the common man—farmers, craftsmen, and debtors. Jackson called the bank an "irresponsible power" and a threat to the Republic. Its power and financial resources, he thought, allowed the bank to become a "vast electioneering engine" with the "power to control the Government and change its character."

Aware of Jackson's hostility, Clay and Webster persuaded Biddle to ask Congress to recharter the bank in 1832, four years ahead of schedule. They reasoned that in an election year, Jackson would not risk a veto. The bill to recharter the bank swept through Congress and landed on the president's desk one hot, muggy day in July. Jackson took up the challenge. Rather than implement the "milk & water half way veto" recommended by his advisers, Jackson forcefully said: "The bank . . . is trying to kill me, but I will kill it."

Jackson determined not only to veto the bill but also to carry his case to the public. His veto message, condemning the bank as undemocratic, un-American, and unconstitutional, was meant to stir up voters. He presented the bank as a dangerous monopoly that gave the rich special privileges and harmed "the humble members of society." He also pointed to the high percentage of foreign investors in the bank. Jackson's veto message turned the rechartering issue into a struggle between the people and the aristocracy. His oversimplified analysis made the bank into a symbol of everything that worried Americans in a time of change.

The bank furor helped to clarify party differences. In the election of 1832, the National Republicans, now calling themselves Whigs to show their opposition to "King Andrew," nominated Henry Clay. Biddle and the Whigs spent thousands of dollars trying to ensure Clay's election over Jackson, whom they labeled a "tyrant." Democratic campaign rhetoric pitted Jackson, the people, and democracy against Clay, the bank, and aristocracy. The Anti-Masons, the first third party in American political life and the first to hold a nominating convention, expressed popular resentments against the elitist Masonic order (Jackson was a member) and other secret societies.

Jackson won handsomely, with 124,000 more popular votes than the combined total for Clay and the Anti-Mason candidate, William Wirt. "He may be President for life if he chooses," said Wirt of Jackson.

Jackson saw the election as a victory for his bank policy and made plans to finish his war with Biddle. The bank still had four years before the charter expired. Jackson announced that "the hydra of corruption is only scotched, not dead" and declared that it must be killed. He and his advisers decided to weaken the bank by transferring $10 million in government funds to state banks. Although two secretaries of the treasury balked at the removal request as financially unsound, Jackson persisted until he found one, Roger Taney, willing to do it. When Chief Justice John Marshall died in 1835, Jackson replaced him with Taney.

Jackson's war with Biddle and the bank had serious economic consequences. A wave of speculation in western lands and ambitious new state internal improvement schemes in the mid-1830s produced inflated land prices and a flood of paper money. Even Jackson was concerned, and he tried to curtail irresponsible economic activity. In July 1836, he issued the Specie Circular, announcing that the government would accept only gold and silver in payment for public lands. Panicky investors rushed to change paper notes into specie, while banks started calling in loans. The result was the Panic of 1837. Jackson was blamed for this rapid monetary expansion followed by sudden deflation, but international trade problems with Britain and China probably contributed more to the panic and to the ensuing seven years of depression.

Whatever the primary cause, Jackson left his successor, Martin Van Buren, who was elected in 1836 over a trio of Whig opponents, with an economic crisis. Van Buren had barely taken the oath of office in 1837 when banks and businesses began to collapse. "Martin Van Ruin's" presidency was dominated by a severe depression. As New York banks suspended credit and began calling in loans, some $6 million was lost on defaulted debts. In 1838, wealthy merchant and New York mayor Philip Hone wrote in his diary that half his friends were deeply in debt. By 1840, he noted, his three grown sons were out of work and "business of all kinds [was] completely at a stand."

As Hone knew well, however, the laboring poor suffered most in a depression. By the fall of 1837, one-third of America's workers were unemployed, and thousands of others found only sporadic part-time work. For those fortunate enough to retain their jobs, wages fell by 30 to 50 percent within two years. Meanwhile, the price of necessities like flour, pork, and coal nearly doubled. As winter neared in late 1837, a journalist estimated that 200,000 in New York City were "in utter hopeless distress with no means of surviving the winter but those provided by charity." Not surprisingly, they took to the streets, demanding, "Bread! Meat! Rent! Fuel! Their prices must come down!" One worker told newspaperman Horace Greeley that most laborers called "not for the bread and fuel of charity, but for Work!"

The pride of workers was dampened as soup kitchens and bread lines grew faster than jobs. Laboring families found themselves defenseless, for the depression destroyed the trade union movement begun a decade earlier. Many employers hastened the process of killing trade unionism by imposing longer hours, cutting wages and piece rates, and dividing workers. One New England hat manufacturer offered to hire only those untouched by the "moral gangrene of Trades' Union principles." As the hardships of the depression grew worse, violence increased. In 1842, when Philadelphia textile employers lowered wages below subsistence levels, angry hand-loom weavers broke machinery, destroyed cloth, and wrecked the homes of Irish strikebreakers. Job competition, poverty, and ethnic animosities led to violent clashes in other eastern cities as well, as we saw in Chapter 10.

"How is it," a Philadelphia mechanic asked in 1837, that in a country as rich as the United States so many people were "pinched for the common necessaries of life . . . [and] bowed down with gloom and despair?" President Van Buren's responses to the social misery behind this question were sympathetic but limited and even made things worse. An executive order in 1840 declaring a ten-hour day for federal employees affected few workers. Despite inadequate measures, political participation, as well as church membership, reached new heights during the depression, as Americans sought to alleviate their "gloom and despair."

The Second American Party System

By the mid-1830s, a new two-party system and a lively participatory national political culture had emerged

THE SECOND AMERICAN PARTY SYSTEM

	Democrats	Whigs
Leaders	Andrew Jackson John C. Calhoun Martin Van Buren Thomas Hart Benton	Henry Clay Daniel Webster John Quincy Adams William Henry Harrison
Political tradition	Republican party (Jefferson, Madison	Federalist party (Hamilton, John Adams
	Major Political Beliefs	
	State and local autonomy Opposition to monopoly and privilege Low land prices and tariffs Freedom from government interference	National power Support for U.S. Bank, high tariff Internal improvements Broad government role in reforming America
	Primary Sources of Support	
Region	South and West	New England, Middle Atlantic, Upper Midwest
Class	Middle-class and small farmers, northeastern urban laborers and artisans	Big southern planters and wealthy businessmen, pockets of middling farmers in Midwest and South, artisans
Ethnicity	Scots-Irish, Irish, French, German, and Canadian immigrants	English, New England old stock
Religion	Catholics, frontier Baptists and Methodists, free thinkers	Presbyterians, Congregationalists, Quakers, moralists, reformers

in the United States. The parties had taken shape amid the conflicts of Jackson's presidency and the religious fervor of the Second Great Awakening. Although both parties included wealthy and influential leaders and mirrored the growing diversity of a changing nation, the Democrats had the better claim that they were the party of the common man with strength in all sections of the country.

Whigs represented greater wealth than Democrats and were strongest in New England and in areas settled by New Englanders across the Upper Midwest. In an appeal to businessmen and manufacturers, Whigs generally endorsed Clay's American System, which meant that they favored a national bank, federally supported internal improvements, and tariff protection for industry. Many large southern cotton planters joined the Whig party because of its position on bank credit and internal improvements. Whigs ran almost evenly with Democrats in the South for a decade, and artisans and laborers belonged equally to each party. The difficulty in drawing clear regional or class distinctions between Whigs and Democrats suggests that other factors, such as ethnic, religious, and cultural background, also influenced party choice. Because each party offered its own vision of the good society and notions on the role of government in private lives, broad cultural and social perspectives helped to determine party affiliation.

In the Jeffersonian tradition, the Democrats espoused liberty and local rule. They wanted freedom from legislators of morality, from religious tyranny, from special privilege, and from too much government. For them, the best society was one in which all Americans were free to follow their own individual interests. Those who wanted to maintain religious or ethnic traditions found a home in the Democratic party. So, too, did many members of denominations that had suffered discrimination in the colonies and states that had had an established church. The Scots-Irish, German, French, and Irish Catholic immigrants, as well as free thinkers and labor organizers, tended to be Jacksonians. Although they zealously promoted their social vision, Democrats were less moralistic than Whigs. Especially on matters like temperance and slavery, their religious background generally taught the inevitability of sin and evil in the world. Therefore, Democrats sought to keep politics separate from moral issues.

By contrast, for many Whigs, the line between reform and politics was hazy. Indeed, politics seemed an appropriate arena for cleansing society of sin. Calling themselves the party of law and order, most Whigs did not think Americans needed more freedom, but rather they needed to learn to use the freedom they already had. If all men were to vote, they required a "system of general education" that would teach them to use their political privileges. Old-stock New England Yankee Congregationalists and Presbyterians were usually Whigs. So were Quakers and evangelical Protestants, who believed that positive government action could change moral behavior and eradicate sin. Whigs supported a wide variety of reforms, such as temperance, antislavery, public education, and strict observance of the Sabbath, as well as government action to promote economic development.

Party identification played an increasingly large part in the lives of American men. The flamboyant new electioneering styles and techniques were designed to recruit new voters into the political process and to ensure continued loyalty. Party activities offered excitement, entertainment, and camaraderie. They offered a way to shape the changing world.

The election of 1840 illustrated the new style of political culture. Passing over Henry Clay, the Whigs nominated William Henry Harrison of Indiana, the aging hero of the Battle of Tippecanoe (Kithtippecanoe), fought nearly 30 years earlier. A Virginian, John Tyler, was nominated as vice president to underline the regional diversity of the party. The Democrats had no choice but to renominate Van Buren, who conducted a quiet campaign. The Whig campaign, however, featured every form of popularized appeals for votes—barbecues, torchlight parades, songs, and cartoons. Political symbolism was exploited by posing Harrison (who lived in a mansion) in front of a rural log cabin with a barrel of hard cider. Jugs of cider and coonskin caps inscribed with clever slogans were lavishly dispensed to grateful voters.

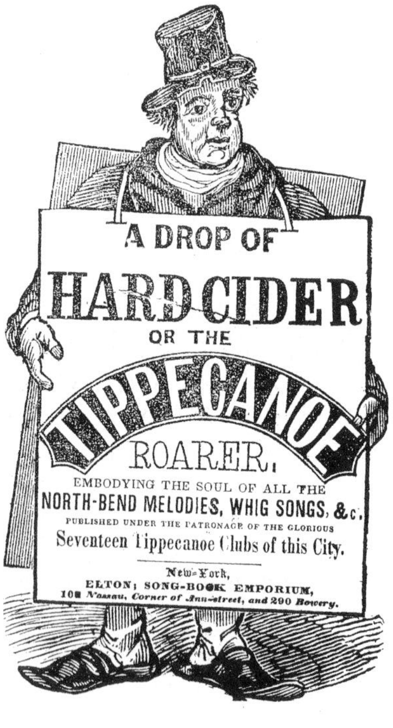

(Left) In the election of 1840, the Whigs "out-Jacksoned the Jacksonians" by playing to the popular political style of slogans, songs, and cider. They touted their candidate as a backwoodsy Indian fighter, the hero of the battle of Tippecanoe who lived in a log cabin and drank hard cider. *(Cincinnati Historical Society)* (Below) Louisiana Democrats responded to the Whig use of the log cabin and cider campaign with this cartoon, titled the "Federal-Abolition-Whig Trap to Catch Voters In," which shows an unwary voter, a member of the "industrious laboring classes," being lured under the log cabin by the promise of hard cider. "Just let him get a taste, " the text said, "and they come down at once upon him, hard and heavy, swig after swig, until they get him in a ranting way, shouting and bawling for Tip. and Ty." *(Library of Congress)*

The Whigs reversed conventional images by labeling Van Buren an aristocratic dandy and contrasting him with their simple candidate sitting in front of his cabin. Harrison reminded voters of General Jackson, and they swept him into office, 234 electoral votes to Van Buren's 60. In one of the largest turnouts in American history, over 80 percent of eligible voters marched to the polls. Commenting on the defeat, a Democratic party journal acknowledged that the Whigs had out-Jacksoned the Jacksonians: "We taught them how to conquer us."

Concern over the new politics outlasted Harrison, who died only a month after taking office. One man complained during the campaign that he was tired of all the hoopla over "the Old Hero. Nothing but politics . . . mass-meetings are held in every groggery." His comment about the combination of politics and drinking was especially telling. For many Americans, usually Whigs and often women, it was precisely the excesses of Jacksonian politics, most notably intemperance and the inherent violence of slavery, that led them to seek other ways than politics of imposing order and morality on American society. To gain a measure of control over their lives and reshape their changing world, the American people turned also to religion, social reform, and utopianism.

PERFECTIONIST REFORM AND UTOPIANISM

"Be ye therefore perfect even as your Father in heaven is perfect," commanded the Bible. Mid-nineteenth-century reformers, inspired by the Finney revivals, took the challenge seriously. Eventually, a perfected millennial era of 1,000 years of peace, harmony, and Christian brotherhood on earth would bring the Second Coming of Christ.

The perfectionist thrust in religion fit America's sense of itself as a redeemer nation chosen by God to reform the entire world. Religious commitment fused with patriotic duty. The motivating impulse to reform in the 1830s, then, had many deep-rooted causes. These included the Puritan idea of American mission; the secular examples of founding fathers like Benjamin Franklin to do good, reinforced by Republican ideology and romantic beliefs in the natural goodness of human nature; the social activist tendencies in Whig political ideology; anxiety over shifting class relationships and the need to achieve some control over one's life as a result of the socioeconomic changes of recent years; family influence and the desire of young people to choose careers of principled service; and the direct influence of the Finney revivals in the early 1830s.

The Dilemmas of Reform

Religious reformers and Whig politicians both faced timeless dilemmas about how best to effect change. Does one, for example, try to change attitudes first and then behavior, or the reverse? Which is more effective, to appeal to people's minds and hearts to change bad institutions, or to change institutions first, assuming that altered behavior will then change attitudes? Taking the first path, the reformer relies on education, on the moral suasion of sermons, tracts, literature, argument, and personal testimony. Following the second, the reformer acts politically and institutionally, seeking to pass laws, win elections, form unions, boycott tainted goods, and create or abolish institutions.

Reformers, moreover, have to decide whether to attempt to bring about limited, piecemeal practical change on a single issue or go for perfection. Should they improve on a partly defective system or tear down the entire system to build a utopian new one? Reformers must further decide whether to use or recommend force and whether to enter into coalitions with less principled potential allies. They also face the difficult challenge of making sure that their own attitudes and actions are thoroughly consistent with the principles of behavior they would urge on others, as Thoreau had demonstrated.

These challenging problems fill the lives of reformers with turmoil. Advocates of change in the status quo experience enormous pressures, recriminations, and economic or physical persecution from the majority. As Marius and Emily Robinson understood,

MOTIVATIONS AND CAUSES OF REFORM IN AMERICA, 1830–1850

- Changing relationships between men and women, masters and workers as a result of the market economy, growth of cities, and increasing immigration
- Finney and other religious revivals in the Second Great Awakening
- Social activist and ethical impulses of the Whig party
- Psychological anxieties over shifting class and ethnic relationships
- Family traditions and youthful idealism
- Puritan and Revolutionary traditions of the American mission to remake the world
- Republican ideology and Enlightenment emphasis on virtue and good citizenship
- Romantic literary influences such as Transcendentalism

promoting change has its costs. What is more, reformers invariably do not agree on appropriate ideology and tactics, so they end up quarreling with one another as well as with representatives of the established order they wish to change. Although reformers suffer pressure to conform and to cease questioning things, their duty to themselves, their society, and their God sustains their commitment.

Utopian Communities: Oneida and the Shakers

Thoreau tried to lead an ideal solitary life. Other reformers sought to create perfect communities. Emerson noted in 1840 that he hardly met a thinking, reading man who did not have "a draft of a new community in his waistcoat pocket." One way to redeem a flawed society, one that seemed to be losing the cohesion and traditional values of small community life, was to create miniature utopian societies. These would offer alternatives to a world characterized by factories, foreigners, flawed morals, and greedy entrepreneurship.

In 1831, as President Jackson and South Carolina approached their confrontation over the tariff and nullification, as Nat Turner planned his slave revolt in Virginia, and as the citizens of Rochester sought ways of controlling their workers' drinking habits, a young man in Putney, Vermont, heard Charles Finney on one of his whirlwind tours of New England. John Humphrey Noyes was an instant, if unorthodox, convert.

Noyes believed that the act of final conversion led to absolute perfection and complete release from sin. However spiritually blessed, Noyes's earthly happiness was soon sorely tested. In 1837, a woman he loved rejected both his doctrine and his marriage offer. Despondent, Noyes wrote a friend that "when the will of God is done on earth as it is in heaven there will be no marriage." Among those who were perfect, he argued, all men and women belonged equally to each other. For Noyes, complete sharing in family relationships was a step toward perfect cooperation, as was shared wealth in socioeconomic relationships. Others called his heretical doctrines "free love" and socialism. Noyes recovered from his unhappy love affair and married a loyal follower. When she delivered four stillborn children within six years, Noyes revised even further his unconventional ideas about sex.

In 1848, Noyes and 51 devoted followers founded a "perfectionist" community at Oneida, New York. Under his strong leadership, Oneida grew and prospered. Sexual life at the commune was subject to many regulations, including sexual restraint and male continence except under carefully prescribed conditions. In a system of

In this sacred Shaker dance, sin is being shaken out of the body through the fingertips. Note the separation of women and men. *(Shakertown at Pleasant Hill, Kentucky)*

planned reproduction, only certain spiritually advanced males (usually Noyes) were allowed to father children. Other controversial practices included communal child rearing, sexual equality in work, the removal of the competitive spirit from both work and play, and an elaborate program of "mutual criticism" at community meetings presided over by "Father" Noyes.

Though creating considerable tension, these unorthodox sexual and social rules gave Oneidans a sense of uniqueness. Wise economic decisions also bound community members in mutual prosperity. Forsaking the nostalgic agricultural emphasis that typified most other communes, Noyes opted for modern manufacturing. Oneida specialized at first in the fabrication of steel animal traps and later diversified into making silverware. Eventually abandoning religion to become a joint-stock company in which individual members held shares, Oneida thrived for many years and continues today as a silverware company.

Noyes greatly admired another group of communitarians, the Shakers, who also believed in perfectionism, surrendering worldly property to the community, and the devotion of one's labor and love to bringing about the millennial kingdom of heaven. Unlike the Oneidans, Shakers condemned sexuality and demanded absolute chastity, so that only conversions could bring in new members. Founded by an Englishwoman, Mother Ann Lee, Shaker conversions grew in the Second Great Awakening and peaked around 6,000 souls by the 1850s, with communities from Maine to New York to Kentucky. They believed that God had a dual personality, male and female, and that Ann Lee was the female counterpart to the masculine Christ. The Shaker worship service featured frenetic dancing intended to release (or "shake") sin out through the fingertips. Shaker communities, some of which survived long into the twentieth century, were known for their communal ownership of property, equality of women and men, simplicity, and beautifully crafted furniture.

Other Utopias

Over 100 utopian communities like Oneida and the Shaker colonies were founded. Some were religiously motivated; others were secular. Most were small and lasted only a few months or years. All eventually collapsed, though giving birth to significant social ideas.

Pietist German-speaking immigrants founded the earliest utopian communities in America, to preserve their language, spirituality, and ascetic lifestyle. The most notable of these were the Ephrata colonists in Pennsylvania, the Harmonists in Indiana, the Zoar community in Ohio, and the Amana Society in Iowa. Some antebellum utopian communities focused less on otherworldly contemplation than on the regeneration of this world. In 1840, Adin Ballou founded Hopedale in Massachusetts as a "miniature Christian republic" based on the ethical teachings of Jesus. Hopedale's newspaper, *The Practical Christian,* advocated temperance, pacifism, women's rights, and other reforms.

Other communities, founded on the secular principles of reason inherited from the Enlightenment, responded more directly to the social misery and wretched working conditions accompanying the Industrial Revolution. These communities differed from religious ones in assuming that evil came from bad environments rather than individual acts of sin. They consequently believed that altered environ-

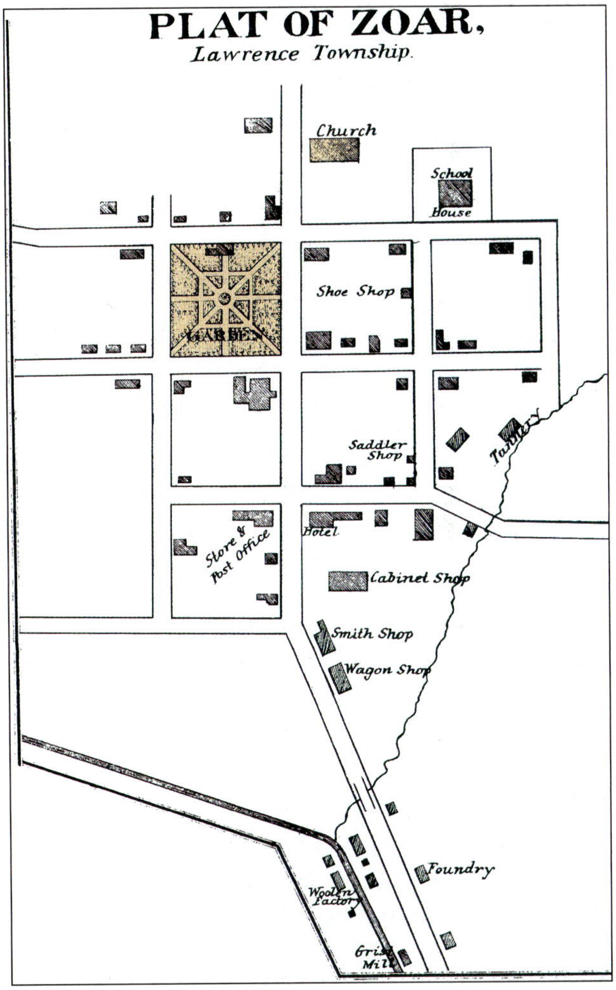

The Zoar community was founded by Pietist Germans in 1817 and lasted until 1898. This type of map, or plat, shows the ordered plan for the town, the prominence of the public gardens (land was not held individually but in common), and the artisan and commercial shops built along the river and the Ohio and Erie Canal, which passed through Zoar in 1832. Note that despite the importance of religion, the church is on the edge of town, while commercial sites, including a hotel welcoming visitors, are in the center. *(Danzer Map Collection)*

ments rather than new morals would eliminate or reduce poverty, ignorance, intemperance, and other ugly by-products of industrialism.

Robert Owen was the best known of the secular communalists. A Scottish industrialist who saw the miserable lives of cotton millworkers, he envisioned a society of small towns—"Agricultural and Manufacturing Villages of Unity and Mutual Cooperation"—with good schools and healthy work for all citizens. Unemployment, poverty, and vice would be unknown in Owen's model communities. In 1824, he established his first town in America at New Harmony, Indiana, a former Pietist community. But little harmony prevailed, and it failed within three years.

Brook Farm, founded by two Concord friends of Emerson, tried to integrate "intellectual and manual labor." Residents would hoe in the fields and shovel manure for a few hours each day and then study literature and recite poetry. Although the colony lasted less than three years, it produced some notable literature in a journal, *The Dial*, edited by Margaret Fuller. Nathaniel Hawthorne briefly lived at Brook Farm and wrote a novel, *The Blithedale Romance* (1852), criticizing the utopians' naive optimism.

The utopian communities all failed for similar reasons. Americans seemed ill-suited to communal living and work responsibilities and were unwilling to share either their property or their spouses. Nor did celibacy arouse much enthusiasm. Other recurring problems included unstable leadership, financial bickering, local hostility toward sexual experimentation and other unorthodox practices, the indiscriminate admission of members, and waning enthusiasm. Emerson pinned the failure of the communities on their inability to confront the individualistic impulses of human nature. As he said of Brook Farm, an epitaph suitable for all utopian communities: "It met every test but life itself."

Millerites and Mormons

If utopian communities failed to bring about the millennium, an alternative hope was to leap directly past the thousand years of peace and harmony to the Second Coming of Christ. William Miller, a shy farmer from upstate New York, became so absorbed with the idea of the imminent coming of Christ that he figured out mathematically the exact time of the event in March 1843. A religious sect, the Millerites, gathered around him to prepare for Christ's return and the Day of Judgment.

A mixture of excitement and fear grew as the day of the predicted return came closer. Some people gave away all their worldly belongings, neglected business, put on robes, and flocked to high hills and rooftops to be nearest the blessed event. When 1843 passed without the expected end, Miller and his followers recalculated and set a series of alternative dates. Each new disappointment diminished Miller's followers, and he died in 1848 a discredited man. But a small Millerite sect, the Seventh-Day Adventists, had already taken root and continues to this day.

Other groups that emerged from the same religiously active area of upstate New York were more successful. As Palmyra, New York, was being swept by Finney revivalism, young Joseph Smith, a recent convert, claimed to be visited by the angel Moroni. According to Smith, Moroni led him to golden tablets buried in the ground near his home. On these plates were inscribed more than 500 pages of *The Book of Mormon,* which described the one true church and a "lost tribe of Israel" missing for centuries. The book also predicted the appearance of an American prophet who would establish a new and pure kingdom of Christ in America. Smith published his book in 1830 and soon founded the Church of Jesus Christ of Latter-Day Saints (the Mormons). His visionary leadership attracted thousands of ordinary people trying to escape what they viewed as social disorder, religious impurity, and commercial degradation in the 1830s.

Smith and a steadily growing band of converts migrated successively to Ohio and Missouri and then back to Illinois, where they met ridicule, persecution, and violence. The hostility stemmed in part from their active missionary work, in part from their beliefs and support for local Indian tribes, and in part from rumors of unorthodox sexual practices.

Despite external persecution and internal dissension caused by Smith's strong leadership style, the Mormons prospered and increased. Converts from England and northern Europe added substantially to their numbers. By the mid-1840s, Nauvoo, Illinois, with a thriving population of nearly 15,000, was the showplace of Mormonism. Smith petitioned Congress for separate territorial status and ran for the presidency in 1844. This was too much for the citizens of nearby towns. Violence escalated and culminated in Smith's trial for treason and his murder by a mob. Under the brilliant leadership of Smith's successor, Brigham Young, the Mormons headed westward in 1846 in their continuing search for the "land of promise."

REFORMING SOCIETY

The Mormons and the utopian communitarians had as their common goal, in Brigham Young's words, "the spread of righteousness upon the earth." Most people,

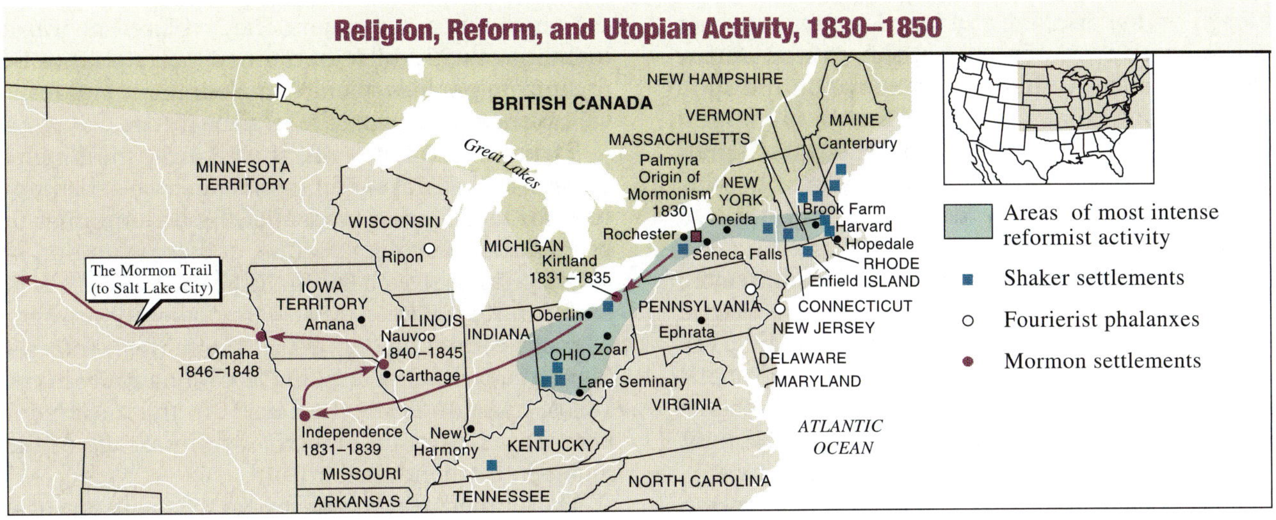

Reformist activity followed both religious revival areas and the Erie Canal into the growing states of the Old Northwest.

however, preferred to spread righteousness by focusing on a specific social evil rather than embracing whole new religions or joining utopian colonies.

"We are all a little wild here," Emerson wrote in 1840, "with numberless projects of social reform." Mobilized in part by their increased participation in the political parties of Jacksonian America, the reformers created and joined all kinds of societies for social betterment. The reform ranks were swelled by thousands of women, stirred to action by the religious revivals and freed from domestic burdens by delayed marriage and smaller families. Organized in hundreds of voluntary societies, women such as Emily Rakestraw joined men such as Marius Robinson in directing their energies to numerous social issues. These included alcohol consumption; diet and health; sexuality; institutional treatment of the mentally ill, the disabled, paupers, and criminals; education; the rights of labor; slavery; and women's rights.

Temperance

On New Year's Eve in 1831, a Finney disciple, Theodore Dwight Weld, delivered a four-hour temperance lecture in Rochester. In graphic detail, he described the awful fate of those who

The temperance movement of the 1830s and 1840s used the tactics of religious revivalists to scare drinkers into taking the "teetotal" pledge. Who could resist this poignant 1846 portrayal of *The Drunkard's Progress*? *(Library of Congress)*

refused to stop drinking and urged his audience not only to cease their tippling but also to stop others. Several were converted to abstinence on the spot. The next day, Elijah and Albert Smith, the largest providers of whiskey in Rochester, rolled their barrels out onto the sidewalk and smashed them. Cheering Christians applauded as the whiskey ran out into Exchange Street.

Americans in the nineteenth century drank heavily. One man observed that "a house could not be raised, a field of wheat cut down, nor could there be a log rolling, a husking, a quilting, a wedding, or a funeral without the aid of alcohol." The corrosive effects of drinking were obvious: poverty, crime, illness, insanity, battered and broken families, and corrupt politics.

Early efforts at curbing alcohol consumption emphasized moderation. Forming local societies, groups of people agreed to limit how much they drank or to imbibe only beer and wine. Some societies even met in local taverns to toast their commitment to moderation. But under the influence of the Beecher and Finney revivals, the movement achieved better organization and clearer goals. The American Temperance Society, founded in 1826, was dedicated not just to moderation but to total abstinence. Within a few years, thousands of local and state societies had formed, though some refused to prohibit drinking of hard cider and communion wine.

Temperance advocates copied successful revival techniques. Fiery lecturers expounded on the evil consequences of drink and urged group pressure on the weak-willed. Mass meetings were accompanied by a deluge of graphic and sometimes gory temperance tracts. Who would not cringe at descriptions of drinkers: "Some are killed instantly; some die a lingering, gradual death; some commit suicide in fits of intoxication; and some are actually burnt up." One "intemperate man," it was claimed, died when his "breath caught fire by coming in contact with a lighted candle." The accumulated pressure of both written and oral testimony, capped off by a sermon like Weld's, was intended to convince people to take the "teetotal" pledge.

By 1840, disagreements over goals and methods split the temperance movement into many separate organizations. In depression times, when jobs and stable families were harder to find than whiskey and beer, laboring men and women moved more by practical concerns than religious fervor joined the crusade. The Washington Temperance Society, founded in a Baltimore tavern in 1840, was enormously popular with unemployed young workers and grew to an estimated 600,000 members in three years. The Washingtonians, arguing that alcoholism was a disease rather than moral failure, changed the shape of the temperance movement. They replaced revivalist techniques with those of the new party politics by organizing parades, picnics, melodramas, and festivals to encourage people to take the pledge.

Tactics in the 1840s also shifted away from moral suasion to political action. Temperance societies lobbied for local option laws, allowing communities to prohibit the sale, manufacture, and consumption of alcohol. The first such law in the nation was passed in Maine in 1851. Fifteen other states followed with similar laws before the Civil War. Despite weak enforcement, the per capita drinking fell dramatically in the 1850s. Interrupted by the Civil War, the movement reached its ultimate objective with passage of the Eighteenth Amendment in 1919.

The temperance crusade reveals the many practical motivations for Americans to join reform societies. For some, as in Rochester, temperance provided an opportunity for the Protestant middle classes to exert some control over laborers, immigrants, and Catholics. Perfectionists saw abstinence as a way of practicing self-control. For many women, the temperance effort was a respectable way to control the behavior of drunken men who beat wives and daughters. For many young men, especially after the onset of the depression of 1837, a temperance society provided entertainment, fellowship, and contacts to help their careers. In temperance societies as in political parties, Americans found jobs, purpose, support, spouses, and relief from the loneliness and uncertainty of a changing world.

Health and Sexuality

It was a short step from the physical and psychological ravages of drink to other potentially harmful effects on the body. Reformers were quick to attack too much eating, too many stimulants, and, above all, too much sex. Many endorsed a variety of special diets and exercise programs for maintaining good health. Some promoted panaceas. One of these was hydropathy: clients sojourned at one of 70 special resorts for bathing and water purges of the body. Many of these resorts especially attracted women who not only found an escape from daily drudgery in the home but also found cures for chronic and untreated urogenital infections. Other panaceas, including hypnotism, phrenology (the study of bumps on the head), and various "spiritualist" seances, sought to cure problems of the mind.

Sylvester Graham, inventor of the Graham cracker, combined all these enthusiasms into a focus on sexual purity. In 1834 he delivered a series of lectures on chastity, later published as an advice book. To those "troubled" by sexual desire, he recommended "cold baths" and "more active exercise in the open air. Graham advised women, apparently not as "passionless" as the Victorian stereotype suggested, to "have intercourse only for procreation." Although females learned to control sexuality for their own purposes, as we shall see, male "sexual purity" advocates urged sexual restraint to protect various male interests. One doctor argued that women ought not to be educated because blood needed for the womb would be diverted to the head, thus breeding "puny men."

The authors of antebellum "health" manuals advocated abstinence from sexual activity as vehemently as from alcohol. The body, they argued, was a closed energy system in which each organ had particular and limited functions to perform. Semen must be saved for reproductive purposes and should not be wasted in masturbation or intercourse only for pleasure. Such waste would cause enervation, disease, insanity, and death. Some argued further that the "expenditure" of sperm meant a loss of needed energy from the economy.

With strong religious roots, the frail Dorothea Dix tirelessly waged a courageous and creative campaign to improve conditions for the insane throughout the nation. "I encounter nothing which a determined will created by the necessities of the cause does not enable me to vanquish," she wrote, reflecting her irrepressible spirit on behalf of public support for humane hospitals for "hundreds of wailing, suffering creatures." *(The Granger Collection, New York)*

Humanizing the Asylum

In their effort to restore order to American society, some reformers preferred to work not for private influence over individuals but toward public changes in institutions. They wanted to transform such social institutions as asylums, almshouses, prisons, schools, and even factories. Horace Mann, who led the struggle for common schools in Massachusetts (see Chapter 10), was a typical antebellum reformer. He blended dedicated idealism with a canny, practical sense of how to institutionalize educational improvements in one state: teacher training schools, higher teachers' salaries, and compulsory attendance laws.

Other reformers were less successful in achieving their goals. This was especially true in the treatment of society's outcasts. In the colonial era, the family or the local community cared for orphans, paupers, the insane, and even criminals. Beginning early in the nineteenth century, various states built asylums, houses of refuge, reform schools, jails, and other institutions to uplift and house social victims. In some of these institutions, such as prisons and almshouses, the sane and insane, children and hardened adult criminals were thrown together in terrible conditions. In 1843, Dorothea Dix, a frail New Englander, horrified the Massachusetts legislature with her famous report that imprisoned insane people in the state were subject to the "extremest state of degradation and misery." They were confined in "cages, closets, stalls, pens! Chained, naked, beaten with rods, and lashed into obedience!" Dix recommended special hospitals, or asylums, where the insane could be "humanly and properly controlled" by trained attendants.

Many perfectionist reformers like Dix believed that asylums could reform society's outcasts. Convinced that bad institutions corrupted basically good human beings, they reasoned that reformed institutions could rehabilitate them. In 1853, Charles Loring Brace started a Children's Aid Society in New York City that was a model of change through effective education and self-help. Reformers like Dix and Brace, as well as Samuel Gridley Howe and Thomas Gallaudet, who founded institutions for the care and education of the blind and deaf, achieved remarkable results.

But all too often, results were disappointing. Prison reformers believed that a properly built and administered penitentiary could bring a hardened criminal "back to virtue." They argued intensely over the most appropriate structural design for rehabilitating criminals. Some preferred the rectangular prison at Auburn, New York, with its tiny cells and common workrooms, whereas others pointed to the Pennsylvania star-shaped system, where each inmate was in solitary confinement, though in a fairly modern cell. Whichever system was preferred, prison reformers assumed that if "penitents" were put into isolated cells to study the Bible and reflect on their wrongdoing,

A popular workingmen's form of entertainment was the minstrel show, where whites would blacken their faces with burnt cork and perform songs and skits that negatively stereotyped blacks. Two oft-depicted types were thick-lipped, dim-witted slavish clowns and faithful "old Darkies," both incapable of coping with plantation life. Another was the northern pseudo-suave dandy like "Zip Coon," shown here who, despite his airs, was always humiliated so as to reassure white workers that free blacks posed no threat to take either their women or their jobs. *(The Harvard Theatre Collection, The Houghton Library)*

they would eventually decide to become good citizens. In practice, many criminals simply went mad or committed suicide. The institutions built by well-intentioned reformers became dumping places for society's outcasts. By mid-century, American prisons and mental asylums had become sadly impersonal, understaffed, overcrowded institutions.

Working-Class Reform

Efforts to improve the institutional conditions of American life were not all top-down movements initiated and led by middle-class reformers. For working-class Americans, the social institution most in need of transformation was the factory. Workers, many of whom were involved in other issues such as temperance, peace, and abolitionism, tried to improve their own lives. As labor leader Seth Luther told a meeting of New England mechanics and laborers, "We must take our business into our own hands. Let us awake." And awake they did, forming both trade unions and workingmen's parties as Andrew Jackson neared the presidency.

Between 1828 and 1832, dozens of workingmen's parties arose. They advocated free, tax-supported schools, free public lands in the West, equal rights for the poor, and elimination of monopolistic privilege. Trade union activity began in Philadelphia in 1827 as skilled workers organized journeymen carpenters, plasterers, printers, weavers, tailors, and other tradesmen. That same year, 15 unions combined into a city-wide federation, a process followed in other cities. The National Trades Union, founded in 1834, was the first attempt at a national labor organization.

Trade unions fared better than labor parties, as Jacksonian Democrats siphoned off workers' votes. Union programs set more practical goals, including shorter hours, wages that would keep pace with rising prices, and ways (such as the closed shop) of warding off the competitive threat of cheap labor. In addition, both workers and their middle-class supporters called for the abolition of imprisonment for debt and of compulsory militia duty (both of which often cost workers their jobs), free public education, improved living conditions in workers' neighborhoods, and the right to organize. Discouraged by decisions of New York State courts, which denied the right to organize in 1835 and again in 1836, workers argued that unions were necessary to "resist the oppressions of avarice" and compared themselves with the Americans who dumped British tea in Boston's harbor in 1773.

Fired by revolutionary tradition, by increasing political influence, and by a union membership of near 300,000, workers struck some 168 times between 1834 and 1836. Over two-thirds of the strikes were over wages (see Chapter 10); the others were for shorter hours. Identifying with the "blood of our fathers" shed on the battlefields of the American Revolution, Boston tradesmen struck in 1835 for a ten-hour day. They failed, but their attempt heralded the subsequent resurgence of a successful ten-hour-day movement in the 1850s. The Panic of 1837 ushered in a depression that dashed the hopes and efforts of American workers. But the organizational work of the 1830s promised that the labor movement would reemerge, strengthened, later in the century.

ABOLITIONISM AND THE WOMEN'S RIGHTS MOVEMENT

As American workers struggled in Lowell and other eastern cities for better wages and hours in 1834, Emily and Marius Robinson arrived in Cincinnati to fight for their causes. They and many other young idealists had been attracted by the newly founded Lane Seminary, a school to train abolitionist leaders. Financed by two wealthy New York brothers, Arthur and Lewis Tappan, Lane soon became a center of reformist activity. When nervous local residents persuaded President Lyman Beecher to crack down on the students, 40 "Lane rebels," led by Theodore Weld, fled to Oberlin in northern Ohio. The rebels turned Oberlin College into the first institution in the United States open to women and men, blacks and whites. Thus, the movements to abolish slavery and for equal rights to women and free blacks were joined.

The goals of the struggle against slavery and subtle forms of racism and sexism often seemed as distant and unrealizable as the millennium itself. Yet antislavery and feminist advocates persisted in their efforts to abolish what they believed were concrete, visible, institutionalized social wrongs. Whether seeking to eliminate coercion in the cotton fields or in the kitchen, they faced the dual challenge of pursuing elusive goals while achieving practical changes in everyday life.

Tensions within the Antislavery Movement

Although the antislavery movement was smaller than temperance advocacy, it revealed more clearly the difficulties of pursuing significant social change in America. As a young man of 22, William Lloyd Garrison passionately desired to improve, if not to perfect, the flawed world in which he lived. He was also ambitious and said that his name would "one day be known to the world." He was right. On January 1, 1831, eight months before Nat Turner's revolt, Garrison published the first issue of *The Liberator,* soon to become the leading antislavery journal in the United States. "I am in earnest," he wrote. "I will not equivocate—AND I WILL BE HEARD." After first organizing the New England Anti-Slavery Society with a group of blacks and whites in a church basement in Boston, in 1833 Garrison and 62 others established the American Anti-Slavery Society.

Before Garrison, most antislavery whites, dominated by southerners like Henry Clay, had advocated gradual emancipation by individual slave owners. Many joined the American Colonizationist Society, founded in 1816, which sent a few former slaves to Liberia, on the West Coast of Africa. But these efforts were woefully inadequate and were racist, the main goal being to rid the country of free blacks rather than slavery itself.

Garrison furiously opposed the colonizationists. "I do not wish to think, or speak, or write, with moderation," he wrote. "No! no! tell a man whose house is on fire to give a moderate alarm; tell him to moderately rescue his wife from the hands of the ravisher." For Garrison, compromise was unthinkable. There would be "no Union with slaveholders," he cried, condemning the Constitution that perpetuated slavery as "a covenant with death, an agreement with Hell." The American Anti-Slavery Society called for the immediate and total abolition of slavery. After escaping slavery, Frederick Douglass agreed: "Power concedes nothing without a demand. It never did and it never will." But the abolitionists did not always agree, splitting into colonizationists, gradualists, and immediatists.

Abolitionists also differed over the tactics of ending slavery. Their primary method was moral suasion, by which they sought to convince slaveholders and their supporters that slavery was a sin. In an outpouring of sermons, petitions, resolutions, pamphlets, and speeches, abolitionists tried to overwhelm slaveholders with moral guilt so that, repentant, they would free their slaves. But as Marius wrote to Emily Robinson, "The spirit of slavery is not confined to the South." His Ohio trip suggests that northerners were equally guilty in providing the support necessary to maintain the slave system.

The abolitionists by 1837 flooded the nation with over a million pieces of antislavery literature. Their writing described slave owners as "manstealers" who gave up all claim to humanity. A slaveholder, Garrison wrote, led a life "of unbridled lust, . . . of haughty domination, of cowardly ruffianism, of boundless dissipation, of matchless insolence, of infinite self-conceit, of unequalled oppression, of more than savage cruelty." In 1839, Weld published *American Slavery as It Is,* which described in the goriest possible detail the inhumane treatment of slaves.

Other abolitionists preferred more direct methods. The main alternative lay in political action by bringing antislavery petitions before Congress and forming third parties. Boycotting goods made by slave labor was a third tactic.

A fourth approach was to call for slave rebellion, as did two northern blacks, David Walker in a pamphlet in 1829 and Henry Highland Garnet in a speech at a convention of black Americans in 1843. Walker, a North Carolina free black living in Boston, published a powerful essay, "Walker's Appeal." He called upon other free blacks to "enlighten your brethren" to their ignorant "wretched condition" and upon slaves themselves to cease their submissiveness and rise up and throw off the yoke of slavery. "Now I ask you," Walker wrote, "had you not rather be killed than to be a slave to a tyrant, who takes the life of your mother, wife, and dear little children? Look upon your mother, wife and children, and answer God almighty; and believe this,

Recovering the Past

SLAVE NARRATIVES

In the 1840s and 1850s, male and female abolitionists eagerly sought out, subsidized, and published book-length accounts of slavery written by runaway slaves themselves. These chilling stories of captivity and successful escapes, in the voices of former slaves, had enormous emotional power and were instrumental by abolitionists in their effort to influence public opinion and end slavery. According to one estimate, nearly 100 book-length "slave narratives" have been published, selections from two of which are included here.

The slave narratives combined three American autobiographical traditions: spiritual confessionals characteristic of Puritans such as Jonathan Edwards; the rags-to-riches individualistic success story of Benjamin Franklin; and Indian captivity narratives. The last tradition, popular reading in the early nineteenth century, described the adventures of white captives who were dragged away from their villages by Indians; suffered the trials, tortures, and sometimes harmonious adaptations to living in an Indian village; and were finally freed and returned ("redeemed") home to white civilization.

The African American slave narratives followed a similar three-stage pattern, beginning either with an idyllic childhood in a West African village or the relative innocence of childhood on a southern plantation. Aimed at northern white readers, the bulk of the story described, in vivid detail, the brutal oppressions of captivity and slavery, dwelling on the horrors of the slave ships, slave sales and the breakup of families, and the daily beatings, punishments, and harsh rigors of life on the plantation. But the narratives also described heroic struggles to survive and even "sass" one's owners and cunning strategies for avoiding work, connecting with loved ones, and learning how to read and write. The narratives concluded with the story of escape and the taking on of a new identity—and often a new name as well—in freedom.

In fact, for many former slaves, the actual process of writing the narrative marked the attainment of their identity and freedom, often involving a ritual of self-naming. As William L. Andrews put it in *To Tell a Free Story,* for blacks to write their story was "in some ways uniquely self-liberating, the final, climactic act in the drama of their lifelong quests for freedom." Other typical themes included poignant appeals to white readers to agitate for the abolition of slavery; contrasts between the slaveholder's use of religion to justify slavery and the simple, spiritually based Christianity of the slaves themselves; and the supportive strength of the slave community and the white and black underground network in facilitating a successful runaway.

Although not the first, the prototypical slave narrative was that of Frederick Douglass, whose story is told in Chapter 11. You have seen how he grew up witnessing the horrors of slavery on a Maryland plantation and as an urban slave in Baltimore, learned to read and write, successfully defied the cruel Mr. Covey's efforts to break his will as a slave, and finally escaped to become a leading abolitionist. Similar stories were told by Henry Bibb, William Welles Brown, Olaudah Equiano, Josiah Henson, Harriet Jacobs, Mattie Jackson, Solomon Northup, Sojourner Truth, and many many others, all of whom provided gory details of whippings and the wrenching loss of loved ones.

The two short selections here—from James W. C. Pennington's *Fugitive Blacksmith* (1849) and Harriet Jacobs's *Incidents in the Life of a Slave Girl* (1861)—focus not on white oppression but on the initial process of planning an escape. Jacobs wrote under the pseudonym Linda Brent and as background to this passage discovers that her two children are to be brought to her master's plantation to be "broke in." As you read, look for restraints on running away, anticipated difficulties, sources of support, and the intelligent cleverness of the runaways. What role does religion play in their efforts? What about issues of family, trust, safety, and self-reliance? What do you learn about slavery in these brief descriptions of the first moments of self-emancipation? Can you imagine the impact they had on northern readers, and why abolitionists avidly used the narratives as part of their attack on slavery?

The Flight

It was the Sabbath: the holy day which God in his infinite wisdom gave for the rest of both man and beast. In the state of Maryland, the slaves generally have the Sabbath, except in those districts where the evil weed, tobacco, is cultivated; and then, when it is the season for setting the plant, they are liable to be robbed of this only rest.

It was in the month of November, somewhat past the middle of the month. It was a bright day, and all was quiet. Most of the slaves were resting about their quarters; others had leave to visit their friends on other plantations, and were absent. The evening previous I had arranged my little bundle of clothing, and had secreted it at some distance from the house. I had spent most of the forenoon in my workshop, engaged in deep and solemn thought.

It is impossible for me now to recollect all the perplexing thoughts that passed through my mind during that forenoon; it was a day of heartaching to me. But I distinctly remember the two great difficulties that stood in the way of my flight: I had a father and mother whom I dearly loved,—I had also six sisters and four brothers on the plantation. The question was, shall I hide my purpose from them?

moreover, how will my flight affect them when I am gone? Will they not be suspected? Will not the whole family be sold off as a disaffected family, as is generally the case when one of its members flies? But a still more trying question was, how can I expect to succeed, I have no knowledge of distance or direction. I know that Pennsylvania is a free state, but I know not where its soil begins, or where that of Maryland ends? Indeed, at this time there was no safety in Pennsylvania, New Jersey, or New York, for a fugitive, except in lurking-places, or under the care of judicious friends, who could be entrusted not only with liberty, but also with life itself.

With such difficulties before my mind, the day had rapidly worn away; and it was just past noon. One of my perplexing questions I had settled—I had resolved to let no one into my secret; but the other difficulty was now to be met. It was to be met without the least knowledge of its magnitude, except by imagination. Yet of one thing there could be no mistake, that the consequences of a failure would be most serious. Within my recollection no one had attempted to escape from my master; but I had many cases in my mind's eye, of slaves of other planters who had failed, and who had been made examples of the most cruel treatment, by flogging and selling to the far South, where they were never to see their friends more. I was not without serious apprehension that such would be my fate. The bare possibility was impressively solemn; but the hour was now come, and the man must act and be free, or remain a slave for ever. How the impression came to be upon my mind I cannot tell; but there was a strange and horrifying belief, that if I did not meet the crisis that day, I should be self-doomed—that my ear would be nailed to the door-post for ever. The emotions of that moment I cannot fully depict. Hope, fear, dread, terror, love, sorrow, and deep melancholy were mingled in my mind together; my mental state was one of most painful distraction. When I looked at my numerous family—a beloved father and mother, eleven brothers and sisters, &c.; but when I looked at slavery as such; when I looked at it in its mildest form, with all its annoyances; and above all, when I remembered that one of the chief annoyances of slavery, in the most mild form, is the liability of being at any moment sold into the worst form; it seemed that no consideration, not even that of life itself, could tempt me to give up the thought of flight. And then when I considered the difficulties of the way—the reward that would be offered—the human blood-hounds that would be set upon my track—the weariness—the hunger—the gloomy thought, of not only losing all one's friends in one day, but of having to seek and to make new friends in a strange world. But, as I have said, the hour was come, and the man must act, or for ever be a slave.

Harriet Jacobs—from Incidents in the Life of a Slave Girl

Again and again I had traversed those dreary twelve miles, to and from the town; and all the way, I was meditating upon some means of escape for myself and my children. My friends had made every effort that ingenuity could devise to effect our purchase, but all their plans had proved abortive. Dr. Flint was suspicious, and determined not to loosen his grasp upon us. I could have made my escape alone; but it was more for my helpless children than for myself that I longed for freedom. Though the boon would have been precious to me, above all price, I would not have taken it at the expense of leaving them in slavery. Every trial I endured, every sacrifice I made for their sakes, drew them closer to my heart, and gave me fresh courage to beat back the dark waves that rolled and rolled over me in a seemingly endless night of storms. . . .

My plan was to conceal myself at the house of a friend, and remain there a few weeks till the search was over. My hope was that the doctor would get discouraged, and, for fear of losing my value, and also of subsequently finding my children among the missing, he would consent to sell us; and I knew somebody would buy us. I had done all in my power to make my children comfortable during the time I expected to be separated from them. . . .

Mr. Flint was hard pushed for house servants, and rather than lose me he had restrained his malice. I did my work faithfully, though not, of course, with a willing mind. They were evidently afraid I should leave them. Mr. Flint wished that I should sleep in the great house instead of the servants' quarters. His wife agreed to the proposition, but said I mustn't bring my bed into the house, because it would scatter feathers on her carpet. I knew when I went there that they would never think of such a thing as furnishing a bed of any kind for me and my little one. I therefore carried my own bed, and now I was forbidden to use it. I did as I was ordered. But now that I was certain my children were to be put in their power, in order to give them a stronger hold on me, I resolved to leave them that night. I remembered the grief this step would bring upon my dear old grandmother; and nothing less than the freedom of my children would have induced me to disregard her advice. I went about my evening work with trembling steps. Mr. Flint twice called from his chamber door to inquire why the house was not locked up. I replied that I had not done my work. "You have had time enough to do it," said he. "Take care how you answer me!"

I shut all the windows, locked all the doors, and went up to the third story, to wait till midnight. How long those hours seemed, and how fervently I prayed that God would not forsake me in this hour of utmost need! I was about to risk every thing on the throw of a die; and if I failed, O what would become of me and my poor children? They would be made to suffer for my fault.

At half past twelve I stole softly down stairs. I stopped on the second floor, thinking I heard a noise. I felt my way down into the parlor, and looked out of the window. The night was so intensely dark that I could see nothing. I raised the window very softly and jumped out. Large drops of rain were falling, and the darkness bewildered me. I dropped on my knees, and breathed a short prayer to God for guidance and protection. I groped my way to the road, and rushed towards the town with almost lightning speed. I arrived at my grandmother's house, but dared not see her. She would say, "Linda, you are killing me;" and I knew that would unnerve me. I tapped softly at the window of a room, occupied by a woman, who had lived in the house several years. I knew she was a faithful friend, and could be trusted with my secret. I tapped several times before she heard me. . . . I told her I had a hiding-place, and that was all it was best for her to know.

. . . The tidings made the old doctor rave and storm at a furious rate. It was a busy day for them. My grandmother's house was searched from top to bottom. As my trunk was empty, they concluded I had taken my clothes with me. Before ten o'clock every vessel northward bound was thoroughly examined, and the law against harboring fugitives was read to all on board. At night a watch was set over the town. Knowing how distressed my grandmother would be, I wanted to send her a message; but it could not be done. Every one who went in or out of her house was closely watched. The doctor said he would take my children, unless she became responsible for them; which of course she willingly did. The next day was spent in searching. Before night, the following advertisement was posted at every corner, and in every public place for miles round:—

$300 Reward! Ran away from the subscriber, an intelligent, bright, mulatto girl, named Linda, 21 years of age. Five feet four inches high. Dark eyes, and black hair inclined to curl; but it can be made straight. Has a decayed spot on a front tooth. She can read and write, and in all probability will try to get to the Free States. All persons are forbidden, under penalty of law, to harbor or employ said slave. $150 will be given to whoever takes her in the state, and $300 if taken out of the state and delivered to me, or lodged in jail.

Dr. Flint

Note: James Pennington successfully escaped to New York, where he became a Presbyterian minister and later performed Frederick Douglass's marriage rites. Harriet Jacobs hid for seven years in a cramped, tiny garret in her grandmother's house before finally escaping in disguise by ship; she eventually was reunited with her children. To mislead Dr. Flint as to her location, she wrote letters to him secreted to and postmarked from the North begging him to free her children.

that it is no more harm for you to kill a man, who is trying to kill you, than it is for you to take a drink of water when thirsty." It was Walker, however, who was mysteriously found dead on a Boston street a year after the publication of his "Appeal." Garnet's call for rebellion was clear: "Brethren arise, arise! Strike for your lives and liberties. Now is the day and the hour. . . . You cannot be more oppressed than you have been—you cannot suffer greater cruelties than you have already. RATHER DIE FREEMEN, THAN LIVE TO BE SLAVES. Remember that you are THREE MILLIONS!"

Abolitionists' tactical disagreements helped splinter the movement. Garrison's unyielding personal style and his commitment to even less popular causes such as women's rights offended many abolitionists. In 1840, at its annual meeting in New York, intended as a unity convention to heal growing divisions, the American Anti-Slavery Society split. Several delegates walked out when a woman, Abby Kelley, was elected to a previously all-male committee. One group, which supported multiple issues and moral suasion, stayed with Garrison; the other followed James Birney and the Tappans into the Liberty party and political action.

Class differences and race further divided abolitionists. Northern workers, though fearful of the potential job competition implicit in emancipation, nevertheless saw their "wage slavery" as similar to chattel slavery. Both violated fundamental republican values of freedom and equality. Strains between northern labor leaders and middle-class abolitionists, who minimized the seriousness of workingmen's concerns, were similar to those between white and black antislavery forces. Whites like Wendell Phillips decried slavery as a moral blot on American society, and blacks like Douglass were more concerned with the effects of slavery and discrimination on black people. Moreover, white abolitionists tended to see slavery and freedom as absolute moral opposites: a person was either a slave or free. Blacks, however, knew that there were degrees of freedom and that discriminatory restrictions on freedom existed for blacks in the North just as did relative degrees of servitude in the South.

Furthermore, black abolitionists themselves experienced prejudice, not just from ordinary northern citizens but also from their white abolitionist colleagues. Many antislavery businessmen refused to hire blacks. The antislavery societies usually provided less than full membership rights for blacks, permitted them to do only menial tasks rather than form policy, and perpetuated black stereotypes in their literature. One free black, in fact, described a white abolitionist as one who hated slavery, "especially that slavery which is 1,000 to 1,500 miles away," but who hated even more "a man who wears a black skin."

The celebrated conflict between Garrison and Douglass reflected these tensions. The famous runaway slave was one of the most effective orators in the movement. But after a while, rather than simply describing his life as a slave, Douglass began skillfully to analyze abolitionist policies. Garrison warned him that audiences would not believe he had ever been a slave, and other whites told him to stick to the facts and let them take care of the philosophy.

It was dangerous to be a public abolitionist in this period. In this Winslow Homer engraving for *Harper's Weekly,* titled "Expulsion of Negroes and Abolitionists from Tremont Temple, Boston, Massachusetts, on December 3, 1860," Homer shows Frederick Douglass being forced from the stage by pro-southern demonstrators, who interrupted the meeting called to debate "How can American slavery be Abolished?" The policeman removing Douglass for his safety was reported to have told him that he "must instantly leave," thus ending the debate and meeting before it had hardly begun. *(The Museum of Fine Arts, Houston; The Mavis P. Wilson Kelsey Collection of Winslow Homer Graphics)*

Douglass gradually moved away from Garrison's views, endorsing political action and sometimes even slave rebellion. Garrison's response, particularly when Douglass came out for the Liberty party, was to denounce his independence as "ungrateful . . . and malevolent in spirit." In 1847, Douglass started his own journal, the *North Star,* later called *Frederick Douglass's Paper.* In it, he expressed his appreciation for the help of that "noble band of white laborers" but declared that it was time for those who "suffered the wrong" to lead the way in advocating liberty.

Moving beyond Garrison, a few black nationalists, like the fiery Martin Delany, totally rejected white American society and advocated emigration and a new destiny in Africa. Most blacks, however, agreed with Douglass to work to end slavery and discrimination in the United States. They believed that for better or worse, their home was America and not some distant land they had not known for generations.

These black leaders were practical. David Ruggles in New York and William Still in Philadelphia led black vigilance groups that helped fugitive slaves escape to Canada or to safe northern black settlements. Ministers, writers, and orators such as Douglass, Henry Highland Garnet, William Wells Brown, Samuel Cornish, Lewis Hayden, and Sojourner Truth lectured and wrote journals and slave narratives on the evils of slavery. They also organized a National Negro Convention movement, which began annual meetings in 1830. These blacks met not only to condemn slavery but also to discuss concrete issues of discrimination facing free blacks in the North.

Flood Tide of Abolitionism

Black and white abolitionists, however, agreed more than they disagreed and usually worked together well. They supported each other's publications. The first subscribers to Garrison's *Liberator* were nearly all black, and an estimated 80 percent of the readers of Douglass's paper were white. Weld and Garrison often stayed in the homes of black abolitionists when they traveled. Black and white "stations" cooperated on the Underground Railroad, too, passing fugitives on from hiding places in a black church to a white farmer's barn to a Quaker meetinghouse to a black carpenter's shop.

The two races worked together fighting discrimination as well as slavery. When David Ruggles was dragged from the "white car" of a New Bedford, Massachusetts, railway in 1841, Garrison, Douglass, and 40 other protesters organized what may have been the first successful integrated "sit-in" act of civil disobedience in American history. Blacks and whites also worked harmoniously in protesting segregated schools. After several years of joint boycotts and legal challenges in Massachusetts, in 1855 that state became the first to outlaw segregated public education. Almost exactly 100 years later, the Supreme Court would begin the desegregation of schools throughout the country.

White and black abolitionists were united perhaps most closely by defending themselves against the attacks of people who regarded them as dangerous fanatics bent on disrupting an orderly society. As abolitionists organized to rid the nation of slavery, they aroused many, northerners as well as southerners, who were eager to rid the nation of abolitionists. Mob attacks like the one on Marius Robinson in Ohio in 1836 occurred frequently in the mid-1830s. Abolitionists were stoned, dragged through streets, ousted from their jobs and homes, and reviled by northern mobs, often led or encouraged by leading citizens. Theodore Weld, known as "the most mobbed man in the United States," could hardly finish a speech without disruption. Douglass endured similar attacks, and Garrison was saved from a Boston mob only by being put in jail. In 1837, an antislavery editor in Illinois, Elijah Lovejoy, was murdered and his printing press destroyed.

Anti-abolitionists were as fervid as the abolitionists themselves and equally determined to publicize their cause. "I warn the abolitionists, ignorant and infatuated barbarians as they are," growled one South Carolinian, "that if chance shall throw any of them into our hands, they may expect a felon's death." One widely circulated book in 1836 described opponents of slavery, led by the "gloomy, wild, and malignant" Garrison, as "crack-brained enthusiasts" and "female fanatics" with "disturbed minds." President Jackson joined in, denouncing the abolitionists in his annual message in 1835 as "incendiaries" who deserved to have their "unconstitutional and wicked" activities broken up by mobs. The president went on to urge Congress to ban antislavery literature from the U.S. mails. A year later, southern Democratic congressmen, with the crucial support of Van Buren, succeeded in passing a "gag rule" to stop the flood of abolitionist petitions in Congress.

By the 1840s, despite factionalism and opposition, the antislavery movement had gained significant strength in American life. Many northerners, including many workers otherwise unsympathetic to the goal of ending slavery, decried the mob violence, supported the right of free speech, and denounced the South and its northern defenders as undemocratic. The gag rule, interference with the mails, and the killing of Lovejoy seemed proof of the growing pernicious influence of slave power. Former president John Quincy Adams, who had returned to Washington as a congressman, devoted himself for several years to the

This marriage certificate from 1848, detailing the respective marital requirements of husband and wife, makes clear male dominance and female subservience ("the wife hath not power of her own body"). In that same year, however, women's rights activists began their long struggle for equality at Seneca Falls, New York. *(Library of Congress)*

repeal of the gag rule, which he finally achieved in 1844. In this way, he kept the matter in the public eye until the question of slavery in the territories became the dominant national political issue of the 1850s (see Chapter 14). Meanwhile, black and white abolitionists continued their struggle, using many different tactics without knowing that the only one that would work, and indirectly at that, would be civil war.

Women's Rights

As a young teacher in Massachusetts in 1836, Abby Kelley circulated petitions for the local antislavery society. She came to reform from revivalism and in 1837 wrote, "'Tis a great joy to see the world grow better. . . . Indeed I think endeavors to improve mankind is the only object worth living for." A year later, she braved the threats of an angry crowd in Philadelphia by delivering an abolitionist speech to a convention of antislavery women. Her speech was so eloquent that Weld told her that if she did not join the movement full-time, "God will smite you." Before the convention was over, a mob, incensed by both abolitionists and women speaking in public, attacked with stones and torches and burned the hall to the ground.

After a soul-searching year, Kelley left teaching to devote all her efforts to the antislavery movement and women's rights. When she married Stephen Foster, she retained her own name and went on lecture tours of the West while her husband stayed home to care for their daughter. Other young women were also defining unconventional new relationships while illustrating the profound difficulty of both fulfilling traditional roles and speaking out for change. Angelina and Sarah Grimké, two demure but outspoken Quaker sisters from Philadelphia who had grown up in slaveholding South Carolina, went to New England in 1837 to lecture to disapproving audiences on behalf of abolitionism and the rights of women. After the tour, Angelina married Theodore Weld and stopped her public speaking to show that she could also be a good wife and mother. At the same time, she and Sarah, who moved in with her, undertook the task of compiling most of the research and doing most of the writing for Weld's book attacking American slavery.

Young white couples like the Robinsons, Kelley and Foster, and Grimké and Weld, while pursuing reform, also experimented with equal private relationships in an age that assigned distinctly unequal roles to husbands and wives. The cult of domesticity told women that their sphere was the home, where they served as guardians of piety and virtue, influencing their husbands and children to lead morally upright lives in a harsh, changing economic world. As one clergyman said, although women were not expected to "step beyond the threshold" of the home, their ethical influence would be "felt around the globe." Given moral responsibilities like this, it is not surprising that many women joined the perfectionist movement to cleanse

(Far Left) Elizabeth Cady Stanton (1815–1902) and (Left) Lucretia Mott (1793–1880) were the leaders of the 1848 gathering for women's rights at Seneca Falls, New York. "The acquaintance of Lucretia Mott, who was a broad, liberal thinker on politics, religion, and all questions of reform," Stanton wrote in her autobiography, "opened to me a new world of thought." *(Sophia Smith Collection, Smith College, Northampton, Massachusetts)*

America of its sins. Active in every reform movement, women discovered the need to improve their own condition.

To achieve greater personal autonomy in the antebellum era, American women pursued several paths. The choice depended on class, cultural background, and situation. Thus, in 1834, the Lowell textile workers went on strike to protest wage reductions while looking to marriage as an escape from millwork. Catharine Beecher argued that it was by accepting marriage and the home as a woman's sphere and by mastering domestic duties there that women could best achieve power and autonomy. In another form of "domestic feminism," American wives exerted considerable control over their own bodies by convincing their husbands to practice abstinence, coitus interruptus, and other forms of birth control.

Other women found an outlet for their role as moral guardians by attacking the sexual double standard. In 1834, a group of Presbyterian women formed the New York Female Moral Reform Society. Inspired by revivalism, they visited brothels and opened up a house of refuge in an effort to convert prostitutes to evangelical Protestantism. They went even further, seeking to limit men's sexual behavior by trying to close houses of prostitution and by publicly identifying men who visited them. Within five years, 445 auxiliaries of the Female Moral Reform Society had blossomed.

The Lowell millworkers and New York moral reformers generally accepted the duties—and attractions—of the cult of female domesticity. Other women, usually from upper-middle-class families, did not. They sought control over their lives by working directly for more legally protected equal rights with men. Campaigns to secure married women's control of their property and custody of their children involved many of them. Others, like Kelley and the Grimkés, labored in the abolitionist movement and garnered not only valuable experience in organizational tactics but also a growing awareness of the striking similarities between the oppression of women and that of slaves. As they collected antislavery signatures and spoke out in churches and public meetings, they continually faced denials of their right to speak or act politically. American women "have good cause to be grateful to the slave," Kelley wrote, for in "striving to strike his iron off, we found most surely, that we were manacled *ourselves*."

The more active women became in antislavery activities, the more hostility they encountered, especially from clergymen, who quoted the Bible to justify female inferiority and servility. Sarah Grimké was criticized once too often for her outspoken views. She struck back in 1837 with a series called *Letters on the Condition of Women and the Equality of the Sexes,* claiming that "men and women were created equal" and that "whatever is right for man to do, is right for woman." Arguing that men ought to be satisfied with 6,000 years of dominion based on a false interpretation of the creation story, Grimké concluded that she sought "no favors for my sex. I surrender not our claim to equality. All I ask of our brethren is, that they will take their feet from off our necks and permit us to stand upright on that ground which God designed us to occupy."

Technology Changes the American People

THE SEWING MACHINE

Probably no technological innovation changed everyday life for American women in the second half of the nineteenth century more than the sewing machine. In 1860, *Godey's Lady's Book* hailed the sewing machine as the "queen of invention," crediting it not only with the power to transform the work of American women but also with the ability to "do a hundred times more toward clothing the indigent and feeble than the united fingers of all the [world's] charitable and willing ladies." Like many innovations, the marvelous machine that could fasten two pieces of cloth or leather together using either one thread (the chain stitch) or two (the lock stitch), resulted from 50 years of experimentation on both sides of the Atlantic. The first successful machine may have been one devised by a French tailor, Barthelemy Thimonnier, in 1829. Constructed mostly of wood, the machine had a hooked needle and made a chain stitch. Thimonnier, with the backing of the French government, established a factory with 80 machines. His success in the garment industry, however, was short lived; outraged Paris tailors, who rightly saw that Thimonnier's enterprise threatened their livelihood, attacked the factory and destroyed all the machines.

In the United States, experiments started at least as early as 1818. One of the first significant American technological breakthroughs came in the 1840s. Elias Howe, a former worker at a Massachusetts textile mill, and an apprentice to a Boston maker of precision instruments devised a machine that used an eye-pointed needle that pulled one thread through the cloth to make a loop through which a shuttle with another thread passed, thus producing a lock stitch. Both the eye-pointed needle and the moving shuttle became standard features of the commercial sewing machine.

Singer came up with a device in which the needle moved vertically rather than horizontally (as Howe's machine had done) and where power came from a treadle rather than a handcrank. *(The Granger Collection, New York)*

Howe's first sewing machines were extremely expensive ($300 when the yearly wage of a fully employed and well-paid factory girl might be only $165). Despite his successful demonstration of the machine's abilities (using it, he was able to sew faster than five able seamstresses), he was not able to sell any in the United States. While Howe was in England trying to promote his invention there, Isaac Singer, a one-time mechanic and cabinetmaker, was trying to solve some of the problems connected with the new machine. Securing a patent in 1851, Singer began to manufacture and market his machines.

The basic Singer machine was both practical and complex. Special features made the machine relatively easy to operate but also contributed to its cost. Clothing and shoe manufacturers quickly acquired the machines because they could afford to pay the high prices and recognized the obvious benefits of using them. The introduction of the sewing machine stimulated a period of expansion. By 1858, in Troy, New York, alone 3,000 machines were turning out men's shirts and collars. Larger and more important than the clothing industry, the shoe industry had an immense demand for sewing machines, the first application of technology to the shoe manufacturing process. By 1860, one female worker, using a machine, was able to stitch together enough shoe uppers to keep 20 shoemakers busy.

Despite their marketing success with clothing and shoe manufacturers, sewing machine makers dreamed of selling their wares to the many thousands of women who were sewing by hand for their families. But the purchase price was too high for most family budgets. In 1856, Singer's partner, Edward Clark, came up with the idea of allowing buyers to pay for their machines in installments. The plan succeeded brilliantly. The very next year, sales of Singer machines almost tripled. Clark then hit upon another marketing concept—the trade-in. The Singer Company offered $50 for "old Sewing Machines of any kind" that could be used to finance a new machine. Sales took another leap upward. Profits produced by these innovative schemes allowed improvements in the production of sewing machines that halved prices by 1859. Technological and marketing innovations combined to put machines into the hands of ordinary Americans.

As sewing machines entered American households, they relieved women of their most time-consuming domestic chore: sewing by hand. Harriet Kidder, mother of five, welcomed her new "very valuable household article," which made "sewing a pleasure rather than a toil." The calico dress that once demanded over six hours of hand sewing now could be finished in less than an hour.

Some women ended up doing more and fancier sewing than they had done without their new machines. If one calico dress took only an hour, why not make several? Ruffles, pleats, tucks, and other embellishments could all be made with the machine, and women's fashions reflected the ornamental possibilities now within reach. Sewing machines also transformed other sewing tasks. Quilting became more elaborate, and many quilters during the second half of the nineteenth century used their machines to create complex works of art.

Many women did not have the luxury of using their machines to create elaborate clothes or colorful quilts. Instead, sewing machines became their means of support, as they labored as machine operators in factories or as piece workers at home.

Like most successful innovations, the development of the sewing machine had some surprising consequences. In what ways could you argue that the sewing machine improved women's lives? In what ways could you suggest that it did not? Did the sewing machine have effects on all members of the family or just the women of the household? In what ways did the sewing machine have an impact on the larger society? What does the development of the sewing machine reveal about the process of technological change?

In this competition with five New York seamstresses, Elias Howe demonstrated the superiority of his machine over hand sewing. *(© Collection of the New-York Historical Society)*

Male abolitionists were divided about women's rights. At the World Anti-Slavery Convention in 1840, attended by many American abolitionists, the delegates refused to let women participate. Two upstate New Yorkers, Elizabeth Cady Stanton and Lucretia Mott, were compelled to sit behind curtains and not even be seen, much less be permitted to speak. When they returned home, they resolved to "form a society to advocate the rights of women." In 1848, in Seneca Falls, New York, their intentions, though delayed, were fulfilled in one of the most significant protest gatherings of the antebellum era.

In preparing for the meeting, Mott and Stanton drew up a list of women's grievances. They discovered that even though some states had awarded married women control over their property, they still had none over their earnings. Modeling their "Declaration of Sentiments" on the Declaration of Independence, the women at Seneca Falls proclaimed it a self-evident truth that "all men and women are created equal" and that men had usurped women's freedom and dignity. A man, the Declaration of Sentiments charged, "endeavored in every way he could, to destroy [woman's] confidence in her own powers, to lessen her self-respect, and to make her willing to lead a dependent and abject life." The remedy was expressed in 11 resolutions calling for equal opportunities in education and work, equality before the law, and the right to appear on public platforms. The most controversial resolution called for women's "sacred right to the elective franchise." The convention approved Mott and Stanton's list of resolutions.

Throughout the 1850s, led by Stanton and Susan B. Anthony, women continued to meet in annual conventions, working by resolution, persuasion, and petition

Timeline

1824	New Harmony established
1825	John Quincy Adams chosen president by the House of Representatives
1826	American Temperance Society founded
1828	Calhoun publishes "Exposition and Protest"
	Jackson defeats Adams for the presidency
	Tariff of Abominations
1828–1832	Rise of workingmen's parties
1830	Webster–Hayne debate and Jackson–Calhoun toast
	Joseph Smith, *The Book of Mormon*
	Indian Removal Act
1830–1831	Charles Finney's religious revivals
1831	Garrison begins publishing *The Liberator*
1832	Jackson vetoes U.S. Bank charter
	Jackson reelected
	Worcester v. *Georgia*
1832–1833	Nullification crisis
1832–1836	Removal of funds from U.S. Bank to state banks
1833	Force Bill
	Compromise tariff
	Calhoun resigns as vice president
	American Anti-Slavery Society founded
1834	New York Female Moral Reform Society founded
	National Trades Union founded
	Whig party established
1835–1836	Countless incidents of mob violence
1836	"Gag rule"
	Specie Circular
	Van Buren elected president
1837	Financial panic and depression
	Sarah Grimké, *Letters on the Equality of the Sexes*
	Emerson's "American Scholar" address
1837–1838	Cherokee "Trail of Tears"
1840	William Henry Harrison elected president
	American Anti-Slavery Society splits
	World Anti-Slavery Convention
	Ten-hour day for federal employees
1840–1841	Transcendentalists found Hopedale and Brook Farm
1843	Dorothea Dix's report on treatment of the insane
1844	Joseph Smith murdered in Nauvoo, Illinois
1846–1848	Mormon migration to the Great Basin
1847	First issue of Frederick Douglass's *North Star*
1848	Oneida community founded
	First women's rights convention at Seneca Falls, New York
1850	Nathaniel Hawthorne's *Scarlet Letter* is published
1851	Maine prohibition law
	Herman Melville's *Moby Dick* is published
1853	Children's Aid Society established in New York City
1854	Thoreau's *Walden* is published
1855	Massachusetts bans segregated public schools

campaign to achieve equal political, legal, and property rights with men. The right to vote, however, was considered the cornerstone of the movement. It remained so for 72 years of struggle until 1920, when passage of the Nineteenth Amendment made woman suffrage part of the Constitution. The Seneca Falls convention was crucial in beginning the campaign for equal public rights. The seeds of psychological autonomy and self-respect, however, were sown in the struggles of countless women like Abby Kelley, Sarah Grimké, and Emily Robinson. The struggle for that kind of liberation continues today.

Conclusion

Perfecting America

Inspired by religious revivalism, advocates for women's rights and temperance, abolitionists, and other reformers carried on very different crusades from those waged by Andrew Jackson against Indians, nullificationists, and the U.S. Bank. In fact, Jacksonian politics and antebellum reform were often at odds. Most abolitionists and temperance reformers were anti-Jackson Whigs. Jackson and most Democrats repudiated the passionate moralism of reformers.

Yet both sides shared more than either side would admit. Reformers and political parties were both organized rationally. Both mirrored new tensions in a changing, growing society. Both had an abiding faith in change and the idea of progress yet feared that sinister forces jeopardized that progress. Whether ridding the nation of alcohol or the national bank, slavery or nullification, mob violence or political opponents, both forces saw these responsibilities in terms of patriotic duty. Whether inspired by religious revivalism or political party loyalty, both believed that by stamping out evil forces, they could shape a better America. In this effort, they turned to politics, religion, reform, and new lifestyles. Whether politicians like Jackson and Clay, religious community leaders like Noyes and Ann Lee, or reformers like Garrison and the Grimkés, these antebellum Americans sought to remake their country politically and morally as it underwent social and economic change.

As the United States neared mid-century, slavery emerged as the most divisive issue. Against much opposition, the reformers had made slavery a matter of national political debate by the 1840s. Although both major political parties tried to evade the question, westward expansion and the addition of new territories to the nation would soon make avoidance impossible. Would new states be slave or free? The question increasingly aroused the deepest passions of the American people. For the pioneer family, who formed the driving force behind the westward movement, however, questions involving their fears and dreams seemed more important. We turn to this family and that movement in the next chapter.

Recommended Reading

Religious Revival and Reform Philosophy

Robert Abzug, *Cosmos Crumbling: American Reform and the Religious Imagination* (1994); Richard J. Carwardine, *Evangelicals and Politics in Antebellum America* (1993); Jay P. Dolan, *Catholic Revivalism: The American Experience, 1830–1890* (1978); Charles E. Hambrick-Stowe, *Charles G. Finney and the Spirit of American Evangelicalism* (1996); Mark Y. Hanley, *Beyond a Christian Commonwealth: The Protestant Quarrel with the American Republic, 1830–1860* (1994); Paul Johnson, *A Shopkeeper's Millennium: Society and Revivals in Rochester, New York, 1815–1837* (1978); William McLoughlin, *Revivals, Awakenings, and Reform: An Essay on Religion and Social Change in America* (1980); Stephen Mintz, *Moralists and Modernization: American Pre–Civil War Reformers* (1995); Richard Rabinowitz, *The Spiritual Self in Everyday Life: The Transformation of Personal Religious Experience in 19th Century New England* (1989); Mary Ryan, *Cradle of the Middle Class: The Family in Oneida County, New York, 1790–1865* (1981).

The Political Response to Change: Politics and Parties in the Age of Jackson

Jean Baker, *Affairs of Party* (1983); Donald B. Cole, *The Presidency of Andrew Jackson* (1993); Richard Ellis, *The Union at Risk: Jacksonian Democracy, States Rights, and the Nullification Crisis* (1987); Ronald Formisano, *The Transformation of Political Culture* (1983); Lawrence F. Kohl, *The Politics of Individualism: Parties and the American Character in the Jackson Era* (1989); Richard Latner, *The Presidency of Andrew Jackson: White House Politics, 1829–1837* (1979); Theda Perdue and Michael D. Green, eds., *The Cherokee Removal: A Brief History with Documents* (1995); Michael Paul Rogin, *Fathers and Children: Andrew Jackson and the Subjugation of the American Indian* (1975); Arthur M. Schlesinger, Jr., *The Age of Jackson* (1945); Charles Sellers, *The Market Revolution: Jacksonian America, 1815–1846* (1992); Joel H. Silbey, *The Partisan Imperative: The Dynamics of American Politics Before the Civil War* (1985); Harry L. Watson, *Liberty and Power: The Politics of Jacksonian America* (1990); Major L. Wilson, *The Presidency of Martin Van Buren* (1984).

The Political Response to Change: Political Biographies of the Jacksonian Era

Maurice G. Baxter, *One and Inseparable: Daniel Webster and the Union* (1984); Richard Current, *Daniel Webster and the Rise of National Conservatism* (1955); Clement Eaton, *Henry Clay and the Art of American Politics* (1957); John Niven, *John C. Calhoun and the Price of Union* (1988); Merrill O. Peterson, *The Great*

Triumvirate: Webster, Clay, and Calhoun (1987); Robert Remini, *Life of Andrew Jackson* (1988), *Andrew Jackson and the Course of American Freedom, 1822–1832* (1981), and *Andrew Jackson and the Course of American Democracy* (1984); John William Ward, *Andrew Jackson: Symbol for an Age* (1955).

Perfectionist Reform and Utopianism

Arthur Bestor, *Backwoods Utopias* (1950); Priscilla Brewett, *Shaker Communities, Shaker Lives* (1986); Michael Fellman, *The Unbounded Frame: Freedom and Community in Nineteenth-Century American Utopianism* (1973); Robert Fogarty, ed., *American Utopianism* (1972); Lawrence Foster, *Women, Family, and Utopia: Communal Experiments of the Shakers, the Oneida Community, and the Mormons* (1991); William Kephart and William Zellner, *Extraordinary Groups: An Examination of Unconventional Life Styles,* 4th ed. (1991); Carol A. Kolmerten, *Women in Utopia: The Ideology of Gender in the American Owenite Communities* (1990); Grant Underwood, *The Millenarian World of Early Mormonism* (1993); Kenneth H. Winn, *Exiles in a Land of Liberty* (1989).

Reforming Society

Susan Cayleff, *Wash and Be Healed: The Water-Cure Movement and Women's Health* (1987); Teresa Anne Murphy, *Ten Hours' Labor: Religion, Reform, and Gender in Early New England* (1992); Stephen Nissenbaum, *Sex, Diet, and Debility in Jacksonian America: Sylvester Graham and Health Reform* (1980); W. J. Rorabaugh, *The Alcoholic Republic: An American Tradition* (1979); David Rothman, *The Discovery of the Asylum: Social Order and Disorder in the New Republic* (1971); Alice Felt Tyler, *Freedom's Ferment* (1944); Ian Tyrrell, *Sobering Up: From Temperance to Prohibition in Antebellum America, 1800–1860* (1979); Ronald Walters, *American Reformers, 1815–1860* (1978); Sean Wilentz, *Chants Democratic: New York City and the Rise of the American Working Class, 1788–1850* (1983).

Abolitionism and the Women's Rights Movement

Robert Abzug, *Passionate Liberator: Theodore Dwight Weld and the Dilemma of Reform* (1980); Ellen DuBois, *Feminism and Suffrage: The Emergence of an Independent Women's Movement in America, 1848–1869* (1978); Lawrence Friedman, *Gregarious Saints: Self and Community in American Abolitionism, 1830–1870* (1982); Paul Goodman, *Of One Blood: Abolitionism and the Origins of Racial Equality* (1998); Elisabeth Griffith, *In Her Own Right: The Life of Elizabeth Cady Stanton* (1984); Julie Roy Jeffrey, *The Great Silent Army of Abolitionism: Ordinary Women in the Antislavery Movement* (1998); Gerda Lerner, *The Grimké Sisters from South Carolina: Rebels Against Slavery* (1967); Henry Mayer, *All on Fire: William Lloyd Garrison and the Abolition of Slavery* (1998); Keith Melder, *Beginnings of Sisterhood: The American Woman's Rights Movement, 1800–1850* (1977); Jane A. and William H. Pease, *They Who Would Be Free: Blacks' Search for Freedom, 1830–1861* (1974).

Fiction and Film

Nathaniel Hawthorne's *Blithedale Romance* (1852), a novel set in a utopian community much like Brook Farm, reveals the challenges of perfecting America through socialistic communal experiments and other reforms such as woman suffrage, spiritualism, and prison reform. Hawthorne's *Celestial Railroad and Other Stories* (1963 edition, reprinting stories written in the 1830s and 1840s)—in particular, "The Birthmark," "Rappaccini's Daughter," and the title story—and *The Scarlet Letter* (1850) show the author's struggles to balance the head and the heart, scientific and romantic perfectionism. *The Scarlet Letter* is also a 1995 Hollywood film, but not a particularly good adaptation of Hawthorne's novel. A better version is a four-episode *Scarlet Letter* produced in 1979 by Boston public television station WGBH and available from PBS. Although not fiction, *Walden* (1854), Henry David Thoreau's account of living for two years in a small cabin by Walden Pond, is one of the great creative, imaginative, and naturalistic expressions of the age, exemplifying the transcendentalist message of Ralph Waldo Emerson's "Self-Reliance," "Nature," "The American Scholar," and other essays. *Not for Ourselves Alone: The Story of Elizabeth Cady Stanton and Susan B. Anthony* is a superb documentary produced by Ken Burns for PBS in 1999.

Suggested Web Sites

http://memory.loc.gov/ammem/daghtml/daghome.html

America's First Look into the Camera: Daguerreotype Portraits and Views, 1839–1864. The Library of Congress' daguerreotype collection consists of more than 650 photographs. Portraits, architectural views, and some street scenes make up most of the collection.

http://memory.loc.gov/ammem/naw/nawshome.html

NAWSA Home Page. This Library of Congress site is called "Votes for Women: Selections from the National American Woman Suffrage Association Collection, 1848–1921." It contains 167 books, pamphlets, and other artifacts documenting the suffrage campaign.

http://memory.loc.gov/ammem/vfwhtml/vfwhome.html

Votes for Women: 1850–1920. Portraits, suffrage parades, picketing suffragists, an anti-suffrage display, and cartoons commenting on the movement make up this Library of Congress site.

http://xroads.virginia.edu/~HYPER/DETOC/FEM/home.htm

Women in America. This University of Virginia site takes a look at women in antebellum America, 1820–1842.

http://www.history.rochester.edu/godeys/

Godey's Lady's Book Online Home Page. Here is on-line text of this interesting nineteenth-century journal.

http://www.loc.gov/exhibits/african/influ.html

Influence of Prominent Abolitionists. This Library of Congress exhibit site, with pictures and text, discusses some key African American abolitionists and their efforts to end slavery.

http://www.tocqueville.org/

In Search of Tocqueville's Democracy in America. Text, images, and teaching suggestions are part of this companion site to C-SPAN's recent programming on de Tocqueville.

http://www.ushistoryplace.com

the history place A richly detailed on-line learning environment complete with interactive maps, timelines, history activities, primary source documents, and links to related American history sites.

13

MOVING WEST

CHAPTER OUTLINE

By the 1840s, the frontier was retreating across the Mississippi. As Americans contemplated the lands west of the great river, they debated the question of expansion. Some, like Michigan's senator Lewis Cass, saw the Pacific Ocean as the only limit to territorial expansion. Cass believed that the West represented not only economic opportunity for Americans but also political stability for the nation as well. People crowded into cities and confined to limited territories endangered the Republic, he told fellow senators in a speech. But if they headed west to convert the "woods and forests into towns and villages and cultivate fields" and to extend the "dominion of civilization and improvement over the domain of nature," they would find rewarding personal opportunities that would ensure political and social harmony.

Cass's arguments supporting the righteousness and necessity of westward expansion were echoed again and again in the 1840s. Thousands of men seconded his sentiments by volunteering to join American forces in the war against Mexico in the summer of 1845. Largely untrained, dressed in fanciful uniforms, and called by names like Eagles, Avengers, and Tigers, the companies hurried south. But before long, these supporters of expansion saw the ugly side of territorial adventures: insects, bad weather, poor food, and unsanitary conditions. They discovered that such illnesses as the "black vomit" (yellow fever), dysentery, and diarrhea could kill more men than Mexican bullets. As a member of the American occupying army, Henry Judah also experienced the hostility of conquered peoples. In his diary, he reported, "It is dangerous to go out after night. . . . Four of our men were stabbed today." Not only, he wrote, was a man "by the name of Brown" stabbed in the back, but an "infernal villain cut his throat."

Like Henry Judah, Thomas Gibson, a captain of Indiana volunteers, also paid some of the costs of winning new territories. Less than a month after Cass's speech, he wrote to his wife, Mary, in Charlestown, Indiana. Although glad to report news of an American victory, he described a battlefield "still covered with [Mexican] dead" where "the stench is most horrible." Indiana friends had been killed, and Gibson himself had narrowly escaped. "The ball struck me a glancing blow on the head and knocked me down, but it did not harm me." As for the rest, the weather was foul, and so too was the food—"hard biscuit full of bitter black bugs."

Despite the harsh realities of war, Gibson did not challenge the enterprise. He bragged to Mary that "our little army could go out tomorrow in a fair field of battle and whip fifty thousand of the best Mexican troops that ever were on a field of battle. One thing is certain, we would be willing to try it."

Like other wives and family members at home, Mary was less interested in heroics than in the simple truth: Was Tommy dead or alive? As she anxiously awaited news, she wrote of her great hope: "May God bless you and send you home." Yet even with all her worries and prayers for the war's rapid conclusion, she could not escape the heady propaganda for national expansion. She had heard that Indiana soldiers had "shode themselves great cowards by retreating during battle," and she disapproved. "We all would rather you had stood like good soldiers," she told her husband.

Lewis Cass, Henry Judah, Thomas and Mary Gibson, and thousands of other Americans played a part in the nation's expansion into the trans-Mississippi West. The differences and similarities in their perspectives and in their responses to territorial growth unveil the complex nature of the western experience. Lewis Cass's speech illustrates the hold the West had on people's imagination and shows how some linked expansion to the American belief in individual opportunity and national progress. His reference to its riches reminds us of the gigantic contribution western resources made to national development and wealth. Yet his assumption that the West was vacant points to the costs of white expansion for Mexican Americans and Native Americans and the challenge non-Anglo groups would pose to the inclusiveness of American ideals. The Gibsons' letters show similar preconceptions and racial prejudices. They also portray the winning of the West on a human level: the anxieties, deprivation, enthusiasm, and optimism felt by those who fought for and settled in the West.

This chapter concerns movement into the trans-Mississippi West between 1830 and 1865. First we will consider how and when Americans moved west, by what

This painting by Albert Bierstadt captures the majesty of the western landscape, which dwarfs the Native Americans depicted in the foreground. (The Rocky Mountains, Lander's Peak, *1863, The Metropolitan Museum of Art, Rogers Fund, 1907 (07.123) Photograph by Geoffrey Clements)*

means the United States acquired the vast territories that in 1840 belonged to other nations, and the meaning of "Manifest Destiny," the slogan used to defend the conquest of the continent west of the Mississippi River. Then we explore the nature of life on the western farming, mining, and urban frontiers. Finally, the chapter examines responses of Native Americans and Mexican Americans to expansion and illuminates the ways different cultural traditions intersected in the West.

PROBING THE TRANS-MISSISSIPPI WEST

Until the 1840s, most Americans lived east of the Mississippi. The admission of new states between 1815 and 1840 symbolized the steady settlement of the eastern half of the continent. As frontier log cabins gave way to brick and clapboard houses, farmers cleared and planted land earlier settlers had ignored. Roads replaced tracks, and new churches, schools, stores, and banks attested to the march of settlement toward the Mississippi. By 1860, some 4.3 million Americans had moved west of the great river.

Foreign Claims and Possessions

With the exception of the Louisiana Territory, Spain held title to most of the trans-Mississippi region in 1815. For hundreds of years, explorers, soldiers, settlers, and missionaries had marched north from Mexico to explore and settle the lands lying beyond the Rio Grande and to spread Spanish culture to native peoples. Eventually, Spanish holdings included present-day Texas, Arizona, New Mexico, Nevada, Utah, western Colorado, California, and small parts of Wyoming, Kansas, and Oklahoma. Spanish rulers had tried to keep foreigners out of its northern frontier areas, but increasingly they found this policy difficult to enforce. When Mexico won its independence from Spain in 1821, it inherited this vast area with 75,000 Spanish-speaking inhabitants and numerous Native Americans living there. These people confronted the avid American appetite for expansion that Spain had tried to curb.

To the north of California was the Oregon country, a vaguely defined area extending from California to Alaska. Both Great Britain and the United States claimed the Oregon country on the basis of explorations in the late eighteenth century and fur trading in the early nineteenth. Joint occupation, agreed on in the Convention of 1818 and the Occupation Treaty of 1827, temporarily avoided settling the boundary question.

Early Interest in the West

Americans penetrated the trans-Mississippi West long before the great migrations of the 1840s and 1850s and were familiar with some of its people and terrains. Commercial goals fueled early interest as traders first sought beaver skins in Oregon territory and then bison robes prepared by the Plains tribes in the area around the upper Missouri River and its tributaries.

As early as 1811, Americans engaged in the fur trade in Oregon, and within ten years, fur trappers and traders were actively exploiting the resources of the Rocky Mountain region. Many of the men in the fur business married Indian women, thereby making valuable connections with Indian tribes involved in trapping. They and their wives occupied a cultural middle ground, adopting elements from both American and native ways of life. When the beaver was all but exterminated in the mid-1830s, some of the early traders and trappers acted as guides for Americans who would have little tolerance for the hybrid ways of the mountain men and their families.

Religious idealism also drew some Americans to the West. Two Presbyterian missionary couples, Marcus and Narcissa Whitman and Henry and Eliza Spalding, were among the first to travel to Oregon territory with help from fur traders. Like Methodist and Roman Catholic missionaries (sent from Europe), the Presbyterians hoped to convert Oregon Indians to Christianity. Their fervor drew strength from the fires of the Second Great Awakening and their conviction that without conversion, the Indians were doomed to everlasting torment in hell. Less successful initially in converting the Indians than their Catholic counterparts who were more tolerant of Indian culture, American missionaries also tried to teach Indians how to live like white people. Their missions became early outposts of Americanism.

In the Southwest, the collapse of the Spanish Empire in 1821 gave American traders an opportunity they had long sought. Each year, caravans from "the States" followed the Santa Fe Trail over the plains and mountains, loaded with weapons, tools, and brightly colored calicoes. New Mexico's 40,000 inhabitants proved eager buyers, exchanging precious metals and furs for manufactured goods. Eventually, some "Anglos" settled there. Their economic activities prepared the way for military conquest.

To the south, in Texas, land for cotton rather than trade or missionary fervor attracted settlers and squatters in the 1820s at the very time that the Hispanic population of 2,000 was adjusting to their country's new independence. The lure of cheap land drew more Americans to that area than to any other. By 1835, almost 30,000 Americans were living in Texas. As the largest group of Americans living outside the nation's boundaries at that time, their numbers dwarfed that of Tejanos.

On the Pacific, a handful of New England traders carrying sea otter skins to China anchored in the harbors of Spanish California in the early nineteenth century. By the 1830s, as the near extermination of the animals ruined this trade, a commerce based on California cowhides and tallow developed. New England ships tied up in California ports while hides were collected from local ranches in exchange for clothes, boots, hardware, and furniture manufactured in the East.

Among the earliest easterners to settle in the trans-Mississippi West were tribes from the South and the Old Northwest whom the American government forcibly relocated in present-day Oklahoma and Kansas. Ironically, some of these eastern tribes acted as agents of white civilization by introducing cotton, the plantation system, black slavery, and schools. Other tribes triggered conflicts that weakened the western tribes with whom they came into contact. The Cherokee, Shawnee, and Delaware forced the Osage out of their Missouri and Arkansas hunting grounds, and tribes from the Old Northwest successfully claimed hunting areas long used by Kansas plains tribes. These disruptions foreshadowed white incursions later in the century.

The facts that much of the trans-Mississippi West lay outside U.S. boundaries and that the government had guaranteed Indian tribes permanent possession of some western territories did not curtail American economic or missionary activities. By the 1840s, a growing volume of published information fostered dreams of possession. Government reports by explorers Zebulon Pike and John C. Frémont, among others, provided detailed information about the interior, and guidebooks and news articles described the routes that such fur trappers as Jim Bridger, Kit Carson, and Jedediah Smith had mapped out. Going west was clearly possible. Lansford Hastings's *Emigrants' Guide to Oregon and California* (1845) provided not only the practical information that emigrants would need but also the encouragement that heading for the frontier was the right thing to do.

In his widely read guide, Hastings minimized the importance of Mexican and British sovereignty. California, as a Mexican possession, presented a problem, he conceded, but Oregon did not. "So far from having any valid claim to any portion of it," Hastings argued, Great Britain "had no right even to occupy it." Furthermore, American settlers were already trickling into the Pacific Northwest, bringing progress with them. Surely the day could not be far distant, he wrote approvingly, "when genuine Republicanism and unsophisticated Democracy shall be reared up . . . upon the now wild shores, of the great Pacific," to replace "ignorance, superstition, and despotism."

Hastings's belief that Americans would obtain rights to foreign holdings in the West came true within a decade. In the course of the 1840s, the United States, through war and diplomacy, acquired Mexico's territories in the Southwest and on the Pacific (1,193,061 square miles, including Texas) as well as title to the Oregon country up to the 49th parallel (another 285,580 square miles). Later, with the Gadsden Purchase in 1853, the country incorporated another 29,640 square miles of Mexican territory.

Manifest Destiny

What explained the feverish desire to expand? Bursts of florid rhetoric accompanied territorial growth, and Americans used the slogan "Manifest Destiny" to justify and account for it. The phrase, coined in 1845 by John L. O'Sullivan, editor of the *Democratic Review*, expressed the conviction that the country's superior institutions and culture gave Americans a God-given right, even an obligation, to spread their civilization across the entire continent. Lewis Cass, Henry Judah, the Gibsons, Lansford Hastings, and most other Americans agreed.

This sense of uniqueness and mission was a legacy of early Puritan utopianism and the republicanism of the Revolutionary era. By the 1840s, however, an argument for territorial expansion merged with the belief that the United States possessed a unique civilization. The successful absorption of the Louisiana Territory, rapid population growth, and advances in transportation, communication, and industry bolstered the idea of national superiority and the notion that the United States could successfully absorb new territories. Publicists of Manifest Destiny proclaimed that the nation must do so.

WINNING THE TRANS-MISSISSIPPI WEST

Manifest Destiny justified expansion but did not cause it. Concrete events in Texas triggered the national government's determination to acquire territories west of the Mississippi River. The Texas question originated in the years when Spain held most of the Southwest. Although some settlements such as Santa Fe, founded in 1609, were almost as old as Jamestown, the Spanish considered the sparsely populated and underdeveloped Southwest primarily a buffer zone for Mexico. The main centers of Spanish settlement were geographically distant from one another and thousands of miles from Mexico City. Although these northern borderlands formed a weak defensive perimeter of the Spanish Empire that was increasingly vulnerable as Spain weakened, their legal status was recognized internationally in the Transcontinental Treaty. Moreover, in its treaty negotiations with Spain in 1819, the United States, in return for Florida, accepted a southern border excluding Texas, to which the Americans had vague claims stemming from the Louisiana Purchase.

Annexing Texas, 1845

By the time the treaty was ratified in 1821, Mexico had won its independence from Spain but had scarcely had the opportunity to cope effectively with the borderlands, their people, and their problems or to develop powerful bonds of national identity. Mexicans soon had reason to wonder whether the American disavowal of any claim to Texas in the Transcontinental Treaty would last, for political leaders like Henry Clay began to cry out for "reannexation." Fear about American expansionism, fueled by several attempts to buy Texas and by continuing aggressive American statements, permeated Mexican politics.

In 1823, the Mexican government resolved to strengthen border areas by increasing population. To attract settlers, it offered land in return for token payments and pledges to become Roman Catholics and Mexican citizens. Stephen F. Austin, whose father had gained rights from Spain to bring 200 families into Texas two years earlier, was among the first of the American impresarios, or contractors, to take advantage of this opportunity from the new Mexican government. His call for settlers brought an enthusiastic response, as Mary Austin Holley recalled. "I was a young thing then, but 5 months married, my husband . . . failed in Tennessee, proposed to commence business in New Orleans. I ready to go anywhere . . . freely consented. Just then Stephen Austin and Joe Hawkins were crying up Texas—beautiful country, land for nothing, etc.—Texas fever rose then . . . there we must go. There without much reflection, we did go." Like the Holleys, most of the American settlers came from the South, and some brought slaves. By the end of the decade, some 15,000 white Americans and 1,000 slaves lived in Texas, far outnumbering the 5,000 Tejano inhabitants.

Mexican officials soon questioned the wisdom of their invitation. Although Stephen Austin converted to Roman Catholicism, few settlers gave signs of honoring their bargain with the Mexican government. Most remained far more American than Mexican. Some were malcontents who disliked Mexican laws and customs and limitations on their economic and commercial opportunities. In late 1826, a small group of them raised the flag of rebellion and declared the Republic of

This 1872 painting by John Gast—with its large, goddesslike figure trailing telegraph lines, its parade of settlers, its depiction of technological progress—captures the confidence of white Americans that the acquisition of the West was a positive and inevitable event. It also presents the conventional picture of the settlement of the frontier as a process generated by the movement of people from east to west. In fact, the West was also settled by emigrants moving from Mexico northward and by Indian tribes moving south. *(The Museum of the City of New York)*

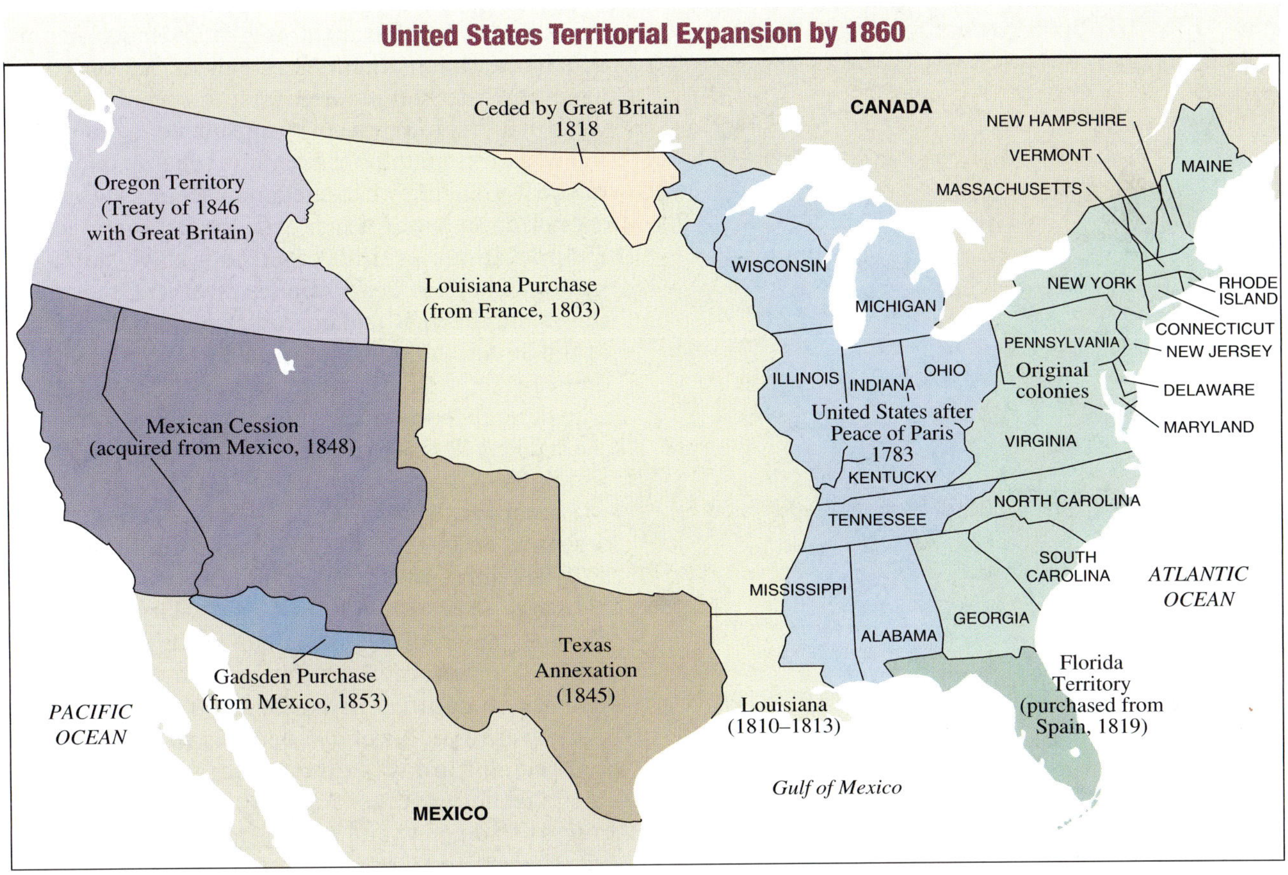

This map reveals that it took over 100 years for the United States to expand from the original 13 colonies to Mississippi. You can see the substantial gains Americans won as a result of the Revolution. Then, as the map shows, within the span of a lifetime, the United States acquired the vast territories across the Mississippi River.

Fredonia. Although Stephen Austin and others assisted in putting down the brief uprising, American newspapers hailed the rebels as "apostles of democracy" and called Mexico an "alien civilization."

Mexican anxiety grew apace. Secretary of Foreign Relations Lucas Aláman accused American settlers of being advance agents of the United States. "They commence by introducing themselves into the territory which they covet," he told the Mexican Congress, "grow, multiply, become the predominant party in the population. . . . These pioneers excite . . . movements which disturb the political state of the country . . . and then follow discontents and dissatisfaction."

In 1829, the Mexican government altered its Texas policy. Determined to curb American influence, the government abolished slavery in Texas in 1830 and forbade further emigration from the United States. Officials began to collect customs duties on goods crossing the Louisiana border. But little changed in Texas. American slave owners freed their slaves and then forced them to sign life indenture contracts. Emigrants still crossed the border and continued to outnumber Mexicans.

Tensions escalated to the brink of war. In October 1835, a skirmish between the colonial militia and Mexican forces signaled the beginning of hostilities. Sam Houston, onetime governor of Tennessee and army officer, became commander in chief of the Texas forces. Although Texans called the war with Mexico a revolution, a Vermont soldier perhaps more accurately observed, "It is in fact a rebellion."

Mexican dictator and general Antonio López de Santa Anna hurried north to crush the rebellion with an army of 6,000 conscripts. Although he had a numerical advantage, many of his soldiers were Mayan Indians who had been drafted unwillingly, spoke no Spanish, and were exhausted by the long march. Supply lines were spread thin. Nevertheless, Santa Anna and his men won the initial engagements of the war: the Alamo at San Antonio fell to him, taking Davy Crockett and Jim Bowie with it. So, too, did the fortress of Goliad, to the southeast.

As he pursued Houston and the Texans toward the San Jacinto River, carelessness proved Santa Anna's undoing. Although fully anticipating an American attack, the Mexican general and his men settled down

This map shows the significance of the American settlement in Texas and the major military engagements of the war. The map also suggests how far the Mexican army had traveled before meeting the Texans on the battlefield.

to their usual siesta on April 21, 1836, without posting an adequate guard. As the Mexicans dozed, the Americans attacked. With cries of "Remember the Alamo! Remember Goliad!" the Texans overcame the army, captured its commander in his slippers, and won the war within 20 minutes. Their casualties were minimal: 8 or 9 dead, 17 wounded. But 630 Mexicans lay dead.

With the victory at San Jacinto, Texas gained its independence. Threatened with lynching, Santa Anna saw little choice but to sign the treaty of independence setting the republic's boundary at the Rio Grande. When news of the disastrous events reached Mexico City, however, the Mexican Congress repudiated an "agreement carried out under the threat of death." Mexico maintained that Texas was still part of Mexico.

The new republic started off shakily. It was financially unstable, unrecognized by its enemy, rejected by its friends. Although Texans immediately sought admission to the Union, their request failed. Jackson, whose agent in Texas had reported that the republic was so weak that "her future security must depend more upon the weakness and imbecility of her enemy than upon her own strength," was reluctant to act quickly and run the risk of war with Mexico. Many northerners violently opposed annexation of another slave state. The Union was precariously balanced, with 13 free and 13 slave states. Texas would upset that equilibrium in favor of the South. Petitions poured into Congress in 1837 opposing annexation, and John Quincy Adams repeatedly denounced the idea. Annexation was too explosive a political issue to pursue; debate finally died down and then disappeared.

For the next few years, the Lone Star Republic led a precarious existence. Mexico refused to recognize its independence but could send only an occasional raiding party across the border. Texans skirmished with Mexican bands, did their share of border raiding, and suffered an ignominious defeat in an ill-conceived attempt to capture Santa Fe in 1841. Diplomatic maneuvering in European capitals for financial aid and recognition was only moderately successful. Financial ties with the United States increased, however, as trade grew and many Americans invested in Texas bonds and lands.

Texas became headline news again in 1844. "It is the greatest question of the age," an Alabama expansionist declared, "and I predict will agitate the country more than all the other public questions ever have." He was right. Although President John Tyler (who assumed office after Harrison's sudden death) reopened the question of annexation hoping that Texas would ensure his reelection, the issue exploded. It brought to life powerful sectional, national, and political tensions and demonstrated how divisive the questions connected to the expansion of slavery into the West could be. Southern Democrats insisted that the South's future hinged on the annexation of Texas. "Now is the time to vindicate and save our institutions," John C. Calhoun insisted. His supporters hoped that by exploiting the Texas issue, Calhoun would win the White House.

Other wings of the Democratic party capitalized more successfully on the issue, however. Lewis Cass, Stephen Douglas of Illinois, and Robert Walker of Mississippi vigorously supported annexation, not because it would expand slavery, a topic they carefully avoided, but because it would spread the benefits of American civilization. Their arguments, classic examples of the basic tenets of Manifest Destiny, put the question into a national context of expanding American freedom. So powerfully did they link Texas to Manifest Destiny and avoid sectional issues that their candidate, James Polk of Tennessee, secured the Democratic nomination in 1844. Polk called for "the reannexation of Texas at the earliest practicable period" and the occupation of the Oregon Territory. Manifest Destiny had come of age.

Whigs tended to oppose annexation, fearing slavery's expansion and the growth of southern power with the addition of another slave state. They accused the Democrats of exploiting Manifest Destiny, more as a means of securing office than of bringing freedom to Texas.

The Whigs were right that the annexation issue would bring victory to the Democrats. Polk won a close election in 1844. But by the time he took the oath of office in March 1845, Tyler had resolved the question of annexation. In his last months in office, Tyler pushed through Congress a joint resolution admitting Texas to the Union. Unlike a treaty, which required the approval of two-thirds of the Senate and which Tyler had failed to win in 1844, a joint resolution needed only majority support. Nine years after its revolution, Texas finally became part of the Union. The agreement gave Texas the unusual right to divide into five states if it chose to do so.

War with Mexico, 1846–1848

When Mexico learned of Texas's annexation, it promptly severed diplomatic ties with the United States. It was easy for Mexicans to interpret the events from the 1820s on as part of a gigantic American plot to steal Texas. During the war for Texas independence, American papers, especially those in the South, had enthusiastically hailed the efforts of the rebels, while southern money and volunteers had aided the Texans in their struggle. Now that the Americans had gained Texas, would they want still more?

In his inaugural address in 1845, President Polk pointed out "that our system may easily be extended to the utmost bounds of our territorial limits, and that as it shall be extended the bonds of our Union, so far from being weakened will become stronger." What were those territorial limits? Did they extend into the territory the Mexican government considered its own?

Polk, like many other Americans, failed to appreciate how the annexation of Texas humiliated Mexico and increased pressures on its government to respond belligerently. Aware of its weakness, the president anticipated that Mexico would grant his grandiose demands: a Texas bounded by the Rio Grande rather than the Nueces River 150 miles to its north, as well as California and New Mexico.

Even before the Texans could accept the long-awaited invitation to join the Union, rumors of a Mexican invasion were afloat. As a precautionary move, Polk ordered General Zachary Taylor to move "on or near the Rio Grande." By October 1845, Taylor and 3,500 American troops had reached the Nueces River. The positioning of an American army in Texas did not mean that Polk actually expected war. Rather, he hoped that a show of military force, coupled with secret diplomacy, would bring the desired concessions. In November, the president sent his secret agent, John L. Slidell, to Mexico City with instructions to secure the Rio Grande border and to buy Upper California and New Mexico. When the Mexican government refused to receive Slidell, an angry Polk decided to force Mexico into accepting American terms. He ordered Taylor south of the Rio Grande. To the Mexicans, who insisted that the Nueces River was the legitimate boundary, their presence constituted an act of war. Democratic newspapers and expansionists enthusiastically hailed Polk's provocative decision; the Whigs opposed it.

It was only a matter of time before an incident occurred to serve as the American justification for hostilities. In late April, the Mexican government declared a state of defensive war. Two days later, a skirmish broke out between Mexican and American troops, resulting in 16 American casualties. When Polk received Taylor's report, he quickly drafted a war message for Congress. The president claimed that Mexico had "passed the boundary of the United States . . . invaded our territory and shed American blood upon American soil." "War exists," he claimed, and, he added untruthfully, "notwithstanding all our efforts to avoid it, exists by act of Mexico."

Although Congress declared war, the conflict bitterly divided Americans. Many Whigs, including Abraham Lincoln, questioned the accuracy of Polk's initial account of the events, and their opposition grew more vocal as time passed. Lincoln called the war one "of conquest brought into existence to catch votes." The American Peace Society revealed sordid examples of army misbehavior in Mexico, and Frederick Douglass accused the country of "cupidity and love of dominion." Many workers also were critical of the war.

Debate continued as American troops swept into Mexico and advanced toward the capital. Although the Mexicans were also fighting Indian tribes on their northern border, the government refused to admit defeat and negotiate an end to the hostilities. The war dragged on and on. The *American Review,* a Whig paper, proclaimed that the conflict was a "crime over which angels may weep." In 1847, a month after General Winfield Scott took Mexico City, Philadelphian Joseph Sills wrote in his diary, "There is a widely spread conviction . . . that it is a wicked & disgraceful war."

In February 1847, American forces, depleted by the departure of 9,000 troops for the Vera Cruz campaign, met Santa Anna's much larger army several miles north of the hacienda of Buena Vista. The Americans, largely inexperienced volunteers, dug themselves into the valley's gullies and ravines. After bitter conflict, the Americans won the day with far fewer casualties than their Mexican opponents. This victory secured northeastern Mexico for the Americans and helped make General Zachary Taylor into a popular hero and potential political candidate. *(Frances Flora Bond Palmer after Joseph H. Eaton,* Battle of Buena Vista. View of the Battle-Ground of "The Angostura" fought near Buena Vista, Mexico February 23rd. 1847. (Looking S. West) *Amon Carter Museum, Fort Worth, Texas 1971.48)*

Yet Polk enjoyed the enthusiastic support of expansionists. Thomas Gibson's men, like most other soldiers, were eager volunteers. Some expansionists even urged permanent occupation of Mexico. Illinois Democratic Senator Sidney Breese told the Senate, "The avowed objects of the war . . . [were] to obtain redress of wrongs, a permanent and honorable peace, and indemnity for the past and security for the future." To secure these goals, Breese could even contemplate permanent occupation with "great ultimate good" to the United States, to Mexico, "and to humanity."

Inflated rhetoric did not win the war, however. In the end, chance helped draw hostilities to a close. Mexican moderates approached Polk's diplomatic representative, Nicholas Trist, who accompanied the American army in Mexico. In Trist's baggage were detailed, though out-of-date, instructions outlining Polk's requirements: the Rio Grande boundary, Upper California, and New Mexico. Although the president had lost confidence in Trist and had ordered him home in chains, Trist stayed in Mexico to negotiate an end to the war. Having obtained most of Polk's objectives, Trist returned to Washington to an ungrateful president. Apparently Polk had wanted more territory from Mexico for less money. Firing him from his job at the State Department, Polk denounced Trist as an "impudent and unqualified scoundrel."

California and New Mexico

Although Texas and Mexico dominated the headlines, Polk made it clear from the early days of his presidency that California and New Mexico were part of any resolution of the Mexico crisis. Serious American interest in California dated only from the late 1830s. A few Americans, mostly traders and shopkeepers, had settled in California during the 1820s and 1830s, but they constituted only a small part of the Spanish-speaking Californio population that had reached 3,200 by 1821. Many had married into Californio families and taken Mexican citizenship. But gradual recognition of California's fine harbors, its favorable position for the China trade, and the suspicion that other countries, especially Great Britain, had designs on the region nourished the conviction that it must become part of the United States.

In 1842, a comic dress rehearsal for rebellion occurred when a U.S. naval commodore, Thomas

The Mexican-American War

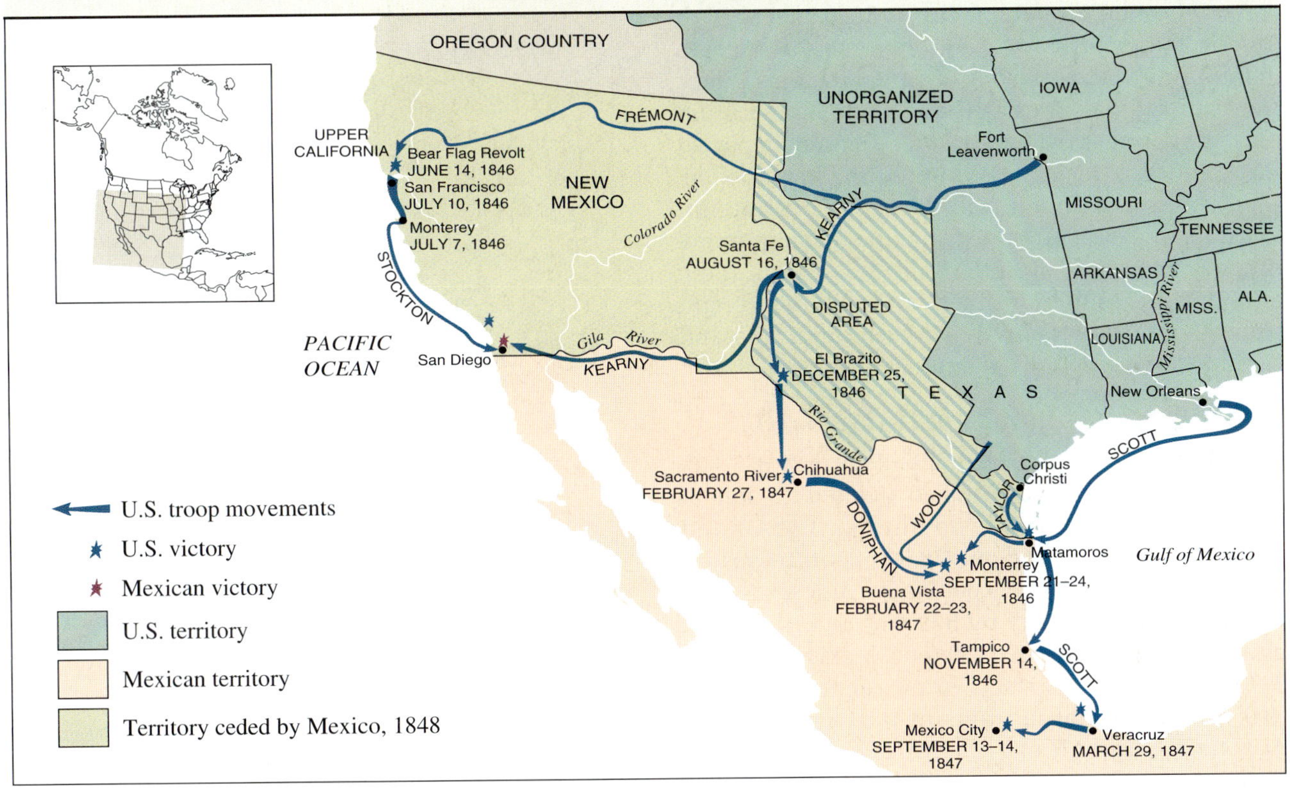

This map shows not only the movements of American troops during the Mexican-American War but also the large area that was in dispute. Note how far into Mexico American troops penetrated during the conflict.

Catsby Jones, believing that war had broken out with Mexico, sailed into Monterey, forced the Mexican commander to surrender, and proclaimed California's annexation. When Jones learned of his error, he apologized and watched the Mexican flag hoisted once more. Yet the arrival of 1,500 American overland emigrants in a three-year period intensified the friction. These newcomers had little interest in blending into Californio society. They and their families wanted an American California. As one resident realized, "The American population will soon be sufficiently numerous to play the Texas game."

In 1845, Polk appointed Thomas Larkin, a successful American merchant in Monterey, as his confidential agent. Larkin had clear instructions should Californians decide to break with Mexico. "While the President will make no effort and use no influence to induce California to become one of the free and independent states of the Union," wrote Polk's secretary of state, James Buchanan, to Larkin, "yet if the people should desire to unite their destiny with ours, they would be received as brethren." Polk's efforts to purchase California suggested that he was sensitive to the fragility of American claims to the region. But Santa Anna, who bore the burden of having lost Texas, was in no position to sell. Thus, in 1846, a few armed American settlers rose up against Mexican "tyranny" and established the "Bear Flag Republic."

New Mexico was also on Polk's list. Ties with the United States began in the 1820s, when American traders began to bring their goods to Santa Fe. Economic profits stimulated American territorial appetites. As the oldest and largest Mexican group in North America (60,000 out of 75,000), however, New Mexicans had little desire for annexation. The unsuccessful attempt by the Texans to capture Santa Fe in 1841 and border clashes in the two following years did not enhance the attractiveness of their Anglo neighbors. But, standing awkwardly in the path of westward expansion and further isolated from Mexico by the annexation of Texas in 1846, New Mexico had an uncertain future as a Mexican province.

In June 1846, shortly after the declaration of war with Mexico, the Army of the West, led by Colonel Stephen W. Kearney, left Fort Leavenworth, Kansas, for New Mexico. Kearney had orders to occupy Mexico's northern provinces and to protect the lucrative Santa Fe trade. Two months later, the army took Santa Fe without a shot, although one eyewitness noticed the "surly countenances" and the "wail of grief . . . above the din of our horses' tread." New Mexico's upper class, who had already begun to intermarry with American merchants and send some sons to colleges in the United States, readily accepted the new rulers. However, ordinary Mexicans and Pueblo Indians did not take conquest so lightly. After Kearney departed for California, resistance erupted in New Mexico. Californios also fought the American occupation force. Kearney was wounded, and the first appointed American governor of New Mexico was killed. In the end, however, superior American military strength won the day. By January 1847, both California and New Mexico were firmly in American hands.

The Treaty of Guadalupe Hidalgo, 1848

Negotiated by Trist and signed on February 2, 1848, the Treaty of Guadalupe Hidalgo dictated the fate of most people living in the Southwest. The United States absorbed the region's 75,000 Spanish-speaking inhabitants and its 150,000 Native Americans and increased its territory by 529,017 square miles, almost a third of Mexico's extent. Mexico received $15 million and in 1853 would receive another $10 million for large tracts of land in southern Arizona and New Mexico (the Gadsden Purchase). In the treaty, the United States guaranteed the civil and political rights of former Mexican citizens and their rights to land and also agreed to satisfy all American claims against Mexico.

If the territorial gains were immense, some costs were equally huge: 13,000 American lives lost, mostly to diseases such as measles and dysentery, and $97 million expended for military operations. Although sporadic violence would continue for years in the Southwest as Mexicans protested the new status quo, the war was over, and the Americans had won.

The Oregon Question, 1844–1846

Belligerence and war secured vast areas of the Southwest and California for the United States. In the Pacific Northwest, the presence of mighty Great Britain rather than the weak, crisis-ridden Mexican government suggested more cautious tactics. There diplomacy became the means for territorial gains. Despite the disputed nature of claims to the Oregon Territory, Polk assured the inauguration day crowd huddled under umbrellas that "our title to the country of Oregon is 'clear and unquestionable,' . . . already our people are preparing to perfect that title by occupying it with their wives and children." Polk's words reflected American confidence that settlement carried the presumption of possession. But the British did not agree. As the *London Times* warned, "Ill regulated, overbearing, and aggressive . . . [Polk's] pretensions amount, if acted upon, to the clearest

The Oregon Country

This map highlights the extravagant claims to Oregon voiced during the election of 1844 and the eventual boundaries established with Great Britain. The major trails that brought American settlers to the West suggest the population movements that lay behind the Oregon controversy.

causa belli which has yet arisen between Great Britain and the American Union."

Though the British considered the president's speech belligerent, Polk was correct in saying that Americans had not hesitated to settle the disputed territories. Between 1842 and 1845, the number of Americans in Oregon grew from 400 to over 5,000. Most located south of the Columbia River in the Willamette valley. By 1843, these settlers had written a constitution and soon after elected a legislature. At the same time, changing conditions set the stage for an eventual compromise. British interests in the area were declining as the near destruction of the beaver caused the fur trade to dwindle. Attractive commercial opportunities elsewhere were opening up; New Zealand and other colonies lured English settlers away from the Pacific Northwest.

Polk's flamboyant posture and the expansive American claims made mediation difficult, however. The Democratic platform and the slogan that had helped elect Polk laid claim to a boundary of 54°40′. In fact, Polk was not willing to go to war with Great Britain for Oregon. Privately, he considered reasonable a boundary at the 49th parallel, which would extend the existing Canadian-American border to the Pacific and secure the harbors of Puget Sound for the United States. But Polk could hardly admit this to his

Democratic supporters, who had so enthusiastically shouted "Fifty-four forty or fight" during the recent campaign.

Soon after his inaugural, Polk offered his compromise to Great Britain. But his tone offended the British minister, who rejected the offer at once. Polk compounded his error by gracelessly withdrawing the suggestion. In his year-end address to Congress in 1845, the president created more diplomatic difficulties. Urging the protection of American settlers in Oregon, he again publicly claimed that Oregon belonged to the United States. In addition, he asked Congress to give Britain the one-year notice required by previous agreements to terminate joint occupation there.

Discussions about Oregon occupied Congress for months in early 1846. Debate, however, gradually revealed deep divisions about Oregon and the possibility of war with Great Britain. Despite slogans, most Americans did not want to fight for Oregon and preferred to resolve the crisis diplomatically. As war with Mexico loomed, this task became more urgent.

The British, too, were eager to settle. In June 1846, the British agreed to accept the 49th-parallel boundary if Vancouver Island remained British. Polk took the unorthodox step of forwarding this proposal to the Senate for a preliminary response. Within days, the Senate overwhelmingly approved the compromise. Escaping some of the responsibility for retreating from slogans by sharing it with the Senate, Polk ended the crisis just a few weeks before the declaration of war with Mexico.

As these events show, Manifest Destiny was an idea that supported and justified expansionist policies. It corresponded, at the most basic level, to what Americans believed, that expansion was both necessary and right. As early as 1816, American geography books pictured the nation's western boundary at the Pacific and included Texas. Poems, essays, and stories about winning the West, enlivened with illustrations of covered wagons and Indian fighters, were standard reading fare. Popular literature typically described Indians as a dying race that had failed in the basic tasks of cultivating the soil and conquering the wilderness. Mexicans were dismissed as "unjust and injurious neighbor[s]." Only whites could make the wilderness flower. Thus, as lands east of the Mississippi filled up, Americans automatically called on familiar ideas to justify expansion.

GOING WEST

After diplomacy and war clarified the status of the western territories, Americans lost little time in moving there. What had been a trickle of emigrants became a flood. During the 1840s, 1850s, and 1860s, thousands of Americans left their homes for the frontier. By 1860, California alone had 380,000 settlers.

Some chose to migrate by sea. Although the trip was expensive, one could sail from Atlantic or Gulf Coast ports around South America to the West Coast or embark for Panama, cross the isthmus by land, and then continue by sea. Most emigrants, however, chose land routes. In 1843, the first large party succeeded in crossing the plains and mountains to Oregon. More followed. Between 1841 and 1867, some 350,000 traveled the overland trails to California or Oregon, while others trekked part of the way to intermediate points like Colorado and Utah.

The Emigrants

Most of the emigrants who headed for the Far West, where slavery was prohibited, were white and American-born. They came from the Midwest and the Upper South. A few free blacks made the trip as well. Pioneer Margaret Frink remembered seeing a "Negro woman . . . tramping along through the heat and dust, carrying a cast iron black stove on her head, with her provisions and a blanket piled on top . . . bravely pushing on for California." Emigrants from the Deep South usually selected Arkansas or Texas as their destination, and many took their slaves with them. By 1840, over 11,000 slaves toiled in Texas and 20,000 in Arkansas.

The many pioneers who kept journals during the five- to six-month overland trip captured the human dimension of emigrating. Their journals, usually their only contribution to the historical record, focused on day-to-day events and expressed some of the thoughts and emotions experienced on the long journey west. One migrant, Lodisa Frizzell, described her feelings at parting in 1852:

> Who is there that does not recollect their first night when started on a long journey, the well known voices of our friends still ring in our ears, the parting kiss feels still warm upon our lips, and that last separating word farewell! sinks deeply into the heart! It may be the last we ever hear from some or all of them, and to those who start . . . there can be no more solemn scene of parting only at death.

Most emigrants traveled with family and relatives. Only during the gold rush years did large numbers, usually young men, travel independently. Migration was a family experience, mostly involving men and women from their late twenties to early forties. A sizable number of them had recently married. And for most, migration was a familiar experience. Like other geographically mobile Americans, emigrants to the Far West had earlier moved to other frontiers, often as children or as newlyweds. The difference was the vast distance to this frontier and the seemingly final separation from home.

Migrants' Motives

What led so many Americans to sell most of their possessions and embark on an unknown future thousands of miles away? Many believed that frontier life would offer rich opportunities. A popular folk song expressed this widespread conviction:

Since times has been hard, I'll tell you sweetheart,
I've a notion to leave off my plow and my cart,
Away to Californy a journey pursue,
To double my fortunes as other men do.

Western Population Advance, 1830–1850

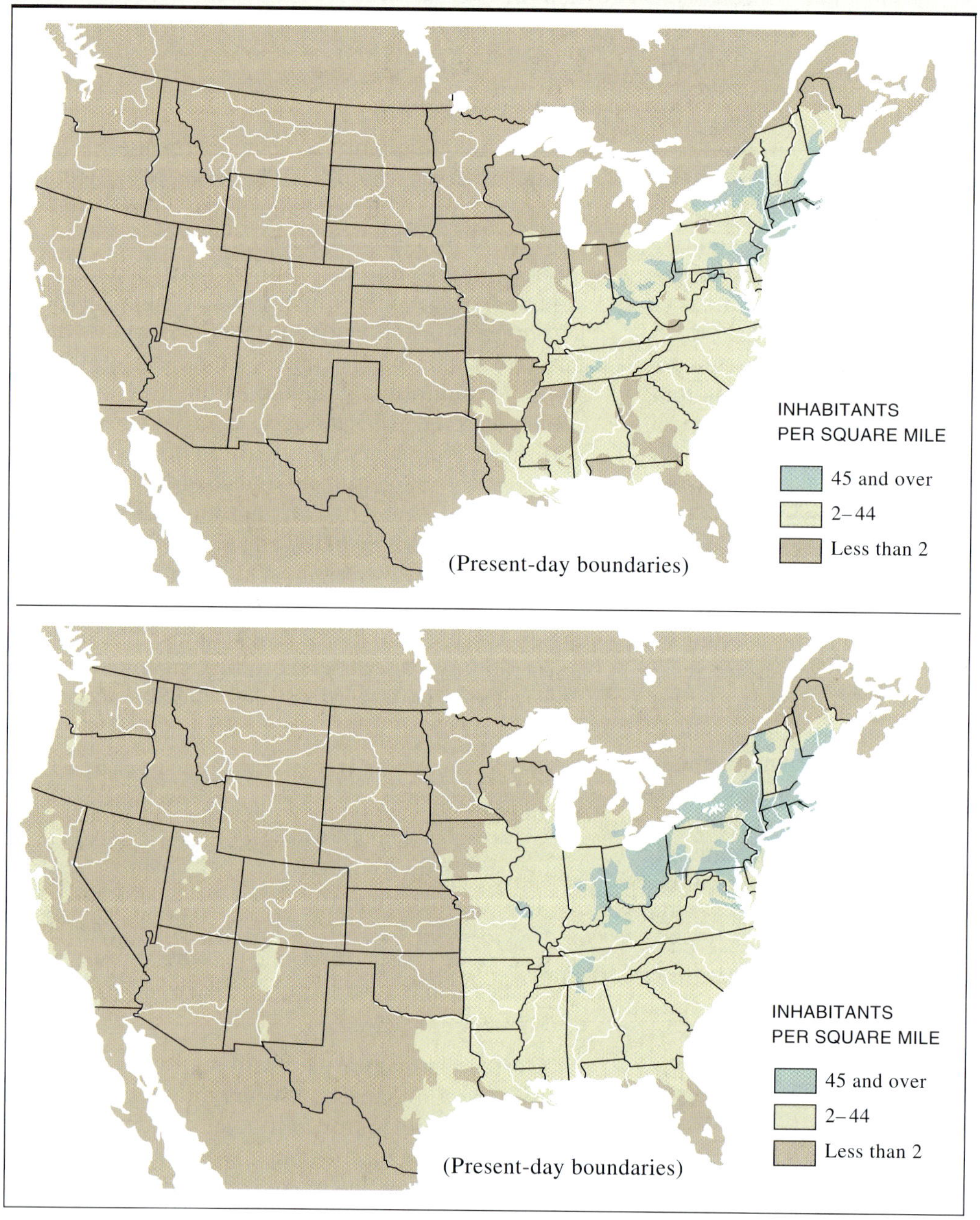

Within a 20-year period, as this map shows, the eastern half of the nation was almost completely settled, while some areas of the trans-Mississippi West acted as magnets for emigrants. Despite the considerable disruption to nature and the peoples living near the overland trails caused by emigrant trains, many parts of the West were little touched by white settlement until after the Civil War.

The kinds of opportunities emigrants expected varied widely. Thousands sought riches in the form of gold. Others anticipated making their fortune as merchants, shopkeepers, and peddlers. Some intended to speculate in land, acquiring large blocks of public lands and then selling them later to settlers at a handsome profit. The possibility of professional rewards gained from practicing law or medicine on the frontier attracted still others.

Most migrants dreamed of bettering their life by cultivating the land. As one settler explained, "The motive that induced us to part with pleasant associates and dear friends of our childhood days, was to obtain from the government of the United States a grant of land that 'Uncle Sam' had promised." Federal and state land policies made the acquisition of land increasingly alluring. Preemption acts during the 1830s and 1840s gave "squatters" the right to settle public lands before the government offered them for sale and then allowed them to purchase these lands at the minimum price once they came on the market. At the same time, the amount of land a family had to buy shrank to only 40 acres. In 1862, the Homestead Act went further by offering 160 acres of government land free to citizens or future citizens over 21 who lived on the property, improved it, and paid a small registration fee. Oregon's land policy, which predated the Homestead Act, was even more generous. It awarded a single man 320 acres of free land and a married man 640 acres provided he occupied his claim for four years and made improvements.

Some emigrants hoped the West would restore them to health. Settlers from the Mississippi valley wished to escape the region's debilitating agues and fevers. Doctors advised those suffering the dreaded tuberculosis that the long out-of-doors trip and the western climate might cure them. Even invalids grasped at the advice offered by one doctor in 1850, who urged them to "attach themselves to the companies of emigrants bound for Oregon or Upper California."

Others pursued religious or cultural missions in the West. Missionary couples like David and Catherine Blaine, who settled in Seattle when it was a frontier outpost, determined to bring Protestantism and education west. Stirred by the stories they had heard of the "deplorable morals" on the frontier, they willingly left the comforts of home to evangelize and educate westerners. Still others, like the Mormons, made the long trek to Utah to establish a society in conformity with their religious beliefs.

Not everyone who dreamed of setting off for the frontier could do so, however. Unlike the moves to earlier frontiers, the trip to the Far West involved considerable expense. The sea route, while probably the most comfortable, was the most costly. Guidebooks estimated that the trip around Cape Horn came to $600 per person. For the same sum, four people could make the overland trip. And if the emigrants sold their wagons and oxen at the journey's end, the final expenses might amount to only $220. Clearly, however, the initial financial outlay was considerable enough to rule out the trip for the very poor. Despite increasingly liberal land policies, migration to the Far West (with the exception of group migration to Utah) was a movement of middle-class Americans.

This illustration of a young woman being carried away by a Comanche chief came from a book entitled *Thrilling Adventures Among the Indians,* published in 1850. An increasingly racist view of Native Americans, nourished by popular accounts of Indians as "savage brute[s]," colored emigrants' views of Indians they encountered in the trans-Mississippi West and seemed to justify disregarding native rights. *(The Newberry Library)*

The Overland Trails

The trip started for most emigrants in the late spring when they left their homes and headed for starting points in Iowa and Missouri: Council Bluffs, Independence, Westport, St. Joseph. There, companies of wagons gathered, and when grass was up for the stock, usually by the middle of May, they set out. Emigrant trains first followed the valley of the Platte

Recovering the Past

PERSONAL DIARIES

Nineteenth-century journals kept by hundreds of ordinary men and women traveling west on the overland trails constitute a rich source for exploring the nature of the westward experience. They are also an example of how private sources can be used to deepen our understanding of the past. Diaries, journals, and letters all provide us with a personal perspective on major happenings. These sources tend to focus on the concrete, so they convey the texture of daily life in the nineteenth century, daily routines and amusements, clothing, habits, and interactions with family and friends. They also provide evidence of the varied concerns, attitudes, and prejudices of the writers, thus providing a test of commonly accepted generalizations about individual and group behavior.

Like any historical source, personal documents must be used carefully. It is important to note the writer's age, sex, class, and regional identification. Although this information may not be available, some of the writer's background can be deduced from what he or she has written. It is also important to consider for what purpose and for whom the document was composed. This information will help explain the tone or character of the source and what has been included or left out. It is, of course, important to avoid generalizing too much from one or even several similar sources. Only after reading many diaries, letters, and journals is it possible to make valid generalizations about life in the past.

Here we present excerpts from two travel journals of the 1850s. Few of the writers considered their journals to be strictly private. Often, they were intended as a family record or as information for friends back home. Therefore, material of a personal nature has often been excluded. Nineteenth-century Americans referred to certain topics, such as pregnancy, only indirectly or not at all.

One excerpt comes from Mary Bailey's 1852 journal. Mary was 22 when she crossed the plains to California with her 32-year-old doctor husband. Originally a New Englander, Mary had lived in Ohio for six years before moving west. The Baileys were reasonably prosperous and were able to restock necessary supplies on the road west. The other writer, Robert Robe, was 30 when he crossed along the same route a year earlier than the Baileys, headed for Oregon. Robert was a native of Ohio and a Presbyterian minister.

As you read these excerpts, notice what each journal reveals about the trip west. What kinds of challenges did the emigrants face on their journey? Do these correspond to the picture you may have formed from novels, television, and movies? What kinds of work needed to be done, and who did it? Can you see any indication of a division of work based on sex? What kinds of interactions appear to have occurred between men and women on the trip? What does the pattern tell us about nineteenth-century society? How does the painting of the "emigrant train" reinforce the journal accounts of men's and women's roles?

Even these short excerpts suggest that men and women, as they traveled west, may have had different concerns and different perspectives on the journey. In what ways do the two accounts differ, and in what ways are they similar?

(Benjamin Reinhardt, The Emigrant Train Bedding Down for the Night, *1867, 40 x 70 in. oil on canvas. In the Collection of the Corcoran Gallery of Art, Washington, D.C., Gift of Mr. and Mrs. Landsell K. Christie, 59.21)*

Journal of Mary Stuart Bailey

Wednesday, April 13, 1852 Left our hitherto happy home in Sylvania amid the tears of parting kisses of dear friends, many of whom were endeared to me by their kindness shown to me when I was a stranger in a strange land, when sickness and death visited our small family & removed our darling, our only child in a moment, as it were. Such kindness I can never forget. . . .

Friday, 21st [May] Rained last night. Slept in the tent for the first time. I was Yankee enough to protect myself by pinning up blankets over my head. I am quite at home in my tent.

12:00 Have traveled in the rain all day & we are stuck in the mud. I sit in the wagon writing while the men are at work doubling the teams to draw us out....

Sunday, 23rd. Walked to the top of the hill where I could be quiet & commune with nature and nature's God. This afternoon I was annoyed by something very unpleasant & shed many tears and felt very unhappy. . . .

Thursday, 4th [June] Very cold this morning after the shower. . . . We stopped on the banks of the Platte to take dinner. I am sitting on the banks of the Platte with my feet almost in the water. Have been writing to my Mother. How I wish I had some of my own relations with me....

Sunday, 4th [July] Started at 3 o'clock to find feed or know where it was. Had to go 4 or 5 miles off the road. Found water & good grass. Camped on the sand with sage roots for fuel. It is wintery, cold & somewhat inclined to rain, not pleasant. Rather a dreary Independence Day. We speak of our friends at home. We think they are thinking of us. . . .

Monday, 12th. Stayed in camp another day to get our horse better. He is much improved. It is cold enough. Washed in the morning & had the sick headache in the afternoon. . . .

Thursday, 12th [August] Very warm. Slept until we stopped to take breakfast. Mr. Patterson starts as soon as light & stops in the heat of the day to rest the animals. We do not have much time to do anything except 4 or 5 hours in the middle of the day. . . .

Friday, 17th [September] Have been confined ever since Monday with ague in my face which is very much swollen. Have suffered very much. We are now in Carson Valley. Plenty of trees but the country is very barren.

Saturday, 18th. Very pleasant, delightful weather. Feel much better today. We are not stirring this afternoon. We have heard to a great deal of suffering, people being thrown our on the desert to die & being picked up & brought to the hospital. . . .

Source: Sandra L. Myers, ed., Ho for California! Women's Overland Diaries from the Huntington Library *(San Marino, CA: Henry F. Huntington Library, 1980).*

Journal of Robert Robe

[May] 19, [1851] A fine day. The first spent in travelling on the plains of the Platte river.

20. Continue our journey up the Platte valley which I would judge to be here some 12 miles wide on this side of the river. The only game seen here are the antelope and wolf beside some wild fowl.

21. A rainy morning started early passed an old Pawnee village in ruins. The houses are constructed by placing timbers in forks and upon these without placing upright poles then rushes bound with [illegible] and finally earth. Chimney in center. Day became more & more rainy and wound up with a storm which beggared description.

22. Bluff approach the river—travelling less monotonous river finely skirted with timber.

23. Roads very muddy in afternoon. Today our wagon severed itself from our former companions & joined a company of Californians.

24. Before starting a trader direct from Ft. Kearney arrived at our camp. He informs us it is yet 25 miles thither. Travelling is by no means dangerous a waggon of provisions passing with only three guards. In the afternoon passed the entrance of the Independence Weston & St. Jo. roads. Emigrants became more numerous.

25. Passed Fort Kearney this morning and after a short drive encamped. Having conversed with some of the soldiers I find they consider life very monotonous.

26. Roads heavy—short drive—a storm.

27. High Bluffs on the opposite side of river approach and present a beautiful appearance. At night a fearful storm.

28. Roads heavy nothing singular.

29. Have arrived in the region abounding in Buffalo. At noon a considerable herd came in sight. The first any of us had ever seen. Thus now for the chase—the horsemen proved too swift in pursuit and frightened them into the Bluffs without capturing any—the footmen pursued however and killed three pretty good success for the first.

30. Nothing remarkable today.

31. Game being abundant we resolved to rest our stock and hunt today—Started in the morning on foot. Saw probably 1,000 Buffalo. Shot at several and killed one. Where ever we found them wolves were prowling around as if to guard them. Their real object is however no doubt to seize the calves as their prey. Saw a town of Prairie dogs, they are nearly as large as a gray squirrel. They bark fiercely when at a little distance but on near approach flee to their holes. Wherever they are we see numerous owls. After a very extensive ramble and having seen a variety of game we returned at sunset with most voracious appetites.

June 1. The Bluffs became beautifully undulating losing their precipitous aspect and the country further back is beautifully rolling prairie.

2. In the evening camped beside our old friends Miller and Dovey. They had met with a great loss this morning their 3 horses having taken fright at a drove of buffalo and ran entirely away. Some of our company killed more buffalo this evening & a company went in the night with teams to bring them in.

Source: Pacific Northwest Quarterly 19 *(January 1928): 52–63.*

Overland Trails to the West

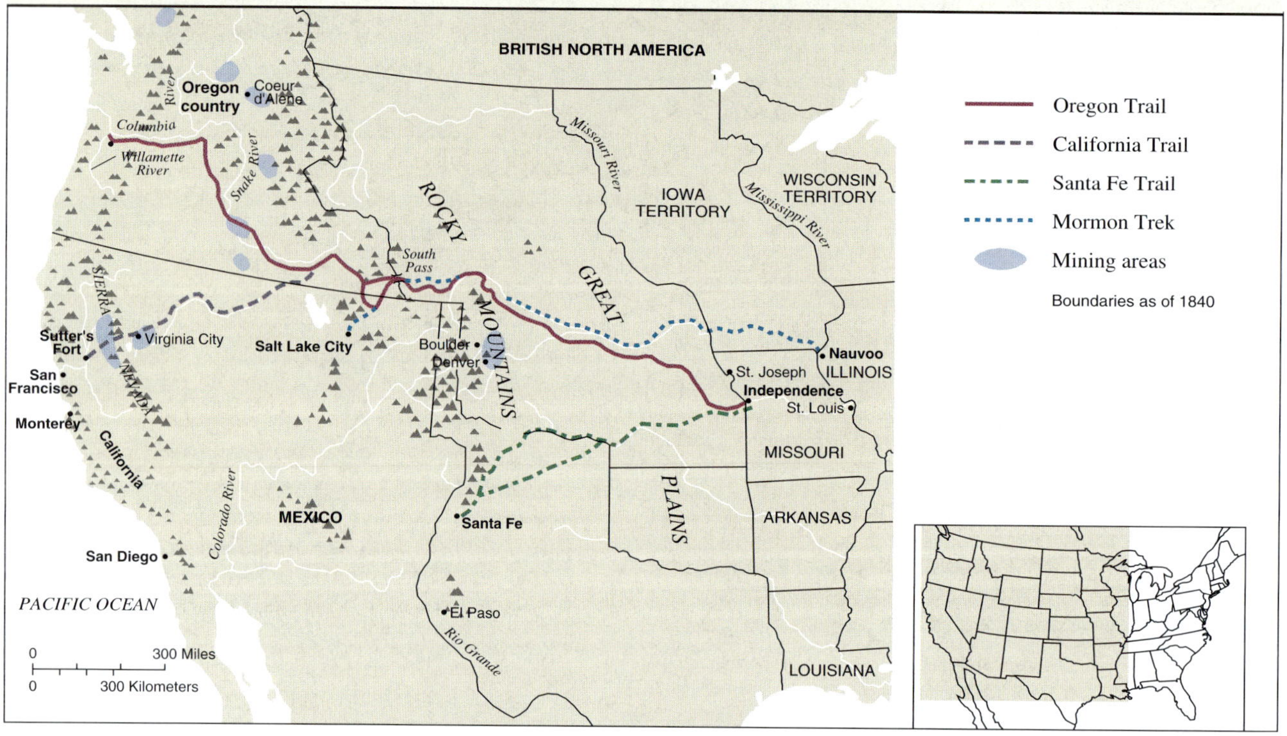

The various trails over which thousands of Americans traveled during the 1840s, 1850s, and 1860s are depicted on this map. The geographic features begin to suggest the increasing number of natural obstacles that travelers faced during the last months of their trip.

River. Making only 15 miles a day, they slowly wound their way through the South Pass of the Rockies, heading for destinations in California or Oregon.

Emigrants found the first part of the trip novel and even enjoyable. The Indians, one woman noted, "proved better than represented"; some even helped emigrants cross rivers swollen by spring rains. The scenery, with its spring and early summer flowers, was new. Familiar chores were a challenge out in the open. The traditional division of labor known at home persisted. Generally, men did the "outdoor" work. They drove and repaired the wagons, ferried cattle and wagons across rivers, hunted, and stood guard at night. Women labored at domestic chores, caring for children, cooking meals, and washing clothes. As they had at home, women procured small treats, trading with each other and with Indians for buffalo meat, fish, or moccasins. During travel, young children stayed out of the way in the wagons, while older brothers and sisters walked alongside and lent a hand to their elders. Many of the children later remembered the trip as an exciting adventure. Sometimes a day off from traveling provided a chance for fun. Wagon trains might stop to observe the Sabbath, allowing men and animals time to rest and women an opportunity to catch up on the laundry.

As the trip lengthened, difficulties multiplied. Cholera often took a heavy toll. Conflict with Indians became a problem only in the 1850s and made emigrants jumpy during the second half of the trip. (Between 1840 and 1860, Indians killed about 400 emigrants, most during the second half of the trip; the emigrants themselves killed at least that many Indians.) Traveling grew more arduous as deserts and mountains replaced rolling prairies.

Emigrants had to cross the final mountain ranges of the Sierras and the Cascades before the first snowfall, so there was a pressing need to push ever onward. Animals weakened by constant travel, poor feed, and bad water sickened, collapsed, and often died. As families faced the harsh realities of travel, they had to lighten their wagons by throwing out possessions lovingly brought from home. Food grew scarce.

The familiar division of responsibilities often broke down. Women found themselves driving wagons, loading them, even helping to drag them over rocky mountain trails. Their husbands worked frantically with the animals and the wagons as the time of the first snowfall drew closer. Tempers frayed among tired, overworked, and anxious families. Finally, five or six months after setting out, emigrants arrived, exhausted and often penniless, in Oregon or

This view of a Mormon wagon train in the 1850s gives some idea of the rough terrain that emigrant families encountered as they went west. The Mormon migrations were the most organized of the migrations into the trans-Mississippi West, although not all Mormons were lucky enough to travel by wagon. Some emigrants to Utah pushed handcarts across the plains to their destination. *(Used by permission, Utah State Historical Society, all rights reserved. Photo no. 10077)*

California. As one wrote on a September day in 1854, her journey had ended, "which for care, fatigue, tediousness, perplexities and dangers of various kinds, can not be excelled."

The strains of the trip led some groups to draw up rules and elect officers. This did not prevent dissension, however. Many companies split because of arguments over the pace of travel or the number of rest stops or because some changed their minds about their eventual destination. Family harmony often collapsed under the strain of increased workloads, the irritations of travel, and crises of sickness and even death. Mary Power, who with her husband and three children crossed in 1853, revealed exasperation and depression in her journal: "I felt my courage must fail me, for there we were in a strange land, almost without anything to eat, [with] a team that was not able to pull an empty wagon." In a letter she was even more candid: "I felt as though myself and the little ones were at the mercy of a madman." Men, too, lost nerve as they confronted the hazards of travel. Oregon-bound John Minto described coming upon a father of four, "lying on his back upon a rock, taking the rain in his face, seemingly given up all thought of manly struggle," while the cry of Indians sent some men in another train into their wagons to hide.

LIVING ON THE FRONTIER

When emigrants finally reached their destinations, their feelings ranged from acute disappointment to buoyant enthusiasm. But whether elated or depressed, they had no choice but to start anew. As they turned toward building a new life, they naturally drew on their experiences back East. "Pioneers though we are, and proud of it, we are not content with the wilds . . . with the idleness of the land, the rudely construct[ed] log cabin," one Oregon settler explained. "Pioneers are not that kind of folks."

Farming on the Frontier

Pioneer farmers faced the urgent task of establishing their homesteads and beginning farming. First, the family had to locate a suitable claim. Clearing the land and constructing a crude shelter followed. Only then could crops be planted.

As farmers labored "to get the land subdued and the wilde nature out of it," they repeated a process that had occurred on earlier frontiers. Felling timber, pulling out native plants that seemed to have no value, and planting familiar crops began a transformation of the landscape (see the final section of Chapter 10). The results were often unanticipated. When they planted their crops, for example, farmers unknowingly introduced weeds whose seeds were mixed in with plant seeds from home. Some of the weeds, like the Canadian thistle, might do even better than the intended crops. Over time, the weeds could become much more than a nuisance to be pulled out of the ground. The Canadian thistle, for example, moved from field to pasture, where it gradually displaced grass and rendered the land useless for livestock grazing.

As they began their agricultural operations, emigrants did not recognize the ecological patterns that seem so clear to us today. The goal of taming nature was so central and the task so challenging that there was little time or inclination to question long-range consequences.

Because emigrants brought so few of their possessions west, the work of getting started was even more difficult than it would have been in the East. A young Oregon bride who set up housekeeping in the 1840s with only a stew kettle and three knives was not unusual. A letter from Sarah Everett to her sister-in-law in the East told the tale of hardship. Pleased with a gift of pretty trimmings, Sarah confessed, "I am a very old woman. My face is thin sunken and wrinkled, my hands bony and withered and hard—I shall look strangely I fear with your nice undersleeves and coquettish cherry bows." Sarah was 29 years old.

After months of intense interaction with other travelers, families were now alone on their claims. The typical frontier household consisted of parents with one to four children. Although frontier families might interact with nearby Indians, cultural biases made close friendships difficult. No wonder the pioneers often felt lonely and thought longingly of old friends. No wonder either that women helped men with their work and men assisted their wives in domestic chores such as washing.

For several years, such isolation was the rule. One pioneer remembered, "We were . . . 'all told,' eleven families within a radius of six or eight miles, widely separated by our holdings and three hundred and twenty acres to each family. In those days anyone residing within twenty miles was considered a neighbor." But the isolation usually ended within a few years as most areas attracted new emigrants and old settlers seeking better claims.

As rural communities grew, settlers worked to establish schools, churches, and clubs. These organizations drew together people from different places and backgrounds and helped mold them into a new community. They also served to redefine acceptable forms of behavior and remind members of conventional standards and beliefs.

The determination to reestablish familiar institutions was most apparent in politics and law. In Oregon, for example, the pioneers set up a political system based on eastern models before the status of the territory was resolved. Before permanent schools or churches existed, men resumed the familiar political rituals of voting, electioneering, and talking politics. They were also going to court to resolve controversies and to ensure law and order. Although modern movies and novels suggest that violence was a part of everyday life on the frontier, this was not true on the farming frontier. Courts, rather than rough-and-ready vigilante groups, usually handled the occasional violence.

Setting up a common school system was more difficult and less urgent in the eyes of many frontier communities than beginning political life. Few settlers initially thought education important enough to tax themselves for permanent public schools. There were some schools, of course. But most operated sporadically and only for students who could pay at least part of the fees.

Various obstacles hindered organized religion. Although settlers often attended early church services no matter what the denomination, community growth proved a mixed blessing. When confirmed believers gathered in their own churches, they often discovered to their dismay that the congregation was too small to sustain the new church financially. Nor were converts plentiful, for many settlers had grown out of the habit of regular churchgoing. In early Seattle, Catherine and David Blaine were shocked. "Observation and experience have taught us since we left home," David remarked, "the unwelcome lesson that separation from gospel influences has rendered them quite indifferent to gospel truth." Catherine believed, "This is an awfully wicked country."

The chronic shortage of cash on the frontier retarded the growth of both schools and churches. Until farmers could send their goods to market, they had little cash to spare. Geographic mobility also contributed to institutional instability. Up to three-quarters of the population of a frontier county might vanish within a ten-year period as emigrants left to seek better land. Some farmed in as many as four locations until they found a satisfactory claim. Institutions relying on continuing personal and financial support suffered accordingly.

Yet even if their efforts to re-create familiar institutional life often faltered, settlers did not lose sight of their goals. Newspapers, journals, and books, which circulated early on the frontier, reinforced familiar values and norms and kept determination strong. As more and more settlers arrived, the numbers willing to support educational, religious, and cultural institutions grew. In the end, as one pioneer pointed out, "We have a telegraph line from the East, a daily rail road train, daily mail and I am beginning to feel quite civilized. And here ended my pioneer experience." Only 16 years had passed since she had crossed the Plains.

Although the belief in the frontier's special economic and social opportunities encouraged emigration, the dream was often illusory. Western society rapidly acquired a social and economic structure similar to that of the East. Frontier newspapers referred to leading settlers as the "better" sort, giving voice to an emerging world of social and economic distinctions. The appearance of workers for hire and tenant farmers also pointed to real economic differences and hinted at the difficulties those on the bottom would face as they tried to improve their situation.

Their widespread geographic mobility also indicates that many found it difficult to capitalize on the benefits of homesteading. Census data show that those who moved were generally less successful than the core of stable residents, who became the community's economic and social leaders. Of course, those on the move may have believed that fortune would finally smile on them at their next stop. But one wife was not so hopeful. When her husband announced that they were to move once again, she commented, "Perhaps I was not quite so enthusiastic as he. I seemed to have heard all this before."

Mining Western Resources

The mineral riches of the trans-Mississippi West prompted people to leave their ordinary lives behind and set out to make their fortunes. News of the discovery of gold in 1848 in California swept the country like "wildfire," according to one Missouri emigrant. Thousands raced to cash in on the bonanza. Within a year, California's population ballooned from 14,000 to almost 100,000. By 1852, that figure had more than doubled.

Like migrants who planned to establish farms in the West, the "forty-niners" were mostly young (in 1850, over half the people in California were in their twenties). Unlike pioneers headed for the rural frontier, however, the gold seekers were unmarried, predominantly male, and heterogeneous. Of those pouring into California in 1849, about 80 percent came from the United States, 8 percent from Mexico, and 5 percent from South America. The rest came from Europe and Asia. Few were as interested in settling the West as they were in extracting its precious metals and returning home rich.

California was the first and most dramatic of the western mining discoveries. But others followed. Rumors of gold propelled between 25,000 and 30,000 emigrants, many from California, to British Columbia

Charles Nalil's 1856 painting *Saturday Night at the Mines* creates a rather cozy picture of the men. But the presence of the bottle, the miners' rough clothing and beards, all show that the miners made little pretense of upholding eastern manners. Miners went west to get rich, not to advance civilization. *(Stanford University Museum of Art, 12083, Gift of Jane Lathrop Stanford)*

in Canada in 1858. A year later, news of gold strikes in Colorado set off another frantic rush for fortune. Precious metals unearthed in the Pacific Northwest early in the decade and in Montana and Idaho a few years later kept dreams alive and prospectors moving. In the mid-1870s, more gold, this time in the Black Hills of North Dakota, attracted hordes of fortune seekers.

In contrast to the agricultural settlements, where early residents were isolated and the community expanded gradually, the discovery of gold or silver spurred rapid, if usually short-lived, growth. Mining camps, ramshackle and often hastily constructed, soon housed hundreds or even thousands of miners and people serving them. Merchants, saloonkeepers, cooks, druggists, gamblers, and prostitutes hurried into boom areas as fast as prospectors. Usually, about half the residents of any mining camp were there to prospect the miners rather than the mines.

Given the motivation, character, and ethnic diversity of those flocking to boomtowns and the feeble attempts to set up local government in what were perceived as temporary communities, it was hardly surprising that mining life was often disorderly. Racial antagonism between American miners and foreigners, whom they labeled "greasers" (Mexicans), "chinks" (Chinese), "keskedees" (Frenchmen), and lesser "breeds," led to ugly riots and lynchings. Miners had few qualms about eliminating those who interfered with the race for riches. Fistfights, drunkenness, and murder occurred often enough to become part of the lore of the gold rush. Wrote one woman, "In the short space of twenty four days, we have had murders, fearful accidents, bloody deaths, a mob, whippings, a hanging, an attempt at suicide, and a fatal duel."

If mining life was usually not this violent, it tolerated behavior that would have been unacceptable farther east. Miners were not trying to re-create eastern communities but to get rich. Married men, convinced of the raucous and immoral character of mining communities, hesitated to bring wives and families west. As one declared, "I would much prefer that a wife of mine should board in a respectable bawd house in the city of New York than live anywhere in the city of San Francisco."

Although the lucky few struck it rich or at least made enough money to return home with pride intact, miners' journals and letters reveal that many made only enough to keep going. Wrote one, "Everybody in the States who has friends here is always writing for them to come home. Now they all long to go home. . . . But it is hard for a man to leave . . . with nothing. . . . I have no pile yet, but you can bet your life I will never come home until I have something more than when I started." The problem was that easily mined silver and gold deposits soon ran out. Although Chinese miners proved adept at finding what early miners overlooked, the remaining rich deposits lay deeply embedded in rock or gravel. Extraction required cooperative efforts, capital, technological experience, and expensive machinery. Eventually, mining became a corporate industrial concern, with miners as wage earners. As early as 1852, the

This 1852 photograph of miners and the constructions they built on the American River hints at some of the environmental consequences of mining activity. The formal clothing of the woman contrasts sharply with that worn by the men and suggests that she has not forgotten the standards of civilized life. *(California State Library)*

This picture of the near ghost town of Ophir City, Nevada, taken in the 1870s, points to the way the mining frontier left its mark on the landscape and suggests the unstable nature of such a frontier. *(Denver Public Library, Western History Department)*

changing nature of mining in California had transformed most of the shaggy miners into wage workers.

Probably 5 percent of early gold rush emigrants to California were women and children. Many of the women also anticipated getting "rich in a hurry." Because there were so few of them, the cooking, nursing, laundry, and hotel services women provided had a high value. When Luzena Wilson arrived in Sacramento, a miner offered to pay her $10 for a biscuit. That night, Luzena dreamt she saw "crowds of bearded miners striking gold from the earth with every blow of the pick, each one seeming to leave a share for me." Yet it was wearying work, and some wondered if the money compensated for the exhaustion. As Mary Ballou thought it over, she decided, "I would not advise any Lady to come out here and suffer to toil and fatigue I have suffered for the sake of a little gold." As men's profits shrank, so, too, did those of the women who served them.

Some of the first women to arrive on the mining frontier were prostitutes. They rejected the hard labor of cooking and washing that "respectable" women performed, hoping that the sex ratio would make their profession especially profitable. Prostitutes may have constituted as much as 20 percent of California's female population in 1850, and they probably vastly outnumbered other women in early mining camps. During boom days, they made good money and sometimes won a recognized place in society. But prostitutes always ran risks in a disorderly environment. They were more often the victims of murder and violence than the recipients of courtesy.

The Mexicans, South Americans, Chinese, and small numbers of blacks seeking their fortunes in California soon discovered that although they contributed substantially to California's growth, racial discrimination flourished vigorously in the land of golden promise. At first, American miners hoped to force foreigners out of the gold fields altogether. But an attempt to declare mining illegal for all foreigners failed. A high tax on foreign miners proved more successful. Thousands of Mexicans left the mines, while the Chinese found other jobs in San Francisco and Sacramento. As business stagnated in mining towns, however, white miners had second thoughts about the levy and reduced it. By 1870, when the tax was declared unconstitutional, the Chinese, who had paid 85 percent of it, had "contributed" $5 million to California for the right to prospect. The hostility that led to this legislation also fed widespread violence against the Chinese and Mexicans.

Black Americans found that their skin color placed them in a situation akin to that of foreigners. Deprived of the vote, forbidden to testify in civil or criminal cases involving whites, excluded from the bounties of the state's homestead law, blacks led a precarious existence. When news arrived of the discovery of gold in British Columbia in the late 1850s, hundreds of blacks as well as thousands of Chinese left the state, hoping that the Canadian frontier would be more hospitable than California.

For the Native American tribes of the interior, the mining frontier was a disaster. Used to foraging for food, they found fish and game increasingly scarce as miners diverted streams, hunted game, or drove it from mining areas altogether. When Indians responded by raiding mining camps, miners erupted with fury. They stalked and killed native men and women, sometimes collecting bounties offered by some mining communities for their scalps. Indian women were raped; children were kidnapped and offered as apprentices. As one miner pointed out, "Indians seven or eight years old are worth $100 . . . [and] it is a damn poor Indian that's not worth $50." Without legal recourse because of their skin color, Native Americans could not withstand the onslaught of white society. Subjected not only to violence but to white disease, Indians died by the thousands. In 1849, there had been about 150,000 Indians in California. In just over 20 years, numbers had tumbled to fewer than 30,000.

Although the mining frontier was never as brutal for whites as for people of color, white men's and women's fantasies of dazzling riches rarely came true. The ghost towns of the West testify to the typical pattern: boom, bust, decay, death. The empty streets and rotting buildings stood as symbols of dashed hopes and disappointed dreams. Also left behind were other physical signs recalling the presence and passing of the mining frontier. Mining operations left an indelible mark on the land. Forests were decimated to provide timber for the flumes miners constructed to divert rivers from their channels in the hopes of exposing rich gold deposits in the dry river beds. They built slurries and ditches and created mounds of debris that during floods or heavy rains oozed over fields and choked rivers and streams. Consumed by visions of glittering metal, miners were blind to the realities of eroding soil, deforested mountains, diverted waterways, and silt.

It was difficult, however, to recognize some of the negative consequences of the discovery of gold, for it had many positive effects on the West as a whole. Between 1848 and 1883, California mines supplied two-thirds of the country's gold. Gold transformed San Francisco from a sleepy town into a bustling metropolis. It fueled the agricultural and commercial development of California and Oregon, as miners provided a market for goods and services. Gold built harbors, railroads, and irrigation systems not just in California and Oregon but all over the West. Though few people made large fortunes, both the region and the nation profited from gold.

The Mormon Frontier

In the decades before 1860, many emigrants heading for the Far West stopped to rest and buy supplies in Salt Lake City, the heart of the Mormon state of Deseret. There they encountered a society that seemed familiar and orderly, yet foreign and shocking. Visitors admired the attractively laid out town with its irrigation ditches, gardens, and tidy houses. But as they noted the decorous nature of everyday life, they gossiped about polygamy and searched for signs of rebellion in the faces of Mormon women. Emigrants who opposed slavery were fond of equating the position of the Mormon wife with that of the black slave. They were amazed that so few Mormon women seemed interested in escaping from the bonds of plural marriage.

Violent events had driven the Mormons to the arid Great Basin area. Joseph Smith's murder in 1844 marked no end to the persecution of his followers. By the fall of 1846, angry mobs had chased the last of the "Saints" out of Nauvoo, Illinois. As they struggled to join their advance groups at temporary camps in Iowa, Smith's successor, Brigham Young, realized that flight from the United States represented the best hope for survival. The Saints must create the kingdom of God anew, somewhere in the West, far removed from the United States, that "Babylon" of corruption and injustice.

The Mexican-American war unexpectedly furthered Mormon plans. At first, most Mormons probably agreed with Hosea Stout, who was glad "to learn of the war," hoping it "might never end until the States were entirely destroyed, for they had driven us into the wilderness, and now were laughing at our calamities." But Brigham Young realized that war might provide capital needed for the new Mormon kingdom. By raising 500 Mormon young men for Kearney's Army of the West, Young acquired vital resources. The battalion's advance pay bought wagonloads of supplies for starving and sick Mormons strung out along the trail between Missouri and Iowa and helped finance the impending great migration.

Young selected the Great Basin area, technically part of Mexico, as the best site for his future kingdom. It was arid and remote, 1,000 miles from its nearest "civilized" neighbors. But if irrigated, Mormon leaders concluded it might prove as fertile as the fields and vineyards of ancient Israel.

In April 1847, Young led an exploratory expedition of 143 men, 3 women, and 2 children to this promised land. In late July, after reaching Salt Lake, Young exclaimed, "This is the place." Before returning to Iowa to prepare Mormons for the trip to Utah, he announced his land policy. Settlers would receive virtually free land on the basis of a family's size and its

C. A. A. Christensen painted this picture of the Mormon Temple in Nauvoo, Illinois, in 1844. Despite the dignified and substantial nature of the building, which almost could be an academy or a New England church, the Mormons appeared to their neighbors to harbor unacceptable and un-American ideas. *(Museum of Art, Brigham Young University)*

ability to cultivate it. After Young left, the expeditionary group followed his directions to construct irrigation ditches and begin planting.

The following months and years tested Young's organizational talents and his followers' cooperative abilities. By September 1847, fully 566 wagons and 1,500 of the Saints had made the arduous trek to Salt Lake City. Still more Mormons came the next year, inspired by visions of a new Zion in the West. Their trip was also a collective venture, planned and directed by Church leaders. By 1850, the Mormon frontier had attracted over 11,000 settlers. Missionary efforts in the United States and abroad, especially in Great Britain and Scandinavia, drew thousands of converts to the Great Basin. The Church emigration society and a loan fund facilitated the journey for many who could never have otherwise undertaken the trip. By the end of the decade, over 30,000 Saints lived in Utah, not only in Salt Lake City but also in more than 90 village colonies Young had planned. Though hardship marked these early years, the Mormons thrived. As one early settler remarked, "We have everything around us we could ask."

Non-Mormon, or "Gentile," emigrants passing through Utah found much that was recognizable. The government had familiar characteristics. Most Mormons were farmers; many of them came originally from New England and the Midwest and shared many of the same customs and attitudes. But outsiders perceived profound differences, for the heart of Mormon society was not the individual farmer living on his own homestead but the cooperative village.

Years of persecution had nourished a strong sense of group identity and acceptance of Church leadership. Organized by the Church leaders, who made the essential decisions, farming became a collective enterprise. All farmers were allotted land. All had irrigation rights, for water did not belong to individuals but to the community. During Sunday services, the local bishop might give farming instructions to his congregation along with his sermon. As Young explained, "I have looked upon the community of Latter-day Saints in a vision and beheld them organized as the great family of heaven, each person performing his several duties in his line of industry, working for the good of the whole more than for individual aggrandizement." In this vast communal effort, every Mormon was expected to work for success, men and women alike. "We do not believe in having any drones in the hive," one woman said tartly.

The Church was omnipresent in Utah; in fact, nothing separated Church and state. Despite familiar government forms, Church leaders occupied all important political posts. Brigham Young's Governing Quorum contained the high priests of the Church, who made both religious and political decisions.

When it became clear that Utah would become a territory, Mormon leaders drew up a constitution that divided religious and political power. But once in place, powers overlapped. As one Gentile pointed out, "This intimate connection of church and state seems to pervade everything that is done. The supreme power in both being lodged in the hands of the same individuals, it is difficult to separate their two official characters, and to determine whether in any one instance they act as spiritual or merely temporal officers."

The Treaty of Guadalupe Hidalgo officially incorporated Utah into the United States, but little affected political and religious arrangements. Brigham Young became territorial governor. Local bishops continued to act as spiritual leaders as well as civil magistrates in Mormon communities. Mormons had come to Utah to establish a kingdom rather than a republic. Their motives dictated the unique politicoreligious nature of the Utah experience.

Other aspects of the Mormon frontier were distinctive. Mormon policy toward the Indian tribes was remarkably enlightened. As one prominent Mormon pointed out, "It has been our habit to shoot Indians with tobacco and bread biscuits rather than with powder and lead, and we are most successful with them." After two expeditions against the Timpanago and Shoshone in 1850, Mormons concentrated on converting rather than killing Native Americans. Mormon missionaries learned Bannock, Ute, Navajo, and Hopi languages to bring the faith to these tribes. They also encouraged Native Americans to ranch and farm.

Although most Gentiles could tolerate some of the differences they encountered on the Mormon frontier, few could accept polygamy and the seemingly immoral extended family structure that plural marriage entailed. Although Joseph Smith and other Church leaders had secretly practiced polygamy in the early 1840s, Brigham Young publicly revealed the doctrine only in 1852, when the Saints were safely in Utah. Smith believed that the highest or "celestial" form of marriage brought special rewards in the afterlife. Because wives and children contributed to these rewards, polygamy was a means of sanctification. From a practical standpoint, polygamy served to incorporate into Mormon society single female converts who had left their families to come to Utah.

Although most Mormons accepted the doctrine and its religious justification, some found it hard to follow. One woman called it a "great trial of feelings." Actually, relatively few families were polygamous. During the 40-year period in which Mormons practiced plural marriage, only 10 to 20 percent of Mormon families were polygamous. Few men had more than two wives. Because of the expense of maintaining several families and the personal strains involved, usually only the most successful and visible Mormon leaders practiced polygamy.

Polygamous family life was a far cry from the lascivious arrangement outsiders fantasized. Jealousy among wives could destroy the institution of plural marriage, so Mormon leaders minimized the role of romantic love and sexual attraction in courtship and marriage. Instead, they encouraged marriages founded on mutual attachment, with sex for the purposes of procreation rather than pleasure.

To the shock of outsiders, Mormon women did not consider themselves slaves but rather highly regarded members of the Mormon community. Whether plural wives or not, they saw polygamy as the cutting edge of their society and defended it to the outside world. Polygamy was preferable to monogamy, which left the single woman without the economic and social protection of family life and forced some of them into prostitution, Brenda Pratt explained. "Polygamy . . . tends directly to the chastity of women, and the sound health and morals . . . of their children."

Although they faced obvious difficulties, many plural wives found rewards in polygamy. Without the constant presence of husbands, they had an unusual opportunity for independence. Many treated husbands when they visited as revered friends; their children, not their spouses, provided them with day-to-day emotional satisfaction. Occasionally, plural wives lived together and shared domestic work, becoming close friends. As one such wife put it, "We three . . . loved each other more than sisters" and would "go hand in hand together down till eternity."

Although the Mormon frontier seemed alien to outsiders, it succeeded in terms of its numbers, its growing economic prosperity, and its group unity. Long-term threats loomed for this community, however, once the area became part of the United States. Attacks on Young's power as well as heated verbal denunciations of polygamy proliferated. Efforts began in Congress to outlaw polygamy. In the years before the Civil War, Mormons withstood these assaults on their way of life. But as Utah became more connected to the rest of the country, the tide would turn against them.

Cities in the West

Many emigrants went west not to claim farmland or to pan for gold but rather to settle in cities like San Francisco, Denver, and Portland. There they hoped to find business and professional opportunities or, perhaps, the chance to make a fortune by speculating in town lots.

Cities were an integral part of frontier life and, in some cases, preceded agricultural settlement. Some communities turned into bustling cities as they catered to the emigrant trade. St. Joseph, Missouri, outfitted families setting out on the overland journey. Salt Lake City offered weary pioneers headed for California an opportunity to rest and restock. Portland was the destination of many emigrants and became a market and supply center for homesteaders.

Some cities grew so rapidly that they have been called "instant cities." San Francisco and Denver turned into cities almost overnight; in a mere 12 years, San Francisco's population zoomed from 812 to 56,802. The discovery of precious metals sent thousands of miners with diverse demands and desires to and through these places. And once the strike ran out, many miners returned to these cities to make a new start. Still other places supplied frontier farmers and

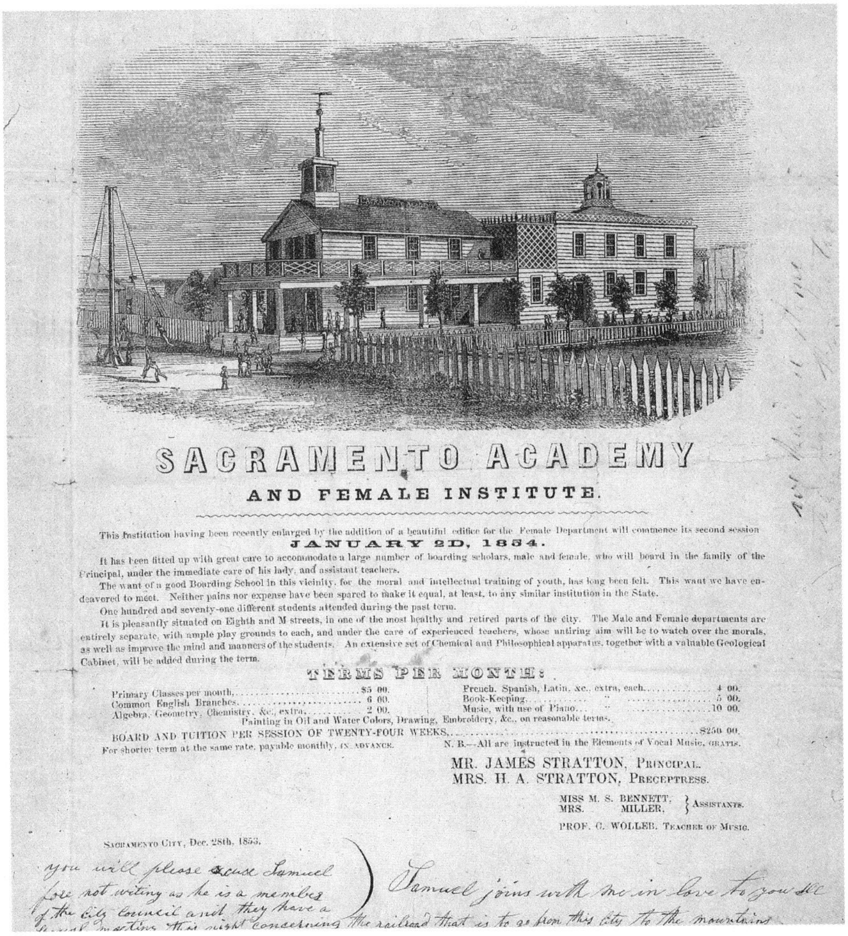

SACRAMENTO ACADEMY

AND FEMALE INSTITUTE.

This Institution having been recently enlarged by the addition of a beautiful edifice for the Female Department will commence its second session

JANUARY 2D, 1854.

It has been fitted up with great care to accommodate a large number of boarding scholars, male and female, who will board in the family of the Principal, under the immediate care of his lady, and assistant teachers.

The want of a good Boarding School in this vicinity, for the moral and intellectual training of youth, has long been felt. This want we have endeavored to meet. Neither pains nor expense have been spared to make it equal, at least, to any similar institution in the State.

One hundred and seventy-one different students attended during the past term.

It is pleasantly situated on Eighth and M streets, in one of the most healthy and retired parts of the city. The Male and Female departments are entirely separate, with ample play grounds to each, and under the care of experienced teachers, whose untiring aim will be to watch over the morals, as well as improve the mind and manners of the students. An extensive set of Chemical and Philosophical apparatus, together with a valuable Geological Cabinet, will be added during the term.

TERMS PER MONTH:

Primary Classes per month,	$5 00.	French, Spanish, Latin, &c., extra, each	4 00.
Common English Branches,	6 00.	Book-Keeping, "	5 00.
Algebra, Geometry, Chemistry, &c., extra,	2 00.	Music, with use of Piano... "	10 00.

Painting in Oil and Water Colors, Drawing, Embroidery, &c., on reasonable terms.

BOARD AND TUITION PER SESSION OF TWENTY-FOUR WEEKS, ... $250 00.

For shorter term at the same rate, payable monthly, IN ADVANCE.

N. B.—All are instructed in the Elements of Vocal Music, GRATIS.

MR. JAMES STRATTON, PRINCIPAL.
MRS. H. A. STRATTON, PRECEPTRESS.

MISS M. S. BENNETT, } ASSISTANTS.
MRS. MILLER,

PROF. C. WOLLEB, TEACHER OF MUSIC.

SACRAMENTO CITY, Dec. 28th, 1853.

you will please excuse Samuel
fore not writing as he is a member
of the City Council and they have a

Samuel joins with me in love to you all

the railroad that is to go from this City to the mountains

This circular advertising Sacramento Academy and Female Institute shows settlers' desire to re-create familiar patterns of life. The circular informs interested parents that the school's teachers would watch over "the morals, as well as improve the minds and manners of our students." It was possible to study French, Latin, and Spanish and to study piano for an extra fee. *(Courtesy of the California History Room, California State Library, Sacramento, California)*

served as their markets. They only gradually acquired urban characteristics.

Commercial life bustled on the urban frontier, offering residents a wide range of occupations and services. As a Portland emigrant remarked in 1852, only a few years after that community's beginning, "In many ways life here . . . was more primitive than it was in the early times in Illinois and Missouri. But in others it was far more advanced. . . . We could get the world's commodities here which could not be had then, or scarcely at all, in the interior of Illinois or Missouri."

Young, single men seeking their fortunes made up a disproportionate share of the urban population. Frontier Portland had more than three men for every woman. Predictably, urban life was often noisy, rowdy, and occasionally violent. The presence of so many young men could not help but affect urban family life. Mothers worried that their children would fall into bad company. Some attempted to reform the atmosphere by pressing for Sunday store closings or prohibition. Other women, of course, enjoyed all the attention that came with the presence of so many young men. As one observed with gusto, "There is plenty of men here. They cast sheeps eyes at Lib and Lucy's girl but have not popt the question yet." Eventually, the sex ratio became balanced, but as late as 1880, fully 18 of the 24 largest western cities had more men than women.

Although western cities began with distinctive characters, they soon resembled eastern cities. As a western publication boasted, "Transport a resident of an Eastern city and put him down in the streets of Portland, and he would observe little difference between his new surroundings and those he beheld but a moment before in his native city."

The history of Portland suggests the common pattern of development. In 1845, Portland was only a clearing in the forest, large enough for four streets and 16 blocks. Speculation in town lots was lively. By the early 1850s, Portland had grown into a small trading center with a few rough log structures and muddy tracks for streets. As farmers poured into Oregon, the city became a regional commercial center. More permanent structures were built, giving the city an "eastern" appearance.

The belief that urban life in the West abounded with special opportunities initially drew many young men to Portland and other western cities. Many of them did not find financial success there.

This 1853 view of San Francisco reveals the rapid transformation of the city. Brick buildings, several stories high, with elaborate cornices, board sidewalks, kerosene street lamps, and the inevitable grid street pattern give San Francisco the appearance of an eastern city rather than a raw western community, only four years after the gold rush. *(The Bancroft Library, University of California, Berkeley)*

Opportunities were greatest for newcomers who brought assets with them. These residents became the elite of the community. By the 1860s, when the city's population had reached 2,874, Portland's Social Club symbolized the emergence of that city's elite. Portland's businessmen, lawyers, and editors controlled an increasing share of the community's wealth and set its social standards. Their elaborate parties, summer trips, and exclusive clubs showed how far Portland had come from its raw frontier beginnings.

CULTURES IN CONFLICT

Looking at westward expansion through the eyes of white emigrants provides only one view of the frontier experience. An entry from an Oregon Trail journal suggests other perspectives. On May 7, 1864, Mary Warner, a bride of only a few months, described a frightening event. That day, a "fine-looking" Indian had visited the wagon train and tried to buy her. Mary's husband, probably uncertain how to handle the situation, played along, agreeing to trade his wife for two ponies. The Indian generously offered three. "Then," wrote Mary, "he took hold of my shawl to make me understand to get out [of the wagon]. About this time I got frightened and really was so hysterical [that] I began to cry." Everyone laughed at her, she reported, though surely the Indian found the whole incident no more amusing than she had.

This ordinary encounter on the overland trail only begins to hint at the social and cultural differences separating white Americans moving west and the peoples with whom they came in contact. Confident of their values and rights, emigrants had little regard for those who had lived in the West for centuries and no compunction in seizing their lands. Many even predicted that the Indian race would disappear from the continent, a just reward for tribal "degeneracy."

Confronting the Plains Tribes

During the 1840s, white Americans, for the first time, came into extensive contact with the powerful Plains tribes, whose culture differed from that of the more familiar eastern Woodlands tribes. Probably a quarter million Native Americans occupied the area from the Rocky Mountains to the Missouri River and from the Platte River to New Mexico. Nearest the Missouri and Iowa frontier lived the "border" tribes—the Pawnee, Omaha, Oto, Ponca, and Kansa. These Indians, unlike other Plains tribes, lived in villages and raised crops, though they supplemented their diet with buffalo meat during the summer months. On the Central Plains lived the Brulé and Oglala Sioux, the Cheyenne, the Shoshone, and the Arapaho, aggressive tribes who followed the buffalo and often raided the border tribes. In the Southwest were the Comanche, Ute, Navajo, and some Apache bands; the Kiowa, Wichita, Apache, and southern Comanche claimed northern and western Texas as their hunting grounds. Many of the southwestern tribes had adopted aspects of Spanish culture and European domestic animals like cattle, sheep, and horses.

Although there were differences between the Plains tribes, they shared certain characteristics. Most had adopted a nomadic way of life after the introduction of Spanish horses in the sixteenth century increased their seasonal mobility from 50 to 500 miles. Horses allowed Indian braves to hunt the buffalo with such success that tribes (with the exclusion of the border groups) came to depend on the beasts for food, clothing, fuel, teepee dwellings, and trading purposes. Because women were responsible for processing buffalo products, some men had more than one wife to tan skins for trading.

Mobility also increased tribal contact and conflict. War played a central part in the lives of the Plains tribes. No male became a fully accepted member of

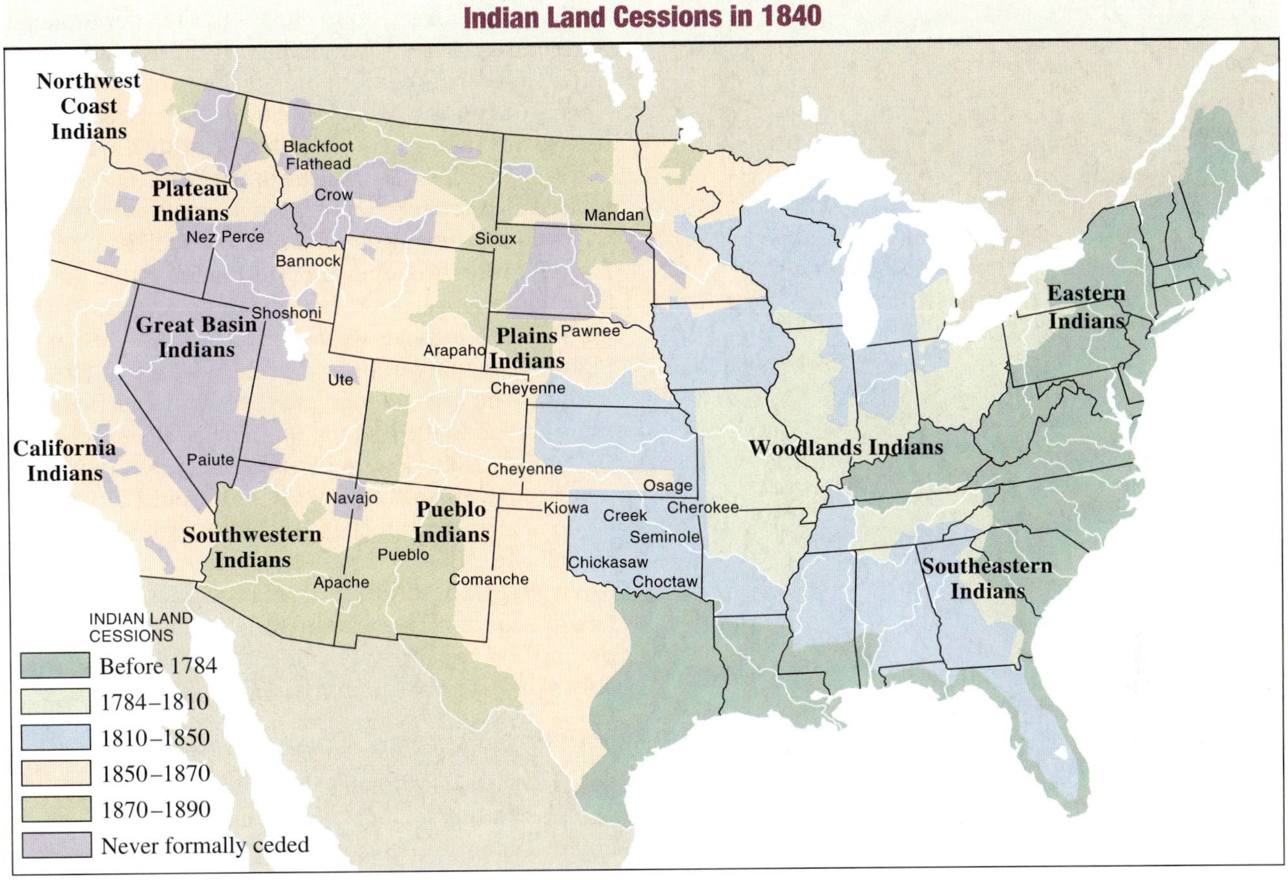

This map of Indian tribes and groupings reveals locations in 1840, but it presents too static a picture of tribal territories. Some of the Indian groups in the West had been forced across the Mississippi by events in the Midwest. What the map does make obvious, however, is the rapid pace of Indian land cessions in the nineteenth century, especially in the trans-Mississippi West.

his tribe until he had proved himself in battle. But tribal warfare was not like the warfare of white men. Indians sought not to exterminate their enemies or to claim territory but rather to steal horses and to prove individual prowess. They considered it braver to touch an enemy than to kill or scalp him. This pattern of conflict on the Plains discouraged political unity. Moreover, individual tribes were loosely organized. Chiefs enjoyed only limited authority over their followers. As Chief Low Horn, a Blackfoot, explained, chiefs "could not restrain their young men . . . their young men were wild, and ambitious, in their turn to be braves and chiefs. They wanted by some brave act to win the favor of their young women, and bring scalps and horses to show their prowess."

Armed with guns, mounted on fast ponies, and skilled in warfare and raiding, the Plains tribes, though disunified, posed a fearsome obstacle to white expansion. They had signed no treaties with the United States and had few friendly feelings toward whites. Their contact with white society had brought gains through trade in skins, but the trade had also brought alcohol and destructive epidemics of smallpox and scarlet fever.

When the first emigrants drove their wagons across the plains and prairies in the early 1840s, relations between Indians and whites were peaceable. But the intrusion of whites set in motion an environmental cycle that eventually drew the two groups into conflict. Indian tribes depended on the buffalo but respected this source of life. The Teton Sioux performed rituals to ensure a continuing supply of the animals, while hunters often ritualistically apologized to the Great Unseen Buffalo for slaughtering what the tribe needed. The grasses that nourished the buffalo also sustained the Indians' own ponies and the animals that supported horse traders like the Cheyenne.

Whites, however, fed their oxen and horses on the grass both the Indians' ponies and the buffalo needed. And they adopted the "most exciting sport," the buffalo hunt. As the great herds began to shrink, Native American tribes began to battle one another for hunting grounds and food. The powerful Sioux swooped down into the hunting grounds of their enemies and

This drawing, done by an unknown Indian artist sometime in the 1840s, contrasts the traditionally clad Indians and the wild animals they hunted with the formally dressed white men and their stock animals. Has the artist depicted whites in a sympathetic manner? *(Archives de Jesuites, St. Jerome Quebec)*

mounted destructive raids against the Pawnee and other smaller tribes. In an 1846 petition to President Polk, the Sioux explained that "for several years past the Emigrants going over the Mountains from the United States, have been the cause that Buffalo have in great measure left our hunting grounds, thereby causing us to go into the Country of Our Enemies to hunt, exposing our lives daily for the necessary subsistence of our wives and Children and getting killed on several occasions." Despite their difficulties, the Sioux had "all along treated the Emigrants in the most friendly manner, giving them free passage through our hunting grounds."

The Sioux requested compensation for damages caused by whites. When the president denied their request, they tried to extract taxes from the emigrants passing over their lands. Emigrants were outraged at what they considered Indian effrontery. After all, the United States had won these lands. Frontier newspapers printed letters denouncing the Sioux, demanding adequate protection for travelers and some chastening of the "savages." However, little was done to relieve the suffering of the tribes bearing the brunt of Sioux aggression, the dismay of the Sioux at the white invasion, or the fears of the emigrants themselves.

The discovery of gold in California, which lured over 20,000 across the Plains in 1849 alone, became the catalyst for federal action. The vast numbers of gold seekers and their animals wrought such devastation in the Platte valley that it rapidly became a wasteland for the Indians. The dreaded cholera that whites carried with them spread to the Indians, killing thousands.

To meet the crisis, government officials devised a two-pronged plan. The government would construct a chain of forts to protect emigrants and, simultaneously, call the tribes to a general conference. Officials expected that in return for generous presents, Indians would end tribal warfare and limit their movements to prescribed areas. They instructed tribes to select chiefs to speak for them at the conference.

The Fort Laramie Council, 1851

In 1851, the tribal council convened at Fort Laramie. As many as 10,000 Indians, hopeful of ending the destruction of their way of life and eager for the promised presents, gathered at the fort. Tribal animosities simmered, however. Skirmishes occurred on the way to the fort, and the border tribes, fearful of the Sioux, declined to participate. The Comanche, Kiowa, and Apache also refused to come, because their enemies, the Sioux and the Crow, were to be there.

At the conference, whites told the gathered tribes that times had changed. In the past, "you had plenty of buffalo and game . . . and your Great Father well knows that war has always been your favorite amusement and pursuit. He then left the question of peace and war to yourselves. Now, since the settling of the districts West . . . by the white men, your condition has changed." There would be compensation for the destruction of their grass, timber, and buffalo and annual payments of goods and services. But in return, the tribes had to give up their rights of free movement. The government drew tribal boundaries, and chiefs made promises to stay within them. In most cases, some tribal lands were sold.

The Fort Laramie Treaty was the first agreement between the Plains tribes and the U.S. government. It expressed the conviction of whites that Indians must stay in clearly defined areas apart from white civilization.

But this system of isolation and its purported benefits were still in the future. During the conference, ominous signs appeared that more trouble would precede any "resolution" of Indian–white affairs. Sioux Chief Black Hawk told whites, "You have split the country and I do not like it." His powerful tribe refused to be restricted to lands north of the Platte, for south of the river lay their recently conquered lands. "These lands once belonged to the Kiowas and the Crows," one Sioux explained, "but we whipped those nations out of them and in this we did what the white men do when they want the lands of the Indians." The words suggested that Indians, despite agreements, would not willingly abandon their traditional way of life for confinement. In the following years, it would become evident that Americans and Sioux had conflicting interests south of the Platte. Elsewhere in the trans-Mississippi West, other tribes, like the fierce Navajo of New Mexico, also resisted white attempts to confine them.

Overwhelming the Mexicans

In the Southwest, in Texas, and in California, Americans encountered a Spanish-speaking population and Hispanic culture. Expansionist Lewis Cass expressed Americans' scorn for both. Speaking in a congressional debate on the annexation of New Mexico, Cass stated, "We do not want the people of Mexico, either as citizens or as subjects. All we want is a portion of territory . . . with a population, which would soon recede, or identify itself with ours." Americans regarded Mexicans as lazy, ignorant, and cunning, the "dregs of society." Although Mexicans easily recognized such cultural arrogance, they lacked the numbers to fend off American aggression.

Although Anglo–Mexican interaction differed from place to place, few Anglos heeded the Treaty of Guadalupe Hidalgo's assurances that Mexicans would have citizens' rights and the "free enjoyment of their liberty and property." The greatest numbers of Spanish-speaking people lived in New Mexico, and, of all former Mexican citizens, they probably fared the best. Most were of mixed blood, living marginally as ranch hands for rich landowners or as farmers and herdsmen in small villages dominated by a *patron,* or headman. As the century wore on, Americans produced legal titles and took over lands long occupied by peasant farmers and stock raisers. But despite economic reversals, New Mexicans survived, carrying their rural culture well into the twentieth century.

Light-skinned, upper-class landowners fared better. Even before the conquest, rich New Mexicans had protected their future by establishing contracts with American businessmen and by sending their sons east to American schools. When the United States annexed New Mexico, this substantial and powerful class contracted strategic marriage and business alliances with the Anglo men who slowly trickled into the territory. During the 1850s, they maintained their influence and prestige and their American connections. Only rarely did they bother with the plight of their poor countrymen. Class outweighed ethnic or cultural considerations.

In Texas, the Spanish-speaking residents, only 10 percent of the population in 1840, shrank to a mere 6 percent by 1860. Although the upper class also intermarried with Americans, they lost most of their power, as Germans, Irish, French, and Americans poured into the state. Poor, dark-skinned Hispanics clustered in low-paying and largely unskilled jobs.

In California, the discovery of gold radically changed the situation for the Californios. In 1848, there were 7,000 Californios and about twice as many Anglos. By 1860, the Anglo population had ballooned to 360,000. Hispanic-Americans were hard-pressed to cope with the rapid influx of outsiders. At first, Californios and several thousand Mexicans from Sonora joined Anglos and others in the gold fields. But competition there fed antagonism and finally open conflict. Posters warned foreigners out of the gold fields. In Anglo eyes, one Hispanic was much like another, even if one claimed to be a Californio with political rights and another a Sonoran. Taxes and terrorism ultimately succeeded in forcing most Spanish speakers out of the mines and established the racial contours of the new California.

Other changes were even more disastrous. In 1851, Congress passed the Gwinn Land Law, supposedly a measure for validating Spanish and Mexican land titles. The law violated the pledge contained in a Statement of Protocol accompanying the Treaty of Guadalupe Hidalgo that stated the government "did not in any way" intend to annul the grants of lands made by Mexico, for it forced California landowners to defend what was already theirs and encouraged squatters to settle on land in the hopes that the Californios' titles would prove false. The process was slow—it took an average of 17 years to establish clear title to land—and unfamiliar. As one woman explained, her mother had been "totally unprepared for the problems that came with American rule. Not only was the language foreign to her, but also the concept of property taxes, mortgages and land title regulations." Landowners found themselves paying American lawyers large fees, often in land, and borrowing at high interest rates to pay for court proceedings. A victory at court often turned into a defeat when legal expenses forced owners to sell their lands to pay debts. In the South, where Anglos judged land less valuable than in the mining North, the process of dispossession was slower. But by the early 1860s, the ranching class there had also lost most of its extensive holdings and slid into relative poverty.

This painting presents an idyllic picture of the lives of the elite Mexican landowners. Their way of life would disappear with the arrival of hordes of American settlers. Both the former elite and more ordinary Mexicans would find themselves, in the words of Pablo la Guerra, "foreigners in their own land." *(Charles Christian Nahl,* The Fandango, *1873/Crocker Art Museum, E. B. Crocker Collection, Sacramento, California,)*

For working-class Hispanic-Americans, who became laborers for Anglo farmers or mining or railroad companies, the arrival of Anglos was the start of a steadily deteriorating situation. Whatever their employment, Hispanic-Americans earned less and did more unpleasant jobs than Anglo workers. By 1870, the average Hispanic-American worker's property was worth only about a third of its value of 20 years earlier. As newspaper editor and champion of the Mexican–American cause, Francisco Ramírez pointed out in the Los Angeles newspaper *El Clamor Publico* in 1856, "California has fallen into the hands of the ambitious sons of North America who will not stop until they have satisfied their passions, by driving the first occupants of the land out of the country, villifying their religion and disfiguring their customs."

Western movies and novels, with their images of sheriffs in hot pursuit of outlaws and bandits, some wearing sombreros, hint at the reality of resistance to American expansion into the Southwest. The exploits of Tiburcio Vásquez, a notorious *bandido* in southern California, reveal that some Hispanics responded to events through violence:

> My career grew out of the circumstances by which I was surrounded. . . . As I grew to manhood I was in the habit of attending balls and parties given by the native Californians, into which the Americans, then beginning to become numerous, would force themselves and shove the native born men aside, monopolizing the dance and the women. This was about 1852. A spirit of hatred and revenge took possession of me. I had numerous fights in defense of my countrywomen. The officers were continually in pursuit of me. I believed we were unjustly and wrongfully deprived of the social rights that belonged to us.

Other Hispanics tried different tactics. In New Mexico, members of Las Gorras Blancas ripped up railroad ties and cut the barbed-wire fences of Anglo ranchers and farmers. The religiously oriented Penitentes tried to work through the ballot box. Ordinary men, women, and children resisted efforts to convert them to Protestantism and clung to familiar customs and beliefs even as they learned some of the skills needed to survive in a changing culture.

Timeline

1803–1806	Lewis and Clark expedition
1818	Treaty on joint U.S.–British occupation of Oregon
1819	Spain cedes Spanish territory in United States and sets transcontinental boundary of Louisiana Purchase, excluding Texas
1821	Mexican independence
	Opening of Santa Fe Trail
	Stephen Austin leads American settlement of Texas
1821–1840	Indian removals
1830	Mexico abolishes slavery in Texas
1836	Texas declares independence
	Battles of the Alamo and San Jacinto
1840s	Emigrant crossings of Overland Trail
1844	James Polk elected president
1845	"Manifest Destiny" coined
	United States annexes Texas and sends troops to the Rio Grande
	Americans attempt to buy Upper California and New Mexico
1846	Mexico declares defensive war
	United States declares war and takes Santa Fe
	Resolution of Oregon question
1847	Attacks on Veracruz and Mexico City
	Mormon migration to Utah begins
1848	Treaty of Guadalupe Hidalgo
1849	California gold rush begins
1850	California admitted to the Union
1851	Fort Laramie Treaty
1853	Gadsden Purchase
1862	Homestead Act

Conclusion

Fruits of Manifest Destiny

Like Lewis Cass, many nineteenth-century Americans were convinced that the country had merely gained western territories to which it was entitled. Although the process of acquiring the western half of the continent was swift, the prospect of winning the West loomed large in the imagination of the American people for many years. A number of western settlers became folk heroes. All white Americans could be thankful for the special opportunities, the new chance for success, that the West seemed to offer.

The expanding nation did gain vast natural wealth in the trans-Mississippi West. But only a small fraction of the hopeful emigrants heading for the frontier realized their dreams of success. And the move west had a dark side, as Americans clashed with Mexicans and Native Americans in their drive to fulfill their "Manifest Destiny" and as the acquisition of new territories fueled the controversy over the future of slavery.

Recommended Reading

Probing the Trans-Mississippi West

Norman A. Graebner, ed., *Manifest Destiny* (1968); Theodore J. Karamanski, *Fur Trade and Exploration: Opening the Far Northwest, 1821–1852* (1983); Patricia Nelson Limerick, *The Legacy of Conquest: The Unbroken Past of the American West* (1987); Anders Stephanson, *Manifest Destiny: American Expansionism and the Empire of Right* (1995).

Winning the Trans-Mississippi West

Gene Brack, *Mexico Views Manifest Destiny, 1821–1846* (1975); Robert H. Ferrell, ed., *Monterrey Is Ours! The Mexican War Letters of Lieutenant Dana, 1845–1847* (1990); Neal Harlow, *California Conquered* (1982); Robert W. Johanssen, *To the Halls of Montezuma: The Mexican War in the American Imagination* (1985); Ernest M. Lander Jr., *Reluctant Imperialists: Calhoun, the South Carolinians, and the Mexican War* (1980); David Pletcher, *The Diplomacy of Annexation: Texas, Oregon, and the Mexican War* (1973); Cecil Robinson, ed., *The View from Chapultepec: Mexican Writers on the Mexican-American War* (1989); David J. Weber, *The Mexican Frontier, 1821–1846* (1982).

Going West

John Mack Faragher, *Women and Men on the Overland Trail* (1978); Sandra Myres, ed., *Ho for California! Women's Overland Diaries from the Huntington Library* (1980); John D. Unruh Jr., *The Plains Across: The Overland Emigrants and the Trans-Mississippi West, 1840–1860* (1979).

Living on the Frontier

Peter G. Boag, *Environment and Experience: Settlement Culture in Nineteenth-Century Oregon* (1992); Richard L. Bushman, *Joseph Smith and the Beginnings of Mormonism* (1984); Arrell Morgan Gibson, *Yankees in Paradise: The Pacific Basin Frontier* (1993); Julie Roy Jeffrey, *Frontier Women: "Civilizing" the West? 1840–1880* (1998); William Loren Katz, *The Black West* (1971); Lawrence H. Larson, *The Urban West at the End of the Frontier* (1978); Laurie F. Maffly-Kipp, *Religion and Society in Frontier California* (1994); Dean L. May, *Three Frontiers: Family, Land, and Society in the American West, 1850–1900* (1994); Adolf E. Schroeder and Carla Schulz-Geisberg, eds., *Hold Dear, As Always: Jette, a German Immigrant Life in Letters* (1988).

Cultures in Conflict

Albert Camarillo, *Chicanos in a Changing Society: From Mexican Pueblos to American Barrios in Santa Barbara and Southern California, 1848–1930* (1979); Albert L. Hurtado, *Indian Survival on the California Frontier* (1988); Julie Roy Jeffrey, *Converting the West: A Biography of Narcissa Whitman* (1991); Timothy M. Marovina, *Tejano Religion and Ethnicity: San Antonio, 1821–1860* (1995); M. S. Meir and Feliciano Rivera, *The Chicanos: A History of Mexican-Americans* (1972); Alfredo Mirande and Evangeline Enriquez, *La Chicana: The Mexican-American Woman* (1979); Peter Nabakov, ed., *Native American Testimony: An Anthology of Indian and White Relations* (1978); Jacqueline Peters, *Sacred Encounters: Father DeSmet and the Indians of the Rocky Mountain West* (1993); Leonard Pitt, *The Decline of the Californios: A Social History of the Spanish-Speaking Californians, 1846–1890* (1970); Robert J. Rosenbaum, *Mexicano Resistance in the Southwest: "The Sacred Right of Self-Preservation"* (1981); Theodore Stern, *Chiefs & Chief Traders: Indian Relations at Fort Nez Perces, 1818–1855 (1993);* Sylvia Van Kirk, *Many Tender Ties: Women in the Fur Trade Society, 1670–1870* (1983); David J. Wishart, *An Unspeakable Sadness: The Dispossession of the Nebraska Indians* (1994).

Fiction and Film

Mark Twain's *Roughing It* is often humorous, but through the humor you can see Twain's insightful comments about westerners' values and standards. James C. Work's *Gunfight!* (1996) contains a selection of gunfight stories originally printed in popular magazines. For an example of an early dime novel, see Ann Sophia Winterbotham Stephens's *Malaeska: Indian Wife of the White Hunter* (1861, but use any edition).

The West is a nine-part series by Ken Burns, first shown on television. The films provide a sympathetic and critical account of the settlement of the West and its impact on Native Americans. *The Donner Party* (1992) is a PBS video of the disastrous experience of a party of emigrants who were caught in the Sierra Nevadas during the winter of 1846–1847. One critic notes a dark tone to the film, which is characteristic of the New Western History.

Suggested Web Sites

http://memory.loc.gov/ammem/umhtml/umhome.html

Pioneering the Upper Midwest: Books from Michigan, Minnesota, and Wisconsin, ca. 1820–1910. This Library of Congress site looks at first-person accounts, biographies, promotional literature, local histories, ethnographic and antiquarian texts, colonial archival documents, and other works from the seventeenth to the early twentieth century. It covers many topics and issues that affected Americans in the settlement and development of the Upper Midwest.

http://sunsite.unam.mx/revistas/1847

The Mexican-American War Memorial Homepage. Images and text at this site explain the causes, courses, and outcomes of the Mexican-American War.

http://www.ukans.edu/carrie/kancoll/galtrl.htm

Gallery: On the Trail . . . This Kansas Collection site holds several good primary sources with images concerning the Oregon Trail and America's early movement westward.

http://www.xmission.com/~drudy/amm.html

Mountain Men and the Fur Trade. Private letters can speak volumes about the concerns and environment of the writers and recipients. Letters from early settlers west of the Mississippi River are offered on this site, which is an on-line research center devoted to the trappers, explorers, and traders known as the Mountain Men.

http://members.aol.com/danmrosen/donner/index.htm

The Donner Party. This site includes logs from the infamous party that resorted to extreme measures to survive. It also has images of the region.

http://www.si.edu/organiza/museums/amerind/start.htm

National Museum of the American Indian. The Smithsonian Institution maintains this site, providing information about the museum. The museum is dedicated to everything about Native Americans.

http://www.ushistoryplace.com

the History place A richly detailed on-line learning environment complete with interactive maps, timelines, history activities, primary source documents, and links to related American history sites.

14

The UNION *in* PERIL

CHAPTER OUTLINE

The autumn of 1860 was a time of ominous rumors and expectations. The election was held on November 6 in an atmosphere of crisis. In Springfield, Illinois, Abraham Lincoln, taking coffee and sandwiches prepared by the "ladies of Springfield," waited as the telegraph brought in the returns. By 1 A.M., victory was certain. He reported later, "I went home, but not to get much sleep, for I then felt, as I never had before, the responsibility that was upon me." And with good cause. He and the American people faced the most serious crisis since the founding of the Republic.

Lincoln won an unusual four-party election with only 39 percent of the popular vote. He had appealed almost exclusively to northern voters in a blatantly sectional campaign, defeating his three opponents by carrying every free state except New Jersey. Of the candidates, only Illinois Senator Stephen Douglas campaigned actively in every section of the country. For his efforts, he received the second-highest number of votes. Douglas's appeal, especially in the closing days of the campaign, was "on behalf of the Union," which he feared—correctly—was in imminent danger of splitting apart.

Other Americans sensed the mood of crisis that fall and faced their own fears and responsibilities. A month before the election, plantation owner Robert Allston wrote his oldest son, Benjamin, that "disastrous consequences" would follow from a Lincoln victory. Although his letter mentioned the possibility of secession, he dealt mostly with plantation concerns: a new horse, the mood of the slaves, ordering supplies from the city, instructions for making trousers on a sewing machine. After Lincoln's election, Allston corresponded with a southern colleague about the need for an "effective military organization" to resist "Northern and Federal aggression." In his shift from sewing machines to military ones, Robert Allston prepared for what he called the "impending crisis."

Frederick Douglass greeted the election of 1860 with characteristic optimism. Not only was this an opportunity to "educate . . . the people in their moral and political duties," he said, but "slaveholders know that the day of their power is over when a Republican President is elected." But no sooner had Lincoln's victory been determined than Douglass's hopes turned sour. He noted that Republican leaders, in their desire to keep southern border states from seceding, sounded more antiabolitionist than antislavery. They vowed not to touch slavery in areas where it already existed, which included the District of Columbia, and they promised to enforce the hated Fugitive Slave Act and to put down slave rebellions. Slavery would, in fact, Douglass bitterly concluded, "be as safe, and safer" with Lincoln than with a Democrat.

Michael Luark, an Iowa farmer, was not so sure. Born in Virginia, Luark was a typically mobile nineteenth-century American. After growing up in Indiana, he followed the mining booms of the 1850s to Colorado and California before returning to the Midwest to farm. Luark sought a good living and resented all the furor over slavery. He could not, however, avoid the issue. Writing in his diary on the last day of 1860, Luark looked ahead to 1861 with a deep sense of fear. "Startling" political changes would occur, he predicted, perhaps even the "Dissolution of the Union and Civil War with all its train of horrors." He blamed abolitionist agitators, perhaps reflecting his Virginia origins. On New Year's Day, he expressed his fears that Lincoln would let the "most ultra sectional and Abolition" men disturb the "vexed Slavery question" even further, as Frederick Douglass wanted. But if this happened, Luark warned, "then farewell to our beloved Union of States."

Within four months of this diary entry, the guns of the Confederate States of America fired on a federal fort in South Carolina, and the Civil War began. Luark's fears, Douglass's hopes, and Lincoln's and Allston's preparations for responsibility all became realities. The explanation of the peril and dissolution of the Union forms the theme of this chapter.

Such a calamitous event as Civil War had numerous causes, large and small. The reactions of Allston, Douglass, and Luark to Lincoln's election suggest some of them: moral duties, sectional politics, growing apprehensions over emotional agitators, and a concern for freedom and independence on the part of blacks, white southerners, and western farmers. But as Douglass understood, by 1860, it was clear that "slavery is the real issue, the single bone of contention between all parties and sections. It is the one disturbing force, and explains the confused and irregular motion of our political machine."

George Caleb Bingham's *Stump Speaking* (1856) captures the democratic energy of politics at mid-century. Note the Lincolnlike figure sitting to the right. *(From the Art Collection of Bank of America)*

This chapter analyzes how the momentous issue of slavery disrupted the political system and eventually the Union itself. We will look at how four major developments between 1848 and 1861 contributed to the Civil War: first, a sectional dispute over the extension of slavery into the western territories; second, the breakdown of the political party system; third, growing cultural differences in the views and lifestyles of southerners and northerners; and fourth, intensifying emotional and ideological polarization between the two regions over losing their way of life and sacred republican rights at the hands of the other. A preview of civil war, bringing all four causes together, occurred in 1855-1856 in Kansas. Eventually, emotional events, mistrust, and irreconcilable differences made conflict inevitable. The election of Lincoln was the spark that touched off the conflagration of civil war, with all its "train of horrors."

SLAVERY IN THE TERRITORIES

Senator Lewis Cass (chapter 13) had been wrong when he predicted that the western territories were areas of individual freedom where civilization would advance and political and social harmony would prevail. As many migrants and residents discovered, personal costs attended the American march westward. White migrations threatened both the safety and the cultural integrity of Native Americans and Mexicans whose land stood in the way. They also caused a collision of Yankees and slaveholders.

The North and the South had contained their differences over slavery, with only occasional difficulties, during the 60 years after the Constitutional Convention. Compromise in 1787 had resolved questions of the slave trade and the matter of counting slaves for congressional representation. Although slavery threatened ("like a fireball in the night," Jefferson had said) the uneasy sectional harmony in 1820, the Missouri Compromise had established a workable balance of free and slave states and had defined a geographic line (36°30') to determine future decisions. In 1833, compromise had defused South Carolina's attempt at nullification, and the gag rule in 1836 had kept the abolitionists' petitions off the floor of Congress.

Each apparent resolution, however, raised the level of emotional conflict between North and South and postponed ultimate settlement of the slavery question. One reason why these compromises temporarily worked was the two-party system, with Whigs and Democrats in both North and South. Party loyalties served as an "antidote," as Van Buren put it, to sectional allegiance. The parties differed over cultural and economic issues, but the volatile issue of slavery was largely kept out of political campaigns and congressional debates. This changed in the late 1840s, and the change would prove catastrophic to the Union.

Free Soil or Constitutional Protection?

When the war with Mexico broke out in 1846, it seemed likely that the United States would acquire new territories in the Southwest. Would they be slave or free? To an appropriations bill to pay for the war, David Wilmot, a congressman from Pennsylvania, added a short amendment declaring that "neither slavery nor involuntary servitude shall ever exist" in any territories acquired from Mexico. The debates in Congress over the Wilmot Proviso were significant because legislators voted not as Whigs and Democrats but as northerners and southerners.

A Boston newspaper prophetically observed that Wilmot's resolution "brought to a head the great question which is about to divide the American people." When the Mexican-American War ended, several solutions were presented to deal with this question of slavery in the territories. The first was the "free soil" idea of preventing any extensions of slavery. But did Congress have the power or right to do so? Two precedents suggested that it did. One was the Northwest Ordinance, which had prohibited the entry of slaves into states created in the Upper Midwest; the other was the Missouri Compromise.

Supporters of free soil had mixed motives. For some, slavery was a moral evil to be attacked and destroyed because it trampled on principles of liberty and equality. But for many northern white farmers looking to move westward, the threat of economic competition with an expanding system of large-scale slave labor was even more serious. Neither did they wish to compete for land with free blacks. As Wilmot put it, his proviso was intended to preserve the area for the "sons of toil, of my own race and own color." Other northerners supported the Wilmot Proviso as a means of restraining what seemed to them the growing political power and "insufferable arrogance" of the "spirit and demands of the Slave Power."

Opposed to the free-soil position were the arguments of Senator John C. Calhoun of South Carolina, expressed in several resolutions introduced in the Senate in 1847. Not only did Congress lack the constitutional right to exclude slavery from the territories, Calhoun argued, but it had a positive duty to protect it. The Wilmot Proviso, therefore, was unconstitutional, as was the Missouri Compromise, and any other federal act that prevented slaveholders from taking their slave property into the territories of the United States.

Economic, political, and moral considerations stood behind the Calhoun position. Many southerners hungered for new cotton lands in the West and Southwest, even in Central America and the Caribbean. Politically, southerners feared that northerners wanted to trample on their liberties—namely, the right to protect their institutions against abolitionism. Southern leaders saw the Wilmot Proviso as a moral issue that raised questions about basic republican principles. One congressman called it "treason to the Constitution," and Senator Robert Toombs of Georgia warned that if Congress passed the proviso, he would favor disunion rather than "degradation."

Popular Sovereignty and the Election of 1848

With such divisive potential, it was natural that many Americans sought a compromise solution to keep slavery out of politics. Polk's secretary of state, James Buchanan of Pennsylvania, proposed that the Missouri Compromise line be extended through the lands acquired from Mexico to the Pacific Ocean, avoiding thorny questions about the morality of slavery and the constitutionality of congressional authority. So would "popular sovereignty," Senator Cass's proposal to leave decisions about permitting slavery to the local territorial legislature, avoid these issues. The idea appealed to the American democratic belief in local self-government but left many details unanswered. At what point in the progress toward statehood could a territorial legislature decide about slavery? Cass preferred to leave such questions ambiguous, reasoning that both northern and southern politicians would conclude that popular sovereignty favored their interests.

The Democratic party, liking popular sovereignty because it could mean all things to all people, nominated Cass for president in 1848. Cass denounced abolitionists and the Wilmot Proviso but otherwise avoided the issue of slavery. The Democrats, however, cleverly printed two campaign biographies of Cass, one for the South and one for the North.

The Whigs found an even better way to hold the party together by evading the slavery issue. Rejecting

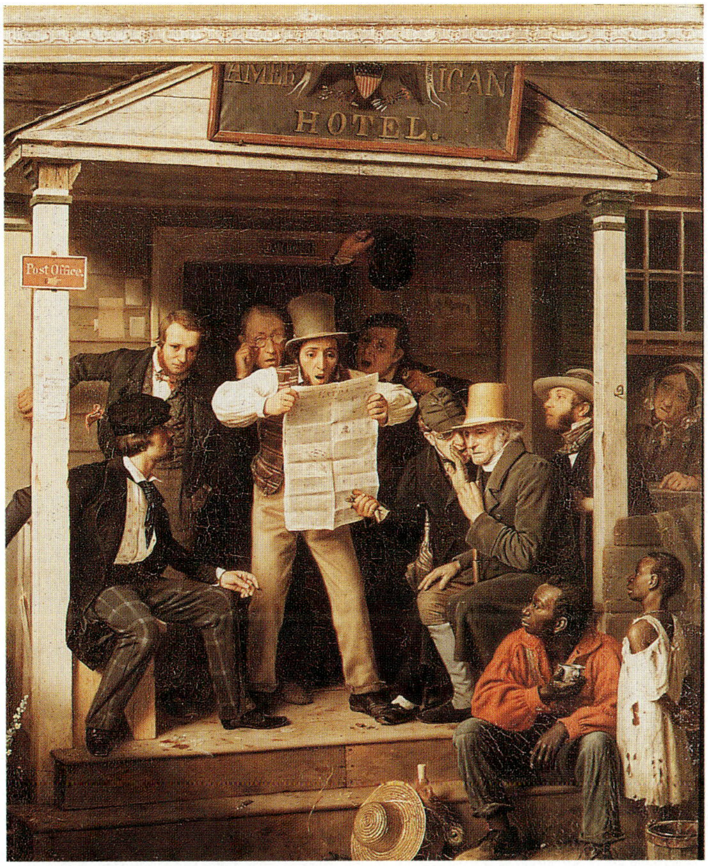

This 1848 painting by Richard Caton Woodville, titled *War News from Mexico,* captures the mood of the period from the Mexican-American War through the Civil War; in towns across the country, outside of countless "American Hotels," the American people listened eagerly to the latest news in an era of steadily worsening political, socioeconomic, and constitutional crises. Separate from the men on the porch, but clearly a part of the picture, are a black father and daughter in rags; they await the war news with special interest, for black Americans would have most to lose by an outcome of the war that led to the expansion of slavery into the territories. *(National Academy of Design, New York)*

Recovering the Past

SENATE SPEECHES

The history of average, anonymous Americans can be recovered in letters, diaries, folktales, and other nontraditional sources. But in times of political conflict with enormous implications for all Americans, as in the years before the Civil War, historians turn to more conventional sources such as congressional speeches. Recorded in the *Congressional Globe,* these speeches are a revealing means of recovering the substance, tone, and drama of political debate.

Despite the cynical view of American politics held by some European visitors, the mid-nineteenth century was an era of giants in the U.S. Senate: Daniel Webster, Henry Clay, Thomas Hart Benton, John C. Calhoun, William Seward, and Stephen Douglas. When Congress debated a major issue, such as the tariff, nullification, or the extension of slavery, large crowds would pack the Senate galleries. The speeches would then be quickly printed and widely distributed. These spectacular oratorical encounters provided mass entertainment and political instruction. Such was the case with the Senate speeches over the Compromise of 1850. The three principal figures early in the debates were Clay (Kentucky), Calhoun (South Carolina), and Webster (Massachusetts), each of whom delivered a great address crowning a long, distinguished career.

Born within five years of each other as the American Revolution was ending (1777–1782), each man began his political career in the House of Representatives in the era of the War of 1812. Each served a term as secretary of state; in addition, Clay was speaker of the House and Calhoun secretary of war and vice president. Each served for over a decade in the Senate (Clay, 13 years; Calhoun, 15 years; Webster, 19 years). Each was a party leader, Clay and Webster of the Whigs and Calhoun of the Democrats. During their 40 years of public service, they represented strong nationalistic positions as well as their various states and sections. All three were candidates for president between 1824 and 1844. All three spent most of their careers in the political shadow of Andrew Jackson, and all three had serious conflicts with him.

Many years of political and ideological conflict with each other not only sharpened their oratorical skills but also led to mutual respect. Webster said of Calhoun that he was "the ablest man in the Senate. He could have demolished Newton, Calvin, or even John Locke as a logician." Calhoun said of Clay, "He is a bad man, but by god, I love him." And "Old Man Eloquent" himself, John Quincy Adams, said of Webster that he was "the most consummate orator of modern times."

It was therefore a momentous event when they each prepared speeches and met for one last encounter early in 1850. Clay was over 70 years old and in failing health, but he came out of retirement to try to keep the Union together. He defended his compromise proposals in a four-hour speech spread over two days, February 5 and 6. The Senate galleries were so packed that listeners were pushed into hallways and even into the rotunda of the Capitol. Copies of his speech were in such demand that over 100,000 were printed.

A month later, on March 7, the scene was repeated as Webster rose to join Clay in defending the compromise. Three days earlier, although too ill to deliver the speech himself, Calhoun had "tottered into the Senate" on the arm of a friend to hear James Mason of Virginia read his rejection of the compromise. Within a month, Calhoun was dead. Clay and Webster followed him to the grave two years later, and Senate leadership passed on to Seward, Douglas, and a new generation of Senate giants.

As you read the excerpts from each speech, try to imagine yourself sitting in the gallery overlooking the Senate floor, listening to each man and absorbing the drama of the moment. How do the oratorical styles differ? Which passages convey the most emotional power? Which speaker is most persuasive to you? Why? To what extent do the three agree on the fugitive slave issue?

John C. Calhoun

March 4, 1850
Having now, Senators, explained what it is that endangers the Union, and traced it to its cause, and explained its nature and character, the question again recurs—How can the Union be saved? To this I answer, there is but one way by which it can be—and that is—by adopting such measures as will satisfy the States belonging to the Southern section, that they can remain in the Union consistently with their honor and their safety. . . .

But will the North agree to this? It is for her to answer the question. But, I will say, she cannot refuse, if she has half the love of the Union which she professes to have, or without justly exposing herself to the charge that her love of power and aggrandizement is far greater than her love of the Union. At all events, the responsibility of saving the Union rests on the North, and not on the South. . . .

Henry Clay

February 5–6, 1850
I have seen many periods of great anxiety, of peril, and of danger in this country, and I have never before risen to address any assemblage so oppressed, so appalled, and so anxious; and sir, I hope it will not be out of place to do here, what again and again I have done in my private chamber, to implore of Him who holds the destinies of nations and individuals in His hands, to bestow upon our country His blessing, to calm the violence and rage of party, to still passion, to allow reason once more to resume its empire. . . .

Mr. President, it is passion, passion-party, party, and intemperance—that is all I dread in the adjustment of the great questions which unhappily at this time divide our distracted country. Sir, at this moment we have in the legislative bodies of this Capitol and in the States, twenty old furnaces in full blast, emitting heat, and passion, and intemperance, and diffusing them throughout the whole extent of this broad land. Two months ago all was calm in comparison to the present moment. All now is uproar, confusion, and menace to the existence of the Union, and to the happiness and safety of this people. . . .

Sir, when I came to consider this subject, there were two or three general purposes which it seemed to me to be most desirable, if possible, to accomplish. The one was, to settle all the controverted questions arising out of the subject of slavery. . . . I therefore turned my attention to every subject connected with this institution of slavery, and out of which controverted questions had sprung, to see if it were possible or practicable to accommodate and adjust the whole of them. . . .

We are told now, and it is rung throughout this entire country, that the Union is threatened with subversion and destruction. Well, the first question which naturally rises is, supposing the Union to be dissolved,—having all the causes of grievance which are complained of,—How far will a dissolution furnish a remedy for those grievances? If the Union is to be dissolved for any existing causes, it will be dissolved because slavery is interdicted or not allowed to be introduced into the ceded territories; because slavery is threatened to be abolished in the District of Columbia, and because fugitive slaves are not returned, as in my opinion they ought to be, and restored to their masters. These, I believe, will be the causes; if there be any causes, which can lead to the direful event to which I have referred. . . .

Mr. President, I am directly opposed to any purpose of secession, of separation. I am for staying within the Union, and defying any portion of this Union to expel or drive me out of the Union.

Daniel Webster

March 7, 1850
Mr. President: I wish to speak to-day, not as a Massachusetts man, nor as a Northern man, but as an American, and a member of the Senate of the United States. . . .

I speak to-day for the preservation of the Union. "Hear me for my cause." I speak to-day, out of a solicitous and anxious heart, for the restoration to the country of that quiet and that harmony which make the blessing of this Union so rich, and so dear to us all. . . . I shall bestow a little attention, Sir, upon these various grievances existing on the one side and on the other. I begin with complaints of the South . . . and especially to one which has in my opinion just foundation; and that is, that there has been found at the North, among individuals and among legislators, a disinclination to perform fully their constitutional duties in regard to the return of persons bound to service who have escaped into the free States. In that respect, the South, in my judgment, is right, and the North is wrong. Every member of every Northern legislature is bound by oath, like every other officer in the country, to support the Constitution of the United States; and the article of the Constitution which says to these States they shall deliver up fugitives from service is as binding in honor and conscience as any other article. . . .

Where is the line to be drawn? What States are to secede? What is to remain American? What am I to be? An American no longer? Am I to become a sectional man, a local man, a separatist, with no country in common with the gentlemen who sit around me here, or who fill the other house of Congress? Heaven forbid! Where is the flag of the republic to remain? Where is the eagle still to tower? or is he to cower, and shrink, and fall to the ground?

Henry Clay, they nominated the Mexican-American War hero, General Zachary Taylor, a Louisiana slaveholder. Taylor compared himself with Washington as a "no party" man above politics. This was about all he stood for. Southern Whigs supported Taylor because they thought he might understand the burdens of slaveholding, and northern Whigs were pleased that he took no stand on the Wilmot Proviso.

The evasions of the two major parties disappointed Calhoun, who tried to create a new unified southern party. His "Address to the People of the Southern States" threatened secession and called for a united stand against further attempts to interfere with the southern right to extend slavery. Although only 48 of 121 southern representatives signed the address, Calhoun's argument raised the specter of secession and disunion.

Warnings also came from the North. A New York Democratic faction bolted to support Van Buren for president. At first, the split had more to do with internal state politics than moral principles, but it soon involved the question of slavery in the territories. Disaffected "conscience" Whigs from Massachusetts, unhappy with a slaveholder as their party standard-bearer, also explored a third-party alternative. These groups met in Buffalo, New York, to form the Free-Soil party and nominate Van Buren for president. The platform of the new party, an uneasy mixture of ardent abolitionists and opponents of free blacks moving into western lands, pledged to fight for "free soil, free speech, free labor and free men."

General Taylor won easily, largely because defections from Cass to the Free-Soilers cost the Democrats New York and Pennsylvania. Although weakened, the two-party system survived. Purely sectional parties had failed. The Free-Soilers took only about 10 percent of the popular vote, and no electoral votes.

The Compromise of 1850

Taylor won by avoiding slavery questions. But as president he had to deal with them. As he was inaugurated in 1849, four compelling issues faced the nation. First, the rush of some 80,000 unruly gold miners to California qualified it for statehood. But California's entry as a free state would upset the balance between slave and free states in the Senate that had prevailed since 1820.

The unresolved status of the Mexican cession in the Southwest posed a second problem. The longer the area remained unorganized, the louder local inhabitants called for an application of either the Wilmot Proviso or the Calhoun doctrine. The Texas–New Mexico boundary was also disputed, Texas claiming everything east of Santa Fe. Northerners feared that Texas might split into five or six slave states.

A third problem, especially for abolitionists, was the existence of slavery and one of the largest slave markets in North America in the nation's capital.

Henry Clay argues for the compromise package of 1850 in this painting by R. Whitechurch, titled *The United States Senate, 1850.* Clay warned that failure to adopt his bill would lead to "furious" and "bloody" civil war. *(Library of Congress)*

Fourth, southerners resented the lax federal enforcement of the Fugitive Slave Act of 1793. They called for a stronger act that would end protection for runaways fleeing along the Underground Railroad to Canada.

Although Taylor was a newcomer to politics (he had never even voted in a presidential election before 1848), he tackled these problems in a statesmanlike, if evasive, manner. Sidestepping the issue of slavery in the territories, he invited California and New Mexico to apply immediately for statehood, presumably as free states. But soon he alienated both southern supporters like Calhoun and mainstream Whig leaders like Clay and Webster.

Early in 1850, the old compromiser Henry Clay sought to regain control of the Whig party by proposing solutions to the divisive issues before the nation. With Webster's support, Clay introduced a series of resolutions in an omnibus package intended to settle these issues once and for all. The stormy debates, great speeches, and political maneuvering that followed provided a crucial and dramatic moment in American history. Yet despite some 70 speeches on behalf of the compromise, the Senate defeated Clay's Omnibus Bill. The tired and disheartened 73-year-old Clay left Washington, hoping to regain his strength. He never did, and soon died. Into the gap stepped a new compromiser, Senator Stephen Douglas of Illinois, who saw that Clay's resolutions had a better chance of passing if voted on individually. Under Douglas's leadership, and with the support of Millard Fillmore, who succeeded to the presidency upon Taylor's sudden death, a series of bills was finally passed.

The so-called Compromise of 1850 put Clay's resolutions, slightly altered, into law. First, California entered the Union as a free state, ending the balance of free and slave states, 16 to 15. Second, territorial governments were organized in New Mexico and Utah, letting the people there decide whether to permit slavery. The Texas–New Mexico border was settled, denying Texas the disputed area. In return, the federal government gave Texas $10 million to pay debts owed to Mexico. Third, the slave trade, but not slavery, was abolished in the District of Columbia.

The fourth and most controversial part of the compromise was the Fugitive Slave Act, containing many provisions that offended northerners. One denied alleged fugitives a jury trial, leaving special cases for decision by commissioners (who were paid $5 for setting a fugitive free but $10 for returning a fugitive). An especially repugnant provision compelled northern citizens to assist in the enforcement of the act by hunting down runaway slaves and turning them in.

Consequences of Compromise

The Compromise of 1850 was the last attempt to keep slavery out of politics. How well it succeeded in doing so is debatable. Voting behavior on the several bills

The Compromise of 1850

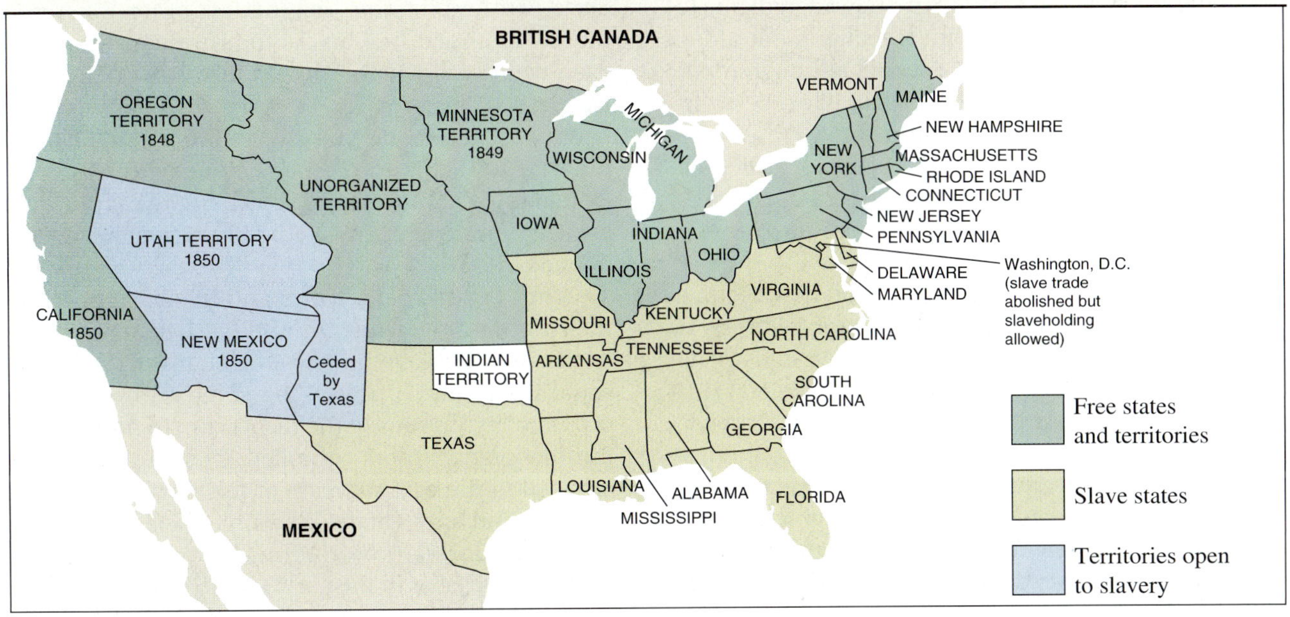

"I have seen many periods of great anxiety, of peril, and of danger in this country," Henry Clay told the Congress in February 1850, "and I have never before risen to address any assemblage so oppressed, so appalled, and so anxious." What followed were the debates that led eventually to the passage of his great compromise. Can you find three of the four major parts of the bill on the map?

CAUTION!!

COLORED PEOPLE

OF BOSTON, ONE & ALL,

You are hereby respectfully CAUTIONED and advised, to avoid conversing with the

Watchmen and Police Officers of Boston,

For since the recent ORDER OF THE MAYOR & ALDERMEN, they are empowered to act as

KIDNAPPERS

AND

Slave Catchers,

And they have already been actually employed in KIDNAPPING, CATCHING, AND KEEPING SLAVES. Therefore, if you value your LIBERTY, and the *Welfare of the Fugitives* among you, *Shun* them in every possible manner, as so many *HOUNDS* on the track of the most unfortunate of your race.

Keep a Sharp Look Out for KIDNAPPERS, and have TOP EYE open.

APRIL 24, 1851.

THEODORE PARKER'S PLACARD

Placard written by Theodore Parker and printed and posted by the Vigilance Committee of Boston after the rendition o

As a group of runaways makes its way north in this painting by Theodor Kaufmann, *On to Liberty* (1867) *(The Metropolitan Museum of Art, gift of Erving and Joyce Wolf, 1982 (1982.443.3))*, the peril of the journey, even if successful, is reflected in this broadside published by Boston abolitionist Theodore Parker, which alerted the city's black community in 1851 to the dangers posed by the Fugitive Slave Act. *(Chicago Public Library)*

varied, with legislators following sectional lines on some issues and party lines on others. Douglas had good reason to feel pleased, celebrating the acts of 1850 as a "final settlement" of the slavery question.

But the compromise only delayed more serious sectional conflict, and it added two new ingredients to American politics. First, political realignment along sectional lines moved closer. Second, although repudiated by most ordinary citizens, ideas like secessionism, disunion, and a "higher law" than the Constitution entered political discussions. People wondered whether the question of slavery in the territories could be compromised away the next time it arose.

Others were immediately upset. The new fugitive slave law angered many northerners because it brought the evils of slavery right into their midst. The owners of runaway slaves hired agents, labeled "kidnappers" in the North, to hunt down fugitives. In a few dramatic episodes, most notably in Boston, literary and religious intellectuals led mass protests to resist slave hunters' efforts to return alleged fugitives to the South. When Senator Webster supported the law, New England abolitionists denounced him as "indescribably base and wicked." Theodore Parker called the new law a "hateful statute of kidnappers," and Ralph Waldo Emerson said it was a "filthy law" that he would not obey.

Frederick Douglass would not obey it either. As a runaway slave himself, he was threatened with arrest and return to the South until friends overcame his objections and purchased his freedom. Douglass still risked harm by his strong defiance of the Fugitive Slave Act. Arguing the "rightfulness of forcible resistance," he urged free blacks to arm themselves and even wondered whether it was justifiable to kill kidnappers. "The only way to make the Fugitive Slave Law a dead letter," he said in Pittsburgh in 1853, "is to make a half dozen or more dead kidnappers." Douglass raised money for black fugitives, hid runaways in his home, and helped hundreds escape to Canada.

Other northerners, white and black, stepped up their work for the Underground Railroad in response to the fugitive slave law. Several states passed "personal liberty laws" that prohibited the use of state officials and institutions in the recovery of fugitive slaves. But most northerners complied. Of some 200 blacks arrested in the first six years of the law, only 15 were rescued, and only 3 of these by force. Failed rescues, in fact, had more emotional impact than successful ones. In two cases in the early 1850s (Thomas Sims in 1851 and Anthony Burns in 1854), angry mobs of abolitionists in Boston, reminiscent of the Revolutionary days of the Tea Party, failed to prevent the forcible return of blacks to the South. These celebrated cases aroused antislavery emotions in more northerners than the abolitionists had been able to do in all their tracts and speeches. Amos Lawrence, a textile tycoon in Massachusetts, wrote of the trial of Anthony Burns that sent him back to the South: "We went to bed one night old fashioned, conservative Compromise Union Whigs and waked up stark mad abolitionists."

Longtime abolitionists escalated their rhetoric, fueling emotions over slavery in the aftermath of the Fugitive Slave Act. In an Independence Day speech in 1852, Frederick Douglass wondered, "What, to the American slave, is your 4th of July?" It was, he said, the day that revealed to the slave the "gross injustice and cruelty to which he is the constant victim." To a slave, the American claims of national greatness were vain and empty; the "shouts of liberty and equality" were "hollow mockery, . . . mere bombast, fraud, deception, impiety, and hypocrisy." Douglass's speeches, like those of another former slave, Sojourner Truth, took on an increasingly strident tone in the early 1850s.

At a women's rights convention in Akron, Ohio, in 1851, Truth made one of the decade's boldest statements for minority rights. The convention was attended by some clergymen who kept interrupting the proceedings to heckle female speakers. Up stood Sojourner Truth to speak in words still debated by historians. She pointed to her many years of childbearing and hard, backbreaking work as a slave, crying out in a repetitive refrain, "And ar'n't I a woman?" Referring to Jesus, she asked where he came from: "From God and a woman: Man had nothing to do with Him." Referring to Eve, she concluded, "If the first woman God ever made was strong enough to turn the world upside down all alone, these women together ought to be able to turn it back, and get it right side up again! And now they is asking to do it, the men better let them." Her brief speech silenced the hecklers.

As Truth spoke, another American woman, Harriet Beecher Stowe, was finishing a novel, *Uncle Tom's Cabin,* that would go far toward turning the world upside down and trying to right it again. As politicians were hoping the American people would forget slavery, Stowe's novel brought it to the attention of thousands. She gave readers an absorbing indictment of the horrors of slavery and its immoral impact on both northerners and southerners. Published initially in serial form, each month's chapter ended at a nail-biting dramatic moment. Readers throughout the North cheered Eliza's daring

The hypocrisy of the Fugitive Slave Act (part of the Compromise of 1850) and Henry Clay's mixed motives are the focus of this 1851 cartoon. Whites preach the "blessings of liberty" at a free black man they are holding back from freedom as Clay turns his back on the fugitive slave and talks to a northerner about the tariff. *(Library of Congress)*

escape across the ice floes on the Ohio River, cried over Uncle Tom's humanity and Little Eva's death, suffered under the lash of Simon Legree, and rejoiced in the reuniting of black family members.

Although outraging the South when published in full in 1852, *Uncle Tom's Cabin* became one of the all-time best-sellers in American history. In the first year, over 300,000 copies were printed, and Stowe's novel was eventually published in 20 languages. When President Lincoln met Stowe in 1863, he is reported to have said to her: "So you're the little woman who wrote the book that made this great war!"

POLITICAL DISINTEGRATION

The response to *Uncle Tom's Cabin* and the Fugitive Slave Act indicated that politicians had congratulated themselves too soon for saving the Republic in 1850. Political developments, not all dealing with slavery, were already weakening the ability of political parties—and ultimately the nation—to withstand the passions slavery aroused.

The Apathetic Election of 1852

Political parties, then and now, thrive on their ability to convince voters that their party stands for moral values and economic policies crucially different from those of the opposition. In the period between 1850 and 1854, these differences were blurred, thereby undermining party loyalty. First, both parties scrambled to convince voters that they had favored the Compromise of 1850. In addition, several states rewrote their constitutions and remodeled their laws in the early 1850s, standardizing many political and economic procedures. One effect of these changes was to reduce the number of patronage jobs available for party victors to dispense. Another effect was to regularize the process, begun in the 1830s, for securing banking, railroad, and other corporate charters, removing the role formerly played by the legislature. Both of these weakened the importance of the party in citizens' lives.

The third development that weakened parties was economic. For almost a quarter of a century, Whigs and Democrats had disagreed over such issues as the tariff, money and banking systems, and government support for internal improvements. But economic conditions improved markedly in the early 1850s. In a time of prosperity, party distinctions over economic policies seemed less important. An ample money supply made the revenues of a high tariff less necessary. Moreover, in the rush for railroad charters during the boom of the early 1850s, local connections were more important than national party politics.

Economic issues persisted, but the battles were fought at the local rather than national level. Thus Georgia voters in 1851 disagreed over commercial banking laws, taxes for internal improvements, and, as an Augusta newspaper put it, "the jealousies of the poor who owned no slaves, against the rich slaveholder." In Indiana, where Congressman George Julian observed that people "hate the Negro with a perfect if not a supreme hatred," legislators rewrote the state constitution in 1851, depriving blacks of the rights to vote, attend white schools, and make contracts. Those who could not post a $500 bond were expelled from the state, and an 1852 law made it a crime for blacks to settle in Indiana. In Massachusetts, temperance reform and a law limiting the working day to ten hours were hot issues. Fleeting political alliances developed around particular issues and local personalities. As a Baltimore businessman said, "The two old parties are fast melting away."

CHANGING POLITICAL PARTY SYSTEMS AND LEADERS

It is characteristic of American politics that when the two major parties fail to respond to the pressing issues of the day, third parties are born and major party realignment occurs. This happened in the 1850s over the issue of slavery and its extension into the territories, which resulted in the collapse of the Whigs and the emergence of the Republican party. Note that the "Republican" party begins in one tradition and ends up in the other. Is political realignment happening again in American politics?

First Party System: 1790s–1820s

Republican	Federalist
Jefferson	Hamilton
Madison	John Adams
Monroe	

Transition: 1824 and 1828

Democrat-Republican	National Republican
Jackson	J. Q. Adams

Second Party System: 1830s–1850s

Democrat	Whig
Jackson	Clay
Van Buren	Webster
Calhoun	W. H. Harrison
Polk	

Third Party System: 1856–1890s

Democrat	Republican
Douglas	Lincoln
Pierce	Seward
Buchanan	Grant

The election of 1852 illustrated the lessening significance of political parties. The Whigs nominated General Winfield Scott, another Mexican-American War hero, whom they hoped would repeat Taylor's success four years earlier. With Clay and Webster both dead, party leadership had passed to Senator William Seward of New York, who wanted a president he could influence more successfully than the pro-southern Fillmore. Still, it took 52 ballots to nominate Scott over Fillmore, with serious costs to the party allegiance of southern Whigs. Democrats had their own problems deciding on a candidate. After 49 ballots, in which Cass, Douglas, and Buchanan each held the lead for a time, the party turned to the lackluster Franklin Pierce of New Hampshire as a compromise candidate.

The two parties offered little choice. Both played down issues so as not to widen intraparty divisions. Voter interest diminished. "Genl. Apathy is the strongest candidate out here," was the report from Ohio, while the Baltimore *Sun* remarked that "there is no issue that much interests the people." Democratic prospects were aided by thousands of new Catholic immigrants from Ireland and Germany. Eligible for naturalization and, therefore, the right to vote after only three years, they were influenced by party officials, usually Democrats, who bought their votes with bribes and drinks. Internal conflicts and defections seriously weakened the Whigs, and Pierce won easily, 254 to 42 electoral votes.

The Kansas-Nebraska Act

The Whig party's final disintegration came on a February day in 1854 when southern Whigs stood to support Stephen Douglas's Nebraska bill, thus choosing to be more southern than Whig. The Illinois senator had many reasons for introducing a bill organizing the Nebraska Territory (which included Kansas). As an ardent nationalist and chairman of the Committee on Territories, he was concerned for the continuing development of the West. As a solid citizen of Illinois in a period of explosive railroad building, he wanted the eastern terminus for a transcontinental railroad in Chicago rather than in rival St. Louis. This meant organizing the lands west of Iowa and Missouri.

Politics also played a role. Douglas wanted to recapture the party leadership he had held when he led the fight to pass the Compromise of 1850. He also harbored presidential ambitions. Although he had replaced Cass as the great advocate of popular sovereignty, which won him favor among northern Democrats, he needed the support of southern Democrats. Many southerners, especially slaveholders from Missouri, just east of the Nebraska Territory, opposed the organization of the territory unless it were open to slavery. The problem, as Douglas knew well, was that the entire Nebraska Territory lay north of the line where slavery had been prohibited by the Missouri Compromise.

In George Caleb Bingham's *Verdict of the People* (after 1855), the American flag flies proudly over a happy throng celebrating the outcome of the political process. However, the process of deciding the Kansas-Nebraska Act marked the collapse of the second party system and moved the Union a step closer to disruption and civil war. In an earlier version of the painting, the women on a hotel balcony in the upper right display a banner announcing (ironically?) "Freedom for Virtue." *(Courtesy of the R.W. Norton Art Gallery, Shreveport, Louisiana)*

Douglas's bill, introduced early in 1854, recommended using the principle of popular sovereignty in organizing the Kansas and Nebraska territories. This meant that inhabitants could vote slavery in, thereby violating the Missouri Compromise. Douglas reasoned, however, that the climate and soil of the prairies in Kansas and Nebraska would never support slavery-based agriculture, and the people would decide to be a free state. Therefore, he could win the votes he needed for the railroad without also getting slavery. His bill, then, ignored the Missouri Compromise, simply stating that the state or states created out of the Nebraska Territory would enter the Union "with or without slavery, as their constitution may prescribe at the time of their admission."

Douglas miscalculated. Northerners from his own party immediately attacked him and his bill as a "criminal betrayal of precious rights" and as part of a plot promoting his own presidential ambitions by turning free Nebraska over to "slavery despotism." The outrage among Whigs and abolitionists was even greater. Frederick Douglass branded the act a "hateful" attempt to extend slavery, the result of the "audacious villainy of the slave power."

But Stephen Douglas was a fighter. The more he was attacked, the harder he fought. Eventually his bill passed, but not without seriously damaging the political party system. What began as a railroad measure ended in reopening the question of slavery in the territories that Douglas and others had thought was finally settled in 1850. What began as a way of avoiding conflict ended up in violence over whether Kansas would enter the Union slave or free. What began as a way of strengthening party lines over issues ended up destroying one party (the Whigs), planting deep, irreconcilable divisions in another (the Democrats), and creating two new ones (Know-Nothings and Republicans).

Expansionist "Young America"

The Democratic party was weakened in the early 1850s not only by the Kansas-Nebraska Act but also by an ebullient, expansive energy that led Americans to adventures far beyond Kansas. As republican revolutions erupted in Europe in 1848, Americans greeted them as evidence that the American model of free republican institutions was the wave of the future. Those dedicated to the idea of this continuing national mission, which ironically included the spread of slavery, were called "Young America." An early expression of the spirit of Young America was the enthusiastic reception given the exiled Hungarian revolutionary Louis Kossuth while on a tour of the United States in 1851.

Pierce's platform in 1852 recalled the successful expansionism of the Polk years, declaring that the war with Mexico had been "just and necessary." Many Democrats took their overwhelming victory as a mandate to continue adding territory to the Republic. A Philadelphia newspaper in 1853 described the United States as a nation bound on the "East by sunrise, West by sunset, North by the Arctic Expedition, and South as far as we darn please." Southward expansion into Latin America looked most attractive.

Many of Pierce's diplomatic appointees were southerners interested in adding new cotton-growing lands to the national domain. As ambassador to Mexico, for example, Pierce sent James Gadsden of South Carolina to negotiate with Mexican President Santa Anna for the acquisition of large parts of northern Mexico. Gadsden failed to get all the land he wanted, but he did manage to purchase a strip of desert along the southwest border to build a transcontinental railroad linking the Deep South with the Pacific Coast.

The failure to acquire more territory from Mexico legally did not discourage expansionist Americans from pursuing illegal means. During the 1850s, Texans and Californians staged dozens of raids (called "filibusters") into Mexico. The most daring adventurer of the era was William Walker, a 100-pound Tennessean with a zest for danger and power. After migrating to southern California, Walker made plans to add slave lands to the country. In 1853, he invaded Lower California (the Baja Peninsula) with fewer than 300 men and declared himself president of the independent Republic of Sonora. Although eventually arrested and tried in the United States, he was acquitted after eight minutes of deliberation.

Back Walker went, invading Nicaragua two years later. He overthrew the government, proclaimed himself to have been elected dictator, and issued a decree legalizing slavery. When the Nicaraguans, with British help, acted to regain control of their country, the U.S. Navy rescued Walker. After a triumphant tour in the South, he tried twice more to conquer Nicaragua. Walker came to a fitting end in 1860 when he was captured and shot by a Honduran firing squad after invading that country.

Undaunted by failures in the Southwest, the Pierce administration looked to the acquisition of Cuba, a Spanish colony many Americans thought destined to be a part of their country. One expansionist even suggested that Cuba physically belonged to the United States because it had been formed by alluvial deposits from the Mississippi River. "What God has joined together let no man put asunder," he said. The acquisition of Cuba was necessary, many maintained, as an extension of America's Manifest Destiny and as an ideal place for expanding the slave-based economy of the southern states.

A decade earlier, the Polk administration had offered $10 million for Cuba, but Spain had refused the offer. Unsuccessful efforts were then made to foment a revolution among Cuban sugar planters, who would then request annexation by the United States. One Latin adventurer organized an invasion of Cuba, launched from New Orleans in 1850. When his attempt failed, he was executed, and hundreds of captured comrades were sent to Spain. The citizens of New Orleans rioted in protest, storming the Spanish consulate, which forced an embarrassed Congress to pay an indemnity. A few years later, a former governor of Mississippi, with the support of his friend, Secretary of War Jefferson Davis, planned to raise $1 million and 50,000 troops to invade the island. The proposed expedition, intended to carve Cuba into several new slave states, was aborted.

Although President Pierce did not support these illegal efforts, his administration did want Cuba. Secretary of State William Marcy instructed the emissary to Spain, Pierre Soulé, to offer $130 million for Cuba. If that failed, Marcy suggested stronger measures. In 1854, the secretary arranged for Soulé and the American ministers to France and England to meet in Belgium to consider options. The result was the Ostend Manifesto, a document intended to pressure Spain to sell Cuba to the United States. It also provides a fascinating glimpse of American expansionist attitudes.

The manifesto argued that Cuba "belongs naturally" to the United States. Both geographically and economically, the fortunes and interests of Cubans and southerners were so "blended" that they were "one people with one destiny." Trade and commerce in the hemisphere would "never be secure" until Cuba was part of the United States. Moreover, southern slaveholders feared that a slave rebellion would "Africanize" Cuba, like Haiti, suggesting all kinds of "horrors to the white race" in the nearby southern United States. The American acquisition of Cuba was necessary, therefore, to "preserve our rectitude and self-respect."

If Spain refused to sell the island, the ministers threatened a revolution in Cuba with American support. If that should fail, the manifesto warned, "we should be justified in wresting it from Spain." Even Secretary Marcy was shocked when he received the document from Belgium, and he quickly rejected it. Like the Kansas-Nebraska Act, Democrats who advocated the expansion of slavery urged approval of the Ostend Manifesto. The outraged reaction of northerners in both cases divided and further weakened the Democratic Party.

Nativism, Know-Nothings, and Republicans

Foreign immigration damaged an already enfeebled Whig party and created concern among many native-born Americans. To the average hardworking Protestant American, the foreigners pouring into the cities and following the railroads westward spoke

The American (Know-Nothing) party campaign against the immigrants is dramatically shown in this cartoon of a whiskey-drinking Irishman and beer-barreled German stealing the ballot box while native-born Americans fight at the election poll in the background. The Know-Nothing flag (right) makes starkly clear the origin of the danger. One can only imagine what American Indians thought of this banner. *(New York Public Library, Astor, Lenox & Tilden Foundations)*

unfamiliar languages, wore funny clothes, drank alcohol freely in grogshops, and increased crime and pauperism. Moreover, they seemed content with a lower standard of living and would work for lower wages than American workers, thus threatening their jobs.

Still worse, these Irish and German immigrants were part of an unprecedented growth in the Catholic Church. By the 1850s, there were nearly three million Catholics in the United States, not only in eastern cities but expanding westward into the Ohio valley (Germans in Wheeling, Cincinnati, and St. Louis) and south along old French Canadian trade routes through Detroit, Green Bay, and Vincennes. A surprising and, to many, disturbing development was the Catholic success in converting Protestants. As one Catholic put it, it was "a time when great throngs of Americans began to flock to the Roman Catholic Church despite bitterly intense propaganda and overt opposition." Although overstated, two notable conversions in 1844 compelled Protestant Americans to take the threat seriously. Orestes Brownson, a lifelong Jacksonian Democrat and spiritual seeker, moved successively through Congregationalism, Presbyterianism, Unitarianism, and Transcendentalism until finally converting to a Catholicism he argued was fully compatible with democracy. His disciple, the Methodist German immigrant Isaac Hecker, converted to Catholicism two months earlier in 1844. Joining the Redemptorist order, Hecker served poor German immigrants and, with papal permission, shifted in the 1850s to the active recruiting of Protestants.

Led by the Redemptorists and Jesuits, over 400 parish mission revivals and retreats were held in the 1850s in an aggressive effort to convert urban American Protestants to Roman Catholicism. "All America can be reformed," one religious superior told a group of seminarians in 1856, calling them "instruments in the hands of God which He will use to effect a wonderful change—a spiritual revolution in this country." Sending their children to Catholic schools offended Protestants. Perhaps worst of all, many charged that Catholic immigrants corrupted American politics.

Most Catholics preferred the Democratic party out of traditional loyalties and because Democrats were less inclined than Whigs to interfere with religion, schooling, drinking, and other aspects of personal behavior. It was mostly former Whigs, therefore, who in 1854 founded the American party to oppose the new immigrants. Members wanted a longer period of naturalization to guarantee the "vital principles of Republican Government" and pledged themselves never to vote for Irish Catholics for public office, because it was assumed that their highest loyalty was to the pope in Rome. They also agreed to keep information about their order secret. If asked, they would say, "I know nothing." Hence, they were dubbed the Know-Nothing party.

The Know-Nothings were overwhelmingly a party of the middle and lower classes, workers who worried about their jobs and wages and farmers and small-town Americans who worried about disruptive new forces in their lives. As one New Yorker put it in 1854, "Roman Catholicism is feared more than American slavery." It was widely believed that Catholics slavishly obeyed the orders of their priests, who represented a Church associated with European despotism. The opposition of the Catholic Church to the revolutionary movements of 1848 in Europe intensified the fears of many Protestant Americans that Catholic voters and the Catholic revivals deeply threatened their democratic order. The call to parish missions by Hecker to "make Yankeedom the Rome of the modern world" confirmed their fears. In the 1854 and 1855 elections, the Know-Nothings gave anti-Catholicism a national political focus for the first time.

Although nativists argued that papism would subvert freedom and other republican values, others maintained that the slave power of the South was the chief danger. No sooner had the debates over Nebraska ended than a group of former Whigs and Free-Soilers met and formed the nucleus of another new party, called the Republican party. Concerned about southern expansionism, as reflected in the Kansas-Nebraska Act debates, the Ostend Manifesto, and plans to build a transcontinental railroad from the South to California on land acquired in the Gadsden Purchase, the party sought to respond to popular sentiments by mobilizing sectional fears and ethnic and religious concerns.

Composed almost entirely of northerners, former "conscience" Whigs, and disaffected Democrats, the Republican party combined four main elements. The first group—led by William Seward, Senators Charles Sumner of Massachusetts and Salmon P. Chase of Ohio, and Congressmen Joshua Giddings of Ohio and George Julian of Indiana—was fired by a moral fervor to prohibit slavery in the territories. They also sought to divorce the federal government from the support of slavery by freeing slaves in the District of Columbia, repealing the Fugitive Slave Act, and eliminating the internal slave trade. There were, however, limits to the idealism of most Republicans. A more moderate and larger group, typified by Abraham Lincoln of Illinois, opposed slavery in the western territories only but would not interfere with it where it already existed. This group also indicated that it would not support efforts to achieve equal rights for northern free blacks.

Republicans were anti-Catholic as well as antislavery. This third element of the party, reflecting the tra-

THE EMERGING THIRD PARTY SYSTEM: PRESIDENTIAL ELECTIONS, 1852–1860

Year	Candidates	Party	Popular Vote	Electoral Vote
1852	FRANKLIN PIERCE	Democrat	1,601,474 (51%)	254
	Winfield Scott	Whig	1,386,578 (44%)	42
	John P. Hale	Free-Soil	156,149 (5%)	0
1856	JAMES BUCHANAN	Democrat	1,838,169 (45%)	174
	John C. Frémont	Republican	1,335,264 (33%)	114
	Millard Fillmore	American	874,534 (22%)	8
1860	ABRAHAM LINCOLN	Republican	1,866,352 (40%)	180
	Steven A. Douglas	Democrat	1,375,157 (29%)	12
	John C. Breckinridge	Democrat	847,953 (18%)	72
	John Bell	Constitutional Union	589,581 (13%)	39

Note: Winners' names appear in capital letters.

ditional Whig reformist impulse, felt responsible for cleansing America of its sins of intemperance, impiety, parochial schooling, and other forms of immorality. Another sin included voting for Democrats, who were accused of catering to the "grog shops, foreign vote, and Catholic brethren" by combining the "forces of Jesuitism and Slavery."

The fourth element of the Republican party, a Whig legacy from the American System of Henry Clay, included those who wanted the federal government to

This map was part of a Frémont campaign handbill in 1856, which contrasted the white "free soil" states (including Canada) with the slave states shown in black. Frémont and the Republicans advocated "the extension of free labor" in contrast to his rival, James Buchanan, who championed the extension of slavery. The use of gray for all of the U.S. territories (and Mexico and Cuba) seems to anticipate the Dred Scott decision in 1857, which opened those areas to slavery. Although Minnesota and Oregon would soon come into the Union as "white" free states, taken together, the vastness of the black and the gray areas posed an ominous threat to liberty, according to Republican northerners. The written messages, which are difficult to read, reinforce the Republican point that the slave states, because of the 3/5s rule (which counted slaves in figuring representatives in the House), were overrepresented in Congress. *(Danzer Map Collection)*

promote commercial and industrial development and the dignity of labor. This fourth group, like the antislavery and anti-Catholic elements, had a strong ideological faith that a system of free labor led to progress. At the heart of both the new party and the future of America were hardworking, middle-class, mobile, free white laborers—farmers, small businessmen, and independent craftsmen. As the Springfield *Republican* said in 1856, the Republican party's strength came from "those who work with their hands, who live and act independently, who hold the stakes of home and family, of farm and workshop, of education and freedom—these as a mass are enrolled in the Republican ranks."

The strengths of the Republican and Know-Nothing (American) parties were tested in 1856. Which party could best oppose the Democrats? The American party nominated Fillmore, who had strong support in the Upper South and border states. The Republicans chose John C. Frémont, a Free-Soiler from Missouri with virtually no political experience. The Democrats nominated James Buchanan of Pennsylvania, commonly known as a "northern man with southern principles." Frémont's strength in the North helped him carry several free states, while Fillmore won only Maryland. Buchanan, taking advantage of the divided opposition, won the election, but with only 45 percent of the popular vote.

After 1856, the Know-Nothings died out, largely because Republican leaders cleverly redirected nativist fears—and voters—into their broader program, but also because Know-Nothing secrecy, hatreds, and occasional violent attacks on Catholic voters damaged their image. The Know-Nothings represented a powerful current in American politics that would return each time social and economic changes seemed to threaten the nation. It became convenient to label certain people "un-American" and seek to root them out. Thus, the Know-Nothing party disappeared after 1856, but nativism did not.

KANSAS AND THE TWO CULTURES

However appealing nativist issues were for many Americans, the problem of slavery was the issue that would not disappear. As Democrats sought ways of expanding slavery and other American institutions westward across the Plains and south into Cuba in the mid-1850s, Republicans wanted to halt the advance of slavery to prove to the world, as Seward said, that the American "experiment in self-government" still worked. In 1854, Lincoln worried that it was slavery that "deprives our republican example of its just influence in the world." The specific cause of his concern was the likelihood that slavery might be extended into Kansas as a result of the passage that year of Stephen Douglas's Kansas-Nebraska Act.

Competing for Kansas

During the congressional debates over the Kansas-Nebraska bill, Seward had accepted the challenge of slave-state senators to "engage in competition for the virgin soil of Kansas." The passage of the Kansas-Nebraska Act in 1854 opened the way for proslavery and antislavery forces to meet physically and to compete over whether Kansas would become a slave or free state. No sooner had the bill passed Congress than Eli Thayer founded the Massachusetts Emigrant Aid Society to recruit free-soil settlers to go to Kansas. From New York, Frederick Douglass called for "companies of emigrants from the free states . . . to possess the goodly land." By the summer of 1855, about 1,200 New England colonists had migrated to Kansas.

One of the migrants was Julia Louisa Lovejoy, a Vermont minister's wife. As a Mississippi riverboat carried her into a slave state for the first time, she described the dilapidated plantation homes of the monotonous Missouri shore as reflecting the "blighting mildew of slavery." By the time Julia and her husband arrived in the Kansas Territory, she had concluded that the "inhabitants and morals" of slaveholding Missourians who had moved into Kansas were of an "*undescribably repulsive* and undesirable character." To Julia Lovejoy, northerners came to bring the "energetic Yankee" virtues of morality and economic enterprise to the drunken, unclean slaveholders of the Southwest.

Perhaps she had in mind David Atchison, Democratic senator from Missouri. Atchison believed that Congress had an obligation to protect slavery in the territories, thereby permitting Missouri slaveholders to move into Kansas. As early as 1853, he pledged himself "to extend the institutions of Missouri over the Territory at whatever sacrifice of blood or treasure." He described New England migrants as "negro thieves" and "abolition tyrants." He recommended to fellow Missourians that they defend their property and interests "with the *bayonet* and with *blood*" and, if need be, "to kill every God-damned abolitionist in the district."

Under Atchison's inflammatory leadership, secret societies sprang up in the Missouri counties adjacent to Kansas. They vowed to combat the Free-Soilers. One editor exclaimed that northerners came to Kansas "for the express purpose of stealing, running off and hiding runaway negroes from Missouri [and] taking to their own bed . . . a stinking negro wench." It was not slaveholders but New Englanders, he said, who were immoral, uncivilized, and hypocritical. Rumors of 20,000 such Massachusetts migrants spurred Missourians to action. Thousands poured across the border late in 1854 to vote on whether to permit slavery in the territory. Twice as many ballots were cast as the number of registered voters, and in one polling place only 20 of over 600 voters were legal residents.

The proslavery forces overreacted to their fear of the New England migrants and their intentions. The permanent population of Kansas consisted primarily of migrants from Missouri and other border states who were more concerned with land titles than slavery. They opposed any blacks—slave or free—moving into their state. As one clergyman put it, "I kem to Kansas to live in a free state and I don't want niggers a-trampin' over my grave."

In March 1855, a second election was held to select a territorial legislature. The pattern of border crossings, intimidation, and illegal voting was repeated. Atchison himself, drinking "considerable whiskey" along the way, led a band of armed men across the state line to vote and frighten would-be Free-Soil voters away. Not surprisingly, a small minority of eligible voters elected a proslavery territorial legislature. Free-Soilers, meanwhile, staged their own constitutional convention in Lawrence and created a Free-Soil government at Topeka. It banned blacks from the state. The proslavery legislature settled first in Shawnee Mission and then in Lecompton, giving Kansas two governments.

The struggle shifted to Washington, where President Pierce, who could have nullified the illegal election, did nothing. Congress debated the wrongs in Kansas and sent an investigating committee, which further inflamed passions. Throughout 1855, the call to arms grew more strident. One proslavery newspaper invited southerners to bring their weapons and "send the scoundrels" from the North "back to whence they came, or . . . to hell, it matters not which." In South Carolina, Robert Allston wrote his son Benjamin that he was "raising men and money . . . to counteract the effect of the Northern hordes. . . . We are disposed to fight the battle of our rights . . . on the field of Kansas."

Both sides saw Kansas as a holy battleground for their version of moral right. An Alabaman, Colonel Jefferson Buford, sold his slaves to raise money to hire an army of 300 men to fight for slavery in Kansas, promising free land to his recruits. A Baptist minister blessed their departure from Montgomery, promised them God's favor, and gave each man a Bible. Northern Christians responded in kind. At Yale University, the noted minister Henry Ward Beecher presented 25 Bibles and 25 Sharps rifles to young men who would go fight for the Lord in Kansas. "There are

Led by Senator David Atchison, thousands of gun-toting Missourians crossed into Kansas in 1854 and 1855 to vote illegally for a proslavery territorial government. The ensuing bloodshed made Kansas a preview of the Civil War. *(The Newberry Library, Chicago)*

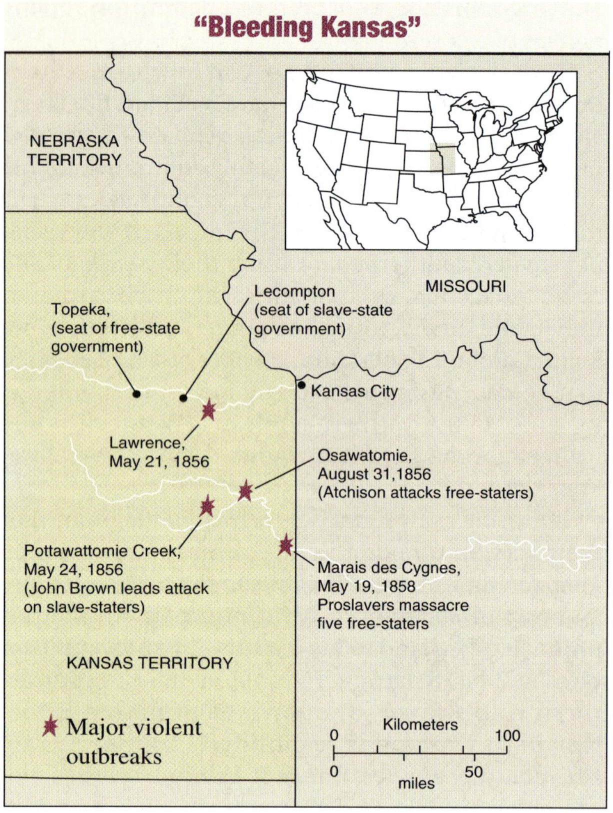

times," he said, "when self-defense is a religious duty. If that duty was ever imperative it is now, and in Kansas." Beecher suggested that rifles would be of greater use than Bibles. Missourians dubbed them "Beecher's Bibles" and vowed, as one newspaper put it, "Blood for Blood! . . . for each drop spilled, we shall require one hundred fold!"

"Bleeding Kansas"

As civil war threatened in Kansas, a Brooklyn poet, Walt Whitman, heralded American democracy in his epic poem *Leaves of Grass* (1855). Whitman identified himself as the embodiment of average Americans "of every hue and caste, . . . of every rank and religion." Ebulliently, Whitman embraced urban mechanics, southern woodcutters, planters' sons, runaway slaves, mining camp prostitutes, and a catalog of others in his poetic celebration of "the word Democratic, the word En-Masse." At the same time, Whitman's faith in the American masses faltered in the mid-1850s. He worried that a knife plunged into the "breast" of the Union would bring on the "red blood of civil war."

As Whitman feared, blood flowed in Kansas. In May 1856, supported by a prosouthern federal marshal, a mob entered Lawrence, smashed the offices and presses of a Free-Soil newspaper, fired several cannonballs into the Free State Hotel, and destroyed homes and shops. Three nights later, motivated by vengeance and a feeling that he was doing God's will, John Brown led a small New England band, including four of his sons, to a proslavery settlement near Pottawatomie Creek. There they dragged five men out of their cabins and despite the terrified entreaties of their wives, hacked them to death with swords.

Violence also entered the halls of Congress. That same week, abolitionist Senator Charles Sumner delivered a tirade that became known as "The Crime Against Kansas." He lashed out at the "murderous robbers" and "incredible atrocities of the Assassins and . . . Thugs" from the South. With nasty invective, he accused proslavery Senate leaders, especially Atchison and Andrew Butler of South Carolina, of cavorting with the "harlot, Slavery." Two days later, Butler's nephew, Congressman Preston Brooks, avenged the honor of his colleague by beating Sumner senseless with his cane as he sat at his Senate desk.

The sack of Lawrence, the massacre at Pottawatomie Creek, and the caning of Sumner set off a minor civil war, which historians have called "Bleeding Kansas." It lasted throughout the summer. Crops were burned, homes were destroyed, fights broke out in saloons and streets, and night raiders tortured and murdered their enemies. For residents like Charles Lines, who just wanted to farm his land in peace, it was impossible to remain neutral. Lines hoped his neighbors near Lawrence would avoid "involving themselves in trouble." But when proslavery forces seized a mild-mannered neighbor, bound him, tortured him, and left him to die, Lines joined the battle. He wrote to a friend that "blood must end in the triumph of the right."

Even before the bleeding of Kansas began, the New York *Tribune* warned, "We are two peoples. We are a people for Freedom and a people for Slavery. Between the two, conflict is inevitable." As the moral rhetoric and violence in Kansas demonstrated, competing visions of two separate cultures for the future destiny of the United States were at stake. Despite many similarities between the North and the South, the gap between the two sides widened as the hostilities of the 1850s increased.

Northern Views and Visions

The North saw itself, as Julia Lovejoy suggested, as a prosperous land of bustling commerce and expanding, independent agriculture. Northern farmers and workers were self-made free men who believed in individualism and democracy. The "free labor system" of the North, as both Seward and Lincoln often said, offered equality of opportunity and upward mobility. Both generated more wealth. Although the North contained many growing cities, northerners revered the values of the small towns that spread from New England across the Upper Midwest. These values included a respect for the rights of the people, tempered by the rule of law; individual enterprise, balanced by a concern for one's neighbors; and a fierce morality rooted in Calvinist Protestantism. Northerners would regulate morality—by persuasion if possible but by legislation if necessary—to remove the sins of irreligion, illiteracy, and intemperance from American society. It was no accident that the ideas of universal public education and laws against the sale and consumption of alcohol both began in New England.

Northerners valued the kind of republican government that guaranteed the rights of free men, enabling them to achieve economic progress. Specifically, this meant supporting government action to promote free labor, industrial growth, some immigration, foreign trade (protected by tariffs), and the development of railroads and free farm homesteads westward across the continent. Energetic mobility both westward and upward would dissolve state, regional, and class loyalties and increase the sense of nationhood. A strong Union could achieve national and even international greatness. These were the conditions, befitting a chosen people, that would, as Seward put it, spread American institutions around the world and "renovate the condition of mankind." These were also the ideological principles of the Republican party.

Only free men could achieve economic progress and moral society. Therefore, the worst sin in the northerner's view was the loss of one's freedom. Slavery was the root of all evil. It was, Seward said, "incompatible with all . . . the elements of the security, welfare, and greatness of nations." The South, then, represented the antithesis of everything that northerners saw as good. Southerners were unfree, backward, economically stagnant, uneducated, lawless, immoral, and out of harmony with the values and ideals of the nineteenth century. Julia Lovejoy's denunciation of slaveholding Missourians was mild. Her fellow migrants to Kansas described southerners as subhuman, unclean, and uncivilized. They were, as one put it, "drunken ourangoutans," "wild beasts" who drank whiskey, ate dirt, uttered oaths, raped slave women, and fought or dueled at the slightest excuse. In the popular language of the day, they were known as "Pukes."

The Southern Perspective

Epithets aside, southerners were a diverse people who, like northerners, shared certain broad values, generally those of the planter class. If in the North the values of economic enterprise were most important, southerners revered social values most. Like the English gentry they sought to emulate, they saw themselves as courteous, refined, hospitable, and chivalrous. By contrast, they saw northerners as coarse, ill-mannered, aggressive, materialistic "Yankees." In a society where one person in three was a black slave, racial distinctions and paternalistic relationships were crucial in maintaining order and white supremacy. Fear of slave revolt was ever present. The South had five times more military schools than the North. Northerners educated the many for economic utility, but southerners educated the few for grace and character. In short, the South saw itself as a genteel, ordered society guided by the aristocratic code of the gentleman planter.

Southerners agreed with northerners that sovereignty in a republic rested in the people, who created a government of laws to protect life, liberty, and property. But unlike people in the North, southerners believed that the democratic principle of self-government was best preserved in local political units such as the state. Southerners were ready to fight to defend their sacred rights against any tyrannical encroachment on their liberty, as they had in 1776. They saw themselves, in fact, as true revolutionary patriots. Like northerners, southerners cherished the Union. But they preferred the loose confederacy of the Jeffersonian past to the centralized nationalism Seward kept invoking.

To southerners, Yankees were in too much of a hurry—to make money, to reform the behavior of others, to put dreamy theories (like racial equality) into practice. Two images dominated the South's view of northerners: either they were stingy, hypocritical, moralizing Puritans, or they were grubby, slum-dwelling, Catholic immigrants. A Georgia paper combined both images in an 1856 editorial: "Free society! we sicken at the name. What is it but a conglomeration of greasy mechanics, filthy operatives, small-fisted farmers, and moon-struck theorists?" These northerners, the paper said, "are devoid of society fitted for well-bred gentlemen."

Each side, then, saw the other threatening its freedom and infringing on its view of a proper republican society. Each saw the other imposing barriers to its vision for America's future, which included the economic systems described in Chapters 10 and 11. As hostilities increased, the views each section had of the other grew steadily more rigid and conspiratorial. Northerners saw the South as a "slave power," determined to foist the slave system on free labor throughout the land. Southerners saw the North as full of "black Republicanism," determined to destroy the southern way of life.

These scenes illustrate the contrasting socioeconomic cultures of the antebellum North and South. Chicago (top) was a rapidly growing, bustling northern city in the 1850s; situated on the Great Lakes and a developing railroad hub, Chicago became the distribution center for industrial and agricultural goods throughout the Midwest. The vital unit of southern commerce was, by contrast, the individual plantation (bottom), with steamboats and flatboats carrying cotton and sugar to port cities for trade with Europe. *(top: Corbis; bottom: Library of Congress)*

POLARIZATION AND THE ROAD TO WAR

Because of the national constituencies of the two major political parties, northern and southern cultural stereotypes and conspiratorial accusations had been largely held in check. But events in Kansas solidified the image of the Republicans as a northern party and seriously weakened the Democrats. Further events, still involving the question of slavery in the territories, split the Democratic party irrevocably into sectional halves: the Dred Scott decision of the Supreme Court (1857), the constitutional crisis in Kansas (1857), the Lincoln–Douglas debates in Illinois (1858), John Brown's raid in Virginia (1859), and Lincoln's election (1860). These incidents further polarized the negative images each culture held of the other and set the nation on the final road to civil war.

The Dred Scott Case

The events of 1857 reinforced the arguments of those who believed in a slave power conspiracy. Two days after James Buchanan's inauguration, the Supreme Court finally ruled in *Dred Scott* v.

Sandford. The case had been pending before the Court for nearly three years, but the slave family of Dred Scott had been waiting longer for the decision. In 1846, Dred and Harriet Scott had filed suit in Missouri for their freedom. They argued that their master had taken them into Minnesota, Wisconsin, and other territories where the Missouri Compromise prohibited slavery, and therefore they should be freed. By the time the case reached the Supreme Court, the issue of slavery in the territories had become a heated political issue.

When the Court, with a majority of southern judges, issued its decision, by a vote of 7 to 2, it made three rulings. First, because blacks were, as Chief Justice Roger Taney put it, "beings of an inferior order [who] had no rights which white men were bound to respect," Dred Scott was not a citizen and had no right to sue in federal courts. Justice Peter Daniel of Virginia was even more indelicate in his consenting opinion, saying that the "African Negro race" did not belong "to the family of nations," but rather was a subject for "commerce or traffic." The second ruling stated that the Missouri Compromise was unconstitutional because Congress did not have the power to ban slavery in a territory. And third, the fact that the Scotts had been taken in and out of free states did not affect their status. Despite two eloquent dissenting opinions, Dred and Harriet Scott remained slaves.

The implications of these decisions went far beyond the Scotts' personal freedom. The arguments about black citizenship infuriated many northerners. Frederick Douglass called the ruling "a most scandalous and devilish perversion of the Constitution, and a brazen misstatement of the facts of history." Many citizens worried about the few rights free blacks still held. Even more troublesome was the possibility hinted at in the decision that slavery might be permitted in the free states of the North, where it had long been banned. People who suspected a conspiracy were not calmed when Buchanan endorsed the Dred Scott decision as a final settlement of the right of citizens to take their "property of any kind, including slaves, into the common Territories . . . and to have it protected there under the Federal Constitution." Rather than settling the political issue of slavery in the territories, as Buchanan had hoped, the Dred Scott decision threw it back into American politics. It opened up new questions and increased sectional hostilities.

Douglas and the Democrats

The Dred Scott decision and Buchanan's endorsement fed northern suspicions of a slave power conspiracy to impose slavery everywhere. Events in Kansas, which still had two governments, heightened these fears. In the summer of 1857, Kansas had still another election, with so many irregularities that only 2,000 out of a possible 24,000 voters participated. They elected a proslavery slate of delegates to a constitutional convention meeting at Lecompton as a preparation for statehood. The convention decided to exclude free blacks from the state, to guarantee the property rights of the few slaveholders in Kansas, and to ask voters to decide in a referendum whether to permit more slaves.

The proslavery Lecompton constitution, clearly unrepresentative of the wishes of the majority of the people of Kansas, was sent to Congress for approval. Eager to retain the support of southern Democrats, Buchanan endorsed it. Stephen Douglas challenged the president's power and jeopardized his own standing with southern Democrats by opposing it. Facing reelection to the Senate from Illinois in 1858, Douglas needed to hold the support of the northern wing of his party. Congress sent the Lecompton constitution back to the people of Kansas for another referendum. This time they defeated it, which meant that Kansas remained a territory rather than becoming a slave state. While Kansas was left in an uncertain status, the larger political effect of the struggle was to split the Democratic party almost beyond repair.

No sooner had Douglas settled the Lecompton question than he faced reelection in Illinois. Douglas's opposition to the Lecompton constitution had restored his prestige in the North as an opponent of the slave power. This cut some ground out from under the Republican party claim that it was the only force capable of stopping the spread of southern power. Republican party leaders from the West, however, had a candidate who understood the importance of distinguishing Republican moral and political views from those of the Democrats.

Lincoln and the Illinois Debates

Although he was relatively unknown nationally and had not held elected office in several years, by 1858, Abraham Lincoln of Illinois had emerged to challenge William Seward for leadership of the Republican party. Lincoln's character was shaped on the Midwestern frontier, where he had educated himself, developed mild abolitionist views, and dreamed of America's greatness.

Douglas was clearly the leading Democrat, so the Senate election in Illinois appeared to be a preview of the presidential election of 1860. The other Douglass, Frederick, observed that "the slave power idea was the ideological glue of the Republican party." Lincoln's handling of this idea would be crucial in distinguishing him from Stephen Douglas. The Illinois campaign featured a series of seven debates between Lincoln and Douglas in different cities. With a national as well

The overwhelming stress of leading the nation through the Civil War is evident in these two images of Abraham Lincoln. To the left is a portrait from 1860 *(Chicago Historical Society)* and on the right is an April 1865 photograph taken just before his assassination. *(Library of Congress)*

as a local audience, the debates provided a remarkable opportunity for the two men to state their views on the heated racial issues before the nation.

Lincoln set a solemn tone when he accepted the Republican senatorial nomination in Chicago in June. The American nation, he said, was in a "crisis" and building toward a worse one. "A House divided against itself cannot stand. I believe this government cannot endure, permanently half *slave* and half *free.*" Lincoln said he did not expect the Union "to be dissolved" or "the house to fall," but rather that "it will become *all* one thing, or *all* the other." Then he rehearsed the history of the South's growing influence over national policy since the Kansas-Nebraska Act, which he blamed on Douglas. Lincoln stated his firm opposition to the Dred Scott decision, which he believed part of a conspiracy involving Pierce, Buchanan, Taney, and Douglas. People like himself, who opposed this conspiracy, wished to place slavery, he said, on a "course of ultimate extinction."

In the ensuing debates with Douglas, Lincoln reiterated these controversial themes. He also expressed his views on race and slavery, formed from a blend of experience, principle, and politics. Although far from a radical abolitionist, in these debates Lincoln skillfully staked out a moral position not only in advance of Douglas but well ahead of his time.

Lincoln was also very much a part of his time. He believed that whites were superior to blacks and opposed granting specific equal civil rights to free blacks. He believed, furthermore, that the physical and moral differences between whites and blacks would "forever forbid the two races from living together on terms of social and political equality" and recommended "separation" and colonization in Liberia or Central America as the best solution to racial differences.

Lincoln, however, differed from most contemporaries in his deep commitment to the humane principles of the equality and essential dignity of all human beings, including blacks. Douglas, by contrast, arguing against race mixing in a blatant bid for votes, continually made racial slurs. Lincoln believed not only that blacks were "entitled to all the natural rights . . . in the Declaration of Independence" but also that they had many specific economic rights as well, like "the right to put into his mouth the bread that his own hands have earned." In these rights, blacks were, Lincoln said, "my equal and the equal of Judge Douglas, and the equal of every living man."

Unlike Douglas, Lincoln hated slavery. At Galesburg, he said, "I contemplate slavery as a moral, social, and political evil." In Quincy, he said that the difference between a Republican and a Democrat was quite simply whether one thought slavery wrong or right. Douglas was more equivocal and dodged the issue in Freeport by pointing out that slavery would not exist if favorable local legislation did not support it. Douglas's moral indifference to slavery was clear in his admission that he did not care if a territorial legislature voted it "up or down." A white supremacist, Douglas was democratic enough to want white people to be able to create whatever type of society they wanted. Republicans did care, Lincoln affirmed, sounding a warning that by stopping the expansion of slavery, the course toward "ultimate extinction" had begun. Although barred by the Constitution from doing anything about slavery where it already existed, Lincoln said that because Republicans believed slavery to be wrong, "we propose a course of policy that shall deal with it as a wrong."

What Lincoln meant by "policy" was not yet clear, even to himself. However, in the debates, he did succeed in affirming that the Republican party was the only moral and political force capable of stopping the slave power. It seems ironic now, though not at the time, that Douglas won the election. When he and Lincoln met again two years later, the order of their finish would be reversed. Elsewhere, in 1858, however, Democrats did poorly, losing 18 congressional seats to the Republicans.

John Brown's Raid

Unlike Lincoln, John Brown was prepared to act decisively against slavery. On October 16, 1859, he and a band of 22 men attacked a federal arsenal at Harpers Ferry, Virginia (now West Virginia). He hoped that the action might provoke a general uprising of slaves throughout the Upper South or at least provide the arms by which slaves could make their way to freedom. Although he seized the arsenal, federal troops soon overcame him. Nearly half his men were killed, including two sons. Brown himself was captured, tried, and hanged for treason. So ended a lifetime of failures.

In death, however, Brown was not a failure. His daring if foolhardy raid, and his impressively dignified behavior during his trial and speedy execution, unleashed powerful passions, further widening the gap between North and South. Northerners responded to his death with an outpouring of sympathy; memorial rallies, parades, and prayer meetings were

This modern mural captures both the madness and passionate larger-than-life commitment of John Brown against a backdrop of flag-covered wagon trains across the Great Plains, a raging tornado and angry sky (God's wrath?), struggling slaves (by his left knee), and a violent confrontation between those for and against slavery. *(Kansas State Historical Society)*

In the aftermath of John Brown's raid, passions fed by fear were unleashed throughout the South against northern sympathizers, and vice versa. A year later, the editor of a Massachusetts newspaper who expressed Democratic, southern sympathies found himself the victim of the time-honored mob punishment of tarring and feathering. *(The New York Public Library, Astor, Lenox & Tilden Foundations)*

held. Admirers wrote poems, songs, and speeches in Brown's honor. Thoreau compared him to Christ and called him an "angel of light." Abolitionist William Lloyd Garrison, though a pacifist, was moved to wish "success to every slave insurrection" in the South. Ministers called slave revolt a "divine weapon" and glorified Brown's treason as "holy."

Brown's raid, Frederick Douglass pointed out, showed that slavery was a "system of brute force" that would only be ended when "met with its own weapons." Southerners were filled with "dread and terror" over the possibility of a wave of slave revolts led by hundreds of imaginary John Browns and Nat Turners and concluded that northerners would stop at nothing to free the slaves. This atmosphere of suspicion eroded freedom of thought and expression. A North Carolinian described a "spirit of terror, mobs, arrests, and violence" in his state. Twelve families in Berea, Kentucky, were evicted from the state for their mild abolitionist sentiments. A Texas minister who criticized the treatment of slaves in a sermon was given 70 lashes.

In response to the Brown raid, southerners also became more convinced, as the governor of South Carolina put it, that a "black Republican" plot in the North was "arrayed against the slaveholders." In this atmosphere of mistrust, southern Unionists lost their influence, and power became concentrated in the hands of those favoring secession. Only one step remained to complete the southern sense of having become a permanent minority within the United States: withdrawal to form a new nation. Senator Robert Toombs of Georgia, insistent that northern "enemies" were plotting the South's ruin, warned fellow southerners late in 1859, "Never permit this Federal government to pass into the traitorous hands of the black Republican party."

The Election of 1860

The conflict between Buchanan and Douglas took its toll on the Democratic party. When the nominating convention met in Charleston, South Carolina, a hotbed of secessionist sentiments, it sat for a record ten days and went through 59 ballots without being able to name a candidate. Twice, southern delegates withdrew, forcing adjournments. Reconvening in Baltimore, the Democrats acknowledged their irreparable division by choosing two candidates at two separate conventions: Douglas for northern Democrats and John C. Breckinridge, Buchanan's vice

The Presidential Election of 1860

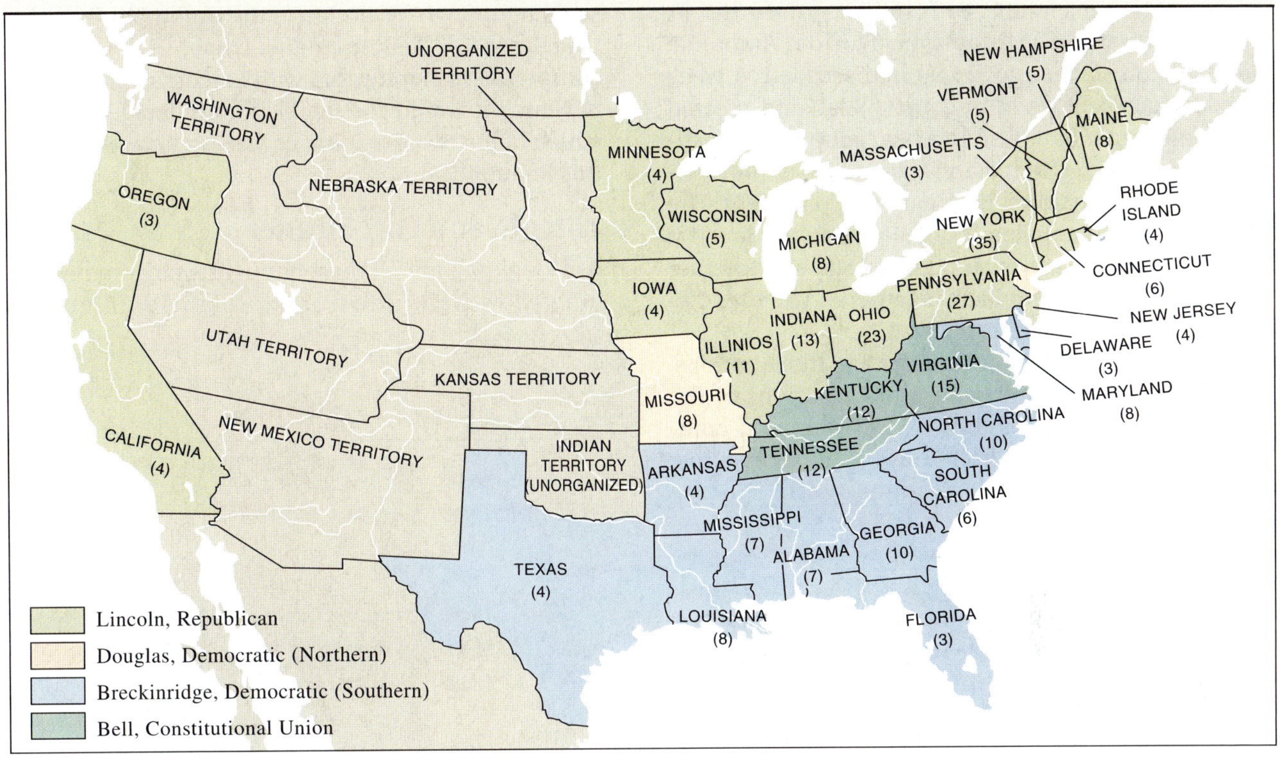

Lincoln's election, the first by a Republican, was on the basis of a totally northern sectional victory, and with only 40 percent of the popular vote.

president, for the proslavery South. The Constitutional Union party, made up of former southern Whigs and border-state nativists, claimed the middle ground and nominated John Bell, a slaveholder from Tennessee favoring compromise.

With Democrats split and a new party in contention, the Republican strategy aimed at keeping the states carried by Frémont in 1856 and adding Pennsylvania, Illinois, and Indiana. Seward, the leading candidate for the nomination, had been tempering his antislavery views to appear more electable. So had Abraham Lincoln, who seemed more likely than Seward to carry those key states. After shrewd maneuvers emphasizing his "availability" as a moderate with widespread appeal, Lincoln was nominated.

The Republican platform also reflected moderation, opposing only slavery's extension. Most of it spoke of tariff protection, subsidized internal improvements, free labor, and a homestead bill. Above all, the Republicans, like southern Democrats, defended their view of what republican values meant for America's future. It did not include the equal rights envisioned by Frederick Douglass. An English traveler in 1860 observed that in America "we see, in effect, two nations—one white and another black—growing up together within the same political circle, but never mingling on a principle of equality."

The Republican moderate strategy worked as planned. Lincoln was elected by sweeping the entire Northeast and Midwest. Although he got less than 40 percent of the popular vote nationwide, his triumph in the North was decisive. Even a united Democratic party could not have defeated him. With victory assured, Lincoln finished his sandwich and coffee on election night in Springfield and prepared for his awesome new responsibilities. They came even before his inauguration.

THE DIVIDED HOUSE FALLS

The Republicans overestimated the extent of Unionist sentiment in the South. They could not believe that the secessionists would prevail after Lincoln's victory. A year earlier, some southern congressmen had walked out in protest of the selection of an antislavery speaker of the House. A Republican leader, Carl Schurz, recalling this act, said that the southerners had taken a drink and then come back. Now, Schurz predicted, they would walk out, take two drinks, and come back again. He was wrong.

Secession and Uncertainty

On December 20, 1860, South Carolina seceded from the Union, declaring the "experiment" of putting people with "different pursuits and institutions" under one government a failure. By February 1, the other six Deep South states (Mississippi, Florida, Alabama, Georgia, Louisiana, and Texas) had seceded. A week later, delegates met in Montgomery, Alabama, created the Confederate States of America, adopted a constitution, and elected Jefferson Davis, a Mississippi senator and cotton planter, its provisional president. The divided house had fallen, as Lincoln had predicted it would. What was not yet certain, though, was whether the house could be put back together or whether disunion necessarily meant civil war.

The government in Washington had three options. The first was compromise, but the emotions of the time ruled out that possibility. Most proposed compromises were really concessions to the secessionist states. The second option, suggested by Horace Greeley, editor of the New York *Tribune,* was to let the seven states "go in peace," taking care not to lose the border states. But this was opposed by northern businessmen, who would lose profitable economic ties with the South, and by those who believed in an indissoluble Union. The third option was to compel secessionist states to return, which probably meant war.

Republican hopes that southern Unionism would assert itself and make none of these options necessary seemed possible in February 1861. The momentum toward disunion slowed, and no other southern states seceded. The nation waited and watched, wondering what Virginia and the border states would do, what outgoing President Buchanan would do, and what Congress would do. Prosouthern and determined not to start a civil war in the last weeks of his already dismal administration, Buchanan did nothing. Congress made some feeble efforts to pass compromise legislation, waiting in vain for the support of the president-elect. And as Union supporters struggled with secessionists, Virginia and the border states, like the entire nation, waited for Abraham Lincoln.

Frederick Douglass waited, too, without much hope. He wanted nothing less than the "complete and universal *abolition* of the whole slave system," as well as equal suffrage and other rights for free blacks. His momentary expectation during the presidential campaign, that Lincoln and the Republicans had the will to do this, had been thoroughly dashed. In November, the voters of New York State had defeated a referendum for black suffrage by more votes than a similar measure 14 years earlier. Moreover, Douglass saw northern politicians and businessmen "granting the most demoralizing concessions to the Slave Power."

In his despair, Douglass began to explore possibilities for emigration and colonization in Haiti, an idea he had long opposed. To achieve full freedom and citizenship in the United States for all blacks, he said in January 1861, he would "welcome the hardships consequent upon a dissolution of the Union." In February, Douglass said, "Let the conflict come." He opposed all compromises, hoping that with Lincoln's inauguration in March it would "be decided, and decided forever, which of the two, Freedom or Slavery, shall give law to this Republic."

Lincoln and Fort Sumter

As Douglass penned these thoughts, Lincoln began a long, slow train ride from Springfield, Illinois, to

Timeline

1832	Nullification crisis
1835–1840	Intensification of abolitionist attacks on slavery
	Violent retaliatory attacks on abolitionists
1840	Liberty party formed
1846	Wilmot Proviso
1848	Free-Soil party founded
	Zachary Taylor elected president
1850	Compromise of 1850, including Fugitive Slave Act
1850–1854	"Young America" movement
1851	Women's rights convention in Akron, Ohio
1852	Harriet Beecher Stowe publishes *Uncle Tom's Cabin*
	Franklin Pierce elected president
1854	Ostend Manifesto
	Kansas-Nebraska Act nullifies Missouri Compromise
	Republican and Know-Nothing parties formed
1855	Walt Whitman publishes *Leaves of Grass*
1855–1856	Thousands pour into Kansas, creating months of turmoil and violence
1856	John Brown's massacre in Kansas
	Sumner–Brooks incident in Senate
	James Buchanan elected president
1857	Dred Scott decision legalizes slavery in territories
	Lecompton constitution in Kansas
1858	Lincoln–Douglas debates
1859	John Brown's raid at Harpers Ferry
1860	Democratic party splits
	Four-party campaign
	Abraham Lincoln elected president
1860–1861	Seven southern states secede
1861	Confederate States of America founded
	Attack on Fort Sumter begins Civil War

THE CAUSES OF THE CIVIL WAR

Date	Issues and Events	Deeper, Underlying Causes of Civil War
1600s–1860s	Slavery in the South	Major underlying pervasive cause
1700s–1860s	Development of two distinct socioeconomic systems and cultures	Further reinforced slavery as fundamental socioeconomic, cultural moral issue
1787–1860s	States' rights, nullification doctrine	Ongoing political issue, less fundamental as cause
1820	Missouri Compromise (36°30')	Background for conflict over slavery in territories
1828–1833	South Carolina tariff nullification crisis	Background for secession leadership in South Carolina
1831–1860s	Antislavery movements, southern justification	Thirty years of emotional preparation for conflict
1846–1848	War with Mexico (Wilmot Proviso, Calhoun, popular sovereignty)	Options for issue of slavery in territories

Date	Issues and Events	Specific Impact on the Road to War
1850	Compromise of 1850	Temporary and unsatisfactory "settlement" of divisive issue
1851–1854	Fugitive slaves returned and rescued in North; personal liberty laws passed in North; Harriet Beecher Stowe's *Uncle Tom's Cabin*	Heightened northern emotional reactions against the South and slavery
1852–1856	Breakdown of Whig party and national Democratic party; creation of a new party system with sectional basis	Made national politics an arena where sectional and cultural differences over slavery were fought
1854	Ostend Manifesto and other expansionist efforts in Central America	Reinforced image of Democratic party as favoring slavery
	Formation of Republican party	Major party identified as opposing the extension of slavery
	Kansas-Nebraska Act	Reopened "settled" issue of slavery in the territories
1856	"Bleeding Kansas"; Senator Sumner physically attacked in Senate	Foretaste of Civil War (200 killed, $2 million in property lost) inflamed emotions and polarized North and South
1857	Dred Scott decision; proslavery Lecompton constitution in Kansas	Made North fear a "slave power conspiracy," supported by President Buchanan and the Supreme Court
1858	Lincoln-Douglas debates in Illinois; Democrats lose 18 seats in Congress	Set stage for election of 1860
1859	John Brown's raid and reactions in North and South	Made South fear a "black Republican" plot against slavery; further polarization and irrationality
1860	Democratic party splits in half; Lincoln elected president; South Carolina secedes from Union	Final breakdown of national parties and election of "northern" president; no more compromises
1861	Six more southern states secede by February 1; Confederate Constitution adopted February 4; Lincoln inaugurated March 4; Fort Sumter attacked April 12	Civil War begins

Washington, writing and rewriting his inaugural address. Lincoln's quietness in the period between his election and his inauguration had led many to wonder if he were not weak and indecisive. He was not. Lincoln was firmly opposed to secession and to any compromises with the principle of stopping the extension of slavery. He would neither conciliate secessionist southern states nor force their return.

But Lincoln believed in his constitutional responsibility to uphold the laws of the land, and on this significant point he would not yield. The focus of his attention was a federal fort in the harbor of Charleston,

South Carolina. Major Robert Anderson, the commander of Fort Sumter, was running out of provisions and had requested new supplies from Washington. Lincoln would enforce the laws and protect federal property at Fort Sumter.

As the new president rose to deliver his inaugural address on March 4, he faced a tense and divided nation. Federal troops, fearing a Confederate attack on the nation's capital, were everywhere. Lincoln asserted his unequivocal intention to enforce the laws of the land, arguing that the Union was constitutionally "perpetual" and indissoluble. He reminded the nation that the "only substantial dispute" was that "one section of our country believes slavery is *right,* and ought to be extended, while the other believes it is *wrong,* and ought not to be extended." Still hoping to appeal to Unionist strength among southern moderates, Lincoln indicated that he would make no attempts to interfere with existing slavery or the law to return fugitive slaves.

Nearing the end of his address, Lincoln urged against rash actions and put the burden of initiating a civil war on the "dissatisfied fellow-countrymen" who had seceded. As if aware of the horrible events that might follow, he said in an eloquent conclusion:

> I am loath to close. We are not enemies, but friends. We must not be enemies. Though passion may have strained, it must not break our bonds of affection. The mystic chords of memory, stretching from every battlefield, and patriot grave, to every living heart and hearthstone, all over this broad land, will yet swell the chorus of the Union, when again touched, as surely they will be, by the better angels of our nature.

Frederick Douglass was not impressed with Lincoln's "honied phrases" and accused him of "weakness, timidity and conciliation." Also unmoved, Robert Allston wrote his son from Charleston, where he was watching the developing crisis over Fort Sumter, that the Confederacy's "advantage" was in having a "much better president than they have."

On April 6, Lincoln notified the governor of South Carolina that he was sending "provisions only" to Fort Sumter. No effort would be made "to throw in men, arms, or ammunition" unless the fort were attacked. On April 10, Jefferson Davis directed General P. G. T. Beauregard to demand the surrender of Fort Sumter. Davis told Beauregard to reduce the fort if Major Anderson refused.

On April 12, as Lincoln's relief expedition neared Charleston, Beauregard's batteries began shelling Fort Sumter, and the Civil War began. Frederick Douglass was about to leave for Haiti when he heard the news. He immediately changed his plans: "This is no time . . . to leave the country." He announced his readiness to help end the war by aiding the Union to organize freed slaves "into a liberating army" to "make war upon . . . the savage barbarism of slavery." The Allstons had changed places, and it was Benjamin who described the events in Charleston harbor to his father. On April 14, Benjamin reported exuberantly the "glorious, and astonishing news that Sumter has fallen." With it fell America's divided house.

Conclusion

The "Irrepressible Conflict"

Lincoln had been right. The nation could no longer endure half-slave and half-free. The collision between North and South, William Seward said, was not an "accidental, unnecessary" event but an "irrepressible conflict between opposing and enduring forces." Those forces had been at work for many decades, but they developed with increasing intensity after 1848 in the conflict over the extension of slavery into the territories. Although economic, cultural, political, constitutional, and emotional forces all contributed to the developing opposition between North and South, slavery was the fundamental, enduring force that underlay all others, causing what Walt Whitman called the "red blood of civil war."

Recommended Reading

Overviews of the Imperiled Union and Crises of the 1850s

Eric Foner, ed., *Politics and Ideology in the Age of the Civil War* (1980); James McPherson, *Ordeal by Fire: The Civil War and Reconstruction* (1982); David Potter, *The Impending Crisis, 1848–1861* (1976); Brian Holden Reid, *The Origins of the American Civil War* (1996); Richard Sewall, *A House Divided: Sectionalism and Civil War, 1848–1865* (1988); Kenneth Stampp, *The Imperilled Union: Essays on the Background of the Civil War* (1980); Kenneth Stampp, ed., *The Causes of the Civil War, rev. ed.* (1974); Mark Summers, *The Plundering Generation: Corruption and the Crisis of the Union, 1849–1861* (1987).

Slavery in the Territories

Eugene Berwanger, *The Frontier Against Slavery: Western Anti-Negro Prejudice and the Slavery Extension Controversy* (1967); William W. Freehling, *The Road to Disunion: I. Secessionists at*

Bay, 1776–1854 (1990); Hamilton Holman, *Prologue to Conflict: The Crisis and Compromise of 1850* (1964); Willard C. Klunder, *Lewis Cass and the Politics of Moderation* (1996); Michael A. Morrison, *Slavery and the American West: The Eclipse of Manifest Destiny and the Coming of the Civil War* (1997); Mark J. Stegmaier, *Texas, New Mexico, and the Compromise of 1850: Boundary Dispute & Sectional Crisis* (1996); Albert J. Von Frank, *The Trials of Anthony Burns* (1998).

Political Disintegration and Realignment

Eric Foner, *Free Soil, Free Labor, Free Men: The Ideology of the Republican Party Before the Civil War* (1970); William E. Gienapp, *The Origins of the Republican Party, 1852–1856* (1987); William E. Gienapp, Thomas B. Alexander, Michael F. Holt, Stephen E. Mazlish, and Joel H. Silbey, *Essays on American Antebellum Politics, 1840–1860* (1982); Anthony Gronowicz, *Race and Class Politics in New York City Before the Civil War* (1997); Michael Holt, *The Political Crisis of the 1850s* (1978); Robert W. Johanssen, *The Frontier, the Union, and Stephen A. Douglas* (1989); Robert Remini, *Daniel Webster: The Man and His Time* (1997); E. Smith, *The Presidencies of Zachary Taylor and Millard Fillmore* (1988); Geoffrey Wolff, *The Kansas-Nebraska Bill: Party, Section and the Origin of the Civil War* (1977).

Kansas, Two Cultures, and Polarized Emotions

William J. Cooper, *The South and the Politics of Slavery* (1978) and *Liberty and Slavery: Southern Politics to 1860* (1983); Donald Fehrenbacher, *Slavery, Law, and Politics: The Dred Scott Case in Historical Perspective* (1981); Thomas F. Gossett, *Uncle Tom's Cabin and American Culture* (1985); David S. Heidler, *Pulling the Temple Down: The Fire-Eaters and the Destruction of the Union* (1994); Nell Irvin Painter, *Sojourner Truth: A Life, A Symbol* (1996); James Rawley, *Race and Politics: "Bleeding Kansas" and the Coming of the Civil War* (1969); Richard Sewell, *Ballots for Freedom: Antislavery Politics in the United States, 1837–1865* (1976).

Lincoln and the Divided House: The Road to Civil War

David H. Donald, *Lincoln* (1995); Don Fehrenbacher, ed., *Abraham Lincoln: A Documentary Portrait Through His Speeches and Writings* (1977); Maury Klein, *Days of Defiance: Sumter, Secession, and the Coming of the Civil War* (1997); Mark E. Neely, *The Last Best Hope of Earth: Abraham Lincoln and the Promise of America* (1993); Kenneth Stampp, *America in 1857: A Nation on the Brink* (1990) and *And the War Came* (1950); David Zarefsky, *Lincoln, Douglas and Slavery in the Crucible of Public Debate* (1990).

Fiction and Film

Russell Banks's *Cloudsplitter* (1998) is an exciting novel on John Brown's antislavery activities in the 1850s. Ken Burns's *Civil War,*, part 1, sets the slavery and 1850s background for his haunting documentary portrayal of the Civil War. Herman Melville's *Moby Dick* (1850), an immense novel published at the time of the Senate debates over the disposition of slavery in the territories, tells the story of Ahab's pursuit of the great white whale. *Moby Dick* is about giant polar forces facing each other, good and evil, nature and man, and, perhaps, North and South. Harriet Beecher Stowe wrote *Uncle Tom's Cabin* (1852) in serial form, with each episode stopping at a nail-biting moment. Stowe's romantic novel strongly influenced northern readers and had an impact on the antislavery politics of the 1850s. Walt Whitman's collection of poems, *Leaves of Grass* (1855), celebrates not only the poet's own ego but also the common people and democratic American values in a decade that sorely tested those values.

Suggested Web Sites

http://history.furman.edu/~benson/docs/

Furman: Secession Era Editorials Project. Furman University is digitizing editorials about the secession crisis and already includes scores of them on this site.

http://www.law.umkc.edu/faculty/projects/ftrials/Brown.html

John Brown Case. For information about the trial of John Brown, this site provides a list of excellent links.

http://grid.let.rug.nl/~usa/H/1990/ch5_p6.htm

USA: Lincoln Attacks Slavery. This site discusses Lincoln's views and action concerning slavery, especially the Lincoln–Douglas debate.

http://www.ukans.edu/carrie/kancoll/galbks.htm

Gallery: Bleeding Kansas. Contemporary and later accounts of America's rehearsal for the Civil War make up this University of Kansas site.

http://www.pbs.org/wgbh/aia/part4

The Compromise of 1850 and the Fugitive Slave Act. From the series on Africans in America, an analysis of the Compromise of 1850 and of the effects of the Fugitive Slave Act on black Americans.

http://nac.gmu.edu/mmts/50proto.html

The 1850s: An Increasingly Divided Union. A tutorial skills development site focusing on the events in the 1850s leading to the Civil War; from MMTS, the Multi-Media Thinking Skills project.

http://lcweb2.loc.gov/ammem/mcchtml/corhome.html

Words and Deeds in American History. A Library of Congress site containing links to Frederick Douglass, the Compromise of 1850, speeches by John C. Calhoun, Daniel Webster and Henry Clay, and other topics from the Civil War era.

http://www.ushistoryplace.com

the History place

A richly detailed on-line learning environment complete with interactive maps, timelines, history activities, primary source documents, and links to related American history sites.

15

The UNION SEVERED

CHAPTER OUTLINE

In his remarks to Congress in 1862, Abraham Lincoln reminded congressmen that, "We cannot escape history. We of this Congress and this administration will be remembered in spite of ourselves. No personal significance, or insignificance, can spare . . . us. The fiery trial through which we pass, will light us down, in honor or dishonor, to the latest generation." Lincoln's conviction that Americans would long remember him and other major actors of the Civil War was correct. Jefferson Davis, Robert E. Lee, Ulysses S. Grant—these are the men whose characters, actions, and decisions have been the subject of continuing discussion and analysis, whose statues and memorials dot the American countryside and grace urban squares. Whether seen as heroes or villains, great men have dominated the story of the Civil War.

Yet from the earliest days, the war touched the lives of even the most uncelebrated Americans. From Indianapolis, 20-year-old Arthur Carpenter wrote to his parents in Massachusetts begging for permission to enlist in the volunteer army: "I have always longed for the time to come when I could enter the army and be a military man, and when this war broke out, I thought the time had come, but you would not permit me to enter the service . . . now I make one more appeal to you." The pleas worked, and Carpenter enlisted, spending most of the war fighting in Kentucky and Tennessee.

In that same year, in Tennessee, George and Ethie Eagleton faced anguishing decisions. Though not an abolitionist, George, a 30-year-old Presbyterian preacher, was unsympathetic to slavery and opposed to secession. But when his native state left the Union, George felt compelled to follow and enlisted in the 44th Tennessee Infantry. Ethie, his 26-year-old wife, despaired over the war, George's decision, and her own forlorn situation.

> Mr. Eagleton's school dismissed—and what for? O my God, must I write it? He has enlisted in the service of his country—to war—the most unrighteous war that ever was brought on any nation that ever lived. Pres. Lincoln has done what no other Pres. ever dared to do—he has divided these once peaceful and happy United States. And Oh! the dreadful dark cloud that is now hanging over our country—'tis enough to sicken the heart of any one. . . . Mr. E. is gone. . . . What will become of me, left here without a home and relatives, a babe just nine months old and no George.

Both Carpenter and the Eagletons survived the war, but the conflict transformed each of their lives. Carpenter had difficulty settling down. Filled with bitter memories of the war years in Tennessee, the Eagletons moved to Arkansas. Ordinary people such as Carpenter and the Eagletons are historically anonymous. Yet their actions on the battlefield and behind the lines helped to shape the course of events, as their leaders realized, even if today we tend to remember only the famous and influential.

For thousands of Americans, from Lincoln and Davis to Carpenter and the Eagletons, war was both a profoundly personal and a major national event. Its impact reached far beyond the four years of hostilities. The war that was fought to conserve two political, social, and economic visions ended by changing familiar ways of life in both North and South. War was a transforming force, both destructive and creative in its effect on the structure and social dynamics of society and on the lives of ordinary people. This theme underlies this chapter's analysis of the war's three stages: the initial months of preparation, the years of military stalemate between 1861 and 1865, and, finally, resolution.

Artist Winslow Homer captured a Union sharpshooter in one of his early paintings. *(Portland Museum of Art, Maine. Gift of Barbro and Bernard Osher, 3.1993.3)*

ORGANIZING FOR WAR

The Confederate bombardment of Fort Sumter on April 12, 1861, and the surrender of Union troops the next day ended the uncertainty of the secession winter. The North's response to Fort Sumter was a virtual declaration of war as President Lincoln called for state militia volunteers to crush southern "insurrection." His action pushed several slave states (Virginia, North Carolina, Tennessee, Arkansas) off the fence and into the southern camp. Other states (Maryland, Kentucky, and Missouri) agonizingly debated which way to go. The "War Between the States" was now a reality.

Many Americans were unenthusiastic about the course of events. Southerners like George Eagleton only reluctantly followed Tennessee out of the Union. When he enlisted, he complained of the "disgraceful cowardice of many who were last winter for secession and war . . . but are now refusing self and means for the prosecution of war." Robert E. Lee of Virginia was equally hesitant to resign his federal commission but finally decided that he could not "raise [a] hand against . . . relatives . . . children . . . home." Whites living in the southern uplands (where blacks were few and slaveholders were heartily disliked and envied), yeomen farmers in the Deep South (who owned no slaves), and many residents of border states were dismayed at secession and war. Many would eventually join the Union forces.

In the North, large numbers had supported neither the Republican party nor Lincoln. Irish immigrants who feared the competition of free black labor and southerners now living in Illinois, Indiana, and Ohio harbored misgivings about the war. Indeed, northern Democrats at first blamed Lincoln and the Republicans almost as much as the southern secessionists for the nation's crisis.

Nevertheless, the days following Fort Sumter and Lincoln's call for troops saw an outpouring of support on both sides, fueled in part by relief at decisive action, in part by patriotism and love of adventure, in part by unemployment. Northern blacks and even some southern freedmen proclaimed themselves "ready to go forth and do battle," while whites like Carpenter enthusiastically flocked to enlist. In some places, workers were so eager to join up that trade unions collapsed. Sisters, wives, and mothers set to work making uniforms. A New Yorker, Jane Woolsey, described the drama of those early days "of terrible excitement."

> Outside the parlor windows the city is gay and brilliant with excited crowds, the incessant movement and music of marching regiments and all the thousands of flags, big and little, which suddenly came fluttering out of every window and door. . . . In our little circle of friends, one mother has just sent away an idolized son; another, two; another, four. . . . One sweet young wife is packing

In May 1861, the first Michigan Regiment mustered in Detroit before boarding the train to Washington. The people crowded in the square, on the porches of the Rail-Road Hotel and on rooftops suggest the patriotic enthusiasm of the send-off. Many women shared the fervor for the coming conflict. Thousands of them would be involved in war work at home or in army hospitals or camps. As one explained, "As the soldiers went from among us, there came the yearning wish to lessen somewhat the hardships of their lonely camp life, especially when sick in hospital or wounded." *(Courtesy of the Burton Historical Collection, Detroit Public Library)*

a regulation valise for her husband today, and doesn't let him see her cry.

The war fever produced so many volunteers that neither northern nor southern officials could handle the throng. Northern authorities turned aside offers from blacks to serve. Both sides sent thousands of white would-be soldiers home. The conviction that the conflict would rapidly come to a glorious conclusion fueled the eagerness to enlist. "We really did not think that there was going to be an actual war," remembered Mary Ward, a young Georgia woman. "We had an idea that when our soldiers got upon the ground and showed, unmistakably that they were really ready and willing to fight . . . the whole trouble would be declared at an end." Lincoln's call for 75,000 state militiamen for only 90 days of service, and a similar enlistment term for Confederate soldiers, supported the notion that the war would be short.

The Balance of Resources

Despite the bands, parades, cheers, and confidence, the outcome of the approaching civil conflict was much in doubt. Statistics of population and industrial development suggested that the North would win. But Great Britain had also enjoyed enormous statistical advantages in 1775 and yet had lost the War of American Independence. Many of the North's assets would become effective only with time. The military stalemate in 1861 and 1862 proved that in the short term, North and South were evenly matched.

In the North, state militia volunteers called up in April 1861 supplemented the small federal army of 16,000. Probably a quarter of the regular army officers, however, had followed Lee's example and resigned. The Confederate Army, authorized in March 1861, could count on the service of able military men like Robert E. Lee, Joseph E. Johnston, and Albert Sidney Johnston. Its president, Jefferson Davis, was an 1828 graduate of West Point.

The North's white population greatly exceeded that of the South, giving the appearance of a military advantage. Yet in the early days of war, the armies were not unevenly matched. Almost 187,000 Union troops bore arms in July 1861, while just over 112,000 men marched under Confederate colors. Even if numerically inferior, southerners believed that their population would prove the superior fighting force because it was more accustomed to outdoor life and the use of firearms. Many northerners feared that southerners were better natural warriors. True or not, slaves could carry on vital work behind the lines, freeing most adult white males to serve the Confederacy. Slavery, southerners thought, would prove to be a "tower of strength . . . at the present crisis."

Resources for War: North Versus South

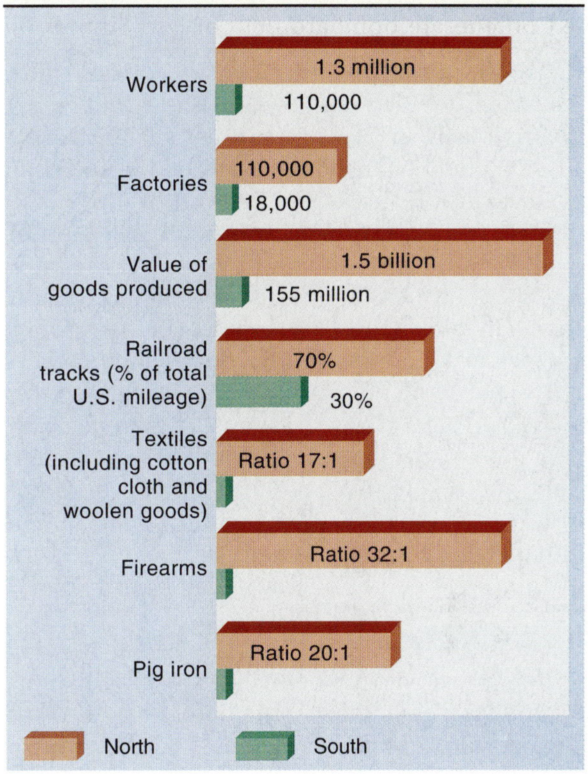

This chart shows the long-range advantages the North enjoyed in the war, but the length and destruction of the conflict suggest that the North was not able to capitalize on its strengths effectively to bring the war to a quick end.

The Union also enjoyed impressive economic advantages. In the North, 1.3 million workers in 110,000 manufacturing concerns produced goods valued at $1.5 billion annually, while 110,000 southern workers in 18,000 manufacturing concerns produced goods valued at only $155 million a year. The North had one factory for every southern industrial worker, and 70 percent of the nation's railroad tracks were in the North. Producing 17 times as much cotton cloth and woolen goods, 32 times as many firearms, and 20 times as much pig iron as the South, the North could clothe and arm troops and move them and their supplies on a scale that the South could not match. But to be effective, northern industrial resources had to be mobilized for war. That would take time, especially because the government did not intend to direct production. Furthermore, the depleted northern treasury made the government's first task the raising of funds to pay for military necessities.

The South traditionally depended on imported manufactured goods from the North and from Europe. If Lincoln cut off that trade, the South would face the enormous task of creating its industry almost from scratch. Moreover, its railroad system was organized to move cotton, not armies and supplies. Yet the agricultural South did have important resources of food, draft animals, and, of course, cotton, which southerners believed would secure British and French support. Finally, in choosing to wage a defensive war, the South could tap regional loyalty and would enjoy protected lines of supply and support.

Union forces, however, were embarked on an expensive and difficult war of conquest. Because many parts of the South raised cotton and tobacco rather than food crops, Union armies could not forage for necessary food and fodder. Supplying northern forces in the South presented significant logistic problems and dangers. Extended supply lines were always vulnerable to attack, rendering northern armies less mobile and secure than southern troops. The Union had to win a war of conquest and occupation. The South merely had to survive until its enemy tired and gave up.

The Border States

Uncertainty over the war's outcome and divided loyalties produced indecision in the border states. When the seven states of the Deep South seceded during the winter of 1860–1861, the border states adopted a wait-and-see attitude. Delaware identified with the Union camp, but the others vacillated. Their decisions were critically important to both North and South.

The states of the Upper South could provide natural borders for the Confederacy along the Ohio River, access to its river traffic, and vital resources, wealth, and population. The major railroad link to the West ran through Maryland and western Virginia. Virginia boasted the South's largest ironworks, and Tennessee was the region's principal source of grain. Missouri provided the road to Kansas and the West and was strategically placed to control Mississippi River traffic. It was difficult to imagine the long- or short-term success of the Confederacy without the border states.

For the North, every border state that elected to remain loyal represented a psychological triumph for the idea of Union. Nor was the North indifferent to the economic and strategic advantages of keeping the border states with the Union. Lincoln's call for troops precipitated decisions in several states, however. Between April 17 and May 20, 1861, Virginia, Arkansas, Tennessee, and North Carolina joined the Confederacy.

The significance of border state loyalty was soon dramatized in Maryland. Slave-owning tobacco and wheat planters from the state's southern counties and eastern shore favored secession. Confederate enthusiasts abounded in Baltimore. But in the western and northern parts of the state, small farmers, often of German background, opposed slavery and supported the Union cause.

On the morning of April 19, the 6th Massachusetts Regiment arrived in Baltimore headed for Washington. Because the regiment had to change railroad lines, the soldiers set out across the city on foot and in horsecars. As they marched through the streets, a mob of some 10,000 southern sympathizers, flying Confederate flags, attacked them with

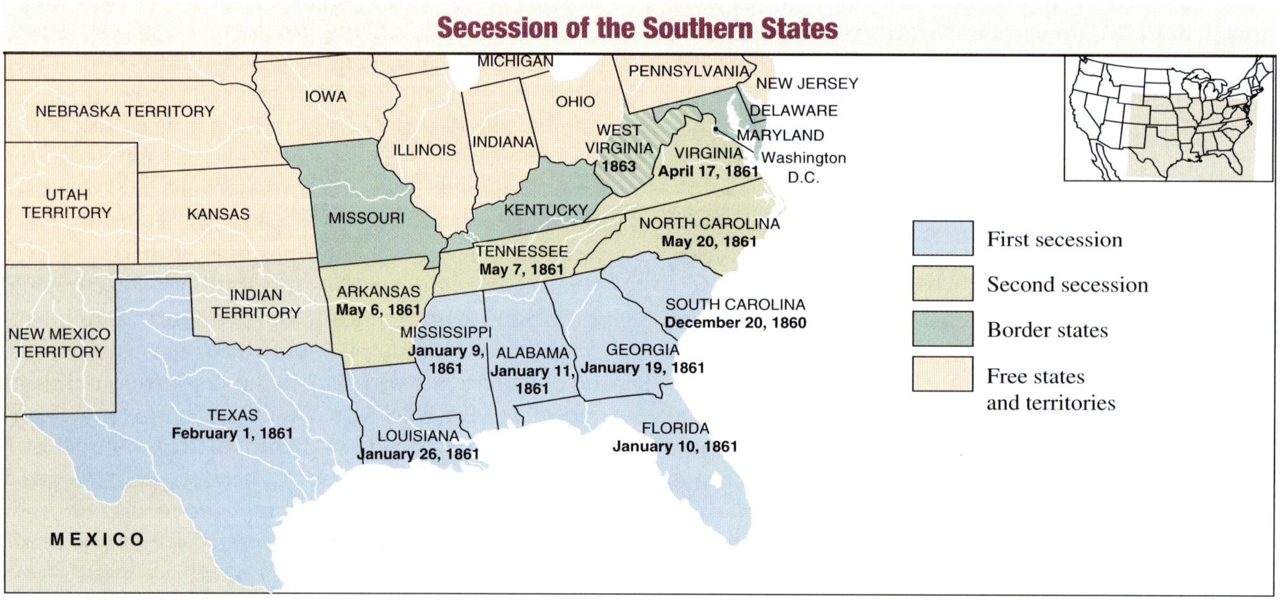

This map provides a chronology of secession and shows the geographic importance of the border states. The map also highlights the vulnerable position of Washington and explains many of Lincoln's actions in the early days of the war.

paving stones, then bayonets and bullets. Finally, as a contemporary explained, the "patience of their commander was . . . exhausted. He cried out in a voice, which was heard even above the yells of the mob, 'Fire!' . . . A scene of bloody confusion followed." In the commotion, would-be secessionists burned the railroad bridges connecting Baltimore to the North and to the South. Washington found itself cut off from the rest of the Union, an island in the middle of hostile territory.

Lincoln took stern measures to secure Maryland. The president agreed temporarily to route troops around Baltimore. In return, the governor called the state legislature into session at Frederick, a center of Union sentiment in western Maryland. This action and Lincoln's swift violation of civil rights damped secessionist enthusiasm. Hundreds of southern sympathizers, including 19 state legislators and Baltimore's mayor, were arrested and languished in prison without trial. Although the chief justice of the United States, Roger B. Taney, challenged the legality of the president's action and issued a writ of habeas corpus for the release of John Merryman, a southern supporter, Lincoln ignored him. A month later, Taney ruled in *Ex parte Merryman* that if the public's safety was endangered, only Congress had the right to suspend a writ of habeas corpus. By then, Lincoln had secured Maryland for the Union.

Though Lincoln's quick and harsh response ensured Maryland's loyalty, he was more cautious elsewhere. Above all, he had to deal with slavery prudently, for any hasty action would push border states into the waiting arms of the Confederacy. Thus, when General John C. Frémont, in a burst of enthusiasm, issued an unauthorized declaration of emancipation in Missouri in August 1861, Lincoln revoked the order and recalled the general. As the president explained, he expected a chain reaction if certain key states left the Union. "I think to lose Kentucky is nearly the same as to lose the whole game. Kentucky gone, we cannot hold Missouri, nor, as I think, Maryland. These all against us, and the job on our hands is too large for us." In the end, after some fighting and much maneuvering, Kentucky and Missouri, like Maryland, stayed in the Union.

Challenges of War

The tense weeks after Fort Sumter spilled over with unexpected challenges. Neither North nor South could handle the floods of volunteers. Both faced enormous organizational problems as they readied for war. In the South, a nation-state had to be created and its apparatus set in motion. Everything from a constitution and government departments to a flag and postage stamps had to be devised. As one onlooker observed, "The whole country was new. Everything was to be done—and to be made."

In February 1861, the original seceding states sent delegates to Montgomery, Alabama, to begin work on a provisional framework and to select a provisional president and vice president. The delegates swiftly wrote a constitution, much like the federal constitution of 1787 except in its emphasis on the "sovereign and independent character" of the states and its explicit recognition of slavery. The provisional president, Jefferson Davis of Mississippi, tried to put together a geographically and politically balanced cabinet with a moderate face for the outside world. He succeeded in creating a balanced cabinet, but it had few of his friends and, more serious, few men of political stature. As time passed, it turned out to be unstable as well. In a four-year period, 14 men held six positions.

Davis's cabinet appointees faced the formidable challenge of creating government departments from scratch. They had to hire employees and initiate administrative procedures with woefully inadequate resources. The president's office was in a hotel parlor. The Confederate Treasury Department was housed in a room in an Alabama bank "without furniture of any kind; empty . . . of desks, tables, chairs or other appliances for the conduct of business." Treasury Secretary Christopher G. Memminger bought furniture with his own money; operations lurched forward in fits and starts. In those early days, when an army captain came to the treasury with a warrant from Davis for blankets, he found only one clerk. After reading the warrant, the clerk offered the captain a few dollars of his own, explaining, "This, Captain, is all the money that I will certify as being in the Confederate Treasury at this moment." Other departments faced similar difficulties.

Inheriting the federal government, Lincoln did not have to set up a postal system or decide whether laws passed before 1861 were valid. Without administrative experience, however, the new president, like his Confederate counterpart, faced organizational problems. Military officers and government clerks daily left the capital for the South. The treasury was empty. The Republicans had won their first presidential election, and floods of office seekers who had worked for Lincoln now thronged into the White House looking for rewards.

Nor could Lincoln, who did not know many of the "prominent men of the day," easily select a cabinet. Finally, he appointed important Republicans from different factions of the party to cabinet posts whether they agreed with him or not. Most were almost strangers to the president. Several scorned him as a bumbling backwoods politician. Treasury Secretary Salmon P. Chase actually hoped to replace Lincoln as president in four years' time. Soon after the inauguration, Secretary of State William Seward sent Lincoln a memo condescendingly offering to oversee the formulation of presidential policy.

Lincoln and Davis

A number of Lincoln's early actions illustrated that he was no malleable backcountry bumbler. As his Illinois law partner, William Herndon, pointed out, Lincoln's "mind was tough—solid—knotty—gnarly, more or less like his body." In his reply to Seward's memo, the president firmly indicated that he intended to run his own administration. After Sumter, he swiftly called up the state militias, expanded the navy, and suspended habeas corpus. He ordered a naval blockade of the South and approved the expenditure of funds for military purposes, all without congressional sanction, because Congress was not in session. As Lincoln told legislators later, "The dogmas of the quiet past are inadequate to the stormy present. . . . As our case is new, so must we think anew, and act anew . . . and then we shall save our country." This willingness to "think anew" was a valuable personal asset, even though some critics called his expansion of presidential power despotic.

By coincidence, Lincoln and his rival, Jefferson Davis, were born only 100 miles apart in Kentucky. However, the course of their lives diverged radically. Lincoln's father had migrated north and eked out a simple existence as a farmer in Indiana and Illinois. Abraham had only a rudimentary formal education and was largely self-taught. Davis's family, however, had moved south to Mississippi and become cotton planters. Davis grew up in comfortable circumstances, went to Transylvania University and West Point, and fought in the Mexican-American War before his election to the U.S. Senate. In recognition of his social, political, and economic prominence, Davis served as secretary of war under Franklin Pierce (1853–1857). Tall, distinguished-looking, and very rich, he appeared every inch the aristocratic southerner.

Although Davis had not been eager to accept the presidency, he had loyally responded to the call of the provisional congress in 1861 and worked tirelessly as the chief executive of the Confederacy until the war's end. His wife, Varina, observed that "the President hardly takes time to eat his meals and works late at night." Some contemporaries suggested that Davis's inability to let subordinates handle details explained this schedule. Others observed that he was sickly, reserved, humorless, too sensitive to criticism, and hard to get along with. But Davis, like Lincoln, found it necessary to "think anew." He reassured southerners in his inaugural address that his aims were conservative, "to preserve the Government of our fathers in spirit." Yet under the pressure of events, he moved toward creating a new kind of South.

CLASHING ON THE BATTLEFIELD, 1861–1862

The Civil War was the most brutal and destructive conflict in American history. Much of the bloodshed resulted from changing military technology coupled with inadequate communications. By the opening of hostilities, the range of rifles had increased from 100 to 500 yards, in part owing to the new French minié bullet, which traveled with tremendous velocity and accuracy. The greater reach of the new rifles meant that it was no longer possible to position the artillery close enough to enemy lines to allow it to support an infantry charge. During the Civil War, then, attacking infantry soldiers faced a final, often fatal, dash of 500 yards in the face of deadly enemy fire.

As it became clear that infantry charges resulted in horrible carnage, military leaders increasingly valued the importance of the strong defensive position. Although Confederate soldiers criticized General Lee as "King of Spades" when he first ordered them to construct earthworks, the epithet evolved into one of affection as it became obvious that earthworks saved lives. Union commanders followed suit. By the end of 1862, both armies dug defensive earthworks and trenches whenever they interrupted their march.

War in the East

The war's brutal character only gradually revealed itself. The Union commanding general, 70-year-old Winfield Scott, at first pressed for a cautious, long-term strategy, known as the Anaconda Plan. Scott proposed weakening the South gradually through blockades on land and at sea until the northern army was strong enough for the kill. The excited public, however, hungered for action and quick victory. So did Lincoln, who knew that the longer the war lasted, the more embittered the South and the North would both become, making reunion ever more difficult. Under the cry of "Forward to Richmond!" 35,000 partially trained men led by General Irwin McDowell headed out from Washington in sweltering July weather.

On July 21, 1861, only 25 miles from the capital at Manassas Creek, or Bull Run, as it is also called, inexperienced northern troops confronted 25,000 raw Confederate soldiers commanded by Brigadier General P. G. T. Beauregard, a West Point classmate of McDowell's. Although sightseers, journalists, and politicians accompanied the Union troops, expecting only a Sunday outing, the encounter at Bull Run was no picnic. The course of battle swayed back and forth before the arrival of 2,300 fresh Confederate troops, brought by trains, decided the day. Union soldiers and sightseers fled toward Washington in terror and confusion. An English journalist, William Russell, described the troops as they poured into Washington on July 22:

> I saw a steady stream of men covered with mud, soaked through with rain . . . pouring irregularly, without any semblance of order, up Pennsylvania Avenue toward the Capitol. . . . I perceived they belonged to different regiments . . . mingled pell-mell together. . . . Hastily [I] . . . ran downstairs and asked an officer . . . a pale young man who looked exhausted to death and who had lost his sword . . . where the men were coming from. "Where from? Well, sir, I guess we're all coming out of Virginny as far as we can, and pretty well whipped too. . . . I know I'm going home. I've had enough of fighting to last my lifetime."

"Pretty well whipped" the Union forces certainly were. Yet inexperienced Confederate troops had lost their chance to turn the rout into the quick and decisive victory they sought. As General Joseph E. Johnston pointed out, his men were disorganized, confused by victory, and not well enough supplied with food to chase the Union army back toward Washington.

In many ways, the Battle of Bull Run was prophetic. Victory would be neither quick nor easy. As the disorganization and confusion of both sides suggested, the armies were unprofessional. And it was becoming obvious that bravado would not win the war. Then, too, both sides faced problems with short-term enlistments. Finally, logistic problems connected with mass armies plagued both sides. The Civil War put more men in the field than any previous American engagement. Supplying and moving so many men and ensuring adequate communication, especially during battle, were tasks of an unprecedented kind. It was hardly surprising that the armies floundered trying to meet these logistic challenges.

Robert Allston, the prominent South Carolina rice planter, viewed the battlefield at Bull Run and decided it had been a "glorious tho bloody" day. For the Union, however, the loss at Bull Run was sobering. Replacing McDowell with 34-year-old General George McClellan, Lincoln began his search for a northern commander capable of winning the war. McClellan, formerly an army engineer, confronted the task of

Eastern Theater of the Civil War, 1861–1862

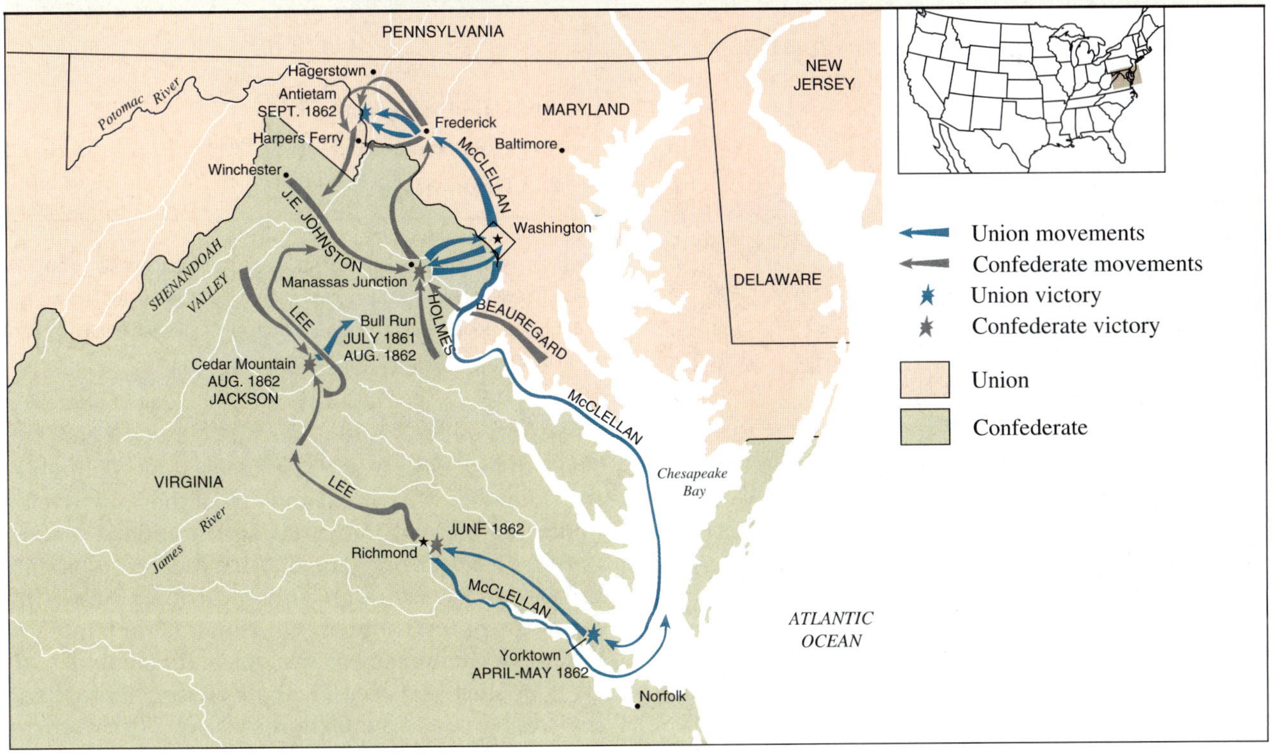

This map reveals the military actions in the East during the early years of the war. Initially, military planners hoped to end the war quickly by capturing Richmond. They soon discovered that the Confederate army was too powerful to allow them an easy victory. Eventually, Lincoln decided to combine military pressure on Virginia with an effort in the West aimed at cutting the Confederacy in two.

transforming the Army of the Potomac into a fighting force. Short-term militias went home. When Scott retired in the fall of 1861, McClellan became general in chief of the Union armies.

McClellan had considerable organizational ability but no desire to be a daring leader on the battlefield. Convinced that the North must combine military victory with efforts to persuade the South to return to the Union, he sought to avoid unnecessary and embittering loss of life and property. He intended to win the war "by maneuvering rather than fighting."

In March 1862, pushed by an impatient Lincoln, McClellan finally led his army of 130,000 toward Richmond, now the Confederate capital. By late June, his army was close enough to hear Richmond's church bells pealing. But just as it seemed that victory was within grasp, Lee counterattacked and slowly drove the Union forces away from the city. Finally, orders came from Washington: abandon the Peninsula campaign.

Other Union defeats followed in 1862 as commanders came and went. In September, the South took the offensive with a bold invasion of Maryland. But after a costly defeat at Antietam, in which more than 5,000 soldiers were slaughtered and another 17,000 wounded on the grisliest day of the war, Lee withdrew his army to Virginia. Victory eluded both sides. The war in the East was stalemated.

This dying horse, stripped of saddle and bridle, was the mount of a Confederate officer killed during the battle of Antietam. The stark character of the picture reveals the devastating nature of the Civil War battlefield. *(Library of Congress)*

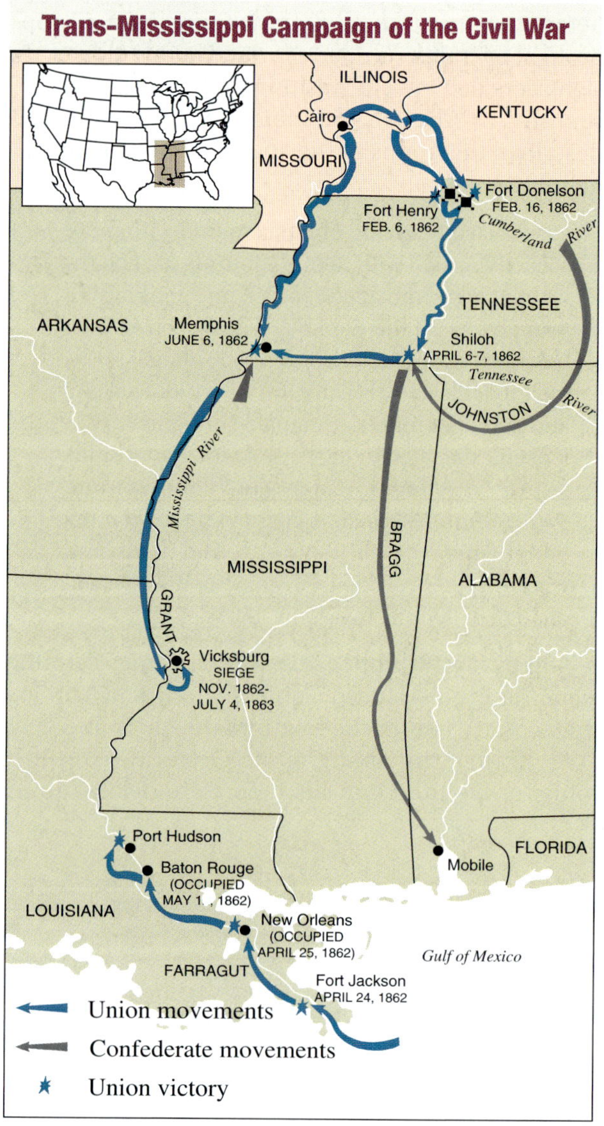

The military movements in the trans-Mississippi West appear here. Union forces operating in the Mississippi valley were attempting to separate Texas, Arkansas, and Louisiana from other southern states as part of an attempt to squeeze the Confederacy.

War in the West

The early struggle in the East focused on Richmond, the Confederacy's capital and one of the South's most important railroad, industrial, and munitions centers. But the East was only one of three theaters of action. Between the Appalachian Mountains and the Mississippi lay the western theater, the states of Kentucky, Tennessee, Mississippi, and Alabama. At its edge lay the Mississippi, with its vital river trade and its great port, New Orleans. Here both George Eagleton and Arthur Carpenter served. Beyond lay the trans-Mississippi West—Louisiana, Arkansas, Missouri, Texas, and the Great Plains—where Native American tribes joined the conflict on both sides.

This photograph taken at a field hospital in Virginia during a battle in the summer of 1862 shows surgeons trying to attend to the crowds of wounded lying on the ground. Many deaths resulted from inadequate care for the wounded and sick of both armies. Although there was initial resistance to the idea of women becoming nurses in such hospitals, the dreadful shortage of qualified medical men and the huge workload that they faced eventually resulted in allowing women nurses into hospitals. One described her first reaction to the scene that greeted her eyes: "A strange sense of suffocation oppressed me, as the air by which I was surrounded was filled with poisonous vapors, and for a few minutes I doubted my own strength." *(Library of Congress)*

In the western theater, the Union had two strategic objectives: the domination of Kentucky and eastern Tennessee, the avenues to the South and West, and control of the Mississippi River to split the South in two. Major campaigns sought strategic points along rivers and railroads.

It was in the western theater that Ulysses S. Grant rose to prominence. His modest military credentials included a West Point education, service in the Mexican-American war, and an undistinguished stint in the peacetime army. After his resignation, he went bankrupt. At the war's opening, he was working in his family's leather store in Illinois. Soon after Fort Sumter, Grant enlisted as a colonel in an Illinois militia regiment. Within two months, he was a brigadier general.

Grant's military genius consisted of an ability to see beyond individual battles to larger goals. In 1862, he realized that the Tennessee and Cumberland Rivers were the paths for the successful invasion of Tennessee. A premature Confederate invasion of Kentucky allowed Grant to bring his forces into that state without arousing sharp local opposition. Assisted by gunboats, Grant was largely responsible for the capture of Fort Henry and Fort Donelson, key points on the rivers, in February 1862. His successes there raised fears among Confederate leaders that southern mountaineers, loyal to the Union, would rush to Grant's support.

Despite Grant's grasp of strategy, his army was nearly destroyed by a surprise Confederate attack at Shiloh Church in Tennessee. The North won this battle, but victory proved enormously costly. In that two-day engagement, the Union suffered over 13,000 casualties, while 10,000 Confederates lay dead or wounded. More men fell in this single battle than in the American Revolution, the War of 1812, and the Mexican-American War combined. Because neither army offered sufficient care on the battlefield, untreated wounds caused many of the deaths. A full day after the battle had ended, nine-tenths of the wounded still lay in the rain. Many died of exposure; others drowned in the downpour. Those who survived the weather had infected wounds by the time they received medical attention. Though more successful than efforts in the East, such devastating Union campaigns failed to bring decisive results. Western plans were never coordinated with eastern military activities. Victories there did not force the South to its knees.

The war in the trans-Mississippi West was a sporadic, far-flung struggle for control of the manpower and natural resources of this vast area. California was one prize that lured both armies into the Southwest. Confederate troops from Texas held Albuquerque and Santa Fe briefly in 1862. Volunteer soldiers from the Colorado mining fields, joined by Mexican Americans and other soldiers, drove the Texas Confederates from New Mexico. A Union force recruited in California arrived after the Confederates were gone. They spent the remainder of the Civil War years fighting the Apache and the Navajo and with brutal competence crushed both Native American nations.

Farther east was another prize, the Missouri River, which flowed into the Mississippi River, bordered Illinois, and affected military campaigns in Kentucky and Tennessee. Initially, Confederate troops were successful here, as they had been in New Mexico. But in March 1862, at Pea Ridge in northern Arkansas, the balance tilted in favor of the Union. There the Union forces defeated a Confederate army of 16,000 that included a brigade of Native Americans from the Five Civilized Nations. Missouri entered the Union camp for the first time in the war, and fierce guerrilla warfare continued in the region.

Naval Warfare

At the beginning of the war, Lincoln had decided to strangle the South with a naval blockade. But an effective blockade proved elusive. With no more than 33 ships, the Union navy tried to close up 189 ports along a 3,500-mile coastline. In 1861, the navy intercepted only about one blockade runner in ten and in 1862 one in eight. In the short run, the blockade did little damage to the South.

More successful were operations to gain footholds along the southern coast. In November 1861, a Union expedition took Port Royal Sound, where it freed the first slaves, and the nearby South Carolina sea islands. A few months later, the navy defeated a Confederate force on Roanoke Island, North Carolina. By gaining fueling stations and other important coastal points, the navy increased the possibility of making the blockade effective. The Union's greatest naval triumph in the early war years was the capture of New Orleans in 1862. The loss of the South's greatest port seriously weakened the Confederacy. The success of this amphibious effort stimulated other joint attempts to cut the South in two.

The Confederate leadership, recognizing that the South could not match the Union fleet, concentrated on developing new weapons like torpedoes and formidable ironclad vessels, a concept already successfully tested by the French navy. Because the Union fleet consisted primarily of wooden ships, iron ships might literally crash through the Union blockade.

The *Merrimac* was one key to southern naval strategy. Originally a U.S. warship sunk as the federal navy hurriedly abandoned the Norfolk Navy Yard early in the war, the Confederates raised the vessel and covered it with heavy iron armor. Rechristened the *Virginia,* the ship steamed out of Norfolk in March 1862, heading directly for the Union ships blocking the harbor. Using its 1,500-pound ram and guns, the *Virginia* drove a third of the ships aground and destroyed the squadron's largest ships. Victory was short-lived. The next day, the *Virginia* confronted the *Monitor,* a newly completed and better designed Union iron vessel. While the *Virginia* survived the crash, it withdrew and was burned during the evacuation of Norfolk that May. Southern attempts to buy and produce ironclad ships failed and southern hopes of evading the northern noose faded.

Though technological innovation failed to break the blockade, the Confederate navy's policy of harming northern commerce brought some success. Confederate raiders, many of them built in England, wreaked havoc on northern shipping. In its two-year career, the raider *Alabama* destroyed 69 Union mer-

This painting of the battle between the Confederate *Virginia* (stubbornly called the *Merrimac* by northerners) and the Union *Monitor* captures the dramatic impact of the new iron ships. During this engagement, the *Monitor* showed it could manuever more easily than the Confederate vessel. Both navies eventually used these innovative iron ships, but the Confederacy could never match the pace of northern production. *(Chicago Historical Society)*

chant vessels valued at more than $6 million. But while such blows were costly to the North, they did not seriously damage its overall war effort.

Throughout the first two years of conflict, both sides achieved victories, but the war remained deadlocked. Although the South was far from being defeated, the North was as far from giving up or accepting southern independence. The costs of war, in manpower and supplies, far exceeded what either side had anticipated. The need to replace lost men and supplies thus loomed ever more serious at the end of 1862.

Cotton Diplomacy

Both sides in the Civil War realized that attitudes in Europe could be critical. European diplomatic recognition of the Confederacy would give the nation credibility in the eyes of the rest of the world. Furthermore, European loans and assistance might bring the South victory just as French and Dutch aid had helped the American colonies win their independence. If the European nations refused to recognize the South, however, the fiction of the Union was kept alive, undermining Confederate chances for long-term survival. The European powers, of course, consulted their own national interests. Neither England nor France, the two most important nations, wished to back the losing side. Nor did they wish to upset Europe's delicate balance of power by hasty intervention in American affairs. One by one, therefore, the European states declared a policy of neutrality.

Southerners were sure that cotton would be their trump card. English and French textile mills needed cotton, and southerners believed that their owners would eventually force government recognition of the Confederacy and an end to the North's blockade. But a glut of cotton in 1860 and 1861 left foreign mill owners oversupplied. As stockpiles dwindled, European industrialists found cotton in India and Egypt. The conviction that cotton was "the king who can shake the jewels in the crown of Queen Victoria" proved false.

Union Secretary of State Seward sought above all else to prevent diplomatic recognition of the Confederacy. The North had its own economic ties with Europe, so the Union was not as disadvantaged as southerners thought. Seward daringly threatened Great Britain with war if it interfered in what he insisted was an internal matter. Some called his boldness reckless, even mad. Nevertheless, his policy succeeded. Even though England allowed the construction of Confederate raiders in its ports, it did not intervene in American affairs in 1861 or 1862. Nor did the other European powers. Unless the military situation changed dramatically, the Europeans were willing to sit on the sidelines.

Common Problems, Novel Solutions

As the conflict dragged on into 1863, unanticipated problems appeared in both the Union and the Confederacy, and leaders devised novel approaches to solve them. War acted as a catalyst for changes that no one could have imagined in the heady spring days of 1861.

The problem of fighting a long war was partly monetary. Both treasuries had been empty initially, and the war proved extraordinarily expensive. Neither side considered trying to finance the war by imposing direct taxes. Such an approach violated custom and risked alienating support. Nevertheless, each side was so starved for funds that it initiated taxation on a small scale. Ultimately, taxes financed 21 percent of the North's war expenses (but only 1 percent of southern expenses). Both treasuries also tried borrowing. Northerners bought over $2 billion worth of bonds, but southerners proved reluctant to buy their government's bonds.

As in the American Revolution, the unwelcome solution was to print paper money. In August 1861, the Confederacy put into circulation $100 million in

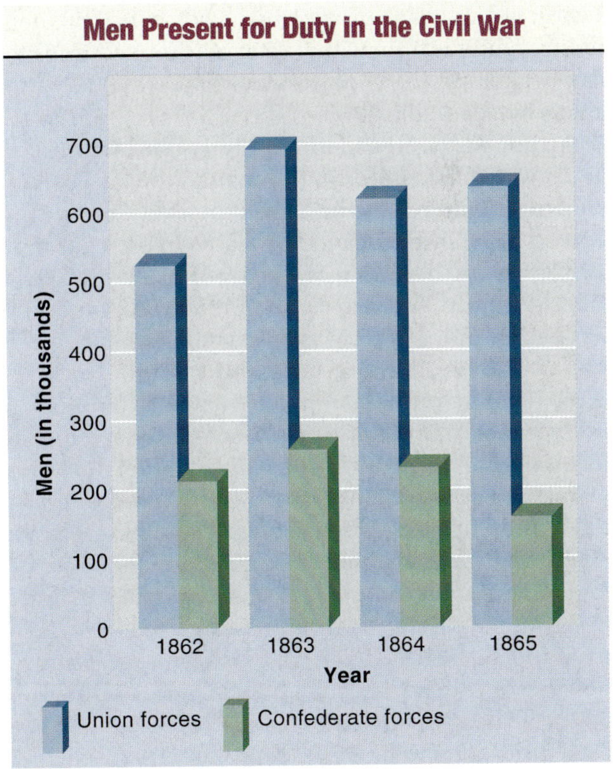

This chart demonstrates the growing superiority of the North in terms of manpower and the impact of draft laws. After 1863, blacks, like native-born Americans and Irish and German immigrants, served in the armed forces.

crudely engraved bills. Millions more followed the next year. Five months later, the Union issued $150 million in paper money, soon nicknamed "greenbacks" because of their color. Although financing the war with paper money was unexpected, the resulting inflation was not. Inflation was particularly troublesome in the Confederacy, but a "modest" 80 percent increase in food prices brought Union city families near starvation and contributed to urban unhappiness during the war.

Both sides confronted similar manpower problems as initial enthusiasm for the war evaporated. Soldiering, it turned out, was nothing like the militia parades and outings familiar to most American males. Young men were shocked at the deadliness of diseases that accompanied the army wherever it went and were unprepared for the boredom of camp life. As one North Carolina soldier explained, "If anyone wishes to become used to the crosses and trials of this life, let him enter camp life." None was prepared for the vast and impersonal destruction of the battlefield, which made a mockery of values like courage and honor. It was with anguish that Robert Carter of Massachusetts saw bodies tossed into trenches "with not a prayer, eulogy or tear to distinguish them from so many animals." Those in the service longed to go home. The swarm of volunteers disappeared. Rather than fill their military quotas from within, rich northern communities began offering bounties of $800 to $1,000 to outsiders who would join up.

Arthur Carpenter's letters give a good picture of life in the ranks and a young man's growing disillusionment with the war. As Carpenter's regiment moved into Kentucky and Tennessee in the winter of 1862, his enthusiasm for army life evaporated. "Soldiering in Kentucky and Tennessee," he complained, "is not so pretty as it was in Indianapolis. . . . We have been half starved, half frozen, and half drowned. The mud in Kentucky is awful." Soldiering often meant marching over rutted roads carrying 50 or 60 pounds of equipment with insufficient food, water, or supplies. One blanket was not enough in the winter. In the summer, stifling woolen uniforms attracted lice and other vermin. Poor food, bugs, inadequate sanitation, and exposure invited disease. Carpenter marched through Tennessee suffering from diarrhea and then fever. His regiment left him behind in a convalescent barracks in Louisville, which he fled as soon as he could. He feared the hospital at least as much as the sickness. "99 Surgeons out of a hundred," he wrote his parents, "would not know whether his patient had the horse distemper, lame toe, or any other disease."

Confederate soldiers, even less well supplied than their northern counterparts, complained similarly. In 1862, a Virginia captain described what General Lee called the best army "the world ever saw":

> During our forced marches and hard fights, the soldiers have been compelled to throw away their knapsacks and there is scarcely a private in the army who has a change of clothing of any kind. Hundreds of men are perfectly barefooted and there is no telling when they can be supplied with shoes.

In such circumstances, desertion was common. An estimated one of every nine men enlisting in the Confederate armies and one of every seven in the Union armies deserted.

As the manpower problems became critical, both governments resorted to the draft. Despite the sacrosanct notion of states' rights, the Confederate Congress passed the first conscription act in American history in March 1862. Four months later, the Union Congress also approved a draft measure. Both laws sought to encourage men already in the army to reenlist and to stimulate volunteers rather than to force men to serve. Ultimately, over 30 percent of the Confederate army and 6 percent of the Union forces were draftees.

The Confederacy relied more heavily on the draft than the Union did because the North's initial manpower pool was larger and growing. During the war, 180,000 foreigners of military age poured into the northern states. Some came specifically to claim bounties and fight. Immigrants made up at least 20 percent of the Union army.

Necessary though they were, draft laws were very unpopular. The first Confederate conscription declared all able-bodied men between 18 and 35 eligible for military service but allowed numerous exemptions and the purchase of substitutes. Critics complained that the provision entitling every planter with more than 20 slaves to one exemption from military service favored rich slave owners. Certainly, the legislation fed class tension in the South and encouraged disloyalty and desertion among the poorer classes, particularly among southern mountaineers. The advice one woman shouted after her husband as he was dragged off to the army was hardly unique. "You desert again, quick as you kin. . . . Desert, Jake!" The law, as one southerner pointed out, "aroused a spirit of rebellion."

Northern legislation was neither more popular nor fair. The 1863 draft allowed the hiring of substitutes, and $300 bought an exemption from military service. Workers, already suffering from inflation, resented the ease with which moneyed citizens could avoid army duty. In July 1863, the resentment boiled over in New York City in the largest civil disturbance of the nineteenth century.

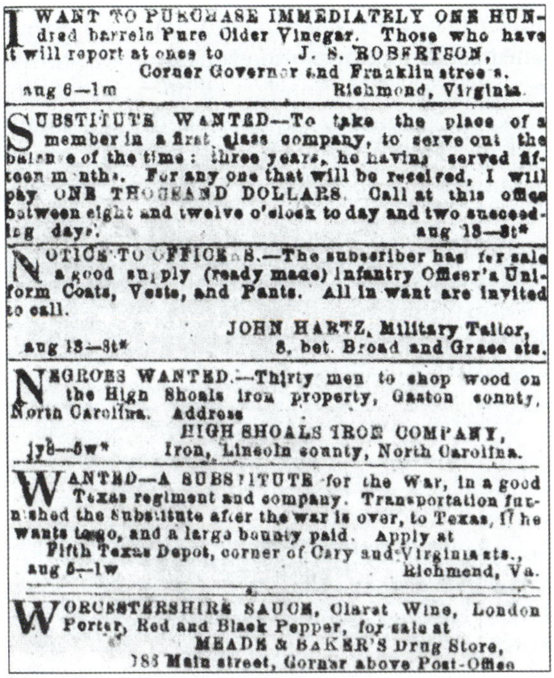

I WANT TO PURCHASE IMMEDIATELY ONE HUNdred barrels Pure Cider Vinegar. Those who have it will report at once to J. S. ROBERTSON,
Corner Governor and Franklin streets.
aug 6—1m Richmond, Virginia.

SUBSTITUTE WANTED—To take the place of a member in a first class company, to serve out the balance of the time: three years, he having served fifteen months. For any one that will be received, I will pay ONE THOUSAND DOLLARS. Call at this office between eight and twelve o'clock to day and two succeeding days.
aug 18—3t*

NOTICE TO OFFICERS.—The subscriber has for sale a good supply (ready made) Infantry Officer's Uniform Coats, Vests, and Pants. All in want are invited to call.
JOHN HARTZ, Military Tailor,
aug 18—3t* 8, bet. Broad and Grace sts.

NEGROES WANTED.—Thirty men to chop wood on the High Shoals Iron property, Gaston county, North Carolina. Address
HIGH SHOALS IRON COMPANY,
jy8—6w* Iron, Lincoln county, North Carolina.

WANTED—A SUBSTITUTE for the War, in a good Texas regiment and company. Transportation furnished the Substitute after the war is over, to Texas, if he wants to go, and a large bounty paid. Apply at
Fifth Texas Depot, corner of Cary and Virginia sts.,
aug 5—1w Richmond, Va.

WORCESTERSHIRE SAUCE, Claret Wine, London Porter, Red and Black Pepper, for sale at
MEADE & BAKER'S Drug Store,
183 Main street, Corner above Post-Office

These advertisements from a Virginia newspaper include two for substitutes, indicating the advantages money provided for those who wished to avoid military service. *(Virginia Historical Society, Richmond)*

The three-day riot came only a month after a work stoppage on the New York waterfront. The process of selecting several thousand conscripts began on a weekend in early July. By Monday, workers opposed to the draft were parading through the streets. Several Irish members of the Black Joker Volunteer Fire Company whose names had been listed were determined to go further than peaceful protest by destroying draft records and the Enrollment Office. Events spun out of control as a mob also burned the armory, plundered the houses of the rich, and looted jewelry stores. Blacks, whom the Irish hated as economic competitors and the cause of the war, became special targets. Mobs shouting, "Vengeance on every nigger in New York," beat and lynched blacks and even burned the Colored Orphan Asylum. More than 100 people died in the violence. There was much truth in the accusation that the war on both sides was a rich man's war but a poor man's fight.

Political Dissension, 1862

As the war continued, rumbles of dissension grew louder. On February 24, 1862, the *Richmond Examiner* summarized many southerners' frustration. "The Confederacy has had everything that was required for success but one, and that one thing it was and is supposed to possess more than anything else, namely Talent." As victory proved elusive, necessitating unpopular measures like the draft, criticism of Confederate leaders mounted. Jefferson Davis's vice president, Alexander Stephens of Georgia, became one of the administration's bitterest accusers. Public criticism reflected private disapproval. Wrote one southerner to a friend, "Impeach Jeff Davis for incompetency & call a convention of the States. . . . West Point is death to us & sick Presidents & Generals are equally fatal."

Because the South had no party system, dissatisfaction with Davis and his handling of the war tended to be factional, petty, and personal. No party mechanism existed to channel or curb irresponsible criticism. Detractors rarely felt it necessary to offer programs in place of Davis's policies. Davis suffered personally from the carping comments of his detractors. More important, the Confederacy suffered. Without a party leader's traditional weapons and rewards, Davis had no mechanism to generate enthusiasm for his war policies.

Although Lincoln has since become a folk hero, at the time, many northerners derided his performance and eagerly looked forward to a new president in 1864. Peace Democrats, called Copperheads, claimed that Lincoln betrayed the Constitution and that working-class Americans bore the brunt of his policy of conscription. New York Democrats warned the city's Irish residents that freed blacks would "steal the work and bread of honest Irish." Immigrant workers in eastern cities and those who lived in the southern parts of the Midwest had little sympathy for abolitionism or blacks, and they supported the antiwar stance of the Copperheads. Even Democrats favoring the war effort found Lincoln arbitrary and tyrannical. Fearing his expansion of presidential power, they also worried that extreme Republicans would push Lincoln into making the war a crusade for the abolition of slavery.

Republicans were themselves divided. Moderates favored a cautious approach toward winning the war, fearing the possible consequences of emancipating the slaves, confiscating Confederate property, or arming blacks. The radicals, however, urged Lincoln to make emancipation a wartime objective. They hoped for a victory that would revolutionize southern social and racial arrangements.

Lincoln had been moderate on the issue of slavery before the war, advocating the end of its expansion in the West but not its abolition in the South. He began changing his mind in early 1862. The reduction of the congressional Republican majority in the fall elections of 1862 made it imperative that Lincoln listen not only to both factions of his party but also to the Democratic opposition.

THE TIDE TURNS, 1863–1865

Hard political realities as well as Lincoln's sense of the public's mood help explain why he delayed an emancipation proclamation until 1863. Like congressional Democrats, many northerners supported a war for the Union but not one for emancipation. Not only did many, if not most, whites see blacks as inferior, but they also suspected that emancipation would trigger a massive influx of former slaves who would steal white men's jobs and political rights. Race riots in New York, Brooklyn, Philadelphia, and Buffalo dramatized white attitudes. In Cincinnati, Irish dockworkers attacked blacks who were offering to work for less pay with the cry, "Let's clear out the niggers." Arthur Carpenter's evaluation of blacks was typical of many northern soldiers confronting blacks for the first time. In December 1861, he wrote to his parents:

> No one who has ever seen the nigger in all its glory on the southern plantations . . . will ever vote for emancipation. . . . If emancipation is to be the policy of the war (and I think it will not) I do not care how quick the country goes to pot. The negro never was intended to be equal with the white man.

The Emancipation Proclamation, 1863

If the president moved too fast on emancipation, he risked losing the allegiance of people like Carpenter, offending the border states, and increasing the Democrats' chances for political victory. Moreover, he had at first hoped that pro-Union sentiment would emerge in the South and compel its leaders to abandon their rebellion. But if Lincoln did not move at all, he would alienate abolitionists and lose the support of radical Republicans, which he could ill afford.

For these reasons, Lincoln proceeded cautiously. At first, he hoped the border states would take the initiative. In the early spring of 1862, he urged Congress to pass a joint resolution offering federal compensation to states beginning a "gradual abolishment of slavery." Border state opposition killed the idea and indicated reluctance to believe, as Lincoln did, that the "friction and abrasion" of war would finally end slavery. Abolitionists and northern blacks, however, greeted Lincoln's proposal with a "thrill of joy."

That summer, Lincoln told his cabinet he intended to emancipate the slaves. Secretary of State Seward urged the president to delay any general proclamation until the North won a decisive military victory. Otherwise, he warned, Lincoln would appear to be urging racial insurrection behind the Confederate lines to compensate for northern military bungling.

Lincoln followed Seward's advice, using that summer and fall to prepare the North for the shift in the war's purpose. To counteract white racial fears of free blacks, he promoted various schemes for establishing free black colonies in Haiti and Panama. Seizing unexpected opportunities, he lay the groundwork for the proclamation itself. In August, Horace Greeley, the influential abolitionist editor of the New York *Tribune*, printed an open letter to Lincoln attacking him for failing to act on slavery. In his reply, Lincoln linked the idea of emancipation to military necessity. His primary goal, he wrote, was to save the Union:

> If I could save the Union without freeing any slave, I would do it; and if I could save it by freeing all the slaves, I would do it; and if I could do it by freeing some and leaving others alone, I would also do that. What I do about Slavery and the colored race, I do because I believe it helps to save this Union.

If Lincoln attacked slavery, then, it would be only because emancipation would save white lives, preserve the democratic process, and win the conflict for the Union.

In September 1862, the Union victory at Antietam gave Lincoln the opportunity to issue a preliminary emancipation proclamation. It stated that unless rebellious states (or parts of states in rebellion) returned to the Union by January 1, 1863, the president would declare their slaves "forever free." Although supposedly aimed at bringing the southern states back into the Union, Lincoln never expected the South to lay down arms after two years of bloodshed. Rather, he was preparing northerners to accept the eventuality of emancipation on the grounds of necessity. Frederick Douglass greeted the president's action with jubilation. "We shout for joy," he wrote, "that we live to record this righteous decree."

Not all northerners shared Douglass's joy. In fact, the September proclamation probably harmed Lincoln's party in the fall elections. As one Democratic ditty put it:

> *"De Union!" used to be de cry—*
> *For dat we want it strong;*
> *But now de motto seems to be,*
> *"De nigger, right or wrong."*

Although the elections of 1862 weakened the Republicans' grasp on the national government, they did not destroy it. Still, cautious cabinet members begged Lincoln to forget about emancipation. His refusal demonstrated his vision and humanity, as did his efforts to reduce racial fears. "Is it dreaded that the freed people will swarm forth and cover the whole land?" he asked. "Are they not already in the land? Will liberation make them any more numerous? Equally distributed among the whites of the whole country, and there would be but one colored to seven whites. Could the one, in any way, greatly disturb the other?"

Finally, on New Year's Day, 1863, Lincoln issued the final Emancipation Proclamation as he had promised. It was an "act of justice, warranted by the Constitution upon military necessity." Thus, what had started as a war to save the Union now also became a struggle that, if victorious, would free the slaves. Yet the proclamation had no immediate impact on slavery. It affected only slaves living in the unconquered portions of the Confederacy. It was silent about slaves in the border states and in parts of the South already in northern hands. These limitations led Elizabeth Cady Stanton and Susan B. Anthony to establish the woman's Loyal National League to lobby Congress to emancipate all southern slaves.

Though the Emancipation Proclamation did not immediately liberate southern slaves from their masters, it had a tremendous symbolic importance. On New Year's Day, blacks gathered outside the White House to cheer the president and tell him that if he would "come out of that palace, they would hug him to death." They realized that the proclamation had changed the nature of the war. For the first time, the government had committed itself to freeing slaves. Jubilant blacks could only believe that the president's action heralded a new era for their race. More immediately, the proclamation sanctioned the policy of accepting blacks as soldiers into the military. Blacks also hoped that the news would reach southern slaves, encouraging them either to flee to Union lines or to subvert the southern war effort by refusing to work for their masters.

Diplomatic concerns also lay behind the Emancipation Proclamation. Lincoln and his advisers anticipated that the commitment to abolish slavery would favorably impress foreign powers. European statesmen, however, did not abandon their cautious stance toward the Union. The English prime minister called the proclamation "trash." But important segments of the English public who opposed slavery now came to regard any attempt to help the South as immoral. Foreigners could better understand and sympathize with a war to free the slaves than they could with a war to save the Union. In diplomacy, where image is so important, Lincoln had created a more attractive picture of the North. The Emancipation Proclamation became the North's symbolic call for human freedom.

Unanticipated Consequences of War

The Emancipation Proclamation was but another example of the war's surprising consequences. Innovation was necessary for victory. In the final two years of the war, both North and South experimented on the battlefields and behind the lines in desperate efforts to conclude the conflict successfully.

One of the Union's experiments involved using black troops for combat duty. Blacks had offered

This depiction of African Americans celebrating the Emancipation Proclamation appeared in the French publication *Le Monde Illustre.* The artist has provided a triumphant and sympathetic picture of rejoicing freed people. The appearance of such a picture in France points to the importance of the Emancipation Proclamation in legitimizing the Union cause in Europe. *(Public Domain)*

themselves as soldiers in 1861 but had been turned away. They were serving as cooks, laborers, teamsters, and carpenters in the army, however, and composed as much as a quarter of the navy. But as white casualties mounted, so did the interest in black service on the battlefield. The Union government allowed states to escape draft quotas if they enlisted enough volunteers, and they allowed them to count southern black enlistees on their state rosters. Northern governors grew increasingly interested in black military service. One piece of doggerel reflected changing attitudes:

Some tell us 'tis a burnin' shame
To make the naygers fight;
And that the thrade of bein' kilt
Belongs but to the white:
But as for me, upon my soul!
So liberal are we here.
I'll let Sambo be murthered instead of myself
On every day in the year.

Beyond white self-interest lay the promises of the Emancipation Proclamation and the desire to prove blacks' value to the Union. Black leaders like Frederick Douglass pressed for military service. "Once let the black man get upon his person the brass letter, U.S., let him get an eagle on his button, and a musket on his shoulder and bullets in his pocket," Douglass believed that "there is no power on earth that can deny that he has earned the right to citizenship." By the war's end, 186,000 blacks (10 percent of the army) had served the Union cause, 134,111 of them escapees from slave states.

Enrolling blacks in the Union army was an important step toward citizenship and acceptance of blacks by white society. But the black experience in the army highlighted some of the obstacles to racial acceptance. Black soldiers, usually led by white officers, were second-class soldiers for most of the war, receiving lower pay ($10 a month as compared with $13), poorer food, often more menial work, and fewer benefits than

Newspaper engravings provided civilians with images of the conflict. This colored lithograph by Currier & Ives was produced a generation after the war, but it is very much like the journalistic images of the time. The picture shows a famous black regiment, the 54th Massachusetts, valiantly storming Fort Wagner, South Carolina. James Gooding, a member of the volunteer regiment and a free black from New Bedford, Massachusetts, described the assault. "We went at it, over the ditch and on to the parapet through a deadly fire; but we could not get into the fort. We met the foe on the parapet of Wagner with the bayonet—we were exposed to a murderous fire. . . . Mortal men could not stand such a fire, and the assault on Wagner was a failure." The experiences of the 54th form the basis for the Hollywood movie *Glory*. *(Library of Congress)*

whites. Even whites who were working to equalize black and white pay often considered blacks inferior. Many white soldiers, including an entire regiment from Illinois, quit the service rather than fight alongside blacks.

The army's racial experiment had mixed results. But the faithful and courageous service of black troops helped modify some of the most demeaning white racial stereotypes of blacks. The black soldiers, many of them former slaves, who conquered the South felt a sense of pride and dignity as they performed their duties. Wrote one, "We march through these fine thoroughfares where once the slave was forbid being out after nine P.M. . . . Negro soldiers!—with banners floating."

As the conflict continued, basic assumptions about how it should be waged weakened. One wartime casualty was the courtly idea that war involved only armies. Early in the war, many officers tried to protect civilians and their property. In the Richmond campaign, General McClellan actually posted guards to prevent stealing. Such concern for rebel property soon vanished, and along with it went chickens, corn, livestock, and, as George Eagleton noted with disgust, even the furnishings of churches, down to the binding of the Bible in the pulpit. Southern troops, on the few occasions when they came North, also lived off the land. War touched all of society, not just the battlefield participants.

Changing Military Strategies, 1863–1865

In the early war years, the South's military strategy combined defense with selective maneuvers. Until the summer of 1863, the strategy seemed to be succeeding, at least in the eastern theater. But an occasional victory over the invading northern army, such as at Fredericksburg in December 1862, did not change the course of the war. Realizing this, Lee reviewed his strategy and concluded, "There is nothing to be gained by this army remaining quietly on the defensive." Unless the South won victories in the North, he believed, it could not gain the peace it so desperately needed.

In the summer of 1863, Lee led the Confederate army of Northern Virginia across the Potomac into Maryland and southern Pennsylvania. His goal was a victory that would threaten both Philadelphia and Washington. He even dreamed of capturing a northern city. Such spectacular feats would surely bring diplomatic recognition and might even force the North to sue for peace.

At Gettysburg on a hot and humid July 1, Lee came abruptly face-to-face with a Union army led by General George Meade. During three days of fighting, the fatal obsession with the infantry charge returned as Lee ordered costly assaults that probably lost him the battle. On July 3, Lee sent three divisions, about 15,000 men in all, against the Union center. The assault, known as Pickett's Charge, was as futile as it was gallant. At 700 yards, the Union artillery opened fire. One southern officer described the scene: "Pickett's division just seemed to melt away in the blue musketry smoke which now covered the hill. Nothing but stragglers came back."

Lee's dreams of victory died that hot week, with grave consequences for the southern cause. Fighting in the eastern theater dragged on for another year and a half, but Lee's Gettysburg losses were so heavy that he could never mount another southern offensive. Instead, the Confederacy committed itself to a

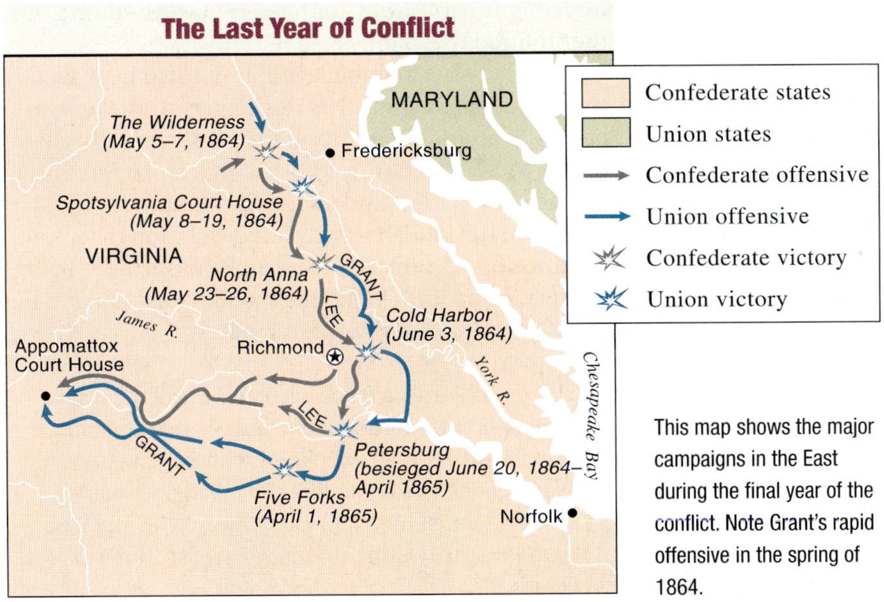

This map shows the major campaigns in the East during the final year of the conflict. Note Grant's rapid offensive in the spring of 1864.

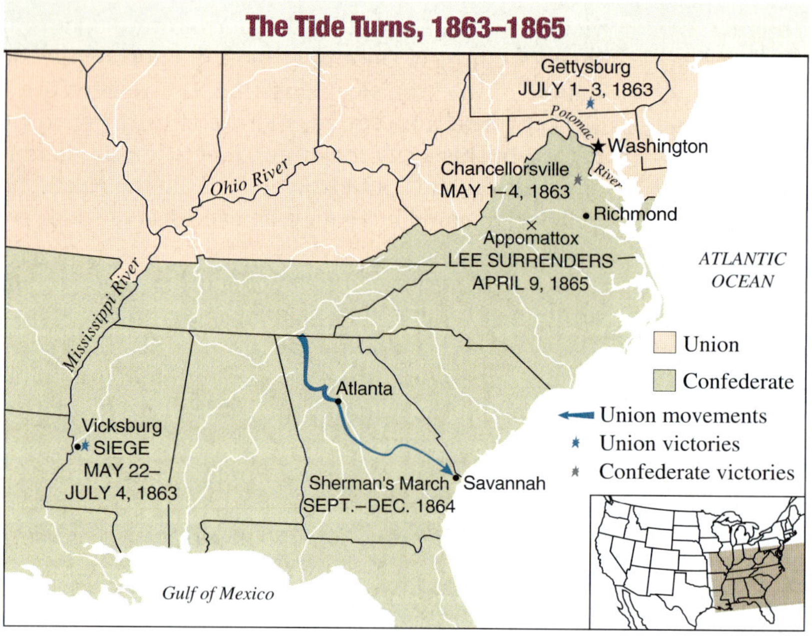

This map highlights important military events during the war's final two years. In the West, Union forces took Vicksburg, and in the East at the battle of Gettysburg they defeated the Confederacy's final effort to bring the war north. During the final stages of the war, Sherman and his army cut a swath through Georgia and then marched north through the Carolinas.

desperate defensive struggle. Gettysburg marked the turn of the military tide in the East.

Despite the Gettysburg victory, Lincoln was dissatisfied with General Meade, who had failed to finish off Lee's demoralized and exhausted army as it retreated. His disappointment soon faded with news of a great victory at Vicksburg in the western theater. The commander, Ulysses S. Grant, would soon solve Lincoln's leadership problem. His July 4 triumph at Vicksburg was thus doubly significant. Vicksburg represented the completion of the Union campaign to gain control of the Mississippi River and to divide the South. Grant's successful capture of the city illustrated the boldness and flexibility that Lincoln sought in a commander.

By the summer of 1863, the military situation finally looked promising for the North. The Union controlled much of Arkansas, Louisiana, Mississippi, Missouri, Kentucky, and Tennessee. In March 1864, Lincoln recognized Grant as the commander to conclude the war and appointed him general in chief of the Union armies. Grant planned for victory within a year. "The art of war is simple enough," he reasoned. "Find out where your enemy is. Get at him as soon as you can. Strike at him as hard as you can, and keep moving on."

As an outsider to the prewar military establishment, Grant had no difficulty rejecting conventional military wisdom. "If men make war in slavish observance of rules, they will fail," he asserted. He sought not one decisive engagement but rather a grim campaign of annihilation, using the North's superior resources of men and supplies to wear down and defeat the South. Although Grant's plan entailed large casualties on both sides, he justified the strategy by arguing that "now the carnage was to be limited to a single year."

A campaign of annihilation involved the destruction not only of enemy armies but also of the resources that fueled the southern war effort. Although the idea of cutting the enemy off from needed supplies was implicit in the naval blockade, economic or "total" warfare was a relatively new and shocking idea. Grant, however, "regarded it as humane to both sides to protect the persons of those found at their homes, but to consume everything that could be used to support or supply armies." Following this policy, he set out after Lee's army in Virginia. General William Tecumseh Sherman, who pursued General Joseph Johnston from Tennessee toward Atlanta, further refined this plan.

The war, Sherman believed, must also be waged in the minds of civilians. His desire was to make southerners "fear and dread" their foes. Therefore, his campaign to seize Atlanta and his march to Savannah spread destruction and terror. Ordered to forage "liberally" on the land, his army left desolation in its wake. "Reduction to poverty," Sherman asserted, "brings prayers for peace." A Georgia woman described in her diary the impact of Sherman's march:

> There was hardly a fence left standing all the way from Sparta to Gordon. The fields were trampled down and the road was lined with carcasses of horses, hogs and cattle that the invaders, unable either to consume or to carry away with them, had wantonly shot down, to starve out the people. . . .

This albumen print by Timothy H. O'Sullivan is entitled "A Harvest of Death, Gettysburg, Pennsylvania, July, 1863." It captures the quiet and misery of the battlefield and suggests the important role photography was coming to play in recording the sweep of American life. *(Rare Books Division, The New York Public Library, Astor, Lenox and Tilden Foundations)*

> The dwellings that were standing all showed signs of pillage, and on every plantation we saw . . . charred remains.

This destruction, with its goal of total victory, showed once more how conflict produced the unexpected. The war that both North and South had hoped would be quick and relatively painless was ending after four long years with great cost to both sides. But the bitter nature of warfare during that final year threatened Lincoln's hopes for reconciliation.

CHANGES WROUGHT BY WAR

As bold new tactics emerged both on and off the battlefield, both governments took steps that changed their societies in surprising ways. Of the two, the South, which had left the Union to conserve a traditional way of life, experienced the more radical transformation.

A New South

The expansion of the central government's power in the South, starting with the passage of the 1862 Conscription Act, continued in the last years of the war. Secession grew out of the concept of states' rights, but, ironically, winning the war depended on central direction and control. Many southerners denounced Davis as a tyrant and a despot because he recognized the need for the central government to take the lead. Despite the accusations, the Confederate Congress cooperated with him and established important precedents. In 1863, it enacted a comprehensive tax law and an impressment act that allowed government agents to requisition food, horses, wagons, and other necessary war materials, often for only about half their market price. These were prime examples of the central government's power to interfere with private property. Government impressment of slaves for war work in 1863 affected the very form of private property that had originally driven the South from the Union.

The Conscription Act of 1862 did not solve the Confederate army's manpower problems. By 1864, the southern armies were only a third the size of the Union forces. Hence, in February 1864, an expanded conscription measure made all white males between the ages 17 and 50 subject to the draft. By 1865, the necessities of war had led to the unthinkable: arming slaves as soldiers. Black companies were recruited in Richmond and other southern towns. However, because the war soon ended, no blacks actually fought for the Confederacy.

In a message sent to Congress in November 1864, Davis speculated on some of the issues involved in arming slaves. "Should a slave who had served his country" be retained in servitude, he wondered, "or should his emancipation be held out to him as a reward for faithful service, or should it be granted at once on the promise of such service . . . ?" The war fought by the South to preserve slavery ended in the contemplation of emancipation.

Recovering the Past

PHOTOGRAPHY

The invention of photography in 1839 expanded the visual and imaginative world of nineteenth-century Americans. For the first time, Americans could visually record events in their own lives and see the images of people and incidents from far away. Photographs, of course, also expand the boundaries of the historian's world. As photographic techniques became simpler, more and more visual information about the nineteenth century was captured. Historians can use photographs to discover what nineteenth-century Americans wore, how they celebrated weddings and funerals, and what their families, houses, and cities looked like. Pictures of election campaigns, parades, strikes, and wars show the texture of public life. But historians can also study photographs, as they do paintings, to glean information about attitudes and norms. The choice of subjects, the way people and objects are arranged and grouped, and the relationships between people in photographs are all clues to the social and cultural values of nineteenth-century Americans.

Some knowledge of the early history of photography helps place the visual evidence in the proper perspective. The earliest type of photograph, the daguerreotype, was not a print but the negative itself on a sheet of silver-plated copper. The first daguerreotype required between 15 and 30 minutes for the proper exposure. This accounts for the stiff and formal quality of many of these photographs. Glass ambrotypes (negatives on glass) and tintypes (negatives on gray iron bases), developed after the daguerreotype, were easier and cheaper

Mathew Brady, *Confederate Captives, Gettysburg, (National Archives)*

Mathew Brady, *Burial Party at Cold Harbor. (Chicago Historical Society)*

to produce. But both techniques produced only one picture and required what to us would seem an interminable time for exposure.

A major breakthrough came in the 1850s with the development of the wet-plate process. In this process, the photographer coated a glass negative with a sensitive solution, exposed the negative (i.e., took the picture), and then quickly developed it. The new procedure required a relatively short exposure time of perhaps five seconds out of doors and one minute inside. Action shots, however, were still not feasible. The entire process tied the photographer to the darkroom. Traveling photographers carried their darkrooms with them. The advantage of the wet-plate process was that it was possible to make many paper prints from one negative, opening new commercial vistas for professional photographers.

Mathew Brady, a fashionable Washington photographer, realizing that the camera was the "eye of history," asked Lincoln for permission to record the war with his camera. He and his team of photographers left about 8,000 glass negatives, currently stored in the Library of Congress and the National Archives, as their record of the Civil War. Shown here are two photographs, one of three Confederate soldiers captured at Gettysburg, the other of the battlefield of Cold Harbor in Virginia.

In the first photograph, study and describe the three soldiers. How are they posed? What kind of clothes are they wearing? What about their equipment? What seems to be their physical condition? Using this photograph as evidence, what might you conclude about the southern soldier—his equipment, uniforms, shoes? How well fed do the men in the picture appear? What attitudes are conveyed through their facial expressions and poses? Finally, what kind of mood was the northern photographer trying to create? What might a northern viewer conclude about the South's war effort after looking at this picture?

The second picture was taken in April 1865, about a year after the battle at Cold Harbor. In the background, you can see two Union soldiers digging graves. In the foreground are the grisly remains of the battle. What do you think is the intent of the photograph? The choice of subject matter shows clearly that photography reveals attitudes as well as facts. What attitude toward war and death is conveyed in this picture? Why is the burial taking place a full year after the battle? What does this tell us about the nature of civil warfare? Notice that the soldiers ordered to undertake this ghastly chore are black, as was customary. What might this scene suggest about the experience of black soldiers in the Union army?

These photographs just begin to suggest what can be discovered from old photographs. Your local historical society and library probably have photograph collections available to you. In addition, at home or in a relative's attic you may find visual records of your family and its history.

Southern agriculture also changed under the pressure of war. Earlier, the South had imported food from the North, concentrating on the production of staples such as cotton and tobacco for market. Now, more and more land was turned over to food crops. Some farmers voluntarily shifted crops, but others responded only to state laws reducing the acreage permitted for cotton and tobacco cultivation. These measures never succeeded in raising enough food to feed southerners adequately. But they contributed to a dramatic decline in the production of cotton, from 4.5 million bales in 1861 to 300,000 bales in 1864.

The South had always depended on imported manufactured goods. Even though some blockade runners were able to evade the Union ships, the noose tightened after 1862. The Confederacy could not, in any case, rely on blockade runners to arm and equip the army. Thus, war triggered the expansion of military-related industries in the South. Here, too, the government played a crucial role. The war and navy offices directed industrial development, awarding contracts to private manufacturing firms like Richmond's Tredegar Iron Works and operating other factories themselves. The number of southerners working in industry rose dramatically. In 1861, the Tredegar Iron Works employed 700 workers; two years later, it employed 2,500, more than half of them black. The head of the Army Ordnance Bureau reflected on the amazing transformation. "Where three years ago we were not making a gun, pistol nor a sabre, no shot nor shell . . . we now make all these in quantities to meet the demands of our large armies." At the end of the war, the soldiers were better supplied with arms and munitions than with food.

Although the war did not transform the southern class structure, relations between the classes began to change. The pressures of the struggle undermined the solidarity of whites, which was based on racism and supposed political unanimity. Draft resistance and desertion reflected growing alienation from a war perceived as serving only the interests of upper-class plantation owners. More and more yeoman families suffered grinding poverty as the men went off to war and government officials and armies requisitioned needed resources. A poor farmer from Georgia, Harlan Fuller, explained his family's situation in the spring of 1864. Fuller was 50 but now eligible for the draft. "I am liable at any time to be taken away from my little crops leaving my family almost without provisions & no hope of making any crop atal. I have sent six sons to the war & now the seventh enrolled he being the last I have no help left atal." This new poverty was an ominous hint of the decline of the yeoman farming class in postwar years.

The Victorious North

Although changes in the South were more noticeable, the Union's government and economy also responded to the demands of war. Like Davis, Lincoln was accused of being a dictator. Although he rarely tried to control Congress, veto its legislation, or direct government departments, Lincoln did use executive power freely. He violated the writ of habeas corpus by suspending the civil rights of over 13,000 northerners, who languished in prison without trials; curbed the freedom of the press because of supposedly disloyal and inflammatory articles; established conscription; issued the Emancipation Proclamation; and removed army generals. Lincoln argued that this vast extension of presidential power was temporarily justified because, as president, he was responsible for defending and preserving the Constitution.

Many of the wartime changes in government proved more permanent than Lincoln had imagined. The financial necessities of war helped revolutionize the country's banking system. Ever since Andrew Jackson's destruction of the Bank of the United States, state banks had served American financial needs. Treasury Secretary Chase found this banking system inadequate and chaotic and proposed to replace it. In 1863 and 1864, Congress passed banking acts that established a national currency issued by federally chartered banks and backed by government bonds. The country had a federal banking system once again.

The northern economy also changed under wartime demands. The need to feed soldiers and civilians stimulated the expansion of agriculture and new investment in farm machinery. With so many men off soldiering, farmers were at first short of labor. McCormick reapers performed the work of four to six men, and farmers began to buy them. During the war, McCormick sold 165,000 of his machines. Northern farming, especially in the Midwest, was well on the way to becoming mechanized. Farmers not only succeeded in growing enough grain to feed civilians and soldiers but also gathered a surplus to export as well.

The war also selectively stimulated manufacturing. Although it is easy to imagine that northern industry as a whole expanded during the Civil War, in fact, the war retarded overall economic growth. War consumed rather than generated wealth. Between 1860 and 1870, the annual rate of increase in real manufacturing value added was only 2.3 percent, in contrast with 7.8 percent for the years between 1840 and 1860 and 6 percent for the period 1870 to 1900. Some important prewar industries, like cotton textiles, languished without a supply of southern cotton.

However, industries that produced for the war machine, especially those with advantages of scale, expanded and made large profits. Each year, the Union army required 1.5 million uniforms and 3 million pairs of shoes; the woolen and leather industries grew accordingly. Meatpackers and producers of iron, steel, and pocket watches all profited from wartime opportunities. Cincinnati was one city that flourished from supplying soldiers with everything from pork to soap and candles.

On the Home Front, 1861–1865

In numerous, less tangible ways, the war transformed northern and southern society. The very fact of conflict established a new perspective for most civilians. War news vied with local events for their attention. They read newspapers and national weekly magazines with a new eagerness. The use of the mails increased dramatically as they corresponded with faraway relatives and friends. Wrote one North Carolina woman, "I never liked to write letters before, but it is a pleasure as well as a relief now." Distant events became almost as real and vivid as those at home. The war helped make Americans less parochial, integrating them into the larger world.

For some Americans, like John D. Rockefeller and Andrew Carnegie, war brought army contracts and unanticipated riches. The New York *Herald* reported that New York City had never been "so gay, . . . so crowded, so prosperous," as it was in March 1864. Residents of Cincinnati noted people who "became suddenly immensely wealthy, and in their fine equipages, with liveried servants, rolled in magnificence along the city streets." In the South, blockade runners made fortunes slipping luxury goods past Union ships.

For the majority of Americans, however, war meant deprivation. The war effort gobbled up a large part of each side's resources, and ultimately ordinary people suffered. To be sure, the demand for workers ended unemployment and changed employment patterns. Large numbers of women and blacks entered the workforce, a phenomenon that would be repeated in all future American wars. But whereas work was easy to get and wages appeared to increase, real income actually declined. Inflation, especially destructive in the South, was largely to blame. By 1864, eggs sold in Richmond for $6 a dozen; butter brought $25 a pound.

This photograph of workers in front of a Washington, D.C., shop points to the vital role the home front workers played in the war. The manpower advantages enjoyed by the North are suggested here. *(Library of Congress)*

The dislocations caused by the war were many. These southerners, forced to leave their home by invading troops, have packed what few belongings they could transport and stand ready to evacuate their homestead. *(Library of Congress)*

Strikes and union organizing pointed to working-class discontent.

Low wages compounded the problem of declining income and particularly harmed women workers. Often forced into the labor market because husbands could save little or nothing from small army stipends, army wives and other women took what pay they could get. As more women entered the workforce, employers cut costs by slashing wages. In 1861, the Union government paid Philadelphia seamstresses 17 cents per shirt. At the height of inflation, three years later, the government reduced the piecework rate to 15 cents. Private employers paid even less, about 8 cents a shirt. Working women in the South fared no better. War may have brought prosperity to a few Americans, North and South, but for most it meant trying to survive on an inadequate income.

Economic dislocation caused by the war reduced the standard of living for civilians. Shortages and hardships were severe in the South, which bore the brunt of the fighting. Most white southerners did without food, manufactured goods, and medicine during the war. Farming families who had no slaves to help with work in the fields fared poorly. As one Georgia woman explained, "I can't manage a farm well enough [alone] to make a suporte." Conditions were most dismal in cities, where carts brought in vital supplies, because trains were reserved for military use. Hunger was rampant. Food riots erupted in Richmond and other cities; crowds of hungry whites broke into stores to steal food. The very cleanliness of southern cities pointed to urban hunger. As one Richmond resident noted, everything was so "cleanly consumed that no garbage or filth can accumulate."

Thousands of southerners who fled as Union armies advanced suddenly found themselves homeless. "The country for miles around is filled with refugees," noted an army officer in 1862. "Every house is crowded and hundreds are living in churches, in barns and tents." Caught up in the effort of mere survival, worried about what had happened to homes and possessions left behind and whether anything would remain when they returned, these southerners must have wondered if the cause was worth their sacrifices. Life was probably just as agonizing for those who chose to stay put when Union troops arrived. Virginia Gray, an Arkansas woman, wrote in her diary of her fear of the "Feds" and the turmoil they caused when they suddenly appeared and then disappeared.

White flight also disrupted slave life. Even the arrival of Union forces could prove a mixed blessing. One slave described the upsetting behavior of the Yankees at his plantation in Arkansas: "Them folks stood round there all day. Killed hogs . . . killed cows . . . . Took all kinds of sugar and preserves. . . . Tore all the feathers out of the mattresses looking for money. Then they put Old Miss and her daughter in the kitchen to cooking." So frightened was this slave's mother that she hid in her bed, only to be roused by the lieutenant, who told her, "We ain't a-going to do you no hurt. . . . We are freeing you." But the next day, the Yanks were gone and the Confederates back. During Sherman's march through Georgia in 1864, his troops stole not only from whites but from slaves as well. Indeed some soldiers flogged blacks who tried to stop the looting.

Wartime Race Relations

The journal kept by Emily Harris in South Carolina conveys some of the character of life behind the lines. She revealed not only the predictable story of shortages, hardships, and the psychological burdens of those at home but also the subtle social changes the war stimulated. Emily and her husband David lived on a 500-acre farm with their seven young children and ten slaves. When David went to war, Emily had to manage the farm, even though David worried that she would be "much at a loss with the . . . farm and the negroes."

Emily's early entries establish two themes that persist for the years she kept her diary. She was worried about how David would survive the "privation and hardships" of army life and was also anxious about her own "load of responsibilities." Her December 1862 entry provides a poignant picture of a wife's thoughts. "All going well as far as I can judge but tonight it is raining and cold and a soldier's wife cannot be happy in bad weather and during a battle." The dozens of tasks she had to do depressed her. "I shall never get used to being left as the head of affairs," she wrote in January 1863. "I am not an independent woman nor ever shall be." As time passed and the war went badly, the dismal news and mounting list of casualties heightened her concern about David's safety.

Her relations with her slaves compounded Emily's problems. As so many southerners discovered, war transformed the master–slave relationship. Because Emily was not the master David had been, her slaves gradually began to take unaccustomed liberties. At Christmas in 1864, several left the farm without her permission; others stayed away longer than she allowed. "Old Will" boldly requested his freedom. Worse yet, she discovered that her slaves had helped three Yankees who had escaped from prison camp.

The master–slave relationship was crumbling, and Emily reported in her journal the consequences for whites. "It seems people are getting afraid of negroes." Although not admitting to fear, she revealed that she could no longer control the blacks, who were increasingly unwilling to play a subservient role.

Understanding what was at stake, slaves, in their own way, often worked for their freedom. Said one later, "Us slaves worked den when we felt like it, which wasn't often." Emily's journal entry for February 22 confessed a "painful necessity." "I am reduced," she said, "to the use of a stick but the negroes are becoming so impudent and disrespectful that I cannot bear it." A mere two weeks later she added, "The Negroes are all expecting to be set free very soon and it causes them to be very troublesom."

Similar scenes occurred throughout the South. Insubordination, refusal to work, and refusal to accept punishment marked the behavior of black slaves, especially those who worked as fieldhands. Thousands of blacks (probably 20 percent of all slaves), many of them women who had been exploited as workers and as sexual objects, fled toward Union lines after the early months of the war. Their flight pointed to the changing nature of race relations and the harm slaves could do to the southern cause. Reflected one slaveowner, "The 'faithful slave' is about played out."

Women and the War

If Emily Harris's journal reveals that she was sometimes overwhelmed by her responsibilities and shocked by the changes in dealings with her slaves, it also illustrates how the war affected women's lives. Nineteenth-century ideology promoted women's domestic role and minimized their economic importance. But the war made it impossible for many women to live according to conventional norms of behavior. So many men on both sides had gone off to fight that women had to find jobs and carry on farming operations. During the war years, southern women who had no slaves to help with the farmwork and northern farm wives who labored without the assistance of husbands or sons carried new physical and emotional burdens.

Women also participated in numerous war-related activities. In both North and South, they entered government service in large numbers. In the North, hundreds of women became military nurses. Under the supervision of Drs. Emily and Elizabeth Blackwell; Dorothea Dix, superintendent of army nurses; and Clara Barton, northern women nursed the wounded and dying for low pay or even for none at all. They also attempted to improve hospital conditions by attacking red tape and bureaucracy. The diary of a volunteer, Harriet Whetten, revealed the activist attitude of many others:

> I have never seen such a dirty disorganized place as the Hospital. The neglect of cleanliness is inexcusable. All sorts of filth, standing water, and the embalming house near the Hospital. . . . No time had to be lost. Miss Gill and I set the contrabands at work making beds & cleaning.

Although men largely staffed southern military hospitals, Confederate women also played an important part in caring for the sick and wounded in their homes and in makeshift hospitals behind the battle lines. Grim though the work was, many women felt that they were participating in the real world for the first time in their lives.

Women moved outside the domestic sphere in other forms of volunteer war work. Some women gained administrative experience in soldiers' aid societies and in the U.S. Sanitary Commission. Many others made bandages and clothes, put together packages for soldiers at the front, and helped army wives and disabled soldiers find jobs. Fund-raising activities realized substantial sums. By the end of the war, the Sanitary Commission had raised $50 million for medical supplies, nurses' salaries, and other wartime necessities.

Many of the changes women experienced during war years ended when peace returned. Jobs in industry and government disappeared when the men came to reclaim them. Women turned over the operation of farms to returning husbands. But for women whose men came home maimed or not at all, the work had not ended. Nor had the discrimination. Trying to pick up the threads of their former lives, they found it impossible to forget what they had done to help the war effort. At least some of them were sure they had equaled their men in courage and commitment.

The Election of 1864

In the North, the election of 1864 brought some of the transformations of wartime into the political arena. The Democrats, seeking to regain power by capitalizing on war weariness, nominated General George McClellan for president. The party proclaimed the war a failure and demanded an armistice with the South. During the campaign, Democrats accused Lincoln of arbitrarily expanding executive power and denounced sweeping economic measures such as the banking bills. Arguing that the president had transformed the war from one for Union into one for emancipation, they tried to inflame racial passions by insinuating that if the Republicans won, a fusion of blacks and whites would result.

Although Lincoln easily gained the Republican renomination because of his tight control over party machinery and patronage, his party did not unite behind him. Lincoln seemed to please no one. His veto of the radical reconstruction plan for the South, the Wade-Davis bill, led to cries of "usurpation." The Emancipation Proclamation did not sit well with conservatives. In August 1864, a gloomy Lincoln told his cabinet that he expected to lose the election. As late as September, some Republicans actually hoped to reconvene the convention and select another candidate.

Sherman's capture of Atlanta in September 1864 and the march through Georgia to Savannah helped swing voters to Lincoln. In the end, Republicans had no desire to see the Democrats oust their party. Lincoln won 55 percent of the popular vote and swept the electoral college.

Why the North Won

In the months after Lincoln's reelection, the war drew to an agonizing conclusion. Sherman moved north from Atlanta to North Carolina, while Grant pummeled Lee's forces in Virginia. The losses Grant would sustain were staggering: 18,000 in the Battle of the Wilderness, over 8,000 at Spotsylvania, and another 12,000 at Cold Harbor. New recruits stepped forward to replace the dead. On April 9, 1865, Grant accepted Lee's surrender at Appomattox. Southern soldiers and officers were allowed to return home with their personal equipment after promising to remain there peaceably. The war was finally over.

Technically, the war was won on the battlefield and at sea. But Grant's military strategy succeeded because the Union's manpower and economic resources could survive staggering losses of men and equipment while the Confederacy's could not. As Union armies pushed back the borders of the Confederacy, the South lost control of territories essential for their war effort. Finally, naval strategy eventually paid off because the North could build enough ships to make its blockade work. In 1861, fully 90 percent of the blockade runners were slipping through the naval cordon. By the war's end, only half made it.

The South had taken tremendous steps toward meeting war needs. But despite the impressive growth of manufacturing and the increasing acreage devoted to foodstuffs, the southern army and the southern people were poorly fed and poorly clothed. As one civilian realized, "The question of bread and meat . . . is beginning to be regarded as a more serious one even than that of War." Women working alone or with disgruntled slaves on farms could not produce enough food. Worn-out farm equipment was not replaced. The government's impressment of slaves and animals cut production. The half million blacks who fled to Union lines also played their part in pulling the South down in defeat.

New industries could not meet the extraordinary demands of wartime, and advancing Union forces destroyed many of them. A Confederate officer in northern Virginia observed, "Many of our soldiers are thinly clothed and without shoes and in addition to this, very few of the infantry have tents. With this freezing weather, their sufferings are indescribable." Skimpy rations, only a third of a pound of meat for each soldier a day by 1864, weakened the Confederate force, whose trail was "traceable by the deposit of dysenteric stool" it left behind. By that time, the Union armies were so well supplied that soldiers often threw away heavy blankets and coats as they advanced.

The South's woefully inadequate transportation system also contributed to defeat. Primitive roads deteriorated and became all but impassable without repairs. The railroad system, geared to the needs of cotton, not war, was inefficient. When tracks wore out or were destroyed, they were not replaced. Rails were too heavy for blockade runners to bother with, and as the Confederate railroad coordinator observed in

This photograph of the South Side Railroad at Appomattox Station, Virginia, shows the condition of a southern railroad at the end of the war. You can see the poor condition of the tracks and the destroyed train lying beside the tracks. The breakdown of the Confederate transportation system through battle, sabotage, and simple wear and tear contributed to the defeat of the Confederacy. *(Library of Congress)*

1865, "Not a single bar of railroad iron has been rolled in the Confederacy since the war, nor can we hope to do better." Thus, food intended for the army rotted awaiting shipment. Supplies were tied up in bottlenecks and soldiers went hungry. Food riots in southern cities pointed to the hunger, anger, and growing demoralization of civilians.

Ironically, measures the Confederacy took to strengthen its ability to win the war, as one Texan later observed, "weakened and paralyzed it." Eventually, the Confederacy could no longer "command and control its moral resources." Conscription, impressment, and taxes all contributed to resentment and sometimes open resistance. They fueled class tensions already strained by the poverty war brought to many yeoman farmers and led some of them to assist the invaders or to join the Union army. The proposal to use slaves as soldiers called into question the war's purpose. The many southern governors who refused to contribute men, money, and supplies on the scale Davis requested implicitly condoned disloyalty to the cause. The belief in states' rights and the sanctity of private property that gave birth to the Confederacy also helped kill it.

By the final months of the war, Jefferson Davis had recognized how dangerous opposition to government measures and defeatist attitudes were to the Confederacy's cause. "The malcontents, seizing on the restlessness consequent upon long and severe pressure," he pointed out, "have created a feeling hostile to the execution of the rigorous laws which were necessary to raise and feed our armies, then magnifying every reverse and prophesying ruin, they have produced public depression and sown the seeds of disintegration." But such realization did not result in any vigorous attempts to influence public opinion or to control internal dissent.

It is tempting to compare Lincoln and Davis as war leaders. There is no doubt that Lincoln's humanity, his awareness of the terrible costs of war, his determination to save the Union, and his eloquence set him apart as one of this country's most extraordinary presidents. Yet the men's personal characteristics were probably less important than the differences between the political and social systems of the two regions. Without the support of a party behind him, Davis failed to engender enthusiasm or loyalty. Even though the Republicans rarely united behind Lincoln, they uniformly wanted to keep the Democrats from office. Despite all the squabbles, Republicans tended to support Lincoln's policies in Congress and back in their home districts. Commanding considerable resources of patronage, Lincoln was able to line up federal, state, and local officials behind his party and administration.

Just as the northern political system provided Lincoln with more flexibility and support, its social system also proved more able to meet the war's extraordinary demands. Although both societies adopted innovations in an effort to secure victory, northerners were more cooperative, disciplined, and aggressive in meeting the organizational and production challenges of wartime. In the southern states, old attitudes, habits, and values impeded the war effort. Southern governors, wedded to states' rights, refused to cooperate with the Confederate government. North Carolina, the center of the southern textile industry, actually kept back most uniforms for its own regiments. At the war's end, 92,000 uniforms and thousands of blankets, shoes, and tents still lay in its warehouses. When Sherman approached Atlanta, Georgia's governor would not turn over the 10,000 men in the state army to Confederate commanders. Even slaveholders, whose property had been the cause for secession, resisted the impressment of their slaves for war work.

In the end, the Confederacy collapsed, exhausted and bleeding. Hungry soldiers received letters from their families revealing desperate situations at home. They worried and then slipped away. By December 1864, the Confederate desertion rate had passed 50 percent. Replacements could not be found. Farmers hid livestock and produce from tax collectors. Many southerners felt their cause was lost and resigned themselves to defeat. But some fought on till the end. One northerner described them as they surrendered at Appomattox:

> Before us in proud humiliation stood the embodiment of manhood: men whom neither toils and sufferings, nor the fact of death, nor disaster, nor hopelessness could bend from their resolve; standing before us now, thin, worn, and famished, but erect, and with eyes looking level into ours, waking memories that bound us together as no other bond.

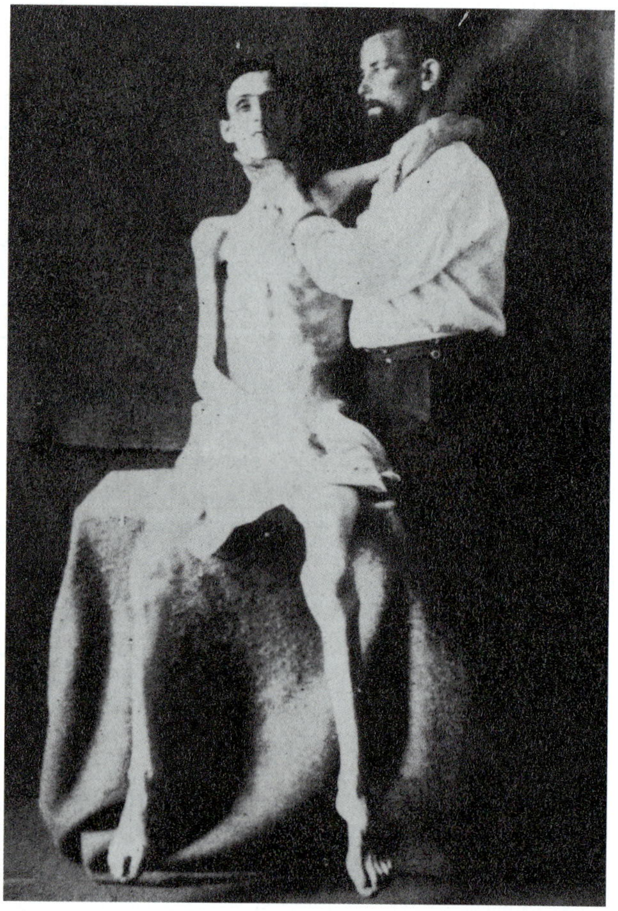

The emaciated state of this prisoner of war, who was incarcerated in Belle Isle Prison, Richmond, shows the fearsome conditions experienced by some Union prisoners. A Union surgeon who inspected the prison's inmates claimed that 90 percent weighed less than 90 pounds when freed. *(Library of Congress)*

The Costs of War

The long war was over, but the memories of that event would fester for years to come. About 3 million American men, a third of all free males between the ages of 15 and 59, had served in the army. Each would remember his own personal history of the war. For George Eagleton, who had worked in army field hospitals, the history was one of "Death and destruction! Blood! Blood! Agony! Death! Gaping flesh wounds, broken bones, amputations, bullet and bomb fragment extractions." Of all wars Americans have fought, none has been more deadly. The death rate during this war was over five times as great as the death rate during World War II. About 360,000 Union soldiers and another 258,000 Confederate soldiers died, about a third of them because their wounds were either improperly treated or not treated at all. Disease claimed more lives than combat. Despite the efforts of men like Eagleton and the women army nurses, hospitals could not handle the scores of wounded and dying. "Glory is not for the private soldier, such as die in the hospitals," reflected one Tennessee soldier, "being eat up with the deadly gangrene, and being imperfectly waited on."

Thousands upon thousands of men would be reminded of the human costs of war by the injuries they carried with them to the grave, by the missing limbs that marked them as Civil War veterans. About 275,000 on each side were maimed. Another 410,000 (195,000 northerners and 215,000 southerners) would recall their time in wretchedly overcrowded and unsanitary prison camps. The lucky ones would remember only the dullness and boredom. The worst memory was of those who rotted in prison camps, such as Andersonville in Georgia, where 31,000 Union soldiers were confined. At the war's end, over 12,000 graves were counted there.

Some Americans found it hard to throw off wartime experiences and adjust to peace. As Arthur Carpenter's letters suggest, he gradually grew accustomed to army life. War provided him with a sense of purpose. When it was over, he felt aimless. A full year after the war's end, he wrote, "Camp life agrees with me better than any other." Many others had difficulty returning to civilian routines and finding a new focus for life. Even those who adjusted successfully discovered that they looked at life from a different perspective. The experience of fighting, of mixing with all sorts of people from many places, of traveling far from home had lifted former soldiers out of their familiar local world and widened their vision. Fighting the war made the concept of national union real.

Unanswered Questions

What, then, had the war accomplished? On the one hand, death and destruction. Physically, the war devastated the South. Historians have estimated a 43 percent decline in southern wealth during the war years, exclusive of the value of slaves. Great cities like Atlanta, Columbia, and Richmond lay in ruins. Fields lay weed-choked and uncultivated. Tools were worn out. A third or more of the South's stock of mules, horses, and swine had disappeared. Two-thirds of the railroads had been destroyed. Thousands were hungry, homeless, and bitter about their four years of what now appeared a useless sacrifice. Over four million slaves, a vast financial investment, were free.

On the other hand, the war had resolved the question of union and ended the debate over the relationship of the states to the federal government. During the war, Republicans seized the opportunity to pass legislation that would foster national union and economic growth: the Pacific Railroad Act of 1862, which set aside huge tracts of public land to finance the transcontinental railroad; the Homestead Act of 1862, which was to provide yeoman farmers cheaper and easier access to the public domain; the Morrill Act of 1862, which established support for agricultural (land-grant) colleges; and the banking acts of 1863 and 1864.

The war had also resolved the issue of slavery, the thorny problem that had so long plagued American life. Yet uncertainties outnumbered certainties. What would happen to the former slaves? When blacks had fled to Union lines during the war, commanders had not known what to do with them. Now the problem became even more pressing. Were blacks to have the same civil and political rights as whites? In the Union army, they had been second-class soldiers. The behavior of Union forces toward liberated blacks in the South showed how deep the stain of racism went. One white soldier, caught stealing a quilt by a former slave, shouted, "I'm fighting for $14 a month and the Union"—not to end slavery. Would blacks be given land, the means for economic independence? What would be their relations with their former owners?

What, indeed, would be the status of the conquered South in the nation? Should it be punished for the rebellion? Some people thought so. Should southerners keep their property? Some people thought not. There were clues to Lincoln's intentions. As early as December 1863, the president had announced a generous plan of reconciliation. He was willing to recognize the government of former Confederate states established by a group of citizens equal to 10 percent of those voting in 1860, as long as the group swore to support the Constitution and to accept the abolition of slavery. He began to restore state governments in three former Confederate states on that basis. But not all northerners agreed with his leniency, and the debate continued.

In his 1865 inaugural address, Lincoln urged Americans to harbor "malice towards none . . . and charity for all." "Let us strive," he urged, "to finish the work we are in; to bind up the nation's wounds . . . to do all which may achieve a just and lasting peace." Privately, the president said the same thing. Generosity and goodwill would pave the way for reconciliation. On April 14, he pressed the point home to his cabinet. His wish was to avoid persecution and bloodshed. That same evening, only five days after the surrender at Appomattox, the president

Timeline

1861	Lincoln calls up state militia and suspends habeas corpus
	First Battle of Bull Run
	Union blockades the South
1862	Battles at Shiloh, Bull Run, and Antietam
	Monitor and *Virginia* battle
	First black regiment authorized by Union
	Union issues greenbacks
	South institutes military draft
	Pacific Railroad Act
	Homestead Act
	Morrill Land-Grant College Act
1863	Lincoln issues Emancipation Proclamation
	Congress adopts military draft
	Battles of Gettysburg and Vicksburg
	Union Banking Act
	Southern tax laws and impressment act
	New York draft riots
	Southern food riots
1864	Sherman's march through Georgia
	Lincoln reelected
	Union Banking Act
1865	Lee surrenders at Appomattox
	Lincoln assassinated; Andrew Johnson becomes president
	Congress passes Thirteenth Amendment, abolishing slavery

attended a play at Ford's Theatre. There, as one horrified eyewitness reported,

> a pistol was heard and a man . . . dressed in a black suit of clothes leaped onto the stage apparently from the President's box. He held in his right hand a dagger whose blade appeared about 10 inches long. . . . Every one leaped to his feet, and the cry of "the President is assassinated" was heard—Getting where I could see into the President's box, I saw Mrs. Lincoln . . . in apparent anguish.

John Wilkes Booth, a southern sympathizer, had killed the president.

Conclusion

An Uncertain Future

As the war ended, many Americans grieved for the man whose decisions had so marked their lives for five years. "Strong men have wept tonight & the nation will mourn tomorrow," wrote one eyewitness to the assassination. Many more wept for friends and relations who had not survived the war but whose actions had in one way or another contributed to its outcome. Perhaps not all Americans realized how drastically the war had altered their lives, their futures, their nation. It was only as time passed that the war's impact became clear to them. And it was only with time that they recognized how many problems the war had left unsolved. It is to these years of Reconstruction that we turn next.

Recommended Reading

Organizing for War

David Donald, *Liberty and Union* (1978); Joseph T. Glatthatt, *Partners in Command: The Relationship between Leaders in the Civil War* (1994); James McPherson, *Battle Cry of Freedom: The Civil War Era* (1988); Phillip S. Paludan, *"A People's Contest": The Union and the Civil War, 1861–1865* (1989); Peter J. Parrish, *The American Civil War* (1985); Emory M. Thomas, *The Confederate Nation, 1861–1865* (1979).

Clashing on the Battlefield, 1861–1862

Thomas B. Buell, *The Warrior Generals Combat Leadership in the American Civil War* (1996); Benjamin Frankling Colling, *Fort Donelson's Legacy: War and Society in Kentucky and Tennessee, 1862–1863* (1997); Perry D. Jamieson, *Attack and Die: Civil War Tactics and the Southern Heritage* (1982); Russell F. Weigley, *The American Way of War: A History of U.S. Military Strategy and Policy* (1973); T. Harry Williams, *The History of American Wars* (1981).

The Tide Turns, 1863–1865

Richard E. Beringer, Herman Hattaway, Archer Jones, and William N. Still, Jr., *Why the South Lost the Civil War* (1986) and *The Elements of Confederate Defeat: Nationalism, War Aims, and Religion* (1988); Robert F. Durden, *The Gray and the Black: The Confederate Debate on Emancipation* (1972); Laurence M. Hauptman, *The Iroquois in the Civil War: From Battlefield to Reservation* (1993); Randall C. Jimerson, *The Private Civil War* (1988); Gerald F. Linderman, *Embattled Courage: The Experience of Combat in the American Civil War* (1987); Malcolm C. McMillan, *The Disintegration of a Confederate State* (1986); James M. McPherson, *For Cause and Comrades: Why Men Fought in the Civil War* (1997); Reid Mitchell, *The Vacant Chair: The Northern Soldier Leaves Home* (1993).

Changes Wrought by War

Ira Berlin, ed., *Freedom: A Documentary History of Emancipation, 1861–1867,* Series I and II (1979, 1982); David W. Blight and Brooks D. Simpson., eds., *Union & Emancipation: Essays on Politics and Race in the Civil War Era* (1997); Michael Burlingame, *The Inner World of Abraham Lincoln* (1994); Catherine Clinton, *Tara Revisited: Women, War, and the Plantation Legend* (1995); Catherine Clinton and Nina Silber, *Divided Houses: Gender and the Civil War* (1992); Mary A. Decredico, *Patriotism for Profit: Georgia's Urban Entrepreneurs and the Confederate War Effort* (1990); David Donald, *Lincoln* (1995); Wayne K. Durrell, *War of Another Kind: A Southern Community in the Great Rebellion* (1990); Drew Gilpin Faust, *Mothers of Invention: Women of the Slaveholding South in the American Civil War* (1997); Eric Foner, *Politics and Ideology in the Age of Civil War* (1980); J. Matthew Gallman, *Mastering Wartime: A Social History of Philadelphia During the Civil War* (1990); Theodore J. Karamanski, *Rally 'Round the Flag: Chicago and the Civil War* (1993); Elizabeth D. Leonard, *Yankee Women: Gender Battles in the Civil War* (1994); Glenn M. Lindend and Thomas J. Pressly, eds., *Voices from the House Divided* (1995); Leon F. Litwack, *Been in the Storm So Long: The Aftermath of Slavery* (1979); David E. Long, *The Jewel of Liberty: Abraham Lincoln's Re-Election and the End of Slavery* (1994); Clarence L. Mohr, *On the Threshold of Freedom* (1986); John L. Thomas, ed., *Abraham Lincoln and the American Political Tradition (1986);* Wendy Hamand Venet, *Neither Ballots Nor Bullets: Women Abolitionists and the Civil War* (1991).

Fiction and Film

Stephen Crane's *The Red Badge of Courage* (any edition) examines the soldier's experience during the war, while MacKinlay Kantor's novel, *Andersonville* (1955), provides an insight into the Civil War's worst prison camp.

The film *Glory,* a feature film, focuses on a black regiment, the 54th Massachusetts, that demonstrated its heroism in the midst of battle. You will get a better sense of the character of warfare and race relations if you see this film. The classic *Gone with the Wind* offers a romanticized but powerful picture of southern life before, during, and after the Civil War. Ken Burns's famous series, *The Civil War,* is a powerful evocation of that period with ample use of period photographs and documents.

Suggested Web Sites

http://sunsite.utk.edu/civil-war/warweb.html

The American Civil War Homepage. This site has a great collection of hypertext links to the most useful identified electronic files about the American Civil War.

http://jefferson.village.virginia.edu/vshadow/vshadow.html

The Valley of the Shadow: Living the Civil War in Pennsylvania and Virginia. This project tells the histories of two communities on either side of the Mason-Dixon line during the Civil War. It includes narrative and an electronic archive of sources.

http://www.awod.com/gallery/probono/cwchas/cwlayout.html

Civil War @ Charleston. This site covers the history of the Civil War in and around Charleston, South Carolina.

http://www.alincolnassoc.com/

Abraham Lincoln Association. This site allows you to search digital versions of Lincoln's papers.

http://www.ruf.rice.edu/~pjdavis/jdp.htm

The Papers of Jefferson Davis Home Page. This site tells about the collection of Jefferson Davis Papers and includes a chronology of his life, a family genealogy, some key Davis documents on-line, and a collection of related links.

http://www.tulane.edu/~latner/CrisisMain.html

Crisis at Fort Sumter. This well-crafted use of hypermedia with assignments and problems explains and explores the events in and around the start of the Civil War.

http://www.cwc.lsu.edu/

U.S. Civil War Center. This is a site whose mission is to "locate, index, and make available all appropriate private and public data on the Internet regarding the Civil War" and to promote the study of the Civil War from the perspectives of all professions, occupations, and academic disciplines.

http://scriptorium.lib.duke.edu/collections/civil-war-women.html

Civil War Women—On-line Archival Exhibits at Duke University. This site includes original documents, links, and biographical information about several women and their lives during the Civil War.

http://www.itd.nps.gov/cwss/history/aa_history.htm

History of African-Americans in the Civil War. This National Park Service site explores the history of the United States Colored Troops.

http://memory.loc.gov/ammem/alhtml/alrintr.html

Mr. Lincoln's Virtual Library. Part of the American Memory series, this site explores the assassination of Abraham Lincoln, with introduction, timeline, and gallery.

http://lcweb2.loc.gov/ammem/cwphome.html

Selected Civil War Photographs Home Page. This is a Library of Congress site, with over 1,000 photographs, many from Mathew Brady.

http://www.historyplace.com/civilwar/index.html

The History Place—U.S. Civil War 1861–1865. This gives a complete timeline of the Civil War, well-illustrated with photographs.

http://www.ushistoryplace.com

the History place A richly detailed on-line learning environment complete with interactive maps, timelines, history activities, primary source documents, and links to related American history sites.

16

The UNION RECONSTRUCTED

CHAPTER OUTLINE

In April 1864, one year before Lincoln's assassination, Robert Allston died of pneumonia. His daughter, Elizabeth, was left with a "sense of terrible desolation and sorrow" as the Civil War raged around her, and she and her mother took over the affairs of their many rice plantations. With Yankee troops moving through coastal South Carolina in the late winter of 1864–1865, Elizabeth's sorrow turned to "terror" as Union soldiers arrived seeking liquor, firearms, and hidden valuables. The Allston women endured an insulting search and then fled. In a later raid, Yankee troops encouraged the Allston slaves to take furniture and other household goods from the Big Houses, some of which the blacks returned when the Yankees were gone. But before they left, the Union soldiers, in their role as liberators, gave the keys to the crop barns to the semifree slaves.

When the war was over, Adele Allston took an oath of allegiance to the United States and secured a written order commanding the blacks to relinquish these keys. She and Elizabeth made plans to return in the early summer of 1865 to resume control of the family plantations, thereby reestablishing white authority. She was assured that although the blacks had guns and were determined to have the means to a livelihood, "no outrage has been committed against the whites except in the matter of property." But property was the key issue. Possession of the keys to the barns, Elizabeth wrote, would be the "test case" of whether former masters or their former slaves would control land, labor and its fruits, and even subtle aspects of interpersonal relations.

Not without some fear, Adele and Elizabeth Allston rode up in a carriage to their former home, Nightingale Hall, to confront their former slaves. To their surprise, a pleasant reunion took place. The Allston women greeted the blacks by name, inquired after their children, and caught up on the affairs of those with whom they had lived closely for many years. A trusted black foreman handed over the keys to the barns. This harmonious scene was repeated elsewhere.

In this Winslow Homer painting, *A Visit from the Old Mistress,* imagine Adele Allston returning to her plantation to reunite with former slaves. What kind of new relationships would they form in the transformed world after a wrenching Civil War? *(National Museum of American Art, Smithsonian Institution)*

But at Guendalos, a plantation owned by a son absent during most of the war fighting with the Confederate army, the Allston women met a very different situation. As their carriage arrived and moved slowly toward the crop barns, a defiant group of armed former slaves lined both sides of the road, following the carriage as it passed by. Tension grew when the carriage stopped. A former black driver, Uncle Jacob, was unsure whether to yield the keys to the barns full of rice and corn, put there by black labor. Mrs. Allston insisted. As Uncle Jacob hesitantly began to hand the keys to her, an angry young man shouted out: "Ef yu gie up de key, blood'll flow." Uncle Jacob slowly slipped the keys back into his pocket.

The tension increased as the blacks sang freedom songs and brandished hoes, pitchforks, and guns in an effort to discourage anyone from going to town for help. Two blacks, however, left the plantation to find some Union military officers to come settle the issue of the keys, most likely on the side of the Allstons. As Adele and Elizabeth waited, word finally arrived that the Union officers, who were difficult to locate, would no doubt be found the next day and would come to Guendalos. The Allstons spent the night safely, if restlessly, in their house. Early the next morning, they were awakened by a knock at the unlocked front door. Adele slowly opened the door, and there stood Uncle Jacob. Without a word, he gave her the keys.

The story of the keys reveals most of the essential human ingredients of the Reconstruction era. Despite defeat and surrender, southern whites were determined to resume control of both land and labor. Rebellion aside, the law, property titles, and federal enforcement were generally on the side of the original owners of the land. The Allston women were friendly to the blacks in a genuine but maternal way and insisted on the restoration of the deferential relationships that existed before the war. Adele and Elizabeth, in short, both feared and cared about their former slaves.

The black freedmen likewise revealed mixed feelings toward their former owners. At different plantations, they demonstrated a variety of emotions: anger, loyalty, love, resentment, and pride. Respect was paid to the person of the Allstons but not to their property and crops. The action of the blacks indicated that what they wanted was not revenge but economic independence and freedom.

In this encounter between former slaves and their mistresses, the role of the northern federal officials is also revealing. The Union soldiers, literally and symbolically, gave the keys of freedom to the blacks but did not stay around long enough to guarantee that freedom. Although encouraging the freedmen to plunder the master's house and take possession of the crops, in the crucial encounter, northern officials had disappeared. Understanding the limits of northern help, Uncle Jacob handed the keys to land and liberty back to his former owner. The blacks at Guendalos knew that if they wanted to ensure their freedom, they had to do it themselves.

The theme of this chapter is the story of what happened to the conflicting goals and dreams of three groups as they sought to form new social, economic, and political relationships during the Reconstruction era. Amid devastation and divisions of class and race, Civil War survivors sought to put their lives back together again. Victorious but variously motivated northern officials, defeated but defiant southern planters, and impoverished but hopeful black freedmen—all had strong needs and dreams. In no way could all fulfill their conflicting goals, yet each had to try. This situation guaranteed that the Reconstruction era would be divisive, leaving a mixed legacy of human gains and losses.

THE BITTERSWEET AFTERMATH OF WAR

"There are sad changes in store for both races," the daughter of a Georgia planter wrote in her diary early in the summer of 1865, adding, "I wonder the Yankees do not shudder to behold their work." To understand the bittersweet nature of Reconstruction, we must look at the state of the nation in the spring of 1865, shortly after the assassination of President Lincoln.

The United States in 1865

The "Union" faced constitutional crisis in April 1865. What was the status of the 11 former Confederate states? The North had denied the South's constitutional right to secede but needed four years of civil war and over 600,000 deaths to win the point. Were the 11 southern states part of the Union or not? Lincoln's official position had been that they had never left the Union, which was "constitutionally indestructible." As a result of their rebellion, they were only "out of their proper relation" with the United States. The president, therefore, as commander in chief, had the authority to decide how to set relations right again.

Lincoln's congressional opponents argued that by declaring war on the Union, the Confederate states had broken their constitutional ties and reverted to a kind of pre-statehood status, like territories or "conquered provinces." Congress, therefore, which decided on the admission of new states, should resolve the constitutional issues and assert its authority over the reconstruction process. Differences between Congress and the White House mirrored a wider struggle between two branches of the national government. During war, as has usually been the case, the executive branch assumed broad powers necessary for rapid mobilization of resources and domestic security. Many believed, however, that Lincoln had far exceeded his constitutional authority. As the war ended, Congress sought to reassert its authority, as it would do after every subsequent war.

In April 1865, the Republican party ruled virtually unchecked. Only 11 years old, the Republicans had made immense achievements in the eyes of the northern public: winning the war, preserving the Union, and freeing the slaves. The party had enacted sweeping economic programs on behalf of free labor and free enterprise. These included a high protective tariff, a national banking system, broad use of the power to tax and to borrow and print money, generous federal appropriations for internal improvements, the Homestead Act, and an act to establish land-grant colleges to teach agricultural and mechanical skills. Alexander Hamilton, John Quincy Adams, and Henry Clay might all have applauded. Despite these achievements, the Republican party was still an uneasy grouping of former Whigs, Know-Nothings, Unionist Democrats, and antislavery idealists.

The Democrats, by contrast, were in shambles. Republicans depicted southern Democrats as rebels, murderers, and traitors, and they blasted northern Democrats as weak-willed, disloyal, and opposed to economic growth and progress. Nevertheless, in the elections of 1864 the Republicans, needing to show that the war was a bipartisan effort, nominated a Unionist Tennessee Democrat, Andrew Johnson, as Lincoln's vice president. Now the tactless Johnson headed the government.

The United States in the spring of 1865 presented stark contrasts. Northern cities hummed with productive activity; many southern cities were piles of rubble. Northern factories produced railroad tracks and

CONFLICTING GOALS DURING RECONSTRUCTION

Victorious Northern ("Radical") Republicans
- Justify the war by remaking southern society in the image of the North
- Inflict political but not physical or economic punishment on Confederate leaders
- Continue programs of economic progress begun during the war: high tariffs, railroad subsidies, national banking
- Maintain the Republican party in power
- Help the freedmen make the transition to full freedom by providing them with the tools of citizenship (suffrage) and equal economic opportunity

Northern Moderates (Republicans and Democrats)
- Quickly establish peace and order, reconciliation between North and South
- Bestow on the southern states leniency, amnesty, and merciful readmission to the Union
- Perpetuate land ownership, free labor, market competition, and other capitalist ventures
- Promote local self-determination of economic and social issues; limit interference by the national government
- Provide limited support for black suffrage

Old Southern Planter Aristocracy (Former Confederates)
- Ensure protection from black uprising and prevent excessive freedom for former slaves
- Secure amnesty, pardon, and restoration of confiscated lands
- Restore traditional plantation-based, market-crop economy with blacks as cheap labor force
- Restore traditional political leaders in the states
- Restore traditional paternalistic race relations as basis of social order

New "Other South": Yeoman Farmers and Former Whigs (Unionists)
- Quickly establish peace and order, reconciliation between North and South
- Achieve recognition of loyalty and economic value of yeoman farmers
- Create greater diversity in southern economy: capital investments in railroads, factories, and the diversification of agriculture
- Displace the planter aristocracy with new leaders drawn from new economic interests
- Limit the rights and powers of freedmen; extend suffrage only to the educated few

Black Freedmen
- Secure physical protection from abuse and terror by local whites
- Achieve economic independence through land ownership (40 acres and a mule) and equal access to trades
- Receive educational opportunity and foster the development of family and cultural bonds
- Obtain equal civil rights and protection under the law
- Commence political participation through the right to vote

engines, steel, textiles, farm implements, and building materials; southern factory chimneys stood silent above the rubble. Roadways and railroad tracks laced the North; southern railroads and roads lay in ruins. Northern banks flourished; southern financial institutions were bankrupt. Increasingly mechanized northern farms were more productive than ever before, and free farmers took pride that they had amply fed the Union army and urban workers throughout the war. They saw the Union victory as evidence of the superiority of free over slave labor. By contrast, southern farms and plantations, especially those that had lain in the path of Sherman's march, were like a "howling waste." Said one resident, "The Yankees came through . . . and just tore up everything."

Despite pockets of relative wealth, the South was largely devastated as soldiers demobilized and returned home in April 1865. Rare was the family, North or South, that had not suffered a serious casualty in the war. Missing limbs and suffering from hunger (a half-million southern whites faced starvation), the ragtag remains of the Confederate army experienced widespread sickness and social disorder as they traveled home. Yet, as a later southern writer, Wilbur Cash, explained, "If this war had smashed the Southern world, it had left the essential Southern mind and will . . . entirely unshaken." Many white southerners braced to resist Reconstruction and restore their former life, but the minority who had remained quietly loyal to the Union dreamed of reconciliation.

Whatever the extremes of southern white attitudes, the dominant social reality in the spring of 1865 was that nearly four million former slaves were on their own, facing the challenges of freedom. After an initial

THE UNITED STATES IN 1865: CRISES AT THE END OF THE CIVIL WAR

- **Military Casualties**
  360,000 Union soldiers dead
  260,000 Confederate soldiers dead
  620,000 Total dead
  375,000 Seriously wounded and maimed
  995,000 Casualties nationwide in a total male population of 15 million (nearly 1 in 15)
- **Physical and Economic Crises**
  The South devastated; its railroads, industry, and some major cities in ruins; its fields and livestock wasted
- **Constitutional Crisis**
  Eleven former Confederate states not a part of the Union, their status unclear and future states uncertain
- **Political Crisis**
  Republican party (entirely of the North) dominant in Congress; a former Democratic slaveholder from Tennessee, Andrew Johnson, in the presidency
- **Social Crisis**
  Nearly four million black freedmen throughout the South facing challenges of survival and freedom, along with thousands of hungry demobilized white southern soldiers and displaced white families
- **Psychological Crisis**
  Incalculable stores of resentment, bitterness, anger, and despair throughout North and South

reaction of joy and celebration, expressed in jubilee songs, the freedmen quickly became aware of their continuing dependence on former owners. A Mississippi woman stated the uncertainty of her new status this way:

> I used to think if I could be free I should be the happiest of anybody in the world. But when my master come to me, and says—Lizzie, you is free! it seems like I was in a kind of daze. And when I would wake up in the morning I would think to myself, Is I free? Hasn't I got to get up before day light and go into the field of work?

For Lizzie and four million other blacks, everything—and nothing—had changed.

Hopes Among the Freedmen

Throughout the South in the summer of 1865, optimism surged through the old slave quarters. As Union soldiers marched through Richmond, prisoners in slave-trade jails chanted: "Slavery chain done broke at last! Gonna praise God till I die!" The slavery chain, however, was not broken all at once but link by link. After Union soldiers swept through an area, Confederate troops would follow, or master and overseer would return, and the slaves learned not to rejoice too quickly or openly. "Every time a bunch of No'thern sojers would come through," recalled one slave, "they would tell us we was free and we'd begin celebratin'. Before we would get through somebody else would tell us to go back to work, and we would go." Another slave recalled celebrating emancipation "about twelve times" in one North Carolina county. So former slaves became cautious about what freedom meant.

Gradually, though, freedmen began to test the reality of freedom and express a vision of what life beyond bondage and the plantation might be like. Typically, the first test was to leave the plantation, if only for a few hours or days. "If I stay here I'll never know I am free," a South Carolina woman said, and off she went to work as a cook in a nearby town. Some former slaves cut their ties entirely, leaving cruel and kindly masters alike. Some returned to an earlier master, but others went to towns and cities to work and to find schools, churches, and association with other blacks, where they would be safe from whippings and retaliation.

Many freedmen left the plantation in search of members of their families. The quest for a missing spouse, parent, or child, sold away years before, was a powerful force in the first few months of emancipation. Advertisements detailing these sorrowful searches filled black newspapers. For those who found a spouse and those who had been living together in slave marriages, freedom meant getting married legally. Wedding ceremonies involving many couples were common in the first months of emancipation. Legal marriage was important morally, but it also served such practical purposes as establishing the legitimacy of children and gaining access to land titles and other

Both white southerners and their former slaves suffered in the immediate aftermath of the Civil War, as illustrated by this engraving from *Frank Leslie's Illustrated Newspaper,* February 23, 1867. *(The Granger Collection, New York)*

economic opportunities. Marriage also meant special burdens for black women who took on the now familiar double role as housekeeper and breadwinner. For many newly married blacks, however, the initial goal was to create a traditional family life, resulting in the widespread withdrawal of women from plantation field labor.

Freedmen also demonstrated their new status by choosing surnames. Names connoting independence, such as Washington, were common. As an indication of the mixed feelings the freedmen had toward their former masters, some would adopt their master's name, and others would pick "any big name 'ceptin' their master's." Emancipation changed black manners around whites as well. Masks were dropped, and old expressions of humility—tipping a hat, stepping aside, feigning happiness, addressing whites with titles of deference—were discarded. For the blacks, these were necessary symbolic expressions of selfhood; they proved that things were now different. To whites, these behaviors were seen as acts of "insolence," "insubordination," and "puttin' on airs."

However important were choosing names, dropping masks, moving around, getting married, and testing new rights, the primary goal for most freedmen was the acquisition of their own land. "All I want is to git to own fo' or five acres ob land, dat I can build me a little house on and call my home," a Mississippi black said. Only through economic independence, the traditional American goal of controlling one's own labor and land, could former slaves prove to themselves that emancipation was real.

During the war, some Union generals had placed liberated slaves in charge of confiscated and abandoned lands. In the Sea Islands off the coast of South Carolina and Georgia, blacks had been working 40-acre plots of land and harvesting their own crops for several years. Farther inland, most freedmen who

In the early months of freedom, the daily life of former slaves was both changed and unchanged. Here (above) we see a photograph of freedmen, led by a crew leader much like during slavery days, leaving the cotton fields after a full day of gang labor carrying cotton on their heads, and a sketch (below) of a Freedmen's Bureau school in 1866, which many men, women, and children attended at night. *(Above, © Collection of The New-York Historical Society; Below, The Newberry Library)*

The Promise of Land: 40 Acres

Note the progression in the various documents in this chapter from promised lands (this page), to lands restored to whites (page 501), to work contracts (page 508), to semiautonomous tenant farms (page 510). Freedom came by degrees to the freedmen.

To All Whom It May Concern

Edisto Island, August 15th, 1865

George Owens, having selected for settlement forty acres of Land, on Theodore Belab's Place, pursuant to Special Field Orders, No. 15, Headquarters Military Division of the Mississippi, Savannah, Ga., Jan. 16, 1865; he has permission to hold and occupy the said Tract, subject to such regulations as may be established by proper authority; and all persons are prohibited from interfering with him in his possession of the same.

By command of R. SAXTON
Brev't Maj. Gen.,
Ass't. Comm.
S.C., Ga., and Fla.

received land were the former slaves of Cherokees and Creeks. Some blacks held title to these lands. Northern philanthropists had organized others to grow cotton for the Treasury Department to prove the superiority of free labor over slavery. In the Davis Bend section of Mississippi, thousands of former slaves worked 40-acre tracts on leased lands formerly owned by Jefferson Davis. In this highly successful experiment, they made profits sufficient to repay the government for initial costs, then lost the land to Davis's brother.

Many freedmen expected a new economic order as fair payment for their years of involuntary work on the land. "It's de white man's turn ter labor now," a black preacher in Florida told a group of fieldhands. Whites would no longer own all the land, he went on, "fur de Guverment is gwine ter gie ter ev'ry Nigger forty acres of lan' an' a mule." Other freedmen were willing to settle for less: One in Virginia offered to take only one acre of land—"Ef you make it de acre dat Marsa's house sets on." Another was more guarded, aware of how easy the power could shift back to white planters: "Gib us our own land and we take care ourselves; but widout land, de ole massas can hire us or starve us, as dey please." However cautiously expressed, the freedmen had every expectation, fed by the intensity of their dreams, that the promised "40 acres and a mule" was forthcoming. Once they obtained land, reunited families, and education, they looked forward to civil rights and the vote.

The White South's Fearful Response

White southerners had equally mixed goals and expectations at the war's end. Yeoman farmers and poor whites stood side by side with rich planters in bread lines, as together they looked forward to the restoration of their land and livelihood. Suffering from "extreme want and destitution," as a Cherokee County, Georgia, resident put it, white southerners responded to the immediate postwar crises with feelings of outrage, loss, and injustice. "I tell you it is mighty hard," said one man, "for my pa paid his own money for our niggers; and that's not all they've robbed us of. They have taken our horses and cattle and sheep and everything." Others felt the loss more personally, as former slaves whom they thought were faithful or for whom they felt great affection suddenly left. "Something dreadful has happened dear Diary," a Florida woman wrote in May 1865. "My dear black mammy has left us. . . . I feel lost, I feel as if someone is dead in the house. Whatever will I do without my Mammy?"

A more dominant emotion than sorrow, however, was fear. The entire structure of southern society was shaken, and the semblance of racial peace and order that slavery had provided was shattered. Many white southerners could hardly imagine a society without blacks in bondage. It was the basis not only of social order but of a lifestyle the larger slaveholders, at least, had long regarded as the perfect model of gentility and civilization. Having lost control of all that was familiar and revered, whites feared everything from losing their cheap labor supply to having to sit next to blacks on trains.

The mildest of their fears was the inconvenience of doing various jobs and chores they had rarely done before, like housework. A Georgia woman, Eliza Andrews, complained that it seemed to her a "waste of time for people who are capable of doing something better to spend their time sweeping and dusting while scores of lazy negroes that are fit for nothing else are

The black codes, widespread violence against freedmen, and President Johnson's veto of the Civil Rights Bill gave rise to the sardonic question “Slavery Is Dead?” Note the irony of blind justice presiding over two violations of the freedmen's rights (described in the newspaper headings at the bottom on either side of a death's head encircled by “state rights”). *(The Newberry Library, Chicago)*

lying around idle.” Worse yet was the “impudent and presumin'” new manners of former slaves, as a North Carolinian put it, worrying, with others, that blacks wanted social equality.

The worst fears of southern whites were of rape and revenge. Impudence and pretensions of social equality, some thought, would lead to legal intermarriage, which in turn would produce mulattoes, “Africanization,” and the destruction of the purity of the white race. The presence of black soldiers touched off fears of violence and revenge. Although demobilization occurred rapidly after Appomattox, a few black militia units remained in uniform, parading with guns in southern cities. Acts of violence by black soldiers against whites, however, were extremely rare.

Believing that their world was turned upside down, the former planter aristocracy tried to set it right again. Their goal was to restore the old plantation order and appropriate racial relationships. The key to reestablishing white dominance was in the “black codes” that state legislatures passed in the first year after the end of the war. Many of the codes granted freedmen the right to marry, sue and be sued, testify in court, and hold property. But these rights were qualified. Complicated passages in the codes explained under exactly what circumstances blacks could testify against whites or own property (mostly they could not) or exercise other rights of free people. Some rights were denied, including racial intermarriage and the right to bear arms, possess alcoholic beverages, sit on trains except in baggage compartments, be on city streets at night, or congregate in large groups.

Many of the qualified rights guaranteed by the black codes—testimony in court, for example—were passed only to induce the federal government to withdraw its remaining troops from the South. This was a crucial issue, for in many places marauding groups of whites were assaulting and terrorizing virtually defenseless freedmen. In one small district in Kentucky, for example, a government agent reported in 1865:

> Twenty-three cases of severe and inhuman beating and whipping of men; four of beating and shooting; two of robbing and shooting; three of robbing; five men shot and killed; two shot and wounded; four beaten to death; one beaten and roasted; three women assaulted and ravished; four women beaten; two women tied up and whipped until insensible; two men and their families beaten and driven from their homes, and their property destroyed; two instances of burning of dwellings, and one of the inmates shot.

Freedmen clearly needed protection and the right to testify in court against whites.

For white planters, the violence was another sign of social disorder that could be eased only by restoring a plantation-based society. More significant, they needed the freedmen's labor. The crucial provisions of the black codes were thus intended to regulate the freedmen's economic status. "Vagrancy" laws provided that any blacks not "lawfully employed," which usually meant by a white employer, could be arrested, jailed, fined, or hired out to a man who would assume responsibility for their debts and future behavior. The codes regulated the work contracts by which black laborers worked in the fields for white landowners, including severe penalties for leaving before the yearly contract was fulfilled and rules for proper behavior, attitude, and manners. Thus, southern leaders sought to reestablish their dominance. Although thwarted in perpetuating slavery or even in a program for gradual emancipation, many southerners believed, like this Texan, that "we will be enabled to adopt a coercive system of labor." A Kentucky newspaper was more direct: "The tune . . . will not be 'forty acres and a mule,' but . . . 'work nigger or starve.'"

NATIONAL RECONSTRUCTION

The black codes directly challenged the national government in 1865. How would it use its power—to uphold the codes and impose racial intimidation in the South, or to defend the newly sought rights of the freedmen? Would the federal government stress human liberty and the democratic reform impulse in American history, or would it emphasize property rights, order, and self-interest? Although the primary drama of Reconstruction pitted white landowners against black freedmen over land and labor in the South, in the background of these local struggles raged the debate over Reconstruction policy among politicians in Washington. This dual drama would extend well into the twentieth century.

The Presidential Plan

After initially demanding that the defeated Confederates be punished for "treason," President Johnson soon adopted a more lenient policy. On May 29, 1865, he issued two proclamations setting forth his reconstruction program. Like Lincoln's, it rested on

Promised Land Restored to Whites

Richard H. Jenkins, an applicant for the restoration of his plantation on Wadmalaw Island, S. C., called "Rackett Hall," the same having been unoccupied during the past year and up to the 1st of Jan. 1866, except by one freedman who planted no crop, and being held by the Bureau of Refugees, Freedmen and Abandoned Lands, having conformed to the requirements of Circular No. 15 of said Bureau, dated Washington, D. C., Sept. 12, 1865, the aforesaid property is hereby restored to his possession.

. . . The Undersigned, Richard H. Jenkins, does hereby solemnly promise and engage, that he will secure to the Refugees and Freedmen now resident on his Wadmalaw Island Estate, the crops of the past year, harvested or unharvested; also, that the said Refugees and Freedmen shall be allowed to remain at their present houses or other homes on the island, so long as the responsible Refugees and Freedmen (embracing parents, guardians, and other natural protectors) shall enter into contracts, by leases or for wages, in terms satisfactory to the Supervising Board.

Also, that the undersigned will take the proper steps to enter into contracts with the above described responsible Refugees and Freedmen, the latter being required on their part to enter into said contracts on or before the 15th day of February, 1866, or surrender their right to remain on the said estate, it being understood that if they are unwilling to contract after the expiration of said period, the Supervising Board is to aid in getting them homes and employment elsewhere.

the claim that the southern states had never left the Union.

Johnson's first proclamation continued Lincoln's policies by offering "amnesty and pardon, with restoration of all rights of property" to most former Confederates who would take an oath of allegiance to the Constitution and the Union of the United States. Johnson revealed his Jacksonian hostility to "aristocratic" planters by exempting former Confederate government leaders and rich rebels with taxable property valued over $20,000. Any southerners not covered by the amnesty proclamation, however, could apply for special individual pardons, which Johnson granted to nearly all applicants.

In his second proclamation, Johnson accepted the reconstructed government of North Carolina and prescribed the steps by which other southern states could reestablish state governments. First, the president would appoint a provisional governor, who would call a state convention representing "those who are loyal to the United States," including persons who took the oath of allegiance or were otherwise pardoned. The convention must ratify the Thirteenth Amendment, which abolished slavery; void secession; repudiate all Confederate debts; and elect new state officials and members of Congress.

Under this lenient plan, all southern states successfully completed Reconstruction and sent representatives to the Congress that convened in December 1865. Southern voters defiantly elected dozens of former officers and legislators of the Confederacy, including a few not yet pardoned. Some state conventions hedged on ratifying the Thirteenth Amendment, and some asserted former owners' right to compensation for the loss of slave property. No state convention provided for black suffrage, and most did nothing to guarantee civil rights, schooling, or economic protection for the freedmen.

Less than eight months after Appomattox, the southern states were back in the Union, former slaves were returning to work for their former masters under annual contracts, and the new president seemed firmly in charge. Reconstruction of the southern states seemed to be over. But northern Republicans were far from satisfied with President Johnson's efforts. Georges Clemenceau, a young French newspaper reporter covering the war, wondered if the North, having made so many "painful sacrifices," would "let itself be tricked out of what it had spent so much trouble and perseverance to win."

Congressional Reconstruction

Late in 1865, northern leaders painfully saw that almost none of their postwar goals—moral, political, or psychological—were being fulfilled. The South seemed far from reconstructed and was taking advantage of the president's program to restore the power of the prewar planter aristocracy. The freedmen were receiving neither equal citizenship nor economic independence. And the Republicans were not likely to maintain their political power and stay in office. Would Democrats and the South gain by postwar elections what they had been unable to achieve by civil war?

A song popular in the North in 1866 posed the question: "Who shall rule this American Nation?"—those who would betray their country and "murder the innocent freedmen" or those "loyal millions" who had shed their "blood in battle"? The answer was obvious. Congressional Republicans, led by Congressman Thaddeus Stevens of Pennsylvania and Senator Charles Sumner of Massachusetts, decided to assert their own policies for reconstruction. Although labeled "radicals," the vast majority of Republicans were moderates on the issues of the economic and political rights of the freedmen.

Rejecting Johnson's notion that the South had already been reconstructed, Congress exercised its constitutional authority to decide on its own membership. It refused to seat the new senators and representatives from the old Confederate states. It also established the Joint Committee on Reconstruction to investigate conditions in the South. Its report documented disorder, resistance, and the appalling treatment and conditions of the freedmen.

Even before the report came out in 1866, Congress passed a civil rights bill to protect the fragile rights of the blacks and extended for two more years the Freedmen's Bureau, an agency providing emergency assistance at the end of the war. Johnson vetoed both bills and called his congressional opponents "traitors." His actions drove moderates into the radical camp, and Congress passed both bills over his veto—both, however, watered down by weakening the power of enforcement. Southern courts, therefore, regularly disallowed black testimony against whites, acquitted whites charged with violence against blacks, and sentenced blacks to compulsory labor. In this judicial climate, racial violence erupted with discouraging frequency.

In Memphis, for example, a race riot occurred in May 1866 that typified race relations during the Reconstruction period. In the months before the riot, local Irish policemen frequently unleashed unprovoked brutality on black Union soldiers stationed at nearby Fort Pickering. A Memphis newspaper suggested that "the negro can do the country more good in the cotton field than in the camp" and criticized what it called the "dirty, fanatical, nigger-loving Radicals of this city" who thought otherwise.

A white mob burned this freedmen's school during the Memphis riot of May 1866. *(Library Company of Philadelphia)*

In this inflamed atmosphere, a street brawl erupted between the police and some recently discharged but armed black soldiers. After some fighting and an exchange of gunfire, the soldiers went back to their fort. That night, white mobs, led by prominent local officials (one of whom urged the mob to "go ahead and kill the last damned one of the nigger race"), invaded the black section of the city. With the encouragement of the Memphis police, the mobs engaged in over 40 hours of terror, killing, beating, robbing, and raping virtually helpless residents and burning houses, schools, and churches. When it was over, 48 people, all but two of them black, had died in the riot. The local Union army commander took his time intervening to restore order, arguing that his troops had a "large amount of public property to guard [and] hated Negroes too." A congressional inquiry found that in Memphis, blacks had "no protection from the law whatever."

A month later, Congress sent to the states for ratification the Fourteenth Amendment, the single most significant act of the Reconstruction era. The first section of the amendment sought to provide permanent constitutional protection of the civil rights of freedmen by defining them as citizens. States were prohibited from depriving "any person of life, liberty, or property, without due process of law," and all people were guaranteed the "equal protection of the laws." In Section 2, Congress granted black male suffrage in the South by making blacks whole people eligible to vote (thus canceling the Constitution's "three-fifths" clause). States that denied this right would have their "basis of representation reduced" proportionally. Other sections of the amendment denied leaders of the Confederacy the right to hold national or state political office (except by act of Congress), repudiated the Confederate debt, and denied claims of compensation to former slave owners. Johnson urged the southern states to reject the Fourteenth Amendment, and ten states immediately did so.

The Fourteenth Amendment was the central issue of the 1866 midterm election. Johnson barnstormed the country asking voters to throw out the radical Republicans and trading insults with hecklers in a nasty campaign of low forms of electioneering. Democrats north and south appealed openly to racial prejudice in attacking the Fourteenth Amendment. The nation would be "Africanized," they charged, with black equality threatening both the marketplace and the bedroom.

Republicans responded in kind, calling Johnson a drunkard and a traitor. Bitter Civil War memories were revived as Republicans "waved the bloody shirt," reminding voters of Democrats' treason and draft

RECONSTRUCTION AMENDMENTS

Constitutional Seeds of Dreams Deferred for 100 Years (or More)

Substance	Outcome of Ratification Process	Final Implementation and Enforcement
Thirteenth Amendment—Passed by Congress January 1865		
Prohibited slavery in the United States	Ratified by 27 states, including 8 southern states, by December 1865	Immediate, although economic freedom came by degrees
Fourteenth Amendment—Passed by Congress June 1866		
(1) Defined equal national citizenship; (2) reduced state representation in Congress proportional to number of disenfranchised voters; (3) denied former Confederates the right to hold office	Rejected by 12 southern and border states by February 1867; radicals made readmission depend on ratification; ratified in July 1868	Civil Rights Act of 1964
Fifteenth Amendment—Passed by Congress February 1869		
Prohibited denial of vote because of race, color, or previous servitude	Ratification by Virginia, Texas, Mississippi, and Georgia required for readmission; ratified in March 1870	Voting Rights Act of 1965

dodging. Governor Oliver P. Morton of Indiana described the Democratic party as a "common sewer and loathsome receptacle, into which is emptied every element of treason . . . inhumanity and barbarism which has dishonored the age." Although voters were moved more by self-interest and local issues rather than by such speeches, the result was an overwhelming Republican victory. The mandate was clear. The presidential plan for reconstruction had not worked, and Congress must suggest another.

Early in 1867, Congress passed three Reconstruction acts. The southern states were divided into five military districts, whose military commanders had broad powers to maintain order and protect civil and property rights. Congress also defined a new process for readmitting a state. Qualified voters—including blacks but excluding unreconstructed rebels—would elect delegates to state constitutional conventions that would write new constitutions guaranteeing black suffrage. After the new voters of the states had ratified these constitutions, elections would be held to choose governors and state legislatures. When a state ratified the Fourteenth Amendment, its representatives to Congress would be accepted, completing readmission to the Union.

The President Impeached

Congress also restricted presidential powers and established legislative dominance over the executive branch. The Tenure of Office Act, designed to prevent Johnson from removing the outspoken Secretary of War Edwin Stanton, limited the president's appointment powers. Other measures trimmed his power as commander in chief.

Johnson responded exactly as congressional Republicans had anticipated. He vetoed the Reconstruction acts, limited the activities of military commanders in the South, and removed cabinet officers and other officials sympathetic to Congress. The House Judiciary Committee investigated, charging the president with "usurpations of power" and of acting in the "interests of the great criminals" who had led the southern rebellion. It was evident, however, that Johnson was guilty only of holding principles, policies, and prejudices different from those of congressional leaders, and moderate House Republicans defeated the impeachment resolutions.

In August 1867, Johnson dismissed Stanton and asked for the consent of the Senate. When the Senate refused, the president ordered Stanton to surrender his office, which he refused, barricading himself inside. Now the House quickly approved impeachment resolutions, charging the president with "high crimes and misdemeanors," mostly alleged violations of the Tenure of Office Act. The three-month trial in the Senate early in 1868 featured impassioned oratory, similar to that heard in the Clinton impeachment and trial proceedings in 1998–1999. Evidence was skimpy, however, that Johnson had committed any crime justifying his removal. With seven moderate Republicans joining Democrats against conviction, the effort to find the president guilty fell exactly one vote short of the required two-thirds majority. Not until Nixon in the 1970s would a president again face removal from office through impeachment.

Moderate Republicans, satisfied with the changes wrought by the Civil War, may have feared the consequences of removing Johnson, for the next man in line for the presidency, Senator Benjamin Wade of Ohio, was a leading radical Republican. Wade had endorsed woman suffrage, rights for labor unions, and civil rights for blacks in both southern and northern states. As moderate Republicans gained strength in 1868 through their support of the presidential election winner, Ulysses S. Grant, radicalism lost much of its power within Republican ranks.

Congressional Moderation

The impeachment crisis revealed that most Republicans were more interested in protecting themselves than the freedmen and in punishing Johnson rather than the South. Congress's political battle against the president was not matched by an idealistic resolve on behalf of the rights and welfare of the freedmen. As early as the state and local elections of 1867, it was clear that voters preferred moderate reconstruction policies. It is important to look not only at what Congress did during Reconstruction but also at what it did not do.

With the exception of Jefferson Davis, Congress did not imprison Confederate leaders, and only one person, the commander of the infamous Andersonville prison camp, was executed. Congress did not insist on long probation before southern states could be readmitted to the Union. It did not reorganize southern local governments. It did not mandate a national program of education for the four million former slaves. It did not confiscate and redistribute land to the freedmen, nor did it prevent President Johnson from taking land away from freedmen who had gained titles during the war. It did not, except indirectly, provide economic help to black citizens.

What Congress did do, and that only reluctantly, was grant citizenship and suffrage to the freedmen. Northerners were no more prepared than southerners to make blacks equal citizens. Between 1865 and 1869, several states held referendums proposing black suffrage. Voters in Kansas, Ohio, Michigan, Missouri, Wisconsin, Connecticut, New York, and the District of Columbia (by a vote of 6,521 to 35!) all turned the proposals down. Only in Iowa and Minnesota (on the third try, and then only by devious wording) did northern whites grant the vote to blacks.

Proposals to give black men the vote gained support in the North only after the election of 1868, when General Grant, a military hero regarded as invincible, barely won the popular vote in several states. To ensure grateful black votes, congressional Republicans, who had twice rejected a suffrage amendment, took another look at the idea. After a bitter fight, the Fifteenth Amendment, forbidding all states to deny the vote to anyone "on account of race, color, or previous condition of servitude," became part of the Constitution in 1870. A black preacher from Pittsburgh observed that "the Republican party had done the Negro good, but they were doing themselves good at the same time."

Congress, therefore, gave African Americans the vote but not the land, the opposite priority of what the freedmen wanted. Almost alone, Thaddeus Stevens argued that "forty acres . . . and a hut would be more valuable . . . than the . . . right to vote." But Congress never seriously considered his plan to confiscate the land of the "chief rebels" and to give a small portion of it, divided into 40-acre plots, to the freedmen. This would have violated deeply held beliefs of the Republican party and the American people in the sacredness of private property. Moreover, northern business interests looking to develop southern industry and invest in southern land liked the prospect of a large pool of propertyless black workers.

Most Americans, North and South, opposed land confiscation and the right of independent blacks to own land. Congress did, however, pass the Southern Homestead Act of 1866, proposed by George Julian of Indiana, making public lands available to blacks and loyal whites in five southern states. But the land was

PRESIDENTIAL ELECTIONS, 1864–1868

Year	Candidate	Party	Popular Vote	Electoral Vote
1864	ABRAHAM LINCOLN	Republican	2,206,938 (55.0%)	212
	George B. McClellan	Democratic	1,803,787 (45.0%)	21
1868	ULYSSES S. GRANT	Republican	3,013,421 (52.7%)	214
	Horatio Seymour	Democratic	2,706,829 (47.3%)	80

Note: Winners' names are in capital letters.

poor and inaccessible; no transportation, tools, or seed was provided; and most blacks were bound by contracts that prevented them from moving onto claims before the deadline. Only about 4,000 black families even applied for the Homestead Act lands, and fewer than 20 percent of them saw their claims completed. White claimants did little better. Congressional moderation, therefore, left the freedmen economically weak as they faced the challenges of freedom.

Women and the Reconstruction Amendments

One casualty of the Fourteenth and Fifteenth Amendments was the goodwill of women who had been petitioning and campaigning for suffrage for two decades. They had hoped that grateful male legislators would recognize their wartime service in support of the Union effort and the willing temporary suspension of their own campaign for rights in order to work on behalf of blacks. They would be deeply disappointed.

During the war the Woman's Loyal League, headed by Elizabeth Cady Stanton and Susan B. Anthony, gathered nearly 400,000 signatures on petitions asking Congress to pass the Thirteenth Amendment. They were therefore shocked when the Fourteenth Amendment, in referring to a citizen's right to vote, for the first time inserted the word *male* into the Constitution. To one senator who supported adding woman suffrage at the same time, a colleague said that for "negroes" the ballot "is necessary for their protection; but to extend the right of suffrage to women is not necessary."

Some suffragists such as Lucy Stone were willing to accept delay, recognizing the plea of Frederick Douglass, a longtime proponent of woman suffrage, that this was "the Negro's hour." But Stanton, Anthony, and other women campaigned against an amendment that left them out, arguing against having to continue to rely on their fathers and husbands to protect their rights. Anthony vowed to "cut off this right arm of mine before I will ever work for or demand the ballot for the Negro and not the woman." Largely abandoned by Reconstruction social activists, women had few champions in Congress, and their efforts were put off for half a century.

Disappointment over the suffrage issue helped split the women's movement in 1869. Anthony and Stanton continued their fight for a national amendment for woman suffrage and a long list of property, educational, and sexual rights, while other women focused their hopes on securing the vote state by state. But African Americans would also be disappointed. Events in coming decades showed that the Reconstruction amendments did not change the fact that specific requirements for the suffrage were still in the hands of states, and that southern states would find many ingenious ways to prevent blacks from voting.

LIFE AFTER SLAVERY

Union army major George Reynolds boasted to a friend late in 1865 that in the area of Mississippi under his command, he had "kept the negroes at work, and in a good state of discipline." Clinton Fisk, a well-meaning white who helped found a black college in Tennessee, told freedmen in 1866 that they could be "as free and as happy" working again for their "old master . . . as any where else in the world." Such pronouncements reminded blacks of white preachers' exhortations during slavery to work hard and obey their masters. Ironically, Fisk and Reynolds were agents of the Freedmen's Bureau, the agency intended to ease the transition from slavery to freedom for the four million former slaves.

The Freedmen's Bureau

Never in American history has one small agency—underfinanced, understaffed, and undersupported—been given a harder task than was the Bureau of Freedmen, Refugees and Abandoned Lands. Its purposes and mixed successes epitomized the tortuous course of Reconstruction.

The Freedmen's Bureau performed many essential services. It issued emergency food rations, clothed and sheltered homeless victims of the war, and established medical and hospital facilities. It provided funds to relocate thousands of freedmen and white refugees. It helped African Americans search for relatives and get legally married, and it served as a friend in local civil courts to ensure that the freedmen got fair trials. Although not initially empowered to do so, the agency was responsible for educating the former slaves in schools staffed by other blacks and idealistic northerners.

The bureau's largest task was to serve as an employment agency, tending to blacks' economic well-being. This included settling them on abandoned lands and getting them started with tools, seed, and draft animals, as well as arranging work contracts with white landowners. As we shall see, in the area of work contracts, the Freedmen's Bureau served more to "reenslave" the freedmen as impoverished fieldworkers than to set them on their way as independent farmers.

The Freedmen's Bureau had fewer resources in relation to its purpose than any agency in the nation's history. *Harper's Weekly* published this engraving of freedmen lining up for aid in Memphis in 1866. *(Library of Congress)*

Although some agents were idealistic young New Englanders eager to help slaves adjust to freedom, others were Union army officers more concerned with social order than social transformation. Working in a postwar climate of resentment and violence, Freedmen's Bureau agents were constantly accused of partisan Republican politics, corruption, and partiality to blacks by local white residents. But even the best-intentioned agents would have agreed with General O. O. Howard, commissioner of the bureau, in a belief in the traditional nineteenth-century American values of self-help, minimal government interference in the marketplace, the sanctity of private property, contractual obligations, and white superiority. The bureau's work served to uphold these values.

On a typical day, these overworked and underpaid agents would visit courts and schools in their district, supervise the signing of work contracts, and handle numerous complaints, most involving contract violations between whites and blacks or property and domestic disputes among blacks. One agent sent a man who had complained of a severe beating back to work with the advice, "Don't be sassy [and] don't be lazy when you've got work to do." Another, reflecting his growing frustrations, complained that the freedmen were "disrespectful and greatly in need of instruction." Although helpful in finding work for the freedmen, more often than not the agents found themselves defending white landowners by telling the blacks to obey orders, to trust their employers, and to sign and live by disadvantageous contracts.

Despite mounting pressures to support white landowners, personal frustrations, and even threats on their lives, the agents accomplished a great deal. In little more than two years, the Freedmen's Bureau issued 20 million rations (nearly one-third to poor whites); reunited families and resettled some 30,000 displaced war refugees; treated some 450,000 people for illness and injury; built 40 hospitals and hundreds of schools; provided books, tools, and furnishings—and even some land—to the freedmen; and occasionally protected their economic and civil rights. Black historian W. E. B. Du Bois's epitaph for the bureau might stand for the whole of Reconstruction: "In a time of perfect calm, amid willing neighbors and streaming wealth," he wrote, it "would have been a herculean task" for the bureau to fulfill its many purposes. But in the midst of hunger, sorrow, spite, suspicion, hate, and cruelty, "the work of any instrument of social regeneration was . . . foredoomed to failure."

Economic Freedom by Degrees

The economic failures of the Freedmen's Bureau, symbolic of the entire congressional program, forced the freedmen into a new economic dependency on their former masters. Although the planter class did not lose its economic and social power in the postwar years, the character of southern agriculture went through some major changes. First, a land-intensive system replaced the labor intensity of slavery. Land ownership was concentrated into fewer and even larger holdings than before the Civil War. From South Carolina to Louisiana, the wealthiest tenth of the population owned about 60 percent of the real estate in the 1870s. Second, these large planters increasingly concentrated on one crop, usually cotton, and were tied into the international market. This resulted in a steady drop in food production (both grains and livestock) in the postwar period. Third, reliance on one-crop farming meant that a new credit system emerged whereby most farmers—black and white—depended on local merchants for renting seed, farm implements and animals, provisions, housing,

A Freedman's Work Contract

As you read this rather typical work contract defining the first economic relationship between whites and blacks in the early months of the postwar period, note the regulation of social behavior and deportment, as well as work and "pay" arrangements. How different is this from slavery? As a freedman or freedwoman, would you have signed such an agreement? Why or why not? What options did you have?

State of South Carolina
Darlington District
Articles of Agreement

This Agreement entered into between Mrs. Adele Allston Exect of the one part, and the Freedmen and Women of The Upper Quarters plantation of the other part Witnesseth:

That the latter agree, for the remainder of the present year, to reside upon and devote their labor to the cultivation of the Plantation of the former. And they further agree, that they will in all respects, conform to such reasonable and necessary plantation rules and regulations as Mrs. Allston's Agent may prescribe; that they will not keep any gun, pistol, or other offensive weapon, or leave the plantation without permission from their employer; that in all things connected with their duties as laborers on said plantation, they will yield prompt obedience to all orders from Mrs. Allston or his *[sic]* agent; that they will be orderly and quiet in their conduct, avoiding drunkenness and other gross vices; that they will not misuse any of the Plantation Tools, or Agricultural Implements, or any Animals entrusted to their care, or any Boats, Flats, Carts or Wagons; that they will give up at the expiration of this Contract, all Tools & c., belonging to the Plantation, and in case any property, of any description belonging to the Plantation shall be willfully or through negligence destroyed or injured, the value of the Articles so destroyed, shall be deducted from the portion of the Crops which the person or persons, so offending, shall be entitled to receive under this Contract.

Any deviations from the condition of the foregoing Contract may, upon sufficient proof, be punished with dismissal from the Plantation, or in such other manner as may be determined by the Provost Court; and the person or persons so dismissed, shall forfeit the whole, or a part of his, her or their portion of the crop, as the Court may decide.

In consideration of the foregoing Services duly performed, Mrs. Allston agrees, after deducting Seventy five bushels of Corn for each work Animal, exclusively used in cultivating the Crops for the present year; to turn over to the said Freedmen and Women, one half of the remaining Corn, Peas, Potatoes, made this season. He *[sic]* further agrees to furnish the usual rations until the Contract is performed.

All Cotton Seed Produced on the Plantation is to be reserved for the use of the Plantation. The Freedmen, Women and Children are to be treated in a manner consistent with their freedom. Necessary medical attention will be furnished as heretofore.

Any deviation from the conditions of this Contract upon the part of the said Mrs. Allston or her Agent or Agents shall be punished in such manner as may be determined by a Provost Court, or a Military Commission. This agreement to continue till the first day of January 1866.

Witness our hand at The Upper Quarters this 28th day of July 1865.

Sharecroppers and tenant farmers, though more autonomous than contract laborers, remained dependent on the landlord for their survival. *(Brown Brothers)*

and land. These changes affected race relations and class tensions among whites.

This new system, however, took a few years to develop after emancipation. At first, most freedmen signed contracts with white landowners and worked in gangs in the fields as farm laborers very much as during slavery. Watched over by superintendents, who still used the lash, they toiled from sunrise to sunset for a meager wage and a monthly allotment of bacon and meal. All members of the family had to work to receive their rations. The freedmen resented this new form of semiservitude, preferring small plots of land of their own to grow vegetables and grains. Moreover, they wanted to be able to send their children to school and insisted on "no more outdoor work" for women. What the freedmen wanted, a Georgia planter correctly observed, was "to get away from all overseers, to hire or purchase land, and work for themselves."

Many blacks therefore broke contracts, ran away, engaged in work slowdowns or strikes, burned barns, and otherwise expressed their displeasure with the contract labor system. One white landowner expressed his frustration over having "to bargain and haggle with our servants about wages." In the Sea Islands and rice-growing regions of coastal South Carolina and Georgia, where slaves had long held a degree of autonomy, resistance was especially strong. On the Heyward plantations, near those of the Allstons, the freedmen "refuse work at any price," a Freedman's Bureau agent reported, and the women "wish to stay in the house or the garden all the time." The Allstons' former slaves also refused to sign their contracts, even when offered livestock and other favors, and in 1869, Adele Allston was forced to sell much of her vast landholdings.

Blacks' insistence on autonomy and land of their own was the major impetus for the change from the contract system to tenancy and sharecropping. As a South Carolina freedman put it, "If a man got to go crost de riber, and he can't git a boat, he take a log. If I can't own de land, I'll hire or lease land, but I won't contract." Families would hitch a team of mules to their old slave cabin to drag it to their assigned plot of land as far away from the Big House as possible. Sharecroppers received seed, fertilizer, implements, food, and clothing. In return, the landlord (or a local merchant) told them what to grow and how much and he took a share—usually half—of the harvest. The half retained by the cropper usually went to pay for goods bought on credit (at high interest rates) at the landlord's store. Thus, sharecroppers remained only semiautonomous, tied to the landlord's will for economic survival.

Tenant farmers had only slightly more independence. Before a harvest, they promised to sell their crop to a local merchant in return for renting land, tools, and other necessities. From the merchant's store they also had to buy goods on credit (at a higher price than whites paid) against the harvest. At "settling up" time, income from sale of the crop was compared with debts accumulated at the store. It was possible, especially after an unusually bountiful season, to come out ahead and eventually to own one's own land. But tenants rarely did; in debt at the end of each year, they had to pledge the next year's crop. World cotton prices remained low, and whereas big landowners still generated profits through their large scale of operation, sharecroppers rarely made much money. When they were able to pay their debts, landowners frequently altered loan agreements. Thus, a system of debt peonage replaced slavery, ensuring a continuing cheap labor supply to grow cotton and other staples in the South. Only a very few blacks became independent landowners—about 2 to 5 percent by 1880, but closer to 20 percent in some states by 1900.

These changes in southern agriculture affected yeoman and poor white farmers as well, and planters worried about a coalition between poor black and pro-Unionist white farmers. As a yeoman farmer in Georgia said in 1865, "We should tuk the land, as we did the niggers, and split it, and giv part to the niggers and part to me and t'other Union fellers." But confiscation and redistribution of land was no more likely for white farmers than for the freedmen. Whites, too, were forced to concentrate on growing staples, to pledge their crops against high-interest credit from local merchants, and to face the inevitability of perpetual indebtedness. In the upcountry piedmont area of Georgia, for example, the number of whites who worked their own land dropped from nine in ten before the Civil War to seven in ten by 1880. During the same period, the production of cotton doubled.

Larger planters' reliance on cotton meant fewer food crops, which necessitated greater dependence on local merchants for provisions. In 1884, Jephta Dickson of Jackson County, Georgia, purchased over $50 worth of flour, meal, meat, syrup, peas, and corn

The Rise of Tenancy in the South, 1880

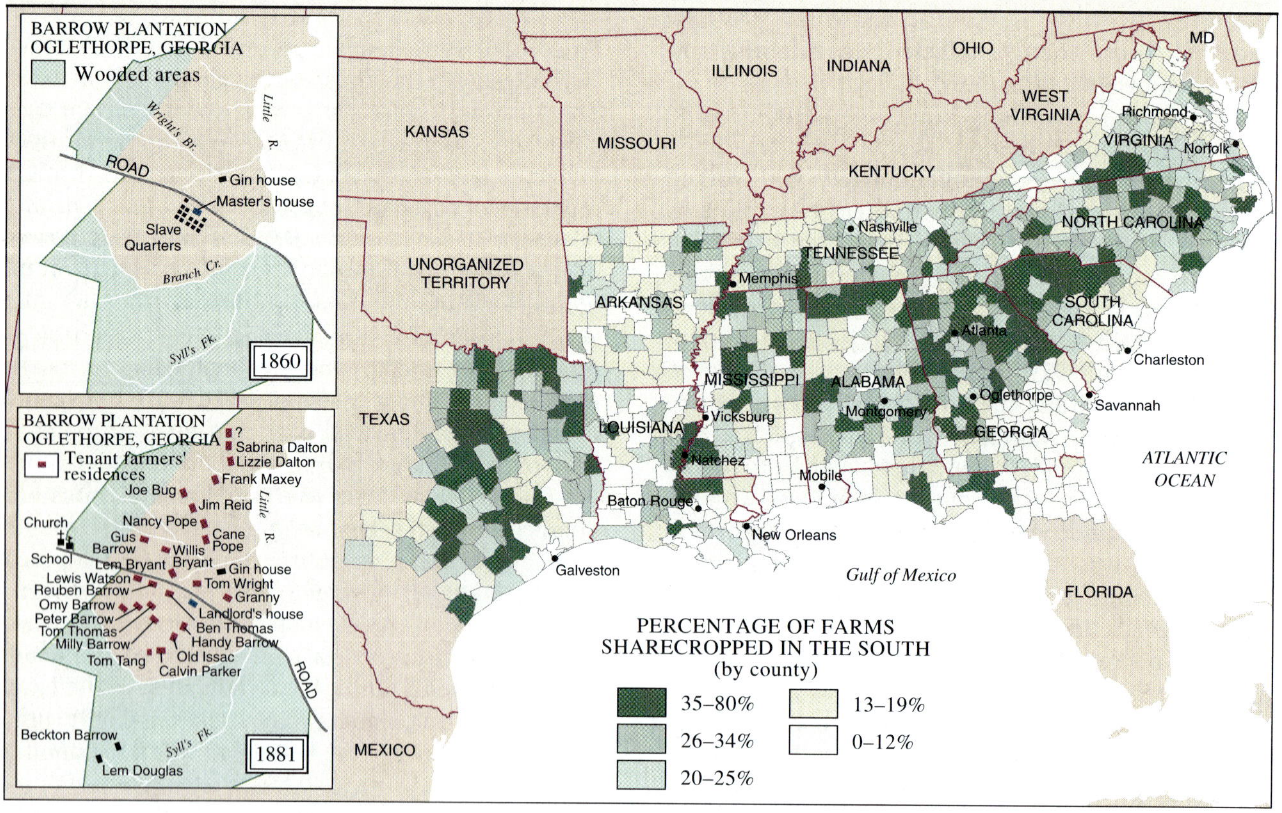

Although no longer slaves and after resisting labor contracts and the gang system of field labor, the freedmen (as well as many poor whites) became tenant farmers, working on shares, in the New South. The former slaves on the Barrow Plantation in Georgia, for example, moved their households to individual 25–30 acre tenant farms, which they rented from the Barrow family in annual contracts requiring payment in cotton and other cash crops. Note that the highest percentage of tenants were in the "black belt."

from a local store, an almost unthinkable situation 25 years earlier, when he would have needed to buy almost no food to supplement his homegrown fare. Fencing laws seriously curtailed the livelihood of poor whites raising pigs and hogs, and restrictions on hunting and fishing reduced the ability of poor whites and blacks alike to supplement their income and diet.

In the worn-out flatlands and barren mountainous regions of the South, poor whites faced diminishing fortunes in the era of Reconstruction. Their antebellum heritage of poverty, ill health, and isolation worsened in the years after the war. A Freedmen's Bureau agent in South Carolina described the poor whites in his area as "gaunt and ragged, ungainly, stooping and clumsy in build." They lived a marginal existence, hunting, fishing, and growing corn and potato crops that, as a North Carolinian put it, "come up puny, grow puny, and mature puny." Many poor white farmers, in fact, were even less productive than black sharecroppers. Some became farmhands at $6 a month and board. Others fled to low-paying jobs in cotton mills, where they would not have to compete against blacks.

The cultural life of poor southern whites reflected both their lowly position and their pride. Their emotional religion centered on camp meeting revivals. Their ballads and folklore told of debt, chain gangs, and deeds of drinking prowess. In backwoods clearings and bleak pine barrens, men and women told tall tales of superhuman feats and exchanged folk remedies for poor health. In Alabama, there were over 90 superstitious sayings for calling rain. Aesthetic expression, in quilt making and house construction, for example, reflected a marginal culture in which everything was saved and reused.

In part because their lives were so hard, poor whites persisted in their belief in white superiority. As a federal officer reported in 1866, "The poorer classes of white people . . . have a most intense hatred of the Negro, and swear he shall never be reckoned as part of the population." Many poor whites, therefore, joined the Ku Klux Klan and other southern white terror groups that emerged between 1866 and 1868. But however hard life was for poor whites, blacks were far more often sentenced to chain gangs for the slightest crimes and were bound to a life of debt, degradation, and dependency. The high hopes with which the freedmen had greeted emancipation turned slowly to resignation and disillusionment. Felix Haywood, a former Texas slave, recalled:

> We thought we was goin' to be richer than white folks, 'cause we was stronger and knowed how to work, and the whites . . . didn't have us to work for them anymore. But it didn't turn out that way. We soon found out that freedom could make folks proud but it didn't make 'em rich.

Black Self-Help Institutions

Felix Haywood understood the limitations of government programs and efforts on behalf of the freedmen. It was clear to many black leaders, therefore, that because white institutions could not fulfill the promises of emancipation, black freedmen would have to do it themselves. Fortunately, the tradition of black community self-help survived in the organized churches and schools of the antebellum free Negro communities and in the "invisible" cultural institutions of the slave quarters. Religion, as usual, was vital. Emancipation brought an explosion in the growth of membership in black churches. The Negro Baptist Church grew from 150,000 members in 1850 to 500,000 in 1870. The various branches of the African Methodist Episcopal Church increased fourfold in the decade after the Civil War, from 100,000 to over 400,000 members.

Black ministers continued their tradition of community leadership. Many led efforts to oppose discrimination, some by entering politics. Over one-fifth of the black officeholders in South Carolina were ministers. Most preachers, however, focused on traditional religious themes of sin, conversion, and salvation. An English visitor to the South in 1867 and 1868, after observing a revivalist preacher in Savannah arouse nearly 1,000 people to "sway, and cry, and groan," noted the intensity of black "devoutness." Despite some efforts by urban elite blacks to restrain the emotionalism characteristic of black worship, most congregations preferred their traditional forms of religious expression. One black woman, when urged to pray more quietly, complained: "We make noise 'bout ebery ting else . . . I want ter go ter Heaben in de good ole way."

The freedmen's desire for education was as strong as for religion. A school official in Virginia echoed the observation of many when he said that the freedmen were "down right crazy to learn." A Mississippi farmer vowed, "If I nebber does do nothing more, I shall give my children a chance to go to school, for I consider education next best ting to liberty." The first teachers of these black children were unmarried northern women, the legendary "Yankee schoolmarms." Sent by groups such as the American Missionary Association, these idealistic young women sought to convert blacks to Congregationalism and to white moral values of cleanliness, discipline, and dutiful

Along with equal civil rights and land of their own, what the freedmen wanted most was education. Despite white opposition and limited facilities for black schools, one of the most positive outcomes of the Reconstruction era was education in freedmen's schools. *(Valentine Museum, Richmond, Virginia)*

work. In October 1865, Esther Douglass found "120 dirty, half naked, perfectly wild black children" in her schoolroom near Savannah, Georgia. Eight months later, she reported that "their progress was wonderful." They could read, sing hymns, and repeat Bible verses and had learned "about right conduct which they tried to practice."

Glowing reports like this one changed as white teachers grew frustrated with crowded facilities, limited resources, local opposition, and the absenteeism that resulted from the demands of fieldwork. In Georgia, for example, only 5 percent of black children went to school for part of any one year between 1865 and 1870; this contrasted with 20 percent of white children. Furthermore, blacks increasingly preferred their own teachers, who could better understand former slaves. To ensure the training of black preachers and teachers, northern philanthropists founded Howard, Atlanta, Fisk, Morehouse, and other black universities in the South between 1865 and 1867.

Black schools, like churches, became community centers. They published newspapers, provided training in trades and farming, and promoted political participation and land ownership. A black farmer in Mississippi founded both a school and a society to facilitate land acquisition and better agricultural methods. These efforts made black schools objects of local white hostility. A Virginia freedman told a congressional committee that in his county, anyone starting a school would be killed and that blacks were "afraid to be caught with a book." In 1869, in Tennessee alone, 37 black schools were burned to the ground.

White opposition to black education and land ownership stimulated black nationalism and separatism. In the late 1860s, Benjamin "Pap" Singleton, a former Tennessee slave who had escaped to Canada, observed that "whites had the lands and . . . blacks had nothing but their freedom." Singleton urged them to abandon politics and migrate westward. He organized a land company in 1869, purchased public property in Kansas, and in the early 1870s took several groups from Tennessee and Kentucky to that prairie state to establish separate black towns. In following years, thousands of "exodusters" from the Lower South bought some 10,000 infertile acres in Kansas. But natural and human obstacles to self-sufficiency often proved insurmountable. By the 1880s, despairing of ever finding economic independence in the United States, Singleton and other nationalists urged emigration to Canada and Liberia. Other black leaders, notably Frederick Douglass, continued to press for full citizenship rights within the United States.

RECONSTRUCTION IN THE STATES

Douglass's confidence in the power of the ballot seemed warranted in the enthusiastic early months under the Reconstruction Acts of 1867. With President Johnson neutralized, national Republican leaders were finally in a position to accomplish their political goals. Local Republicans, taking advantage of the inability or refusal of many southern whites to vote, overwhelmingly elected their delegates to state constitutional conventions in the fall of 1867. With guarded optimism and a sense of the "sacred importance" of their work, black and white Republicans turned to the task of creating new state governments.

Republican Rule

Despite popular belief, the southern state governments under Republican rule were not dominated by illiterate black majorities intent on "Africanizing" the South by passing compulsory racial intermarriage laws, as many whites feared. Nor were these governments unusually corrupt or financially extravagant. Nor did they use massive numbers of federal troops to enforce their will. By 1869, only 1,100 federal soldiers remained in Virginia, and most federal troops in Texas were guarding the frontier against Mexico and hostile Indians. Without the support of a strong military presence, then, these new state governments tried to do

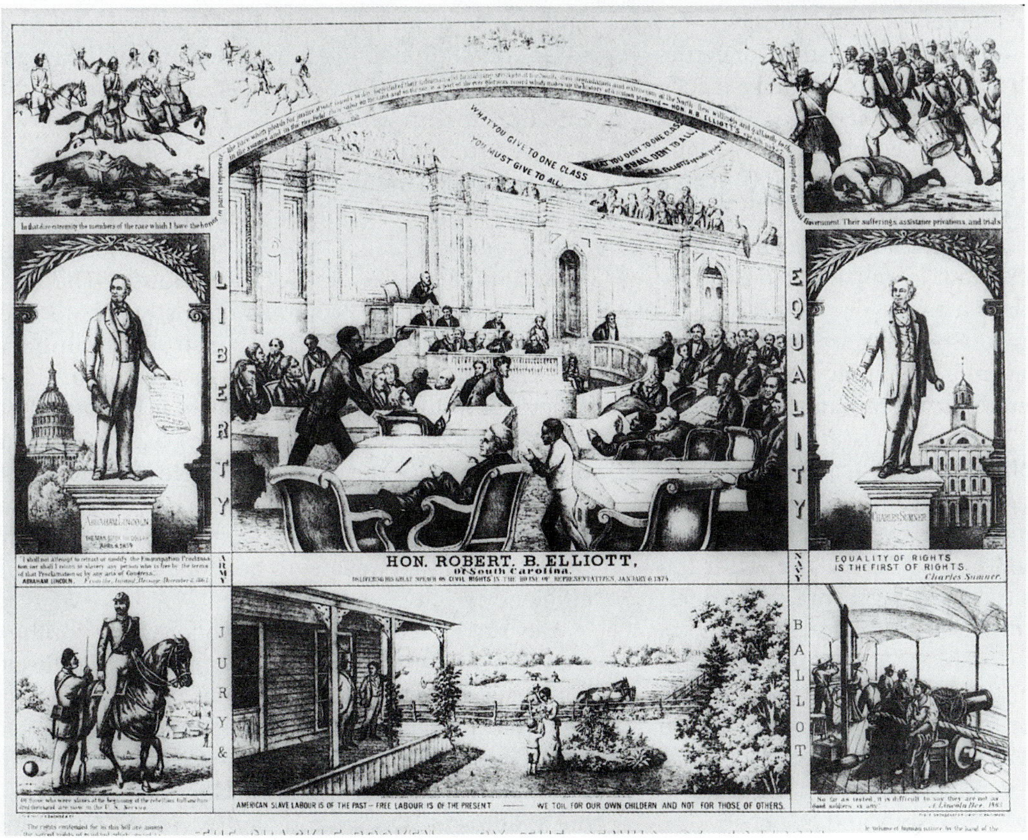

A talented, articulate, well-educated lawyer and Civil War veteran, Robert B. Elliott was elected to the South Carolina legislature in 1868, where he later was Speaker of the House, and served two terms in the U.S. Congress, from 1871 to 1874. This 1874 lithograph is titled "The Shackle Broken by the Genius of Freedom." The banner quotes Elliott, saying: "What you give to one class you must give to all. What you deny to one class you shall deny to all." *(Chicago Historical Society)*

their work in a climate of economic distress and increasingly violent harassment.

A diverse combination of political groups made up the new governments elected under congressional Reconstruction. Labeled the "black and tan" governments by their opponents to suggest domination by former slaves and mulattoes, they were actually predominantly white, with the one exception of the lower house of the South Carolina legislature. One part of the new leadership consisted of an old Whiggish elite class of bankers, industrialists, and others interested far more in economic growth and sectional reconciliation than in radical social reforms. A second group consisted of northern Republican capitalists who headed south for investments in land, railroads, and new industries. Others included retired Union veterans seeking a warmer climate for health purposes and missionaries and teachers pursuing an outlet for their idealism in the Freedmen's Bureau schools. Such people were unfairly labeled "carpetbaggers."

Moderate blacks made up a third group participating in the Republican state governments. A large percentage of black officeholders were mulattoes, many of them well-educated preachers, teachers, and soldiers from the North. Others, such as John Lynch of Mississippi, were self-educated tradesmen or representatives of the small landed class of southern blacks. In South Carolina, for example, of some 255 black state and federal officials elected between 1868 and 1876, two-thirds were literate and one-third owned real estate. Only 15 percent owned no property at all. This class composition meant that black leaders often supported land policies that largely ignored the economic needs of the black masses.

These black politicians were more interested in pursuing a political agenda of gaining access to government influence and education than an economic agenda of land redistribution or state aid to black peasants. They fashioned their political goals squarely in the American republican tradition. Black leaders reminded whites that they, too, were southerners and Americans, attached both to the land of the South and to the white families they had lived with for generations: "The dust of our fathers mingles with yours in the same grave yards. . . . This is your country, but it is ours too." Because of this intermingled past, blacks sought no revenge or reversal of power, only, as an 1865 petition said, "that the same laws which govern white men shall govern black men [and that] we be dealt with as others are—in equity and justice."

The primary accomplishment of Republican rule in the South was in eliminating the undemocratic features of earlier state constitutions. All states provided universal men's suffrage and loosened requirements for holding office. The basis of state representation was made fairer by apportioning more legislative seats to the interior regions of southern states. Social legislation included the abolition of automatic imprisonment for debt and laws for the relief of poverty and for the care of the handicapped. The first divorce laws in many southern states were passed, as were laws granting property rights to married women. Penal laws were modernized by reducing the list of crimes punishable by death, in one state from 26 to 5.

Republican governments undertook the task of financially and physically reconstructing the South, overhauling tax systems, and approving generous railroad and other capital investment bonds. Harbors, roads, and bridges were rebuilt. Hospitals, asylums, and other state institutions were established. Most important, the Republican governments provided for a state-supported system of public schools, absent before in most of the South. As in the North, these schools were largely segregated, but for the first time, rich and poor, black and white alike had access to education. As a result, black school attendance increased from 5 to over 40 percent, and white from 20 to over 60 percent by the 1880s. All this cost money, and the Republicans did indeed greatly increase tax rates and state debts. All in all, the Republican governments "dragged the South, screaming and crying, into the modern world."

These considerable accomplishments were achieved in the midst of opposition like that expressed at a convention of Louisiana planters, which labeled the Republican leaders the "lowest and most corrupt body of men ever assembled in the South." There was some corruption, to be sure, but mostly in land sales, fraudulent railway bonds, and construction contracts, the kind of graft that had become a way of life in American politics, South and North, in the aftermath of the Civil War. Given their lack of experience with politics, the black role was remarkable. As Du Bois put it, "There was one thing that the White South feared more than negro dishonesty, ignorance, and incompetence, and that was negro honesty, knowledge, and efficiency."

Despite its effectiveness in modernizing southern state governments, the Republican coalition did not last very long. In fact, as the map nearby indicates, Republican rule lasted for different periods of time in different states. In some states—Virginia, for example—the Republicans ruled hardly at all. Situated in the shadow of Washington, conservatives in Virginia professed their agreement with Congress's Reconstruction guidelines while doing as they pleased. As one of the states most devastated by the war, Virginia looked almost immediately to northern

The Return of Conservative Democratic Control in Southern States During Reconstruction

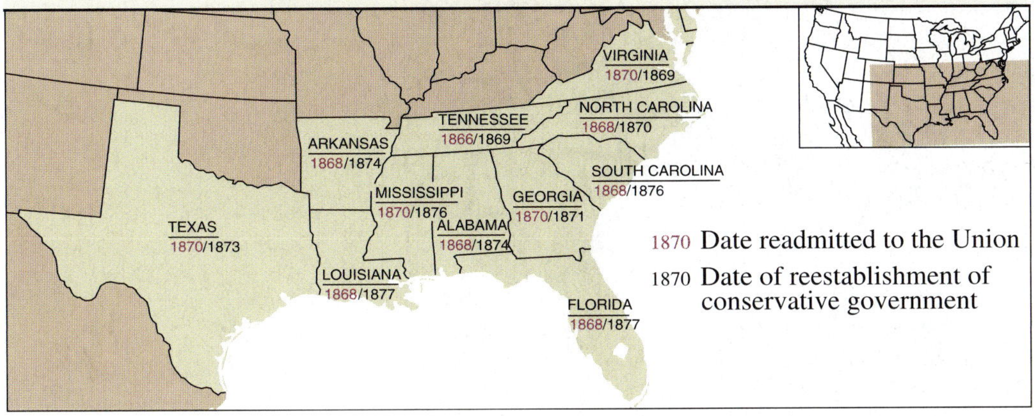

Note that the length of time Republican governments were in power to implement even moderate Reconstruction programs varied from state to state. In North Carolina and Georgia, for example, Republican rule was very brief, while in Virginia it never took place at all. "Redemption," the return of conservative control, took longest in the three Deep South states where electoral votes were hotly contested in the election of 1876.

investors to rebuild its cities and to develop industry. Blacks and whites alike flocked to the cities for work. In South Carolina, the unwillingness of black leaders to use their power to help black laborers contributed to their loss of political control to the Democrats. Class tensions and divisions among blacks in Louisiana helped to weaken that Republican regime as well.

Republican rule lasted the longest in the black belt states of the Deep South, where the black population was equal to or greater than the white. In Louisiana, Reconstruction began with General Ben Butler's occupation of New Orleans in 1862. Although he insisted on granting civil rights to blacks, he was quickly replaced by a succession of Republican governors in the late 1860s more interested in graft, election laws, and staying in office than in the rights and welfare of poor black Louisianans. Alabama received a flood of northern capital to develop the rich coal, iron ore, and timber resources of the northern third of the state. Republican rule in Alabama, as in other states, involved a greater role for towns and merchants, the endorsement of generous railroad bonds, and an emergent class structure that replaced the old planter aristocracy with a new industrial one.

Violence and "Redemption"

A Georgia newspaper in 1868 charged that Republican rulers would "see this fair land drenched in blood from the Potomac to the Rio Grande rather than lose their power." In fact, it was the Democrats who used racial violence, intimidation, and coercion to restore their power. As one southern editor put it, "We must render this either a white man's government, or convert the land into a Negro man's cemetery." The Ku Klux Klan was only one of several secret organizations that used force and violence against black and white Republicans to drive them from power. The cases of North Carolina and Mississippi are representative in showing how conservative Democrats were able to regain control.

After losing a close election in North Carolina in 1868, conservatives waged a concentrated campaign of terror in several counties in the piedmont area. If the Democrats could win these counties in 1870, they would most likely win statewide. In the year before the election, several prominent Republicans were killed, including a white state senator, whose throat was cut, and a leading black Union League organizer, who was hanged in the courthouse square with a sign pinned to his breast: "Bewar, ye guilty, both white and black." Scores of citizens were flogged, tortured, fired from their jobs, or forced to flee in the middle of the night from burning homes and barns. The courts consistently refused to prosecute anyone for these crimes. Local papers, in fact, charged that "disgusting negroes and white Radicals" had committed the crimes. The conservative campaign worked. In the election of 1870, some 12,000 fewer Republicans voted in the two crucial counties than had voted two years earlier, and the Democrats swept back into power.

In the state election in Mississippi in 1875, Democrats used similar tactics, openly announcing that "the thieves . . . robbers, and scoundrels, white

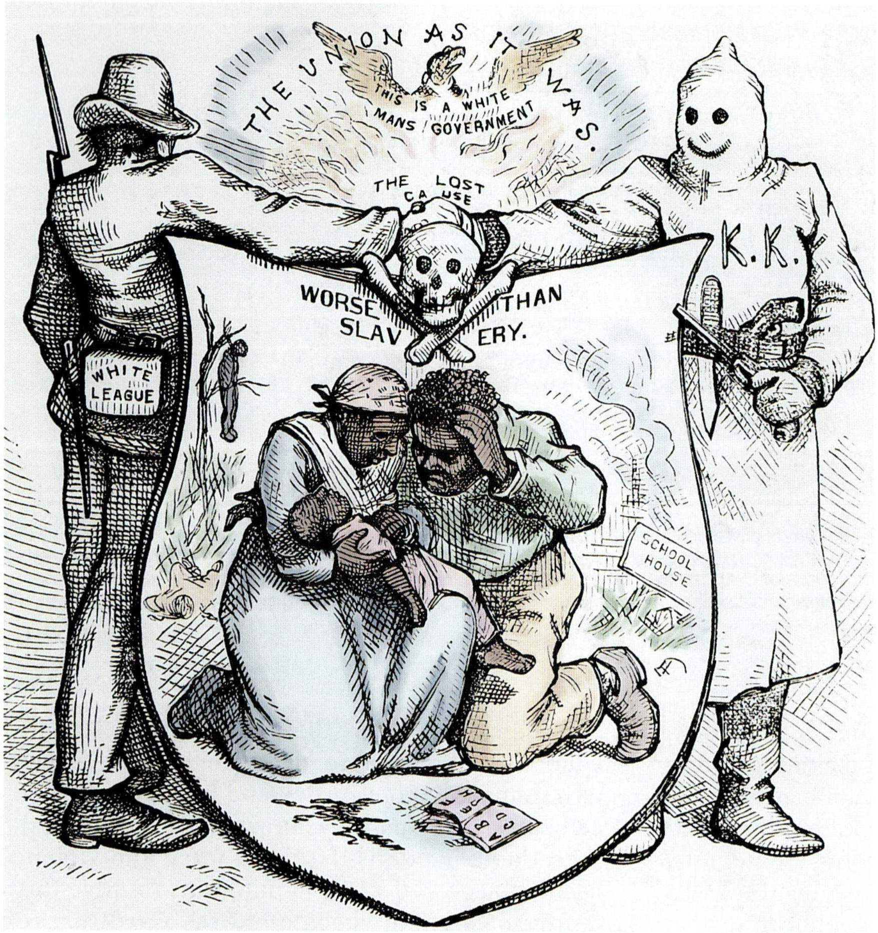

As shown in this Thomas Nast cartoon, "Worse Than Slavery," to restore a "white man's government" and redeem the noble "lost cause," white groups such as the Ku Klux Klan and the White League used every form of terror, violence, and intimidation. (Harper's Weekly, *October 24, 1874)*

and black," in power "deserve death and ought to be killed." In what was called the Mississippi Plan, local Democratic clubs organized themselves into armed militias, marching defiantly through black areas, breaking up Republican meetings, and provoking riots to justify the killing of hundreds of blacks. Armed men were posted during voter registration to intimidate Republicans. At the election itself, anyone still bold enough to attempt to vote was either helped by gun-toting whites to cast a Democratic ballot or driven away from the polls with cannon and clubs. Counties that had earlier given Republican candidates majorities in the thousands in 1875 managed a total of less than a dozen votes!

Democrats called their victory "redemption." As conservative Democratic administrations resumed control of each state government, Reconstruction came to an end. Redemption resulted from a combination of the persistence of white southern resistance, including violence and other coercive measures, and a loss of will to persist in the North. Albion Tourgée summed up the Reconstruction era in his novel *A Fool's Errand* (1879): "The spirit of the dead Confederacy was stronger than the mandate of the nation to which it had succumbed in battle."

Congress and President Grant did not totally ignore the violence in the South. Three force acts, passed in 1870 and 1871, gave the president strong powers to use federal supervisors to make sure that citizens were not prevented from voting by force or fraud. The third act, known as the Ku Klux Klan Act, declared illegal secret organizations that used disguise and coercion to deprive others of equal protection of the laws. Congress created a joint committee to investigate Klan violence, which reported in 1872 in 13 huge volumes of horrifying testimony. Grant, who had supported these measures, delivered special messages to Congress proclaiming the importance of the right to vote, issued proclamations condemning lawlessness, and sent some additional troops to South Carolina. However, as reform Republicans realized that black voters supported Grant, they lost interest in defending those voters. Regular Republicans were also not very supportive, because many felt that they could do

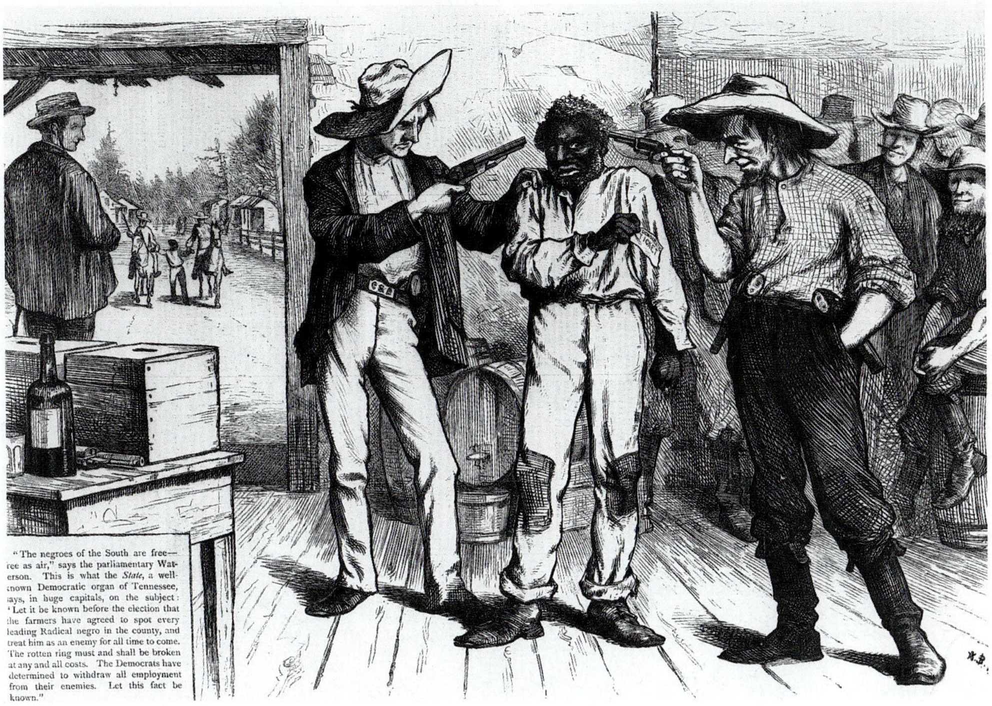

Although the Fourteenth and Fifteenth Amendments gave African American males the right to vote in the late 1860s, by the 1870s white southerners opposed to black suffrage found many illegal ways of influencing and eventually depriving that vote, thus returning white Democrats to office. In this cartoon, titled "Of course he wants to vote the Democratic Ticket," one of the two pistol-wielding men is saying: "You're as free as air, ain't you? Say you are, or I'll blow your black head off!" Note that another freedmen is being led down the street to the polling place, no doubt to vote Democratic also. *(Corbis)*

without black voters. Both groups were much more concerned with northern issues. In 1875, Grant's advisers told him that Republicans might lose important Ohio elections if he continued to protect blacks. Thus, he decided that year to reject appeals by Mississippi blacks that troops be stationed in their state to guarantee free elections. Grant declared instead that he and the nation "had tired of these annual autumnal outbreaks."

The success of the Mississippi Plan in 1875, imitated a year later in South Carolina and Louisiana, indicated that congressional reports and presidential proclamations did little to stop the reign of terror against black and white Republicans throughout the South. The force acts were wholly inadequate and weakly enforced. Although there were hundreds of arrests, all-white juries were reluctant to find their fellow citizens guilty of crimes against blacks. The U.S. Supreme Court backed them. In two decisions in 1874, the Court threw out cases against whites found guilty of preventing blacks from voting and declared key parts of the force acts unconstitutional. In Hamburg, South Carolina, in 1876, several blacks were killed in a riot that started in a courtroom when a white mob came to provide its own form of "justice" to some black militiamen who had been arrested for parading on Independence Day. Although the Ku Klux Klan's power was officially ended, the attitudes (and tactics) of Klansmen would continue long into the next century.

Reconstruction, Northern Style

Most northerners, like their leaders, were never committed to the principle of guaranteeing constitutional rights to African Americans. It was easy, therefore, to shift their attention to other matters than helping the freedmen. Frustrated with the difficulties of trying to transform an unwilling South, the easiest course was to give blacks citizenship and the vote, and wash their hands of the whole thing. Americans of increasing ethnic diversity were interested primarily in starting families, finding work, and making money. Thus, German immigrants fired furnaces in new steel plants in Wheeling, West Virginia; Chinese men pounded in

These two scenes vividly contrast family life during Reconstruction in the North and South. For most white northerners, as shown in this 1868 Currier & Ives print (top), the end of the Civil War meant renewing the good life of genteel middle-class values. *(Museum of the City of New York, The Harry T. Peters Collection)* For many black freedmen, however, family life was constantly threatened by the intrusion of Klan violence. *(The Granger Collection, New York)*

railroad ties for the Central Pacific over the Sierra Nevada mountains and across the Nevada desert; female teachers struggled to teach in one-room schoolhouses in Vermont for $23 a month; Mexican vaqueros drove Texas cattle herds to Kansas; and Scandinavian families battled heat, locusts, and high railroad rates on farmsteads in the Dakotas.

At both the individual and national levels, Reconstruction, northern style, meant the continuation of the enormous economic revolution of the nineteenth century. Northern Republicans were able to accelerate and solidify their program of economic growth and industrial and territorial expansion. The sad, practical consequence of this focus, however, was the abandonment of efforts to help four million freedmen to secure their freedom.

Thus, as the Central Pacific and Union Pacific railroads met at Promontory Point, Utah, in 1869, linking the Atlantic and the Pacific by rail, Klansmen met in dark forests to plan their next raid in North Carolina. As southern cotton production revived, northern iron and steel manufacturing and western settlement of the mining, cattle, and agricultural frontiers also surged. As black farmers were "haggling" over work contracts with white landowners in Georgia, white workers were organizing the National Labor Union in Baltimore. As Elizabeth and Adele Allston demanded the keys to their crop barns in the summer of 1865, the Boston Labor Reform Association was demanding that "our . . . education, morals, dwellings, and the whole Social System" needed to be "reconstructed." If the South would not be reconstructed, labor relations might be.

The years between 1865 and 1875 featured not only the rise (and fall) of Republican governments in the South but also the spectacular rise of working-class activity and organization. Stimulated by the Civil War to improve working conditions in northern factories, trade unions, labor reform associations, and labor parties flourished, culminating in the founding of the National Labor Union in 1866. Before the depression of 1873, an estimated 300,000 to 500,000 American workers enrolled in some 1,500 trade unions, the largest such increase in the nineteenth century.

This growth inevitably stirred class tensions. In 1877, thousands of railroad workers in Pittsburgh, St. Louis, Omaha, and other northern cities went out in a nationwide wave of strikes over wage cuts, clashing with local police and the National Guard. As we will see in Chapter 18, union activity and strikes exploded in the last two decades of the century. But southern black workers also protested worsening labor conditions. A year before the northern railroad strikes, hundreds of freedmen in the rice region along the Combahee River in South Carolina had organized a strike to protest a 40-cent-per-day wage cut. They clashed not only with local sheriffs but also with unofficial white Democratic rifle clubs, and no friendly Union troops were there to defend them.

As economic relations changed, so did the Republican party. Heralded by the moderate tone of the state elections of 1867 and Grant's election in 1868, the Republicans changed from a party of moral reform to one of material interest. In the continuing struggle in American politics between "virtue and commerce," commercial self-interest was again winning.

Abandoning the Freedmen's Bureau, Republican politicians had no difficulty handing out huge grants of money and land to the railroads. As blacks were told to go to work and help themselves, the Union Pacific was getting subsidies of between $16,000 and $48,000 for each mile of track laid across western plains and mountains. As Susan B. Anthony and others tramped through the snows of Upstate New York with petitions for rights of suffrage and citizenship, Boss Tweed and other machine politicians defrauded New York taxpayers of millions of dollars. As Native Americans in the Great Plains struggled to preserve their sacred Black Hills from greedy gold prospectors and U.S. soldiers, government officials in the East "mined" public treasuries by various forms of graft.

By 1869, the year financier Jay Gould almost succeeded in cornering the gold market, the nation was increasingly defined by materialistic "go-getters" and by sordid grasping for wealth and power. Henry Adams, descendant of two presidents, was living in Washington, D.C., during this era. As he wrote later in his autobiography, *The Education of Henry Adams* (1907), he had high expectations in 1869 that Grant, like another "great soldier" and president, George Washington, would restore moral order and peace. But when Grant announced the members of his cabinet, a group of army cronies and rich friends to whom he owed favors, Adams felt betrayed, complaining that "a great soldier might be a baby politician."

Ulysses Grant himself was an honest man, but his judgment of others was flawed. The scandals of his administration touched his relatives, his cabinet, and two vice presidents. Under Grant's appointments, outright graft, as well as loose prosecution and generally negligent administration, flourished in a half dozen departments. Most scandals involved large sums of public money. The Whiskey Ring affair, for example, cost the public millions of dollars in lost tax revenues siphoned off to government officials. Gould's gold scam received the unwitting aid of Grant's Treasury Department and the knowing help of the president's brother-in-law.

Nor was Congress pure. Crédit Mobilier, a dummy corporation supposedly building the transcontinental

Recovering the Past

NOVELS

We usually read novels, short stories, and other forms of fiction for pleasure, for the enjoyment of plot, style, symbolism, and character development. "Classic" novels such as *Moby Dick, Huckleberry Finn, The Great Gatsby, The Invisible Man,* and *Beloved,* to name a few American examples, are not only written well but also explore timeless questions of good and evil, innocence and knowledge, noble dreams fulfilled and shattered. Often, we enjoy novels because we find ourselves identifying with one of the major characters. Through that person's problems, joys, relationships, and search for identity, we gain insights about our own.

We can also read novels as historical sources, for they reveal much about the attitudes, dreams, fears, and ordinary everyday experiences of human beings in a particular historical period. They also show how people reacted to and felt about the major events of that era. The novelist, like the historian, is a product of time and place and has an interpretive point of view. Consider the two novels about Reconstruction quoted here. Neither is reputed for great literary merit, yet both reveal much about the various interpretations and impassioned attitudes of the post–Civil War era. *A Fool's Errand* was written by Albion Tourgée, a northerner; *The Clansman,* by Thomas Dixon, Jr., a southerner.

Tourgée was a young northern teacher and lawyer who fought with the Union army at several major battles during the Civil War. After the war, he moved to North Carolina, partly for health reasons and partly to begin a legal career. He became a judge and was an active Republican, supporting black suffrage and helping shape the new state constitution and the codification of North Carolina laws in 1868. With jurisdiction over eight counties, Tourgée earned a reputation as one of the fairest judges in the state. Because he boldly criticized the Ku Klux Klan for its campaign of terror against blacks, his life was threatened many times. When the fearless judge finally left North Carolina in 1879, he published an autobiographical novel about his experiences.

The "fool's errand" in the novel is that of the northern veteran, Comfort Servosse, who like Tourgée seeks to fulfill humane goals on behalf of both blacks and whites in post–Civil War North Carolina. His efforts are thwarted, however, by threats, intimidation, a campaign of violent "outrages" against Republican leaders in the county, and a lack of support from Congress. Historians have verified the accuracy, down to the smallest details, of the events in Tourgée's novel. While exposing the brutality of the Klan, Tourgée features loyal southern Unionists, respectable planters ashamed of Klan violence, and even guilt-ridden poor white Klansmen who try to protect or warn intended victims.

In the year of Tourgée's death, 1905, another North Carolinian published a novel with a very different analysis of Reconstruction and its fate. Thomas Dixon was born during the Civil War. He was a lawyer, North Carolina state legislator, Baptist minister, lecturer, and novelist. *The Clansman,* subtitled *A Historical Romance of the Ku Klux Klan,* reflects turn-of-the-century attitudes most white southerners still had about Republican rule during Reconstruction. According to Dixon, once the "Great Heart" Lincoln was gone, a power-crazed, vindictive radical Congress, led by scheming Austin Stoneman (Thaddeus Stevens), sought to impose corrupt carpetbagger and brutal black rule by bayonet on a helpless South. Only through the inspired leadership and redemptive role of the Ku Klux Klan was the South saved from the horrors of rape and revenge.

Dixon dedicated *The Clansman* to his uncle, a Grand Titan of the Klan in North Carolina during the time when two crucial counties were being transformed from Republican to Democratic through intimidation and terror. No such violence shows up in Dixon's novel. When the novel was made the basis of D. W. Griffith's film classic, *Birth of a Nation,* in 1915, the novel's attitudes were firmly imprinted on the twentieth-century American mind.

Both novels convey the events and attitudes of the era by creating clearly defined heroes and villains. Both include exciting chase scenes, narrow escapes, daring rescues, and tragic, heart-rending deaths. Both include romantic subplots in which a young white southern man falls in love with a young white northern woman. In each novel, however, the author's primary purpose was to convey his views of the politics of Reconstruction. Examining brief excerpts is a poor substitute for reading the novels in their entirety. Notice the obvious differences of style and attitude in the descriptions of Uncle Jerry and Old Aleck.

A Fool's Errand

Albion Tourgée (1879)

When the second Christmas came, Metta wrote again to her sister:

"The feeling is terribly bitter against Comfort on account of his course towards the colored people. There is quite a village of them on the lower end of the plantation. They have a church, a sabbath school, and are to have next year a school. You can not imagine how kind they have been to us, and how much they are attached to Comfort. . . . I got Comfort to go with me to one of their prayer-meetings a few nights ago. I had heard a great deal about them, but had never attended one before. It was strangely weird. There were, perhaps, fifty present, mostly middle-aged men and women. They were singing in a soft, low monotone, interspersed with prolonged exclamatory notes, a sort of rude hymn, which I was surprised to know was one of their old songs in slave times. How the chorus came to be endured in those days I can not imagine. It was

'Free! free! free, my Lord, free!
An' we walks de hebben-ly way!'

"A few looked around as we came in and seated ourselves; and Uncle Jerry, the saint of the settlement, came forward on his staves, and said, in his soft voice,

"'Ev'nin', Kunnel! Sarvant, Missus! Will you walk up, an' hev seats in front?'

"We told him we had just looked in, and might go in a short time; so we would stay in the back part of the audience.

"Uncle Jerry can not read nor write; but he is a man of strange intelligence and power. Unable to do work of any account, he is the faithful friend, monitor, and director of others. He has a house and piece of land, all paid for, a good horse and cow, and, with the aid of his wife and two boys, made a fine crop this season. He is one of the most promising colored men in the settlement: so Comfort says, at least. Everybody seems to have great respect for his character. I don't know how many people I have heard speak of his religion. Mr. Savage used to say he had rather hear him pray than any other man on earth. He was much prized by his master, even after he was disabled, on account of his faithfulness and character."

The Clansman

Thomas Dixon, Jr. (1905)

At noon Ben and Phil strolled to the polling-place to watch the progress of the first election under Negro rule. The Square was jammed with shouting, jostling, perspiring negroes, men, women, and children. The day was warm, and the African odour was supreme even in the open air. . . .

The negroes, under the drill of the League and the Freedman's Bureau, protected by the bayonet, were voting to enfranchise themselves, disfranchise their former masters, ratify a new constitution, and elect a legislature to do their will. Old Aleck was a candidate for the House, chief poll-holder, and seemed to be in charge of the movements of the voters outside the booth as well as inside. He appeared to be omnipresent, and his self-importance was a sight Phil had never dreamed. He could not keep his eyes off him. . . .

[Aleck] was a born African orator, undoubtedly descended from a long line of savage spell-binders, whose eloquence in the palaver houses of the jungle had made them native leaders. His thin spindle-shanks supported an oblong, protruding stomach, resembling an elderly monkey's, which seemed so heavy it swayed his back to carry it.

The animal vivacity of his small eyes and the flexibility of his eyebrows, which he worked up and down rapidly with every change of countenance, expressed his eager desires.

He had laid aside his new shoes, which hurt him, and went barefooted to facilitate his movements on the great occasion. His heels projected and his foot was so flat that what should have been the hollow of it made a hole in the dirt where he left his track.

He was already mellow with liquor, and was dressed in an old army uniform and cap, with two horse-pistols buckled around his waist. On a strap hanging from his shoulder were strung a half-dozen tin canteens filled with whiskey.

railroad, received generous bonds and contracts in exchange for giving congressmen gifts of money, stocks, and railroad lands. An Ohio congressman described the House of Representatives in 1873 as an "auction room where more valuable considerations were disposed of under the speaker's hammer than any place on earth." Henry Adams spoke for many Americans when he said that Grant's administration "outraged every rule of decency."

In *Democracy* (1880), a novel written by Henry Adams about Washington life during this period, Adams's main character, Mrs. Madeleine Lee, sought to uncover "the heart of the great American mystery of democracy and government." What she found were corrupt legislators and lobbyists in an unprincipled pursuit of power and wealth. "Surely something can be done to check corruption?" Mrs. Lee asked her friend one evening, "Are we forever to be at the mercy of thieves and ruffians? Is a respectable government impossible in a democracy?" The answer she heard was hardly reassuring: "No responsible government can long be much better or much worse than the society it represents."

The election of 1872 marked the decline of public interest in moral issues. A "liberal" faction of the Republican party, unable to dislodge Grant and disgusted with his administration, formed a third party with a reform platform and nominated Horace Greeley, editor of the New York *Tribune*, for president. The liberal Republicans advocated free trade, which meant lower tariffs and fewer grants to railroads; honest government, which meant civil service reform; and noninterference in southern race relations, which meant the removal of federal troops from the South. Democrats, lacking notable presidential candidates, also nominated Greeley, even though he had spent much of his earlier career assailing Democrats as "rascals." Despite his wretched record, Grant easily won a second term. Greeley was beaten so badly, he said, that "I hardly knew whether I was running for the Presidency or the Penitentiary."

The End of Reconstruction

Soon after Grant's second inauguration, a financial panic, caused by railroad mismanagement and the collapse of some eastern banks, started a terrible depression that lasted throughout the mid-1870s. In these times of hardship, economic issues dominated politics, further diverting attention from the freedmen. As Democrats took control of the House of Representatives in 1874 and looked toward winning the White House in 1876, politicians talked about new Grant scandals, unemployment and public works projects, the currency, and tariffs.

No one, it seemed, said much about the rights and conditions of southern freedmen. In 1875, a guilt-ridden Congress passed Senator Charles Sumner's civil rights bill, intended to put teeth into the Fourteenth Amendment. But the act was not enforced and after eight years was declared unconstitutional by the Supreme Court. Congressional Reconstruction, long dormant, had ended. The election of 1876 sealed the conclusion.

As their presidential candidate in 1876, the Republicans nominated a former governor of Ohio, Rutherford B. Hayes. Hayes had a reputation for honesty and had been an officer in the Union army, a necessity for post–Civil War candidates. But he was also, as Henry Adams put it, "obnoxious to no one." The Democrats nominated Governor Samuel J. Tilden of New York, who achieved national recognition as a civil service reformer in breaking up the corrupt Tweed ring.

Tilden won a majority of the popular vote and appeared to have enough electoral votes for victory. Twenty more electoral votes were disputed, all but one in the Deep South states of Louisiana, South Carolina, and Florida, where some federal troops still remained on duty and where Republicans still controlled the voting apparatus. Democrats, however, had applied various versions of the Mississippi Plan to intimidate voters. To settle the disputed electoral votes, Congress created a special electoral commission of five senators, five representatives, and five Supreme Court justices—eight of whom were Republicans and seven Democrats. The vote in each disputed case was eight to seven along party lines. Hayes was given all 20 votes, enough to win, 185 to 184.

Outraged Democrats threatened to stop the Senate from officially counting the electoral votes, thus preventing Hayes's inauguration. The country was in a state of crisis, and some Americans wondered if civil war might break out again. But unlike the 1850s, when passions over slavery erupted, this time a compromise was drawn between northerners and southerners mutually interested in modernization of the southern economy through capital investments. They focused on a Pacific railroad linking New Orleans with the West Coast. Northern investors wanted the government to help pay for the railroad. Southerners wanted northern dollars but not northern political influence—no social agencies, no federal enforcement of the Fourteenth and Fifteenth Amendments, and no military occupation, not even the small symbolic presence left in 1876.

As the March 4 inauguration date approached and newspapers echoed outgoing President Grant's call for "peace at any price," the forces of mutual self-interest concluded the "compromise of 1877." Democrats agreed to suspend resistance to the counting of the electoral votes, and on March 2, Rutherford B. Hayes was declared president. After his inauguration, he ordered the last federal troops out of the South, appointed a former Confederate general to his cabinet, supported federal aid for economic and railroad development in the South, and promised to let southerners handle race relations themselves.

On a goodwill trip to the South, Hayes told blacks in Atlanta that "your rights and interests would be safer if this great mass of intelligent white men were let alone by the general government." The message was clear: Hayes would not enforce the Fourteenth and Fifteenth Amendments, thus initiating a pattern of presidential inaction and white northern abandonment of African Americans that would last for nearly a hundred years. Thus ended the era of Reconstruction.

Under a caption quoting a Democratic party newspaper, "This is a white man's government," this Thomas Nast cartoon from 1868 shows three white groups, stereotyped as apelike northern Irish workers, unrepentant former Confederates, and rich northern capitalists, joining hands to bring Republican Reconstruction to an end almost before it began. The immigrant's vote, the Kluxer's knife, and the capitalist's dollars would restore a "white man's government" on the back of the freedman, still clutching the Union flag and reaching in vain for the ballot box. No single image better captures the story of the end of Reconstruction. (Harper's Weekly, *September 5, 1868/ The Granger Collection, New York)*

Timeline

1865	Civil War ends
	Lincoln assassinated; Andrew Johnson becomes president
	Johnson proposes general amnesty and reconstruction plan
	Racial confusion, widespread hunger, and demobilization
	Thirteenth Amendment ratified
	Freedmen's Bureau established
1865–1866	Black codes
	Repossession of land by whites and freedmen's contracts
1866	Freedmen's Bureau renewed and Civil Rights Act passed over Johnson's veto
	Southern Homestead Act
	Ku Klux Klan formed
	Tennessee readmitted to Union
1867	Reconstruction Acts passed over Johnson's veto
	Impeachment controversy
	Freedmen's Bureau ends
1868	Fourteenth Amendment ratified
	Senate fails to convict Johnson of impeachment charges
	Ulysses Grant elected president
1868–1870	Ten states readmitted under congressional plan
1869	Georgia and Virginia reestablish Democratic party control
1870	Fifteenth Amendment ratified
1870s–1880s	Black "exodusters" migrate to Kansas
1870–1871	Force acts
	North Carolina and Georgia reestablish Democratic control
1872	Grant reelected president
1873	Crédit Mobilier scandal
	Panic causes depression
1874	Alabama and Arkansas reestablish Democratic control
1875	Civil Rights Act passed
	Mississippi reestablishes Democratic control
1876	Hayes–Tilden election
1876–1877	South Carolina, Louisiana, and Florida reestablish Democratic control
1877	Compromise of 1877; Rutherford B. Hayes assumes presidency and ends Reconstruction
1880s	Tenancy and sharecropping prevail in the South
	Disfranchisement and segregation of southern blacks begins

Conclusion

A Mixed Legacy

In the 12 years between Appomattox and Hayes's inauguration, victorious northern Republicans, defeated white southerners, and hopeful black freedmen each wanted more than the others would give. But each saw some fulfillment of their dreams. The compromise of 1877 cemented the reunion of South and North, providing new opportunities for economic development in both regions. The Republican party achieved its economic goals and preserved its political hold on the White House, though not Congress, until 1932. The former Confederate states came back into the Union, and southerners retained their firm grip on southern lands and black labor, though not without struggle and some changes.

And the freedmen? In 1880, Frederick Douglass wrote:

> Our Reconstruction measures were radically defective. . . . To the freedmen was given the machinery of liberty, but there was denied to them the steam to put it in motion. They were given the uniform of soldiers, but no arms; they were called citizens, but left subjects; they were called free, but left almost slaves. The old master class . . . retained the power to starve them to death, and wherever this power is held there is the power of slavery.

The wonder, Douglass said, was "not that freedmen have made so little progress, but, rather, that they have made so much; not that they have been standing still, but that they have been able to stand at all."

The freedmen had made admirable gains in education and economic and family survival. Despite sharecropping and tenancy, black laborers organized themselves to achieve a measure of autonomy and opportunity in their lives that could never be diminished. The three great Reconstruction amendments to the Constitution, despite flagrant violation over the next 100 years, held out the promise of equal citizenship and political participation.

And yet, there was still an underlying tragedy to Reconstruction, as a short story by W. E. B. Du Bois, written a few years later, makes sadly clear. Two boyhood playmates, both named John, one black and one white, are sent from the fictional town of Altamaha, Georgia, north to school to prepare for leadership of their respective communities, the black John as a teacher and the white John as a judge and possible governor of the state. While they were away, the black and white people of Altamaha, each race thinking of its own John and not of the other, waited for "the coming of two young men, and dreamed . . . of new things that would be done and new thoughts that all would think."

After several years, both Johns returned to Altamaha, but a series of tragic events shattered the hopes and dreams of a new era of racial justice and harmony. Neither John understood the people of the town, and each was in turn misunderstood. Black John's school was closed because he was teaching ideals of liberty. Heartbroken and discouraged as he walked through the forest near town, he surprised the white John in an attempted rape of his sister. Without a word, black John picked up a fallen limb, and with "all the pent-up hatred of his great black arm," killed his boyhood friend. Within hours he was lynched.

Du Bois's story captures the human cost of the Reconstruction era. The black scholar's hope for reconciliation by a "union of intelligence and sympathy across the color-line" was smashed in the tragic encounter between the two Johns. Both young men, each once filled with glorious dreams, lay dead under the pines of the Georgia forest. Dying with them were hopes that interracial harmony, intersectional trust, and equal opportunities and rights for the freedmen might be the legacies of Reconstruction. Conspicuously absent in the forest scene was the influence of the victorious northerners. They had turned their attention to other, less noble, causes.

Recommended Reading

The Bittersweet Aftermath of War

Dan T. Carter, *When the War Was Over: The Failure of Self-Reconstruction in the South* (1985); W. E. B. Du Bois, *Black Reconstruction* (1935); Laura Edwards, *Gendered Strife & Confusion: The Political Culture of Reconstruction* (1997); Eric Foner, *Nothing but Freedom: Emancipation and Its Legacy* (1983) and *Reconstruction: America's Unfinished Revolution, 1863–1877* (1988); John Hope Franklin, *Reconstruction after the Civil War* (1961); Leon Litwack, *Been in the Storm So Long: The Aftermath of Slavery* (1980).

National Reconstruction

Richard H. Abbott, *The Republican Party and the South, 1855–1877* (1986); Michael Les Benedict, *A Compromise of Principle: Congressional Republicans and Reconstruction, 1863–1869* (1974); Frederick J. Blue, *Charles Sumner and the Conscience of the North* (1994); James E. Bond, *No Easy Walk to Freedom: Reconstruction and the Ratification of the Fourteenth Amendment* (1997); David Donald, *The Politics of Reconstruction* (1965); William Gillette, *Retreat from Reconstruction, 1869–1879* (1979); Brooks D. Simpson, *Let Us Have Peace: Ulysses S. Grant and the Politics of War and Reconstruction, 1861–1868* (1991); Hans Trefousse, *Thaddeus Stevens: Nineteenth-Century Egalitarian* (1997); C. Vann Woodward, *The Strange Career of Jim Crow* (1974) and *Reunion and Reaction* (1956).

Life After Slavery

W. E. B. Du Bois, *The Souls of Black Folk* (1903); Jacqueline Jones, *Soldiers of Light and Love: Northern Teachers and Georgia Blacks, 1865–1873* (1980); Leon Litwack, *Been in the Storm So Long: The Aftermath of Slavery* (1980); William E. Montgomery, *Under Their Own Vine and Fig Tree: The African-American Church in the South, 1865–1900* (1993); Donald Nieman, *To Set the Law in Motion: The Freedmen's Bureau and the Legal Rights of Blacks, 1865–1868* (1979); Claude Oubré, *Forty Acres and a Mule: The Freedmen's Bureau and Black Land Ownership* (1978); Nell I. Painter, *Exodusters: Black Migration to Kansas after Reconstruction* (1977); Roger Ransom and Richard Sutch, *One Kind of Freedom: The Economic Consequences of Emancipation* (1977); Edward Royce, *The Origins of Southern Sharecropping* (1993); Julie Saville, *The Work of Reconstruction: From Slave to Wage Laborer in South Carolina, 1860–1870* (1994).

Reconstruction in the States

W. Fitzhugh Brundage, *Lynching in the New South: Georgia and Virginia, 1880–1930* (1993); Paul Cimbala, *Under the Guardianship of the Nation: The Freedmen's Bureau and the Reconstruction of Georgia, 1865–1870* (1997); Thomas Holt, *Black over White: Negro Political Leadership in South Carolina During Reconstruction* (1977); Edward Miller, *Gullah Statesman: Robert Smalls from Slavery to Congress, 1839–1915* (1995); George C. Rable, *But There Was No Peace: The Role of Violence in the Politics of Reconstruction* (1984); Allen Trelease, *White Terror: The Ku Klux Klan Conspiracy and Southern Reconstruction* (1971); Richard Zuczek, *State of Rebellion: Reconstruction in South Carolina* (1996).

Fiction and Film

Toni Morrison's *Beloved* (1988), an extraordinary novel set near Cincinnati in 1873, is about the lasting traumas of slavery and the trials of blacks putting new lives together and pursuing their dreams in freedom. The film by the same name, though long and slow moving, follows the time disconnections of the novel well, with some powerfully effective acting. *Birth of a Nation,* the classic 1913 film by D. W. Griffith portraying heroically the rise of the Ku Klux Klan as the defender of white supremacy, is based on Thomas Dixon's *The Clansman* (1905), described in the "Recovering the Past" section of this chapter. A quite different film portrayal is seen in Oscar Micheaux's *Within Our Gates* (1919), the first feature film by an African American, available from the Library of Congress early American film collection. W. E. B. Du Bois's *The Quest of the Silver Fleece* (1911) is a little-known novel by the sociologist-historian about the lives of sharecroppers during Reconstruction. Howard Fast's *Freedom Road* (1944) is a novel about the heroic but ultimately failed efforts of poor whites and blacks to unite politically during the Reconstruction era. Ernest Gaines's *The Autobiography of Miss Jane Pittman* (1971), framed as an autobiography, is actually a gripping fictional account of a proud centenarian black woman who lived from the time of the Civil War to the era of civil rights. Albion Tourgée in *A Fool's Errand* (1879), as described in the "Recovering the Past" section of this chapter, takes the viewpoint of a sympathetic white judge toward helping the freedmen in North Carolina during Reconstruction.

Suggested Web Sites

http://www.ohiohistory.org/places/hayes/search/index.cfm

Hayes Diary Search. The Rutherford B. Hayes Presidential Center in Fremont, Ohio, maintains this searchable database of Hayes's writing.

http://digital.nypl.org/schomburg/images_aa19/

Images of African Americans from the 19th Century. The New York Public Library–Schomburg Center for Research in Black Culture site contains visuals by artists, engravers, and photographers capturing elements of African-American life in the nineteenth century.

http://www.inform.umd.edu/ARHU/Depts/History/Freedman/home.html

Freedmen and Southern Society Project. This site contains a chronology and sample documents from several print collections and primary sources about emancipation and freedom in the 1860s.

http://www.whitehouse.gov/WH/glimpse/presidents/html/aj17.html

Andrew Johnson. This is a White House web site that presents a history of Andrew Johnson.

http://www.whitehouse.gov/WH/glimpse/presidents/html/ug18.html

Ulysses S. Grant. This White House site gives a history of Ulysses Grant.

http://www.ncwa.org/info.html

National Civil War Association Home Page. The NCWA is one of the many Civil War reenactment organizations in the United States. Its site includes a Civil War and history links page.

http://www.ushistoryplace.com

A richly detailed on-line learning environment complete with interactive maps, timelines, history activities, primary source documents, and links to related American history sites.

Appendix

THE DECLARATION OF INDEPENDENCE IN CONGRESS, JULY 4, 1776

The Unanimous Declaration of the Thirteen United States of America

When, in the course of human events, it becomes necessary for one people to dissolve the political bonds which have connected them with another, and to assume, among the powers of the earth, the separate and equal station to which the laws of nature and of nature's God entitle them, a decent respect to the opinions of mankind requires that they should declare the causes which impel them to the separation.

We hold these truths to be self-evident: That all men are created equal; that they are endowed by their Creator with certain unalienable rights; that among these are life, liberty, and the pursuit of happiness; that, to secure these rights, governments are instituted among men, deriving their just powers from the consent of the governed; that whenever any form of government becomes destructive of these ends, it is the right of the people to alter or to abolish it, and to institute new government, laying its foundation on such principles, and organizing its powers in such form, as to them shall seem most likely to effect their safety and happiness. Prudence, indeed, will dictate that governments long established should not be changed for light and transient causes; and accordingly all experience hath shown that mankind are more disposed to suffer, while evils are sufferable, than to right themselves by abolishing the forms to which they are accustomed. But when a long train of abuses and usurpations, pursuing invariably the same object, evinces a design to reduce them under absolute despotism, it is their right, it is their duty, to throw off such government, and to provide new guards for their future security. Such has been the patient sufferance of these colonies; and such is now the necessity which constrains them to alter their former systems of government. The history of the present King of Great Britain is a history of repeated injuries and usurpations, all having in direct object the establishment of an absolute tyranny over these states. To prove this, let facts be submitted to a candid world.

He has refused his assent to laws, the most wholesome and necessary for the public good.

He has forbidden his governors to pass laws of immediate and pressing importance, unless suspended in their operation till his assent should be obtained; and, when so suspended, he has utterly neglected to attend to them.

He has refused to pass other laws for the accommodation of large districts of people, unless those people would relinquish the right of representation in the legislature, a right inestimable to them, and formidable to tyrants only.

He has called together legislative bodies at places unusual, uncomfortable, and distant from the depository of their public records, for the sole purpose of fatiguing them into compliance with his measures.

He has dissolved representative houses repeatedly, for opposing, with manly firmness, his invasions on the rights of the people.

He has refused for a long time, after such dissolutions, to cause others to be elected; whereby the legislative powers, incapable of annihilation, have returned to the people at large for their exercise; the state remaining, in the mean time, exposed to all the dangers of invasions from without and convulsions within.

He has endeavored to prevent the population of these states; for that purpose obstructing the laws for naturalization of foreigners; refusing to pass others to encourage their migration hither, and raising the conditions of new appropriations of lands.

He has obstructed the administration of justice, by refusing his assent to laws for establishing judiciary powers.

He has made judges dependent on his will alone, for the tenure of their offices, and the amount and payment of their salaries.

He has erected a multitude of new offices, and sent hither swarms of officers to harass our people and eat out their substance.

He has kept among us, in times of peace, standing armies, without the consent of our legislatures.

He has affected to render the military independent of, and superior to, the civil power.

He has combined with others to subject us to a jurisdiction foreign to our constitution, and unacknowledged by our laws, giving his assent to their acts of pretended legislation:

For quartering large bodies of armed troops among us;

For protecting them, by a mock trial, from punishment for any murder which they should commit on the inhabitants of these states;

For cutting off our trade with all parts of the world;

For imposing taxes on us without our consent;

For depriving us, in many cases, of the benefits of trial by jury;

For transporting us beyond seas, to be tried for pretended offenses;

For abolishing the free system of English laws in a neighboring province, establishing therein an arbitrary government, and enlarging its boundaries, so as to render it at once an example and fit instrument for introducing the same absolute rule into these colonies;

For taking away our charters abolishing our most valuable laws, and altering fundamentally the forms of our governments;

For suspending our own legislatures, and declaring themselves invested with power to legislate for us in all cases whatsoever.

He has abdicated government here, by declaring us out of his protection and waging war against us.

He has plundered our seas, ravaged our coasts, burned our towns, and destroyed the lives of our people.

He is at this time transporting large armies of foreign mercenaries to complete the works of death, desolation, and tyranny already begun with circumstances of cruelty and perfidy scarcely paralleled in the most barbarous ages, and totally unworthy the head of a civilized nation.

He has constrained our fellow-citizens, taken captive on the high seas, to bear arms against their country, to become the executioners of their friends and brethren, or to fall themselves by their hands.

He has excited domestic insurrection among us, and has endeavored to bring on the inhabitants of our frontiers the merciless Indian savages, whose known rule of warfare is an undistinguished destruction of all ages, sexes, and conditions.

In every stage of these oppressions we have petitioned for redress in the most humble terms; our repeated petitions have been answered only by repeated injury. A prince, whose character is thus marked by every act which may define a tyrant, is unfit to be the ruler of a free people.

Nor have we been wanting in our attentions to our British brethren. We have warned them, from time to time, of attempts by their legislature to extend an unwarrantable jurisdiction over us. We have reminded them of the circumstances of our emigration and settlement here. We have appealed to their native justice and magnanimity; and we have conjured them, by the ties of our common kindred, to disavow these usurpations, which would inevitably interrupt our connections and correspondence. They, too, have been deaf to the voice of justice and of consanguinity. We must, therefore, acquiesce in the necessity which denounces our separation, and hold them, as we hold the rest of mankind, enemies in war, in peace friends.

We, therefore, the representatives of the United States of America, in General Congress assembled, appealing to the Supreme Judge of the world for the rectitude of our intentions, do, in the name and by the authority of the good people of these colonies, solemnly publish and declare, that these United Colonies are, and of right, ought to be, FREE AND INDEPENDENT STATES; that they are absolved from all allegiance to the British crown, and that all political connection between them and the state of Great Britain is, and ought to be, totally dissolved; and that, as free and independent states, they have full power to levy war, conclude peace, contract alliances, establish commerce, and do all other acts and things which independent states may of right do. And for the support of this declaration, with a firm reliance on the protection of Devine Providence, we mutually pledge to each other our lives, our fortunes, and our sacred honor.

JOHN HANCOCK

BUTTON GWENNETT
LYMAN HALL
GEO. WALTON
WM. HOOPER
JOSEPH HEWES
JOHN PENN
EDWARD RUTLEDGE
THOS. HEYWARD, JUNR.
THOMAS LYNCH, JUNR.
ARTHUR MIDDLETON
SAMUEL CHASE
WM. PACA
THOS. STONE
CHARLES CARROLL OF CARROLLTON
GEORGE WYTHE
RICHARD HENRY LEE
TH. JEFFERSON
BENJA. HARRISON

THS. NELSON, JR.
FRANCIS LIGHTFOOT LEE
CARTER BRAXTON
ROBT. MORRIS
BENJAMIN RUSH
BENJA. FRANKLIN
JOHN MORTON
GEO. CLYMER
JAS. SMITH
GEO. TAYLOR
JAMES WILSON
GEO. ROSS
CAESAR RODNEY
GEO. READ
THO. MíKEAN
WM. FLOYD
PHIL. LIVINGSTON
FRANS. LEWIS
LEWIS MORRIS

RICHD. STOCKTON
JNO. WITHERSPOON
FRAS. HOPKINSON
JOHN HART
ABRA. CLARK
JOSIAH BARTLETT
WM. WHIPPLE
SAML. ADAMS
JOHN ADAMS
ROBT. TREAT PAINE
ELBRIDGE GERRY
STEP. HOPKINS
WILLIAM ELLERY
ROGER SHERMAN
SAMíEL. HUNTINGTON
WM. WILLIAMS
OLIVER WOLCOTT
MATHEW THORNTON

THE CONSTITUTION OF THE UNITED STATES OF AMERICA*

PREAMBLE

We the People of the United States, in Order to form a more perfect Union, establish Justice, insure domestic Tranquility, provide for the common defence, promote the general Welfare, and secure the Blessings of Liberty to ourselves and our Posterity, do ordain and establish this Constitution for the United States of America.

ARTICLE I.

Section 1 All legislative Powers herein granted shall be vested in a Congress of the United States, which shall consist of a Senate and House of Representatives.

Section 2 The House of Representatives shall be composed of Members chosen every second Year by the People of the several States, and the Electors in each State shall have the Qualifications requisite for Electors of the most numerous Branch of the State Legislature.

No Person shall be a Representative who shall not have attained to the Age of twenty five Years, and been seven Years a Citizen of the United States, and who shall not, when elected, be an Inhabitant of that State in which he shall be chosen.

Representatives and direct Taxes shall be apportioned among the several States which may be included within this Union, according to their respective Numbers, *which shall be determined by adding to the whole Number of free Persons, including those bound to Service for a Term of Years, and excluding Indians not taxed, three fifths of all other Persons.* The actual Enumeration shall be made within three Years after the first Meeting of the Congress of the United States, and within every subsequent Term of ten Years, in such Manner as they shall by Law direct. The Number of Representatives shall not exceed one for every thirty Thousand, but each State shall have at Least one Representative; *and until such enumeration shall be made, the State of New Hampshire shall be entitled to chuse three, Massachusetts eight, Rhode-Island and Providence Plantations one, Connecticut five, New-York six, New Jersey four, Pennsylvania eight, Delaware one, Maryland six, Virginia ten, North Carolina five, South Carolina five, and Georgia three.*

When vacancies happen in the Representation from any State, the Executive Authority thereof shall issue Writs of Election to fill such Vacancies.

The House of Representatives shall chuse their Speaker and other Officers; and shall have the sole Power of Impeachment.

Section 3 The Senate of the United States shall be composed of two Senators from each State, chosen by the Legislature thereof, for six Years; and each Senator shall have one Vote.

Immediately after they shall be assembled in Consequence of the first Election, they shall be divided as equally as may be into three Classes. The Seats of the Senators of the first Class shall be vacated at the Expiration of the second Year, of the second Class at the Expiration of the fourth Year, and of the third Class at the Expiration of the sixth Year, so that one third may be chosen every second Year; and if Vacancies happen by Resignation, or otherwise, during the Recess of the Legislature of any State, the Executive thereof may make temporary Appointments until the next Meeting of the Legislature, which shall then fill such Vacancies.

No Person shall be a Senator who shall not have attained to the Age of thirty Years, and been nine Years a Citizen of the United States, and who shall not, when elected, be an Inhabitant of that State for which he shall be chosen.

The Vice President of the United States shall be President of the Senate, but shall have no Vote, unless they be equally divided.

The Senate shall choose their other Officers, and also a President *pro tempore,* in the Absence of the Vice President, or when he shall exercise the Office of President of the United States.

The Senate shall have the sole Power to try all Impeachments. When sitting for that Purpose, they shall be on Oath or Affirmation. When the President of the United States is tried the Chief Justice shall preside: And no Person shall be convicted without the Concurrence of two thirds of the Members present.

Judgment in Cases of Impeachment shall not extend further than to removal from Office, and disqualification to hold and enjoy any Office of honor, Trust or Profit under the United States: but the Party convicted shall nevertheless be liable and subject to Indictment, Trial, Judgment and Punishment, according to Law.

Section 4 The Times, Places and Manner of holding Elections for Senators and Representatives, shall be prescribed in each State by the Legislature thereof; but the Congress may at any time by Law make or alter such Regulations, except as to the Places of chusing Senators.

The Congress shall assemble at least once in every Year, and such Meeting *shall be on the first Monday in December, unless they shall by Law appoint a different Day.*

Section 5 Each House shall be the Judge of the Elections, Returns and Qualifications of its own Members, and a Majority of each shall constitute a Quorum to do Business; but a smaller Number may adjourn from day to day, and may be authorized to compel the Attendance of absent Members, in such Manner, and under such Penalties as each House may provide.

Each House may determine the Rules of its Proceedings, punish its Members for disorderly Behaviour, and, with the Concurrence of two thirds, expel a Member.

Each House shall keep a Journal of its Proceedings, and from time to time publish the same, excepting such Parts as may in their Judgment require Secrecy; and the Yeas and Nays of the Members of either House on any question shall, at the Desire of one fifth of those Present, be entered on the Journal.

Neither House, during the Session of Congress, shall, without the Consent of the other, adjourn for more than

*The Constitution became effective March 4, 1789. Any portion of the text that has been amended is printed in italics.

three days, nor to any other Place than that in which the two Houses shall be sitting.

Section 6 The Senators and Representatives shall receive a Compensation for their Services, to be ascertained by Law, and paid out of the Treasury of the United States. They shall in all Cases, except Treason, Felony and Breach of the Peace, be privileged from Arrest during their Attendance at the Session of their respective Houses, and in going to and returning from the same; and for any Speech or Debate in either House, they shall not be questioned in any other Place.

No Senator or Representative shall, during the Time for which he was elected, be appointed to any civil Office under the Authority of the United States, which shall have been created, or the Emoluments whereof shall have been encreased during such time; and no Person holding any Office under the United States, shall be a Member of either House during his Continuance in Office.

Section 7 All Bills for raising Revenue shall originate in the House of Representatives; but the Senate may propose or concur with Amendments as on other Bills.

Every Bill which shall have passed the House of Representatives and the Senate, shall, before it become a Law, be presented to the President of the United States; If he approve he shall sign it, but if not he shall return it, with his Objections to that House in which it shall have originated, who shall enter the Objections at large on their Journal, and proceed to reconsider it. If after such Reconsideration two thirds of that House shall agree to pass the Bill, it shall be sent, together with the Objections, to the other House, by which it shall likewise be reconsidered, and if approved by two thirds of that House, it shall become a Law. But in all such Cases the Votes of both Houses shall be determined by yeas and Nays, and the Names of the Persons voting for and against the Bill shall be entered on the Journal of each House respectively. If any Bill shall not be returned by the President within ten Days (Sundays excepted) after it shall have been presented to him, the Same shall be a Law, in like Manner as if he had signed it, unless the Congress by their Adjournment prevent its Return, in which Case it shall not be a Law.

Every Order, Resolution, or Vote to which the Concurrence of the Senate and House of Representatives may be necessary (except on a question of Adjournment) shall be presented to the President of the United States; and before the Same shall take Effect, shall be approved by him, or being disapproved by him, shall be repassed by two thirds of the Senate and House of Representatives, according to the Rules and Limitations prescribed in the Case of a Bill.

Section 8 The Congress shall have Power:

To lay and collect Taxes, Duties, Imposts and Excises, to pay the Debts and provide for the common Defence and general Welfare of the United States; but all Duties, Imposts and Excises shall be uniform throughout the United States;

To borrow Money on the credit of the United States;

To regulate Commerce with foreign Nations, and among the several States, and with the Indian Tribes;

To establish an uniform Rule of Naturalization, and uniform Laws on the subject of Bankruptcies throughout the United States;

To coin Money, regulate the Value thereof, and of foreign Coin, and fix the Standard of Weights and Measures;

To provide for the Punishment of counterfeiting the Securities and current Coin of the United States;

To establish Post Offices and post Roads;

To promote the Progress of Science and useful Arts, by securing for limited Times to Authors and Inventors the exclusive Right to their respective Writings and Discoveries;

To constitute Tribunals inferior to the supreme Court;

To define and punish Piracies and Felonies committed on the high Seas, and Offences against the Law of Nations;

To declare War, grant Letters of Marque and Reprisal, and make Rules concerning Captures on Land and Water;

To raise and support Armies, but no Appropriation of Money to that Use shall be for a longer Term than two Years;

To provide and maintain a Navy;

To make Rules for the Government and Regulation of the land and naval Forces;

To provide for calling forth the Militia to execute the Laws of the Union, suppress Insurrections and repel Invasions;

To provide for organizing, arming, and disciplining, the Militia, and for governing such Part of them as may be employed in the Service of the United States, reserving to the States respectively, the Appointment of the Officers, and the Authority of training the Militia according to the discipline prescribed by Congress;

To exercise exclusive Legislation in all Cases whatsoever, over such District (not exceeding ten Miles square) as may, by Cession of particular States, and the Acceptance of Congress, become the Seat of the Government of the United States, and to exercise like Authority over all Places purchased by the Consent of the Legislature of the State in which the Same shall be, for the Erection of Forts, Magazines, Arsenals, dock-Yards, and other needful Buildings;-And

To make all Laws which shall be necessary and proper for carrying into Execution the foregoing Powers, and all other Powers vested by this Constitution in the Government of the United States, or in any Department or Officer thereof.

Section 9 *The Migration or Importation of such Persons as any of the States now existing shall think proper to admit, shall not be prohibited by the Congress prior to the Year one thousand eight hundred and eight, but a Tax or duty may be imposed on such Importation, not exceeding ten dollars for each Person.*

The Privilege of the Writ of Habeas Corpus shall not be suspended, unless when in Cases of Rebellion or Invasion the public Safety may require it.

No Bill of Attainder or ex post facto Law shall be passed.

No Capitation, or other direct, Tax shall be laid, unless in Proportion to the Census or Enumeration herein before directed to be taken.

No Tax or Duty shall be laid on Articles exported from any State.

No Preference shall be given by any Regulation of Commerce or Revenue to the Ports of one State over those of another: nor shall Vessels bound to, or from, one State, be obliged to enter, clear, or pay Duties in another.

No Money shall be drawn from the Treasury, but in Consequence of Appropriations made by Law; and a regular Statement and Account of the Receipts and Expenditures of all public Money shall be published from time to time.

No Title of Nobility shall be granted by the United States: And no Person holding any Office of Profit or Trust under them, shall, without the Consent of the Congress, accept of any present, Emolument, Office, or Title, of any kind whatever, from any King, Prince, or foreign State.

Section 10 No State shall enter into any Treaty, Alliance, or Confederation; grant Letters of Marque and Reprisal; coin Money; emit Bills of Credit; make any Thing but gold and silver Coin a Tender in Payment of Debts; pass any Bill of Attainder, ex post facto Law, or Law impairing the Obligation of Contracts, or grant any Title of Nobility.

No State shall, without the Consent of the Congress, lay any Imposts or Duties on Imports or Exports, except what may be absolutely necessary for executing it's inspection Laws: and the net Produce of all Duties and Imposts, laid by any State on Imports or Exports, shall be for the Use of the Treasury of the United States; and all such Laws shall be subject to the Revision and Controul of the Congress.

No State shall, without the Consent of Congress, lay any Duty of Tonnage, keep Troops, or Ships of War in time of Peace, enter into any Agreement or Compact with another State, or with a foreign Power, or engage in War, unless actually invaded, or in such imminent Danger as will not admit of delay.

ARTICLE II.

Section 1 The executive Power shall be vested in a President of the United States of America. He shall hold his Office during the Term of four Years, and, together with the Vice President, chosen for the same Term, be elected, as follows

Each State shall appoint, in such Manner as the Legislature thereof may direct, a Number of Electors, equal to the whole Number of Senators and Representatives to which the State may be entitled in the Congress: but no Senator or Representative, or Person holding an Office of Trust or Profit under the United States, shall be appointed an Elector.

The Electors shall meet in their respective States, and vote by Ballot for two Persons, of whom one at least shall not be an Inhabitant of the same State with themselves. And they shall make a List of all the Persons voted for, and of the Number of Votes for each; which List they shall sign and certify, and transmit sealed to the Seat of Government of the United States, directed to the President of the Senate. The President of the Senate shall, in the Presence of the Senate and House of Representatives, open all the Certificates, and the Votes shall then be counted. The Person having the greatest Number of Votes shall be the President, if such Number be a Majority of the whole Number of Electors appointed; and if there be more than one who have such Majority, and have an equal Number of Votes, then the House of Representatives shall immediately chuse by Ballot one of them for President; and if no Person have a Majority, then from the five highest on the List the said House shall in like Manner chuse the President. But in chusing the President, the Votes shall be taken by States, the Representation from each State having one Vote; A quorum for this Purpose shall consist of a Member or Members from two thirds of the States, and a Majority of all the States shall be necessary to a Choice. In every Case, after the Choice of the President, the Person having the greatest Number of Votes of the Electors shall be the Vice President. But if there should remain two or more who have equal Votes, the Senate shall chuse from them by Ballot the Vice President. The Congress may determine the Time of chusing the Electors, and the Day on which they shall give their Votes; which Day shall be the same throughout the United States.

No Person except a natural born Citizen, *or a Citizen of the United States, at the time of the Adoption of this Constitution,* shall be eligible to the Office of President; neither shall any Person be eligible to that Office who shall not have attained to the Age of thirty five Years, and been fourteen Years a Resident within the United States.

In Case of the Removal of the President from Office, or of his Death, Resignation, or Inability to discharge the Powers and Duties of the said Office, the Same shall devolve on the Vice President, and the Congress may by Law provide for the Case of Removal, Death, Resignation or Inability, both of the President and Vice President declaring what Officer shall then act as President, and such Officer shall act accordingly, until the Disability be removed, or a President shall be elected.

The President shall, at stated Times, receive for his Services, a Compensation, which shall neither be encreased nor diminished during the Period for which he shall have been elected, and he shall not receive within that Period any other Emolument from the United States, or any of them.

Before he enter on the Execution of his Office, he shall take the following Oath or Affirmation: "I do solemnly swear (or affirm) that I will faithfully execute the Office of President of the United States, and will to the best of my Ability, preserve, protect and defend the Constitution of the United States."

Section 2 The President shall be Commander in Chief of the Army and Navy of the United States, and of the Militia of the several States, when called into the actual Service of the United States; he may require the Opinion, in writing, of the principal Officer in each of the executive Departments, upon any Subject relating to the Duties of their respective Offices, and he shall have Power to grant Reprieves and Pardons for Offences against the United States, except in Cases of Impeachment.

He shall have Power, by and with the Advice and Consent of the Senate, to make Treaties, provided two thirds of the Senators present concur; and he shall nominate, and by and with the Advice and Consent of the Senate, shall appoint Ambassadors, other public Ministers and Consuls, Judges of the supreme Court, and all other Officers of the United States, whose Appointments are not herein otherwise provided for, and which shall be established by Law: but the Congress may by Law vest the Appointment of such inferior

Officers, as they think proper, in the President alone, in the Courts of Law, or in the Heads of Departments.

The President shall have Power to fill up all Vacancies that may happen during the Recess of the Senate, by granting Commissions which shall expire at the End of their next Session.

Section 3 He shall from time to time give to the Congress Information of the State of the Union, and recommend to their Consideration such Measures as he shall judge necessary and expedient; he may, on extraordinary Occasions, convene both Houses, or either of them, and in Case of Disagreement between them, with Respect to the Time of Adjournment, he may adjourn them to such Time as he shall think proper; he shall receive Ambassadors and other public Ministers; he shall take Care that the Laws be faithfully executed, and shall Commission all the Officers of the United States.

Section 4 The President, Vice President and all civil Officers of the United States, shall be removed from Office on Impeachment for, and Conviction of, Treason, Bribery, or other high Crimes and Misdemeanors.

ARTICLE III.

Section 1 The judicial Power of the United States, shall be vested in one supreme Court, and in such inferior Courts as the Congress may from time to time ordain and establish. The Judges, both of the supreme and inferior Courts, shall hold their Offices during good Behaviour, and shall, at stated Times, receive for their Services, a Compensation which shall not be diminished during their Continuance in Office.

Section 2 The judicial Power shall extend to all Cases, in Law and Equity, arising under this Constitution, the Laws of the United States, and Treaties made, or which shall be made, under their Authority;—to all Cases affecting Ambassadors, other public Ministers and Consuls;—to all Cases of admiralty and maritime Jurisdiction;—to Controversies to which the United States shall be a Party;—to Controversies between two or more States;*—between a State and Citizens of another State;*—between Citizens of different States;—between Citizens of the same State claiming Lands under Grants of different States, and between a State, or the Citizens thereof, and foreign States, Citizens or Subjects.

In all Cases affecting Ambassadors, other public Ministers and Consuls, and those in which a State shall be Party, the supreme Court shall have original Jurisdiction. In all the other Cases before mentioned, the supreme Court shall have appellate Jurisdiction, both as to Law and Fact, with such Exceptions, and under such Regulations as the Congress shall make.

The Trial of all Crimes, except in Cases of Impeachment, shall be by Jury; and such Trial shall be held in the State where the said Crimes shall have been committed; but when not committed within any State, the Trial shall be at such Place or Places as the Congress may by Law have directed.

Section 3 Treason against the United States, shall consist only in levying War against them, or in adhering to their Enemies, giving them Aid and Comfort. No Person shall be convicted of Treason unless on the Testimony of two Witnesses to the same overt Act, or on Confession in open Court.

The Congress shall have Power to declare the Punishment of Treason, but no Attainder of Treason shall work Corruption of Blood, or Forfeiture except during the Life of the Person attainted.

ARTICLE IV.

Section 1 Full Faith and Credit shall be given in each State to the public Acts, Records, and judicial Proceedings of every other State. And the Congress may by general Laws prescribe the Manner in which such Acts, Records and Proceedings shall be proved, and the Effect thereof.

Section 2 The Citizens of each State shall be entitled to all Privileges and Immunities of Citizens in the several States.

A Person charged in any State with Treason, Felony, or other Crime, who shall flee from Justice, and be found in another State, shall on Demand of the executive Authority of the State from which he fled, be delivered up, to be removed to the State having Jurisdiction of the Crime.

No Person held to Service or Labour in one State, under the Laws thereof, escaping into another, shall, in Consequence of any Law or Regulation therein, be discharged from such Service or Labour, but shall be delivered up on Claim of the Party to whom such Service or Labour may be due.

Section 3 New States may be admitted by the Congress into this Union; but no new State shall be formed or erected within the Jurisdiction of any other State; nor any State be formed by the Junction of two or more States, or Parts of States, without the Consent of the Legislatures of the States concerned as well as of the Congress.

The Congress shall have Power to dispose of and make all needful Rules and Regulations respecting the Territory or other Property belonging to the United States; and nothing in this Constitution shall be so construed as to Prejudice any Claims of the United States, or of any particular State.

Section 4 The United States shall guarantee to every State in this Union a Republican Form of Government, and shall protect each of them against Invasion; and on Application of the Legislature, or of the Executive (when the Legislature cannot be convened) against domestic Violence.

ARTICLE V.

The Congress, whenever two thirds of both Houses shall deem it necessary, shall propose Amendments to this Constitution, or, on the Application of the Legislatures of two thirds of the several States, shall call a Convention for proposing Amendments, which, in either Case, shall be valid to all Intents and Purposes, as Part of this Constitution, when ratified by the Legislatures of three fourths of the several States, or by Conventions in three fourths thereof, as the one or the other Mode of Ratification may be proposed by the Congress; Provided *that no Amendment which may be made prior to the Year One thousand eight hundred and eight shall in any Manner affect the first and fourth Clauses in the Ninth Section of the first Article; and* that no State, without its Consent, shall be deprived of its equal Suffrage in the Senate.

ARTICLE VI.

All Debts contracted and Engagements entered into, before the Adoption of this Constitution, shall be as valid against the United States under this Constitution, as under the Confederation.

This Constitution, and the Laws of the United States which shall be made in Pursuance thereof; and all Treaties made or which shall be made, under the Authority of the United States, shall be the supreme Law of the Land; and the Judges in every State shall be bound thereby, any Thing in the Constitution or Laws of any State to the Contrary notwithstanding.

The Senators and Representatives before mentioned, and the Members of the several State Legislatures, and all executive and judicial Officers, both of the United States and of the several States, shall be bound by Oath or Affirmation, to support this Constitution; but no religious Test shall ever be required as a Qualification to any Office or public Trust under the United States.

ARTICLE VII.

The Ratification of the Conventions of nine States, shall be sufficient for the Establishment of this Constitution between the States so ratifying the Same.

Done in Convention by the Unanimous Consent of the States present the Seventeenth Day of September in the Year of our Lord one thousand seven hundred and Eighty seven and of the Independence of the United States of America the Twelfth IN WITNESS whereof We have hereunto subscribed our Names,

GEORGE WASHINGTON,
President and Deputy from Virginia

North Carolina
WILLIAM BLOUNT
RICHARD DOBBS SPRAIGHT
HU WILLIAMSON

Pennsylvania
BENJAMIN FRANKLIN
THOMAS MIFFLIN
ROBERT MORRIS
GEORGE CLYMER
THOMAS FITZSIMONS
JARED INGERSOLL
JAMES WILSON
GOUVERNEUR MORRIS

Delaware
GEORGE READ
GUNNING BEDFORD, JR.
JOHN DICKINSON
RICHARD BASSETT
JACOB BROOM

South Carolina
J. RUTLEDGE
CHARLES C. PINCKNEY
PIERCE BUTLER

Virginia
JOHN BLAIR
JAMES MADISON, JR.

New Jersey
WILLIAM LIVINGSTON
DAVID BREARLEY
WILLIAM PATERSON
JONATHAN DAYTON

Maryland
JAMES MCHENRY
DANIEL OF ST. THOMAS JENIFER
DANIEL CARROLL

Massachusetts
NATHANIEL GORHAM
RUFUS KING

Connecticut
WILLIAM S. JOHNSON
ROGER SHERMAN

New York
ALEXANDER HAMILTON

New Hampshire
JOHN LANGDON
NICHOLAS GILMAN

Georgia
WILLIAM FEW
ABRAHAM BALDWIN

Amendments to the Constitution*

Amendment I

Congress shall make no law respecting an establishment of religion, or prohibiting the free exercise thereof; or abridging the freedom of speech, or of the press; or the right of the people peaceably to assemble, and to petition the Government for a redress of grievances.

Amendment II

A well regulated Militia, being necessary to the security of a free State, the right of the people to keep and bear Arms, shall not be infringed.

Amendment III

No Soldier shall, in time of peace be quartered in any house, without the consent of the Owner, nor in time of war, but in a manner to be prescribed by law.

Amendment IV

The right of the people to be secure in their persons, houses, papers, and effects, against unreasonable searches and seizures, shall not be violated, and no Warrants shall issue, but upon probable cause, supported by Oath or affirmation, and particularly describing the place to be searched, and the persons or things to be seized.

Amendment V

No person shall be held to answer for a capital, or otherwise infamous crime, unless on a presentment or indictment of a Grand Jury, except in cases arising in the land or naval forces, or in the Militia, when in actual service in time of War or public danger; nor shall any person be subject for the same offence to be twice put in jeopardy of life or limb; nor shall be compelled in any criminal case to be a witness against himself, nor be deprived of life, liberty, or property, without due process of law; nor shall private property be taken for public use, without just compensation.

Amendment VI

In all criminal prosecutions, the accused shall enjoy the right to a speedy and public trial, by an impartial jury of the State and district wherein the crime shall have been committed, which district shall have been previously ascertained by law, and to be informed of the nature and cause of the accusation; to be confronted with the witnesses against him; to have compulsory process for obtaining witnesses in his favor, and to have the Assistance of Counsel for his defence.

*The first ten amendments (the Bill of Rights) were adopted in 1791.

Amendment VII
In Suits at common law, where the value in controversy shall exceed twenty dollars, the right of trial by jury shall be preserved, and no fact tried by a jury, shall be otherwise re-examined in any Court of the United States, than according to the rules of the common law.

Amendment VIII
Excessive bail shall not be required, nor excessive fines imposed, nor cruel and unusual punishments inflicted.

Amendment IX
The enumeration in the Constitution, of certain rights, shall not be construed to deny or disparage others retained by the people.

Amendment X
The powers not delegated to the United States by the Constitution, nor prohibited by it to the States, are reserved to the States respectively, or to the people.

Amendment XI [Adopted 1798]
The Judicial power of the United States shall not be construed to extend to any suit in law or equity, commenced or prosecuted against one of the United States by Citizens of another State, or by Citizens or Subjects of any Foreign State.

Amendment XII [Adopted 1804]
The Electors shall meet in their respective states, and vote by ballot for President and Vice-President, one of whom, at least, shall not be an inhabitant of the same state with themselves; they shall name in their ballots the person voted for as President, and in distinct ballots the person voted for as Vice-President, and they shall make distinct lists of all persons voted for as President, and of all persons voted for as Vice-President, and of the number of votes for each, which list they shall sign and certify, and transmit sealed to the seat of the government of the United States, directed to the President of the Senate;—The President of the Senate shall, in the presence of the Senate and House of Representatives, open all the certificates and the votes shall then be counted;—The person having the greatest number of votes for President, shall be the President, if such number be a majority of the whole number of Electors appointed; and if no person have such majority, then from the persons having the highest numbers not exceeding three on the list of those voted for as President, the House of Representatives shall choose immediately, by ballot, the President. But in choosing the President, the votes shall be taken by states, the representation from each state having one vote; a quorum for this purpose shall consist of a member or members from two thirds of the states, and a majority of all the states shall be necessary to a choice. And if the House of Representatives shall not choose a President whenever the right of choice shall devolve upon them, before the *fourth day of March* next following, then the Vice-President shall act as President, as in the case of the death or other constitutional disability of the President.

The person having the greatest number of votes as Vice-President, shall be the Vice-President, if such number be a majority of the whole number of Electors appointed, and if no person have a majority, then from the two highest numbers on the list, the Senate shall choose the Vice-President; a quorum for the purpose shall consist of two thirds of the whole number of Senators, and a majority of the whole number shall be necessary to a choice. But no person constitutionally ineligible to the office of President shall be eligible to that of Vice-President of the United States.

Amendment XIII [Adopted 1865]

Section 1 Neither slavery nor involuntary servitude, except as a punishment for crime whereof the party shall have been duly convicted, shall exist within the United States, or any place subject to their jurisdiction.

Section 2 Congress shall have power to enforce this article by appropriate legislation.

Amendment XIV [Adopted 1868]

Section 1 All persons born or naturalized in the United States, and subject to the jurisdiction thereof, are citizens of the United States and of the State wherein they reside. No State shall make or enforce any law which shall abridge the privileges or immunities of citizens of the United States; nor shall any State deprive any person of life, liberty, or property, without due process of law; nor deny to any person within its jurisdiction the equal protection of the laws.

Section 2 Representatives shall be apportioned among the several States according to their respective numbers, counting the whole number of persons in each State, excluding Indians not taxed. But when the right to vote at any election for the choice of electors for President and Vice-President of the United States, Representatives in Congress, the Executive and Judicial officers of a State, or the members of the Legislature thereof, is denied to any of the male inhabitants of such State, being twenty-one years of age, and citizens of the United States, or in any way abridged, except for participation in rebellion, or other crime, the basis of representation therein shall be reduced in the proportion which the number of such male citizens shall bear to the whole number of male citizens twenty-one years of age in such State.

Section 3 No person shall be a Senator or Representative in Congress, or elector of President and Vice-President, or hold any office, civil or military, under the United States, or under any State, who, having previously taken an oath, as a member of Congress, or as an officer of the United States, or as a member of any State legislature, or as an executive or judicial officer of any State, to support the Constitution of the United States, shall have engaged in insurrection or rebellion against the same, or given aid or comfort to the enemies thereof. But Congress may by a vote of two thirds of each House, remove such disability.

Section 4 The validity of the public debt of the United States, authorized by law, including debts incurred for payment of pensions and bounties for services in suppressing insurrection or rebellion, shall not be questioned. But neither the United States nor any State shall assume or pay any debt or obligation incurred in aid of insurrection or rebellion against the United States, or any claim for the loss or emancipation of any slave; but all such debts, obligations and claims shall be held illegal and void.

Section 5 The Congress shall have power to enforce, by appropriate legislation, the provisions of this article.

Amendment XV [Adopted 1870]

Section 1 The right of citizens of the United States to vote shall not be denied or abridged by the United States or by any State on account of race, color, or previous condition of servitude

Section 2 The Congress shall have power to enforce this article by appropriate legislation.

Amendment XVI [Adopted 1913]

The Congress shall have power to lay and collect taxes on incomes, from whatever source derived, without apportionment among the several States, and without regard to any census or enumeration.

Amendment XVII [Adopted 1913]

The Senate of the United States shall be composed of two Senators from each State, elected by the people thereof, for six years; and each Senator shall have one vote. The electors in each State shall have the qualifications requisite for electors of the most numerous branch of the State legislatures.

When vacancies happen in the representation of any State in the Senate, the executive authority of such State shall issue writs of election to fill such vacancies: *Provided,* That the legislature of any State may empower the executive thereof to make temporary appointments until the people fill the vacancies by election as the legislature may direct.

This amendment shall not be so construed as to affect the election or term of any Senator chosen before it becomes valid as part of the Constitution.

Amendment XVIII [Adopted 1919; Repealed 1933]

Section 1 After one year from the ratification of this article the manufacture, sale, or transportation of intoxicating liquors within, the importation thereof into, or the exportation thereof from the United States and all territory subject to the jurisdiction thereof for beverage purposes is hereby prohibited.

Section 2 The Congress and the several States shall have concurrent power to enforce this article by appropriate legislation.

Section 3 This article shall be inoperative unless it shall have been ratified as an amendment to the Constitution by the legislatures of the several States, as provided in the Constitution, within seven years from the date of the submission hereof to the States by the Congress.

Amendment XIX [Adopted 1920]

Section 1 The right of citizens of the United States to vote shall not be denied or abridged by the United States or by any State on account of sex.

Section 2 Congress shall have power to enforce this article by appropriate legislation.

Amendment XX [Adopted 1933]

Section 1 The terms of the President and Vice-President shall end at noon on the 20th day of January, and the terms of Senators and Representatives at noon on the third day of January, of the years in which such terms would have ended if this article had not been ratified; and the terms of their successors shall then begin.

Section 2 The Congress shall assemble at least once in every year, and such meeting shall begin at noon on the third day of January, unless they shall by law appoint a different day.

Section 3 If, at the time fixed for the beginning of the term of the President, the President elect shall have died, the Vice-President elect shall become President. If a President shall not have been chosen before the time fixed for the beginning of his term, or if the President elect shall have failed to qualify, then the Vice-President elect shall act as President until a President shall have qualified; and the Congress may by law provide for the case wherein neither a President elect nor a Vice-President elect shall have qualified, declaring who shall then act as President, or the manner in which one who is to act shall be selected, and such person shall act accordingly until a President or Vice-President shall have qualified.

Section 4 The Congress may by law provide for the case of the death of any of the persons from whom the House of Representatives may choose a President whenever the right of choice shall have devolved upon them, and for the case of the death of any of the persons from whom the Senate may choose a Vice-President whenever the right of choice shall have devolved upon them.

Section 5 Sections 1 and 2 shall take effect on the 15th day of October following the ratification of this article.

Section 6 This article shall be inoperative unless it shall have been ratified as an amendment to the Constitution by the legislatures of three fourths of the several States within seven years from the date of its submission.

Amendment XXI [Adopted 1933]

Section 1 The eighteenth article of amendment to the Constitution of the United States is hereby repealed.

Section 2 The transportation or importation into any State, Territory, or possession of the United States for delivery or use therein of intoxicating liquors, in violation of the laws thereof, is hereby prohibited.

Section 3 This article shall be inoperative unless it shall have been ratified as an amendment to the Constitution by conventions in the several States, as provided in the Constitution, within seven years from the date of the submission hereof to the States by the Congress.

Amendment XXII [Adopted 1951]

Section 1 No person shall be elected to the office of the President more than twice, and no person who has held the office of President, or acted as President, for more than two years of a term to which some other person was elected President shall be elected to the office of the President more than once. But this Article shall not apply to any person holding the office of President when this Article was proposed by the Congress, and shall not prevent any person who may be holding the office of President, or acting as President, during the term within which this Article becomes operative from holding the office of President or acting as President during the remainder of such term.

Section 2 This article shall be inoperative unless it shall have been ratified as an amendment to the

Constitution by the legislatures of three fourths of the several States within seven years from the date of its submission to the States by the Congress.

Amendment XXIII [Adopted 1961]

Section 1 The District constituting the seat of Government of the United States shall appoint in such manner as the Congress may direct:

A number of electors of President and Vice-President equal to the whole number of Senators and Representatives in Congress to which the District would be entitled if it were a State, but in no event more than the least populous State; they shall be in addition to those appointed by the States, but they shall be considered, for the purposes of the election of President and Vice-President, to be electors appointed by a State; and they shall meet in the District and perform such duties as provided by the twelfth article of amendment.

Section 2 The Congress shall have power to enforce this article by appropriate legislation.

Amendment XXIV [Adopted 1944]

Section 1 The right of citizens of the United States to vote in any primary or other election for President or Vice-President, for electors for President or Vice-President, or for Senator or Representative in Congress, shall not be denied or abridged by the United States or any State by reason of failure to pay any poll tax or other tax.

Section 2 The Congress shall have power to enforce this article by appropriate legislation.

Amendment XXV [Adopted 1967]

Section 1 In case of the removal of the President from office or his death or resignation, the Vice-President shall become President.

Section 2 Whenever there is a vacancy in the office of the Vice-President, the President shall nominate a Vice-President who shall take the office upon confirmation by a majority vote of both houses of Congress.

Section 3 Whenever the President transmits to the President pro tempore of the Senate and the Speaker of the House of Representatives his written declaration that he is unable to discharge the powers and duties of his office, and until he transmits to them a written declaration to the contrary, such powers and duties shall be discharged by the Vice-President as Acting President.

Section 4 Whenever the Vice-President and a majority of either the principal officers of the executive departments, or of such other body as Congress may by law provide, transmit to the President pro tempore of the Senate and the Speaker of the House of Representatives their written declaration that the President is unable to discharge the powers and duties of his office, the Vice-President shall immediately assume the powers and duties of the office as Acting President.

Thereafter, when the President transmits to the President pro tempore of the Senate and the Speaker of the House of Representatives his written declaration that no inability exists, he shall resume the powers and duties of his office unless the Vice-President and a majority of either the principal officers of the executive department, or of such other body as Congress may by law provide, transmit within four days to the President pro tempore of the Senate and the Speaker of the House of Representatives their written declaration that the President is unable to discharge the powers and duties of his office. Thereupon Congress shall decide the issue, assembling within 48 hours for that purpose if not in session. If the Congress, within 21 days after receipt of the latter written declaration, or, if Congress is not in session, within 21 days after Congress is required to assemble, determines by two-thirds vote of both houses that the President is unable to discharge the powers and duties of his office, the Vice-President shall continue to discharge the same as Acting President; otherwise, the President shall resume the powers and duties of his office.

Amendment XXVI [Adopted 1971]

Section 1 The right of citizens of the United States, who are eighteen years of age or older, to vote shall not be denied or abridged by the United States or any state on account of age.

Section 2 The Congress shall have power to enforce this article by appropriate legislation.

Amendent XXVII [Adopted 1992]

No law, varying the compensation for the services of Senators and Representatives, shall take effect until an election of Representatives have intervened.

PRESIDENTIAL ELECTIONS

Year	Candidates	Parties	Popular Vote	Electoral Vote	Voter Participation
1789	GEORGE WASHINGTON		*	69	
	John Adams			34	
	Others			35	
1792	GEORGE WASHINGTON		*	132	
	John Adams			77	
	George Clinton			50	
	Others			5	
1796	JOHN ADAMS	Federalist	*	71	
	Thomas Jefferson	Democratic-Republican		68	
	Thomas Pinckney	Federalist		59	
	Aaron Burr	Dem.-Rep.		30	
	Others			48	
1800	THOMAS JEFFERSON	Dem.-Rep.	*	73	
	Aaron Burr	Dem.-Rep.		73	
	C. C. Pinckney	Federalist		64	
	John Jay	Federalist		1	
1804	THOMAS JEFFERSON	Dem.-Rep.	*	122	
	C. C. Pinckney	Federalist		14	
1808	JAMES MADISON	Dem.-Rep.	*	122	
	C. C. Pinckney	Federalist		47	
	George Clinton	Dem.-Rep.		6	
1812	JAMES MADISON	Dem.-Rep.	*	128	
	De Witt Clinton	Federalist		89	
1816	JAMES MONROE	Dem.-Rep.	*	183	
	Rufus King	Federalist		34	
1820	JAMES MONROE	Dem.-Rep.	*	231	
	John Quincy Adams	Dem.-Rep.		1	
1824	JOHN Q. ADAMS	Dem.-Rep.	108,740 (10.5%)	84	26.9%
	Andrew Jackson	Dem.-Rep.	153,544 (43.1%)	99	
	William H. Crawford	Dem.-Rep.	46,618 (13.1%)	41	
	Henry Clay	Dem.-Rep.	47,136 (13.2%)	37	
1828	ANDREW JACKSON	Democratic	647,286 (56.0%)	178	57.6%
	John Quincy Adams	National Republican	508,064 (44.0%)	83	
1832	ANDREW JACKSON	Democratic	687,502 (55.0%)	219	55.4%
	Henry Clay	National Republican	530,189 (42.4%)	49	
	John Floyd	Independent		11	
	William Wirt	Anti-Mason	33,108 (2.6%)	7	
1836	MARTIN VAN BUREN	Democratic	765,483 (50.9%)	170	57.8%
	W. H. Harrison	Whig		73	
	Hugh L. White	Whig	739,795 (49.1%)	26	
	Daniel Webster	Whig		14	
	W. P. Magnum	Independent		11	
1840	WILLIAM H. HARRISON	Whig	1,274,624 (53.1%)	234	80.2%
	Martin Van Buren	Democratic	1,127,781 (46.9%)	60	
	J. G. Birney	Liberty	7069	—	
1844	JAMES K. POLK	Democratic	1,338,464 (49.6%)	170	78.9%
	Henry Clay	Whig	1,300,097 (48.1%)	105	
	J. G. Birney	Liberty	62,300 (2.3%)	—	
1848	ZACHARY TAYLOR	Whig	1,360,967 (47.4%)	163	72.7%
	Lewis Cass	Democratic	1,222,342 (42.5%)	127	
	Martin Van Buren	Free-Soil	291,263 (10.1%)	—	
1852	FRANKLIN PIERCE	Democratic	1,601,117 (50.9%)	254	69.6%
	Winfield Scott	Whig	1,385,453 (44.1%)	42	
	John P. Hale	Free-Soil	155,825 (5.0%)	—	
1856	JAMES BUCHANAN	Democratic	1,832,955 (45.3%)	174	78.9%
	John C. Fremont	Republican	1,339,932 (33.1%)	114	
	Millard Fillmore	American	871,731 (21.6%)	8	

Year	Candidates	Parties	Popular Vote	Electoral Vote	Voter Participation
1860	ABRAHAM LINCOLN	Republican	1,865,593 (39.8%)	180	81.2%
	Stephen A. Douglas	Democratic	1,382,713 (29.5%)	12	
	John C. Breckinridge	Democratic	848,356 (18.1%)	72	
	John Bell	Union	592,906 (12.6%)	39	
1864	ABRAHAM LINCOLN	Republican	2,213,655 (55.0%)	212	73.8%
	George B. McClellan	Democratic	1,805,237 (45.0%)	21	
1868	ULYSSES S. GRANT	Republican	3,012,833 (52.7%)	214	78.1%
	Horatio Seymour	Democratic	2,703,249 (47.3%)	80	
1872	ULYSSES S. GRANT	Republican	3,597,132 (55.6%)	286	71.3%
	Horace Greeley	Democratic; Liberal Republican	2,834,125 (43.9%)	66	
1876	RUTHERFORD B. HAYES	Republican	4,036,298 (48.0%)	185	81.8%
	Samuel J. Tilden	Democratic	4,300,590 (51.0%)	184	
1880	JAMES A. GARFIELD	Republican	4,454,416 (48.5%)	214	79.4%
	Winfield S. Hancock	Democratic	4,444,952 (48.1%)	155	
1884	GROVER CLEVELAND	Democratic	4,874,986 (48.5%)	219	77.5%
	James G. Blaine	Republican	4,851,981 (48.2%)	182	
1888	BENJAMIN HARRISON	Republican	5,439,853 (47.9%)	233	79.3%
	Grover Cleveland	Democratic	5,540,309 (48.6%)	168	
1892	GROVER CLEVELAND	Democratic	5,556,918 (46.1%)	277	74.7%
	Benjamin Harrison	Republican	5,176,108 (43.0%)	145	
	James B. Weaver	People's	1,041,028 (8.5%)	22	
1896	WILLIAM McKINLEY	Republican	7,104,779 (51.1%)	271	79.3%
	William J. Bryan	Democratic People's	6,502,925 (47.7%)	176	
1900	WILLIAM McKINLEY	Republican	7,207,923 (51.7%)	292	73.2%
	William J. Bryan	Dem.-Populist	6,358,133 (45.5%)	155	
1904	THEODORE ROOSEVELT	Republican	7,623,486 (57.9%)	336	65.2%
	Alton B. Parker	Democratic	5,077,911 (37.6%)	140	
	Eugene V. Debs	Socialist	402,283 (3.0%)	—	
1908	WILLIAM H. TAFT	Republican	7,678,908 (51.6%)	321	65.4%
	William J. Bryan	Democratic	6,409,104 (43.1%)	162	
	Eugene V. Debs	Socialist	420,793 (2.8%)	—	
1912	WOODROW WILSON	Democratic	6,293,454 (41.9%)	435	58.8%
	Theodore Roosevelt	Progressive	4,119,538 (27.4%)	88	
	William H. Taft	Republican	3,484,980 (23.2%)	8	
	Eugene V. Debs	Socialist	900,672 (6.0%)	—	
1916	WOODROW WILSON	Democratic	9,129,606 (49.4%)	277	61.6%
	Charles E. Hughes	Republican	8,538,221 (46.2%)	254	
	A. L. Benson	Socialist	585,113 (3.2%)	—	
1920	WARREN G. HARDING	Republican	16,152,200 (60.4%)	404	49.2%
	James M. Cox	Democratic	9,147,353 (34.2%)	127	
	Eugene V. Debs	Socialist	919,799 (3.4%)	—	
1924	CALVIN COOLIDGE	Republican	15,725,016 (54.0%)	382	48.9%
	John W. Davis	Democratic	8,386,503 (28.8%)	136	
	Robert M. La Follette	Progressive	4,822,856 (16.6%)	13	
1928	HERBERT HOOVER	Republican	21,391,381 (58.2%)	444	56.9%
	Alfred E. Smith	Democratic	15,016,443 (40.9%)	87	
	Normal Thomas	Socialist	267,835 (0.7%)	—	
1932	FRANKLIN D. ROOSEVELT	Democratic	22,821,857 (57.4%)	472	56.9%
	Herbert Hoover	Republican	15,761,841 (39.7%)	59	
	Norman Thomas	Socialist	881,951 (2.2%)	—	
1936	FRANKLIN D. ROOSEVELT	Democratic	27,751,597 (60.8%)	523	61.0%
	Alfred M. Landon	Republican	16,679,583 (36.5%)	8	
	William Lemke	Union	882,479 (1.9%)	—	
1940	FRANKLIN D. ROOSEVELT	Democratic	27,244,160 (54.8%)	449	62.5%
	Wendell L. Willkie	Republican	22,305,198 (44.8%)	82	

Year	Candidates	Parties	Popular Vote	Electoral Vote	Voter Participation
1944	FRANKLIN D. ROOSEVELT	Democrat	25,602,504 (53.5%)	432	55.9%
	Thomas E. Dewey	Republican	22,006,285 (46.0%)	99	
1948	HARRY S TRUMAN	Democratic	24,105,695 (49.5%)	304	53.0%
	Thomas E. Dewey	Republican	21,969,170 (45.1%)	189	
	J. Strom Thurmond	State-Rights Democratic	1,169,021 (2.4%)	38	
	Henry A. Wallace	Progressive	1,156,103 (2.4%)	—	
1952	DWIGHT D. EISENHOWER	Republican	33,936,252 (55.1%)	442	63.3%
	Adlai E. Stevenson	Democratic	27,314,992 (44.4%)	89	
1956	DWIGHT D. EISENHOWER	Republican	35,575,420 (57.6%)	457	60.5%
	Adlai E. Stevenson	Democratic	26,033,066 (42.1%)	73	
	Other	—	—	1	
1960	JOHN F. KENNEDY	Democratic	34,227,096 (49.9%)	303	62.8%
	Richard M. Nixon	Republican	34,108,546 (49.6%)	219	
	Other	—	—	15	
1964	LYNDON B. JOHNSON	Democratic	43,126,506 (61.1%)	486	61.7%
	Barry M. Goldwater	Republican	27,176,799 (38.5%)	52	
1968	RICHARD M. NIXON	Republican	31,770,237 (43.4.%)	301	60.6%
	Hubert H. Humphrey	Democratic	31,270,633 (42.7%)	191	
	George Wallace	American Indep.	9,906,141 (13.5%)	46	
1972	RICHARD M. NIXON	Republican	47,169,911 (60.7%)	520	55.2%
	George S. McGovern	Democratic	29,170,383 (37.5%)	17	
	Other	—	—	1	
1976	JIMMY CARTER	Democratic	40,828,587 (50.0%)	297	53.5%
	Gerald R. Ford	Republican	39,147,613 (47.9%)	241	
	Other	—	1,575,459 92.1%)	—	
1980	RONALD REAGAN	Republican	43,901,812 (50.7%)	489	52.6%
	Jimmy Carter	Democratic	35,483,820 (41.0%)	49	
	John B. Anderson	Independent	5,719,722 (6.6%)	—	
	Ed Clark	Libertarian	921,188 (1.1%)	—	
1984	RONALD REAGAN	Republican	54,455,075 (59.0%)	525	53.3%
	Walter Mondale	Democratic	37,577,185 (41.0%)	13	
1988	GEORGE H. W. BUSH	Republican	48,886,000 (45.6%)	426	57.4%
	Michael S. Dukakis	Democratic	41,809,000 (45.6%)	111	
1992	WILLIAM J. CLINTON	Democratic	43,728,375 (43%)	370	55.0%
	George H. W. Bush	Republican	38,167,416 (38%)	168	
	Ross Perot	—	19,237,247 (19%)	—	
1996	WILLIAM J. CLINTON	Democratic	45,590,703 (50%)	379	48.8%
	Robert Dole	Republican	37,816,307 (41%)	159	
	Ross Perot	Independent	7,866,284 (9%)		

SUPREME COURT JUSTICES

Name	Service	Appointed by
John Jay*	1789–1795	Washington
James Wilson	1789–1798	Washington
John Blair	1789–1796	Washington
John Rutledge	1790–1791	Washington
William Cushing	1790–1810	Washington
James Iredell	1790–1799	Washington
Thomas Johnson	1791–1793	Washington
William Paterson	1793–1806	Washington
John Rutledge†	1795	Washington
Samuel Chase	1796–1811	Washington
Oliver Ellsworth	1796–1799	Washington
Bushrod Washington	1798–1829	J. Adams
Alfred Moore	1799–1804	J. Adams
John Marshall	1801–1835	J. Adams
William Johnson	1804–1834	Jefferson
Henry B. Livingston	1806–1823	Jefferson
Thomas Todd	1807–1826	Jefferson
Gabriel Duval	1811–1836	Madison
Joseph Story	1811–1845	Madison
Smith Thompson	1823–1843	Monroe
Robert Trimble	1826–1828	J.Q. Adams
John McLean	1829–1861	Jackson
Henry Baldwin	1830–1844	Jackson
James M. Wayne	1835–1867	Jackson
Roger B. Taney	1836–1864	Jackson
Philip P. Barbour	1836–1841	Jackson
John Catron	1837–1865	Van Buren
John McKinley	1837–1852	Van Buren
Peter V. Daniel	1841–1860	Van Buren
Samuel Nelson	1845–1872	Tyler
Levi Woodbury	1845–1851	Polk
Robert C. Grier	1846–1870	Polk
Benjamin R. Curtis	1851–1857	Fillmore
John A. Campbell	1853–1861	Pierce
Nathan Clifford	1858–1881	Buchanan
Noah H. Swayne	1862–1881	Lincoln
Samuel F. Miller	1862–1890	Lincoln
David Davis	1862–1877	Lincoln
Stephen J. Field	1863–1897	Lincoln
Salmon P. Chase	1864–1873	Lincoln
William Strong	1870–1880	Grant
Joseph P. Bradley	1870–1892	Grant
Ward Hunt	1873–1882	Grant
Morrison R. Waite	1874–1888	Grant
John M. Harlan	1877–1911	Hayes
William B. Woods	1880–1887	Hayes
Stanley Matthews	1881–1889	Garfield
Horace Gray	1882–1902	Arthur
Samuel Blatchford	1882–1893	Arthur
Lucious Q. C. Lamar	1888–1893	Cleveland
Melville W. Fuller	1888–1910	Cleveland
David J. Brewer	1889–1910	B. Harrison
Henry B. Brown	1890–1906	B. Harrison
George Shiras	1892–1903	B. Harrison
Howell E. Jackson	1893–1895	B. Harrison
Edward D. White	1894–1910	Cleveland
Rufus W. Peckham	1896–1909	Cleveland
Joseph McKenna	1898–1925	McKinley

Name	Service	Appointed by
Oliver W. Holmes	1902–1932	T. Roosevelt
William R. Day	1903–1922	T. Roosevelt
William H. Moody	1906–1910	T. Roosevelt
Horace H. Lurton	1910–1914	Taft
Charles E. Hughes	1910–1916	Taft
Willis Van Devanter	1910–1937	Taft
Joseph R. Lamar	1911–1916	Taft
Edward D. White	1910–1921	Taft
Mahlon Pitney	1912–1922	Taft
James C. McReynolds	1914–1941	Wilson
Louis D. Brandeis	1916–1939	Wilson
John H. Clarke	1916–1922	Wilson
William H. Taft	1921–1930	Harding
George Sutherland	1922–1938	Harding
Pierce Butler	1923–1939	Harding
Edward T. Sanford	1923–1930	Harding
Harlan F. Stone	1925–1941	Coolidge
Charles E. Hughes	1930–1941	Hoover
Owen J. Roberts	1930–1945	Hoover
Benjamin N. Cardozo	1932–1938	Hoover
Hugo L. Black	1937–1971	F. Roosevelt
Stanley F. Reed	1938–1957	F. Roosevelt
Felix Frankfurter	1939–1962	F. Roosevelt
William O. Douglas	1939–1975	F. Roosevelt
Frank Murphy	1940–1949	F. Roosevelt
Harlan F. Stone	1941–1946	F. Roosevelt
James F. Byrnes	1941–1942	F. Roosevelt
Robert H. Jackson	1941–1954	F. Roosevelt
Wiley B. Rutledge	1943–1949	F. Roosevelt
Harold H. Burton	1945–1958	Truman
Frederick M. Vinson	1946–1953	Truman
Tom C. Clark	1949–1967	Truman
Sherman Minton	1949–1956	Truman
Earl Warren	1953–1969	Eisenhower
John Marshall Harlan	1955–1971	Eisenhower
William J. Brennan, Jr.	1956–1990	Eisenhower
Charles E. Whittaker	1957–1962	Eisenhower
Potter Stewart	1958–1981	Eisenhower
Byron R. White	1962–1993	Kennedy
Arthur J. Goldberg	1962–1965	Kennedy
Abe Fortas	1965–1969	Johnson
Thurgood Marshall	1967–1991	Johnson
Warren E. Burger	1969–1986	Nixon
Harry A. Blackmun	1970–1994	Nixon
Lewis F. Powell, Jr.	1972–1988	Nixon
William H. Rehnquist	1972–1986	Nixon
John Paul Stevens	1975–	Ford
Sandra Day O'Connor	1981–	Reagan
William H. Rehnquist	1986–	Reagan
Antonin Scalia	1986–	Reagan
Anthony M. Kennedy	1988–	Reagan
David H. Souter	1990–	Bush
Clarence Thomas	1991–	Bush
Ruth Bader Ginsberg	1993–	Clinton
Stephen Breyer	1994–	Clinton

*Chief Justices appear in bold type.
†Acting Chief Justice; Senate refused to confirm appointment.

STATES OF THE UNITED STATES

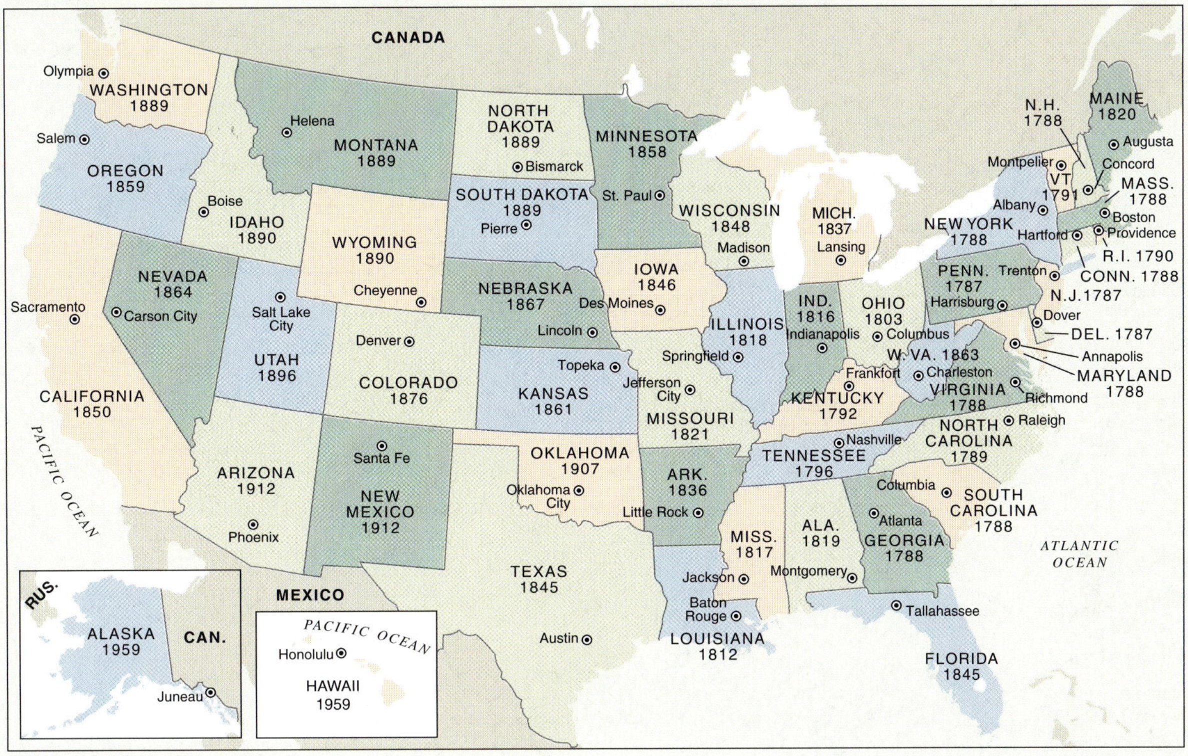

State	Date of Admission	State	Date of Admission
Delaware	December 7, 1787	Michigan	January 16, 1837
Pennsylvania	December 12, 1787	Florida	March 3, 1845
New Jersey	December 18, 1787	Texas	December 29, 1845
Georgia	January 2, 1788	Iowa	December 28, 1846
Connecticut	January 9, 1788	Wisconsin	May 29, 1848
Massachusetts	February 6, 1788	California	September 9, 1850
Maryland	April 28, 1788	Minnesota	May 11, 1858
South Carolina	May23, 1788	Oregon	February 14, 1859
New Hampshire	June 21, 1788	Kansas	January 29, 1861
Virginia	June 25, 1788	West Virginia	June 19, 1863
New York	July 26, 1788	Nevada	October 31, 1864
North Carolina	November 21, 1789	Nebraska	March 1, 1867
Rhode Island	May 29, 1790	Colorado	August 1, 1876
Vermont	March 4, 1791	North Dakota	November 2, 1889
Kentucky	June 1, 1792	South Dakota	November 2, 1889
Tennessee	June 1, 1796	Montana	November 8, 1889
Ohio	March 1, 1803	Washington	November 11, 1889
Louisiana	April 30, 1812	Idaho	July 3, 1890
Indiana	December 11, 1816	Wyoming	July 10, 1890
Mississippi	December 10, 1817	Utah	January 4, 1896
Illinois	December 3, 1818	Oklahoma	November 16, 1907
Alabama	December 14, 1819	New Mexico	January 6, 1912
Maine	March 15, 1820	Arizona	February 14, 1912
Missouri	August 10, 1821	Alaska	January 3, 1959
Arkansas	June 15, 1836	Hawaii	August 21, 1959

TERRITORIAL EXPANSION OF THE UNITED STATES

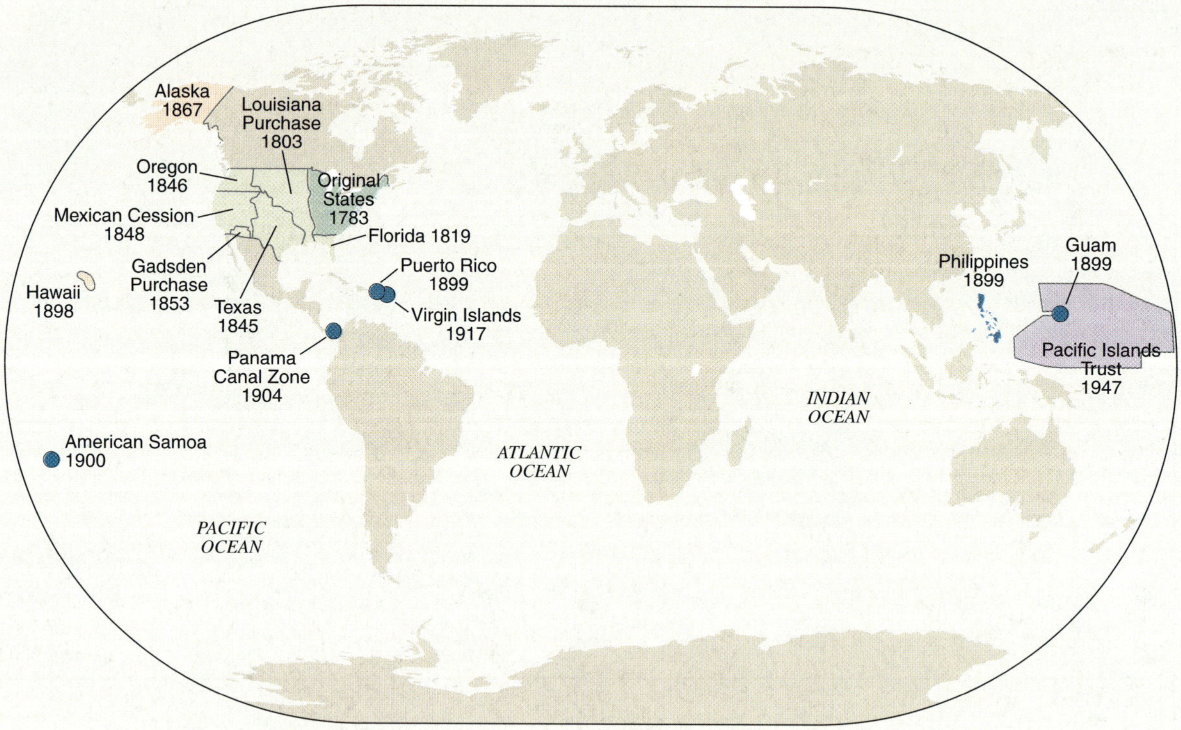

Date	Territory	Area (sq. mi.)	Cumulative Total (sq.mi.)
1793	Original states	888,685	888,685
1803	Louisiana Purchase	827,192	1,715,877
1819	Florida	72,003	1,787,880
1845	Texas	390,143	2,178,023
1846	Oregon	285,580	2,463,603
1848	Mexican Cession	529,017	2,992,620
1853	Gadsden Purchase	29,640	3,022,260
1867	Alaska	589,757	3,612,017
1898	Hawaii	6,450	3,618,467
1899	Philippines	115,600	3,734,067
1899	Puerto Rico	3,435	3,737,502
1899	Guam	212	3,737,714
1900	American Samoa	76	3,737,790
1904	Panama Canal Zone	553	3,738,343
1917	Virgin Islands	133	3,738,476
1947	Pacific Islands Trust	8,489	3,746,965
	All others	46	3,747,011

POPULATION OF THE UNITED STATES

Year	Number of States	Population	Percent Increase	Population per Square Mile
1790	13	3,929,214		4.5
1800	16	5,308,483	35.1	6.1
1810	17	7,239,881	36.4	4.3
1820	23	9,638,453	33.1	5.5
1830	24	12,866,020	33.5	7.4
1840	26	17,069,453	32.7	9.8
1850	31	23,191,876	35.9	7.9
1860	33	31,443,321	35.6	10.6
1870	37	39,818,449	26.6	13.4
1880	38	50,155,783	26.0	16.9
1890	44	62,947,714	25.5	21.2
1900	45	75,994,575	20.7	25.6
1910	46	91,972,266	21.0	31.0
1920	48	105,710,620	14.9	35.6
1930	48	122,775,046	16.1	41.2
1940	48	131,669,275	7.2	44.2
1950	48	150,697,361	14.5	50.7
1960	50	179,323,175	19.0	50.6
1970	50	203,235,298	13.3	57.5
1980	50	226,545,805	11.5	64.1
1990	50	248,709,873	9.8	70.3

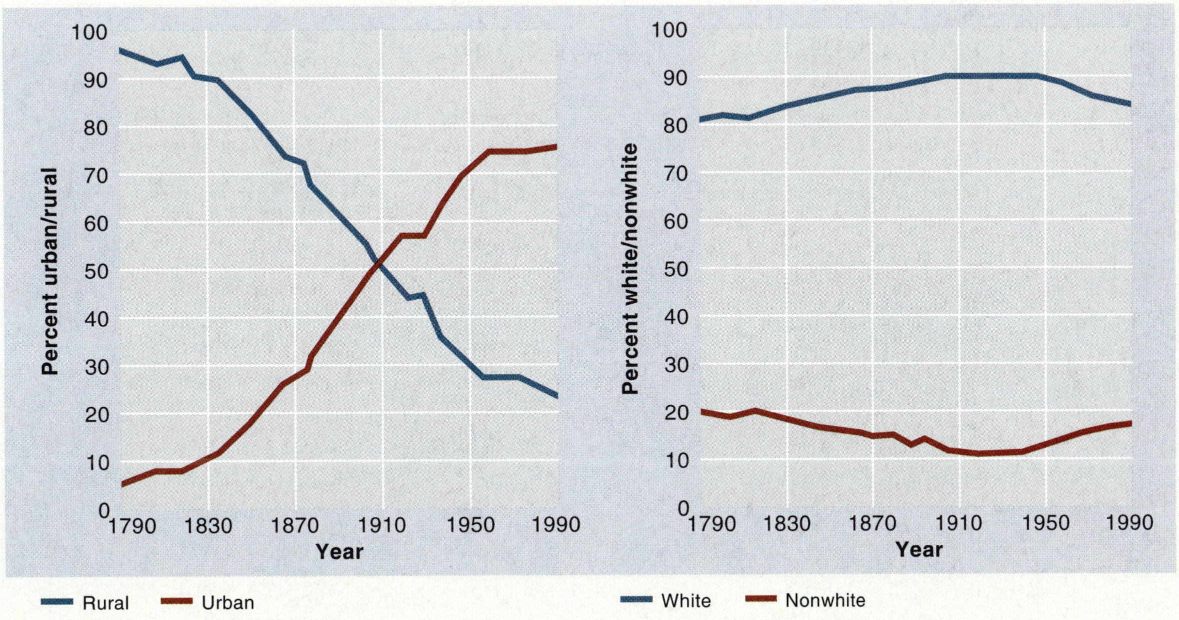

Source: U.S. Bureau of the Census estimates.

Index

The World

Central America and the Caribbean

Southwest Asia

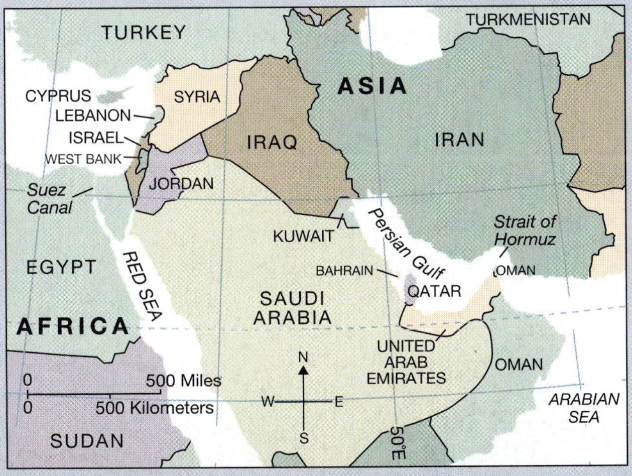

Europe

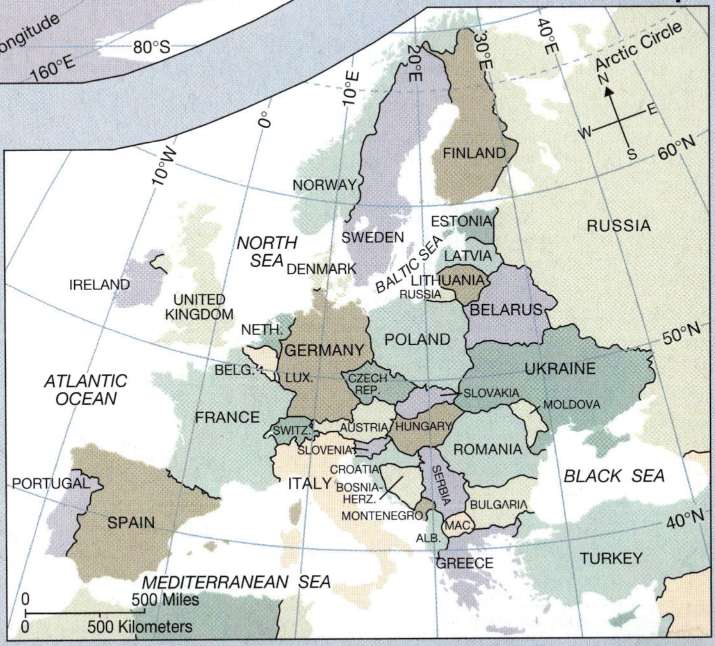